May 1996

A

Abbott MRS Alice Reid (Alice F Reid)
  CtCol'69.Ne'74 . . . . ☎ (317) 743-4374
  MISS Laurel S—at Yale . . . . 220 W Stadium Av,
  JUNIORS MISS Sally N . . . . West Lafayette, IN
                                          47906
Abbott MR & MRS James S 4th (Nancy A Hamilton) Woos'92.Ofp.Woos'91
  ☎ (216) 423-3875 . . PO Box 171, 1795 Epping Rd, Gates Mills,
  OH *44040*
Abbott DR R Tucker . . . . Died at
                                               Sanibel, FL Nov 3'95
Abercrombie CAPT (RET) & MRS Daniel W (MacMullan—White—
  Rachel M Horak) USN.Cvc.Y'38
  ☎ (941) 261-4430 . . 1285 Gulf Shore Blvd N, Apt 8C, Naples,
  FL *33940*
Acheson MRS Dean (Alice Stanley) . . . . Died at
                                        Washington, DC Jan 20'96
Achilles MISS Frances M . . . . Died Dec 12'95
Ackerman MR Allan D—Dth'68.H'74 . . . . ☎ (312) 871-8681
  MISS Mary F—H'92 . . . . 905 W Willow St,
  MR Samuel K—at RI Sch of Design . . . . Chicago, IL *60614*
Adams MR & MRS Andrew M (Charlotte M Whann) Va'91.Col'85.CalSt'88
  1107 Arabella St, New Orleans, LA *70115*
Adams DR & MRS James L (Player—Marian B Leib) ☎ (415) 324-0200
  Stan'64.CalTech'52.Stan'60 . . . . 740 Santa Ynez St,
  MR Robert L—Stan'86.Stan'88—at . . . . Stanford, CA *94305*
  1325 Bryant St, Palo Alto, CA *94301* . . . .
    MISS Elizabeth C Player—Ty'93—at
    ☎ (415) 462-1139 . . 505 Hawthorne St,
    Palo Alto, CA *94301* . . . .
    MR Samuel L Player—Wes'91—at
    ☎ (415) 321-3528 . . 200 Waverly St, Apt 1,
    Menlo Park, CA *94025* . . . .
Adams MISS P Lee Hamilton—Woos'89.Bost'95
  ☎ (617) 887-2528 . . 27 Pembroke St, Apt 1, Chelsea, MA *02150*
Addis MRS Roland Taylor (Virginia Downes) . . . . Died at
                                            West Orange, NJ Jan 29'96
Ahearne MISS Marion Connolly (John J) . . . . Born Jly 5'95

Ahn MR & MRS Sangwoo (Alison Donald)   ☎ (203) 869-4875
  Ln.Wms'60.Y'63 . . . . 106 Patterson Av,
  MISS Laura . . . . Greenwich, CT
  MISS Ginger *06830*
  MR Woodrow—at ☎ (212) 628-8404
  30 E 68 St, New York, NY *10021* . . . .
Albright MISS Martina B (Nile L) . . . . Married at Boston, MA
  Bernstein MR Jon A (Yale) . . . . Oct 7'95
Alcott MRS Franklyn L 3d (Virginia A Slaven) . . . . Died at
                                            Blue Hill, ME Apr 3'95
Alcott COL & MRS Henry S (Mary J Charlton)   ☎ (612) 825-9585
  USA.Minn'72.Web'86.FlaIT'89 . . . . 4636 Oakland Av S,
  MISS Catherine A . . . . Minneapolis, MN
  MR Michael B *55407*
Aldrich MR & MRS John Winthrop (Middleton—   ☎ (914) 758-5895
  Katharine D Ryan) SL'64.Hn.H'65 . . . . "Good Hap"
  MISS Margaret L—at Columbia . . . . Barrytown, NY
  MISS Katharine D—at U of Tex Austin *12507*
    MISS Laura D R Middleton—Sth'86.
    Wash'87.AmU'94—at ☎ (202) 328-3721
    3000 Connecticut Av NW, Washington, DC
    20008 . . . .
    MR Daniel T Middleton—Stan'87—at
    ☎ (415) 567-7841 . . 601 Van Ness Av,
    San Francisco, CA *94102* . . . .
Alessio MASTER Matthew Dominic (Marco D) . . . . Born at
                                            San Diego, CA Jan 6'96
Alexander MRS Frederick B JR (Dorothy Schierenberg) V'31
  ☎ (214) 750-9117 . . 7831 Park Lane, Apt 144C, Dallas, TX *75225-2041*
Alexander MRS J Forsyth (Elizabeth D Allen) . . . . Died at
                                            Philadelphia, PA Aug 20'95
Alexander MR & MRS Quentin (Elisabeth S Hadden)
  Un.Kt.Tv.Cv.Pk.Sar.Pa'41 . . of
  ☎ (216) 423-4763 . . "Eutrophia Farm" 2657 River Rd, Chagrin Falls,
  OH *44022*
  ☎ (561) 278-9345 . . 901 S Ocean Blvd, Delray Beach, FL *33483*
Alexander MR & MRS William B 5th (Sarajane P   ☎ (202) 234-3694
  Smith) Cvc.Me.Cry.Rv.Ll.StA.Pn.P'41 . . . . 1834 Kenyon St
  MR William B 6th—Cvc.StA.Rv.Ll.StLaw'91.   NW, Washington,
  GeoW'95 . . . . DC *20010-2619*
Alford MRS J Edwin (Mary-Louise Kittinger) St.G.
  ☎ (716) 885-7475 . . 33 Gates Circle, Buffalo, NY *14209*
Alger MISS Roxana S . . see H Robinson JR

Allen MR & MRS A Clinton 3d (Lawson Prince) B.Un.Ny.Hn.H.'67 . . . . ☎ (617) 449-3365
710 South St, Needham, MA 02192
   MISS Samantha L—at Harvard . . . .
   MISS Walker P—at Harvard . . . .
   MISS Lawson K . . . .

Allen MISS Fredericka L . . . . Died at Darien, CT Jan 5'96

Allnatt MISS Madeline Ruth (Matthew J) . . . . Born Dec 22'93

Allnatt MR & MRS Matthew J (Margaret Sculley) Cal'85.Ealing'84
   ☎ (310) 573-9250 . . 959 Fiske St, Pacific Palisades, CA 90272

Almy MRS George Blair (Potter—Seabury—Virginia E Shrigley) . . . . Died at Marblehead, MA Jan 7'96

Ambrus DR & MRS (DR) Julian L (Clara M Bayer) Zürich'49.Jef'55.St.Cos.G.Zürich'49. Jef'54 . . . ☎ (716) 883-8382
143 Windsor Av, Buffalo, NY 14209-1020
   MR Julian L JR—at 4328 Laclede Av, St Louis, MO 63108 . . . .
   MR Steven G—at Carrera 2, Torna 11-72, Apt 102, Bogotá, Colombia . . . .
   MR Charles T G . . . .

Ames MRS Alden JR (Jane H Campiglia) Tcy.Sfy.Cp.
   ☎ (415) 424-4341 . . 501 Portola Rd, Box 8024, Portola Valley, CA 94028

Ames MR Frederick L—Sm.Ub.Bost'86.Bab'92
   ☎ (508) 768-3222 . . 79 Western Av, Essex, MA 01929

Ames MRS R Gardner (Rebecca B Gardner) . . Married at Manchester, MA
   Campbell MR Samuel R (John P) . . . . Sep 23'95

Anderson MR & MRS David C (A Elizabeth Long) NCar'87.Campb'91.NCar'87
   ☎ (803) 748-1066 . . 120 S Shandon St, Columbia, SC 29205

Anderson MISS Eleanor A (Warren H) . . . . Married at Princeton, NJ
   Shanahan LT Daniel P—USN. (James F) . . . . Sep 30'95

Anderson MISS Elizabeth S . . see E L Meinfelder 2d

Andrews MRS Mark E (Lavone L Dickensheets) Rice'33.Rice'34.Ln.Ri.Fic.Fiy.Cly.
   ☎ (713) 522-8234 . . 2121 Kirby Dv, Apt 109, Houston, TX 77019

Andrews MRS T Hollingsworth 3d (Patricia Vauclain) . . . . Died at Princeton, NJ Sep 29'95

Angelo MRS Marjorie G (Marjorie T Gold) Dick'72.Ht. . . . . ☎ (908) 920-9668
186 Cartagena Dv, Brick, NJ 08723-7005
   MR Hunter B—Cw.Rv.Wt.Ht.StA.Fw. . . . .

Anikeeff MR Anthony H (Nicholas M) . . . . . . Married at Washington, DC
   Wu MISS Tung-lin (late Heuna-sen) . . . . Oct 21'95

Annibali MR & MRS Philip A (Mary-Louise Richmond) On.Wms'55 . . of
   ☎ (847) 234-4923 . . 1388 N Green Bay Rd, Lake Forest, IL 60045
   ☎ (561) 546-2356 . . Coquina, 112 N Beach Rd, Hobe Sound, FL 33455

Annibali MRS William (Guglielmina Decker) . . . . Died at Charleston, SC Oct 7'95

Anthon MR Donald W JR (Donald W) . . . . Married at Nashville, TN
   Williams MISS Melissa T (James A) . . . . Jly 22'95

Anwyl MISS Pandora H C . . see MRS A Sheffield

Apple MR & MRS Raymond Walter JR (Brown—Betsy G Pinckney) BMr'65.C.An.Pn.Cl'61.Denis'69.Knox'93 . . of
   ☎ (202) 333-6974 . . 1509—28 St NW, Washington, DC 20007
   ☎ (717) 642-5035 . . "Copper Top Farm" Orrtanna, PA 17353

Archer MR & MRS Pierce (Cynthia R Hill) Wit'74.Me.Rc.Colby'78
   ☎ (610) 293-7655 . . 750 Harrison Rd, Villanova, PA 19085

Archie MASTER Samuel Gray Ward (g—George Rublee 2d) . . . . Born Dec 28'95

Armstrong MR & MRS James M (Elizabeth M Hill) P'90.P'90
   431 Briarhill Lane NE, Atlanta, GA 30324

Armstrong MR & MRS Richard M JR (Susan T Dole) Ph.Pe.Me.StA.Ac.Ncd.Yn.Wes'60.Pa'62 . . . . . . ☎ (610) 696-2797
"Some Chance Farm" Box 633, West Chester, PA 19381-0633
   MISS Katrina A—Ws'93.Me.—at ☎ (303) 543-0166 . . 2750 Moorhead Av, Apt 208, Boulder, CO 80303 . . . .
   MR Richard M 3d—Me.Colby'85—at ☎ (303) 442-7160 . . 710—35 St, Boulder, CO 80303 . . . .

Armstrong MR & MRS Thomas N 3d (V Whitney Brewster) K.Ri.Fic.Cr'54 . . . . ☎ (212) 734-2688
36 E 72 St, New York, NY 10021
   MISS Amory A—Hlns'92—at 666 Greenwich St, New York, NY 10014 . . . .
   MR Thomas N 4th—at 306 E 71 St, New York, NY 10021 . . . .
   MR Whitney B—Y'87—at ☎ (215) 351-6312 336 Lombard St, Philadelphia, PA 19147 . . . . . .

Armstrong-Götz MRS Leila L M (Götz—Leila L M Armstrong) . . . Married at Phoenix, AZ
   Winssinger MR Reginald A H (Guy) . . . . Jun 19'93

Arnold COL (RET) & MRS Joseph C (Mary B Sethness) Wa.USA'64 . . . . ☎ (703) 356-3899
6500 Anna Maria Court, McLean, VA 22101
   MISS Mary S—LakeF'94 . . . .
   MR Joseph C JR . . . .
   JUNIORS MISS Emily E—at Madeira . . . .
   JUNIORS MR Michael B . . . .

Arrison CAPT & MRS James M 3d (Susan C Sheppard) Pa'65.An.Rv.USN'64 . . . . ☎ (703) 519-7656
118 Madison Place, Alexandria, VA 22314
   MISS Anne D—at U of Va . . . .
   LT James M 4th—USN'92—aboard USS Ingersoll, DD-990, Pearl Harbor, Honolulu, HI 96818 . . . .

Arthur MR & MRS Stuart G (Ellen L Tanenbaum) Pa'75.Cl'76
   ☎ (212) 772-2230 . . 301 E 78 St, Apt 11F, New York, NY 10021

Ashton MR & MRS David G JR (Dorothy M Wilson) Snc.Cw.Myf.Rv.Ncd.Pn.P'50.Cl'58
   ☎ (802) 867-4133 . . Box 737, West Rd, Dorset, VT 05251

Atherholt MASTER Kyle Thomas (g—MRS Charles C Harrison 4th) . . . Born at Bryn Mawr, PA Jly 9'95

Atkeson MISS Lindsay (g—Jonathan G Wells 3d) . . . . Born at Hartford, CT Aug 22'95

Atkins MR & MRS James H (Kathleen L Wright) Ark'65.Ark'54
   ☎ (501) 663-6075 . . 42 Edgehill Rd, Little Rock, AR 72207

Atterbury MISS Katherine Close (W W Atterbury 3d & E C Redfield) . . . . Born at West Palm Beach, FL Jan 24'96

Atterbury MR William W 3d (late William Wallace) . . . . Married at Palm Beach, FL
   Redfield MISS Elizabeth C (Cowles—Elizabeth C Redfield) . . Nov 11'95

Atterbury, William W 3d & Redfield, Elizabeth C (Cowles—Elizabeth C Redfield) RISD'79.BtP. NCar'69 . . . . ☎ (407) 848-4861
300 Queen Lane, Palm Beach, FL 33480
   JUNIORS MR Story A Cowles . . . .

Atterbury MR William Wallace . . . . Died at Palm City, FL Dec 14'95
Atwood MRS Philip Trowbridge (June D Beebe) Wa. . . . . ☎ (847) 251-9262
  MR James T—Pa'63—at 1408 Strand St, | 626 Warwick Rd,
  Manhattan Beach, CA 90266 . . . . | Kenilworth, IL 60043-1150
Atwood MR & MRS William C (Elizabeth R Baker) U'84.H'89.H'95.BostColl'84.Cl'90
  ☎ (617) 696-6674 . . 46 Brandon Rd, Milton, MA 02186
Aubry MR & MRS Jules W (Moon—Julia D Andrus) Sth'37.Cs. . .of
  ☎ (212) AT9-4667 . . 17 E 89 St, New York, NY 10128
  ☎ (203) 488-9623 . . 88 Notch Hill Rd, Apt 219, North Branford, CT 06471
Auchincloss MR Conrad McI . . see H D Sedgwick
Auchincloss MISS Hilary M . . see H D Sedgwick
Auclair MR & MRS Nicholas C (Alison C Virgin) ☎ (301) 870-4549
  OState'81.OState'80.Philip'88 . . . . | 9570 Ironsides Rd,
  JUNIORS MR Austin W . . . . | Nanjemoy, MD 20662
Augsbury MR & MRS Frank A JR (Howard-Smith—Foster—Imogen R Snowden) USMMA'45 . . of
  ☎ (315) 393-0434 . . 7713 State H'way 68, Ogdensburg, NY 13669
  ☎ (941) 262-1484 . . "Duck Cottage" 360 Bald Eagle Dv, Naples, FL 33942
Austin MISS Alexandra—V'91 . . see T Cohen
Austin MR & MRS James P 3d (Britt—A Tudor McBride) Ill'74.Coe'71.NIa'73 . . . . ☎ (207) 439-0593
  JUNIORS MISS Amanda L Walther . . . . | "Phyllis Cove" Lawrence Lane, Box 278, Kittery Point, ME 03905
Austin MASTER Michael Davis (James E) . . . . Born at Portsmouth, NH Jun 21'94
Austin MRS Oliver L JR (Rich—Edythe A Paisons) BMr'27.GeoW'64
  ☎ (202) 237-7048 . . 5420 Connecticut Av NW, Washington, DC 20015
Auten MR & MRS David C (Suzanne C Plowman) ☎ (215) 627-2535
  Denis'64.Pe.Ph.R.Fst.Ac.Sdg.Pa'60.Pa'63 . . . . . | 120 Delancey St,
  MISS Anne C—at 850 W Newport Av, Apt 3W, | Philadelphia, PA
  Chicago, IL 60657 . . . . | 19106
  MISS Meredith S . . . .
Aydelotte MR William O . . . . Died at Iowa City, IA Jan 17'96
Ayer MR James C JR (James C) . . . . Married at New York, NY
  Boody MISS Margaret L (late David A) . . . . Dec 9'95
Ayers MRS Aileen B (Van der Las—Aileen A Bruch) . . . . ☎ (954) 764-4124
  MR Joseph B 3d—at ☎ (216) 397-0706 | 333 Sunset Dv,
  2915 Fairfax Rd, Cleveland Heights, OH 44118 . | Apt 103, Ft Lauderdale, FL 33301
Ayres MR & MRS Richard E (Symington—Merribel S Levis) BMr'72.Dub'73.P'64.Y'69 . . . . ☎ (202) 966-4668
  MISS Alice E H—P'95—at Peizheng School, | 3040 Foxhall Rd
  2 Peizheng Rd, Dongshan, Guangzhou 510080, | NW, Washington,
  China . . . . | DC 20016
  JUNIORS MR Richard A—at Landon . . . .

B

Babcock MR & MRS Henry D JR (James—Erica Hohner) Y'62.Cl'70 . . . . | of ☎ (516)367-3268
  MISS K Chauncey—Y'94 . . . . | 48 Snake Hill Rd,
  MISS Laura S—at U of Colo Boulder . . . . | Cold Spring Harbor, NY 11724
  ☎ (307) 739-9230 755 N Bar Y Rd, Jackson, WY 83001
Babcock MR & MRS Orville Elias 3d (Judith I Jones) ☎ (860) 395-0137
  Col'60.On.LakeF'64 . . . . | 19 Otter Brook Dv,
  MISS Alison Ely—StLaw'93 . . . . | Old Saybrook, CT 06475-4313
Babcock MR & MRS William N (Victoria M Plimpton) Ws'78.Pqt.Ncd.H'78.Cl'80 . . . . | of ☎ (603)673-0100
  JUNIORS MR Charles N . . . . | 80 Mack Hill Rd, Amherst, NH 03031
  ☎ (203) 255-7974 1289 Burr St, Fairfield, CT 06430
Bacon MR Leonard Lee . . . . Died Nov 27'94
Badger MISS Elizabeth A . . . . Married at South Freeport, ME
  Quinby MR Thomas M . . . . Jly 17'93
Bahlman MISS Edith Walker (Baker DeC) . . . . Born at Cincinnati, OH Dec 17'95
Bahlman MISS Leah DeCamp (Baker DeC) . . . . Born at Cincinnati, OH Dec 17'95
Baines MISS Grace Ann (Robert A) . . . . Born at West Chester, PA Dec 27'95
Baines MR & MRS Robert A (Ann M Armstrong) Colby'88.Duke'90.Rm'88.Duke'89
  ☎ (610) 273-2868 . . 235 Hill Rd, Honey Brook, PA 19344
Baker MR Brinton E—Tufts'78.H'83
  ☎ (415) 345-9422 . . 1153 Foster City Blvd, Apt 4, Foster City, CA 94404
Baker MR David S JR . . . . Died at Greenwich, CT Feb 19'96
Baker MRS David S JR (Ethel Prosser)
  ☎ (203) TO9-5327 . . 32 French Rd, Greenwich, CT 06831
Baker MRS George P (Jones—Osher—Mary E Wyeth) . . . Died Sep 12'95
Baker MRS Harold W (Charlotte B Tindle) . . . . Died Oct 22'95
Baker MRS Ross W (Penelope Winslow) . . . . Died at Oyster Bay, NY Sep 11'95
Bakewell MISS Ann E (Henry P JR) . . . . Married at Irvington, NY
  Woodward MR Gordon H (John H) . . . . Dec 9'95
Balaguer MISS Katherine Evans (g—John Butterworth) . . Born Oct 31'95
Baldwin MR James French 3d (James F JR) . . . Married at East Chop, MA
  Reed MISS Katheryn M (late Timothy) . . . . Sep 23'95
Baldwin MR Richard 3d (Richard JR) . . . . Married at St Louis, MO
  Johnson MISS Deborah B (Robert C) . . . . Dec 31'95
Baldwin MR & MRS Richard 3d (Deborah B Johnson) Rv.P'90
  ☎ (314) 862-5554 . . 665 S Skinker Blvd, Apt 9T, St Louis, MO 63105
Ball MR & MRS Stephen F W (Elaine P Boschen) ☎ (603) 643-8227
  Skd'62.Rv.P'58 . . . . | 2 Algonquin Trail,
  MISS Sarah W—CtCol'93—at U of N Mex . . . . . | Etna, NH 03750
  JUNIORS MR Stephen F W JR—at St Andrew's . . .

Ball MR & MRS Thomas J (Turben—Catherine C Eppinger) V'59.Woos'75..of
   ☎ (216) 423-4578..Battles Rd, Gates Mills, OH *44040*
   ☎ (011-39-41) 522-4035..1677F Dorsoduro, Venice, Italy

Ballantine MR & MRS Andrew Van B (McChristian—D Dené A Binnié) Cw.Col'70.Rut'78
   ☎ (201) 786-5274.."Tor Moria Farm" 49 Ballantine Rd, Andover, NJ *07821*

Ballantine MASTER Ian Pratt (John H 2d) .... Born at Carmel, NY May 13'95

Ballantine MASTER Peter Wilgus (John H 2d) .... Born at Carmel, NY May 13'95

Ballantine MR Robert W .... Died at Tucson, AZ Sep 17'95

Ballard DR & MRS Ian M (Hoffman—Helen Clothier) Rose'79.M.Me.Laf'58.Temp'62 .....
   MR Ian M JR—Me.Bow'90.Va'95—at
   ☎ (215) 627-1733..622 S Hancock St, Apt 3, Philadelphia, PA *19147* ....
   ☎ (610) 688-2004 529 County Line Rd, Radnor, PA *19087*

Ballard MRS Martha M (Martha M Muzzey) ......
   MRS Wendy F R (Swindell—Gourd—Wendy F R Ballard) Cly.—at ☎ (561) 234-3493
   PO Box 3832, Vero Beach, FL *32964* ....
   ☎ (908) 974-9332 1912C Old Mill Rd, Spring Lake, NJ *07762*

Ballentine MRS Michael (Stettinius—Reynolds—Mary Ballou Handy) Swb'59 ....
   MISS Mary Stuart Stettinius—Va'89—at
   ☎ (212) 254-9047..56 W 12 St, Apt 4, New York, NY *10011* ....
   MR Joseph Stettinius JR—at
   ☎ (540) 364-3212..PO Box 1712, Middleburg, VA *22117* ....
   MR Edward R Stettinius—Va'84—Box 278, Upperville, VA *22176* ....
   MR R Roland Reynolds—P'93—at
   ☎ (212) 799-8307..11 W 69 St, Apt 7A, New York, NY *10023* ....
   ☎ (804) 288-1273 6317 Three Chopt Rd, Richmond, VA *23226*

Balliet MASTER William Hill (g—Michael Balliet) ...... Born Jan 25'96

Ballou MR & MRS F Remington (Frothingham—Priscilla W West) Y'50
   ☎ (401) 272-4368..25 John St, Providence, RI *02906*

Bancroft MISS Elizabeth S (William W) ..... Married at Skurup, Sweden
   Pettersson MR Dan A .... Jun 10'95

Bandler MISS Elise de Struvé
   ☎ (415) 381-1065..435 E Blithdale Av, Mill Valley, CA *94941*

Bandler MR & MRS Richard (Eleanor S Trenholm) ..
   MISS Tatiana S—at ☎ (305) 868-9230
   9133 Collins Av, Surfside, FL *33154* ....
   ☎ (305) 538-1669 5266 Fisher Island Dv, Fisher Island, FL *33109*

Banta MR & MRS Philip L (Pei—Susan G Johnson) GeoW'76.S.H'72..of
   ☎ (510) 654-3255..6050 Hollis St, Emeryville, CA *94608*
   ☎ (415) 460-0965.."Sleepy Hollow" San Anselmo, CA *94960*

Barbour MRS Warren (F Deborah Platt) .... Died at Bronxville, NY Nov 29'95

Barclay MR & MRS Rutgers (di Carpegna—Leslie Boocock) K.Y'57 ....
   MISS Allegra di Carpegna—at London, England ....
   MR Guelfo di Carpegna—at
   ☎ (212) 541-5319..35 W 54 St, New York, NY *10019*..........................
   MR Rufo di Carpegna—at ☎ (505) 982-8337 616 Washington Av, Santa Fe, NM *87501* ...
   ☎ (505) 982-1000 Rabbit Junction, Rte 9, Box 66, Santa Fe, NM *87505*

Barker MISS Bridget Lauren (John JR) .... Born Feb 2'95

Barker MR & MRS John JR (Maureen E Kelly) Sth'78.ColC'80
   ☎ (303) 388-4614..440 Eudora St, Denver, CO *80220*

Barlerin MISS Caroline P—V'95..see MRS P M Patterson

Barlow MR & MRS Joel (Eleanor Livingston Poe) Cvc.Mt.Ds.Ncd.Alma'29.GeoW'35 ....
   MISS Eleanor Poe—Sth'61—at "Lands Away" HC 68, Box 418, Friendship, ME *04547* ......
   ☎ (561) 272-8211 Harbours Edge 369, 401 E Linton Blvd, Delray Beach, FL *33483*

Barrell MR Nathaniel A .... Died at Schroon Lake, NY Aug 28'95

Barrett MR C Francis
   3136 Victoria Av, Cincinnati, OH *45208*

Barriger MR & MRS John W 5th (Marianne C Fox)
   ☎ (602) 905-7230..Briarwood Place, 6265 N 73 Way, Scottsdale, AZ *85253*

Barron MR & MRS Hugh D (Sarah M Moore) Cal'88.Vt'86
   ☎ (415) 332-5212..5 Josephine St, Apt 3, Sausalito, CA *94965*

Barrows MISS Lily Carver (William D) .... Born at Newburyport, MA Jun 27'95

Barrows MR & MRS Mercer B (Connolly—Joy T Price) Pa'63.Gm.Me.Rc.Ac.Pa'51 ....
   MISS L Nichols
   MR William K—at 1402 E Orange St, Tempe, AZ *85281*..........................
   MR Joseph C Connolly—Dick'95—at
   ☎ (717) 241-5142..140 W Louther St, Apt 3, Carlisle, PA *17013* ....
   ☎ (610) 353-1530 825 Briarwood Rd, Newtown Square, PA *19073*

Bartholet MRS E Ives (Elizabeth Ives) .... Died Oct 26'95

Bartlett DR & MRS Frederick H 3d (Melanie W Roden) MtH'79.Wms'77.Jef'81
   2200 Inverness Lane, Huntingdon Valley, PA *19006*

Bartlett MASTER Samuel Kinnicutt (Henry P) .... Born at Cambridge, MA Jly 20'95

Bartol MR John H 3d (John H JR) .... Married at Spring Lake, NJ
   Gilmore MISS Katherine L .... Oct 14'95

Bartolec MR & MRS Thomas A (Corinne DeL Morris) Md'61.Md'64
   ☎ (561) 694-3044..8164 Quail Meadow Trace, West Palm Beach, FL *33412*

Barton MR Reginald McCarroll JR—David'73.NCar'77
   ☎ (910) 484-0771..119 Hillside Av, Fayetteville, NC *28301*

Bartow MR & MRS Philip K JR (Madeleine R Cresap) Csh.Wms'70..........................
   MISS Madeleine C—at Williams ....
   JUNIORS MR Philip K 3d—at Westminster ......
   ☎ (516) 271-4762 101 Woodchuck Hollow Rd, Cold Spring Harbor, NY *11724*

Bartram MR & MRS Brent E (Glenny L Dunlop) .. of
☎ (606) 441-5208 .. 32 Brigadier Court, Wilder, KY *41076*
☎ (502) 451-3795 .. 206 Flanders Court, Apt 5, Louisville, KY *40218*
Bartram MASTER Carter Henry (Brent E) .... Born at Louisville, KY Sep 28'95
Baskett MR & MRS Charles E (von Raab—Mary R Lambert) Un.
MISS Alexandra L von Raab—Denis'95—at ☎ (415) 474-5989 .. 2733 Bush St, San Francisco, CA *94115* .... of ☎ (212)755-2783 300 E 57 St, New York, NY *10022*
☎ (860) 434-8261 66 Hedlund Rd, East Haddam, CT *06423*
Bass MRS Edith McB (Edith McBride) V'54 ......
MISS Claire McB—Ken'79—at ☎ (818) 980-5222 10741 Camarillo St, Apt 111, North Hollywood, CA *91602* ....
MR Jack M 3d—Tul'93—at ☎ (615) 385-5606 714 Clearview Av, Nashville, TN *37205* ......
☎ (615) 383-7555 202 Moultrie Park, Nashville, TN *37205*
Bassett MR & MRS John W (Lillian McC Friend) Sth'78.Stan'77.Hast'80
☎ (510) 655-0422 .. 148 Ronada Av, Piedmont, CA *94611*
Bastedo MRS Philip (Helen C Wilmerding) Csn. ....
MISS Cecily—at ☎ (603) 563-7036 PO Box 1051, Dublin, NH *03444* ....
MR Christopher K—at ☎ (212) 722-3202 1641 Third Av, Apt 15JE, New York, NY *10128*
☎ (603) 924-2112 144 River Mead, Peterborough, NH *03458*
Bates MRS Susan Hastings—Stan'78.Myf.
☎ (212) 879-2313 .. 360 E 72 St, Apt B505, New York, NY *10021*
Baumann MR & MRS Richard M (Katharine C Kinsolving) V'82.P'81
7A Courtfield Gardens, London SW5 0PA, England
Baxter MISS Edith P (Cope—Edith P Baxter) Wheat'65.Ch'66 ....
MR Jonathan B Cope—at Princeton ....
☎ (617) 271-1571 7 Hawthorne Lane, Bedford, MA *01730*
Bayne MASTER Jonathan Golden (David F) .... Born at New York, NY Oct 6'95
Beale MRS Edward F (Margaret Y Allen) .... Died Sep 14'93
Beard MR & MRS Alexander R (Margaret A Over) StLaw'52.Va'50 ....
MISS Mary Stuart—SCar'81.SCar'87—at ☎ (404) 365-8729 .. 55 Pharr Rd NW, Apt 104B, Atlanta, GA *30305* ....
MR Alexander R JR—Penn'81.Penn'83—at ☎ (303) 442-6099 .. 6148 Red Hill Rd, Boulder, CO *80302* ....
☎ (610) 688-7319 427 Conestoga Rd, St Davids, PA *19087-4811*
Beck MISS Virginia C
☎ (215) 545-7185 .. 1228 Spruce St, Apt 709, Philadelphia, PA *19107*
Becker MASTER Alexander de Marneffe (Terrence C) .... Born at San Francisco, CA Feb 24'96
Becker MRS E Lovell (Gernerd—Pontius—M Eleanor Holden) Ri.Bcs.
☎ (617) 326-6144 .. 10 Longwood Dv, Apt 448, Westwood, MA *02090-1123*
Beckett MR & MRS William J (Juliet M Thomas) SFr'92 ....
MISS Heather E—at Lawrence U..............
☎ (415) 494-6922 4189 Baker Av, Palo Alto, CA *94306*
Beckner MRS Bruce A (Mary F Brawner) .... Died at Annapolis, MD Feb 4'95

Bedford MR & MRS Erskine L (Benitz—Nancy L Gerry) Cr'55..............
MISS Cynthia L Benitz—Box 640, Upperville, VA *22176*..............
MR Bryan M Benitz—at 2 Sloan Court E, London SW3 4TF, England ....
☎ (540) 253-5080 "Old Whitewood" 3760 Whitewood Rd, The Plains, VA *22171*
Behn MR William C ....
MR William S ....
MRS Aphra (Lesoeur—Aphra Behn) ....
MR & MRS Franck Le Pelletier (Monica Behn) .. MR absent ....
☎ (305) 661-6946 746 Benevento Av, Coral Gables, FL *33146*
Belgaumi MISS Salena Harriet (g—Jonathan G Wells 3d) .... Born at Philadelphia, PA May 14'95
Belin MRS Peter (Mary E D Cootes) .... Died at Washington, DC Jan 10'96
Belknap MR & MRS Robert E 3d (Mary J Sloan) StFran'95.Chr.Rby.Ne.Y.Va'61 ....
MISS Elizabeth T—F&M'91—at 202 Quarry Rd, Stamford, CT *06903*..............
MISS Berkeley S—Y'92—at 60 E 8 St, Apt 5F, New York, NY *10003* ....
MISS Mary C—P'92—at 10 Jones St, Apt 4H, New York, NY *10010* ....
of 128 Willow St, Brooklyn, NY *11201* ☎ (441) 292-3119 6 Robin Hood Dv, Pembroke HM 13, Bermuda
Bell MISS Barbara C (Bryan) .... Married at New Orleans, LA
Barrett MR John H .... May 27'95
Bell MRS Harry E (Caroline P Matthews) .... Died at Tucson, AZ Sep 11'95
Bell MR & MRS James B (Miriam S Reay) Minn'57.Minn'55.Ox'64 ....
MISS Vanessa M S—at 165 Griggs Dv, Princeton, NJ *08540* ....
MR James B JR ....
MR Elliott M ....
☎ (609) 924-2125 689 Mercer Rd, Princeton, NJ *08540*
Bellingrath MR & MRS Ferdinand McM (Frances H Martin) Hendrix'51.Ark'50
☎ (501) 534-8817 .. 30 Longmeadow St, Pine Bluff, AR *71603*
Bellis MISS Alexandra (G Gordon) .... Married at San Francisco, CA
Kromelow MR Justin M (Marc) .... Dec 12'95
Belt MISS Elizabeth H (John H K) .... Married at Glen Cove, NY
McGregor MR William E (W Ellsworth) .... Oct 7'95
Benedict MISS Elizabeth Helen (William J JR) .... Born Mch 28'95
Benenson MR & MRS Marcius K (Letizia Pitigliani) CUNY'51.Cl'56 ....
MISS Daniela ....
MR Alexander ....
of ☎ (212)799-7862 585 West End Av, New York, NY *10024-1715* ☎ (011-39-6) 322-7406 via Antonio Allegri 13, 00196 Rome, Italy
Benét MRS Thomas C (Joan Gregory) .... Died at San Francisco, CA Jan 28'96
Benitz MR Bryan M .. see E L Bedford
Benitz MISS Cynthia L .. see E L Bedford
Benkhart MRS Bruce S (Carlyne R Rosati) RISD'75.Wes'79
☎ (401) 847-8104 .. "Daybreak" Atlantic Av, Newport, RI *02840*

Benkhart MR Bruce S—Cal'77
☎ (401) 849-1773 . . 455 Tuckerman Av, Middletown, RI *02842*

Bennett MR Alexander J R—Vt'91 . . see MRS J F Bruno JR

Bennett MISS Christina deT . . see MRS J F Bruno JR

Benoit MR Constant A JR . . . . Died at
West Palm Beach, FL May 24'95

Bentley MRS Robert A L (Charlotte M Fowler)
Sth'30.Plg.StA.Snc.Dar.Ne.StJ.
☎ (212) 254-4199 . . 390 First Av, New York, NY *10010*

Berger MR & MRS John Torrey JR (H Lee Thompson) Wash'61.Nd.Wash'63 . . . .
MISS Helen E—Swb'88. . . . .
DR John T 3d—Va'85.Wash'89 . . . .
☎ (314) 579-9227
1257 Takara Court,
Town & Country,
MO *63131*

Bergmann MASTER George Bayard (Michael R) . . . . Born at
Reston, VA Feb 21'96

Berkowitz MASTER Hayward Manice (Mortimer 3d) . . . . Born at
New York, NY Feb 14'96

Berkowitz MASTER Thomas Goelet (Mortimer 3d) . . . . Born at
New York, NY Feb 14'96

Bermingham, David C & Searle, Marion S (Chandler—Marion S Searle) ColC'77.On. Ithaca'77 . . . .
JUNIORS MR William K Chandler . . . .
☎ (847) 295-9245
209 N Green Bay
Rd, Lake Forest, IL
60045

Bernann MR Bruce K—Colg'61
☎ (203) 869-3774 . . 20 Church St, Greenwich, CT *06830*

Bernard MR & MRS Matthew L (Hilary M Lea) Ws'82.Cl'88.CtCol'83.Cl'88
☎ (203) 869-2260 . . Belle Haven, 83 Meadow Wood Dv, Greenwich,
CT *06830*

Bernhard MISS Adèle Catlin (Jason Ruggles) . . . . Born at
New York, NY Sep 10'95

Bernhard MR & MRS Jason Ruggles (Ashley C Briggs)
Pa'88.Rc.Pa'88.Pa'93
☎ (718) 596-9486 . . 1 Pierrepont St, Brooklyn, NY *11201*

Bertish MISS Jane M . . see MRS W T Stewart JR

Bertish MISS Suzanne C . . see MRS W T Stewart JR

Betancourt MR Raul . . . . Died at
Philadelphia, PA Oct 16'95

Bethea MRS Osborne JR (Martha H Mann) CtCol'64
MISS Martha A . . . .
☎ (919) 408-8025
35 Bloomsbury
Court, Chapel Hill,
NC *27514*

Bethea MR Osborne JR—David'63 . . . .
MISS Laura E . . . .
☎ (704) 896-2863
PO Box 1391,
Davidson, NC *28036*

Bethell MRS E Knode (M Ellen Knode) . . . .
MR Hugh A H—at 9307 SW 1 St, Plantation, FL *33324* . . . .
2895 Kalakaua Av,
Apt 303, Honolulu,
HI *96815*

Beuttell MRS Richard C (Isabelle P Manger)
☎ (561) 567-0586 . . PO Box 2367, Vero Beach, FL *32961*

Beyer MR Edward M . . . . Died at
New York, NY Dec 25'95

Bicket MR & MRS Robert M (Katherine P Hedger) ⚓
☎ (011-44-1983) 281-388 . . 1 Union Rd, Cowes, Isle of Wight
PO34 7TW, England

Biddle MR Ernest L 3d (Ernest L JR) . . . . Married at Ossetawgua, NY
Heely MISS Hilary (George) . . . . Sep 30'95

Biddle MR & MRS Nicholas JR (Joan A Moore) Swb'64.Csh.H'63 . . . .
MISS Virginia M—Nu'91—at ☎ (213) 938-2119 339 S Detroit St, Apt 3, Los Angeles, CA *90036*
MISS Barbara MacL—H'93—at
☎ (212) 633-9640 . . 394 West St, Apt 4, New York, NY *10014*
MISS Katherine M—H'93—at ☎ (212) 734-4096 193 Bleecker St, Apt 10, New York, NY *10012* .
☎ (804) 979-1117
Ivy Farm,
2040 Foal Lane,
Charlottesville, VA
22901

Biddle MR & MRS Willing L (Catherine C Urstadt) Colby'85.Ken'83
☎ (914) 234-7585 . . 816 S Bedford Rd, Bedford, NY *10506*

Bielenstein MR & MRS Hans (Gabrielle C Maupin) Un.StA.Lm.Ncd.Dc.Ds.Ht.Stock'54 . . . .
MISS Danielle E M—at ☎ (703) 845-1963
2425 S Walter Reed Dv, Arlington, VA *22206* .
MISS Andrea J G—at ☎ (718) 802-1180
70 Remsen St, Brooklyn, NY *11201* . . . .
☎ (212) 663-3479
21 Claremont Av,
New York, NY
10027

Bigelow DR & MRS Bradley (Michelle Cousturier) H'44 . . . .
MISS Claire E—at ☎ (212) 243-0630
77 Christopher St, New York, NY *10014* . . . . .
445 E 84 St,
New York, NY
10028

Biggs MISS Melissa E (Jeremy H) . . . . Married at New York, NY
Bradley MR Michael T (E Michael) . . . . Nov 4'95

Billings MR Charles A JR—Bost'89.CarnM'94
☎ (303) 413-0148 . . 3845C Northbrook Dv, Boulder, CO *80304*

Bilodeau MR & MRS Harrison Otis C (Alessia Ortolani) Hampshire'90.Hampshire'91
1843 Biltmore St NW, Washington, DC *20009*

Binger MRS Walter (Beatrice Sorchan) . . . . Died at
New York, NY Dec 27'95

Bingham MRS Charles T (Kathleen W Howell) . . . . Died at
Essex, CT Feb 22'96

Bingham MR J Reid—Mlsps'67. . . . .
MR Joseph R JR. . . . .
JUNIORS MR Robert L . . . .
☎ (305) 444-8141
915 Palermo Av,
Apt 207,
Coral Gables, FL
33134

Bingham MR & MRS Robert K (Anne Fairfax Carr) Hb.Y'65.Bost'68 . . . .
MR Robert K JR—Wes'93—at ☎ (212) 260-8346 270 E 10 St, Apt 4B, New York, NY *10009* . . .
☎ (860) 889-4381
42 Round Hill Rd,
Salem, CT *06420*

Birmingham MR & MRS John M (Littell—Mary Lee Monroe) Roch'50.FlaAtl'66.Rv.Sar.Ht.Ofp.Dar. Dc.Cda.Dcw.Temp'49 . . . .
MISS Georgia A—Ht.Dar.Dcw.—at N Ariz U . . .
MR John Monroe—Ht.Sar.Rv.—at
☎ (303) 202-1802 . . 5242 W Ninth Av, Lakewood, CO *80214* . . . .
☎ (520) 527-0369
5025 E Hawthorne
Dv, Flagstaff, AZ
86004-7376

Bishop MR Brooks O
☎ (407) 629-7694 . . 1048 N Kentucky Av, Winter Park, FL *32789*

Bishop MR & MRS Thomas B JR (Martha C Smith) Va'69 . . . .
MISS Maria R—at Hollins . . . .
MISS Marianna R . . . .
☎ (804) 295-6568
The Barracks,
518 Barracks Farm
Rd, Charlottesville,
VA *22901*

Bishop MRS Thomas Benton (Dorothea Roeding) Tcy.
☎ (408) 626-4879 . . Carmel Valley Manor, 8545 Carmel Valley Rd, Carmel, CA *93923*

Bishop MISS Wilder O (Warner B) . . . . Married at Palm Beach, FL
Regalbuto MR Jason R (late Robert R) . . . . Feb 24'96

Bishopric MR Allison—Dyc.Sa.Y.'23
PO Box BQ, Amagansett, NY *11930*

Black MR Andrew A . . see A W Perry

Black MISS Heather S . . see A W Perry

Black MR Luther F (Robert L JR) . . . . Married at Seattle, WA
Wright MISS Catherine C (Winslow W) . . . . Oct 7'95

Blackmun MR JUSTICE & MRS Harry A (Dorothy E Clark)
1—1 St NE, Washington, DC *20543*

Blackwell MRS Nigel S (Eliza P Mauran) . . . . Died at
Oxford, England Sep 23'95

Blackwell MR Nigel S—Ox'69
☎ (011-44-1367) 870-659 . . "Low Dow" Lake House, Pusey, nr Faringdon, Oxfordshire SN3 8QB, England

Blacutt MR & MRS Sergio X (Gail L Sawyer) Ariz'87.SEMoSt'85
Camino del Pregonero 2799, Lo Barnechea, Santiago, Chile

Blain MR Daniel JR (late Daniel) . . . . Married at
Chester, Nova Scotia, Canada
Forbes MISS Sheila . . . . Jan 6'96

Blain MR P Travis (Daniel JR) . . . . Married at Jupiter, FL
Leinweber MISS Kristen . . . . Nov 19'94

Blain MISS Stacy W (Daniel JR) . . . . Married at Jupiter, FL
Mraz MR Jason . . . . Nov 11'95

Blair MR & MRS Watson K (Wallace—Ford—Valerie M Hollmann) Rcn.K.Cysl.Y'49
☎ (561) 546-1241 . . PO Box 218, Hobe Sound, FL *33475*

Blair MR & MRS William D JR (Jane F Coleman) Cvc.Mt.P'48.AmU'74
☎ (202) 362-5966 . . 5006 Warren St NW, Washington, DC *20016*

Blair MR Wolcott R—Cy.Ne'79. . . . . | ☎ (314) 991-8755
MISS Aloyse M . . . . | 9119 Clayton Rd,
| St Louis, MO *63124*

Blanc MRS Jose M (Elizabeth Hunt) Hlns'83
☎ (011-44-171) 221-3777 . . 45 Matlock Court, Kensington Park Rd, London W11 3BS, England

Blanc MR Jose M—Hn.Madrid'78.Madrid'79.H'85
☎ (011-44-171) 371-1937 . . 72 Elsham Rd, Apt 1, London W14, England

Blanchard MR & MRS James A 2d (June Peterson) Myf.Cw.Ofp.Rv.Pa'33
Ocean View Tower 4C, 7601 N Ocean Blvd, Myrtle Beach, SC *29572*

Bland MR & MRS Michael G (Laura S Miller) Hlns'87.Pc.Va'87
☎ (804) 784-5804 . . 302 Hill Point Rd, Richmond, VA *23233*

Blau MR & MRS Andrew McD (Leslie F Hodges) Denis'85.Cly.Denis'85
☎ (212) 644-9501 . . 417 Park Av, Apt 10E, New York, NY *10022*

Blevins MR (DR) Pengwynne Potter (Pengwynne E C Potter) BMr'64
☎ (847) 864-2466 . . 1320 Mulford St, Evanston, IL *60202*

Bliss MRS Cornelius N (Haskins—Mary Lovering) . . . . Died at
Kennett Square, PA Dec 15'95

Blodget MISS Alexandra K—Colby'94 . . see T P Briney

Blossom MRS Dudley B (Henrietta F Clark) . . . . Died at
Greenwich, CT Oct 24'95

Blow MR John M—Hob'62
☎ (954) 491-1491 . . 3200 Port Royale Dv N, Apt 1506, Ft Lauderdale, FL *33308-7806*

Blue MRS E Stuart (Jackson—Economakis—E | ☎ (202) 298-5942
Stuart Blue) Cvc.Dc.Ncd. . . . . | 2801 New Mexico
 MISS Elizabeth L Jackson—RISD'90 . . . . . . | Av NW,
 MR Richard L Jackson JR—ColC'90 . . . . | Washington, DC
 | *20007*

Blundon MR & MRS Carroll M (Felicity H Sargent) Pa'75.Ny.Csn.Ariz'72
☎ (540) 672-0585 . . "Sunnybrook Farm" Box 54, Somerset, VA *22972*

Boardman MRS Gerard (Eleanor R Davis) . . . . Died at
New York, NY Dec 25'95

Bockmann MISS Jill O—Bow'89 . . see R G Smith

Bockmann MR Nathaniel V . . see R G Smith

Bodine MISS Marian T (late Samuel T) . . . . Married at
Upper Saranac Lake, NY
Tomaino MR Peter R (Peter R) . . . . Aug 5'95

Bodman MR & MRS Taylor S (April A Ward) Sm.P'83
☎ (617) 259-1823 . . 75 Todd Pond Rd, Lincoln, MA *01773-3836*

Boland MRS M Gillette (Hubbard—Myra H Gillette) . . . . Died Jan 22'96

Bole MRS Joseph K (Bole—Bidle—Bonnell—Emily M King) . . . . . . Died
Jly 22'95

Bolt MR Eugene A JR—Fi.Rc.Wt.Rv.Pa'88.Pa'92
☎ (215) 735-9414 . . 2008 Spruce St, Philadelphia, PA *19103*

Bolton MR & MRS Earle W 3d (Katharine G Dall) | ☎ (803) 838-4242
Mid'55 . . . . | "Yard Farm"
 MISS Susanna B . . . . | PO Box 2442,
 MR Timothy W . . . . | Beaufort, SC *29901*
 MR Samuel H . . . . |

Bolton MR & MRS John Wood (Nancy J Van Zandt) | ☎ (804) 979-4229
Hlns'61.Y'57 . . . . | 2267 Garth Rd,
 MISS Catherine C—Hlns'92 . . . . | Charlottesville, VA
 MR Richard K Van Z—Va'88.Madrid'89.DU'92 | *22901*

Bolton MR & MRS John Wood JR (Cynthia H Lockhart) Lynch'88.Ct.Cw.Rr.Pg.Lynch'88
☎ (703) 917-9228 . . 6325 Kellogg Dv, McLean, VA *22101*

Bomeisler MASTER Trey Kniffin (Douglass T) . . . . Born at
Stuart, FL Sep 28'95

Bonbright MRS Eleanor L (Eleanor Van Rensselaer Lipson) . . . . Married at
New Canaan, CT
Naess MR Michael R . . . . Sep 23'95

Bond MR & MRS Langhorne McC (Enriqueta P | ☎ (919) 545-0125
Carter) Ws'61.Mt.Cvc.Va'59 . . . . | 1066 Fearrington
 MISS Prescott McC—at Wofford . . . . | Post, 27 E Madison,
 MR Langhorne C . . . . | Pittsboro, NC *27312*

Boney MR & MRS Leslie N JR (Lillian M Bellamy) NCarSt'40
☎ (910) 763-6013 . . 2305 Gillette Dv, Wilmington, NC *28403*

Boring MISS Brooke Noelle (Douglas D) . . . . Born Dec 19'95

Boring MASTER Cody Jonathan Douglas (Douglas D) . . . . . Born Feb 4'94

Boring MR & MRS Dix (Marilyn Moore) Cal'56.Bhm.Fr.Cal'54
☎ (415) 922-0582 . . 2519 Broadway St, San Francisco, CA *94115*

Boring MR & MRS Douglas D (Judy A Rogers) Cal'83
☎ (916) 791-5395 . . 5980 Reba Dv, Granite Bay, CA *95746*

Borst MISS Kathryn Reilly (gg—MRS Nelson B Sackett) . . . . Born at
New York, NY Aug 2'94

Borst MASTER Kyle Noble Leonard (gg—MRS Nelson B Sackett) . . . . Born
at Englewood, NJ Apr 7'95

Bos MR & MRS Gerard A (Harriet W Pierpoint) ☎ (704) 442-9848
NCar'73.WashColl'73.Tul'76 . . . . 3051 Ferncliff Rd,
JUNIORS MISS Abigail S . . . . Charlotte, NC *28211*
JUNIORS MR Gerard P . . . .

Boss DR & MRS Jack F 3d (Grace P Hammond)
NH'74.PTheo'85.Hawaii'89.Cly.Cda.OState'79. OState'81.Y'91
"Evergreen Vista" 2520 Hayes St, Eugene, OR *97405*

Boss MASTER Timothy Palmer (Jack F 3d) . . . . Born at
Eugene, OR Nov 2'95

Bowditch MR & MRS James L (Felicity J Sexton) ☎ (215) 247-3904
Tvb.Y'61 . . . . 712 St Andrew's
MR Matthew S—at 200 South Av, Weston, MA Rd, Philadelphia, PA
02193 . . . . *19118*
MR Andrew R—at ☎ (617) 964-4789
75 Hunnewell Av, Newton Corner, MA *02158* .

Bowditch MR & MRS Nathaniel R (Margaret S ☎ (215) 248-0753
Parsons) V'56.Temp'78.Ph.Cs.Cr'55.Stan'59 . . . 5 E Hampton Rd,
MR William P—Roch'89.Mich'93—at Philadelphia, PA
1400 Worcester Rd, Apt 7204, Framingham, MA *19118*
01701 . . . .

Bowditch MISS (DR) P Lowell (late Richard L JR) . . . . Married at
Eugene, OR
Sibley MR Andrew B (Clayton) . . . . Sep 1'95

Bowen MISS Blair A (John de K 3d) . . . . Married at Ivy, VA
Bedell MR Kevin B . . . . Nov 11'95

Bowers MRS Cynthia S-H (Sinclair—Place— ☎ (212) 288-2860
Cynthia Smith-Hutton) . . . . 145 E 74 St,
MISS Sabrina C Place—Skd'89—at New York, NY
330 E 54 St, New York, NY *10022* *10021*

Bowers MRS Frances C (Grand-Jean—Frances C ☎ (847) 234-3057
Bowers) . . . . 211 N Maple Court,
MISS Laura R Grand-Jean . . . . Lake Forest, IL
60045

Bowers MR & MRS J Ros JR (Deborah E Rogers) Wash'88.Va'87.NCar'93
755 Boylston St, Apt 402, Boston, MA *02116*

Bowles MR J Laing JR (John L) . . . . Married at Washington, DC
Galvan MISS Maria C (Juan R) . . . . Nov 18'95

Bowron MR Paul J JR
2139 Avenida De La Playa, La Jolla, CA *92037*

Boyce MASTER Roger Fleming Hagerty (John C G JR) . . . . Born at
Baltimore, MD Aug 7'95

Boyd MR & MRS A Shapleigh 3d (Jennifer H Dodge) ☎ (941) 485-7530
So'62 . . . . 840 The Esplanade,
MISS Jennifer D—So'88 . . . . Apt 602, Venice, FL
34285

Boyd MR & MRS A Shapleigh 4th (Elizabeth L Garcia)
So'85.So'85.MidTennSt'87
☎ (615) 598-2800 . . 735 University Av, Sewanee, TN *37383-1000*

Boyd MR Allen R—P'55.JHop'60
☎ (941) 779-2122 . . 2101 Bay Dv N, PO Box 117, Bradenton Beach,
FL *34217*

Boyd MR Andrew C—NH'91
☎ (617) 859-7257 . . 27 Bay State Rd, Apt 6, Boston, MA *02115*

Boyd MISS Emma Richards (Robert S) . . . . Born at
London, England Nov 8'95

Boyd MR Ingram F JR . . . . Died at
Clayton, MO Feb 8'96

Boyd MASTER James Hallam 4th (J Hallam 3d) . . . . Born at
Memphis, TN Feb 1'96

Boyd MRS K Busselle (Katherine Scott Busselle) . . . . . . name changed to
Busselle

Boyd MISS Katherine Wheeler (g—MISS Katherine Scott Busselle) . . Born
at West Falmouth, MA Feb 15'95

Boyd MISS Nancy N (Crosby N JR) . . . . Married at Grosse Pointe, MI
Clark MR Charles R . . . . Jly 8'95

Boyd MR & MRS Robert S (Katherine D Royes) Wes'87.Mid'83
☎ (011-44-181) 747-3601 . . 146 Park Rd, Chiswick, London W4 3HP,
England

Boyden MRS W Lincoln 3d (Nancy Cummings) . . . . Died at
Belmont, MA Aug 16'95

Boyden MR W Lincoln 3d—Tv.H'53 . . . . | ☎ (617) 484-4091
MISS Ruth E—at ☎ (617) 893-5572 | 24 Oak St,
111 Woerd Av, Waltham, MA *02154* . . . . | Belmont, MA *02178*
MR Geoffrey L—at 52 Foster St, Cambridge, MA
02138 . . . .

Boykin MASTER Coulter Stone (Robert I M) . . . . Born Jun 12'95

Boykin MR & MRS Robert I M (Marcia Fail) . . . . | ☎ (970) 925-3389
JUNIORS MR Robert I M JR . . . . | 926 Willoughby
Way, Aspen, CO
81612

Boykin MR Samuel M JR—Ala'84
☎ (404) 355-4354 . . 2265 Riada Dv NW, Atlanta, GA *30305*

Boyse MR & MRS Matthew G (Eleanore H Kuhn)
Tul'79.JHop'85.Hav'79.Cl'85
☎ (011-48-2) 642-1990 . . American Embassy, Warsaw, Poland,
Dept of State, Washington, DC *20521-5010*

Bozarth MR & MRS Robert S (Marsha Ketcham) | ☎ (804) 288-3695
Swb'67.Va'67.Va'75 . . . . | 1103 E Durwood
MR Howard A—Va'93—at ☎ (703) 892-1689 | Crescent, Richmond,
1111 Army-Navy Dv, Arlington, VA *22202* . . . . | VA *23229*
JUNIORS MR Robert B . . . .

Bozesky MASTER Edmund Philip (g—MRS Melissa H Chamberlain) . . . Born
at St Louis, MO Feb 6'94

Bradbury MR Charles R . . . . Died at
Lexington, KY May 21'95

Bradbury MRS Charles R (Charlotte M Lyon)
☎ (606) 266-9141 . . 3625 Humphrey Lane, Lexington, KY *40502-3603*

Bradford MISS Eleanor Howe (g—MRS Le Baron Turner) . . . . . . Born at
Walnut Creek, CA Oct 26'94

Bradford MISS Madeleine Jackson (Robert W) . . . . Born at
Ann Arbor, MI Apr 7'95

Bradford MISS Marion R (Cooper—Marion R Bradford) . . . . . Married at
Norton Shores, MI
Battreall MR Marc A (Wilson D JR) . . . . Dec 16'95

Bradley MR Michael T (E Michael) . . . . Married at New York, NY
Biggs MISS Melissa E (Jeremy H) . . . . Nov 4'95

Bradley MR & MRS Michael T (Melissa E Biggs)
☎ (212) 628-3790 . . 200 E 71 St, New York, NY *10021*

Bradley MR & MRS Montgomery S (Joanne Freytag)
L&C'55.Mt.Sl.Hn.H'40 . . of
☎ (301) 229-5161 . . 4974 Sentinel Dv, Bethesda, MD *20816*
1919 Gulf Shore Blvd N, Naples, FL *33940*

Brady MISS Anna E C (William J JR) . . . . Married at Punta Arenas, Chile
Evans MR Samuel S (Spencer) . . . . Dec 23'95

Brady MR & MRS George T (Hope C V Tarpey) Pcu.Cp.Fr.Ncd.Dar.SFr'32
☎ (415) 346-3334 . . 1200 California St, Apt 7B, San Francisco, CA *94109*
Brady MR & MRS James H (Julia L Trotman) H'89.Ayc.Ny.
☎ (617) 876-3668 . . 205 Mt Auburn St, Apt 2B, Cambridge, MA *02138*
Brady MR William J B 3d—Pc.P'87
☎ (415) 674-9779 . . 2438 Clay St, San Francisco, CA *94115*
Bragdon MR David L—H'82
2566 NW Marshall St, Portland, OR *97210*
Brandin MRS Donald N (Keyes—Mary A Elliott) . . . . Married at Nantucket, MA
Bentele MR Raymond F . . . . Jly 22'95
Brandon MRS B Douglas JR (Elizabeth L Riggs) Ark'55
☎ (501) 221-2121 . . 5000 Country Club Blvd, Little Rock, AR *72207*
Brandt MR & MRS Frederick A (Margaret Delafield) | ☎ (518) 785-9553
Stan'64.Stan'63.LIU'71.ArizSt'76.SUNY'86 . . . | 11 Vandenburgh
MR Matthew A—at 1750 Swann St NW, | Lane, Latham, NY
Washington, DC *20009* . . . . | *12110*
CAPT Edward R—USAF.
Brant MR & MRS John R JR (Wendella L Kelsey) . . MRS C C Kelsey
Brazer MR & MRS Wilson M (Mohn—Anne M M | PO Box 2507,
Wickham) Sth'47.Rv.W.Y'37. . . . . | New London, NH
MISS Susan W Mohn . . . . | *03257*
Breasted MRS Martha M F (Martha M Ferguson) . . . . Died at Tuscon, AZ Dec 31'94
Breckenfeld MR William G . . see MRS P W Travell
Breed MR William B JR—H'55.H'60
1978 Picabo St, Park City, UT *84098*
Breed MR & MRS William B 3d (Stephanie C Smith) Tul'84.Van'86
☎ (802) 867-2531 . . 1226 Danby Mountain Rd, Dorset, VT *05251*
Brey MISS M Cynthia (Robert N JR) . . . . Married at Philadelphia, PA
Nissen MR John C 3d . . . . Sep 10'94
Brick MR James E 2d . . of
☎ (407) 627-9570 . . ''Steeplechase'' 5771 Dixie Belle Rd, Palm Beach Gardens, FL *33418*
☎ (305) 674-1809 . . Bell Isle 10F, 3 Island Av, Miami Beach, FL *33139*
Bricken MR & MRS Jonathan M (Madeleine D Seaman)
Cl'82.Mds.Cly.Denis'77
8 Bayberry Hill Rd, Ridgefield, CT *06877*
Brickley MR & MRS Richard L JR (Nancy P Stanley) | ☎ (617) 262-4534
Ws'75.Bost'86.Tr.Srb.Ofp.U'69.Suff'73 . . . . . . | 4 W Cedar St,
MISS Katherine Hickox—at Occidental . . . . | Boston, MA *02108*
Bright MR & MRS (DR) William B (Theresa T H Nguyen)
☎ (610) 347-9712 . . 1399 Doe Run Rd, Coatesville, PA *19320*
Brinckerhoff MR & MRS (DR) William B (Theresa T H Nguyen)
JHop'90.Nu'94.JHop'90
☎ (410) 560-5619 . . 800 Roundtop Court, Apt 2D, Lutherville, MD *21093*
Briney MR & MRS Timothy P (Blodget—A Dallas | ☎ (518) 794-9089
Collingwood) Y.'69 . . . . | PO Box 129,
MISS Alexandra K Blodget—Colby'94—at | Old Chatham, NY
128 E 85 St, New York, NY *10028* . . . . | *12136*

Britton MR & MRS J Boyd (Pillsbury—Frances C | ☎ (561) 569-0958
Garvin) D.Ncd.Wash'29 . . . . | 2400 Indian Creek
MR Charles S B Pillsbury—at | Blvd, Apt E218,
☎ (603) 563-8420 . . Dublin, NH *03444* . . . . | Vero Beach, FL
 | *32966*
Brodhead MRS Robert Stafford (Alice Kinsman) Pa'33
☎ (302) 655-9534 . . 162 Stonegates, 4031 Kennett Pike, Greenville, DE *19807*
Brokaw MR Clifford V 4th (Clifford V 3d) . . . . Married at New York, NY
Bedrick MISS Catherine B (Melvin L) . . . . Sep 16'95
Brooke MR & MRS Peter F (Dorothy J Swanson) | ☎ (718) 834-9595
Me.Cspa.Rv.NCar'59 . . . . | 1 Pierrepont St,
MISS Marion C—P'92—at 1 Fifth Av, New York, | Brooklyn, NY *11201*
NY *10003* . . . . |
Brooke MR & MRS Robert Z (Helen Chase Kimball)
Mass'70.Paris'76.INSEAD'84.Camb'79.INSEAD'84
☎ (011-44-181) 998-1204 . . 35 Castlebar Rd, Ealing, London W5 2DJ, England
Brooke MRS Sarah M (Sarah A McDougal)
2857 Westwood Lane, Apt 4, Carmichael, CA *95608-4141*
Brooks MR J Judson . . . . Died at Sewickley, PA Sep 16'95
Brooks MR John I—Me.M.Pa'94
☎ (610) 251-0109 . . 483 School House Lane, Devon, PA *19333*
Brooks DR & MRS John R (Dorothy Kalbfleisch) Sth'41.Tv.H'40
Fox Hill Village 138, 10 Longwood Dv, Westwood, MA *02090*
Brooks MRS John W (Strong—Margaret O Magoun) . . . . . Died Nov 2'95
Brooks MR & MRS Kyle C (Anne C Boyd)
☎ (513) 321-5565 . . 3533 Holly Lane, Cincinnati, OH *45208*
Brooks MASTER Timothy Clinton (Clinton C) . . . . Born at Wynnewood, PA May 8'95
Brooks-Baker MR & MRS Harold Brooks (Irène | of ☎ (011-44-1722)
du Luart de Montsaulnin) Cvc.Mt.Gi.Ty'57 . . . . | 782-635
MISS Nadia E . . . . | 3 Dv Great Durnford
MISS Natasha Y D . . . . | Manor, Great
 | Durnford, Salisbury,
 | Wiltshire, England
 | ☎ (011-44-171)
 | 730-2342
 | 23A Holland Villas
 | Rd, London W14,
 | England
 | . . MRS absent
Bross MISS Marie Suzette deM—Nw'90
☎ (212) 689-6134 . . 31 E 31 St, Apt 2A, New York, NY *10016*
Brown MISS Catherine Duer (Stanley N JR) . . . . Married at New York, NY
Stanton MR Gordon R (Louis L JR) . . . . Jan 6'96
Brown MISS Clara Warner (g—W L Lyons Brown JR) . . . . Born at Louisville, KY Oct 22'95
Brown MR Clinton B D . . . . Died at Washington, DC Feb 1'96
Brown MRS Clinton H (Catharine K Smith) . . . . Died at Newtown Square, PA May 24'94
Brown MR & MRS Duncan F (Olivia Ramsey) H'42 . | 801 Wake Robin
MISS Melissa—at 1748 N Verdugo Rd, Glendale, | Dv, Shelburne, VT
CA *91208* . . . . | *05482*

Brown MR Georges P (William G) . . . . Married at Hobe Sound, FL
  Hamilton MISS Ann Louise H . . . . Nov 4'95
Brown MR & MRS Georges P (Ann Louise H Hamilton)
  ☎ (617) 837-7916 . . 321 Congress St, Duxbury, MA *02332*
Brown MR & MRS H Templeton JR (Suzanne C Olsen) Y'52
  14 Birch Mill Rd, Lyme, CT *06371*
Brown MR & MRS J Stuart 3d (Carroll—Jones—Ann C Reber) Ph.Y'51 . . .of
  PO Box 831, York Harbor, ME *03911*
  ☎ (207) 363-6770 . . "Moonfleet" 131 Cider Hill Rd, York, ME *03909*
Brown MR & MRS James M 4th (Eyvonne K Melemai) Hawaii'84.Y'81
  ☎ (808) 373-7717 . . 5018 Poola St, Honolulu, HI *96821*
Brown MR Jeremy . . . . Died at
  Naples, FL Feb 13'96
Brown MR John A . . . . Died at
  Wayne, PA Nov 30'95
Brown MR John R JR—Va'90 ⚓
  ☎ (540) 586-6807 . . Roaring Run Farm, Rte 1, Box 273, Goode,
  VA *24556*
Brown MR & MRS Michael M (Renée M Mullen) SUNY'83.Ore'84
  abroad
Brown MASTER Peter Rust (William F L) . . . . Born at
  Morristown, NJ Jly 28'95
Brown MRS R Manning JR (Margrette L Burnham) . . . . Died at
  Warrington, PA Nov 11'95
Brown MISS Regina Devlin Kennedy (William J W) . . . . . Born Sep 20'95
Brown MR & MRS Wilding G (Solange M F Pezon) | ☎ (561) 546-1970
  Poitiers'66.On.P'64.H'67 . . . . | 207 S Beach Rd,
  MISS Solange S P—at 1 Emerson Place, Apt 12A, | Hobe Sound, FL
  Boston, MA *02114* . . . . | *33455*
  MISS Sophie S P—at Princeton . . . . |
Browne MR Philip K . . . . Died Dec 25'95
Brownell MRS Frederic H (Hust—Nora Mead) Sg. . | ☎ (215) 646-3670
  MISS Samantha B—at ☎ (212) 988-2501 | "Woodbridge
  44 East End Av, Apt 4F, New York, NY *10028*. . | Meadow"
  MISS Alexa B—at U of Va . . . . | 4 Timberfare Place,
  MR Peter M. . . . . | Spring House, PA
                                                       | *19477*
Brownell MR Frederic H—Sg.DU'67
  ☎ (415) 543-5575 . . 525—4 St, San Francisco, CA *94107*
Bruce MRS David K E (Evangeline Bell) . . . . Died at
  Washington, DC Dec 13'95
Brune MISS Constance T . . see G A Nordmann
Brune MR Timothy H N . . see G A Nordmann
Brune MR William H N 2d—StLaw'91 . . see G A Nordmann
Bruno MRS James Francis JR (Bennett—Sandra | ☎ (802) 867-4476
  Isabella Skinker) Skd'63 . . . . | PO Box 753,
   MISS Christina deT Bennett—at | West Rd, Dorset,
   ☎ (212) 831-7676 . . 171 E 88 St, Apt 2B, | VT *05251*
   New York, NY *10128* . . . . |
   MR Alexander J R Bennett—Vt'91—at |
   ☎ (212) 794-1153 . . 219 E 69 St, Apt 10M, |
   New York, NY *10021* . . . . |
Bruno MR James Francis JR—Pa'61. . . . . | PO Box 980,
  MISS Michelle E—Bost'90 . . . . | Manchester, VT
  MISS Jennifer L—Vt'93 . . . . | *05254*
Buchanan MR & MRS Calumb J (Mary B Turner) Alf'93.Va'85.GeoM'90
  4910 W Franklin St, Richmond, VA *23226*

Buchanan DR & MRS J Robert (Susan T Carver) | ☎ (860) 663-1211
  Swth'52.Cl'56.Unn.Sm.Csn.Aht'50.Cr'54 . . . . . | 5 Chestnut Hill Rd,
  MISS Allyn H—Col'90—at ☎ (303) 393-1769 | PO Box 669,
  1628 Detroit St, Denver, CO *80206* . . . . | Killingworth, CT
                                                     | *06419*
Buck MISS Elinor A (g—J Mahlon Buck JR) . . . . Born at
  Bryn Mawr, PA Sep 14'95
Buckley MR & MRS William F JR (Patricia A Taylor) Bhm.Ny.C.Km.Y'50
  Wallacks Dv, Stamford, CT *06902*
Bucklin MISS Caroline M (late Charles M) . . . . Married at Naples, FL
  Bossi MR Robert F JR . . . . Dec 30'93
Bucklin MRS Charles M (Martha S Jackson) Wheat'60 . . of
  ☎ (603) 526-6675 . . "Meadow House" PO Box 183, New London,
  NH *03257*
  ☎ (941) 262-2452 . . 3420 Gulf Shore Blvd N, Apt 36, Naples, FL *33940*
Bucklin MISS Jennifer C (late Charles M) . . . . . Married at Claremont, NH
  Roy MR Leo V . . . . Aug 12'95
Bucknell MR Nathaniel S
  ☎ (212) 481-3120 . . 140 E 28 St, Apt 5E, New York, NY *10016*
Buell MISS N Catherine . . see C A Volmert
Burden MR & MRS Childs F (Elaine C Siker) Mt.Va'73
  ☎ (540) 687-6940 . . "Seven Springs Farm" 22857 Carters Farm Lane,
  Middleburg, VA *22117*
Burden MR S Carter . . . . Died at
  New York, NY Jan 23'96
Burger MR F Gregg (late Frank G) . . . . Married at Bay Head, NJ
  Kirkland MRS Charles A (Koeniger—Martha G Weimar) . . . . Aug 4'95
Burger MR & MRS F Gregg (Koeniger—Kirkland—Martha G Weimar)
  Nw'45.W&L'42 ⚓
  ☎ (941) 966-5529 . . "Oaks Preserve" 151 Bishopscourt Rd, Osprey,
  FL *34229*
Burke MR Edwin M 3d—Geo'95 . . see H L Clark JR
Burke MR James Van V . . see H L Clark JR
Burkham MR & MRS Elzey G JR (Nancy Floyd) Sth'48.P'50
  ☎ (603) 964-5415 . . 42 Straws Point, PO Box 247, Rye Beach,
  NH *03871*
Burnap MR Wilder Luke—Col'49
  ☎ (011-33-1) 39-37-20-39 . . 118 av Aristide Briand, 60230 Chambly,
  France
Burnett MR & MRS Robert R (Elizabeth A Bole) | ☎ (540) 347-4921
  Y'59 . . . . | 5114 Laurel Lane,
  MR Alexander P—J&W'89—at | Broan Run, VA
  ☎ (540) 347-3882 . . 8464 Elway Lane, | *22014*
  Warrenton, VA *22186* . . . . |
  MR Anthony C—Cl'89—at ☎ (415) 346-3664 |
  1369A Greenwich St, San Francisco, CA *94109* |
Burpee MR & MRS George B (Callanan—Hughes—Jane A Porter)
  Temp'72.Pc.Dar.Rens'46.Cr'48
  ☎ (610) 584-8563 . . PO Box 1, Lafayette Hill, PA *19444*
Burr MR & MRS Benjamin M (Virginia Monks) | ☎ (561) 283-5710
  Hn.Hb.H'45 . . . . | 5630 SE Miles
  MISS Sarah M—at ☎ (718) 875-2963 | Grant Rd, Stuart, FL
  45 Grace Court, Apt 4C, Brooklyn, NY *11201* . . | *34997*
  MR Benjamin M JR . . . . |
  MR John E . . . . |
Burr MR Walter T—Bvl.H'84
  27 Ned's Point Rd, Mattapoisett, MA *02739-2198*

Burroughs MR & MRS Vincent DeP (Deuel—Marta D Nagel) SUNY'73 . . . . ☎ (716) 243-3394
2605 Genesee St, Piffard, NY *14533*
  MISS Maggie D Deuel—at Niagara U . . . . . .
  JUNIORS MISS Sarah G Deuel . . . .
Burwell MR John T 3d—H'72 . . see MRS A Page
Burwell MISS Lesslie B . . MRS A Page
Bushnell MRS Kipp (Drum—Reed—Margaret Kipp) . . . . Married at Newtown Square, PA
  Kelsey MR Stephen T JR (late Stephen T) . . . . Sep 9'95
Busselle MISS Katherine Scott (Boyd—Katherine Scott Busselle) MtH'95
☎ (508) 540-4822 . . Box 27, 24 Bowline Rd, West Falmouth, MA *02574*
Butcher MASTER Thomson Keen (g—W W Keen Butcher) . . . . Born Dec 15'95
Butler MR & MRS Edwin F A (Patricia E Whitney) Md'57 . . . . ☎ (410) 377-5284
106 Thicket Rd, Baltimore, MD *21212*
  MISS Jennifer W—NotreD'93—at 616 Woodbine Av, Towson, MD *21204* . . . .
Butler MR Pierce J . . . . Died Feb 10'96
Butler HON & MRS Piers J R (Laura B Gary) Cl'80.Rcch.
☎ (011-44-171) 924-6900 . . 44 Stanmer St, London SW11 3EG, England
Butler MR Shane Lloyd—Cp.Loy'41 . . . .
  MR S Michael—SFr'72 . . . .
2201 Laguna St, Apt 302, San Francisco, CA *94115*
Butler MR & MRS Sidney M G (Aileen S Taylor) Plg. . . . . ☎ (802) 387-2683
"Hewitt House" PO Box 213, Main St, Putney, VT *05346*
  MISS Laura S—at ☎ (011-81-98) 956-9658 Dodds PSC 79, Box 20979, APO AP, *96364-0979* . . . .
Butsch DR & MRS John L (Lucy J Butt) Wheat'62.Ts.G.P.'56.McG'60 . . . . ☎ (716) 886-1210
174 Soldiers Place, Buffalo, NY *14222*
  MISS Mary C . . . .
  MR John L O'B . . . .
  MR Winfield S . . . .
Buttenheim MR & MRS Richard M (Meta C Boykin) Wms'63 . . . . ☎ (518) 794-7328
Box 179, Old Chatham, NY *12136*
  MISS Melissa H . . . .
  JUNIORS MISS Paulette B . . . .
Butterworth MR & MRS James E 3d (Shawn L Gray) NCar'83.NCar'83
☎ (704) 366-4847 . . 5823 Doncaster Dv, Charlotte, NC *28211*
Butterworth MISS Julia Marley (James E 3d) . . . . Born May 12'95
Buttrick MISS Samantha Cox (Samuel C) . . . . Born at Bronxville, NY Nov 1'95
Buxton DR & MRS Jorge N (Amalia Gonzalez) Bcs.Cly.StGeo'40.BuenosA'47
☎ (212) 861-1866 . . 857 Fifth Av, New York, NY *10021*
Byczkowski MISS Anne—V'79 . . see MRS K M Dibble
Byczkowski MISS Leila M (Jurek) . . . . Married at Sonoma, CA
  Blodgett MR D Ward JR (Donald W) . . . . Oct 8'95
Byington MRS Clarke (Dorothy Jeanne Clarke) . . . . Died at Baltimore, MD Dec 18'95

Byron DR & MRS H Thomas JR (E Lee Kimball) Sth'67.MontI'72.Stone'65.Fla'73.Aub'77 . . . . . . ☎ (941) 371-4588
653 Sinclair Dv, Sarasota, FL *34240*
  MISS Lee Hayes—at Stanford . . . .
  MR Chase K—at ☎ (941) 349-4588
129 Edmondson Av, Sarasota, FL *34242* . . . . . .

C

Cabaniss DR J Allen—Ht.Cw.Sar.Rhodes'32.Ch'39
17 N Woods Dv, Grenada, MS *38901*
Cabell MRS Charles Pearré (Jacklyn O de Hymel) . . . . Died at McLean, VA Nov 4'95
Cabot MR James S (Walter M) . . . . Married at Topsfield, MA
  Theriault MISS Shannin C (Omer C) . . . . Oct 15'95
Cabot MR Timothy P (Lewis P) . . . . . Married at Glynde, Sussex, England
  Snow MISS Sara R E (late Peter) . . . . Feb 10'96
Cabot MR & MRS Timothy P (Sara R E Snow) ClCol'89
☎ (011-44-1244) 346-546 . . 4D Kings Bldg, Kings St, Chester CH1 2HA, England
Cain MRS Walker O (Houghton—Elizabeth D McCall) . . . Died Feb 13'96
Caldwell MR & MRS Kenneth S 3d (Dixon—Teresa L Major) SanDiego'80.SanDiego'83.Sdy.Tex'81
☎ (805) 482-6810 . . 5235 Mission Oaks Blvd, Apt 673, Camarillo, CA *93012*
Calil MRS Frances C (Frances B Condon)
☎ (901) 454-4898 . . Chickasaw Gardens, 2979 Gardens Way, Memphis, TN *38111*
Callaway MR & MRS Trowbridge 3d (Phyllis J Anderson) Cho.On.Br'60 . . . . ☎ (407) 369-0028
67 Spanish River Dv, Ocean Ridge, FL *33435*
  MISS Leslie A—at ☎ (614) 799-0639 4728F Heathstead Dv, Dublin, OH *43017* . . . . .
  MR William T—at 208 S 3 St, Philadelphia, PA *19106* . . . .
Callen MR & MRS John H JR (Carolyn P Coleman) Rm.Stc.Ty'55 . . . . ☎ (802) 325-3039
"Mettowee Valley Farm" Box 55, Rupert Mountain Rd, Pawlet, VT *05761*
  MR John H 3d—at ☎ (617) 928-0844 75 Brookside Av, Newtonville, MA *02160* . . . .
  MR J Hunter . . . .
Calvocoressi MISS Ameya Lee (Thomas J) . . . . Born at Middletown, CT Nov 17'95
Cameron MRS C Lindsley (Butler—C Lindsley Cameron) B'gton'69
☎ (212) 989-3992 . . 300 W 23 St, Apt 16I, New York, NY *10011*
Cameron MR Daniel D JR—NCar'73
☎ (919) 942-5554 . . 1003 Lamond Av, Durham, NC *27701*
Cameron MR & MRS Douglas W (Tara L Warrick) NCar'94.Rol'88.AmU'93
☎ (212) 447-1624 . . 151 E 31 St, Apt 7F, New York, NY *10016*
Cameron MR & MRS John J G (Manley—Sheila M Hickey) . . . . ☎ (914) 738-4552
169 Hudson St, Pelham Manor, NY *10803*
  MISS Jennifer A Manley—at 332 E 67 St, Apt 14A, New York, NY *10021* . . . .
  MISS Alexandra C Manley—at 109 Bartlett St, Apt 2, Charlestown, MA *02129* . . . .
Cameron MISS Laura H—Denis'91.Sim'94
☎ (203) 661-8297 . . 20 Fairfield Rd, Greenwich, CT *06830*

Cameron MRS Nicholas G (Katherine M Rogers) .... Died at Princeton, NJ Dec 27'95
Cammann MR Hamilton F..................... ☎ (508) 693-1512
  JUNIORS MR Nicholas F .... "Mill Pond Farm" PO Box 150, West Tisbury, MA *02575*

Camp MRS Ehney A JR (Mildred T Tillman) B'hamS'30.Cy.
  ☎ (205) 967-5200 . . 3605 Ratliff Rd, Birmingham, AL *35210*
Campbell MRS Anne M (Anne L Meigs) ☎ (603) 643-9410
  MtH'63.Hb................................ PO Box 287,
  MISS Camilla K—MtH'91..................... Etna, NH *03750*
  MISS Meriweather W—at Colo Coll ....
  MR Andrew R—at U of Cal Berkeley ....
Campbell MR Douglas K—Knox'74
  ☎ (312) 664-8729 . . 1310 N Ritchie Court, Apt 19B, Chicago, IL *60610*
Campbell MRS George J JR (Cross—Inez Perpall) ...... Died May 8'95
Campbell MRS James A (Elda S Crichton) .... Died at Chicago, IL Jly 2'95
Campbell MRS John C E (Valerie T Parry) ☎ (610) 358-4813
  Temp'76.VillaN'81 .... 220 Wawa Rd,
  JUNIORS MR Angus C...................... Wawa, PA *19063*
  JUNIORS MR Shane P ....
Campbell MR John C E—Ph.Rc.Ll.Syr'67
  ☎ (215) 928-5581 . . Residences at Pier Five, 7 N Christopher Columbus Blvd, Philadelphia, PA *19106-1422*
Campbell MRS M Schuyler (McPherson—Mary ☎ (864) 233-1160
  Schuyler Campbell) Dar.Lm................ 420 Belmont Av,
  MISS E Schuyler—at ☎ (803) 577-0451 Greenville, SC
  200 Grove St, Charleston, SC *29403* *29601-4306*
Campbell MR Morrow G—Ds.Fw.StA. .... ☎ (610) 436-8993
  MR E Graham—at ☎ (310) 547-3530 449 Eaton Way,
  2733 Gaffey St, San Pedro, CA *90731* .... Hershey's Mill,
  MR G Ross—at ☎ (714) 496-7855 West Chester, PA
  33781 Alcazar Dv, Dana Point, CA *92629* *19380*
  MRS Katherine C (Millard—Teisan—Katherine C Campbell)—at ☎ (310) 305-1611
  520 Washington Blvd, Apt 590, Marina Del Rey, CA *90292*...................................
Campbell MR Samuel R (John P) .... Married at Manchester, MA
  Ames MRS R Gardner (Rebecca B Gardner) .... Sep 23'95
Campbell MR Samuel R (Ames—Rebecca B Gardner)
  HRdc'76.Bost'86.My.H.Hn.H'73
  ☎ (508) 526-7887 . . 9 Old Neck Rd, Manchester, MA *01944*
Campbell MR & MRS Thomas R B (Barbara H Hunt) ☎ (518) 392-2490
  Ws'63.Cl'95.Au.P'61 .... Box 232,
  MISS Elizabeth H—Ober'92 .... Ghent, NY *12075*
  MR Thomas E H—P'91 ....
  MR John R B—Ober'90 ....
Campbell MR William D .... Died at New York, NY Oct 20'95
Canfield MRS Befani (Gabriella Befani) Nu'72 .... ☎ (212) 533-1511
  MR Temple Emmet—Colg'91— 129 W 22 St,
  ☎ (212) 777-0453 .... New York, NY
  MR Lewis Cass—Wes'91 .... *10011*

Cannell MISS Josephine Rose (James C) .... Born at Boston, MA Jun 21'95
Carchidi MR & MRS (DR) Bruce G (Victoria S E Kirkland) Pa'80.Pa'84.Pa'87.Pa'77
  "Possom Hollow" 20 Anderson St, Palmerston North, New Zealand
Carey MR G Cheston JR .... Died at Baltimore, MD Oct 25'95
Carey MRS G Cheston JR (Le Boutillier—Carroll—Clelia Delafield) Bnd'51.Elk.Cda.
  ☎ (410) 435-1445 . . 5710 Stony Run Dv, Baltimore, MD *21210*
Carlisle MRS Henry C (Mary Gorgas) .... Died at Tiburon, CA Jan 10'96
Carlson MR & MRS Richard W (Hunt—Patricia C of ☎ (703)506-7718
  Swanson) Mt.Plg.......................... "Tulip Hill"
  MR Buckley S P—at 420 Burges Dv, Nashville, 7718 Georgetown
  TN *37209*.............................. Pike, McLean, VA
                                          22102
                                          ☎ (410) 643-0041
                                          "Swan Haven"
                                          111 Carlson Lane,
                                          Kent Island, MD
                                          21666
Carlton MRS Winslow (Margaret M Gillies) ☎ (508) 548-0625
  C.Csn.Hn.H............................. 80 Church St,
  MISS Ann W—Sth'62—at 304 W 88 St, Woods Hole, MA
  New York, NY *10024* *02543*
Carmine MISS Anne Winton (Benjamin C JR) ... Married at Blue Bell, PA
  McFarlane MR Ronn (Lee) .... Sep 23'95
Carney MR Gardner L G (James H 2d) .... Died in Colorado Sep 12'95
Carpenter MISS Frederica L
  ☎ (508) 627-9232 . . "Garden House" 8 High St, PO Box 1213, Edgartown, MA *02539*
Carpenter MR & MRS Peter R (Janet R Buck) Penn'62.ArizSt'93.Sar.Penn'62
  ☎ (602) 860-9370 . . 13076 N 101 St, Scottsdale, AZ *85260*
Carr MISS Margaret T—L&C'93.Ct.
  ☎ (404) 367-9871 . . 1 Biscayne Dv NW, Apt 712, Atlanta, GA *30309*
Carroll MR & MRS Lucius W 2d (Cullet—Lucie L ☎ (615) 297-7907
  Miller) NCar'71.Van'63 ⚓ .... "Sugartree"
  MISS Sarah A—at ☎ (615) 292-7178 139 Prospect Hill,
  Box 50765, Nashville, TN *37205* .... Nashville, TN *37205*
  MR Christopher A—at ☎ (615) 255-8922
  710 Fatherland St, Nashville, TN *37206*.......
  JUNIORS MISS Catherine B ....
Carta MISS Kayla Elizabeth (g—MRS William B White) .. Born Mch 6'95
Carter MISS Julia D (Richard J) .... Married at West Falmouth, MA
  Hoar MR Roger S 2d (late Sherman) .... Sep 9'95
Carter MR & MRS M Hill (Judy E Temple) Millers'85.GeoW'91.Cvc.Md'86
  ☎ (301) 593-1938 . . 10111 Portland Rd, Silver Spring, MD *20901*
Carton MISS Barbara W . . see P B Hemp
Case MR Colin J (late John M) .... Married at San Francisco, CA
  Ricks MISS Ann E (Barker—Ann E Ricks) .... Feb 17'96

Casey MR & MRS James J (Claudia Prout)
Rc.B.Nrr.Ny.Shcc.Srb.Cly.Cl'37 . . . .
  MISS Edith B—at ☎ (212) 874-7751
  15 W 81 St, New York, NY *10024* . . . .
  of ☎ (908)234-0531
  "Dower Farm"
  PO Box 18,
  25 Highland Av,
  Peapack, NJ *07977*
  ☎ (212) 713-0925
  17 W 54 St,
  New York, NY
  10019
Cashman MRS Eugene R (Pauline Lenihan) . . . . Died at
  Wilmington, DE Jan 13'96
Casscells DR S Ward . . . . Died at
  Houston, TX Feb 8'96
Castellini MR & MRS Robert H (Susan S Fox) Bnd'63.Qc.Geo'63
  ☎ (513) 533-0984 . . 2180 Grandin Rd, Cincinnati, OH *45208*
Casto MR & MRS Don Monroe 3d (Ann Harrison)
  Stan'68.Stan'71.Stan'66.Stan'69 . . . .
  MISS Katherine A . . . .
  ☎ (614) 253-7600
  10 Sessions Dv,
  Columbus, OH
  43209
Caswell MRS William W 3d (Maryann B Shields) . . . . Died at
  Gloucester, MA Oct 29'95
Caulkins MR Dan Platt . . . . Died at
  Hobe Sound, FL Sep 25'95
Caulkins MRS Dan Platt (Collier—Carhart—Dixie Thompson) StJ.
  ☎ (561) 546-8691 . . 350 S Beach Rd, Hobe Sound, FL *33455*
Cayley MRS E Ward (Francis—Elinor Ward) . . . name changed to Francis
Chace MR Arthur F . . . . Died at
  Fairfield, CT Feb 24'96
Chadsey MRS Murrell R (Bowden—Patrick—F Murrell Rickards)
  Swb'44.Cly.Ncd.
  ☎ (804) 640-1338 . . 512 Mowbray Arch, Norfolk, VA *23507*
Chandler MISS Blake . . see J B Sibley
Chandler MASTER Levi Graves (Peter C) . . . . Born at
  Boulder, CO Sep 26'95
Chandler MR & MRS Nathan (Phyllis A Russell) Yn.Y'44
  ☎ (207) 666-5595 . . RR 3, Box 3120, Bowdoinham, ME *04008*
Chandler MR & MRS Peter C (S Blair Nichols) CtCol'83.Bgt.Cly.Bow'83
  ☎ (303) 442-0403 . . 740 S 41 St, Boulder, CO *80303*
Chandler JUNIORS MR William K . . see D C Bermingham
Channing MR William E . . . . Died at
  London, England Sep 9'95
Chapin MR & MRS Christopher K (Carroll H Thornton)
  Miss'69.H'82.Mt.Cvc.Yn.Y'67.Pa'72
  ☎ (202) 387-7830 . . 2136 Leroy Place NW, Washington, DC *20008*
Chapin MR Schuyler G (late L H Paul) . . . . Married at New York, NY
  Mortimer MRS Catia Z (Catia S Zoullas) . . . . Sep 15'95
Chapin MR & MRS Schuyler G (Mortimer—Catia S
  Zoullas) Ws'60.C.Mto.Cly. . . . .
  MISS Liza Mortimer—at ☎ (212) 446-9043
  245 E 62 St, New York, NY *10021* . . . .
  MR E Nicholas Mortimer—at
  ☎ (212) 388-7405 . . 151 First Av, Apt 49,
  New York, NY *10003* . . . .
  ☎ (212) 734-5553
  655 Park Av,
  New York, NY
  10021
Chapman MR & MRS James P (Lillian Anne Dinning) Wesley'94
  ☎ (410) 836-3595 . . "October Mist" 3405 Mill Green Rd, Street,
  MD *21154*

Chapman MASTER Nicholas Coste (Gilbert W 3d) . . . . Born at
  New York, NY Oct 1'95
Chase MISS Christine D . . see H C Robbins
Chase MR Eric H . . see H C Robbins
Chase MRS Mary J (Mary B Jennings) . . . . Died at
  Glen Head, NY Nov 12'95
Cheek MISS Katharine DeW (Leslie 3d) . . . . Married at Boston, MA
  Mast MR Robert D JR (Robert D) . . . . Sep 30'95
Chéhab MRS C Riker (Cornelia Riker) Stc. . . . .
  MISS Randa . . . .
  MISS Carina . . . .
  MR Eric L—H'91 . . . .
  ☎ (908) 842-8066
  18 Lennox Av,
  Rumson, NJ *07760*
Chellis MISS Dana E . . . . Married at Wellesley, MA
  Keel MR Norwood S JR . . . . Jly 29'95
Cheney MASTER Christopher Matthew (g—Julian L Ambrus) . . . . Born at
  Spokane, WA Nov 23'95
Cherouny MR Arthur S . . . . Died Jly 28'95
Cherouny MRS Arthur S (Janet R Little)
  20 Devonwood Lane, Apt 333S, Farmington, CT *06032*
Cheshire MR & MRS William P (Lucile Geoghegan) MaryW'58.Cc.NCar'58
  "Riverside" Rte 5, Box 51, Washington, NC *27889*
Chewning MR & MRS E Taylor JR (Hernstadt—
  Prince—Jonna R Leonard) K.Ny.Srb.Mt.Cas.
  Y'45 . . . .
  MR Scott C Wood Prince—at
  ☎ (312) 871-8551 . . 4135 N Greenview Av,
  Chicago, IL *60613* . . . .
  MR Patrick B Wood Prince—at
  ☎ (312) 486-3609 . . 1621 N Paulina St,
  Chicago, IL *60622* . . . .
  ☎ (561) 388-0178
  10645 Fife Av,
  Vero Beach, FL
  32963
Childress MRS Fielding T (Ruth B E McElroy) Cy.
  ☎ (314) 367-3517 . . 16 Homewood Dv, St Louis, MO *63122*
Chinn MR & MRS Garretson W (Nancy Deering) OState'66.Y'62.Mit'68
  ☎ (212) 472-1315 . . 34 E 75 St, New York, NY *10021*
Choumenkovitch MR Iliya A M—Roch'85
  ☎ (612) 542-8280 . . 12700 Sherwood Place, Apt 200, Wayzata,
  MN *55305*
Choumenkovitch MR Nicolas M (late Milorad) . . . . Married at
  Charlottesville, VA
  Furlong MISS Silvina M (Guillermo) . . . . Dec 30'95
Choumenkovitch MR & MRS Nicolas M (Silvina M Furlong)
  BuenosA'90.Occ'86.Va'92
  ☎ (617) 441-5170 . . 29 Concord Av, Apt 411, Cambridge, MA *02138*
Chrisman MR & MRS William H (Craig—Margaret M Baker)
  Nw'52.H'58.H'55
  ☎ (602) 948-3666 . . 6235 E Catesby Rd, Paradise Valley, AZ *85253*
Christ MR & MRS M Hallsted (Ann C Gilbert)
  Colg'53.Nu'55 . . . .
  MISS Marian G—Col'90 . . . .
  MR John R—Guil'90 . . . .
  ☎ (410) 476-5050
  "Mallard Point
  Farm" 32123
  Clark's Wharf Rd,
  Trappe, MD *21673*
Chronis MR & MRS Gregory G (Jean E Carpenter)
  Ariz'88.ArizSt'93.Colby'88.ArizSt'91
  ☎ (602) 451-3776 . . 9019 E Corrine Dv, Scottsdale, AZ *85260*
Chrystie MR James McD—Skd'88
  407 W Koch, Bozeman, MT *59715*

Church MISS Caroline W (Gunnell—Caroline W Church) AmU'91
☎ (540) 347-7973 .. PO Box 297, Warrenton, VA *22186*
Claghorn MR & MRS Edward T (Katrina Van Buren) | 457 Weadley Rd,
NCar'75.Ofp.Rv.Dh.NCar'74 .... | Wayne, PA *19087*
JUNIORS MR Edward T JR ....
Claiborne MRS John T 3d (Cox—Cornelia D Sharp)
☎ (561) 753-6083 .. 11679 Wimbledon Circle, West Palm Beach,
FL *33414*
Clancy MR & MRS Andrew O (Denyse R Finn) Y'89.Cl'92.Aht'88.Nw'94
☎ (214) 827-2184 .. 5201 Goodwin Av, Dallas, TX *75206*
Clark MASTER Benjamin Garfield (Laurance R) .... Born at
Cambridge, MA Jan 16'96
Clark MRS Caulkins (Bliss Caulkins) Mich'66.Mich'90
☎ (313) 886-5007 .. 40 Tonnancour Place, Grosse Pointe Farms,
MI *48236-3033*
Clark MRS Elise C—Colg'93
☎ (415) 775-7019 .. 1181 Green St, San Francisco, CA *94109*
Clark MR & MRS Ernest C JR (Mary C Fahnestock) D.Pa'42
☎ (603) 772-1782 .. 7 River Woods Dv, Exeter, NH *03833-4373*
Clark MR Gordon T—Y'62 .... | ☎ (212) 206-7913
MISS Alexandra C—at St Margaret's School, | 55 W 11 St, Apt 6G,
PO Box 158, Tappahannock, VA *22560* ...... | New York, NY
MR Timothy B—at 470 Argyle Av, PO Box 187, | *10011*
Garrett Park, MD *20896* ....
Clark MRS Grenville JR (Barnum—Hansen—Elizabeth Lamb)
Ws'87.Bost'90.Sm.My.Myc.Cy.K ... of
☎ (212) 799-4890 .. 35 W 90 St, Apt 7J, New York, NY *10024*
85 Grove St, Wellesley, MA *02181*
Clark MR & MRS Howard L JR (Burke—Karen M | of ☎ (203)869-3508
Kaess) Rcn.Ln.Ri.Bost'67.Cl'68 .... | 404 Round Hill Rd,
MR Howard L 3d—at Tulane | Greenwich, CT
MR Edwin M Burke 3d—Geo'95—at | *06831*
515 E 72 St, Apt 16D, New York, NY *10021* | ☎ (561) 546-0385
MR James Van V Burke—at Georgetown ... | "Seaview"
| 9 N Beach Rd,
| Hobe Sound, FL
| *33475*
Clark MRS John Bigelow (Heath—Eves—Johanna V Smith)
☎ (860) 526-5098 .. Chester Village W, Apt 2203, 317 W Main St,
Chester, CT *06412*
Clark MR William H .... Died at
Shelburne, VT Jan 24'96
Clarke MR Dumont—Myf.P'34
Highland Farms Apt D57, 200 Tabernacle Rd, Black Mountain,
NC *28711*
Clarke MRS George M (Jeannette G Litchfield) .... Died at
Bryn Mawr, PA Oct 6'95
Clarke MR & MRS George M 3d (Sally K Larson) | 984 Springdale Rd
AmU'68.GaSt'72 .... | NE, Atlanta, GA
MISS Elizabeth L..................... | *30306*
MR G Marshall—at Presby Coll ....
Clarke MR & MRS Thomas C (Tullis—Schurz— | ☎ (410) 819-0304
Robin S Rowan) V'60.H'53.H'59 .... | "The Reach"
MISS Tracy Tullis—Br'86—at | 8850 Marengo Farm
148 Sterling Place, Brooklyn, NY *11217* .... | Rd, Easton, MD
MR Paul R Tullis—Cal'92—at 1641—18 St, | *21601*
San Francisco, CA *94107* ....

Clattenburg MR & MRS Richard N (Henrietta R Battle) H'35.Pa'38
☎ (603) 924-7338 .. 243 River Mead Rd, Peterborough, NH *03458*
Clay MR John W 3d (John W JR) .... Married at Franklin, TN
Shavers MISS Ashley E (James) .... Aug 19'95
Clayman MR & MRS John M (Lalande L Keeshan) Bost'75.Ny.Nyc.Dth'75
☎ (508) 921-1659 .. 804 Hale St, Beverly Farms, MA *01915*
Claytor MRS Richard (Mary Ingersoll) .... Died at
King of Prussia, PA Oct 31'95
Clein MR & MRS Mark P (Nancy E Lemann)
210 W 101 St, Apt 10G, New York, NY *10025*
Clement MR & MRS Charles F 3d (Sadtler—Barbara A Koltes)
Minn'61.Me.Wt.Rv.P'65.Cl'67
655 Augusta Court, Berwyn, PA *19087*
Clement MR Edward S—Bab'71
☎ (860) 923-2899 .. 47 Chase Rd, PO Box 423, Thompson, CT *06277*
Clement MRS Jill (Stephenie G Baughman) .... | ☎ (401) 348-2172
MR Edward S JR—Vt'91 | 199 Watch Hill Rd,
MR Taylor W—Mont'95 | Watch Hill, RI
| *02891-5030*
Clement DR Stephen M 2d .... Died at
Tryon, NC Sep 12'95
Close MR & MRS Edward B (Anne Merryweather) | of ☎ (303)771-0216
Sth'50.Ln.Y'49 | 4875 S Fairfax
MR Montgomery B—at 2172 Pacific Av, Apt 2, | Lane, Littleton, CO
San Francisco, CA *94115* .... | *80121*
| ☎ (970) 926-2017
| 0028 Eagle Crest
| Rd, Edwards, CO
| *81632*
Clothier MRS George B (Muller—Dorothea M Helbig) .. Died Sep 17'95
Clough MR Peter A (Anson W) .... Married at Ridgefield, CT
Grant MISS Lisa J (David A) .... Oct 28'95
Clough MR & MRS Peter A (Lisa J Grant) Mid'86
☎ (215) 545-8164 .. 2210 Mt Vernon St, Philadelphia, PA *19130*
Clow MR Matthew (Gerald C) .... Married
Weinberg MISS Hillary .... Oct 13'95
Cluett MR & MRS Mark S (Elizabeth A Gummey) | ☎ (912) 598-7043
Hlns'61.Pcu.Fr.Wms'55.Va'61 ⚓ .... | 13 Magnolia
MISS Julia S .... | Crossing, Savannah,
| GA *31411-1417*
Clyde MR & MRS Thomas M (Christine S MacIver) | ☎ (617) 227-8964
V'61.Sm.Tr.Myf.P'58.H.'61................ | 23 Chestnut St,
MISS Alexandra T .... | Boston, MA *02108*
MR Thomas MacI ....
MR William C......................
Cobb MR & MRS Brodie L (Frances S Daniels) Tul'84.Tul'84.Tex'85
275 Mallorca Way, San Francisco, CA *94123*
Cobb MR & MRS Winthrop C (Mary H Sullivan) MtVern'81.Va'72
☎ (703) 823-0535 .. 2211 Belle Haven Rd, Alexandria, VA *22307*
Cochrane MR & MRS James A 4th (Biddle—Sarah Gamwell) Pkg.Dth'56
☎ (610) 363-7033 .. 651 Nantmeal Rd, Glenmoore, PA *19343*
Coe MR & MRS Robert L (Mariella R Cartwright) Rens'31
☎ (314) 863-3408 .. 900 S Hanley Rd, Clayton, MO *63105*
Coe MR Robert S—T.H'56..................... | ☎ (970) 487-3055
MISS Cassandra H—H'85.Cal'89—at | PO Box 137C,
☎ (415) 366-2984 .. 439 Woodside Dv, | RD 1, Collbran, CO
Woodside, CA *81624* .... | *81624*

Coffin DR & MRS Lewis A 3d (Angeline J W Glass) Va'52.Duke'56.......... ☎ (404) 815-0943 1027 St Charles Av NE, Apt A, Atlanta, GA *30306-4271*
MISS Jennifer N..........
MR Jared S..........
Coggeshall MRS John (Barbara A Bredt).......... Died Dec 17'95
Cohen MR & MRS Ted (Austin—Ann R Collier) V'57.Ch'62.H'65.H'72.......... ☎ (312) 288-4694 4950 S Chicago Beach Dv, Chicago, IL *60615*
MISS Alexandra Austin—V'91—at ☎ (312) 752-7573.. 5550 S Dorchester Av, Chicago, IL *60637*..........
Cole MRS Bonnie L—Dar.Wt.
☎ (601) 734-2482.. 2418 H'way 583 SE, Bogue Chitto, MS *39629*
Cole MRS Henry P (Katherine S Bullock).......... Died at Royalston, MA Oct 9'95
Cole DR Henry P JR—Wms'59.MichSt'63.Alaska'78
☎ (907) 488-3493.. Box 71490, Fairbanks, AK *99707*
Cole MR John Y JR—Stan'58.......... ☎ (817) 921-3006 2521 Rogers Av, Ft Worth, TX *76109*
MISS Valerie S—TCU'86..........
MR John Y 3d—Miss'89..........
Colket MRS Carl C (Peggie M Dushane).......... Died at Bryn Mawr, PA Nov 7'95
Colladay MISS Constance L (Edgar B JR)..... Married at San Mateo, CA
Hooker MR Michael G (late R Lent).......... Sep 30'95
Collier MISS Dorothy B—NH'41.Cwr'49.Dar.
☎ (301) 879-0987.. 101 Carlisle Dv, Silver Spring, MD *20904*
Collier MRS Sargent (Elizabeth H Moore) Madrid'68.Sm.My.......... ☎ (508) 768-7575 PO Box 927, Essex, MA *01929*
MISS Leandra M—at Holderness..........
JUNIORS MISS Eliza D..........
JUNIORS MR Sargent M McC..........
Collier MR Sargent—Sm.My.Bow'64
☎ (508) 282-4394.. PO Box 549, Essex, MA *01929*
Collins MISS Adele A (Farnham F).......... Married at Millbrook, NY
Legerski MR Gregory P (Donald).......... Jun 17'95
Collins MR Daniel Wills—Myf.H'54
☎ (609) 235-0066.. 633 E Main St, Apt B2, Moorestown, NJ *08057*
Collins MRS Edward R (Elizabeth D Conklin) Hood'58.Gi.Ht.Cda.
☎ (410) 255-1250.. Box 34, Broadwater Way, Gibson Island, MD *21056-0034*
Collins MR & MRS Farnham F (E Anne Archbold) Gchr'60.Un.P'57
☎ (914) 677-3822.. "Skyward" RR 1, Box 64, Millbrook, NY *12545*
Colmore MISS Julia C.......... Died at New York, NY Feb 14'96
Colt MASTER Samuel Crane (Zenas M C).......... Born at Atlanta, GA Jun 2'94
Colt MR & MRS William W (Melody K Schultz) NCar'82.Va'69
☎ (704) 283-8061.. 404 S Church St, Monroe, NC *28112-5611*
Colt MR Zenas M C—Va'71.......... ☎ (401) 783-2557 697 Post Rd, Wakefield, RI *02879*
JUNIORS MISS Susannah..........
JUNIORS MR Zenas C 2d..........
Colvocoresses MRS Harold L (Josephine R Rice).......... Died at West Hartford, CT Nov 1'95
Colwell MR David H (Kent L).......... Married at San Anselmo, CA
Wood MISS Katherine M (Ashford D).......... Jly 15'95
Colyer MRS Ralph C (Townsend—Virginia T Bottomley) V'45.Cs.
☎ (516) 692-7095.. 55 Harbor Rd, Oyster Bay, NY *11771*

Compton MR & MRS Douglass M (Marie Eugenie Thébaud) Y'32
☎ (203) 245-1859.. 23 Aylesbury Circle, Madison, CT *06443*
Congdon MR & MRS Jeffrey H (Katherine C Burkett) Briar'70.Bhm.Tcy.Dar.Cal'67.......... ☎ (415) 921-1145 3675 Washington St, San Francisco, CA *94118*
MISS Elizabeth B—at U of Cal Berkeley..........
JUNIORS MISS Katherine C..........
JUNIORS MR Chester A 3d..........
Conger MR & MRS Clement E (Lianne B Hopkins) Evg.Mt.Cvc.Sl.GeoW'44.......... of ☎ (703)276-3131 The Jefferson Apt 2112, 900 N Taylor St, Arlington, VA *22203*
MR William R..........
MISS Shelley Louise (Dabrowski—Shelley Louise Conger) CtCol'76—at 3054 Donna Marta Dv, Studio City, CA *91604-4324*.......... ☎ (561) 274-3444 Seagate Towers S, Apt 505S, 220 Macfarlane Dv, Delray Beach, FL *33483*
Conner MR Thomas D JR
☎ (334) 262-4152.. 2562 College St, Montgomery, AL *36106*
Connolly MR Edward P (Joseph G J).......... Married at Hale, Cheshire, England
Purvis MISS Sara L (Bryan J).......... Aug 12'95
Connolly MR Joseph C—Dick'95.. see M B Barrows
Connolly MR & MRS Joseph G J (Patricia A Quinn) BMr'91.Pa'93.Ph.R.Rc.Gm.Cry.Ac.Pa'62.Pa'65.. ☎ (610) 642-4621 836 Buck Lane, Haverford, PA *19041*
MR James J—Me.Pa'88—at Columbia Grad....
Connolly MASTER Peter Boggs (Christopher C).......... Born at Baltimore, MD Dec 19'95
Connors MASTER Hamilton Phillips (Timothy P).......... Born at Denver, CO Jly 14'94
Connors MR & MRS Timothy P (Elsie C Hamilton) Clare'82.Vt'83
☎ (303) 698-2655.. 1015 S Gilpin St, Denver, CO *80209*
Conrad MR David C—Br'90.Juilliard'95
☎ (212) 473-8074.. 29 Av B, Apt 5E, New York, NY *10009*
Conrad MR & MRS Elbert A (Louisa L Vaughan) Chi.
☎ (508) 927-0091.. 454 Hale St, Box 245, Prides Crossing, MA *01965* Jan 1.. ☎ (809) 450-8525.. Manteca, Box 400, Castries, St Lucia
Consagra MR & MRS George D (Louisa J Moore) Cal'86.CtCol'84
☎ (415) 292-4689.. 1580 Filbert St, Apt 16, San Francisco, CA *94123*
Constable MR & MRS James W (Chamberlin—Lott—Katherine M McLean) Paris'66.Md.Nyc.Va'65.Md'68
☎ (410) 771-4568.. "Brerewood" 2300 Sheppard Rd, Monkton, MD *21111*
Constable MR & MRS Richard D J (Anne P Arnold) Snc........... ☎ (310) 541-6121 85 Yacht Harbor Dv, Palos Verdes, CA *90275*
MISS Ashley A..........
Cook MRS Camilla W (Camilla S Wright) Ala'44.Ala'47.Cda.
☎ (205) 345-6720.. 32 Ridgeland, Tuscaloosa, AL *35406*
Cook MISS Lida B (Kevit R).......... Married at Northeast Harbor, ME
Fay MR William F JR (William F).......... Jly 1'95
Cooke MR & MRS Bradford (Marion P Mundy) Vt'80.Ham'72
☎ (914) 738-7879.. 421 Stellar Av, Pelham Manor, NY *10803*
Cooke MASTER James Warren McKean (James W 3d).......... Born at Columbia, MD Jun 11'95

Coolidge MR Roger S . . . . Died at
Epsom, NH Nov 7'95
Coolidge MRS Winthrop K (Cook—Catherine J Beresford-Owen) Sc.
☎ (520) 529-6361 . . 4532 N Via Entrada, Tuscon, AZ *85718*
Cooper MRS Angus R 2d (Wadick—Miriam Walmsley) . . . . Died at
Point Clear, AL Oct 16'95
Cooper MR & MRS Charles T (Nancy S Hovey)
  Nf.Ny.My.Hob'72 . . . . | ☎ (508) 768-6969
  JUNIORS MR Chandler H . . . . | "Lilac Hill"
  JUNIORS MR Charles L . . . . | 8 John Wise Av,
  | Essex, MA *01929*
Cooper MR & MRS Joseph W J JR (Dorothea-Louise
  Phelps) P'53.Va'58 . . . . | ☎ (212) 517-6522
  MISS Dorothea Grier—at 2665 Pine St, Apt 1, | 1035 Fifth Av, Apt
  San Francisco, CA *94115* . . . . | 3B, New York, NY
  MR Joseph W J 3d . . . . | *10028*
  MR James H—at N'eastern . . . . |
  MR Brendon P. . . . . |
Coords MRS Deane M (Priscilla S Todd) Lm.Dar. . . | ☎ (904) 423-4314
  MISS Barbara S—Lm.Dar.—at ☎ (860) 364-1130 | 3501 S Atlantic Av,
  144 East St, Sharon, CT *06069* . . . . | New Smyrna Beach,
  | FL *32169*
Cope MRS E Baxter (Edith P Baxter) . . . . name changed to Baxter
Cope MR Jonathan B . . see MISS E P Baxter
Corbin MRS Justine M (Justine B Montgomery) . . . | of ☎ (516)283-5532
  MR R Beverley 3d—Vt'83—at ☎ (212) 688-5706 | "Potpourri"
  200 E 66 St, Apt D1503, New York, NY *10021* | PO Box 1276,
  MR C Suydam Cutting—at ☎ (970) 920-6870 | 224 Great Plains Rd,
  PO Box 12046, Aspen, CO *81612* . . . . | Southampton, NY
  | *11969*
  | ☎ (212) 688-3793
  | 200 E 66 St,
  | New York, NY
  | *10021*
  | ☎ (809) 494-2730
  | Wyndcliffe, Havers,
  | Tortola, BVI
Corcoran MR John B—Ck.Rc.Mid'86
  ☎ (212) 427-9264 . . 182 E 95 St, Apt 20A, New York, NY *10128*
Corey MR & MRS Alan L 3d (Raezer—Wetzel—Patricia Ellis)
  Sim'63.Cardoza'83.Unn.Pr.Y'65
  ☎ (803) 649-2075 . . 129 Easy St, Aiken, SC *29801*
Corey MR Alan L 4th . . see P J Pell
Corey MISS Christine M . . see P J Pell
Corey MISS Cynthia E . . see P J Pell
Corey MR R William . . see P J Pell
Cormier MISS Naomi Claudia (g—Clayton P Cormier) . . . . Born at
Kamagawa-gun, Hokkaido, Japan Jly 25'94
Cornell MR & MRS James K (Shields—E Sara Rowbotham)
  Lawr'85.Cy.NCar'85
  ☎ (617) 424-9373 . . 416 Commonwealth Av, Boston, MA *02215*
Cornell MISS Schuyler Van Rensselaer (James K) . . . . Born Oct 7'94
Corning MISS Ursula—Csn.
  ☎ (011-39-75) 932135 . . Civitella Ranieri, Umbertide, 06109 Perugia,
  Italy

Corroon MRS Robert F (Helen V Maitland) Csn. . . . | ☎ (203) 869-0771
  MISS Andrée B . . . . | 27 Greenbriar Lane,
  MR Richard F 2d—at ☎ (212) 369-6807 | Greenwich, CT
  110 E 87 St, New York, NY *10128* . . . . | *06831*
  MSRS Peter M & Christopher L—at
  ☎ (801) 654-4874 . . 743 S Southfield Dv,
  Heber City, UT *84032* . . . . |
Corscaden MR James A JR . . . . Died at
Houston, TX Feb 9'96
Corse MR & MRS Dean McN C (Bell—Roberta A Patrick)
  Cc.Ll.Fw.Cw.Rv.Sar.Ne'70.Emer'78
  ☎ (603) 430-1055 . . 42 Beechstone St, Apt 1, Portsmouth, NH *03801*
Corts DR & MRS Thomas E (Marla R Haas) H'ton'63.Cy.Geo'63
  ☎ (205) 969-0350 . . 2829 Overton Rd, Birmingham, AL *35223*
Cossé Brissac CTSS Anita de (PRCSS Anita O Lobkowicz) . . . .
name changed to Lobkowicz
Cossé Brissac CT Charles L de—Cc. . . . . | ☎ (011-33)
  MISS Diane M de . . . . | 37-26-81-25
  | "Château de
  | Blanville" 28190
  | St Luperce, France
Côté MASTER Pierce Lamb (Edward T JR) . . . . Born at
New York, NY Oct 9'95
Cottafavi MR Francesco L—Pr.Rome'69 . . . . | of ☎ (516)922-5010
  MR Vittorio E—at Georgetown . . . . | 127 Cove Rd,
  | Oyster Bay, NY
  | *11771*
  | ☎ (011-39-6)
  | 333-8219
  | via Guido Banti 33,
  | 00191 Rome, Italy
Cowell MR & MRS Richard C (Sullivan—Jacqueline | ☎ (407) 655-4911
  McKissick) FlaSo'52.Rcn.Ri.Evg.BtP.H'52 . . . . | 240 El Vedado Way,
  MR Richard C JR—at 177 E 75 St, Apt 4A, | Palm Beach, FL
  New York, NY *10021* . . . . | *33480*
  MR Christopher—at Fla State . . . . |
Cowles MISS Charlotte Ainsley Winnifred (James C) . . . . Born at
New York, NY Jan 28'95
Cowles MR & MRS James C (Kathryn C Maney)
  VPI'77.Cl'82.So.Denis'77.Pa'79
  ☎ (212) 794-0711 . . 8 E 83 St, Apt 2B, New York, NY *10028*
Cowles JUNIORS MR Story A . . see W W Atterbury 3d
Cowley MR & MRS Nicholas P T (Page K Ayres)
  Nu'75.OxPoly'76.Cl'79.Rc.Cs.
  ☎ (212) 877-0124 . . 169 W 88 St, New York, NY *10024*
Cox MRS Raymond E (Margaret Berwind) . . . . Died at
Washington, DC Dec 17'95
Coxe MR Weld—Rcp.Hp. ⚓ . . . . | ☎ (401) 466-2865
  MISS Sally M—Lin'76.Ore'85—at | "Block Island
  ☎ (541) 345-1272 . . 991 Polk St, Eugene, OR | Studio" PO Box
  97402 . . . . | 515, Block Island,
  MR Philip A Hayden—Conn'84.Del'89—at | RI *02807*
  ☎ (609) 921-8259 . . 38 Washington St,
  Rocky Hill, NJ *08553* . . . . |
Coyne MASTER Joseph Darby (g—MRS Marshall B Walthour) . . . Born at
Baltimore, MD Jan 2'96

Coyne MISS Susan O'Neil (g—MRS Marshall B Walthour) ...... Born at Baltimore, MD Jly 27'93
Craig MR & MRS Berton A (Denton—Elizabeth C Russel) Cin'63.Ncd.Ken'52 ....
  MR Michael S—Hob'93—at ☎ (212) 501-8924 313 W 75 St, Apt 4B, New York, NY *10023* ...
    MISS Elizabeth C Denton—SL'90.Cin'94—at ☎ (614) 299-6153 .. 65 Clark Place, Columbus, OH *43201* ....
    MR E Castner Denton 3d—BowlG'92—at ☎ (513) 961-7670 .. 410 Ludlow Av, Apt 52, Cincinnati, OH *45220* ....
☎ (561) 335-4583 2867 SE Wiltshire Terr, Port St Lucie, FL *34952-5734*

Craig MRS Howard R (Agnes C Broward) .... Died at Sharon, CT Nov 14'95
Crawford MISS Arabella Moseley (Harden L 4th) ...... Born Sep 11'95
Crawford MASTER George Carroll (W Michael) .... Born at Southampton, NY Jan 9'96
Crawford MRS Harden L (Stone—Hélène Sartorelli) .... Died at Vero Beach, FL Jan 31'95
Crawford MR & MRS Harden L 3d (Ailsa Moseley) B.Ny.Myc.Rv.Ll.StA.Eh.Cly.Ncd.Cl'56 ⚓
  ☎ (908) 234-0126 .. "Longrun" PO Box 365, Far Hills, NJ *07931*
Crawford MR & MRS Harden L 4th (Kersti E Magi) UWash'86.Bost'85
  ☎ (203) 259-2239 .. "Summerfield" 195 Greens Farms Rd, Greens Farms, CT *06436*
Crawford MR & MRS Steven C (Pesquera—Danielle P André) Spgfd'76.NH'77
  ☎ (703) 538-2141 .. 6905 Hutchison St, Falls Church, VA *22043*
Creel MISS Alexandra Coleman (Lawrence G) .... Born at New York, NY Sep 12'95
Creel MR & MRS Lawrence G (Jennifer M Coleman) PineM'86.Rc.Mb.Fic.LakeF'85
  ☎ (212) 327-4263 .. 155 E 72 St, New York, NY *10021*
Crimmins MR & MRS Martin Lalor 3d (House—Martha P Thomson) V'53.Cly.Ncd.Cda.Cal'51
  ☎ (212) 472-1571 .. 125 E 72 St, New York, NY *10021*
Crisler MR & MRS Edgar Theodore JR (Emma Flautt) Miss'61.Sar.Wt.Rhodes'56
  ☎ (601) 437-4410 .. 1108 Church St, PO Box 1002, Port Gibson, MS *39150-1002*
Crisler MR Richard C .... Died at Cincinnati, OH Aug 28'95
Crivelli MRS Gioconda M K (Colapinto—Rippel—Gioconda M K Crivelli) .. of
  ☎ (212) 988-7872 .. 117 E 71 St, Apt 5C, New York, NY *10021*
  ☎ (011-39-55) 47-42-17 .. "I Colombi" Vicolo San Marco Vecchio 34, La Pietra, 50139 Firenze, Italy
Crocker MR & MRS Arthur M (Putnam—Barbara J Stout) Unn.Pr.Csn.P'31.H'33
  ☎ (941) 261-2580 .. 126 Moorings Park Dv, Apt I204, Naples, FL *33942*
Cronin MR & MRS Paul D (E Ann Swift) Rdc'62.Cr'81.Nyc.An.Stone'60.Pitt'67 ....
  MR Peter F—Denis'91—at ☎ (415) 781-0630 350 Union St, Apt 609, San Francisco, CA *94133*
  MR David R—Ken'93—at ☎ (703) 379-8351 4884 S 28 St, Arlington, VA *22206* ....
☎ (804) 381-5966 "The Farmhouse" Farmhouse Rd, Sweet Briar, VA *24595*

Crosby MR George de F—Unn.NH'80 7-11 av Pasteur, L-2311 Luxembourg, Luxembourg
Crosier MR Louis M—Dth'87 .. see R N Pyle
Crossman MR & MRS William L (Alison L Vietor) LakeF'79.Shcc.LakeF'78 Spring Island, Rte 6, Box 284, Okatie, SC *29910*
Cruice MISS Kathryn W (late John M) .... Married Francis MR Charles A (late William A) .... Nov 25'95
Cruice MR Robert B .... Died at Philadelphia, PA Jan 9'96
Cruice MISS Sydney F (late John M) .... Married at Philadelphia, PA Dixon MR Terence A (Victor F) .... Oct 7'95
Cruickshank MISS Carol W (William H) .... Married at Lincoln, MA Ostenson MR Steen (Raymond) .... Oct 16'95
Culley MR & MRS Peter M (Elizabeth E Hohmann) Ariz'51
  ☎ (602) 945-4841 .. 5102 N Casa Blanca Rd, Paradise Valley, AZ *85253*
Culver MRS H Harrison (Elizabeth Jenney) .... Died Nov 25'95
Cumings MR J Bradley 3d .... Died at Toronto, Ontario, Canada Jan 24'96
Cumings MASTER Thayer Edward (g—MRS J Bradley Cumings 3d) ... Born at Toronto, Ontario, Canada Oct 21'95
Cummin MRS Arch W (Diane Kidman Young) Me.
JUNIORS MISS Chandra K F ....
☎ (212) 289-3225 1120 Fifth Av, New York, NY *10128*

Cummin MR Arch W—Rc.B.Me.H'66.Pa'70
  ☎ (516) 537-3328 .. 41 Quimby Lane, Box 253, Bridgehampton, NY *11932*
Cumming MR & MRS Edward G (Fagan—Paulson—Patricia McMillan) Snc.Ht.H'52 ....
  MR Charles K Fagan ....
  MR John F Paulson ....
of ☎ (011-33-1) 47-34-25-05 71 quai Branly, 75007 Paris, France ☎ (910) 777-1484 1257 Kent Place Lane, Winston-Salem, NC *27104*

Cummings DR & MRS Harlan G (Robinson—Virginia De B Hinman) Eyc.Plg.Cly.Mid'58.Tufts'61 ....
  MR Sanger P Robinson II—at ☎ (213) 467-7133 .. 5710 Waring Av, Los Angeles, CA *90038* ....
☎ (802) 296-5087 PO Box 892, Norwich, VT *05055-0892*

Cummings MR & MRS Walter J 3d (Pauline Field) Bur.Y'69.Stan'74
  ☎ (617) 278-9719 .. 219 Buckminster Rd, Brookline, MA *02146-5805*
Cunningham MR & MRS John J (Miller—Gordon—Karen R Kreidler) WChesU'82.Me.Leh'60.Pa'65
  MISS Amy—at 231 E Main St, Bozeman, MT *59715* ....
  MR James A—Leh'94 ....
☎ (610) 520-1250 "Wrenfield" 335 Wrenfield Way, Villanova, PA *19085*

Curcio MISS Samantha Morgan (g—E Frederick Wheelock) ..... Born at Philadelphia, PA Oct 6'94
Currey MR & MRS Christian B (Ashley A Trapp) Bcs.Van'84
  ☎ (615) 371-8896 .. 1041 Sneed Rd, Franklin, TN *37064*
Currier MR & MRS E Gray (Mary J Pfile) Rv.Bel'72
JUNIORS MISS Katharine E ....
☎ (970) 223-7277 1426 Red Oak Court, Ft Collins, CO *80525*

Curry DR & MRS Charles M JR (Susanne T McGuire) | ☎ (908) 234-1285
B.L.Wk.HolyC'65.Pa'85 . . . . | PO Box 17,
MR C MacNeil 3d—at U of Pa . . . . | Oldwick, NJ *08858*
MR Fraser MacL 2d—at U of Pa . . . .
Curry MRS Henry M 3d (Kennedy—Margaretta duP Tatnall) . . . . . Died at Sewickley, PA Jan 21'96
Curtis MR & MRS Charles F JR (Corinne W Collins) StLaw'84.NEng'83
185 Woodbury St, Hamilton, MA *01983*
Curtis MR & MRS John R JR (Christine W | ☎ (203) 264-4675
von Goeben) Sth'51.GeoW'50.JHop'51 . . . . | 353A Heritage
MR Allen R—Box 1129, South Bend, WA *98586* | Village, Southbury,
MR Robert F—at 4040 Synott Rd, Apt 209, | CT *06488-1710*
Houston, TX *77082*
Curtis MISS Laura B—StLaw'84
☎ (303) 543-9690 . . 3439 Cripple Creek Square, Boulder, CO *80303*
Curtis MRS McCall (Ward—Beachboard—Anne L Curtis)
Tex'57.Me.Ac.Dar.Ncd.
Cuadrante 8A, San Miguel de Allende, GTO 37700, Mexico
Cushing MR & MRS Edward B (Philio E | ☎ (508) 526-9934
Wigglesworth) SL'80.Sim'91.My.Myc. . . . . . . | 44 Masconomo St,
MISS Amelia C—at Northfield-Mt Hermon . . . . . | Manchester-By-The-
JUNIORS MISS Mae L . . . . | Sea, MA *01944*
Cushman MISS Christina M—Tul'92
9167 W 3 St, Beverly Hills, CA *90210*
Cushman MRS John G (Katharine M Adams) . . . . Died Aug 29'95
Cutler MR Donald F 4th . . see E N Vestner
Cutler MR & MRS L Bradley 2d (Ebner—Linda A Beech)
Miami'75.Cyb.H'71
4010 Wycombe Dv, Sacramento, CA *95864*
Cutler MRS Louisa R (Louisa R Baptiste) . . . . Married at Hamilton, MA
Vestner MR Eliot N (late Eliot N) . . . . Aug 11'95
Cutler MR Q A Shaw . . see E N Vestner
Cutter MR & MRS Bruce A (Claudia M Steers) Stone'79.Conn'72
☎ (203) 461-8173 . . 34 Ethan Allen Rd, North Stamford, CT *06903*
Cuvelier MR & MRS Guillaume (Andrea N Rizzo) Geo'89.Va'91
☎ (011-33-1) 42-88-95-79 . . 65 rue de Passy, 75016 Paris, France

D

Daley REV DR Alexander S—Cw.H'57.EpiscTheo'71.PittTheo'84
☎ (508) 686-6858 . . 390 Main St, North Andover, MA *01845*
Daley MRS Robert F (Louisa Watson) . . . . Died Aug 28'95
Daly MRS J Holmes (Bliss—Katharine Boston)
☎ (619) 551-8378 . . The Cloisters, 7160 Fay Av, La Jolla, CA *92037*
Dalzell MISS (DR) Victoria P (Robert F JR) . . . . . . Married at Amherst, MA
Dundon MR Sean T (late Thomas) . . . . Sep 23'95
Dandy MASTER Robert Praeger (Walter E 3d) . . . . Born at Vail, CO Dec 20'95
Danforth MR & MRS Thomas H (Rachel G Weaver) Cr'45.St.G.Cr'43
☎ (716) 626-4968 . . 193 Oakgrove Dv, Buffalo, NY *14221*
Daniels MR & MRS Frank A 3d (Teresa A Davidson) Kas'78.Duke'78
☎ (919) 836-1231 . . 2342 Churchill Rd, Raleigh, NC *27608*
Darman MASTER Christopher Temple Emmet (Richard G) . . . . . . Born at Washington, DC Dec 5'95

Darrell MR & MRS Norris JR (Henriette M Haid) | ☎ (516) 692-9654
Ri.Eyc.Csh.Plg.H.'51.H'54 . . . . | 44 Walnut Tree
MR Andrew H—Ri.Eyc.Csh.Geo'85.Tufts'88. | Lane, Cold Spring
Va'91—at ☎ (212) 580-0108 . . 127 W 79 St, | Harbor, NY *11724*
Apt 11D, New York, NY *10024* . . . .
Davidge MISS Dorsey—Tufts'80.Cvc.
☎ (202) 387-0558 . . 2740 Cortland Place NW, Washington, DC *20008*
Davidge MR & MRS Nicholas A (Jill Rabon) Char'ton'82.Mt.Mid'77
☎ (203) 245-9361 . . "Prospect Farm" 7 Fence Creek Dv, Madison, CT *06437-3113*
Davidge MASTER William G (Nicholas A) . . . . Born Feb 2'93
Davidson MR Allen D (Malcolm) . . . . Married at Lake Forest, IL
Grumhaus MISS Leslie (Peter) . . . . Oct 14'95
Davis MRS A Meyers (Dillen—Alice E Meyers) . . . . Died Sep 15'95
Davis MISS Alexandra Victoria (Michael J) . . . . Born at Wilmington, DE Feb 8'96
Davis MISS Julianne—PCTS'84
☎ (616) 975-3832 . . 3304 S Creek Dv SE, Apt 103, Kentwood, MI *49512-8382*
Davis MISS Margareta Evarts (J Staige 3d) . . . . Born at Burlington, VT Oct 14'95
Davis MR & MRS Mark A H (Michelle S Heydenreich)
Va'90.Va'94.Va'90.W&M'92
☎ (804) 378-8007 . . 1900 Swamp Fox Rd, Midlothian, VA *23112*
Davis MR & MRS Nathaniel (Elizabeth K Creese) | ☎ (909) 624-5293
Ober'54.Cos.Br'44 . . . . | 1783 Longwood Av,
MR James C—at Brown Grad . . . . | Claremont, CA
MR Thomas R—at NYU Law . . . . | *91711*
Davis MASTER Nicholas Charles (Michael J) . . . . Born at Wilmington, DE Aug 28'93
Davis JUNIORS MR Robert E . . see MRS K E Jackson
Davis MR & MRS Scott L (Martin—Christina | ☎ (509) 747-6724
Williams) LIU'68.Dar.Cal'61.Cl'68 . . . . | 2114 W Riverside
MR Scott L JR—at 30272 Rainbow Hill Rd, | Av, Spokane, WA
Golden, CO *80401* . . . . | *99201*
Davison MR & MRS George P (Judith F Rivkin) Y'79.Y'79.Cl'84
☎ (212) 877-7979 . . 255 W 90 St, Apt 5A, New York, NY *10024*
Davlin MR & MRS William E B (F Tracy Wenzell) Laf'88.Ford'94
☎ (212) 327-2990 . . 167 E 67 St, Apt 8A, New York, NY *10021*
Day MR & MRS Ethan S (Teresa M Tapia) NMexSt'89
☎ (505) 820-7617 . . 1660 Old Pecos Trail, Apt A308, Santa Fe, NM *87505*
Day MISS Savannah Bixby (Ethan S) . . . . Born at Santa Fe, NM Sep 9'94
Day MRS Statter (Voorhees—Frances Statter) . . . . Died at Short Hills, NJ Nov 30'95
Dean MR & MRS J Simpson JR (McConnell—Margaret A Mahler)
Wil.BtP.Evg.Rv.Cw.Bab'49
☎ (407) 832-8888 . . 291 El Vedado Way, Palm Beach, FL *33480*
Deane MISS Susan R (Daniel Thomas) . . . . Married at Narberth, PA
Hunter MR Robert McA 3d . . . . Jly 8'95
de Branges de Bourcia VCTSSE Elise (Groesbeck—VCTSSE Elise
de Branges de Bourcia) . . . . Died at Pompano Beach, FL Jan 6'96
Decker LT COL (RET) Arnold F A—USA . . . . Died at Moorestown, NJ Oct 21'95
Deeds JUNIORS MR Blake . . see D R Taylor

Deering MISS Alexandra K (Robinson A) ..... Married at New York, NY
  Haigney MR Dayton P 3d (Dayton P JR) .... Oct 14'95
de Fontnouvelle MR & MRS Patrick Y de F (Nathalie Nespoulous-Neuville) P'87
  ☎ (515) 292-7746 .. 2114 Hughes Av, Ames, IA *50014*
de France HRH PRCSS Chantal .. see F-X de Sambucy
Defty MRS S Bixby (Sarah T Bixby) V'53 .... | ☎ (011-49-30)
  MR Matthew B—V'82.Rice'88 .... | 324-0357
  | Schiller Strasse 73,
  | 10627 Berlin,
  | Germany
de Labar MRS Margot (Grill—Margot A Hoagland de Labar) Paris'79.Ht.Hl.
  ☎ (619) 682-7138 .. 9528 Miramar Rd, Apt 27, San Diego, CA *92126*
Delafield MRS B Reed (Barbara de S Reed) | ☎ (609) 466-3043
  Wheat'58 .... | 4 Cotswold Lane,
  MR M Livingston JR—at 1515 Montecito Rd, | Princeton, NJ *08540*
  Ramona, CA *92065* ....
Delafield MRS Edward C (Clelia B Benjamin) .... Died at
  Baltimore, MD Oct 17'95
Delafield MISS Susan E (J Dennis) .... Married at New York, NY
  Thornberry MR James K (James T) .... Oct 21'95
Delafield MRS William F (Brengle—Helen W Fox) Sg.
  ☎ (215) 984-8401 .. 600 E Cathedral Rd, Apt L106, Philadelphia, PA *19128*
de Laire MISS Anne M L (late Antoine R) .... Married at
  Poughkeepsie, NY
  Mulgrew MR George F JR .... Mch 18'95
de Laire MRS Antoine R (Mohl—Maria-Hélène | of ☎ (603)643-6647
  Manville) K.Cly. .... | 3 Balch Hill Lane,
  MR Georges F—StLaw'88—at St John's | Hanover, NH
  Seminary .... | *03755-1623*
  MISS Catherine M Mohl—V'81—at | ☎ (011-33)
  ☎ (011-33) 66-80-42-89 .. La Source, | 31-65-22-77
  rue des Pouzes, 30250 Junas, France ...... | "Le Petit
  | Bonneville" 14800
  | Englesqueville-en-
  | Auge, France
de Mailly MISS Diane B—BMr'76
  ☎ (310) 821-0920 .. 14000 Tahiti Way, Apt 312, Marina Del Rey, CA *90292*
de Marneffe DR & MRS Francis (Hopkins—Barbara | ☎ (617) 354-6300
  C Rowe) Va'52.Cy.Sm.Chi.Ncd.H.Lond'50 .... | 126 Coolidge Hill
  MR Peter L—at ☎ (602) 922-1436 | Rd, Cambridge, MA
  5877 N Granite Reef Rd, Scottsdale, AZ *85250* . | *02138*
de Meaux VCTE & VCTSSE Marc (Katherine D M Tuck) Gen'82.Strasbourg'86
  ☎ (011-33-1) 43-06-15-18 .. 13 bis rue Carrier Belleuse, 75015 Paris, France
de Mello MR & MRS Michael E S S (Deborah Fiuza) Rcn.Cl'79.Cl'81
  ☎ (011-351-1) 467-2966 .. Avenida de Inglaterra 30, 2765 Estoril, Portugal
DeMicheli MR & MRS Robert J (Judith R MacLean) LondDsgn'75.Ant'86.Sfy.SFrSt'74.CenMich'80
  ☎ (415) 668-9978 .. 747 Twelfth Av, San Francisco, CA *94118-3620*
Demmler MR Ralph H .... Died at
  Pittsburgh, PA Dec 23'95

DeMott MISS Beatrice Leigh (g—Richard W DeMott) ... Born Dec 24'94
DeMott MR Garret P (Richard W) .... Married
  Hickey MISS Madeleine .... May 24'93
DeMoville MRS Margaret Jock (Carnathan—Margaret Jock DeMoville) MissSt'70.Dar.Dcw.
  ☎ (601) 842-7913 .. 2309 Parkway Dv, Tupelo, MS *38801-1113*
Denebeim MR & MRS Keith Webster (Marie L O'Dea) Cal'82.Sfy.SFrSt'85
  ☎ (415) 388-7271 .. 413 Maple St, Mill Valley, CA *94941*
de Neufville MR Robert E—Hn.H'92
  ☎ (510) 841-4058 .. 2821 Hillegass Av, Apt 8, Berkeley, CA *94705*
Denison MISS Sandra M .... Married at Plainfield, NH
  Mallett MR Edmund E 3d .... Jly 29'95
Dennis DR & MRS (DR) Daniel A 3d (Roxanna | ☎ (334) 343-1210
  Stewart) TroySt'75.SAla'76 .... | 4105 Ridgelawn Dv,
  JUNIORS MR Daniel A 4th | Mobile, AL *36608*
  JUNIORS MR Joseph S ....
Dennis MR Richmond B .... Died Dec 19'95
Denny MRS George M (Spaulding—Blanche Staniland) .... Died at
  Buffalo, NY Apr 28'95
Denton MR E Castner 3d—BowlG'92 .. see B A Craig
Denton MISS Elizabeth C—SL'90.Cin'94 .. see B A Craig
de Peyster MR & MRS F Ashton 3d (Margo M Donahue) BtP.Va'67.Stan'71
  ☎ (407) 835-8126 .. 306 Worth Av, Palm Beach, FL *33480*
de Rham MR J Christopher—McG'83
  ☎ (212) 534-1321 .. 345 E 93 St, Apt 20G, New York, NY *10128*
de Ropp MRS Alfred (Zoé B Belt) .... Died Sep 13'95
DeRosa MASTER Brian Gorman (Thomas J) .... Born at
  Baltimore, MD Jly 3'94
DeRosa MR & MRS Thomas J (Leslie R Gorman) Geo'82.Md.Geo'80.Cl'88
  ☎ (410) 467-7283 .. 7 Whitfield Rd, Baltimore, MD *21210*
de Sambucy BRN François-Xavier & de France | 4 rue Denis Poisson,
  HRH PRCSS Chantal .... | 75017 Paris, France
  JUNIORS BRNSS Kildine ....
  JUNIORS BRN Axel ....
  JUNIORS BRN Alexandre ....
de Sibour MR Raoul L—Duke'82
  ☎ (561) 833-1829 .. 2800 N Flagler Dv, West Palm Beach, FL *33407*
Despard MRS Douglas C JR (White—Janet Harwood) .... Died at
  Carmel, CA Sep 5'95
Detweiler MRS Lynn L (Irene B McCune) Pc. ..... | Bishop White
  MISS Anne L .... | Lodge,
  | 600 E Cathedral Rd,
  | Philadelphia, PA
  | *19128*
Deuel MISS Maggie D .. see V DeP Burroughs
Deuel JUNIORS MISS Sarah G .. see V DeP Burroughs
Devens MR Richard M .... Died at
  Olney, MD Nov 4'95
Dewart MR Brian—Hob'64.Cr'67.SUNY'92 ...... | 350 Ellis Hollow
  MISS Elizabeth A—at SUNY Buffalo .... | Creek Rd, Ithaca,
  | NY *14850*
Dewey MISS Olivia Alexandra (Paul C G JR) .... Born at
  New London, CT Aug 31'95
Dewing MR John P JR .... Married at Palm Beach, FL
  Diedrich MISS Carol L (Wesley) .... Jun 25'95
De Witt MR H Sanford .... Died at
  Cincinnati, OH Jan 4'96

De Witt MRS H Sanford (Annette M Kite) . . . . ☎ (513) 782-6410
    MISS Jessica S—Wells'79—at ☎ (718) 389-4220   643 Maple Trace,
    182 Norman Av, Brooklyn, NY *11222* . . . .   Springdale, OH
                                                                                45246
Dibble MRS Kathleen M (Byczkowski—Kathleen C   ☎ (415) 931-0575
    Moulder) Hlns'50 . . . .   1000 Green St,
    MISS Anne Byczkowski—V'79—at   Apt 1101,
    105 Lake St, San Francisco, CA *94118* . . . . .   San Francisco, CA
                                                                                94133
di Carpegna MISS Allegra . . see R Barclay
di Carpegna MR Guelfo . . see R Barclay
di Carpegna MR Rufo . . see R Barclay
Dick MR John H . . . . Died at
                                                                                Meggett, SC Sep 22'95
Dickason MRS Livingston T (Katherine H Maxwell) . . . . Died at
                                                                                Short Hills, NJ Sep 20'95
Dickerman MR Watson B—Sm.H'69
    ☎ (617) 354-6100 . . 19 Chauncy St, Cambridge, MA *02138*
Dickey MRS Lucy Baker (Harfield—Lucy Baker) ⚓
    ☎ (011-599-5) 55-288 . . "Morning Glory" Simpson Bay, St Maarten,
    Netherlands Antilles
Dickson MRS Dennis C (Platt—Dennis Covel) Sth'58
    ☎ (203) 629-4370 . . 249 Milbank Av, Apt 326, Greenwich, CT *06830*
Diederichs MR John K . . . . Died at
                                                                                Chicago, IL Jly 29'95
Diesel MASTER Elliot Armour (John H 2d) . . . . Born at
                                                                                Houston, TX Jun 2'93
Diesel MR & MRS John H 2d (M Brooks Armour) P'85.On.Rice'82
    ☎ (409) 532-4252 . . Pierce Ranch, Pierce, TX *77467*
Diffenderffer MR C Rich (late Clarence R) . . . Married at Montchanin, DE
    Thouron MRS C Kitchell (McCoy—Carol V Kitchell) . . . . . . Dec 9'95
Diffenderffer MR & MRS C Rich (McCoy—Thouron   ☎ (302) 654-0509
    —Carol V Kitchell) Me.Ste.Cts.Rcp.Md.Wil.   PO Box 141,
    Va'55 . . . .   190 Rockland Rd,
    MISS Anne W—at ☎ (011-44-1865) 242-550   Montchanin, DE
    Manor Farm, North Hinksey, Oxfordshire   *19710*
    ONX2 0NA, England . . . .
    JUNIORS MR George G Thouron 3d—at
    Randolph-Macon . . . .
Diffenderffer MR Michael K—Me.
    ☎ (011-44-1666) 822-518 . . Park House, Charlton Park, Malmesbury,
    Wiltshire SN16 9OJ, England
Dillon MRS Hardenbergh (Elizabeth K Hardenbergh) Shcc.
    1127 Fellowship Rd, Basking Ridge, NJ *07970*
Dillon MR Herbert L JR—P'47
    ☎ (805) 969-6708 . . 1967 Inverness Lane, Santa Barbara, CA *93108*
Dillon MR R Forrest—So'70
    73 River Rd, Brunswick, ME *04011*
Dimond MR F Ronald—Yn.Y'58.Cl'60 . . . .   ☎ (203) 329-7440
    MISS Allison B—at Lindsley Rd, West Falmouth,   789 Riverbank Rd,
    MA *02574* . . . .   Stamford, CT *06903*
    JUNIORS MR James L—at Lindsley Rd,
    West Falmouth, MA *02574* . . . .
Dimond MR & MRS Renwick De G JR (Ellen B Doyle) Denis'91.Denis'89
    ☎ (804) 358-3558 . . 4517 W Franklin St, Richmond, VA *23221*
Dingman MR Robert J—StLaw'63
    ☎ (208) 336-0474 . . 1376 E Braemere Rd, Boise, ID *83702*

Dinkins MRS Philip M (Ella K Uppercu) . . . . Died at
                                                                                Palm Beach, FL Nov 17'95
Dixon MR & MRS Bruce De W (Barbara Engel) Sth'55.Uncl.Tvcl.Ihy.H'55
    ☎ (203) 629-1043 . . 20 Greenbriar Lane, Greenwich, CT *06831*
Dixon MRS Morris H (Linn—Mary E Lewis) . . . . Died at
                                                                                Kennett Square, PA Apr 16'95
Dixon MR & MRS Stewart S JR (Catherine A Miller) Nw'87.Ithaca'87
    ☎ (847) 295-0562 . . 55 E Witchwood Lane, Lake Bluff, IL *60044*
Dixon MASTER Stewart Strawn 3d (Stewart S JR) . . . . Born at
                                                                                Chicago, IL Jan 14'96
Dixon MR & MRS Terence A (Sydney F Cruice)
    Penn'81.Drex'92.TyDub'87.Cl'93
    ☎ (212) 799-7040 . . 20 W 64 St, Apt 17N, New York, NY *10023*
D'Lauro MR Frank A JR—Pc.Rc.Rv.W&L'62.Pa'65
    ☎ (610) 584-1601 . . "Long Lane Farm" Box 674, Worcester, PA *19490*
Dodge MR Marshall J JR—Fic.Fiy.Y'33
    ☎ (941) 377-2930 . . B417 Kobernick, 1955 N Honoré Av, Sarasota,
    FL *34235*
Dohan MISS Marguerite Van Dyke (Thomas R JR) . . . . Married
    Hecking MR Dirck J 2d . . . . Dec 16'95
Donahoe MR Daniel J 4th—Bost'92
    ☎ (415) 474-5852 . . 964 Central Av, San Francisco, CA *94115*
Donald MR & MRS Glenn H JR (M Kenneith Wilson) Aub'86.Cy.Aub'85
    ☎ (205) 879-7769 . . 7 Honeysuckle Lane, Mountain Brook, AL *35213*
Donaldson MR William H (late Eames) . . . . . . Married at Waccabuc, NY
    Morrison MRS J W Phillips (Jane W Phillips) . . . . Dec 23'95
Donnell MR & MRS John R (Caraboolad—Maureen Nahas)
    Ursul'54.BtP.Evg.Srb.Nrr.Cv.Cy.Un.Rr.Case'34. H'56 . . of
    ☎ (407) 655-2297 . . "Villa Contenta" 300 Parc Monceau, Palm Beach,
    FL *33480*
    ☎ (216) 851-2297 . . 1 Bratenahl Place, Apt 1401, Bratenahl, OH *44108*
Dorland MR & MRS Dodge O (Bonita G Zeese)
    Nu'76.Nu'78.Snc.Hl.Cw.Rv.Vca.Y.Colg'70
    ☎ (212) 628-6067 . . 755 Park Av, New York, NY *10021*
Dorn MR Christopher H—Cl'86
    ☎ (212) 348-1088 . . 305 E 86 St, Apt 5BW, New York, NY *10028*
Dorrance MR & MRS Bennett (Jacquelynn B Williams) Ariz'69.Bcs.Ariz'69
    ☎ (602) 596-5000 . . 7400 N Shadow Mountain Rd, Paradise Valley,
    AZ *85253-3381*
Dorsey MISS Elizabeth C—Gonzaga'96 . . see A D Terry
Doub MISS Victoria Elizabeth Fenger (George C 3d) . . . . Born at
                                                                                Palos Verdes, CA Nov 21'94
Doucette MR Donald F JR . . see MRS C E Kinkade
Dougherty MR John K . . . . Died May 19'95
Douglas MRS Archibald G (BRNSS Margareta C H Lagerfelt) Sl.
    ☎ (804) 978-2002 . . Rivanna Farm, 2973 Stony Point Rd,
    Charlottesville, VA *22911-9140*
Douglas MR Barclay JR—Nrr.Wk.Snc.Ford'73
    3 Division St, Newport, RI *02840*
Douglas MRS Eleanor Dick (Eleanor S Dick)   ☎ (617) 242-8260
    Wk.Ncd. . . . .   197—8 St,
    MISS Dorothy H . . . .   Charlestown, MA
    MISS Emilie D. *02129*
Douglas MISS Sharman (Hay—Sharman Douglas) . . . . Died at
                                                                                New York, NY Feb 3'96
Douglass MR Archibald G . . . . Died at
                                                                                Fish Creek, WI Sep 14'95

Downing MR & MRS James B JR (Patricia A Del Piano) Gv.P'53 . . . . ☎ (561) 286-3697
47 S Sewalls Point Rd, Stuart, FL *34996*
   MISS Katherine M . . . .
   MISS Megan E . . . .
Downing MISS Lily de J (James B JR) . . . . Married at Watch Hill, RI
   Burke MR John S 3d (John S JR) . . . . Oct 7'95
Doyle MR & MRS J Carol (Louise duP Rhinelander) Bnd'60.NotreD'57.Cl'60 . . . . ☎ (407) 855-2156
5012 St Denis Court, Orlando, FL *32812*
   MR Christopher H H . . . .
   MR Andrew C R—at ☎ (404) 888-0628 1207 Renaissance Way NE, Atlanta, GA *30308* .
Doyle MRS Jesse I (Johnstone—Curtis—Christy Mann) . . . . Died at Peterborough, NH Nov 17'95
Drake MR & MRS Lawrence (Morris—Cassandra S Franklin) V'47.Pkg.Me.P'41.Pa'52
   ☎ (610) 645-8681 . . 1400 Waverly Rd, Villa 32, Gladwyne, PA *19035*
Drayton MR & MRS Whitney (Catherine J Mactier) Syd'84.ColC'80
   ☎ (203) 637-8492 . . 16 Shore Acre Dv, Old Greenwich, CT *06870*
Drew MRS Thayer Hoffstot (Unterman—Thayer Drew Hoffstot) Cly. . . . . of ☎ (540)832-7284
Old Blue Ridge Tpke, Gordonsville, VA *22942*
☎ (407) 585-4089
2100 S Ocean Blvd, Palm Beach, FL *33480*
   JUNIORS MISS Megan D Unterman—at Kent . .
   JUNIORS MR Ian H Unterman—at Kent . . . . . .

Drowne MR & MRS Rhodes F (Lisa A Dinallo) AmU'91.AmU'85
   ☎ (610) 525-1229 . . 917 Old Gulph Rd, Bryn Mawr, PA *19010*
Drum COL & MRS J Hunter (Kenney—Elizabeth A Burke) Cvc.Sl.USA'37
   ☎ (860) 767-2433 . . 311 Essex Meadows, Essex Meadows, CT *06426*
Drummond MR Kenneth (Rachel L Cuendet)
   ☎ (609) 219-0115 . . Morris Hall, Apt M208, 1 Bishop's Dv, PO Box 6498, Lawrenceville, NJ *08648-0498*
Drury MR & MRS Andrew S JR (Margaret M Reeves) Yh.Cc.Ne.Cw.GeoW'77.Cit'82
   ☎ (307) 684-7000 . . PO Box 157, Buffalo, WY *82834*
Duble MR David Q . . . . Married Rock MISS Victoria . . . . Jly 1'95
DuBois MR & MRS Raymond F JR (Helen R Runnells) Y'78.Cvc.An.P'72 . . of
   ☎ (202) 342-1974 . . 1545—35 St NW, Washington, DC *20007*
   ☎ (540) 987-9212 . . "Lone Oak" 50 Manahoac Lane, Sperryville, VA *22740*
Du Bose MR & MRS Charles F (Sarah R Peters) Va'81.DU'82.Cc.NCar'80
   ☎ (804) 971-7261 . . "Ruddington" 4042 Ivy Rd, Charlottesville, VA *22903*
Du Bose MISS Elizabeth Porcher (Charles F) . . . . Born at Charlottesville, VA Aug 23'95
Du Bose MISS Sarah Robinson (Charles F) . . . . Born at Charlottesville, VA Feb 2'94
Duemling MR & MRS Robert W (Biddle—Louisa d'A duP Copeland) Cvc.C.Mt.Cly.Sl.Y'50.Y'53 . . of
   ☎ (202) 364-4690 . . 2950 University Terr NW, Washington, DC *20016*
   ☎ (410) 778-3568 . . 11966 Andelot Farm Lane, Worton, MD *21678*
Dugdale MR & MRS William Matthew S (Fisk—Paige S Perkins) SL'83
   ☎ (011-44-1827) 711-653 . . "Merevale Hall" Atherstone, Warwickshire CV9 2HG, England

Duggan MRS Stephen P (Beatrice V Abbott) . . . . Died Feb 18'96
Duke MR & MRS Anthony Drexel (Longaray—Maria L Alcebo) LIU'89.Rc.Ri.Pr.Mds.P'41 . . . . ☎ (516) 324-1596
"Harbor House" Box 177, East Hampton, NY *11937*
   MISS Lulita C—at Duke
   JUNIORS MR Washington A—at Pomfret . . . . .
   JUNIORS MR James B—at Rumsey Hall . . . .
Duke MR Nicholas R—Van'69
   ☎ (804) 971-3763 . . 1419 Old Ballard Rd, Charlottesville, VA *22901*
Duke MASTER William Angier Biddle (A Biddle JR) . . . . Born at Buenos Aires, Argentina Nov 11'95
Duncan MR Graham P (Ransom H) . . . . Married at Paul Smiths, NY La Torre MISS Laura M (James) . . . . Aug 19'95
Dunn MISS E Shawn (Stewart A JR) . . . . Married at Canadensis, PA Gardner MR Michael J (John J) . . . . Sep 9'95
Dunn MR & MRS Edward K JR (Janet Evans) Gchr'81.Elk.Md.Mv.P'57.H'60
   ☎ (410) 377-5641 . . "Vesper Hill" 7315 W Bellona Av, Baltimore, MD *21212*
Dunn MR & MRS Sydney B JR (Nelson—Mary M Knox) ColbyS'57.WChesU'86.Me.Wt.Rv.Ac. Ncd.Cr'40. . . . . of ☎ (610)688-5623
204 Hermitage Dv, Radnor, PA *19087*
☎ (803) 671-6957 "Dunn Inn" 1913 S Beach Rd, Hilton Head Island, SC *29928*
   MISS E Pegge Nelson—PugetS'90.Pitt'96. Me.—at ☎ (412) 687-7650 . . 5437 Ellsworth Av, Pittsburgh, PA *15232-1851* . . . .

du Pont MR Edmond . . . . Died at Kennett Square, PA Jan 15'96
du Pont MASTER Nicholas Randolph Powers (g—Pierre S du Pont) . . . Born at London, England Aug 28'95
Duryee MRS Kittie M S (Kittie Mills Sylvester) . . . . Died Jly 30'95
Dutterer MISS Debra C (late Downing Huber) . . . . Married at Westminster, MD
Bullock MR Jeffery . . . . Oct 1'95
Du Val MR & MRS Philip L R (Emmons—Janis L Lee) Plg.StA.Yn.Y'43 . . . . ☎ (203) 966-0695
193 Park St, New Canaan, CT *06840*
   MR David W Emmons . . . .
D'Wolf MRS F Lewis (Holmes—King—Frances H Lewis) . . name changed to King

E

Earle MASTER Henry Owens (g—MRS Eleanor F O Earle) . . . . Born Jun 13'94
Earle MASTER Thomas Vincent (g—MRS Eleanor F O Earle) . . . . . . Born May 18'94
Easter MRS Donald (Virginia Follett) . . . . Died at Charlottesville, VA Oct 25'95
Easterby LT & MRS David E (Rebecca P Webb) USN.Ws'89.Mit'87
   ☎ (713) 852-0269 . . 20810 Lake Park Trail, Kingwood, TX *77345*
Eberts MR Frederick W . . . . Died at Delray Beach, FL Oct 20'95

Eckman MRS John W (Ziesing—Jane Haussman) Nyc. . . . . ☎ (610) 469-6648
  "Heatherlea Farm"
  MISS Jane D Ziesing. . . . . 101 Iron Bridge Rd,
  MISS Heather W Ziesing . . . . Glenmoore, PA *19343*

Eddison MRS (DR) Grace G (Eddison—Dunne—Grace B Gere)
  Ws'49.Cl'60
  ☎ (803) 237-2679 . . PO Box 507, 202 Wyndham Rd, Pawleys Island, SC *29585-0507*

Edelen MR & MRS William B (Marian E Harvey) . . . . . ☎ (410) 377-3382
  Elk.Md. . . . . 6436 Cloister Gate
  MISS Wendy N—at Boston, MA . . . . Dv, Baltimore, MD *21212*

Edgar MR & MRS James A JR (Mary D Saunders) of ☎ (914)724-3557
  Wms'56.Cl'60 . . . . "Blueberry Hill"
  MR David S . . . . 100 Deer Hollow
  MR Christopher W . . . . Rd, Poughquag, NY *12570*
  "Allamanda" Windermere Island, Eleuthera, Bahamas

Edgerton MR Carter H (Albert S) . . . . Married at San Francisco, CA
  Foehr MISS Stephanie D . . . . Mch 4'95

Edgeworth MR & MRS Arthur B JR (Elizabeth D Walker)
  Cvc.Mt.Ncd.Wms'51.Va'54.Geo'57
  ☎ (301) 907-9111 . . 3907 Thornapple St, Chevy Chase, MD *20815-5039*

Edinger MR John S—Sar.Aht'51.H'53 . . of
  ☎ (302) 654-5791 . . 1002 Kensington Lane, Greenville, DE *19807-2540*
  ☎ (561) 274-0827 . . 1209 Crestwood Dv, PO Box 1806, Delray Beach, FL *33447*

Edmonston MR William E 3d (William E) . . . . Died Nov 14'95
Edson MISS Mary Trinity (Green—Mary Trinity Edson) Ariz'87
  ☎ (410) 235-1381 . . 110 W 39 St, Apt 171D, Baltimore, MD *21210*

Edwards MISS Deirdre (g—John Munroe) . . . . Born at Alexandria, VA May 17'94

Eells MR Jonathan W (William H) . . . . Married at Columbus, OH
  Grogg MISS Brenda L (Ronald) . . . . Dec 17'93

Eells MR & MRS Jonathan W (Brenda L Grogg) Wit'92.OWes'89
  ☎ (970) 395-0491 . . 5133 W 11 St, Apt 712, Greeley, CO *80634*

Egan MRS Burgevin (Illiaschenko—Julia D Burgevin) Chr.Dar.Cda.Dc.
  ☎ (904) 280-0677 . . 1000 Vicar's Landing Way, Apt I206, Ponte Vedra Beach, FL *32082*

Egan MRS Richard M (Mary Haskell) . . . . Died Jan 9'96

Eggleston MR & MRS Richard H JR (Gretchen G Hatfield)
  Pa'65.Sa.Ac.Pa'65.Geo'71 . . of
  ☎ (215) 438-3469 . . 308 Carpenter Lane, Philadelphia, PA *19119*
  ☎ (212) 861-8037 . . 229 E 80 St, New York, NY *10021*

Eichorn MR & MRS Mark D (Jane deD Kidd) Va'87.Rc.Fic.H'86
  ☎ (212) 876-7403 . . 1150 Fifth Av, Apt 11E, New York, NY *10128*

Eidt MR & MRS Edward Duncan (Mary Bellan) NELa'79.Miss'50
  ☎ (601) 442-7219 . . 211 S Rankin St, Natchez, MS *39120*

Eldridge MR Huntington . . . . Died at Lake Forest, IL Sep 23'95

Elebash CAPT LeGrand—USMC. . . . . Married at Cashiers, NC
  Barron MISS Allison . . . . Jun 10'95

Eliott DR Matthew S—Purd'79.Purd'83 . . see H Luce 3d

Elliott MR & MRS Gregory R (Henrietta C Judson) OWes'90.Dar.
  149 W Northwestern Av, Philadelphia, PA *19118* . . MR absent

Elliott MR Virgil L . . . . Died at San Francisco, CA Dec 2'95

Ellis MR & MRS G Corson 3d (Marion F Freeman)
  P'73.Y'80.Stc.Yn.Aht'77.Cl'84
  ☎ (207) 865-0799 . . 10 Cushing Briggs Rd, Freeport, ME *04032*

Elmer DR David B—Tufts'80.Tufts'84 . . . . ☎ (508) 362-1156
  JUNIORS MR Peter D—at Winchendon Sch . . . . . 568 Shoot Flying Hill Rd, Centerville, MA *02632*

Elmore MR S Churchill . . . . Died at Washington, DC Nov 1'95

Eltz CT Franz J—Vien'82
  52 Sagamore Rd, Bronxville, NY *10708*

Eltz CTSS Katharine (Katharine E O'Donoghue) . . ☎ (914) 337-4193
  Ken'73 . . . . 7 Midland Gardens,
  JUNIORS MISS Fiona F—at Indian Mtn Sch . . . . . Apt 03, Bronxville,
  JUNIORS MR Philipp A . . . . NY *10708*

Emery MR George I . . . . Died at Newton, MA Mch 17'95

Emery MASTER James David (g—MRS George I Emery) . . Born Nov 7'94

Emery MRS Rose B (Rose B Burks) Swb'61
  ☎ (804) 977-3767 . . 12 Oak Circle, Charlottesville, VA *22901*

Emery MRS Willard (Elizabeth Marvin) . . . . Died at Sarasota, FL Dec 18'95

Emery MR & MRS William 3d (Shelley H Dwight) ☎ (203) 966-3433
  Sth'57.San.Y'56 . . . . 677 Weed St,
  MR Nicholas D—at ☎ (303) 258-7813 . . . . PO Box 1222,
  PO Box 386, Nederland, CO *80466* . . . . New Canaan, CT *06840-1222*

Emmet MISS Caroline—Bnd'86
  ☎ (011-33-1) 48-74-43-04 . . 48 rue Notre Dame de Lorette, 75009 Paris, France

Emmet MISS Katharine Temple (True—Katharine of ☎ (212)255-4553
  Temple Emmet) Cly. . . . . 104 Bedford St, Apt
    MISS Gabriella M True—at ☎ (212) 966-5709 4C, New York, NY
    472 Broome St, New York, NY *10012* *10014*
  ☎ (802) 325-3098 Herrick Brook Rd, Pawlet, VT *05761*

Emmons MR David W . . see P L R Du Val
Emmons MASTER William Bacon 4th (g—MRS William B Emmons JR) . . . . Born Jly 1'95

Emory MRS Morris S (Mary P Leisenring) . . . . Died Sep 20'95
Ennis MRS Alfreda W (Alfreda L Wallace) . . . . Died at Mt Dora, FL Sep 10'95

Epstein DR & MRS Stephen E (Lee—Alice C Brown) Va'84.SL'81
  ☎ (804) 979-4622 . . "Tandem" Rte 10, Box 266, Charlottesville, VA *22903*

Erker MISS Marianna S—Cda.
  ☎ (404) 325-7617 . . 3100 Briarcliff Rd NE, Atlanta, GA *30329*

Ertman MISS Emilie Alexandra (C Eric) . . . . Born Jan 17'96
Eshleman MRS B Franklin 2d (Eshleman—Potts—Phoebe L Davis)
  Bnd'37.Sg.
  ☎ (508) 693-4456 . . 78 Franklin St, Box 2037, Vineyard Haven, MA *02568*

Eskridge MR & MRS William I (Josephine P Haas) Ala'91.Ala'91
☎ (205) 870-8002 . . 129 Cherry St, Birmingham, AL *35213*
Evans MASTER Charles Anthony JR (C Anthony) . . . . Born at Chicago, IL Jan 13'94
Evans MRS Harold G (Wagley—Lucas—M Elizabeth Raible) . . . . Died at Nantucket, MA Jun 18'95
Evans MISS Kathryn M (J Hart) . . . . Married at Newton Center, MA
Lagunowich MR Mark J (John) . . . . Jly 15'95
Evans MISS Lucretia B . . . . Died at Bronx, NY Jan 29'96
Evans MISS Margaret MacColl (Thomas G JR) . . . . Born Dec 27'95
Evans MR & MRS Thomas G JR (Emily W Eastlake) Hlns'92.W&L'91
☎ (413) 498-5459 . . 187 Main St, Apt 1, Northfield, MA *01360*
Evans MRS Thomas Goodwin (Juliet I Merryweather)
☎ (215) 836-2546 . . 6 Haws Lane, Apt C2, Flourtown, PA *19031*
Evans MR Thomas Goodwin—Pc.Bab'64 | ☎ (215) MI6-4013
MR Andrew M—WashColl'94—at New York, | "Merrywin"
NY . . . . | 335 Skippack Pike,
MR Charles H—at U of Pittsburgh . . . . | Ft Washington, PA *19034*
Evans MR Thomas M 3d (Thomas M JR) . . . . Married at Boston, MA
Duncan MISS Julia . . . . Dec 23'95
Evans MR William J (late John J) . . . . Married at New York, NY
Jones MRS Christina C (Christina P Clare). . . . . Oct 27'95
Evans MR & MRS William J (Jones—Christina P | ☎ (212) 876-3030
Clare) Rc.Ncd.Va'54 . . . . | 17 E 89 St,
JUNIORS MR Elliott S . . . . | New York, NY
MISS Palmer D Jones—at Trinity . . . . | *10128*
JUNIORS MR Oliver H Jones . . . . |
JUNIORS MR Frederick K Jones . . . . |
Everett MR & MRS Chandler H (Wiegand—Hoffman—
Marsha Crandall Brayton) Cent'y'59.Cv.Kt.Tv.Yn.Y'60.Cwr'70
☎ (216) 932-0363 . . 12546 Cedar Rd, Apt 2, Cleveland Heights, OH *44106*
Everett MR & MRS Frank E (Margaret C Bryant) Miss'34.Ncd.Miss'34
☎ (601) 636-4617 . . 4 Glenwood Circle, Vicksburg, MS *39180*
Ewald MISS Jessie Benton (Charles R) . . . . Born Nov 7'95
Ewald MISS Mary Adeline (Charles R) . . . . Born Nov 7'95
Ewing MR J G Blaine JR . . . . Died at Charleston, SC Sep 17'95
Ewing MR Patrick C (William) . . . . Died at Philadelphia, PA Nov 8'95
Ewing MR & MRS William Sanford (Sandra H Wickenden) Plg.
☎ (410) 876-5429 . . 2606 Jeffrey Lori Dv, Finksburg, MD *21048*
Eyre MR Alan E (Stephen C) . . . . Married at Rockville, MD
De Pree MISS Anita L (Willard) . . . . Sep 23'95
Eyre MR & MRS F Beverley 2d (Jennifer L Tullos) Cal'94.Cal'95
☎ (310) 839-0203 . . 9053 3-4 Hubbard St, Culver City, CA *90232*
Eyre MISS Riley Elizabeth (F Beverley 2d) . . . . Born at Los Angeles, CA Jun 30'95

F

Faber MR Albert H . . . . Died at Miami Beach, FL Oct 24'95

Faerber MISS Alexis (g—Douglas M Leale) . . . . Born at Seattle, WA Dec 29'95
Faesy MISS (DR) Lydia (A Robert) . . . . Married at Peacham, VT
Wanzer MR Charles T (Sidney H) . . . . Aug 19'95
Faesy MISS Mia Marcella (Richard) . . . . Born at Starksboro, VT Aug 12'95
Fagan MR Charles K . . see E G Cumming
Fair MISS Florence B (J Henry JR) . . . . Died at Telluride, CO Mch 9'95
Fair MR & MRS J Henry JR (Ravenel—Mary T | ☎ (803) 884-9181
Curtis) Sth'63.Ht.Ncd.GaTech'52. . . . . | 101 Mary St,
MISS Tiphaine T Ravenel . . . . | Mt Pleasant, SC
MR Curtis deSt Julien Ravenel—at | *29464*
☎ (803) 883-9141 . . 2867 Brownell St, |
Sullivans Island, SC *29482* . . . . |
MR Ramsay M Ravenel . . . . |
Fairbank MISS Elsa . . see MISS M Mahon
Fairbank MISS Wendy (Hatch—Wendy Fairbank) . . see MISS M Mahon
Fairchild MR Peter T—Snc. . . . . | ☎ (508) 699-6729
MR Peter T JR—at ☎ (203) 977-7042 | 89 Circular St,
11 Hoyt St, Darien, CT *06820* . . . . | North Attleboro, MA *02766*
Fanjul MR & MRS Alexander L (Leidy—Nicole Von G Redfield) Evg.BtP.Miami'74 ⚓
☎ (407) 835-3882 . . 110 Chateaux Dv, Palm Beach, FL *33480*
Farman-Farmaian MR & MRS Alexander (Patricia P Barlerin) Bnd'89.Cl'95.Ri.P.'87
☎ (212) 472-6711 . . 300 E 74 St, PH-A, New York, NY *10021*
Farmer MISS Suzanne (Fryer—Suzanne Farmer) . . . . | ☎ (717) 394-5515
MISS Amanda Fryer . . . . | 205 Heatherstone
JUNIORS MISS Abigail Fryer . . . . | Way, Lancaster, PA *17601*
Farr MRS Hollon W (Anne V Mathews) | ☎ (407) 647-4938
Bnd'46.C.Csn. . . . . | 1005 S Lakemont
MR James W—Dowl'79.LIU'81.Ford'86—at | Circle, Winter Park,
☎ (516) 447-6681 . . 77-405 Waverly Av, | FL *32792*
Patchogue, NY *11772* . . . . |
MR John M—GeoW'79.GeoW'81—at |
☎ (617) 969-5718 . . 206 Sumner St, |
Newton Center, MA *02159* . . . . |
Farr MR & MRS Thomas A (Lawrence—M Terry | ☎ (803) 524-9071
Livingston) P'54. . . . . | 78 Dolphin Point
MR Kenneth H—at ☎ (505) 820-6054 | Dv, Beaufort, SC
601 W San Mateo Rd, Santa Fe, NM *87505*. . . . | *29902*
MR Edward L—at ☎ (212) 879-5944 |
434 E 75 St, New York, NY *10021* . . . . |
Farrell MR & MRS W Mason (Julia L Pattison) Cal'86.NCar'85
☎ (805) 684-6460 . . 5412 Granada Way, Carpinteria, CA *93013*
Faunce MR John H JR . . . . Died Nov 10'95
Fay MR & MRS Paul B JR (Anita R Marquez) Bhm.Pcu.Cvc.Sfg.Stan'41 . . of
☎ (415) 752-9596 . . 3766 Clay St, San Francisco, CA *94118*
☎ (619) 862-2267 . . 74-641 Arroyo Dv, Indian Wells, CA *92210*
Feder MR & MRS Andrew M (Abigail L Jones) V'85.Co.Ny.S.Cda.V'85 ⚓
☎ (516) 922-2804 . . 5 Mill River Rd, Upper Brookville, NY *11771*
Fedor MR & MRS David A (Katherine S Stone) Sth'93.Br'91
☎ (408) 446-1416 . . 20749 Celeste Circle, Cupertino, CA *95014*

Fenton MR & MRS Martin JR (Griffith—Majella K Clark) Y'56 . . . . ☎ (619) 456-1938
  MISS Lauren W—at 5635 E Sixth Avenue P'kway, Apt F, Denver, CO 80220 . . . . 8070 La Jolla Shores, Apt 446,
  MR Walker—at 3519 South Court, Palo Alto, CA 94306 . . . . La Jolla, CA 92037
    MISS Caroline C Griffith—at Middlebury . . . .

Fenzl MR & MRS Terry E (Barbara L Pool) Wis'67.Wis'66
  ☎ (602) 266-0071 . . 6610 N Central Av, Phoenix, AZ 85012

Ferguson MR & MRS J Howard 3d (Johnson—Patricia L Zoch) A.Ri.
  ☎ (210) 828-7080 . . 350 Argyle Av, San Antonio, TX 78209

Ferrarini LT & MRS Brant G (Tawni Hunt) USAF.SIll'85.Wash'88.Wash'93.UWash'88
  15034 SW 91 Av, Tigard, OR 97224

Ferrarini MR & MRS Steven P (Jennifer A Callies) Seattle'90.UWash'89
  2444 SE Tibbetts St, Portland, OR 97202

Ferrer MRS C O'Hara (Catherine E O'Hara) Cal'65.Cwr'91 . . . . ☎ (216) 371-5177
  MR Hugh G—P'90 . . . . 2303 Scholl Rd, University Heights, OH 44118

Ferrer MAJ & MRS Robert N JR (Elizabeth Gravatt) USMC.VaCmth'82.An.Rv.Cspa.Fw.Cit'82
  ☎ (804) 633-6862 . . "Chase's End Farm" 17237 Antioch Rd, Milford, VA 22514

Ferrer MR Thomas H—Unn.Kt.P'64
  ☎ (216) 491-9371 . . 3208 Warrensville Center Rd, Apt 308, Shaker Heights, OH 44122

Fessenden MRS Alexandra I (Meehan—Alexandra D Irving) So. . . . . ☎ (516) 283-8614
  MR Michael J Meehan 3d . . . . 25 Ochre Lane, PO Box 2686,
  MR Alexander D Meehan . . . . Southampton, NY 11969

Fessenden MR Jerald D—Un.Plg.Y'60.Pa'66
  ☎ (212) 348-5583 . . 1060 Fifth Av, New York, NY 10128

Fessenden MRS Sewall H (Crowninshield—Elizabeth Taylor) . . . . Died at Sherborn, MA Jan 2'96

Fetcher MRS Edwin S (Fetcher—Marguerite Foster) . . . . . Died May 5'95

Fiechter MISS Olivia Hayward (Bayard R) . . . . Born at Chestnut Hill, PA Sep 15'95

Field MR Augustus B 3d . . . . Married at Naples, FL
  Rynne MISS Susan E . . . . Jun 18'94

Field MR & MRS Augustus B 3d (Susan E Rynne) T.H'55
  ☎ (803) 432-9356 . . 1819 Brevard Place, Camden, SC 29020

Field MR & MRS James A (Lila R Breckinridge) Ws'40.H'37
  3500 West Chester Pike, CH5, Newtown Square, PA 19073

Field MRS Robert M (Mary L Gardner) . . . . Died at Atlanta, GA Dec 12'95

Fielding MISS Margaret Fairfax
  ☎ (410) 539-0761 . . 1425 Haubert St, Baltimore, MD 21230

Fink MRS Bruce W (Rodzianko—Patricia H Boyd)
  ☎ (202) 332-1932 . . 2370 Champlain St NW, Washington, DC 20009-2634

Finley MISS Milbourne S (Knox H) . . . . Married at Collonge-Bellerive, Switzerland
  Mowery MR Thomas . . . . Oct 5'95

Fiorato MR & MRS Hugo (Pogue—Scott—Gilchrist —Joelyn S Littauer) Bnd'46.Pqt.Cly . . . . ☎ (203) 259-0888
  MISS Stephanie S Gilchrist—at PO Box 886,
    ☎ (802) 253-2893 . . 43 Shawhill Rd, Stowe, 459 Hull's H'way,
    VT 05672 . . . . Southport, CT 06490-0886

Fischer MR Edwin G JR (Edwin G) . . . . Married at Newport, RI
  Grow MISS Amanda B (Virgil B) . . . . Oct 7'95

Fischer MR & MRS George W (Suzannah C White) DeP'91.Wab'91
  ☎ (718) 834-8328 . . 53 Dean St, Apt 1, Brooklyn, NY 11201

Fischer MASTER John Edwards (George W) . . . . Born at New York, NY Oct 29'95

Fish MR Frederick . . . . Died at Chatham, NJ Jan 30'96

Fish MRS Richard R (Heckert—Callender—Margaret Gibbons) Woos'44.SUNY'52
  ☎ (619) 744-8696 . . 1508 Circa Del Lago, Apt B111, San Marcos, CA 92069

Fisher MR & MRS Chester G 3d (Laura E Smith) Geo'77.Pitt'80.Rr.Pqt.Pa'74
  ☎ (412) 688-8595 . . 5540 Dunmoyle St, Pittsburgh, PA 15217

Fisher MISS Helen E (Bergquist—Helen E Fisher) Nu'68.Col'75
  ☎ (212) 744-9870 . . 4 E 70 St, New York, NY 10021

Fisher DR & MRS John R S (Marianna S O'Donovan) Srr.Wil.Ac.Pa'61 . . . . ☎ (610) 384-3902
  MISS Katharine S—at ☎ (202) 333-8099 "Glenderro Farm"
  3008 R St NW, Apt 2, Washington, DC 20007 . RD 3, Coatesville, PA 19320

Fisk MRS Shirley C (Mary A Harriman) . . . . Died at Arden, NY Jan 6'96

FitzGerald MRS Philip J (Hortense E Chatillon) . . . . Died at Carmel, CA Oct 22'95

Flaherty MISS Jennifer deB (Francis E) . . . . . . Married at Palo Alto, CA
  Galey MR David W . . . . Oct 21'95

Flather-Morgan MISS (DR) Alexandra W—P'85.Y'89 . . see H S Morgan

Fleck MRS Francis E (Sweeney—Isabelle M Seltzer) ☎ (717) 762-1388
  BMr'37.Ny.Sl.Dar. . . . . 201 Clayton Av,
  MISS Elaine C—at 4100 Cathedral Av NW, Waynesboro, PA
  Washington, DC 20016 17268

Fleitas MRS Allison F (Maddock—Ruth M Quigley) BtP.Evg.
  ☎ (407) 659-7371 . . 369 S Lake Dv, Apt 5G, Palm Beach, FL 33480

Fletcher MR & MRS Andrew JR (Vincel—Frank— ☎ (516) 283-2975
  Ann S Burford) Un.So.B.Srb.Chr.Snc.StJ.Ne . . . . "Caramar IV"
  MISS Carolyn A Vincel . . . . 420 Hill St, Southampton, NY 11968

Flint MRS John Gardiner (Laura M Hancock)
  ☎ (309) 694-7016 . . Riverview 315, 500 Centennial Dv, East Peoria, IL 61611-6767

Flint MR & MRS Peter H (Karen R Gebhart) ☎ (302) 652-7642
  Ober'64.Wil.Y'64 . . . . 205 Center Meeting
  MR Peter H JR . . . . Rd, Box 3971, Greenville, DE 19807

Flood MR & MRS David B (Georgia A Clark) Pa'82.Del'78.Pitt'79
  ☎ (508) 356-3602 . . 141 County Rd, Ipswich, MA 01938

Flowers MISS C Leigh (Samuel R) . . . . Married at Birmingham, AL
  Gannaway MR Bryan W (George T) . . . . Feb 24'96

Fogarty MISS Elizabeth E (Edward T) . . . . Married at Darien, CT
    Foote MR Joel D 2d (Joel B) . . . . Oct 21'95
Foley MRS James E 3d (Jennifer A Seymour) Stan'84.Srb.Ncd.
    ☎ (415) 986-6267 . . 840 Powell St, Apt 501, San Francisco, CA *94108*
Foley MR James E 3d—L.Wk.Pcu.Srb.Me'75
    ☎ (401) 848-9709 . . ''Brenton Cottage'' 125 Brenton Rd, Newport, RI *02840-7207*
Follett MASTER Benjamin Branch 4th (William R) . . . . Born at
    Stamford, CT Jly 24'93
Follett MR & MRS William R (Barbara D Wickersham)
    Sim'83.Snc.Sar.Ofp.Dar.GreenMt'83
    ☎ (203) 978-0644 . . 30 Birchwood Rd, Stamford, CT *06907*
Fooshee MRS Malcolm (Taylor—Green—Wynne Byard) . . . . Died at
    Gig Harbor, WA Nov 15'95
Foote MR Douglass G—Cr'43
    ☎ (615) 352-3764 . . 105 Lincoln Court, Nashville, TN *37205*

Forbes MR & MRS Christopher C (BRNSS Astrid M von Heyl) K.C.Eh.Gr.Plg.StJ.P'72 . . . .
    MISS Charlotte A M . . . .
☎ (908) 234-9483
''Timberfield''
95 Old Dutch Rd,
Far Hills, NJ *07931*

Forbes MR Richard M . . . . Died at
    Baltimore, MD Oct 6'95

Forbes MR & MRS Robert L (Raurell-Soto—Lydia S Appel) Cl'95.Rc.Shcc.Eh.NCar'71 . . . .
    MR A Miguel Raurell-Soto . . . .
☎ (212)620-2460
211 Central Park W,
New York, NY
10024
''Timberfield''
95 Old Dutch Rd,
Far Hills, NJ *07931*

Forbes MRS W Stuart (Godley—Katharine H Fitch) . . . . Died at
    Gloucester, MA Aug 11'95

Forbes DR & MRS William I 3d (Barbara L Frederick) P'64.TJef'72.TJef'73. . . . .
    MR David S—at U of Rochester . . . .
    MR William F—at Lafayette . . . .
☎ (315) 629-5754
27815 Call Rd,
PO Box 309,
Evans Mills, NY
13637

Forcier MR Guy S . . . . Died at
    St Louis, MO Jly 7'95

Ford MR & MRS Brin R (Joy Winder) H'64 . . . .
    MISS Brinley S—at ☎ (203) 966-9982
    6 Ledge Av, New Canaan, CT *06840* . . . .
    MISS Jennifer M—at ☎ (505) 820-2495
    836A E Palace Av, Santa Fe, NM *87501* . . . . . .
☎ (203) 776-9532
411 Temple St,
New Haven, CT
06511

Ford MR Christopher P (F Richards 3d) . . . . Married
    Noonan MISS Laura A . . . . Oct 14'95
Ford MRS Frank Hewitt JR (Butler—Barbara W Cowan) . . . . . . Married at
    Mobile, AL
    Peebles MR Emory B JR . . . . Mch 24'95
Ford MR & MRS Gerald R (Warren—Elizabeth Bloomer) Bhm.Mich'35.Y'41
    ☎ (619) 324-1763 . . Rancho Mirage, CA *92270*

Ford MR & MRS Peter B (Amanda C Millspaugh) Bost'78 ⚓ . . . .
    MISS Jessica B . . . .
☎ (561) 234-4749
1789 Coral Way S,
Vero Beach, FL
32963

Fordyce MR Robert D . . . . Died at
    New York, NY Jun 7'95

Fordyce MR S Wesley 5th—Geo'78.Pa'84
    ☎ (314) 831-2223 . . ''Beaux Eaux'' 2701 Shackelford Rd, Florissant, MO *63031*
Fordyce MR William C . . . . Died at
    St Louis, MO Oct 12'95

Forrester MR & MRS Peter C (Edith W Brooks) D.Un.Bost'66 . . . .
    MISS Melinda B—LakeF'90—at
    ☎ (617) 536-4120 . . 233 Beacon St, Boston, MA *02116* . . . .
☎ (617) 536-0225
136 Beacon St,
Boston, MA *02116*

Forster MR & MRS Christopher A (Elizabeth M Cheston) Sth'56.Y.'54 . . . .
    MISS Emily C—Colg'90—at ☎ (206) 729-0651
    6522 Fourth Av NE, Seattle, WA *98115* . . . . . .
    MR David A—Y'86—at ☎ (011-44-171)
    373-1172 . . 58 Lexham Gardens, London W8 JA, England . . . .
☎ (212) AT9-2193
1105 Park Av,
New York, NY
10128

Fortenbaugh MASTER William Wall 2d (Michael W) . . . . Born at
    New York, NY Jly 2'95
Foss MR Eugene N 2d . . . . Died at
    Franconia, NH Nov 14'95
Foster MR David V (Giraud Vernam) . . . . . Married at Washington, DC
    Listzwan MISS Olivia (Thomas) . . . . Dec 5'94
Foster MISS Gail M—Cr'82.Geo'95
    ☎ (703) 558-0448 . . 2100 Lee H'way, Apt 119, Arlington, VA *22201*
Foster MRS Howard H (Dorothy J Ernst)
    ☎ (908) 224-7670 . . 40 Riverside Av, Apt 6B, Red Bank, NJ *07701*
Foster MRS Lyn O (Lyn Oliva) . . . . Married at Orlando, FL
    MacVane MR Phillip F . . . . Dec 31'95

Fouke MR & MRS Lucien R JR (Becky W Jones) Cy.Y'63.Wash'70. . . . .
    MR Lucien R III—at ☎ (314) 725-3290
    6253 Northwood Av, St Louis, MO *63105* . . . . .
    MR Edward W—at ☎ (212) 889-7236
    200 E 33 St, Apt 3I, New York, NY *10016* . . . .
☎ (314) 997-4042
66 Briarcliff,
St Louis, MO *63124*

Fowler MISS Angela W—Franklin'75.Bost'78.Va'88.Cly.
    ☎ (212) 722-1561 . . 49 E 96 St, Apt 7A, New York, NY *10128*

Fowler MR & MRS Conrad Murphree JR (Rachel Brown) Ala'69.Ala'91.Ala'69.Ala'72 . . . .
    MISS Catherine L . . . .
    MISS Elizabeth B . . . .
☎ (205) 669-6887
121 Bolton Lane,
Columbiana, AL
35051

Fowler MR Eric A . . . . Died at
    Westtown, PA Aug 22'95

Fowler MRS F Hunter (Frances A Hunter) Me . . . . . .
    MR E Anderson JR—Ty'77—at
    ☎ (610) 622-4075 . . 7236 Glenthorne Rd,
    Upper Darby, PA *19082* . . . .
☎ (610) 356-6881
505 Waters Edge,
Newtown Square,
PA *19073*

Fowler MASTER Gordon Michael Berkeley (Gordon B JR) . . . . Born at
    Stamford, CT Oct 8'95

Fowler MR & MRS Howland A (Shirley J Boers) P'51.Br'57 . . . .
    MISS Amy A—P'90—at ☎ (617) 876-1330
    27 Garfield St, Apt 3, Cambridge, MA *02138* . .
☎ (301) 320-4820
4924 Sentinel Dv,
Apt 203, Bethesda,
MD *20816*

Fowler MR Hunter A—Ty'78.Rens'79
    ☎ (410) 385-2323 . . PO Box 20509, Baltimore, MD *21223*
Fowler MASTER Kyle Anderson (g—MRS F Hunter Fowler) . . . . . Born at
    New York, NY Nov 14'95

Fowler MR Lindsay Anderson—Wms'75
  PO Box 232592, Pleasant Hills, CA *94523*
Fox MR B Wilmsen 2d—CtCol'92 . . see S C Graves JR
Fox MR Caleb F 3d . . . . Died Nov 5'95
Fox MRS Caleb F 3d (Mary A Phipps) Pc.Sg.Fst.Ac.
  ☎ (215) 984-8177 . . Cathedral Village K004, 600 E Cathedral Rd,
  Philadelphia, PA *19128*
Fox MISS Nell C . . see S C Graves JR
Fox MR Porter T—Mid'94 . . see S C Graves JR
Fox MR & MRS Richard L 2d (Ashton F W Lilly) NCar'68.MethCol'68
  ☎ (910) 868-1498 . . 240 Summertime Rd, Fayetteville, NC *28303*
Fox MR S Crozer—Pa'64
  7 East St, Newport, RI *02840*
Francis MR Charles A (late William A) . . . . Married
  Cruice MISS Kathryn W (late John M) . . . . Nov 25'95
Francis MR & MRS Charles A (Kathryn W Cruice) MaryW'75.OWes'74
  ☎ (610) 695-9265 . . 48 Manchester Court, Berwyn, PA *19312*
Francis MRS George T JR (Francis—Cayley—Elinor Ward)
  Swb'37.Me.Gm.Ac . . . of
  ☎ (610) 527-3355 . . 409 Caversham Rd, Bryn Mawr, PA *19010*
  ☎ (561) 276-4259 . . 582 Palm Way, Gulf Stream, FL *33483*
Frank MR Walter N JR . . . . Died at
  New York, NY Sep 28'95
Frank MRS Walter N JR (Oesch—Margaret G Douglas) Pr.Cly . . . . | of ☎ (516)671-8020
  MISS Melinda M—at Duke Law . . . . | 99 Factory Pond Rd, Locust Valley, NY *11560*
    MISS Stephanie E Oesch—at U of Ore . . . . . . |
    MR Peter I Oesch . . . . | ☎ (212) 734-3503
                                                         | 3 E 77 St,
                                                         | New York, NY
                                                         | *10021*
Frankenhoff MR & MRS William P (Jill T Hyland) | ☎ (212) 249-6908
  Ln.Ri.Y'45w . . . . | 19 E 72 St,
  MISS Christine H—Dth'95—at ☎ (212) 861-0906 | New York, NY
  200 E 72 St, New York, NY *10021* . . . . | *10021*
  MR William P JR—ColC'92—at
  ☎ (212) 876-3851 . . 200 E 89 St, New York, NY
  10128
Franklin MRS C Crosby (Cynthia de F Crosby) . . . . Died Feb 15'96
Frazer MISS Jean Riley (g—Nimrod T Frazer) . . . . Born at
  Atlanta, GA Feb 8'95
Frazer MISS Sloan G (Persifor JR) . . . . Married at Marblehead, MA
  Pendleton MR Charles K (Lea B) . . . . Oct 14'95
Frazier MISS Elizabeth Darling (B Graeme 4th) . . . . Born at
  Philadelphia, PA May 27'95
Frazier MRS J Rollins (Joan P Rollins) | 218 Strafford Av,
  Ant'80.Me.Gm. . . . . | Wayne, PA *19087*
  MISS Ramsey R—at Cornell . . . . |
Frazier DR Thomas G—Me.Gm.W&J'64.Pa'68
  ☎ (610) 525-1155 . . 607 Winsford Rd, Bryn Mawr, PA *19010*
Frederick MRS Walter S (Christine P Brooke) . . . . Died at
  Monterey, CA Aug 23'95
Freeman MR William W Keen . . . . Died Jan 19'95
Frelinghuysen MRS Henry O H (Seherr-Thoss—Marian C Kingsland)
  BtP.Evg.Lx.
  ☎ (908) 439-2058 . . ''Primrose House'' 11 King St, Oldwick, NJ *08858*

Fremantle MR & MRS Hugh D (Susan F Stevens) Ore'72.Geo'66 . . of
  ☎ (212) 410-1082 . . 1082 Park Av, Apt 3, New York, NY *10128*
  ☎ (415) 928-7707 . . 2525 Union St, San Francisco, CA *94123*
French MR Alexander (John R) . . . . Married
  Lewis MISS Stacy . . . . Aug 26'95
French MR & MRS G Remick (Marianne Sysak) Conn'84.WorPoly'82
  ☎ (207) 767-2703 . . 6 Roundabout Lane, Cape Elizabeth, ME *04107*
French MASTER Garrett Keen (John S) . . . . Born Aug 21'95
French MR & MRS Hollis 3d (Rosemary Spier) Ty'81.Ec.H'83
  191 Main St, Wenham, MA *01984*
French MISS Virginia D—Wis'70.Md'75
  ☎ (410) 628-2559 . . 40 Somers Court, Cockeysville, MD *21030*
Frey MR & MRS Frank G 3d (Madeline P Becker) | 5 Joining Brook,
  Pa'64.Sg.Pa'67 . . . . | Spring House, PA
  MISS Cleaves M . . . . | *19477*
  MISS Sydney B—at Skidmore . . . . |
Fries MISS Emma E . . . . Died at
  Bronx, NY Dec 31'95
Fritz MR & MRS Arthur Joseph JR (Barbara F Carr) | ☎ (415) 922-2741
  Pcu.Sfy.Fr.Dth'62.Stan'65 . . . . | 2006 Washington St,
  MISS Jenner Lee . . . . | San Francisco, CA
  MR Arthur J 3d . . . . | *94109*
  MR Clayton B . . . . |
Frobes MR & MRS David Bruce (Carole E Battey) DeP'62.DeP'62
  ☎ (602) 998-4037 . . 7520 E McLellan Lane, Scottsdale, AZ *85250*
Fryer JUNIORS MISS Abigail . . see MISS S Farmer
Fryer MISS Amanda . . see MISS S Farmer
Fryer MRS S Farmer (Suzanne Farmer) . . . . name changed to Farmer
Fuller MR & MRS Benjamin A G (Roberta L Tayloe) Cda.Dar.P'40.H'52
  ☎ (508) 688-1364 . . New Pond Village, Apt B112, 180 Main St,
  Walpole, MA *02081*
Fullerton MISS Sallie Mallan (Stuart L) . . . . Born at
  Philadelphia, PA Oct 20'95
Fulweiler MR Spencer B . . . . Died at
  South Norwalk, CT Feb 20'96
Fusz MR Philip R—Nwood'87
  9549 Park Lane, St Louis, MO *63124*

G

Gaillard MISS Schuyler Larkin (William D) . . . . Born at
  Washington, DC May 11'95
Gaines MR Kellogg C (L Ebersole) . . . . Married at Rector, PA
  Allison MISS Kerry S (Paul J) . . . . Oct 29'94
Gaines MRS L Ebersole (Sheila Kellogg) . . . . Born at
  Washington, DC Nov 6'95
Galatti MR & MRS Stephen (Hall—Correll Clancy) H'52.Va'56
  ☎ (914) 677-5000 . . PO Box 1433, Millbrook, NY *12545*
Galbraith MRS George S R (Helen N Boyle) Bnd'38
  ☎ (914) 722-4811 . . 120 E Hartsdale Av, Apt 4G, Hartsdale, NY *10530*
Gallagher MR Peter R . . . . Died at
  Cupertino, CA Apr 19'95
Gallagher MRS Thomas A (Eleanor S Donahue)
  Cathedral Village A316, 600 E Cathedral Rd, Philadelphia, PA *19128*

Galt MISS Judith B—Wash'40
☎ (314) 821-9973 . . 123 E Washington Av, St Louis, MO *63122*
Gambee MRS A Sumner (Eleanor E Brown) . . . . Died at
Englewood, NJ Dec 2'95
Gammill MR & MRS Lee M JR (Jane Houchin)
Okla'58.Bhm.Ln.Pcu.Cly.Dth'56 . . . .
  MISS Sarah L—at ☎ (415) 456-3055
  PO Box 1148, Ross, CA *94957* . . . .
  MR Christopher M—at ☎ (212) 758-6408
  200 E 66 St, Apt B1002, New York, NY *10021*.
☎ (212) 759-3273
200 E 66 St, Apt
C2103, New York,
NY *10021*
Gannaway MR & MRS Bryan W (C Leigh Flowers) RMWmn'93
☎ (205) 879-7011 . . 2650 Beverly Dv, Birmingham, AL *35223*
Gardiner MR & MRS Henry (Bramwell—Katharine H Emmet)
Unn.Au.C.Pn.P'38
7 Meadow Lakes, 04-06U, Hightstown, NJ *08520-0070*
Gardner MR & MRS David T (Dana L Mericle) ClmbusC'95.Stan'84
☎ (706) 569-8869 . . 5508 Southlea Lane, Columbus, GA *31909*
Gardner MISS Elinor Mericle (David T) . . . . Born at
Traverse City, MI Jly 14'95
Gardner MR & MRS John R (McPherron—Dorothy S
Hannon) Cas.Cho.Ih.Wa.Y'65.Ch'67 . . . .
  MISS Elizabeth F—StLaw'86.Mid'88—at
  ☎ (312) 226-5458 . . 835 N Wood St, Apt 305,
  Chicago, IL *60622* . . . .
  MISS Dorcas W—Cl'90—at 147 Broadway,
  Brooklyn, NY *11211* . . . .
  MISS Melissa D—NEng'93—at 500 E-Ku-Sumee
  Dv, Candor, NC *27229* . . . .
  MR William A H—at New England Coll . . . . . .
of ☎ (847)251-3758
94 Indian Hill Rd,
Winnetka, IL *60093*
☎ (970) 926-2786
Box 1318, Edwards,
CO *81632*
Garesché MR Richard L . . . . Died at
St Louis, MO Dec 10'95
Garrison MISS Margaret S (Maynard) . . . . . Married at San Francisco, CA
Murphy MR James R (James L) . . . . Oct 21'95
Garroway MRS David C (Sarah Lee Lippincott) . . . . Married
Zimmerman MR Christian B . . . . Jly 18'95
Garver MRS Chauncey B (Virginia Rook) . . . . Died Nov 11'95
Gaston MR & MRS Benjamin McT JR (Dawn S Bates) Va'55.Pa'60 ⚓
☎ (305) 289-7313 . . 1466 Overseas H'way, Marathon, FL *33050*
Gaston MR John JR—Fic.Cl'70 . . . .
  MISS Deven D—at ☎ (804) 293-3450
  327 Campbell Rd, Keswick, VA *22947* . . . .
☎ (305) 294-1731
Truman Annex,
520 Emma St,
Key West, FL *33040*
Gates MR & MRS Courtlandt D (Natalie S Bigelow) H'81.Cr'85.H'81.H'86
☎ (415) 461-5524 . . PO Box 1524, Ross, CA *94957*
Gates MRS Edward L SR (J Jane Powning)
☎ (941) 263-1875 . . 4760 West Blvd, Apt F102, Naples, FL *33940*
Gates MR & MRS Peter R (Deborah P Marshall) Sth'73.Cy.P'73
155 Summer St, Weston, MA *02193*
Gates MASTER William Gillet (Courtlandt D) . . . . Born at
San Francisco, CA Nov 3'94
Gawthrop MRS Kathleen (Kathleen Tansey) Col'61
  MISS Blair—at 3002 Pacific Av, Apt 2, Venice,
  CA *90291* . . . .
  MR Alfred 3d—at 2116 S Humboldt St, Denver,
  CO *80210* . . . .
☎ (415) 789-0066
25 Corinthian Court,
31, Tiburon, CA
94920
Gebhard MR Karl T E . . . . Married at Upperville, VA
Powell MISS Joy L . . . . Oct 15'95

Geddes MR Eugene M . . . . Died Mch 1'96
Gee MRS M Moulton (Matilda Moulton) . . . . Died at
St Louis, MO Aug 10'95
Geer MRS Irving S (Virginia B Taggart) . . . . Died at
Bryn Mawr, PA Aug 1'92
Geer MR Irving S . . . . Died at
Bryn Mawr, PA Nov 12'95
Geer DR & MRS R Taggart (Juliana Ernst)
Pkg.Sfh.Nyc.P'61.Va'65 . . . .
  MISS Jacqueline E—Mid'90—at 26 Linwood St,
  Arlington, MA *02174-6622* . . . .
  MISS Emily B
  MR Ralph T JR—Ken'93—at 328 W 88 St,
  New York, NY *10024* . . . .
☎ (610) 827-7267
1944 Conestoga Rd,
Chester Springs, PA
19425
Geist MR Bradley B—Rc.Dick'66
☎ (212) 433-1200 . . 1025 Park Av, New York, NY *10028*
Geist MRS Nancy S (Nancy L Sands) . . . .
  MISS Tyler L—at 210 E 73 St, New York, NY
  10021 . . . .
  MR Bradley B JR—Rc.Dick'89—at 218 E 79 St,
  New York, NY *10021* . . . .
  MR Nicholas Van V—at U of Vt . . . .
101 W 81 St,
New York, NY
10024-7237
Gemes MISS Charlotte Bettle (Kenneth E) . . . . Born at
New York, NY Jan 1'96
Gemes MR & MRS Kenneth E (Marian B Thayer) MaryW'84.Ga'78
4 Sunnybrae Place, Bronxville, NY *10708*
Gengler MRS Arthur (Joan A Kinney) . . . . Died at
Southport, CT Oct 2'95
George MRS Samuel K 3d (Kail—Margaret E Rastetter)
☎ (803) 342-2870 . . 11 Birdsong Way, Apt 103E, Hilton Head Island,
SC *29926*
Germic MISS Eloise Ravenel (Stephen A) . . . . Born at
Grosse Pointe, MI Sep 5'95
Germic MR & MRS Stephen A (Catherine R Boomer) Alb'90.Alb'89
☎ (313) 885-6674 . . 482 Neff Rd, Grosse Pointe, MI *48230*
Gerrity MR & MRS Robert T (Judith Van Daam)
ColC'70.LaTrobe'76.DU'69.LaTrobe'75
PO Box 15, Chatham, NY *12037*
Geupel MRS John C (Hamilton—Ann H Mulville)
Ty'58 . . . .
  MISS Sarah Hamilton—Box 23662, Flagstaff,
  AZ *86002* . . . .
  MR William C Hamilton 3d—at 444 Arden Rd,
  Columbus, OH *43214* . . . .
☎ (561) 546-1276
53 S Beach Rd,
Hobe Sound, FL
33455
Giard MR & MRS George P JR (Thomas—Wendell Adams) Evg.BtP.
☎ (407) 655-3889 . . 312 Worth Av, Apt C, Box 453, Palm Beach,
FL *33480*
Gibb MRS Charles A R (Mary L Johnson) . . . . Died at
Chevy Chase, MD Nov 1'95
Gibb CDR Charles A R—RN. . . . . Died at
Chevy Chase, MD Jly 13'94
Gibbons-Neff MR & MRS Grellet (Phyllis Barba)
☎ (610) MU8-4105 . . 225 Old Lancaster Rd, Devon, PA *19333*
Gignoux MISS Hollister H (Frederick E 3d) . . . Married at New York, NY
McDonnell MR David R (James F) . . . . Sep 16'95
Gilchrist MISS Stephanie S . . see H Fiorato
Gildemeister MRS Carl John (Davis—Robbie E Peyton) . . Died Dec 21'95

Gilfillan MR & MRS Graeme A (Constance Elizabeth Lewis) Cal'77.Vh.Cal'75 . . . . ☎ (818) 585-0022
JUNIORS MISS Sarah E . . . . 1290 Hillcrest Av, Pasadena, CA *91106*

Gill MRS Abigail S (Abigail B Stanton) . . . . . Married at Weirs Beach, NH
Mercer MR Philip W (H Hubert) . . . . Jun 10'95

Gillespie MRS C Waring (Jane Baldwin) Mds.
☎ (912) 927-8257 . . John-Wesley Villas, 231 W Montgomery Crossroads, Savannah, GA *31406*

Gillespie MRS Harold E (Mary M Kress)
☎ (804) 264-6669 . . Westminster-Canterbury 548, 1600 Westbrook Av, Richmond, VA *23227*

Gilmor MASTER Michael Samuel (Robert 3d) . . . . Born Sep 8'95

Gilmor MR & MRS Robert 3d (Janet L Charzuk) SUNY'86.Csh.Woos'87
☎ (516) 266-2203 . . 303 Cuba Hill Rd, Huntington, NY *11743*

Gilmour MR & MRS (DR) David L (Anula K Jayasuriya) H'80.Camb'82.H'89.H'91.H'93.H'80.H'82.H'84
☎ (415) 949-2248 . . 26010 Torello Lane, Los Altos Hills, CA *94022-2041*

Gilpin MASTER Alexander Vincent (David V) . . . . Born at Christiana, DE Jun 20'95

Gilpin MR & MRS David V (Sharon V Guthrie) Towson'82.Duke'86.Ty'81.Duke'86
☎ (610) 430-1205 . . 1906 New Market Court, West Chester, PA *19382*

Gilpin MISS Eliza Rough (David V) . . . . Born at Christiana, DE Aug 13'93

Gilpin MISS Megan Crosson (g—Vincent Gilpin JR) . . . . Born at White Plains, NY Oct 25'95

Gimbel MR & MRS Thomas S T (Lesley Bush-Brown) Bow'76.Pr.B.Rv.Cly.Bow'76.Cl'78 . . of
☎ (516) 759-6467 . . 22 Duck Pond Rd, Glen Cove, NY *11542*
☎ (212) 249-7376 . . 205 E 77 St, New York, NY *10021*

Gladsky MISS Katherine Kennedy (g—St George Holden) . . . . Born Jly 31'94

Glancy MASTER Benjamin Cabell (Richard D JR) . . . . Born at Richmond, VA Sep 1'95

Glancy MR & MRS Richard D JR (H Keyser Harris) Hlns'89.W&M'89
☎ (804) 360-7639 . . 6001 Melcroft Court, Glen Allen, VA *23060*

Glascock MASTER William Brewster (John W) . . . . Born Dec 18'95

Glass MR Laurence d'A M—P'58.P'59 . . see MRS D B Sherman

Glen MRS Alixe R (Alixe C Reed) Hlns'79
5810 Madaket Rd, Bethesda, MD *20816*

Glen MR Robert M—Ln.Mt.NCar'78.JHop'87
67 E 11 St, Apt 518, New York, NY *10003*

Glenn MR & MRS Lawrence R (Anne D Dunlaevy) S.Ny.Pa'60.GeoW'65 . . . . ☎ (516) 676-5339
MISS D'Arcy A—Rm'90—at ☎ (212) 932-8539 "Robin Hill"
230 Riverside Dv, New York, NY *10025* . . . . . . Town Cocks Lane,
MISS Allison L—at Bowdoin . . . . Locust Valley, NY
MR Lawrence R JR—Bow'89—at 259 W 10 St, *11560*
New York, NY *10014* . . . .

Gober MISS Margaret W—Rut'90
☎ (610) 873-8954 . . "P Patch Farm" 1206 E Lancaster Av, Downingtown, PA *19335*

Goddard MR & MRS Preston L (Ashley W King) Rich'83.LakeF'79
☎ (203) 857-4818 . . 8 Stephen Mather Rd, West Norwalk, CT *06850*

Godfrey MR & MRS Raymond H JR (Susan J Schoch) Wheat'65.P.Y'67.H'69
☎ (212) 876-3043 . . 9 E 93 St, New York, NY *10128*

Godfrey MRS Robert H (Rachel A Ogilvie) SL'90.SL'92 . . . . ☎ (914) 232-6229
MISS Nicola H—NCar'89—at 707 Van Buren St, 21-16 Croton Lake
Raleigh, NC *27604* . . . . Rd, Katonah, NY
MISS Emma E—NCar'87—at 614 Polk St, *10536*
Raleigh, NC *27604* . . . .

Godfrey MR Robert H—Ty'57
☎ (914) 764-5401 . . 41 Cradle Rock Rd, Pound Ridge, NY *10576*

Goessling MASTER Christopher McComas (John G JR) . . . . Born at St Louis, MO Jly 7'95

Goffinet MR François M P J—K.
☎ (804) 979-9495 . . PO Box 4381, Charlottesville, VA *22905*

Goiran MR Roger—Paris'30 . . . . ☎ (813) 734-8269
MISS (DR) Anne F—FtWr'74.Col'79.Col'83—at 634 Edgewater Dv,
8147 W Virginia Av, Lakewood, CO *80226* . . . Dunedin, FL
MISS Jo Lucie—Nu'75—at 9 Monroe Lane, *34697-1044*
Topsham, ME *04086* . . . .

Gold MR & MRS William B (Marjorie F Tonner) Pc.R.Pe.Fi.An.Plg.Cw.Wt.Rv.StA.Ht.Ne.Vca.Ll. Coa.Cspa.Sar.Fw.Snc.Ac.Sdg.Dll.Pn.P'35.H'38
☎ (609) 753-2358 . . Harvest Village D102, 114 Hayes Mill Rd, Atco, NJ *08004*

Golding MR & MRS Colin F M (Laura B Wheeler)
☎ (610) 296-5545 . . RD 3, Box 126, Swedesford Rd, Malvern, PA *19355*

Goldsmith MR & MRS Robert H (Kathryn R Boyl) . . . . ☎ (415) 924-0282
Mls'66.Bhm.Pcu.Sfy.Cp.Cal'66 ⚓ . . . . 40 Blue Ridge Rd,
MISS Leigh J—at 247 Newbury St, Boston, MA Kentfield, CA *94904*
02116 . . . .

González MR Eugene R—B.Ri.Rc.Ct.Pcu.Mt.Y'51
☎ (212) 744-5685 . . 165 E 66 St, Apt 6B, New York, NY *10021*

Goodale MR & MRS John B (Martha H Lowe) Va'77.Bost'75
☎ (508) 448-2277 . . 30 Drumlin Hill Rd, Groton, MA *01450*

Goodall MR & MRS (DR) McChesney 3d (Anne H Horst) Va'86.Va'96
920 Rosser Lane, Charlottesville, VA *22903-1623*

Goodrich MRS Hunter (Kendall—Mary L Netterville) . . . . Married at Natchez, MS
Shields DR Joseph Dunbar JR (late Joseph D) . . . . Feb 10'96

Goodwin MRS Hamlin (Goodwin—Brooks—Mary Hamlin) . . . . Died at Santa Fe, NM Nov 29'95

Goodyear MRS Carolyn L (Wyeth—Carolyn S Levering) . . . . Died at Boca Grande, FL Dec 24'95

Goodyear MR & MRS Frank H JR (Elizabeth W Balis) K.Sg.Ssk.Y'66 . . . . ☎ (307) 527-5239
MISS Grace W—at ☎ (703) 671-8995 1323 Sunset Blvd N,
4666 S 34 St, Arlington, VA *22206* . . . . Box 2048, Cody,
MR Frank H 3d—at ☎ (512) 482-0581 WY *82414*
809B E 30 St, Austin, TX *78705* . . . .

Gordon MR Nicholas T . . . . Died at Philadelphia, PA Oct 18'94

Gordon MR Nicholas T JR—Pars'67
☎ (609) 263-5510 . . 31 Tecumseh Av, Strathmere, NJ *08248*

Gordon MR William D . . . . Died at Hilton Head Island, SC May 9'95

Gore MRS Philip Larner (Anne M Wyant) . . . . Died at Washington, DC Feb 16'96

Gorman MR Paul A . . . . Died at
Delray Beach, FL Jan 11'96
Gould MRS Lyttleton B P JR (Jackson—Mary E Krech) . . . . Died at
Hadlyme, CT Nov 20'95
Gowen MR & MRS George F JR (Karen L Jordan) HWSth'86.Rc.
☎ (610) 388-0136 . . 391 Spring Mill Rd, Chadds Ford, PA *19317*
Gowen MASTER Samuel Claus (George F JR) . . . . Born at
West Chester, PA Nov 12'95
Graebner MR & MRS Clark E JR (Kendall L Losee) MtVern'90
☎ (202) 244-7089 . . 4395 Embassy Park Dv NW, Washington,
DC *20016*
Graff MISS Marla Lynn (William E) . . . . Married at Richmond, VA
Decker MR Richard H 3d (Richard H JR) . . . . Oct 14'95
Graham MISS Samantha S (Robert L) . . . . Married at Westwood, CA
Vura MR Richard G (Richard) . . . . May 28'95
Granbery MR & MRS E Carleton JR (Diana Allyn)
B'gton'41.Yn.Y'35.Y'38 . . . .
MISS Pamela (Foley—Pamela Granbery)
B'gton'70.CUNY'82.Srb.—at ☎ (401) 331-9249
362 Lloyd Av, Providence, RI *02906* . . . .
☎ (203) 453-2449
111 Old Quarry Rd,
Leetes Island,
Guilford, CT *06437*
Grand MRS Gordon (Ruth Young) . . . .
MR Timothy W—Y'85 . . . .
☎ (203) 972-8083
Leefair East,
21 Bank St,
New Canaan, CT
06840
Grand-Jean MISS Laura R . . see MRS F C Bowers
Grandy MR Jeffrey McK—Rens'87 . . . .
MR Edward B—at ☎ (801) 364-4937
15 S 300 E, Apt 5, Salt Lake City, UT *84111* . .
MR A Stuart—at Evergreen State . . . .

Grannis MRS Adrienne E (Adrienne H Ely) . . . .
MR Anthony E—at ☎ (305) 295-0506
1611 Venetian Dv, Key West, FL *33040* . . . . . .
☎ (510) 443-1150
1192 Portola
Meadows, Apt 172,
Livermore, CA
94550
☎ (608) 249-4009
51 Golf P'kway,
Madison, WI
53704-7024
Grant MR & MRS Francis C 3d (Sands—Jean B
Minskoff) Nu'76.Nu'79.Nf.Pe.Ph.Pa'71.Pa'72 . .
MR Francis C 4th—at Coll of Charleston . . . . . .

of ☎ (212)486-6783
500 Park Av,
New York, NY
10022
☎ (914) 967-4554
55 Stratford Rd,
Harrison, NY *10528*
Grant DR & MRS Joseph L (Mary Drayton)
Nf.H'43.Pa'46 ⚓ . . . .
MISS (REV) Priscilla R—Swb'83.VaTheo'92—at
☎ (703) 912-3913 . . 8120 Kingsway Court,
Springfield, VA *22152* . . . .
☎ (802) 649-1273
Box 285, Norwich,
VT *05055*
Grant MISS Lisa J (David A) . . . . Married at Ridgefield, CT
Clough MR Peter A (Anson W) . . . . Oct 28'95
Grant MR & MRS Thomas W (Mary F Ingram)
Rc.Pr.Cly.Cda.NCar'63 . . . .
MISS Mary F—Roan'92—at ☎ (212) 593-1508
357 E 57 St, New York, NY *10022* . . . .
MR Thomas W JR—HWSth'96 . . . .
☎ (516) 626-1055
Box 93,
Locust Valley, NY
11560
Grantham MR Ward Heeth . . . . Died at
Greenwich, CT Dec 25'95

Gratz MR Clifford B—Curry'74
☎ (508) 526-7182 . . 3 School St, Apt 1, Manchester, MA *01944*
Graves MR & MRS John H (Kathleen G Carskadon) Rdc'60.H'57
☎ (617) 899-8297 . . "Trapelo Farm" 470 Forest St, Waltham,
MA *02154-5725*
Graves MR & MRS Sidney C JR (Fox—Robin Reath)
Nf.H'58.RISD'65 . . . .
MISS Monica W—Vt'87.Un.—at
☎ (617) 731-1082 . . 55 Boylston St, Brookline,
MA *02146* . . . .
MR Sidney C 3d—at 710 E Harbor Circle,
Grand Junction, CO *81506* . . . .
MR Martin F—Ne'94—at ☎ (617) 661-5387
79 Hampshire St, Cambridge, MA *02138* . . . . . .
  MISS Nell C Fox—at Middlebury . . . .
  MR B Wilmsen Fox 2d—CtCol'92—at
  ☎ (617) 864-0268 . . 86 Kirkland St,
  Cambridge, MA *02138* . . . .
  MR Porter T Fox—Mid'94—at
  ☎ (307) 734-8048 . . Box 1286,
  Jackson Hole, WY *83001* . . . .
☎ (617) 326-6565
20 Woods End Rd,
Dedham, MA *02026*
Gray MR & MRS Alexander L (Elizabeth M Wagg) NCar'91.StLaw'90
Box 532, Canaan, NH *03741*
Gray MR Carl A . . . . Died at
Durham, NC Jan 23'91
Gray MASTER Carter S (g—Walter F Gray) . . . . Born at
Philadelphia, PA Aug 28'94
Gray MRS David D (Lucile R Ralston) . . . . Married at Greenwich, CT
Northrop MR Johnston F (late Filmer S C) . . . . Sep 15'95
Gray MR & MRS Robert L 3d (Elizabeth D Elkins)
Sth'59.Rc.Y.'59.Pa'63 . . . .
MR James E—at 3804 Florence Dv, Alexandria,
VA *22305* . . . .
1229 Denbigh Lane,
Radnor, PA *19087*
Grayson MR & MRS Eric D (Natasha Justina Pray)
Hartw'86.Ihy.StLaw'79.Tul'82
☎ (203) 869-5535 . . 65 Buckfield Lane, Greenwich, CT *06831*
Graziano MR & MRS Anthony W JR (Robin L
Ryckman) HolyC'63.Bg.Va'66 . . . .
MISS R Virginia—Buck'95—at ☎ (201) 377-4472
17 Waverly Place, Madison, NJ *07940* . . . .
☎ (317) 966-5480
3913 Backmeyer Rd,
Richmond, IN *47374*
Greaves MASTER Christopher Austin (g—Harry B Greaves JR) . . . Born at
San Diego, CA Dec 31'95
Green DR Bernard . . . . Died at
New York, NY Dec 16'95
Green MR & MRS Michael P (Karen C Andretta) UWash'65.Y'63
☎ (602) 956-0536 . . 6544 N 36 St, Phoenix, AZ *85018*
Green MR & MRS Thomas M 3d (du Pont—Dulcinea H Lee) Sth'55.P'48
☎ (912) 598-8150 . . 6 Captain Kirk Lane, Savannah, GA *31411*
Greene MR Philip G . . . . Died at
San Francisco, CA May 11'95
Greenleaf MR James M (late John M) . . . . Married at Hood River, OR
Clay MISS Natalie . . . . Aug 12'95
Greenleaf MISS Victoria S—Hampshire'83.Pr.Cly . . of
☎ (212) 369-6278 . . 1225 Park Av, PH-B, New York, NY *10128*
☎ (516) 922-7565 . . 37 Frost Mill Rd, Mill Neck, NY *11765*
Greenway MR John S . . . . Died at
Tucson, AZ Sep 13'95

Greenway MISS Sarah D (Hugh D S) . . . . Married at Dover, MA
    Lawson MR Jonathan W (John W) . . . . May 6'95
Greer MISS Elizabeth (Alexander P) . . . . Married at Spokane, WA
    Edwards MR J Jeffrey (James T) . . . . Oct 7'95
Greer MR & MRS John T (Sara C Gotcher) Cal'79.Bur.Wms'77
    ☎ (415) 341-0321 . . 1035 Vista Rd, Hillsborough, CA *94010*
Gregg MR & MRS James G (Martha H Bellis) Ty'78
    ☎ (415) 752-4280 . . 281 Sixteenth Av, San Francisco, CA *94118-1018*
Gregg MR & MRS Robert E 3d (Katherine E Dorr) NH'93.NH'90
    ☎ (413) 527-1520 . . Williston Northampton School, 19 Payson Av,
    Easthampton, MA *01027*
Grew MR Christopher A—Unn.Plg.Mich'84.Camb'86
    ☎ (011-44-171) 704-8238 . . 15 Noel Rd, London N1 8HQ, England
Grew MR & MRS Robert R (Anne G Bailey) Mich'54.Un.Plg.Cs.Mich'53
    ☎ (212) 688-0994 . . 139 E 63 St, New York, NY *10021*
Gridley MR Henry M (late William G) . . . . Married
    Veitch MRS Mary F (Mary Fismer) . . . . Sep 27'95
Grieves MASTER Patrick Deering (James R JR) . . . . Born at
    Baltimore, MD Oct 13'95
Griffin MR & MRS Andrew (Wyman—Sharon Crary)
    Cal'59.Sfg.Pcu.Cal'58
    MR Sherman G—at 2875 Greenwich St,
    San Francisco, CA *94123* . . . .
    MR Mark C—at 107 Queensbury St, Apt 10,
    Boston, MA *02215* . . . .
    ☎ (415) SK1-2227
    151 Commonwealth
    Av, San Francisco,
    CA *94118*
Griffith MISS Caroline C . . see M Fenton JR
Griffith MR & MRS Thomas G (Susan A Hackett)
    Bhm.Bur.Sfy.Cp.Fr.Cal'64
    MR Charles L III—at U of Pacific . . . .
    MR Millen VI—at Salisbury . . . .
    ☎ (415) 342-9993
    532 Maple St,
    San Mateo, CA
    94402
Grimball MR & MRS William H JR (Frieda S
    Benson) Cc.So'68 . . . .
    MISS Marian S . . . .
    JUNIORS MR William H . . . .
    ☎ (904) 434-7203
    111 W Gonzales St,
    Pensacola, FL *32501*
Grimm MRS Sara H (Mahone—Villalba—Griffin—
    Sara H Grimm) . . . .
    MISS Sonia M Villalba—at ☎ (505) 699-5601
    1111 Buckman Rd, Santa Fe, NM *87501* . . . .
    ☎ (207) 729-9991
    Rte 1 & I-95,
    Brunswick, ME
    04011
Grindinger MR & MRS Kent J (Sharon E Nichols) Stan'79.Cr'82
    ☎ (214) 713-7209 . . 6630 Duffield Dv, Dallas, TX *75248*
Grinnell MR & MRS Alexander (Bodman—Helen K Dunn) Cs.Y'57.Y'60
    ☎ (212) 369-6933 . . 25 E 86 St, New York, NY *10028*
Griswold MR H Bridgman—Ny.
    ☎ (561) 234-0086 . . 100 Cowry Lane, John's Island, Vero Beach,
    FL *32963*
Griswold MR Kent C (Lincoln T) . . . . Married at Chestnut Hill, PA
    Rosenquist MISS (DR) Lori L (James A) . . . . Oct 7'95
Groat MRS Robert A (Smith—Jane D Durston) Hl.Myf.
    ☎ (860) 739-0109 . . 10 Francis Lane, Old Black Point, Niantic,
    CT *06357*
Groome MR & MRS Harry C 3d (Evelyn S
    Richardson) Pa'68.Pa'74.VillaN'81.Ph.Cts.
    Me.Au.Pa'63 . . . .
    MISS Evelyn S—H'88—at U of So Cal . . . .
    MR Harry C—Ham'86—at 1539 Shradee St,
    San Francisco, CA *94111* . . . .
    MR Peter Z—Ham'90—at 18 W 95 St, Apt 1B,
    New York, NY *10015* . . . .
    ☎ (610) 525-2763
    964 Conestoga Rd,
    Rosemont, PA
    19010
Grose MR & MRS Thomas Pierpont (Herlin—Eleanor
    F Evans) Bost'65.Hof'62 ⛵
    MISS Signe P . . . .
    MISS Vanessa P . . . .
    MISS Heather B . . . .
    JUNIORS MR William F P . . . .
    ☎ (011-44-171)
    603-7046
    7 St Mary Abbot's
    Place, London
    W8 6LS, England
Grosjean MISS Maria Emlen—Cs.
    ☎ (516) 725-2292 . . "Watch Case House" PO Box 1482, 67 Suffolk St,
    Sag Harbor, NY *11963-0056*
Gross MR Charles Edward
    ☎ (334) 821-7508 . . 433 N College St, Auburn, AL *36830*
Gross MR George Mason . . . . Died at
    Delray Beach, FL Apr 2'95
Grote MR Otto F—Ri.H'53.H'57
    ☎ (603) 427-2022 . . PO Box 640, New Castle, NH *03854*
Grow MASTER Sawyer McCoy (g—C Rich Diffenderffer) . . Born Jly 5'95
Gruber MR Matthew J—Rc.Ch'84
    ☎ (212) 957-1670 . . 200 Central Park S, Apt 21F, New York, NY *10019*
Gubelmann MISS Marjorie Barton—NEng'91.Srb.Cda.
    ☎ (212) 758-0508 . . 188 E 64 St, Apt 702, New York, NY *10021*
Guinness HON & MRS Sebastian (Margaret H Stephaich) . . of
    451 Broome St, Apt 8W, New York, NY *10013-2644*
    ☎ (011-34-72) 25-86-90 . . Ermita St Sebastian, Cadaques, 17488 Girona,
    Spain
Gunnell MRS C Church (Caroline W Church) . . . name changed to Church
Gunnell MR T Nelson
    ☎ (540) 687-4168 . . Covington Farm, Box 2061, Middleburg,
    VA *22117*
Gunter MRS Davis (Alice R Davis)
    3219 Audubon Rd, Montgomery, AL *36106*
Gunter MR W Davis . . . . Died Dec 13'95
Gunter MR William A 4th—Ala'80
    ☎ (334) 264-2778 . . 1110 Westmoreland Av, Montgomery, AL *36106*
Guntharp MR Alfred E JR . . see MRS E Van R Stires

H

Haack MR & MRS Frederick L (Hobson—Ann Kendall) Ri.Cly.Wyo'48
    ☎ (504) 522-6622 . . 1224 Jackson Av, New Orleans, LA *70130*
Haas MR Walter A JR . . . . Died at
    San Francisco, CA Sep 20'95

Hachman MR & MRS Timothy J (Judith K Musto) Cal'65.Bhm.Fr.Cal'63.Hast'66 . . . . ☎ (209) 465-2270
  MISS Carter K—Cal'91—at ☎ (415) 563-6562 3621 Country Club
  1245 California St, Apt 402, San Francisco, CA Blvd, Stockton, CA
  94109. 95204
  MR Timothy D M—Cp.Cal'95—at
  ☎ (415) 386-7471 . . 3010 Turk St,
  San Francisco, CA 94118. . . . .
Hackett MRS B Peterson (Barbara J Peterson) Wells'68
  570 Park Av, New York, NY 10021
Hackett MR Montague H JR—Rc.Bcs.Ng.So.P'54.H'59
  ☎ (212) 838-0875 . . 550 Park Av, New York, NY 10021
Hadden MR & MRS John W 3d (Victoria S Hillebrand) Pars'95.Tul'91
  ☎ (617) 661-0208 . . 6 Soldiers Field Park, Apt 603, Boston, MA 02163
Hadley MRS Hamilton (Emily Morris) . . . . Died at
  Hamden, CT Dec 20'95
Hagen MASTER Harry Talbott (Lee R) . . . . Born at
  Princeton, NJ Jun 30'94
Hagen MR & MRS Lee R (Mary G Mead) Va'86
  ☎ (609) 497-2943 . . 27 Armour Rd, Princeton, NJ 08540
Haigler MR & MRS Charles Brightman JR (Susan of ☎ (334)227-8886
  McC Foster) Ala'61.Dar.Ala'57 . . . . 1221 Old Fort Rd,
  MR Charles B 3d. . . . . Ft Deposit, AL
                                                                                 36032
                                                                                 ☎ (334) 961-7557
                                                                                 "Blue Bayou"
                                                                                 30498 Magnolia St,
                                                                                 Perdido Beach, AL
                                                                                 30650
Haigney MR & MRS Dayton P 3d (Alexandra K Deering)
  Scripps'85.FIT'88.StLaw'84.W&L'87
  ☎ (212) 535-6742 . . 501 E 87 St, Apt 1B, New York, NY 10128
Haines MASTER Cameron Galloway (g—Henry J Maresi) . . . . Born at
  Greenwich, CT Feb 10'96
Haines MRS Harold A JR (Emily L Richards) Me.Ac.Ncd.
  PO Box 747, Buckingham, PA 18912
Haines MRS William W (Frances S Tuckerman)
  ☎ (714) 450-5392 . . The White Sands, 7450 Olivetas Av, La Jolla, CA 92037
Halberstadt MR & MRS Robert LeC (Eda C Nelson)
  Okla'34.Cspa.Cw.Rv.Wt.Ll.Fw.Ncd.Dll.Dar.Hav'30
  ☎ (215) 575-9583 . . Logan Square E, Apt 1403, 2 Franklin Town Blvd, Philadelphia, PA 19103
Hale MISS Abigail Frances (Bradley H) . . . . Born Jun 9'94
Hale MR Prentis Cobb . . . . Died at
  San Francisco, CA Feb 16'96
Hale MRS Richard W JR (Elisabeth Fairbanks) . . . . Died at
  Boston, MA Oct 22'95
Hale MR & MRS Thomas H (Nancy Brooks) of ☎ (303)839-5530
  Card'60.Minn'68 . . . . 930 Humboldt St,
  MR Mark C—at Wittenberg . . . . Apt 4, Denver, CO
  JUNIORS MR Christopher R F—at Pomfret 80218-3518
                                                                                 ☎ (719) 539-4253
                                                                                 "Can Doo"
                                                                                 604 Crestone Av,
                                                                                 Salida, CO 81201

Hall MR & MRS C Barrows (Eleanor L Crosby) The Cliff,
  Ty'73.Unn.Pa'69.P'76 . . . . 11 Carmichael Rd,
  JUNIORS MISS Letitia L—at Groton . . . . Bombay 400 026,
                                                                                 India
Hall MR & MRS Newell N (Jane N Gallagher) TyU'77.Bow'77.H'89
  ☎ (617) 698-1564 . . 215 Canton Av, Milton, MA 02186
Hall MR & MRS Nicholas H J (Mary Lou Mullen)
  Geo'79.K.Cly.Ox'79.Ox'85
  ☎ (212) 249-7031 . . 21 E 67 St, New York, NY 10021
Hall MR & MRS Thomas Cartwright (Garber—Louise C Simrall)
  ☎ (513) 771-9425 . . 850 Van Nes Dv, Glendale, OH 45246
Hall MR Virginius C—P'54 . . . . 1071 Celestial St,
  MISS Maria A—at 161 Gilbert St, Apt 16, Apt 2004,
  San Francisco, CA 94118. . . . . Cincinnati, OH
  MISS Susannah M—at 2400—41 St NW, Apt 309, 45202
  Washington, DC 20007 . . . .
Hallock MASTER Samuel David (g—MRS Robert Scott Noone) . . . Born at
  Cincinnati, OH Nov 28'95
Halsey MRS Donald H (Virginia K Logan) . . . . Died at
  New Orleans, LA in May 1993
Hamann MR Edmund T (Charles M) . . . . . . Married at Kansas City, MO
  Bockrath MISS Susan E . . . . May 20'95
Hamilton MISS Ann Louise H . . . . Married at Hobe Sound, FL
  Brown MR Georges P (William G) . . . . Nov 4'95
Hamilton MR John W (late Ferris F) . . . . Married at Denver, CO
  Driscoll MISS Elizabeth A (Dennis D) . . . . Nov 18'95
Hamilton JUNIORS MR Rylan . . see T G Stemberg
Hamilton MR S Laird . . . . Died Nov 16'95
Hamilton MISS Sarah . . see J C Geupel
Hamilton MR William C 3d . . see J C Geupel
Hammer MR & MRS Joseph W (Katherine L Carton) ☎ (617) 734-8582
  Sm.Ln.Cy.Srb.H'64 . . . . 173 Woodland Rd,
  JUNIORS MISS Alexandra C . . . . Chestnut Hill, MA
                                                                                 02167
Hammett MR & MRS Philip M (Palmer—Mary Jane ☎ (215) 790-0014
  Dowd) Man'vl'48.Rc.H'42.Pa'48 . . . . 1914 Spruce St,
  MISS Ann W—Gchr'84—at ☎ (206) 782-5044 Philadelphia, PA
  518 Fourteenth Av E, Seattle, WA 98117 19103
  MR Christopher D Palmer—Colg'86.Nu'88—
  at ☎ (011-44-171) 460-2518
  8A Marloes Rd, Kensington, London W8 5LJ,
  England . . . .
Hammond REV & MRS James A (Gina B Bronkie) ☎ (703) 754-0259
  V'70.Md'58 . . . . 4240 Berry Rd,
  MISS Carolyn E—at 401 Westshire Rd, Baltimore, Gainesville, VA
  MD 21229 22065
Hammond MR William C JR . . . . Died at
  Hancock Point, ME Jan 19'96
Hancock MR & MRS William P W (Patricia Clay) Me.Rb.Ac.Pa'53
  ☎ (802) 824-6851 . . RR 1, Box 35, Brook Rd, South Londonderry, VT 05155
Hanley MRS William Lee (Elizabeth W Niles) Evg.BtP.Cly.
  ☎ (407) 655-0725 . . 155 Hammon Av, Palm Beach, FL 33480
Hanna MR Richard R . . . . Died at
  San Mateo, CA Jan 16'96
Hanneken MASTER Christopher Fagan (Christopher L) . . . . Born at
  Pleasanton, CA Nov 24'95

Hansen MRS H Leighton (Katharine D Baird) Cda.
☎ (561) 231-3787 . . 240 Sabal Palm Lane, Vero Beach, *32963*
Hansen MASTER William Holger (g—William A Chisolm) . . . . . . Born at Worcester, MA Jun 2'95
Harder MR Douglas W (late George A JR) . . Married at Bernardsville, NJ
Prieto MISS Patricia D (Joseph) . . . . Nov 5'95
Harder MRS George A JR (Sally Knight) Skd'56
☎ (201) 890-1178 . . 1147 Stephanie Dv, North Caldwell, NJ *07006*
Hardie MR & MRS William H JR (Harris—C Alix Winter) Y'59.Va'63
JUNIORS MR Frank W. . . . .
☎ (334) 344-5231
3267 Stein St,
Mobile, AL *36608*
Hardiman MR & MRS Joseph R (Katherine McCampbell) Gchr'63.Ln.Mt.Md.Elk.Rr.Md'59.Md'62
☎ (410) 377-6428 . . 8 Bowen Mill Rd, Baltimore, MD *21212*
Hargrave MR Homer P JR—Cho.Rcch.Cant'48
☎ (812) 988-9355 . . 762 Helmsburg Rd, Nashville, IN *47448*
Harmar MISS A Ashley (William 3d) . . . . . . Married at Chestnut Hill, PA
Rappoport MR Jason E (James E) . . . . Nov 18'95
Harmsworth HON Esmond V—Br'90.H'95 . . of
☎ (617) 247-2098 . . 359 Beacon St, Apt 4, Boston, MA *02116*
46 Rutland Gate, Apt 1, London SW1, England
Harper MR Fletcher (late Fletcher M) . . . . Married at Flippin, AR
Rueb MISS Jennifer L (Robert) . . . . Oct 10'92
Harper MR Stuart L—Bab'74
MISS Lindsay A—Box P32, South Dartmouth, MA *02748* . . . .
MR Benjamin M—at Hobart . . . .
JUNIORS MISS Anna W—Box P32, South Dartmouth, MA *02748* . . . .
☎ (716) 648-1707
3257 Queens Lane,
Hamburg, NY *14075*
Harrah MR Eric—H'50
☎ (401) 783-5672 . . 14 Dobson St, Wakefield, RI *02879*
Harris MISS Ann B . . . .
MR Percival van R—Pa'48—at
☎ (212) FI8-6386 . . 1199 Park Av, New York, NY *10128* . . . .
MR Lawrence C—Pa'47—at ☎ (415) 332-2232
553 Sausalito Blvd, Sausalito, CA *94965* . . . . . .
☎ (908) 295-0083
Box 17,
Bay Head, NJ *08742*
Harris MR & MRS Christopher H (Talbot Chamberlin) Ham'92.Hob'92
☎ (203) 673-6768 . . 24 Irvine Rd, Old Greenwich, CT *06870*
Harrison MASTER Charles Albert (Charles C 5th) . . . . Born Nov 13'94
Harrison MASTER Charles Avery (Philip D) . . . . Born at Chestnut Hill, PA Apr 16'95
Harrison MR & MRS Charles C 5th (J Leanne Prillaman) Roan'88.Roan'82
8315 Saddle Ridge Terr, Ellicott City, MD *21043*
Harrison MRS J Randolph (Fox—Elizabeth B Cary) . . . . Died at Hightstown, NJ Nov 25'95
Harrison MISS Lucy Gurnee—Rol'89
☎ (407) 659-6015 . . PO Box 3375, 161 Clarke Av, Palm Beach, FL *33480*
Harrower MRS Lyle (Léontine Lyle)
☎ (619) 759-5610 . . PO Box 7213, 3805 Avenida Feliz, Rancho Santa Fe, CA *92067-7213*
Harsch MR J William M (Joseph C) . . . . Married at Newport, RI
Ticknor MRS Michael P (A Christine Thayer) . . . . Aug 26'95
Hart MR & MRS David E (Caroline H Gold) Dar.Dll.Ht.
☎ (908) 974-0439 . . 311 Jersey Av, Spring Lake, NJ *07762*

Hart MRS John G (Moore—Cummings—Scammell—Eva C Lathrop) . . . . . Died at Boynton Beach, FL Jan 4'96
Hart MRS Thornley W (Joan F Johnson)
☎ (212) YU8-2069 . . 114 E 72 St, New York, NY *10021*
Hartley MR & MRS James R (Hillyard—Barbara Johnson) . . of
☎ (303) 830-1400 . . 14 Cheesman Gardens, 1510 E Tenth Av, Denver, CO *80218*
☎ (303) 674-4257 . . 160 County Rd 480, Evergreen, CO *80439*
Hartman MR & MRS William R JR (Barbara C Cauffman) Ken'86.Pa'91.Ken'86.Pa'91
☎ (610) 647-4376 . . 57 Knox Av, Berwyn, PA *19312*
Hartshorne MR Harold—Cho.P'40
☎ (803) 449-8459 . . Gator Gap Apt 614, 100 Lands End Blvd, Myrtle Beach, SC *29572*
Harvey MR & MRS C Randolph (Rouvina—Elizabeth Raney) Rv.Hav'48.Pa'51 . . . .
MISS Julia E Rouvina—Mich'83—at
☎ (610) 983-0367 . . 32 Sheffield Court, Collegeville, PA *19426* . . . .
☎ (610) 644-4479
314 N Fairfield Rd,
Devon, PA *19333*
Harvey MR & MRS Cyrus I JR (Rebecca P Miller) Hb.H'47 . . . .
MISS Natasha—Pa'92.Ste—at ☎ (202) 338-1029
1657—31 St NW, Apt B5, Washington, DC *20007* . . . .
☎ (860) 928-0092
PO Box 50,
Woodstock, CT *06281*
Harvey MR Eldon JR . . . . Died at Stonington, CT Jan 28'96
Hastings MR & MRS Caryl C B (Katherine L Sherman) Skd'67.Cc.H'62.H'66 . . . .
JUNIORS MR Craig C B . . . .
JUNIORS MR Richard O M
50 Colchester Rd,
Weston, MA *02193*
Hastings MR & MRS Matthew T (Linda F Steele) Rdc'72.Va'75.Ne.Ht.Ncd.H.Pots'74.Penn'78 . . of
☎ (540) 338-7667 . . "Maple Hill" Philomont, VA *22131*
115 E 90 St, New York, NY *10128*
Hastings DR & MRS Peter L (Rosina M de Barros Gomes) Rio'84.Berklee'83.H'85.Stan'88.P'92.Mit'95 . . of
2590 Dearborn Dv, Hollywood, CA *90068*
"Vente Du Fromage" rue des Cheveux, Céret, France
Hawkes MRS (REV) Dudley F (Daphne W Parker) Penn'60.PTheo'75.Ds.Ncd. . . . .
MISS Jennifer D—at 4454 Reservoir Rd NW, Washington, DC *20007* . . . .
MR Andrew F—at 217 South St, Sausalito, CA *94965* . . . .
MR Timothy W . . . .
☎ (609) 921-2404
50 Patton Av,
Princeton, NJ *08540*
Hawkins MISS Jennifer Lee (David A) . . . . Born at Woodland, CA Aug 10'93
Hawkins MASTER William Burbank (David A) . . . . Born at Davis, CA Jly 30'95
Hawley MRS Clifford B (Sarah A Clark)
☎ (704) 859-9547 . . 217 Chestnut St, Tryon, NC *28782*
Hay MR & MRS Richard J (Lucinda A Smith) Ws'78.Tor'77
Cranley Grange, Cranley Rd, Burwood Park, Walton-on-Thames, Surrey KT12 5BP, England

Hayden MRS Curtiss JR (Alice B Dollar) . . . . ☎ (415) 453-3526
  MISS Alice D . . . . 15 Morrison Rd,
  MISS Mara Lisa . . . . Box 487, Ross, CA
  94957
Hayden MR Philip A—Conn'84.Del'89 . . see W Coxe
Hayes MR & MRS Geoffrey N (Cox—Rosane B   ☎ (505) 822-7967
  André) NMex'82.Myf.NMex'83 . . . . 7404 Vivian Dv NE,
  MISS Jocelyn J . . . . Albuquerque, NM
  87109
Hayes MRS Henry G (Katharine H Collins) BMr'29
  ☎ (415) 461-9729 . . 15 Wolfe Glen Way, Kentfield, CA *94904*
Hayes MR Nicolas—Unn.Ct.Ty'69
  PO Box 240, Rectortown, VA *22140*
Heberton MR & MRS Robert M JR (Kathryn R Perris) MtH'51.Pc.
  235 Lancaster Av, Devon, PA *19333*
Hecking MR & MRS Dirck J 2d (Marguerite Van Dyke Dohan) Miss'96
  ☎ (601) 234-6906 . . 2112 Old Taylor Place, Apt H2, Oxford, MS *38655*
Heckman MR William Guy . . . . Died at
  Hobe Sound, FL Nov 26'95
Hefter MISS Allison Claire (J Scott) . . . . Born at
  Greenwich, CT Dec 23'94
Hefter MR & MRS J Scott (Anne H Crocker) Br'88.Pa'93.CtCol'81 . . of
  ☎ (203) 622-0792 . . 11 Birch Lane, Greenwich, CT *06830*
  ☎ (212) 708-6165 . . 121 W 73 St, Apt 8D, New York, NY *10023*
Heiner MRS William G JR (Frances C Lyne) Fcg.Ncd.
  ☎ (412) 963-8887 . . 302 Fox Chapel Rd, Apt 210, Pittsburgh, PA *15238*
Heiserman MR Hewitt JR—Ken'82
  10 Central St, Southborough, MA *01772*
Heiserman MR Robert B 3d . . see J B Sibley
Hellauer MR & MRS Joseph F 3d (Katrine S Otto) StLaw'83.Assumption'82
  ☎ (314) 963-9883 . . 238 Park Rd, St Louis, MO *63119*
Hellauer MASTER Thomas Robert (Joseph F 3d) . . . . Born Feb 3'95
Helme MRS Karen R (Karen J Rundell) WmSth'78
  6 Willing Way, Wilmington, DE *19807*
Hemp MISS Catharine Carton (P B Hemp & B W Carton) . . . . Born at
  Boston, MA Sep 1'95
Hemp, Paul B & Carton, Barbara W—Pa'72.Bost'74.Whit'75.H'82
  ☎ (617) 720-2802 . . 12 Chestnut St, Apt 5, Boston, MA *02108*
Hemphill MASTER Garret DeWitt (William R JR) . . . . Born at
  Austin, TX Aug 9'95
Hemphill MR & MRS William R JR (Abigail Lounsbery)
  Hlns'86.W&L'86.Smu'91
  ☎ (512) 452-5092 . . 3504 Lakeland Dv, Austin, TX *78731*
Hemphill MASTER William Rushing 3d (William R JR) . . . . Born at
  Austin, TX May 30'93
Henderson MRS (DR) Anne Atkinson (Anne Atkinson) Rhodes'62
  ☎ (601) 833-1377 . . 421 Perkins Dv, Brookhaven, MS *39601*
Henderson MR & MRS Charles F (Pamela T Fenton) Witt'65.Dth'64
  ☎ (847) 256-3133 . . 133 Lawndale Av, Wilmette, IL *60091*
Henderson MR & MRS G L Cabot (Elliott—Sarah G | 76 West St,
  Bever) Mass'84.Mid'73 . . . . Beverly Farms, MA
  MISS Davina M—at Occidental *01915*
Henkels MISS Lindsay H . . . . Married at Elkton, MD
  Confer MR James . . . . Oct 10'95
Henrici MR Rafael . . . . Died at
  Berkeley, CA Sep 11'95

Henry de Tessan MRS Joan C T (Joan   ☎ (415) 921-5431
  Chatfield-Taylor) Sth'62 . . . . 2066 Green St,
  MISS Christina . . . . San Francisco, CA
  JUNIORS MR Matthew *94123*
Hepburn MR & MRS Austin Barry JR (Hannah C Wood) AppSt'82.SCar'80
  ☎ (610) 688-4335 . . 253 Upper Gulph Rd, Radnor, PA *19087*
Hepburn MASTER Austin Barry 3d (Austin Barry JR) . . . . Born Sep 28'95
Hermann MASTER Robert Ringen 3d (Robert R JR) . . . . . Born Feb 19'96
Herod MRS William Rogers (Thompson—Fries—Caroline Klotz) . . Died at
  New York, NY Jan 21'96
Herrick MR Bayard B . . . . Died at
  Greenbrae, CA Nov 22'95
Herrick MISS Helene M (g—Thomas G Herrick) . . . . Born Jan 10'96
Hervey-Bathurst SIR Frederick P . . . . Died at
  Middletown, NJ Dec 27'95
Hess-Childs MASTER Alan Kane (g—Timothy W Childs) . . . . Born at
  Seattle, WA Apr 29'95
Hesser MRS Paul M JR (Ritter—Eleanor C Gillespie) . . . . Died at
  Philadelphia, PA Dec 6'95
Hetherington MR & MRS Arthur F JR (Betty A Smith) V'38.Edg.Yn.Y'37
  316 Beaver St, Apt 401, Sewickley, PA *15143*
Hickox JUNIORS MR James A B . . see MISS (DR) D S Shaw
Higgins MR & MRS James H 3d (Martha M Robinson)
  Bow'78.Unn.Eh.Shcc.NCar'71.Dth'74
  ☎ (201) 539-8488 . . ''Peacemeal'' 140 Washington Valley Rd,
  Morristown, NJ *07960*
Higgins MRS Lawrence (Roberts—Angela G Honan)
  ☎ (011-52) 280-1155 . . Av Cicerón 608, Los Morales,
  11510 Mexico 5, DF, Mexico
Higley DR Stephen R—Drake'71.Ill'75.Ill'92
  ☎ (205) 322-8699 . . 3350 Altamont Rd, Birmingham, AL *35205*
Hildesley REV & MRS C Hugh (Constance C Palmer) | ☎ (212) 772-3239
  Rc.Pr.StJ.StJTheo'76 . . . . 570 Park Av,
  MISS Melissa M . . . . New York, NY
  MR Mark A *10021*
Hilgenberg MR & MRS C Edward (Carlisle—Alexandre—F Gilbert Tucker)
  Md.Dc.Va'32
  ☎ (410) 822-3065 . . 20 Lynnebrook Terr, Easton, MD *21601*
Hilgenberg MR Carl R . . . . Died at
  Baltimore, MD Oct 12'95
Hilgenberg MR & MRS John C (Twells—Evelyn B   ☎ (410) 235-4593
  Handy) Elk.Md.Y'63.Va'65 . . . . 810 Drohomer
  MISS Elizabeth Crady . . . . Place, Baltimore,
  MD *21210*
Hill MASTER Ethan (g—MRS Robert B Meyer JR) . . . . . . Born May 23'94
Hill MRS John J 3d (Crew—Mary Marsh) Rd.
  ☎ (610) 469-6778 . . ''Nantmeal Hunt Farm'' 3111 Horseshoe Trail,
  Glenmoore, PA *19343*
Hill MASTER Jordan Russell Howe (g—Nathaniel S Howe) . . . . . . Born at
  Berkeley, CA Feb 8'95
Hillman MR & MRS Robert S (Sandra L Schwartz) Penn'62.JHop'60.H'63
  ☎ (410) 664-1654 . . 5514 S Bend Rd, Baltimore, MD *21209*
Hills MISS Sarah L (Carter H) . . . . Married at Washington, DC
  DeCocco MR Philip M (Philip) . . . . Oct 7'95
Hinckley MISS Annalisa M (G F Steedman) . . . . . . Married at Orlean, VA
  Savin MR Adam M (Howard A) . . . . Sep 9'95

Hinken DR & MRS Michael Van D (Joan L Otis) Ill'52.Loy'55 . . . . ☎ (501) 922-5603
MR Michael Van D JR . . . . 7 Aldaya Lane, Hot Springs Village, AR *71909*

Hitschler MRS Diana T (Diana Timmerman) Me. . . . ☎ (610) 527-8336
MISS W Rehn—at ☎ (215) 731-1592
2028 Delancey Place, Philadelphia, PA *19103* . . 730 Woodleave Rd, Bryn Mawr, PA
MISS Pamela B *19010*

Hoar MR John JR . . . . Died Nov 16'95

Hoar MR Roger S 2d (late Sherman) . . . . . Married at West Falmouth, MA
Carter MISS Julia D (Richard J) . . . . Sep 9'95

Hoar MR & MRS Roger S 2d (Julia D Carter)
☎ (508) 563-7169 . . 67 Glen Av, North Falmouth, MA *02556*

Hobbs MASTER David Whitehead JR (David W) . . . . Born Feb 8'96

Hobbs MISS Marilyn . . . . Died Jly 21'95

Hoblitzell MR & MRS Alan P JR (Prentice—M Louise Perkins) Nu'71.P'53
☎ (410) 828-1906 . . 326 S Wind Rd, Baltimore, MD *21204*

Hobson MR J Kendall (late John B 3d) . . . . . Married at New Orleans, LA
Friel MISS Kathleen L (Ketchum—Kathleen L Friel) . . . . Jun 17'95

Hobson MR & MRS J Kendall (Ketchum—Kathleen L Friel) Tul'73.Tul'87 . . . . ☎ (504) 891-4571
JUNIORS MR John K JR . . . . 5207 Chestnut St, New Orleans, LA *70115*

Hodges MISS Madeleine Foulke (Stuart T) . . . . Born Nov 12'95

Hodges MISS Sarah L (Lorin C) . . . . Married at Malibu, CA
Newton MR Charles I (Edwin Anthony T) . . . . Oct 14'95

Hoeffner MASTER Colin James (Jeff D) . . . . Born at Helena, MT Mch 6'93

Hoeffner MR & MRS Jeff D (Marie T Belson) Gettys'87.MontSt'84
☎ (406) 458-5817 . . 1340 Ranch View Rd, Helena, MT *59601*

Hoeffner MASTER Kenneth Griffin (Jeff D) . . . . Born at Helena, MT Apr 7'95

Hoffman MR & MRS David F (Gale Hayman) Skd'78.Wms'74
☎ (610) 527-4432 . . 511 Lynmere Rd, Bryn Mawr, PA *19010*

Hoffman MISS Mary F
☎ (561) 272-5704 . . 716 N Lake Av, Delray Beach, FL *33483*

Hoffman MASTER Rush Stockton (David F) . . . . Born at Greenwich, CT Dec 31'94

Hoffman MR & MRS Thomas J (Janet Van W Stanley) LakeF'63.Ih.Cnt.Ncd.Ken'62.Mich'63.GeoW'67
☎ (206) 286-8607 . . 341 W Olympic Place, Apt 3, Seattle, WA *98119-3791*

Holden MISS Ellen B—Pa'74.Cal'83
☎ (310) 477-0016 . . 10517 Rountree Rd, West Los Angeles, CA *90064*

Holden MISS Helen W (Green—Helen W Holden) . . . . Married at Santa Rosa, CA
Gladsky MR John J JR . . . . Apr 22'93

Holder MR Albin O . . . . Died at Palm Beach, FL Apr 15'95

Hole MR & MRS James W B (Heidi D Thiermann) Pa'88.Me.Cry.F&M'87 Valley Brooke Farm, PO Box 609, Wayne, PA *19087*

Hollingsworth MR & MRS William I 3d (Pickett—Marilyn D Seaman) Finch'62.B.Pr.Mb.Clare'63 .
MISS Jocelyn M Pickett—Ty'93—at 245 E 72 St, New York, NY *10021* . . . . of ☎ (212)737-3573 155 E 72 St, New York, NY *10021*
☎ (516) 922-7770 Box 572, Oyster Bay Rd, Locust Valley, NY *11560*

Hollister MRS Robert (Ellenor R McCombs) . . . . Died at Dennis, MA Dec 11'95

Hollstein COL (RET) & MRS Jean W (Kistler—Dell W Proctor) USA.NCar'47.OreSt'41
☎ (910) 484-6318 . . 323 Birnam Dv, Fayetteville, NC *28305*

Hooff MR Charles R JR . . . . Died at Alexandria, VA Mch 3'95

Hooker MR & MRS Henry G (Janine A Roeth) Br'85.Stan'68.Cal'84 . . . . ☎ (408) 457-0332
MISS Elizabeth R . . . . 407 Ocean View Av, Santa Cruz, CA *95062*

Hooker MR Michael G (late R Lent) . . . . Married at San Mateo, CA
Colladay MISS Constance L (Edgar B JR) . . . . Sep 30'95

Hooker MISS Simone Roeth (Henry G) . . . . Born Jly 29'95

Hopkins MR & MRS R Stockton B (Elizabeth W Drayton) Sa.Rb.Cts.Me.Pa'50 . . . . ☎ (610) 725-9944
MISS Mary B—Pa'82—at ☎ (201) 692-8463 1367 Academy Lane, Teaneck, NJ *07666* . . . . 53 Cabot Dv, Chesterbrook, PA *19087*
MISS Elizabeth D—Cent'y'88.Me.—at
☎ (610) 964-8609 . . 116 N Aberdeen Av, Wayne, PA *19087* . . . .
MR R Stockton B JR—at ☎ (610) 964-0349 121 Old Forge Crossing, 1027 Valley Forge Rd, Devon, PA *19333* . . . .

Hoppin MRS Mariana F (Mariana Field) . . . . ☎ (212) 289-4665
MISS Ashley G—Pom'89—at ☎ (212) 751-1403 200 E 66 St, New York, NY *10021* . . . . 1133 Park Av, New York, NY
MR David F—Ham'87—at ☎ (703) 243-3121 *10128*
1125 N Vernon St, Arlington, VA *22201* . . . . . .

Horan MR Daniel D H (John R) . . . . Married at Westfield, NJ
Beglin MISS Julie Ann (Edward) . . . . May 27'95

Horn MR Fraser M . . see R R Plum

Horn MR Geoffrey M . . see R R Plum

Horn MR & MRS Richard A (Rothman—Hope H Miller) Br'76.Tex'74
☎ (404) 982-9414 . . 2240 Heritage Dv NE, Atlanta, GA *30345*

Horn MASTER Samuel Anderson (Richard A) . . . . Born Feb 15'94

Hornor MR Gurdon W—AmInt'l'83
113 W Bluegill Lane, Suffield, CT *06078-1951*

Hornor MR John W—Ham'77.Pa'83
☎ (413) 584-5403 . . 46 Ladyslipper Lane, Northampton, MA *01060*

Hornsey MR & MRS John W 3d (Sewall Gibbons-Neff) Cry.VillaN'62 . . . . 1121 Seven Oaks Rd, Chester Springs,
MISS Katherine H—at 168 Sutherland Av, Apt 7, London W9 1HR, England . . . . PA *19425*
MR John W . . . .

Hosmer MISS Alicia Watts—Md'88.Wis'91
☎ (301) 365-2559 . . 7545 Spring Lake Dv, Bethesda, MD *20817*

Hostetler MR & MRS Charles A (D Anne Gore) Duke'53.WakeF'49
☎ (910) 875-2745 . . 305 W Elwood Av, Raeford, NC *28376*
Houghton MR Charles G 3d—Cysl.H'67
☎ (914) 384-6148 . . "Octagonal House" Frog Hollow Farm, Box 111, Esopus, NY *12429-0111*
Houghton MR William M . . . . Died at Concord, MA Sep 18'95
Houston MRS Howard E (Frances G Crawford) . . . . Died at Hartford, CT Dec 12'95
Hovey MRS Charles F (Anita C Hinckley) | ☎ (617) 566-0795
  Sm.Cy.Chi.Ncd. . . . . | 334 Newton St, Apt
  MR Benjamin . . . . | C, Chestnut Hill, MA *02167-2715*
Howard MR & MRS Morton (Susan McInnes) | ☎ (610) 649-4226
  Pa'60.Me.Y'56. . . . . | 411 Fishers Rd,
  MISS Anne B—Bow'87. . . . . | Bryn Mawr, PA
  MR Robert M—Bow'84 . . . . | *19010*
  MR Nicholas—Mid'85 . . . . |
  MR Alexander McI—at Skidmore . . . . |
Howard MRS Thomas Clark (Frances M Hall) . . . . Died at Boston, MA Jly 23'95
Howe MASTER Tobias (g—Nathaniel S Howe) . . . . Born at Dover, MA Jan 11'94
Howland DR Murray S JR . . . . Died at Buffalo, NY Nov 14'95
Hubbell MRS Howard H (Hubbell—Bryant—Lanham—Mary H Betts) . . . . Died at University City, MO Sep 30'95
Hubby MR & MRS David G (Sarah P Foote) | ☎ (919) 942-4465
  Va'59.Geo'63. . . . . | 1252 Falmouth
  MISS Elizabeth A—at 5010 Keokuk St, Bethesda, MD *20816* . . . . | Court, Chapel Hill, NC *27514*
  MR Peter K—at S Beach Marina Apt 1-703, 2 Townsend St, San Francisco, CA *94107* . . . . . |
Huber MISS Allison Rose (John Y 4th) . . . . Born at Phoenix, AZ Aug 30'95
Huddleston MR & MRS C Elsworth (Watson— | ☎ (410) 819-8771
  Dorothy H Burnett) WmW'ds'35.Cr'29 . . . . | Easton Club,
  MISS May C—GlasSt'75—at Atlantic City, NJ . . | 28525 Augusta Court, Easton, MD *21601*
Hudson MR & MRS William P C (Kolowitz—M | ☎ (210) 504-6650
  Antonia R Ramirez) Tex'75 . . . . | "Casa Tonio"
  JUNIORS MISS Vanessa L . . . . | 2300 Coffee Port
  JUNIORS MR John H P . . . . | Rd, Brownsville, TX
    MISS Emma H Kolowitz. . . . . | *78521*
Hughes MR Joseph D . . . . Died Sep 6'95
Hughes MASTER Matthew McVay (Thomas M) . . . . Born at New York, NY Oct 20'95
Hughes MR & MRS Robert David (Carlissa K Richards)
  Nw'90.Nw'95.Nw'88.Loy'96
☎ (847) 864-3592 . . 3224 Otto Lane, Evanston, IL *60201*
Hughes MR Theodore M JR . . . . Died at Worcester, PA Jan 5'94
Hughes MRS Theodore M JR (Callanan—Jane A Porter) . . . . . Married at Chestnut Hill, PA
  Burpee MR George B . . . . Apr 8'95

Hughes MR & MRS Thomas L (Kuczynski—Jane D Casey) Ws'60.Pg.Cvc.
☎ (301) 656-1420 . . 5636 Western Av, Chevy Chase, MD *20815*
Hulme MR Alfred P JR . . . . Died at New York, NY Jan 31'96
Humphrey MR William D—Dick'61
☎ (314) 825-2044 . . 1561 Autumn Leaf Dv, Ballwin, MO *63021*
Hungerford MR Charles S JR—Cw.Wms'43
☎ (203) 966-2362 . . 153 East Av, New Canaan, CT *06840*
Hungerford MISS Sally-Byrd (Breeney—Sally-Byrd Hungerford) Bost'78
☎ (860) 567-2233 . . 3 Tapping Reeve Village, Litchfield, CT *06759*
Hunnewell MISS Clarissa Gaylord (Walter JR) . . . . Born at Boston, MA Mch 2'95
Hunnewell MISS Sarah F—Ty'75.Pa'84 ⚓ . . of
☎ (516) 726-4656 . . 99 Halsey Lane, PO Box 75, Water Mill, NY *11976-0075*
☎ (212) 362-3264 . . 176 W 87 St, New York, NY *10024*
Hunt MRS E Norton (Catharine E Montgomery) Ac.Cda.
☎ (610) 687-8551 . . 505 E Lancaster Av, Apt 301, St Davids, PA *19087*
Hunt MR William O JR—Cho.Rcch.Sc.Cas.Y'61 | PO Box 7951,
⚓ . . . . | Aspen, CO *81612*
  MISS Hilary B . . . . |
  MISS Fiona McC . . . . |
  MR Ian C . . . . |
  MR Christopher . . . . |
Hunter MR & MRS Robert D (Elizabeth I Valsam) | ☎ (508) 668-6073
  McG'67.Sb.Nh.Chi. | 492 Lincoln Rd,
  JUNIORS MISS Catherine B . . . . | Walpole, MA *02081*
Huntington MR & MRS Charles G (Correa—Elizabeth Winchester) Scripps'41.Cly.Dc.Ncd.Myf.
☎ (619) 742-1202 . . PO Box 87, Pauma Valley, CA *92061*
Hurd MR Eliot P . . . . Died at Baltimore, MD Jly 15'95
Hurd MR & MRS H Ward (Cox—Elizabeth Hertz) . . | 787 Jackson Valley
  MISS Claire L . . . . | Rd, Oxford, NJ
  MR Holcombe W JR . . . . | *07863*
Hurley MASTER William Pumroy (Stephen Nash) . . . . Born at Boston, MA Sep 8'95
Hustead MR & MRS Walter Bugh 3d (Mary P S | of 11019 N 75 St,
  McCormick) SFr'72 . . . . | Scottsdale, AZ
  MR Walter Bugh 4th . . . . | *85260*
 | ☎ (520) 527-3981
 | 2265 Valley View
 | Dv, 10122,
 | Flagstaff, AZ *86001*
Husted MR & MRS John G W (Keeling—Elizabeth | ☎ (508) 228-5511
  Hanbury-Williams) B.Nyc.Plg.Y'49 . . . . | 2 Wannacomet Rd,
  MR Patrick J Keeling— | PO Box 896,
  27 Pembridge Square, London W2 4DS, | Nantucket, MA
  England . . . . | *02554*
Hutz MASTER Michael Benjamin (Rudolf E) . . . . Born at Christiana, DE Jan 27'96

I

Igleheart MR & MRS Edgar A (Shinkle—Marie Elizabeth Benoist)
Pn.P'45..of
☎ (812) 426-1951.. 4021 Fairfax Rd, Evansville, IN *47710*
☎ (502) 436-5397.. ''Isabella'' Rte 6, Box 219, Murray, KY *42071*
Ingalls MISS Lynn K (Melville E JR) .... Married at Danbury, CT
Latterman MR Arnold .... Sep 4'95
Ingham MISS Ames—Pitzer'92
☎ (213) 468-9177.. 314 N Curson Av, Apt 103, Los Angeles,
CA *90036*
Irvine MR & MRS Kenneth A (Bettina S Brown) | ☎ (203) 869-5271
Wis'65.Hn.Mich'63.H'66 .... | 147 Cat Rock Rd,
JUNIORS MR K Andrew JR .... | Cos Cob, CT *06807*
Irving MISS Sarah Torrey (g—Frederick F Irving) .... Born at
Jacksonville, FL Dec 25'95
Irwin MR D King .... Died at
New York, NY Nov 21'95
Irwin MR & MRS Henry M (Cunningham—H Chauncy Lloyd)
Pc.Ph.P'47.Pa'51
PO Box 1237, 5 Freeman St, Mattapoisett, MA *02739*
Irwin MR & MRS Robert J A JR (Donna V Henwood) | ☎ (716) 885-7960
St.Cw.G.Dh.Colg'49 ⚓ | 6 St Andrews Walk,
MR Ronald H—Ty'92—at 1 Highstead Flats, | Buffalo, NY *14222*
1 Highstead Rd, 7700 Rondebosch, Cape Town,
South Africa ....
MR Derrick M—Colg'93—at 91-97 Fitzroy St,
St Kilda, Victoria 3182, Australia ....
Ivison MR Thayer .... Died at
New Canaan, CT Aug 13'95

J

Jackman MR & MRS George A (Lucinda U Ritter) Mid'86.Tr.Tor'82.Tex'87
☎ (508) 263-3345.. 14 Minuteman Rd, Acton, MA *01720*
Jacks MISS Elizabeth B—Duke'91.Nw'96.. see A L Scott
Jacks MR Robert LeRoy JR—Duke'94.Stan'95.. see A L Scott
Jackson MISS Elizabeth L—RISD'90.. see MRS E S Blue
Jackson MRS Katharine E (Patty—Davis— | ☎ (404) 955-9152
Katharine F Evans) BMr'61.Rd. .... | 3210C Post Woods
MR William A Patty 4th—at Middlebury .... | Dv NW, Atlanta,
JUNIORS MR Robert E Davis—at | GA *30339*
Trinity-Pawling .... |
Jackson MISS Margaret (James H) .... Married at Nonquitt, MA
Gottsegen MR Daniel A (Robert) .... Jly 4'95
Jackson MR & MRS Patrick T JR (Christina C | ☎ (207) 846-5472
Converse) Sth'63.Chi.Bab'61 .... | PO Box 642,
MISS Mary E—at ☎ (617) 859-7944 | Brown's Point Rd,
696 Tremont St, Apt 1, Boston, MA *02116* .... | Yarmouth, ME
 | *04096*
Jackson MR Richard L JR—ColC'90.. see MRS E S Blue
Jackson MISS Riley Gaines (g—L Ebersole Gaines) ...... Born Feb 9'96
Jacobs MR & MRS Charles Clark JR (Alley—Rosemary Wilson)
Miss'42.Miss'47
☎ (601) 843-5719.. 514 Robinson Dv, Cleveland, MS *38732*

Jacobson MR Edward—Carl'42.H'43.Ariz'46
☎ (602) 252-2511.. 2201 N Central Av, Phoenix, AZ *85004-1424*
James MR Ian R (Leland T) .... Married at Darien, CT
Cox MISS Wendy L (Bruce B) .... Sep 17'94
Jansing MR Christopher C—Roan'90
☎ (212) 879-4323.. 310 E 65 St, Apt 4A, New York, NY *10021*
Janvier MISS Eleanor Scullin (William P) .... Born at
Raleigh, NC Aug 31'95
Jay MISS Anne O (Robert D) .... Married at St James, NY
Vieth MR Erich .... Jly 8'95
Jeffress MRS Gardner N (Janet A Hollands) | ☎ (804) 784-6728
Camb'66 .... | 4 Buck Branch Dv,
MR Stanley G—W&M'94 .... | Richmond, VA
MR Alan S—at Auburn U .... | *23233*
Jeffress MR Gardner N—Rv.
10100B Palace Way, Richmond, VA *23233*
Jenkins MR & MRS Hyde Rust 2d (Beverly Phillips) | ☎ (601) 446-7842
Miss'74.Sar.Miss'71 .... | PO Box 1747,
JUNIORS MR Lemuel P .... | Natchez, MS *39120*
JUNIORS MR Hyde D |
Jenkins MISS Marion W—Cal'84.Cal'91
☎ (916) 753-0106.. 1806 Birch Lane, Davis, CA *95616*
Jenkins MR Reginald Courtenay .... Died at
Stanford, CA Dec 10'95
Jenney MRS Reginald (Baird—Margaretta S Gibbons) Cy.Chi.
10 Longwood Rd, Baker 380, Westwood, MA *02090*
Jennings MR & MRS Christopher R (Cordelia A | ☎ (717) 566-5560
Willis) WashColl'76.Rut'79.Ste.Myf.Pa'65. | 1051 Knoll Dv,
Pa'67.H'93 .... | Hummelstown, PA
MISS Elise B—Denis'95—at ☎ (617) 536-2714 | *17036*
725 Boylston St, Apt 5, Boston, MA *02115* ....
MR Christopher R JR—at ☎ (215) 628-9942
3 Joining Brook, Spring House, PA *19477* .....
Jennison MR & MRS David R (Joëlle M T N Husson) Parnasse'77.Hob'80
☎ (011-44-171) 937-9658.. 26 Kelso Place, London W8 5QG, England
Jennison MASTER Nicolas Philip Roger (David R) .... Born at
London, England Mch 11'94
Jennison MR & MRS Peter H (Alexandra J Curran)
☎ (212) 831-7098.. 201 E 87 St, New York, NY *10128*
Jewett MR & MRS Edgar B 3d (Frances B Appleton) Ny.St.Buf'50
☎ (716) 447-0476.. 92 Middlesex Rd, Buffalo, NY *14216*
Jobson MR Mark deV—Cp.Ll.Cal'83
☎ (619) 299-9737.. 1043 University Av, Apt 150, San Diego,
CA *92103*
Johnson MR F Lincoln .... Died at
Greenwich, CT Jan 28'96
Johnson MRS Patricia Z (Patricia L Zoch) ... Married at San Antonio, TX
Ferguson MR J Howard 3d .... Oct 28'95
Johnson MRS Sallie B (Sallie B Moore) SL'46.Cda.
☎ (212) 758-1362.. 424 E 52 St, Apt 10D, New York, NY *10022*
Johnson MISS Theodora L—GeoW'41
Santa Cruz Av, Menlo Park, CA *94025*
Johnston MR & MRS Edwin M JR (Schoellkopf—Susan Fiske Surdam)
St.G.Y'55
☎ (716) 874-3722.. 161 Middlesex Rd, Buffalo, NY *14212*
Johnston MR & MRS Henry O (Sally F Curby) Cy.
☎ (314) 993-0860.. 4 Town & Country Dv, St Louis, MO *63124*

Johnston MRS Hugh McB (Sheffield—Ellen J Wacker) Cly.StJ.
☎ (847) 735-0771 . . PO Box 826, Lake Forest, IL *60045*
Johnston MR John W—Rcn.Cl'66 . . . . ☎ (561) 731-2969
  MISS Dana C—at U of Vt . . . . 902 SW 34 Av,
  MISS Alix V—at St George's . . . . Boynton Beach, FL
  33435
Johnston MISS Julia S (Thomas S) . . . . Married at Rosemont, PA
  Umberger MR Max J (Douglas B) . . . . Sep 23'95
Johnston MRS Lisa A (Lisa A Oliver) . . . . ☎ (360) 563-2400
  JUNIORS MISS Rochelle R . . . . 6011—157 Av SE,
  Snohomish, WA
  98290
Johnston DR & MRS Thomas S (Jettie L Bergman) ☎ (912) 598-7488
  Dick'58.Me.Rd.Ac.Buck'57.Temp'61 . . . . 2 Pennystone
  MISS Jettie L—PCTS'86.Me.—at Retreat, Savannah,
  ☎ (610) 525-2516 . . Rosemont Apt 302, GA *31411*
  1062 Lancaster Av, Rosemont, PA *19010* . . . . .
  MR Thomas S JR—Me.Buck'93—at
  ☎ (706) 560-0439 . . 1210 Huntington Dv,
  Augusta, GA *30909* . . . .
Jones MRS Andrieus A (Rona M Longinotto) . . . . Died at
  Hillsborough, CA Oct 22'95
Jones, Bryan D & Packard, Elise B—Br'88.Br'89
  ☎ (703) 379-4613 . . 5708 S 4 St, Arlington, VA *22204*
Jones MR & MRS Charles H JR (Hope Haskell) ☎ (407) 881-7124
  BMr'56.Rcn.Rm.Stc.BtP.Rv.Cc.Cda.Va'56 . . . . 218 Via Linda,
  MR Henry M T—HampSydney'94—at Palm Beach, FL
  ☎ (212) 249-7122 . . 451 E 83 St, Apt 1A, *33480*
  New York, NY *10028* . . . .
Jones MR Charles H 3d—Rm.Stc.P'90
  ☎ (703) 671-7641 . . 1200 N Quaker Lane, Alexandria, VA *22302-3000*
Jones MRS Christina C (Christina P Clare) . . . . Married at New York, NY
  Evans MR William J (late John J) . . . . Oct 27'95
Jones JUNIORS MR Frederick K . . see W J Evans
Jones MR & MRS Howard Lee JR (Cook—Sherry D Scarbrough)
  Houst'75.Dar.LSU'60
  ☎ (601) 442-3091 . . Providence Plantation, 91 Providence Rd, Natchez,
  MS *39120*
Jones JUNIORS MR Oliver H . . see W J Evans
Jones MISS Palmer D . . see W J Evans
Jones MR & MRS Patrick S JR (Katherine H Mellon)
  StLaw'86.Eh.Macalester'86
  Box 310, 24 Hill & Dale Rd, Oldwick, NJ *08858*
Jones MR & MRS Peter R (Margot Potter Kiser) DU'82.DU'84.Mds . . . of
  ☎ (011-255-57) 8547 . . Ndarakwai Reserve, PO Box 49,
  Arusha, Tanzania
  ☎ (406) 932-6212 . . "Twisted Stick" W Boulder Rd, McLeod,
  MT *59052*
Jordan MRS F Peter (Beatrice L Renwick) Ac.
  ☎ (610) 933-8441 . . "Rolling Acres" Box 127, Valley Forge,
  PA *19481-0127*
Jordan MR & MRS Philip H JR (Sheila A Gray) ☎ (614) 427-2171
  Ws'55.P'54.Y'56.Y'62 . . . . 401 Gaskin Av,
  MR Philip H 3d—Wms'89 Gambier, OH *43022*
  MR John G 2d—at Colby . . . .
Judson MR & MRS Gilbert H (Mohr—Blair B Bellis) LakeF'77
  ☎ (415) 507-9268 . . 25 Circle Rd, San Rafael, CA *94903*

K

Kahle MR Jeffrey L (late Julian L) . . . . Married at New York, NY
  Goulian MISS Elizabeth J (Dicran) . . . . Nov 4'95
Kahle MR & MRS Jeffrey L (Elizabeth J Goulian) Y.'84
  ☎ (212) 875-1933 . . 10 W 80 St, Apt 3E, New York, NY *10024*
Kaiser MR Franck H JR . . . . ☎ (407) 768-2299
  MISS Courtenay A—at ☎ (508) 993-7780 605 Sheridan Woods
  378 Cottage St, New Bedford, MA *02740* . . . . . Dv, West
  Melbourne, FL
  32904-3303
Karlson MR Douglas E . . . . Married at Harwich Port, MA
  Smith MISS Wendy L (Marvin) . . . . Jly 8'95
Kauders MR Erick . . . . Died at
  Bedford, MA Oct 24'95
Kay MRS William G JR (Chellis—Marcia Quale) Nw'61.H'79.Hb.
  ☎ (407) 832-8320 . . La Casita, 200 N Ocean Blvd, Palm Beach,
  FL *33480*
Keady MR & MRS Robert R (Kathryn M Updegraff) of ☎ (408)338-6122
  Cal'56.Me.Wash'60 . . . . "Quail Haven"
  MR Kevin I PO Box 63,
  MR Michael G . . . . Quail Haven Lane,
  MR Robert R JR . . . . Boulder Creek, CA
  95006
  ☎ (011-44-1)
  43-29-32-20
  13 rue Jacob,
  75006 Paris, France
Kean MR Stewart B—Unn.Lm.Rv.Va'57
  ☎ (702) 454-5387 . . 3258 Brookfield Dv, Las Vegas, NV *89120*
Keeling MR Patrick J . . see J G W Husted
Keen MR George W . . . . Died at
  Annapolis, MD May 12'95
Keidel MR & MRS Albert JR (Justine F Lewis) of 404 Brightwood
  V'37.Md.Gv.Elk.Mv.Ncd.Pn.P'33 ⚓ . . . . Club Dv,
  MISS Anne G—Bost'68.Van'69—at Lutherville, MD
  Goethestrasse 4, 8700 Würzburg, Germany *21093*
  ☎ (305) 367-3190
  004 Andros Rd,
  Ocean Reef Club,
  North Key Largo,
  FL *33037*
Keil MR & MRS Bryant L (Shelia K Swift) StLaw'91.Geo'86
  1320 N State P'kway, Chicago, IL *60610*
Keil DR & MRS Francis C (Eleanor Schalck)
  Occ'39.Mls'41.Pr.Csh.Cl'31.Cr'37
  ☎ (607) 257-4301 . . 312 Savage Farm Dv, Ithaca, NY *14850*
Keleher MR & MRS Walter D (Wendy K Webster) ☎ (617) 934-5867
  Ub.Chi.Dc.Ncd.Cl'66 . . . . 7 Freeman Place,
  MR Christopher D—Alf'86—in Indonesia . . . . . Box 262,
  Snug Harbor,
  Duxbury, MA *02331*
Kelley MR Albert J . . . . Died at
  Boyce, VA Jan 14'96
Kelly MASTER Charles James (John F JR) . . . . Born Oct 10'94

Kelly MR & MRS John F JR (Emilie P Barton) Br'83.StLaw'86
☎ (303) 697-0658 . . 215 S Park Av, Morrison, CO *80465*
Kelly MR John W (late John S) . . . . Married at Ipswich, MA
Barrett MRS Jennifer B (Jennifer Benson) . . . . Jun 24'95
Kelly MR & MRS John W (Barrett—Jennifer Benson)
Mass'84.H'89.K.S.Bost'80
☎ (508) 468-1544 . . PO Box 2460, 14 Pleasant St, Hamilton, MA *01982*
Kelly MR & MRS Richard B (Jerilyn Tabbert) | ☎ (602) 945-3738
MichSt'69.H'67 . . . . | 5320 N Casa Blanca
MISS Colleen M . . . . | Dv, Paradise Valley,
JUNIORS MISS Kimberly S . . . . | AZ *85253*
Kelsey MISS Caroline Olivia (Henry B JR) . . . . Born at
Louisville, KY Jly 6'95
Kelsey MRS Charles C (Dorothy Bugbee) . . . . | ☎ (317) 769-6200
MR Charles C JR—at Houston, TX . . . . | 9240 E 350 S,
MR & MRS John R Brant JR (Wendella L | Zionsville, IN *46077*
Kelsey) . . . . |
Kelsey MR & MRS Henry B JR (Deborah L Hightower) Ky'88.Cent'85
☎ (502) 327-9268 . . 2306 Donleigh Court, Louisville, KY *40222*
Kelsey MR Peter B (H Burr) . . . . Married at Oakton, VA
DeLonga MRS Mary P (Mary Purzycki) . . . . Jly 9'95
Kelsey MR Stephen T JR (late Stephen T) . . . . Married at
Newtown Square, PA
Bushnell MRS Kipp (Drum—Reed—Margaret Kipp) . . . . . . Sep 9'95
Kelsey MR & MRS Stephen T JR (Drum—Reed—Bushnell—Margaret Kipp)
Bgt.Fic.Y'39
☎ (610) 647-8173 . . 360 Keller Rd, Berwyn, PA *19312*
Kemble MR Peter—Ty'61.H'67
☎ (617) 864-9182 . . 6½ Grant St, Cambridge, MA *02138*
Kemble MR William . . . . Died at
Mt Kisco, NY Oct 5'95
Kendall MRS Donna Lee (Warren—Model—Donna Lee Kendall) Whit'70
☎ (803) 577-5378 . . 17 Meeting St, Charleston, SC *29401*
Kendrick MR & MRS Stephen L 2d (Helenanne Page)
Ty'83.Ncd.Ne'77.Bentley'83
☎ (708) 904-4684 . . 3531 Eliot Lane, Naperville, IL *60564*
Kenna MR & MRS Timothy C (Laura A Moorhouse) RISD'90.V'88
17 McGregor Rd, Woods Hole, MA *02543*
Kennedy MR & MRS Gregory D (Victoria S Reese) V'90.Stan'88.Stan'92
105 Duane St, New York, NY *10007*
Kennedy MISS Lin
☎ (215) 732-8121 . . Lenox Apt 3E, Box 31, 250 S 13 St, Philadelphia,
PA *19107*
Kent MR & MRS A Atwater 3d (Williams—Pamela Gamage) Rd . . .of
☎ (610) 353-2090 . . PO Box 183, Newtown Square, PA *19073*
☎ (407) 833-8797 . . "Lemmon Tree Cottage" 410 Australian Av,
Palm Beach, FL *33480*
Kent MISS Ann Alexander (Mark B) . . . . Born at
Greenville, SC Dec 28'95
Kent MASTER Mark Thompson (Mark B) . . . . Born at
Greenville, SC Dec 28'95
Kenyon MR W Houston JR . . . . Died Jan 22'96
Keogh MR George P . . see N N Solley
Ker MASTER David Angus Longhurst (g—David S I Ker) . . . . . . Born at
Vancouver, BC, Canada Sep 21'95

Ker MISS Hannah Wren McCulloch (g—David S I Ker) . . . . Born at
Vancouver, BC, Canada Feb 11'96
Kernan MR Henry S—H'38.Y'41 . . . . | ☎ (607) 397-8805
MISS Patricia McC—Wis'85.RISD'88—at | 300B County Rte
☎ (518) 426-7537 . . 602 Madison Av, Albany, | 40, South Worcester,
NY *12208* . . . . | NY *12197*
MR Henry D—☎ (607) 397-9446 . . . . |
MR Christopher N—Cr'77.Tex'92—at |
☎ (305) 661-0627 . . Box 560273, Miami, FL |
38256 . . . . |
Kerr MRS Constance B (Constance J Barkan) Cal'68
☎ (415) 349-9621 . . 5 Creekridge Court, San Mateo, CA *94402*
Kester MASTER Joshua Banning Eyre (g—John L Eyre) . . . . Born at
Ottawa, Ontario, Canada Aug 19'94
Kestler MRS Manuel S (Kneedler—Pauline Perry)
☎ (510) 947-5558 . . 1580 Geary Rd, Apt 148, Walnut Creek, CA *94596*
Kew MISS Christina E . . see MISS L B Watson
Key MR Frank L . . . . Died at
Clayton, MO Sep 27'95
Key MISS Julia Bowdoin (g—Albert L Key) . . . . Born at
New York, NY Dec 5'94
Keyes MR & MRS Charles Griffith (E Kenan Jones) RMWmn'68.Rhodes'66
☎ (501) 664-1814 . . 2904 N Pierce St, Little Rock, AR *72207*
Keys MR A de Forest—Pn.P'40 . . . . | ☎ (011-44-1380)
MR David de F—Bost'93—at ☎ (213) 954-1343 | 828-518
1226 S Highland Av, Los Angeles, CA *90019* . . | Cleeve Lodge,
| SEEND, Wilshire
| SN12 6PG, England
Kidder MR Christopher H—W&M'87
☎ (011-44-171) 924-7008 . . 1 Battersea Bridge Rd, London SW11 3BZ,
England
Kidder MRS Randolph A (Dorothy D Robinson) . . . . Died at
Washington, DC Sep 18'95
Kidder MR Randolph A . . . . Died Jan 4'96
Killiam MR Paul—Hn.H'37 . . . . | ☎ (203) 966-2479
MR Timothy S—at Kerkstraat 211, 1017 GJ | 115 Bayberry Rd,
Amsterdam, The Netherlands . . . . | New Canaan, CT
MR Theodore R—at ☎ (203) 458-3922 | *06840*
185 Dennison Dv, Guilford, CT *06437* . . . . |
Kimball MR & MRS Daniel M (Lydia C Fitler) Mid'84.H.'92.Nf.Me.Conn'63
☎ (617) 354-6768 . . 9 Poplar Rd, Cambridge, MA *02138*
Kimball MRS Mary Eliza (Stanley—Mary Eliza | ☎ (212) 688-4516
Kimball) Sth'73.GeoW'76 . . . . | 303 Rivercross,
JUNIORS MR Arthur E Kimball Stanley . . . . . . | 531 Main St,
| New York, NY
| *10044*
King MR James D JR
☎ (410) 628-1741 . . 10311 Malcolm Circle, Cockeysville, MD *21030*
King MISS Katharine H
☎ (215) 836-7173 . . 519 Filbert Rd, Oreland, PA *19075*
King MISS Marina LeRoy (George G) . . . . Born at
New York, NY Jun 21'95
King MR Philip R (Jonathan LeR) . . . . Married at
Paray-le-Monial, Burgundy, France
Thévenin MISS Elisabeth (Jean) . . . . Sep 2'95

King MR & MRS Robert M (Laura T Bethea) Cly.P'57.CTech'58.H'65 . . . . ☎ (203) 762-9926
MISS Caroline P—at DePaul . . . . 9 English Dv,
MR Donald M—at ☎ (203) 838-5708 Wilton, CT *06897*
208 Flax Hill Rd, Apt 9, Norwalk, CT *06854* . .

King MISS Sara Louise (Caleb K) . . . . Born at
Boston, MA Sep 30'95

King MRS Willard van B (Holmes—King—D'Wolf—Frances H Lewis) Cy.
☎ (314) 721-3700 . . 709 S Skinker Blvd, Apt 302, St Louis, MO *63105*

Kinkade MRS Charles E (Doucette—Patricia G ☎ (207) 985-7928
  King) Cyb.Ec. 16 Grove St,
  MISS Sheila A . . . . Kennebunk, ME
  MISS Susan M *04043*
  MISS Nancy A . . . .
  MISS Patricia H (Boymer—Patricia H Kinkade) .
  MR Donald F Doucette JR . . . .

Kinney MR Jeremy F (late Francis S) . . . . Married at Denver, CO
  Arnold MISS Holly (McNulty—Holly Arnold) . . . . Feb 3'96

Kinney MR & MRS Jeremy F (McNulty—Holly Arnold)
  Rc.Ng.Ny.Y'68.H'73 . . of
  ☎ (303) 333-3551 . . 1177 Race St, Denver, CO *80206*
  ☎ (212) 580-2203 . . 33 W 70 St, New York, NY *10023*

Kinsella MR Eugene Benoist (late J Reid) . . . . Married at
West Palm Beach, FL
  Lindsey MRS Christopher F (Ethel P du Pont) . . . . Feb 6'96

Kinsella MR & MRS Eugene Benoist (Lindsey—Ethel ☎ (407) 659-2436
P du Pont) BtP.Cda. . . . . 243 Seaspray Av,
  MISS Marina H Lindsey—ColC'91 . . . . Palm Beach, FL
  33480

Kinsella MR & MRS William A 3d (Eleanor L ☎ (508) 785-0207
Watson) Van'79.Va'81.D.Conn'72 . . . . 14 Juniper Lane,
  MR William S—at Hamilton . . . . Dover, MA *02030*
  JUNIORS MR Christopher B—at Yale . . . .

Kinslow MRS Pamela M S (Pamela M Scott) Cal'76
  ☎ (011-44-1488) 648-683 . . Jasmine Cottage, East Garston,
  nr Hungerford, Berkshire RG17 7EX, England

Kinsolving MR Thomas B . . . . Died at
Arlington, VA Dec 8'95

Kipp MRS Harold A (Margarita Boettger) . . . . Died Feb 19'95

Kirkland MR Craig E . . . . Married at Orlando, FL
  Counts MISS Carol . . . . Sep 23'95

Kirkwood MISS Alexandra Hayne (John H) . . . . Born at
San Francisco, CA Sep 3'95

Kirkwood MISS Elisabeth Packard (John H) . . . . Born at
San Francisco, CA Sep 3'95

Kiser MISS Margot Potter (late John W JR) . . . . Married at
West Kilimanjaro, Tanzania
  Jones MR Peter R (Schuyler) . . . . Oct 22'95

Kissel MISS Rosalie Thorn (Michael Case) . . . . Born at
New York, NY Jun 12'95

Kissinger MR & MRS Henry A (Nancy Maginnes) Bhm.
  350 Park Av, New York, NY *10022*

Klenk DR Eugene L . . . . Died at
Denver, CO Nov 7'95

Kloman MR & MRS Christopher R (Pamela W ☎ (703) 356-9142
Brown) GeoW'69 . . . . 1403 Kurtz Rd,
  MISS Sibyl W—P'94—at 183 Thompson St, McLean, VA *22101*
  New York, NY *10012*
  MR Christopher A T—at U of Va . . . .
  JUNIORS MR Peter J—at Potomac Sch . . . .

Kloman MR & MRS H Felix 2d (Ann B Stern) ☎ (860) 434-5356
Pn.P'55 ⚓ . . . . 61 Ely's Ferry Rd,
  MISS Sarah P—at ☎ (718) 856-1895 Lyme, CT *06371*
  369 Parkside, Brooklyn, NY *11226* . . . .
  MR Edward F—Ty'81—at ☎ (508) 463-6904
  14 Buck St, Newburyport, MA *01950* . . . .

Klotz MR George Meredith
  ☎ (904) 775-6264 . . 120 Southlake Dv, Apt 319C, Orange City,
  FL *32763*

Knight MR & MRS James E (Alison W Rogers) StLaw'91
  1037 North St, Greenwich, CT *06831*

Knight MRS Peyton H (Claudine M Tillier) ☎ (212) 861-4336
Bnd'50.Un.Cly.Y. . . . . 325 E 79 St,
  MISS Cornelia C—Man'vl'93.Cly. . . . . New York, NY
  10021

Knoll MRS Alvin H (Martha Irving) . . . . Died at
Cincinnati, OH Sep 19'95

Knott MR F Stuart (Francis X) . . . . Married at Omaha, NE
  Tamisiea MISS Mary C (Paul E) . . . . Nov 10'95

Knowles MRS James H (Reed—Elizabeth McCullough) Pg.Rr.
  ☎ (520) 684-5484 . . Rancho de los Caballeros, 1551 S Vulture Mine Rd,
  Wickenburg, AZ *85390*

Knowlton MISS Jessica (g—MRS Eben Knowlton) . . . . Born at
Bronxville, NY Oct 24'95

Knox DR & MRS J H Mason 3d (Frances Apthorp Vaughan)
  Mv.Ncd.Y'34.JHop'38
  ☎ (410) 823-3089 . . 1407 W Joppa Rd, PO Box 23, Riderwood,
  MD *21139*

Koberg MR & MRS Heino C F (Charlotte W Baker) ☎ (610) 525-4373
OsnU'63. . . . . 217 Landover Rd,
  MR Heino F—at Pottsville, PA *17901* . . . . Bryn Mawr, PA
  MR David S—at Blue Bell, PA *19422* *19010*
  MR Franz P—at San Diego, CA . . . .

Kobusch MR Nicholas Cabell—Cysl.Lc.TCU'87
  1106 W 6 St, Austin, TX *78703*

Koehler MR Warren B . . . . Died at
Colorado Springs, CO Nov 8'95

Kolowitz MISS Emma H . . see W P C Hudson

Koppelman MR John Van C . . . . Died at
Baltimore, MD Feb 3'96

Koppelman MR Walter JR . . . . Died Jly 3'95

Koppelman MRS Walter JR (Barbara R M Tschudi) ☎ (410) 435-0703
Mv. . . . . 100C Cross Keys
  MR Jay Van C—Frost'82 . . . . Rd, Baltimore, MD
  MR Baker R—Guil'90 . . . . *21210*

Kopper MRS Juliette Starr (Bidlack—Juliette Starr Kopper)
  Ober'52.AmU'78
  ☎ (301) 972-7425 . . PO Box 217, 22331 Mt Ephraim Rd, Dickerson,
  MD *20842*

Kratovil MR Emil A JR—Unn.San.Eyc.Wms'62
  ☎ (203) 532-1171 . . 206 W Lyon Farm Dv, Greenwich, CT *06831-4353*

Kriz MR Christopher J—Myf.Rich'91 . . . . ☎ (202) 338-7838
  MR Andrew S—Rich'93—at "Turkoise" 1061—31 St NW,
  Providenciales, Turks & Caicos . . . . Washington, DC
  20007

Krone MRS Robert C (Mary L Ewing) Bv.
  230 S Brentwood Blvd, Apt 8A, St Louis, MO *63105*

Kuczynski MISS Alexandra L—Bnd'90
  ☎ (212) 684-4592 . . 235 E 22 St, Apt 7N, New York, NY *10010*

Kuczynski MRS Jane C (Jane D Casey) . . . . Married at Chevy Chase, MD
  Hughes MR Thomas L . . . . Nov 25'95

Kuehn MR & MRS George W (Katherine Rust) Un.Cy.Cho.Chi.Hn.H'32
  ☎ (617) 329-4852 . . 10 Longwood Dv, Apt 146, Westwood, MA *02090*

Kulikowski MRS Edward (F Lorillard Ronalds) . . . . ☎ (813) 896-4455
  MISS M Josephine L . . . . MLS Towers Apt
  709, 540 Second Av,
  St Petersburg, FL
  33701

Kunhardt MR Christopher C (late Kenneth B) . . . . Married at
  Old Lyme, CT
  Erni MISS Robin E (Ronald) . . . . Oct 8'94

Kuser MISS Suzanne D—Cvc.Sl.
  ☎ (202) FE8-1849 . . 2225—46 St NW, Washington, DC *20007*

Kyte MR & MRS Lawrence H JR (Marjorie A Meyer) ☎ (513) 561-5180
  Qc.NotreD'60.Va'63 . . . . 5805 Mohican Lane,
  MISS Megan E . . . . Cincinnati, OH
  MR Ryan L—at 535 Tusculum Av, Cincinnati, *45243*
  OH *45226* . . . .

L

Lacey DR & MRS Stephen H (Kathleen O'N Henney) ☎ (216) 321-2287
  Ws'64.May.Y'64 . . . . 2277 Chatfield Dv,
  MISS Margaret C—at 154 W 70 St, Apt 3A, Cleveland Heights,
  New York, NY *10023* . . . . OH *44106-3655*
  MISS Elizabeth H . . . .

Ladd MR Carleton R JR (Carleton R) . . . . . Married at Little Compton, RI
  Swayze MISS Samantha K (Robert G) . . . . May 27'95

Lafferty MISS Ashlyn Kennard (F Wayne JR) . . . . Born Dec 30'95

La Haye Jousselin MR & MRS Edmond de (Anne G of ☎ (011-33-1)
  Manice) 47-20-98-46
  MISS Alix de . . . . 17 rue de l'Amiral
  MISS Amélie de . . . . d'Estaing, 75116
  JUNIORS MR George de . . . . Paris, France
  ☎ (011-33)
  32-35-87-01
  Château de St Aubin
  d'Ecrosville, 27110
  St-Aubin-
  d'Ecrosville, Eure,
  France

Laimbeer MR & MRS Richard B (Mary A Kotecki) ☎ (810) 932-3362
  Cata'67 . . . . 30465 Rushmore
  MR Jonathan W . . . . Circle, Franklin, MI
  JUNIORS MISS Kate A *48025*

Lakeman MR & MRS David J (Susanne E Collier)
  W'mont'80.Birm'ham'86.Lond'76
  2546 E Lynwood St, Simi Valley, CA *93065*

Lamb MR & MRS David R (Daria K Pace) Ch'86.Ck.Pars'79.Pa'84
  ☎ (516) 922-6478 . . PO Box 391, 52 Frost Mill Rd, Mill Neck,
  NY *11765-0391*

Lamb MASTER William Miner (David R) . . . . Born Jly 13'95

Lambert MR & MRS J Laird (M Susan Mahoney) Fontb'77.Wash'73
  ☎ (815) 633-3231 . . 2505 Bradley Rd, Rockford, IL *61107*

Lamberton MR & MRS Benjamin Paulding 3d (Mary ☎ (202) 362-3997
  P Riches) AmU'66.U'62.Va'65 . . . . 4418 Lowell St NW,
  MISS Eleanor M B . . . . Washington, DC
  JUNIORS MR Derek H R *20016*

Lamberton MR & MRS Harry C JR (Margaret M Schaefer) Ct . . .of
  ☎ (202) 483-6161 . . 2230 Massachusetts Av NW, Washington,
  DC *20008*
  ☎ (717) 794-2493 . . "Margaret's Place" Charmian Lane, Blue Ridge
  Summit, PA *17214*

Lamberton MISS M Rawlings (Harry C JR) . . . Married at Washington, DC
  Miller MR Jonathan R (Raymond F JR) . . . . Dec 30'95

Lammers MRS Suzanne K (E Suzanne Kaiser) ☎ (610) 525-3538
  Buck'55.Me.Rd. . . . . "Moro Manor"
  MISS Suzanne K—Temp'81.Me.—at 1618 Hepburn Dv,
  442 Rte 202-206 N, Apt 173, Bedminster, NJ Villanova, PA *19085*
  07921 . . . .
  MISS Alexandra V—Franklin'88.Mich'90.Rd.Me.

Lamont MRS Donald B (Noble—Louise Lyndon) . . . . Died at
  Hobe Sound, FL Dec 27'95

Landers DR & MRS James H (Linda J Pipe) Okla'65.Okla'66
  ☎ (501) 664-1216 . . 1910 Country Club Lane, Little Rock, AR *72207*

Landreth MRS Betty W (Stevens—Landreth— ☎ (212) 355-7004
  O'Neill—Betty A Wright) . . . . 325 E 57 St,
  MISS Ann W—at ☎ (847) 475-9966 New York, NY
  820 Grey Av, Evanston, IL *60202* *10022*
  MISS Nancy W—Box 586463, Oceanside, CA
  92058-6463 . . . .

Lane MR George Bliss JR
  ☎ (617) 277-5225 . . 258 Harvard St, Apt 303, Brookline,
  MA *02146-2904*

Lane MRS Glenn (Bishop—Frankie A Wallace) . . . . Died at
  Portland, OR Jan 6'96

Lane MRS Peggy O (Peggy A Offutt) Pn . . . . ☎ (941) 263-5872
  MISS Heather W—Dth'91.Va'96 . . . . 4796 Crayton Court,
  MR Christopher—Ham'93—at 119 W 71 St, Naples, FL
  New York, NY *10023* *33940-3012*

Langdon MR & MRS George D JR (Domandi—Agnes Körner)
  V'59.Nu'66.C.H'54.Y'61
  124 W 60 St, Apt 17H, New York, NY *10023*

Langenberg MR & MRS Roy T (Patricia I Cole) Wash'62.K.Br'60
  ☎ (603) 772-9093 . . 140 High St, Exeter, NH *03833*

Lanier MISS Katherine C
  ☎ (914) 277-5059 . . 130B Heritage Hills, Somers, NY *10589*

Lanius MR P Baxter 3d—Rc.Ub.Y.Dth'72
  30 E 95 St, New York, NY *10128*

Lanius MRS R Ripley (Rosemary L Ripley) . . . . name changed to Ripley

Lannamann MR Richard S—Ln.Yn.Y'69.H'73
  ☎ (203) 637-9337 . . 21 Willowmere Circle, Riverside, CT *06878*

Lanni MRS Allison D (Allison B Day) Duke'85
☎ (610) 526-9955 . . 900 Montgomery Av, Apt 602, Bryn Mawr, PA *19010*
Lansbury MASTER Galen Kean (James E) . . . . Born at
Los Angeles, CA Oct 31'94
Lansbury MR & MRS James E (Susan A Snorf) SCal'78
☎ (310) 459-8900 . . 16388 Shadow Mountain Dv, Pacific Palisades, CA *90272*
Lapham MR Lewis A . . . . Died at
Greenwich, CT Dec 20'95
Lapin MISS Emma Rebecca (David A) . . . . Born at
Los Angeles, CA Jan 29'96
Lapin MASTER John David (David A) . . . . Born at
Los Angeles, CA Jan 29'96
Lapsley MR Robert W (John W) . . . . Married at Springwater, MN
Dekker MISS Elisabeth (Hans) . . . . Dec 30'95
La Roche MRS Chester J (Rasmussen—Warren— | ☎ (561) 655-9333
Clark—Ritchey C Farrell) Evg.BtP.Cly. . . . . | 529 S Flagler Dv,
MISS Leslie Warren . . . . | Apt 25E,
| West Palm Beach,
| FL *33401*
Larrabee MRS Sterling L (Constance Stuart)
501 E Campus Av, Apt 311, Chestertown, MD *21620-1671*
Lathrop MR & MRS Walter W JR (Anne Alexander) | of ☎ (419)893-7650
Mich'64.Cr'56 . . . . | "Grassy Creek"
MISS Susan C—at London, England . . . . | 9684 Carnoustie Rd,
MR John E—at 180 Beacon St, Apt 8A, Boston, | Perrysburg, OH
MA *02116* . . . . | *43551*
MR George W—at 8609 Ponte Vedra, Holland, | ☎ (941) 964-1260
OH *43528*. . . . . | "Osprey Nest"
| Boca Grande Club,
| PO Box 476,
| Boca Grande, FL
| *33921*
Laub MR David C—Cy.Bf.Br'60.Buf'65
☎ (716) 877-0479 . . 81 Middlesex Rd, Buffalo, NY *14216*
Law MR Hartland . . . . Died Nov 16'94
Lawrence MISS Barbara K (Train—Barbara K Lawrence)
B'gton'65.Nu'69 . . of
☎ (617) 247-9474 . . 34 Upton St, Boston, MA *02118*
☎ (207) 276-5108 . . PO Box 168, Northeast Harbor, ME *04662*
Lawrence MR & MRS David T (Susan L Hadden) | Regent Court 16B,
Wh'lck'69.Pr.K.Cly.H'67 . . . . | 4 Sankuaiban
MISS Katharine P—at Colby . . . . | Yonganli,
MR John H—at Trinity . . . . | Jianguomenwai,
JUNIORS MISS Sarah T—at Groton . . . . | Dajie, Beijing
| 100022, China
Lawrence MRS James (Hallowell—Frances L Weeks) Cy.Tv.Ub.Chi.Ncd.
585A Gay St, Westwood, MA *02090*
Lawrence MRS James F (Barbara R Childs) Yh.Cly.Cda.
☎ (860) 542-5495 . . "South Pole Farm" 57 Windrow Rd, Norfolk, CT *06058*
Lawrence MR Robert C 4th—Rc.Stc.Y'89
☎ (212) 807-9639 . . 615½ Hudson St, Apt 9, New York, NY *10014*
Lawrence MRS Robert L (Janet S Plummer) . . . . Died at
Wilmington, NC Jun 2'95

Lawrence MR & MRS Robert L (Joan E Hilseberg) Seton'65
☎ (910) 256-0230 . . 1221 Arboretum Dv, Wilmington, NC *28405*
Lawson MR & MRS Richard L (Carolyn P Thomas) OState'68.H'71
120 Newark Lane, Mooresville, NC *28115*
Lawson MR & MRS W David IV (Constance T Carter)
Nw'79.Cvc.Rr.W&L'75
☎ (212) 426-1346 . . 1150 Fifth Av, New York, NY *10128*
Lay MRS Elizabeth N (Elizabeth L Nager) . . . . Married at New York, NY
Thompson MR Anthony de V (Henry B 3d) . . . . Nov 18'95
Leachman MR & MRS William H 3d (Kelsey K Drowne)
MtVern'85.Unn.Cvc.W&L'83
1312—35 St NW, Washington, DC *20007*
Le Boutillier MR Philip JR . . . . Died at
Toledo, OH Dec 10'95
Le Day MASTER Mark Thomas 2d (gg—Thomas P Faulconer) . . . . Born
Oct 12'95
Lee MRS Aubrey F (Mary G Hammond) . . . . Died Jly 10'95
Lee DR & MRS Charles T JR (Caroline T Lawson) Au.Rb.Sg.Ac.Pa'47
☎ (215) 247-8189 . . 8882 Norwood Av, Philadelphia, PA *19118*
Lee MR & MRS D Day (Nancy A Mills) Sth'49.Au.H'45.Pa'56
☎ (505) 299-6292 . . 10821 Central Park Dv NE, Albuquerque, NM *87123*
Lee MR & MRS P O'Donnell (Jean R Gibb) | ☎ (410) 228-3892
Elk.Pr.Mv. . . . . | 5301 Cassons Neck
MISS Virginia D . . . . | Rd, Cambridge, MD
MR O'Donnell. . . . . | *21613*
Lee MR R Bland 5th (late Philip H) . . . . Married at Richmond, VA
White MRS Edwin Borden JR (Marsh—M Ann Carter) . . . . . Feb 10'96
Lee MR & MRS R Bland 5th (Marsh—White—M Ann Carter)
Cvc.Sl.Ncd.Va'55 . . of
☎ (804) 435-3636 . . "Cedar Point" PO Box 288, White Stone, VA *22578*
☎ (804) 435-0984 . . "Cobbs Hall" Rte 1, Box 1777, Kilmarnock, VA *22482*
Lee MRS Robert H (Florence A Fell) . . . . Died at
Philadelphia, PA Dec 31'95
Lee MR William Justice—R.Me.Fw.
☎ (610) 359-1035 . . 3500 West Chester Pike, Apt E205, Newtown Square, PA *19073*
Leedom MRS Charles L (Varrell Drew) . . . . Died Aug 19'95
Leeson MASTER Nathaniel Hazard (Robert 3d) . . . . Born at
Beverly, MA Aug 29'95
LeFevre MISS Ann Elizabeth (A Scott) . . . . Born at
San Francisco, CA Oct 27'95
Leggett MRS John D JR (O'Connell—Catharine M Bracher)
Swb'43.Yh.Ncd.
☎ (860) 767-8952 . . 25T Essex Meadows, Essex, CT *06426*
Legier MR & MRS David A JR (Jane Cunningham) StMDom'74.SoLa'68
☎ (504) 897-2682 . . 1401 Exposition Blvd, New Orleans, LA *70118-6037*
Lemmon MRS Nancy O (Nancy Overton)
4241 Westway Av, Dallas, TX *75205-3725*
Lemon MR & MRS L Gene (Catherine D Lanier)
Salem'63.ArizSt'95.Ill'62.Ill'64
☎ (602) 997-0568 . . 1136 W Butler Dv, Phoenix, AZ *85021-4428*
Leness MISS Amanda V—HRdc'89.Cl'93
PO Box 339, Quogue, NY *11959*

Lennig MRS Charles K JR (Annette Brogden Cheston) . . . . Died at Gwynedd, PA Jan 11'96
Leonard MR Maurice B . . . . Died at North Kingstown, RI Jan 11'96
Leonard MR Richard R (Anthony C) . . . . Married
   Turk MISS Gayle K . . . . Nov 11'95
Le Pelletier MR & MRS Franck (Monica Behn) . . MR absent
   see W C Behn
Leslie MR & MRS George R (Smith—Catherine M McIntire)
   Fic.Fiy.Cly.Dar.Ncd.Ht.
   10 Longwood Dv, Apt 309, Westwood, MA *02090*
Lester MISS Katherine A (g—MRS Gioconda M K Crivelli) . . . . . Born at Killingworth, CT May 25'95
Levick MISS Claudia Elizabeth (g—Dudley A Levick JR) . . . . Born at Charlotte, NC Jun 15'95
Levine MISS Jessica Rachel (g—MRS Margaret A Mills) . . . . Born at Baltimore, MD Jun 5'95
Levine MISS Samantha Brooke (g—MRS Margaret A Mills) . . . . . Born at Baltimore, MD Jun 5'95
Levy MR Irvin L—Smu'50
   ☎ (214) 599-9885 . . 2801 Turtle Creek Blvd, Apt 11, Dallas, TX *75219*
Lewis MISS Annabel Phelps (Andrew L 4th) . . . . Born at Wynnewood, PA Jun 22'95
Lewis MISS Elizabeth Aird (Andrew A) . . . . Born at Philadelphia, PA Oct 28'95
Lewis MR & MRS Griffith E (Anne M Kiernan) CtCol'85.Bab'85
   ☎ (518) 436-5960 . . 19 Wildwood Dv, Loudonville, NY *12211*
Lewis MR & MRS H Hunter (Elizabeth Sidamon-Eristoff)
   Y'83.Mt.K.Ub.H'69
   ☎ (804) 973-9003 . . Trearne Farm, 6747 Blackwells Hollow Rd, Crozet, VA *22932*
Lewis MR John N (John B JR) . . . . Married at Bellport, NY
   Lewis MISS Laura C (Richard A) . . . . Sep 23'95
Lewis MASTER Michael Ryan (Griffith E) . . . . Born at Albany, NY Dec 29'95
Lewis MASTER Peter McCauley (Griffith E) . . . . Born at Albany, NY Dec 29'95
Lewis MR Stuart A . . . . Died at Washington, DC Aug 10'95
Lewis MRS Stuart A (Elizabeth R Fankhauser)   ☎ (202) 363-9225
   Cal'43.Cvc. . . . . 5035 Lowell St NW,
   MISS Mary Margaret—at 2984 Clay St,   Washington, DC
   San Francisco, CA *94115* *20016*
Limpert MRS John H JR (Michelle Van Der Leur) . .   ☎ (718) 601-7589
   MISS Alexandra Michelle—at ☎ (718) 387-9126   2475 Palisade Av,
   63 S 3 St, Brooklyn, NY *11211* . . . . Apt 5D, Bronx, NY
   MR John H 3d—Cl'91—at ☎ (212) 539-1472   *10463*
   315 E 12 St, New York, NY *10003* . . . .
Limpert MR John H JR—H'55
   ☎ (908) 753-7289 . . 1111 Park Av, Plainfield, NJ *07060*
Lindblad MRS Elizabeth T (Abbott—Elizabeth L   ☎ (212) 722-2559
   Tysen) Cl'84   27 E 95 St,
   JUNIORS MR Justin T—at St George's . . . .   New York, NY
    10128
Lindsay MR & MRS Alvin F (Jameson—Webster—Helen V Kiendl)
   Srr.Cly.Dc.Ncd.Mo'43
   ☎ (305) 864-5203 . . 6645 Pinetree Lane, Miami Beach, FL *33141*

Lindsey MRS Christopher F (Ethel P du Pont) . . . . Married at West Palm Beach, FL
   Kinsella MR Eugene Benoist (late J Reid) . . . . Feb 6'96
Lindsey MISS Marina H—ColC'91 . . see E B Kinsella
Lindsley MR Robert C—LakeF'66
   ☎ (610) 687-3665 . . 222 W Lancaster Av, PO Box 205, Devon, PA *19333*
Lindsley MRS Van Sinderen (Dick—Anne Child) . . . . Died at San Antonio, TX Dec 27'95
Littell MISS Lisa
   ☎ (520) 298-0945 . . 2025 N Camino De La Cienega, Tucson, AZ *85715*
Little MISS Christine Charlotte (Gary R) . . . . Born at Palo Alto, CA Jan 3'96
Little MR & MRS George F 2d (Claudia A Randel)   of ☎ (212)988-6094
   Skd'74.Bgt.Cw.Ham'71 . . . . 1 Gracie Square,
   JUNIORS MR Bradford C . . . . New York, NY
    10028
   ☎ (203) 655-9889
   57 Contentment
   Island Dv, Darien,
   CT *06820*
Little MISS Melinda L—Wes'75.Nw'78
   ☎ (518) 891-0197 . . 18 Shepard Av, Saranac Lake, NY *12983*
Littlefield MR & MRS Arthur S 3d (Cecelia M Blaine) Det'84.DeP'93.Ind'75
   213 W 9 St, Hinsdale, IL *60521*
Livingston MR & MRS Deryck Van V (Serena T Ritter)
   Gordon'83.Iona'92 ⚓
   ☎ (860) 355-5404 . . 191 Carmen Hill Rd, Apt 2, New Milford, CT *06776*
Lloyd MR & MRS David (Hollenbeck—Susan B   ☎ (215) 836-0458
   Lattner) Msq.Why.Ty'66 . . . . 6009 Cricket Rd,
   MR Jordan S—at 246 Tulip Tree Rd, Blue Bell,   Flourtown, PA
   PA *19422* *19031*
Lobaugh MR & MRS Garry M (Diane H Beales)   529 E Snow Rd,
   Cent'y'68.Rcch.IaState'67 . . . . Baroda, MI *49101*
   MISS Molly B
   JUNIORS MR Christopher M
Lobkowicz PRCSS Anita O (Cossé Brissac—PRCSS Anita O Lobkowicz)
   ☎ (011-33) 37-26-78-69 . . 2 rue de la Croix Blanche,
   28190 St-Luperce, France
Locke REV Bradford B—Va'49.VaTheo'52 . . . .   ☎ (203) 453-2479
   MISS Suzanne G—at ☎ (203) 453-1376   75 Stepstone Hill
   23 Davis Dv, Guilford, CT *06437* . . . . Rd, Guilford, CT
   MISS Nancy A—at 241 Sunrise Hill Lane,   *06437*
   Norwalk, CT *06851* . . . .
Locke MISS Elaine Sommer (Mark D) . . . . Born at Chicago, IL Nov 8'95
Lockwood MR & MRS Roy H (Nina S Hunsicker)   ☎ (716) 385-1232
   Dick'61.Dick'59.AmU'64 . . . . 48 Astor Dv,
   MISS Christina C—Dick'94—at   Rochester, NY
   ☎ (716) 256-1921 . . 2141 East Av, Rochester,   *14610*
   NY *14610* . . . .
Loeb MISS Alexandra S (John L JR) . . . . Married at New York, NY
   Driscoll MR Joseph E (John P JR) . . . . Oct 15'94
Loebs MR Peter S S—Srb.CtCol'82 . . of
   ☎ (540) 456-6988 . . "Sundance" Rte 1, Box 346, Afton, VA *22920*
   ☎ (540) 456-6989 . . "Point de Vue" Rte 1, Box 347, Afton, VA *22920*

Logan MISS Alice L—NCar'43
☎ (919) 918-3472 . . 750 Weaver Dairy Rd, Apt 2106, Chapel Hill, NC *27514*
Logan MR & MRS Francis D (Claude Rivière de Colommès) Ch'50.Ox'54.H'55 . . . .
 MR Francis D JR—Dth'86 . . . .
☎ (818) 796-8020
1726 Linda Vista Av, Pasadena, CA *91103*
Lohmann MISS Olivia Dunn (Charles P 3d) . . . . Born at West Chester, PA Jun 30'95
Loomis MR & MRS Alfred F 2d (Stephanie A Neuhaus) Cin'88.Cc.Roch'80.Nu'94
☎ (212) 734-9791 . . 420 E 79 St, Apt 15B, New York, NY *10021*
Loomis MRS Macleod (Mary P Macleod) My.
☎ (508) 526-9652 . . 37 Forster Rd, Manchester, MA *01944*
Loomis MR Robert L—Y'50 . . . .
 MISS Julia W—V'83—at ☎ (312) 274-7882
 6307 N Lakewood Av, Chicago, IL *60660* . . . . .
 MR Timothy L . . . .
☎ (860) 738-2721
PO Box 210, Colebrook, CT *06021*
Lord DR & MRS George de F JR (Sharon M Allen) GaSt'86.Emory'90.Wash'76.LCC'80 . . . .
 MISS Amelia T—at ☎ (860) 691-0538
 11 S Ridge Rd, Niantic, CT *06357* . . . .
 MR Miguel W—at ☎ (860) 691-0538
 11 S Ridge Rd, Niantic, CT *06357* . . . .
 JUNIORS MISS Juliette K—at ☎ (860) 691-0538
 11 S Ridge Rd, Niantic, CT *06357* . . . .
☎ (706) 678-1863
116 S Elijah Clark Dv, Washington, GA *30673*
Lord MRS Herbert G (Norton—Anne D Bingham) V'23 North Hill D307, 865 Central Av, Needham, MA *02192*
Lord MR & MRS J Couper (Barbara S Hartley) St.So.H'41.Duke'48 . . . .
 MR J Couper JR—Rol'72 . . . .
☎ (516) 283-1882
Box 1446, S Hill St, Southampton, NY *11969*
Lord MASTER James Edward Carpenter (g—Charles Goodwin) . . . . Born at Danbury, CT Jly 25'95
Lotsch MISS Pamela King . . of
 400 E 59 St, New York, NY *10022*
 Carysbrook Plantation, RR 1, Box 57D, Fork Union, VA *23055*
Lott MR & MRS Edward M 3d (Tamara J Neufeld) Biola'84.Biola'86
☎ (510) 661-9391 . . 2222 Valorie St, Fremont, CA *94539*
Lott MR & MRS John Benjamin (Monica L Sims) Htdon'90.Htdon'89
☎ (334) 244-9340 . . 1812 Llanfair Rd, Montgomery, AL *36106*
Lott MASTER John Tyson (John Benjamin) . . . . Born Jan 21'93
Loud MR & MRS Douglass N (Smith—Erin H Farrell) Ck.Y'64.Cal'67 . . . .
 JUNIORS MR Douglass N JR . . . .
  MR Thurston H Smith 3d—at Lynchburg Coll
  MR Townsend U Smith—at Trinity . . . .
23 Abbott Lane, Wilton, CT *06897*
Loud MR & MRS Theodore E (Deering—Eager— R Keith Kerr) Ne.Cly.Yn.Y'57.Pa'60 . . . .
 MISS Amanda K . . . .
☎ (804) 295-4242
1253 Maple View Dv, Willow Lake, Charlottesville, VA *22902*
Loughlin JUNIORS MISS Anna M . . see J T Witherspoon
Loughlin MISS Clare M . . see J T Witherspoon
Loughlin MR John J JR . . see J T Witherspoon
Love MRS George H (Lindenmeyr—McClintic—Lorraine McArthur)
☎ (561) 278-0776 . . 3524 Oleander Way, Delray Beach, FL *33483*
Love MISS Talis Marguerite Thorndike (g—George I Reynolds) . . . Born at Boston, MA Dec 23'95
Low MR & MRS Christian C (O'Brien—Julie F Chu) Hawaii'81.H'82 26 Ewen-Alison Rd, Devonport, Auckland, New Zealand
Low MR & MRS John M (Julie S Henderson) StLaw'87
☎ (203) 259-4220 . . 110 Figlar Av, Fairfield, CT *06430*
Lowe MISS Avery Higbie (David M) . . . . Born Oct 17'95
Lowe MR & MRS David M (Katrina K Higbie) AmU'83.Law'81
☎ (617) 367-5835 . . 23 Joy St, Apt 3, Boston, MA *02114*
Lowe MASTER Oliver Chapin (David M) . . . . Born at New York, NY Aug 14'93
Lowe MR Stephen . . . .
 MR Stephen G . . . .
 MR Oliver W . . . .
☎ (510) 835-8424
424—2 St, Oakland, CA *94607*
Lowrey MASTER Jameson Rodriguez (Charles F JR) . . . . Born at New York, NY Nov 8'95
Lowry MR Arthur S (late John B) . . . . Married at Washington, DC Smith MISS Julie A (Gary T) . . . . Jan 15'95
Lucas MRS C Clement JR (Sawyer—Marcia H Clare) DU'71.Nf.Csn.Ncd.Ne.Myf.
☎ (803) 722-0955 . . 24 Limehouse St, Charleston, SC *29401*
Lucas DR C Clement JR—Un.Nf.NCar'69.Duke'72
☎ (914) 834-6411 . . 2039 Palmer Av, Larchmont, NY *10538-2405*
Luce MR & MRS Henry 3d (Hadley—Smitter—Musham—Leila Eliott Burton) Fic.Plg.Y'45 . . . .
 DR Matthew S Eliott—Purd'79.Purd'83 . . . . . .
of ☎ (212)759-8640
4 Sutton Place, New York, NY *10022*
☎ (516) 922-0356
"Wychwood"
Mill Hill Rd, Mill Neck, NY *11765*
Luckie MR & MRS Robert E 3d (Jill Harris) Ala'71.Ala'91.Cy.Ala'69
☎ (205) 970-2226 . . 137 Queensberry Crescent, Birmingham, AL *35223*
Luebke MISS Marie K . . see G Schwab 5th
Lum MISS Sheerah Shelby (William Douglas JR) . . . . . . Born May 30'95
Lydon MR Douglas K—Wash'77
☎ (312) 943-1133 . . 301 W Superior St, Chicago, IL *60610*
Lyman MRS Arthur T (Joan M Lincoln)
☎ (803) 648-8658 . . 1290 Richardson Lake Rd, Aiken, SC *29803*
Lyman MR Arthur T 3d—Ny.Cl'68.H'71
☎ (617) 523-3321 . . 85 E India Row, Boston, MA *02110*
Lyman MRS John L (Cynthia Forbes) Chi.Ncd.
☎ (617) 235-0351 . . "Descrie" 636 Charles River St, Needham, MA *02192*
Lynch MRS Francis R V (Helen A Barrett) . . . . Died at Greenwich, CT Oct 27'95
Lynch MRS Hilary G (Marian P Tenaglia) Pg.Rr. . . . .
 MR Kevin McK . . . .
 MISS Michelle G (Asselineau—Michelle G Lynch)
☎ (412) 683-3266
Royal York Apt 816, 3955 Bigelow Blvd, Pittsburgh, PA *15213*
Lynch MR & MRS Robert F 3d (Robin M Keefe) Tul'78.Cda.Colg'73
☎ (718) 543-6362 . . 4663 Palisades Av, Bronx, NY *10471*
Lynn MRS Henry S (Fariss Gambrill) . . . . Died at Birmingham, AL Oct 21'95

M

McAllister MR & MRS Alexander B (Owen—Elizabeth M Ustvedt) Cal'54.Bur.Bhm.Sfg.Cp.
☎ (619) 341-6242 . . 46-795 E El Dorado Dv, Indian Wells, CA *92210*

McAniff MR & MRS John Edward (Carey Theresa Lewis) SCal'81.Vh.HolyC'83
☎ (818) 796-4818 . . 1406 Wellington Av, Pasadena, CA *91103*

McBride DR Raymond A—Tul'52 . . . . of ☎ (011-39-6) 68-30-08-87 Palazzo Lancellotti CBM, via Lancellotti 18, 00186 Rome, Italy
MR Andrew Gore—SFrArt'92—at
☎ (303) 443-3099 . . 1530—8 St, Boulder, CO *80302* . . . .
☎ (713) 888-0659 5001 Woodway Dv, Apt 1404, Houston, TX *77056*

McBryde MR & MRS J Bolton (Landreth—Tinney—Ethel M Wilson)
☎ (803) 521-9034 . . 821 Ribault Rd, Beaufort, SC *29902*

McBurney MR F Lane (late Andrew M) . . . . . . Married at New York, NY
Marotti MISS Ondine L (Victor M) . . . . Sep 23'95

McCabe MRS Annette P (Annette J Prophet) Km.Dar . . . .
MR Edward J 3d . . . .
☎ (617) 237-9851 137 Hampshire Rd, Wellesley Hills, MA *02181*

McCandless MRS Rosemary Van L (Ross—Fri—Rosemary Van L McCandless) ColC'71.Tex'88.Dar.W.
☎ (216) 752-0400 . . PO Box 192, Chagrin Falls, OH *44022*

McCargo MRS David (Standish—Dorothy L Cabell) . . . . . Died Nov 6'95

McCargo MR Thomas W—Eyc.
☎ (412) 749-0565 . . Little Sewickley Creek Rd, Sewickley, PA *15143*

McCarrens MISS Constance (Schwerin—Constance McCarrens) Man'vl'71
☎ (617) 742-1416 . . 66 Chestnut St, Boston, MA *02108*

McCarthy MASTER William Fox (David G) . . . . Born at Lafayette, CA Jun 27'95

McClenahan MR & MRS Robert W JR (Ann Rebecca Freeman) NCar'69.Ty'58.NCar'74 . . . .
MISS Amanda W—at ☎ (212) 370-1078 300 E 46 St, Apt 4J, New York, NY *10017* . . . .
JUNIORS MR Edward P—at Ohio Wesleyan . . . . .
☎ (203) 782-0459 72 Cottage St, New Haven, CT *06511*

McClintic MASTER Alastair William Stanley (g—Richard W Murphy) . . . . . Born at London, England May 15'95

McClintic MR & MRS David W (Denise L Arcand) Tufts'80.Suff'83.Bost'86.Rr.Pg.Ne'84.NH'92
☎ (603) 523-7876 . . RR 2, PO Box 56A, Canaan, NH *03751*

McCloud MRS Kimberly S (Kimberly A Sherman) CalInst'82 . . . .
MR Cory S—Reed'92—at Paris, France . . . . . .
☎ (415) 434-3419 22 Vandewater St, Apt 108, San Francisco, CA *94133*

McCollum MR & MRS T Bonner (Edwene Stevens) Ark'60.Ark'55
☎ (501) 633-3622 . . 2 Ridgewood Lane, Forrest City, AR *72335*

McCormack MR & MRS Brian P (Barbara D Juergens) Prov'65 . . . .
MR M Scott—H'90 . . . .
MR Brian P JR—H'92 . . . .
☎ (512) 392-5568 2912 Maravillas Loop, Austin, TX *78735*

McCormick MR & MRS Levering (Brown—Judith L Talcott) Denis'71.DU'74.Vt'69 . . . .
MISS Wynne K—Vt'94—at 327 NE 57 St, Seattle, WA *98105* . . . .
MR John W—at Ohio Wesleyan . . . .
☎ (802) 362-3201 PO Box 116, West Rd, Manchester, VT *05254*

McCoy MISS Lindsey Jay (Timothy J) . . . . Born at St Louis, MO Sep 10'95

McCoy MISS Sophia Marie (g—C Rich Diffenderffer) . . . . Born Jan 8'95

McCrindle MR Joseph F R—Rc.Gr.C.H'44.H'48
☎ (212) 362-4052 . . 91 Central Park W, Apt 14A, New York, NY *10023*

McElhiney MR & MRS Richard L (Lucie Lee Kinsolving) Br'75.Nu'88.Y'75.Y'79
☎ (212) 316-3203 . . 7 W 96 St, New York, NY *10025*

McFadden MR & MRS Ashton S dos S (Camilla Corballis) Rol'88.Rc.Cr'87
☎ (212) 280-0208 . . 3 E 71 St, Apt 5E, New York, NY *10021*

McFarland MR Alan R . . . . Died at Gladwyne, PA Aug 19'95

McFarland MR & MRS George C JR (Elizabeth L Kennedy) NH'81.Me.Rc.P.'81.Duke'84
☎ (610) 689-8848 . . 215 Cheswold Lane, Haverford, PA *19041*

McGehee MR & MRS Carden C JR (Kristine E Miller) Hlns'78.Dar.Skd'76.Va'80
☎ (301) 320-2858 . . 4907 Rockmere Court, Bethesda, MD *20816*

McGehee MISS Elizabeth Ann Bacot (Michael H) . . . . Born at Charleston, SC Dec 14'95

McGehee MASTER John Van Wyck Hoke (Michael H) . . . . Born at Charleston, SC Apr 28'94

McHugh MISS Ernestine L (Suwal—Poole—Ernestine L McHugh) Cal'76.Cal'85
☎ (716) 473-4928 . . 120 Hampshire Dv, Rochester, NY *14618*

McKay MR James C . . . . Died at Latrobe, PA Dec 13'95

McKechnie MR D Eric—Rd.Nyc.
☎ (508) 228-9163 . . 76 N Liberty St, Nantucket, MA *02554*

McKechnie MRS Deborah S (Deborah N Smith) Rd.Nyc. . . . .
MR Christopher W—at ☎ (415) 921-8363 1801 Beach St, San Francisco, CA *94123* . . . .
MR Gregory E . . . .
MR Andrew N . . . .
☎ (610) 647-4284 707 Hillview Rd, Malvern, PA *19355*

McKee MR Paul W—Mich'58
☎ (202) 333-1108 . . 2502 I St NW, Washington, DC *20037-2210*

McKim MRS Anthony L (Mabel Geer) . . . . Died Sep 28'95

McKinley MISS Rayna Leone (g—MRS (REV) Ellen B McKinley) . . . . . Born at Philadelphia, PA Jun 30'95

McKinney MRS Laurence (Strain—Betsy Marvin) . . . . Died at Loudonville, NY Oct 17'92

McKinney MR & MRS W Richardson (Jie Cao) Sichuan'84.Guam'90.Pa'79.Cal'81.ColSt'92
☎ (414) 830-2226 . . 1321 Montclaire Court, Appleton, WI *54915*

McKnight MRS Agnes H (Agnes Hanes) 3 Coniston Dv, West Chester, PA *19382*

McKnight MR & MRS Philip R (Kathleen E Lord) ☎ (860) 435-2068
V'66.Rcn.Wms'65.Ch'68 . . . . 59 Old CNE Rd,
MISS Sarah L—Wms'93.Man'vl'95 . . . . Lakeville, CT *06039*
McLanahan MR Ellery S (late Duer) . . . . Married at Houston, TX
Colson MISS Kay D . . . . Feb 11'95
McLean MISS Ann (Ephraim R 3d) . . . . Married at Los Angeles, CA
McCabe MR John G . . . . Jly 15'95
McLean MR Stuart L—Rc.Fic.Ham'91
☎ (212) 517-9672 . . 321 E 79 St, New York, NY *10021*
McLean MR & MRS William H (Vesta B Tittmann)
Unn.Bg.Cysl.Plg.Hn.Stv'31.H'33
☎ (201) 379-2017 . . 50 Birch Lane, Short Hills, NJ *07078*
McLenegan MR Alan G . . . . Died at
Greenbrae, CA Sep 6'95
McManus MISS Clare E D . . see T E Miller
McManus JUNIORS MR Henry J . . see T E Miller
McMillan MR & MRS S Sterling 3d (Judith E Knight) | ☎ (216) 256-8224
Un.Tv.P'60.H'63 | 9044 Metcalf Rd,
  MISS Victoria M—at ☎ (206) 643-0722 | Waite Hill, OH
  6061 E 16 St, Bellevue, WA *98008* . . . . | *44094*
  MR S Sterling 4th—at ☎ (312) 327-0504
  434 W Roscoe St, Apt 5A, Chicago, IL *60657*. .
McMillen MR James JR—Va'53 . . . . | ☎ (516) 749-0255
  MISS Shelley—Les'91—at ☎ (617) 783-1243 | 29 Nostrand P'way,
  56 Brighton Av, Apt 48, Allston, MA *02134* . . . | PO Box 545, Shelter
  MR Bryan—Ariz'90—at ☎ (213) 851-2650 | Island Heights, NY
  1605 W Martel Av, Apt 18, Los Angeles, CA | *11965-0545*
  90046 . . . .
McMillen MRS Louis A (Koch—Persis White) . . . . Died at
Gloucester, MA Jly 31'95
McMullin MR & MRS David B (Sandra F Keefe) | ☎ (610) 356-5633
Pa'62.Me.P.'59.Va'64 . . . . | 813 Malin Rd,
  MISS Anita L—Pa'85.Me.—at ☎ (410) 997-7464 | Newtown Square,
  1034 Hickory Ridge Rd, Apt 337, Columbia, MD | PA *19073-3515*
  21044 . . . .
  MISS (DR) Dana F—W&M'87.Penn'96—at
  ☎ (717) 531-8852 . . Hershey Medical Center,
  38 University Manor E, Hershey, PA *17033* . . .
  MR David B JR—Me.Denis'92—at
  ☎ (610) 526-2868 . . 1429 County Line Rd,
  Rosemont, PA *19010* . . . .
McNeil MR Robert L 3d (Robert L JR) . . . . . . Married at Bryn Mawr, PA
Bangert MISS Jane A (late George H) . . . . Sep 16'95
McNulty MR & MRS T Stanley JR (Jean G Hartsell) Cl'59.Ark'57
☎ (501) 535-8025 . . 605 W 34 Av, Pine Bluff, AR *71603*
McPherson MR & MRS Aaron F (Amy B Lankenau) Ws'93.Mit'89
☎ (617) 787-1726 . . 16 Ransom Rd, Apt 14, Brighton, MA *02135-4914*
McPherson MR & MRS John W (Rupp—Jane M Dubbs)
V'36.Me.Rc.Gm.Cw.Rv.Cc.Ac.H.'29
☎ (610) 527-1818 . . 79 Pasture Lane, Bryn Mawr, PA *19010*
McSweeney MISS A Thayer . . see W J Strawbridge JR
McSweeney JUNIORS MISS Catherine B D . . see W J Strawbridge JR
McSweeney MISS Christine S . . see W J Strawbridge JR
McWilliams MISS Marcia Reed
☎ (603) 964-5534 . . PO Box 476, Rye Beach, NH *03871-0476*
McWilliams MISS Saba—SL'59
949 F St, Salida, CO *81201-2501*

Mabon MR Kingsley . . . . Died at
New York, NY Dec 2'95
MacCracken MISS Nell E
☎ (919) 398-4222 . . 420 Lakeview Dv, Murfreesboro, NC *27855*
MacDonald MASTER Alexander William (g—MRS Le Baron Turner) . . Born
at Boston, MA Jan 11'96
MacDonald MASTER Benjamin Makepeace (g—MRS Le Baron Turner) . . .
Born at Boston, MA Jan 11'96
MacDonald MISS Julia Turner (g—MRS Le Baron Turner) . . . . . . Born at
Boston, MA Jan 11'96
MacDonald MRS William G (Margaret Sweeney) . . . . Died at
Manchester, NH May 26'95
MacEwan MR Nigel S (late Nigel S) . . . . . . Married at Dark Harbor, ME
Beavers MRS J Sperry (Elliman—Judith G Sperry) . . . . Sep 2'95
MacEwan MR & MRS Nigel S (Elliman—Beavers—Judith G Sperry)
Ln.Ny.Yn.Y'55.H'59 ⚓
☎ (203) 972-9253 . . 153 Oenoke Lane, New Canaan, CT *06840*
Macey MISS Mary P (James G) . . . . Married at San Rafael, CA
Butler MR Robert C . . . . Oct 15'95
MacGuire MISS Mary J—Man'vl'87 . . . . | see F R Reinecke
MR Sean M . . . . |
MacKay MR Edward H . . . . Died Oct 23'95
MacKay MRS Edward H (Whitman—Cynthia | ☎ (415) 346-5625
Vansittart) StJ. . . . . | 2655 Clay St,
  MR Edward H 3d—at ☎ (510) 256-6347 | San Francisco, CA
  275 Stevenson, Pleasant Hill, CA *94523* . . . . . . | *94115*
  MR Robert V—at ☎ (707) 776-2701
  1609 Andover Way, Petaluma, CA *94954* . . . . .
MacKay MR John F 3d (John F JR) . . . . Married at Short Hills, NJ
Brazill MISS Kelly A (Burt) . . . . Aug 5'95
Mackay MRS Malcolm S (V Gray | ☎ (612) 473-8302
von Grebenstein) . . . . | PO Box 667,
  MR Malcolm S 3d . . . . | Long Lake, MN
   | *55356*
MacKenzie MR & MRS David O (Deborah W | ☎ (847) 234-9249
Williams) On.Sr.Cas.Ncd.Ty'54 . . . . | 1180 N Elm Tree
  MR Douglas S—at Chicago, IL . . . . | Rd, Lake Forest, IL
  MR David W—Col'92. . . . . | *60045*
MacKenzie MASTER Eamon (Jared D) . . . . Born at
Wareham, MA May 8'95
Mackey MISS Emily Claire (g—B Franklin Mackey JR) . . . . Born at
Little Rock, AR Oct 25'95
Mackey MISS Katherine Isabel (g—B Franklin Mackey JR) . . . . . . Born at
Columbia, MD Jun 12'94
Mackey MR & MRS Michael V (Wendy E Dorsaneo) WChesU'85 . . . .
☎ (610) 449-4637 . . 127 Strathmore Rd, Havertown, PA *19083*
Mackey MASTER Ryan James (Michael V) . . . . Born at
Bryn Mawr, PA Apr 29'93
Mackey MISS Taylor Marie (Michael V) . . . . Born at
Bryn Mawr, PA Jun 8'95
Maclaurin MR Peter J—Lawr'67
☎ (617) 423-5930 . . 9 Melrose St, Apt 3, Boston, MA *02116*
MacLean DR William A H—Y'61.Cl'65 . . . . | 2305 English
MISS Kathryn E—Wms'93.Cl'94—at | Village Lane,
1401 St Andrew St, New Orleans, LA *70130*. . . | Birmingham, AL
MISS Stephanie H—Ty'96—at 401 Holland Av, | *35223*
San Antonio, TX *78212* . . . . |

MacNair MR Andrew P—P.'69.Cl'73
☎ (212) 334-2132 . . 426 W Broadway, New York, NY *10012-3775*
MacNair MISS Caroline P (Tauranac—Caroline P MacNair) BMr'65
☎ (212) 388-7188 . . 141 E 88 St, Apt 2C, New York, NY *10128*
Macpherson MISS Marian . . see P L Payson
MacRae MRS Cameron F (Jane B Miller) . . . . Died at Hobe Sound, FL Jan 9'96
Macy MR & MRS John H D JR (Janice A Kettlety) Cyb.
☎ (602) 391-9833 . . 9209 N 117 Way, Scottsdale, AZ *85259*
Madden MR & MRS Robert L (Frazer—Butler—Diana Dunning) Myf.Dll.Ncd.Pitt'37
☎ (561) 286-2711 . . 1600 SE St Lucie Blvd, Apt 115, Stuart, FL *34996*
Madeira MRS Mary V (Mullet—Mary V Madeira) Pac'76
☎ (408) 626-6585 . . 25500 Shafter Way, Carmel, CA *93923*
Madsen MASTER Benton Howard (Stephen S) . . . . Born at New York, NY Dec 27'95
Maebius MR & MRS Jed B JR (Nancy B Kingsland) Mich'63.Tex'90.Mich'63.GeoW'66.Tex'67 . . | ☎ (210) 822-3651 200 Belvidere Dv, San Antonio, TX *78212*
MISS Elizabeth F—at 1527—1 St, Coronado, CA *92118* . . . .
MR Stephen B—at 114—21 St S, Arlington, VA *22202* . . . .
MR Brian G—at 1756 E 4620 S, Salt Lake City, UT *84117* . . . .
MR Andrew K—at 200 McCauley St, Chapel Hill, NC *27516* . . . .
Mahon MISS Marinna (Fairbank—Marinna Mahon) Rose'63 . . . . | ☎ (216) 420-7086 12493 Cedar Rd, Apt 16, Cleveland Heights, OH *44106*
MISS Elsa Fairbank . . . .
MISS Wendy Fairbank (Hatch—Wendy Fairbank) . . . .
Mail MISS Miranda Ann (gg—MRS G Allen Mail) . . . . Born at Trumbull, CT Oct 1'94
Makepeace MR Charles R . . . . Died at Pawtucket, RI Feb 24'96
Malabre MR & MRS Alfred L JR (Mary P Wardropper) Durham'53.Ng.Un.Plg.Y'52 . . . . . | ☎ (212) 988-9262 150 E 73 St, New York, NY *10021*
MISS E Ann—Ty'85.Sim'90—at ☎ (207) 824-3050 . . PO Box 1097, Bethel, ME *04217* . . . .
MR John A—at ☎ (212) 650-9442 1587 Second Av, New York, NY *10021* . . . . .
Mali MRS H Allen (Jane A Lawrence) . . . . Died at Norfolk, CT Oct 2'95
Mallory MR & MRS Clifford D (Pauline Cropper) Unn.Ny.StJ.Cly.
☎ (860) 535-2258 . . 76 Water St, Stonington, CT *06378*
Malloy MISS Elizabeth G—H'69.Cvc.Hn.
☎ (303) 278-6706 . . 1301 Arapahoe St, Apt 303, Golden, CO *80401*
Manheim MR Grant C—Pa'67 . . of
☎ (011-44-171) 280-5000 . . New Court, St Swithin's Lane, London EC4P 4DU, England
☎ (212) 744-1600 . . 35 E 76 St, New York, NY *10021*
Manice MR & MRS Robert G (Heidi G Knollenberg) RISD'80.Bost'76 . . . . | ☎ (508) 785-8068 229 Dedham St, Dover, MA *02030*
JUNIORS MISS Emily P . . . .
Manigault MR & MRS Pierre (Elizabeth L Van Alen) Bnd'92
☎ (803) 722-8787 . . 33 King St, Charleston, SC *29401-2734*

Manley MISS Alexandra C . . see J J G Cameron
Manley MISS Jennifer A . . see J J G Cameron
Manley MRS Sheila H (Sheila M Hickey) . . . . Married at Pelham Manor, NY Cameron MR John J G . . . . Dec 2'95
Mann MR Donegan (late Ephriam D) . . . . Married at Potomac, MD Jenkins MRS Stephen (Frances M Mann) . . . . Jan 7'95
Mann MRS Henry B (Nancy L Mersfelder) Skd'67.Conn'70.Yn. . . . . | ☎ (203) 245-7627 PO Box 940, Madison, CT *06443*
JUNIORS MR David W . . . .
JUNIORS MR Michael L . . . .
Mann DR Henry B—Yn.Tufts'60.Y'66
☎ (860) 873-3510 . . "The Old Bank House" 90 Old East Haddam Rd, East Haddam, CT *06423*
Mann MR & MRS William H (Wilkins—Sewall—Patricia Leighton) Ncd.Ch'40 . . of
☎ (603) 563-8371 . . "Spur House II" PO Box 273, Dublin, NH *03444*
☎ (561) 744-7351 . . 353 US H'way 1, Jupiter, FL *33477*
Mannel MRS Janice H (Peake—Janice H Mannel)
☎ (215) 233-4299 . . 7809 Pine Rd, Wyndmoor, PA *19038*
Manning MISS Anne G (William D JR) . Married at Willoughby Hills, OH de Dios MR Gonzalo (Horacio L) . . . . Sep 30'95
Mannion MR & MRS William F (H Langdon Manley) Ty'59
☎ (561) 234-1515 . . 761 Manatee Cove, Vero Beach, FL *32963*
Marani MR & MRS Paul P (Carole du P Wickes) F&M'87.Ford'85
☎ (615) 377-6248 . . 9008 Demery Court, Brentwood, TN *37027*
Marckwald MR A Hunt (late Albert H JR) . . . . . Married at Quogue, NY Palumbo MISS Catherine (late John) . . . . Aug 26'95
Marckwald MR & MRS A Hunt (Catherine Palumbo) SHall'74.Rol'74 . . . . | ☎ (516) 653-4795 11 Club Lane, Box 879, Quogue, NY *11959*
MISS Morgan N . . . .
JUNIORS MR A Hunt JR . . . .
JUNIORS MR Nicholas K . . . .
Mark MR Peter C—Woos'90
☎ (312) 944-4422 . . 1120 N Lake Shore Dv, Apt 9A, Chicago, IL *60611*
Markham MRS George F JR (Marianne Elser) . . . . Died in Oct 1994
Marr DR William G . . . . Died Feb 10'95
Marron MISS Serena Elizabeth (Donald B) . . . . Born at New York, NY Oct 17'95
Marsh MISS A Carter—Cvc . . . of
☎ (804) 282-4296 . . 8260 W Greystone Circle, Richmond, VA *23229*
☎ (804) 435-3838 . . "Cedar Point" PO Box 288, White Stone, VA *22578*
Marsh MASTER Clayton Farnsworth (Alan R JR) . . . . Born at Port Chester, NY Dec 12'95
Marsh MRS Helen H (Helen C Hewitt) Sth'52.Cl'73
☎ (203) 661-7730 . . 3 Cat Rock Rd, Cos Cob, CT *06807*
Marsh MR Michael—K.Rc.Ph.Cl'93 . . . . | ☎ (212) 799-9786 101 Central Park W, New York, NY *10023*
MISS Sarah K . . . .
JUNIORS MR William A . . . .
Marshall MR & MRS Allerton D (Pollard—Mary Markley) Nw'58.Cl'65.P'53
☎ (803) 689-6263 . . 33 Old Fort Dv, Hilton Head Island, SC *29926*

Marshall MR & MRS John R (Virginia N Corbett) RMWmn'64.Cc.Ncd.P'60.Va'65.Geo'95 . . . . . . of ☎ (703)821-2249 "Crow's Nest" 7508 Royal Oak Dv, McLean, VA 22102
   MISS Peyton M—Reed'96—at ☎ (503) 239-5707 21 SE 18 St, Portland, OR 97214 . . . .
   MR Fielding C—Va'93—at ☎ (703) 521-0187 519 S Courthouse Rd, Arlington, VA 22204 . . .
☎ (804) 529-5435 Bright Meadow Farm, Lodge Creek, PO Box 80, Lottsburg, VA 22511

Marsteller MISS Emily Bolling (Robert W) . . . . Born at Washington, DC Feb 1'95
Martin MR David B H . . . . Died at Barnstable, MA Sep 27'95
Martin MISS Leslie—MtH'58
   18 Bissell Lane, Norwalk, CT 06850
Martin MR & MRS R David (Bonnie J Allen) MichSt'68
   ☎ (602) 945-2100 . . 6020 E Calle del Media, Scottsdale, AZ 85251
Martinez MR & MRS James M JR (Kathleen M Gurren) VaCmth'83.W&L'74.Va'77
   ☎ (804) 359-2735 . . 1504 Palmyra Av, Richmond, VA 23227
Martinez MISS Patricia (Baker—Patricia Martinez) Alf'73
   ☎ (805) 834-4118 . . 5807 Stacey St, Bakersfield, CA 93313
Martinez MR Peter M—CtCol'78
   ☎ (617) 326-7852 . . "Lowder Brook Hollow" 82 Highland St, Dedham, MA 02026
Marting MRS Walter A (Margaret Brown) Ky'34.Kt.
   ☎ (216) 831-2009 . . 3911-3 Lander Rd, Chagrin Falls, OH 44022-1328
Marvin MR & MRS Timothy S (Jones—D Faye Mann) Myf.Emory'79
   ☎ (205) 978-9360 . . 2638 Greenmont Dv, Birmingham, AL 35226
Mashek MRS Chandler C (Montgomery—A Chandler Cox) Smu'72.BtP.Evg.Srb.Cly. . . . . . .
   JUNIORS MR Grant E . . . .
of ☎ (407)659-4999 1290 S Ocean Blvd, Palm Beach, FL 33480
☎ (212) 223-2044 40 E 61 St, Apt 19B, New York, NY 10022

Masland MR James G . . . . Died Jly 5'95
Mason MR & MRS Charles E (Geraldine Ridgway) Rad'62.Sewanee'61
   ☎ (301) 248-3806 . . 7518 Glade Dv, Ft Washington, MD 20744
Massey MRS Loren J (Eleanor B Rogers) . . . . Died at Bloomington, IN Jly 3'95
Massey MRS Paul H (Dorothy T Doubleday) Csn. . .
   MISS Mary Elizabeth—Pom'91 . . . .
   MR Paul D—at 744 Spruce, Boulder, CO 80302 . .
☎ (505) 982-6170 831 Los Lovatos Rd, Santa Fe, NM 87501

Mastin REV & MRS Charles O'F (Georgann Logsdon) Ill'46.Sar.Ncd.Del'59.VaTheo'61
   3925 Muhlenberg Court, Burlington, NC 27215
Mather MR Charles E 4th (Charles E 3d) . . . . . Married at New York, NY
   Sigler MISS Elizabeth M (Andrew C) . . . . Feb 3'96
Mathews MR & MRS Adam A (Cheryl A Beach) Vt'80
   ☎ (954) 389-9369 . . 555 Cambridge Dv, Ft Lauderdale, FL 33326
Mathews MR & MRS Charles P (Wendy E Graham) Denis'83.Mid'85.Dar.CtCol'80.Nu'91
   ☎ (201) 701-9424 . . 74 Fairmount Av, Chatham, NJ 07928

Mattes MISS Laura L—Sth'82.Cly.Dar.
   ☎ (914) 835-4681 . . 40 Bradford St, Harrison, NY 10528
Matthews MISS Susan T (R Timothy) . . . . Married at Coronado, CA
   Regan MR Robert J (James R) . . . . Nov 25'95
Maull MR Baldwin . . . . Died Dec 14'95
Mauran MISS Margaret T (Duncan H) . . . . Married at Strafford, VT
   Zuccotti MR John A . . . . Aug 5'95
Maurer MR & MRS Donald E (Clark—Ann L Outhwaite) Briar'68.Col'64.CalTech'68 . . . .
   MISS Stephanie L—at Moore Coll of Art . . . . . .
   JUNIORS MISS Laura A . . . .
☎ (410) 381-7432 7160 Lasting Light Way, Columbia, MD 21045

Maury MR & MRS John M (Rosalie L Brown) Ny. . .
   MR Richard L—San.NCar'68—at
   ☎ (307) 687-7750 . . 813 Wagon Trail, Gillette, WY 82716 . . . .
☎ (203) 838-0218 24 Indian Spring Rd, Rowayton, CT 06853

Maxwell MRS Allison R JR (Douglass—Margaret Taylor) . . . . Died Nov 18'95
May MISS Julia Wells (Herbert A 3d) . . . . Born at Owings Mills, MD Jan 10'96
Mayhew MR Clarence W W . . . . Died at San Rafael, CA Feb 13'94
Mayne MR & MRS Stephen S (Linda Furst) Cal'75.Bhm.Br'63.Geo'66 . . . .
   MR Michael . . . .
☎ (415) 931-0900 2240 Jackson St, San Francisco, CA 94118

Means MRS Blanchard W (Louise C Rich) Myf. . . .
   MISS Louise B . . . .
☎ (508) 867-3844 "Elm Hill Farm" RR 1, Box 307, Brookfield, MA 01506-9764

Meehan MR Alexander D . . see MRS A I Fessenden
Meehan MR Michael J 3d . . see MRS A I Fessenden
Meek MR & MRS George H (Cynthia A Martin) Cal'67.Pac'65 . . . .
   MISS Lissa H—at ☎ (805) 594-0939 476 South St, Apt D, San Luis Obispo, CA 93401
   MISS Tally A—at ☎ (510) 937-9949 365 Masters Court, Apt 2, Walnut Creek, CA 94598 . . . .
   JUNIORS MR John M—at U of Cal San Diego . . .
☎ (209) 827-4125 1621 S 6 St, Los Banos, CA 93635

Meeker MASTER Jeffrey James (James B) . . . . Born at Greenwich, CT Aug 12'95
Mehran JUNIORS MR Alexander R JR . . see MISS L B Watson
Mehran MISS Annabel M . . see MISS L B Watson
Meier MRS Duncan I JR (Marie P Ball)
   ☎ (314) 256-7788 . . 1131 Jo Carr Dv, Town & Country, MO 63017-8401
Meigs MISS Isabel McCurrach (James B) . . . . Born at Boston, MA Aug 20'93
Meigs MR & MRS James B (Julia M Talcott) Wms'80.Wms'81
   ☎ (617) 630-0377 . . 74 Elmhurst Rd, Newton, MA 02158
Meigs MASTER Stoddard MacDonald (James B) . . . . Born at Boston, MA Aug 20'93
Mein MRS William W (Sarah M Nickel) . . . . Died at Woodside, CA Sep 30'95

Meinfelder MR & MRS Edmond L 2d (Anderson—Edith S Blake) Eyc.Rd.Madrid'63 . . . . | "The Crow's Nest" Barrio Florida, PO Box 1521, Viaquez, Puerto Rico *00765*
    MISS Elizabeth S Anderson—Ty'95.Eyc.—at ☎ (617) 367-1286 . . 2 Brimmer St, Apt B, Boston, MA *02108* . . . .
Mele MR & MRS Joseph F (Butler—M Victoria Leiter) Cvc.Srb.Dyc.Wag'71
    ☎ (301) 656-2323 . . 40 Grafton St, Chevy Chase, MD *20815*
Melen DR & MRS Roger D (Williams—Arlene H Camm) Stan'73.Stan'74.Stan'78.Stan'71 . . . . . . | ☎ (415) 941-5546 12992 Vista Del Valle Court, Los Altos Hills, CA *94022*
    JUNIORS MISS Michelle A . . . .
    JUNIORS MR Samuel A F Williams—Box 4051, Stanford, CA *94305* . . . .
    JUNIORS MR Nicholas C Williams . . . .
Melhado MRS Henry S (Joan I Hoffman) . . . . Died at Tuxedo Park, NY Dec 16'95
Mellon MISS Mary-Louise Adams (Armour N) . . . . Born at Pittsburgh, PA Feb 11'96
Mellor MR Stephen R (late Edward) . . . . Married at Bryn Mawr, PA Wada MISS Anastazya T . . . . Jly 6'92
Melville MR & MRS John W (Jane Akin) Cin'32.Cin'35
    ☎ (513) 821-3070 . . 3113 Evergreen Ridge Dv, Cincinnati, OH *45215*
Menges MISS Serena Lyndon (James C) . . . . Born at Southampton, NY Jan 13'96
Mentzer MISS Lesley A (William V) . . . . Married at Bryn Mawr, PA Findlay MR Joshua P (H Peter) . . . . Oct 28'95
Merle-Smith MR & MRS Grosvenor F (Rosemarie L Wright) ColSt'80.Col'76
    ☎ (804) 295-5339 . . "Paddock Wood" PO Box 185, Keswick, VA *22947*
Merna MRS Thomas F JR (Roberts—Dagmar L Pierce) . . . . Died at Duxbury, MA Jan 15'96
Merrell MISS Caroline C (Stanley W 2d) . . . . . Married at Nantucket, MA Tucker MR Jeffrey P (Richard F) . . . . Sep 9'95
Merriam MR William R—Cvc.Mt.Leh'34
    ☎ (202) 338-7756 . . 2512 Q St NW, Washington, DC *20007*
Merrill MR & MRS Barrant V (Martha E Page) Unn.Why.Msq.Yh.Cr'53 . . . . | ☎ (407) 276-5954 3525 Polo Dv, Gulf Stream, FL *33483*
    MISS Elizabeth M—at ☎ (212) 772-8737 156 E 79 St, New York, NY *10021* . . . .
    MR William D—at ☎ (212) 772-8737 156 E 79 St, New York, NY *10021* . . . .
Merrill MISS Jane M—Tcy.
    ☎ (011-44-171) 589-3652 . . 1 Onslow Gardens, London SW7 3LY, England
Merrill MASTER Thorn King (Peter K) . . . . Born at Salem, MA Dec 29'95
Merwin MRS Davis U (Tailer—Nancy S Smith) . . . . Died at Tucson, AZ Feb 21'95
Mestres MR & MRS Anthony G (Sarah B Ingersoll) Dick'92.Dick'92
    ☎ (404) 816-9801 . . 2590 Acorn Av NE, Atlanta, GA *30305*
Metcalf MRS Elliott F (B Hope Rogers) Conv'42 . . . | ☎ (315) 782-5832 247 Elm St, Watertown, NY *13601*
    MISS Susan L—HWSth'82.Buf'93—at ☎ (617) 899-6851 . . 149 Weston St, Waltham, MA *02154* . . . . |

Metcalf MR & MRS Manton B 3d (Teresa D Peabody) Un.Rm.Stc.Myf.Cly.H'45 . . . . | ☎ (212) 288-0445 21 E 79 St, New York, NY *10021*
    MR John P—at ☎ (970) 626-5399 PO Box 517, Ridgway, CO *81432* . . . .
Metcalfe MR & MRS James W (Elizabeth C Brokaw) Wash'62.Ncd.Wash'57.StL'67 . . . . | ☎ (314) 962-8481 65 Berry Road Park, St Louis, MO *63122*
    MISS Elizabeth C—at Colby . . . .
    MR James K B—K'zoo'95—at ☎ (011-42-47) 526-3287 . . Pension Spolchemie 26, Klisská 53, 400 01 Ústí nad Labem, Czech Republic . . . . . .
Meyer MRS George C JR (Esther P Blodgett) Sth'37.Ck. 135 Beach Bluff Av, Swampscott, MA *01907*
Mezzina MISS Hannah Patricia (g—Robert K Bingham) . . . . . . Born at Lawrence, MA Aug 10'95
Mezzina MASTER Mark Bingham (g—Robert K Bingham) . . . . . . Born at Fairfax, VA May 18'93
Michael MR & MRS Charles A SR (Carole W Neff)
    ☎ (717) 626-8816 . . 209 Oxford Dv, Lititz, PA *17543*
Michel MR Clifford F—Y'90
    ☎ (212) 226-6138 . . 17 White St, Apt 5A, New York, NY *10013*
Michelsen MISS Suzanne R . . . . Married Ward MR George H 2d . . . . Jun 24'95
Mickel MISS Paige Coolidge (Paul J) . . . . Born at New York, NY Jan 24'96
Middleton MR Daniel T—Stan'87 . . see J W Aldrich
Middleton DR & MRS (REV) Elliott JR (Elizabeth Blackford) Cl'48.Col'68.G.P'47.Cl'50
    ☎ (207) 846-6411 . . RR 1, Box 596, Chebeague Island, ME *04017*
Middleton MISS Laura D R—Sth'86.Wash'87.AmU'94 . . see J W Aldrich
Miles MRS Serena W (O'Shaughnessy—Serena W Miles) Gchr'89 . . . . | ☎ (302) 226-0245 70 Park Av, Rehoboth Beach, DE *19971*
    MR Robert M O'Shaughnessy—at Boston U . .
    JUNIORS MR William A O'Shaughnessy . . . . .
Miller MISS Amanda E 104 Golden State Circle, Napa, CA *94558*
Miller MR Andrew Otterson JR . . . . Died at West Palm Beach, FL Nov 8'95
Miller MRS Barbara Duff (Barbara D Duff) . . . . | 224 Dolphin Cove Quay, Stamford, CT *06902*
    MR Prescott C—at U of SCar . . . .
    JUNIORS MR Barclay St J . . . .
Miller MR & MRS Barton H (Marion J Becker) CtCol'58.Lx.Rr.Y'58
    ☎ (617) 267-2522 . . 40 Commonwealth Av, Apt H, Boston, MA *02116*
Miller MRS Carroll T (Ingamni—Sachs—Carroll R Townsend) Ub . . . . | ☎ (617) 423-2088 50 Fayette St, Boston, MA *02116*
    MISS Sarah T . . . .
    JUNIORS MR Andrew D . . . .
    JUNIORS MR Jared W . . . .
Miller MR & MRS Courtlandt G (Gina M Salvatore) Geo'79.Loy'81.Rcn.Ri.Evg.BtP.Pr.Snc.Cly.Ford'76. Tul'80
    ☎ (407) 833-4446 . . 177 Clarke Av, Palm Beach, FL *33480*
Miller MRS Elizabeth S (Elizabeth H Schaff) . . . . Died at Middlesex, CT Oct 2'95
Miller MR & MRS Eric T (Spencer—Susan Williams) Unn.Dth'50 . . . . | ☎ (415) 397-0936 155 Jackson St, Apt 1307, San Francisco, CA *94111*
    MISS Holly Spencer—at 406 S Sherman St, Denver, CO *80209* . . . .

Miller MR & MRS George G (Mary Richardson Buck) Me.Ste.Pa'59.Pa'68 .... ☎ (305) 860-9111
 MISS Cassandra C .... Brickell Bay Club,
 MR Alexander C—Col'93 .... Apt 1506,
2333 Brickell Av,
Miami, FL *33129*
Miller MR & MRS Gerald A (Gail C Benedict) ☎ (847) 234-1041
 On.Rc.Sc.Cas.Wa.Miami'69 .... 1701 Kennedy Rd,
 JUNIORS MISS Brooke B .... Box 936,
 JUNIORS MISS Christina P .... Lake Forest, IL
 JUNIORS MR Stuart H *60045*
Miller MR & MRS Jeffrey K (Mary Armour Reid) Br'83.Br'83
 ☎ (203) 972-6144 . . 92 Woodland Rd, New Canaan, CT *06840*
Miller MR & MRS Jonathan R (M Rawlings Lamberton) U'92.Bost'93
 Redondo Towers 8G, 425 W Paseo Redondo, Tucson, AZ *85701*
Miller DR Kennon S—Wms'82.Dth'87
 ☎ (716) 854-6302 . . 11 Marina Park S, Buffalo, NY *14202*
Miller MR L Don
 ☎ (602) 947-6441 . . 4821 N 70 St, Scottsdale, AZ *85251*
Miller MR & MRS Robert H (Quarton—Cynthia E PO Box 4124,
 Swanson) Cal'68.Wms'70.Stan'74 .... McLean, VA *22103*
 MISS Carolyn D ....
 JUNIORS MR Robert H JR ....
  MISS Anne K Quarton ....
 JUNIORS MR Bradley R Quarton ....
Miller CAPT Robert N 3d—USN. .... Died at
Santa Barbara, CA Jun 13'95
Miller MR & MRS Thomas E (McManus—Emery M ☎ (216) 423-0713
 Norweb) GeoW'71.It .... 2020 Berkshire Rd,
 JUNIORS MISS Eleanora J .... Gates Mills, OH
 JUNIORS MR Thomas E JR *44040*
  MISS Clare E D McManus ....
 JUNIORS MR Henry J McManus ....
Miller MR & MRS Thomas W C (Miller—Loraine ☎ (212) 289-1376
 Laughlin MacDougall) Pa'65.Un.Rr.Chr.Msq. 161 E 90 St,
 Why.Plg.Ll.Cly.P.Hav'60.Cl'64 .... New York, NY
 MISS Katherine A—SCal'90.Rr.—at *10128*
  ☎ (310) 450-8544 . . 2010—3 St, Apt 106,
  Santa Monica, CA *90405* ....
 MR T Wilson C—Unn.Why.Plg.J&W'89—at
  ☎ (704) 362-3745 . . 196 Providence Square Dv,
  Charlotte, NC *28270* ....
 MR Jason E B—Rr.Un.Plg.HWSth'92—at
  ☎ (212) 477-9303 . . 220 Park Av S, Apt 90,
  New York, NY *10003* ....
Millett DR & MRS J Bradford (Kurtz—Constance H Dallas) H'38
 ☎ (315) 392-4780 . . "Hemlock Hill" 3 Newell Rd, Forestport,
 NY *13338*
Milliken MR & MRS John F (Elizabeth P Willcox) Y'42
 ☎ (919) 545-0133 . . 687 Fearrington Post, Fearrington Village,
 Pittsboro, NC *27312*
Mills MASTER Avery William (g—MRS Margaret A Mills) ...... Born at
Wilmington, NC Jly 30'95
Milne MR David 4th—R.Ste.Rv.Pa'58 .... ☎ (215) 922-3311
 MR Caleb .... 118 Church St,
Philadelphia, PA
19106

Milne MRS Walgren (Karen Walgren) Ac. .... ☎ (610) 527-2331
 MR David 5th—at Miller Rd, Chester Springs, PA 332 Greenbank Rd,
 19425 .... Rosemont, PA
19010
Minot MR Otis N .... Died at
Brunswick, ME Dec 16'95
Minot MR Robert E .... Died at
Nantucket, MA Jan 12'96
Minott MR & MRS Owen W (Mary S Vermilye) P'81.Ec.H'80
 ☎ (617) 444-3430 . . 1196 Central Av, Needham, MA *02192*
Missett MR & MRS Joseph V 3d (Topping—Nancy of ☎ (212)744-5319
 Lu Davenport) Va'65.Rc.Mb.Cly.Geo'57.Geo'61 115 E 67 St,
 MR Joseph V 4th—Emory'87—at New York, NY
  ☎ (212) 988-5314 . . 23 E 74 St, Apt 8E, *10021*
  New York, NY *10021* .... ☎ (011-33-1)
 MR Stephen T 47-20-12-73
  MISS Samantha S Topping—at 28 av Montaigne,
   ☎ (212) 472-8631 . . 203 E 72 St, Apt 3H, 75008 Paris, France
   New York, NY *10021* ....
  MR Henry J Topping 4th—Smu'91—at
   ☎ (804) 979-9318 . . 134 Ivy Dv, Apt 3,
   Charlottesville, VA *22903* ....
Mitch DR & MRS William E JR (F Alexandra Fisher) ☎ (404) 239-9064
 Ws'65.Mid'84.Cda.H'63.H'67 .... 3330 W Andrews
 MISS Eleanor B—Pa'90.Paris'96.Dar.—at Dv NW, Atlanta,
  23 rue Rosenwald, 75015 Paris, France ...... GA *30305*
 MR William Armistead—H'93—at 1240—7 St,
  Apt 12, San Francisco, CA *94122* ....
Mitchell MR & MRS W Garry (Valerie Nield) ☎ (508) 362-9794
 Alta'62.Nu'88 .... 450 Main St,
 MISS Heather McC—at Cornell .... Yarmouth Port, MA
02675
Mixter LT CDR (RET) Henry F JR—USN.Bost'68
 10 Shamrock Dv, Mary Esther, FL *32569*
Mixter MRS Nancy W (Nancy Van H Wagner) .... ☎ (904) 651-8652
 MISS Paige R .... 28 Poplar Av,
 MISS Heather E .... Shalimar, FL *32579*
Model MISS Faith . . see J E Nielson
Model MR Robert JR . . see J E Nielson
Moffitt MRS Anne P (Wickersham—Lawton—Anne P Moffitt)
 Wheat'64.Cly . . .of
 ☎ (941) 346-8200 . . 333 Island Circle, Sarasota, FL *34242*
 ☎ (516) 624-9608 . . "Orchard II" 101 Blair Rd, Oyster Bay, NY *11771*
Mohl MISS Catherine M—V'81 . . see MRS A R de Laire
Mohn MISS Susan W . . see W M Brazer
Monmonier MRS Raymond F (Annette Davies) .... Died Sep 5'95
Montgomery MR Austin P JR .... Died at
Bennington, VT Nov 21'95
Montgomery MISS Catherine Binney (Hugh) .... Born Feb 9'93
Montgomery MR Donnell Harry—Vh.SCal'53
 ☎ (818) 795-8093 . . 2040 E Walnut St, Pasadena, CA *91107*
Montgomery MISS Victoria Sanford (J Anthony JR) .... Born at
Greenwich, CT Jan 12'95
Moon MRS Stanley (Julia Lee) .... Died at
St Louis, MO Nov 28'95
Moore MR & MRS Beverly C (Irene W Mitchell) NCar'31.Y'34
 ☎ (910) 274-6519 . . 906 Country Club Dv, Greensboro, NC *27408-5602*

Moore MR & MRS C Atwell JR (Erica E Bauer) Penn'65 . . . . ☎ (941) 486-0225
  MISS Erica F—at ☎ (941) 488-2032
  608 Armada Rd S, Venice, FL 34285 . . . . 712 Valencia Rd, Venice, FL 34285
  MR C Atwell 3d—at U of Va Law . . . .
Moore MR & MRS David A C (Christiane H Citron) Y'71.StJ'67
  ☎ (303) 777-2242 . . 373 Marion St, Denver, CO 80218
Moore MR & MRS Douglas G (Margaret G Gibbs) Bhm.Pcu.Cal'59.H'65 . . . . ☎ (415) 921-5570
  MR Mark A . . . . 15 Walnut St, San Francisco, CA 94118
Moore MR Franklin H—Ty'68 . . . . of ☎ (617)236-6407
  MISS Margaret O—at ☎ (212) 529-9621
  134 E 17 St, New York, NY 10003 . . . . 188 W Canton St, Boston, MA 02116
  MISS Natalie H—at ☎ (508) 248-9783
  65 Worcester Rd, Charlton, MA 01507 . . . . . . ☎ (508) 255-7914
  310 Windjammer Lane, Eastham, MA 02642
Moore MASTER George Charles 3d (g—George C Moore) . . . . . . Born at Westerly, RI Jan 24'96
Moore MRS James R (Jane E Thaler) . . . . Died at Walnut Creek, CA Jan 16'96
Moore MISS Jayne Thaler 24801 Santa Fe St, Carmel, CA 93923
Moore MASTER Jeffrey Cole (g—Henry A Little 3d) . . . . . Born Dec 8'93
Moore MRS Sandra Sizer (Moore—Sandra Sizer)
  ☎ (941) 729-0141 . . 4322—15 Way W, Palmetto, FL 34221
Moorhead MISS Allison F—SCal'93 . . see MRS C E Wood
Moorhead MR Dudley T 3d . . see MRS C E Wood
Moorhead MR Thomas B—Yn.Y'56.Pa'59.Nu'64 . . ☎ (203) 966-0627
  MISS Hannah C—OWes'93—at 215 W 10 St, Apt 2E, New York, NY 10014 . . . . 148 Ramhorne Rd, New Canaan, CT 06840
  MISS Rachel McG—Kenyon . . . .
Moorhead MR & MRS Thomas C JR (Elizabeth S Hundt) Vt'83.Pa'70
  ☎ (412) 741-7397 . . Farmhill Rd, Sewickley, PA 15143
Morehouse MR & MRS Alexander G (Elizabeth W Rasch) Emory'63 . . . . Burge Plantation, 200 Morehouse Rd, Mansfield, GA 30255
  MISS Nancy A . . . .
  MISS Eve G . . . .
Moorhouse MISS Laura A (William H JR) . . . Married at Woods Hole, MA
  Kenna MR Timothy C (Edgar C) . . . . Sep 9'95
Moorhouse MR & MRS William H JR (Margaret C Pew) M.Sfy.Fmy.Me.Fr.Va'70 . . . . of ☎ (610)649-6066
  MISS Nina E—at 2080 Filbert St, Apt 3, San Francisco, CA 94123 . . . . 719 Black Rock Rd, Gladwyne, PA 19035
  ☎ (415) 435-3042 85 Mt Tiburon Rd, Tiburon, CA 94920

Moran MR Joseph H 2d—BtP.Bcs.Pr.Wms'33.H'36 . . of
  ☎ (407) 655-6500 . . 160 Royal Palm Way, Palm Beach, FL 33480
  ☎ (516) 671-2057 . . 24 Prospect Av, Sea Cliff, NY 11579-1004
  ☎ (970) 923-5600 . . Snowmass Club, PO Box G2, Snowmass Village, CO 81615
Moran MISS Mary B (MISS Nina L Large) . . . . Born at Philadelphia, PA Dec 8'94
Morey MRS Joseph H JR (McConaughy—Marion Hancock) . . . . Died Nov 9'95
Morgan MISS Allison Gale (Jonathan C) . . . . Born Aug 14'93
Morgan MRS Edwin Ernest (Freer—Jane B Walker) Vh.
  ☎ (818) 792-7884 . . 842 E Villa St, Apt 323, Pasadena, CA 91101
Morgan MR & MRS George O JR (Marianela Martinez de Eguiluz) Laf'72.Iese'74 . . . . ☎ (305) 663-5607
  MR George O 5th . . . . 11345 SW 63 Av, Miami, FL 33156-4943
  JUNIORS MISS Marianela . . . .
Morgan RR ADM (RET) & MRS Henry S (Flather—J Alexandra McCain) USN.Br'56.GeoW'78.Gi. Ny.Mt.H'44.GeoW'78 . . . . ☎ (410) 360-3432
  MISS Katherine McC—MaryB'89—at 641 Stillwater Rd, PO Box 173, Gibson Island, MA 21056
  ☎ (703) 691-4052 . . 9509 Barcellona Court, Fairfax, VA 22031 . . . .
  MISS (DR) Alexandra W Flather-Morgan— P'85.Y'89—at ☎ (617) 876-6782
  38 Dana St, Cambridge, MA 02138 . . . .
Morgan MASTER Jesse Cory (g—Carl R Withers) . . . . Born in Houston, TX Jan 30'94
Morgan MR John A JR (John A) . . . . Married at Paget, Bermuda
  Groomes MISS Karen H (Joseph N JR) . . . . Aug 12'95
Morgan MR & MRS John M (Andrew—Elizabeth M McPherson) Strat'64.Gi.Elk.Mv.Rv.Cw.Ncd.JHop'51 . . of
  ☎ (410) 523-6771 . . 115 Cross Keys Rd, Baltimore, MD 21210
  ☎ (561) 231-7022 . . 203 N Carmel Court, Vero Beach, FL 32963
Morgan MR & MRS Jonathan C (Carol S Frigo) Ill'84.JHop'96.Ill'83
  ☎ (410) 435-8223 . . 5006 Broadmoor Rd, Baltimore, MD 21212
Morgan DR Kenneth R . . . . Died Dec 11'95
Morgan MR LeRoy Tuttle . . . . Died at Clarksburg, MD Nov 1'95
Morgan MR Thomas N . . . . Died at New York, NY Oct 20'95
Morgan DR & MRS Walter McN 3d (Anne McK Zimmerman) P'78.Van'81.Elk.P'78.Van'82
  ☎ (615) 383-0438 . . ''Greenspring'' 200 Evelyn Av, Nashville, TN 37205
Morosi MR Justin I (Donald J) . . . . Married at Harmony, CA
  Gilles MISS Marji O (John) . . . . Jly 30'95
Morosi MR & MRS Justin I (Marji O Gilles) CalPoly'95
  ☎ (317) 259-0546 . . 7469 Somerset Bay, Indianapolis, IN 46240
Morrell MASTER Alexander Raynor (g—Lee C Alexander) . . . . . . Born at Spring Hill, FL Mch 9'95
Morrin MRS Kevin C (Helen L Clanton) . . . . ☎ (314) 367-0291
  MR Kevin C JR—Wash'61—at Columbus Academy, 4300 Cherry Bottom Rd, PO Box 30745, Gahanna, OH 43230 . . . . 1 McKnight Rd, St Louis, MO 63108
Morris MISS Deirdre L E—Vt'83
  ☎ (802) 459-6389 . . 15 Pine St, Proctor, VT 05765

Morris MR & MRS James S (Eleanor K Smith) Rdc'56.Pa'59.Pc.Cs.Ac.Edin'55.Pa'57 . . . . MR S Houston—H'89—at 30 Brechin Place, London SW7, England . . . . of ☎ (215)248-4553 "Sugar Loaf Orchard" 31 W Bells Mill Rd, Philadelphia, PA *19118* ☎ (011-44-1875) 833-789 "Woodcote Park" Fala & Soutra, Midlothian EH37 57G, Scotland

Morris MRS John McL (Marjorie S Austin) Cda.
☎ (203) 562-5070 . . 4 Edgehill Rd, New Haven, CT *06511*

Morris DR Robert D (late John McL) . . . . Married at Milwaukee, WI Müeller MISS (DR) Astrid D (Alphons) . . . . Jan 20'95

Morrison MISS Isobel Marguerite (James A) . . . . Born at Greenbrae, CA Aug 27'95

Morrison MR & MRS James A (Anne N Wilbur) Geo'87.Cal'82.Dth'87
☎ (415) 459-1747 . . 501 Oak Av, San Anselmo, CA *94960*

Morrison MRS John McF (Eleanor B Morris) V'38
☎ (011-44-131) 447-6373 . . The Elms 23, 148 Whitehouse Loan, Edinburgh EX9 2EZ, Scotland

Morse MR David H (late Charles F) . . . . Married at Boston, MA McNeely MRS S McWhinney (Susan P McWhinney) . . . . . . Dec 29'95

Morse MR & MRS David H (McNeely—Susan P McWhinney) Sth'55.Au.Ub.Sm.H'56.Cl'59 . . of
☎ (617) 227-1570 . . 13 Temple St, Boston, MA *02114*
☎ (617) 698-6870 . . 397 Hillside St, Milton, MA *02186*

Morss MRS Everett (Anne Wentworth) Ncd.
☎ (508) 526-4653 . . Oakwood, 601 Summer St, Manchester, MA *01944*

Morss MR Sherman . . . . Died in Florida Feb 29'96

Mortimer MRS Catia Z (Catia S Zoullas) . . . . . Married at New York, NY Chapin MRS Schuyler G (late L H Paul) . . . . Sep 15'95

Mortimer MR E Nicholas . . see S G Chapin

Mortimer MISS Liza . . see S G Chapin

Mortlock MR David H . . . . Died at Quogue, NY Jly 14'95

Mosle MISS Cornelia B—Cda. . . . . MR Daniel B . . . . 190—72 St, Apt 134, Brooklyn, NY *11209*

Mosle MR William B JR . . . . Died Dec 19'95

Moss MR George F (George K) . . . . Married at Millbrook, NY Chamine MISS Courtney A (Robert J) . . . . Oct 14'95

Motch MR & MRS Elton F JR (Patricia A Pecor) Duke'65.Tvcl.Duke'65 . . . . MISS Lauren S—Sth'87—at ☎ (617) 241-8852 33 Mystic St, Apt 3, Charlestown, MA *02129* . . MR E Franklin 3d—StLaw'91—at ☎ (802) 865-0153 . . 350 Maple St, Apt E, Burlington, VT *05401* . . . . ☎ (802) 425-2423 "Wings Point" RR 2, Box 2442, Charlotte, VT *05445*

Motley MR & MRS John L (Deborah E Benton) VillaN'81.Dar.Vt'73
☎ (703) 734-8588 . . 7703 Carlton Place, McLean, VA *22102-2150*

Motley MR Thomas—H.'63.Cl'66 . . . . MISS Sarah P—NH'93 . . . . MISS Elisabeth C—at Columbia . . . . MR Thomas 3d—McG'91 . . . . ☎ (508) 263-4054 115 School St, Acton, MA *01720-4415*

Moulton MRS H Douglass (Beers—Isobel C Lee) . . . . Died at Hightstown, NJ Dec 2'95

Mower MR & MRS Grove N (Brooke Hummer) Wes'85.Br'80
☎ (312) 871-4419 . . 829 W George St, Chicago, IL *60657*

Mullan MRS Nancy D (Nancy De V Field) Cly. . . . . MR Peter D—P'91—at ☎ (203) 865-2335 8 Edgewood Av, New Haven, CT *06511* . . . . . . ☎ (212) 628-4629 333 E 68 St, Apt 6F, New York, NY *10021*

Muller MR & MRS E Nicholas (Mary F Clay) Y'37 . . MR Richard C . . . . ☎ (520) 760-1066 9225 E Tanque Verde Rd, Apt 13104, Tucson, AZ *85749-8715*

Mulry MISS Cecelia Fox (g—John W Lapsley) . . . . Born Jly 5'95

Mulvihill MRS Francis X (Rosalie G Lamy) . . . . Died Dec 9'95

Munn MRS Charles A (Dupuy—McCarthy—Dorothy C Spreckels) . . of ☎ (407) 844-6766 . . "Amado" 455 N County Rd, Box 269, Palm Beach, FL *33480* 22 rue Barbet de Joux, 75007 Paris, France

Munn MR Mark T (late Mark S) . . Married at Audrieu, Normandy, France Kelly MISS Lisa . . . . Apr 30'94

Munroe MRS Charles L (Miriam U Allen) . . . . Died Jly 6'94

Munroe MR John—H'46
☎ (914) 677-8197 . . PO Box 137, Tyrell Rd, Millbrook, NY *12545* Dec 15 . . ☎ (809) 956-5588 . . "Flint River House" Sandy Bay, Hanover, Jamaica

Murphy MR Edwynne P . . . . Died at St Louis, MO Mch 20'93

Murphy MR George J . . . . Died Nov 9'94

Murphy MRS Grayson M P (Mary E Warren) Cly.Cs.
☎ (212) 838-8096 . . 1 E 66 St, New York, NY *10021*

Murphy MR & MRS James R (Margaret S Garrison) Pac'93.Ariz'87 9225 N 119 Way, Scottsdale, AZ *85259*

Murphy MISS Margaret J—Ia'84 . . . . MR George J 3d . . . . ☎ (312) 404-1622 2658J N Southport Av, Chicago, IL *60614*

Murphy MISS Stephanie Chouteau—StL'68.Dar.
☎ (954) 351-4201 . . 133 N Pompano Blvd, Pompano Beach, FL *33062*

Muse MISS Alexandra V—Geo'89.Rr.Pg.Fcg.
☎ (212) 875-0463 . . 322 W 87 St, Apt 1, New York, NY *10024*

Muse MISS Nancy C—SCal'92.Rr.Pg.Fcg.
☎ (213) 933-8705 . . 630 S Masselin Av, Apt 403, Los Angeles, CA *90036*

N

Naffziger MRS Howard C (Louise McNear) . . . . Died Dec 3'95

Nash MR & MRS Peter W II (Sandra B Nichols) LakeF'84.Ken'83
☎ (508) 266-0013 . . 216 School St, Acton, MA *01720-4468*

Naughton MASTER Albert Stephen 3d (A Stephen JR) . . . . Born Jun 23'94

Neal MRS Kirke A (Dorothy H B Becker) .... Died Jly 19'94
Needham MR George P .... Died May 2'95
Neff MR & MRS Morton Gibbons JR (Florence M Chance) Cry.
   ☎ (410) 778-0775 .. "Clovelly Farm" 421 Clovelly Lane, Chestertown, MD *21620*
Neilson MR Lewis L .... Died at Chester Springs, PA Jly 11'95
Neilson MR Thomas R 3d (late Thomas R JR) .... Married at Geneva, NY
   Kepner MISS Misty Jo (Eugene) .... Jly 29'95
Nelson MISS E Pegge—PugetS'90.Pitt'96.Me ... see S B Dunn JR
Nesbitt MR & MRS Patrick Michael (Hillgren— | ☎ (310) 476-2364
   Williams—Marji Bailey) SCal'74.USAF'67 .... | 273 S Glenroy Av,
   MISS Elizabeth P .... | Los Angeles, CA
   JUNIORS MR Patrick M JR .... | *90049*
Neumeyer MR William E .... Died at McLean, VA Jly 27'95
Neville MR & MRS Penrhyn B (Adams—Barbara A | ☎ (302) 421-9123
   Berger) Myf.P'55.Pa'61 .... | 2206 Fairfield Place,
   MISS Katherine V—Roan'93—at | Wilmington, DE
   ☎ (970) 482-3677 .. 645 S Loomis Av, | *19805*
   Ft Collins, CO *80521* ....
   MISS Emily B—JMad'94—at ☎ (617) 536-8225
   511 Beacon St, Apt 10, Boston, MA *02115* ....
Newbold MRS William T 2d (Mary K Simmons) Ala'80.Temp'94
   ☎ (205) 547-8858 .. 280 Alpine View, Gadsden, AL *35901*
Newbold MR William T 2d—Ala'79.Drex'86.Drex'92
   ☎ (215) 233-9072 .. 401 Hillcrest Av, Wyndmoor, PA *19038*
Newhall MR & MRS Charles W 3d (Amy L Liebno) | ☎ (410) 363-1552
   Sm.Rr.Gv.Cc.Mv.Pa'67.H'71 .... | 2803 Caves Rd,
   MR Charles A .... | Owings Mills, MD
   JUNIORS MR Adair B .... | *21117*
Newhall MISS Hannah Shelburne (Thomas B) .... Born at Boston, MA Dec 6'95
Newlin MRS E Mortimer (Elizabeth B Battles) .... Died at Wayne, PA Jly 15'95
Newman MR & MRS George W 3d (Mary E Kyte) | ☎ (513) 561-8118
   Man'vl'63.Xav'65.Cal'72.My.Ec.Qc.Geo'61. | 9825 Cunningham
   Cin'64 .... | Rd, Cincinnati, OH
   MR George W 4th .... | *45243*
   JUNIORS MISS Mary E K ....
   JUNIORS MR Charles L ....
Newsom MR & MRS Noble (Boldemann—Marjorie S | ☎ (619) 759-0717
   Behneman) Stan'44.Cal'38 .... | PO Box 3787,
   MR Roger Van S—at ☎ (954) 458-0121 | Rancho Santa Fe,
   3331 Farragut St, Apt 8D, Hollywood, FL *33021* | CA *92067*
Newton MISS Barbara L (White—Barbara L Newton) Cal'84
   543 Aliso Av, Newport Beach, CA *92663*
Newton MR Charles I (Edwin Anthony T) ...... Married at Malibu, CA
   Hodges MISS Sarah L (Lorin C) .... Oct 14'95
Newton MR & MRS Charles I (Sarah L Hodges) Br'89
   ☎ (310) 822-5357 .. 2326 Clement Av, Venice, CA *90291*

Nicholl MRS Helen Dale (Helen D Kulik) Bvr'67 ... | of ☎ (212)745-4282
   MISS Ashley A—at St Mark's .... | 435 E 79 St,
   JUNIORS MR Maynard C 3d .... | New York, NY
   | *10021*
   | ☎ (516) 287-5281
   | "Sparrow's Nest"
   | 399 Canoe Place Rd,
   | Southampton, NY
   | *11968*
Nicholl MR Maynard C JR—Va'53.Balt'60
   ☎ (301) 972-6661 .. 12409 Deoudes Rd, Boyds, MD *20841-9022*
Nichols MR & MRS Brett E (D Reed Wessells) Ken'88.RochTech'86
   ☎ (415) 856-7677 .. 425 Margarita Av, Palo Alto, CA *94306*
Nickerson MR Joshua B—Geo'92 .. see W M Riegel
Niedringhaus MRS W Delafield (Effie V Zeibig) ... | ☎ (314) 569-2466
   MISS Adaline H—at ☎ (314) 991-0768 | 10379 Tuxford Dv,
   979 Rue De La Banque, Apt 1, St Louis, MO | Apt 2, St Louis, MO
   63141 .... | *63146*
Niedringhaus MR & MRS W Delafield JR (Linda | ☎ (314) 997-6751
   Van Eck) BostColl'72.BostColl'73.Cy.W&L'66 | 4 Wyndtop Lane,
   MISS Alicia A .... | St Louis, MO *63141*
   MR Charles H—W&L'90—at 8121 Whitburn Dv,
   St Louis, MO *63105* ....
Nielson, James E & Young, Anne N (Model—Anne | ☎ (307) 587-5821
   N Young) Pa'63.Cly.Wyo'54 .... | Sage Creek Ranch,
   MISS Faith Model—at Cornell .... | PO Box 1507, Cody,
   MR Robert Model JR—at U of Wyo .... | WY *82414*
Nigh MRS William H (Kate S Boardman) .... Died Nov 30'95
Nightingale MRS John T (Augusta W Harrison) .... Died at Beverly Farms, MA Dec 16'95
Nimick MASTER Thomas Marshall Howe 3d (g—Thomas M H Nimick JR) . Born at Falls Church, VA Apr 5'95
Niven MRS James G (Fernanda Wanamaker | ☎ (212) 744-5339
   Wetherill) Ng.Sg.BtP.Plg.StJ. .... | 160 E 72 St,
   MISS Fernanda W .... | New York, NY
   MISS Eugenie R .... | *10021*
Niven MR James G—K.Ng.Sg.BtP.Plg.StJ.H'67
   4 E 66 St, New York, NY *10021*
Niver MISS Judson S (Thomas M) .... Married at New York, NY
   O'Hair MR Timothy D (late James P) .... Oct 21'95
Nixon MISS Allison Elizabeth (Jeffrey S) .... Born Nov 24'95
Nixon MISS Amy Catherine (Jeffrey S) .... Born May 31'94
Nixon MR & MRS Jeffrey S (Holly B Walker) Les'89.NewHaven'89
   ☎ (908) 219-6646 .. 4 Forrest Av, Rumson, NJ *07760*
Nixon MISS Jessica Marie (Jeffrey S) .... Born Feb 7'93
Noble MR & MRS Daniel S (Elizabeth A Ream) LakeF'90.LakeF'89
   ☎ (847) 251-4352 .. 2334 Greenwood Av, Wilmette, IL *60091*
Noble MISS Helen Rike (Daniel S) .... Born at Wilmette, IL Jan 3'96
Noble MRS Lawrence M JR (Helen C Rike) .... Died at Woodstock, VT Oct 27'95
Nordmann MR & MRS Gary A (Brune—Caroline S | ☎ (516) 673-4787
   Crary) Mich'63.Cl'65.Purd'64.H'70 .... | 15 Lloyd Harbor Rd,
   MISS Constance T Brune .... | Huntington, NY
   MR William H N Brune 2d—StLaw'91—at | *11743*
   765 Ottawa St, Harbor Springs, MI *49740* ...
   MR Timothy H C Brune ....

Norfleet MASTER John Norwood (Christopher McC) . . . . Born at Norwalk, CT Dec 15'95
Norfleet MR & MRS John V R SR (Sarah F Edwards) Wheat'83.Sar.Cw.
☎ (617) 585-9062 . . "Evergreen" 14 Summer St, Kingston, MA *02364*
Norling MR & MRS Barry Allen (Abigail B Chandler) | ☎ (207) 474-2738
  Bost'67.Bost'67 . . . . | Beech Hill Rd,
  MISS Alesia Fay—RISD'94—at | Norridgewock, ME
  ☎ (401) 351-4895 . . 27 Sycamore St, | *04957*
  Providence, RI *02909* . . . . |
  JUNIORS MISS Rebecca M. . . . . |
Norment MRS Clarence F 3d (Nancy A Richards) . . . . Married at Washington, DC
  McCabe MR Walter C (late Charles D) . . . . Feb 3'96
Norment MR Clarence F 4th (late Clarence F 3d) Married at Bethesda, MD
  Boyer MISS Mary E (late Paul) . . . . Oct 7'95
Northrop MRS Edward H (Christine E B Mueller) . . | Box 808,
  MISS Marjorie C . . . . | Fraser, CO *80442*
  MR Wilhelm E . . . . |
Northrop MR Edward H—T.Ln.Y.Dth'66.Va'71
☎ (914) 351-2809 . . "Innisfree" Box 7, Arden, NY *10910-0007*
Northrop MR Johnston F (late Filmer S C) . . . . Married at Greenwich, CT
  Gray MRS David D (Lucile R Ralston) . . . . Sep 15'95
Northrop MR & MRS Johnston F (Gray—Lucile R Ralston)
Nyc.Ihy.Ne.Chr.Cly.Yn.Y'43
☎ (203) 869-9243 . . 665 Steamboat Rd, Greenwich, CT *06830*
Norton MR Garrison . . . . Died at Washington, DC Sep 9'95
Notides MR & MRS Russell J (Ellanor T Roberts) | ☎ (011-852)
  Bur.Bgt.Nf.LakeF'73 . . . . | 2868-4410
  JUNIORS MISS Elizabeth C | Tavistock 602,
  JUNIORS MR Alexander B . . . . | 10 Tregunter Path,
     | Hong Kong
Notman MR & MRS Donald D (Gertrude L M Raynor-Smith)
Mt.Cvc.Sl.Ncd.Y'49
☎ (207) 967-5129 . . PO Box 527, 15 Summit Av, Kennebunkport, ME *04046*
Nowland MR & MRS David T (Cathleen B Cotter) W&M'89
☎ (212) 832-0998 . . 349 E 49 St, Apt 6K, New York, NY *10017*
Nulsen DR Frank E . . . . Died Jun 30'94
Nyland MRS Katherine S (Katherine S McLenegan) . | ☎ (415) 441-7408
  MISS Leslie S . . . . | 2325 North Point St,
  MR Matthew W—Cal'95 . . . . | San Francisco, CA
     | *94123*

O

O'Brien MISS Bridget Colleen (W Gardnar) . . . . Born at Fullerton, CA Feb 1'96
O'Brien MR Frank 3d (Frank JR) . . . . Married at Edgartown, MA
  Buckley MISS Amybeth (James E) . . . . Jly 29'95
O'Brien MR Miles M . . . . Died Feb 5'96
O'Connor MASTER Kiliaen Van Rensselaer (Michael J) . . . . Born at Morristown, NJ Sep 15'95
O'Connor MISS Perry Martin (Anthony M JR) . . . . Born at New York, NY Mch 15'95

Odom MR & MRS John G (E Lee Scott)
Va'76.An.Cw.Ncd.Y'73.Ox'75.Va'78.Ox'81 . . of
☎ (504) 837-8883 . . 105 Northline St, Metairie, LA *70005*
☎ (912) 794-3420 . . "Old Home Place" 5502 Hall Rd, Hahira, GA *31632*
O'Donnell MISS Nancy S—Srb . . . of
☎ (415) 474-7539 . . 3196 Pacific Av, San Francisco, CA *94115*
☎ (407) 655-5947 . . 325 S Lake Dv, Palm Beach, FL *33480*
Oesch MR Peter I . . see MRS W N Frank JR
Oesch MISS Stephanie E . . see MRS W N Frank JR
O'Grady MASTER Alexander Ladd (Bradford S) . . . . Born at Princeton, NJ Aug 30'95
Ohrstrom MR & MRS Christopher F (Lilla Y Matheson)
☎ (607) 293-7945 . . RR 1, Box 93B2, Hartwick, NY *13348*
Ohrstrom MASTER Finlay Matheson (Christopher F) . . . . Born at Cooperstown, NY Dec 30'95
Ohrstrom MR Kenneth M
☎ (407) 655-6507 . . 150 Chilian Av, Palm Beach, FL *33480*
Ohrstrom MRS Ricard R (Rosse—Allen G Dunnington)
Bnd'50.Cly.Ncd . . . of
☎ (540) 253-5056 . . PO Box 446, 4008 Milestone Rd, The Plains, VA *22171*
☎ (809) 952-5154 . . Round Hill, Montego Bay, Jamaica
☎ (808) 885-5252 . . Mauna Lani Terr, Kohala Coast, Kamuela, HI *96743*
Oliphant MR & MRS Andrew E (Lara M Hall) NCar'87
☎ (704) 849-7949 . . 4514 Candalon Way, Matthews, NC *28105*
Olmsted MR Robert MacC—Au.Pr.Ri.P'63.Cl'65 . . | ☎ (212) TR6-8668
  MISS Alexandra MacC—P'94—at 166 Máy Dèn, | 1100 Park Av,
  Chuong Duong, Hanoi, Vietnam . . . . | New York, NY
     | *10128*
O'Malley MR & MRS Shaun F (S Julia Bernard) | ☎ (215) 247-7785
  BMr'65.B.Ri.Pc.Pa'59 . . . . | 725 Glengary Rd,
  MISS Sibyl H—at 74 Fayette St, Cambridge, MA | Philadelphia, PA
  02139 . . . . | *19118*
  MISS Aine B—at NYU |
Ormrod MRS Reginald M C (Leslie—Pierce—Sarah J Webster) . . . . Died at St Louis, MO Jan 14'96
Orr MISS Jean A—Bnd'79 . . of
☎ (203) 531-6179 . . 18 Connecticut Av, Greenwich, CT *06830*
☎ (518) 854-3287 . . "Todd Hunter Farm" Robinson Rd, Shushan, NY *12873*
Orr MR & MRS P Welles (Ann S Young) Y'80.Pg.Rr.Denis'82
☎ (202) 342-7130 . . 4823 Reservoir Rd NW, Washington, DC *20007*
Orrick CDR DeCourcy W 3d—USNR.Va'73
☎ (404) 816-9179 . . 1180 Kendrick Rd NE, Apt A, Atlanta, GA *30319*
Orrick MR William H JR (late William H) . . . . Married at San Francisco, CA
  Rogers MRS John G (Suzanne V Bensinger) . . . . Jan 19'96
Orrick MR & MRS William H JR (Rogers—Suzanne | ☎ (415) 567-8324
  V Bensinger) BMr'45.Bhm.Pcu.Sfy.Bur.Tcy. | 250 Locust St,
  Y'37.Cal'41 | San Francisco, CA
  MISS Diana V Rogers—at ☎ (510) 548-8433 | *94118*
  20 Stonewall Rd, Berkeley, CA *94705* . . . . . . |
Osborn MR Henry C 4th (Henry C 3d) . . . . . . Married at Brunswick, ME
  Treworgy MISS Sara A . . . . Sep 30'95

Osborn MR James E 2d . . . . Died at Greenwich, CT Dec 15'95
O'Shaughnessy MR Robert M . . see MRS S W Miles
O'Shaughnessy JUNIORS MR William A . . see MRS S W Miles
Ostheimer MR & MRS John M (Nancy J Cushing) Man'vl'60.Myf.Dar.Y'60.Y'67 . . . .
MR William A . . . .
3615 Canada Goose Crossing, Racine, WI *53403*
O'Toole MR & MRS John J 3d (Suzanne Black) Geo'77.GeoW'77.CathU'80
☎ (708) 920-8046 . . 424 N Garfield Av, Hinsdale, IL *60521*
Ottley MR & MRS E Granger (Smith—Judith Morton) Wms'51 . . . .
MR Garrett M Smith—at ☎ (212) 535-0933 510 E 85 St, New York, NY *10028* . . . .
☎ (207) 655-2947 132 Mountain Rd, PO Box 783, Raymond, ME *04071*
Ottley MISS Heidi H—Vt'90
☎ (208) 726-9447 . . PO Box 1444, Sun Valley, ID *83353*
Ottley MR & MRS Philip G (Glenna R Holleran) CtCol'59 ⚓
☎ (561) 546-5465 . . on board Noble Falcon'' PO Box 8530, Hobe Sound, FL *33475*
Ottley MR Philip G JR—Vt'93
☎ (208) 726-9447 . . PO Box 1444, Sun Valley, ID *83353*
Otto MISS Marie Luise—Cal'59.Dom'81.Fr.
☎ (415) 346-1206 . . 1070 Green St, Apt 602, San Francisco, CA *94133*
Ottum MR Philip K—Ore'73 . . . .
JUNIORS MISS Katherine McI . . . .
☎ (503) 226-0433 2377 NW Overton St, Portland, OR *97210*
Owen MRS Frederick H JR (Dayton—Jeanne P Comey) Sth'47.Dyc.
☎ (561) 978-0911 . . 2727 Tenth Av, Vero Beach, FL *32960*
Oyster MRS Maginis (A Patricia Maginis) . . . . Died at Greenbrae, CA Nov 18'94

P

Packard MASTER Daniel George Daubek (George W W) . . . . Born at San Francisco, CA Dec 26'95
Packer MISS Juliet Law (late Charles Wallace) . . . . Married at New York, NY
Kutik MR William M (Paul) . . . . Feb 10'96
Page MRS Anderson (Burwell—Katharine G Despard) . . . .
MISS Lesslie B Burwell—at ☎ (206) 729-0829 326 NE 54 St, Seattle, WA *98105* . . . .
MR John T Burwell 3d—H'72—at
☎ (508) 460-0040 . . St Mark's School, 25 Marlborough Rd, Southborough, MA *01772*
☎ (908) 781-5851 4128 Fellowship Rd, Basking Ridge, NJ *07920*
Page MR & MRS Shelby H (Roberta G Raworth) Hn.H'43
☎ (803) 681-6474 . . 15 Outerbridge Circle, Hilton Head Island, SC *29926*
Pagon MR Marshall W (late Garrett D) . . . . . . Married at Siasconset, MA
Matteson MISS Holly T (William B) . . . . Sep 30'95
Paine MRS Alix E (Seymore—O'Shea—Alix E Paine) SL'69.ChHill'91 . . . .
MISS Chloë B Seymore—RISD'96 . . . .
of ☎ (212)988-6671 157 E 72 St, New York, NY *10021*
☎ (518) 398-5601 ''Old Orchard'' PO Box 162, Pine Plains, NY *12567*
Pakenham HON & MRS Michael Aidan (Lavine—Meta L Doak) Ty'64.Tex'65 . . . .
JUNIORS MISS Alexandra Clio I B . . . .
of ☎ (011-33-1) 42-66-91-42 British Embassy, 35 rue du Faubourg St Honoré, 75383 Paris Cedex 08, France
☎ (011-44-1580) 860-494 Bernhurst, Hurst Green, East Sussex TN19 7QN, England
☎ (011-44-171) 727-8956 34 Aldridge Rd Villas, London W11 1BW, England
Palfrey MASTER Alexander Gorham (g—George G Palfrey) . . . . Born Apr 13'95
Palmer MR Christopher D—Colg'86.Nu'88 . . see P M Hammett
Palmer MRS Franklin H (Mary Hunnewell) . . . . Died Jun 8'95
Palmer MISS Lydia W (Philip) . . . . Married at New York, NY
Chaudhry MR Kashif . . . . Mch 12'94
Palmer MR Morgan—H'55
☎ (508) 650-3586 . . PO Box 133, Natick, MA *01760*
Palmer MR & MRS Raymond N (Joan M Starkey) Ty'75.H'84.P'68.H'78.Bost'85
☎ (512) 263-1879 . . 10012 Circleview Dv, Austin, TX *78733*
Palmer MR Richard M . . . . Died Jan 22'96
Palmer MISS Susannah C (F Timothy) . . . . Married at New York, NY
McCarthy MR Colin . . . . Jan 5'94
Panarese MASTER Bartholomew Magner (Mark J) . . . . Born at Boston, MA Oct 15'95
Panon Desbassayns de Richemont JUNIORS MISS Amélie see C F Smithers JR
Panon Desbassayns de Richemont JUNIORS MR Philippe see C F Smithers
Park MR & MRS Peter G JR (McPherson—Joy J Medley) NEng'74.CathU'75.Wis'67.GeoW'74
1909 Earldale Court, Alexandria, VA *22306-2715*
Parker MRS Comfort T (O'Connor—Lord—Stuart—Comfort T Parker) Cly.
☎ (407) 655-6323 . . The Australian, 429 Australian Av, Palm Beach, FL *33480*
Parker MASTER Devon Walton (Todd K) . . . . Born at Alexandria, VA Oct 24'95
Parker MR J Hutchison (late Richard S) . . . . Married
Pollack MISS Rebecca . . . . Aug 3'92

Parker MRS Richard S (Sarah M Price) . . . . Married at Rye, NY
    Chittenden MR George H . . . . Sep 24'95
Parker MR Sherman C . . . . Died Feb 19'95
Parker MRS Sherman C (Horne—Kathleen Sheldon) Pg.Chi.Cc.
    ☎ (202) 625-2920 . . 2512 Q St NW, Apt 316, Washington, DC 20007
Parmley MR & MRS John R (Shyamala Murugesan)
    ☎ (808) 247-6094 . . 45-082 Waiape Place, Kaneohe, HI 96744
Parr MR & MRS Edward John JR (Adair D Freeman)
    Duke'88.Geo'93.Nu'86.Geo'93
    ☎ (540) 592-3690 . . 22378 Trappe Rd, PO Box 438, Upperville,
    VA 20185
Parry MR Rawdon M C (late Richard) . . . . Married
    Pritchard MISS Leslie A (Biccich—Leslie A Pritchard) . . . . . . Jly 28'95
Parsons MR & MRS I Manning 3d (Fehsenfeld— | ☎ (410) 876-1203
    Cynthia Riley) Sth'56.JHop'63.Nyc.Gv.Mv. | 1701 Western Run
    Ty'52.Md'79 . . . . | Rd, Cockeysville,
    MISS Caroline Harvey E—at ☎ (508) 257-6785 | MO 21030
    PO Box 471, Siasconset, MA 02564 . . . . |
    MR Ira Manning IV—at Columbia Phys & Surg . |
Patch MASTER Benjamin Woodward (g—MRS Howard R Patch JR) . . . Born
    at New York, NY Jly 5'95
Patch MRS Howard R JR (Kathryn V Woodward) | ☎ (860) 434-2450
    Ws'46.Co.Hn. . . . . | 25 McCurdy Rd,
    MR David S R—Cr'88—at ☎ (419) 472-3878 | Old Lyme, CT
    2034 Berden St, Toledo, OH 43613 . . . . | 06371
Patel MISS India Marshall (Sanjay H) . . . . Born at
    New York, NY Jly 7'95
Patel MR & MRS Sanjay H (Leslie S Dickey) Ws'83.H.'83.Stan'87
    ☎ (212) BU8-6599 . . 125 E 72 St, Apt 10D, New York, NY 10021
Patterson MR & MRS David C (Considine—Maria C | ☎ (212) 439-9103
    Wall) Rdc'70.K.Fic.H'70 . . . . | 162 E 66 St,
    JUNIORS MISS Eloise C . . . . | New York, NY
    JUNIORS MR David G . . . . | 10021
Patterson MISS Elena A (Michael E) . . . . Married at Old Lyme, CT
    Tyree MR Walter P 4th (Walter P 3d) . . . . Oct 7'95
Patterson MRS Patricia M (Barlerin—Lebermann— | ☎ (214) 521-9940
    Patricia M Patterson) Sth'60.Cl'70.Ri. . . . . | 3831 Turtle Creek
    MISS Caroline P Barlerin—V'95—at | Blvd, Apt 23C,
    329—25 Av, Apt 2, San Francisco, CA 94121 | Dallas, TX 75219
Patterson MASTER Robert Bermingham (Lloyd A) . . . . Born at
    Lubbock, TX Oct 10'95
Patty MR William A 4th . . see MRS K E Jackson
Paul DR & MRS Oglesby (Hatch—Paul—Jean D | 10 Longwood Dv,
    Lithgow) Sb.Sm.Cw.StJ.Csn.H'38.H'42 . . . . | Apt 322, Westwood,
    MISS Marguerite—at ☎ (404) 377-4871 | MA 02090
    269 Mt Vernon Dv, Decatur, GA 30030 . . . . |
Paull MISS Sarah Christian (Robert C) . . . . Born at
    Santa Cruz, CA Jly 26'95
Paulson MR John F . . see E G Cumming
Payson, Parker L & Macpherson, Marian—So'87.Ch'93
    ☎ (703) 768-3676 . . 2403 Daphne Lane, Alexandria, VA 22306
Pease MR Roland F—Un.Chr.Mto.Plg.Myf.Vca. | 45 E 72 St,
    Rv.Cw.Ne.StJ.Cl'48 . . . . | New York, NY
    MISS Deborah S . . . . | 10021
Peck MR H Rollinson JR . . . . Died Feb 9'94
Peck MR & MRS William H (Mary Q Weeks) Y'36.H'39
    ☎ (203) 264-1861 . . 632B Heritage Village, Southbury, CT 06488

Pedley MRS Eric L (McGettigan—Molly Fay) . . . . Died at
    Belvedere, CA Dec 30'95
Peebles MR & MRS Emory B JR (Butler—Ford—Barbara W Cowan)
    Ala'45.Dar.Cit'39
    ☎ (334) 476-0546 . . 110 Canongate, 2404 Springhill Av, Mobile,
    AL 36607
Peet MR Robert M . . . . Died at
    Hanover, NH Oct 23'95
Pell MR & MRS Peter J (Corey—Christine Benson) | ☎ (516) 671-1971
    Post'84.Rc.Pr.Post'67 . . . . | 6 Libby Dv,
    MISS Christine M Corey—at | Glen Cove, NY
    ☎ (360) 943-4010 . . 1262 NE Glass St, | 11542
    Olympia, WA 98506 . . . . |
    MISS Cynthia E Corey—at 6 Windsor Dv, |
    Old Westbury, NY 11568 . . . . |
    MR Alan L Corey 4th . . . . |
    MR R William Corey . . . . |
Pendergast MR Jeffrey R
    ☎ (610) 525-0768 . . 17 Hawthorne Lane, Rosemont, PA 19010
Pennington MR & MRS James Sutton 3d (Jennie R Collis) Stan'65.Stan'64
    ☎ (518) 372-7503 . . 2276 Sweetbriar Rd, Niskayuna, NY 12309
Pennington MR & MRS Stuart W (Mary Melonakis) | ☎ (206) 885-1054
    DU'70.DU'69 . . . . | 14502 NE 61 St,
    MR Mark . . . . | Redmond, WA
    JUNIORS MISS Christine . . . . | 98052-4680
    JUNIORS MR Daniel . . . . |
Perkins MISS Courtney Lee-Anne (g—Frederic B Perkins) . . . . . . Born at
    Austin, TX Mch 10'95
Perkins MR & MRS Gilman (Rebecca D Mastin)
    ☎ (716) 264-9985 . . 14 Tobey Court, Pittsford, NY 14534
Perkins MR & MRS Gilman C (Deborah S Hower) Van'84.StLaw'77
    ☎ (203) 222-0663 . . 375 Sasco Hill Rd, Fairfield, CT 06430
Perkins MR & MRS Stephen L (Vause—Paula J | ☎ (610) 293-1001
    Wiltshire) Va'74.Me.Cry.Ac.Pa'89 . . . . | 609 S Valley Forge
    JUNIORS MR Ryan W . . . . | Rd, Wayne, PA
    | 19087
Perkins MR & MRS William Whittington (Betty A Malvaney) LSU'49
    ☎ (601) 833-1748 . . 1595 Smith Lake Rd NE, Brookhaven, MS 39601
Perot MR Edward S 3d
    ☎ (714) 347-8466 . . 25834 Avatar, Laguna Niguel, CA 92677
Perrier MASTER Lucas Wright (g—MRS Barbara W Gatje) . . . . . . Born at
    New York, NY Jly 1'95
Perry MR & MRS Allen Wade (Black—Judith | ☎ (617) 259-0336
    Sinclair) Bost'68.Cv.H.'62.Cl'65.Y'72 . . . . | 97 Lincoln Rd,
    MISS Heather S Black—at ☎ (212) 535-1469 | Lincoln, MA 01773
    1360 York Av, Apt 3D, New York, NY 10021 |
    MR Andrew A Black—at Colby . . . . |
Perry MR I Newton JR . . . . Died at
    Santa Barbara, CA Feb 13'95
Perry DR J Mitchell—Pac'80
    ☎ (209) 477-9494 . . 3379 Fairway Dv, Stockton, CA 95204-1107
Perry MR & MRS Winston C (Zahnzinger—Andrea J Hiller) Ty'58
    ☎ (617) 934-2411 . . ''Perrydise'' 66 Elder Brewster Rd, Duxbury,
    MA 02332
Pershing COL John W—USA. (late F Warren) . Married at New York, NY
    Bergen MRS S Sinclair (Lloyd—Sandra Sinclair) . . . . Oct 25'95

Peterkin MR & MRS Patrick O'B (Jennifer M Wieland) CarnM'86.Nu'95.Yn.W&L'85
☎ (203) 655-0359 . . 33 Brookside Rd, Darien, CT *06820*
Peters MR James G
☎ (520) 648-8314 . . 501 La Posada Circle, Apt 190, Green Valley, AZ *85614*
Peters MISS Marjorie S—Bab'89
☎ (703) 418-1010 . . 801 N Pitt St, Alexandria, VA *22314*
Peters MR Preston H—Cl'64
☎ (860) 824-5088 . . 2 Puddlers Lane, Falls Village, CT *06031*
Petersen MR Howard C . . . . Died at Radnor, PA Dec 28'95
Pettit DR Horace . . . . Died at Gladwyne, PA Sep 11'95
Pettus MR & MRS Robert C (Sharon A Wright) Wash'63 . . . .
MISS Airlia W—at 9515 Park Lane, St Louis, MO *63124* . . . .
☎ (520) 624-5330 PO Box 85293, Tucson, AZ *85754-5293*
Petty MRS Lee M (H Lee Mills) V'52.Cvc.T . . . .
MISS Victoria L—at ☎ (503) 635-4378 1 Jefferson P'kway, Apt 105, Lake Oswego, OR *97035* . . . .
☎ (301) 654-1813 37 W Lenox St, Chevy Chase, MD *20815*
Petty MASTER Russell Morgan (L Talmage) . . . . Born at Rockville, MD Mch 4'95
Peyton REV & MRS F Bradley 4th (Joan A D'Adamo) Md'81.Md'89.Cc.Va'72.Va'75.VaTheo'84 . . . . .
JUNIORS MISS K Ashby—at Marvelwood . . . .
JUNIORS MR F Bradley 5th . . . .
☎ (301) 609-8596 1020 Wiltshire Dv, La Plata, MD *20646-3510*
Pfeil MRS (REV) Susan M (Susan Magro) Y'94.Yn . . .
MISS Anneliese—Dth'92—at 284 Mott St, Apt 9P, New York, NY *10012* . . . .
☎ (203) 966-7271 275A Park St, New Canaan, CT *06840*
Pfingst MR & MRS Osborne JR (Eleanor F Cannon) Pc.
☎ (215) 643-7388 . . 9 High Gate Lane, Blue Bell, PA *19422*
Pflager MR Charles D (Godfrey H) . . . . Married at Bronx, NY Boutsolis MISS Alexandra (Christos) . . . . Oct 15'95
Phelps MRS Reginald H (Julia G Sears) . . . . Died at Cambridge, MA Oct 4'95
Phelps MR Taylor . . . . Died at Half Moon Bay, CA Oct 14'95
Phelps MRS Thomas W (Cameron—Christine Reed) . . . . Died at Nantucket, MA Jan 14'96
Phillips MR Asa E JR . . . . Died at Boston, MA Sep 24'95
Phillips MR & MRS Francis F (Chara D Church)
☎ (908) 363-8858 . . Harrogate B2200, 400 Locust St, Lakewood, NJ *08701*
Phillips, Steven P & Siegman, Jessica L—Cal'80.SanJ'88
☎ (916) 971-0878 . . 4220 Boone Lane, Sacramento, CA *95821*
Phillips MRS William M (Elizabeth P Colahan)
☎ (215) 984-8355 . . Cathedral Village I505, 600 E Cathedral Rd, Philadelphia, PA *19128*
Phipps MR Frank H 4th
☎ (904) 362-3015 . . 11193—198 Terr, O'Brien, FL *32071*
Phister MRS Lispenard B (Fox—Eunice Jameson) . . . . Died at Clearwater Beach, FL Feb 15'96

Phyfe MISS Edith A (Churchill B) . . . . Married at Darien, CT Walsh DR Arthur W (late John K) . . . . Oct 13'95
Pickett MISS Jocelyn M—Ty'93 . . see W I Hollingsworth 3d
Pierce MR & MRS Robert W JR (Carroll C Driscoll) HWSth'86.Col'75
☎ (617) 720-3923 . . 35 Brimmer St, Boston, MA *02108-1001*
Pilkington MR & MRS Charles F (Katherine B Scott) StLaw'92.Rcn.Mb.WashColl'91
☎ (610) 975-0705 . . 1255 Gulph Creek Dv, Radnor, PA *19087*
Pilling MRS J Ross (Bettie Keen) . . . . Died at Philadelphia, PA Nov 13'95
Pilling CAPT (RET) J Ross—USN.H'47
☎ (610) 645-8975 . . 1400 Waverly Rd, Apt A223, Gladwyne, PA *19035*
Pilling MISS Margaret E (John F) . . . . Married at Mantoloking, NJ Rux MR William L (late William L) . . . . Sep 23'95
Pillsbury MR Charles S B . . see J B Britton
Pingeon MR & MRS Hendon C (Kate C Mali) Ken'84.Roan'84
☎ (617) 259-8849 . . 9 Baker Bridge Rd, Lincoln, MA *01773*
Pinkard MRS Walter D (Anne M Merrick) Gchr'46.Elk.Md.Mv.
613 Brightwood Club Dv, Lutherville, MD *21093*
Pinkham MR & MRS Arthur D JR (Margaret H Merker) Rcn.Cly.Chi.Ncd . . .of
☎ (617) 266-8885 . . 160 Commonwealth Av, Boston, MA *02116*
"Pumpkin Hill Farm" 106 Colts Pond Rd, Ashford, CT *06278*
Piro DR & MRS Philip A JR (Marion W Jones) Hlns'75.Bcs.So.Unn.Myf.Cda.Y'74
☎ (203) 661-0802 . . Conyers Farm Dv, Greenwich, CT *06831*
Pitou MR David W—Wag'56 . . . .
MR Jeremy D . . . .
☎ (718) 984-0900 20 Edgewood Rd, Staten Island, NY *10308*
Pitts MASTER Alexander Morgan (Paris T) . . . . Born at Kirkland, WA Nov 28'95
Pitts MR & MRS Paris T (Lynn E Ferrarini) Whit'91.Van'88
☎ (206) 957-0428 . . 16949 NE 19 Place, Bellevue, WA *98008*
Pizzinat MR & MRS Arthur Franklin (Julia Wingfield) Stan'52.Vh.Stan'56
☎ (805) 969-3868 . . 1419 Sea Meadow Place, Montecito, CA *93108*
Pizzinat MASTER Emerson Christopher (g—Arthur Franklin Pizzinat) . . . . Born at Santa Barbara, CA Dec 10'95
Place MISS Sabrina C—Skd'89 . . see MRS C S-H Bowers
Player MISS Elizabeth C—Ty'93 . . see J L Adams
Player MR Samuel L—Wes'91 . . see J L Adams
Plum MR & MRS Roy R (Horn—Katherine F Foshay) Ng.Cly.Y'60 . . . .
MR Richard R—at ☎ (212) 879-6146 340 E 72 St, New York, NY *10021* . . . .
MR Fraser M Horn—at ☎ (970) 827-9353 Box 75, Minturn, CO *81645* . . . .
MR Geoffrey M Horn—at ☎ (212) 288-5527 315 E 70 St, New York, NY *10021* . . . .
☎ (561) 546-7646 6 Isle Ridge W, Hobe Sound, FL *33455*
Poinier MRS John (Lawrence—Lois P Wodell) Shcc.Msq.
☎ (908) 781-6522 . . "Vixen's Lair" Box 192, Gladstone, NJ *07934*
Pollock MISS Deborah W . . . . Married at Denver, CO Parkman MR John M (James) . . . . Aug 28'93
Pollock MR Edward L (Oren T) . . . . Married at Lake Forest, IL Wittig MISS Elizabeth S (Robert V) . . . . Oct 1'95
Ponvert MRS Joan L (Joan C Lynott) . . . . Died at Locust Valley, NY Nov 6'95

Pool MR Charles Chauncey—Y'35
Caller 9000, Water Mill, NY *11976*
Pool MR & MRS Eugene H (L Parrish Dobson) ☎ (617) 489-2829
Y'71.Brand'80.H.'64 . . . . 263 Payson Rd,
MR Nathan B—at San Ramon, CA *94583* . . . . . Belmont, MA *02178*
Pool MRS G Hansen (Gillette K Hansen) . . . . ☎ (303) 333-2220
MR Fred W 3d 401 Gilpin St,
MR Henry B . . . . Denver, CO *80218*
JUNIORS MR Wyllys L . . . .
Poole MRS E McHugh (Suwal—Ernestine L McHugh) . . . . name changed to McHugh
Poole MR Fitz John P—Nu'68.Cr'70.Cr'76
☎ (619) 944-9668 . . 2358 Cambridge Av, Cardiff-By-The-Sea, CA *92007-2002*
Poole MISS Sara Elisabeth (Edward G) . . . . Born at
San Francisco, CA Jan 22'96
Pooley MR & MRS John A (Mary L Gardner) D.
☎ (704) 884-5645 . . 17 Tsisdu Court, Connestee Falls, Brevard, NC *28712*
Pope MR Edward J . . . . Died at
Washington, DC Dec 23'95
Pope MISS Laura Marie (g—Eric Hoffman) . . . . Born at
Portland, OR Jun 21'95
Porter MR C Burnham . . . . Died at
Danvers, MA Sep 6'95
Porter MISS Deborah A (Frank B JR) . . . . Married at Cambridge, MA
Glenn MR Cooper L Oct 28'95
Post MR & MRS Christopher C (Jennifer Fortenbaugh) Hlns'76.Wash'77
☎ (518) 851-5950 . . PO Box 521, Claverack, NY *12513*
Post MR & MRS Edward Everett (Smith—Harriet C ☎ (802) 985-9242
Bottomley) V'40.C.Cs.H.'33.Nu'41 . . . . 610 Wake Robin
MISS Dorothy S—at ☎ (617) 527-1862 Dv, Shelburne, VT
24 Brookdale Rd, Newtonville, MA *02160* *05482*
Potter MISS Alexandra Peabody (Charles S JR) . . . . Born at
Billings, MT Oct 11'95
Potter MR & MRS Charles S JR (Julia B Peabody) DU'83.On.Rcch.Nw'82
☎ (406) 655-9155 . . "The Rims" 4626 Arapaho Lookout, Billings, MT *59106*
Potter DR & MRS Robert T (Helena A Wolfe) Sth'52.H'46.H'52
☎ (941) 475-6385 . . 8270 Manasota Key Rd, Englewood, FL *34223*
Potts MRS Frederic (Eshleman—Phoebe L Davis) . . . . . . name changed to Eshleman
Powell MR & MRS John (Margaret L Proper) Mid'56.Colg'52.Cl'58
☎ (602) 991-0212 . . 5347 E Royal Palm Rd, Paradise Valley, AZ *85253*
Powers MR John M JR . . . . Died at
Radnor, PA Jan 15'96
Pratt MR & MRS Carl E (M Julie Hogan) ☎ (513) 231-6332
Cin'70.Xav'77.Cc.Xav'67.Xav'75.Cin'77.Xav'86 1159 Sutton Rd,
JUNIORS MR Carl E JR . . . . Cincinnati, OH
MRS Everard S JR (Susan C Slough)— *45230-3538*
☎ (513) 231-7930 . . . .
Pratt MR Everard S JR . . . . Died Apr 12'91
Pratt MR Henry C . . . . Died at
Ft Washington, PA Aug 18'95
Prentice MR Bryant H JR . . . . Died at
Santa Barbara, CA Jan 29'96
Prentice MRS Pierrepont Isham (Pflieger—Janet McNeir) . . . . Died at
Belleair, FL Oct 25'95
Preyer MR & MRS Britt Armfield (Alice C Dockery) ☎ (910) 275-6442
Salem'77.Cda.David'75 . . . . 1508 Kirkpatrick
JUNIORS MR Britt A JR . . . . Place, Greensboro, NC *27408*
Price MRS Gregory F (Helen Piersol)
Mediplex, 162 S Britain Rd, Southbury, CT *06488*
Prince MR Patrick B Wood . . see E T Chewing JR
Prince MR Scott C Wood . . see E T Chewning JR
Prince MR William N W—Rcn.Sr.Rc.Cho.Srb.Van'64
☎ (312) 787-2832 . . 303 W Wisconsin St, Chicago, IL *60614*
Prockop MR & MRS David J (Hope S Nichols) H'90.Wms'87.Tufts'93 . . of
☎ (860) 651-4336 . . Westminster School, 995 Hopmeadow St, Simsbury, CT *06070*
☎ (802) 365-9105 . . River Rd, Box 448, Newfane, VT *05345*
Proctor MR & MRS Kenneth C (Baker—Margaret Leonard)
Swb'42.Mv.JHop'28.Md'32
☎ (410) 323-8081 . . 101 Cross Keys Rd, Apt B, Baltimore, MD *21210*
Proctor MASTER Trey Williams (Robert W) . . . . Born at
Hartford, CT Nov 5'95
Prout MR & MRS John R T (Weldon—Judith de Barany)
Ws'77.H'80.Cly.H'75 . . of
☎ (011-33-1) 47-42-22-69 . . 52 rue du Faubourg St Honoré, 75008 Paris, France
☎ (011-33) 37-47-20-99 . . 2 rue des Ormes, Vilsix, 28800 Pré-St-Evroult, France
Prouty MISS Honor H—Pitzer'93
☎ (310) 207-6764 . . 11959 Mayfield Av, Apt 5, Los Angeles, CA *90049*
Prouty MR Nicholas A—Pitzer'92
☎ (212) 987-9829 . . 55 E 93 St, New York, NY *10128*
Prouvost MR & MRS Amédée S (Clare H Cushman)
Mid'84.Paris'94.Paris'82.Pa'90
3615 Spring St, Chevy Chase, MD *20815*
Pryor MR & MRS Edward R (Beverly B Jones) Va'56
☎ (860) 536-9746 . . 6 Hickory Ledge, Mason's Island, Mystic, CT *06355*
Pryor MRS Luanne W (Van Norden—Luanne R Williamson)
CalSt'71.H'84.Cly.H.
☎ (617) 247-2366 . . 181 Marlborough St, Boston, MA *02116*
Psoroyannis MISS Ioanna R . . see MRS P A Taylor
Pugh MISS (DR) Elizabeth W (Schwarckoff—Elizabeth W Pugh)
Rens'80.Tul'89.Tul'93
☎ (410) 666-5276 . . 10702 Cardington Way, Apt 202, Cockeysville, MD *21030*
Pugh MR & MRS William W (Elizabeth J Ritter) Sth'41.Mit'44
☎ (513) 533-4476 . . 3509 Forestoak Court, Cincinnati, OH *45208*
Pulling MR Edward L—P'89
☎ (011-852-5) 849-7451 . . 3-5 Plunketts Rd, Modreenagh Apt 3A, The Peak, Hong Kong
Pumphrey MR & MRS Edward A 3d (Elisabeth A A Ehrhorn) Cda.Ithaca'76
537 Aberdeen Rd, Frankfort, IL *60423*
Purser MR & MRS Carr R JR (Susan W Hunter) 4511 Windsor Park,
Pa'66 . . . . Sarasota, FL *34236*
JUNIORS MR Carr R 3d . . . .
Purviance MRS Akeroyd (Edith Akeroyd) Sg.
☎ (610) 645-8842 . . 1400 Waverly Rd, Apt 116, Gladwyne, PA *19035*

Purvis MR & MRS J Oliver JR (Clover Du Val) StJ'34
☎ (410) 832-1736 . . Pickensville Apt 1422, 615 Chestnut Av, Towson, MD *21204*
Putnam MR Alfred W . . . . Died at Philadelphia, PA Nov 12'95
Putnam MR Gerald R . . . . Died Jun 18'94
Pyle MR & MRS Robert N (Crosier—Claire Thoron)
B'gton'65.Ct.Dick'48 . . . .
MR Louis M Crosier—Dth'87 . . . .
☎ (202) 338-9039
2613 Dumbarton St NW, Washington, DC *20007*

Q

Quarton MISS Anne K . . see R H Miller
Quarton JUNIORS MR Bradley R . . see R H Miller
Quist MR & MRS Robert L (Leslie P Madeira)
Cal'75.Bhm.Pcu.Cal'75 . . . .
JUNIORS MISS Lauren S . . . .
JUNIORS MR William G . . . .
☎ (415) 851-7572
219 Albion Av, Woodside, CA *94062*

R

Raffetto REV & MRS Edward C JR (Elizabeth D Purnell) Gv.Geo'64 . . . .
JUNIORS MR Charles P . . . .
☎ (410) 778-6694
301 Main St, Church Hill, MD *21623-1278*
Ramsey MRS Mercy Essig (Prader—Mercy L R Essig) . . . . Married at Stockton, NJ
Freeman MR Melvin . . . . Dec 23'95
Rankin MR & MRS Alfred M JR (Victoire C Griffin)
Man'vl'64.Kt.Mt.Cv.Tv.Un.Rr.Sl.Y'63 . . . .
MISS Clara T—at 2600 N Southport Av, Chicago, IL *60614*
☎ (216) 269-8222
7421 Markell Rd, Waite Hill, OH *44094*
Ratcliffe MRS Myron F (Margaret E Archibald) Cho.Ih.Cas.Cnt.
"La Casa Pequeña" 1008 Fairway Rd, Montecito, CA *93108*
Rathborne MRS Carol S (Carol Simmons) Man'vl'69.Mds.
☎ (212) 223-0022 . . 485 Park Av, New York, NY *10022*
Rauch MR & MRS R Stewart (Frances S Brewster)
Ph.Gm.Me.Fic.Rb.Ri.Pn.P.'36
☎ (610) 527-3321 . . 13 Pond Lane, Bryn Mawr, PA *19010*
Raurell-Soto MR A Miguel . . see R L Forbes
Ravenel MR Curtis deSt Julien . . see J H Fair JR
Ravenel MR Ramsay M . . see J H Fair JR
Ravenel MISS Tiphaine T . . see J H Fair JR
Rawls MR & MRS William H (Mary M Holmes) H'57
MR Timothy F—at ☎ (206) 782-3998
2641 NW 57 St, Seattle, WA *98107* . . .
Beaver Pond, Beverly, MA *01915*
Reardon DR & MRS James J JR (Miller—Robin A Arbon) S.Ck.Mto.Cly.StJ'61.SUNY'65 . . . .
JUNIORS MISS J Alexes—at Marymount Sch . . . . .
JUNIORS MR J Ashe—at Browning . . . .
☎ (212) 722-2152
128 E 95 St, New York, NY *10128*
Reardon MR & MRS Mark C (Elizabeth K Rich) Pac'89.Pac'87.Cal'93
☎ (847) 735-1321 . . 775 E Illinois Rd, Lake Forest, IL *60045*

Redfield MR & MRS Christopher McK (Carol A Holmes)
Duke'83.Mit'87.P'85.Mit'87
☎ (415) 917-8754 . . 1101 Los Altos Av, Los Altos, CA *94022*
Redfield MISS Elizabeth C (Cowles—Elizabeth C Redfield) . . . . . Married at Palm Beach, FL
Atterbury MR William W 3d (late William Wallace) . . . . . . Nov 11'95
Redfield MISS Emily Holmes (Christopher McK) . . . . Born Sep 19'95
Redpath MISS Christine P (Frederick L) . . . . . . Married at Gladwyne, PA
Soleau MR William C . . . . Aug 7'95
Redpath MR & MRS Frederick L (Long—Deborah B Law) Pn.P'39 . . . .
MR Bruce L . . . .
☎ (610) 645-8652
1400 Waverly Rd, Villa 3, Gladwyne, PA *19035*
Reece MR & MRS Christopher S (Elizabeth L Riemer)
Ty'78.Cy.San.Cw.Chi.Pa'72
☎ (617) 320-8577 . . 1061 High St, Dedham, MA *02026*
Reed MR Adrian W (Nathaniel P) . . . . Married at Park City, UT
Roberts MISS Michelle (Sonnie) . . . . Mch 27'93
Reed MASTER Benjamin Whitaker (g—Nathaniel P Reed) . . . . Born Nov 24'95
Reed MRS C Lawson (Dorothy Whittaker) Qc.Cm.Yn.
☎ (513) 321-6833 . . 419 Torrence Court, Cincinnati, OH *45202*
Reed MR & MRS H Mason JR (Marguerite Mann) Rr.P'54
☎ (203) 966-5494 . . 141 Hemlock Hill Rd, New Canaan, CT *06840*
Reed MASTER Nathaniel Pryor 3d (Nathaniel P JR) . . . . Born at Charlottesville, VA Mch 1'96
Reed MRS Robert Lafayette (Susan Albright) . . . . Died at Madison, WI Oct 9'95
Reeve MISS Cintra Lowell (Rossi—Cintra L Reeve) Briar'68
☎ (508) 927-3994 . . "Rockmarge" Prides Crossing, MA *01965*
Reeves MR & MRS William H 4th (Suzanne Evans) Swb'68.NCar'66.Pa'71 . . . .
MISS Elizabeth S—at ☎ (415) 673-7427
1550 Bay St, Apt 258, San Francisco, CA *94123*
MR William Evans—at ☎ (415) 292-7369
1312 Fulton St, San Francisco, CA *94117* . . . . .
☎ (401) 621-8848
175 Upton Av, Providence, RI *02906*
Regalbuto MR & MRS Jason R (Wilder O Bishop) PineM'91.BtP.
☎ (407) 655-1886 . . 160 Seabreeze Av, Palm Beach, FL *33480*
Reich MR & MRS Christopher V (Eleanor M Paschal) Nu'91.Dth'80
☎ (914) 253-8336 . . 70 Westerleigh Rd, Purchase, NY *10577*
Reich MASTER George Scoville (Christopher V) . . . . Born at New York, NY Feb 5'94
Reichner MR Aiken—Cw.Sar.Cc.P'47 . . . .
MISS Cristina—P'95—at Georgetown Med . . . . .
☎ (561) 659-7479
LaFontana Apt 105, 2800 N Flagler Dv, West Palm Beach, FL *33407*
Reid MRS B Trowbridge (Sheriff—White—Barbara W Trowbridge) Va'63 . . . .
MISS Nathalie H Sheriff—at 7 Lewis St, Portland, ME *04101* . . . .
☎ (860) 535-4135
75 Main St, Stonington, CT *06378-1222*
Reid MR Bagley—Fic.Va'59
☎ (212) 371-0821 . . 400 E 57 St, New York, NY *10022*
Reid LT & MRS Daniel F M (Andrea R McEuen)
USN.SwTex'86.CalSt'89.Leh'85
3323 Hickory Falls Dv, Kingwood, TX *77345*

Reid MRS Dorian F (Betty G Sharley) . . . . Died at
    Atherton, CA Apr 9'95
Reinicke MR & MRS F Rogers (Dalais—Judith A | ☎ (212) 427-3681
    MacGuire) Woos'49.Cl'51 . . . . | 1100 Park Av,
    MISS Mary J MacGuire—Man'vl'87 . . . . | New York, NY
    MR Sean M MacGuire . . . . | *10128*
Reiniger MASTER Alexander Graham (Harlan deC) . . . . Born at
    Winchester, MA Mch 16'95
Reiniger MR & MRS Harlan deC (Jane D Maurer) AMag'78.Bost'80.Emer'87
    ☎ (617) 631-3180 . . 4 Linden St, Marblehead, MA *01945*
Remer MRS John H JR (Mary F Scott) Bost'73
    ☎ (610) 688-0516 . . "Ardrossan" 811 Newtown Rd, Villanova,
    PA *19085*
Remer MR John H JR—Col'73 . . of
    ☎ (302) 995-1559 . . PO Box 3720, Wilmington, DE *19807*
    ☎ (212) 355-1214 . . 340 E 52 St, New York, NY *10022*
Remington MR & MRS David F (Chelsey A Carrier) | ☎ (508) 456-8889
    Br'61.H'64 . . . . | 3 Depot Rd,
    MISS Chelsey A—Br'89.Pa'95—at | General Delivery,
    1840 Jefferson St, Apt 201, San Francisco, CA | Still River, MA
    94123 . . . . | *01467*
Remington MR & MRS Thomas R (Frances Whitehead)
    Cy.Nd.P'51.H'56 . . of
    9 Cedar Crest, St Louis, MO *63132-4205*
    ☎ (941) 697-5985 . . "Tween Waters Cottage" Palm Island,
    7092 Placida Rd, Cape Haze, FL *33946*
Reno DR & MRS Stephen J (Catherine R Motley)
    Elmira'74.StJColl'65.Cal'66
    ☎ (541) 482-3044 . . 610 Elkander St, Ashland, OR *97520*
Reque DR & MRS Paul G (Barbara T Britton) | 3850 Galleria
    Duke'33 . . . . | Woods Dv, Apt 215,
    MR Peter A—at 1073 Bush St, San Francisco, CA | Birmingham, AL
    94109 . . . . | *35244*
    MISS Susan B (Aldridge—Susan B Reque)—at
    312 E Glenwood Dv, Birmingham, AL *35209* . .
Resnik MR & MRS Michael D (Janet M Depping) | ☎ (919) 929-3324
    V'60.Y'60 . . . . | "Pegasus Farm"
    MISS Sarah L—NCar'92 . . . . | 132 Collins
    MR Dimitri—NCar'88 . . . . | Mountain Rd,
    | Chapel Hill, NC
    | *27516*
Reuben MR & MRS Michael B (Susan B Miller)
    Ford'76.H'79.H'73.Stan'77.Stan'80.H'82
    ☎ (212) 570-9486 . . 70 E 77 St, Apt 7A, New York, NY *10021*
Reynolds MR R Roland—P'93 . . see MRS M Ballentine
Rezny MRS Catherine M (Read—Catherine | 2120 Sonoma Av,
    Minnick) Pa'41 . . . . | Apt 19, Santa Rosa,
    MISS Karen K—at ☎ (512) 472-3329 | CA *95405*
    2500 Nueces St, Austin, TX *78705* . . . .
Rhein MRS Jean-Pierre F (Wills—BRNSS Ludmilla M Forani)
    Brussels'59.Duke'66.Rut'72
    ☎ (011-33-1) 42-23-51-91 . . 102 Chemin du Puy du Roy,
    13090 Aix-en-Provence, France
Rhinelander MR Philip M (late Philip H) . . . . . Married at Falmouth, ME
    Sears MRS S White (Sonzski—Susannah White) . . . . Jan 6'96
Rhinelander MR & MRS Philip M (Sonzski—Sears— | ☎ (207) 846-4970
    Susannah White) Sth'62.H'65 . . . . | RR 3, Box 403D,
    MISS Katharine C Sears—at Stanford . . . . . . | Browns Point Rd,
    MR Edmund H Sears JR . . . . | Yarmouth, ME
    | *04096*
Rhinelander MRS T J Oakley (Brainard—Kelley—Tatiana Holmsen) . Died
    at Newport, RI Dec 14'95
Rhodes MRS Augustine J (McKinney—Augustine W Janeway) Pa'51
    520 Fearrington Post, Pittsboro, NC *27312*
Rial MR William S JR . . . . Died at
    Pittsburgh, PA Oct 6'95
Rianhard MR Perry D JR (Perry D) . . . . Married at Burlington, VT
    Thomas MISS Kelly J . . . . Jun 18'95
Rice MRS Anton H JR (Lydia Sands) . . . . Died at
    Ardsley-on-Hudson, NY Jun 21'95
Richards MR John T L JR (John T L) . . . . Married at Alexandria, VA
    Bruns MISS H Jordan (Eugene) . . . . Feb 17'96
Richards MISS Raquel L (Alfred L 3d) . . . . Married at Malvern, PA
    Meyer MR Todd J . . . . Apr 8'95
Richards MR William B—Me.Denis'67 . . . . | ☎ (212) 684-7595
    MR William B JR—at ☎ (916) 925-5003 | 38 E 37 St, PH,
    1100 Howe Av, Apt 426, Sacramento, CA *95825* | New York, NY
    MR Robert A—at U of Cal Santa Barbara . . . . . . | *10016*
Richardson MRS Harris S JR (Albach—Margaret Kent) . . Died Jan 20'95
Richardson DR & MRS William C (Nancy Freeland)
    Sth'62.Cos.Ty'62.Ch'64.Ch'71
    ☎ (616) 671-5175 . . 4392 E Gull Lake Dv, Hickory Corners, MI *49060*
Richey MR & MRS John M (Barbara Bray) Gchr'56.Rcn.Mds.Ty'43
    2810 Cardinal Dv, Vero Beach, FL *32963*
Riegel MR & MRS William M (Nickerson—Nancy C | of ☎ (617)934-5161
    Bailey) V'57.H.'61.Chi.Wms'50 . . . . | 14 Surplus St,
    MR Joshua B Nickerson—Geo'92—at | Duxbury, MA *02332*
    U of Va Law . . . . | ☎ (602) 481-6024
    | 5101 N Casa Blanca
    | Rd, Scottsdale, AZ
    | *85253*
    | ☎ (901) 761-4328
    | 5400 Park Av,
    | Apt 217, Memphis,
    | TN *38119*
Riepe MR & MRS James S (Gail N Petty) Pa'68.Gv.Md.Mv.Pa'65.Pa'67
    ☎ (410) 329-3925 . . 14921 Tanyard Rd, Sparks, MD *21152*
Riggs MR Lawrason JR . . . . Died at
    Nantucket, MA Jan 22'96
Ringe MR & MRS Henry Ralph 2d (Sarah T Funk) | ☎ (609) 596-0599
    RI'71.Sap.F&M'62 . . . . | 605 Westerly Dv,
    MISS Jennifer T—Mid'88 . . . . | Marlton, NJ *08053*
    MISS V Alexandra—Wes'92—at 272 Sixth Av,
    Apt 2L, Brooklyn, NY *11215* . . . .
    MR Benjamin Rhoads—Del'93—at 1026 Pine St,
    Apt 3, Philadelphia, PA *19107* . . . .
Ripley MISS Rosemary L (Lanius—Rosemary L Ripley) Y.'76.Y'80.Cly.
    ☎ (212) 860-9051 . . 55 E 86 St, New York, NY *10028*
Rippel MRS G Crivelli (Colapinto—Gioconda M C Crivelli) . . . .
    name changed to Crivelli

Ritchie MR & MRS John B (Suzanne Raisin) B.Fr.Y'46.Cal'49 . . . .
   MR Randolph B . . . .
   MR Mark H—at ☎ (415) 771-9474
   1055 California St, San Francisco, CA *94104* . .
   MISS Charlotte S (Hogan—Charlotte S Ritchie)— at 21 Marinero Circle, Apt 203, Tiburon, CA *94920* . . . .
   of ☎ (415)921-2250 1201 Greenwich St, Apt 400, San Francisco, CA *94109*
   ☎ (808) 926-5515 Niihau Penthouse, 247 Beach Walk, Waikiki, Honolulu, HI *96815*

Ritter MISS Lucinda U (William B) . . . . Married at Jamestown, RI Jackman MR George A (Frank T) . . . . Sep 16'95

Robb MR James S . . . . Died at Bealeton, VA Oct 17'95

Robbins MR & MRS Hanson C (Chase—Linda H Morrison) MaryW'63.H'59.Cl'64 . . . .
   MISS Christine D Chase—at New York, NY .
   MR Eric H Chase—at Bethlehem, NH *03574* .
   ☎ (617) 266-1321 207 Commonwealth Av, Apt 9, Boston, MA *02116*

Robbins MR Noel . . . . Died Jan 14'96

Robe MR & MRS Robert S JR (Lucy B Barry) Rdc'55.S.StA.Va'56.NYTech'76.LIU'86 . . . . . .
   MISS Parrish C—Rol'95 . . . .
   ☎ (407) 627-6815 509 Sea Oats Dv, Apt D1, Juno Beach, FL *33408-1433*

Roberts MRS H Radcliffe (E Hazel Warden) ☎ (610) 645-8653 . . Waverley Heights, Villa 4, 1400 Waverley Rd, Gladwyne, PA *19035*

Roberts MRS John M 3d (Arminta Kapphahn) . . . . Died at Sewickley, PA Sep 11'94

Roberts MASTER Zachary John (g—John R Burdick) . . . . Born at Chester, SC May 30'94

Robertson MRS Edward L JR (Pearsall—Jean Taussig) ☎ (561) 278-6469 . . Harbours Edge 461, 401 E Linton Blvd, Delray Beach, FL *33483*

Robertson MR & MRS William R (Anne Tuck) Sth'36.Cw.Cr'34 ☎ (603) 924-8654 . . 55 Colonial Square, Peterborough, NH *03458*

Robinson MR & MRS C David (Mary P Leonard) Bur.P'57.Pa'65 . . . .
   MISS Anne H—P'88.H'92—at 223 N Guadalupe St, Santa Fe, NM *87501* . . . .
   MR Edward B . . . .
   MR Steven L—Colg'95—at 30 W 63 St, New York, NY *10023* . . . .
   ☎ (415) 332-1470 54 Spencer Av, Sausalito, CA *94965*

Robinson MISS Elizabeth C—Col'90 ☎ (212) 628-9321 . . 303 E 83 St, Apt 105, New York, NY *10028*

Robinson MR & MRS H Ivens (Dodge Hobson) Ncmb'74.H'73 ☎ (504) 895-7555 . . 6028 Pitt St, New Orleans, LA *70118*

Robinson MR & MRS Hamilton JR (Alger—Roxana Barry) Ri.Bgt.C.P'55.H'60 ⚓ . . . .
   MISS Roxana S Alger—at ☎ (718) 768-8581 425—14 St, Brooklyn, NY *11215* . . . .
   of ☎ (212)421-8598 400 E 52 St, New York, NY *10022*
   ☎ (914) 232-9061 Willow Green Farm, 159 N Salem Rd, Katonah, NY *10536*

Robinson MASTER Jonathan Snowden (Samuel S JR) . . . . Born at Morristown, NJ Sep 2'93

Robinson MR & MRS Randall S (Charlotte U Hitchcock) Mit'55 ☎ (410) 472-4633 . . 12 Sparks Station Rd, Sparks, MD *21152*

Robinson MR Sanger P II . . see H G Cummings

Robinson MRS Wolcott de W JR (Jane C Bunn) . . . . Died Oct 25'95

Robinson MR Wolcott de W JR—Sap.Rv.Pa'63 ☎ (212) 725-0952 . . 40 Park Av, New York, NY *10016*

Robson MASTER Frederick Lawrence William (Rupert W) . . . . . . Born at London, England Jly 14'95

Robson MR & MRS Rupert W (E K Alexandra G Morris) Camb'91.Stan'93.Camb'89 ☎ (011-44-171) 603-1084 . . 15 Hofland Rd, London W14, England

Roche MR & MRS Thomas K (Knapp—Beverly Brady) S.P'39.Y'41 ⚓ . . . .
   MISS Barbara M . . . .
   ☎ (516) WA1-7543 "Poverty Pocket" 1782 Oyster Bay Rd, Syosset, NY *11791*

Rockwell MR & MRS Charles E JR (Madeline B Neilson) Mid'71.Mid'71 . . . .
   JUNIORS MISS Katherine L . . . .
   ☎ (802) 325-3534 Sykes Hollow Rd, Pawlet, VT *05761*

Rockwell MR & MRS Thorson (Melinda de W Highley) F'klinSwitz'82.Nyc.Srb. ☎ (212) 288-8167 . . 28 E 73 St, New York, NY *10021*

Rockwood MAJ & MRS Robert K (Margaret E Dolan) Geo'89.Ill'91.USA'82.Ill'91 ☎ (913) 784-4787 . . 435 Carpenter Av, Apt A, Ft Riley, KS *66442*

Rodd MISS Audrey Edith (g—David C Fuchs) . . . . Born at Cornwall, NY Nov 11'95

Rodiger MASTER Jonathan Amory (William K) . . . . Born at Newton, MA Jan 11'95

Rodiger MR & MRS William K (Heather L McKinney) Roch'86.SUNY'88.Dick'84.Syr'86 ☎ (508) 443-9435 . . 193 Morse Rd, Sudbury, MA *01776*

Roell REV Rudolph—D.P'33 . . of 600 Riomar Dv, Apt 5, Vero Beach, FL *32963* ☎ (617) 326-2342 . . 52 Village Av, Box 223, Dedham, MA *02026*

Roesler MRS Edward JR (Marshall—Frances E Kerr) ☎ (415) 851-1930 . . 501 Portola Rd, Box 8007, Portola Valley, CA *94028-7601*

Rogers MISS Beverly J . . . . Died at Burbank, CA Oct 24'95

Rogers MISS Diana V . . see W H Orrick JR

Rogers MR Edmund C . . . . Died in St Louis Co, MO Jan 10'96

Rogers MR H Elliott . . . . Died at Hilton Head Island, SC Dec 28'95

Rogers MR & MRS James H 3d (Margaret Frost) Col'59.Br'56.H'65 . . . .
   MISS Whitney H—Br'88—at 45 Tilden Av, Newport, RI *02840* . . . .
   MISS Jessica H—Br'93—at 247 W 87 St, Apt 10J, New York, NY *10024* . . . .
   ☎ (207) 326-8020 "Dotten House" Perkins St, PO Box 281, Castine, ME *04421*

Rogers MRS John G (Susanne V Bensinger) . . . . Married at San Francisco, CA
   Orrick MR William H JR (late William H) . . . . Jan 19'96

Rogers MR Peter M—H'76 ☎ (860) 379-3932 . . 153 Chapel Rd, Winchester Center, CT *06094*

Rohrbach MISS Emily Elizabeth (Gammon E) . . . . Born at
Alexandria, VA Dec 10'93
Rohrbach MR & MRS Gammon E (Mary E Carmichael) V'81
☎ (540) 255-9460 . . 9927 Steeple Run Court, Vienna, VA *22181*
Rolfe MISS Leslie Welch (Robert O) . . . . Born Mch 23'95
Rolfe MR & MRS Robert O (Kathy G Welch) Ala'82.Ala'82.Van'88
☎ (615) 385-4346 . . 505 Park Center Dv, Nashville, TN *37205-3429*
Romine MR David E (John R JR) . . . . Married at Southbury, CT
Kopple MISS (DR) Kathryn A (Alexander) . . . . Oct 7'95
Romine MR & MRS (DR) David E (Kathryn A Kopple)
B'gton'84.Nu'94.Hn.Cl'86.H'93
☎ (610) 617-7980 . . 300 N Essex Av, Apt 210B, Narberth, PA *19072*
Roosevelt MISS (DR) Anna C—Stan'68.Cl'77
☎ (847) 869-0422 . . 1028 Judson Av, Evanston, IL *60202*
Roosevelt MRS Quentin (Frances B Webb) . . . . Died at
Glen Cove, NY Sep 11'95
Root MR & MRS Anthony (Pamela J Peglau) BMr'76.Nu'80.Hav'75.Nu'82
☎ (011-852) 2849-8233 . . Mt Austin Estates H-D, 5 Mt Austin Rd,
The Peak, Hong Kong
Rork MR & MRS Allen Wright (Marilyn Greene) of ☎ (203)259-5322
Sth'67.Nu'71.Ford'95.Wms'66.H'68 . . . . 410 Galloping Hill
MISS Jennifer—Wms'95—at 181 North St, Rd, Fairfield, CT
Williamstown, MA *01267* *06430*
MISS Tamara—at Lafayette . . . . ☎ (802) 464-8910
"Greenspring"
Rte 100,
West Dover, VT
05356
Rose MISS Elizabeth L (R Peter) . . . . Married at Tucson, AZ
Picoli MR Robert C JR (Robert C) . . . . Nov 18'95
Rosenfeld MR & MRS Michael A (Bettina I Wulfing) Wash'83.Wes'83
☎ (213) 467-2372 . . 920 N Wilcox Av, Los Angeles, CA *90038*
Ross MRS Andrea C (Andrea G Courchene) ☎ (201) 543-2551
Shcc.Eyc.Mo.Eh. . . . . 14 Corey Lane,
MISS Allyson H . . . . Mendham, NJ *07945*
Ross MR & MRS Donald F (Elizabeth H Boardman)
Stan'42.Bhm.Fr.Cal'41.Stan'47
☎ (415) 854-4031 . . 125 Alta Vista Dv, Atherton, CA *94027*
Ross DR & MRS Donald F JR (Jeanne F Martin) ☎ (617) 244-3592
Woos'69.Wms'65.Tufts'66.Tufts'67.Tufts'74 . . 211 Winslow Rd,
JUNIORS MISS Elizabeth S . . . . Waban, MA *02168*
JUNIORS MASTER Anne N . . . .
Ross MR E Burke JR—Rcn.Shcc.Eyc.Mo.Eh.Pn.P'73.Ch'82
☎ (908) 766-0083 . . 85 Crest Dv, Bernardsville, NJ *07924*
Ross MASTER Morgan Channing (Thomas H) . . . . Born at
Bryn Mawr, PA Dec 18'95
Rouvina MISS Julia E—Mich'83 . . see C R Harvey
Rowan MISS Dorothy G—Br'82
☎ (212) 627-8578 . . 99 Bank St, Apt 4L, New York, NY *10014-2125*
Rowan MR Paul . . of
☎ (410) 819-8193 . . 27337 Rest Circle, Easton, MD *21601*
☎ (561) 231-0944 . . 550 Beach Rd, John's Island, Vero Beach,
FL *32963*
Rowley MR & MRS E Davis JR (Maria Cristina Pope) Cy.
42 Ogden Rd, Chestnut Hill, MA *02167-3732*

Roxby MAJ GEN (RET) & MRS William C JR (Corinne ☎ (215) 836-0121
T Romig) USAF.MtH'57.R.Pc.Rv.Wt.P. "Chantilly"
Leh'53.Cl'59 . . . . 701 Hunt Lane,
MISS Elisabeth C—P.'89.Pp.—at Flourtown, PA
☎ (212) 243-3501 . . 9 E 13 St, Apt 2J, *19031-1001*
New York, NY *10003* . . . .
MISS Susanna T—Roan'92.Pc.P.—at
☎ (215) 283-3258 . . 200 Tupelo Grove, Ambler,
PA *19002*
Royster DR Hubert A JR . . . . Died at
Blue Hill, ME Dec 22'95
Rudinger MRS Charles R (Kappler—Coe—Lillian C Norton) . . . . . Died at
Nassau, Bahamas Dec 18'95
Rumbough MR & MRS Stanley M JR (Janson—Janne Herlow)
Copen'64.Rcn.BtP.Mds.Ng.Evg.Y'42
☎ (407) 659-2230 . . 655 Island Dv, Palm Beach, FL *33480*
Rumery MR & MRS John R (Hall—Nancy Kluge) B'gton'46.Va'40
☎ (910) 295-6376 . . Box 1584, Linden Rd, Pinehurst, NC *28374*
Rundlett MRS Donald H (Mary Jane Keller) Skd'57 ☎ (407) 694-6750
MISS Elizabeth H—at ☎ (212) 982-9512 11666 Lost Tree
7 Lexington Av, Apt 7C, New York, NY *10010* Way, North Palm
Beach, FL *33408*
Rundlett MR Donald H JR—SL'91
☎ (503) 221-6239 . . 2014 NW Glison St, Apt 404, Portland, OR *97209*
Russell MR & MRS A Douglas JR (Marie-Caroline M ☎ (301) 299-5920
Masson) Paris'70.P'55.Pa'60 . . . . 9709 Sotweed Dv,
MISS Eugenia Isabelle C . . . . Potomac, MD *20854*
MR Alexis A Douglas . . . .
JUNIORS MR Adrien Philippe M M . . . .
JUNIORS MR Pierre-Alexandre O . . . .
Rutgers MR & MRS Anthony L (Diane G Lipshultz) ☎ (970) 925-8229
Cal'75.Cal'75 . . . . 512 Spruce St,
JUNIORS MISS Anthony L JR . . . . Aspen, CO *81611*
Rutherfurd MRS Hugo (Francesca L Villa) . . . . Died at
Hobe Sound, FL Nov 13'95
Rutherfurd MR & MRS Winthrop JR (Mary S ☎ (212) 348-6051
Kernan) Rc.Fic.Cly.P'64.Va'67 . . . . 1115 Fifth Av,
MISS Leslie H—Skd'92 . . . . New York, NY
MISS Elizabeth P—P'93 . . . . *10128*
MISS Emily K—at U of So Cal . . . .
Ruxton MRS Ruth M (Chapin—Harvey—Ruth M Ruxton) . . . . Died at
Vero Beach, FL Jly 19'95
Ryan MR C Gregg—Rcn.StLaw'83
☎ (540) 253-7402 . . 7234 Fleming Farm Rd, The Plains, VA *22171*
Ryan MR John B
☎ (415) 661-2533 . . 1233 Willard St, San Francisco, CA *94117*
Ryan MR William H . . . . Died at
Stockbridge, MA Sep 29'95
Ryland MR W Bradford 2d—Cw.Cc.Br'62
☎ (619) 360-9139 . . "Castello Rylando" 77120 Delgado Dv,
Indian Wells, CA *92210*

S

Sack MRS Topping (Sandra E Topping) . . . . . . name changed to Topping

Sack MISS Whitney Baker (A Albert) . . . . Married at Washington, DC
  Corderi MR Joseph E JR (Joseph E) . . . . Oct 7'95
St Claire REV & MRS Elbert K (Schmidt—Jean | ☎ (610) 658-0220
  Maxwell) Syr'50.Me.P'41.EpiscDiv'43 . . . . | The Quadrangle
    MISS Helene M Schmidt—Fla'86—at | H101, 3300 Darby
    ☎ (610) 688-7940 . . 220 Ithan Creek Rd, | Rd, Haverford, PA
    Villanova, PA *19085* . . . . | *19041*
Salas MRS Caroline W (Caroline W Trevor) | ☎ (516) 922-0620
  Ws'78.Mb.Pr.Cly.Dc.Ht. . . . . | 367 Split Rock Rd,
  JUNIORS MISS Caroline T . . . . | Syosset, NY *11791*
Salem MR & MRS David A (Eleanor B Shannon)
  Dth'79.H'84.Hn.Mid'78.H'83
  ☎ (603) 643-2004 . . 6 Rope Ferry Rd, Hanover, NH *03755*
Salisbury MRS Lorraine L (Burke—Salisbury—Colvin—
  Lorraine Littlefield)
  ☎ (561) 655-0704 . . 1001 S Flagler Dv, Apt 201, West Palm Beach,
  FL *33401*
Saltonstall MR & MRS Robert (Hannah G Ayer) H.'33
  Carleton-Willard Village, Essex 77, 100 Old Billerica Rd, Bedford,
  MA *01730*
Saltzman MRS C Myrick (Cynthia S Myrick) . . . . Died at
  New York, NY Feb 7'96
Samuel MISS Barbara Elisabeth Jane (James R JR) . . . . . . Born Aug 4'94
Samuel MR & MRS James R JR (M Jane C Murphy) | ☎ (314) 993-4145
  Mar'vil'73.StL'68 . . . . | 2800 Stonington
  JUNIORS MISS Clara P . . . . | Place, St Louis, MO
  JUNIORS MISS Catherine L . . . . | *63131*
Sanders MR & MRS Theodore R (Elizabeth D Parker) G.Buf'50
  ☎ (716) 886-7653 . . 50 Cleveland Av, Buffalo, NY *14222*
Sands MISS Katherine Cory (Geoffrey K) . . . . Born at
  New York, NY Sep 25'95
Sanford MR & MRS Terry (Margaret R Knight)
  NCar'41.Cos.NCar'39.NCar'46
  ☎ (919) 489-0700 . . 2500 Auburn St, Durham, NC *27706*
San Román MR & MRS José L (Pauline F Marshall) | Calle Adelfas 53,
  Madrid'56 . . . . | Monteprincipe,
  MISS Lola . . . . | Boadilla del Monte,
  MR José F . . . . | 28668 Madrid, Spain
  MR David . . . . |
  MR Jacabo . . . . |
Santy MR & MRS Ross C (Lucia L Elmore) | ☎ (207) 439-4649
  P'60.H'63 . . . . | 42 Goodwin Rd,
  MISS Leigh—at U of Cal Santa Cruz . . . . | Kittery Point, ME
  | *03904*
Sargent MASTER John Alling (Thomas A) . . . . Born at
  Boston, MA Apr 18'95
Saunders MISS Elenore Holden (g—MRS Harriet M Saunders) . . . Born at
  Hyannis, MA Jan 19'96
Saunders MR & MRS Thomas A III (M Jordan | of ☎ (516)671-4143
  Horner) VaCmth'64.Ln.Pr.Ri.Cly.Vmi'58.Va'67 | 180 Piping Rock Rd,
  MR Thomas A IV—Cc.—at ☎ (212) 734-2752 | Locust Valley, NY
  176 E 77 St, New York, NY *10021* . . . . | *11560*
  | ☎ (212) 288-1236
  | 130 E 75 St,
  | New York, NY
  | *10021*

Sawers MRS William B (Amy B Hayward) Gchr'31.Ncd.
  ☎ (410) 377-7572 . . 830 W 40 St, Baltimore, MD *21211*
Scannell MR Christopher G—Geo'91.CathU'92
  ☎ (703) 960-7954 . . 5990 Richmond H'way, Apt 1109, Alexandria,
  VA *22303*
Scarlett MRS L Landon—Pa'64.Cl'67.Pa'84
  ☎ (615) 377-3999 . . 1133 Holly Tree Farms Rd, Brentwood, TN *37027*
Scarlett MR & MRS Lindley C (Christine P | ☎ (201) 267-9822
  Kenworthy) Cent'y'69.Shcc.Mvh.Ty'66 . . . . . . | "Tempe Hollow
  MISS Whitney B—at Trinity . . . . | Farm" Tempe Wick
  MR Beecher C—at Denison . . . . | Rd, Morristown, NJ
  | *07960*
Scattergood MR & MRS J Henry (M Augusta Russel) | ☎ (201) 635-7370
  NCar'67.NCar'67 . . . . | 53 Lincoln Av,
  MISS Caroline I—Tul'89—at 1219 Peniston St, | Chatham, NJ *07928*
  New Orleans, LA *70115* . . . . |
  MISS Katherine C . . . . |
Scharlotte MRS Robert B (Barbara A Wieser) . . . . Died at
  Hudson, OH Jan 9'96
Schauffler MR Frederick A—Vca.Wt.SUNY'82 | ☎ (212) 410-1806
  MISS Nancy A—Ober'81—at ☎ (212) 876-1791 | 66 E 93 St, Apt 2R,
  66 E 93 St, Apt 5R, New York, NY *10128* . . . | New York, NY
  | *10128*
Scheerer MR Thomas I—Mds.CooperU'85
  ☎ (803) 723-0210 . . 60 Anson St, Charleston, SC *29401*
Scheetz MR & MRS William Cramp JR (Snyder—Stouffer—Mary A Biddle)
  Me.Pe.Rv.Fw.Ll.Ac.Sdg.Ncd.Pa'34
  3500 West Chester Pike, CH124, Newtown Square, PA *19073-4168*
Schiffeler DR & MRS John Wm (Katherine Y Chang)
  Cc.Myf.Cal'66.Cal'67.Hawaii'69.Ind'74.Cal'79 . . of
  ☎ (415) 221-0511 . . 511 El Camino Del Mar, San Francisco,
  CA *94121-1041*
  ☎ (011-86-21) 5854-4014 . . Jianping-21st Century High School,
  275 Gu Shan Rd, Pudong, Shanghai 200135, China
Schlafly MR Thomas F (Daniel L) . . . . Married at St Louis, MO
  Kärst MISS Ulrike G (late Carl) . . . . Sep 2'95
Schlafly MR & MRS Thomas F (Ulrike G Kärst)
  Cologne'77.Rc.Nd.Cy.Geo'70.Geo'77
  ☎ (314) 361-0361 . . 8 Portland Place, St Louis, MO *63108*
Schmader MR & MRS J Peter (Rachel L Ijams) WmSth'81.VillaN'73
  ☎ (410) 727-5935 . . 38 E Montgomery St, Baltimore,
  MD *21230* . . MRS absent
Schmidt MASTER Benjamin Lapsley (g—L F Boker Doyle) . . . . . . Born at
  Paris, France Sep 15'95
Schmidt MISS Helene M—Fla'86 . . see E K St Claire
Schneeberger MISS Katherine Lee (John A) . . . . Born at
  New York, NY Aug 4'95
Schoettle MR Ferdinand P—Ayc.P'55.H'60.H'78 | ☎ (410) 263-1804
  H'83 . . . . | Shearwater,
  MR Michael K . . . . | 15B3 Spa Creek
  MR Derek C . . . . | Landing, PO Box
  | 4935, Annapolis,
  | MD *21403-6935*
Scholle MISS Elizabeth Parsons (Oliver C JR) . . . . Born at
  Greenwich, CT Mch 12'95

Scholle MR & MRS Oliver C (Diana deB Parsons) Bur.Cc.H'49 . . . . ☎ (415) 347-8790
MR Palmer H—at 21 Kinross Rd, Apt 1R, Brighton, MA *02135* . . . . 535 Laurent St, Hillsborough, CA *94010*
Schotz MR & MRS Jon P (Patricia F Wheeler) Y'77.Y'77
☎ (310) 458-9402 . . 148 Georgina Av, Santa Monica, CA *90402*
Schoyer MR Timothy R
☎ (512) 992-0268 . . 4645 Ocean Dv, Apt 1B, Corpus Christi, TX *78415*
Schuster MR Charles J . . . . Died Sep 29'95
Schutt MR & MRS C Porter (Layton—Greta B Brown) Wil.Cry.Ny.Ac.Cly.Ncd.Va'35
☎ (302) 658-4421 . . 302 Hillside Rd, Box 3694, Greenville, DE *19807*
Schuyler MR & MRS David B (Lynn E McCormac) NIll'85.NIll'85
☎ (847) 726-1106 . . 6 Summit Terr, Lake Zurich, IL *60047*
Schuyler MASTER Jacob William (David B) . . . . Born at Libertyville, IL Mch 4'95
Schuyler MR & MRS William M (Katherine K Groman) Ch'31.Hl.Cnt.Dth'31.Ch'39
☎ (312) 573-1456 . . 680 N Lake Shore Dv, Apt 518, Chicago, IL *60611*
Schwab MR & MRS Gustav 5th (Luebke—Mary E Klein) Col'60.Y'36 . . . . ☎ (904) 285-7309
MISS Marie K Luebke—at 108 E 38 St, Apt 200, New York, NY *10016* . . . . The Carlyle 407, 600 Ponte Vedra Blvd, Ponte Vedra Beach, FL *32082*
Schwab MR & MRS Stuart T (Vicki A McClendon) Tex'53.Duke'81.Tex'86
☎ (210) 828-0135 . . 112 Sheraton Dv, San Antonio, TX *78209*
Schwartz MR & MRS Alexander C JR (Perry—Glorvina H Rodewald) Wk.T.K.BtP.Cl'56
☎ (407) 848-6238 . . 995 Adam Rd, Palm Beach, FL *33480*
Schwartz MRS Peter A (Alice C Sinclair) . . . . Died at Charleston, SC Feb 3'95
Scott MR & MRS Alfred L (Jacks—Elizabeth Bond Hunter) V'62.Ch'65.UnTheo'9.CUNY'92.Ri.Un. Myf.Cs.Cly.Ncd.Dc.U'53.Nu'56 . . . . ☎ (212) 534-5148
MR Alexander L—Un.CtCol'89.Pa'94—at ☎ (212) 816-5869 . . 131 E 66 St, New York, NY *10021* . . . . 1160 Park Av, New York, NY *10128*
MISS Elizabeth B Jacks—Duke'91.Nw'96 . . .
MR Robert LeRoy Jacks JR—Duke'94.Stan'95 —at ☎ (910) 251-7711 . . 201½ S Front St, Wilmington, NC *28401* . . . .
Scott MISS Diana M—LakeF'78.Nyc.
☎ (508) 228-2651 . . 4 Capaum Rd, Nantucket, MA *02554*
Scott MR & MRS Edgar JR (Lindsay C Febiger) Srr.Ph.H'49
☎ (610) 347-2235 . . PO Box 431, Unionville, PA *19575*
Scott MR & MRS John H (Avern—Jean McDougall) Pg.P'45.Cr'51 . . . . ☎ (412) 361-2556
MR Hugh McD—Nyc.Ken'80 . . . . 1275 Beechwood Blvd, Pittsburgh, PA *15206*
Scribner MR Charles JR . . . . Died at New York, NY Nov 11'95
Scully MR David B (John A) . . . . Married at Madison, CT Christensen MISS Erika (P Erik) . . . . Sep 16'95
Scully MR & MRS David B (Erika Christensen) HWSth'91.B.Shcc.Rcn.Ty'83
☎ (011-44-171) 721-3574 . . 20 Campden St, London W8 7EP, England
Seabright MASTER James Walter (Thomas W) . . . . Born Jly 7'94

Searle MISS Charlotte Sibley (Robert S) . . . . Born at Greenwich, CT Jan 17'95
Searle MISS Marion S (Chandler—Marion S Searle) . . . . Married at Lake Forest, IL
Bermingham MR David C . . . . Feb 25'95
Searle MISS Marion S (Chandler—Marion S Searle) see D C Bermingham
Sears MISS Alice G
☎ (202) 362-1577 . . 3287D Sutton Place NW, Washington, DC *20016*
Sears MR Edmund H JR . . see P M Rhinelander
Sears MR Frederick F JR—Bost'90
☎ (617) 639-8530 . . 66 Front St, Marblehead, MA *01945*
Sears MISS Katharine C . . see P M Rhinelander
Sears MRS Richard (M Christiane Linas) . . . . Died at Paris, France Dec 4'91
Sears MR Richard—Sm.H'38 . . . . ☎ (011-33-1) 47-23-49-11
MISS Stephanie . . . . 2 rue Gaston de St Paul, 75016 Paris, France
Sears MR & MRS Robert M (Erica B Leisenring) Pa'78.Ant'77.Nf.ColC'68.Bost'71
☎ (314) 361-1478 . . 5095 Westminster Place, St Louis, MO *63108*
Sears MRS S White (Sonzski—Susannah White) . . . . Married at Falmouth, ME
Rhinelander MR Philip M (late Philip H) . . . . Jan 6'96
Sedgwick MR & MRS Henry D (Auchincloss—Robin Dike) Wheat'65.Hb.H'51.MgmtInst'53 . . . . of ☎ (212)427-9380
MR Robert B . . . . 163 E 94 St, New York, NY *10128*
MR Nicholas J . . . .
MISS Hilary M Auchincloss . . . . ☎ (860) 434-2114
MR Conrad McI Auchincloss . . . . 23 Ferry Rd, Old Lyme, CT *06371*
Seggerman MRS Kenneth M (Helen L K Simpson) . . . . Died Dec 8'95
Seipp MR Paul E (Edwin A) . . . . Married at Portola Valley, CA
Clarke MISS Julie (Richard A) . . . . Apr 22'95
Selby MR Christopher H M F (Frederick P) . . . . . Married in Wakaia, Fiji
Sutton MISS Melinda . . . . Jly 24'95
Selden MR James K (George L) . . . . Married in Barbados
Hart MISS Jessica L . . . . Jan 16'96
Sellers MISS Sabine Marie Weightman (Coleman VI) . . . . Born at Wilmington, DE Mch 8'95
Sellman MR & MRS Charles R (Patricia M M Barroll) Va'86.Pom'87
☎ (212) 875-1614 . . 114 W 70 St, New York, NY *10023*
Seltzer MISS Cassandra Lewis (Jonathan H) . . . . Born at Philadelphia, PA Mch 22'95
Seltzer DR & MRS Jonathan H (Elizabeth D Nickerson) Geo'84.Tufts'88.Hav'80.Mich'82.Pa'88
216 Pine St, Philadelphia, PA *19106*
Seymore MISS Chloë B—RISD'96 . . see MRS A E Paine
Shafer MISS Emily Pindell (g—MRS Gail P Shafer) . . . . Born at New Haven, CT Jan 31'96
Sharp MRS Frederick D 3d (Fleckinger—Eugenia C van de Water) . . . . . . Died at Portland, ME Aug 3'95
Sharples MR & MRS Thomas D (Renate H A Backhausen) SFr'75.SFr'77
☎ (415) 324-4848 . . 128 Heather Dv, Atherton, CA *94027*

Sharretts MR & MRS Amos B JR (Jeanne M McMillan) Vt'80.CasSt'79
  ☎ (201) 644-0674 . . 76 Washington Av, Morristown, NJ *07960*
Sharretts MASTER Edward Patrick (Amos B JR) . . . . Born at Morristown, NJ Nov 22'95
Shaw MR & MRS Alan W 3d (Ingree A Griffin) LSU'66.SWLa'66 . . . .
  MISS Amidie E—Austin'95—at
  ☎ (214) 521-8871 . . 3911 Holland Av, Apt 105, Dallas, TX *75219* . . . .
  JUNIORS MR Alan W 4th . . . .
  ☎ (615) 353-7900
  3802 Hillmeade Court, Nashville, TN *37221*
Shaw MISS (DR) Deborah S (Passarella—Hickox—Tankoos—Deborah S Shaw) Ga'74.Ga'79 . . . . .
  JUNIORS MR James A B Hickox . . . .
  ☎ (303) 322-2828
  450 Clermont P'kway, Denver, CO *80220*
Shaw MR & MRS Robert G (Cass L Ruxton) Un.T.Lm.Myf.Cly.Dc.Cda.Dh.Ty'51 . . . .
  MISS (REV) Cass L—Sth'77.PTheo'80 . . . .
  of ☎ (914)351-2210 ''Highland'' PO Box 106, Tuxedo Park, NY *10987-0106*
  ☎ (212) 751-1912 200 E 66 St, New York, NY *10021*
Shaw MR & MRS S Parkman JR (Lisa A Geissenhainer) NH'80.Sm.H'66
  ☎ (617) 731-5261 . . 89 Carlton St, Brookline, MA *02146*
Shaw MRS Z George (Bingham—Mary Ann Pearce) Dar.
  ☎ (601) 453-5734 . . 406 Crockett Av, Greenwood, MS *38930*
Shea MRS Stephanie W (Stephanie Wilds) Cly . . .of
  ☎ (011-55-11) 247-2937 . . Rua Cassiano Ricardo 83, São Paulo 04640-200 SP, Brazil
  ☎ (212) 249-8383 . . 20 E 68 St, Apt 10G, New York, NY *10021*
Sheehan MR Mark A—Pg.Va'84.Pitt'89
  ☎ (215) 545-2268 . . 1420 Locust St, Philadelphia, PA *19102-4217*
Sheffield MRS Anne (Anwyl—Anne Sheffield) V'51
  MISS Pandora H C Anwyl—at
  ☎ (305) 867-0429 . . 710—86 St, Miami Beach, FL *33141* . . . .
  ☎ (212) 319-4232 136 E 64 St, New York, NY *10021*
Shehan MR John T—Cy.Loy'55 . . . .
  MISS Margaret H . . . .
  505 Epsom Rd, Apt 2A, Towson, MD *21286*
Sheriff MISS Nathalie H . . see MRS B T Reid
Sherman MR Dallas B . . . . Died at Scottsdale, AZ Dec 24'95
Sherman MRS Dallas B (Glass—Beatrice Schaenen) Nu'32.Nu'67.Chr.StJ . . . .
  MISS Cordelia C—V'71—at 111 Elm St, Somerville, MA *02144* . . . .
  MR Laurence d'A M Glass—P'58.P'59—at 704 Cathedral St, Baltimore, MD *21201* . . . . .
  9 E 84 St, New York, NY *10028*
Sherwin MR Peter M JR
  ☎ (408) 625-9652 . . PO Box 381, Carmel, CA *93921*
Sherwin MRS Robert P (Thayer—Katherine V Barr)
  ☎ (610) 525-5891 . . 312 Thornbrook Rd, Rosemont, PA *19010*
Shields MR & MRS Charles W (Catherine C Kernott) Pep'86
  ☎ (805) 969-4417 . . 558 San Ysidro Rd, Montecito, CA *93108*

Shields MR & MRS Day R (M Elaine Hamrick) Y'69 . . of
  ☎ (203) 762-9849 . . 155 Hulda Hill Rd, Wilton, CT *06897*
  ☎ (809) 332-6003 . . ''Sundowner'' Windermere Island, Eleuthera, Bahamas
Shields DR & MRS Joseph Dunbar JR (Kendall—Goodrich—Mary L Netterville) So.Cly.Dar.Tul'33
  ☎ (601) 445-5674 . . ''Montaigne'' PO Box 886, 200 Liberty Rd, Natchez, MS *39121*
Shober MRS Pemberton H (Georgiana F Harris) 301 Stenton Av, Plymouth Meeting, PA *19462*
Shore MR F Croft JR—W&J'75
  ☎ (513) 241-7138 . . 231 W 4 St, Apt 501A, Cincinnati, OH *45202*
Shorey MISS Laura Fairbank (MISS Nathalie E Ames) . . . . Born at Cleveland, OH Jun 3'94
Shumlin MISS Julia Lovett (Jeffrey P) . . . . Born at Putney, VT Jly 15'95
Sibley MR & MRS John B (Heiserman—Shirley D Cook) Pa'45 . . . .
  MISS Mariah W—OWes'87—at
  ☎ (610) 356-9322 . . 618 Andover Rd, Newtown Square, PA *19073* . . . .
    MISS Blake Chandler . . . .
    MR Robert B Heiserman 3d—at
    ☎ (212) 749-0382 . . 878 West End Av, New York, NY *10025*
  ☎ (610) 353-2523 627 Glendale Rd, Newtown Square, PA *19073*
Sibley MR & MRS Thomas (Jean C Eagleson) Fla'67.H'62 . . . .
  MISS Erin W—at U of Colo Boulder . . . .
  MR Thomas S—at Art Inst Chicago . . . .
  ☎ (941) 688-9802 1400 Grasslands Blvd, Lakeland, FL *33803*
Siegman MISS Jessica L . . see S P Phillips
Siems MISS Shelby D—Mid'84
  ☎ (206) 528-4746 . . 8060 Ridge Dv NE, Seattle, WA *98115*
Sigety MR & MRS Cornelius E (Virginia White) H'86.Unn.Cly.Hn.Roch'80.H'85 ⚓
  7145 Old Easton Rd, PO Box 369, Pipersville, PA *18947*
Sigety MR & MRS Robert G (Elizabeth P Donnem) Y'86.Ch'89.Duke'80.H'90 . . of
  ☎ (215) 766-6208 . . 3820 Secondwoods Dv, PO Box 1090, Doylestown, PA *18901*
  ☎ (212) 517-6208 . . 333 E 80 St, Apt 6F, New York, NY *10021*
Silbert THE REVS John C R & Marion N (Marion G Nimick) NH'76.PTheo'82.Gordon'78.PTheo'82
  ☎ (412) 327-5826 . . 4016 Remaley Rd, Murrysville, PA *15668*
Silver MR Duncan M—FairD'82 ⚓
  ☎ (716) 626-9085 . . 12 Spindrift Dv, 3, Williamsville, NY *14221*
Simenstad MRS Susan O (Susan A Oyster) Stph'65
  ☎ (415) 454-9553 . . 366 Forbes Av, San Rafael, CA *94901*
Simmons MR & MRS William E 3d (Bolles—Eliza A Atkinson) SoMiss'69.Cda.Dar.Mlsps'78
  ☎ (601) 736-1763 . . 1 Hugh White Place, Columbia, MS *39429*
Simon MR & MRS Robert S (Margaret D Turnbull) SL'68.Tcy.Cl'64 . . . .
  JUNIORS MISS Abigail T . . . .
  ☎ (415) 986-3642 45—21 Av, San Francisco, CA *94121*
Simpson JUNIORS MISS Melanie S . . see MRS M Trevor
Simpson MRS Sandra S (Sandra Stingily) Swb'57
  3796 Glencoe Dv, Birmingham, AL *35213*

Simpson MR & MRS William 4th (Charlene Amidon) Tex'43.Gm.Rc. . . . . of ☎ (610)296-4004
MR James A—Gm.Bab'87—at ☎ (610) 431-7105 38 Manchester
605 W Market St, West Chester, PA *19382* . . . . Court, Berwyn, PA *19312*
☎ (602) 471-7536
18810 Chinle Dv,
Rio Verde, AZ *85263*

Sincerbeaux MRS Richard M (Katherine A Connell) Ws'66.Cly. . . . . ☎ (212) 860-2973
MISS Caroline C—at Princeton . . . . 1088 Park Av, New York, NY *10128*

Sincerbeaux MR Richard M—Ck.P'64. . . . . ☎ (212) 734-4053
MR Richard M JR—Vt'90 . . . . 520 E 76 St, New York, NY *10021*

Sinclair MRS Winkler (Gretchen A Winkler)
☎ (603) 228-6921 . . 5 Hanover St, Apt 2, Concord, NH *03301*
Skeele MR & MRS James B (Constance E C Moss) Fic.
☎ (508) 541-1422 . . 76 Cleveland St, Norfolk, MA *02056*
Skvarch MR & MRS Jeffrey P (Cynthia A Bradford) Stph'86
☎ (616) 335-3364 . . 4766 Wildwood Rd, Holland, MI *49423*
Slaughter MR & MRS D French 3d (Marcie L Mott) ☎ (804) 979-0331
MtVern'80.Va'77.Va'80. . . . . "Holly Hollow"
JUNIORS MISS Caroline M . . . . 2330 Owensville Rd,
JUNIROS MISS Karin E . . . . Charlottesville, VA *22901*

Sloan MISS Berkeley C . . . . Died at
St Louis, MO Nov 4'95

Sloan MR & MRS Julian R (Cecile C Kelly) Br'51 . . ☎ (508) 945-3639
MISS H Edesse—Conn'80—at ☎ (203) 454-1915 "Wicked Hill Barn"
12 Wild Rose Rd, Westport, CT *06880* . . . . 106 Highland Av,
MISS Margot S—at ☎ (508) 240-0595 . . RR 2,   Box 453, Chatham,
Herringbrook Rd, Eastham, MA *02640* . . . . MA *02633*
MR Julian R 3d—WNEng'82—at
☎ (513) 923-1612 . . 3473 Oakmeadow Lane,
Apt 2, Cincinnati, OH *45239* . . . .

Sloane MRS James Ross (Hammond—Helen C Stuart) Sth'45.Csn.Lx.
☎ (413) 443-4625 . . 311 Washington Mountain Rd, Becket, MA *01223*
Smith MRS Catherine Z (Catherine B Zick) Smu'75
☎ (703) 528-2667 . . 1506 N 22 St, Arlington, VA *22209*
Smith MISS Dana V (Richard L) . . . . Married at Prouts Neck, ME
Haskell MR Charles JR . . . . Sep 9'94
Smith MR & MRS David L (Leslie A Gerardo) Va'84.AmU'87.Dick'82.Bost'87
☎ (703) 671-6852 . . 4618A S 36 St, Arlington, VA *22206*
Smith MR Garrett M . . see E G Ottley
Smith MR & MRS George Putnam (Llewellyn S ☎ (508) 526-1935
Parsons) Sth'60.Y'58.H'67. . . . . "Masconomo
MISS Abigail A—Bow'91—at Harvard Divinity . House"
MR G Putnam JR—Bow'94 . . . . 8 Masconomo St,
Manchester, MA *01944*

Smith MRS Patricia M (Patricia M White) . . . . Died Sep 3'95
Smith MR & MRS Prentice K JR (Sheilah L Thorn) Nw'73.DU'73 *abroad*

Smith MR & MRS R Gordon (Bockmann—Catherine ☎ (804) 288-2658
C Baird) Va'60.H'64 . . . . 5 Spicer Rd,
MISS Jill O Bockmann—Bow'89—at Richmond, VA *23226*
☎ (203) 699-1213 . . 1308 S Meridan Rd,
Cheshire, CT *06410* . . . .
MR Nathaniel V Bockmann—at
☎ (503) 235-7361 . . 3022 SE Main St,
Portland, OR *97217* . . . .

Smith MR & MRS Richard A JR (Catherine C ☎ (011-82-2)
Munnell) Ws'64.Cvc.Sl.Ty'65 397-4114
MR Carter McC. . . . . American Embassy,
Seoul, Korea,
Unit 15550, APO
AP, *96205-0001*

Smith MR Richard B—Pn.P'34
☎ (908) 842-1447 . . 11 Linden Lane, Rumson, NJ *07760*
Smith MASTER Richard Ferree 3d (Richard F JR) . . . . Born at
Philadelphia, PA Jly 17'95
Smith MRS Robinson (Alice P Robinson) . . . . Died Oct 3'95
Smith MISS Shelley D (Richard L) . . . . Married at Philadelphia, PA
Edalatpour MR Timothy F . . . . Apr 22'95
Smith MR Sidney S . . . . Died at
New Canaan, CT Sep 30'95
Smith MR Thurston H 3d. . see D N Loud
Smith MR Townsend U. . see D N Loud
Smith MR & MRS W N Harrell 4th (Mary Oakes ☎ (202) 338-2630
Skinner) Sth'63.Mit'77.Cvc.Mt.Sl.Wms'60. 2630 Foxhall Rd
Ox'62.H'65 . . . . NW, Washington,
MISS Caroline Doswell—at 1611 Anacapa St, DC *20007*
Apt 6, Santa Barbara, CA *93101* . . . .

Smith MR & MRS Winthrop D (Claire V A de Tarr) Mid'74.Mid'80.Mid'75.Mit'81 . . of
☎ (603) 436-5516 . . 485 FW Hartford Dv, Portsmouth, NH *03801-5890*
☎ (603) 278-5516 . . 100 Mt Washington Place, Bretton Woods, NH *03595*

Smithers MR & MRS Charles F JR (Panon ☎ (212) 289-1535
Desbassayns de Richemont—Anne M Hart 1175 Park Av,
Green) Un.Ny.Plg.Hob'52 . . . . New York, NY *10128*
JUNIORS MISS Amélie Panon Desbassayns
de Richemont—at Wycombe Abbey England .
JUNIORS MR Philippe Panon Desbassayns
de Richemont—at Winchester Coll England. .

Smyth MISS Anne C (D Grahame) . . . . Married at Colorado Springs, CO
Renfrow MR Seadon T (J Royce) . . . . Jly 8'95
Snead MR Phillip H—W&M'55
☎ (860) 525-2227 . . 525 Brown St, B9 Apt 193, Meriden, CT *06450*
Snowdon MRS Henry Taft (Nancy C Buckingham) Mt.Cvc.Ncd.
☎ (202) 337-6316 . . 4000 Cathedral Av NW, Apt 852B, Washington, DC *20016*
Snyder MASTER Richard Elliott (g—Parker G Montgomery) . . . . Born
Aug 12'94
Soffel MISS Christie A—EMich'77
4607 Kenmore Dv NW, Washington, DC *20007*
Sokoloff MRS Kiril (Catherine H Miller) Bgt.Ri.
Cider Mill Farm, Bouton Rd, South Salem, NY *10590*

Sokoloff MR Kiril—Rcn.Bgt.Ri.Geo'69 .... ☎ (208) 726-4334
   JUNIORS MISS Emily D...................... 109 Boulder View
   JUNIORS MR Kiri St J........................ Lane, Ketchum, ID *83340*

Solley MISS Katherine Denison (Nicholas N) .... Born at Stamford, CT Oct 13'95

Solley MR & MRS Nicholas N (Keogh—Wierdsma— ☎ (860) 868-0092
  Pamela D Clark) IaWes'72.................... 17 Judea Cemetery
   MISS Emily F Wierdsma—at Gunnery ...... Rd, Washington, CT
   MR George P Keogh—at Columbia *06793*
   MR Clark R Wierdsma—at Gunnery ....

Solley MASTER Nicholas Noyes JR (Nicholas N) .... Born at Stamford, CT Oct 13'95

Sommaripa MR & MRS George (Eva A Coifman) ☎ (617) 661-3800
  Ws'63.H'51.Cl'60 .... 17 Bishop Allen Dv,
   MR Leo M—at Corps de la Paix, BP 1282, Cambridge, MA
  Cidex 01, Abijan 06, Côte d'Ivoire........... *02139*
   JUNIORS MR Nicholas C R—at Northfield-Mt Hermon ....

Sommerfield MRS Mark J (Carvette—Katharine K ☎ (908) 449-2256
  Gold) UMiami'69.Ac.Chr.Sdg.Dll.Dar.Ht.Ne. .. 501 Jersey Av,
   MISS Megan A .... Spring Lake, NJ
   JUNIORS MISS Laura B *07762*

Sommerfield MR Mark J—Pe.Pars'69
  ☎ (704) 556-7141 .. 6332-3C Cameron Forest Lane, Charlotte, NC *28210*

Soule MASTER Thomas Winsor (Edgar W) .... Born at Newton, MA Nov 12'95

Soutendijk MR & MRS Dirk R (Mary M Tremaine) Chath'77.Y'60 .. of
  ☎ (201) 334-9237 .. 52 Briarcliff Rd, Mountain Lakes, NJ *07046*
  ☎ (212) 722-0726 .. 1755 York Av, New York, NY *10128*

Spaeth MR & MRS Christopher P (Julie L Bartelme) ColSt'94.Pc.ColSt'95
  ☎ (970) 484-6618 .. 1015 W Prospect Rd, Apt 2, Ft Collins, CO *80526*

Spalding MRS Charles F (Janet F Haskell) ☎ (914) 424-3030
  CUNY'65.Marist'76 .... PO Box 139,
   MISS Bethany P—Wms'89.H'93—Box 84619, Garrison, NY *10524*
  Fairbanks, AK *99708* ....
   MR Mark F—Ken'91.FlaIT'94 ....

Sparkman MR & MRS Thorne 3d (Lane H Talbot) P'89.H'89
  ☎ (510) 848-7261 .. 2912 Claremont Av, Apt 32, Berkeley, CA *94705*

Spear MISS Sarah Eddy (g—John S Kerns JR) .... Born at Charlotte, NC Apr 1'95

Spears MR & MRS Daniel B (Margaret E Williams) Bow'81.Gv.Bow'81
  ☎ (410) 584-2904 .. Old Orchard Farm, 14640 Falls Rd, Cockeysville, MD *21030*

Speers MASTER Carter Patrick Kinney (William S) .... Born at Wilmington, DE Nov 11'94

Speers REV & MRS T Guthrie JR (Susan Savage) BMr'51.C.Csn.P'50.UnTheo'53
  ☎ (603) 284-7770 .. RR 1, Box 67, 36 Taylor Rd, Center Sandwich, NH *03227-9703*

Speers MR & MRS William S (Donna E Kinney) Mid'83.Mid'87.Pp.P'79.Mid'84
  ☎ (302) 378-4205 .. 350 Noxontown Rd, Middletown, DE *19709*

Spencer MISS Ellery Price (Scott R) .... Born at Bernardsville, NJ Feb 18'93

Spencer MR & MRS Henry B 2d (Phillips—Helen M Walker) K.Mt.Cvc.H'62 "The Greenhouse" Great Island, Noroton, CT *06820*

Spencer MISS Holly .. see E T Miller

Spencer MISS Katherine King (Scott R) .... Born at Bernardsville, NJ May 18'95

Spencer MR & MRS Scott R (Elizabeth K Ballantine) Gettys'87.Smu'85
  ☎ (908) 953-0324 .. 9 Bodnar St, Bernardsville, NJ *07924*

Spofford MR & MRS C Nicholas (Martha F ☎ (914) 234-7924
  McKown) Bgt.Fic.Y.'56 .... 472 Bedford Center
   MISS Jennifer B—Vt'92—at ☎ (617) 354-4285 Rd, Bedford, NY
  24 Chauncy St, Apt 15, Cambridge, MA *02138* . *10506*

Spradling LT & MRS Brock A (Hannah A T Lee) Md'93.USN'93
  ☎ (360) 598-6995 .. 6004 Gudgeon Av, Apt A, Silverdale, WA *98315*

Spradling MASTER Jake Andrew (Brock A) .... Born at Bremerton, WA Dec 5'95

Sprague MRS Julie H (Minot—Talmage—Julie H Sprague)
  ☎ (407) 833-4944 .. 354 Chilean Av, Apt 2A, Palm Beach, FL *33480*

Stackelburg MRS Constantine (Gardiner—Garnett Butler)
  ☎ (202) 667-6520 .. 1673 Columbia Rd NW, Washington, DC *20009*

Stamm MRS G Edward (Berdell—Alida S Freeborn) ...... Died Nov 9'95

Stanley JUNIORS MR Arthur E Kimball .. see M E Kimball

Stanley (DR) Emily H—Y'84.ArizSt'93
  ☎ (405) 372-5743 .. 2108 N Husband St, Stillwater, OK *74075*

Stanton MR Gordon R (Louis L JR) .... Married at New York, NY
  Brown MISS Catherine Duer (Stanley N JR) .... Jan 6'96

Stanton MR & MRS Gordon R (Catherine Duer Brown) Colby'86.Cly.Y'82.Nu'92
  ☎ (212) 249-6160 .. 230 E 73 St, New York, NY *10021*

Stark MISS Alison C (Robert W JR) .... Married at Nantucket, MA
  Sendelbach MR Peter .... Sep 30'95

Staub MR John H 3d—Cw.Va'74
  721 Fifth Av, Apt 46H, New York, NY *10022*

Stauffer MASTER Thomas Christian (John C) .... Born at Larchmont, NY Mch 1'96

Steadman MR & MRS Charles W (Artini—Consuelo Matthews) Rcn.Uncl.Evg.Hn.Neb'35.H'38 .. of
  ☎ (407) 833-2487 .. 425 Worth Av, Apt 3E, Palm Beach, FL *33480*
  ☎ (202) 333-1770 .. 700 New Hampshire Av NW, Apt 1202, Washington, DC *20037*

Stearns MR & MRS Peter C (Cordelia P Dunlaevy) of ☎ (307)733-8090
  Pr.Ri.Chr.Ncd.Ne.Y'56 .... 3465 Arrowleaf
   MR John C—Va'85........................ Lane, Box E4,
     Jackson, WY *83001*
     ☎ (212) 249-3959
     785 Park Av,
     New York, NY
     10021

Stearns MISS Sarah W (James P JR) .... Married at Washington, CT
  Fey DR Christopher P V (Philip) .... Sep 9'95

Steavenson MR & MRS David H M J (Foshay— ☎ (011-44-181)
  Wendell E Miller) B. 960-9172
   MISS M Wendell E—Camb'92—at 23 Bassett Rd,
  ☎ (212) 614-0666 .. 245 E 10 St, New York, NY London W10 6LA,
  10009 .... England
   MR D H Michael McL—at ☎ (212) 614-0666
  245 E 10 St, New York, NY *10009* ....
   MR Alexander M H......................

Stebbins MR & MRS Rowland 3d (Dick—Carla M Cole) K.Plg.Y'59.H'62
  ☎ (607) 936-8952 . . 1 North Rd, Corning, NY *14830*

Steel MR & MRS Alfred JR (Hannah D Butler) Ty'64 . | ☎ (860) 521-3557
  MISS Loretta D—Bow'95 . . . . | 147 Stoner Dv,
  MISS Amy H—at Bowdoin . . . . | West Hartford, CT *06107*

Steen MR & MRS John T JR (Ida L Clement) | ☎ (210) 824-7999
  TyU'74.A.P'71 . . . . | 207 Ridgemont Av,
  JUNIORS MISS Ida L—at St Mary's Hall . . . . | San Antonio, TX
  JUNIORS MR John T 3d—at Deerfield . . . . | *78209-5431*

Steers MR & MRS John C (Claudia A Peaquin) McG'53.Ford'49
  ☎ (203) 531-9330 . . 200 Byram Shore Rd, Greenwich, CT *06830*

Steever MR N Beaumont—Syr'70
  ☎ (401) 466-8643 . . "Cielo" 781 Lakeside Dv, Box 1281, Block Island, RI *02807*

Stefani MR & MRS Jeffrey J (Emily E Todd) Stph'79.Cda.Purd'79
  5926 Lengwood Dv, Cincinnati, OH *45244*

Stemberg MR & MRS Thomas G (Hamilton—Zarins | ☎ (617) 227-5293
  —Dola S Davis) V'74.Pa'76.H.'71.H'73 . . . . . . | 5 Louisburg Square,
  JUNIORS MR Rylan Hamilton . . . . | Boston, MA *02108*

Stephaich MISS Margaret H . . . . Married at New York, NY
  Guinness HON Sebastian . . . . Nov 18'95

Stephens MR & MRS James Thomas (Julia F | ☎ (205) 322-5279
  McDonald) Y'61.H'64 . . . . | 3710 Redmont Rd,
  MISS Trent McD . . . . | Birmingham, AL
  MISS Alys F . . . . | *35213*
  MR Bryson D D . . . . |
  MR Bart W R . . . . |

Stephens MRS Robert B (Mignon J Rozier) . . . . Died at
  Washington, DC Jan 29'95

Stephens MR Robert B . . . . Died in
  Colorado Jan 16'96

Stephenson MISS Sarah Elizabeth (g—Nelson D Hooe JR) . . . . . . Born at
  Boston, MA Jun 26'95

Sterling MR & MRS Robert Lee JR (Milner—Joyce Lanier)
  Ga'53.BtP.Eyc.Plg.Srb.Evg.StA.Cc.Snc.Ne.Br'56. Cl'62 . . of
  ☎ (212) 288-1379 . . 907 Fifth Av, Apt 5C, New York, NY *10021*
  ☎ (407) 655-5981 . . 200 Regent Park, Palm Beach, FL *33480*
  "Wakefield" 2724 Peachtree Rd NE, Atlanta, GA *36305*

Stettinius MR Edward R—Va'84 . . see MRS M Ballentine
Stettinius MR Joseph JR . . see MRS M Ballentine
Stettinius MISS Mary Stuart—Va'89 . . see MRS M Ballentine

Stevens MR & MRS Lemuel B JR (Caroline A Boyd) Van'54.H'56
  ☎ (615) 269-6136 . . 4422 Warner Place, Nashville, TN *37205*

Stevens MRS William J JR (Kathleen A T Harris)
  ☎ (610) 942-2818 . . "Bally Cloon" 221 Highspire Rd, Glenmoore, PA *19343-1711*

Stevenson MR & MRS Frederick J 3d (Elizabeth M Tarasi) Pitt'82.Duq'91
  ☎ (412) 741-8909 . . 620 Sewickley Heights Dv, Sewickley, PA *15143*

Stevenson MR Frederick J 3d
  312 Breading Av, Ben Avon, Pittsburgh, PA *15202*

Stevenson MR & MRS John R (Johnson—Ruth Carter)
  SL'45.Ln.Mt.Cvc.Cly.Sl.P'42
  ☎ (817) 737-9582 . . 1200 Broad St, Ft Worth, TX *76107*

Stewart MR Henry B . . . . Died at
  Abilene, TX Sep 18'95

Stewart MISS Mary A (Zeph) . . . . Married at St Helena, CA
  Holland MR Francis K JR (late Francis K) . . . . Apr 22'95

Stewart MRS William T JR (Bertish—Cecile B | ☎ (908) 534-6918
  Bridgett) Eh.Shcc. . . . . | "Hedgerow"
  MISS Suzanne C Bertish . . . . | PO Box 116,
  MISS Jane M Bertish . . . . | Far Hills, NJ *07931*

Stick MR Gordon M F JR—Rv.Cc.Wt.Cw.Lm.Ht. | ☎ (410) 243-5555
  JHop'57.Nw'70 . . . . | A308 Evans Chapel
  MISS Anne H F . . . . | Rd, Baltimore, MD
  MISS Sarah W . . . . | *21211-1616*
  JUNIORS MISS Fair E B . . . . |
  JUNIORS MISS Margaret G W . . . . |

Stillman MRS Margaret R (Margaret D Riley) Cs.
  ☎ (212) 831-4625 . . 145 E 92 St, New York, NY *10128*

Stillman MR Peter Gordon B . . . . Died at
  New York, NY Dec 11'95

Stimpson MISS Alexandra Rose (Alexander F) . . . . Born Mch 15'94

Stimpson MR & MRS Phillip E (Brita E Schlosser) Rc.Y.Vt'81
  ☎ (212) 996-7271 . . 115 E 87 St, Apt 30A, New York, NY *10128*

Stires MRS Ernest Van R (Guntharp—Nell Kilgore) | ☎ (912) 638-4628
  MR Alfred E Guntharp JR . . . . | 28 E DeSoto,
  | PO Box 30006,
  | Sea Island, GA
  | *31561-0006*

Stocker MRS David B (Wendy Townsend) Pa'74
  ☎ (508) 369-0317 . . 702 Lowell Rd, Concord, MA *01742-5510*

Stocker MR David B—H'57.H'59
  ☎ (206) 453-9959 . . 10022 Meydenbauer Way SE, Apt 217, Bellevue, WA *98004*

Stockwell MISS Katharine W—H'92
  ☎ (617) 666-1172 . . 26 Campbell Park, Somerville, MA *02144*

Stokes MR & MRS John W 2d (Alice H Enos) | ☎ (203) 259-2750
  Me.Nrr.Hn.H'54.H'58 . . . . | 221 Willow St,
  MISS Ellery T—Vt'89.JHop'94—at Dakar, | Southport, CT *06490*
  Senegal . . . . |
  MISS Anne Kemble—at Wash'n U . . . . |

Stonesifer MR Geary L 3d (Geary L JR) . . . . Married at Coral Gables, FL
  Bowen MISS Shelley A (Barry M) . . . . Nov 4'95

Storey MR & MRS Charles Mills (Marie-Armide L Ellis)
  Br'81.Va'87.H'82.H'89
  ☎ (508) 768-6300 . . 143 John Wise Av, Essex, MA *01929*

Storrs MR & MRS David K (Young—Landon R | ☎ (203) 255-4969
  Thorn) Ny.Pqt.Yn.Y'67.H'71 . . . . | 65 Southgate Lane,
  MR David K JR—at 330 W 72 St, New York, NY | Southport, CT *06490*
  10023 . . . . |

Strain MR Robert M JR—Ny.Cin'64.Cin'65
  ☎ (516) 371-6731 . . 1635 Ocean Blvd, PO Box 476, Atlantic Beach, NY *11509*

Strand MASTER Henry Augustus (John G) . . . . Born May 30'94

Straub MR & MRS W Watson (Cheryl L Sterner) FlaSo'88.M.Me.FlaSo'91
  ☎ (610) 527-3339 . . 103B Summit Dv, Bryn Mawr, PA *19010*

Straus MR & MRS Michael S (Philippa McC Bainbridge)
  3004 Brookwood Rd, Birmingham, AL *35223*

Straus MISS Philippa Bainbridge (Michael S) . . . . Born at
  Birmingham, AL Sep 13'95

Straus MR Ralph I . . . . Died at
  Carefree, AZ Feb 5'96

Strawbridge MISS Catharine Skylar (John N) .... Born at Stamford, CT Apr 16'95
Strawbridge MR & MRS George JR (Neilson—Nina G Stewart) Srr.Ph.Rcp.Ty'60
  ☎ (302) 571-8340 . . 3801 Kennett Pike, Apt B100, Greenville, DE *19807*
Strawbridge MR & MRS William J JR (McSweeney—Christine S Penniman) Nf.Chr.Cly.Br'60 ......
  MISS Sabrina V—at 90 Victoria St, Windsor, CT *06095* ....
  MR Geoffrey T ....
  MR Michael R—at 812 Gerald St, Missoula, MT *59801* ....
    MISS A Thayer McSweeney—at 206 E 81 St, New York, NY *10028* ....
    MISS Christine S McSweeney—at Roanoke Coll ....
    JUNIORS MISS Catherine B D McSweeney....
  ☎ (410) 822-8228
  "Hippo"
  6860 Travelers Rest Circle, Easton, MD *21601-7668*
Strebeigh MISS Barbara .... Died Sep 22'94
Street MASTER Thomas Mercer JR (g—Thomas A Street) .... Born at Concord, MA Mch 23'95
Strong MR Frederick L .... Died at Bangor, ME Feb 17'96
Strong MRS Phebe (H Phebe Drayton) Pc. ....
  MR John P.........................
  ☎ (215) 836-9217
  8125 Eastern Av, Wyndmoor, PA *19038*
Stuart MRS C Parker (O'Connor—Lord—Comfort T Parker) .... name changed to Parker
Stuart MR Robert D JR (late Robert D) .... Married at Lake Forest, IL Lovenskiold MRS Harold (Inggjerd Andvord).............. Oct 7'95
Stuart MR & MRS Robert D JR (Lovenskiold—Ingegjerd Andvord) Bhm.Mt.Cho.On.Sr.Cas.Ri.Myf.P'37.Y'46 . . of
  ☎ (847) 234-3894 . . "Topsfield Farm" 1601 Conway Rd, Lake Forest, IL *60045*
  "Vaekero" Drammensveien 250, 0277 Oslo, Norway
Stuart MR Robert W W—Unn.Evg.
  ☎ (561) 334-6268 . . 1424 SE Macarthur Blvd, Stuart, FL *34996*
Studwell MISS Susannah Healy (g—William T Healy) .... Born at San Francisco, CA Jun 30'95
Sturges MR Hollister 3d—Cr'62.Cal'65
  ☎ (203) 869-4012 . . 40 Field Point Park, Greenwich, CT *06830*
Sulger MR Thomas C (late Alden H JR) ..... Married at New Orleans, LA Winingder MISS Dana L (Thomas K)..................... Nov 4'95
Sullivan MISS Eugenia C—Ac.
  ☎ (215) 542-9122 . . 239 Tulip Tree Court, Blue Bell, PA *19422*
Sullivan MR & MRS Jeremiah J 3d (Jane Mather)
  ☎ (610) 793-1157 . . "Cockaigne" 1046 Birmingham Rd, West Chester, PA *19382*
Sumner MR & MRS William O (Nancy Dry) Sth'57.Bur.H'54 ....
  MISS Allison F ....
  MR Robert M ....
  MR Stephen S ....
  ☎ (602) 488-5767
  Sincuidados 27, 30600 N Pima Rd, Scottsdale, AZ *85262-1856*
Sutherland MISS Julie P (Donald J) .... Married at Locust Valley, NY DeLalio MR John T (late Louis)....................... Sep 16'95

Sutro MRS Katharine B (Katharine S Barbour) Mds. MR Andrew H—Skd'93—at ☎ (617) 288-6323 56 Granite Av, Dorchester, MA *02124* ....
  ☎ (561) 231-8436
  600 Indian Harbor Rd, Vero Beach, FL *32963*
Sutro MRS Victor (Margherita Colucci) .... Died at Nantucket, MA Mch 13'95
Sutton MISS Elizabeth H—Winth'91.Dar.
  150 Howell Circle, Apt 226, Greenville, SC *29615*
Swan MR & MRS Henry (Freda Theopold) Stph'55.Bost'57.Me'57.H'63
  ☎ (603) 353-9834 . . "Butternut Farm" 133 Breck Hill Rd, Lyme, NH *03768*
Swan MRS Kingsley JR (Stewart—E Frances Rice)............. Died at Locust Valley, NY Dec 4'95
Swartwood MR & MRS Slater W (Kathryn H Pécot) Tr.SELa'67.
  MISS Heather W—Ala'95—at 6550 Bridgewater Valley Rd NW, Atlanta, GA *30328* ....
  MR Slater W JR—at U of Ala ....
  JUNIORS MISS Effie B ....
  ☎ (404) 255-2980
  13 Ridgemere Trace NE, Atlanta, GA *30328*
Sweatt MRS L Woodville (Louisa Woodville) .... name changed to Woodville
Swetland MR & MRS Eli B (Michelle Garnette) Miami'71.NMex'70 ....
  MR Eli B JR—at Tex Christian U ....
  JUNIORS MR Luke V—at Mercersburg ....
  ☎ (011-571) 341-9059
  Carrera 13, 27-98 Torre B, Apt 1701, Bogotá, Colombia
Swetland MR & MRS Frederick L JR (Anita M Fellner) V'40.Wms'35
  ☎ (513) 767-2541 . . Hawk Hill Farm, 170 E Hyde Rd, Yellow Springs, OH *45387*
Swett MR & MRS Steven C (Shiela L Chanler) Rdc'57.C.Hn.H'56
  ☎ (802) 649-2121 . . 1062 Bragg Hill Rd, Norwich, VT *05055*
Swift MASTER Alexander Harvey (Donald S) .... Born Sep 5'94
Swift MR & MRS Donald S (Marjorie M Harvey) NEng'83.Eh.Mg.Denis'79
  ☎ (908) 781-2465 . . PO Box 205, Old Farm Rd, Bedminster, NJ *07921*
Swift MISS Sheila K (Hampden M)............. Married at Lake Forest, IL Keil MR Bryant L (Herbert B) .... Oct 7'95
Swindell MISS Kathryn Prince (Robert H 3d)................. Born at Greenwich, CT Nov 19'95
Swope MR & MRS Gerard L (Mary G Carlton) Rdc'59.H'66.Unb.Csn.Bab'61.H'70 ....
  MR Timothy W C ....
  MR Ian G—at ☎ (215) 925-8562 . . 329 S 12 St, Philadelphia, PA *19107* ....
  ☎ (202) 363-1394
  3927 Idaho Av NW, Washington, DC *20008*
Symington MASTER Duncan McFarland (John S) .... Born Jan 3'96
Symington MR & MRS James McKim JR (Susan M Ratcliff) NwColl'76.AmU'78.Y'74.Geo'82
  ☎ (703) 356-2340 . . 1712 Birch Rd, McLean, VA *22101-4729*
Symington DR & MRS (DR) John S (Margaret J McFarland) Y'82.P'84.P'87.Y'82.StL'86
  4674 Garfield St NW, Washington, DC *20007*
Symington MRS Maud L (Van Alen—Ives—Gray—Crosby—Maud L Symington)
  ☎ (602) 314-0714 . . PO Box 12414, Scottsdale, AZ *85267*
Symington MR & MRS W Stuart 4th (Susan Ide) Bnd'74.Br'74 . . of
  ☎ (314) 994-3233 . . 745 Cella Rd, St Louis, MO *63124*
  ☎ (703) 256-7913 . . 6423 Lakeview Dv, Falls Church, VA *22041*

Symmers MRS Ann T (Ann M Trenary) Rk.
☎ (804) 984-5840 . . 73E Barclay Place Court, Charlottesville, VA *22901*

T

Taft MRS Charles N (Weu—Virgiline Thomas) . . . . Died at
Sun City, AZ Jun 20'94
Tagatac MR & MRS Christopher J (Ashley H Jones)
Geo'86.Rc.Bcs.Cly.Col'86
☎ (212) 475-0428 . . 34 Gramercy Park E, New York, NY *10003*
Tait MR & MRS Thomas (Patricia E Ritter) ArizSt'64
☎ (602) 944-6667 . . 511 W Northview Av, Phoenix, AZ *85021*
Tait MR & MRS William E (Jill S Maurer) NAriz'91.NAriz'89
☎ (602) 861-2979 . . 65 W State Av, Phoenix, AZ *85021*
Tait MASTER William Matthew (William E) . . . . Born Mch 14'95
Talley MISS Melanie DeV (Truman M) . . . . Married at New York, NY
Whatley MR Harlan D (Stanford B SR) . . . . Nov 18'95
Taney MISS Sara E (J Charles 3d) . . . . Married at Riverside, CT
Humphreys MR William F (Henry) . . . . Sep 10'95
Tasman MR & MRS W Graham (Amy L Thomas)
MmtVa'91.Pc.Rv.Ht.Duke'89
☎ (215) 86-6557 . . 702 Winding Way, Glenside, PA *19038*
Tasman DR & MRS William (Alice Lea Mast)
Bnd'55.Pc.Rv.Ht.Ac.Ncd.Dar.Dcw.Hav'51 . . . . ☎ (215) 247-3055
MISS Alice L M—Br'89.Pc.Ncd.—at 550 E Gravers Lane,
☎ (212) 780-9473 . . 140 W 4 St, Apt 10, Wyndmoor, PA
New York, NY *10012* *19038*
MR James B—Pc.Rv.Ht.Penn'87—
☎ (215) 233-3080 . . . .
Taylor MR Augustus R (William O) . . . . Married at Hanalei, Kauai, HI
Soos MISS Gabriella (Josef) . . . . Oct 4'95
Taylor MR & MRS B Loyall JR (Nancy S Harkins) ☎ (610) 725-1122
DeP'72.Cwr'74.Me.NCar'69 600 Cedar Hollow
MISS Brooke S . . . . Rd, Paoli, PA *19301*
JUNIORS MR B Loyall 3d . . . .
Taylor MR Carter S D (David W) . . . . Married at Ithan, PA
Alleva MISS Ann C (late F Alexander) . . . . Oct 7'95
Taylor MR & MRS Duncan R (Deeds—E Kathleen ☎ (520) 529-6671
Brewer) Van'70.PacRel'74.Ariz'85.Ariz'66. 3575 N Calle
Bost'69 . . . . Rosario, Tucson, AZ
MR Duncan R JR—at 1505 Virginia St, Berkeley, *85750*
CA *94703* . . . .
MR Nathaniel B—at 2639 E 9 St, Apt 7, Oakland,
CA *94601* . . . .
JUNIORS MR Blake Deeds . . . .
Taylor MRS E Hope (Thompson—E Hope Palmer) . ☎ (603) 924-9258
JUNIORS MR Robert S JR . . . . 53 Grove St,
Peterborough, NH
03458
Taylor MR & MRS Henry W JR (Sekula—Ann L Dayton) Leh'56.Nu'61
☎ (561) 575-5667 . . 953 Dolphin Court, Jupiter, FL *33458-4343*
Taylor MR & MRS John K (Delle Ernst)
☎ (513) 533-0162 . . 3580 Shaw Av, Apt 412, Cincinnati, OH *45208*
Taylor DR & MRS John Martin (Billie Minx) LSU'46
☎ (601) 442-0201 . . 311 Jefferson St, Natchez, MS *39120*

Taylor MISS Katherine Ann (Robert C JR) . . . . Born at
Winfield, IL Oct 20'95
Taylor MISS Madeline McGregor (Edmund C) . . . . Born Nov 23'95
Taylor MRS Pamela A (Psoroyannis—Pamela A ☎ (011-30-289)
Taylor) 25469
MISS Ioanna R Psoroyannis—at "L'Hameau"
☎ (718) 721-5138 . . 22-59—26 St, PO Box 606,
Long Island City, NY *11105* . . . . 84 600 Mykonos,
Greece
Taylor MISS Piper Anna (g—William O Taylor) . . . . Born Dec 24'95
Taylor MASTER Robert Carroll 3d (Robert C JR) . . . . Born at
Winfield, IL Oct 20'95
Taylor MR Robert S . . . . ☎ (603) 924-7027
MISS Lisa K—at ☎ (207) 799-7657 Old Town Farm,
7 Orchid Rd, Cape Elizabeth, ME *04107* . . . . . . Peterborough, NH
MR William C *03458*
Taylor MR Thomas . . . . Died at
Manchester-By-The-Sea, MA Nov 26'95
Taylor MRS William Davis (Ann C Macy) Tv.D.Cy.Chi.
☎ (617) 329-2621 . . 10 Longwood Dv, Apt 241, Westwood, MA *02090*
Taylor MR William Davis—Tv.D.Cy.Cw.H.'31
Burrage House, 314 Commonwealth Av, Boston, MA *02116*
Taylor MR & MRS Wilson H (Gaumer—Barbara A Bacon) Ty'64
1980 Rochambeau Dv, Malvern, PA *19355-9723*
Teller MR Andrew JR . . . . Married at Dallas, TX
Chapman MISS Carrie Christine (Robert L) . . . . Nov 4'95
Teller MR & MRS Andrew JR (Carrie Christine Chapman) Smu'86
☎ (214) 369-8584 . . 6630 Stefani Dv, Dallas, TX *75225*
Tenney MRS Charles H (Joan P Lusk) Ny.Cly.Cw.Y.
☎ (516) 581-1251 . . "The Cove" 46 Elder Rd, Islip, NY *11751*
Terry MR & MRS Anthony Denison (Dorsey— ☎ (520) 721-8788
Cecelia L Sullivant) Houst'68.Ariz'53 . . . . 7021 E Calle
MISS Elizabeth C Dorsey—Gonzaga'96—at Tolosa, Tucson, AZ
☎ (509) 325-2791 . . 224 E Sinto Av, Spokane, *85715*
WA *99202* . . . .
Terry MR Robert Cushing . . . . Died at
Boston, MA Aug 28'95
Tetzeli MRS Frederick E (Margaret L Weld) . . . . Died at
Summerton, SC Dec 28'95
Tetzeli MR Frederick E—Geo'52 . . . . ☎ (609) 921-8609
MR William G—at ☎ (804) 296-3841 336 Rosedale Rd,
912B Coleman St, Charlottesville, VA *22901* . . Princeton, NJ *08540*
MR Christopher W—at ☎ (804) 295-9973
Rte 2, Box 308, Charlottesville, VA *22901* . . .
Thieriot MR Juan P (Richard T) . . . . Married at San Francisco, CA
Brady MISS Leslie C (William J) . . . . Jan 27'96
Thieriot MR & MRS Juan P (Leslie C Brady)
3655 Clay St, San Francisco, CA *94115*
Thomas MRS Alexandra Stokes (Wheeler—Lloyd— ☎ (803) 648-1944
Alexandra C Stokes) . . . . 816 S Boundary Av,
MISS Frances P Wheeler—at Aiken, SC *29801*
1050 King of Prussia Rd, Radnor, PA *19087* .
Thomas DR & MRS James Henry (Fitts—Fitts—Cynthia I Ford)
Ala'46.Ncd.H'47 . . of
☎ (205) 553-3824 . . 1 Fairmont Woods, Tuscaloosa, AL *35405-1711*
☎ (205) 758-2664 . . "Fordland" Fosters, AL *35463*

Thomas MISS Julia K (Donald W) . . . . Married at Bedford, MA
  Bucklin MR Timothy S (Edward R) . . . . Aug 26'95
Thomas MR & MRS Robert J JR (Katherine McC Miller)
  Pg.Fcg.Rr.Ncd.Leh'72.Nw'74
  3 Deep Woods Dv, Latham, NY *12110*
Thomas MISS Sarah W (Henry M 3d) . . . . Married at
                                                  Hastings-on-Hudson, NY
  Maldonado MR Robert T (Tomas) . . . . Sep 9'95
Thomas MR Williamson . . . . Died Oct 2'95
Thompson MR & MRS Anthony de V (Lay—Elizabeth L Nager)
  MtVern'86.Pr.Ct.Emory'87
  ☎ (212) 772-7648 . . 125 E 74 St, New York, NY *10021*
Thompson MR & MRS Bruce R (Eleanor E Southworth)
  Ws'83.Del'85.Cly.Wes'83.Pa'87
  ☎ (713) 666-4461 . . 4146 Swarthmore St, Houston, TX *77005*
Thompson MRS Carolyn C (Morrison—Carolyn C Thompson)
  ☎ (713) 789-1806 . . 1806D Potomac Dv, Houston, TX *77057*
Thompson MRS Charles W (Elizabeth A Nichols) . . . . Died at
                                                Cabin John, MD Nov 14'95
Thompson DR Charles W . . . . Died at
                                                  Cabin John, MD Oct 23'95
Thompson MR Charles W JR—Del'66.Va'68
  ☎ (212) 879-8198 . . 12 E 72 St, Apt 2A, New York, NY *10021*
Thompson MR & MRS Christopher (Margaret B
  Meyer) Pitzer'74
  MISS Felicity B—at Loomis Chaffee . . . .
  MR Noel B—at "Wit's End" Old Turnpike,
  Fareham, Hampshire PO16 7HA, England . . . . .
  ☎ (707) 965-1531
  PO Box 166,
  Pope Valley, CA
  94567
Thompson MISS Eleanor S (Bruce R) . . . . Born at
                                                      Houston, TX Feb 5'96
Thompson MRS Frank L (Eleanore H Hall) . . . . Died at
                                                   St Louis, MO Apr 13'92
Thompson MR Frank L . . . . Died at
                                                   St Louis, MO Sep 30'95
Thompson MRS (DR) James E JR (Francesca Morosani) . . . Died Feb 15'96
Thompson MR & MRS John Miles JR (Williams—
  Wanda I Rolston) Rv.
  MR John Miles 3d—Chr.Rv.V'82—at
  ☎ (212) 979-1689 . . 625 E 14 St, Apt 1C,
  New York, NY *10009*
  ☎ (612) 473-7064
  1194 Weston Lane
  N, Plymouth, MN
  55447
Thompson MISS Lindsay Warrington (Stuart D) . . . . Born at
                                                 Toronto, Ontario, Canada Nov 9'95
Thompson MR Michael A (Harry A 2d) . . . . . Married at Jacksonville, FL
  Perry MISS Elisabeth D (James McL) . . . . Oct 21'95
Thompson MR & MRS Neil L (Kathleen Cox)
  Ws'80.Cy.Tvcl.Uncl.Yn.Y'64.H'66
  JUNIORS MISS Caroline R . . . .
  ☎ (617) 232-2757
  155 Chestnut Hill
  Rd, Chestnut Hill,
  MA *02167*
Thompson REV & MRS Paul M (Sallie H
  McClenahan) Sw'58.EpiscTheo'62 . . . .
  MR Ian A . . . .
  MISS Sallie H (Moore—Sallie H Thompson)—at
  67 Sea St, Apt H6, Hyannis, MA *02601* . . . .
  ☎ (802) 254-9619
  3 Bradley Av,
  Brattleboro, VT
  05301
Thompson MR Peter S—Ln.Md.H'40
  ☎ (410) 822-1640 . . "Dorsey Farm" Box 396, Rte 1, Easton,
  MD *21601-9801*

Thompson MR & MRS Robert T (Frances Bush-Brown)
  Br'77.Cyb.H'76.Stan'83
  ☎ (203) 972-1668 . . 2 Wahackme Lane, New Canaan, CT *06840*
Thomson MRS Richard S (Inez C Heidelberg) . . . . Died at
                                                    Hattiesburg, MS Nov 2'95
Thomson MR & MRS Schuyler W (Heather S Neal)
  Wms'76.Conn'85.Conn'69
  ☎ (860) 542-5081 . . 15 Pine Ledge Way, Norfolk, CT *06058*
Thorndike MISS Amanda W (Richard K 3d) . . . . Married at
                                                    South Hamilton, MA
  Landry MR Paul A (Arthur L) . . . . Dec 2'95
Thorndike MR & MRS David N (Karin E Lunde) RogerW'88.J&W'91
  ☎ (540) 955-4288 . . "Andley Farm" PO Box 510, Berryville,
  VA *22611*
Thorndike MR & MRS Richard K 3d (Myers—Margaret J Eyre)
  Drex'62.Lx.Sar.Dar.Burd'59
  ☎ (508) 922-3618 . . Box 189, 71 Paine Av, Prides Crossing, MA *01965*
Thorndike MASTER Samuel Augustus (David N) . . . . Born at
                                                    Winchester, VA Aug 25'95
Thorne MISS Susan T . . . . Died at
                                                   Hastings, MN Jun 26'95
Thouron JUNIORS MR George G 3d . . see C R Diffenderffer
Timbal MRS Paul J (Carlsund—Barbro de Jounge) . . . . Died at
                                                   Brussels, Belgium in Jly 1995
Timberlake MRS Frank S (Spencer—Winters—Bluford Richardson) . . . . . .
                                                  Died at Berryville, VA Dec 14'95
Timbers MASTER Brendan Charles (Stephen B) . . . . Died at
                                                   Durham, NC Nov 27'95
Timbers MASTER Christopher Bryan (Stephen B) . . . . Died at
                                                   Durham, NC Feb 1'96
Timpson MR & MRS Carl W JR (Patricia White) Rcn.Pr.Ln.Ng.Cly.H'52 ⚓
  ☎ (561) 243-1835 . . 725 Palm Trail, Apt 13, Delray Beach, FL *33483*
Timpson MR Ogden W (Carl W JR) . . . . Married at Prouts Neck, ME
  Hefferan MISS Frances L (George B) . . . . Nov 25'95
Tingue MASTER John Morrison (David M) . . . . Born at
                                                   Evanston, IL May 27'95
Tirrell MISS Angela
  ☎ (707) 963-2040 . . 1415 Hudson Av, St Helena, CA *94574*
Tobin MR Richard L . . . . Died at
                                                   Southbury, CT Sep 10'95
Todd MR Anderson (late Forde A) . . . . Married at Stonington, CT
  Lawrence MRS I Gracey (Iris B Gracey) . . . . Jly 4'92
Todd MR & MRS Anderson (Lawrence—Iris B Gracey)
  Rice'49.Rice'9.Dar.Pn.P'43.P'49
  ☎ (713) 529-1932 . . 1932 Bolsover Rd, Houston, TX *77005-1614*
Todd MR James—Plg.P'27.Cl'53
  ☎ (914) BE4-3382 . . "High Tor" 80 Mianus River Rd, Bedford,
  NY *10506*
Todd MR James de P JR (James de P) . . . . Married at Hamilton, NY
  Ashbaugh MISS Kyra A (Craig) . . . . Jly 24'93
Todd MR Jeffrey B (Robert C JR) . . . . Married
  McEnroe MISS Ann Marie . . . . Jun 3'95
Tolan MR & MRS Henry L (Anita M Carroll) Pa'40
  ☎ (410) 653-1605 . . 725 Mount Wilson Lane, Apt 231, Baltimore,
  MD *21208*
Toland MASTER Amos Livingston (John G) . . . . Born Dec 1'94
Toland MASTER Henry Wickser (John G) . . . . Died Sep 11'94

Tolson MRS John I (Abigail C Jones) . . . . Died
Tolson MR John I . . . . Died
Topping MR Henry J 4th—Smu'91 . . see J V Missett 3d
Topping MISS Samantha S . . see J V Missett 3d
Topping MRS Sandra E (Sack—Sandra E Topping)
   PO Box 2377, Georgetown, SC *29442*
Torrance MRS Doreen M (Doreen J Morris) F&M'79
   ☎ (610) 688-7277 . . 418 N Bellevue Av, Wayne, PA *19087*
Torrey MISS Ella King—Y'80.Miss'84
   ☎ (415) 771-9107 . . 950 Lombard St, San Francisco, CA *94133*

Tower MR & MRS Whitney (Lucy N Lyle) K.Ri.Srr.H'45 . . . . JUNIORS MISS Aurora de S	☎ (518) 584-0538 249 Clinton St, Saratoga Springs, NY *12866*

Townsend MR & MRS David G (Helen I Gaylord) Stan'52.L. . . . . MISS Sheila C—at 4795 Easley Rd, Golden, CO *80403* . . . . MISS Lila G—at ☎ (207) 775-0758 42 Alton St, Portland, ME *04102*	☎ (860) 824-5653 "River House" River Rd, Box 257, Falls Village, CT *06031*

Townsend MR Edward L—VaCmth'86
   ☎ (804) 573-5763 . . "Maserville Farm" 3435 Musket Dv, Midlothian, VA *23113*
Townsend MR Rodman . . . . Died at
   Knoxville, TN Dec 6'95

Townsend MR & MRS Steven S JR (Jones—Baxter— Lucia P Whitman) Bur.Cal'68.H'75 . . . . JUNIORS MR John L	☎ (415) 668-1148 136 Third Av, San Francisco, CA *94118*

Trautman MRS Mary Lee (Mary Lee Love)
   ☎ (508) 748-2480 . . 555 Delano Rd, Marion, MA *02738*

Travell MRS Philippa W (Harlan—Breckenfeld— Philippa L Walter) . . . . MR William G Breckenfeld—at Villanova Law	☎ (860) 767-3307 Heritage Cove C6, 85 River Rd, Essex, CT *06426*

Treadwell MR & MRS Louis Mead 2d (Carol A Walsh) SUNY'80.Y'78.H'82
   528 N St, Anchorage, AK *99501*

Treat MRS L Smith (Lucinda Luce Smith) Cvc. . . . . MISS Lucinda K . . . . MR Charles E . . . . MR John T E	☎ (202) 337-1718 3851 Newark St NW, Apt 457, Washington, DC *20016*

Trenholm MRS Elena de S (Bullock—Bowyer—Elena de Struve)
   ☎ (305) 868-9230 . . 9133 Collins Av, Surfside, FL *33154*
Trevor MR & MRS Bronson (Eleanor D Fisher)
   Un.Rc.K.BtP.Pr.Cw.Sar.Cly.Dc.Ht.Cl'31
   ☎ (516) 759-1264 . . 125 Shu Swamp Rd, Locust Valley, NY *11560*
Trevor MASTER John Bond 5th (gg—John B Trevor JR) . . . . Born at
   Providence, RI Dec 8'95

Trevor MRS Michele (Simpson—Michele M Safley) Ariz'75 . . . . JUNIORS MISS Melanie S Simpson—at Choate Rosemary	☎ (602) 948-9680 5029 Roadrunner Rd, Paradise Valley, AZ *85253*

Trimble MISS Delia Moher (g—Francis de Marneffe) . . . . Born at
   Philadelphia, PA Feb 24'96

Trimble MR & MRS Francis Elliott (Elizabeth H Rudolph) Van'38.Van'40
   ☎ (601) 442-7529 . . 24 Homochitto St, Natchez, MS *39120*
Trink MRS B Zilkha (Bettina L Zilkha) . . . . name changed to Zilkha

Tripp MRS Robert J (Audrey D Shortlidge) . . . . MR Stephen R 3d—at ☎ (408) 476-0795 4780 Porter Gulch Rd, Aptos, CA *95003*	☎ (415) 324-7487 850 Webster St, Palo Alto, CA *94301*

Trippe MR & MRS Charles W (Pamela J Reid) Ny.Ln.Yn.Y'57.H'59
   ☎ (561) 388-9822 . . 12376 N A1A, Vero Beach, FL *32963*
True MISS Amy Ballantine (Jeffrey R) . . . . Born Nov 20'95
True MISS Gabriella M . . see MISS K T Emmet
True MR & MRS Jeffrey R (Carolyn D Ballantine) Hood'83
   ☎ (301) 371-8509 . . 6827 Maryland Av, PO Box 220, Braddock Heights, MD *21714*
True MISS K Emmet (Katharine T Emmet) . . . . . . name changed to Emmet
Trueblood MRS Wilbur T (Anne C Taussig)
   ☎ (941) 597-1790 . . 6060 Pelican Bay Blvd, Apt B201, Naples, FL *33963*

Trump MR & MRS Robert Townshend (Sandra F Snowden) Cda. . . . . MISS Lillie F—Ithaca'90—at ☎ (770) 449-7509 Peachtree Corners Circle, Norcross, GA *30092* . MR Michael—Syr'93—at ☎ (818) 797-9896 280½ E Mendocino St, Altadena, CA *91001* . . .	☎ (215) 233-1707 "Hayloft" 668 Bethlehem Pike, Whitemarsh, Flourtown, PA *19031*

Truslow MASTER Austen Riggs (Peter C) . . . . Born at
   Ft Lauderdale, FL Feb 13'96

Truslow MR & MRS William A (Miriam P Kellogg) Rdc'62.Sim'82.C.Sb.Tv.Y'58.H'64 . . . . MR Hugh K—Vt'91—at ☎ (212) 229-9240 120 Christopher St, Apt 16, New York, NY *10014* . . . . MR Samuel B—H'94—at ☎ (617) 742-2312 144 Chestnut St, Boston, MA *02108*	of ☎ (617)864-1327 4 Hawthorn St, Cambridge, MA *02138* ☎ (802) 234-9000 Box 104, Barnard, VT *05031*

Truslow MR William A 3d (William A) . . . . Married at New London, CT
   Cairns MISS Jennifer A (George E) . . . . Aug 12'95
Tuck MISS Katherine D M (J Marshall) . . . . Married at Paris, France
   de Meaux VCTE Marc (Maurice) . . . . Sep 23'95
Tucker MR & MRS Daniel J (Lucy Thornton Lennon) Colby'87
   ☎ (207) 772-7127 . . 9 Wellstone Dv, Portland, ME *04103*
Tucker MR Marshall O—Cvc.Vt'84.Cl'91
   ☎ (212) 242-4118 . . 351 W 22 St, New York, NY *10011-2601*
Tucker MRS Mayson H (Welton—Tucker—Selma A Badenhop) . . . . Died Oct 28'95
Tucker MR & MRS Peter J (Sara A Glover) Geo'82.Cl'89.Geo'82
   ☎ (203) 222-7625 . . 151 Imperial Av, Westport, CT *06880*
Tucker MR & MRS Sterling Woodward 3d (Ann Hancock) NCar'46.Duke'43
   ☎ (501) 663-4051 . . 6 Armistead Rd, Little Rock, AR *72207*
Tucker MRS Toinette (Randell—King—Toinette Tucker) MmtMhn'80.Ri.Ds.
   ☎ (860) 364-0004 . . "Rosewood Farm" 6 Herb Rd, Sharon, CT *06069*
Tucker MASTER Tristan James (Daniel J) . . . . Born at
   Portland, ME Jun 30'95
Tuckerman MRS Alfred G (Kerr—Anne O Clark) . . . . Died at
   Needham, MA Jan 9'96
Tullis MR Paul R—Cal'92 . . see T C Clarke
Tullis MISS Tracy—Br'86 . . see T C Clarke

Turman MRS Christopher M JR (Elisabeth F Morris)
☎ (215) 643-1162 . . Spring House Estates F122, 728 Norristown Rd, Lower Gwynedd, PA *19002*
Turner MR Burton B . . . . Died at San Francisco, CA Sep 19'95
Turner MRS Gardner C (Virginia Wells) . . . . Died at Chesham, NH Nov 8'95
Turner MISS Maria M (Le Baron) . . . . Married at Danville, CA Gerard MR Scott T (William U) . . . . Jan 13'96
Turnure MISS Barbara F—Hartw'84
☎ (310) 399-8566 . . 245 Main St, Apt 108, Venice, CA *90291*
Tweedy MRS Gordon B (Mary Johnson) . . . . Died Dec 2'95
Tyler MR & MRS Harold R JR (Barbara L Eaton) C.Csn.P'43.Cl'49
☎ (860) 435-8053 . . 14 Tokone Hills Rd, Lakeville, CT *06039*

U

Uihlein MISS Linda R—Swb'77
☎ (804) 973-6015 . . Little Owl Farm, 1842 Davis Shop Rd, Earlysville, VA *22936*
Umberger MR & MRS Max J (Julia S Johnston) Penn'92
☎ (610) 695-8972 . . 207 Charleston Greene, Malvern, PA *19355*
Unruh MR & MRS Charles L (Mary L Sexton) NH'92.NH'91
☎ (011-49-6221) 351286 . . 10-1 Botheplatz, 69126 Heidelberg, Germany
Unterman JUNIORS MR Ian H . . see MR T H Drew
Unterman JUNIORS MISS Megan D . . see MR T H Drew
Unterman MRS T Hoffstot (Thayer Drew Hoffstot) . . . . name changed to Drew

Upson MR Thomas F—Sar.Cw.W&J'63.Conn'68 . . | ☎ (203) 753-1193
MR Secor . . . . | 827 Oronoke Rd,
MR Chauncey J . . . . | Apt 10-1, Waterbury, CT *06708*

Urban MR & MRS Henry Z JR (Margaret A Kroth) SUNY'83.St.Cy.Ham'77.Suff'80
95 Wagon Wheel Dv, East Amherst, NY *14051*

V

Valentine MR & MRS E Massie (Van Alen—Virginia Guest) Srr.BtP.Va'56
☎ (804) 353-1579 . . 204 Lockgreen Court, Richmond, VA *23226*
Valentine MR & MRS H Stuart 4th (Kara K Mulcahy) VillaN'92.Shcc.Yn.Y'86
☎ (908) 234-1388 . . 47 E Fox Chase Rd, Chester, NJ *07930*

Van Cleave MR & MRS John P (Margaret M Prigmore) Hlns'75.Tenn'73 . . . . | ☎ (423) 821-5662
JUNIORS MISS Margaret G . . . . | 202 W Brow Oval, Lookout Mountain, TN *37350*

Vandam MRS Albert R (Carolyn T Laughlin) Br'67.Ub. | ☎ (617) 749-1474
MISS Hilary R—Br'96 . . . . | 33 Fearing Rd,
LT Todd P—USA.Ub.Br'92—at | Hingham, MA *02043*
☎ (617) 424-1210 . . 124 Beacon St, Boston, MA *02116* . . . . |

Vandam MR Albert R—Ub.Br'64
☎ (617) 545-1153 . . 63 Tilden Rd, Scituate, MA *02066*

Vandeveer MR & MRS Jay W (Jeanette A Jenkins) Ws'76.DU'73 . . . . | ☎ (402) 393-4630
JUNIORS MISS Elizabeth C . . . . | 1415 S 84 St,
JUNIORS MR William W . . . . | Omaha, NE *68124*
JUNIORS MR Austin C . . . . |

Vanneck MASTER William James (g—William P Vanneck) . . . . . Born at Rye, NY Jun 1'94
Vanneck MR & MRS William P (Scroggins—Margaret R Heffington) AthSt'72.BtP.Evg.U'62
☎ (407) 833-5018 . . 315 Southlake Dv, Palm Beach, FL *33480*
Van Ness MR & MRS Lewis W (Janis S Wren) Ark'78.Ark'78
☎ (501) 227-4711 . . 28 Huntington Rd, Little Rock, AR *72207*
Van Vranken MR & MRS J Frederick JR (Nancy J Sharp) MHBaylor'60.Ri.Mb.Mid'57
☎ (516) 681-4077 . . "Black Walnut Farm" PO Box 264, Cedar Swamp Rd, Jericho, NY *11753*
Vasquez MISS Alexandra (g—MRS Robert B Meyer JR) . . . . . Born Sep 5'95
Vasquez MISS Elliott (g—MRS Robert B Meyer JR) . . . . Born Oct 5'93
Vaughan MR Todd K—Rcp.B.Nyc.Ste.Md'66.Pa'71
☎ (410) 820-6033 . . Box 1326, Easton, MD *21601*
Vaughn MR & MRS James M JR (Salle A Werner) TexWmn'61.Tex'61 . . of
☎ (713) 524-6574 . . 2235 Brentwood Dv, Houston, TX *77019*
☎ (212) 879-9786 . . 9 E 82 St, Apt 5A, New York, NY *10028*
Vermeule MRS Cornelius C (Catherine S Comstock) . . . . Died at Summit, NJ Jan 13'96
Vestner MR Eliot N (late Eliot N) . . . . Married at Hamilton, MA Cutler MRS Louisa R (Louisa R Baptiste) . . . . Aug 11'95

Vestner MR & MRS Eliot N (Cutler—Louisa R Baptiste) . . . . | ☎ (617) 523-5074
MR Donald F Cutler 4th—at 138 Lerner Rd, Huntington, VT *05462* . . . . | 1 Devonshire Place, Apt 2605, Boston, MA *02109*
MR Q A Shaw Cutler—at 308 Sagamore St, PO Box 2176, South Hamilton, MA *01982* . . |

Victor MISS Jane G (g—Royall Victor 3d) . . . . Born at San Francisco, CA Jun 2'95
Vilas MRS Charles H (Margaret V Van Pelt) . . . . Died at Branford, CT Sep 13'95
Villalba MISS Sonia M . . see MRS S H Grimm
Villard MR Henry S . . . . Died at Los Angeles, CA Jan 21'96
Vincel MISS Carolyn A . . see A Fletcher JR

Vincent MRS Linn Rumsey (M Linn C Rumsey) Tex'67.Dar. . . . . | ☎ (713) 973-7010
JUNIORS MR Kenneth R . . . . | 12644 Huntingwick Dv, Houston, TX *77024*

Vlcek MRS Jan B (Ann E Lewis) Stan'69.Geo'81.Cvc.Sl. . . . . | ☎ (301) 657-2035
MISS Elizabeth A—at Princeton . . . . | 30 Quincy St, Chevy Chase, MD *20815*
JUNIORS MISS Katharine B—at Nat'l Cath Sch . . . |

Vogt MISS Amy Nicole (Peter A) . . . . Born Mch 18'93
Vogt MR Thomas Bulman . . . . | 5900 Old Ocean
    MISS Newell W . . . . | Ridge Blvd, Apt B7,
    | Ocean Ridge, FL
    | *33435*
Vohr MISS Caroline Sheldon (g—John C Jansing) . . . . Born at
    Laurel Hollow, NY Sep 1'95
Volmert, Craig A & Buell, N Catherine—Wash'87
    ☎ (314) 862-4649 . . 85 Greendale Dv, St Louis, MO *63121*
von Briesen MRS Elizabeth S (Moore—Elizabeth S Suydam) . . . . . Died at
    Cold Spring Harbor, NY Feb 12'96
von Estorff MISS (DR) Irene—Ws'62.Mayo'80
    ☎ (914) 534-2878 . . PO Box 505, Deer Hill Rd, Cornwall-on-Hudson,
    NY *12520*
von Raab MISS Alexandra L—Denis'95 . . see C E Baskett
von Russow MISS Katherine Francis (Wolfgang L) . . . . Born at
    Port Jefferson, NY Jly 22'94
von Stade MR F Skiddy JR . . . . Died Sep 29'95
von Stade MR & MRS John T (Sandra K Carnahan) Rcn.Srr.Shcc.Eh.H'60
    ☎ (908) 234-0430 . . 54 Fowler Rd, Peapack, NJ *07977*
von Zweck MR & MRS Heimart (Laura B Pollock)
    Wheat'77.Bvl.Graz'58 ⚓
    ☎ (617) 354-3385 . . 221 Mt Auburn St, Cambridge, MA *02138*
Voorhees MR Peter C Van (Clifford I Van) . . . . Died Sep 30'95
Vulté MR Richard T JR . . . . Died at
    Greenbrae, CA Jan 19'96

W

Wack MR & MRS Patrick J JR (Laura H Sculley) SCal'89.Ihy.P'89
    ☎ (203) 869-5004 . . 21 John St, Greenwich, CT *06831*
Wadsworth MR W Austin—Cr'59 . . . . | ☎ (716) 243-1413
    MISS (LT) Martha C—USAF.ArizSt'93 . . . . | "The Homestead"
    MR Craig P—at ☎ (716) 658-3364 | Box 5, Geneseo, NY
    Box 159, Geneseo, NY *14354* . . . . | *14454*
Wait MR William G . . . . Died at
    Needham, MA Mch 18'94
Waite MR & MRS Parker R (M Florence Wardwell) Me.Myf.
    ☎ (610) 525-3947 . . 74 Pasture Lane, Apt 236, Bryn Mawr, PA *19010*
Wakeman MR & MRS G Wiley (Michele Hallett) BostColl'86.Bvl.
    ☎ (207) 967-5803 . . 78R Beachwood Rd, Kennebunkport, ME *04046*
Walcott MRS Roger C (Maud L Pool) . . . . Died at
    Milwaukee, WI Sep 16'95
Walden MR & MRS Russell T (Natalie L Campbell) ColC'72.Conn'70
    ☎ (513) 561-1071 . . 8675 Camargo Club Dv, Cincinnati, OH *45243*
Waldron MR & MRS Adam A (Susan M Wenzell)
    Geo'85.Pa'89.HampSydney'84
    ☎ (610) 388-3472 . . 212 Fairville Rd, Chadds Ford, PA *19317*
Waldron MASTER Theodore Nelson (Arthur N) . . . . Born Jan 10'96
Walker MR Christopher G P (George G JR) . . . Married at Plymouth, MN
    Keding MISS Susan (Albert) . . . . Dec 30'95
Walker MR John 3d . . . . Died at
    Amberley, West Sussex, England Oct 16'95
Walker MR John B . . . . Died Sep 16'95
Walker MR John Y G . . . . Died at
    Montclair, NJ Jun 3'94
Walker MRS John Y G (Mary L Riter)
    ☎ (201) 633-7420 . . 9 Christopher Court, Lincoln Park, NJ *07035*
Walker MASTER John Yates Gohlson 4th (g—MRS John Y G Walker) . . . .
    Born Oct 19'95
Walker MR & MRS Richard W (Christine M | of ☎ (011-44-171)
    Krumpholz) B.Pcu.Cly. . . . . | 589-2318
    JUNIORS MR Marco C—at Brighton U . . . . | 39 Egerton Crescent,
    | London SW3 2EB,
    | England
    | ☎ (011-43-1)
    | 869-0654
    | Rudolfgasse 9,
    | A2380
    | Perchtoldsdorf,
    | Austria
Walker MR & MRS Robert A JR (Monique M Briend) | ☎ (301) 230-9809
    Rennes'70.Rennes'71.Godd'74.Vt'83.Bost'86 . . . | 10818 Brewer
    JUNIORS MISS Charlotte M E . . . . | House Rd,
    | North Bethesda, MD
    | *20852*
Walker MR Stewart S—Bost'91
    ☎ (401) 247-7489 . . 72 Orchard Av, Barrington, RI *02806*
Wall MRS Ashbel T (Cocroft—Isabel Doolittle) . . . . Died Sep 12'95
Wall MRS Fenwick W (Edmonds—Appleby—Audrey B Ulman) . . . Died at
    New York, NY Aug 10'95
Wallace MR & MRS Christopher G (Margaret F Tucker)
    Lynch'86.Me.Cda.Pa'74
    ☎ (215) 233-8027 . . 208 Yeakel Av, Erdenheim, PA *19038*
Wallace MR Revett B . . . . Died at
    Woodside, CA Oct 12'95
Wallace MRS William Byron (Josephine J Player)
    Tamalpais 317, 501 Via Casitas, Greenbrae, CA *94904*
Waller MR & MRS John W 3d (Alexis P Robinson) MtVern'88.Va'71
    ☎ (212) 534-3242 . . 1112 Park Av, New York, NY *10128*
Waller MASTER John Wickliffe 4th (John W 3d) . . . . Born at
    New York, NY Jun 22'95
Walsh MISS Emily Owens (Eric F) . . . . Born at
    Newport Beach, CA Dec 28'95
Walsh CAPT & MRS Eric F (Caroline E McK Earle) USMC.H'88.Ham'89
    ☎ (401) 273-9288 . . 20 Cooke St, Providence, RI *02906*
Walsh MRS Margaret F (Margaret S Fearey) Me. . . . | ☎ (415) 461-6257
    MISS Samantha A—at 240 W Evergreen Av, | 644 Via Casitas,
    Philadelphia, PA *19118* . . . . | Greenbrae, CA
    | *94904*
Walsh MR & MRS Mark L (Mary B Vail) Skd'76.Hn.U'76.H'80
    ☎ (301) 657-3620 . . 5212 Dorset Av, Chevy Chase, MD *20815*
Walther JUNIORS MISS Amanda L . . see J P Austin 3d
Walton MISS Anne B (Robert E) . . . . . . Married at Gibson Island, MD
    Hanifen LT COL Timothy C—USMC. . . . . Apr 29'95
Walton MR & MRS Henry Foster 3d (Jessie M Delp) EStroud'42
    ☎ (717) 897-5467 . . 3018 N Delaware Dv, PO Box 385, Portland,
    PA *18351*

Walton MR & MRS John M 3d (Cornelia P Parsly) Rc.Sg. . . . . ☎ (215) 646-9320
MISS Elfrida E—HWSth'84—at 5 Fox Pond,
☎ (215) 233-8924 . . 6280 Henry Lane, Spring House, PA
Flourtown, PA *19031* *19477*
Walton MR & MRS Joseph C (Molly Erwin)
Tex'81.Fcg.Pg.Rr.Wms'79.Tex'83
☎ (412) 338-6604 . . 1449 Wightman St, Pittsburgh, PA *15217*
Walton MR & MRS Robert E (Mary K Heyl) Br'50.Gi.Rv.Cspa.W.Pa'43
☎ (410) 255-5765 . . St Giles Rd, Gibson Island, MD *21056*
Wanzer MR & MRS (DR) Charles T (Lydia Faesy)
Vt'86.Bastyr'94.Mid'85.H'92
☎ (802) 229-0701 . . 5 Edwards St, Montpelier, VT *05602*
Ward MR John . . . . Died Feb 21'96
Ward MASTER Owen Thomas Babbott (g—Thomas E Ward JR) . . Born at
Boston, MA Oct 7'95
Ward MR & MRS Seth C (Anne P Bowers) Va'83.My.Y'83.H'88
☎ (617) 723-5460 . . 17 Joy St, Boston, MA *02114*
Warden DR David E . . . . Died Jan 25'96
Ware MR & MRS Charles E (Sample—Kathleen B Calkins) H'34
☎ (603) 924-0902 . . 15 River Mead Rd, Peterborough, NH *03458*
Ware MASTER Thomas Holmes (g—MRS A Gilkey Ware) . . . . Born
Dec 9'94
Ware MR & MRS William (Susan L Fullerton) ☎ (508) 563-5202
H.'59.H'64. . . . . 270 Old Main Rd,
MISS (DR) Elisabeth P—Carl'87.Mass'95—at North Falmouth,
☎ (513) 731-0250 . . 3501 Bellewood Av, MA *02556-2402*
Cincinnati, OH *45213*. . . . .
MISS Anne C—Wes'87
MISS Mary L—Amer'90—at ☎ (916) 642-2737
5821 Farish Rd, Placerville, CA *95667* . . . . . .
MR William JR—Mid'91.Dth'94—at
☎ (415) 368-9024 . . 660 Briar Island Rd, Apt
40, Redwood City, CA *94063* . . . .
Warfield MR John W (Edwin 3d). . . . . Married at Scarborough, ME
Edmondson MISS M Josephine (Robert). . . . . Sep 23'95
Warren MISS Catharine K (Bernstein—Catharine K Warren) SL'69 . . of
☎ (212) 288-9228 . . 145 E 74 St, New York, NY *10021*
☎ (011-33-90) 92-51-13 . . Mas de Mérmbeau, 13210
St Rémy-de-Provence, France
Warren MRS John D (Helen G Lynch) Exy.
☎ (860) 767-1180 . . 134 Essex Meadows, Essex, CT *06426*
Warren MISS Leslie . . see MRS C J La Roche
Warren MASTER Peter Milliken (Peter W) . . . . Born Jun 22'95
Warren MR & MRS Peter W (Harriette M Moore) RISD'85.Rc.Srb.Nrr.H'82
☎ (212) 288-8235 . . 106 E 85 St, Apt 8S, New York, NY *10028*
Warren MRS Ralph A (Meyerink—Kathryn Watkins) . . . . Died Aug 3'95
Washburn MR Charles G III
☎ (612) 291-0014 . . 339 Summit Av, St Paul, MN *55102*

Washburn MR & MRS J Murray 3d (Karen E ☎ (603) 643-2829
Wagner) Thiel'66.Purd'62.Cal'69. . . . . Dogford Rd, Etna,
MISS Wynne C—at 4117 N Albina Av, Portland, NH *03750*
OR *97217*. . . . .
MISS Anne K. . . . .
MR J Murray 4th—ColC'93—at 2126 W Kiowa
St, Colorado Springs, CO *80904* . . . .
MR Peter C—Hampshire'95—at 51 Bay Rd,
Hadley, MA *01035* . . . .
Washburn MRS Patricia W (Sampson—Patricia Weld) . . . Died Dec 31'95
Washburn MISS Sandra L—H'78.Nu'83
☎ (214) 358-3806 . . 5112 Horseshoe Trail, Dallas, TX *75209*
Waterman MRS A Porter (Sterling—Edwards—Patricia G Kenway) . . . . .
Died at Greenwich, CT Nov 12'95
Watkins MR Robert M—Aht'49.Cl'51. . . . . ☎ (212) EN9-2478
MR Richard S—at ☎ (617) 277-9097 520 E 90 St,
5 Gorham Av, Brookline, MA *02146* . . . . New York, NY
10128
Watson MR & MRS George E 3d (Louisa Carter ☎ (202) 244-7033
Johnson) Wheat'62.Cos.Y'53.Y'61.Y'64 . . . . . 4323 Cathedral Av
MISS Elisabeth Carter—Ws'91—at NW, Washington,
☎ (202) 237-7113 . . 3516—34 St NW, DC *20016*
Washington, DC *20008*. . . . .
MR George E IV—Duke'94—at
☎ (704) 342-5756 . . 2108 Park Rd, Apt 1,
Charlotte, NC *28203*. . . . .
Watson MISS Lucinda B (Kew—Mehran—Lucinda ☎ (415) 435-5923
B Watson) SL'77 . . . . 10 Crest Rd,
MISS Christina E Kew . . . . Belvedere, CA
MISS Annabel M Mehran *94970*
JUNIORS MR Alexander R Mehran JR. . . . .
Watterson MRS David G (Jane Van Gorder) Ws'31.May.
☎ (216) 231-8414 . . 2181 Ambleside Dv, Apt 802, Cleveland,
OH *44106*
Watts MR Henry M JR . . . . Died at
Philadelphia, PA Oct 2'95
Watts MISS Louise . . . . Died at
New York, NY Oct 9'95
Waxter MR Arthur L S JR—MdArt'77
5542 Suffield Court, Columbia, MD *21044*
Webb MRS Grant H (Weld—Sally A Duggan). . . . . Died Feb 7'96
Webb MR & MRS Samuel B JR (Weir—Marshall M ☎ (802) 985-4151
Brown) SFr'75.Cl'86.Rc.B.Pr.BtP.So.Cly.Y'61. "Deerhill"
Y'63.Cal'70 Southern Acres
MR Edward W—Vt'92—at ☎ (617) 964-5337 Farm, Harbor Rd,
31 Highland Av, Apt 1, Newton, MA *02160* . . . PO Box 216,
MR William V—at ☎ (802) 865-3801 Shelburne, VT
7 Bradley St, Burlington, VT *05401* *05482*
Webb CAPT & MRS T Ladson JR (Kristin B Dillon) ☎ (703) 750-3512
USN.Tex'72.An.Tul'72.Chap'78 . . . . 680 N Armistead St,
MISS Katherine D—at Wm & Mary . . . . Alexandria, VA
JUNIORS MR T Ladson 3d—at Episcopal *22312*

Weber MRS John C (Charlotte D Colket)
Rd.Ri.Srr.Ac.Cly. . . . .
  MISS Christina C . . . .
  MR John C JR—Srr. . . . .
  MR Chester C . . . .
  of ☎ (352)854-6776
  "Live Oak"
  9275 SW 9 Street
  Rd, Ocala, FL *34481*
  ☎ (212) 517-8833
  3 E 77 St, Apt 4B,
  New York, NY
  10021

Weber DR John C—Rd.Ri.Srr.Colg'61.Cl'65
  ☎ (212) 249-5433 . . 960 Fifth Av, New York, NY *10021*
Weber MISS Megan Elise (Peter B) . . . . Born Dec 5'94
Webster MR & MRS Geoffrey L (Lucy R Anthony) MtVern'87.Cly.Cda.
  ☎ (212) 772-9919 . . 314 E 83 St, New York, NY *10028*
Webster MISS Helen Sherman (Hugh K) . . . . Born at
  Washington, DC Dec 12'95
Webster MRS Herbert S SR (Crowell—Jean Biddle Page) . . . . Died
  Oct 10'95
Weed DR & MRS Timothy (Lucinda Nalle) Ty'87.W&L'83.Aub'94
  ☎ (803) 642-0368 . . 321 Orangeburg St, Aiken, SC *29801*
Weedon MR & MRS Alexander R (Elizabeth L Warner) WmSth'77.Cy.Ty'77
  ☎ (617) 237-5292 . . 6 Woodlawn Av, Wellesley Hills, MA *02181*
Weekes MR & MRS John M (Tamsen A Rideout)
Chico'70.Mid'63 . . . .
  MISS Elizabeth S—at ☎ (208) 622-6528
Box 2974, Ketchum, ID *83340* . . . .
  MR Henry DeF—at ☎ (208) 726-5597
Box 4774, Ketchum, ID *83340* . . . .
  ☎ (208) 788-3833
  PO Box 3784,
  Hailey, ID *83333*

Weeks MISS Carly Allyn (Gerald C) . . . . Born Jun 29'95
Weeks MR & MRS Gerald C (Nancy K Allen) StL'84.StL'85
  ☎ (802) 885-9306 . . 831 Randall Hill Rd, Springfield, VT *05156*
Weicker MISS Alexa Gray (Gray G). . . . . Born at
  Greenwich, CT Sep 2'94
Weicker MR & MRS Gray G (Penne L Brooks) StLaw'85.StLaw'84
  ☎ (203) 655-9432 . . 120 Five Mile River Rd, Darien, CT *06820*
Weicker MASTER Matthew Godfrey (Scot B) . . . . Born at
  Greenwich, CT Feb 16'93
Weicker MR & MRS Scot B (Lisa M Hull) Rich'81.Rich'80
  ☎ (203) 622-6091 . . 475 North St, Greenwich, CT *06830*
Weisberger MRS David (Forbes—Jackson—Alida B Goodwin) . . . . . Died
  Nov 3'95
Weist MISS Helen H . . . . Died Nov 13'95
Welch MR Samuel M (Stuart C) . . . . Married at Santa Barbara, CA
  Goena MISS Mina A . . . . May 7'94
Wellborn MR & MRS John Bennett (Kelly G Dunnam) Tex'88.Okla'90
  ☎ (214) 350-9215 . . 5433 Druid Lane, Dallas, TX *75209*
Welles MR & MRS David W (Marcia L Andersen)
Y'61.Va'64 . . . .
  MISS Dede W—Y'92 . . . .
  MISS Margaret D—at Yale . . . .
  MR Michael L—Ch'94 . . . .
  ☎ (212) TR6-5042
  55 E 76 St,
  New York, NY
  10021

Wells MRS A Turner (Celia S Kreis) . . . . Died at
  Walpole, MA Dec 8'95
Wells MR Christopher J—Ht.Lm.Cl'72
  ☎ (011-44-171) 584-7533 . . 21 Sumner Place, London SW7 3EG,
  England

Wells MASTER George Breckinridge (Mason B 2d) . . . . Born at
  Norwalk, CT Jun 19'95
Wells MR & MRS Gordon Menard (Maxine Richbourg)
  ☎ (601) 373-4407 . . 1564 Wood Glen Dv, Jackson, MS *39204*
Wells MR & MRS L Dana (Regina M Witt) Va'58 . . . .
  MR Geoffrey S—Va'85—at 16 Redwood Dv,
San Rafael, CA *94901* . . . .
  MR Michael D—at ☎ (818) 584-9451
425 Waldo Av, Apt 306, Pasadena, CA *91101* . .
  of ☎ (540)348-5453
  Cloverdale Farm,
  Rte 1, Box 596,
  Raphine, VA *24472*
  ☎ (941) 475-7618
  7365 Manasota Key
  Rd, Englewood, FL
  34223

Wells MR & MRS M Henry (Patricia P Brown)
BMr'44.Ox'49.Pc.Ill'37.Y'47 . . . .
  MISS Emily H—Earl'86.BMr'93—at
☎ (610) 239-0415 . . 1220 Skippack Pike,
Blue Bell, PA *19422* . . . .
  ☎ (215) CH7-7084
  8022 Roanoke St,
  Philadelphia, PA
  19118

Wells MR & MRS Mason B 2d (Kathryn Breslin) Ham'85.Rcn.Mid'84
  ☎ (203) 656-0535 . . 7 Old Stone Rd, Darien, CT *06820*
Wells MR & MRS Roger K (Susan Shaffer)
Hlns'66.Mit'67 . . . .
  MISS Kiley A—at Boulder, CO . . . .
  MISS Louise L . . . .
  ☎ (401) 846-9537
  229 Gibbs Av,
  Newport, RI *02840*

Wells MRS Wellington JR (Hudgins—Vallie K Olson) . . . . Died at
  Marlborough, NH Jan 2'96
Welsh MRS Charles N (Olga Bobrovnikova) . . . . Died at
  Haverford, PA Sep 19'95
Werner MISS Andrée Rozier (Peter G D) . . . . Born Nov 19'93
Wessells MISS D Reed (Daniel B) . . . . Married at Glenmoore, PA
  Nichols MR Brett E (Fred E) . . . . Nov 4'95
Wessells MR & MRS Daniel B (Deborah L Dunn)
Sfh.Ds.P'50 . . . .
  MISS Alexandra B—Syr'90—at 676 Olive Av,
Novato, CA *94947* . . . .
  ☎ (610) 942-4383
  781 Fairview Rd,
  Glenmoore, PA
  19343

Westwater MR & MRS William King (Shirle J Nesbitt) OState'35
  ☎ (614) 253-5559 . . 2371 Commonwealth Park S, Columbus, OH *43209*
Wetzel MASTER Christopher Baldwin (Robert B) . . . . Born at
  Pittsburgh, PA Oct 26'95
Wheeler MRS Alexander JR (Greer—Christina Binney) . . . . Died at
  Sherborn, MA Aug 30'95
Wheeler MRS Edward K (Charlotte Sharp) . . . . Died at
  Washington, DC Jan 14'95
Wheeler MISS Frances P . . see MRS A S Thomas
Wheeler MR Frederic C 3d—Ithaca'80 . . . .
  JUNIORS MISS Kerry W . . . .
  ☎ (610) 574-0707
  605 W Market St,
  Apt 38,
  West Chester, PA
  19380

Wheeler MR Leonard . . . . Died at
  Boston, MA Apr 4'95
Wheeler MR & MRS Thomas B (Anne T Robertson)
Sth'61.Ln.Cly.Yn.Y'58 ⚓ . . . .
  MISS Wendy B—Cr'90—at 17 Gloucester St,
Boston, MA *02115* . . . .
  288 Park Dv,
  Springfield, MA
  01106

Wheeler DR & MRS W Mark 3d (Katherine M Norcross) P'60.Wash'64. . . . . ☎ (207) 443-5712 "Harndon Farm" RR 3, Box 828, Montsweag Rd, Woolwich, ME 04579
MISS Elizabeth F. . . . .
MR Timothy N. . . . .
MR Andrew C. . . . .
MR Geoffrey H. . . . .
Wheeler MR William L. . . . . Died
Wheelock DR & MRS E Frederick (M Jean Lowery) Ala'51.Mit'50.Cl'55.Rock'61 . . . . ☎ (610) LA5-5270 315 Baintree Rd, Rosemont, PA 19010
MISS Cynthia A—at ☎ (313) 761-7239 315 Mulholland Av, Ann Arbor, MI 48103 . . . .
MR Scott F—at ☎ (215) 925-4792 225 Brown St, Philadelphia, PA 19123 . . . .
Wheelock MR Thomas G B—Un.Mto.Clark'65.Wyo'72
☎ (212) 794-4720 . . 7 E 84 St, New York, NY 10028
Wheelwright MISS Elizabeth B—Bost'47
☎ (508) 785-0648 . . 139 Walpole St, Dover, MA 02030
Whisnand MR & MRS R Van Arsdel JR (E Campbell Baker) Unn.Ln.Rm.Stc.Br'66.Va'68 . . . . of ☎ (908)842-9242 973 River Rd, Fair Haven, NJ 07704-3317
MR Tyler S—Va'90 . . . .
MR Carter Van A—Va'94. . . . .
☎ (941) 591-8653 6131 Pelican Bay Blvd, Naples, FL 33963

White MR & MRS A Ridgely (Mary W Davy)
☎ (540) 687-8741 . . "Chilton Farm" 23028 St Louis Rd, Box 54, Middleburg, VA 22117
White MR & MRS Christopher M (Cornish—Alice L Johnson) Wash'73.Mass'79.Cl'89 ⚓ . . . . ☎ (617) 424-1081 390 Commonwealth Av, Apt 610, Boston, MA 02215
MR Nathaniel T—at U of Chicago . . . .
JUNIORS MR Gavin W—at Buxton . . . .
White MISS Cynthia (Cobb—Cynthia White) . . . . Married at Port Washington, NY
Rossini MR Paul L N . . . . Dec 23'95
White MR & MRS Edward P (Katherine E Wilson) Wells'42.Cr'41
☎ (919) 933-0738 . . 379 Carolina Meadows Villa, Chapel Hill, NC 27514-7521
White MRS Edwin Borden JR (Marsh—M Ann Carter) . . . . Married at Richmond, VA
Lee MR R Bland 5th (late Philip H) . . . . Feb 10'96
White MISS Elizabeth S (F L Peter) . . . . Married
Lieber DR Arnold . . . . Jan 26'94
White MR Fred Rollin JR . . . . Died at Shaker Heights, OH Dec 10'95
White MR H Wade . . . . Died at Fairfield, CT May 11'95
White MRS Henry Bowen (Susanne Crocker) . . . . Died at Jacksonville, FL Oct 15'95
White MR Henry Bowen . . . . Died at Ponte Vedra Beach, FL Oct 25'95
White MRS John O (Bartlett—Anita B Martin) . . . . Died Oct 4'95
White MISS Mary B—CalArt'69
☎ (510) 848-3932 . . 2327—5 St, Berkeley, CA 94710

White MR & MRS Stephen H (Ann R Kelly) Col'71.Col'68. . . . . ☎ (203) 761-8550 35 Branch Brook Rd, Wilton, CT 06897
MISS Hillary Ann . . . .
MISS Jessica R. . . . .
JUNIORS MISS Emily H. . . . .
White MISS Virginia (Edgar P E) . . . . Married at New York, NY
Sigety MR Cornelius E (Charles E) . . . . Oct 28'95
White MRS William B (Virginia L Rutter) . . . . ☎ (904) 278-8155 2643 Whipple Av, Orange Park, FL 32073
MISS Mary A—at ☎ (404) 262-2835 999 Northrope Dv NE, Atlanta, GA 30324 . . . . .
Whitehead MR & MRS Charles E 2d (Lydia M Thompson) SL'71.P'69.H'72 . . . . ☎ (301) 656-3823 4824 Chevy Chase Blvd, Chevy Chase, MD 20815
MISS Amanda P. . . . .
MISS Molly T . . . .
JUNIORS MISS Anna M M
Whitehead MRS Jean F H (Jean F R Heiberg) . . . . Died at Washington, DC Feb 19'96
Whitelaw MR & MRS George P JR (Nancy F O'Donnell) Cy.Aht'43
6 Kingston Manor, St Louis, MO 63124-1913
Whiteside MR Thomas—H'32
☎ (617) 320-8423 . . Fox Hill Village, Clark House, 30 Longwood Dv, Westwood, MA 02090
Whitman MRS Peter M (F Elizabeth Blodget) Nyc.Cly.
☎ (610) 321-7221 . . 506 Brightwood Club Dv, Lutherville, MD 21093
Whitney MRS Caroline H B (Caroline H Blake) SL'59.Cy. . . . . ☎ (617) 354-9073 31 Linnaean St, Apt 3, Cambridge, MA 02138-1530
MISS Vanessa C . . . .
Whitney MR & MRS Edward B (Stover—Martha C Howell) Geo'66.Cl'79.H'66.H'69 . . . . of ☎ (212)662-5124 307 W 102 St, New York, NY 10025
☎ (914) 424-4772 Cat Rock Rd, Garrison, NY 10524
JUNIORS MR William H . . . .
JUNIORS MR John H . . . .
Whitney MISS Nancy M
☎ (860) 868-9598 . . "Hightops" 106 Church Hill Rd, Washington, CT 06794
Whitney MR Robert B—H'65.Stan'76 . . . . ☎ (970) 487-3277 PO Box 268, 204 Plateau Av, Collbran, CO 81624
MR Stephen W . . . .
MR Jason—at U of Colo . . . .
Whitney MRS Sarah Cross (Chewing—Sarah W Cross) . . . . . Married at San Anselmo, CA
Neill MR Richard P L . . . . Feb 3'96
Whitson MR & MRS Christopher C (Julia C Higdon) Fla'84.Van'87.NCar'83.Van'87
☎ (615) 386-9372 . . 4300 Sneed Rd, Nashville, TN 37215
Whitson MASTER John Morford (Christopher C) . . . . Born Oct 21'93
Whittemore VERY REV & MRS H Lawrence JR (Elizabeth Eschmann) Dar.Cda.Wms'39. . . . . . . ☎ (802) 388-1349 14 Nedde Lane, Middlebury, VT 05753-2107
MISS Elizabeth B—Sth'77.Sth'81—at
☎ (617) 646-1196 . . 37 Hamlet St, Arlington, MA 02174 . . . .

Wichman MR & MRS Herman L 3d (Cook—Wichman—Betty J Morse) Wash'46.Wash'42
☎ (619) 341-9519.. 75114 Concho Dv, Indian Wells, CA *92210*
Wickersham REV & MRS George W 2d (Elizabeth W Craighill) H'35
☎ (540) 348-5847.. McCurdy Lane, Rockbridge Baths, VA *24473*
Wickersham MR & MRS Walter M (Allison M Mills) Ne'93.Bos'91.Bost'95
☎ (617) 926-8154.. 15 Chauncey St, Watertown, MA *02172*
Wickes MR & MRS W Forman 4th (Nicola L Le Clair) Mid'87
☎ (011-44-181) 946-1240.. 47 Pepys Rd, London SW20 8NL, England
Wieler MR & MRS Scott A (Mary M Baily) Geo'79.BostColl'81.Pa'87
☎ (410) 323-6417.. 811 St George's Rd, Baltimore, MD *21210*
Wiener MRS Alexander L (Ellanore S Brown) .... Died Oct 21'95
Wierdsma MR Clark R.. see N N Solley
Wierdsma MISS Emily F.. see N N Solley
Wilbur MR Peter I S .... Died at
Menlo Park, CA Feb 6'96
Wiles MASTER Charles Gilman (Christopher C) .... Born at
Woodland Hills, CA May 24'95
Wiles MR & MRS Ellis W (Natalie W Huston) Pa'75.NMMI'70.ClCol'89 .... | ☎ (011-49-711) 853388
JUNIORS MR Geoffrey H................... | Heidloch Strasse 159, B4, 70376 Stuttgart, Germany
Wiley MR & MRS Richard M (Zimmerman— Margaret A Palmer) Col'73.ArizSt'67 .... | ☎ (909) 676-8292 3140 Corte Montiel, Temecula, CA
MISS Abigail P Zimmerman................ |
JUNIORS MR Casey K Zimmerman........... | *92592*
Wilgis MR & MRS Herbert E 3d (Linda J Mason) Skd'81.P'83
☎ (206) 524-6817.. 326 NE 59 St, Seattle, WA *98105*
Wilgis MASTER Herbert Elijah 4th (Herbert E 3d) .... Born at
Seattle, WA Apr 11'95
Wilgis MASTER Nicholas Blackman (Herbert E 3d) .... Born at
Seattle, WA May 9'93
Wilking MASTER Eliot Andrew (Leo F J 3d) .... Born Jan 16'95
Wilking MR & MRS Leo F J 3d (Martha K Leclerc) Geo'82.H'74.Ford'78
☎ (701) 293-7026.. 1115 S 8 St, Fargo, ND *58103*
Wilkinson MRS H Bernard (Wharton—Josephine Dodge) .... Died at
Bailey's Bay, Bermuda Mch 14'95
Willard MR John O—Pitt'66
☎ (215) 732-8814.. 326 S 19 St, Apt 5A, Philadelphia, PA *19103*
Willard MRS Le Baron S JR (Lawson—Alice Kistler) Gv.BtP.So.Evg.Elk.Md.Plg.Mv.Myf.Dar.Cda...of
☎ (410) 532-7490.. 405 Brightwood Club Dv, Lutherville, MD *21093*
☎ (407) 835-0293.. 129 Woodbridge Rd, Palm Beach, FL *33480*
Willcox MISS Alexandra Rose (J Keating) .... Born at
Boston, MA Jun 28'95
Willcox MR & MRS J Taney JR (Catherine E Goldschmidt) StJos'50.Temp'58 .... | ☎ (610) 525-5613 800 Harriton Rd, Bryn Mawr, PA *19010*
MISS Catherine E—at 232 Dudley Av, Narberth, PA *19072* .... |
MR Bryan C—at "Ivy Mills" 109 Ivy Mills Rd, Glen Mills, PA *19342* .... |
Williams MISS Claire Louise (g—Henri W Emmet) .... Born at
Columbus, OH May 17'95
Williams MR David B .... Died at
Point O'Woods, NY Oct 1'95
Williams MR David B (Benjamin J) .... Married at Huntington, NY
McGuinness MISS Martha (William G) .... Sep 9'95
Williams MR & MRS Francis H (Susan B Martin) Cyb.. | ☎ (212) 737-9206 175 E 70 St, New York, NY *10021-5109*
MR Francis H JR—StLaw'93—at ☎ (212) 717-4046.. 326 E 65 St, New York, NY *10021* .... |
Williams MR Henry C—Y'40 .... | ☎ (914) 234-6931 RFD 1, PO Box 622, Guard Hill Rd, Bedford, NY *10506*
MR H Martyn—Geo'73..................... |
Williams MRS Huntington (Kreykamp—Isabelle Van Wessem) ... Died at
Baltimore, MD Apr 14'95
Williams VERY REV (DR) J Lawrence B—Chi.Unn.Mt.An. Cc.Cw.Rv.Va'36.. of
☎ (540) 687-8090.. "Huntland" 35955 Huntland Farm Rd, Middleburg, VA *22117*
☎ (407) 659-2257.. 334 Chilean Av, Palm Beach, FL *33480*
Williams MR & MRS Lloyd E JR (M Anne Miller) Ill'56.Ih.Y'56
☎ (847) 251-5803.. 714 Forrest, Wilmette, IL *60091*
Williams JUNIORS MR Nicholas C.. see R D Melen
Williams MRS Robert Hugh (Alice N Tuckerman) Sl.Cda.
☎ (202) 337-1230.. 3900 Watson Place NW, Apt 7HB, Washington, DC *20016*
Williams JUNIORS MR Samuel A F.. see R D Melen
Williamson MR Harold L JR .... Died at
New York, NY Sep 25'95
Williamson MR & MRS James G JR (Carole R McCann) Emory'66
☎ (501) 474-0511.. 1009 Azure Hills W, Van Buren, AR *72956*
Williamson MISS Julia N—LakeF'84
☎ (847) 735-1876.. 1510 N Green Bay Rd, Lake Forest, IL *60045*
Williamson MR & MRS Norman B (Victoria W Andrew) Scripps'58.Vh.Clare'59 ⚓
1550 Orlando Rd, Pasadena, CA *91106*
Willis MISS Amanda Janet (Richard S) .... Born at
Willow Grove, PA Dec 21'95
Willis MRS Benjamin G (Whipple—Eugenia Jennings) .... Died at
Houston, TX Jan 20'95
Willis MR & MRS Richard S (Bowers—Cynthia Gardner) Ne'82.Bost'78
☎ (215) 657-4725.. 1636 Twining Rd, Willow Grove, PA *19090*
Wilmerding MR Henry A JR—Rc.Pr.Ln.Ng.Mb. Colby'61.Cl'63............................. | ☎ (516) 671-8107 Piping Rock Rd, Locust Valley, NY *11560*
MISS Kathryn H........................... |
MISS Patsy R.............................. |
MISS Daphne H........................... |
Wilmerding MR & MRS Patrick R (Elsie Storm) Nf. ⚓ .... | ☎ (617) 232-4555 35 Crafts Rd, Chestnut Hill, MA *02167-1823*
MISS Eliza R—at Bowdoin .... |
MR Patrick S—at Apoquindo 6960, Los Condes, ST 60 Santiago, Chile .... |
MR Michael R—Box 123D, Rte 19, Santa Fe, NM *87501* .... |
Wilshire MR & MRS W Murray (Beresford—Kingsbury— Charlotte E Meyer) Err.Eyc.Cly.P'22
☎ (941) 924-7593.. Lake Pointe Woods 153, 7979 S Tamiami Trail, Sarasota, FL *34231*

Wilson MRS A Morton (Mary H Marsh) .... Died at
    Paoli, PA Nov 18'95
Wilson MRS Anne Sears (Anne Ware Sears) Rdc'53 | ☎ (508) 371-0047
    MISS Erica Sears—at 504 Nashua St, Box 717, | 100 Newbury Court,
    Milford, NH *03055*..................... | Apt 202, Concord,
    | MA *01742*
Wilson MRS Edward G (Jane H Johnson) Chr.Mt.Csn.
    Noble Horizons, 17 Cobble Rd, Salisbury, CT *06068*
Wilson MRS George A (Elisabeth H Dent) .... Died at
    New York, NY Sep 14'95
Wilson MR & MRS Holden JR (Sally E Sampson) | of ☎ (513)961-1939
    Yh.Cw.Miami'52 | 1901 Madison Rd,
    MISS Caroline P—at 1236 Eads Rd, Crittenden, | Cincinnati, OH
    KY *41030*........................ | *45206*
    MISS Laura W—at 3521 Pembroke Av, | "Seven Oaks"
    Cincinnati, OH *45226*.................. | Yeamans Hall Club,
    | PO Box 9455,
    | Charleston, SC
    | *29410*
Wilson MR John M B (David Gordon) .... Married at Troy, NY
    Rachidy MISS Judy..................... Jly 24'95
Wilson MR John R—Cv.Pn.P'49.Md'54
    ☎ (216) 442-5810 . . 6800 Mayfield Rd, Apt 709, Cleveland, OH *44124*
Wilson MRS Judith G (Hinckley—Judith C Goncza) Man'vl'59
    ☎ (505) 660-2295 . . 509 Webber St, Santa Fe, NM *87501*
Wilson MASTER Nicholas Alexander (g—Dennis K Wilson) .... Born
    Apr 20'95
Wilson MR Perkins .... Died at
    Richmond, VA Nov 2'95
Wilson MRS Robert W (Sarah J Leslie) .... Died at
    St Louis, MO Dec 12'95
Wilson MR & MRS Stephen A (Smith—Campbell—
    Elizabeth C de Cravioto) Dar.Yn.Ga'24.Y'27
    ☎ (802) 362-2684 . . "Point O'View" PO Box 454, Manchester,
    VT *05254*
Wilson LT William W—USN.ECar'85
    2283 London Bridge Rd, Virginia Beach, VA *23456*
Winchester MR John G 2d—Y.V'83
    1435 Lexington Av, Apt 2B, New York, NY *10128*
Winslow MR Albert F .... Died at
    Tuxedo Park, NY Sep 24'95
Winsor MR & MRS Philip (Marion Steyn) | ☎ (814) 234-6943
    H'50.Col'55 | 507 Crickwood Dv,
    MISS Marina .... | State College, PA
    | *16803*
Winthrop MR H Grenville—NEng'89
    ☎ (803) 757-7379 . . PO Box 22792, Hilton Head Island, SC *29925-2792*
Winthrop MR & MRS John (Elizabeth Goltra) | ☎ (803) 722-8480
    K.Hn.H'58 | 9 Ladson St,
    MR Bayard—at ☎ (415) 928-4713 | Charleston, SC
    2428A California St, San Francisco, CA *94115* . | *29401*
Winthrop MR & MRS John JR (Louisa L Daley) Duke'87.H'86.H'92
    ☎ (212) 988-4885 . . 527 E 72 St, Apt 5A, New York, NY *10021*
Winthrop MR & MRS Robert (Haas—Halfparn—Wilkes—
    Floreine J Nelson) Rc.Pr.B.Mb.Ri.Sm.Msq.H'26
    ☎ (516) 626-3942 . . 40 Piping Rock Rd, Upper Brookville, Box 306,
    Glen Head, NY *11545*

Wise MR & MRS D Scott (Linden Havemeyer) K.C.Y.'74
    ☎ (212) 249-9203 . . 133 E 80 St, New York, NY *10021*
Wise MR & MRS John H JR (Margaret R Hinckley) B.Chi.Ncd.Stan'43
    ☎ (540) 364-3532 . . "Tasmania" PO Box 239, Orlean,
    VA *20128-0239*
Wise MISS Louisine Havemeyer (D Scott) .... Born at
    Ft Worth, TX Oct 3'95
Witherspoon MR & MRS John T (Loughlin—Dorothy | ☎ (314) 726-5674
    M Mudd) Rose'69.Denis'63 | 57 Ridgemoor Dv,
    MISS Clare M Loughlin .... | St Louis, MO *63105*
    MR John J Loughlin JR ....
    JUNIORS MISS Anna M Loughlin ....
Wodell MRS W Page (Arndt—Margaret R Stroud) .... Died Mch 28'95
Wolcott MR Oliver III—My.OWes'75
    ☎ (508) 468-2001 . . 18 Lake Av, Wenham, MA *01984*
Wolf MR Christopher R—K.Ri.OWes'78.Y.'83 . . of
    ☎ (212) 807-8775 . . 233 W 26 St, New York, NY *10001*
    ☎ (011-52) 376-60278 . . "Villa Los Suenos" Apdo Postal 604, Ajijic,
    45920 Jalisco, Mexico
Wolf MR Dwight E.............................. Died at
    Hilton Head Island, SC Oct 27'95
Wolf MRS Dwight E (Elizabeth W Dandridge) Dar.
    ☎ (803) 785-7841 . . 300 Woodhaven Dv, Apt 2403, Hilton Head Island,
    SC *29928*
Wolf MR & MRS Richard A (Christine Marburg) Msq.Pa'69 . . of
    1481 E Mountain Dv, Montecito, CA *93108*
    ☎ (212) 772-2955 . . 12 E 86 St, New York, NY *10028*
Wolfe MR Albert B—Cw.Hb.P'31.H'34
    ☎ (603) 924-0854 . . 133 Rivermead Rd, Peterborough, NH *03458*
Wolfe MRS John W (Lovelace—Norina Vannucci)
    ☎ (614) 231-2952 . . 485 Columbia Place, Columbus, OH *43209*
Wolfensperger MRS Hans R (Diana L Potter) .... Died at
    Orinda, CA Aug 10'94
Wood MRS Carolyn E (Moorhead—Carolyn F | ☎ (206) 454-4641
    Wood) CtCol'64 .... | 2719—93 Av NE,
    MISS Ariel K (Tomeny—Ariel K Wood) | Clyde Hill, WA
    Syr'93.Syr'94—at 6522 Ambrosia Dv, Apt 5314, | *98004*
    San Diego, CA *92124* .... |
        MISS Allison F Moorhead—SCal'93—at |
        1860 McGilvra Blvd, Seattle, WA *98112* .... |
        MR Dudley T Moorhead 3d—at U of Mont . . |
Wood MR & MRS Charles R (Anna S Farnum) | ☎ (610) 649-3590
    BMr'58.Sg.Me.Rc.Yn.Y'53 .... | 229 Rose Lane,
    MISS Sarah S—Y.'93.Me.—at ☎ (212) 787-9142 | Haverford, PA
    200 W 79 St, Apt 17M, New York, NY *10024* .. | *19041*
    MISS Hannah D—at Davidson................ |
Wood MISS Charlotte Lee (g—David M Hinckley) .... Born at
    Falls Church, VA Aug 6'95
Wood MR & MRS Harvard C 3d (Sandra B | ☎ (610) 688-3521
    Sanderson) Pars'67.Cry.Rv.Pars'67 .... | 66 Sullivan Rd,
    MISS Laura H—Penn'94—at ☎ (215) 438-7204 | Wayne, PA *19087*
    3529 Indian Queen Lane, Philadelphia, PA *19129* |
    MR Harvard C 4th—WestSt'95 .... |
Wood MR & MRS Malbon R (Anne R Slingluff) Cda. | ☎ (504) 945-8630
    MISS Cynthia B—at ☎ (504) 943-4659 | 4219 Burgundy St,
    4019 Royal St, New Orleans, LA *70117* ...... | New Orleans, LA
    | *70117*

Wood MRS Richard D (Margaretta C Duane) . . . . Died Feb 6'96
Wood MR Richard D . . . . Died at
Newtown Square, PA Jun 14'95
Wood MISS Rowena A F—FIT'79 . . of
☎ (212) 988-7363 . . 167 E 82 St, New York, NY *10028*
☎ (513) 281-2681 . . 2706 Cleinview Av, Cincinnati, OH *45206*
Wood MISS Sarah Elizabeth (g—David M Hinckley) . . . . Born at
Falls Church, VA Jan 30'93
Wood MR William P . . . . Died Feb 23'96
Woodbridge MR Henry S . . . . Died at
Pomfret, CT Nov 2'95
Woodford MRS Walter DeW (Beatrice C Smith) . . . . Died at
Cleveland, OH Jan 20'94
Woodville MISS Louisa (Sweatt—Louisa Woodville) Bost'76.Va'79.Nu'85
☎ (540) 364-4435 . . 7025 Owl Lane, Marshall, VA *22015*
Woodward MR & MRS Gordon H (Ann E Bakewell) Y'91.Rut'92.H'92
☎ (914) 693-7034 . . 49 Clinton Av, Dobbs Ferry, NY *10522*
Woodward MISS (DR) Kate S—Towson'66.SUNY'69.Cr'86 . . of
☎ (315) 364-7057 . . PO Box 88, Aurora, NY *13026*
☎ (803) 671-2648 . . 8 Gull Point Rd, Sea Pines, Hilton Head Island, SC *29928*
Woodward MR & MRS Robert F JR (Mary J Reilly) | ☎ (301) 229-6376
Geo'67 . . . . | 17 Ericsson Rd,
MR Jonathan F—at 62020 E Cottonwood, | Cabin John, MD
Brightwood, OR *97011-0024* . . . . | *20818*
Wooldridge MRS William P (Van Stralen—C Elizabeth Tubby)
100 Thorndale Rd, Apt 426, San Rafael, CA *94903*
Worrall MRS William E (Elizabeth C Hubbard) . . . . Died at
Middleburg, VA Jan 19'96
Worth MR & MRS David McAlister (Laurenze Jones) | ☎ (910) 273-5414
Stph'76.NCar'72 . . . . | 1604 Granville Rd,
JUNIORS MR Alexander McA 3d . . . . | Greensboro, NC
 | *27408*
Worthington MRS Sarah G (Price—Sarah Gilmer)
☎ (804) 977-6695 . . Box 274, 977 Seminole Trail, Charlottesville, VA *22901*
Wright CAPT Benjamin T—USMC.An.USN'85
☎ (617) 942-2720 . . 129 Woburn St, Apt 2, Reading, MA *01867*
Wright MR & MRS George I 3d (M Ann Kyle) | ☎ (610) 524-9463
Bvr'66.StA.Rv.VillaN'66 . . . . | 408 Balderston Dv,
MISS Jessica M—at ☎ (704) 822-6531 | Exton, PA *19341*
2428 Belsite Dv, Belmont, NC *28012* . . . . |
Wright MR Henry De F . . . . Died at
Gulf Stream, FL Sep 6'95
Wurts MR & MRS John S (Roberta P Ray) Sth'46
☎ (941) 484-7471 . . 146 Inlets Blvd, Nokomis, FL *34275*
Wurts MR & MRS John W JR (Tracy T Johnson) | ☎ (610) 644-6938
V'64.Me.Pa'61 . . . . | 831 Forest Lane,
MISS M Wister . . . . | Malvern, PA *19355*

Y

Yardley MR & MRS John L McK (Mikkelsen—Leaf | ☎ (011-44-171)
V Heathcote) Plg.Cw.P'50.Pa'56 . . . . | 235-1442
MR Michael A . . . . | 31 Pont St, Apt 10,
 | London SW1X 0BB,
 | England
Yerkes MISS Caroline Woodward (g—Harry Estile Yerkes 3d) . . . Born at
New York, NY Sep 1'95
Yerkes MR & MRS Harry Estile 3d (Nancy Spofford) | ☎ (212) 876-1353
V'52.Un.Fic.P.'48 ⛵ . . . . | 1192 Park Av,
MISS Nathalie S—Conn'88—at | New York, NY
☎ (212) 427-8754 . . 245 E 93 St, New York, NY | *10128*
10128 . . . . |
MR J Nicholas—Fic.Rol'92—at
☎ (617) 639-3231 . . 39 High St, Marblehead, MA *01945*
Yerkes MASTER Tristan Nicholas Goldstein (g—Harry Estile Yerkes 3d) . . .
Born at Hanover, NH Apr 30'94
Yonce MR Clifford M—Rr.Fic.Cw.Yn.Va'91
☎ (804) 296-9586 . . Liberty Hall Farm, Rte 5, Box 341K, Charlottesville, VA *22901*
Yonce MASTER Samuel McClay 3d (S McClay JR) . . . . Born at
Wayzata, MN Oct 10'95
York MR & MRS John W (Eleanor Rulon-Miller) | ☎ (207) 883-2440
P'46 . . . . | 3 Acorn Lane,
MR John W JR—at ☎ (207) 799-0843 | Scarborough, ME
18 Ocean St, South Portland, ME *04106* . . . . . . | *04074*
Young MISS Anne N (Model—Anne N Young) . . see J E Nielson
Young MR Arthur M (Paine—Thomas—Ruth Forbes) Ph.
☎ (510) 848-8385 . . 2924 Benvenue Av, Berkeley, CA *94705*
Young MISS Margaret A C—LakeF'89
☎ (617) 266-1106 . . 469 Beacon St, Boston, MA *02115*
Youtsey MASTER Adam Taylor (Thomas H) . . . . Born at
Bellevue, WA Jan 1'96

Z

Zantzinger MRS C Clark (Mary A Cook) Csp.
☎ (610) 645-8985 . . 1400 Waverly Rd, Andrews 322, Gladwyne, PA *19035*
Zara MR & MRS George A (Kand—Patricia A | ☎ (602) 451-6041
Teeter) Kas'73.DU'71.Pitt'77 . . . . | 10115 E Paradise
JUNIORS MISS Elizabeth A . . . . | Dv, Scottsdale, AZ
JUNIORS MISS Kellie M . . . . | *85260*
JUNIORS MR Michael T . . . . |
Zembrzuski MAJ & MRS Michael A (Wendy L Phillips)
USA.Ariz'90.An.Ty'84
US Embassy, Rome, Italy, PSC 59, Box 60, APO AE, *09264*
Ziegler MR Frederick S—Harvey'91
☎ (408) 746-2971 . . 979 Pinto Palm Terr, Apt 21, Sunnyvale, CA *94087-3740*
Ziesing MISS Heather W . . see MRS J W Eckman
Ziesing MISS Jane D . . see MRS J W Eckman

Zilkha MISS Bettina L (Trink—Bettina L Zilkha) P'82.So.Pn.
   ☎ (011-33-1) 47-27-33-54 . . 80 av Victor Hugo, 75116 Paris, France
Zimmerman MISS Abigail P . . see R M Wiley
Zimmerman JUNIORS MR Casey K . . see R M Wiley
Zimmerman MR & MRS Christian B (Garroway—Sarah Lee Lippincott) Pa'42.Penn'43
   ☎ (609) 829-2099 . . 306 Bell Rd, Cinnaminson, NJ *08077*
Zimmerman MR & MRS Paul M (Gwen H Drum) BallSt'73
   ☎ (941) 489-1483 . . 16016 Forest Oaks Dv, Ft Myers, FL *33908*
Zimmerman MR Victor Eric van Engelen (Robert W JR) . . . . Died at Ensenada, Mexico Feb 25'96

Social Register
Summer 1996

VOL. CX   May, 1996

THE SUMMER SOCIAL REGISTER records the addresses of
families where they may be reached during the season.
A listing of Yachts and Their Owners is included
for the convenience of subscribers.

SOCIAL REGISTER ASSOCIATION
381 PARK AVENUE SOUTH, NEW YORK, N.Y. 10016

©Copyright 1996 by THE SOCIAL REGISTER ASSOCIATION

ISBN 0 940281 09 0

DILATORY DOMICILES under front cover of this book should be consulted first for all changes.

The Social Register is issued in November and its accuracy is maintained by Dilatory Domiciles and the Summer Edition.

The Social Register records the full names and addresses of members of prominent families grouped together, any change of address, the clubs to which they belong, and the birth, marriage or death of each person as it may occur.

Names of Juniors $\begin{cases} \text{MISSES} & \text{12 to 17} \\ \text{MSRS} & \text{14 to 20} \end{cases}$ appear under the names of adult members of their families.

The subscription is $96.00 per annum and includes the Summer Edition, Dilatory Domiciles and the *Social Register Observer*.

The listings of Births, Marriages and Deaths now appear in the *Social Register Observer*.

1996

A

Aall MR & MRS Christian H (Ely—Sally Sample)
☎ (011-33-50) 58-60-84 . . Le Starvan, 74920 Combloux, France
Abbey MR & MRS Clifford L (Clare M Luce)
☎ (707) 963-7431 . . ''Due Passioni'' 2893 St Helena H'way N, St Helena, CA *94574*
Abbott MRS John A (Diana A Ballin)
☎ (508) 545-9387 . . The Glades, Glades Rd, Minot, MA *02055*
Abdulrazak MR & MRS Fawzi (Caroline D Wendell) | ☎ (508) 548-1321
  MISS Caroline Earle . . . . | Box 363,
  JUNIORS MISS Nadia Wendell . . . . | Chapoquoit Island, West Falmouth, MA *02574*
Abeles MR & MRS Charles C (Mehitable | ''Sundance''
  Mackay-Smith) . . . . | 132 Payson St,
  MISS Damaris S . . . . | Corolla, NC *27927*
  MISS Jessica A K . . . . |
  MR Nathaniel C . . . . |
Abercrombie CAPT (RET) & MRS Daniel W (MacMullan—White—Rachel M Horak) USN.
☎ (704) 966-4666 . . ''Point of View'' Box 432, Lake Toxaway, NC *28747*
Abreu MR & MRS Jean Claude (Mann—Farr—Georgiana W Manly) . . of
☎ (011-33-1) 42-22-52-80 . . 55 rue de Verneuil, 75007 Paris, France
☎ (212) 794-9877 . . 315 E 72 St, New York, NY *10021*
Acheson MR & MRS David C (Patricia J Castles)
☎ (508) 398-2919 . . 162B Pleasant St, South Yarmouth, MA *02664*
Adair MRS John A (Carroll—Grace L Shumway)
☎ (508) 420-0641 . . 24 York Terr, Osterville, MA *02655*
Adam MR & MRS Laszlo (Eleanor J Furlaud)
☎ (516) 329-1097 . . 26 Pondview Lane, East Hampton, NY *11937*
Adams MR & MRS Charles C 3d (Leith McLean)
☎ (704) 645-5111 . . ''Brookside Farm'' 8 Morgan Cove Rd, Weaverville, NC *28787*
Adams MR & MRS Charles S 3d (Elise T Dewey)
☎ (301) 241-3585 . . 14615 Hilltop Rd, Cascade, MD *21719*
Adams MR D Nelson
☎ (315) 896-2780 . . ''Partridge Hill'' 327 Partridge Hill Rd, Barneveld, NY *13304*

Adams MR & MRS Daniel N JR (Siglow—Camilla A | ☎ (315) 896-2780
  Sloat) . . . . | ''Partridge Hill''
  MR Daniel N 3d . . . . | 327 Partridge Hill
  MR Bryan G . . . . | Rd, Barneveld, NY
  MR Bruce H . . . . | *13304*
    MR Jesse W Siglow JR . . . . |
    MR Zachary H Siglow . . . . |
Adams MR & MRS Dayton W JR (Shelley A West)
☎ (714) 499-0021 . . ''Three Arch Bay'' 83 S La Senda Dv, Laguna Beach, CA *92677*
Adams MRS F Jackson (Frances M Jackson)
☎ (802) 276-3150 . . ''My House'' West St, Brookfield, VT *05036*
Adams MISS Martha L
☎ (508) 548-1711 . . 168 Shore St, Falmouth, MA *02540*
Adams MR Mitchell
☎ (207) 734-8306 . . Dark Harbor, Islesboro, ME *04848*
Adams MR & MRS Peter B (Sharon K Pruett) . . . . . . | ☎ (508) 545-5082
  MR Charles F . . . . | The Glades,
  JUNIORS MR Reid B . . . . | Glades Rd, Minot,
  JUNIORS MR Jarrett M . . . . | MA *02055*
Adams MRS Scarritt (Beatrice M Agnew)
☎ (206) 462-8903 . . ''Sunnybrook Farm'' 7808 NE 12 St, Medina, WA *98039*
Adams MR & MRS Warren S 2d (Wheeler—Clinton—Romaine Bristow) . . of
☎ (802) 362-2676 . . ''Samphire'' Upland Hollow Rd, Box 1962, Manchester Center, VT *05255*
☎ (401) 847-1704 . . ''Baldwin Cottage'' 420 Bellevue Av, Newport, RI *02840*
Adams MRS Weston W (Gordon—Nancy E Atkins)
☎ (617) 631-1677 . . 67 Harbor Av, Marblehead, MA *01945*
Adamson MR Ames
☎ (401) 294-3420 . . 80 Ferry Rd, Saunderstown, RI *02874*
Adamson SIR Campbell & LADY (Chandler— | ☎ (011-44-1491)
  Josephine L Lloyd) . . . . | 575-271
  MISS Hilary K Chandler . . . . | ''Orchard Cottage'' Binfield Heath, nr Henley-on-Thames, Oxfordshire, England
Adamson MR & MRS Gary (Millicent W Ames)
''The Arboretum'' PO Box 5, Everton, MO *65646*

Adamson MR & MRS William JR (Keyser—Helen H Angier)
☎ (508) 748-0033 .. "Hermitage" Box 56, Marion, MA *02738*

Adda MR & MRS Michael E S (Judith B Henderson) . | "The White
JUNIORS MISS Alexia M E .... | Cottage" East
JUNIORS MR Gavin J E.................... | Boldre, Beaulieu,
JUNIORS MR Benjamin R L .... | Hampshire, England

Addison MR & MRS Christopher C (Sylvia McN Ripley)
☎ (860) 567-4667 .. 61 Duck Pond Rd, Litchfield, CT *06759*

Addison MR & MRS Francis G 3d (Sherrard C Marthinson)
☎ (302) 539-7134 .. "Beach House" Sussex Shores, Bethany Beach, DE *01990*

Adelizzi MR & MRS Robert Frederick (Thomasine S | ☎ (619) 934-6413
Lane) .... | Mammoth Estates,
MISS Judith A .... | 215 Lakeview Dv,
MR James F .... | Mammoth Lakes, CA *93546*

Adibi DR & MRS Siamak A (Joan W Foedisch) ..... | ☎ (508) 627-4807
MISS Elise W .... | Star Rte 109,
MISS Jennifer J .... | Edgartown, MA
MR Camron F .... | *02539*

Adler MR & MRS Allen (Frances F L Beatty)
☎ (516) 653-4014 .. Box 565, Quogue, NY *11959*

Adsit MR & MRS Willcox B (Harriet J McNulty)
☎ (802) 867-4484 .. Upper Hollow Rd, PO Box 295, Dorset, VT *05251*

Agnew MR & MRS Donald (Shields—Rebecca W Tenney)
☎ (516) 676-2708 .. 94 Ryefield Rd, Locust Valley, NY *11560*

Agnew MR & MRS James Q (Barbara L Rossiter)
☎ (540) 348-1111 .. PO Box 23, Brownsburg, VA *24415*

Agnew MRS Seth M (Nancy Longley)
☎ (508) 257-9993 .. "Betide" Box 272, Siasconset, MA *02564*

Ahern MR & MRS F Gregory (Vivian M Spencer)
☎ (401) 847-4050 .. "Chastellux" Chastellux Av, Newport, RI *02840*

Aidinoff MR M Bernard
☎ (516) 267-3435 .. Box 187, Bluff Rd, Amagansett, NY *11930*

Aitken MR & MRS Russell B (McAlpin—Roosevelt—Irene E Boyd)
☎ (401) 847-2252 .. "Champ Soleil" Bellevue Av, Newport, RI *02840*

Albano MRS Salvatore A (Stillman—Spier—Frances D Johnson)
☎ (516) 288-1067 .. "Mudjekewis" Homans Av, PO Box 344, Westhampton Beach, NY *11978*

Alden MR & MRS John J W (Llewellyn P Hall) ..... | ☎ (902) 542-9541
MISS Mary S .... | 76 Highland Av,
MISS Sarah L P .... | Wolfville, Nova Scotia B0P 1X0, Canada

Aldrich MR & MRS Alexander (Watts—Phyllis | ☎ (207) 734-6402
Williamson) .... | "Grindle Point"
MISS Sarah F .... | Islesboro, ME *04848*
MR William C .... |

Aldrich MRS Nelson W (Frances E Turner)
☎ (617) 631-0130 .. 6 Crowninshield Rd, Marblehead, MA *09145*

Alexander DR & MRS J Deaver (Flood—Susanna | ☎ (610) 857-3444
Boylston Bolton) .... | Glen Rose Rd,
MISS Helen C .... | RD 3, Coatesville,
MISS Caroline R .... | PA *19320*
MISS Henrietta K ....|
MISS Dorothy D ....|
MR John D JR ....|

Alexander MR & MRS John S (G Elizabeth Bakewell)
☎ (207) 244-7141 .. Mt Desert, ME *04660*

Alford MR & MRS Robertson F (M Paige Cartmell)
☎ (860) 542-5114 .. 624 Doolittle Dv, Norfolk, CT *06058*

Alford MR & MRS W Stewart (Mary W Randall).... | ☎ (860) 542-5275
MR J Winslow................................... | "Manchester"
MR Joseph S .... | Box 551, Norfolk, CT *06058*

Alig MR Wallace Baird
☎ (011-44-131) 337-40-40 .. "Linton Court" Murieston Rd, Edinburgh EH11 2JJ, Scotland

Allen MR Armin B .... | of ☎ (401)846-7178
JUNIORS MR A William B .... | "Pagoda House" 36 Church St, Newport, RI *02840*
                                              | ☎ (518) 589-5763 "Wildwood" Onteora Park, Tannersville, NY *12485*

Allen MR & MRS Arthur Yorke (Towner—Mary Stewart Hammond)
☎ (508) 627-5004 .. "Athearn House" Planting Field Way, Edgartown, MA *02539*

Allen MR Barton B .. see R U Jelinek

Allen MR & MRS Frederick H S (Annelyse M Fiaux) | ☎ (802) 446-2394
JUNIORS MISS Emily M .... | "Sugar Hill Farm"
JUNIORS MR Julian M C H .... | Wallingford, VT *05773*

Allen MR & MRS George V JR (Josephine E | Squirrel Island,
Tetreault) .... | ME *04570*
MR Theodore T ....|

Allen MISS Jennifer S .. see R U Jelinek

Allen MR Joshua C .. see R U Jelinek

Allen MR Kevin S
☎ (909) 796-6310 .. "Casa Irene" 11223 Bellaire St, Loma Linda, CA *92354*

Allen MISS Laura C
☎ (518) 483-1979 .. "Halcyon" Box 334, Malone, NY *12953*

Allen MR & MRS Louis La B (Annette T Hadley)
☎ (705) 762-5142 .. "Gem Island" Box 456, Bala, Ontario P0C 1A0, Canada

Allen MR & MRS Nathan R JR (Mathilde E Thébaud) . | 9 Quince St,
MR Matthew T .... | Nantucket, MA *02554*

Allen MR & MRS Philip D (Elisabeth H Fell) .... | ☎ (207) 734-8869
MISS Alexandra F .... | Shipyard Point Rd,
MR Christopher D .... | Dark Harbor,
MR Andrew D .... | Box 78, Islesboro,
MR Nicholas E .... | ME *04848*

Allen MRS W Cottingham (Smith—Alloo—Howell—Ethel D Sloan)
☎ (616) 547-4788 .. "Woodbine" Cottage 111, Belvedere Club, Charlevoix, MI *49720*

Allen DR & MRS Yorke 3d (C Lee Jones) .... | Box 682,
JUNIORS MR Yorke 4th.......................... | Edgartown, MA *02539*

Allen MR Zachariah 3d
☎ (011-48-22) 25-29-14 . . ul Raszyńska 3 M 19, 02-026 Warsaw, Poland

Alley MRS James B (Lowe—Esther Hall)
☎ (518) 576-4429 . . "The Shanty" Ausable Club, St Huberts, NY *12943*

Allis MRS Frederick S JR (Hughes—Laura Reasor) . .
  MISS Frances M D'O Hughes . . . .
☎ (508) 432-9121
340 Long Pond Rd, RD 1, Harwich, MA *02645*

Allis MR William P
☎ (603) 563-8691 . . "Yonder Farm" Page Rd, Dublin, NH *03444*

Allison MR & MRS Donald G (Janet L Wright) . . . . .
  JUNIORS MR Charles S . . . .
☎ (516) 653-8959
"Allison Wonderland" Box 652, 12 Ogden Lane, Quogue, NY *11959*

Allison MR & MRS Peter (Barbara L Nowland)
☎ (304) 497-2037 . . Cave Creek Farm, Box 36, Frankford, WV *24938*

Allport MR & MRS Walter F P (Ann E Snyder)
"Tinker Ridge Farm" RD 3, Box 285, Norwich, NY *13815*

Allyn DR Compton
☎ (508) 945-3909 . . 156 Chatham Bars Av, Chatham, MA *02633*

Almy MR William 4th
☎ (508) 993-9520 . . Nonquitt, MA *02748*

Alsdorf MRS James W (Markham—Marilynn Bruder)
☎ (847) 446-1078 . . 301 Woodley Rd, Winnetka, IL *60093-3740*

Amato BRN Carlo C B & BRNSS (De Bergendal—Lorraine M Dresselhuys)
☎ (902) 643-2581 . . "Shangri-La Farm" PO Box 70, RR 1, Glenwood, Nova Scotia B0W 1W0, Canada

Ambler MR & MRS Michael Nash (Marsha W Dancy) . . . .
  MR Christian D . . . .
☎ (516) 653-4581
8 Foster Rd, Box 692, Quogue, NY *11959*

Ambrus DR & MRS (DR) Julian L (Clara M Bayer) . . .
  MR Julian L JR . . . .
  MR Charles T G . . . .
☎ (716) 941-3394
"West Hill Farms" 9943 Emerling Rd, Boston, NY *14025*

Ames MR Amyas
☎ (508) 693-1164 . . Seven Gates Farm, Vineyard Haven, MA *02568*

Ames MRS Azel (Josephine E Church)
☎ (705) 366-5032 . . Ojibway, Pointe au Baril, Ontario P0G 1K0, Canada

Ames MR & MRS Lawrence C JR (Smith—Betty Mitchell)
☎ (702) 831-0721 . . 58 Mountain Shadows, Incline Village, NV *89450*

Ames MR & MRS Sanford S (Elizabeth Clarke)
☎ (616) 869-4151 . . Pentwater, MI *49449*

Ames MRS Van Meter (Betty C Breneman)
Pentwater, MI *49449*

Ammidon MR & MRS Hoyt JR (Ashley Moore)
☎ (441) 232-1059 . . "Glencoe" 11 Salt Kettle Rd, Paget PG 02, Bermuda

Amory MRS Carolyn P (Geddes—Amory—Milbank—Haile—Carolyn M Pesnell)
☎ (508) 228-3993 . . "The East Brick" 93 Main St, Nantucket, MA *02554*

Amory MR & MRS Harcourt JR (Trudeau—Jean D Moore)
☎ (212) 754-4514 . . 45 Sutton Place S, New York, NY *10022*

Amory MR & MRS John S (Porter—Marcelle E Eason) . . . .
  MISS Wendy B . . . .
☎ (619) 569-8773
6378 Caminito Del Pastel, San Diego, CA *92111*

Amory MRS Robert JR (Mary Armstrong)
☎ (207) 867-4839 . . North Haven, ME *04853*

Anable MRS Anne C S (Henriques—Anne C Steinert)
☎ (603) 563-8455 . . "Field House" Old Harrisville Rd, Dublin, NH *03444*

Anathan MR & MRS Thomas J (Patricia K Scott) . . .
  MISS Leah K . . . .
  MISS Elizabeth B . . . .
☎ (508) 228-1840
"Hillside" 68 Monomoy Rd, Nantucket, MA *02554*

Anderson MR & MRS Daniel G (Miller—Margot S West) . . . .
  MISS Jennifer West . . . .
  MR Robert J Miller 3d . . . .
☎ (302) 227-0655
22 Ocean Av, Rehoboth Beach, DE *19971*

Anderson MR David K . . . .
  MR D Reed . . . .
  JUNIORS MR John S B . . . .
☎ (705) 654-3684
Munro Island, Stoney Lake, Ontario K0L 2H0, Canada

Anderson MR & MRS E Forrest (Alice E Charleston)
  MISS Lisa . . . .
  MR Timothy F . . . .
  MR Peter E . . . .
☎ (916) 525-6542
PO Box 916, Tahoma, CA *96142*

Anderson MISS Elizabeth S . . see E L Meinfelder 2d

Anderson MR & MRS Ellis B (Mueller—Andrews—Jermain D Johnson)
☎ (908) 899-6573 . . 1084 Barnegat Lane, Mantoloking, NJ *08738*

Anderson DR & MRS Frank H (Constance D Miller) . .
  MISS Christina H . . . .
  MR Robert B . . . .
  JUNIORS MR David P . . . .
☎ (508) 228-5557
39 India St, Nantucket, MA *02554*

Anderson MR & MRS (REV) James M (Marjorie H Caldwell) . . . .
  MISS Marjorie C . . . .
  MR Joseph H . . . .
  JUNIORS MR Hilding F . . . .
"Camp Island" PO Box 176, Stonington, ME *04681*

Anderson MR & MRS John B (Phillips—Ruth E Coppersmith)
☎ (609) 494-5258 . . "Greene Cananea" 11 E 57 St, Brant Beach, NJ *08008*

Anderson MRS Joseph C (Eugenie W Riley)
☎ (207) 528-2018 . . Point of Pines, Box 534, Patten, ME *04765*

Anderson MR & MRS McCutchen B (Ellen H Few)
☎ (518) 962-4375 . . "Stonysides" Westport, NY *12993*

Anderson MR & MRS O Kelley JR (Biggs—Brenda A Bolton)
233 S Main St, Southampton, NY *11968*

Anderson MRS Robert Gardner (Doris Tansill)
☎ (508) 775-0403 . . "Lilac Hedge" Box 367, Hyannis Port, MA *02647*

Anderson MR & MRS Robert Gardner JR (Catherine H Olian)
"Lilac Hedge" Hyannis Port, MA *02647*

Anderson MR & MRS Thomas D (Helen L Sharp)
☎ (409) 836-4168 . . "Hunt-Hardy House" Old Gay Hill Texas, Rte 5, Brenham, TX *77833*

Anderson MR & MRS William G (Bergland—Dorothy H Mower) ⛵
☎ (207) 284-4915 .. "Wind Song" St Martins Lane, Biddeford Pool, ME *04006*

Anderson MR & MRS William W 5th (Rosemary Wire)
"Wadefield" Box 34, Washington, VA *22747*

Anderson-Bell MR Andrew— ⛵
☎ (207) 867-2238 .. "The Leadbetter House" North Haven, ME *04853*

Andresen MRS John E (Alice Farnsworth)
☎ (617) 585-3732 .. 290 Kings Town Way, Duxbury, MA *02332*

Andrew MR & MRS Lucius A D 3d (Kellogg—Phoebe L Haffner)
☎ (604) 653-4328 .. Musgrave Farm, Box 64, Fulford Harbour, BC V0S 1C0, Canada

Andrews MR & MRS Adolphus JR (Emily P Taylor)
☎ (916) 546-2158 .. "Porcupine Point" Box 1161, Kings Beach, CA *95719*

Andrews MR & MRS Mark E 3d (Elizabeth M Quay) | ☎ (516) 788-7281
JUNIORS MISS Elizabeth Q .... | "Sea Wynde"
JUNIORS MR Mark E 4th .... | Fishers Island, NY *06390*

Andrews MR & MRS Schofield 3d (Eleanor G Bowne)
☎ (207) 276-3751 .. "Copper Beeches" Northeast Harbor, ME *04662*

Andrews MR & MRS Stuart B (G Devereux Hunter)
☎ (207) 276-5578 .. Tennis Club Rd, Northeast Harbor, ME *04662*

Andrews MR & MRS William T (Suzanne W Evans) ⛵
"Gravesend" Skinners Neck, Rock Hall, MD *21661*

Andrews MRS Wolcott Erskine (Anne K Lord) .... | ☎ (207) 882-5578
MRS Penelope A Sprague (Penelope Andrews) | Bath Rd,
 | PO Box 746,
 | Wiscasset, ME
 | *04578*

Angell MR & MRS Christopher C (Margaret J | ☎ (207) 883-8177
Blettner) .... | PO Box 3132,
MISS Elizabeth M .... | Prouts Neck, ME
MISS Margaret B .... | *04074*
JUNIORS MR Christopher E .... |

Angell MR & MRS I Jackson (A Lea Osborne) ...... | ☎ (401) 635-2941
MISS Jessica N .... | Grange Av,
MR I Jackson 3d .... | Little Compton, RI
JUNIORS MISS Sarah O .... | *02837*

Angle MR & MRS Richard W (Jean Hobbs) ⛵
☎ (508) 748-0211 .. "Long Wharf" 0 Main St, Box 428, Marion, MA *02738-0428*

Angle MR & MRS Richard W JR (Barbara | ☎ (203) 453-6065
Buddington) .... | 52 Uncas Circle,
MISS Amanda F .... | Guilford, CT *06437*
MISS Hilary H .... |
MR Eliot P .... |

Anker-Simmons MRS Ronald S (Ferguson—F Bay Echols)
☎ (212) 754-9382 .. 188 E 64 St, New York, NY *10021*

Annan MR & MRS John W (Kent—Hope H | ☎ (970) 925-5012
Parkhurst) .... | Box 313, Aspen,
MR Peter A Kent .... | CO *81612*

Annan MRS M Barbara (Hanson—M Barbara | ☎ (715) 356-7099
Annan) .... | "Bobcat"
MISS Phaedra A Hanson .... | PO Box 82,
 | Minocqua, WI
 | *54548*

Anstey JUNIORS MR Christopher L .. see MISS J M Lamy

Anthony MR & MRS Edward L 2d (Constance Foss) . | ☎ (617) 235-2819
MR Richard G D .... | 68 Woodcliff Rd,
 | Wellesley Hills, MA
 | *02181-1320*

Anthony MR & MRS Silas R JR (Anne C Sampsell) | ☎ (516) 288-4175
⛵ | "Privet Rock"
MISS Wendy C .... | 72 Potunk Lane,
MR Silas R 3d .... | Box 377,
 | Westhampton
 | Beach, NY *11978*

Antoli-Candela DR & MRS Francisco (Elizabeth W | 24 E Rosebud Rd,
Arndt) .... | Roscoe, MT *59071*
JUNIORS MISS Stephanie .... |
JUNIORS MISS Irene .... |

Appell MR & MRS George N (Laura W Reynolds)
☎ (207) 833-5550 .. Barnes Island, South Harpswell, ME *04079*

Applegate MR & MRS A Lowrie (Elizabeth A Eighmy)
☎ (705) 375-2351 .. "Rocky Roost" Iron City Fishing Club, Box 308, Parry Sound, Ontario P2A 2X4, Canada

Applegate MR & MRS L Thomas 3d (Cathleen H | ☎ (508) 627-4183
Sullivan) .... | 61 S Summer St,
MISS Claire S .... | Edgartown, MA
JUNIORS MR William T .... | *02539*

Appleton MRS Benjamin B (Betty A Schaefer)
☎ (905) 835-2589 .. RR 1, Pinecrest Rd, Port Colborne, Ontario L3K 5V3, Canada

Appleton MR Benjamin B
4255 SW Washouga Av, Portland, OR *97201-1375*

Appleton MRS Phebe G (Phebe Grauer)
☎ (905) 468-2802 .. 292 Johnson St, Niagara-on-the-Lake, Ontario L0S 1J0, Canada

Archbold MRS Phoebe W (van Beuren—Phoebe R | ☎ (610) 827-1146
Wildman) .... | "Summerfield"
MISS Jennifer D .... | PO Box 38,
 | Birchrunville,
 | PA *19421*

Archibald MR Fred J
☎ (301) 865-5155 .. "Armadale Farms" PO Box 74, Frederick, MD *21705-0074*

Arensberg MR & MRS Charles C (Gertrude H Hays)
☎ (412) 443-1368 .. "Boot Hill" 85 Shepard Rd, Gibsonia, PA *15044*

Armentrout MR & MRS Alexander Van Dyke (Packard—Paula F Goodridge)
☎ (207) 367-5003 .. "Rabbit Hill" Crockett Cove, Stonington, ME *04681*

Armistead MR & MRS Henry T (Mary E Mallam) ... | ☎ (410) 745-2764
MISS Anne T .... | "Rigby's Folly"
MISS Mary D .... | 25124 W Ferry
MR George L .... | Neck Rd,
 | Royal Oak, MD
 | *21662*

Armour MR & MRS Norman 3d (Isabelle Ferté)
1 rue du Cleux, Ressons le Long, 02290 Vic-sur-Aisne, France

Armour MRS Philip D 3d (MacDonald—M Kerstin M Lindberg)
☎ (415) 775-0578 .. 1466 Greenwich St, San Francisco, CA *94109*

Armour MR Philip D 3d
　MR Philip D 4th
　MR D A Maximillian
　JUNIORS MR Nicholas E A .... ☎ (209) 753-6350 1221 Bear Valley Rd, PO Box 5398, Bear Valley, CA *95223*
Armstrong MISS Anne C
　☎ (517) 479-6790 .. "Chipmunkery" Cottage 28, Harbor Beach, MI *48441*
Armstrong MRS Donald (Wilmot—Rachel D Buntin)
　☎ (304) 536-4040 .. The Greenbriar, 334 Creekside Cottage, White Sulphur Springs, WV *24986*
Armstrong MRS Edward McP (Sheila H Starr)
　General Delivery, Edgartown, MA *02539*
Armstrong MRS Hamilton Fish (Christa von Tippelskirch)
　☎ (516) 537-0999 .. Box 14, Wainscott, NY *11975*
Armstrong MR & MRS J Sinclair (Faircloth—Charlotte P Horwood)
　☎ (508) 627-8927 .. "Topmast Head" 6 Armstrong Lane, Star Rte 14, Edgartown, MA *02539*
Armstrong MR & MRS John C (Hurlimann—Mary H Post)
　☎ (207) 372-8096 .. Glenmere Rd, Box 771, Tenants Harbor, ME *04860*
Armstrong MR & MRS John K (A Maria E van Haersma Buma)
　MISS Marca C van H
　MR Jeb S .... ☎ (860) 435-9792 "Bird Peak" Box 190, Lakeville, CT *06039*
Armstrong MISS Katherine StJ .. see J M Brown 3d
Armstrong MISS Leigh T .. see J M Brown 3d
Armstrong MR & MRS Richard M (Katherine A Maynard)
　☎ (518) 327-3212 .. Camp Underpines, Upper St Regis, NY *12945*
Armstrong MR & MRS Thomas N 3d (V Whitney Brewster)
　☎ (516) 788-7091 .. "Hoover Hall" Box 582, Fishers Island, NY *06390*
Arndt MR Willis C JR .. see W P Wodell
Arnold MR & MRS David B JR (Dorothy Q Warren) ⚓
　☎ (508) 281-1860 .. 966 Washington St, Gloucester, MA *01930*
Arnold MRS George C JR (Stark—Louise S Wolf)
　☎ (508) 228-0278 .. 90 Main St, Nantucket, MA *02554*
Arnone DR & MRS Andrea (Elise M Chapin)
　☎ (908) 439-3445 .. Cold Brook Farm, PO Box 56, Oldwick, NJ *08858*
Arnot MRS Nathaniel du B (Alice C Bowie)
　☎ (315) 482-9695 .. "Cliff Cottage" Summerland Island, Alexandria Bay, NY *13607*
Arnot MR & MRS Nathaniel du B JR (Mary H Sands)
　MISS Mary E
　MR Nathaniel du B III
　MR John S
　JUNIORS MISS Rachel B .... ☎ (315) 482-9695 "Cliff Cottage" Summerland Island, Alexandria Bay, NY *13607*
Arrott MR & MRS Anthony S (Patricia Graham)
　MISS Helen G .... ☎ (604) 734-1843 1445 Marpole Av, Apt 508, Vancouver, BC V6H 1S5, Canada
Arthur MR & MRS D Richardson (Mathews—Barbara R Shultz)
　MISS Barbara R Mathews .... ☎ (914) 254-4195 Winnisook Club, Oliverea, NY *12462*
Arthur MR & MRS James R (Kelton M Himsl)
　☎ (970) 845-9843 .. 134 N Fairway Dv, Beaver Creek, CO *81620*

Arundel MR & MRS Arthur W (Margaret C McElroy)
　MR Thomas B .... ☎ (508) 627-4126 "Eagle's Landing" 105 N Water St, PO Box 5173, Edgartown, MA *02539*
Ashdown MR & MRS Cecil Spanton JR (Gartman—Suffel—Marie A Matranga)
　MR Cecil Spanton 3d
　MR Charles C
　　MISS Vivian M Gartman
　MR John S Gartman .... ☎ (860) 354-2342 "Frascati" 17 Birch Lane, Candlewood Lake Club, New Milford, CT *06776*
Ashforth MRS H Adams (Madden—Elsie R Little)
　☎ (203) 869-0104 .. 1 Milbank Av, Greenwich, CT *06830*
Ashley MRS Constance B (Wick—Constance Bowman)
　☎ (520) 368-8354 .. The Shores, Pinetop, AZ *85935*
Ashmead MR & MRS Duffield 3d (Aspinwall—Mary T Saunders)
　☎ (518) 576-4396 .. "High Tee" Ausable Club Rd, St Huberts, NY *12943*
Ashton MR & MRS Thomas G (Ann V Lahéns)
　MISS Rebecca H
　MR Thomas G JR .... ☎ (207) 326-4305 "The Dwyer House" Water St & Dwyer Lane, Castine, ME *04421*
Aspegren MRS John B (Lois F Barstow)
　MR John B JR .... ☎ (516) 283-1324 "Sunnymead" 49 Ox Pasture Rd, Box 643, Southampton, NY *11968*
Astor MRS W Vincent (Kuser—Marshall—Brooke Russell)
　"Cove End" Northeast Harbor, ME *04662*
Atkinson MR & MRS Matthew S 3d (Leipold—Atkinson—Cromwell—Martha S Egerton)
　☎ (207) 359-4630 .. "Emwilauka" Box 306, Sargentville, ME *04673*
Atterbury MR & MRS Boudinot P (Katharine T Talcott)
　114 Elena St, Santa Fe, NM *87501*
Attride MR & MRS Roy R B JR (M Helen Hayes)
　MR Roy R B 3d
　MR Thomas J H .... ☎ (703) 777-3353 "Oatlands Hamlet" Rte 2, Box 363, Leesburg, VA *22075*
Atwell MR & MRS Anthony (Susan Lay)
　☎ (704) 898-7788 .. Grandfather Golf & Country Club, PO Box 785, Linville, NC *28646*
Atwood MR & MRS John C 3d (Mary E Sanford)
　☎ (517) 386-2493 .. "Wild Turkey Acres" 207 W Wheaton Av, Clare, MI *48617*
Atwood DR William G
　☎ (860) 355-0480 .. "Haiku" 81 South St, Roxbury, CT *06783*
Auchincloss MR & MRS Douglas (Kelly—Larkin—Winston—Catherine M Hannon)
　☎ (207) 734-2263 .. Shipyard Point, Dark Harbor, Islesboro, ME *04848*
Auchincloss MR Edgar S
　☎ (802) 362-4103 .. PO Box 870, Manchester Center, VT *05255*

Auchincloss MR Hugh D 3d . . . . | ☎ (401) 846-0307
MISS Maya L . . . . | "The Castle"
MR Cecil L . . . . | Hammersmith Farm,
| 203 Harrison Av,
| Newport, RI *02840*

Auchincloss MRS John W (Audrey Maynard)
 ☎ (207) 244-3413 . . "Juniper Farm" Seal Cove, ME *04674*
Augsbury MR & MRS Frank A JR (Howard-Smith—Foster—
 Imogen R Snowden)
 ☎ (315) 686-3063 . . "Roughlands" Grindstone Island, Box 249,
 Clayton, NY *13624*
Augur MRS Newell A (L Trimble Hoblitzelle)
 ☎ (207) 883-9985 . . "Eastcliff" Prouts Neck, ME *04074*
Ault MR & MRS Lee A (Laura H Leonard)
 ☎ (207) 763-3138 . . "The Camp" Beaucaire Av, PO Box 4218,
 Camden, ME *04843*
Austin MR & MRS C Lee JR (McEvoy—McGleughlin—Diane Pollitz)
 ☎ (508) 385-8945 . . 1099 Main St, Dennis, MA *02638*
Austin MRS Francis R (Barbara K Hall)
 ☎ (508) 992-2559 . . Salters Point, South Dartmouth, MA *02748*
Austin MR & MRS James P 3d (Britt—A Tudor | Gooseberry Island,
 McBride) . . . . | Portsmouth Harbor,
 JUNIORS MISS Amanda L Walther . . . . | Kittery Point, ME
 | *03905*

Austin MR John F JR
 ☎ (508) 548-6174 . . "Cedar Crest" 10 Lummis Lane, PO Box 408,
 West Falmouth, MA *02574*
Austin MR & MRS Stephen D W (Linda P Garvin) | ☎ (508) 428-7852
⚓ . . . . | on board Intrepid"
 MISS Sarah R . . . . | Oyster Harbor
 JUNIORS MISS Emily B P . . . . | Marine, Osterville,
 JUNIORS MR Stephen D . . . . | MA *02655*

Averell MR John B . . see H Meigs
Avery MRS Victoria J (Victoria J Jelke) ⚓ | ☎ (401) 848-0579
 MISS Jillian F . . . . | 3 Brenton's Cove,
 MISS Alexandra F . . . . | 229 Harrison Av,
 MISS Elizabeth A . . . . | Newport, RI *02840*
 MR Christopher A . . . . |

Aydelotte MRS William O (Myrtle E Kitchell)
 ☎ (860) 443-7123 . . 149 Oswegatchie Rd, Waterford, CT *06385*
Aye HON Lobsang N & LADY (Phillips—Jane B Werner)
 ☎ (518) 239-4717 . . "Kailash House" Travis Hill Rd, Preston Hollow,
 NY *12469*
Ayer MR & MRS Anthony J (Larsson—Nancy Sumwalt)
 ☎ (360) 376-4980 . . Orcas Island, Eastsound, WA *98245*
Ayers MRS Aileen B (Van der Las—Aileen A Bruch)
 7341 Markell Rd, Waite Hill, OH *44094*
Azoy MR & MRS Philip L (Elizabeth M Fowler) . . . . | ☎ (508) 775-3715
 MISS Katrina de P . . . . | Lake Elizabeth Dv,
 | Craigville, MA
 | *02636*

B

Babcock MR & MRS Hugh H (Marion Somerville)
 ☎ (805) 565-5609 . . Valley Club, 1901 E Valley Rd, Santa Barbara,
 CA *93108*
Bacon MR & MRS Louis Moore (Cynthia I Pigott)
 Robins Island, PO Box 301, New Suffolk, NY *11956*
Bacon MR & MRS Robert H JR (Moore—Juliette W Fentress)
 ☎ (401) 322-0407 . . "Twilight" 30 Meadow Av, Weekapaug, RI *02891*
Bacon MR & MRS William T JR (Margaret L Hoyt)
 ☎ (715) 588-3733 . . Camp Wipigaki, Lac du Flambeau, WI *54538*
Baddour MR & MRS Raymond F (Anne M Bridge)
 ☎ (603) 525-4783 . . "The Aerie" Ledge Rd, Hancock, NH *03449*
Badger MRS Helen W (Helen F Webster) . . . . | ☎ (717) 676-4438
 MR Mark C . . . . | "Hid 'N Timber"
 | Lake Paupac Club,
 | Greentown, PA
 | *18426*

Baer MR & MRS Richard H (Silvia M Sager)
 ☎ (716) 834-1164 . . 58 Ruskin Rd, Eggertsville, NY *14226*
Bafford MR & MRS Joseph E (Margaret A Brand) . . . | ☎ (516) 537-0076
 MISS M Angeline B . . . . | "High Cotton"
 MR J Edmonds JR . . . . | Sagaponack Rd,
 | Bridgehampton, NY
 | *11932*

Bailey MR & MRS Glenn W (Cornelia L Tarrant)
 ☎ (203) 655-3228 . . Contentment Island, Darien, CT *06820*
Bailey MR Irving W 2d
 ☎ (802) 228-5210 . . 24 Lake Rescue, Ludlow, VT *05149*
Bailey MR & MRS Samuel JR (Janet E Gaw) ⚓ . . . | ☎ (508) 228-1341
 JUNIORS MR David P . . . . | "Silflay"
 JUNIORS MR John S W . . . . | 11 Mill St,
 | Nantucket, MA
 | *02554*

Bailey MR & MRS William P D (Madeleine H Reilly) | ☎ (413) 229-8639
 MR William P R . . . . | "Signal Hill"
 | Southfield, MA
 | *01259*

Baillière MR & MRS Thomas H G JR (Anne J | ☎ (908) 892-1224
 Dobbin) ⚓ . . . . | 1053 Ocean Av,
 MISS Elisabeth J . . . . | Mantoloking, NJ
 MISS Alexandra R . . . . | *08738*

Bainbridge MR & MRS Robert P (Mary Hastings)
 ☎ (508) 945-2472 . . "Turtle Hill" 353 Barn Hill Rd, West Chatham,
 MA *02669*
Baird MISS Abi A
 ☎ (908) 892-4782 . . on board Dunraven III" Canal Point Harbor,
 Bay Av, Point Pleasant, NJ *08742*
Baker MR & MRS Anthony K (Carol V Oelsner) ⚓
 ☎ (516) 922-7419 . . "Georgia Hill" Box 381, Frost Mill Rd, Mill Neck,
 NY *11765*
Baker MRS David S JR (Ethel Prosser)
 ☎ (401) 789-9434 . . Whale Rock Point, Narragansett, RI *02882*
Baker DR & MRS George P JR (Katharine H Elliott)
 ☎ (603) 367-8762 . . "Pebble Farm" N Division Rd, Silver Lake,
 NH *03875*

Baker MR & MRS Harold d'O (Little—Nancy Stevenson)
☎ (401) 789-4401 . . 44 Baker Rd, Box 201, Narragansett, RI *02882*
Baker MRS Henry S (Frances I Robinson)
☎ (609) 368-2318 . . 9335 First Av, Stone Harbor, NJ *08247*
Baker MR & MRS Hollis MacL (Betsy J Brown) ⛵
☎ (616) 458-2001 . . 330 Plymouth Rd, East Grand Rapids, MI *49506*
Baker MRS John B (Caroline P Hoar)
☎ (508) 627-9982 . . "Martin House" Star Rte 136, Edgartown, MA *02539*
Baker MRS Marianna J (Marianna Johnson) . . . . | ☎ (401) 423-1097
JUNIORS MISS Joanna J . . . . | "Mackeral Cove"
JUNIORS MR George F 2d . . . . | PO Box 344, Beavertail Rd, Jamestown, RI *02835*
Bakewell MRS Alexander McN (Elizabeth Stevens)
☎ (518) NH4-3201 . . "Fallen Arches" PO Box 1184, Bolton Landing, NY *12814*
Bakewell MR & MRS Anderson D (Francine L Stone) | Isle of Scarp, Harris, Scotland
MISS Petra . . . . |
JUNIORS MR Lorenzo . . . . |
Bakewell MRS Sarah (Cannon—Sarah Bakewell)
☎ (518) 644-9022 . . "Mohigan Point" N Shore Rd, Bolton Landing, NY *12814*
Bakker MR & MRS Peter A (Quinlan—Katharine L Murdock) . . . . | ☎ (011-33-31) 98-13-08
MR Anton W . . . . | "Deaucal" 6 quai Marchands, Deauville SM, France
Balboni MRS Victor G (Marjorie C Fletcher)
☎ (401) 635-8822 . . Bailey's Ledge, Little Compton, RI *02837*
Baldini MRS Mario G (Dorothy L Hovey)
☎ (508) 927-0450 . . 24 Paine Av, Prides Crossing, MA *01965*
Baldridge REV & MRS Kempton D (Isabel S Curtis)
☎ (207) 374-5319 . . Parker Point Rd, Blue Hill, ME *04614*
Baldwin MR Alfred W
☎ (441) 293-0856 . . "Out of the Blue" 8 Mid-Ocean Dv, St George's HS 02, Bermuda
Baldwin MRS G Storer (Jenckes—Mollie W Cromwell)
Aug 1 . . North Haven, ME *04238*
Baldwin MRS James French (Moore—Eileen Narizzano)
☎ (516) 676-2332 . . Piping Rock Club, Piping Rock Rd, Locust Valley, NY *11560*
Baldwin MRS Lisa Leonard (Lisa Leonard) . . . . | of ☎ (616)526-2667 44 Beach Dv, Wequetonsing, MI *49740* ☎ (616) 526-2421 Marina Village 7, 524 E Bay St, Harbor Springs, MI *49740*
MISS Almira S . . . . |
MR Lawrence T . . . . |
MR Townsend L . . . . |
Baldwin MRS O H Perry (Elizabeth St J Webb)
☎ (603) 523-4814 . . "Perry House" 28 Canaan St, Canaan, NH *03741*

Baldwin MR & MRS Richard 3d (Deborah B Johnson)
☎ (616) 526-2667 . . PO Box 4261, 44 Beach Dv, Wequetonsing, MI *49740*
Baldwin MR & MRS Roger P (Mary L Stewart)
☎ (207) 244-3569 . . "Eagle Point" Little Cranberry Island, Islesford, ME *04646*
Baldwin MR & MRS Rosecrans (Sarah S Griffin)
☎ (207) 276-3628 . . "Pine Ledge" Seal Harbor, ME *04675*
Balis MRS C Wanton JR (Johnston—Deborah Butler)
☎ (508) 693-4566 . . West Chop, MA *02573*
Ball DR & MRS Eugene R (Sarah J Ashmun)
☎ (914) EL1-4791 . . Tuxedo Club, Tuxedo Park, NY *10987*
Ball MR & MRS Stephen F W (Elaine P Boschen) . . . | ☎ (516) 583-8772 Point O'Woods, NY *11706*
MISS Sarah W . . . . |
JUNIORS MR Stephen F W JR . . . . |
Ballantine MRS Robert W (Fahey—Thomas—Virginia McB Garesché)
Fish Creek Ranch, Wilson, WY *83014*
Ballard MR Alexander R F R . . see L S Huntington
Ballard MR & MRS Robert F R (Talbot—Lucinda M Constable)
☎ (508) 228-0061 . . 7 Darling St, Nantucket, MA *02554*
Ballengee MR & MRS James M (Jo McIlhattan)
☎ (609) 492-2719 . . 122 Fairview Av, Beach Haven, NJ *08008*
Ballenger DR & MRS Peter L (Barbara M Maury) . . . | ☎ (615) 924-2819 "Eagle's Loft" Monteagle Assembly, Monteagle, TN *37356*
MISS F Maury . . . . |
MISS Brooke B . . . . |
Ballinger MRS Robert I JR (de Mohrenschildt—Denton—Wynne Sharples)
☎ (603) 253-6343 . . "Singing Eagle" Box 1044, Center Harbor, NH *03226*
Ballinger DR & MRS Walter F 2d (Mary Randolph G Dickson) . . . . | PO Box 2091, Oyster Harbors, Osterville, MA *02655*
MR Walter F 3d . . . . |
MR Christopher B . . . . |
MR David G . . . . |
Ballman MR & MRS B George (Frances L Hurst) . . . | ☎ (609) 822-0055 "Bayroon" 3 Bay Haven Dv, Longport, NJ *08403*
MISS Lynda H . . . . |
MISS Kimberly S . . . . |
Ballou MR & MRS F Remington (Frothingham—Priscilla W West)
☎ (508) 993-1816 . . "High Tide" 112 Mattarest Lane, South Nonquitt, MA *02748*
Baltazar-Campos MR J Rafael . . see MRS G S Regan
Bancroft MR & MRS Alexander C (Margaret A Armstrong)
☎ (914) 677-5846 . . Tyrell Rd, Millbrook, NY *12545*
Bancroft MR & MRS Frederic M (Suzanne G Coleman)
☎ (516) 788-7879 . . Fishers Island, NY *06390*
Bancroft MRS Harding F (Merrill—Edith C Hall)
☎ (011-353-58) 60332 . . "Avonmore" Ballyduff, Co Waterford, Ireland
Bancroft MR & MRS Harding F JR (Helen H Goodbody) . . . . | ☎ (418) 665-3125 "Darley Fields" CP6, Cap-a-l'Aigle, Charlevoix, Quebec G0T 1B0, Canada
MISS Kelly G . . . . |
JUNIORS MR Alexander P . . . . |

Bancroft MRS Mary Jane (Casey—Collins—Mary Jane Bancroft) .... | ☎ (418) 665-3125 "Darley Fields" CP6, Cap-a-l'Aigle, Charlevoix, Quebec G0T 1B0, Canada
    JUNIORS MR Christian J Collins ....

Bangs MR & MRS Nathaniel S (Jean E Gridley)
    ☎ (715) 747-3561 . . Box 197, La Pointe, WI *54850*

Banta MR & MRS Charles U (Melissa P Wickser)
    ☎ (508) 645-9077 . . Abel's Hill, Chilmark, MA *02535*

Barbey MRS Henry I (Lillian J Manger) .... | ☎ (516) 283-4238 Gin Lane, Southampton, NY *11968*
    MISS Florence F ....
    MR Henry I 3d ....

Barclay MR & MRS J Randell (Dianne E Richoz)
    ☎ (802) 492-3794 . . "Pengwerne" PO Box 332, Cuttingsville, VT *05738*

Barfield MR & MRS Edward D (Alice D Guthrie)
    ☎ (207) 282-6343 . . Box 177, Biddeford Pool, ME *04006*

Barker MRS Theodore R (Nancy Edwards)
    ☎ (715) 354-3615 . . "Wit's End" Rte 2, Birchwood, WI *54817*

Barkhorn MR & MRS Henry C (Jean D Cook)
    ☎ (516) 324-1016 . . 16 Meadow Lane, East Hampton, NY *11937*

Barkus MR & MRS Paul R (Christine G Wilmer)
    ☎ (516) 788-7974 . . Fishers Island, NY *06390*

Barloga MR & MRS Fred R (Sara H Stafford) ...... | ☎ (704) 526-9705 "Hidden Hollow" PO Box 427, Mill Creek Lane, Highlands, NC *28741*
    MISS Cindy Cay (Hall—Cindy Cay Barloga) . . .

Barnard MISS Anne . . see J Timpson

Barnard MR & MRS George B (Frances F Fleming)
    ☎ (508) 627-8400 . . Box 42, Edgartown, MA *02539*

Barnard MISS Phoebe . . see J Timpson

Barnes MRS William 3d (Julia Terry)
    ☎ (616) 526-2533 . . Cottage 69, Harbor Point, MI *49740*

Barnes MR & MRS William S (Mary West)
    ☎ (603) 968-3921 . . "Hampeau" Box 148, Holderness, NH *03245*

Barnett MISS Alexis A . . see N Doubleday

Barnett MR & MRS Benjamin H (Catharine W Thacher)
    ☎ (908) 899-7646 . . 623 East Av, Bay Head, NJ *08742*

Barnett MR Joseph W 3d . . see N Doubleday

Barney MR & MRS William Hadwen (Katherine L Kennedy)
    ☎ (508) 228-5937 . . "The Barnacle" Swain's Wharf, 31 Orange St, Nantucket, MA *02554*

Barngrove MRS Sally Ann (McQuilkin—Sally Ann Barngrove) .... | ☎ (818) 793-4538 310 S San Rafael Av, Pasadena, CA *91105*
    MISS Hilary B McQuilkin................
    MR G J Geoffrey McQuilkin ....

Barnhill MR & MRS Gregory H (Lisa P Angelozzi)
    ☎ (302) 227-1325 . . "Pine Tree Cottage" 13 Oak Av, Rehoboth Beach, DE *19971*

Barnum MR & MRS John W (Nancy R Grinnell) ⚓ | ☎ (508) 548-9618 Waquoit, MA *02536*
    MISS Sarah K ....
    MR Alexander S ....
    MR Cameron L ....

Barrell MRS Nathaniel A (I G Brigitte Steffan) .... | ☎ (518) 532-7409 "Far Hills" Schroon Lake, NY *12870*
    MISS Brigitte A ....

Barrett MRS (DR) Beatrice H (Ribback—van Buren—Beatrice H Barrett) ⚓
    33 Champlain Rd, Chatham, MA *02633-2511*

Barrett MRS Harvey N JR (Taplin—Constance W Huntington)
    ☎ (802) 496-6240 . . "Hit'er Miss" Prickly Mountain, Warren, VT *05674*

Barrett MR & MRS Robert J 3d (Tankoos—Catherine B Moore)
    ☎ (207) 667-9528 . . Barretts' Point, Green Lake, Ellsworth, ME *04605*

Barrington MR & MRS Felix M (Linda V Batten) . . . | ☎ (715) 798-3225 "The Belfry" Lake Owen, Cable, WI *54821*
    MISS Felicity V ....
    JUNIORS MR Anton B ....

Barrows MRS David Nye (Frances L Scoville)..... | ☎ (203) 268-0862 151 Adams Rd, Easton, CT *06612*
    MISS Lila H ....

Barrows MR & MRS Thomas S (Abigail S Liggett)
    ☎ (508) 228-3610 . . "Small Craft" Tennessee Av, Madaket, MA *02554*

Barry MR John L 3d .... | ☎ (508) 693-1525 "Shorwinds" Harthaven, Box 1333, Oak Bluffs, MA *02557*
    MISS Alison S ....

Barry MRS Robert R (Hermann—Anne R Benjamin)
    ☎ (516) 283-5185 . . Halsey Neck Lane, Box 936, Southampton, NY *11969*

Bartholet MRS Elizabeth (Du Bois—Elizabeth Bartholet)
    Stonington, CT *06378*

Bartholomew MR & MRS James R (Elizabeth Oberndorfer)..................... | ☎ (609) 494-8484 24 Maiden Lane, Harvey Cedars, NJ *08008*
    MISS Elizabeth S ....
    MISS Sarah D ....
    JUNIORS MR William B ....

Bartle MR Thomas P 3d . . see F L Buddenhagen

Bartlett MRS Francis G JR (Sara T Hundley)
    ☎ (902) 766-4388 . . Box 74, Riverport, Nova Scotia B0J 2W0, Canada

Bartlett MR Francis G JR
    ☎ (410) 822-0269 . . Box 481, Easton, MD *21601*

Bartlett MR Harry G
    ☎ (302) 227-8562 . . Henlopen Condominium 204, 527 Surf & Boardwalk, Rehoboth Beach, DE *19971*

Bartlett MRS L Dortch (Louisa Bethune Dortch)
    ☎ (610) 388-6769 . . "The Woods" Box 184, Mendenhall, PA *19357*

Bartol MRS John G (Caroline C Schiller)
    ☎ (207) 883-2243 . . "The Bungalow" PO Box 3063, Prouts Neck, ME *04074*

Bartol MR & MRS John Hone (Walker—Norma W Magnus)
    ☎ (516) 788-7866 . . Box 491, Fishers Island, NY *06390*

Bartolec MR & MRS Thomas A (Corinne DeL Morris)
    ☎ (302) 654-9355 . . 8 The Mill, Rockland Mills, Rockland, DE *19732*

Barton MR & MRS David W JR (Cherry—Carol H Urban) . . . . ☎ (603) 823-8512
   MR John M Cherry . . . . 249 Paine Rd,
   MR Henry A Cherry . . . . Franconia, NH
   03580
Barton DR Evan M
   ☎ (616) 334-4844 . . "The Cottage" 7213 SW Glen Lake Rd, Glen Arbor, MI *49636*
Barton MR & MRS H Hudson 5th (Elisa D Menocal) . | Pocono Lake
   JUNIORS MISS Zoë E . . . . | Preserve, PA *18348*
   JUNIORS MISS Ashley J . . . . |
Barton MRS Meta Packard (Meta M Packard)
   ☎ (603) 253-4996 . . "Windfall" Harvard Point Rd, Squam Lake, Center Harbor, NH *03226*
Bartow MRS Clarence W (Woolston—Elizabeth V Ingersoll)
   ☎ (516) 788-7892 . . Box 696, Fishers Island, NY *06390*
Bartram MRS J Burr (Mary S Sheppard)
   ☎ (203) 869-3115 . . 680 Steamboat Rd, Apt 3, Greenwich, CT *06830*
Baruch MR & MRS Fernand (Margery G Wyckoff) . . | ☎ (207) 738-2333
   MISS Lucy D . . . . | Bottle Lake,
   | Springfield, ME
   | *04487*
Barzun MR Jacques
   ☎ (508) 428-2231 . . 135 Putnam Av, Cotuit, MA *02635*
Barzun DR & MRS (DR) James L (Kathleen B Agayoff) . . . . | ☎ (508) 428-2231
   MISS Alice L . . . . | 135 Putnam Av,
   JUNIORS MISS H Kathleen . . . . | Cotuit, MA *02635*
Bass MR George S . . . . | ☎ (207) 276-3782
   MISS Margot S . . . . | "Reef Point"
   MISS Catherine H . . . . | Northeast Harbor,
   MR Steedman L . . . . | ME *04662*
Bass MR & MRS Perkins (Riley—Rosaly Swann)
   ☎ (508) 627-3964 . . Edgartown, MA *02539*
Bassett MRS William B K (Constance Colt)
   ☎ (609) 397-1128 . . "Quarry House" PO Box 329, Stockton, NJ *08559*
Bast MR & MRS William L (Alice-Ann Salomon)
   Cat Bow Farm, RD 2, Lancaster, NH *03584*
Bastedo MR & MRS P Russell (Linda Bullard) . . . . . . | ☎ (603) 563-8924
   MR Nils P . . . . | "The Barn at
   JUNIORS MISS Kip S . . . . | Sky Field"
   JUNIORS MR Spencer C . . . . | Old Harrisville Rd,
   | Dublin, NH *03444*
Bastedo MRS Philip (Helen C Wilmerding)
   ☎ (603) 563-8865 . . "Snow Hill" PO Box 262, Dublin, NH *03444*
Bates MISS Barclay P . . see P C Leach
Bates MR & MRS Nicholas L (Susan P Muirhead)
   ☎ (617) 934-2656 . . 23 Lovers Lane, Duxbury, MA *02332*
Bates MISS Susan Hastings
   ☎ (516) 283-2448 . . "Sohcahtoa" PO Box 734, Pond Lane, Southampton, NY *11969*
Bates MRS Victoria F (Victoria Frelinghuysen)
   ☎ (908) 223-0993 . . PO Box 112, 925 Cole Dv, Brielle, NJ *08730*
Batt MR & MRS Robert R (Mona Nystroem)
   ☎ (207) 244-5257 . . "Lingon Berget" Richtown Rd, West Tremont, ME *04690*

Battey MR & MRS William R JR (Nancy R Hoversten)
   ☎ (401) 596-3153 . . "Briar Rock" 1 Ninigrett Av, Watch Hill, RI *02891*
Battle MR T Westray . . see R M Scaife
Battles MRS Winthrop H (Marjorie Y Gibbon)
   ☎ (207) 244-5223 . . Cranberry Point, Mt Desert, ME *04660*
Bauer MR & MRS Gregory W (Anne V Henderson)
   ☎ (908) 223-5821 . . "T.L.H." 615 Cherokee Lane, Brielle, NJ *08730*
Bauer MR & MRS Joseph A JR (Parlee—Mary E Brown) . . . . | The Islands,
   MISS Elizabeth J Parlee . . . . | Pickerel Pond,
   | Wayne, ME *04284*
Baugh MRS William S (Pauline S Brown)
   ☎ (508) 283-6388 . . 49 Norwood Heights, Gloucester, MA *01930*
Bauman MR & MRS Robert P (Lewis—Patricia A Jones)
   ☎ (207) 967-5591 . . "Harbor Light" 22 Great Hill Rd, Kennebunk Beach, ME *04043*
Baumgartner MR J Peter
   ☎ (702) 832-7380 . . "Winter Palace" 24 Somers Loop, Crystal Bay, NV *89402*
Baxter MISS Anne W
   ☎ (415) 663-1222 . . PO Box 1345, Point Reyes, CA *94956*
Baxter MR & MRS George W (Ruth Reynolds)
   ☎ (704) 733-9383 . . Laurel Lane, Box 1072, Linville, NC *28646*
Bayard MRS James A (Nancy W F Lennig)
   ☎ (410) 885-5525 . . "Bohemia Manor" Chesapeake City, MD *21915*
Bayley MRS James C (Janet C Carr)
   ☎ (617) 598-8813 . . "Box Stall" 61 Phillips Beach Av, Swampscott, MA *01907*
Bayne MR & MRS James E (Mary Lee C Skinner) . . . | ☎ (207) 244-3571
   MISS Laura Lee P . . . . | "Hio Hill"
   MR James E JR . . . . | Box 152, Manset,
   | ME *04656*
Beach MRS George R (Tams—Mary V Finney)
   ☎ (540) 839-2849 . . Fairway Dv, Northridge, Hot Springs, VA *24445*
Beacham MRS E Brand JR (Bessie Keith)
   ☎ (802) 867-4446 . . "Snowfall" Box 906, Dorset, VT *05251*
Beachboard MRS Walter W (Dunn—Cynthia Reed)
   ☎ (207) 644-8404 . . Christmas Cove, South Bristol, ME *04568*
Beadle MR & MRS J Grant 3d (Nancy Lee Oliver)
   ☎ (616) 335-9027 . . "The Beams" 4503 Audubon Dv, Castle Park, Holland, MI *49423*
Beadleston MR & MRS William L (PRCSS Marina Romanov) ⚓ . . . . | ☎ (207) 244-7112
   MISS Tatiana . . . . | "Bayberry Cottage"
   MISS Alexandra . . . . | Bernard, ME *04612*
   JUNIORS MISS Natasha . . . . |
   JUNIORS MR Nicolai . . . . |
Beal MR Alexander M
   ☎ (212) 251-0948 . . 151 E 31 St, Apt 16G, New York, NY *10016*
Beal MR Louis M S
   ☎ (518) 499-1787 . . "The Châlet" Huletts Landing, NY *12841*
Beal MR & MRS Thomas Prince JR (Barbara P Beals) | ☎ (603) 253-4958
   MR Thomas P 3d . . . . | High Haith Rd,
   | Squam Lake,
   | Center Harbor, NH
   | *03226*

Beale MR & MRS John S JR (Louise L Ritchie) . . . . . ☎ (508) 228-1484
 MISS Holly C . . . . 276 Polpis Rd,
 MISS Sarah C . . . . Nantucket, MA
 JUNIORS MISS Katharine S *02554*
 JUNIORS MISS Christina C . . . .
Beals MRS E Mauran (Julia O Blake)
 ☎ (508) 468-3145 . . 59 Walnut St, South Hamilton, MA *01982*
Beard MRS Patricia D (Patricia Dranow) . . . . General Delivery,
 MISS Hillary R . . . . Fishers Island, NY
 MR Alexander *06390*
Bearns MRS Wendy H (Wendy M Hobson)
 ☎ (011-39-575) 70613 . . Il Molinello, Pianezze 20, 52035 Monterchi, Italy
Beattie MRS James H (Olivia von S Cover)
 ☎ (802) 372-8738 . . Camp Longquina, North Hero, VT *05474*
Beaty MR & MRS James C (Julia Corscaden)
 ☎ (518) 543-6424 . . The Boathouse at Island Harbor, Box 542, Rte 9N, Hague, NY *12836*
Beck MISS Elizabeth R F . . see R Hynson
Beck MRS H Brooks (Emily M Morison)
 ☎ (207) 276-5575 . . Good Hope, Northeast Harbor, ME *04662*
Beck MR Robert L . . see R Hynson
Becker MRS Sherburn M 3d (Becker—Clough— . . . . ☎ (970) 479-9339
 Marion E Pitts) . . . . 5123 Black Bear
 MISS Sarah M . . . . Lane, Vail, CO
 MISS Anne S *81657*
 MISS Elizabeth V . . . .
Beck von Peccoz MR & MRS Charles M (Marian W . . ☎ (508) 896-7820
 Larkin) . . . . 95 Stuart St,
 MISS Shellie M . . . . Brewster, MA *02631*
Beckwith MR & MRS James S 3d (Alice W Snodgrass)
 ☎ (412) 238-9257 . . "Twin Fawn Meadows" Star Rte, Laughlintown, PA *15655*
Becton MR & MRS Henry P JR (Jean C Redpath) . . . . ☎ (207) 374-2100
 MISS Sara C . . . . "High Tide"
 JUNIORS MR Wilson P . . . . PO Box 5,
  Blue Hill, ME
  04614
Bédard MRS Pierre (Winter—Gertrude E King)
 ☎ (401) 849-5333 . . 400 Bellevue Av, Newport, RI *02840*
Bedford MR & MRS Frederick T 3d (Jane S Waterman)
 ☎ (603) 643-2524 . . "Partridge Crest" 23 Partridge Rd, Etna, NH *03750*
Begg MR & MRS Charles B JR (Mary L McIlvain) . . . ☎ (517) 479-6216
 MISS Mary L . . . . Cottage 39,
 MISS Carolyn D . . . . Harbor Beach, MI
  48441
Begley MR & MRS Louis (Dujarric de la Rivière— . . . ☎ (516) 537-3098
 Anne Muhlstein) . . . . Sagaponack, NY
 MR Peter H *11962*
  MR Robert Dujarric de la Rivière . . . .
Beha MR & MRS James A 2d (Nancy Ryan) . . . . ☎ (516) 725-3918
 MISS Mary A . . . . "Ryan House"
 JUNIORS MR Christopher R . . . . Woodland Rd,
 JUNIORS MR James J . . . . Sag Harbor, NY
  11963

Behn MRS Sosthènes 2d (Beatrix Nogueira)
 ☎ (011-351-1) 458-1574 . . Praceta do Junqueiro Lote B3, 2o-DTo, Carcavelos, 2775 Parede, Portugal
Behn MR William C . . . . ☎ (011-33-59)
 MR William S 26-15-02
 MRS Aphra (Lesoeur—Aphra Behn) . . . . "Villa Ya-Séou"
  MR & MRS Franck Le Pelletier (Monica 5 av Pellot,
  Behn) . . MR absent . . . . 64500 St-Jean-de-
  Luz, France
Behr MR & MRS Karl H (Howard—Elaine L Oakley)
 ☎ (516) 324-2023 . . 88 Egypt Lane, East Hampton, NY *11937*
Beidler MR & MRS Francis 3d (Prudence L . . . . ☎ (414) 248-2316
 Richardson) . . . . "Robinswood"
 MISS Prudence E . . . . 670 S Lake Shore
 MR Francis 4th . . . . Dv, Lake Geneva,
  WI *53147*
Beinecke MR & MRS Frederick W (Candace L . . . . . ☎ (413) 528-3636
 Krugman) . . . . "Wheelbarrow Hill
 JUNIORS MR Jacob S . . . . Farm"
 JUNIORS MR Benjamin B . . . . Egremont Rd,
  Rte 23, Box 122,
  Great Barrington,
  MA *01230-0122*
Bell MR & MRS Alexander C (Catharine R Johnson)
 ☎ (705) 782-6618 . . "Range Lights" Desbarats, Ontario P0R 1E0, Canada
Bell MRS John C JR (Sarah A Baker)
 ☎ (207) 883-7036 . . "Les Cloches" Prouts Neck, ME *04074*
Bell MR & MRS John C 4th (M Ramsay Gross)
 ☎ (207) 883-5638 . . "Bellhaven" 8 Ferry Rd, Prouts Neck, ME *04074*
Bell MR Marcus L (Landin—Alison Grubb)
 ☎ (540) 347-2770 . . Fauquier White Sulphur Springs, Box 194, RR 2, Warrenton, VA *22186-8517*
Bellinger MRS Dunn (Adrian J Dunn)
 ☎ (508) 693-2080 . . 326 Main St, RFD Box 167A, Vineyard Haven, MA *02568*
Bellis MR & MRS James L (Blair Butler)
 ☎ (616) 335-5498 . . 6705 Audubon, Castle Park, Holland, MI *49423*
Belson MR & MRS James A (Rosemary P Greenslade) ☎ (410) 757-1747
 MISS Elizabeth A . . . . 12 W Severn Ridge
 MR Stephen G . . . . Rd, Annapolis, MD
  21401
Bemberg MRS Edward P (Georgia B Hatch)
 41 rue de Varenne, 75007 Paris, France
Bemis MRS James R (Burke—Jane Simpson)
 ☎ (616) 547-6540 . . 509 Belvedere Club, Charlevoix, MI *49720*
Benacerraf MR Ari
 ☎ (516) 749-0037 . . 8 Shore Rd, Dering Harbor, Shelter Island Heights, NY *11965*
Benasuli MR & MRS Alan (Nancy E Cooley) . . . . ☎ (516) 749-2088
 MISS Marina I . . . . 6 Cobbetts Lane,
 MR Alexandre J . . . . Shelter Island, NY
  11964
Bender MR & MRS Michael A (Martin—Belinda S Gilmer)
 ☎ (518) 734-9764 . . "The Edge" Clarence D Lane Rd, Windham, NY *12496*

Bender MR & MRS Robert G (Carolyn B Jensen)
☎ (712) 337-3333 . . Okoboji, Box 158, RR 3, Milford, IA *51351*
Benedict MR & MRS Neil P (Nancy K Brenizer)
☎ (508) 228-8837 . . 5 Sherburne Tpke, Nantucket, MA *02554*
Benedict MR & MRS Samuel (Elizabeth B Carruthers)
☎ (616) 484-2564 . . "The Nest" Box 393, Cedarville, MI *49719*
Benedict MR & MRS William J (Helen Stiassni)
☎ (802) 824-5285 . . 83 Landgrove Rd, Weston, VT *05161*
Benenson MR & MRS Marcius K (Letizia Pitigliani) . | ☎ (908) 852-4691
  MISS Daniela . . . . | PO Box 99,
  MR Alexander . . . . | Port Murray, NJ
                                                        | *07865*
Benington MRS Arthur (Mathilde M Johnston)
☎ (203) 966-4342 . . 982 Ponus Ridge Rd, New Canaan, CT *06840*
Benjamin MR & MRS Samuel N (Joan S Oakey)
☎ (516) 283-1446 . . "The Studio" Art Village, Box 1409, Southampton, NY *11968*
Benjamin MR & MRS W Hoffman (Joan Ellett)
☎ (914) 424-3340 . . "Lower Hayfields" Avery Rd, Garrison, NY *10524*
Benkard MR & MRS James W B (Margaret W | ☎ (516) 788-7515
  Spofford) . . . . | "Marvin Gardens"
  MISS Margaret M . . . . | Fishers Island, NY
  MR James R . . . . | *06390*
Benkhart MRS Donald R (Nancy S Howe)
☎ (508) 945-9852 . . "Lobster Caper" 22 Cabot Lane, West Chatham, MA *02669*
Benner MR & MRS Robert V A JR (Rebecca M Boyd)
☎ (802) 295-1944 . . Davenport Lane, Quechee, VT *05059*
Bennett MR & MRS Charles P (Catharine DeW | "Bridge Creek"
  Cabell) . . . . | Rte 1, Box 120E,
  MR Charles C . . . . | Reedville, VA
  MR Benjamin P . . . . | *22539*
Bennett MR & MRS Edward H 3d (Sekera—Marcia C | ☎ (705) 782-4229
  Oonk) . . . . | Range Lights Rd,
  MR Christopher E . . . . | Desbarats, Ontario
  MR Timothy R . . . . | P0R 1E0, Canada
  MISS Katherine H Sekera . . . .
  MR Jeffrey O Sekera . . . .
Bennett MR John H JR
☎ (704) 749-1134 . . "The Roost" Crescent Rd, Saluda, NC *28776*
Bennett DR & MRS Joseph S IV (Letty P Knight) . . . | ☎ (609) 967-8216
  MISS Amy Jo . . . . | 45 E 13 St, Avalon,
  MR Wade K . . . . | NJ *08202*
  MR Matthew MacGeorge . . . . |
Bennett MR & MRS Paul H (Sally I Neff)
The Berkshire, 11820 Edgewater Dv, Lakewood, OH *44107*
Benoist MR & MRS Howard 3d (Patricia L Reigle) . . . | ☎ (414) 868-3495
  MISS Sara R . . . . | "Beechwood"
  MR Ian E . . . . | Fish Creek, WI
                                                        | *54212*
Benoist DR & MRS Walter F (Claude V Fouke) . . . . | ☎ (414) 868-3495
  JUNIORS MISS Claude C . . . . | "Beechwood"
                                                         | Fish Creek, WI
                                                         | *54212*

Bensinger MR & MRS (DR) Peter B (Judith A | ☎ (809) 952-1463
  Schneebeck) . . . . | "Hillside"
  MISS Jennifer A . . . . | Round Hill,
  MISS Elizabeth Brooke . . . . | Montego Bay,
  MISS V Brette . . . . | Jamaica
Bent MR & MRS Edward S (Lambert—Rebecca J Fotouhi)
☎ (508) 228-1887 . . 2 S Valley Rd, Nantucket, MA *02554*
Bentley MR & MRS Chester A (Dunham—Angelica Van R Fales)
☎ (518) 576-9715 . . "Heboma" PO Box 584, St Huberts, NY *12943*
Bentley MR & MRS James A (Crowe—Cecily F Teague)
☎ (603) 569-3607 . . "Brick House" Mirror Lake, NH *03853*
Benton MR & MRS Nicholas (Kate Bigelow)
☎ (508) 295-0902 . . "West House" Indian Neck, Wareham, MA *02571*
Berger MRS George R B (Mary M Wurts)
☎ (705) 764-1996 . . Beaumaris, Lake Muskoka, Ontario P0B 1B0, Canada
Berger MR William M B . . . . | of ☎ (303)838-5321
  MISS Katherine M B . . . . | "Estabrook" Park
  MR George B . . . . | County H'way 68,
                                                         | Bailey, CO *80421*
                                                         | ☎ (207) 883-3399
                                                         | "Black Rock"
                                                         | 18 Winslow Homer
                                                          | Rd, Prouts Neck,
                                                         | ME *04074*
Bering MRS Edgar A JR (Harriet C Aldrich)
☎ (207) 734-6710 . . "House on Hill" HC 60, Box 77, Islesboro, ME *04848*
Berkeley MR & MRS Alfred R 3d (Muriel L | ☎ (717) 643-1513
  Van Dusen) . . . . | Pocono Lake
  MISS Cary B . . . . | Preserve, PA *18348*
  MISS Helen E . . . . |
  JUNIORS MISS Muriel Van D . . . . |
Berkey MR & MRS J Addison 3d (Osborn—Marietta | ☎ (207) 963-2558
  H Whittlesey) . . . . | PO Box 102,
  MISS Perrin R . . . . | Corea, ME *04621*
  MR John A 4th . . . . |
Berkheimer DR & MRS George A (Margaret P Yates)
☎ (508) 228-0403 . . 8 Pine St, Nantucket, MA *02554*
Berkley MRS Brown (Constance Brown)
☎ (302) 227-3405 . . North Shores, 59 Anchor Rd, Rehoboth Beach, DE *19971*
Berkowitz MR & MRS Mortimer 3d (Amelia F Manice)
☎ (516) 788-7008 . . Fishers Island, NY *06390*
Berl MR Charles S W . . see P B Brainard
Berl MR Christopher N . . see P B Brainard
Berl MR E Ennalls 4th . . see P B Brainard
Berl MISS Rita S . . see P B Brainard
Berlind MR & MRS Roger S (Brook R Wheeler) . . . . | ☎ (860) 567-9649
  MR William P . . . . | Looking Glass Hill
                                                         | Rd, Bantam, CT
                                                         | *06750*
Bestani MR & MRS Robert M (Marion W Raymond) . | ☎ (207) 363-5047
  JUNIORS MISS Elizabeth D . . . . | Box 238,
  JUNIORS MR William E . . . . | York Harbor, ME
                                                         | *03911*

Bethell MR Ralph A
 ☎ (418) 936-3403 . . ''MacDougall House'' Metis Beach, Quebec, Canada
Betts REV & MRS Darby W (Elaine J Wiswall) . . . . .
 MR Darby W JR. . . . .
 ☎ (207) 326-4332
 Box 247, Perkins St, Castine, ME *04421*
Betts DR & MRS Henry Brognard (Monika C Paul) . .
 MISS Amanda M E . . . .
 ☎ (011-33-93) 59-36-52
 4 rue du Pontail Neuf, Tourrettes sur Loup, 06140 Vence, France
Beuerlein MISS Pamela . . see A V Leness
Beuerlein MR Robert . . see A V Leness
Beuerlein MISS Sandra . . see A V Leness
Bevan MR D R Chandler . . see S A Dunn JR
Bever DR & MRS Christopher T (Josephine J Morton)
 ☎ (207) 422-9077 . . Bay Av, Hancock Point, ME *04640*
Bickel MR & MRS William Croft (Minnette C Duffy)
 ☎ (508) 775-5991 . . ''Hawthorne'' Box 143, Washington Av, Hyannis Port, MA *02647*
Bickford MR & MRS Nathaniel J (Jewelle A Wooten)
 MISS Laura C . . . .
 ☎ (508) 997-3805
 ''Mermaison'' 163 Mishaum Point Rd, South Dartmouth, MA *02748*
Biddle MRS Anne G (Biddle—Mikhalapov—Anne G Biddle)
 ☎ (207) 244-5213 . . ''Twixt-the-Graves'' Beech Hill Rd, Mt Desert, ME *04660*
Biddle MR & MRS Charles M 3d (Morrison—Phyllis Jenkins)
 ☎ (717) 646-0818 . . Pocono Lake Preserve, PA *18348*
Biddle MR & MRS David A T (Diane E Lishon)
 ☎ (609) 368-0617 . . ''The Boat House'' 6338 Heron Cove, Avalon, NJ *08202*
Biddle MR & MRS Edmund R (Frances E Disner)
 ☎ (508) 349-2264 . . ''Bright Mariner'' 610 & 612 Bound Brook Island Rd, Wellfleet, MA *02667*
Biddle MR & MRS Jonathan W (Emily R Boyle)
 ☎ (805) 684-0455 . . 181 Rincon Point Rd, Carpinteria, CA *93013*
Biddle MR & MRS Nicholas JR (Mary Hopkins)
 ☎ (401) 423-0310 . . ''Treetops'' PO Box 212, Jamestown, RI *02835*
Biddle MR & MRS Richard C D (Warfield—Crewe—Jean W Miller)
 ☎ (607) 749-4269 . . PO Box 393, Homer, NY *13077*
Biddle MRS Tania G (Tania P Gopcevic) . . . .
 MISS Tania A . . . .
 MR Christopher L . . . .
 ☎ (401) 423-0479
 53 Conanicus Av, Jamestown, RI *02835*
Biddle MR Wharton
 ☎ (401) 423-2278 . . ''Gull's Nest'' 201 Beavertail Rd, Jamestown, RI *02835*
Bidwell MRS Cynthia B (Cynthia H Barry). . . . .
 MISS Emily P . . . .
 MISS Cristina M R . . . .
 ☎ (516) 283-5185
 PO Box 936, Halsey Neck Lane, Southampton, NY *11969*
Bidwell MR & MRS J Truman JR (O'Neil—Katharine T Thomas)
 ☎ (516) 788-7674 . . North Hill, Fishers Island, NY *06390*
Bidwill MR & MRS William V JR (Nicole G Kugler)
 ☎ (314) 569-2753 . . 2 Country Life Acres, St Louis, MO *63131*
Biegler MR & MRS John C (Greer—A Carol Newman)
 ☎ (540) 466-2510 . . 820 Long Crescent Rd, Bristol, VA *24201*
Bielenstein MR & MRS Hans (Gabrielle C Maupin) . .
 MISS Danielle E M . . . .
 MISS Andrea J G . . . .
 ☎ (804) 397-1625
 328 Court St, Portsmouth, VA *23704*
Bierman MR & MRS Stephen K (Elizabeth Carrington) . . . .
 JUNIORS MR Frederick C . . . .
 ☎ (860) 435-9780
 ''The Schoolhouse'' 552 Twin Lakes Rd, Salisbury, CT *06068*
Bigbie MR & MRS J Taylor (Nadine de Coninck)
 ☎ (011-32-50) 60-14-58 . . ''Green Lodge'' 22 Av C Lemmonier, 8300 Knokke-Heist, Belgium
Bigelow MR & MRS Joseph S 3d (Mary E Brown)
 ☎ (401) 847-0789 . . ''Bois Doré'' Gardener's Cottage, 128 Webster St, Newport, RI *02840*
Billings MR Kenney
 ☎ (508) 693-2567 . . ''The Farm'' Box 17, Middle Rd, West Tisbury, MA *02575*
Billington MRS Nelson (Gaunt—Billington—Chandor—Dorothy Lalor)
 ☎ (207) 359-2234 . . ''Meadow-Reach'' Box 296, Sargentville, ME *04673*
Bilodeau MR & MRS Harrison Otis C (Alessia Ortolani)
 ☎ (011-39-1) 85-26-05-61 . . Villa Bianca, via Del Castellino 18, 16035 Rapallo, Italy
Binger MR & MRS David G (Jane A Wilmerding)
 ☎ (401) 635-8841 . . Quoquonset Lane, Little Compton, RI *02837*
Bingham MR & MRS A Walker 3d (Nicolette S Pathy)
 ☎ (011-41-29) 4-51-25 . . ''Châlet Emeraude'' Les Hauts de Bon Accueil, Châteaux-d'Oex, Switzerland
Bingham MR & MRS C Tiffany JR (Ann S Dickey)
 ☎ (207) 372-8896 . . ''Daly House'' Harts Neck Rd, Tenants Harbor, ME *04860*
Bingham MR & MRS Harry Payne JR (de Bustamante—Helen Ramsdell)
 ☎ (802) 375-6669 . . ''Stone Gate Farm'' Rte 1, Box 226, Shaftsbury, VT *05262*
Bingham MRS Sally Grover (Davies—Davis—Sarah L Grover) . . . .
 JUNIORS MR Wheelock R JR . . . .
 MISS Sarah M Davies . . . .
 MR Stephen T Davies . . . .
 ☎ (415) 851-4659
 2891 Woodside Rd, Woodside, CA *94062*
Bingham LT COL & MRS William L (H Virginia Potter) USAF.
 ☎ (315) 354-4135 . . ''The Cottage'' 1 Brandreth Park, Long Lake, NY *12847*
Binney MISS Caroline Thorn (Dougherty—Caroline Thorn Binney)
 ''Oakleigh'' Rumstick Rd, Barrington, RI *02806*
Binney MR & MRS Robert H (Martha B Billings)
 ☎ (508) 546-3107 . . ''Windywalls'' 11 Athena Way, Rockport, MA *01966*
Binnian MR & MRS William (Jacqueline C Bolling)
 ☎ (207) 348-2391 . . ''Binnacle'' Box 1, Sunset, ME *04683*

Binz MR & MRS Urban G (June H Pynchon)
☎ (516) 283-0703 . . 293 Little Plains Rd, Box 671, Southampton, NY *11968*
Biondi MR & MRS Frank J JR (Carol Oughton) . . . . . | ☎ (508) 645-2877
  MISS Anne O . . . . | Old Farm Rd,
  MISS Jane O . . . . | Chilmark, MA *02535*
Bird MRS Goodwin (Mathilde Goodwin) . . . . | ☎ (508) 349-2162
  MISS Zvia N . . . . | "Thoreau House" Old Country Rd, Truro, MA *02666*
Birney MR & MRS Arthur A (Alison Bean)
☎ (518) 656-9007 . . "Glistening Waters" Assembly Point, Lake George, NY *12845*
Birney THE REV & MRS James G (Acton—Cantrell—Barbara A Sullivan)
☎ (413) 269-6227 . . "Cove's End" PO Box 4042, East Otis, MA *01029*
Bishop MR Andre S
☎ (207) 863-4481 . . "Arey's Cove" Vinalhaven, ME *04863*
Bishop MRS John Harding (Mixter—Lewis Watson)
☎ (508) 548-3017 . . "The Farm House" Nobska Point, Woods Hole, MA *02543*
Bishop MRS Louis Faugères 3d (Alexandra Griggs)
☎ (914) OR7-5433 . . "Igloo" Rte 44, Millbrook, NY *12545*
Bishop MR & MRS Thomas L (Dorothy E Lyon)
☎ (603) 875-2627 . . "Woodlands" Star Rte W, Alton Bay, NH *03810*
Bishop MR & MRS Warner B (Landy—Susan B Howard)
☎ (216) 423-1728 . . "Windgate" Brigham Rd, Gates Mills, OH *44040*
Bispham MR & MRS Thomas P (Barbara C Shea)
☎ (508) 257-4478 . . "Hedge Hog" Box 183, 28 New St, Siasconset, MA *02564*
Bissell MR & MRS E Perot 4th (Melissa D Lighthill)
☎ (207) 276-5539 . . "Ready About" Northeast Harbor, ME *04662*
Bistrian DR & MRS Bruce R (Eleanor A Dix) . . . . . . | ☎ (516) 267-8792
  MISS Tennille R D . . . . | "Little House"
  MISS Jordan B D . . . . | Atlantic Av,
  MISS Britton P D . . . . | Amagansett, NY *11930*
Black MRS Clinton R 3d (Woolman—Gene L O'Brien)
920 Woodland Dv, Glenview, IL *60025*
Black MRS Gary (Adams—Verina Borwick)
☎ (011-44-1488) 648220 . . Shefford Woodlands House, Shefford Woodlands, Hungerford, Berkshire RG17 7AG, England
Black DR & MRS Harrison (Gertrude Diefenbach)
☎ (207) 284-6634 . . "Philip Cove" St Martin's Lane, Biddeford Pool, ME *04006*
Black MR & MRS Robert L JR (Helen H Chatfield)
☎ (207) 236-4279 . . "Kentmoor" 10 Russell Av, Rockport, ME *04856*
Black MISS Virginia B
☎ (516) SH9-0002 . . "Blackacre" Box 115, Shelter Island, NY *11964*
Black MR & MRS William M (Mary E Hubbard)
☎ (603) 563-8170 . . "Hasty Retreat" Frost Pond, Dublin, NH *03444*
Blackwell MR & MRS James M 4th (Anne H Stires) | ☎ (508) 228-5657
  MISS Hillary Van C . . . . | "Small Joy"
  MISS Carolyn T . . . . | Massasoit Village, 44 S Cambridge St, Nantucket, MA *02554*

Blagden MR Crawford
☎ (508) 540-3614 . . Box 667, Chapoquoit Island, West Falmouth, MA *02574*
Blagden MR & MRS George (Josephine C S Swan) | ☎ (207) 374-2475
⚓ . . . . | "Kalmia Knoll"
  MISS Julia W . . . . | HC 64, Box 262, Parker Point Rd, Blue Hill, ME *04614*
Blaine DR & MRS Graham B JR (Lovell—Sandra A H Green)
☎ (508) 349-3315 . . "The Ark" King Philip Rd, Wellfleet, MA *02667*
Blaine MRS Richard G (Biddle—Shields—Katharine Mortimer) . . . . | ☎ (516) 283-9303
  MR Walker . . . . | Box 880,
  MISS Katharine Shields . . . . | Southampton, NY *11969*
Blair MR & MRS Edward McC (Elizabeth G Iglehart)
☎ (207) 276-3946 . . "L'Escale" Northeast Harbor, ME *04662*
Blair MRS John B (Todes—Betty Watkins)
☎ (414) 854-9762 . . 2 Knudson House, 6 Water St, Ephraim, WI *54211*
Blair MR & MRS Michael W (Edith B Moore)
☎ (203) 259-6343 . . 60 Brett Rd, Fairfield, CT *06430*
Blair MR & MRS William D JR (Jane F Coleman)
☎ (207) 863-2014 . . "Quarry Point" Box 822, Vinalhaven, ME *04863*
Blake MRS Brooke (McLean—Elizabeth M Brooke)
☎ (401) 847-0679 . . "Indian Spring" Moorland Rd, Newport, RI *02840*
Blake MISS Elinor L . . see H W English
Blake MR Francis (Caroline A Hunnewell)
☎ (508) 758-3357 . . Ship St, Mattapoisett, MA *02739*
Blake MR & MRS John W (Jennifer J Jack)
2 Ship St, Mattapoisett, MA *02739*
Blake MRS Robert M (Delia D Carrington)
☎ (802) 867-4037 . . Box 735, Dorset, VT *05251*
Blake MR & MRS Robert O (Sylvia Whitehouse)
☎ (207) 244-5715 . . Box 4, Mt Desert, ME *04660*
Blanchard MR & MRS Alan F (Ann S Elliott) . . . . . . | ☎ (860) 535-2164
  MISS Deborah G . . . . | 21 Wall St,
  MR A Elliott . . . . | Stonington, CT *06378*
Blanchard MR & MRS Frederick C JR (Lesley H Finnell)
PO Box 612, Siasconset, MA *02564*
Blanchard MR & MRS James A 2d (June Peterson) . . | "Reverie Cove"
  MR James A 3d . . . . | 7 Harbor Lane, Bar Harbor, ME *04609-1107*
Blanchard MRS Mercer C (Elizabeth D Pagon)
☎ (802) 765-4378 . . Mine Rd, South Strafford, VT *05070*
Bland MR & MRS D Gerald JR (Immacolata B Corsini)
☎ (011-39-564) 833-936 . . "Casa Bianca" Porto Ercole, 58018 Grosseto, Italy
Blaxter MR & MRS G Harold (Barbara R Appleton)
☎ (207) 439-1961 . . "The Trolley Stop" Brave Boat Harbor Rd, Kittery Point, ME *03905*
Bleakley MR & MRS William Jay JR (Gring—Gwendolyn Smith)
☎ (617) 631-3707 . . 39 Wharf Path, Marblehead, MA *01945*
Blewer MRS Sondra G (Sondra Gerdau)
☎ (603) 823-7798 . . Box 541, Sugar Hill, NH *03585*

Blind MR & MRS William C (Peggy A Kauffman)
☎ (207) 967-3481 . . "Respite" Box 825, Kennebunkport, ME *04046*
Blind MR & MRS William C JR (Rebecca D McCoy) . | ☎ (441) 238-0235
   MISS Rebecca C . . . . | "Shanty"
   JUNIORS MR Burroughs C L W . . . . | 138 Middle Rd, Southampton SN 02, Bermuda
Blitzer DR & MRS Seth M (Letitia C Biddle)
☎ (410) 778-5311 . . "Plum Point House" Andelot Lane, Worton, MD *21678*
Block MR & MRS Huntington T (Amie Willard)
☎ (508) 257-6216 . . "Unity" 9 Morey Lane, Nantucket, MA *02564*
Block MR Jonathan C . . of
☎ (518) 537-6305 . . "The Clubhouse" Box 373, Germantown, NY *12526*
☎ (508) 257-6275 . . "Rudder Grange" Box 267, Siasconset, MA *02564*
Block MR & MRS Roger W (Miriam Fulton)
☎ (508) 257-6275 . . "Rudder Grange" Box 267, Siasconset, MA *02564*
Blodget MRS Alden S JR (Louise R French)
☎ (508) 283-8570 . . Adams Hill Rd, Annisquam, MA *01930*
Blodgett MR & MRS Mark W (Helen M Watson)
☎ (207) 867-2214 . . "Oak Hill Farm" North Haven, ME *04853*
Blodgett MR & MRS Thomas N (Annc W Blagden) . . | ☎ (603) 563-8646
   JUNIORS MR Thomas N . . . . | Dublin, NH *03444*
Blomquist MR & MRS Edwin Renken (Carol Joan Powers)
☎ (802) 442-1528 . . "Twin Brooks Farm" RR 1, Box 531, North Bennington, VT *05257*
Blount MRS Mary Katherine (Mary Katherine Archibald)
☎ (334) 857-2244 . . "Lakeside" Rte 2, Eclectic, AL *36024*
Blow MR & MRS Michael (Norfleet—Ayres—Diane C Jones) . . . . | ☎ (516) 788-7765
   MISS Valerie W Norfleet . . . . | "Tower Hill" Fishers Island, NY *06390*
Blundon DR & MRS Montague 3d (Dillon—Juanita Doody)
☎ (410) 819-0663 . . "Seven Swans" 7036 Traveler's Rest Circle, Easton, MD *21601*
Blynn MR & MRS Bryce JR (Maffei—Gulliver—Mary Frances Maresca)
☎ (203) 637-9375 . . 61 Indian Head Rd, Riverside, CT *06878*
Boal MISS Ann A
☎ (616) 547-6020 . . "Stony Point" 09284 Boyne City Rd, Charlevoix, MI *49720*
Boalt MR J Anthony
☎ (910) 363-2227 . . Valley View Rd, Roaring Gap, NC *28668*
Boardman MR & MRS D Dixon (Pauline M Baker) . . | ☎ (516) 671-1223
   MISS Serena . . . . | "Little Vikings Cove" Peacock Lane, Locust Valley, NY *11560*
   MISS Samantha . . . . |
Boardman MR & MRS William H JR (Alice Korff) . . | ☎ (518) 576-4548
   MR William H 3d . . . . | "Freiheit Schloss" Keene Valley, NY *12943*
Bockman DR & MRS Richard S (Darcy B Kelley) . . . | ☎ (516) 725-3578
   MISS Danielle R . . . . | 22 Spring St, Box 568, Sag Harbor, NY *11963*
   MR Alexander C . . . . |

Bodell MR & MRS Joseph J JR (Bayne—Jane R Leigh)
☎ (508) 428-6541 . . "Pine Point" 550 Wianno Av, Osterville, MA *02655*
Bodine MRS William W JR (Louise R Dilworth)
☎ (802) 362-3932 . . Rte 7, Manchester, VT *05254*
Boenning MR & MRS H Dickson S (Anne Wister Garnett)
☎ (401) 423-0720 . . "Kettle Cove" PO Box 246, Jamestown, RI *02835*
Boenning MR & MRS Henry D (Perkins—Sara A Hunt)
☎ (609) 967-7112 . . 36 E 16 St, Avalon, NJ *08202*
Boerke MR & MRS Richard E (Fredricka L von Redlich) ⚓
☎ (902) 766-4894 . . RR 1, Rose Bay, Nova Scotia B0J 2X0, Canada
Boersma MR & MRS Milford (Mary E Lister) ⚓ . . | ☎ (616) 889-4073
   MR Frederick L . . . . | 8141 Portage Point Dv, Onekama, MI *49675*
Bogardus DR & MRS Sidney T JR (Julia B Hunt)
"The Carriage House" Sorrento, ME *04677*
Bogert MRS H Lawrence (Margaret Milbank)
☎ (516) 788-7536 . . "Seascape" Box 427, Fishers Island, NY *06390*
Bogert MR & MRS H Lawrence 3d (Palmer—Eleanor P Wheeler) . . . . | ☎ (516) 726-6789
   MISS Hilary L . . . . | 104 Cobb Isle Rd, PO Box 562, Water Mill, NY *11976*
   MISS Blair W Palmer . . . . |
   MR Lansing R Palmer JR . . . . |
Boghossian MR & MRS David M (Elizabeth D Bartle)
☎ (516) 324-8667 . . 9 Davids Lane, East Hampton, NY *11937*
Bogue MR & MRS (DR) Robert W JR (Lauren Lauck) . | ☎ (802) 822-5586
   MISS Jennifer C . . . . | Averill, VT *05901*
   MISS Kimberley W . . . . |
   MR R Peter . . . . |
Boies MR & MRS David (Eugenia Clark)
Great Hill Rd, Tamworth, NH *03886*
Bolling MR & MRS Robert H JR (Joan Ross)
☎ (508) 228-0646 . . "Lightkeeper's Lodge" 11 Easton St, Nantucket, MA *02554*
Bolling MR & MRS Sterling R (Jane Sharon)
☎ (207) 359-2761 . . "On the Rocks" PO Box 178, Brooklin, ME *04616*
Bollman MR & MRS McWilliam V (Lucile A H Roesler)
☎ (518) 499-2349 . . "Rivendell" Huletts Landing, NY *12841*
Bolton MRS Kenyon C (Mary I Peters)
☎ (207) 883-5518 . . "Juniper Ledge" PO Box 3099, Prouts Neck, ME *04074*
Bolton MRS William B (Katherine J Howard)
"The Haven" Winslow Homer Rd, Prouts Neck, ME *04074*
Bomeisler MR & MRS Douglass M JR (Anne O Kniffen)
☎ (508) 228-1356 . . 28 Crooked Lane, Nantucket, MA *02554*
Bond MR & MRS Arthur D JR (Molly Graham)
☎ (508) 996-8333 . . 452 Potomska Rd, South Dartmouth, MA *02748*
Bond MR & MRS Calhoun (Jane L Piper)
☎ (302) 539-7133 . . "Sea Chance" Cotton Patch Hills, Bethany Beach, DE *19930*
Bondurant MRS William W JR (Carr—Nina M Jenkins)
Bear Lake, Box 127, HC 1, Gouldsboro, PA *18424*
Bonner MR Henry M . . . . | ☎ (802) 496-2140
   MR David S . . . . | Bundy Rd, Box 299, Waitsfield, VT *05673*
   MR Robert P . . . . |
   MR Paul B . . . . |

Bonner MISS Jennifer
 ☎ (301) 863-8121 . . Scotland Beach, MD *20687*
Bonnie MR & MRS Robert F (Cynthia A Polk)
 ☎ (540) 592-3402 . . PO Box 961, Middleburg, VA *22117*
Bonoff MR & MRS Burton L (Barbara J Wasserman)
 PO Box 7206, Warwick, RI *02887*
Bonsal MR & MRS David S (Pisani—Edna O'Brien)
 ☎ (717) 595-3312 . . Cottage 312, Buck Hill Falls, PA *18323*
Bonsal MRS Dudley B (Faithfull—Lucia Turner)
 ☎ (914) 234-7117 . . 24 St Marys Church Rd, Bedford, NY *10506*
Bonsal MR & MRS Frank A JR (Helen Baldwin) . . . . . ☎ (516) 788-7341
 MISS Adair B . . . . "Seven Gables"
 MISS Polly P . . . . Fishers Island, NY
 MR Frank A 3d *06390*
Boocock MRS Kenyon (Glenn H Winnett)
 ☎ (516) 788-7376 . . "Chocomount" Fishers Island, NY *06390*
Booher MR & MRS L Dale (Lisa Stamm)
 ☎ (516) 749-2189 . . "Homestead" 67 N Menantic Rd, PO Box 90, Shelter Island Heights, NY *11965*
Boomer MR & MRS George du P (Palmer—Nola Schafer)
 ☎ (603) 323-8934 . . "Boomerhaven" Fowler's Mill Rd, Chocorua, NH *03817*
Boomer MR & MRS Robert E (Anne E Knapp) . . . . . ☎ (517) 738-8464
 MISS Ellen M . . . . Cottage 44,
  Pointe-aux-Barques,
  Port Austin, MI
  48467
Boone MR & MRS Jonathan O (Danielle M de Boisblanc)
 ☎ (916) 546-7225 . . 577 Tripoli, Agate Bay, CA *96140*
Boone MR William H
 ☎ (304) 645-1059 . . Montescena, Greenbrier, Box 1146, Lewisburg, WV *24901*
Boote MR & MRS A Shepard (Heath Drury)
 "Deer Point" N Lubec Rd, Lubec, ME *04652*
Booth MRS John L (Louise P Camper)
 ☎ (313) 884-3093 . . 309 Lake Shore Rd, Grosse Pointe Farms, MI *48236*
Borden MR & MRS Gail F (Hildegard M Laturnus) . . ☎ (360) 321-3506
 MISS Anna C . . . . "The Cabin"
 MR Gail P . . . . Bayview Beach,
  1964 E Shore Av,
  Freeland, WA *98249*
Borie MR & MRS David B (Mary W Stewart)
 ☎ (508) 228-2414 . . 12 Pine St, Nantucket, MA *02554*
Borie MR & MRS J R McAllister (Helder—Judith A Hallerman)
 "Seaview" 68 Seaview Rd, Point O'Woods, South Lyme, CT *06376*
Bortz MR Richard C
 ☎ (207) 867-4631 . . Wharf House, North Haven, ME *04853*
Bosland MR & MRS Paul C (Helen S Nelson)
 ☎ (802) 253-8012 . . Pinnacle Rd, Stowe, VT *05672*
Bossidy MR B Haig (Alice R Bohmfalk)
 ☎ (914) 666-8398 . . Box 448, Succabone Rd, Bedford, NY *10506*
Bossidy MR & MRS Bruce H (Dorothy C Pickering)
 ☎ (203) 259-9514 . . 298 Harbor Rd, Southport, CT *06490*
Bostwick MRS Albert C (Sage—Eleanor Purviance)
 ☎ (516) 334-0876 . . PO Box 440, 25 Hillside Av, Old Westbury, NY *11568*
Bostwick MR & MRS Albert C JR (Handal—Linda M Barrett)
 ☎ (315) 369-6180 . . Bisby Lake, Thendara, NY *13472*
Botsford MR Blake . . see MRS K Van Rensselaer
Bouras MR & MRS James C (Katharine W Adams) . . ☎ (315) 896-2169
 MR Ian C . . . . Box 326,
  Barneveld, NY
  13304
Bouriez MR & MRS Philippe G (Lynch—Edith W Scott)
 ☎ (508) 228-0409 . . 9 Milk St, Nantucket, MA *02554*
Bourne MRS Philip E (Luette R Close) . . . . ☎ (603) 563-8325
 MISS Luette S . . . . "Dead End"
 MR Philip E JR . . . . Box 56,
  Dublin, NH *03444*
Bourne MR & MRS William N JR (Katherine E Day) . ☎ (603) 585-6854
 MISS Katherine L . . . . "Fitz" RFD 62B,
 MR William A . . . . Fitzwilliam, NH
  03447
Bovey MISS Hilary
 ☎ (508) 945-1455 . . "Quason Lodge" Sears Point, Chatham, MA *02633*
Bovey MR & MRS William K (Katherine R MacLean) ☎ (508) 693-1843
 MISS Julia H . . . . West Chop, MA
 MISS Alexandra K *02573*
 MR Edward H 2d
Bowart MISS Nuria L . . see MISS M M Hitchcock
Bowart MISS Sophia J . . see MISS M M Hitchcock
Bowden MR & MRS Adrian H H (Marjorie W ☎ (011-44-1869)
 Gordan) 247014
 MISS Stephanie F H . . . . Bucknell Manor,
 MR Alexander G H . . . . Bucknell nr Bicester,
 JUNIORS MR Richard W B H . . . . Oxfordshire
  OX6 9LS, England
Bowditch MRS E Francis (Anna M Hale)
 ☎ (203) 245-1771 . . PO Box 844, Madison, CT *06443*
Bowditch MR & MRS Samuel I (Marian P Rogers)
 ☎ (603) 323-7956 . . Box 27, Chocorua, NH *03817*
Bower MRS Robert T (Just—Jean C Ramsay)
 ☎ (516) 653-4538 . . Old Depot Rd, Quogue, NY *11959*
Bowers MR Robert C
 ☎ (603) 526-8457 . . "Chimerical Farm" PO Box 249, Georges Mills, NH *03751*
Bowers MR Spotswood D 3d
 ☎ (603) 863-6629 . . 21 Wedgewood Dv, Box 929, Grantham, NH *03753*
Bowes MR & MRS John Garland (Frances Fay)
 ☎ (707) 939-1092 . . "Casa Bowes" 17500 Carriger Rd, Sonoma, CA *95476*
Bowie MR & MRS Robert R (Theodosia Chapman)
 ☎ (410) 822-5803 . . "Stirling" 6918 Traveler's Rest Circle, Easton, MD *21601*
Bowles MISS Beatrice V (Michael—Beatrice V Bowles)
 ☎ (209) 826-3085 . . "The Cabin" Hereford Rd, Los Banos, CA *93635*
Bowles MR & MRS Chester B JR (Outten—Mary S Phelan)
 ☎ (707) 857-3729 . . "Flower Farm" Box 482, Geyserville, CA *95441*
Bowles MR & MRS John L (Kay D Moore) . . . . ☎ (540) 839-5031
 MR C Houston F . . . . Cobbler Ridge,
  Warm Springs, VA
  24484

Bowles MR & MRS Philip E 3d (Jamie E Nicol)
 ☎ (209) 827-3086 . . "Cottonwood Ranch" 11609 S Hereford Rd, Los Banos, CA *93635*
Bowman MRS John Webster (Eleanor Noyes Hempstone)
 22 Skiff Av, Vineyard Haven, MA *02568*
Bowman MR & MRS Samuel A 3d (Fowler—Grace O Grasselli)
 ☎ (914) 677-8655 . . Maple Av, PO Box 459, Millbrook, NY *12545*
Bowman MR Thomas Merritt
 ☎ (808) 696-2166 . . "Sand Buster" 84-965 Farrington H'way, Makaha, HI *96782*
Bowring MRS Charles W 3d (Julie Webber) . . . . | ☎ (207) 495-2671
 MISS Victoria M . . . . | Clearwater Camp,
 MR Charles W . . . . | Water Rte, Box 235, Belgrade Lakes, ME *04918*
Bowring MR & MRS Douglas B (Emily S Godfrey)
 ☎ (207) 495-2671 . . Clearwater Camp, Water Rte, Box 235, Belgrade Lakes, ME *04918*
Bowring MRS E Bonner (Helen Hulbert)
 ☎ (508) 627-3542 . . "Summer Palace" 16 Garden Cove Rd, Box 778, Edgartown, MA *02539*
Boyce MRS John C G (Barbara A Cobb)
 ☎ (616) 526-5680 . . 5 Pennsylvania Av, Box 4423, Wequetonsing, MI *49740*
Boyce MR & MRS John C G JR (Ann F Hagerty) . . . . | ☎ (616) 526-7433
 MISS L Reid . . . . | 33 Third Av,
 JUNIORS MR Collis H G . . . . | Wequetonsing, MI
 JUNIORS MR Sandford C G . . . . | *49740*
Boyce MR & MRS Sandford C (Mary P Bisig) . . . . . . | ☎ (616) 526-5478
 JUNIORS MISS M Gwendolyn . . . . | 17 Beach Dv, Wequetonsing, MI *49740*
Boyd MR & MRS Nicholas G K JR (Margaret V Clifton) ⚓ . . . . | ☎ (916) 541-0341
 MISS Alexandra C . . . . | "Juniper Ledge"
 MR Nicholas G K 3d . . . . | Fallen Leaf Lake, Lake Tahoe, CA *95708*
Boyd MR & MRS Thomas M (Jane E Clayton)
 ☎ (860) 434-3147 . . 10 Becket Hill, Lyme, CT *06371*
Boyer MR F Alger JR . . see D H Carnahan JR
Boyer MISS G Alexandra . . see D H Carnahan JR
Brackenridge MRS Belinda A (Ward—Wiesen— Belinda A Brackenridge) . . . . | ☎ (516) 324-5775
 MR Gavin B Wiesen . . . . | 30A Woods Lane, East Hampton, NY *11937*
Brackenridge MR & MRS Gavin (Mary Kathryn McDonnell) . . . . | ☎ (516) 324-0543
 JUNIORS MISS Anne K . . . . | 26 Woods Lane, East Hampton, NY *11937*
Bradford MR & MRS James C JR (Lillian F Robertson) . . . . | ☎ (704) 733-5556
 MR James C 3d . . . . | "Shadow Lawn"
 MR Bryan R . . . . | Linville, NC *28646*
Bradford MRS Judith R (Sadler—Judith S Rübel) . . | ☎ (603) 323-7358
 MISS Rebecca E . . . . | Chocorua, NH *03817*
Bradford JUNIORS MR Seth . . see J B Hannum JR

Bradley MR & MRS E Michael (Judith A Thompson) | ☎ (516) 653-6907
 MR Samuel A . . . . | 27 Beach Lane, Quogue, NY *11959*
Bradley MR Frederick W . . . . | ☎ (707) 998-3884
 MR Craig H . . . . | "Rancho Solfa Tara" Sulphur Bank Mine Rd, Clearlake Oaks, CA *95423*
Bradley MR & MRS John L (Gabrielle Wright)
 ☎ (916) 525-7543 . . Box 187, Tahoma, CA *95733*
Bradley MR & MRS Montgomery S (Joanne Freytag)
 ☎ (207) 963-2330 . . West Gouldsboro, ME *04607*
Bradshaw MRS Thornton F (West—Patricia J Salter)
 ☎ (508) 627-8727 . . Box 2003, Edgartown, MA *02539*
Bradway MR & MRS Bruce M (Eleanore M Zeiss)
 Camp Wipigaki, Lac du Flambeau, WI *54538*
Braham MR & MRS W Walter JR (I Ann Haines) . . . . | ☎ (906) 484-3439
 ⚓ . . . . | RR 1, Box 64,
 MISS Nancy S . . . . | Woodland Park, Cedarville, MI
 MR Robert B . . . . | *49719*
Brainard MRS Harold J (Ruth H Bickford)
 ☎ (905) 834-4269 . . RR 1, Lorraine, House 1145, Port Colborne, Ontario L3K 5V3, Canada
Brainard MR & MRS Peter B (Berl—Rosalie D Sellar) . . . . | ☎ (860) 388-3752
 MISS Pamela H . . . . | "Fenwick"
 MR Peter B JR . . . . | Grove Av, Old Saybrook, CT
 MR Newton C . . . . | *06475*
  MISS Rita S Berl—at "Seaweed" Bellevue Av, Newport, RI *02840* . . . .
  MSRS E Ennalls 4th, Charles S W & Christopher N Berl—at "Seaweed" Bellevue Av, Newport, RI *02840* . . . .
Brainerd MRS Anne E (Anne Eddison)
 ☎ (802) 333-4208 . . "Juniper Patch" RR 1, Box 265, Fairlee, VT *05045*
Brainerd MR & MRS Stanford H (Hart—Wendy Morgan Smith) . . . . | ☎ (860) 267-2081
 MR Brooks R . . . . | Quarry Hill Farm, Haddam Neck, CT
  MISS Hilary B Hart . . . . | *06424*
  MR Howard S Hart . . . . |
Brakenridge MRS John W (Brooke Hollister) . . . . | ☎ (803) 768-0130
 MISS Wendy H . . . . | 1380 Pelican Watch
 MISS Bonnie S . . . . | Villa, Seabrook Island, SC *29455*
Bramwell MR & MRS William M JR (Thyra Elizabeth Reed) . . . . | ☎ (516) 653-4812
 MISS Hilary F . . . . | 10 Ocean Av,
 JUNIORS MR Austin W . . . . | PO Box 1343, Quogue, NY *11959*
Branscomb MR & MRS Lewis McA (Anne Wells)
 ☎ (970) 728-5691 . . 132 Double Eagle Dv, Telluride, CO *81435*
Bransome DR & MRS Edwin D JR (Janet L Williams)
 ☎ (803) 671-4121 . . 20 Twin Pines Rd, Sea Pines, Hilton Head Island, SC *29928*
Brash MRS Douglas Reid (Nancy Ludington)
 ☎ (516) 583-5991 . . Point O'Woods, NY *11706*

Bratenahl DR & MRS Alexander (Roberta H Robb)
☎ (415) 669-1138 . . "Drakes Nest" 80 Laurel View Way, Inverness, CA *94937*

Brauer MR & MRS Stephen F (Camilla C Thompson) | ☎ (715) 356-1500
MISS Rebecca R . . . . | "Cedar Gates"
MR Blackford F . . . . | Country Club Rd,
JUNIORS MR Stephen F JR . . . . | Minocqua, WI
 | *54548*

Braun MR & MRS Andrew G (Helen F Osborn)
☎ (516) 788-7486 . . Box 103, Fishers Island, NY *06930*

Brauns MRS Robert A W (Benton—Sandra P Neave)
☎ (516) 788-7511 . . "Falling Shingles" Fishers Island, NY *06390*

Bredin MR & MRS J Bruce (Octavia M du Pont)
☎ (508) 228-0837 . . "Duneover" 75 Hulbert Av, Nantucket, MA *02554*

Breed DR & MRS R Huntington 2d (Lucy B Fowlkes)
☎ (508) 228-1305 . . 11 W Chester St, Nantucket, MA *02554*

Brengle MR & MRS George M (Anne B Blum)
☎ (207) 288-3075 . . "The Farm House" Deer Acres, Mt Desert, ME *04660*

Brengle MR & MRS William C (Agnes C Crocker)
Watermans Cove, North Haven, ME *04853*

Brennan MRS William J JR (Lucy Curley Joyce) . . . | ☎ (516) 653-4004
MISS Joyce L . . . . | "Quail's Run"
MISS Lindsley A . . . . | 29 Shinnecock Rd,
 | PO Box 178,
 | Quogue, NY *11959*

Breslin MRS Louis R JR (Vars—Nancy Kincaid)
☎ (315) 482-9721 . . Box 335E, 45496 Landon Rd, Wellesley Island, NY *13640*

Brett MRS Bruce Y (Jacqueline Dewey)
Jun 1 . . ☎ (518) 327-3103 . . "The Pines" Rainbow Lake Rd, Box 54, Rainbow Lake, NY *12976*

Brett MRS Philip M JR (Pool—Mary B Schwab)
☎ (516) 324-1958 . . Box 957, 4 Lockwood Lane, East Hampton, NY *11937*

Brewer MRS George E (Ann Fraser)
☎ (518) 582-2042 . . Tahawus Club, Sanford Rd, Newcomb, NY *12852*

Brewer MR George E 3d
☎ (561) 655-6952 . . 3705 S Flagler Dv, Apt 39, West Palm Beach, FL *33405*

Brewer MRS Wilbert S (Champ—Hornbeck—Jeannette W Watson)
☎ (216) 991-2341 . . Moreland Courts, 13705 Shaker Blvd, Shaker Heights, OH *44120*

Brewster MR & MRS Benjamin H (Davis—Harriet K Dodson) ⚓
☎ (616) 547-2695 . . 27 Belvedere Club, Charlevoix, MI *49720*

Brewster MR David K . . . . | "La Cache"
MISS Rachel D . . . . | 06230 St Jean-Cap-
MR William M . . . . | Ferrat, France
JUNIORS MISS Mary Elizabeth . . . . |

Brewster MR & MRS Galen (Hathaway Tew) . . . . . . | ☎ (207) 354-6232
MISS Paget . . . . | Pleasant Point Rd,
MR Ivan . . . . | Cushing, ME *04563*

Brewster MRS Walter Rice (Stout—Dorothy W Gatins)
☎ (516) 324-8009 . . "Arcadia" Newtown Lane, East Hampton, NY *11937*

Brewster MR & MRS William S (Brodeur—Hornblower—Malabar Schleiter)
☎ (508) 255-1956 . . "Beachy Head" 371 Tonset Rd, Orleans, MA *02653*

Breyer MR & MRS Henry W 3d (Joanne Braatz) . . . . | ☎ (516) 324-6855
MISS Laura L . . . . | 40 Lee Av,
MR Henry W 4th . . . . | Box 5030,
 | East Hampton, NY
 | *11937*

Bricken MR & MRS Jonathan M (Madeleine D Seaman)
☎ (516) 324-4723 . . 18 Cross H'way, East Hampton, NY *11937*

Brickley MR & MRS Richard L JR (Nancy P Stanley) . | ☎ (401) 847-8456
MISS Katherine Hickox . . . . | "The Carriage
 | House"
 | 30 Chastellux Av,
 | Newport, RI *02840*

Briger MR & MRS Paul H (Keyes—Pauline Gray) . . . | ☎ (860) 739-3650
MISS Annabel G . . . . | 209 Old Black Point
MR Samuel A O . . . . | Rd, Niantic, CT
MR Austin D Keyes . . . . | *06357*

Bright MR & MRS J Reeve (Mellon—Anne S Stokes) . | ☎ (207) 244-5035
JUNIORS MR Nicholas R . . . . | "Grayweather
MR Matthew T Mellon . . . . | Farm" Seal Cove,
 | ME *04674*

Bright MRS Nicholas (Eleanor F Hoey)
☎ (207) 244-5936 . . "Brightside" PO Box 51, Islesford, ME *04646*

Bright MRS Stanley (Elizabeth N Reeve)
☎ (207) 244-3175 . . "Seal Sands" Box A, Islesford, ME *04646*

Brinckerhoff MRS D Beard (Deborah Beard)
☎ (914) 472-8592 . . 187 Garth Rd, Scarsdale, NY *10583*

Brinckerhoff MR & MRS Starr E (Mawicke—A Sandra Kolseth) . . . . | ☎ (802) 375-2704
MISS Laura D . . . . | Sandgate, Arlington,
MR Starr E JR . . . . | VT *05250*
MR Frederick H Mawicke . . . . |

Brinckerhoff MR & MRS William H (Dejoux—Natalie R L Grace)
☎ (516) 329-3209 . . Box 1241, East Hampton, NY *11937*

Brinker MR & MRS Norman E (Leitstein—Nancy L Goodman) . . . . | ☎ (214) 363-6038
MISS Christina . . . . | 9410 Alva Court,
MR Eric B . . . . | Dallas, TX
MR Mark . . . . | *75220-2203*

Britt MR Christopher D
☎ (609) 368-0968 . . 184—26 St, Apt 3, Avalon, NJ *08202*

Brittain MR & MRS John S (Bromley—Anne Brewster)
☎ (508) 627-8966 . . 82 S Water St, Edgartown, MA *02539*

Britton MR & MRS J Boyd (Pillsbury—Frances C Garvin) . . . . | ☎ (603) 563-8420
MR Charles S B Pillsbury . . . . | PO Box 82, Dublin,
 | NH *03444*

Broadbent DR & MRS B Holly JR (Jacqueline Owen) | "Laughing Loon
MISS Elizabeth P . . . . | Cottage"
 | Livingstone Lake,
 | Dorset, Ontario,
 | Canada

Brock MR & MRS Charles Lawrence (Mary Jane Hipp) . . . . ☎ (516) 324-7733
JUNIORS MISS Susanna L . . . . 173 Main St,
JUNIORS MR W Walker . . . . East Hampton, NY
11937

Brock MR & MRS Harry B JR (N Jane Hollock)
☎ (704) 526-9222 . . 2316 Upper Divide Rd, Highland Falls, NC 28741

Brock MR & MRS Mitchell (Gioia F C Connell)
☎ (914) 985-2421 . . ''Yamazakura-So'' PO Box 157, Claryville, NY 12725

Brockway MR & MRS Douglas W (Genevieve M Houdry)
☎ (401) 348-9173 . . ''Rockbound'' 30 Windward Dv, Westerly, RI 02891

Brodeur MR Stephen B
☎ (508) 255-1956 . . ''Beachy Head'' 371 Tonset Rd, Orleans, MA 02653

Brodhead MR & MRS John JR (J Josephine Carr) . . . . ☎ (412) 238-7665
MISS Frances . . . . ''Woodcliff''
Country Club Rd,
Rector, PA 15677

Brodie MR & MRS R Kirkwood 3d (Mary J Fry)
☎ (616) 469-0369 . . ''Ground Zero'' Box 113, RR 1, New Buffalo, MI 49117

Brodsky MR & MRS Daniel J (Estrellita Bograd) . . . . ☎ (516) 324-5855
JUNIORS MISS Katherine A . . . . Lily Pond Lane,
JUNIORS MR Alexander T . . . . East Hampton, NY
11937

Bromberg MR & MRS Frank H JR (Lella H Clayton)
☎ (334) 981-9153 . . ''Perdido Breeze'' 26158 Perdido Beach Blvd, Orange Beach, AL 36561

Bromley MR & MRS Richard N (Lois L Thompson)
☎ (717) 828-2178 . . ''Bathaven'' Edgemere Club, Dingmans Ferry, PA 18328

Bronner MR & MRS Frederick V (Judith S Batzer)
☎ (860) 672-0118 . . ''The Wick'' Great Hollow Rd, Cornwall, CT 06753

Brooke MRS Sarah M (Sarah A McDougal)
☎ (702) 265-2655 . . West Fork Ranch, West Side Lane, Gardnerville, NV 89410

Brookfield MRS Gayle Evans (Gayle F Evans)
Jly 1 . . ☎ (011-44-1631) 562-451 . . ''Bon Accord'' Glenmore Rd, Oban, Argyll PA34 4ND, Scotland

Brookfield MRS Samuel L (Alyce Pressprich)
☎ (315) 369-3484 . . Box 8, Old Forge, NY 13420

Brookfield MR & MRS William Lord (Gillett—Jean N McGraw) . . . . ☎ (860) 542-5402
MISS Marian N Gillett . . . . ''Brooktrout''
Doolittle Dv,
Box 572, Norfolk,
CT 06058

Brooks MR & MRS Arthur H JR (Jean Halladay) . . . . ☎ (508) 526-9345
MR Arthur H 3d . . . . 345 Summer St,
Manchester, MA
01944

Brooks MR George R
☎ (414) 743-2321 . . ''Raibrook'' 4137 Bay Shore Dv, Sturgeon Bay, WI 54235

Brooks MR & MRS Harvey S JR (Bray—Kelly F Gavin)
☎ (609) 884-4938 . . 1315 New Jersey Av, Cape May, NJ 08204

Brooks DR & MRS John R (Dorothy Kalbfleisch)
☎ (207) 244-5260 . . ''Eagle Point'' Islesford, ME 04646

Brooks MRS Kyle F (Bullock—Eleine E Hoffman) . ☎ (401) 322-1313
MR & MRS Kyle C (Anne C Boyd) . . . . 16 Taylor Lane,
Weekapaug, RI
02891

Brooks MR & MRS Scott A (Laura Y Eiman)
☎ (508) 693-0700 . . ''Cousins Corners'' East Chop, Oak Bluffs, MA 02557

Brooks MR & MRS Shelton A (Mary Hope Lupfer)
☎ (203) 938-3451 . . Box 178, Redding Ridge, CT 06876

Brooks MR & MRS W Denison (Reece—Elizabeth B Eshleman) ⚓
☎ (207) 244-5228 . . ''The Head'' Little Cranberry Island, Islesford, ME 04646

Brooks MR & MRS Walter B 3d (Sheedy—Tanya L Widrin) . . of
☎ (516) 283-0494 . . PO Box 1484, Southampton, NY 11969
☎ (212) 249-4211 . . 207 E 74 St, New York, NY 10021

Brown MR & MRS Alexander C JR (Janet D Garfield)
Box 24, Cuttyhunk, MA 02713

Brown MISS Alice C
☎ (516) 653-4542 . . 25 Beach Lane, Quogue, NY 11959

Brown MR & MRS Anthony C (Winifred Lee d'Olier) . . ☎ (516) 324-0870
MISS Leelee d'O . . . . 3 Clover Leaf Lane,
East Hampton, NY
11937

Brown MR & MRS Bruce M (Elaine Eldredge)
☎ (908) 899-8390 . . ''Sea Lain'' 526 East Av, Bay Head, NJ 08742

Brown MR & MRS Charles H JR (Rosamond A Ferguson) . . . . ☎ (011-33)
MR Benjamin H D 53-88-81-31
''Montardit''
Verteuil d'Agenais,
47260 Castelmoron,
France

Brown MRS Cyrus Winthrop 2d (Carol D Williams) . ☎ (616) 845-5367
JUNIORS MISS Laura L D . . . . ''House at Pooh
Corners'' Epworth
Heights, Ludington,
MI 49431

Brown MR Cyrus Winthrop 2d
☎ (212) 362-2798 . . 266 West End Av, New York, NY 10023

Brown MR David S
☎ (315) 369-3788 . . Little Moose Lodge, Adirondack League Club, PO Box 8, Old Forge, NY 13420

Brown MRS Dickerman (Honour R Dickerman)
☎ (860) 868-2970 . . ''Pengilly III'' 41 Buffum Rd, Washington Depot, CT 06794

Brown MRS Donald A K (Mary McB Ryerson)
☎ (802) 362-2515 . . PO Box 958, Dorset, VT 05251

Brown MR & MRS Edward W (Gwendolyn G Cochran)
☎ (207) 276-5557 . . ''Kenjockety'' Northeast Harbor, ME 04662

Brown MR & MRS Francis C JR (Nancy A Leitzow) . ☎ (203) 245-9034
MISS Jennifer N . . . . 28 Grove Av,
MR James H L . . . . Madison, CT 06443

Brown MR & MRS Fred E (Hewetson—Darlington—Enid B Sillcox)
☎ (518) 523-3909 . . ''Brown Boathouse'' PO Box 909, Lake Placid, NY 12946

Brown MR & MRS George Edwin JR (Marian R Morton)
☎ (802) 824-6517 . . Peru, VT *05381*

Brown MRS George Estabrook JR (Lela H Cook) ⚓
☎ (513) 561-3904 . . 9375 Shawnee Run Rd, Cincinnati, OH *45243*

Brown MR & MRS George T (Mary E Donahue)
☎ (302) 227-7425 . . 128 Henlopen Av, Rehoboth Beach, DE *19971*

Brown MISS Helen S . . see G R Wright

Brown MR & MRS Howard H JR (Nancy A Houghton) . . . .
MISS Lowrey R . . . .
MR Howland H . . . .
☎ (508) 645-9494
"Windhover"
Box 85, State Rd, Chilmark, MA *02535*

Brown MRS J Crosby (M Locke P Kennedy)
☎ (207) 374-5283 . . Box 392, Blue Hill, ME *04614*

Brown DR & MRS J Warren (Louise A Williams) . . .
MR Thomas Warren . . . .
MR Peter Schuyler . . . .
☎ (207) 276-3712
"Westview"
Northeast Harbor, ME *04662*

Brown MRS James M JR (Jean H Davis)
☎ (508) 257-6606 . . "Blink Bonnie" 13 Baxter Rd, Siasconset, MA *02564*

Brown MR & MRS James M 3d (Armstrong—Sarah C Webb) ⚓ . . . .
MISS Leigh T Armstrong . . . .
MISS Katherine StJ Armstrong . . . .
☎ (508) 993-4946
"Weathersfield"
Nonquitt, MA *02748*

Brown MR & MRS James M 4th (Eyvonne K Melemai)
☎ (808) 572-0117 . . 967 Hiilani St, Makawao, Maui, HI *96768*

Brown MRS John A (Helen Thacher) ⚓
Aug 1 . . ☎ (908) TW2-0314 . . 809 East Av, Bay Head, NJ *08742*

Brown MRS Katharine C (Jeffers—Katharine C Brown)
☎ (305) 448-9928 . . 3720 Harlano St, Coral Gables, FL *33134*

Brown MR & MRS Leland S (Mary M Mahony)
☎ (508) 627-4739 . . Star Rte 270, Edgartown, MA *02539*

Brown DR & MRS Lloyd (Laura W Dodge)
☎ (207) 326-4542 . . Box 323, Brooksville, ME *04617*

Brown MR & MRS Medford J (Master—Kneass—M Clarissa White) . . of
☎ (609) 967-7155 . . "Belfry House" 3249 First Av, Avalon, NJ *08202*
☎ (610) 525-3286 . . 52 Pasture Lane, Bryn Mawr, PA *19010*

Brown MR & MRS Meredith M (Sylvia L Barnard)
☎ (860) 535-0511 . . "The Barn" 79 Tipping Rock Rd, Stonington, CT *06378*

Brown MRS Moreau D JR (Clark—Cynthia W Manchee)
☎ (508) 428-5249 . . "Mews House" 9 Village Square, Osterville, MA *02655*

Brown CAPT (RET) & MRS Nicholas (Diane Vernes) USN. ⚓
☎ (401) 848-0927 . . Beechbound 8, 127 Harrison Av, Newport, RI *02840*

Brown MR & MRS Owsley 2d (Christina S Lee) . . . .
MISS Augusta W . . . .
☎ (502) 222-9786
"Breeze Hill Farm"
6900 Shrader Lane, Box 168C, La Grange, KY *40031*

Brown REV & MRS P Schuyler (Margaret E Meredith)
☎ (705) 327-5444 . . "The Adytum" Paradise Bay, 43 Olive Crescent, Orillia, Ontario L3V 7M8, Canada

Brown MR & MRS Peter Megargee (Stoddard—Alexandra Johns) . . . .
MISS Alexandra B Stoddard . . . .
MISS Brooke G Stoddard . . . .
☎ (860) 535-1924
"Rev John Rathbone House"
87 Water St, Stonington, CT *06378*

Brown MR & MRS Robert L (Charlotte A Banks) . . .
MR Stuart L . . . .
☎ (704) 743-2721
"High Mitre"
Chatooga Woods Rd, Cashiers, NC *28717*

Brown MR Robert U
☎ (508) 228-0918 . . 24 Cliff Rd, Nantucket, MA *02554*

Brown MR & MRS Stanley N JR (Mary Duer) . . . . . .
MISS Starr de Forest . . . .
MR Henry A de F . . . .
☎ (207) 244-3004
"School House"
Box 275, Main St & Shore Rd, Bass Harbor, ME *04653*

Brown MR Townsend 2d
☎ (516) 537-0131 . . "Green Ridge Cottage" Box 294, Sagaponack, NY *11962*

Brown MR & MRS Travis Taylor (Ann du P Huidekoper)
☎ (508) 999-4020 . . "Aestival" Nonquitt, MA *02748*

Brown MR & MRS Vernon H JR (Ransom—Annette H Bowles) . . . .
MISS Ashley B Ransom . . . .
of ☎ (914)557-6184
"Sand Pond"
Eldred, NY *12732*
☎ (516) 537-0366
Box 1303, Bridgehampton, NY *11932*

Brown MR & MRS W Harman JR (Eleanor D Winslow) . . . .
MR William H 3d . . . .
☎ (609) 492-5213
"The Haven"
109 E 34 St, Long Beach Island, NJ *08008*

Brown MR & MRS W L Lyons JR (Alice Cary Farmer)
☎ (516) 788-7529 . . "Osprey Cove" Fishers Island, NY *06390*

Brown MR & MRS W Thacher (Lloyd A Hall) . . . . . .
MISS Quincy A . . . .
MISS L Lee . . . .
☎ (908) 899-5860
809 East Av, Bay Head, NJ *08742*

Brown MR & MRS William G (Solange M F Pezon) .
MISS Solange S P . . . .
MISS Sophie S P . . . .
☎ (847) 234-5018
1275 N Green Bay Rd, Lake Forest, IL *60045*

Brown MR & MRS William J W (Eliza F Smith) ⚓
☎ (508) 748-0968 . . 54 Main St, Marion, MA *02738*

Brown MR & MRS Zadoc W (H Virginia Lowrey) . .
MR David T . . . .
☎ (808) 572-9994
"Makani'olu"
379 Ho'opalua Dv, Pukalani, Maui, HI *96768*

Brownback MR & MRS John M (Elizabeth L Heppe)
General Delivery, Eagles Mere, PA *17731*

Browne MR & MRS Luis F V (Nathalie P Kuhn)
☎ (505) 988-3066 . . Rte 9, Box 66-3, Santa Fe, NM *87505*

Browne MRS Michael L (Marguerite B Mayer)
☎ (609) 884-3505 . . 20 Queen St, Cape May, NJ *08204*
Browning MR & MRS George W (Ellen E Buck) . . . .
MISS Rebecca B . . . .
MR Carter W . . . .
☎ (207) 371-2502
"Mosquito Point"
Black Rocks Rd,
Georgetown, ME
04548
Bruce MR David C
☎ (508) 548-4329 . . 14 School St, Woods Hole, MA *02543*
Bruen MRS Alexander J (Lorna C Harrah)
☎ (401) 783-4098 . . "Over Yonder" 75 Robinson St, Box 571, Narragansett, RI *02882*
Bruen MR & MRS Edward F L (Marian S Gray)
☎ (603) 495-3243 . . "The Venture" Washington, NH *03280*
Brumder MR & MRS Robert C (Barbara Blakney)
☎ (414) 367-6171 . . 6775 N H'way 83, Hartland, WI *53029*
Brumfield MR & MRS James S (Lasarte—Allaire B Chandor)
MISS Sarah C . . . .
JUNIORS MISS Elizabeth H . . . .
JUNIORS MR James B . . . .
JUNIORS MR Michael M . . . .
☎ (609) 398-2328
"El Mijasar"
71 Morningside Rd,
Ocean City, NJ
08226
Brune MR J T Terry (Anne C Tilney)
☎ (212) 426-1647 . . 245 E 87 St, New York, NY *10128*
Brune MR J T Terry—⚓
☎ (518) 251-3831 . . North Woods Club, Minerva, NY *12851*
Brune MRS William H N (Josephine T Terry)
☎ (518) 251-3831 . . North Woods Club, Minerva, NY *12851*
Brunet MR & MRS Stuart R (Carla J G de Módolo Sacon)
☎ (011-55-11) 731-2685 . . Rua Bom Jesus de Pirapora, Apt 2939, V Rami-cep, Jundiaí, São Paulo 13200, Brazil
Brunner MR & MRS Gordon F (Nadine M Slosar) . . . .
MISS Meggan T . . . .
☎ (616) 352-4292
627 Shorewood Dv,
Frankfort, MI *49635*
Brush DR & MRS Charles F 3d (Ellen K Sparry) . . . .
MISS Karen A . . . .
MR Charles F 4th . . . .
☎ (516) 749-1197
42 Ram Island Rd,
PO Box 2013,
Shelter Island, NY
11964
Bryant MISS Jennifer R . . see J N Byers 3d
Bryant MR Stearns J 3d . . see J N Byers 3d
Bubendey MR & MRS Paul F (Orrick—Holbrook—Minor—Shirley K Smith) . . . .
MR Paul F JR . . . .
17 Rowayton Woods
Dv, Norwalk, CT
06854
Buchanan RR ADM Charles Allen—USN.
☎ (401) 846-7061 . . "Flemish Down" Bellevue Av, Newport, RI *02840*
Buchanan MRS Kenneth H (Van Natta—Jennifer S Harcourt) . . . .
MR Jason Van Natta . . . .
☎ (203) 221-7679
24 Whitney St,
Westport, CT *06880*
Buchanan MR Kenneth H
☎ (516) 537-7942 . . 4 Five Rod H'way, PO Box 98, Sagaponack, NY *11962*
Buchanan MRS Wiley T JR (Ruth E Hale)
☎ (401) 847-4320 . . "Beaulieu" 614 Bellevue Av, Newport, RI *02840*

Buchanan MR & MRS William H JR (Eleanor A Lincoln) . . . .
MISS Diana A . . . .
MISS Jessica R . . . .
☎ (207) 244-3488
"Spruce Bough"
Dirigo Rd,
Southwest Harbor,
ME *04679*
Buck MR & MRS Alexander K (Sara H Long)
☎ (207) 563-8852 . . "The Loonybyn" 600 Mountain Rd, Noleboro, ME *04555*
Buck MR & MRS C Austin (Marguerite A Doubleday)
☎ (908) 766-1181 . . 80 Post Rd, Bernardsville, NJ *07924*
Buck MRS J Mahlon (Grace I Knapp)
☎ (609) 884-4691 . . "Seaview" 1120 New Jersey Av, Cape May, NJ *08204*
Buck MR & MRS N Harrison (Nancy C P Brown)
☎ (508) 428-7622 . . 118 Bridge St, Osterville, MA *02655*
Buck MR Roswell S—⚓
☎ (905) 894-0930 . . "Leeward" 9 Abino Hills Rd, Ridgeway, Ontario L0S 1N0, Canada
Buckley MR & MRS Christopher T (Lucy S Gregg) ⚓
☎ (207) 374-9932 . . Blue Hill, ME *04614*
Buckley MRS Howell (Elizabeth H Howell)
"Ivory Mountain" Maquez, Haria, Lanzarote, Canary Islands, Spain
Bucknall MR & MRS William S (Ann M Hamilton)
☎ (518) 589-5121 . . Onteora Club, Tannersville, NY *12485*
Buddenhagen MR & MRS Frederick L (Bartle—Kathleen I Burns) . . . .
MR Thomas P Bartle 3d . . . .
☎ (516) 324-6027
15 Hither Lane,
East Hampton, NY
11937
Buffum MR & MRS Robert C (Sydney F Hinkle)
☎ (401) 322-1222 . . "Gay Head" 36 Taylor Lane, Weekapaug, RI *02891*
Buffum MR & MRS Robert C JR (Linda A DePatie) . .
JUNIORS MISS Alexa C . . . .
☎ (401) 322-1140
27 Ayers Rd,
Haversham, RI
02891
Buice MR & MRS William T 3d (M Stuart Upchurch)
MISS Merrill S . . . .
MR Charles U . . . .
☎ (516) 749-0499
28 Prospect Av,
Shelter Island
Heights, NY *11965*
Bulkley MR Jonathan D . . . .
MISS Adrienne . . . .
MR Derick M . . . .
☎ (415) 459-8040
"Vulturecrest"
San Anselmo, CA
94960
Bull MR Bartle . . . .
MR Bartle B . . . .
☎ (914) 373-8586
"Brampton"
Amenia, NY *12501*
Bullard MR & MRS Edward D (Sharon C Smith) . . . .
JUNIORS MISS Victoria K . . . .
JUNIORS MR Edward W . . . .
☎ (415) 752-4670
3891 Clay St, PH,
San Francisco, CA
94118
Bullen MR & MRS George H (Joyce A Graham) . . . .
MISS Melissa M . . . .
MISS Alicia G . . . .
East Hampton, NY
11937
Bullerjahn MR John te S
☎ (401) 635-2651 . . 706 W Main Rd, Little Compton, RI *02837*

Bullock MR & MRS A George 2d (Carter—Gertrude B Ely).. of
☎ (518) 327-3220.. "Asanago" Upper St Regis, NY *12988*
☎ (401) 423-0767.. "The Barn" Wolcott Av, Jamestown, RI *02835*

Bullock MR Hugh
☎ (508) 627-8641.. Box 1303, Edgartown, MA *02539*

Bullock MRS Leslie Kitchell (de Braux—Leslie H Kitchell)..................... | ☎ (302) 227-2219
JUNIORS MISS Sabrina C................. | "Shell House"
JUNIORS MISS Karena R................. | Rehoboth Beach,
MISS Ariane de Braux | DE *19971*

Bullock MR & MRS Thomas F (Lucy S L Amerman). | Green Bay Camp,
JUNIORS MR Ethan H T................. | Moody Rd,
| Altamont,
| Tupper Lake, NY
| *12986*

Bundy MR & MRS Harvey H 3d (Blakely Fetridge).. | ☎ (616) GA9-7667
MISS Elizabeth Lowell.................. | 4070 Lake Forest
JUNIORS MR Reed F................. | Path, Stevensville,
| MI *49127*

Bundy MR & MRS Thomas F JR (Royce—Marilyn J Maczko)................. | ☎ (518) 589-5920
| "The Whim"
MISS Jennifer H Royce................. | Onteora Club,
MISS Amanda B Royce................. | Tannersville, NY
MR Charles M Royce JR................. | *12485*

Bunn MR & MRS George R JR (Jane G Adams)..... | ☎ (516) 283-6901
MR George R 3d................. | 27 St Andrews Rd,
JUNIORS MISS Palmer H................. | Southampton, NY
JUNIORS MISS Camilla A................. | *11968*

Bunting MR & MRS Josiah 3d (Diana M Cunningham)................. | ☎ (401) 849-7549
| "Berkeley House"
MISS Elizabeth H................. | Berkeley Av,
MR Josiah 4th................. | Newport, RI *02840*

Bunting MRS Sydney S (Vivian Martin)......... | ☎ (011-44-1828)
CDR Geoffrey C—USNR................. | 640216
| Drumkilbo, Meigle,
| Perthshire, Scotland

Burch MR & MRS John W (Robin N Sinkler)
☎ (803) 768-0615.. "Eagles Eye" 1226 Greenslake, Kiawah, SC *29455*

Burch MR & MRS Robert L 3d (Dale Carter Jones).. | ☎ (516) 324-7077
MR Robert L 4th................. | Terbell Lane,
JUNIORS MISS Catherine C W................ | Box 1331,
| East Hampton, NY
| *11937*

Burchenal DR & MRS Joseph Holland (Joan B Riley)
☎ (518) 576-9845.. "Pinewinds" Keene Valley, NY *12943*

Burden MRS William A M (Margaret L Partridge)
☎ (207) 276-5844.. "Sea Change" S Shore Rd, Northeast Harbor, ME *04662*

Burdick MR & MRS Lalor (Patricia M Norris)....... | ☎ (508) 464-2498
MR Christopher L................. | "Foxglove Farm"
JUNIORS MR William W................. | Ball Hill Rd,
| Princeton, MA
| *01541-2101*

Burdick MR & MRS W Newton (Dorothy R MacArthur)
☎ (715) 856-6496.. "Burdhouse" Wausaukee Club, Athelstane, WI *54104*

Burger MR & MRS F Gregg (Koeniger—Kirkland—Martha G Weimar) ⚓
☎ (908) 892-4548.. "Bay View" 16 Bay Point Harbour, Point Pleasant, NJ *08742*

Burger MR & MRS (DR) Van Vechten JR (Mina Farhad)................. | ☎ (516) 239-1705
MISS Leila E................. | 272 Victoria Place,
MISS Katrina I................. | Lawrence, NY
MR Nicholas F................. | *11516*

Burgwin MRS George C 3d (Lela C Hill)
☎ (412) 593-7954.. "White Flag Farm" Box 375, Star Rte, Rector, PA *15677*

Burke MR & MRS Duncan G (Fitzgerald—Nancy B Brookfield) ⚓................. | ☎ (203) 661-7849
| 4 Perkins Rd,
JUNIORS MISS Brooke A Fitzgerald......... | PO Box 628,
| Greenwich, CT
| *06836*

Burke MR Edwin M 3d.. see H L Clark JR

Burke MR & MRS Edwin Marston (Hutton—Virginia C Smith)
☎ (212) 628-1614.. 19 E 72 St, New York, NY *10021*

Burke MRS Jackson (Mary L Griggs)
☎ (516) 922-4763.. 145 Centre Island Rd, Oyster Bay, NY *11771*

Burke MR James Van V.. see H L Clark JR

Burke MR & MRS Peter G (Virginia G Friedrichs) ⚓................. | ☎ (809) 327-7797
| Box N7763,
MISS Mary-Shea................. | Delaporte Point,
MISS Eleanor S................. | Nassau, Bahamas

Burks MR & MRS D Parker (Marilyn Z Dixon)..... | "The Pasture"
MISS Sarah L................. | PO Box 314,
| Sargentville, ME
| *04673*

Burley MR & MRS Dexter L (Pantaleoni—Hope L Baker)................. | ☎ (508) 564-4571
| 121 South Rd,
MISS Jane W................. | PO Box 387,
JUNIORS MR Benjamin T................. | Pocasset, MA *02559*

Burlew MR & MRS Edward JR (Winslow—Frida Frazer)
☎ (508) 394-8974.. 28 Aunt Edith's Rd, Bass River, MA *02664*

Burling MRS Poe (Cotton—Ella K Poe)
☎ (410) 745-2173.. Rich Neck Manor, Claiborne, MD *21624*

Burlingame MR & MRS John H (Baird—Dorcas G Hodges)
☎ (715) 542-2242.. "Windy Point" Box 151, Sayner, WI *54560*

Burnett DR & MRS Joseph W (Kathleen B D Scarlett)................. | ☎ (410) 974-4140
| "Whitehall
MR P Jefferson................. | Cottage"
MR Mark G................. | 1915 Whitehall Rd,
| Annapolis, MD
| *21401*

Burnett MR & MRS Robert R (Elizabeth A Bole).... | ☎ (809) 333-2582
MR Alexander P................. | "Touchstone"
MR Anthony C................. | Harbour Island,
| Bahamas

Burnham MRS De Witt K (Elizabeth L Stenborg)
☎ (916) 583-3238.. "Burnham Hill" PO Box 507, Tahoe City, CA *96145*

Burnham MISS Kim N.. see H M Robertson JR

Burnham MR & MRS Richard I (Fanchon M Watkins).................... ☎ (401) 846-9011 "Alpond House"
    MISS Helen M........................ 4 Alpond Dv,
    JUNIORS MR John S .... Newport, RI 02840

Burns MR & MRS Edward E JR (Winthrop Reid) ⚓ ☎ (207) 439-1423
    MR Christopher W .... 46 Pocahontas Rd, Kittery Point, ME 03905

Burns MRS Thomas R (Ingrid L Frohlich)
    ☎ (516) 324-1223 .. "Georgica Cove" Box 2006, 6 La Forest Lane, East Hampton, NY 11937

Burns MR & MRS Ward (Cynthia A Butterworth) ... ☎ (508) 627-7549
    MISS H Abby .... 21 Atwood Circle,
    MR David W.......................... Edgartown, MA
    JUNIORS MR Walton L 02539

Burr MR & MRS Benjamin M (Virginia Monks) .... ☎ (207) 371-2515
    MISS Sarah M .... Indian Point Rd,
    MR Benjamin M JR .... Georgetown, ME
    MR John E 04548

Burr MR & MRS Francis H (Devens—Aldrich—Lucy T Aldrich)
    ☎ (207) 734-2257 .. "The Playhouse" Dark Harbor, Islesboro, ME 04848

Burr DR & MRS (DR) Richard M (Patricia A LeMay) . ☎ (210) 598-8334
    MISS Ashley LeMay .... Horseshoe Bay, Marble Falls, TX 78654

Burrage MR & MRS Walter S JR (Helen D Dupee) ☎ (508) 526-4472
    ⚓ .... "Kettledrum"
    MISS Alyssa A........................ Coolidge Point,
    JUNIORS MISS Katharine S .... Manchester, MA
    JUNIORS MISS Amanda B 01944

Burroughs MR & MRS Vincent DeP (Deuel—Marta D Nagel) ☎ (705) 765-3430
    .... Minett, Ontario
    MISS Maggie D Deuel .... P0B 1G0, Canada
    JUNIORS MISS Sarah G Deuel ....

Burrows MR & MRS David D (Mary E Grant)...... ☎ (805) 969-1680
    JUNIORS MISS Jennifer J .... "Stornoway"
    JUNIORS MISS Elisabeth W .... 2755 Bella Vista Dv, Santa Barbara, CA 93108

Burrus MRS Jefferson D JR (Woodville—Mary C Curtis)
    ☎ (401) 847-2818 .. 123 Kane Av, Middletown, RI 02842

Burt MR & MRS James M 3d (Raggio—Olive Y Rousseau)
    ☎ (011-33) 93-75-24-45 .. 12 Castelleras, 06370 Mouans-Sarteux, France

Bush MR & MRS George (Barbara Pierce)
    Kennebunkport, ME 04046

Bush MR & MRS Jonathan J (Josephine C Bradley)
    ☎ (860) 663-1771 .. 128 Chestnut Hill Rd, Killingworth, CT 06419

Bush-Brown MR & MRS David F (Mary C Livingston)
    ☎ (508) 362-3053 .. Pine Lane, Barnstable, MA 02630

Butash MR & MRS Adrian M (Susannah E Rake)
    ☎ (207) 967-4991 .. "Gray Gull Cottage" Box 608, Kennebunkport, ME 04046

Butcher MR & MRS W W Keen (Pagon—Madeleine A Kilvert)
    ☎ (508) 228-3268 .. 8 Prospect St, Nantucket, MA 02554

Butler MR & MRS Frederick J C (Marie-Claude Gervais).......................... ☎ (207) 276-3350
    MISS Julia .... "Villa Maria"
    JUNIORS MISS Daphne .... Northeast Harbor, ME 04662

Butler MRS Gilbert (Mary Kernan)
    ☎ (207) 276-3350 .. "Villa Maria" Northeast Harbor, ME 04662

Butler MR & MRS Jonathan P (Deborah D Rogers).. ☎ (860) 739-7783
    MISS Pauline W...................... 10 Great Wight
    MR Jonathan R .... Way, Niantic, CT
    JUNIORS MISS Cynthia D 06357
    JUNIORS MR Benjamin P ....

Butler MR & MRS Thorne G (Kelly A Allin) .... "Bon Repos"
    MISS Cicely B .... St Gerard des
    JUNIORS MISS Rebecca S .... Laurentides, Quebec G9N 6T6, Canada

Butsch DR & MRS John L (Lucy J Butt)
    ☎ (905) 894-4575 .. Abino Hills, Ridgeway, Ontario L0S 1N0, Canada

Butt MR Charles C—⚓
    "Rosserne" Northeast Harbor, ME 04662

Butt MR Clement van B
    ☎ (860) 434-9108 .. "Bayberry Farm" 83 Joshuatown Rd, Lyme, CT 06371

Butterfield LORD John & LADY (Isabel A Kennedy)
    ☎ (508) 349-3323 .. Box 532, Wellfleet, MA 02667

Butterworth MR & MRS J Warner 2d (Diana B Townsend) .... ☎ (518) 576-4470
    JUNIORS MISS Diana B T .... "Meadow Springs"
    JUNIORS MR James T .... Keene Valley, NY 12943

Butterworth MR & MRS James E JR (Nona M Angel)
    ☎ (518) 576-4470 .. "Meadow Springs" Box 742, Keene Valley, NY 12943

Butterworth MR & MRS John (Elsie W Large)
    ☎ (518) 576-9729 .. "Upper Meadow" Keene Valley, NY 12943-0721

Button MR & MRS Edward N (Daphne E S Purry)... ☎ (216) 247-7857
    MR Graham R .... 70 Pheasant Run, Chagrin Falls, OH 44022

Button MRS William H (Montane—Margarita von Hoffmann)
    ☎ (802) 372-8219 .. "Over Lake" Rte 1, Box 48, North Hero, VT 05474

Buxton DR & MRS Jorge N (Amalia Gonzalez)
    ☎ (516) 283-6563 .. "Remanso" 245 Great Plains Rd, Southampton, NY 11968

Byard MRS D Spencer (Margaret L Mather)
    ☎ (860) 868-7487 .. "Littlewood" 41 East St, Washington, CT 06793

Byers MR David Richmond 3d
    ☎ (410) BE5-7226 .. 3419 Guilford Terr, Baltimore, MD 21218

Byers MR & MRS (REV) James N 3d (Bryant—Finley —Katrina Rauch) .... ☎ (518) 576-9875
    MISS Jennifer R Bryant .... "Icy Brook"
    MR Stearns J Bryant 3d .... St Huberts, NY 12943

Byers MR & MRS Randolph K JR (Eleanor B Atwater) ⚓
    ☎ (401) 635-8984 .. 696K W Main Rd, Little Compton, RI 02837

Byram MR Josiah Nye
    ☎ (518) 576-4411 .. Ausable Club, St Huberts, NY 12943

C

Cabell MR Benjamin 5th . . see D N Garrett
Cabell MR & MRS William D (Ellen E Rolston)
 ☎ (603) 253-4438 . . "Analostan" Box 136, Woodland Rd, Center Harbor, NH *03226*
Cabot MR & MRS Charles C JR (Dale D Pirie) . . . . . . | ☎ (407) 867-4823
 MR Charles C 3d . . . . | North Haven, ME *04853*
Cabot MR & MRS Francis H (Anne Perkins)
 ☎ (418) 665-2474 . . "Les Quatre Vents" 345 rue Fraser, La Malbaie, Quebec G5A 1A2, Canada
Cabot MR & MRS Paul C JR (Saltonstall—Jennifer B Felton) . . . . | ☎ (207) 867-4404
 MISS Cornelia C . . . . | "The Crosstrees"
 MISS Jennifer F . . . . | North Haven, ME *04853*
Cabot MRS Thomas D (Virginia Wellington)
 Garden Point, Swans Island, ME *04685*
Cachera MR & MRS Charles R (Laura G S Farrand)
 ☎ (401) 348-8228 . . "To Windward" 10 Pautipaug Way, Watch Hill, RI *02891*
Cain DR & MRS Marvin J (Parnell—Julia D Thieriot)
 ☎ (513) 448-2605 . . "Homefarm" 9552 Seibt Rd, Versailles, OH *45380*
Calder MR & MRS Donald G (Ann E Martin) . . . . . . | ☎ (516) 283-7337
 MISS Cornelia M . . . . | "Pheasant's Field"
 MISS Isabella S . . . . | First Neck Lane,
 MR Donald G JR . . . . | Southampton, NY *11968*
Calder MRS Joan N (Woolverton—Joan L Newton)
 ☎ (011-52-376) 60939 . . "Las Bodegas" Privada Libertad 38, Ajijic, 45920 Jalisco, Mexico
Cale MR & MRS Charles G (Jessie L Rawn) . . . . | ☎ (970) 479-0733
 JUNIORS MISS Whitney R . . . . | 1710 Sunburst Dv, Vail, CO *81657*
Calfee MR & MRS Peter H (Gift—Janice O'Connell)
 ☎ (419) 285-3901 . . "Pebble Cove" South Bass Island, Put-in-Bay, OH *43456*
Calkins MR John T
 ☎ (707) 865-2311 . . "Romany" Bohemian Grove, Monte Rio, CA *95462*
Callahan MR Robert F . . . . | ☎ (508) 428-5692
 MISS M Carroll Kiernan . . . . | "Clam Shell"
 DR Michael J Kiernan . . . . | Box 2051, Oyster Harbors, Osterville, MA *02655*
Callard MR & MRS George D (Tracy L Taylor)
 East Harpswell, ME *04011*
Callard DR & MRS George M (Linda S Siple) . . . . . . | Box 2605, Oakledge Rd,
 MISS Susan K . . . . | East Harpswell, ME
 MR Henry P . . . . | *04011*
 MR David M . . . . |
 MR William S . . . . |
Callaway MR & MRS Norman T (Hare—Barbara B Rose) . . . . | ☎ (908) 295-4613
 MISS Elizabeth B Hare . . . . | 970 S Lagoon Lane,
 MISS Katherine W Hare . . . . | Mantoloking, NJ
 MR Hobart N Hare . . . . | *08738*
Callaway MR & MRS Tyler S (Melinda G Fisher)
 ☎ (714) 642-5852 . . 5701½ Seashore Dv, Newport Beach, CA *92663*
Camden MR & MRS Andrew L (Gayle P Shaw)
 ☎ (716) 357-3515 . . "Tree Tops" Chatham House, 34 Clark Av, Chautauqua, NY *14722*
Cameron DR & MRS Donald J (Alison S Wright)
 "Restawhile" Point O'Woods, NY *11706*
Cameron DR & MRS J Price JR (Louisa Huger Pringle) . . . . | ☎ (704) 698-8418
 JUNIORS MR J Price 3d . . . . | "Clunes" PO Box 34, Zirconia, NC *28790*
Cameron MISS Laura H
 ☎ (516) 583-5466 . . Cottage 48, Point O'Woods, NY *11706*
Cameron MR & MRS Thomas W L (Carol L Soliday)
 ☎ (803) 524-5151 . . "Sovereign Point" Spring Island, Rte 6, Box 284, Okatie, SC *29910*
Cameron MR & MRS William A (Forkner—Katharine Torrey)
 ☎ (516) 324-2740 . . Egypt Close, East Hampton, NY *11937*
Cammann MRS Schuyler van R (Muir—Mary Lyman Cox)
 ☎ (603) 823-5285 . . Sugar Hill, NH *03585*
Campagna MR & MRS David W (Maria E Garcés-Echavarria)
 ☎ (516) 653-5454 . . PO Box 46, 25 Ogden Lane, Quogue, NY *11959*
Campbell MRS Anne M (Anne L Meigs) . . . . | ☎ (508) 548-0709
 MISS Camilla K . . . . | Box 33,
 MISS Meriweather W . . . . | Woods Hole, MA
 MR Andrew R . . . . | *02543*
Campbell MRS Duncan H (Lee—Canaday—Mary Flagg)
 ☎ (802) 457-3270 . . 39 Elm St, Apt B, Woodstock, VT *05091*
Campbell MR & MRS Gordon C (Judith A Brewer)
 ☎ (609) 368-1305 . . 100-10 First Av, Stone Harbor, NJ *08247*
Campbell MR & MRS Hazard K (Virginia E Klopp)
 ☎ (716) 652-5797 . . 431 Willardshire Rd, East Aurora, NY *14052*
Campbell MRS Howard D 2d (Harriet D Turner)
 ☎ (717) 848-2455 . . 1032 Smallbrook Lane, York, PA *17403*
Campbell MRS John B S (Angela Mitchell)
 ☎ (315) 369-6537 . . Woods Camp, Bisby Lake, Thendara, NY *13472*
Campbell DR & MRS Robert E (Nancy M Johnson) . . | ☎ (508) 240-1918
 MR Robert E JR . . . . | 76 Freeman Lane,
 MR Frederick McK 2d . . . . | Box 802,
 MR Colin A . . . . | East Orleans, MA *02643*
Campbell DR & MRS Rolla D JR (Baker—Stevens—Kim Kendall)
 ☎ (516) 788-7803 . . "Life Saving House" Box 261, East Harbor, Fishers Island, NY *06390*
Campodonico MR & MRS John R (Joan M Johnson)
 ☎ (916) 525-1236 . . 4000 W Lake Blvd, Tahoe Pines, CA *94141*
Canfield MR & MRS Franklin O (Hope Brown)
 ☎ (516) 283-4431 . . PO Box 1225, Southampton, NY *11969*

Cannell MR & MRS Peter B (Ann Van A Eberstadt) . | ☎ (516) 583-5391
MR & MRS Peter F (Amanda J Henderson) . . . . . . | Point O'Woods,
MR & MRS Michael T (Elisabeth W Hartman) . . . | NY *11706*
MR & MRS J Carlo (Jennifer T Bradley) ⚓ . . . .
   MR & MRS Rainer Gross (Cynthia Cannell) . . .
Cannon MR Beekman C
   ☎ (607) 264-8171 . . ''Londonderry Farm'' Cherry Valley, NY *13320*
Cannon MR & MRS J Dormer (Grauer—Jane E Egeressy)
   ☎ (860) 435-2629 . . ''The Farmhouse'' 266 Farnham Rd, Lakeville, CT *06039*
Cantlay MR & MRS D Davison (Patricia J King)
   ☎ (516) 788-7817 . . Box 687, Fishers Island, NY *06390*
Canty MR & MRS Richard H (Hope B Woodhouse)
   ☎ (508) 627-8539 . . Star Rte 99, N Neck Rd, Edgartown, MA *02539*
Caracciolo di Forino CT François & CTSS (Shirley Howell) . . . . | ☎ (011-33) 33-20-36-09
MR Riccardo . . . . | 4 quai Chardon, 50760 Barfleur, France
Carden DR & MRS George A (Constance S Sullivan)
   ☎ (908) 234-0558 . . ''Hayfields'' Box 250, Peapack, NJ *07977*
Carew MR Timothy L
   ☎ (603) 532-7002 . . ''Hardpan II'' 489 Thorndike Pond Rd, Jaffrey, NH *03452*
Carey MRS Churchill G (Juliet G McAdams)
   ☎ (207) 372-6549 . . ''Far Cry'' PO Box 239, Port Clyde, ME *04855*
Carey MR & MRS George G 4th (Anna K Steck) . . . . | Bisby Lodge,
MISS Eugenia M . . . . | Thendara, NY *13472*
MR Frederick R . . . . |
Carey MR James Bayard
   ☎ (505) 983-6524 . . 3233 El Trebol Court, Santa Fe, NM *87505*
Carey MR William Polk
   ☎ (518) 797-3390 . . ''The Thwait'' Pond Hill Rd, Rensselaerville, NY *12147*
Carleton MRS Bukk G (M Elizabeth Tucker)
   ☎ (401) 647-5364 . . ''Bukkskin'' Glocester, RI *02814*
Carleton MR Bukk G 3d . . . . | ☎ (508) 990-1363
MISS Samantha L . . . . | Nonquitt, MA *02748*
MISS Heather T . . . . |
Carlisle MR & MRS Miles (Margo Duer Black) . . . . . | ☎ (508) 228-1319
MR Tristram C . . . . | 75 Main St, Nantucket, MA *02554*
Carlson MR & MRS Richard W (Hunt—Patricia C Swanson) . . . . | ☎ (207) 665-2666
MR Buckley S P . . . . | Island Camp, Bryant Pond, ME *04219*
Carlson MR & MRS Robert F (Badger—Elizabeth B Borden)
   ☎ (802) 649-3535 . . Old Coach Rd, Norwich, VT *05055*
Carlson MR & MRS Tucker S McN (Susan T Andrews)
   ☎ (207) 665-2666 . . Island Camp, General Delivery, Bryant Pond, ME *04219*
Carmalt MR & MRS Woolsey (Sarah L Robbins)
   ☎ (717) 553-2183 . . ''Lakeside Farm'' Friendsville, PA *18818*

Carmany MR & MRS George W 3d (Judith J Lawrence) . . . . | ☎ (516) 653-6802
MISS Elizabeth M J . . . . | 12 Shinnecock Rd, Box 1371, Quogue,
MR G William W . . . . | NY *11959*
Carmichael MR & MRS Frederick H (Marjorie Shelburne)
   ☎ (704) 274-0787 . . 1617 Hendersonville Rd, Asheville, NC *28803*
Carmody MR & MRS Christopher G (Carol A Lovell) . | ☎ (401) 322-7763
JUNIORS MISS Meagan L . . . . | ''Thrupence''
JUNIORS MR Christopher . . . . | 6 Upland Rd, Weekapaug, RI
JUNIORS MR Francis W . . . . | *02891*
Carnahan MR & MRS David H JR (Boyer—Gay M Hedlund) . . . . | ☎ (914) 763-3590
MISS G Alexandra Boyer . . . . | ''Treetops'' 63 Post Office Rd,
MR F Alger Boyer JR . . . . | Waccabuc, NY *10597*
Carnett MR & MRS J Berton 3d (Margaret A Coleman) . . . . | ☎ (609) 884-8548
MISS Alicia S . . . . | 15 Queen St, Cape May, NJ
MR John B 4th . . . . | *08204*
Caron MRS D Welwood (Diana N Welwood)
   ☎ (914) 276-0076 . . 954C Heritage Hills, Somers, NY *10589*
Carothers DR & MRS Charles O (Stern—Lucille Klau)
   ☎ (616) 526-5749 . . 15 Fourth Av, Wequetonsing, MI *49740*
Carpenter MR & MRS Edmund N 2d (Gates—Frances C B Morgan) . . . . | ☎ (516) 788-7852
MISS E Lea . . . . | Fishers Island, NY *06390*
MISS Ashley du Pont Gates . . . . |
Carpenter MRS Francis F (Ellsworth—McClelland—Bickel—Dorothea F Wirth) ⚓
   ☎ (410) 757-0338 . . 221 Beach Dv, Winchester-on-Severn, Annapolis, MD *21401*
Carpenter REV DR & MRS James A (Mary L Dunbar)
   ☎ (802) 533-2953 . . Randolph Rd, Greensboro, VT *05841*
Carr MISS Ellen K
   ☎ (508) 432-0089 . . 60 Harbor Rd, Harwich Port, MA *02646*
Carr MR F William
   ☎ (516) 283-3107 . . Meadow Lane, PO Box 729, Southampton, NY *11968*
Carr MISS Margaret T
   ☎ (508) 432-0077 . . 54 Harbor Rd, Harwich Port, MA *02646*
Carr MR Michael . . see G L Smith
Carr MRS Robert F (Margaret E Rich)
   ☎ (906) 484-3362 . . ''The Point'' Les Cheneaux Club, Cedarville, MI *49719*
Carr MRS Robert N (Harriet K Simonds)
   ☎ (517) 821-8307 . . Lakeside Camp, 517 Lake St, Roscommon, MI *48653*
Carr MR & MRS Walter S (Mary F Baine)
   ☎ (616) 469-5228 . . ''Labs Lair'' 4059 Birchmont St, Michiana, MI *49117*
Carr MR & MRS William Plack JR (Lyde H Wall)
   ☎ (508) 228-3124 . . 22 Cliff Rd, Nantucket, MA *02554*
Carrington COL & MRS George W (Mann—Else L Jorgensen) USMC.
   ☎ (508) 748-0696 . . 11 Rose Cottage Lane, Marion, MA *02738*

Carroll MR & MRS Barry J (Barbara A Pehrson) ⚓ | ☎ (508) 693-6308
  MISS Deirdre H . . . . | "Breezy Chop"
  MISS Colleen P . . . . | Weston & Harrison
  MR Sean P . . . . | Avs, East Chop,
  JUNIORS MISS Oona K . . . . | Oak Bluffs, MA 02557

Carroll MR & MRS John L (Cornelia A Thomas) . . . . | ☎ (410) 827-8143
  MISS Genevieve A . . . . | "Blakeford"
  MR John L JR . . . . | Box 199,
  MR Thomas T . . . . | Queenstown, MD 21658

Carroll MR & MRS Lee Wingate (Madeline St George)
  ☎ (201) 744-3272 . . 31 Wayside Place, Montclair, NJ 07042

Carroll MR & MRS Lucius W 2d (Cullet—Lucie L Miller) ⚓ | ☎ (207) 326-8741
  JUNIORS MISS Catherine B . . . . | "Backshore"
  | 100 Wadsworth Cove Rd, Castine, ME 04421

Carroll DR & MRS Robert E (Clay—Jane C Chace)
  ☎ (508) 771-1354 . . Great Island, Box 516, West Yarmouth, MA 02673

Carruthers MR & MRS John D (Letah H Hickman)
  ☎ (616) 526-2495 . . Cottage 82, Harbor Point, MI 49740

Carruthers MR & MRS Ralph R (Donna J Young) . . | ☎ (616) 526-2867
  MISS Sara Procter . . . . | Cottage 49, Harbor Point, MI 49740

Carruthers MR & MRS Thomas H 4th (Patricia M Dennis) ⚓
  ☎ (616) 526-9445 . . Cottage 84, Harbor Point, MI 49740

Carse MR & MRS Donald R JR (Wickes—Barbara Bain Schwab) . . . . | ☎ (802) 867-4174
  JUNIORS MISS Alexandra R . . . . | PO Box 573, Dorset, VT 05251
  MR Nicholas du P Wickes . . . . |

Carstensen MR & MRS Hans L JR (Toland—Jane B Van Pelt)
  ☎ (401) 847-6558 . . "Whetstone" 455 Tuckerman Av, Middletown, RI 02842

Carter MR & MRS Burnham JR (Sue H McLeod)
  ☎ (860) 434-1678 . . "Meetinghouse Hill" Box 362, Old Lyme, CT 06371

Carter MRS Christopher S (Helen T Deuell) . . . . . . | ☎ (201) 697-7781
  MR David S . . . . | "Rockledge"
  | 17 West Shore, Green Pond, NJ 07435

Carter REV & MRS E Lawrence (Murray—Katrina B Ely)
  ☎ (518) 327-3247 . . "Kayumneh" Upper St Regis, NY 12988

Carter MRS Georgina Woolworth (Niman—Georgina B Woolworth)
  ☎ (207) 933-2326 . . Rte 135, Winthrop, ME 04364

Carter MR H Adams (Ann H Brooks)
  ☎ (603) 586-4498 . . "Boismont" Jefferson, NH 03583

Carter MR & MRS Hugh D (Marie J Dempsey)
  ☎ (418) 665-4613 . . "Ciel sur Mer" Murray Bay, La Malbaie, Quebec G5A 1S5, Canada

Carter MRS Raymond H (Harwood—Nancy W Snow)
  ☎ (207) 867-2023 . . North Haven, ME 04853

Carter MRS Rudolph Ellis (Reed—Mead—Mary M McLain)
  Aug 1 . . ☎ (401) 847-9009 . . "The Windmill" Hammersmith Farm, Newport, RI 02840

Carter MR & MRS William Phelps (Lloyd—M Elizabeth Wiedersheim)
  ☎ (207) 864-5235 . . "Justawhim" Faunce Rd, Rangeley, ME 04970

Cartier MR & MRS John G (Salisbury—Suzanne Jackson)
  ☎ (516) 324-5731 . . 105 Main St, East Hampton, NY 11937

Carton DR & MRS Robert W (Jean A Keating)
  ☎ (401) 423-2135 . . 45 Ledge Rd, Jamestown, RI 02835

Cartwright MRS John W P (Joan Baldwin)
  ☎ (802) 545-2222 . . RD 1, Box 120A, Middlebury, VT 05753

Carver MR Peter M
  ☎ (516) 676-5886 . . 89 Duck Pond Rd, Glen Cove, NY 11542

Carver MRS Richard P (Gordon—Mary L Hathaway)
  ☎ (414) 487-5470 . . "The Pillars" Indian Point, Pelican Lake, WI 54463

Cary MR & MRS William L (Katherine L F Cooper) . . . . . | ☎ (607) 547-8022
  MISS Katherine F C . . . . | "Red Creek Farm"
  | Box 47, Cooperstown, NY 13326

Casey MR & MRS James J (Claudia Prout)
  ☎ (401) 846-5465 . . "Broadlawns" 41 Ridge Rd, Newport, RI 02840

Cashman MR Eugene R JR
  ☎ (508) 257-6588 . . "Mostly C" Baxter Rd, Siasconset, MA 02564

Casini MR & MRS Nicolò (Joan S Coburn) . . . . | ☎ (011-39-578) 274315
  MISS Elisa G . . . . |
  MISS Rebecca . . . . | "Villa Marcianella"
  MISS Alessandra S . . . . | Chiusi Città,
  JUNIORS MR Clemente C . . . . | 53043 Siena, Italy

Casner MR & MRS Andrew J JR (Potter—Gaynor Davol)
  ☎ (508) 228-1103 . . 3 King's Way, Nantucket, MA 02554

Caspersen MR & MRS Finn M W (Barbara W Morris) . . . . | ☎ (401) 322-7189
  MR Finn M W JR . . . . | "Ranvik"
  MR Samuel M W . . . . | 105 Donizetti Rd,
  JUNIORS MR Andrew W W . . . . | Shelter Harbor, Westerly, RI 02891

Casscells MRS S Ward (S Oleda Dyson)
  Guyencourt, Montchanin, DE 19710

Cassiday MR P Richard . . see H Luce 3d

Castroviejo MR Christopher R
  ☎ (516) 726-6883 . . 199 Water Mill Towd Rd, Water Mill, NY 11976

Cate MR William C
  ☎ (908) 899-1260 . . Box 265, Mantoloking, NJ 08738

Cates MRS John M JR (Morales—Lopez—Nelia F Barletta)
  ☎ (011-33-1) 42-66-61-53 . . 18 av Matignon, 75008 Paris, France

Cates MR & MRS William C (de Saint-Remy—M A Guyonne de Fontaine de Logeres)
  ☎ (603) 654-9749 . . Pettingill Hill Rd, South Lyndeborough, NH 03082

Catherwood MRS Cummins (Ault—Littler—Dorothy Smith)
  ☎ (518) 587-5931 . . 85 Pepper Lane, Saratoga Springs, NY 12866

Catlin MR & MRS Avery (Edith J Reed) ⚓
  ☎ (508) 627-4686 . . 66 Fuller St, Edgartown, MA 02539

Catlin DR & MRS Brian (Rosalie Hornblower) . . . . . . | ☎ (508) 999-3873
  MISS Doris . . . . | "Dana House"
  MISS Laine . . . . | 155 Mishaum Point,
  JUNIORS MISS Amy . . . . | South Dartmouth,
  JUNIORS MISS Tracy . . . . | MA 02748

Catlin MR & MRS Daniel JR (Dundeen Bostwick) . . . ☎ (508) 228-9398
   MR Dan W . . . . 12 Jefferson Av,
   MR Blake H . . . . Nantucket, MA
   MR Todd B *02554*

Catlin MR & MRS Loring (Susan C Johnson). . . . . . . ☎ (603) 563-8885
   MISS Elizabeth J . . . . "Redtop"
   MR Loring JR . . . . W Lake Rd, Dublin,
   MR Alexander H . . . . NH *03444*

Cattier MRS Jean (Marianne P Vowels) . . . . ☎ (802) 822-5223
   MR Alan R . . . . Camp Papelousu,
   MR Henri R. . . . . Averill, VT *05901*
   MR Jacques E . . . .

Cauffman MR & MRS D Hughes (Heyward—Josephine M Vincent)
   ☎ (903) 295-2544 . . "Llessys Mhor" Big Harbour, Cape Breton, Nova Scotia B0E 1B0, Canada

Cavanagh MR & MRS Roderick A (Carol J Andrus)
   Box 205, Newport, RI *02840*

Cave MRS Edwin F (Spalding—Lincoln—Joan Tozzer)
   "Westwind" Tamworth, NH *03886*

Cay MR & MRS John E 3d (Mary H Daniel) . . . . ☎ (912) 897-1225
   MISS Catherine P. . . . . "Camellia Cottage"
   MR John E 4th . . . . Turners Rock,
   MR Christopher W . . . . Rte 6, Savannah,
                                                        GA *31410*

Cayzer MAJ & MRS H Stanley (de Holguin—Beatrice F Murray-Jacoby) BA . . .of
   ☎ (011-33-92) 10-45-51 . . Le Golfe Bleu, av Georges Drin, Roquebrune, France
   ☎ (011-44-171) 499-1261 . . Cavalry & Guards Club, 127 Piccadilly, London W1, England

Cecconi MR & MRS Giuseppe E (Erharter—Sarah J Coleman)
   ☎ (011-39-41) 52-07-746 . . "Ca Vendramin" 13 Giudecca, 30123 Venice, Italy

Cecil MR & MRS Charles G (Hilary Halpern) . . . . ☎ (516) 922-1080
   JUNIORS MISS Francesca C . . . . 142 Centre Island
                                                        Rd, Centre Island,
                                                        Oyster Bay, NY
                                                        11771 . . MR absent

Chace MRS Arnold B (Ledyard—Evelyn Thayer)
   ☎ (508) 775-0892 . . Box 846, West Yarmouth, MA *02673*

Chace MR Malcolm G JR
   ☎ (508) 775-2091 . . PO Box 516, Great Island, West Yarmouth, MA *02673*

Chadsey MRS Murrell R (Bowden—Patrick—F Murrell Rickards)
   ☎ (802) 765-4072 . . "Sweetwood" Beacon Hill, Box 260, RR 1, Strafford, VT *05072*

Chadwick MRS Thomas M (Wilkinson—Hannah B Willis)
   ☎ (207) 359-2296 . . Box 66, Brooklin, ME *04616*

Chaffe MR & MRS David B H 3d (Nancy R McIver) . ☎ (601) 255-1161
   MISS Anne M . . . . "Halcyon Days"
                                                        25510 Marchetich
                                                       Lane, De Lisle, MS
                                                       39571

Chamberlain MRS Melissa H (Melissa A Hickey)
   ☎ (616) 547-6796 . . 117 Belvedere Club, Charlevoix, MI *49720*

Chamberlin MR & MRS W Macy (Irma Morell)
   ☎ (518) 589-5460 . . "Robin Hill" Onteora Club, Tannersville, NY *12485*

Chance MR Britton—⚓
   ☎ (908) 898-1078 . . "Manto" 1219 Bay Av, Mantoloking, NJ *08738*

Chance MR & MRS Steven K (Colleen B Meyle). . . . ☎ (908) 295-3158
   MISS Anna Benson . . . . 1208 Ocean Av,
                                                      Mantoloking, NJ
                                                      08738

Chandler MR & MRS Nathan (Phyllis A Russell)
   ☎ (207) 389-2459 . . "High Rocks" Small Point, ME *04567*

Chandor MR & MRS Craig D (Grant—Carol S Johnson)
   ☎ (207) 967-3314 . . 30 Sea Fields, Kennebunkport, ME *04046*

Chandor MR & MRS Jeffrey F (Mary R McDonald) . ☎ (401) 635-8997
   ⚓ . . . . "Beaconsfield"
   MISS Heather J . . . . Old Bull Lane,
   MR Jeffrey M . . . . Little Compton, RI
                                                      02837

Chapin MRS Dorothy B (Chambers—Dorothy H Babcock)
   4 Gull Terr, Westerly, RI *02891*

Chapin MR & MRS Edward W (Ethel D Stout) . . . . . ☎ (908) 842-7842
   MR E Whiting JR . . . . 118 Av of Two
   MR Bayard S . . . . Rivers, Rumson,
   MR Bruce B . . . . NJ *07760*

Chapin MR & MRS Melville (Elizabeth A Parker)
   ☎ (508) 627-5901 . . "Cup House" 70 N Summer St, Edgartown, MA *02539*

Chapin MR & MRS Schuyler G (Mortimer—Catia S Zoullas). . of
   ☎ (508) 224-6283 . . "The Lodge" Morgan Rd, Plymouth, MA *02360*
   ☎ (516) 283-0332 . . S Main St, PO Box 557, Southampton, NY *11969*

Chapman MR & MRS John S JR (Edith K Hine) . . . . "PK Boo"
   MISS Peyton S. . . . . Pond Rd, Nantucket,
   MISS Kathryn D . . . . MA *02554*
   MR John S 3d . . . .

Chapman MR & MRS Peter H (Diane C Clark)
   ☎ (516) 676-0460 . . Piping Rock Club, Piping Rock Rd, Locust Valley, NY *11560*

Chapoton MR & MRS O Donaldson (Mary Jo Kelley) ☎ (516) 788-7532
   MISS Kelley W . . . . PO Box 217,
   JUNIORS MR Hunt D. . . . . Fishers Island, NY
                                                      06390

Chappell MR & MRS Hayward H (Thomas—Olivia L Kloman). . . . . ☎ (207) 372-6239
   MISS Hilleary T Thomas . . . . "The School House
   MR Stephen L Thomas JR . . . . Cottage"
                                                      Harts Neck Rd,
                                                      Box 533,
                                                      Tenants Harbor, ME
                                                      04860

Chappell MR & MRS Richard L (Alice C Merckens) . ☎ (508) 548-7097
   MISS Carol L. . . . . 70 Quissett Av,
   JUNIORS MISS P Dreux . . . . Woods Hole, MA
                                                      02543

Chappell MR & MRS William B JR (Percilla A Lincoln)
   ☎ (914) 855-3250 . . "Wind Meadows Farm" 37 N Quaker Hill Rd, Pawling, NY *12564-1710*

Charles MR & MRS Robert H (Leiter—Marion S Oates)
   ☎ (401) 847-1664 . . "The Whim" 44 Ledge Rd, Newport, RI *02840*

Charman MRS Walter M JR (Virginia McG Osborne)
☎ (216) 464-0118 . . "Blue Spruce Hill" 2755 SOM Center Rd, Hunting Valley, OH *44022*

Charrington MR & MRS Arthur M R 3d (Ardis C Borden)
☎ (609) 967-4683 . . "Munningside" 27 Marine Way, Avalon, NJ *08202*

Chase MR & MRS A Mabis (Mathers—Jane Van Hoven) . . of
☎ (515) 280-9981 . . 3131 Fleur Dv, Apt 202, Des Moines, IA *50321*
☎ (712) 332-2557 . . "Dunroamin" 4605 Lake Shore Dv, Rte 6, Box 6199, Lake Okoboji, IA *51355*

Chase MR & MRS Edward T (Ethelyn Atha)
☎ (516) 324-0206 . . "Cranberry Bog" Box 791, Jones Rd, East Hampton, NY *11937*

Chase MR & MRS Irving H (Bailey—Rebecca C Bradford)
on board Gemini" Isle au Haut, ME *04645*

Chatfield MR & MRS Charles W (Post—Mary C Putnam)
☎ (207) 236-2269 . . Rockport, ME *04856*

Chatfield MR Charlton H
☎ (516) 267-6186 . . "El Paraso" PO Box 304, Amagansett, NY *11930*

Chatfield MRS Frederick H (Fisher—Chandler—M Carter MacRae)
☎ (513) 271-0303 . . 4305 Drake Rd, Cincinnati, OH *45243*

Chatfield MR Frederick H
☎ (207) 236-2413 . . "Aldermere" Rockport, ME *04856*

Chatfield MRS Henry H (Margaret A Rowe) . . . . . . | ☎ (516) 267-6186
MISS Helen H . . . . | PO Box 458, Cross H'way, Amagansett, NY *11930*

Chatfield MR & MRS William H (Anne B Whitney)
305 S Main St, Leland, MI *49654*

Chellas MR & MRS Brian F (Merry E Morehouse) . . . | Woodland Valley Park Association, Phoenicia, NY *12464*
MISS Anne Morehouse . . . . |

Chellis MR Bradford A . . see MRS W G Kay JR

Chen MR & MRS Kimball C (Grazioli-Venier—Patrizia Grill) . . . . | ☎ (011-39-75) 885-3382
JUNIORS MISS Assia Grazioli-Venier . . . . | "La Pietraia"
JUNIORS MR Saverio E Grazioli-Venier . . . . . . | Todi, Italy

Cheney MRS Middleton (Kleeman—Ruth Middleton)
☎ (860) 567-5454 . . "White Oak Farm" 199 E Litchfield Rd, PO Box 1436, Litchfield, CT *06759*

Chester MR & MRS Colby M (Jane P Robinson)
☎ (802) 362-1065 . . "The Cascades" Box 201, River Rd, Manchester, VT *05254*

Cheston MR & MRS George M (McIlvain—de Bragança—Winifred D Seyburn)
☎ (207) 244-5358 . . "Rock Point" Box 124, Mt Desert, ME *04660*

Chew MR & MRS H Richard (Judith Brown) ⚓
☎ (410) 266-8599 . . on board Fair Witness" care "Landfall" 146 Riverview Av, Annapolis, MD *21401*

Chew MR & MRS William D M (J Kendall Eisenbrey) . . . . | ☎ (401) 423-0245
MR William D M JR . . . . | "Brushwood" Racquet Rd, Jamestown, RI *02835*

Chewning MR & MRS E Taylor JR (Hernstadt—Prince—Jonna R Leonard)
☎ (401) 847-7020 . . "Rock Cliff" 670 Bellevue Av, Newport, RI *02840*

Chickering MR & MRS Allen L (Moore—Margaret Roeding)
☎ (541) 822-3202 . . "Brightwater" 56823 McKenzie H'way, Blue River, OR *97413*

Chickering MR Nicholas R
☎ (916) 426-3618 . . Summit Soda Springs, Box 870, Soda Springs, CA *95728*

Chilcote MRS Lee A (White—Virginia Horn)
☎ (216) 591-1383 . . 3877-1 Lander Rd, Chagrin Falls, OH *44022*

Child MR & MRS Josiah H JR (Susan Furlow)
☎ (508) 636-4502 . . 1041 Horseneck Rd, South Westport, MA *02790*

Childres MRS Clare F (Clare F Fooshee) . . . . | ☎ (216) 333-5308
MR Nathaniel . . . . | 361 Darby's Run, Bay Village, OH *44140*

Childs MR & MRS Charles O (Barbara J McGill)
"La Propriété" 160 River Bend Circle, Talladega, AL *35160*

Childs MR & MRS Clinton L JR (Margaret B Orr)
☎ (705) 764-1978 . . "Outlook" Beaumaris, Ontario P0B 1B0, Canada

Childs MR & MRS David M (Anne W Reeve) . . . . . | ☎ (518) 576-4777
MISS Jocelyn R . . . . | "Red Oak" Box 73, Keene Valley, NY *12943*
MR Joshua H . . . . |

Childs MRS Eleanor (Eleanor vom Rath)
☎ (516) 676-2197 . . 29 Valentine Lane, Box 168, Old Brookville, NY *11545*

Childs MRS James H JR (Elizabeth D Littell)
☎ (207) 363-4632 . . "Short Sands" 5 Stage Neck Rd, PO Box 267, York Harbor, ME *03911*

Childs MR Thomas W
☎ (860) 868-2392 . . Painter Ridge Rd, Washington, CT *06793*

Childs DR & MRS Timothy W (Hope S Kane)
☎ (860) 542-5726 . . "Spitehouse" 300 West Side Rd, Norfolk, CT *06058*

Chinn MR & MRS Garretson W (Nancy Deering)
☎ (970) 963-3901 . . Hill Roaring Ranch, Carbondale, CO *81623*

Choate MR & MRS Charles F (Jhan C English)
☎ (207) 372-8060 . . General Delivery, Tenants Harbor, ME *04860*

Choate MR & MRS Thomas H (Jane Harte)
☎ (603) 968-4489 . . Box 212, Holderness, NH *03245*

Choumenkovitch MR Iliya A M
PO Box 55, Islesboro, ME *04848*

Chrismen MR & MRS James J (Leslie S Miller) . . see MRS R N Miller 3d

Christhilf MR & MRS Bryson G (Elizabeth B Myers)
☎ (410) 639-7060 . . "Pig Neck Farm" Rock Hall, MD *21661*

Church MR & MRS John F JR (Edwards—Catherine Neth)
☎ (616) 526-7119 . . "Heather Highlands" 242 Camelot St, Harbor Springs, MI *49740*

Claggett CAPT (RET) & MRS B Dulany (Rhea A Robinson) USN.
"Port Defiance" Sharpsburg, MD *21782*

Claggett MR Charles E
☎ (414) 868-3495 . . "Beechwood" Cottage Row, Fish Creek, WI *54212*

Claggett MR & MRS William M (Rogers—Barbara J Clark) . . . . | ☎ (616) 547-2276
MISS Susan E . . . . | "Claygate by the Sea" 15 Belvedere Club, Charlevoix, MI *49720*

Claghorn MR & MRS Frederic Strawbridge (Katharine Taws)
   ☎ (609) 492-5017 . . "Sandy Sheets" 112 Chatsworth St, Beach Haven, NJ *08008*
Claghorn MR & MRS John W JR (Margery E Richardson)
   ☎ (717) 646-2337 . . Claghorn Camp, Pocono Lake Preserve, PA *18348*
Claghorn MR & MRS John W 3d (Margaret E Jump) . | ☎ (717) 646-2337
  JUNIORS MISS Lila S. . . . . | Claghorn Camp,
  JUNIORS MR John W 4th . . . . | Pocono Lake
                                                                                Preserve, PA *18348*
Claiborne MRS John T 3d (Cox—Cornelia D Sharp)
   ☎ (203) 775-1365 . . 34 Junction Rd, Brookfield, CT *06804*
Clancy MR & MRS John Franklin (Paula Jean | ☎ (210) 761-1709
  Johnson). . . . . | Bridgepoint 201,
  MISS Allison Holmes. . . . . | 334 S Padre Blvd,
                                                                                South Padre Island,
                                                                                TX *78597*
Clapham MR & MRS John H (Dorothy S Hallowell) . | ☎ (609) 368-4167
  MISS Wendy S. . . . . | 110—118 St,
  MISS Holly R . . . . | Stone Harbor, NJ
  MR Andrew H. . . . . | *08247*
Clapp MRS Nathaniel D (Mary B Loring)
   ☎ (508) 927-0180 . . Box 221, 34 Thissell St, Prides Crossing, MA *01965*
Clapp MRS Roger E (Black—Linda Cabot)
   ☎ (207) 526-4414 . . "Garden Cove House" Swans Island, ME *04685*
Clare MRS N Holmes (Barbara A Kepler)
   ☎ (011-52-465) 20413 . . "Las Aves" Calle Barranca 62, San Miguel de Allende, GTO 37700, Mexico
Clarey MR John E
   ☎ (207) 633-4321 . . "Ocean Sweep" 6 Pinkham's Cove Rd, Spruce Point, Boothbay Harbor, ME *04538-0804*
Clark MR & MRS David W (Anne T Newbold) . . . . . | ☎ (207) 276-5486
  MISS Emily R . . . . | "Seaward West"
                                                                                Northeast Harbor,
                                                                                ME *04662*
Clark MRS Florence W (George—Altemus—Florence B Whitney)
   ☎ (401) 348-8177 . . "Minnebama" Ninigret Av, Watch Hill, RI *02891*
Clark MR & MRS Frederick W (Rosalie L Smith)
  Box 216, Macedonia, IA *51549-0216*
Clark MR & MRS George R (May D Howe)
   ☎ (207) 276-3219 . . "The Old Library" Northeast Harbor, ME *04662*
Clark MRS Grenville JR (Barnum—Hansen—Elizabeth Lamb)
   ☎ (508) 283-0716 . . "Mistral" 6 Rouse Rd, Eastern Point, Gloucester, MA *01930*
Clark MR & MRS Howard L JR (Burke—Karen M | ☎ (508) 325-6227
  Kaess) . . . . | "Long Hill"
  MR Howard L 3d . . . . | 30 Orange St,
    MR Edwin M Burke 3d . . . . | Nantucket, MA
    MR James Van V Burke. . . . . | *02554*
Clark MR J Dudley 3d
   ☎ (802) 295-2986 . . 32 Club House Rd, Quechee, VT *05059*
Clark MRS Joseph Sill (Richey—Iris Cole)
   ☎ (307) 733-4257 . . "Diamond Acre" Moose, WY *83012*
Clark MR & MRS Laurance R (Anne H Dyrud) ⚓
  Tuckernuck Island, Nantucket, MA *02554*
Clark MR & MRS Lewis W (Barbara H Hale)
   ☎ (603) 563-8683 . . Box 65, E Lake Rd, Dublin, NH *03444*

Clark MR & MRS Lewis Hamilton JR (Caroline C Addison)
   ☎ (508) 693-3500 . . Box 28, West Chop, MA *02573*
Clark MRS Margaret R (MacElree—Margaret A Robertson)
   ☎ (508) 356-3802 . . "Cable Garden" 100 County Rd, Ipswich, MA *01938*
Clark MR & MRS Marshall (Shepard—Vallory Willis)
   ☎ (516) 324-0887 . . 5 Hook Pond Rd, East Hampton, NY *11937*
Clark MRS Martha S (Martha Hilton Sulzby). . . . . . | ☎ (401) 847-0207
  MISS Melissa W . . . . | "The Brambles"
                                                                                20 Atlantic Av,
                                                                                Newport, RI *02840*
Clark MR & MRS Merrell E JR (V Hollister Logan)
   ☎ (860) 868-0388 . . "The Homestead" 6 Romford Rd, Washington, CT *06793*
Clark MRS Monika F (Grassman—Monika Fetzer) . | "Schloss Moos"
  JUNIORS MISS Antonia H . . . . | 899 Lindau,
                                                                                Lake of Constance,
                                                                                Germany
Clark MR & MRS P Hamilton 3d (P Gail Jackson)
   ☎ (207) 276-5824 . . "Gull's Way" Northeast Harbor, ME *04662*
Clark MRS Percy H JR (Edith Earle)
   ☎ (207) 276-5088 . . "Tree Tops" Northeast Harbor, ME *04662*
Clark MRS Reed (Audrey A Iselin)
   ☎ (516) 621-9376 . . 198 Valentine's Lane, Glen Head, NY *11545*
Clark MRS Reuben B 3d (Arabella Huber) ⚓
  on board Naraka III" Lankford Bay, Rock Hall, MD *21661*
Clark MRS Stephen C JR (McGusty—Leib—Kathryn James)
   ☎ (540) 687-5928 . . PO Box 1180, Middleburg, VA *22117*
Clark MR & MRS Thomas C 3d (Elizabeth C Bartlett)
   ☎ (860) 542-5029 . . "Out O'Bounds" Mountain Rd, Norfolk, CT *06058*
Clark MRS William H (Rosemary Dudley)
   ☎ (802) 867-4012 . . PO Box 508, Nichols Hill Rd, Dorset, VT *05251-0508*
Clarke MR & MRS Arthur R H (Rosanna Schimenz)
   ☎ (607) 547-2148 . . "Houghton House" Box 182, Springfield Center, NY *13468*
Clarke MR & MRS Charles F (Nelson—Katherine H Duffy)
   ☎ (616) 869-7091 . . 8343 N Beach, Pentwater, MI *49449*
Clarkson MR & MRS William M E (Elisabeth A Hudnut)
   ☎ (518) 251-2362 . . "Log House" Windover, North Creek, NY *12853*
Clay MR & MRS Jonathan C (Whitney A Fite)
   ☎ (518) 329-0702 . . 507 Wiltsie Bridge Rd, Ancramdale, NY *12503*
Clay MR & MRS William D (Mary A Rogers)
   ☎ (414) 868-3387 . . "The Birches" Box 24, Fish Creek, WI *54212*
Claytor MRS Norris Vaux (Lynda K Leonard)
   ☎ (410) 867-0946 . . "Emprise Cottage" 5975 Rockhold Creek Rd, Deale, MD *20751*
Claytor MR Norris Vaux . . . . | ☎ (610) 687-2435
  MISS Cassandra Nierncée . . . . | "Roconante Farm"
  MR Thomas Ash . . . . | Brower Rd,
  MR Warren Ingersoll ⚓. . . . . | Radnor, PA *19087*
Clegg MRS Charles B (Jeannette L Huffman)
   ☎ (208) 622-9223 . . Box 545, Sun Valley, ID *83353*
Clement MR & MRS Peter W (Soffer—Stephanie L Doering)
   ☎ (518) 523-3141 . . Gull Rock Camp, West Shore, Lake Placid, NY *12946* . . MRS absent

Clement MR & MRS Peter Wickham (Victoria A Chave)
☎ (203) 245-2420 . . 4 Waterbury Av, Madison, CT *06443*

Clement MR & MRS Stephen M 3d (Sally B Dayton)
☎ (914) 677-3000 . . Box 1164, Millbrook, NY *12545*

Clements MRS Robert M (Helen Teagle)
☎ (207) 374-2206 . . ''Winnecowetts'' Box 801, Blue Hill, ME *04614*

Clements MR & MRS Robert M JR (Gutcheon—Beth M Richardson) . . . .
MISS Alice B . . . .
MR John B . . . .
MR David S Gutcheon . . . .
☎ (207) DR4-9979
''Seven Oaks''
Box 990, Blue Hill, ME *04614*

Clements MR & MRS William W (J Karen Johnson)
MISS Kristin E . . . .
☎ (619) 438-3964
''Carlsbad House''
5021 Tierra del Oro, Carlsbad, CA *92008*

Clemm DR & MRS F Michael von (Louisa B Hunnewell)
☎ (207) 867-2059 . . ''The Tower'' Gnarlwood Meadows, North Haven, ME *04853*

Clephane MRS Caroline Chapin (Caroline Chapin) .
MR David Chapin . . . .
☎ (508) 627-3338
''Dove Cottage''
118 N Water St, Edgartown, MA *02539*

Cleveland MR & MRS Blair (Alward—Geraldine Bartlett)
☎ (401) 423-0119 . . ''Windfall'' 50 Whittier Rd, Box 565, Jamestown, RI *02835*

Cleveland MR & MRS Donald L (Caroline Coley) . . .
MR Donald L JR . . . .
☎ (516) 788-7209
''Pump House''
Fishers Island, NY *06390*

Clews MRS Henrietta T (Henrietta B Thompson) . . .
MISS Margaret T . . . .
MISS Leta H . . . .
MISS Charlotte L . . . .
MR Henry A . . . .
☎ (207) 422-3222
Hancock Point, ME *04640*

Clews MR & MRS M Madison (Margaret Strawbridge)
☎ (401) 846-3223 . . ''The Waves'' 61 Ledge Rd, Newport, RI *02840*

Clifford DR & MRS Milton Henry (Lydia Höst) . . . . .
MISS Vera E . . . .
☎ (207) 422-6703
Hancock Point, ME *04640*

Cline MR & MRS Guernsey C (Whittemore—Florence A Hoskins)
☎ (508) 997-9680 . . 5 Lawn Cluster, Round Hill, South Dartmouth, MA *02748*

Clothier MR & MRS Robert C JR (Maree T Horgan)
Burgoyne Island, Indian Point, Nova Scotia B0J 2E0, Canada

Clow MR & MRS Gerald C (Frazier—Barbara G Hand)
Box 2860, Santa Fe, NM *87504-2860*

Clow MR Harry B
☎ (847) 234-0243 . . ''Out of Bounds'' Shoreacres Rd, Lake Bluff, IL *60044*

Clowes MR Allen W
☎ (508) 540-1348 . . ''White Hill'' Nobska Rd, Box 312, Woods Hole, MA *02543*

Clowes MRS George H A (Margaret G Jackson)
☎ (508) 548-0975 . . 148 Nobska Rd, Woods Hole, MA *02543*

Cluett MRS G Alfred JR (Smith—Virginia Ashcraft)
MR A Tucker . . . .
☎ (207) 374-2189
''Mossledge''
PO Box 445, Blue Hill, ME *04614*

Cluett MR & MRS John S (de Peyster—Maria-Luisa B Duke)
☎ (516) 283-2104 . . ''Wyndecote Cottage'' 45 Gin Lane, Box XXX, Southampton, NY *11969*

Cluett MR & MRS Mark S (Elizabeth A Gummey)
⛵ . . . .
MISS Julia S . . . .
☎ (207) 374-5112
''The Pines''
PO Box 246, Blue Hill, ME *04614*

Clulow MRS Margaretta M (Margaretta Mason Maganini) . . . .
MISS Evelyn K . . . .
☎ (401) 847-1847
''Vernon House''
46 Clarke St, Newport, RI *02840*

Coates MR & MRS Benjamin (Nancy Sloane) ⛵
☎ (011-44-1349) 830-946 . . ''Wyvis Lodge'' Evanton, Ross-Shire IV1 9XW, Scotland

Cobb MRS Ahira 2d (Neville—Hope Fay)
☎ (603) 447-2170 . . ''Turtle Bay'' RR 1, Box 18A, Center Conway, NH *03813*

Cobb MR & MRS Calvin H JR (Olive L Watson)
☎ (410) 255-5066 . . Gibson Island, MD *21056*

Cobb MISS Emily M
239 Old Stone H'way, Amagansett, NY *11930*

Cobb MRS Gallatin (Margaret H Gallatin)
☎ (516) 283-1874 . . 86 Post Lane, Southampton, NY *11968*

Cobb MR & MRS Henry N (Joan S Spaulding)
☎ (207) 867-2231 . . North Haven, ME *04853*

Cobb MR & MRS Howard L (Dewing—Wright—Nancy Goodwin)
☎ (616) 526-5196 . . 3853 S Lake Shore Dv, Harbor Springs, MI *49740*

Cobb MR & MRS John W (H Bayard Hooper) . . . . . .
MR Joshua H . . . .
Pleasant Bay, Inverness, Cape Breton, Nova Scotia B0E 2P0, Canada

Cobb CAPT (RET) & MRS Richard (Marian Van V Colwell) USN . . . of
☎ (207) 244-7169 . . ''Willowbrook'' Somesville, Mt Desert, ME *04660*
☎ (207) 244-3354 . . ''Windiana'' Pond House, Mt Desert, ME *04660*

Coburn MR George M
☎ (304) 258-3229 . . ''Christmas Tree Farm'' Box 231, Great Cacapon, WV *25422*

Coburn MR & MRS John (Joan S Shaw)
☎ (508) 295-2718 . . ''Maywood'' Cedar Point, Wareham, MA *02571*

Coburn MR & MRS Lawrence H (Alexandra Taylor)
☎ (518) 576-5403 . . ''The Runway'' Keene Valley, NY *12943*

Cochran MR & MRS Carlyle Van D (Sheila M Smith)
☎ (207) 276-3670 . . ''The Cabin'' PO Box 194, Mt Desert, ME *04660*

Cochran MRS Caroline B (Caroline A Bump) . . . . .
MR William F 2d . . . .
☎ (011-44-1284) 703873
7 College Lane, Bury St Edmunds, Suffolk IP33 1NN, England

Cochran MR & MRS George N (Barbara K Doepke)
☎ (616) 334-4543 . . 5301 Northwood Dv, Glen Arbor, MI *49636*

Cockman MR & MRS Eric W (Lydia S Dougherty)
☎ (908) 892-1333 . . 1044 Barnegat Lane, Mantoloking, NJ *08738*

Cocroft MR & MRS Duncan H (Christina L Miller) . . | ☎ (612) 359-9524
  MISS Constance G . . . . | 1117 Marquette Av,
  MISS Elizabeth S . . . . | Minneapolis, MN *55403*

Coddington MRS Stewart G (Jane A Bell) . . . . | ☎ (414) 275-2866
  MISS Kimberly A . . . . | Belvidere Park,
  MR James S . . . . | Box 610, Fontana, WI *53125*

Coddington MR Stewart G
☎ (516) 487-0105 . . 1 Overlook Av, Great Neck, NY *11021-3750*

Codman MRS Russell S JR (Jane D Ferguson) . . . . . | ☎ (508) 526-1220
  MISS Jane R . . . . | "Namdoc"
  MISS June F. . . . . | 30 Proctor St, Box 1558, Manchester-By-The-Sea, MA *01944*

Cody MR & MRS Coleman F (Hobbs—Sarah P Meigs)
☎ (508) 563-6787 . . 180 Scraggy Neck Rd, Cataumet, MA *02534*

Coffin MR & MRS David D (Rosemary H Baldwin)
☎ (518) 576-9901 . . "Whistlewood" St Huberts, NY *12943*

Coffin MR & MRS Ralston H JR (Phyllis C Verkamp) | ☎ (516) 288-3821
  MISS Claire R . . . . | "Nuthin' Dune"
  MR Jared R . . . . | 491 Dune Rd, Westhampton Beach, NY *11978*

Cogan REV & MRS Timothy B (Ruth W Mitchell) . . . | ☎ (508) 627-5451
  MR John M . . . . | "Indian Field"
  MR Milo S . . . . | RFD 659, Edgartown, MA *02539*

Coggeshall MR & MRS Clarke (Ethel B Ducey) . . . . | ☎ (508) 362-3912
  MISS Katharine D . . . . | Rendez-vous Lane,
  MISS Natalie M . . . . | Barnstable, MA
  JUNIORS MR David C . . . . | *02630*

Coggill MRS George (Elizabeth M Harris)
☎ (207) 374-2320 . . "Parker Ridge" HC 64, Box 270-106, Blue Hill, ME *04614*

Cohen MR & MRS Ted (Austin—Ann R Collier)
☎ (207) 236-8447 . . 10 Church St, Rockport, ME *04856*

Cohû MRS Henry W (Snowden—Dwight—Adelaide Farr)
☎ (401) 348-8203 . . "Shadybrook" Watch Hill, RI *02891*

Colas MR & MRS Josselin C (Elisa J Cosnard des Closets)
☎ (011-33) 96-31-60-59 . . "Les Garennes" 3 rue du Bocage, 22270 Jugon-les-Lacs, France

Colas MR & MRS Pierre H (Ludington—Maryanne Cantrell) . . . . | ☎ (011-33) 32-36-49-29
  MISS Marie-Noelle . . . . | 33 rue Henri IV,
  MISS Valerie C . . . . | Ivry-la-Bataille, France

Colburn MR & MRS Kenneth H (Crye—Virginia M Ventura) ⚓
☎ (207) 633-2430 . . Green Island, West Southport, ME *04576*

Colby MR & MRS Robert L (Gretchen H Rogers) . . . | ☎ (819) 843-7656
  MISS Jessie H . . . . | Georgeville,
  JUNIORS MR Robert G . . . . | Quebec J0B 1T0,
  JUNIORS MR Anthony L . . . . | Canada

Colcord MR & MRS Bradford P (Helen B Johnson) . . | ☎ (207) 734-6719
  MISS Hilary P . . . . | Seal Harbor Cove,
  MR Avery J . . . . | Islesboro, ME *04848*

Cole MR & MRS Charles J (Margery Manning)
☎ (508) 994-3260 . . Nonquitt, MA *02748*

Cole MRS Helen C
12987 GAR H'way, Chardon, OH *44024*

Cole CAPT & MRS L Fletcher (Anne M Magruder) USA.
☎ (704) 743-2051 . . "Harmony Hall" PO Box 324, Cashiers Valley, NC *28717*

Cole MRS Susan H (Sabet—Susan Heyniger) . . . . . . | ☎ (508) 997-2535
  JUNIORS MR Amman H Sabet . . . . | "The Meadows" 189 Smith Neck Rd, South Dartmouth, MA *02748*

Coleman MR & MRS Daniel T Le V (Irene H Conway) . . see H A Conway

Coleman MR & MRS Francis I G (Seymour—Julia G Montgomery) . . . . | ☎ (207) 276-3237
  MISS Anne M . . . . | "Eastward Way"
  MR Bruce D . . . . | Box 927, Northeast Harbor, ME *04662*

Coleman MR & MRS George L (Soles—Dawn Loomis)
☎ (303) 688-1661 . . "Horizon" Castle Pines Golf Club, 1008 Hummingbird Dv, Castle Rock, CO *80104*

Coleman MRS N Tenney (Lloyd—Nancy C Tenney)
☎ (508) 775-1105 . . "The Ark" Box 336, Hyannis Port, MA *02647*

Coleman MR & MRS T Samuel (Cynthia B Balmer)
PO Box 43, Deer Harbor, WA *98243*

Colesberry MR & MRS Robert F JR (Hallowell—Karen L Thorson) . . of
☎ (208) 622-3168 . . "Juniper Road" PO Box 2210, Sun Valley, ID *83353*
☎ (516) 267-1067 . . Atlantic Av, Amagansett, NY *11930*

Colgan MRS John A JR (Anne T Brown)
124 Ocean St, Beach Haven, NJ *08008*

Colhoun MISS Julia F
☎ (415) 703-0952 . . 230 Castro St, San Francisco, CA *94114*

Coiket MR & MRS Tristram C JR (Ruth M Mueller) . . | ☎ (207) 288-3871
  MISS Carolyn M . . . . | "Kenarden"
  JUNIORS MR Tristram C 3d . . . . | 352 Main St,
  JUNIORS MR Bryan D . . . . | PO Box 707, Bar Harbor, ME *04609*

Colket MR & MRS Tristram C 4th (Kathleen Redman) . . . . | ☎ (902) 235-2399
  JUNIORS MISS R Elizabeth . . . . | Belle Cote,
  JUNIORS MR Tristram C 5th . . . . | Nova Scotia B0E 1C0, Canada

Collier MRS Sargent (Elizabeth H Moore) . . . . | ☎ (207) 288-5873
  MISS Leandra M . . . . | "The Farm House"
  JUNIORS MISS Eliza D . . . . | 7 Highbrook Rd,
  JUNIORS MR Sargent M McC . . . . | Bar Harbor, ME *04609*

Collier MR Sargent
☎ (508) 282-4394 . . PO Box 549, Essex, MA *01929*

Collier MRS Sargent F (Eleanor M McCormick)
☏ (207) 288-3816 . . "Gingerbread House" 8 Barberry Lane, Bar Harbor, ME *04609*

Collings MR & MRS Clifford C JR (Helen C Pennock)
☏ (610) 896-7341 . . 35 Evans Lane, Haverford, PA *19041*

Collins MR & MRS Atwood 2d (Gilbert—Rosemary Worth)
☏ (508) 992-7408 . . 25 Buzzards Bay Av, South Dartmouth, MA *02748*

Collins MR & MRS Atwood 3d (Cynthia M Williams) | ☏ (516) 788-7188
  MR A Porter . . . . | "Beach Cottage"
  JUNIORS MR Dwight M . . . . | Fishers Island, NY *06390*

Collins MR & MRS Bradley I (M Carol Ohmer)
☏ (207) 276-5835 . . "Cove Cottage" PO Box 974, Northeast Harbor, ME *04662*

Collins MR & MRS Bradley I JR (Amy M Fine)
Aug 1 . . ☏ (516) 780-7882 . . General Delivery, Fishers Island, NY *06370*

Collins JUNIORS MR Christian J . . see MRS M J Bancroft

Collins MR & MRS Daniel G (Crawford—Anne F | ☏ (516) 537-1228
  Weld) . . . . | Mitchell Lane,
  MISS Serena W Crawford . . . . | PO Box 32,
  MISS Evelyn F Crawford . . . . | Bridgehampton, NY
  MR W Blake Crawford . . . . | *11932*

Collins MR & MRS David H (S Wendell Wood)
☏ (716) 753-3546 . . Collinswood Villa 13, Shore Dv, Box 146, Point Chatauqua, Mayville, NY *14757*

Collins MR & MRS Henry L 3d (E Suzanne Kline) . . . | ☏ (914) 677-5892
  MR Henry L 4th . . . . | "Knockers Farm"
  MR Alexander C . . . . | 311 N Smith Rd, LaGrangeville, NY *12540*

Collins MRS Phyllis D (Huber—Phyllis E Dillon)
☏ (207) 734-6442 . . Dark Harbor, Islesboro, ME *04848*

Colmery MR & MRS Harry W JR (Sallie E Morphy)
☏ (619) 433-7093 . . 42 St Malo Beach, Oceanside, CA *92054*

Colmore MR & MRS Charles B JR (Davis—Margareta B Erikson)
Barter Creek, Isle au Haut, ME *04645*

Colsman-Freyberger MR & MRS Ulrich (Susan B | ☏ (714) 494-3209
  Painter) . . . . | 1665 Viking Rd,
  MR Charles McKee . . . . | Laguna Beach, CA *92651*

Colt MRS C Learned (Hope C Learned) . . . . | ☏ (518) 576-4366
  MR Alexander D . . . . | Sunset Hill,
  MR Ward S . . . . | Keene Valley, NY *12943*

Colt DR & MRS Edward W D (Nelson—Suzanne | ☏ (860) 542-6068
  Knickerbocker) . . . . | 102 Litchfield Rd,
  JUNIORS MISS Angela . . . . | Norfolk, CT *06058*

Colt MRS H Dunscombe (Walsh—Armida M T Bologna)
☏ (011-44-171) 730-4287 . . 70 Chester Square, London SW1, England

Colt MR & MRS James D (Elizabeth S Reynolds) . . . . | ☏ (508) 299-8024
  MISS Alexandra R . . . . | "Pony Pasture"
  MISS Sarah F . . . . | Box 87, Woods Hole, MA *02543*

Colt MR & MRS S Barclay (Hewitt—Julie G George) | ☏ (908) 899-0606
  MR Edward Cooper Hewitt JR . . . . | 36 Harbour Lane, Point Pleasant, NJ *08742*

Colton MRS Sabin W 5th (Graeme de L Grosvenor)
☏ (207) 244-5878 . . "Faraway" Greening Island, Box 548, Southwest Harbor, ME *04679*

Combes MR & MRS Abbott C 4th (Constance W | Frigate Rd,
  Wardrop) . . . . | George Town,
  JUNIORS MISS M L deRaismes . . . . | Great Exuma,
  JUNIORS MISS Ada Barker . . . . | Bahamas

Commons REV DR Harold T
☏ (518) 543-6553 . . "The Pines" Hague, Lake George, NY *12836*

Commons MR & MRS Harold T JR (Carolyn A | ☏ (518) 543-6553
  Damours) . . . . | "Friends Point"
  MR Richard B . . . . | Hague,
  JUNIORS MR Peter T . . . . | Lake George, NY *12836*

Comstock MRS Clyde N (Adelaide H Mason)
☏ (704) 883-2522 . . Fairway Villas 11B, Sapphire Lakes, Sapphire, NC *28774*

Conant MR & MRS George K JR (Ellen L Ryerson)
☏ (516) 788-7273 . . "Proche-Mer" Fishers Island, NY *06390*

Conaway MRS Howard H (Mary E Mitchell) . . . . . . | ☏ (302) 227-7206
  MR Howard H JR . . . . | "Bayberry" Dewey Beach, DE *19971*

Coney MR & MRS Aims C JR (Rita N Platt)
☏ (518) 352-7364 . . "Towahloondah" Box 242, Blue Mountain Lake, NY *12812*

Conger MR Frederic de P
☏ (207) 359-8569 . . Center Harbor, Brooklin, ME *04616*

Conklin MR & MRS George W (Anne P Thomas)
☏ (518) 585-6273 . . Box 113, Rte 74, Eagle Lake, Ticonderoga, NY *12883*

Conklin MR & MRS Theodore B (Natalie H O'Brien) ⛵
☏ (516) 288-1975 . . 14 Griffing Av, Westhampton Beach, NY *11978*

Conlan MRS Walter A JR (Wilkins—Ellen W Meirs) | ☏ (609) 492-5340
  MR William M . . . . | 125 Glendola Av, Beach Haven, NJ *08008*

Connard MR & MRS Carroll S (Fraker—Anna S Hayes)
"Needufeu Farm" Wardwell Point Rd, RR 1, Box 65, Penobscot, ME *04476*

Connard MR & MRS Frank L JR (Suzette H Waters) . | ☏ (860) 536-6406
  MISS Leila H . . . . | "Knappsack" 8 Club House Point, Groton Long Point, CT *06340*

Connell MRS Henrietta L (Vastine—Gardner—Henrietta Underwood Lizars)
☏ (011-41-30) 46527 . . "Châlet National" 3780 Gstaad, Switzerland

Connell MR & MRS Robert H (Elisabeth E Armstrong)
8 Nantucket Av, Nantucket, MA *02554*

Connett MR & MRS William C IV (Josephine D Fusz)
☏ (616) 547-4144 . . 515 Belvedere, Charlevoix, MI *49720*

Connick MR & MRS Andrew J (Alice M Lamm)
☎ (516) 324-8306 . . Georgica Rd, East Hampton, NY *11937*
Connor MR & MRS F Hayden JR (Louise M Bailey)
Brush Hill Rd, Stowe, VT *05672*
Connor MR & MRS John T (Mary O'Boyle)
☎ (508) 428-6321 . . "Chenequa" 110 Vineyard Rd, Cotuit, MA *02635*
Conrad MR & MRS Elbert A (Louisa L Vaughan)
☎ (207) 244-3100 . . "Silo House" Somes Sound, Box 45, Mt Desert, ME *04660*
Conrad MR & MRS Winthrop B JR (Ellen B Rouse) . . | ☎ (705) 387-3362
JUNIORS MISS Louisa K . . . . | Camp Ulvik,
JUNIORS MR Parker R . . . . | Ahmic Lake,
| Magnetawan,
| Ontario P0A 1P0,
| Canada
Conroy MR & MRS Robert G (Ann B Omara) . . . . . | ☎ (603) 448-1065
MR Curtis H . . . . | "Slayton Hill"
MISS Kimberley A (Tyrer—Kimberley A Conroy) | RR 1, Slayton Hill
| Rd, West Lebanon,
| NH *03784*
Conroy MRS Sheila C (Sheila O S Catling) . . see MRS C A R Crosland
Constantine MR & MRS Richard W (Mallory B | ☎ (401) 322-8875
Merriman) . . . . | "Knowletop"
MR Wells W 3d . . . . | 35 Knowles Av,
MR Thaddeus B . . . . | Weekapaug, RI
JUNIORS MISS Caroline H . . . . | *02891*
Converse MR & MRS Bernard T JR (Shirley G Smith) | ☎ (609) 368-2400
MR David A . . . . | 222—104 St,
| Stone Harbor, NJ
| *08247*
Converse MR & MRS Costello C (Funsten—M deLancey Moser)
☎ (401) 423-2771 . . 23 Standish Rd, Jamestown, RI *02835*
Conway MR & MRS Gerald A (Martine Vilas) . . . . . | ☎ (716) 386-5448
MISS Martine . . . . | Chedwel Club
MR Gerald A JR . . . . | TH-106, Box 1106,
MR Neil P . . . . | Chautauqua, NY
| *14722*
Conway MR & MRS Hewitt A (Jeanne L O'Brien) . . . | ☎ (516) 288-2775
MISS Louise G . . . . | 3010 Mitchell Rd,
MR & MRS Daniel T Le V Coleman (Irene H | Westhampton
Conway) . . . . | Beach, NY *11978*
Conze MR & MRS Peter H (Elizabeth B Powers)
☎ (860) 388-5313 . . 55 N Cove Rd, Old Saybrook, CT *06475*
Cook MRS A Werk (Steele—Jane Bancroft)
☎ (617) 383-1017 . . 230 Sohier St, Box 158, Cohasset, MA *02025*
Cook MR & MRS Arthur F JR (Cornelia McL | ☎ (508) 775-0097
Lombard) . . . . | "Ivy Croft"
MISS Nina . . . . | 110 Irving Av,
MR Laurence L . . . . | Hyannis Port, MA
| *02647*
Cook MR & MRS Bruce Stewart (DeLancey K Hollos)
☎ (401) 348-8223 . . "Ridgecrest" Ridge Rd, Watch Hill, RI *02891*
Cook MR & MRS Charles B JR (Campbell—Barbara | ☎ (603) 253-4542
G Welch) . . . . | Kent Island,
MR Charles B 3d . . . . | Squam Lake,
MR Andrew W . . . . | Center Harbor, NH
| *03226*
Cook MRS Hobart A H (Minot—Molly Cummings)
☎ (508) 627-8643 . . "Highwater" 104 S Water St, Edgartown, MA *02539*
Cook MR John Ransom (Driver—Susan Carlyon-Evans)
☎ (011-44-1962) 855918 . . St Swithun's Cottage, 21 St Swithun's St, Winchester, Hampshire SO23 9JP, England
Cook MR & MRS Kevit R (Gail B Fairman)
☎ (207) 276-3635 . . "Quarry Cove" Sargent Dv, Northeast Harbor, ME *04662*
Cook MRS Peter G (Joan B Folinsbee)
☎ (207) 443-5972 . . "Murphy's Corner" RD 3, Wiscasset, ME *04578*
Cook MR & MRS Peter Trowbridge (Hutton—Anne C | ☎ (516) 788-7171
Blind) . . . . | Box 118,
JUNIORS MR Cutler C T . . . . | Fishers Island, NY
| *06390*
Cook MR & MRS Ransom S (McGinn—Nan Hemphill)
☎ (707) 795-5066 . . "The Ranch" 5307 Lichau Rd, Penngrove, CA *94951*
Cook MR & MRS Stephen A (Cynthia A Parker) ⛵
☎ (516) 788-7384 . . Box 52, Fishers Island, NY *06390*
Cook MR & MRS Thomas McK 3d (Genevieve M Huff)
☎ (609) 884-3390 . . 277 Windsor Av, Cape May, NJ *08204*
Cook MRS (DR) W Leigh JR (Anne H Rush)
☎ (412) 235-2063 . . "Carncairn III" RD 1, Box 173B, New Florence, PA *15944*
Cooke MR & MRS James W 3d (Kimberley A Shryock)
"Tudulla" Upper Dam, Lake Richardson, ME *04216*
Cooke MRS S Graff (Sara M Graff) . . . . | ☎ (609) 492-2935
MISS F Elizabeth . . . . | "Sea Biscuit"
MISS Laina K . . . . | 211 Berkeley Av,
MISS Sara R . . . . | Beach Haven, NJ
| *08008*
Coolidge MR & MRS Nicholas J (Eliska Hasek) . . . . . | Jly 1 . .
JUNIORS MISS Alexandra R . . . . | ☎ (011-42)
| 187-93210
| Castle Kundratice,
| Hartmanice,
| Sumava,
| Czech Republic
| Aug 1 . .
| ☎ (603) 968-7744
| Squam Lake,
| Holderness, NH
| *03245*
Coolidge MR Peter J
☎ (603) 968-9233 . . Long Island, Squam Lake, Holderness, NH *03245*
Coolidge MR Robert T . . . . | ☎ (603) 968-3874
MR Miles C . . . . | Rte 1, Box 38,
MR Matthew P . . . . | Center Sandwich,
| NH *03227*

Coolidge MR & MRS Thomas R (Susan L Freiberg)..
MR Thomas L . . . .
of ☎ (603)968-7088 Utopia Island, Squam Lake, Holderness, NH *03245*
☎ (860) 824-0373 "Red Fox Farm" Falls Village, CT *06031*

Coonan MRS James F (Lurline Roth)
☎ (541) 826-9707 . . "Lakecreek Ranch" 18495 H'way 140, Eagle Point, OR *97524-9436*
Cooper MR Alan A . . see R H Soule
Cooper DR & MRS David Y (Cynthia Laughlin)
☎ (919) 441-5116 . . 1405 N Virginia Dare Trail, Kill Devil Hills, NC *27948*
Cooper MR Douglas C . . see R H Soule
Cooper MR & MRS John L (Marie T McCook)
☎ (401) 635-2609 . . 113 Quicksand Pond Rd, Box 576, Little Compton, RI *02837-0576*
Cooper MR & MRS Joseph W J JR (Dorothea-Louise Phelps) . . . .
MR Joseph W J 3d . . . .
MR James H . . . .
MR Brandon P . . . .
☎ (802) 297-9363 "Coopershaven" High Meadow Rd, Box 428, Stratton, VT *05155*
Cooper MRS Leslie T (Struthers Joyce) . . . .
DR Leslie T JR . . . .
☎ (609) 884-4300 208 Windsor Av, Cape May, NJ *08204*
Coords MRS Deane M (Priscilla S Todd)
☎ (860) 868-2713 . . 145 Angevine Rd, Warren, CT *06754-1818*
Corbett MRS Andrew J JR (Victoria A Phillips) . . . .
MISS Christina D . . . .
MR Andrew J 3d . . . .
JUNIORS MR William P . . . .
☎ (212) 861-3747 150 E 69 St, Apt 3T, New York, NY *10021*
Corbett MR Andrew J JR
☎ (508) 768-7820 . . 76 Eastern Av, Essex, MA *01929*
Corbin MRS Horace K JR (Edith D Milbank)
☎ (908) 892-1113 . . 988 Barnegat Lane, Mantoloking, NJ *08738*
Cormier MR Clayton P
☎ (802) 583-3145 . . Mountainside 61, Sugarbush, Warren, VT *05670*
Cornell MR & MRS James K (Shields—E Sara Rowbotham)
☎ (603) 823-5289 . . "Blue Blinds on Sugar Hill" Lovers Lane, Sugar Hill, NH *03585*
Corsini MR & MRS Russell V JR (Althea T Harty) . . .
MISS Lisa H . . . .
MR Russell V 3d . . . .
☎ (508) 385-4455 315 Sesuit Neck Rd, East Dennis, MA *02641*
Corsini di Laiatico MR & MRS Alessandro (Michelle M de Kwiatkowski)
"Villa Corsini" Porto Ercole, 58018 Grosseto, Italy
Cosnard des Closets MR & MRS Jean Pierre (Mary J McKeon)
☎ (011-33-1) 42-22-84-45 . . 8 rue Récamier, 75007 Paris, France
Coster CAPT (RET) Gerard H JR—USN.
☎ (518) 589-9762 . . "East Cottage" Onteora Club, Tannersville, NY *12485*

Coudert MRS Dale (Hokin—Dale Manowitz). . . . . .
MISS Diana Hokin . . . .
MISS Alexandra Hokin . . . .
☎ (970) 544-0141 Chateau Roaring Fork 17, 1039 E Cooper, Aspen, CO *81611*
Coudert MR Ferdinand W
☎ (860) 526-2032 . . "Observatory Hill" 344 Joshuatown Rd, Lyme, CT *06371*
Coudert MR & MRS Frederic R 3d (Margaret R McInnis). . . . .
MISS Cynthia . . . .
MISS Sandra . . . .
☎ (516) 922-3940 "La Chaumiere" 67 Cove Neck Rd, Oyster Bay, NY *11771*
Coues MR & MRS William Pearce (Mildred C Davidson)
☎ (207) 883-6697 . . "The Briars" 2 Fieldways, Prouts Neck, ME *04074*
Coursen MR & MRS R Dennison (Alford—Carolyn H Yeaw)
☎ (508) 945-0492 . . "Highfield" 121 Harding Lane, Chatham, MA *02633*
Cousins MR & MRS Robert E (Ellen C Cummin)
☎ (860) 535-0976 . . "The Hewitt Farm" 576 Norwich-Westerly Rd, North Stonington, CT *06359*
Cover MRS S Detert (Stiling—Sandra L Detert) . . . .
JUNIORS MR William D . . . .
☎ (707) 944-2306 1500 Walnut Dv, Oakville, CA *94562*
Covington MR George M . . . .
MISS Karen M . . . .
MISS Jean T . . . .
JUNIORS MISS Sarah I . . . .
☎ (906) 484-2839 Les Cheneaux Club, Cedarville, MI *49719*
Cowell MR & MRS Richard C (Sullivan—Jacqueline McKissick)
☎ (716) 396-2456 . . "Summer Wind" 4725 W Lake Rd, Canandaigua, NY *14424*
Cowles MR & MRS James C (Kathryn C Maney)
☎ (516) 283-8294 . . PO Box 967, Southampton, NY *11969*
Cowley MR & MRS Nicholas P T (Page K Ayres)
20 Riverside Court, 20 Nine Elms Lane, London SW8, England
Cowley MR & MRS Robert W (Edith P Lorillard). . . .
JUNIORS MISS Olivia L . . . .
JUNIORS MISS Savannah C L . . . .
☎ (401) 846-6791 18 Dennison St, Newport, RI *02840*
Cowperthwait MISS Sarah M
☎ (541) 563-2207 . . "Pelican Landing" 2606 Oceania Dv, Waldport, OR *97394*
Cox MR & MRS Archibald (Phyllis Ames)
☎ (207) 326-8242 . . "Brookway Farm" Bucks Harbor, Brooksville, ME *04617*
Cox DR Denton Sayer
☎ (508) 563-3393 . . "Beech Knoll" Box 467, Cataumet, MA *02534*
Cox MISS Frances B
☎ (207) 359-2760 . . Box 30, Sedgwick, ME *04676*
Cox MRS Howard E (Anne C Delafield Finch)
☎ (516) 288-1188 . . "Sunswyck" 100 Seafield Lane, Box 3, Westhampton Beach, NY *11978*
Cox MR & MRS Roderick H (Mary Rutledge Burnet)
"Big Pine" Ojibway of Keewaydin, Temagami, Ontario P0H 2H0, Canada
Cox MR & MRS Thomas R JR (Walker—Joan Buckley)
☎ (508) 428-1944 . . 106 Hathaway Rd, Osterville, MA *02655*

Cox MR & MRS William C JR (Martha A Whiting) . .
MISS Heidi . . . .
☎ (508) 228-9247
"The Point"
2 Easton St,
Nantucket, MA
02554

Cox MR & MRS William D JR (Janet K Rasmussen). .
MISS Christina L . . . .
MR David D . . . .
☎ (715) 467-2716
Rasmussen Dv,
Scandinavia, WI
54977

Coy MR & MRS Peter Meldrim (Sally McAdoo)
☎ (508) 693-0791 . . "Elmholm" Box 2345, Vineyard Haven, MA *02568*

Coyle MR & MRS Elliott R (Carolyn H Loeffler) . . . .
MR Elliott R JR . . . .
☎ (412) 741-6144
202 Beaver St,
Sewickley, PA
15143

Crabb MR & MRS David L (Dorothy Fay Mixter) . . .
MISS Laura E . . . .
☎ (508) 548-0636
"Seedling House"
Nobska Point,
Woods Hole, MA
02543

Cragin MR & MRS Stuart W JR (Margaret R Mackall)
MISS Grace S . . . .
MR Reginald W . . . .
MR Geoffrey S . . . .
MR Benjamin M . . . .
☎ (516) AM7-3547
Amagansett, NY
11930

Craig MR & MRS Berton A (Denton—Elizabeth C Russel)
☎ (704) 675-9175 . . "Kingfisher's Craig" Burnsville, NC *28714*

Craig MR & MRS Howard R JR (Elena Socorro Revilla)
El Palomar Alto, via Pacasmayo, Chilete, Peru

Craig MR & MRS Robert L (Elizabeth H Lamphere)
☎ (603) 636-1597 . . "Prospect Lodge" RFD 1, Box 405, Groveton, NH *03582*

Craigmyle MRS M Martin (Mary F Martin)
☎ (516) 653-6755 . . "Merriehaven" 5 Quogue St, Quogue, NY *11959*

Craigmyle MR & MRS Robert de R (McCarter—Nancy K Alker)
☎ (413) 229-8411 . . E Hill Rd, Southfield, MA *01259*

Cram MR Henry Sergeant
☎ (803) 757-3306 . . "Bear's Island Cottage" PO Box 185, Bluffton, SC *29910*

Cramer MRS Ambrose C (Mary Meeker)
☎ (207) 236-3003 . . "The Yellow House" Box 220, Rockport, ME *04856*

Crandon MR & MRS A Seabury JR (Mary A Turner)
"Old Elm" 590 W Main Rd, Little Compton, RI *02837*

Crans MR & MRS Robert R (Doris L Beckwith) ⚓
MR Robert R JR . . . .
☎ (804) 725-7491
"Painted Duck
Farm" Mathews
Court House,
Mathews, VA *23109*
Point O'Woods, NY
11706

Crawford MR & MRS Duncan (Stephanie W Pogue) .
MISS Samantha H . . . .
MR Adam B . . . .

Crawford MISS Evelyn F . . see D G Collins

Crawford MR & MRS George (von Mueffling—Marsha Millard)
☎ (516) 283-9343 . . Ox Pasture Rd, PO Box 525, Southampton, NY *11969*

Crawford MR & MRS George L (Margaret L Kendrick)
☎ (401) 423-1444 . . "The Stable" 361 Highland Dv, Jamestown, RI *02835*

Crawford MISS Serena W . . see D G Collins

Crawford MR W Blake . . see D G Collins

Crawford MR & MRS W Michael (Cynthia H Gowen)
☎ (516) 324-4029 . . 53 Lily Pond Lane, PO Box 763, East Hampton, NY *11937*

Creese MRS James (Margaret V Morton)
☎ (518) 576-4456 . . "Overbrook" Keene Valley, NY *12943*

Creighton MR & MRS Albert M JR (Hilary Holcomb)
☎ (207) 863-4420 . . "Whale Rock" Vinalhaven, ME *04863*

Crimmins MR & MRS Martin Lalor 3d (House—Martha P Thomson)
☎ (914) 677-6122 . . "Deep Hollow Hill" Deep Hollow Rd, Millbrook, NY *12545*

Crisler MRS Richard C (Howard—Lucy Hagin)
☎ (606) 689-7228 . . "Neboshon Farm" 8368 River Rd, Hebron, KY *41048*

Crisp MR & MRS Peter O (Emily S Ridgway) . . . . . .
MISS Tina O . . . .
☎ (516) 788-7234
Box 324,
Fishers Island, NY
06390

Crissman MR & MRS James H (Louisa G Murray) . .
JUNIORS MR William G . . . .
☎ (207) 549-7178
"Gaeloft"
King's Mills,
Whitefield, ME
04353

Crittenden MR & MRS G Lamar (Gertrude B Shaw)
☎ (508) 295-2665 . . "Mosquito Hut" Burgess Point, Wareham, MA *02571*

Crittenden MR & MRS G Lamar JR (Abigail O Brown) . . . .
MISS Sarah M . . . .
☎ (508) 295-2665
"Mosquito Hut"
Burgess Point,
Wareham, MA
02571

Crocker MR & MRS Robert G (Ruth E Cox) . . . .
MISS R Sayre . . . .
MR Andrew G . . . .
MR Peter B . . . .
☎ (508) 526-7732
"Sandy Hollow"
48 Proctor St,
Manchester, MA
01944

Croghan MRS John A (Eileen B Erwin) . . . .
MISS Maeve P . . . .
☎ (906) 847-3859
"White Birches"
Box 177,
Mackinac Island, MI
49757

Crolius MR & MRS Thomas Potter (Patricia L Mosser)
☎ (441) 238-8806 . . "Sandpiper" 50 South Rd, Southampton SN 02, Bermuda

Cromwell MR & MRS Jarvis 2d (Shelby P Tison)
☎ (914) 985-7188 . . "Grey Lodge" Denning, NY *12725*

Cronson MRS Mary Sharp (Mary Sharp)
☎ (508) 627-5529 . . 94 Fuller St, Edgartown, MA *02539*

Cronson MR & MRS Paul (Caroline Milnes)
☎ (508) 627-5529 . . 94 Fuller St, Edgartown, MA *02539*

Crook MR & MRS George W (Emily Keeble) . . . . . . | ☎ (616) 547-6355
   MISS Katherine K . . . . | 502 Belvedere Club,
   JUNIORS MR George W JR . . . . | Charlevoix, MI
   49720
Crooker MR & MRS Robert M JR (Susanne Thamm)
   ☎ (516) 692-7062 . . "Hill House" Box 265, Cold Spring Harbor, NY *11724*
Crosby DR & MRS Everett U (Candace Carter)
   ☎ (508) 228-4025 . . "Pimnys Point" Box 847, Nantucket, MA *02554*
Crosby MR John O
   Box 2408, Santa Fe, NM *87501*
Crosier MR Louis M . . see R N Pyle
Crosland MRS C Anthony R (Catling—Susan B Watson) . . . . | ☎ (011-44-1295) 810340
   MRS Sheila C Conroy (Sheila O S Catling) . . | "Old Mill" Adderbury, Oxfordshire, England
Cross MR & MRS Jackson (Anne Meyer)
   ☎ (802) 295-1553 . . "Crossland" Quechee Hartland Rd, Hartland, VT *05048*
Cross MR & MRS William R JR (Sally C Smith)
   ☎ (508) 645-2642 . . Abel's Hill, RD 1, Box 450, Chilmark, MA *02535*
Cruice MR & MRS Charles S (Kathryn J Wilmarth)
   ☎ (208) 726-8938 . . "Points West" 3009 Warm Springs Rd, Ketchum, ID *83340*
Cruice MR & MRS J Seth H (Barbara A Stine)
   ☎ (302) 658-9507 . . Box 3974, Greenville, DE *19807*
Cryan MRS Eugene W (Alice McAlpin) . . . . | ☎ (705) 764-1958
   MR Bruce McA . . . . | Fairholm Island, Beaumaris, Muskoka Lake, Ontario P0B 1B0, Canada
Cudlip MR & MRS Charles T (Page—Brittain Bardes) | ☎ (401) 846-8029
   MISS Charlotte L . . . . | "Hopedene"
   JUNIORS MISS Mary B . . . . | Cliff Av, Newport, RI *02840*
   MISS Olivia M Page . . . . |
   MR Blakely C Page . . . . |
Cullen MR & MRS George L (Marie E Le Fort)
   ☎ (609) 399-1831 . . 214 N Point Rd, Ocean City, NJ *08226*
Culman MR & MRS Peter W (Anne S La Farge) . . . . | "La Farge House"
   MR John La F . . . . | Tuckernuck Island, Nantucket, MA *02554*
   MR P William S . . . . |
Culver MRS Bertram B JR (Jane Metcalfe)
   ☎ (616) 526-2866 . . Cottage 8, Harbor Point, MI *49740*
Cummings MR & MRS Edward McL (Hélène de Marcellus) . . . . | ☎ (011-33-50) 31-65-40-17
   MISS Rose . . . . | "Maillot" 14130 Bonneville-la-Louvet, France
Cummings MR Francis P
   ☎ (518) 523-3060 . . 56 Stevens Rd, Lake Placid, NY *12946-1124*
Cummings DR & MRS Harlan G (Robinson—Virginia De B Hinman)
   ☎ (508) 627-8316 . . PO Box 1163, Edgartown, MA *02539*
Cummings MRS Minnette H (Minnette L Hunsiker)
   ☎ (207) 422-6707 . . PO Box 126, Sorrento, ME *04677*

Cummings MR & MRS Robert C (Georgia A Donaldson)
   ☎ (905) 894-0855 . . 4407 Erie Rd, Bay Beach, Ridgeway, Ontario L0S 1B0, Canada
Cummings MR & MRS Sean H (Suzanne P Swift) . . . | ☎ (508) 362-3465
   MISS Elizabeth R . . . . | 2934 Main St,
   MISS Caroline H . . . . | Box 15, Barnstable, MA *02630*
Cunningham MR & MRS Colin McA (Evelyn M Soule)
   ☎ (207) 846-4142 . . "Pemasong" Little John Island, Yarmouth, ME *04096*
Cunningham MRS John H (Jill P Storey)
   ☎ (508) 748-0632 . . "The Dolphins" 75 Moorings Rd, Marion, MA *02738*
Cunningham MR & MRS John J (Miller—Gordon—Karen R Kreidler)
   ☎ (908) 892-4790 . . 225 Channel Lane, Mantoloking, NJ *08738*
Curran MRS Ann Pew (Holton—Ann S Pew) . . . . . | ☎ (970) 586-0950
   MR William T . . . . | "Crocker Ranch"
   MR Charles C . . . . | Estes Park, CO *80517*
   MISS Alexandra C Holton . . . . |
   MR John M Holton 3d . . . . |
Curran MR & MRS Maurice J 3d (Kate Ewing Walker) . . . . | ☎ (207) 563-3420 Barroll's Point, Newcastle, ME *04553*
   MR Maurice J 4th . . . . |
   MR Coalter Cabell . . . . |
Curran MR & MRS William G JR (Richards—Paula D Haworth) . . . . | ☎ (011-353-21) 334-149
   MISS Paola V . . . . | "Dereen House"
   MISS Melissa S . . . . | Coachford, Co Cork, Ireland
Currey MR & MRS Brownlee O JR (Agneta Akerlund)
   ☎ (516) 283-5612 . . 569 Ox Pasture Rd, PO Box 1545, Southampton, NY *11969*
Currie MR & MRS Patrick R (Carol W Hedblom) . . . | ☎ (616) 335-5072
   JUNIORS MISS Emily H . . . . | 6700 Cherry St, Holland, MI *49423*
Currier MR & MRS C Bertram (M Catharine Blake)
   ☎ (508) 349-9757 . . Chequesset Neck Rd, Wellfleet, MA *02667*
Currier DR & MRS Charles B JR (Lucille A Anstine) | ☎ (508) 349-6617
   MISS Anna L . . . . | "Friendship Cottage"
   MISS Elizabeth A . . . . | Chequesset Neck Rd, Wellfleet, MA *02667*
   MR Charles B 3d . . . . |
   JUNIORS MR William C . . . . |
Currier MR & MRS E Gray (Mary J Pfile) . . . . | ☎ (970) 223-7277
   JUNIORS MISS Katharine E . . . . | "Shivering Timbers" 416 N Pearl St, Ft Collins, CO *80521*
Curry MR Henry M 3d
   ☎ (941) 262-7652 . . "Whale's Folly" 1963 Gulf Shore Blvd S, Naples, FL *33940*
Curtis MISS Diane
   ☎ (616) 526-5364 . . Box 4436, 36 Beach Dv, Wequetonsing, MI *49740*

Curtis DR & MRS Earnest M JR (Anne D McShane) .
  MR Richard L . . . .
  ☎ (334) 928-8946
  PO Box 341,
  Point Clear, AL
  36546

Curtis MR & MRS John N (Helen Akeroyd) . . . .
  MISS Judith A . . . .
  ☎ (508) 748-0634
  50 Point Rd,
  Marion, MA *02738*

Curtis REV DR & MRS Lawrence R (Helen L Dickey)
  ☎ (518) 494-2477 . . Riparius, NY *12862*

Curtis MRS McCall (Ward—Beachboard—Anne L Curtis)
  ☎ (915) 597-2616 . . Z-Bar Ranch, Brady, TX *76825*

Curtis MR William G 5th . . of
  ☎ (516) 576-9034 . . ''Girl's Cover'' Bobcat Basin, Keene Valley, NY *12942*
  ☎ (401) 846-0327 . . ''Nethercliffe'' 192 Ruggles Av, Newport, RI *02840*

Cushing MR & MRS Howard G JR (Griscom—Nora G Knott) . . . .
  JUNIORS MR Howard G 3d . . . .
  ☎ (401) 847-3322
  ''The Ledges''
  Ocean Av, Newport,
  RI *02840*

Cushing MRS Justine C (Justine B Cutting) . . . .
  MISS Justine B . . . .
  ☎ (516) 283-0863
  53 Meadow Lane,
  Southampton, NY
  11968

Cushing MISS Margaret C
  ☎ (508) 927-0290 . . ''The Cottage'' 171 West St, Beverly Farms, MA *01915*

Cushman MR Allerton
  ☎ (604) 468-9590 . . Box 67, Seacrest, 1400 Dorcas Point Rd, Nanoose Bay, BC V0R 2R0, Canada

Cushman MR & MRS Allerton JR (Gottschalk—
  Carole M D von T Janowski) ⚓ . . . .
  MR Adam W H Gottschalk . . . .
  ☎ (207) 326-4438
  Box 92, Rte 175,
  North Brooksville,
  ME *04617*

Cushman DR & MRS Paul JR (Paulette Bessire) . . of
  ☎ (516) 367-7516 . . 1348 Ridge Rd, Laurel Hollow, Syosset, NY *11791*
  ☎ (508) 790-7863 . . 875 Great Island Rd, West Yarmouth, MA *02673*

Cutler MRS Anne H (Anne W Hoffman)
  ☎ (516) 287-4132 . . 214 Hill St, Southampton, NY *11968*

Cutler MR & MRS E Newton JR (Beverly Waring)
  ☎ (508) 627-4754 . . ''Second Wind'' Box 554, Edgartown, MA *02539*

Cutler MR & MRS E Newton 3d (Pell—Alexandra C Moulton) . . . .
  MISS Allison M Pell . . . .
  JUNIORS MR Peter J Pell JR . . . .
  Box 1439,
  Edgartown, MA
  02539

Cutler MR & MRS Eric (Nancy Ware)
  ☎ (603) 284-6973 . . Metcalf Rd, Center Sandwich, NH *03227*

Cutler MR & MRS John W (Davisson—Marietta Howe)
  ☎ (207) 244-3960 . . ''Wild Wings'' Main St, Box 308, Southwest Harbor, ME *04679*

Cutler MR & MRS Richard M (Mary R Cecil)
  153 Trenholm Rd, Flat Rock, NC *28731*

Cutler MR & MRS Stewart L (Anne W Fox)
  ☎ (516) 788-7366 . . Fishers Island, NY *06390*

Cutter MISS Amanda H . . see W A W Stewart 3d
Cutter MISS Kimberly E . . see W A W Stewart 3d

Cutting MR & MRS George W JR (Lucy Pulling)
  ☎ (907) 235-6494 . . PO Box 1747, Homer, AK *99603*

Cutts DR & MRS Morgan (Cornell—Suzanne J Herrick)
  ☎ (401) 635-1686 . . 73 Quaker Hill Farm Rd, Little Compton, RI *02837*

Czoernig von Czernhausen MR & MRS Carl E JR (Martha F Yeaw)
  ☎ (216) 647-5154 . . 52325 Rte 18 W, Wellington, OH *44090*

D

Daane MR & MRS J Dewey (Barbara W McMann)
  ☎ (616) 264-9250 . . General Delivery, Elk Rapids, MI *49629*

Daine MRS Robert A (Barbara H Hoge) . . . .
  MR James H . . . .
  ☎ (516) 583-8034
  Point O'Woods, NY
  11706

Dale MR & MRS Edwin L JR (Haythorne—Cross—Homet—Meredith A Morgan)
  ☎ (508) 420-1772 . . 7 Blue Heron Dv, Osterville, MA *02655*

Dale MR Neal W
  ☎ (207) 644-8313 . . ''Bayledge'' HC 64, Box 211, Eastside Rd, South Bristol, ME *04568*

Dall MR & MRS Stewart M (Margaret Meyerkort)
  Bisby Lodge, Thendara, NY *13472*

Dallett MR & MRS Matthew C (Mary E Pritchard)
  ☎ (207) 359-4663 . . Naskeag Point, Brooklin, ME *04616*

Dalley MR & MRS Lawrence C (Agnes L Dunn)
  ☎ (508) 693-3966 . . Holly Tree Lane, RD 168, Vineyard Haven, MA *02568*

Dallman COL & MRS James H (Elizabeth W Arnold) USA.
  ☎ (616) 335-8711 . . ''Stack Arms'' 2425 Michigan Walk, Macatawa, MI *49434*

Dalva COL & MRS David L II (Margaret Gelinas) USAR. . . . .
  MR David L III . . . .
  ☎ (516) 288-8529
  ''Toad Hill''
  1 Homans Av,
  Quiogue, NY *11978*

Daly MR & MRS Donald F (Sandra R Godfrey)
  ☎ (516) 583-9249 . . Point O'Woods, NY *11706*

Daly MAJ & MRS Thomas B (Lewis—Patricia H Mueller) USA. . . . .
  MISS Jennifer I . . . .
  MR Michael J . . . .
  JUNIORS MR Timothy M . . . .
  19 Nichols Bay,
  Grand Isle, VT
  05458

Dalzell MR & MRS Robert F JR (Lee Baldwin) . . . . . .
  MR Adams A . . . .
  ☎ (207) 647-2667
  Sweden, Harrison,
  ME *04040*

Dame MR & MRS Thomas J (Alexandra Jensen) . . . .
  MISS Laura . . . .
  ☎ (518) 891-2538
  ''Wa A Wa''
  Onchiota, NY *12968*

Dame MR W Page 3d . . . .
  MISS L Alexandra . . . .
  MR W Page 4th . . . .
  ☎ (819) 842-2477
  ''Beau Pré''
  North Hatley,
  Quebec J0B 2C0,
  Canada

Dame MRS William Page (Harriet C Brent)
 ☎ (819) 842-2477.. "Beau Pré" North Hatley, Quebec J0B 2C0, Canada
Damgard MR John M 2d
 Meadow Club, First Neck Lane, Southampton, NY *11968*
Damgard MISS Julie M.. see R P E Leeds
Damgard MR & MRS Michael T (Lucy G Siewers).. see R P E Leeds
Damon MR & MRS Lawrence B (Elisabeth T Wheeler)
 ☎ (508) 432-0220.. "Tide River" 44 Chase St, West Harwich, MA *02671*
Dana MR & MRS David T (Swasey—Potter—Gladys Crocker)
 ☎ (508) 748-2972.. 10 South St, Box 585, Marion, MA *02738*
Dane MR Edward (Barker—Jean-Lamont Proctor).. of
 ☎ (603) 253-4583.. "Hearthstone" RR 1, Box 108, Center Harbor, NH *03226*
 ☎ (617) 326-3596.. Fox Hill Village D535, 10 Longwood Dv, Westwood, MA *02090*
Dane MR & MRS Herbert P (Sally J Johnson) . . . . . . | ☎ (603) 253-6920
 MISS Harriet P. . . . . | "Bulrush Point"
 MISS Lucy B. . . . . | Center Harbor, NH
 JUNIORS MR Daniel S . . . . | *03226*
Danforth MR & MRS A Edwards (Mary E Wagley)
 ☎ (508) 257-9803.. 10 King St, PO Box 714, Siasconset, MA *02564*
Danforth MR & MRS Murray S 3d (Judith C Pollard) | ☎ (401) 635-4807
 JUNIORS MISS Merebea M . . . . | "Prairie Brook
                                                            | Farm" 16B Old W
                                                            | Main Rd, Little
                                                            | Compton, RI *02837*
Danforth MR & MRS Theodore N (Laura B Walker) . | ☎ (516) 283-2777
 MISS Alexandra S . . . . | 274 Little Plains Rd,
 MR Theodore N JR . . . . | Southampton, NY
 MR Bryan N . . . . | *11968*
 JUNIORS MISS Laura . . . . |
D'Angelo MR & MRS Christopher Scott (Betsy Hart | ☎ (609) 494-0979
 Josephs) . . . . | "Arundel"
 JUNIORS MR J Robert . . . . | Norfolk Place,
                                                            | Harvey Cedars, NJ
                                                            | *08008*
Dangler MR David W
 ☎ (608) 935-5274.. "Tor" Norwegian Hollow Rd, Dodgeville, WI *53533*
Daniel MRS Lewis B (Marjorie L Gibson)
 ☎ (518) 523-3863.. Box 786, Lake Placid, NY *12946*
Daniel MRS Polly Reed (Polly G Reed)
 ☎ (704) 479-3221.. Robbinsville, NC *28771*
Dann MR E Webster—⚓
 ☎ (011-44) 955-9425.. "Windward Cove" Co Caithness, Wick KW1 4LG, Scotland
Dann MRS Joan H (Joan B Harriman)
 ☎ (905) 834-4439.. "The Bog" Lorraine, Port Colborne, Ontario L3K 5V3, Canada
Daras MR & MRS Dimitri J (Wendy H A Brewer)
 ☎ (860) 388-0236.. "Red Barn" 34 Pettipaug Av, Fenwick, CT *06475*

Darby MR & MRS D Weston JR (Margarette A | ☎ (508) 228-2312
 Kortina) . . . . | "Summer's Head"
 MR Bruce R B. . . . . | 3 Pleasant St,
                                                                     | Nantucket, MA
                                                                     | *02554*
D'Arcy MR & MRS William C JR (Lillyblad—June Berkey)
 ☎ (507) 280-0086.. 1710 Lakeview Dv SW, Rochester, MN *55902*
Darling COL (RET) & MRS Joseph W McNab (Egbert | ☎ (609) 884-7106
 —Cynthia A Hearne) USA. . . . . | "Pancoast Cottage"
 JUNIORS MR Joseph H McNab . . . . | 1221 Maryland Av,
 MR Garth L Egbert. . . . . | Cape May, NJ
                                                                     | *08204*
Darlington MR & MRS Harry (Jennie Russell) ⚓ . . | ☎ (207) 276-3769
 MR Harry 4th . . . . | "Sound Edge"
                                                                     | Manchester Rd,
                                                                     | Northeast Harbor,
                                                                     | ME *04662*
Darlington MRS McCullough (Edith F Pearson)
 ☎ (540) 364-2192.. "Grouse House" The Plains, VA *22171*
Darlington MISS Rebecca P
 ☎ (302) 227-0146.. "The Perch" 222 Stockley St, Rehoboth Beach, DE *19971*
Darman MR & MRS Richard G (Kathleen Emmet) .. | "Easter Point"
 MR William T E . . . . | Boldwater,
 JUNIORS MR Jonathan W E . . . . | Edgartown, MA
                                                                     | *02539*
Darneille MRS Hopewell H (Virginia Clark)
 ☎ (207) 647-5524.. "Nawandyn" RR 3, Box 1074, Bridgton, ME *04009*
Darrell MRS George H (Marjorie S Hamill)
 ☎ (860) 535-1227.. Box 409, Stonington, CT *06378*
Darrell MRS Norris (Churchill—Mary D Hand)
 ☎ (914) PO4-5564.. Bedford, NY *10506*
Daub MR & MRS William J 3d (Edith T West)
 ☎ (307) 455-2704.. "Trail Lake Ranch" Box 431, Dubois, WY *82513*
Dauch MRS Alan D (Heezen—Wilmot—E Christine de Schirding)
 ☎ (412) 593-2810.. Pike Run Country Club, Jones Mills, PA *15646*
Davant MR & MRS James W (Mary E Westlake)
 ☎ (516) 674-8130.. PO Box 367, Locust Valley, NY *11560*
Davenport MR & MRS David W (Carol J Babcock)
 ☎ (802) 649-2314.. "The Tepee" Tigertown Rd, Box 1237, Norwich, VT *05055*
Davenport MRS Russell W (Ladd—Natalie Potter)
 ☎ (413) 528-2227.. "Rivendell" Stony Brook Rd, Great Barrington, MA *01230-2100*
Davidge MISS Dorsey
 ☎ (603) 788-2728.. Prospect Farm, Prospect Rd, Lancaster, NH *03584*
Davidge MR & MRS John W 3d (Engel—Deborah M Lott)
 ☎ (603) 788-2728.. Prospect Farm, Prospect Rd, Lancaster, NH *03584*
Davidson MRS Marian J (Marian Q Jackson) . . . . . | ☎ (516) 788-7676
 MISS Helen A . . . . | Fishers Island, NY
 MISS Marian L . . . . | *06390*
 MR Matthew H . . . . |
Davidson MRS Norman L (Frank—Dorothy H Pagenstecher)
 ☎ (610) 388-2642.. Crosslands, Cadbury Apt 49, Kennett Square, PA *19348*

Davidson MR & MRS Philip J (Ward—Gordon—Campbell—Campbell—Winifred E Miller) . . . .
    MISS Katharine G Gordon . . . .
☎ (412) 963-6969
207 Kensington Court, Fox Hall, Pittsburgh, PA *15238*

Davidson MR & MRS Stuart C (Sally L Foulis)
    ☎ (970) 925-7952 . . North of Nell Apt 3K, 555 E Durant Av, Aspen, CO *81611*

David-Weill MR & MRS Michel A (Hélène Lehideux)
    "Vikings Cove" Peacock Lane, Locust Valley, NY *11560*

Davies DR & MRS Edward A (Suzanne E Thompson)
    ☎ (203) 938-3292 . . "Chimney Site" Old Foundry Rd, Redding Ridge, CT *06876*

Davies MR & MRS John H (Nagy—Frances P Roberts) . . . .
    MISS Sarah M . . . .
    MR Daniel B . . . .
☎ (410) 867-1630
Etowah Farm, Rte 2, Harwood, MD *20776*

Davies MISS Sarah M . . see MRS S G Bingham
Davies MR Stephen T . . see MRS S G Bingham
Davis MRS Atkinson (Marguerite P Atkinson)
    ☎ (203) 656-0233 . . 708 Hollow Tree Ridge Rd, Darien, CT *06820*

Davis MR & MRS Chester R JR (Anne Meserve) . . . . .
    MISS Julia S . . . .
    MISS Elizabeth M . . . .
☎ (715) 588-3733
Camp Wipigaki, Lac du Flambeau, WI *54538*

Davis MR Christopher L . . . .
    JUNIORS MR George P . . . .
"Golden Acres" Rte 1, Box 59, Nanjemoy, MD *20662*

Davis MR & MRS Duncan S (Hoffmann—Lenore Fleschler) . . . .
    MR Duncan C . . . .
☎ (916) 546-2019
"Agate Cottage" Box 444, Carnelian Bay, CA *96140*

Davis MR & MRS Dwight F 3d (Anne Marie L Cassinari) . . . .
    MR Christopher P . . . .
☎ (203) 637-8990
333 Palmer Hill Rd, Riverside, CT *06878*

Davis DR E William JR
    ☎ (516) 334-0073 . . Box 227, 36 Old Westbury Rd, Old Westbury, NY *11568*

Davis MR & MRS Edward S (Mueenuddin—Barbara J Thompson)
    ☎ (516) 324-3808 . . 21 Old Stone H'way, East Hampton, NY *11937*

Davis MRS Ferdinand H (Hudson—Jane Rule)
    ☎ (508) 349-3919 . . Box 171, Truro, MA *02666*

Davis MISS Helen H
    ☎ (516) 288-1240 . . "Velkommen Hus" Westhampton Beach, NY *11978*

Davis MR & MRS J Hornor 4th (Frederica M Miller)
    ☎ (401) 348-8994 . . "Tredegar" 22 Plimpton Rd, Watch Hill, RI *02891*

Davis MR & MRS J Staige 3d (Martha A Wolcott)
    ☎ (207) 335-2121 . . "Barter Creek" Isle au Haut, ME *04645*

Davis MISS Kirsten M . . see W P Jones
Davis MR & MRS Michael Hamilton (Daphne D Barnard)
    ☎ (860) 535-0420 . . "The Farmhouse" Tipping Rock Rd, Stonington, CT *06378*

Davis MR & MRS Nathanael V (Lois H Thompson)
    ☎ (508) 428-2109 . . 50 Fox Island Rd, Box 309, Osterville, MA *02655*

Davis MR & MRS Nathaniel (Elizabeth K Creese) . . .
    MR James C . . . .
    MR Thomas R . . . .
☎ (518) 576-4456
Keene Valley, NY *12943*

Davis MRS Newlin F (Elizabeth T Sullivan)
    ☎ (508) 228-9478 . . "Broom Patch" 1 Lincoln Av, Nantucket, MA *02554*

Davis MR & MRS Orlin (Lisa J Mackintosh)
    ☎ (518) 963-7670 . . "Old Brick Shoolhouse" PO Box 25, Elm St, Essex, NY *12936*

Davis MR R Neville
    ☎ (011-351-34) 382-871 . . Largo Conselheiro Queiroz 18, 3810 Aveiro, Portugal

Davis MR Robert E . . see MRS K E Jackson
Davis MR & MRS Robert W (Alice L R Sadtler) . . . .
    MISS Julie S . . . .
    MISS Paige W . . . .
    MR Gavin H II . . . .
☎ (706) 265-3410
"The Consortium" Holly Hill, Dawsonville, GA *30534*

Davis MR & MRS Scott L (Martin—Christina Williams) . . . .
    MR Scott L JR . . . .
"Bears Crossing" West Dover, VT *05356*

Davis MRS Shelby Cullom (Kathryn E Waterman)
    ☎ (207) 276-5519 . . "Crestwood" School House Ledge, Northeast Harbor, ME *04662*

Davis MRS W Bowdoin (Trimper—Savage—Carol Bradley)
    ☎ (607) 547-2346 . . "Annsfield" Lake Rd, Box 662, Cooperstown, NY *13326*

Davis MR W Bowdoin JR
    Isle au Haut, ME *04645*

Davis MR & MRS Wendell JR (Penelope Case) . . . . . .
    MISS Jennifer C . . . .
    MISS Virginia W . . . .
    MR Peter T . . . .
☎ (518) 781-4887
"Sunnycrest" Upper Queechy Rd, Canaan, NY *12029*

Davis REV & MRS William M (Louise McC Eddy)
    ☎ (716) 357-2095 . . "Liberty Hall" 14 McClintock Av, Chautauqua, NY *14722*

Davis MR & MRS William R Q (Carey E Anderson-Talmage)
    ☎ (970) 476-7766 . . 1160 Sandstone Dv, Vail, CO *81657*

Davison MR & MRS Charles H (Lessie H L Busbee)
    ☎ (203) 869-3825 . . 35 Meadow Wood Dv, Greenwich, CT *06830*

Davison MR & MRS Daniel P (Catherine Cheremeteff) ⚓
    ☎ (516) 676-0161 . . 90 Peacock Lane, Locust Valley, NY *11560*

Davison MR & MRS George P (Judith F Rivkin)
    ☎ (516) 674-9138 . . 70 Peacock Lane, Locust Valley, NY *11560*

Davison-Ackley MR George W
    ☎ (914) 677-8405 . . "Overlook Farm" RD 3, Box 201, Millbrook, NY *12545*

Davlin MR H Dalton . . see E M de Windt
Davlin MISS Virginia-Marie . . see E M de Windt
Davol DR & MRS (DR) Peter B (Anna Y C Lo) . . . . . .
    MR Samuel B . . . .
    MR Angus P . . . .
☎ (508) 349-1713
Holsberry Lane, Truro, MA *02666*

Davol DR & MRS Rector T (Evers—Anne Gruen)
    ☎ (203) 531-6134 . . Box 11208, Greenwich, CT *06831*

Davol MR Ward M
    ☎ (508) 228-0413 . . "Bluefish Cottage" Washing Pond Rd, Nantucket, MA *02554*

Dawson MR & MRS Benjamin G (Cornelia A Barrett)
"Wunnegin" 551 W Main Rd, Little Compton, RI *02837*
Dawson MR John S W
☎ (516) 653-5498 . . "The Anchorage" Dune Rd, Quogue, NY *11959*
Dawson MR & MRS Matthew B (Pamela Webb)
☎ (401) 635-8801 . . 551 W Main Rd, Little Compton, RI *02837*
Day MR & MRS H Mason (M Germana D Fabbri)
☎ (805) 565-3820 . . 1650 Moore Rd, Montecito, CA *93108*
Dayton MR & MRS S Grey JR (Slaymaker—Margaret A Munro) ⚓
☎ (902) 275-3416 . . Chester, Nova Scotia B0J 1J0, Canada
Dayton MR & MRS William B 3d (Ruth E MacLaren)
☎ (207) 367-2633 . . "The Flying Bridge" RR 1, Box 2944, Stonington, ME *04681*
Dean MRS Arthur H (Mary T Marden)
☎ (508) 257-6518 . . "Sandpipers" Box 234, Siasconset, MA *02564*
Dean MR & MRS Bruce C (Pamela M Prator)
Shore Rd, Manset, ME *04656*
Dean COL (RET) & MRS Guy K 3d (Victoria Norris) USA . . . .
  MISS Anne T W . . . .
  JUNIORS MR Andrew B N . . . .
  ☎ (717) 595-2058 "Todburn" C408, Buck Hill Falls, PA *18323*
Dean MR & MRS J Simpson JR (McConnell—Margaret A Mahler)
☎ (302) 655-7777 . . "Redley" PO Box 4039, Greenville, DE *19807*
Deane MR & MRS Daniel Thomas (Mary K McMurry) . . . .
  MISS Ann P . . . .
  ☎ (609) 399-6372 22 Corinthian Av, Ocean City, NJ *08226*
Dearie MR & MRS Christopher F (Direxa V Dick) . . .
  MISS Direxa V . . . .
  MISS Honora A . . . .
  MR Christopher F JR . . . .
  JUNIORS MR William D . . . .
  JUNIORS MR John C . . . .
  ☎ (516) 626-9773 "Panda's Ledge" Clock Tower Lane, Old Westbury, NY *11568*
de Bary MR & MRS Marquette (Du Vivier—Gary—Patricia E Murrill)
☎ (516) 283-7812 . . 155-3 Hill St, Southampton, NY *11968*
Debevoise MRS Thomas M 2d (Ann Taylor)
☎ (802) 457-1186 . . "Pinnacle Farm" RR 2, Box 787, Cox Rd, Woodstock, VT *05091*
de Blank MR & MRS Paul M B (Laura T Kennedy) . .
  MISS J Gabriel B . . . .
  MR M J Bastiaan . . . .
  MR Peter M K . . . .
  ☎ (508) 775-3010 "Summer Salt" off Scudder Av, Hyannis Port, MA *02647*
de Bragança MR & MRS Miguel (Barbara H Fales)
☎ (508) 693-9511 . . "Windyhill" Old County Rd, West Tisbury, MA *02575*
de Braux MISS Ariane . . see MRS L K Bullock
de Buys MRS Harry D (Elizabeth P Handy)
☎ (518) 543-8863 . . "Last Resort" Hague, NY *12836*
de Castro MR & MRS J Edmund JR (Melissa P Sullivan) ⚓ . . . .
  MISS Alicia P . . . .
  MR Julian E 3d . . . .
  MR Samuel F . . . .
  Honeymoon Island, Box 9, Chippewa Bay, NY *13623*

de Clairville MR & MRS Raymond (Gwendolyn K Gwynne)
☎ (617) 329-9128 . . Fox Hill Village 125, 10 Longwood Dv, Westwood, MA *02090*
de Cordova MR & MRS Eustace JR (Biddle—Peniston —Aimée H Crossan) . . . .
  MR & MRS E Winchester Peniston (S Lyerly Spöngberg) . . . .
  ☎ (516) 653-6612 "Shad Row" 8 Barker Lane, Box 1368, Quogue, NY *11959*
de Dominicis MR & MRS Danilo M (Averyl S Phipps) . . . .
  JUNIORS MISS Daphne P . . . .
  ☎ (508) 993-7674 Nonquitt, MA *02748*
Deeds JUNIORS MR Blake . . see D R Taylor
Deely MR & MRS James S (Patricia S Johnson)
☎ (413) 298-4904 . . "Ingleside" Stockbridge, MA *01262*
Deely MR & MRS Philip S (Hilary L Somers) . . . .
  MISS Mary S . . . .
  ☎ (207) 767-5815 "Lindamarl" 28 Cloyster Rd, South Portland, ME *04106*
de Forest MRS Taber (Marion Archbald)
☎ (603) 876-4517 . . "Sky Farm" Marlborough, NH *03455*
Defty MRS S Bixby (Sarah T Bixby)
☎ (518) 644-2155 . . Federal Hill Farm, Box 110X, Bolton Landing, NY *12814*
de Grazia MR & MRS Sebastian (Ballantine—Lucia B Heffelfinger) . . . .
  MR Tancredi . . . .
  ☎ (011-39-81) 837-2160 "La Sciucella" via Ceselle 7, 80071 Anacapri, Italy
de Gunzburg BRN & BRNSS Dimitri (Brokaw—Ingham— Shawn McWeeney)
☎ (011-33) 90-72-29-39 . . "Le Mas de Pierredon" rte de Bonnieux D3, Menerbe, France
de Heeren MRS Rodman A (Lopes—Aimée de Sa Sottomaior)
☎ (011-33-59) 24-07-29 . . "Villa La Roseraie" 12 rue Martias, 64200 Biarritz, France
de Hemricourt de Grunne CT Bernard & CTSS (Deming P Beyer)
☎ (011-33) 71-59-40-52 . . "Château de Ribes" F43130 Par Retournac, France
Dejoux MR Jacques H L
"La Sauzée" 07 Albon d'Ardèche, France
de Kay MR & MRS George C (Booke—Miranda Knickerbocker) . . . .
  MISS Sarah H . . . .
  MR Colman D . . . .
  MR Charles A . . . .
  ☎ (860) 535-1094 "The Hill" Grand St, Stonington, CT *06378*
de Kertanguy CTE Loic & CTSSE (Rebecca D Williams) . . . .
  MISS Valerie . . . .
  ☎ (516) 324-8794 Box 1205, East Hampton, NY *11937*
de Labar MRS Margot (Grill—Margot A Hoagland de Labar)
☎ (909) 679-7742 . . 27526 Calle Ganado, Sun City, CA *92586*
Delafield MISS Cecily
☎ (516) 584-5693 . . 62 Moriches Rd, St James, NY *11780*

Delafield MR & MRS J Dennis (Jo Ann M Sawyer) . . of ☎ (516)862-8386
    MR John Dennis JR . . . . 62 Moriches Rd,
St James, NY *11780*
☎ (518) 962-4925
"October Farm"
Box 452, Westport,
NY *12993*

Deland MRS F Stanton JR (Susan R Reeves)
    ☎ (508) 748-0023 . . 498 Point Rd, Marion, MA *02738*

Delaney MR & MRS Timothy G (Farr—Katherine E | PO Box 443,
    Putnam) . . . . Edgartown, MA
    JUNIORS MISS Eleanor L Putnam-Farr *02539*

de la Renta MR & MRS Oscar (Reed—Anne F | ☎ (860) 927-4044
    Engelhard) . . . . "Brook Hill Farm"
    MISS P J Eliza Reed . . . . Skiff Mountain Rd,
    MR Charles V Reed . . . . Kent, CT *06757*

de Lesseps MRS Tauni (Downs—Fougner—Harjes—Schoales—
    Tauni de Lesseps)
    ☎ (203) 661-1717 . . "Sauzir" 80 Oneida Dv, Greenwich, CT *06830*

de Liagre MR & MRS Nicholas (Virginia O'Neil)
    ☎ (516) 324-1144 . . "Swan Cove" H'way-Behind-The-Pond,
East Hampton, NY *11937*

de Limur MR & MRS Charles (Eleanor S Walsh)
    ☎ (707) 963-3726 . . "Limur Winery" 771 Sage Canyon Rd, St Helena,
CA *94574*

Dellenbaugh MR & MRS Geoffrey G (Joanna L | ☎ (603) 253-6959
    Campbell) . . . . "Beechwood"
    MISS Virginia L . . . . High Haith Rd,
    MR Samuel . . . . Center Harbor, NH
    JUNIORS MISS Mary H *03226*

de Lyrot CTE Alain & CTSSE (Mary E Allen) . . . . . . | ☎ (011-33-97)
    MR Antoine 57-31-80
"Ile Renaud"
Locmariaquer,
56740 Morbihan,
France

de Lyrot MR & MRS Hervé J (Katy M Goffre)
    ☎ (011-33-97) 57-31-80 . . "Ile Renaud" Locmariaquer,
56740 Morbihan, France

Demarest MR & MRS William (Millar—Eluned A McLaren)
    ☎ (508) 758-4610 . . Box 1013, Mattapoisett, MA *02739*

de Margitay MR & MRS Gedeon (Harris—Virginia V Martin)
    ☎ (717) 775-7884 . . Locke Farms, Box 1526, Hawley, PA *18428*

de Marneffe DR & MRS Francis (Hopkins—Barbara C Rowe)
    ☎ (603) 563-8434 . . "Skywood" Dublin, NH *03444*

de Mello MR & MRS Michael E S S (Deborah Fiuza)
    ☎ (516) 283-0370 . . "Mayday" Halsey Neck Lane, Box 600,
Southampton, NY *11968*

de Menocal MR & MRS Daniel C (Grace W Niedringhaus)
    ☎ (508) 228-0490 . . 1 Quarter Mile Hill, Nantucket, MA *02554*

de Menocal MR & MRS George W (Sarah S Lyon)
    ☎ (508) 228-0490 . . 1 Quarter Mile Hill, Nantucket, MA *02554*

de Mouchy DUKE & DCHSS (Moseley—Luxembourg—Joan D Dillon)
    ☎ (207) 734-6671 . . "Little Dillon" Box 248, Islesboro, ME *04848*

Dempsey MR & MRS John B 2d (Marie T Gravel) . . . | ☎ (216) 541-1600
    MR James H 3d . . . . 1 Bratenahl Place,
Apt 1107, Bratenahl,
Cleveland, OH
44108-1155
Aug 1 . .
☎ (418) 665-3017
18 Blvd des
Falaises, Box 578,
Murray Bay,
Pointe-au-Pic,
Quebec G0T 1M0,
Canada

de Narvaez MRS Felix (Gimbel—Denney—Fern Tailer)
    ☎ (804) 979-6107 . . Forest Hill Plantation, Rte 9, Box 20A, H'way 729,
Charlottesville, VA *22901*

Denckla MR & MRS C Paul JR (Catherine C Ham)
    ☎ (401) 635-1655 . . 30 Old Bull Lane, Little Compton, RI *02837*

de Neufville MR & MRS Richard (Virginia D Lyons)
    ☎ (508) 636-7266 . . 1101 Horseneck Rd, Westport, MA *02790*

Denham MR & MRS William B JR (Marvel— | ☎ (860) 535-0484
    Margaret S Springer) . . . . "Gull Aerie"
    JUNIORS MISS Margaret S . . . . 42 Quanaduck Rd,
    MR James M D Marvel . . . . Stonington, CT
06378

Denison MRS Julie H (Piper—Julie C Hoffer)
    ☎ (518) 644-2562 . . "High Huddle" Trout Lake, Bolton Landing,
NY *12824*

Dennett MRS Roger H (Barbara A Brown)
189 E Rock Rd, New Haven, CT *06511*

Dennis DR & MRS Michael T B (Phyllis D Harrison) | ☎ (207) 276-3034
    MISS Melinda D . . . . "Little Birches"
    MR Michael T B JR . . . . Box 394,
    MR Phillip S . . . . Northeast Harbor,
ME *04662*

Dennis MR & MRS Samuel S 3d (Lillian E Williamson) ⛵
on board Respite III" Duxbury, MA *02331*

Dennis MR & MRS Thomas G (Makrianes—Diane J Milam)
    ☎ (904) 285-4098 . . "Barn on the Beach" 501 Ponte Vedra Blvd,
Ponte Vedra Beach, FL *32082*

Dennison MR & MRS Charles E P (Wharton—Jane D Russell)
    ☎ (802) 362-4918 . . Box 2, Manchester, VT *05254*

Dennison MR & MRS E Allen (Frances I Ferry) ⛵
    ☎ (508) 693-1005 . . West Chop, MA *02573*

Denny MR & MRS Charles S (Ann M Hodges)
    ☎ (603) 763-4447 . . 12 Davis Hill Rd, New London, NH *03257*

Denny MR & MRS John H (Margaret A McGuinness) | ☎ (518) 576-4738
    MR John H JR . . . . "Highland Cottage"
Keene Valley, NY
12943

DeNormandie MRS Tina Rathborne (Ernestine N Rathborne)
    ☎ (860) 435-0718 . . 69 Selleck Hill Rd, Salisbury, CT *06068*

de Noüe VCTE Jehan-Sébastien & VCTSSE (Leslie L Castle)
    ☎ (011-33) 23-96-01-51 . . "Villa St Nicolas" 19 av de Noüe,
Villers-Cotterêts, 02600 Aisne, France

Dent MR & MRS John Elliott (Sandra Slaughter) .... ☎ (803) 249-2846
MISS Sarah-Rutledge S .... 904 N Ocean Blvd,
JUNIORS MR Elliott Johnstone 3d .... Ocean Drive, SC
29582
de Pedroso MR & MRS José L (Reece—Charlotte Worthen)
☎ (207) 276-5008 .. "Rockend Way" Northeast Harbor, ME *04662*
de Peyster MR & MRS F Ashton 3d (Margo M Donahue)
☎ (516) 287-5158 .. PO Box 635, Southampton, NY *11969*
de Peyster MR & MRS F van Cortlandt (Karen D Kermode)
☎ (415) 332-6437 .. "Little Willow" 4 Sausalito Blvd, Sausalito, CA *94965*
d'Eprémesnil MR & MRS Jacques (Susan Mayes) ... ☎ (910) 686-9635
MISS Nadine Marie (Hesse—Nadine Marie 3 Bayberry Place,
d'Eprémesnil)......................... Figure Eight Island,
Wilmington, NC
28405
Derby MRS Roger A JR (Nash—Corbett—Marie K Baird)
☎ (540) 349-2420 .. "Derbyshire" PO Box 3070, Warrenton, VA *22186*
de Rham MR & MRS Casimir JR (Elizabeth M Evarts)
☎ (603) 746-3374 .. 219 Clough & Sanborn Hill Rd, Webster, NH *03303*
de Rham MR & MRS Charles (Shober—Chandlee—Ellen F Smith)
☎ (603) 823-5267 .. "Mittersill" Box 958, Franconia, NH *03580*
de Rham MRS William (Foristall—Vera K Chapin)
☎ (401) 841-5914 .. The Waves, Apt I, 61 Ledge Rd, Newport, RI *02840*
de Rham MR & MRS William (Glenna L Maduro)... ☎ (406) 763-4643
MISS Lee L .... "Rock Bottom
Ranch"
Gallatin Gateway,
MT *59730*
de Roulet MRS Vincent (Lorinda Payson) ⚓ .... ☎ (441) 293-0800
MISS Sandra .... "Old House"
Tucker's Town
HS 02, Bermuda
de Saint Phalle MR & MRS Thibaut (Smith—Mariana V Mann)
☎ (804) 336-3416 .. "Piney Point" 4408 Williams Lane, Chincoteague, VA *23336*
de San Damián MQS Carlos Figueroa & MQSE (DeWilde—Harrison—
Ross—Barbara Crass)
☎ (011-34-52) 77-17-35 .. "La Bárbara" Puente Romano,
29600 Marbella, Spain
Deshler MRS C Franklin (Nancy E Montgomery)
☎ (508) 283-4609 .. 14 Nashua Av, Gloucester, MA *01930*
Deslogé MR & MRS Stephen F (Ann H Drescher)
☎ (616) 843-4703 .. "Sancliff" Epworth Heights, Ludington, MI *49431*
Detchon MRS Elliott R (Coleman—Patricia Disston)
☎ (207) 276-3775 .. Box 868, Northeast Harbor, ME *04662*
Detchon MRS Susan L M (Susan L McGlothlin) ... ☎ (203) 245-5989
MR Elliott B .... Madison Beach
JUNIORS MR Christopher H .... Club, Madison, CT
JUNIORS MR Peter T *06443*
Detweiler MRS Lynn L (Irene B McCune) .... Bean Rd,
MISS Anne L .... Box 200B, RFD 1,
Center Harbor, NH
03226

Devaney MR & MRS Richard T (Mary G Crowell) ... ☎ (609) 399-2849
⚓ .... 12 Tobago Lane,
MISS Susan P .... Ocean City, NJ
MR Craig W *08226*
De Vault MR & MRS Walter D 3d (Catherine M Pickering)
☎ (207) 372-6625 .. "Porter House" Marshall Point Rd, Port Clyde, ME *04855*
De Vecchi MR & MRS Robert P (Duke—Douglass—Wainwright—
Betsy S Trippe)
☎ (516) 324-0185 .. 12 W Dune Lane, PO Box 1398, East Hampton, NY *11937*
de Vegh MR Pierre J
☎ (516) 653-4159 .. 95 Old Depot Rd, Quogue, NY *11959*
Deuel MISS Maggie D .. see V DeP Burroughs
Deuel JUNIORS MISS Sarah G .. see V DeP Burroughs
Devens MR & MRS Charles (Edith P Wolcott)
☎ (207) 883-2198 .. Prouts Neck, ME *04074*
Devine MRS C Robert (Lichine—Gisèle Edenbourgh)
☎ (011-33-56) 88-36-28 .. "Château Prieuré-Lichine" 33460 Margaux, France
Devine MR & MRS Henry C (Alessandra A Hillman)
☎ (203) 762-1338 .. 111 Chestnut Hill Rd, Wilton, CT *06897*
Devine MR & MRS Robert W JR (Mary K Boland)
☎ (516) 569-0600 .. Rockaway Hunting Club, Ocean Av, Lawrence, NY *11519*
Devine MRS Williams (Louise C Williams)
Star Rte 70, Box 136, Great Barrington, MA *01230*
Devitt MRS James E (Emmet—Judith B Morrell)
☎ (516) 749-0752 .. "Shell House" PO Box 281, Shelter Island Heights, NY *11965*
Dewar MR & MRS James M (Margaret L Cawley)... ☎ (011-33-16)
MISS Leah Maria....................... 85-44-41-58
"Aux Trois
Saisons" Le Prémoy
BP6, Dracy-le-Fort,
71640 Givy, France
Dewar MR & MRS Porter King F (Jennifer Sullivan)
33 Rue Charles, San Antonio, TX *78217*
Dewart REV & MRS Russell (Ann de D Stevenson)
☎ (418) 235-4635 .. 123 Languedoc Park, Tadoussac,
Quebec G0T 2A0, Canada
Dewart MR & MRS Timothy R (Ann L Koval)
☎ (418) 235-4323 .. "Tivoli" Languedoc Park, Tadoussac,
Quebec G0T 2A0, Canada
Dewey MRS Carpenter (Alexandra O'N Davies)
☎ (610) 688-1116 .. 43 Dunminning Rd, Newtown Square, PA *19073*
Dewey MR Carpenter
☎ (717) 595-2412 .. "Mountain Dew" Box 125, Cresco, PA *18326*
Dewey MR & MRS Gordon C (Frances B Dear) ..... ☎ (508) 257-6697
MISS Frances W .... 17 McKinley Av,
MR Frederick R .... Box 63, Siasconset,
MR John H D .... MA *02564*
Dewey MR & MRS Paul C G JR (Alexandra P Sheerar)
☎ (401) 348-1012 .. "Mildew Cottage" 37 Avondale Rd, Watch Hill, RI *02891*

Dewey MR & MRS Thomas E JR (Ann R Lawler) . . . . ☎ (914) 941-4847
   MISS Elizabeth D . . . . "Apple Hill"
   MR George R . . . . Box 31,
Scarborough-on-Hudson, NY *10510*

de Windt MR & MRS E Mandell (Davlin—Ennis— ☎ (603) 544-7213
  Mary D Scheffler) . . . . Spring Hill Rd, Bald
   MISS Virginia-Marie Davlin . . . . Peak Colony Club,
   MR H Dalton Davlin . . . . Melvin Village, NH
   MR Thomas W Ennis *03854*

de Wolf MR & MRS Bradford C (Laylin—Gesine Hittenkirchen,
  Rott) . . . . Bernau, Chiemsee,
   MR B Colt JR . . . . Germany
   MR Buckmaster . . . .

Diana MR & MRS Ronald S (Alix Clark)
  ☎ (207) 276-5645 . . Box 77, Northeast Harbor, ME *04662*

Dick MR & MRS C Mathews JR (Mary A Milholland)
  ☎ (401) 847-8165 . . "Ocean View" Bellevue Av, Newport, RI *02840*

Dickason MR & MRS James Frank (Linda C Stewart)
  ☎ (702) 749-5444 . . PO Box 288, 99 China Garden Court, Glenbrook, NV *89413*

Dickerman MRS William C (Livingston—Marion La B Browne)
  ☎ (508) 257-6310 . . Box 103, Siasconset, MA *02564*

Dickerson MRS John S (Engelina E Cuypers)
  ☎ (207) 439-9190 . . 62 Old Dennett Rd, Kittery, ME *03904*

Dickey MR & MRS B Gordon (Ladue—Joyce N ☎ (302) 537-9490
  Moyle) . . . . "Notion-View"
   MISS Lelia S . . . . 601 Old Post Court,
   MR Douglas G . . . . Bethany Beach, DE *19930*

Dickey MR & MRS Charles D JR (Helen B Lynch)
  ☎ (207) 276-5325 . . "Soundings" Manchester Rd, Northeast Harbor, ME *04662*

Dickey MR & MRS Robert 3d (Elizabeth P Beckwith)
  ☎ (307) 587-6802 . . "D-Key Ranch" Sunlight Basin, WY *82414*

Dickinson MR & MRS Thomas W (Rita M Harkins) . ☎ (818) 889-1167
  JUNIORS MR Joseph H . . . . "Malibou Lake"
29067 S Lakeshore Dv, Agoura, CA *91301*

Dickinson MR & MRS William R JR (Anne L Knowles)
  ☎ (616) 547-6780 . . Chicago Club, Charlevoix, MI *49720*

Dickison MR Matthew P . . see R P Paine

Dickison MISS Sara E . . see R P Paine

Diebold MR & MRS A Richard (Dorothy O Roosen)
  ☎ (860) 354-2135 . . "Toplands Farm" Roxbury, CT *06783*

Diedrick MR & MRS Arthur H JR (Tara I Stacom)
  ☎ (860) 567-5087 . . Indian Hill, Box 37, Litchfield, CT *06759*

Diesel MR & MRS John H 2d (M Brooks Armour)
  ☎ (011-47) 51-52-89-66 . . Orknygata 46, 4009 Stavanger, Norway

Diffenbach MRS John E (June G Douglas) . . . . ☎ (508) 349-2438
  MISS Molly G . . . . Zoheth Smith Way,
  JUNIORS MISS Julie N . . . . Wellfleet, MA *02667*

Diffenderffer MR & MRS C Rich (McCoy—Thouron ☎ (302) 539-2733
  —Carol V Kitchell) . . . . 9 Hampton Lane,
  JUNIORS MR George G Thouron 3d . . . . Bethany Beach, DE *19930*

Diffenderffer MR Michael K
  ☎ (808) 579-9305 . . "Lamalani Cove" 568 Hana H'way, Paia, Maui, HI *96779*

Diggs MRS James B JR (Sally P Strobel)
  ☎ (410) 524-1381 . . 11100 Coastal H'way, Apt 902, Ocean City, MD *21842*

Dike MISS Deborah A
  La Dérobade, 30630 Goudargues, France

Dill DR & MRS James N JR (McCall—Jane M French)
  ☎ (207) 288-3484 . . "Green Court" Bar Harbor, ME *04609*

Dillon MR & MRS C Douglas (Bassett—Buchanan—Sage—
  Susan Slater) . . of
  ☎ (207) 734-2274 . . Islesboro, ME *04848*
  ☎ (207) 276-3694 . . Box 1059, Northeast Harbor, ME *04662*

Dillon MR & MRS George C (Joan A Kent)
  ☎ (508) 945-0230 . . "Dead End" 149 Cotchpinicut Rd, North Chatham, MA *02650*

Dillon MR Herbert L JR
  ☎ (409) 826-6781 . . Sunset Ridge Farm, H'way 290 W, Hempstead, TX *77445*

Dillon MR R Forrest
  ☎ (207) 244-5087 . . "Foothold" Dix Point Rd, West Tremont, ME *04690*

Dillon MR & MRS Sidney G (Dorothy D Hardin)
  ☎ (508) 257-6517 . . 71 Baxter Rd, Nantucket, MA *02554*

Dinkel MISS Sallie C F . . see R M Foster

Dinning MR E Lawrence 3d— ⚓
  ☎ (302) 539-5109 . . 24 Dune Rd, Box 368, Bethany Beach, DE *19930*

Dinning MR & MRS E Lawrence 4th (Carroll F ☎ (410) 639-2820
  Hopkins) ⚓ . . . . 5135 Crosby Rd,
   MR Ernest L . . . . Rock Hall, MD *21661*

Dinsmore MR & MRS Francis William (Sallie M Kite)
  Greening Island, Southwest Harbor, ME *04679*

Ditzen MRS Lowell R (Cheesebrough—Tydings—Eleanor Davies)
  17 Pocomo Rd, Nantucket, MA *02554*

Dix MR George E
  ☎ (011-43-662) 27-37-93 . . Schloss Herrnau, Eschenbachgasse 23, 5020 Salzburg, Austria

Dixon MRS Barbara D (Burck—Barbara B Douglas)
  ☎ (616) 547-2896 . . Box 08211, See Rd, Charlevoix, MI *49720*

Dixon MR & MRS Courtlandt P (Penelope A Harrison)
  ☎ (518) 251-4074 . . "Beaver Pond View" North Woods Club, Minerva, NY *12851*

Dixon MR & MRS Dennis C (Wendy F Cole) . . . . . . ☎ (508) 627-4805
  JUNIORS MISS Caroline C . . . . Box 1338,
94 S Water St, Edgartown, MA *02539*

Dixon MR & MRS Fitz Eugene JR (Edith B Robb)
  ☎ (207) 963-2215 . . "Sou'westerly" Winter Harbor, ME *04693*

Dixon MR & MRS Gilbert W (Spence—Gretchen Woodall)
  ☎ (410) 243-5677 . . 830 W 40 St, Apt 616, Baltimore, MD *21211*

Dixon MR Harold G . . . . ☎ (804) 776-7577
MR H Andrew . . . . "Harmony"
MISS Meredith A (Teague—Meredith A Dixon) . Berryville Shores, Deltaville, VA *23043*

Dixon MR & MRS Peter T (Candida A Mabon) . . . . . ☎ (516) 283-0266
MR Peter M . . . . "Swans' Way"
MR John C . . . . 316 Cooper's Neck
MR Mark C M . . . . Lane, Southampton, NY *11968*

Dixon MR & MRS Piers (Mavroleon—Ann Van V Davenport)
☎ (908) 671-0271 . . "Bayberry Spinney" PO Box 397, Middletown, NJ *07748*

Dober MR & MRS Richard P (Eleanor Lee Lyman)
☎ (508) 228-1584 . . "Angels' Roost" 8 Silver St, Nantucket, MA *02554*

Dodds MR & MRS Robert F (Andrea B Lawrence) . . . ☎ (508) 228-6679
MR Robert F . . . . 27 Walsh St,
MR John E . . . . Nantucket, MA
MR Christopher W *02554*

Dodge MR & MRS Cleveland E JR (Phyllis Boushall)
☎ (613) 385-2162 . . Wild Goose Island, Box 343, Clayton, NY *13624*

Dodge MR & MRS Douglas S (Garfield—Christine Fuller Henriques)
"The Bowling Alley" Box 55, Cuttyhunk Island, MA *02713*

Dodge MR & MRS Geoffrey L (Zoë N Wood)
☎ (207) 867-4860 . . "Nabby House" Crabtree Point Rd, North Haven, ME *04853*

Dodge MR Marshall J JR
☎ (516) 788-7266 . . Box 266, Fishers Island, NY *06390*

Doebler MR Charles H 4th
☎ (401) 635-8697 . . "Flap A" Grange Av, Little Compton, RI *02837*

Doelger MRS William P (Cole—Josephine Warren)
☎ (603) 837-2242 . . "Appledor" Jefferson Rd, RD 1, Whitefield, NH *03598*

Dolan MR & MRS Thomas 4th (Kenworthy—H Elizabeth Gubb)
☎ (406) 222-2647 . . W Boulder Reserve, McLeod, MT *59052*
Aug 1 . . ☎ (717) 646-2477 . . Pocono Lake Preserve, PA *18348*

d'Olier MR Franklin JR
☎ (516) 324-0870 . . Box 1317, Lily Pond Lane, East Hampton, NY *11937*

Doman MR & MRS Nicholas R (Perrin—Judith A Nicely)
☎ (516) 749-0006 . . "Tengerlak" Box 298, Shelter Island, NY *11964*

Domínguez MR & MRS Martín (Alexandra H Rush)
☎ (207) 276-3984 . . Box 191, Northeast Harbor, ME *04662*

Dominick MR & MRS Gayer G 2d (Patricia Coggeshall)
Hastings Mesa, CO *81255*

Dommerich MR & MRS Louis A (K Jane Morgan)
☎ (203) 869-7172 . . 20 Deer Park, Greenwich, CT *06830*

Donald MR David L . . . . ☎ (508) 758-2286
MISS Marian S . . . . 33 Ned's Point Rd, Mattapoisett, MA *02739*

Donald MR Malcolm . . . . ☎ (207) 244-5244
MR Alexandre . . . . Main Rd,
JUNIORS MR Samuel . . . . Cranberry Isles, ME *04625*

Donham MR & MRS Paul JR (Valerie F Lawrence) . . ☎ (207) 236-4632
⚓ . . . . PO Box 757,
MISS Phoebe L . . . . Rockport, ME *04856*
JUNIORS MR Samuel L . . . .

Donlon MR & MRS David D (Suzanne E Saunders) . . ☎ (415) 669-7130
MISS Frances K . . . . "Inver House"
MISS Alexandra E . . . . 11 Woodhaven Rd, Inverness, CA *94937*

Donnan MR & MRS David Hibbs (Elizabeth C Pauly) ⚓
☎ (207) 276-5522 . . "Windover" Manchester Rd, Northeast Harbor, ME *04662*

Donnell MR & MRS John R (Caraboolad—Maureen Nahas)
☎ (401) 848-2626 . . "Ker-Arvor" 275 Harrison Av, Newport, RI *02840*

Donnelly MRS William M (Honoria A Murphy)
☎ (516) 324-0033 . . "The Pink House" E Dune Lane, Box 1022, East Hampton, NY *11937*

Donohoe MR Joseph A 5th
☎ (408) 842-3992 . . "Lion Oaks" PO Box 1085, Gilroy, CA *95021*

Donohue MRS A James (Barbara Le R Sanford) . . . ☎ (914) 537-4368
MISS Claire B . . . . Germantown, NY
MR Benjamin F *12526*

Donovan MR & MRS Lee M (Catherine B McKee) . . ☎ (803) 768-5601
⚓ . . . . 4528 Parkside,
MISS Stacy M . . . . Kiawah Island, SC
MISS Kendall McK *29455*
JUNIORS MISS Megan C . . . .

Doolittle MR & MRS Roy W JR (Cynthia Keating)
☎ (905) 834-9884 . . Lorraine, Port Colborne, Ontario L3K 5V7, Canada

Doran MR & MRS Robert W (Evelyn Hollingsworth) ☎ (508) 693-9512
MISS Eleanor H . . . . "Tide Bells"
MR David L . . . . West Chop, MA *02573*

Dorn MRS Carl S (Sally C Hayes)
☎ (603) 569-3259 . . "The Lake" PO Box 152, Mirror Lake, NH *03853*

Dorn MR Christopher H
☎ (603) 569-3259 . . "The Lake" PO Box 152, Mirror Lake, NH *03853*

Dorn MR John Z
☎ (603) 569-3259 . . "The Lake" PO Box 152, Mirror Lake, NH *03853*

Dorr MR & MRS Glenn Bert III (Eleanor M Waud)
☎ (207) 288-3037 . . "Deep Cove" Mt Desert, ME *04660*

Dorsey DR & MRS J Henderson (Matilda H Woodward) ⚓
☎ (803) 671-1771 . . "Hawks' Nest" 7 Snowy Egret, Hilton Head Island, SC *29928*

Dorsey REV CANON James C
☎ (410) 727-2323 . . Maryland Club, 1 E Eager St, Baltimore, MD *21202*

Dorson MR & MRS William S (Mercedes de G Littlejohn) . . . . ☎ (516) 676-8304
JUNIORS MISS Carolina de G . . . . 44 Overlook Rd, Locust Valley, NY *11560*

Doty MR & MRS James J (Paula P Newell) . . . . ☎ (508) 283-0728
MR James M J . . . . "Red Roof"
79 Eastern Point Blvd, Gloucester, MA *01930*

Doub MR & MRS George C JR (Mary W Tyler)
☎ (315) 354-4653 . . "Bluff Point" Raquette Lake, NY *13436*

Doub MR & MRS William O (Mary G Boggs) ...... ☎ (301) 432-5555
MR J Peyton .... "Dearbought Farm"
MR Albert A 2d .... Box 306,
Keedysville, MD *21756*
Doubleday MR & MRS Nelson (Barnett—Sandra Pine)... ☎ (516) 676-4284
Box 483,
MISS Alexis A Barnett .... Locust Valley, NY
MR Joseph W Barnett 3d *11560*
Dougherty MISS Ann S . . see MRS M T Jenney
Dougherty MR & MRS David J 4th (Julie J Rowe)... W Lake Rd,
MR David J 5th........................ Conesus, NY *14435*
MR James P ....
MR Peter L ....
Dougherty MR & MRS Geoffrey B (Nancy M Taylor) ☎ (908) 892-0825
⛵ .... 1044 Barnegat Lane,
MR Edward W .... Mantoloking, NJ
MR G Bromley JR *08738*
Douglas MRS Isabelle Z (Isabelle F Zimmerman)
☎ (516) 583-5291 . . Point O'Woods, NY *11706*
Douglas MRS Percy L (Katherine S Douglas)
☎ (914) 693-2271 . . "Glenalla" Winding Road Farm, Ardsley, NY *10502*
Douglas MR & MRS Stuart T (Lane—Dorothy Dew) . ☎ (401) 635-2687
MR Andrew G .... "Pineapple Hill"
500 Long H'way,
Box 907,
Little Compton, RI *02837*
Douglas MR & MRS William C (McIlvaine—Manker—Adele E Arrowsmith)
☎ (715) 856-6464 . . Wausaukee Club, Athelstane, WI *54104*
Douthit MR & MRS Philip S (Elizabeth Osborne)
☎ (401) 596-4575 . . "Mini House" Watch Hill, RI *02891*
Dow MR & MRS Peter A (Jane Ottaway) ⛵
2 The Boardwalk, Old Club, Harsens Island, MI *48028*
Dowling MR & MRS John L (Hebe Sanders) .... ☎ (203) 259-0444
MISS Meaghan H........................ 110 Beachside Av,
MR John W .... Greens Farms, CT
JUNIORS MR Peter S *06436*
Downer MR & MRS Joseph P (Mahoney—Louise W Swenson)
☎ (516) 759-4277 . . 16 Rabbit Run, Matinecock Farms, Glen Cove, NY *11542*
Downey MR & MRS Bruce J 3d (Victoria A Stewart) . Seagrove Beach, FL
MISS Victoria Tyler.................... *32459*
JUNIORS MR Bruce J 4th ....
JUNIORS MR John S ....
Downey MR & MRS Robert N (Nancy J Adams) .... ☎ (914) 225-4913
JUNIORS MISS Elizabeth L .... Gipsy Trail Club,
JUNIORS MR Daniel J .... Carmel, NY *10512*
Downing MR & MRS James B 3d (Elizabeth C Armstrong)
Aug 1 . . ☎ (401) 348-8277 . . 27 Westerly Rd, Plimpton Hill Rd, Watch Hill, RI *02891*
Doyle MRS M Dorland (Coonley—Morgan—Sarah B Jackson)
☎ (516) 283-3591 . . Whitefield, 155 Hill St, Southampton, NY *11968*

Doyle MRS William T (Ruth M Sartorius)
☎ (707) 865-2649 . . "Confusion Corner" Box 39, Villa Grande, CA *95486*
Draesel REV & MRS Herbert G JR (Ada D Morey)... ☎ (908) 899-1723
MISS Margaret B .... 411 East Av,
MISS Irene R .... Bay Head, NJ *08742*
Drake MR & MRS Clifford JR (Kathleen M L Sladen)
☎ (802) 295-1085 . . 3 Angell Trail, Quechee, VT *05059*
Drake MR & MRS Franklin G (Harriet Y Bouvy)
☎ (503) 738-6788 . . "Neacoxie" PO Box 2628, Gearhart, OR *97138*
Drake DR & MRS Peter F (Charenton H Zelov)
☎ (717) 646-7521 . . Pocono Lake Preserve, PA *18348*
Drake MR William McC JR .... ☎ (217) 947-2337
MISS Ascha K .... "Old Gillett Farm"
MR Mason H........................... Elkhart, IL *62634*
Drayton MR Frederick R 3d . . see MRS S Thayer 3d
Drescher MR & MRS John M JR (Katherine A White)
☎ (616) 843-4703 . . "Sancliff Cottage" Box 4156 Epworth, Ludington, MI *49431-1047*
Drew MR & MRS Thomas E 3d (Susan L Wearn)
☎ (207) 359-8802 . . PO Box 139, Naskeag Point Rd, Brooklin, ME *04616*
Drewes MRS Robert J (Caroline Clifton) .... ☎ (916) 541-0341
MR Stephen R .... "Juniper Ledge"
Fallen Leaf, CA *96151*
Drewsen MRS Edmond T JR (Eunice L Hull)
☎ (914) 855-3468 . . "Windswept" 44 S Mizzentop Rd, Quaker Hill, Pawling, NY *12564*
Drexel MR & MRS John R 3d (HON M S Noreen Stonor).. ☎ (401) 847-3323
"Stonor Lodge"
MR & MRS John R 4th (M Jacqueline Astor) .... 479 Bellevue Av, Newport, RI *02840*
Driscoll MR & MRS Peter E (Farnum—Melissa L Hunsiker)
☎ (207) 363-8049 . . "Scotch Pines" 34 Argo Point Lane, York, ME *03909*
Driscoll DR & MRS Robert W (Sonya E Dehon) .... ☎ (508) 457-0130
MISS Sonya Elizabeth .... "Winds Aloft"
MR Robert W JR .... 50 Carey Lane,
Falmouth, MA *02540*
Driver MR & MRS William R JR (Barnes—Phoebe Washburn)
☎ (207) 867-4482 . . North Haven, ME *04853*
Druckenmiller MR & MRS Stanley F (Beker—Fiona K Biggs)
☎ (516) 287-0065 . . 233 S Main St, Southampton, NY *11968*
Drury MRS Samuel S (E Tracy Keppel)
☎ (819) 842-2200 . . 2035 Lake Rd, North Hatley, Quebec J0B 2C0, Canada
DuBarry MRS Joseph N 4th (Elizabeth Gardner)
☎ (508) 228-2344 . . 32 Fair St, Nantucket, MA *02554*
Du Bois DR & MRS Arthur B (Roberdeau Callery)... ☎ (508) 548-6117
MISS Anne R........................... Box 552, Penzance
MR James E F .... Point, Woods Hole, MA *02543*

Du Bois MR & MRS Peter C (Helen R Wardwell) ... ☎ (516) CE9-4788
  MISS Laura M ....
  MR Christopher M ....
"Driftwood"
282 Seaview Av,
Lawrence, NY
11559

Du Bose MR & MRS Charles F (Sarah R Peters)
  ☎ (804) 428-1195 . . 114—52 St, Virginia Beach, VA *23451*

DuBose MR & MRS Charles W (Diana B Easter) ....
  MISS Edith W ....
  MR Brooks E ....
"The Wolfhouse"
Easter Island,
Trout Lake,
Woodruff, WI *54568*

Dubow MRS Tatyana Y (Tatyana Yassukovich) . . see S M Yassukovich

Ducas MRS Robert (Meyer—Georgiana de Ropp) ... ☎ (518) 584-0975
  MR Christopher H Meyer ....
"Zareba Farm"
150 Meadowbrook
Rd, Saratoga
Springs, NY *12866*

Ducey MR & MRS John F JR (Hoopes—Marion C Schmidt)
  ☎ (207) 276-5254 . . Sargent Dv, Northeast Harbor, ME *04662*

Dudley MR & MRS Bernard F (Strong—Anne W Rudderow)
  ☎ (802) 763-7848 . . High Lake, Sharon, VT *05065*

Dudley MR & MRS E Alexander JR (Elizabeth D Peters)
  ☎ (804) 428-1195 . . "The Cottage" 114—52 St, Virginia Beach, VA *23451*

Dudley MR & MRS Guilford JR (Jane G Anderson)
  ☎ (615) 665-1571 . . 2201 Harding Place, Nashville, TN *37215*

Dudley MRS Robert W (Cunningham—Hirshhorn—Olga M Zatorsky) . . of
  ☎ (202) 332-1501 . . "Mouse House" 2201 Massachusetts Av NW, Washington, DC *20008*
  ☎ (508) 693-0867 . . "Sow's Ear" 134 Franklin St, Vineyard Haven, MA *02568*

Dudley MR & MRS Wesley C (Lucinda V Nash) ⛵
  ☎ (207) 288-4067 . . "The Fog House" Schooner Head Rd, Box 967, Bar Harbor, ME *04609*

Duer MR & MRS A Adgate (Morgan—Molesworth—MacKay—Katherine Bancroft Poe)
  ☎ (410) 822-1190 . . 28476 Bailey's Neck Rd, Easton, MD *21601*

Duer MR & MRS Beverley C (Helen J M Crandell)
  ☎ (401) 635-8644 . . "The Cottage" 86 Warrens Point Rd, Little Compton, RI *02837*

Duffy MR & MRS John P (Anne Kinney) .... ☎ (401) 322-0549
  MISS Hilary ....
  MR Kevin ....
6 Waxcadowa Av,
Weekapaug, RI
02891

Dugan MRS Hammond J JR (Octavia W Chatard)
  ☎ (302) 537-1142 . . "Le Beguinage" PO Box 903, 1007 W Lake View, Bethany Beach, DE *19930*

Dugan DR & MRS Hammond J 3d (Hildagarde M Petit) .... ☎ (410) 822-4088
  MR Hammond J 4th ....
"Holly House"
9338 Bantry Rd,
Easton, MD *21601*

Duggano MR Stephen P
  ☎ (914) 534-4330 . . "Remote" 69 Deer Hill Rd, Cornwall-on-Hudson, NY *12520*

Duggar DR & MRS Roger S (Judy C Layton) .... ☎ (334) 857-2523
  MISS Cameron C ....
  MR Christopher R ....
  JUNIORS MR William L ....
131 Darby Dv,
Eclectic, AL *36024*

Duhme MR & MRS H Richard JR (Ware—Carol L McCarthy)
  ☎ (716) 357-4474 . . Oak Terr, 88 N Lake Dv, Box 1024, Chautauqua, NY *14722*

Dujardin MR & MRS Yves (Rosalind M Cross)
  ☎ (508) 420-1772 . . 7 Blue Heron Dv, Osterville, MA *02655*

Dujarric de la Rivière MR Robert . . see L Begley

Duke MRS A Biddle (Lynn—Robin C Tippett)
  ☎ (516) 283-2799 . . "Wyndecote Barn" 45 Gin Lane, PO Box 5072, Southampton, NY *11969*

Duke MR & MRS A Biddle JR (Idoline A Scheerer)
  ☎ (516) 283-2104 . . "Wyndecote Cottage" PO Box 5072, Southampton, NY *11969*

Duke MR George StG B
  ☎ (406) 664-3267 . . "The Pheasantry" 304 Yellowstone Av, Belfry, MT *59008*

Dumke MRS Glenn (Dorothy D Robison)
  Newport Beach, CA *92663*

Duncan MR & MRS Charles W JR (Anne Smith)
  ☎ (307) 587-3931 . . "T E Ranch" 222 Rd 6EH, Cody, WY *82414*

Duncan MRS Dyson (Mildred P S Hooker)
  ☎ (518) 327-3237 . . Spring Averill Camp, Upper St Regis, NY *12945*

Duncan MR & MRS Ransom H (Judith S Fenn) ..... ☎ (518) 327-3378
  MISS Barbara S ....
  MISS Judith L ....
  MR Ransom E ....
"Red Pines"
Upper St Regis,
NY *12945*

Dunham MR & MRS Peter (M Patricia Hopkinson)
  ☎ (518) 576-4505 . . St Huberts, NY *12943*

Dunham MR & MRS William P (Nearing—Edith Williams)
  ☎ (518) 576-4390 . . Box 712, Keene Valley, NY *12943*

Dunham MR & MRS Wolcott B (Isabel C Bosworth)
  ☎ (207) 244-7052 . . "Gullsweep" Southwest Harbor, ME *04679*

Dunlap MR & MRS J Gaff (Laura E Keys) .... of ☎ (513)771-7366
  MR John G JR ....
  MR William O.........................
965 Laurel Av,
Glendale, OH *45246*
☎ (616) 238-7393
"Pinestead"
Columbus Beach,
Indian River, MI
49749

Dunlop MR G Thomas
  ☎ (508) 627-4355 . . 40 S Summer St, Edgartown, MA *02539-5075*

Dunlop MR & MRS James N JR (Rosemary Royce) .. ☎ (516) 583-7027
  MR Paul C............................
"Driftwood"
Point O'Woods,
NY *11706*

Dunn MRS Richard P (Sturtevant—Elizabeth P Wheeler)
  ☎ (207) 359-8571 . . Box 158, Brooklin, ME *04616*

Dunn MR & MRS Stewart A JR (Bevan—Anne S McIver) .... ☎ (516) 583-8197
  MISS Anne Renwick McKinne ....
  MR D R Chandler Bevan ....
House 14,
Point O'Woods, NY
11706

Dunn MR & MRS William T JR (Laura M Franklin)
  ☎ (516) 759-5875 . . 75 Maple Av, Locust Valley, NY *11560*

Dunnell MRS William W JR (Ellen Frothingham) . . . ☎ (603) 279-4994
  MR Jacob . . . . Squam Lake,
  Great Island,
  Holderness, NH
  03245

du Pont MR & MRS Alexis I (Anne E Smith)
  ☎ (401) 466-2451 . . ''The Parsonage'' Block Island, RI *02807*

du Pont MR & MRS Charles F (Ransom—Clark—Nedinia T Schutt)
  ☎ (610) 388-0318 . . ''Spar Hill'' 438 Burnt Mill Rd, Chadds Ford, PA *19317*

du Pont MRS Henry B 3d (Joan Wheeler) . . . . ☎ (203) 259-6589
  MR Henry B 4th—⛵ . . . . 303 Hulls Farm Rd,
  Southport, CT *06490*

du Pont MR & MRS Henry E I (Schneider—Martha A ☎ (919) 261-2945
  C Verge) . . . . ''The Sand Castle''
  MISS Sophie M . . . . PO Box 8128,
  MR Henri V . . . . Duck Station,
  MR Henry E I II . . . . Kitty Hawk, NC
  27949-8128

Dupree MR & MRS Frederick F JR (Sunny A Seiler) . ☎ (207) 276-3603
  JUNIORS MISS Lila L S . . . . ''Wasgat Cove''
  JUNIORS MR F Aubin S . . . . Manchester Rd,
  Northeast Harbor,
  ME *04662*

Dupuy MR Arnold C
  ☎ (508) 385-6144 . . Box 487, Dennis, MA *02638*

Dupuy MR & MRS Fielding D (Constance L Hunter)
  ☎ (508) 385-6144 . . Scargo Pines, Dennis, MA *02638*

Durand MR & MRS Harry S (Eldredge—M Killeen ☎ (516) 288-1039
  Swartz) . . . . ''Cricket Hill'' Box
  MR Thomas H . . . . 1285, Westhampton
    MISS Margaret M Eldredge . . . . Beach, NY *11978*
    MISS Melissa F Eldredge . . . .

Durfee MR & MRS Allison B (Virginia G Nyvall)
  Taylor's Lane, Little Compton, RI *02837*

Durling MR & MRS C Correll (Eleanor H White) . . . . ☎ (908) 899-0067
  JUNIORS MR C Chapin . . . . 1079 Ocean Av,
  Mantoloking, NJ
  08738

Duryea MR & MRS George R JR (Marita B Halloran) ☎ (807) 894-3903
  MISS Ellen V . . . . Thunder Bay
  MISS Katharine H . . . . Colony,
  Thunder Bay,
  Ontario, Canada

Duryea MR & MRS William M JR (E Lovejoy ☎ (516) 325-2752
  Reeves) . . . . ''Swan Cottage''
  JUNIORS MR Robert A . . . . 23 Seatuck Lane,
  JUNIORS MR David McS . . . . Remsenburg, NY
  11960

Dush MR & MRS Michael W (Susan D Myers)
  ☎ (401) 596-3334 . . 18 Shore Rd, Westerly, RI *02891*

Du Val MR & MRS Daniel H (Karen L Keys)
  ☎ (401) 789-2651 . . 392A Cards Pond Rd, Matunuck, RI *02879*

Du Vivier MR & MRS Paul F (Margaret E de Ropp) . ☎ (516) 283-4285
  MR & MRS Edwin B Green III (Anne K ''Greencote''
  Du Vivier) . . . . PO Box 1135,
  Southampton,
  NY *11969*

Dwight MR & MRS George H P (Gardiner—Eleanor ☎ (207) 288-5203
  M Collier) . . . . ''The Little House''
  MR Sargent C Gardiner . . . . Barberry Lane,
  Bar Harbor, ME
  04609

Dwyer MRS Thomas R (Guittard—Susie J Quealy)
  ☎ (408) 546-3464 . . Kings Beach, CA *95719*

Dyer MR & MRS Randolph H (Elizabeth Huntington)
  ☎ (413) 337-4928 . . Heath, MA *01346*

Dyett MR & MRS Edmond G JR (Adrienne I Murray)
  ☎ (508) 394-0164 . . off Longview Rd, Yarmouth Port, MA *02675*

E

Eagle MR & MRS J Frederick 3d (Sarah T Vaughan)
  ''Ledge Lodge'' North Haven, ME *04853*

Earle MRS Eleanor F O (Eleanor F Owens)
  ☎ (401) 783-8920 . . ''Twin Gables'' 352 Ocean Rd, Narragansett, RI *02882-1390*

Earle MR & MRS George H 5th (Pearson—Ann E ☎ (518) 327-3286
  Lindley) . . . . New Camp,
  MISS Amy R P . . . . Spitfire Lake,
  Upper St Regis, NY
  12945

Earle MRS Richard (Frances Clement)
  ☎ (207) 361-2580 . . ''High Pasture'' 731 Shore Rd, Cape Neddick, ME *03902*

Easter MR Donald
  ☎ (804) 295-5432 . . 2679 Free Union Rd, Charlottesville, VA *22901*

Easterby MR & MRS Stewart D 3d (Judith G Abbot)
  ☎ (210) 537-5322 . . ''Asheburn'' 410 Mountain Springs, Boerne, TX *78006*

Eastman MR & MRS John L (Josephine L Merrill) . . ☎ (516) 324-5332
  MR John L JR . . . . 152 Lily Pond Lane,
  MR Lee V 2d . . . . Box 372,
  East Hampton,
  NY *11937*

Eaton MR & MRS James H 4th (Elizabeth T Meyer)
  ☎ (207) 967-2515 . . ''Sawoakla'' Box 608, Kennebunkport, ME *04046*

Eaton DR & MRS John M (Mary E Beale)
  ☎ (916) 541-3789 . . Camp Sierra, Fallen Leaf Lake, CA *95716*

Eaton MRS William Mellon (Elizabeth W Witsell) . . ☎ (603) 823-8404
  MISS Sarah E . . . . ''Wecas''
  DR Alexander Mellon . . . . PO Box 96,
  Lafayette Rd,
  Sugar Hill,
  Franconia, NH
  03580

Eberhart MR & MRS Frank 3d (Delphine S Espy) ⛵
  ☎ (207) 867-2075 . . Young's Point, Vinalhaven, ME *04863*

Eberts MRS Frederick W (Frazer—Evelyn S Allen) . | ☎ (616) 547-4788
   MR Dustin W . . . . | "Woodbine" Belvedere Club, Cottage 111, Charlevoix, MI *49720*

Ebright MR & MRS Harold R JR (Katherine A Fairlie)
   ☎ (916) 541-5040 . . Box 7034, South Lake Tahoe, CA *96158*

Eckerberg MR & MRS C Lennart (Willia F Fales) . . . | ☎ (011-46-40)
   MISS Alice R D . . . . | 47-31-14
   MR John F. . . . . | Martornsvägen 3,
   MR Christopher F . . . . | Falsterbo, Sweden

Eckfeldt MRS Theodore E (Mildred O Ross)
   ☎ (717) 646-2739 . . "Thanakonek" Pocono Lake Preserve, PA *18348*

Eckman MRS John W (Ziesing—Jane Haussman) . . | ☎ (508) 228-3954
   MISS Jane D Ziesing. . . . . | 4 Brant Point Rd,
   MISS Heather W Ziesing . . . . | Nantucket, MA *02554*

Eddy MR & MRS David C (Laura G D Hersloff)
   ☎ (410) 822-3418 . . "Cross Cove Cottage" 26398 Presquisle Rd, Easton, MD *21601*

Eddy MR & MRS Ernest A JR (Williams—Marjorie A Cizek)
   ☎ (508) 428-6427 . . "Shore House" 551 Old Post Rd, Cotuit, MA *02635-0306*

Eddy MR & MRS Paul C (Connor—Nancy C
   Culbertson). . . . . | ☎ (401) 849-0707
   MR C Clark . . . . | "The Gardener's Cottage"
   MR Charles F . . . . | 30 Hammersmith Rd, Newport, RI *02840*

Edey MRS Maitland A (Helen W Kellogg)
   ☎ (508) 693-2386 . . "Seven Gates Farm" Vineyard Haven, MA *02568*

Edgar MR & MRS Robert V (Sarah S Osborne) . . . . . | 355 Wadleigh Rd,
   JUNIORS MISS Valentine B . . . . | North Hatley, Quebec J0B 2C0, Canada

Edgar MR & MRS William 3d (Barbara S Smyth) . . . | ☎ (819) 842-2123
   MISS Deborah B . . . . | "High House"
   MR William K. . . . . | 355 Wadleigh Rd, North Hatley, Quebec J0B 2C0, Canada

Edgerly MR Peter DeF
   "Edgewoods" Lewis Hill Rd, Newcastle, ME *04553*

Edgerton MR & MRS Albert S (Diana Hunt) . . . . | 60 Compass Close,
   MISS Kimberly . . . . | Sea Ranch, CA *95459*
   MR Edward J. . . . . |

Edgerton DR & MRS Bradford W (Lynne H Todd)
   ☎ (705) 375-0674 . . Iron City Fishing Club, Georgian Bay, MacTier, Ontario P2A 2X4, Canada

Edgerton MR & MRS Malcolm J JR (Arnold—Jackson—Jane Lowe)
   ☎ (518) 576-4429 . . Ausable Club, St Huberts, NY *12943*

Edgeworth MR & MRS Arthur B JR (Elizabeth D Walker)
   ☎ (302) 227-4481 . . 23 Henlopen Av, Rehoboth Beach, DE *19971*

Edinger MR & MRS John S JR (T Lorraine Mather)
   ☎ (609) 263-8221 . . 22 Seaview Rd, Strathmere, NJ *08248*

Edmeades MR & MRS Michael D (Fabienne H B Mander)
   ☎ (914) 373-8674 . . "Brigand Hill" RR 1, Box 413, Smithfield, Amenia, NY *12501*

Edmonds MRS Catharine L (Catharine van B
   Livingston). . . . . | RD 2, Hudson, NY *12534*
   MISS Olivia L . . . . |
   JUNIORS MISS Eugenia F . . . . |

Edmonds MR & MRS George P JR (Sally L Reeves) . | ☎ (508) 428-2933
   MISS Helen M . . . . | 147 Seaport River Rd, Box 2030, Oyster Harbors, Osterville, MA *02655*

Edmonston MR & MRS William E (Rosemary Finney)
   ☎ (207) 359-2153 . . "Ledge Lodge" Sargentville, ME *04673*

Edson MRS Ann Payne (Soffel—Seymour—Ann Payne)
   ☎ (516) 537-7185 . . "Annie's Place" Sagg Main St, Box 45, Sagaponack, NY *11962*

Edwards MR & MRS James C (Sally A Matson)
   ☎ (516) 324-0162 . . Hook Pond Rd, Box 77, East Hampton, NY *11937*

Edwards MR & MRS James C JR (Barbara H Lord)
   ☎ (516) 324-7868 . . 25 Maidstone Lane, East Hampton, NY *11937*

Edwards MR & MRS Oliver (Anita M Schubeler) . . . | ☎ (516) 862-8715
   JUNIORS MISS Margaret K . . . . | 25 Harbor Rd, St James, NY *11780*

Edwards MR & MRS Stephen A (Mary S Hallock)
   ☎ (705) 366-5038 . . "Ish-Pop-Kah" Island 80A, Pointe-au-Baril, Ontario P0G 1K0, Canada

Egbert MR Garth L . . see J W McN Darling

Eglin MRS Thomas W (Edith H Baird) . . . . | ☎ (401) 348-8907
   MR Edward S . . . . | "Bayridge" 8 Aquidneck Av, Watch Hill, RI *02891*

Ehrlich MRS Delia F (Delia Fleishhacker)
   ☎ (415) 851-7274 . . "Green Gables" 329 Albion Av, Woodside, CA *94062*

Eifler MISS Elin C W . . see K S Fennebresque

Eitel MR & MRS Walter T (Berry Reavis) . . . . | ☎ (860) 232-3516
   MISS Alexandra N . . . . | "Winds West"
   MR Reavis H. . . . . | 59 Fernwood Rd, West Hartford, CT *06119*

Elder MISS Alice L . . see MRS C F Vilter

Eldredge MISS Margaret M . . see H S Durand

Eldredge MISS Melissa F . . see H S Durand

Elias MR & MRS Archibald C JR (Susan W Homans) . | ☎ (617) 545-3318
   MISS Abigail H . . . . | The Glades,
   JUNIORS MISS Margaret W . . . . | Glades Rd, Minot, MA *02055*
   JUNIORS MISS Clara C . . . . |

Eliott DR Matthew S . . see H Luce 3d

Elkins MR & MRS James A III (Mary V Arnold)
   ☎ (303) 449-1264 . . 701 Lupine Lane, Chautauqua Park, Boulder, CO *80302*

Elkus MR & MRS Christopher J (Duryea—Gretchen B Miller) . . . . ☎ (412) 238-9422
MR James M . . . . 624 Kissell Springs Rd, Ligonier, PA *15658*

Ellicott MRS Valcoulon LeM (Mary P Gould)
☎ (717) 525-3331 . . "Ellicott Cottage" Box 33, Eagles Mere, PA *17731*

Elliott MR & MRS Howard JR (Susan J Spoehrer) 37 Westwind, Madaket Beach, Nantucket, MA *02554*

Elliott MR & MRS John JR (Eleanor L Thomas)
☎ (914) 232-3466 . . "Highland Fling" Cross River, NY *10518*

Elliott MRS Mary Jane (Mary Jane Wagner) . . . . ☎ (207) 359-2175
MISS Julia W . . . . "Honeysuckle
MR R Gibbons 3d . . . . Bower" PO Box
MR T Scott . . . . 262, Brooklin, ME *04616*

Elliott MR Thomas R
☎ (704) 696-2323 . . 76 N Lake Summit Dv, PO Box 189, Tuxedo, NC *28784-0189*

Ellis MRS D Rowland (Edith B Wetherill) ⚓
☎ (401) 423-0007 . . "Edgewater" Box 52, 10 High St, Jamestown, RI *02835*

Ellis DR & MRS F Henry JR (Mary J Walsh) . . . . ☎ (207) 276-3629
JUNIORS MR Michael G Walsh . . . . "Hillcrest"
Rowland Rd,
Seal Harbor, ME *04675*

Ellis MR & MRS G Corson (Jewett—Constance C Comly) 26 W Highland Av, Atlantic Highlands, NJ *07716*

Ellis MR & MRS J Wiley (Marguerite C Duane) . . . . . ☎ (704) 526-4042
MISS Marguerite C . . . . Satulah Mountain,
MR Benjamin D . . . . N View Rd,
MR Robb W . . . . Highlands, NC *28741*

Ellis MR John A Fitler
☎ (860) 824-1113 . . "Eureka" Box 313, Falls Village, CT *06031*

Ellis MR & MRS Ralph E (Brewster—Nancy Dickinson Buell) 24 Homestead Circle, Old Lyme, CT *06371*

Elmore MRS S Churchill (Betty R Buchanan) . . . . . ☎ (302) 539-6287
MR Stancliff C JR . . . . 7 Evans Rd,
Sussex Shores,
Bethany Beach, DE *19930*

Eltz CT Franz J
☎ (011-43-7711) 6152-71318 . . "Villa Eltz" 8992 Altaussee 54, Styria, Austria

Eltz CTSS Katharine (Katharine E O'Donoghue) . . . ☎ (914) 266-5283
JUNIORS MISS Fiona F . . . . Schultzville Rd,
JUNIORS MR Philipp A . . . . Box 200A, Clinton Corners, NY *12514*

Ely MR & MRS Duncan Cairnes (Elizabeth C Wickenberg)
☎ (803) TE8-7690 . . "Sea Urchins" Fripp Island, SC *29920*

Ely MR & MRS George W (Bernice A MacKenzie)
☎ (916) 266-3593 . . Star Rte 2, Box 3976, Trinity Center, CA *96091*

Ely MR & MRS John I (Harriet Jackson)
☎ (516) 324-4425 . . "Rose-Gate" 28 Dayton Lane, East Hampton, NY *11937*

El-Yacoubi DR & MRS (DR) Hassan H S (Jane B Merritt) . . . . ☎ (908) 899-0257
JUNIORS MISS Fatima H . . . . 510 East Av,
JUNIORS MR Salime H . . . . Bay Head, NJ *08742*
JUNIORS MR Mohammed H . . . .

Embree MR & MRS Jeb N (Connelly—Dianne Thomson) . . . . ☎ (860) 434-9717
MISS Leslie P . . . . 77 Joshuatown Rd, Lyme, CT *06371*

Embry MR & MRS Talton R (Marguerite Tenney)
☎ (516) 287-3319 . . "Big Pink" 195 Sebonac Rd, Southampton, NY *11968*

Emerson MR & MRS Edward E JR (May Starr) . . . . . May 1 . .
MR Edward E III . . . . ☎ (802) 765-4049
JUNIORS MR Benjamin T . . . . "Tamarack Hill Farm" RR 1, Box 234, Strafford, VT *05072*

Emerson MR & MRS H Truxtun JR (M L Tyler Lewis)
☎ (513) 791-5406 . . 7300 Dearwester Dv, Apt 231, Cincinnati, OH *45236*

Emery MR & MRS James J (Allison B Rumsey) Murphy Point, Manatoulin Island, Ontario, Canada

Emery MR & MRS John M 2d (Patricia C Monroe)
☎ (802) 766-2207 . . Morgan Rd, Derby, VT *05829*

Emmet MRS Grenville T (Gammack—Burden—Elizabeth Chace) 2801 New Mexico Av NW, Washington, DC *20007*

Emmet MR & MRS Grenville T 3d (Beach—Beall—Dita A Holloway) . . . . ☎ (703) 777-8237
MISS Samantha B . . . . "Oatlands Hamlet"
MR Grenville T 4th . . . . Rte 2, Box 363,
MR Bradford C . . . . Leesburg, VA *22075*

Emmet MISS Sheila Dahlgren
☎ (401) 847-0929 . . "Dahlgren House" 5 Touro Park W, Newport, RI *02840*

Emory MRS German H H (Katherine E Riegel)
☎ (207) 359-8347 . . Brooklin, ME *04616*

Ems MR & MRS A Frederick (Sargent—Mary Jewett) . ☎ (970) 468-2374
MR Adolf F JR . . . . 41 Rd O,
Silverthorne, CO *80498*

Endicott MRS Charles M (Marianne R Trombley)
☎ (517) 727-2157 . . "Dog-Wood" 6077 Pine Dv, Hubbard Lake, MI *49747*

Engel MR & MRS Thomas E (Suzanne M Gallaudet) . ☎ (914) 439-5413
MISS Pheobe D . . . . "Maple Farm"
MR Montgomery E . . . . Box 127,
JUNIORS MISS Alice G . . . . Lew Beach, NY *12753*

Engelhard MRS Charles W (Mannheimer—Jane Brian) Jly 1 . . ☎ (508) 228-0178 . . 97 Main St, Nantucket, MA *02554*

England MR & MRS Sanford H (Jacquelin Potts)
☎ (802) 223-6224 . . "England Farm" Towne Hill Rd, Montpelier, VT *05602*

English MR Edwin H 3d . . . . ☎ (401) 783-5808
   MISS Mary E . . . . "Windswept"
   137 Bonnet Shores Rd, Narragansett, RI 02882

English MR Henry W . . . . ☎ (203) 488-1376
   MISS Elinor L Blake . . . . 26 Wood Rd, Johnson Point, Branford, CT 06405

English MR & MRS Oscar B (Carroll Bever)
   ☎ (011-44-171) 402-3784 . . St George's Fields, Hanover Steps 35, Albion St, London W2 2YG, England

Engman MR & MRS William C (Marilyn Berger) . . . ☎ (715) 479-8252
   MR David T . . . . "Engman Cottage" 1147 Wooded Lane, Eagle River, WI 54521

Ennis MR Thomas W . . see E M de Windt

Enos MR & MRS Alanson T 3d (Alice H Plimpton)
   "Mojag" Ojibway of Keewaydin, Temagami, Ontario P0H 2H0, Canada

Epstein DR & MRS Stephen E (Lee—Alice C Brown)
   ☎ (516) 788-7529 . . "Osprey Cove" PO Box 244, Fishers Island, NY 06390

Erhart MR & MRS Charles H JR (Sylvia M Montgomery)
   ☎ (207) 244-5104 . . Seawall Point Lane, Manset, ME 04656

Erisman MR & MRS Otis W (Eleanor W Platt)
   ☎ (508) 228-9160 . . "Oak House" Box 934, Surfside, Nantucket, MA 02554

Erker MISS Marianna S
   ☎ (616) 857-4815 . . 130 Lakeshore Dv, Douglas, MI 49406

Ernst MR Charles A 3d
   166 Cliff Rd, Nantucket, MA 02554

Ernst MR & MRS Charles Augustus JR (Jacqueline E Walker)
   ☎ (508) 228-2287 . . "Quarter Mile Hill" Nantucket, MA 02554

Ervin MISS Adele Q
   ☎ (508) 526-1417 . . "Crow Shack" 92 Ocean St, Manchester-By-The-Sea, MA 01944

Ervin MR & MRS Spencer JR (Florence W Schroeder) ☎ (207) 244-4195
   MISS Miriam R . . . . Bass Harbor, ME 04653
   MISS Helen S . . . .

Espinosa de los Monteros MR & MRS Alvaro F (Eugenia C Carver) ⚓ . . . . "Condo Sol" 51 LaBonte St, Dillon, CO 80435
   MSRS John F & Edward P . . . .
   MSRS James J & Martin A . . . .
   MSRS Michael L & Charles G . . . .

Espy DR & MRS John W (Mary B Fowlkes) . . . . ☎ (508) 228-1020
   JUNIORS MR Peter W . . . . 4 New Dollar Lane, Nantucket, MA 02554

Espy MR & MRS Thomas P (Lisa T Hearst)
   ☎ (516) 287-2344 . . 95 N Sea Mecox Rd, Southampton, NY 11968

Estey MR & MRS John S (Dial—Alexandra Montgomery)
   ☎ (717) 525-3377 . . "Shady Lawn" Eagles Mere, PA 17731

Estill MRS Holland (Tweed—Barbara Banning)
   ☎ (516) 668-2981 . . "Derby House" 139 DeForest Rd, Montauk, NY 11954

Esty MR & MRS Donald C (Mae Welfley)
   ☎ (207) 244-3417 . . "Nearby" Box 38, Greening Island, Southwest Harbor, ME 04679

Esty MR & MRS Robert W (Karen E Kennedy) . . . . . ☎ (207) 244-7269
   JUNIORS MISS Kristen E . . . . "Westview" Greening Island, Southwest Harbor, ME 04679

Etheridge MR & MRS Tammy H (Nora Reagan)
   "Rockport" 4095 Sugar Farm Rd, Hazelhurst, MS 39083

Etherington MR & MRS Burton H JR (Margaret P Lowe)
   ☎ (508) 627-5229 . . 17 Down Harbor Rd, Edgartown, MA 02539

Eustis MR George (Herberta Stone)
   ☎ (508) 428-8642 . . 19 Blue Heron Dv, Osterville, MA 02655

Eustis MR & MRS William E C (Mary H Armstrong) ⚓
   ☎ (508) 563-2901 . . 11 Boulder Rd, Cataumet, MA 02534

Evans MRS Benjamin C JR (Jan A King)
   ☎ (540) 687-6032 . . "Groveton Farm" 37689 Lime Kiln Rd, Middleburg, VA 22117

Evans MR David C
   ☎ (508) 775-9042 . . "Bird's Nest" Hyannis Port, MA 02647

Evans MR Edward P
   ☎ (401) 847-3436 . . "La Plaisance" Ledge Rd, Newport, RI 02840

Evans MR Jeremy A M . . see D F Morley

Evans DR & MRS John A (Odell—King—Runyon—Anne A Wilson) . . . . ☎ (516) 749-1010
   MISS Suzanne W Odell . . . . "Wood Winds" 3 Crescent Way, Box 143, Shelter Island Heights, NY 11965
   MISS Alison W Odell . . . .

Evans MR & MRS John F (Dorothy A Warner)
   ☎ (609) 263-8631 . . 237—79 St, Sea Isle City, NJ 08243

Evans MR Paul R
   ☎ (516) 788-7393 . . PO Box 106, Fishers Island, NY 06390

Evans MR & MRS Raymond F (Elizabeth R Whitney)
   ☎ (216) 942-6012 . . 7100 S Lane Rd, Willoughby, OH 44094

Evans MR & MRS Robert B (Jane C Preston)
   ☎ (313) 881-0458 . . 984 Lake Shore Dv, Grosse Pointe, MI 48236

Evans MR & MRS Samuel M (Patricia M Hodder) . . . ☎ (011-44-1903) 700727
   MISS Claire I . . . . 31 South Dv, Ferring, Sussex BN12 5QU, England

Evans MISS Sarah D . . see R A Gallavan

Evans MR & MRS Thomas M JR (Gyurkey—Morgan—Tania Goss) . . . . ☎ (802) 843-2241
   MR Mark J . . . . RR 3, Box 283, Chester Hill Rd, Grafton, VT 05146

Evans MR & MRS William H (Bindley—Phyllis Hoelzel)
   ☎ (216) 932-2550 . . 19201 S Park Blvd, Shaker Heights, OH 44122

Evans MR & MRS William J (Jones—Christina P Clare) . . . . ☎ (518) 589-5360
   JUNIORS MR Elliot S . . . . "Swallow's Nest" Onteora Club, Tannersville, NY 12485
   MISS Palmer D Jones . . . .
   JUNIORS MR Oliver H Jones . . . .
   JUNIORS MR Frederick K Jones . . . .

Evarts MR & MRS William M JR (Helen R Coleman) | ☎ (207) 867-4496
   MR & MRS Clarence W Bartow JR (Kozloff— | "Fish Head"
     Helen C Evarts) . . . . | North Haven,
   MR & MRS Howard P Schipper (Alice C Evarts) | ME *04853*
Everdell MR & MRS Preston (Sarah K Jayne) . . . . . . | ☎ (207) 359-2048
  JUNIORS MISS Marian P . . . . | "Idle Reach"
  JUNIORS MR Nicholas P . . . . | Carter Point,
                                                                                     Sedgwick, ME *04676*
Everdell MR & MRS William (Bellamy—Eleanore H Darling)
  ☎ (508) 627-8081 . . "Rabbit Hill" RR 1, Box 395, Cow Bay, Edgartown, MA *02539*
Everdell MR & MRS William R (Barbara L Scott) . . . | ☎ (508) 627-5012
   MR Christian R . . . . | Cow Bay, Edgartown, MA *02539*
Everett MR & MRS Oliver S (Susan H Heath) . . . . . . | ☎ (508) 255-7240
   MISS Christy H . . . . | Armour Dv,
   MR Andrew B . . . . | Box 978, Eastham, MA *02642*
Ewart MR & MRS Robert B (Musser—Carol L Reed) | ☎ (216) 777-9141
   MISS Lisa D Musser . . . . | 25151 Brookpark Rd, North Olmsted, OH *44070*
Ewell MRS John W (Nancy V Chapman)
  ☎ (207) 967-5291 . . 47 Long & Winding Rd, Kennebunkport, ME *04046*
Ewing MR & MRS J G Blaine 3d (Phyllis C Walker) . | ☎ (803) 883-3727
  JUNIORS MR James G B 4th . . . . | 2514 I'on Av, Sullivans Island, SC *29482*
Ewing MRS Joseph N (Anne Ashton)
  ☎ (401) 423-0092 . . "Altamira" Box 585, Jamestown, RI *02835*
Ewing MR & MRS L Rumsey (Rosalie McRee)
  ☎ (719) 742-3246 . . "Ute Ranch" La Veta, CO *81055*
Eyre MR Edward E JR
  ☎ (702) 753-8018 . . Talbot Canyon Ranch, PO Box 28-1408, Lamoille, NV *89828*
Eyre MR & MRS William H (Margaret A Lerner)
  ☎ (860) 364-0433 . . "Singing Bird Farm" Gay St, Sharon, CT *06069*

F

Faesy MR & MRS A Robert (Nancy Niles)
  Conary Island, Deer Isle, ME *04627*
Fagan MRS Warren (Mary E Warren)
  ☎ (516) 283-0353 . . 32 S Main St, Southampton, NY *11968*
Fahnestock MRS Harris (Frances C Jeffery)
  Jly 1 . . ☎ (413) 637-0030 . . Lenox Club, Lenox, MA *01240*
  Aug 1 . . ☎ (508) 992-1744 . . "Moorlands" South Nonquitt, MA *02748*
Fahs MRS Raymond Z (Mary E Nichols) . . . . | ☎ (516) 692-4093
   MR Thomas R . . . . | "Applewyck" Box 153, Syosset, NY *11791*

Fahy LT Christian Carter—USCG.
  ☎ (603) 539-7767 . . Conner Pond Rd, Box 102, Center Ossipee, NH *03814*
Fair MRS Frederick M (Claire L Evans) . . . . | ☎ (717) 474-9200
   MR Luke J . . . . | "Windhill" White Birch Rd, Glen Summit, PA *18707*
Fairburn MR & MRS Gordon R (Phoebe G Pier) . . . | ☎ (207) 883-5567
   MISS Ramsay P . . . . | "Kuhtai"
   MISS Phoebe E . . . . | Prouts Neck, ME
   MR Arthur D . . . . | *04074*
   MR James G . . . . |
Fairman MR & MRS Endsley P (Marie B Fraley)
  ☎ (207) 276-5146 . . "Sargent Point" Northeast Harbor, ME *04662*
Fales MR & MRS De Coursey JR (Scott—Iten Noa)
  ☎ (617) 934-6867 . . "Solar House" 63 Upland Rd, Duxbury, MA *02332*
Fales MR & MRS Haliburton 2d (Katharine Ladd)
  ☎ (207) 863-4347 . . North Haven, ME *04853*
Fales MRS Samuel (Barbara Foote)
  ☎ (508) 693-2724 . . "Windyhill" Old County Rd, West Tisbury, MA *02575*
Fallon MR & MRS John T (Pauline A Mayer)
  ☎ (508) 428-8015 . . 359 Seapuit Rd, Osterville, MA *02655*
Fanjul MR & MRS J Pepe (Emilia S May) . . . . | of ☎ (407)655-1814
   MISS Emilia H . . . . | "Casa Alegre"
   MR J Pepe JR . . . . | 105 Jungle Rd, Palm Beach, FL *33480*
                                                                    ☎ (809) 562-6594 "Casa Grande" Casa de Campo, La Romana, Dominican Republic
Fanning MR & MRS Philip F N (Slater—Joy B Landreth)
  ☎ (011-353-62) 72120 . . "Cahervillahow" Golden, Co Tipperary, Ireland
Fantauzzi MISS Samantha F . . see H F Taylor 3d
Farber MR & MRS Brent H JR (Bettie R Field)
  ☎ (609) 884-3747 . . 915 Beach Dv, Cape May, NJ *08204*
Farley MR & MRS David L JR (Carol F Duncan)
  ☎ (802) 875-2462 . . Pond Meadow Farm, Quarry Rd, Chester, VT *05143*
Farley MR & MRS Edward I (Coleman—Peterkin—Helen D Minton)
  ☎ (207) 832-5127 . . 80 Butter Point, Waldoboro, ME *04572*
Farley MR & MRS Philip W (Peters—Phyllis Rothschild)
  ☎ (914) 764-4717 . . 20 Rock Hill Way, Bedford, NY *10506*
Farmer MR & MRS Richard T (Joyce Barnes)
  ☎ (616) 526-0382 . . 16 Beach Dv, Harbor Springs, MI *49740*
Farnum MRS Edward S W (McIlvaine—Louise W Bickley)
  ☎ (207) 833-6093 . . "Sunset Lodge" Orrs Island, ME *04066*
Farr MR & MRS C Sims (Byrnes—Muriel StJ Tobin)
  ☎ (207) 236-6795 . . "Harbor House" 7 Ocean Way, Camden, ME *04843*

Farr MR & MRS Francis B (Susan Andrews)
☎ (516) 283-3033 . . "The Studio II" 194 Sebonac Rd, Southampton, NY *11968*

Farrand MR & MRS A Brady (Jeffery—Katharine L McMillan)
☎ (707) 963-4266 . . "Soda Valley Ranch" 4000 H'way 128, St Helena, CA *94574*

Farrar MR & MRS Clayton A (Van Wyck—Patricia White)
☎ (516) 734-5905 . . 9975 Nassau Point Rd, Cutchogue, NY *11935*

Farrell MR & MRS J Michael (Kegg—Jennison—Virginia K Macdonald)
☎ (516) 583-0223 . . Point O'Woods, NY *11706*

Farrell MISS Kristin A . . see T W Marshall

Farrell MR & MRS Michael J (Carolyn H Morris) . . . | ☎ (609) 398-7546
JUNIORS MR John M . . . . | 904 Pennlyn Place, Ocean City, NJ *08226*

Farrelly MR & MRS Louis C R (Dorothy M Fell) . . . | ☎ (518) 576-2026
MISS Elisabeth W . . . . | "Brookmeade"
MR Stephen R R . . . . | Rte 73 & John's Brook, Keene Valley, NY *12943*

Farrington MR & MRS Douglas F (Veronica M Pease)
☎ (603) 869-3113 . . 71D Village at Maplewood, Bethlehem, NH *03574*

Farrington MRS Phillips (Mary J Hazzard)
☎ (802) 457-1800 . . "Windsway" Hartland Hill Rd, RR 1, Box 673, Woodstock, VT *05091*

Farwell MRS Arthur (Russell—Barbara Korff) . . . . . | ☎ (902) 725-2766
MISS Diana Russell . . . . | "Pony's Point" Iona, CBI, Nova Scotia B0A 1L0, Canada

Farwell MRS F Evans (Lynne P Hecht)
☎ (603) 353-4565 . . Across from Ridge, Orford, NH *03777*

Fates MR & MRS Harold L (Miller—Twining—Margery Gerdes)
☎ (802) 824-3264 . . "Joe's Land" Winhall, VT *05201*

Faunce MR & MRS John H JR (Katherine S Chambers)
☎ (919) 249-0441 . . "Teach's Cove" Box 489, Oriental, NC *28571*

Fawcett MR & MRS Michael S (Dana—Polly V | ☎ (508) 468-2989
 Osborn) . . . . | "Cold Comfort Farm" 862 Bay Rd, Hamilton, MA *01936*
MR Courtney . . . . |
JUNIORS MISS Madeleine J . . . . |

Faxon MRS Henry H (Campbell—Sophia D Doolittle)
☎ (207) 363-3091 . . "Rocky Knoll" York Harbor, ME *03911*

Fay MR Edward H JR
"Seaweed Castle" 22 Crystal Lake Dv, Orleans, MA *02653*

Fay MR & MRS Paul B JR (Anita R Marquez)
☎ (415) 851-8529 . . "Paradise" 205 Winding Way, Woodside, CA *94062*

Fay MR & MRS Paul B 3d (Laura E Merriam) . . . . . . | 90 Almendal,
JUNIORS MISS Alexandra R . . . . | Atherton, CA *94027*
JUNIORS MISS Francesca F . . . . |

Fearey MRS Morton (Mary C Senior)
☎ (508) 627-8632 . . 75 Planting Field Way, PO Box 513, Edgartown, MA *02539*

Fearey MR & MRS Morton JR (Beverly A | ☎ (508) 627-8198
 McMonagle) . . . . | Box 1475, Planting Field Way, Edgartown, MA *02539*
MR Christopher L—☎ (508) 627-3107 . . . . |

Fee MR & MRS Joseph M JR (Elizabeth J Crawford)
☎ (702) 749-5103 . . 2146 The Back Rd, Glenbrook, NV *89413*

Feick MR & MRS William JR (Chisholm—Rosemary Fennell)
33 Niamogue Lane, Quogue, NY *11959*

Feigen MR Richard L . . . . | ☎ (914) 232-8476
MISS Philippa C . . . . | "Cantitoe House" 99 Cantitoe Rd, Katonah, NY *10536*
MR Richard W B . . . . |

Feinstein MR & MRS Martin (James—Marcia E Teller)
☎ (516) 749-0797 . . 86 Peconic Av, Shelter Island Heights, NY *11965*

Felch MR & MRS Robert D (Marianne D Hutton) . . . . | ☎ (508) 257-4348
JUNIORS MISS Sarah P . . . . | 11 Morey Lane, PO Box 339, Siasconset, MA *02564*

Feld MR & MRS Alan David (Anne Sanger)
617 W Bleeker, Aspen, CO *81612*

Fennebresque MR & MRS Kim Samuel (Eifler— | ☎ (516) 671-4994
 Deborah A Johnson) . . . . | 140 Duck Pond Rd, Glen Cove, NY *11542*
MISS Elin C W Eifler . . . . |

Fenton MR & MRS Martin JR (Griffith—Majella K | ☎ (408) 624-6984
 Clark) . . . . | "Brise de Mer" Box 2321, Carmel, CA *93921*
MISS Caroline C Griffith . . . . |

Fenton MR & MRS Wendell (Jeannie H Woolston) . . | ☎ (307) 733-7240
MR Joshua W . . . . | PO Box 447, Teton Village, WY *83025*
MR Nicholas W . . . . |
MR Lewis D . . . . |

Fergus MR & MRS Gary S (Isabelle S Beekman)
☎ (415) 669-1531 . . "House with the Red Door" PO Box 886, 193 Park Av, Inverness, CA *94937*

Ferguson MR & MRS J Howard 3d (Johnson—Patricia L Zoch)
☎ (408) 624-1514 . . "Otter Echo" 3221 Whitman Place, Box 1495, Pebble Beach, CA *93953*

Ferguson DR & MRS James J JR (Martha R Saunders)
☎ (508) 548-0236 . . 21 Quonset Rd, Falmouth, MA *02540*

Fernald MR & MRS Mason (Helen Merriman)
☎ (207) 276-3620 . . Sutton Island, Northeast Harbor, ME *04662*

Fernley MR & MRS Robert C (Alice M Guerin)
☎ (307) 733-5613 . . Box 3937, Jackson, WY *83001*

Ferrarini MR & MRS Steven P (Jennifer A Callies)
"The Island" Camano Island, WA *98292*

Ferris MR & MRS Peter T (Diana P Davis)
14 Daggett Av, Tisbury, MA *02568*

Ferriss MR & MRS David P (Schneider—Ruth F Knight)
☎ (905) 894-0254 . . "Open Gate" Abino Hills, RR 1, Ridgeway, Ontario L0S 1N0, Canada

Ferriss MR & MRS Franklin (Lacey—Nancy L Atkins)
35 Resort Rd, Harbor Beach, MI *48441*

Fessenden MR & MRS Edward E (Bannard—Marion H Sutphen)
☎ (516) 692-6488 . . 21 White Hill Rd, Cold Spring Harbor, NY *11724*

Fessenden MR & MRS Samuel (Catherine Buck)
☎ (717) 646-2172 . . ''Relaxly'' Pocono Lake Preserve, PA *18348*

Fetridge MR & MRS Clark W (Jean H Huebner) . . . . | ☎ (616) 429-3666
JUNIORS MR Clark W 2d . . . . | ''Eagle's Nest''
 | 4055 Lake Forest
 | Path, Stevensville,
 | MI *49127*

Fetridge MRS William Harrison (Bonnie-Jean Clark)
☎ (616) 429-5665 . . ''Quinibeck Cottage'' 3995 Lake Forest Path, Stevensville, MI *49127*
Aug 1 . . ☎ (616) 429-9669 . . ''Rainbow Cabin'' 4050 Lake Forest Path, Stevensville, MI *49127*

Few MR & MRS Lyne S (Ellen Hale) . . . . | ☎ (518) 962-4375
MISS Mary R . . . . | ''Stonysides''
 | Lake Shore Rd,
 | Westport, NY *12993*

Fick MR & MRS Ronald G (Valerie L Peterson) . . . . . | ☎ (011-41-38)
MR David Bovet . . . . | 55-21-22
MR Bradley Borel . . . . | Château de Gorgier,
 | Canton de
 | Neuchâtel,
 | Switzerland

Ficks MRS Gerald J (Katharine B Sutphin) ⚓
☎ (508) 627-5002 . . 9 Atwood Circle, Edgartown, MA *02539*

Field MRS Field (Deirdre D Field)
☎ (011-33) 26-80-41-89 . . ''La Tour de Nesle'' 51120 Nesle-la-Reposte, France

Field MR & MRS H James JR (Janet M Isham) . . . . . . | ☎ (401) 635-4285
MISS Elisabeth I . . . . | 143 Sakonnet Point
JUNIORS MISS Jennifer D . . . . | Rd, Little Compton,
 | RI *02837*

Field MRS Harold J (Hartog—Nancy Doering)
☎ (401) 635-4217 . . ''Meadowlands'' 54 Sakonnet Point Rd, Little Compton, RI *02837*

Field MR & MRS James A (Lila R Breckinridge)
☎ (414) 854-2777 . . Box 58, Ephraim, WI *54211*

Field MR & MRS John E (Jane B Wilmot) . . . . | ☎ (715) 542-2009
MR John E JR . . . . | Field Island, Sayner,
MR Christopher E . . . . | WI *54560*

Field MR & MRS R Henry (Hoover—Rennell—Dodge—Nancy A May)
Box 127, Rte 30, Dorset, VT *05251*

Field MR & MRS Spencer (Frances Pierce)
☎ (508) 563-5560 . . 502 Wings Neck Rd, Pocasset, MA *02559*

Fieve DR & MRS Ronald R (Katia von Saxe) . . . . . . | Aug 1 . .
MISS Lara . . . . | ☎ (516) 283-9653
MISS Vanessa . . . . | S Main St,
 | Southampton, NY
 | *11968*

Filley MR & MRS Oliver D (Moira L Redmond)
HC 61, Box 70, Edgartown, MA *02539*

Findlay MR & MRS Donald R (Glover—Katherine D Wiman)
☎ (315) 369-6610 . . Adirondack League Club, Box 8, Little Moose Lake, Old Forge, NY *13420*

Finletter MRS Thomas K (Geist—Eileen Wechsler)
☎ (207) 288-3142 . . ''French Cottage'' Albert Meadow, Bar Harbor, ME *04609*

Finley MR & MRS John H 3d (Margot M Gerrity) . . . | ☎ (207) 363-6507
MISS Charlotte D . . . . | ''Sea Winds''
MR John H 4th . . . . | Norwood Farms Rd,
JUNIORS MR Samuel W . . . . | Box J,
 | York Harbor, ME
 | *03911*

Finley DR Knox H
☎ (415) 868-1328 . . ''Monarch Halt'' Box 145, Stinson Beach, CA *94970*

Finocchio MRS Sarah Elting (Sarah S Elting) . . . . . . | Desbarats, Ontario
MISS Amy W . . . . | P0R 1E0, Canada
JUNIORS MISS Amanda C . . . . |
JUNIORS MR Leigh E . . . . |

Fiorato MR & MRS Hugo (Pogue—Scott—Gilchrist | ☎ (508) 583-4915
—Joelyn S Littauer) . . . . | ''Tower House''
MISS Stephanie S Gilchrist . . . . | on Lamberts Cove,
 | PO Box 757,
 | West Tisbury, MA
 | *02575*

Fioratti MR & MRS Nereo (Helen E Costantino) . . . . | ☎ (011-39-55)
MISS Arianna C . . . . | 61-30-41
 | via Benedetto da
 | Maiano 22, 50014
 | Fiesole, Italy

Firestone MR David M . . see C Runnells
Firestone MR & MRS Leonard K (Lynch—Caroline Hudson)
☎ (970) 949-7160 . . ''Paweech Kahnee'' Box 2304, Avon, CO *81620*

Firestone MRS Peter S (Julie Nelson) . . . . | ☎ (208) 622-8019
MISS Lisa S . . . . | Box 2729,
 | Sun Valley, ID
 | *83353*

Firth MR & MRS Nicholas L D (Slocum—Neilson— | Aug 1 . .
Edmée C de Montmollin) . . . . | ☎ (516) 788-7531
MISS Katherine V . . . . | PO Box 665,
MISS Marie-Louise C Slocum . . . . | Fishers Island, NY
MISS M Olivia J Slocum . . . . | *06390*
MR John J Slocum 3d . . . . |

Fischelis MR Robert L
Strafford, VT *05072*

Fischer MR & MRS F Wood (Constance Linington Froeb)
☎ (516) 749-0878 . . PO Box 1025, Shelter Island Heights, NY *11965*

Fischer MR & MRS Heinz G (Groesbeek—Burdet—Linda L Gray)
''Brisas Norte'' Lake Rd, Newport Center, VT *05857*

Fischer MR & MRS Julian D (Tatiana C Pertzoff) . . . | Pig Island,
MISS Anastasia I . . . . | Beals, ME *04611*
MISS Alexandra G . . . . |
MISS Ariana S . . . . |

Fischer MR & MRS M Peter (Appell—Suzanne | ☎ (508) 432-6627
Chichester) . . . . | 80 Forest Beach Rd
MISS Martha C . . . . | Ext, South Chatham,
MR Matthew A . . . . | MA *02659*
MR Michael P . . . . |

Fisher MRS A Murray (Lucretia Billings)
☎ (401) 245-5646 . . 33 Samoset Rd, Barrington, RI *02806*

Fisher MR & MRS Aiken W (Jane I Marshall)
☎ (412) 593-7734 . . ''Snowball Hill'' RD 1, Stahlstown, PA *15687*

Fisher MRS Benjamin R (Lilian C Hall)
   ☎ (508) 255-3437 . . 121 Lake Dv, Box 36, South Orleans, MA *02662*
Fisher MR & MRS Bennett L (Susan B Huntington) . . | Sorrento, ME *04677*
   MISS Louisa H . . . . |
   JUNIORS MR James B . . . . |
Fisher MR & MRS David J A (Sarah McA Wheatland)
   ☎ (011-44-1328) 711816 . . 53 High St, Wells-next-the-Sea, Norfolk, England
Fisher MRS George C (Jean K Sprague)
   ☎ (705) 756-8859 . . Island 196, Honey Harbour, Ontario P0E 1E0, Canada
Fisher MR & MRS Kenneth W (Whipple—Mettie R | ☎ (615) 383-8201
   Barton) . . . . | 4406 Honeywood
   MR Sean H . . . . | Dv, Nashville, TN
   | *37205*
Fisher MR & MRS Philip B JR (Clarke—Diana Y Dillon)
   ☎ (207) 963-4083 . . ''Orchard Farm'' Winter Harbor, ME *04693*
Fisher DR & MRS Robert M (Katharine S Morris)
   ☎ (717) 477-2078 . . Ganoga Lake 15, Benton, PA *17814*
Fisher MR & MRS Thomas K (Sandra L Martin) . . . . | ☎ (616) 723-5848
   MISS Stephanie M . . . . | Deer Path, Manistee,
   MISS Sarah K . . . . | MI *49660*
Fiske MRS John (Rosalie A Cheney)
   ☎ (508) 724-3488 . . 82 East St, Petersham, MA *01366*
Fiske MR & MRS John N (Jean-Lamont Barker)
   ☎ (603) 253-6277 . . ''Needle Point'' Center Harbor, NH *03226*
Fiske MR & MRS William J (Diana P Furse)
   ☎ (516) 788-7243 . . Bell Hill Av, Fishers Island, NY *06390*
Fitzgerald JUNIORS MISS Brooke A . . see D G Burke
FitzGerald MR & MRS Gerald J (Katherine Jane | ☎ (702) 831-1484
   Edgerton) . . . . | ''Tahoe House''
   MR Scott T . . . . | 525 Lakeshore Blvd,
   | Incline Village, NV
   | *89451*
Flaccus MR & MRS Charles L III (Moe—Anne L | ☎ (609) 368-2504
   Hall) ⚓ . . . . | 8523 Second Av,
   MISS Lisa L . . . . | Stone Harbor, NJ
   MR Charles L 4th . . . . | *08247*
Flachbarth MR Charles T P
   ☎ (304) 428-5411 . . 7 Meadowcrest, Parkersburg, WV *26101*
Flanigan MR & MRS Peter A (Elizabeth R Engelsman)
   ☎ (616) 547-0574 . . 109 Belvedere Club, Charlevoix, MI *49720*
Fleischmann MR & MRS Charles 3d (Burd B | ☎ (508) 945-2191
   Stevenson) . . . . | Hunter House,
   MISS Louisa B . . . . | 309 Bridge St,
   | Chatham, MA *02633*
Fleishhacker MR & MRS David (Victoria J | ☎ (415) 851-2976
   Escamilla) . . . . | ''Green Gables''
   MISS Eleanor D . . . . | 331 Albion Av,
   JUNIORS MR Jeffrey D . . . . | Woodside, CA
   | *94062*
Fleitas MRS Allison F (Maddock—Ruth M Quigley)
   ☎ (207) 276-3227 . . Sweetbriar Bungalow, Harborside Rd, Northeast Harbor, ME *04662*
Fleming MR & MRS Samuel W 3d (Beverly Cochran)
   ☎ (508) 627-9013 . . RFD 81-5, Edgartown, MA *02539*

Fletcher MRS Henry M (Anne V Beers)
   ☎ (516) 726-5991 . . Cobb Isle Rd, Water Mill, NY *11976*
Fletcher MISS Mary L
   ☎ (516) 676-1481 . . Shelter Lane, Locust Valley, NY *11560*
Flicker MR & MRS Richard H (Jane M Mason) . . . . . | ☎ (516) 653-4185
   MISS Meredith A . . . . | ''The Big House''
   MR John M . . . . | Quogo Neck Lane,
   | Quogue, NY *11959*
Flickinger MR & MRS Geoffrey R (Michelle A Ferrall)
   ☎ (516) 788-7972 . . Fishers Island, NY *06390*
Flickinger MR & MRS Peter B (King—Genevieve Roe)
   ☎ (905) 894-0693 . . 4449 Erie Rd, Ft Erie, Ontario L0S 1N0, Canada
Flickinger MR & MRS Thomas R (Phoebe A Raymond)
   ☎ (905) 834-7994 . . RR 1, Lorraine, Port Colborne, Ontario L3K 5V3, Canada
Flight MR & MRS Curtis C (Barbara F Russell)
   ☎ (603) 763-4664 . . ''Granitehead'' 48 Fisher's Bay, Sunapee, NH *03782*
Flinn MR & MRS Lawrence JR (Stephanie H Strubing) | ☎ (516) 324-0205
   MISS Marion de V . . . . | Spaeth Lane,
   MISS Adriane S . . . . | East Hampton, NY
   MR Lawrence 3d . . . . | *11937*
Flinn MR & MRS Michael de V (Hanes—Ann D | ☎ (516) 788-7970
   Gulliver) . . . . | Fishers Island, NY
   MISS Randall E . . . . | *06390*
   MR Michael de V JR . . . . |
   MR T Rex . . . . |
      MISS Allison P Hanes . . . . |
      MR Jonathan Y Hanes . . . . |
Flood MRS James (Elizabeth Dresser)
   ☎ (805) 937-3616 . . ''Rancho Sisquoc'' Rte 1, Box 147, Santa Maria, CA *93454*
Flood MR & MRS James C (Astrid E Sommer) . . . . . . | PO Box 492,
   MISS Elizabeth . . . . | Teton Village, WY
   MISS Karin . . . . | *83025*
   MISS Christina . . . . |
Flower MR & MRS Walter C 3d (Ella S Montgomery) | ☎ (516) 788-7068
   ⚓ . . . . | ''Darby Cove''
   MISS Lindsey Montgomery . . . . | Fishers Island, NY
   | *06390*
Floyd MRS John Paul (Floyd—Kingsland—Maryan F Chadwick)
   ☎ (202) 244-0574 . . 4201 Cathedral Av NW, Apt 23W, Washington, DC *20016-4903*
Flynn MISS Abigail W . . see J Pulitzer 4th
Fogarty MR & MRS Edward T (Johnson—Mary S | ☎ (203) 655-3041
   Elliott) . . . . | 40 Contentment
   MISS Anne C . . . . | Island Rd, Darien,
   MR Edward A . . . . | CT *06820*
Fogarty MR & MRS Gerald J JR (Sarah J Faile)
   ☎ (802) 672-3680 . . Round Top Mountain, Plymouth, VT *05056*
Fogg MRS George P JR (Frances C Knight)
   ☎ (617) 934-2163 . . 25 Russell Rd, Duxbury, MA *02331*
Fogg MR & MRS George P 3d (Jane T Nichols) . . . . . | ☎ (617) 934-2424
   MISS (DR) Jane F . . . . | 25 Russell Rd,
   | Duxbury, MA *02331*

Fogg MR & MRS Joseph G 3d (Leslie K Solbert) . . . .
  MISS Elizabeth P . . . .
  MR Nathaniel T G . . . .
☎ (207) 276-5268
"Wanakiwin"
Seal Harbor, ME *04675*

Foley MRS Gifford T (April J Hoxie) . . . .
  JUNIORS MISS Catherine L . . . .
  JUNIORS MR Gifford T JR . . . .
☎ (414) 854-5916
"Random Farm"
2016 Wildwood Rd, Sister Bay, WI *54234*

Foley MRS Regula (Regula von Muralt)
  ☎ (516) 922-8108 . . Box 313, Seawanhaka Rd, Centre Island, Oyster Bay, NY *11771*

Foley MR Thomas C—⚓
  ☎ (508) 389-6522 . . on board Glory" Nantucket Boat Basin, Nantucket, MA *02554*

Folger MR & MRS Peter M (Barbara B Waterman) . .
  MISS Katharine B . . . .
  MISS Sarah S . . . .
  MISS Abiah A . . . .
  JUNIORS MR Peter . . . .
  JUNIORS MR James A . . . .
☎ (508) 428-1045
"RRAC"
25 Rambler Rd,
Box 102, Osterville, MA *02655*

Follansbee MRS N Walton (Nancy McM Walton) . .
  MISS Nancy W . . . .
  MISS Brooks W . . . .
☎ (716) 386-2556
"Old Trees Farm"
RD 1, Bemus Point, NY *14712*

Follett MR & MRS William R (Barbara D Wickersham)
  ☎ (860) 739-0105 . . 10 Francis Lane, Old Black Point, Niantic, CT *06357*

Fondaras MR & MRS Anastassios (Miller—Weicker—Elizabeth T Robertson)
  ☎ (516) 324-1362 . . Further Lane, Box 186, East Hampton, NY *11937*

Foote MR & MRS Robert L (Barbara K Austin)
  ☎ (715) 856-6156 . . Wausaukee Club, HCR 1, Box 8A, Athelstane, WI *54104*

Forbes MR & MRS Charles Stewart (Dorothy Lockwood)
  ☎ (508) 994-1544 . . "Birchfield Farm" 4 South Lane, South Dartmouth, MA *02748*

Forbes MR & MRS Christopher C (BRNSS Astrid M von Heyl) . . . .
  MISS Charlotte A M . . . .
☎ (719) 379-3263
Forbes Trinchera Ranch, Ft Garland, CO *81125*

Forbes MR & MRS John Douglas (Mary E Lewis)
  ⚓ . . . .
  JUNIORS MR Michael . . . .
☎ (415) 771-2149
1250 Jones St, Apt 1301, San Francisco, CA *94109*

Forbes MR & MRS Peter (Erica L de Berry) . . . .
  MISS Anne de M . . . .
  MR Alexander J . . . .
☎ (207) 244-3392
"Ravensthorp"
Greening Island, Box 1096, Southwest Harbor, ME *04679*

Forbes MRS Wallace F (Betty A Goldsmith)
  ☎ (207) 529-5207 . . "Far Seas" Round Pound, ME *04564*

Forbes MR Wallace F . . . .
  MISS Alexandra E . . . .
  MR Bruce C . . . .
☎ (914) 941-8341
609 Sleepy Hollow Rd, Briarcliff Manor, NY *10510*

Ford MR & MRS Alfred W (Catharina Skjöldebrand) .
  MISS Christina W . . . .
  MR Thomas W . . . .
☎ (207) 633-6857
"Pine Cliff"
HCR 66, Box 473, Pine Cliff Rd, West Southport, ME *04576*

Ford MR & MRS Jeremiah 3d (Stewardson—Elizabeth M Dana) . . . .
  MISS Caroline C Stewardson . . . .
☎ (508) 228-2644
Quidnet Rd, Nantucket, MA *02554*

Ford MRS John B (Low—Mary Holland)
  ☎ (616) 526-2035 . . PO Box 338, Otis Lane, Harbor Springs, MI *49740*

Ford MR & MRS Mills H (M Elise Mallon)
  ☎ (303) 798-9629 . . 1894 E Orchard Rd, Littleton, CO *80121*

Ford MISS Naneen E
  ☎ (516) 283-0425 . . Meadow Club, First Neck Lane, PO Drawer F, Southampton, NY *11969*

Ford MR & MRS Thomas P (Dolph—Mary L McGovern) . . . .
  MR William McG . . . .
☎ (203) 245-7723
154 Middle Beach Rd, Madison, CT *06443*

Forker MRS David M (Elizabeth Nichols)
  ☎ (616) 547-9005 . . 207 Belvedere Club, Charlevoix, MI *49720*

Forrestel MR & MRS Richard E JR (Annabelle V Irey)
  ☎ (716) 699-5511 . . "Aerie" 7094 High Meadows Rd, Ellicottville, NY *14731*

Forrester MR & MRS Peter C (Edith W Brooks) . . . .
  MISS Melinda B . . . .
☎ (508) 636-8570
103 Howland Rd, Westport Harbor, MA *02790*

Forrester MR & MRS Robert R JR (Lilley—Elena Musto)
  ☎ (516) 324-1967 . . Box 1397, East Hampton, NY *11937*

Forsch MRS Peter D (Barbara W Booth)
  ☎ (441) 238-1346 . . "Wynk Beyond" 20 Riddell's Bay Rd, Warwick WK 06, Bermuda

Forster DR & MRS Robert E 2d (Elizabeth H Day) . .
  MISS Julia B . . . .
☎ (617) 934-0733
"The Boat House"
Snug Harbor Station, Box 163, Duxbury, MA *02331*

Fort MRS William L (Preston—Doris Alford)
  ☎ (802) 362-1207 . . "Carriage House" Box 75, Manchester, VT *05254*

Forté MR & MRS Donald (Mason—Joan Jackson)
  ☎ (508) 748-2236 . . 136 Point Rd, Marion, MA *02738*

Fosburgh MRS Pieter W (Cunningham—M Elizabeth Edmondson)
  ☎ (518) 251-3827 . . "Tamarack Corner" North Woods Club, Minerva, NY *12851*

Foss MRS Eugene N 2d (M Winifred Brown)
  ☎ (603) 823-5956 . . "Ridge Farm" Ridge Rd, Box 126, Franconia, NH *03580*

Foss MRS Wilson P (Mae K Chandlee)
  93 Squam Rd, Nantucket, MA *02554*

Fossel MR & MRS Scott G (Petria M Horner)
☎ (307) 739-2537 . . 3570 N Lake Creek Dv, Jackson, WY *83001*

Foster MR & MRS Benjamin R (Karen J Polinger) . . . "Violin House"
  JUNIORS MISS Constance . . . . Tartiers, 02290
  JUNIORS MISS Ruth . . . . Vic-sur-Aisne, France

Foster MR & MRS David V (Judith N Kurz) . . . . ☎ (914) 424-4240
  JUNIORS MISS Julia K . . . . PO Box 277, Travis Corners Rd, Garrison, NY *10524*

Foster DR & MRS Giraud Vernam (Carolyn E Lindquist) . . of
☎ (207) 529-5856 . . "Toad Hall" Damariscotta, ME *04543*
☎ (803) 768-2307 . . 2247 Catesby's Bluff, Seabrook Island, Johns Island, SC *29455*

Foster MISS Jane de M (Lorber—Reece—Jane de M . . . . ☎ (207) 276-0564
  Foster) . . . . "Treetops"
  JUNIORS MISS Augusta H B Lorber . . . . Cooksey Dv,
  JUNIORS MR Giraud van N F Lorber . . . . Seal Harbor, ME *04675*

Foster MRS Lucy C S (Lucy C Sprague)
☎ (207) 883-5472 . . "Bohemia Corner" 18 Massacre Lane, Prouts Neck, Scarborough, ME *04074*

Foster MR & MRS Paul S JR (Lowe—Barbara Keast)
☎ (707) 433-1022 . . "Maacama Creek Ranch" 10835 H'way 128, Healdsburg, CA *95448*

Foster MR & MRS Richard W (Elizabeth Read)
"Wingate House" RR 1, Center Harbor, NH *03226*

Foster MR & MRS Ridgely M (Dinkel—Leta F . . . . . . ☎ (207) 276-5065
  Austin) . . . . "Cedar Hedges"
  MR Varick P . . . . S Shore Rd,
  JUNIORS MISS India R . . . . Northeast Harbor,
  MISS Sallie C F Dinkel . . . . ME *04662*

Foster MR & MRS Rockwood H (Marguerite Peet)
☎ (508) 748-0044 . . "The Hatchery" 151 Allen Point Rd, Marion, MA *02738*

Foster MR & MRS Timothy (Dorothy Colotte) . . . . . . ☎ (609) 967-3187
  MISS Elizabeth A . . . . "High Dunes" 4028 Bayberry Dv, Avalon, NJ *08202*

Fotterall MR & MRS W W Law 3d (Kathleen A Pannepacker)
☎ (609) 967-3316 . . "Avasea" 63 W 23 St, Avalon, NJ *08202*

Foulke MR & MRS Walter L (Wendy S Taylor) . . . . . ☎ (207) 276-5314
  MISS Laura T . . . . "Thomaston
  MR David P . . . . House" Northeast Harbor, ME *04662*

Foulke MR & MRS William G (Louisa L Wood) ⛵
☎ (207) 276-3905 . . "La Folie" County Rd, Seal Harbor, ME *04675*

Foulke MR & MRS William G JR (Wendy H Robbins) . ☎ (207) 276-3989
  MISS Jennifer R . . . . "The Studio"
  MISS Louisa L . . . . Seal Harbor, ME
  MR Adam W *04675*

Fowler MR & MRS H S Winthrop JR (Gigi A Collins)
Stepan Lake, AK *99652*

Fowler MR & MRS Howland A (Shirley J Boers) . . . . ☎ (616) 795-3040
  MISS Amy A . . . . "The Hermitage" 3990 Hermitage Rd, Middleville, MI *49333*

Fowler MR Lindsay Anderson
Box 738, La Jolla, CA *92038*

Fowler MR & MRS Paul D (Christy B Latham) . . . . . ☎ (516) 537-1042
  MISS Hillary B . . . . Georgica
  JUNIORS MR David I . . . . Association, Wainscott, NY *11975*

Fowler MR & MRS Robert A (Berman—Monica E Hedén)
☎ (207) 563-3580 . . "Cottesbrook" Walpole, ME *04573*

Fowlkes MR & MRS George A (Jeannette C Sanford) . ☎ (508) 228-1093
  MISS Daphne B . . . . 26 Easton St, Nantucket, MA *02554*

Fowlkes MR & MRS J Winston 3d (Isabel . . . . ☎ (860) 868-0402
  Lenkiewicz) . . . . Potash Hill Rd,
  MISS Isabel Blair . . . . Washington, CT
  MR Gregory G *06793*
  MR Stephan W . . . .

Fownes MR & MRS Henry G (Godfrey—Harrison—Paulette Bragg)
☎ (203) 622-4298 . . 680 Steamboat Rd, Greenwich, CT *06830*

Fox MR & MRS Caleb F 4th (Patricia N Wheeler)
☎ (207) 363-5234 . . 6 Simpson Lane, York Harbor, ME *03911*

Fox MR Charles Clayton
☎ (610) 827-7255 . . .1425 Yellow Springs Rd, Chester Springs, PA *19425*

Fox MRS Heywood (Elizabeth Wells)
☎ (508) 428-2323 . . 405 Sea View Av, Osterville, MA *02655*

Fox MR & MRS John B (Julia Garrett) . . . . ☎ (207) 392-1791
  MISS Sarah C . . . . "The Gables"
  MR Thomas B . . . . Box 5, Andover, ME *04216*

Fox MR & MRS Joseph Carrère (MacLean—Alison Barbour)
☎ (207) 244-3927 . . "Renardie" Southwest Harbor, ME *04679*

Fox MR & MRS Reeder R (Marion C Laffey) . . . . ☎ (610) BL2-2202
  MISS Vanessa S . . . . "Branch House"
  MR Drew D . . . . Paxinosa Rd, Easton, PA *18042*

Foy MR & MRS Louis A (Katharine B Schaefer) . . . . ☎ (508) 428-6743
  MR Louis E . . . . "Granli" 923 Sea View Av, Box 387, Osterville, MA *02655*

Fraker MR & MRS Harrison S (Richardson—Riehle—Rulon-Miller—
Barbara A Anderson) ⛵
☎ (508) 228-0365 . . 1 Gardner Court, Nantucket, MA *02554*

Francis MR & MRS Bernard A JR (Katharine L . . . . . ☎ (609) 368-6518
  Hancock) . . . . 7 Marine Way,
  MISS Christina Lea . . . . Avalon, NJ *08202*
  MISS Caroline Elizabeth . . . .

Francis MR & MRS Peter T (Susan L Stanton) . . . . . . ☎ (410) 723-1314
 MR Cameron S . . . . "Gull Watch"
 JUNIORS MR Peter T JR . . . . 132 Georgia Av,
 Ocean City, MD
 21842

Francis MR & MRS Sidney R JR (Mary M Westberg)
 ☎ (207) 526-4352 . . "Rose Hill Farm" Swans Island, ME *04685*

Franck DR & MRS Peter T (Fay M Martin) . . . . Center Lovell,
 MISS Valerie M ME *04016*
 JUNIORS MISS Cynthia S . . . .

Frank MR & MRS Lionel Seaton (M Jane Spangler)
 ☎ (802) 823-7829 . . Verdmont Club, RR 1, Box 335A, Pownal,
 VT *05261*

Frankenthal MR & MRS Charles P A (Ann P Krugler)
 ☎ (715) 545-2088 . . 1406 Bear Tail Point, Phelps, WI *54554*

Franklin MR & MRS George S (Helena Edgell)
 ☎ (516) 922-7559 . . 63 Cove Neck Rd, Oyster Bay, NY *11771*

Fraser MR & MRS Ronald G (Patricia Dodd) . . . . ☎ (516) 324-4095
 MISS Alison M . . . . Apaquogue Rd,
 MR Ian M . . . . East Hampton, NY
 11937

Frazer MR & MRS John G JR (Barbara Bitting)
 ☎ (412) 238-9216 . . "Redstone" Box J, Ligonier, PA *15658*

Frazer MR & MRS Nimrod T (Patricia L Martin) . . of
 ☎ (334) 278-4429 . . "Lighting Rod" Germany Rd, Lowndesboro,
 AL *36752*
 ☎ (904) 231-2861 . . 50 Seawatch Dv, Santa Rosa Beach, FL *32459*

Frazier MRS J Rollins (Joan P Rollins) . . . . ☎ (518) 891-1971
 MISS Ramsey R . . . . 150 Moss Rock Rd,
 MR Gibson . . . . Box 52B, HCR 1,
 Saranac Lake, NY
 12983

Frazier MR Stephen C . . see J T Jackson 3d

Frederick MISS Alexandra C M (Baker—Alexandra C M Frederick)
 ☎ (011-44-1883) 74-3252 . . Blechingley Rectory, Redhill,
 Surrey RH1 4LR, England

Freeman MR & MRS David F (Hazel S Farr)
 ☎ (506) 529-8953 . . "Tobermory" Joe's Point Rd, St Andrews,
 NB E0G 2X0, Canada

Freeman MR & MRS David N (Ellen S Wood)
 ☎ (518) 835-6893 . . 4083 S Shore Rd, Canada Lake, NY *12032*

Freeman MRS E Lavalle (Elaine Lavalle)
 ☎ (516) 283-3093 . . 132 Post Lane, Southampton, NY *11968*

Freeman DR & MRS (DR) Jonathan K (Katharine E O'Donnell)
 4083 S Shore Rd, Canada Lake, NY *12032*

Freeman MR & MRS Joseph S (Thorndike—Cynthia F Lyman)
 ☎ (508) 228-9231 . . "Middle Brick" 95 Main St, Nantucket, MA *02554*

Freeman MR & MRS Louis McDaniel (Judith Waite) . ☎ (601) 452-9249
 MISS (DR) Laura Louise . . . . "Boisdore"
 300 Havana Dv,
 Pass Christian, MS
 39571

Freeman MR & MRS Samuel M 2d (Margaret O
 Davison) . . . . ☎ (609) 494-1207
 MR William H . . . . 48 Maiden Lane,
 MR Jonathan C . . . . Harvey Cedars, NJ
 08008

Freemon MR & MRS Richard D (Merces S de Quevedo Pessanha)
 ☎ (011-351-1) 925-8947 . . "Casal S Pedro" Albarraque, 2735 Cacem,
 Portugal

Fremont-Smith MR & MRS Thayer (Anne R Jeffery) . ☎ (603) 744-9440
 MR James J . . . . "Thayer's Lair"
 MR Phillip H . . . . Ledges at Newfound
 Lake, Alexandria,
 NH *03222*

French MR & MRS Harry B (Phyllis P McLean) . . . . ☎ (609) 368-5746
 MISS (DR) Pamela P . . . . "Sea 'scape"
 MR William McL . . . . 165—70 St, Avalon,
 MR Clayton G . . . . NJ *08202*

French MR & MRS John 3d (Gundlach—Marina
 Kellen) . . . . ☎ (203) 438-3014
 MISS Annabelle K Gundlach . . . . "Log House"
 MR Andrew S Gundlach . . . . 178 Ned's Mountain
 Rd, Ridgefield, CT
 06877

French MR & MRS John R (Quasha—Leigh Catlin) . . ☎ (516) 537-3129
 MISS Jennifer C Quasha . . . . "Windswept"
 Matthews Lane,
 PO Box 817,
 Bridgehampton, NY
 11932

French MR & MRS John S (Alexandra B Pagon)
 ☎ (508) 228-2266 . . 6 Prospect St, Nantucket, MA *02554*

French MR & MRS Raymond A (Joan C Foy)
 ☎ (207) 359-2325 . . Bay Rd, Blue Hill Falls, ME *04615*

French MR & MRS Robert A (Nancy H Woods) . . . . ☎ (207) 288-3484
 JUNIORS MR Grayson P . . . . "Greencourt"
 Harbor Lane,
 Bar Harbor, ME
 04609

French MRS Theodore (Katharine L Dunlop) . . . . . . ☎ (516) 583-5997
 MISS Virginia D . . . . Cottage 81,
 Point O'Woods, NY
 11706

Frenning MRS Alfred B (Blanche B Borden)
 ☎ (401) 635-2279 . . "Bumble Bee Farm" 316 W Main Rd,
 Little Compton, RI *02837*

Freund MR & MRS Gerald (Peregrine W Whittlesey)
 ☎ (802) 457-2118 . . General Delivery, North Pomfret, VT *05053*

Frick-Humes MISS Julia E
 129 Seaview Av, Santa Cruz, CA *95062*

Friedeman MRS William S (Lillian Lampert)
 ☎ (616) 429-5946 . . "The Country" 5082 Notre Dame Av, Stevensville,
 MI *49127*

Fries MR William 2d
 8 Brockway Springs Rd, North Tahoe, CA *95715*

Fritz MR & MRS Arthur Joseph JR (Barbara F Carr) . . ☎ (707) 433-3277
 MISS Jenner Lee . . . . "Camelot Ranch"
 MR Arthur J 3d . . . . 24691 Dutcher
 MR Clayton B . . . . Creek Rd,
 Cloverdale, CA
 95448

Fritz DR & MRS William F (Susan E Baker)
 ☎ (603) 532-7655 . . "Still Pond" 25 Gilson Rd, Jaffrey, NH *03452*

Froelich MR & MRS Robert L (Denise McNamara) .. | ☎ (508) 627-7009
MISS Cecilia C .... | "Black Pines"
MISS Emma E B .... | Planting Field Way,
MISS Helen McN .... | Edgartown, MA
 | 02539
Froelicher MRS Hans JR (Frances H Morton)
 ☎ (717) 642-5118 . . "Strawberry Hill" 1537 Mt Hope Rd, Fairfield,
PA *17320*
Froment MR Frank L
 ☎ (717) 775-7918 . . Blooming Grove Hunt & Fish Club, Hawley,
PA *18428*
Fromson MR & MRS Brett D (Carmel S Wilson)
 ☎ (860) 435-0791 . . 263 Belgo Rd, Lakeville, CT *06063*
Frost MR & MRS Rufus S 3d (Mary Brereton)
 ☎ (603) 876-3810 . . "Colonial Hall" Marlborough, NH *03455*
Frothingham MR & MRS A Michael (Sara Struthers) | ☎ (914) 967-2981
MISS Victoria S .... | 30 Green Av, Rye,
MR Eric .... | NY *10580*
Fuiks MR & MRS Lewis J (Calder—Elizabeth Dodge)
 ☎ (802) 362-2888 . . "Apple Hill" RR 1, Box 657, East Dorset,
VT *05253*
Fuller MRS Andrew P (Spreckels—Geraldine Spreckels) . . of
 ☎ (516) 283-3790 . . "Les Pommiers" PO Box 465, Southampton,
NY *11969*
 ☎ (212) 988-6747 . . 765 Park Av, New York, NY *10021*
Fuller MISS Elizabeth H .... | ☎ (516) 324-5106
MR Frederic J .... | "10A Ranch"
 | Cedar St,
 | East Hampton, NY
 | *11937*
Fuller MR & MRS J Kemp G JR (Barbara A Ciullo)
 ☎ (516) 537-3730 . . Box 91, Bridgehampton, NY *11932*
Fuller MR & MRS Peter D (Joan B Marcotte)
 ☎ (603) 964-8923 . . "Lea House" 23 Willow Av, North Hampton,
NH *03862*
Fuller MR & MRS Robert Gorham (Constance W Bader) ⚓
 ☎ (207) 363-2973 . . Stage Neck Colony, Box 391, York Harbor,
ME *03911*
Fulweiler MRS Spencer B (Patricia L Platt) ⚓
 ☎ (203) 866-6709 . . 3 Hilltop Rd, Wilson Point, South Norwalk,
CT *06854*
Fulweiler MR & MRS Spencer B JR (Rena M Zurn)
 ☎ (207) 288-9894 . . "Tea House" Box 5, Hulls Cove, ME *04644*
Fulweiler MR Thomas B
 "Holiday Ledges" Bremen Long Island, Medomak, ME *04551*
Funk MR & MRS W John (Mary Reath) .... | ☎ (207) 276-5265
JUNIORS MISS Lisa A .... | "White House"
JUNIORS MR James T .... | Northeast Harbor,
 | ME *04662*
Funkhouser MR & MRS A Paul (Eleanor R Gamble)
 ☎ (910) 363-2859 . . Roaring Gap, NC *28668*
Funsten MISS de Lancey
 ☎ (401) 423-2771 . . 23 Standish Rd, Jamestown, RI *02835*
Furlaud MRS Banks (Elspeth H Banks)
 ☎ (508) 627-4647 . . Box 1011, Edgartown, MA *02539*
Furlaud MR & MRS Maxime Jay (Alice E Nelson)
 "Hardy Camp" South Brooksville, ME *04617*
Furlaud MR & MRS Richard M (Allen—Philbin—Isabel G T Phelps)
 ☎ (516) 324-1726 . . PO Box 478, East Hampton, NY *11937*
Furse MR & MRS G Ronald (McKim—C Pamela | ☎ (516) 788-7243
 Fowler) .... | Bell Hill Av,
MISS Elizabeth W .... | Fishers Island, NY
MR William R .... | *06390*

G

Gable MR & MRS Robert E (Emily B Thompson)
 ☎ (616) 845-5994 . . Lake Forest Cottage, 4104 Epworth, Ludington,
MI *49431*
Gadsden MR & MRS Charles C (Marie E Dittmann) . | ☎ (401) 635-8638
MISS Pamela D .... | 66 Bailey's Ledge,
MR Charles C JR .... | Little Compton, RI
 | *02837*
Gagarin MR & MRS Peter S (Nancy E Tyner)
 ☎ (508) 945-3266 . . 126 Shore Rd, Chatham, MA *02633*
Gagné MR & MRS W Roderick (Pamela J Bashore)
 ☎ (609) 368-0891 . . 261—52 St, Avalon, NJ *08202*
Gahagan MR & MRS William G (Katharine H du Pont)
 ☎ (508) 428-2615 . . "Indian Point" Box 2106, Oyster Harbors,
Osterville, MA *02655*
Gaillard MR & MRS E Davis (Allen Van Tine) ..... | ☎ (518) 589-5814
MISS Mary B .... | "Harebell"
 | Onteora Club,
 | Tannersville, NY
 | *12485*
Gaillard MR & MRS William D (Katharine J Freie) . . | ☎ (516) 788-7681
MR David L .... | "Kasita"
MR Jeffrey S .... | Bell Hill Av,
 | Fishers Island, NY
 | *06390*
Gaines MR L Ebersole
 Box 1001, Ketchum, ID *83340*
Galban MR & MRS Leandro S JR (Beverley C Mountain)
 ☎ (516) 537-0089 . . 453 Hedges Lane, Box 453, Sagaponack, NY *11962*
Gales MRS Seaton (Marguerite Decroix)
 ☎ (914) 234-3348 . . "Carefree Cottage" Guard Hill Rd, Bedford,
NY *10506*
Gallagher MRS Charles T (Sarah C Woodworth)
 ☎ (603) 323-7291 . . "Page Hill" Tamworth, NH *03886*
Gallatin MRS James P (Sarah G Heyburn) .... | ☎ (516) 692-7008
MR Andrew H .... | 34 Middle Hollow
 | Rd, Huntington, NY
 | *11743*
Gallavan MR & MRS Richard A (McKown— | ☎ (516) 788-7054
 Evans—Suzanne L Whiting) .... | PO Box 546,
MISS Sarah D Evans .... | Fishers Island, NY
 | *06390*
Galt MRS William M 3d (Huston—Nancy E Gardner)
 ☎ (610) 527-4370 . . "The Hermitage" 1218 Round Hill Rd,
Bryn Mawr, PA *19010*

Galvis MR & MRS Sergio J (Mary Lee White)
☎ (516) 329-1667 . . 911 Springs Fireplace Rd, East Hampton, NY *11937*
Gamble MR & MRS Launce E (Joan Law) . . . . | ☎ (707) 944-2137
MISS Sydney . . . . | ''Locust Hill''
MR Mark D . . . . | 669 Oakville Rd, Oakville, CA *94562*
Gannett MR & MRS William B (Nancy Y Farnam)
☎ (603) 366-5020 . . 258 Edgewater Dv, Gilford, NH *03246*
Gantner MR John O
☎ (707) 963-4240 . . Schoolhouse Vineyards, Spring Mountain Rd, St Helena, CA *94574*
Gardiner MR & MRS E Nicholas P (Bron—Sigrid Becker)
☎ (011-33-94) 97-64-71 . . ''Calandra'' Chemin des Treilles de la Moutte, St Tropez, France
Gardiner MR & MRS Henry (Bramwell—Katharine H Emmet)
☎ (516) 653-4294 . . Box 472, 83 Quogue St, Quogue, NY *11959*
Gardiner MR & MRS Robert D L (Oakes—Eunice J Bailey) . . of
☎ (516) 324-0561 . . ''White House'' 127 Main St, East Hampton, NY *11937*
Manor House, Gardiners Island, NY *11937*
Gardiner MR Sargent C . . see G H P Dwight
Gardner MRS Ainslie A (Farley—Mary Ainslie Anderson) . . of
☎ (011-34-71) 301-872 . . Obispo Torres 11, Ibiza, Spain
☎ (401) 846-2165 . . ''Roselawn'' Bellevue Av, Newport, RI *02840*
Gardner MRS Edward P (Clapp—Ruby N Smith)
☎ (616) 537-2343 . . ''The Four Birches'' Ingleside-Douglas Lake, Levering, MI *49755*
Gardner MRS Edward T JR (Elizabeth Paxton)
☎ (203) 661-5576 . . 9 Woodside Rd, Deer Park, Greenwich, CT *06830*
Gardner MISS Eva
☎ (401) 846-1999 . . ''Roselawn'' Bellevue Av, Newport, RI *02840*
Gardner MR & MRS George P (Tatiana Stepanova)
☎ (508) 922-1377 . . ''Dacha'' 37 Paine Av, Prides Crossing, MA *01965*
Gardner MR & MRS John L (Susan B Kobusch)
☎ (207) 734-8863 . . Sabbathday Harbor, Islesboro, ME *04848*
Gardner CDR & MRS Richmond (Helen M Lovejoy) | ☎ (516) 653-4155
USN . . . . | 33 Elizabeth Lane,
MISS Amy E . . . . | Box 71, Quogue,
MSRS Richmond L & David F . . . . | NY *11959*
Gardner MR Stephen V
☎ (616) 386-5652 . . 40 Northport Point, Northport, MI *49670*
Gardner MR Stewart A
☎ (401) 846-1999 . . ''Roselawn'' Bellevue Av, Newport, RI *02840*
Garesché MR & MRS Edmond A B 3d (C Diane Raith)
☎ (314) 993-6232 . . 11 Portland Dv, St Louis, MO *63131*
Garfield MISS Eleanor
☎ (508) 548-0044 . . Box 72, Fay Rd, Woods Hole, MA *02543*
Garfield MR & MRS Michael R (Mary C Seymour)
☎ (508) 548-0044 . . Box 72, Fay Rd, Woods Hole, MA *02543*
Garlich MR & MRS Greg A (Elizabeth B Smyth)
☎ (417) 779-5127 . . 1000 Paradise Landing, Kimberling City, MO *65686*
Garnett MR & MRS Anthony T (Lucie C Palmer) . . . | ☎ (603) 964-8496
MISS Lucie C . . . . | 31 Atlantic Av,
MR William J . . . . | North Hampton, NH *03862*
Garnett MR & MRS Bradford L (Melanie H Fleischmann)
☎ (508) 945-1124 . . 283 Bridge St, Chatham, MA *02633*
Garretson MR & MRS James 2d (Sara C Panks)
☎ (518) 794-7716 . . ''Fox Hollow'' Hunt Club Rd, Old Chatham, NY *12136*
Garrett MR & MRS Darryl N (Cabell—Janet M | ☎ (717) 794-5034
West) . . . . | ''LeeWay''
MR Benjamin Cabell 5th . . . . | 14729 Charmian Rd, Blue Ridge Summit, PA *17214*
Garrett MRS Thomas Cresson (Adelaide McC Jefferys)
☎ (413) 528-2810 . . ''Moss Ledge'' RD 3, Box 57, Mt Washington, MA *01258*
Garrett MRS William Calvert (Harris P Kramer)
☎ (508) 548-3656 . . ''The Tower'' 488 Central Av, East Falmouth, MA *02536*
Gartman MR John S . . see C S Ashdown JR
Gartman MISS Vivian M . . see C S Ashdown JR
Garvan MRS Anthony N B (Lippincott—Beatrice W Bronson)
☎ (315) 354-4066 . . ''Little Prospect'' Green Point, Raquette Lake, NY *13436*
Garvan MRS Jackson (Hope Jackson)
☎ (516) 283-3591 . . Whitefield 12, 155 Hill St, Southampton, NY *11968*
Garvey DR & MRS James McB JR (Mary Blair Buggie)
☎ (516) 267-6716 . . Box 1632, Oceanview Lane, Amagansett, NY *11930*
Garvey MR John P
☎ (516) 324-1459 . . 36 Settlers Landing Lane, East Hampton, NY *11937*
Garvin MR & MRS B Russell JR (Margaret G Perry) . | ☎ (705) 378-5200
JUNIORS MR Perry R . . . . | The Perry Cabin, Rosseau Rd PO, Ontario P0C 1K0, Canada
Garwood MR John M . . see C Runnells
Gary MR Arthur J
☎ (516) 283-6272 . . 87 Pelletreau St, Southampton, NY *11968*
Gary MRS Wyndham L (Hatch—Shirley D Spaulding)
☎ (908) 747-3578 . . 39 Cheshire Square, Little Silver, NJ *07739*
Gaston MR Alexander
☎ (516) 788-7278 . . ''Windswept Aerie'' Isabella Beach Rd, Box 537, Fishers Island, NY *06390*
Gaston MR & MRS Frederick K 3d (Julia A Yawkey)
☎ (802) 824-6276 . . ''Brightmeadows'' Dale Rd, Weston, VT *05161*
Gates MISS Ashley du Pont . . see E N Carpenter 2d
Gates MRS Edward L SR (J Jane Powning)
☎ (508) 526-4022 . . 31 School St, Manchester, MA *01944*
Gates MR & MRS Geoffrey (Wende E Devlin) . . . . . . | ☎ (516) 283-4507
JUNIORS MR Christopher D . . . . | PO Box 2113, Southampton, NY *11969*
Gates MR & MRS John M JR (Letitia Ambrose)
☎ (516) 283-2966 . . 214 Hill St, Southampton, NY *11968*
Gates MR & MRS John S JR (Eloise R Henkel)
☎ (219) 787-8234 . . ''Dune Acres'' 14 Shore Dv, Chesterton, IN *46304*

Gates MRS Samuel E (Philomène Asher)
  ☎ (516) 288-2722 . . "Ketchaboneck" 40 Beach Rd, Westhampton Beach, NY *11978*
Gates MR & MRS Timothy G (Katerina Salteri) . . . . . | Tzonima Bay,
  JUNIORS MR Michael G . . . . | 4 N Plastira St,
  JUNIORS MR Christopher M . . . . | Nea Erythrea, GR 146 71 Athens, Greece
Gathings MR Wilson Randolph
  ☎ (011-44-133) 336-251 . . "Lahill" Upper Largo, Fife KY8 6JE, Scotland
Gatje MRS Barbara W (Ball—Barbara M Wright) . . | "Restawhile"
  MISS Alexandra L . . . . | Point O'Woods, NY
  MISS Margot K . . . . | *11706*
Gay MR & MRS John JR (Woodard—Gallagher—Deborah Hearst)
  ☎ (516) 283-7788 . . PO Box 1516, Southampton, NY *11969*
Gay MR & MRS Peter A (Evelyn Spencer)
  ☎ (203) 655-1601 . . PO Box 2462, Darien, CT *06820*
Geary MRS John W 2d (Hilary S Roche) . . . . | ☎ (516) 283-4444
  MR Alfred H 2d . . . . | "Fairfield"
  JUNIORS MR John W 3d . . . . | Great Plains Rd, Southampton, NY *11968*
Geddes MR & MRS Gerald K (Knechtel—Annette L | ☎ (516) 287-2167
  Longnon) . . . . | Great Plains Rd,
  JUNIORS MR Adam L . . . . | Box 2399, Southampton, NY *11968*
Geer DR & MRS Francis G (Miriam F Lewis)
  ☎ (908) 842-0970 . . 284 Clearbrook Court, PO Box 236, Little Silver, NJ *07739*
Geer REV & MRS Francis H (Sarah W Davis) . . . . . | "Pineapple Point"
  JUNIORS MISS Phoebe T . . . . | 7 Oar & Line Rd,
  JUNIORS MR Samuel L . . . . | PO Box 1586, Plymouth, MA *02362*
Geer MR Garrow T
  ☎ (516) 283-3438 . . "Redbrook" Noyac Rd, Southampton, NY *11968*
Geisler REV CANON & MRS William F (Barbara A | ☎ (916) 541-0530
  Reichmuth) . . . . | Porcupine Lodge,
  MISS Elizabeth M G . . . . | Fallen Leaf Lake, South Lake Tahoe, CA *95716*
Geissbühler MRS Arnold (Elisabeth Chase)
  ☎ (508) 385-3879 . . "Scargo Pines" Box 202, Dennis, MA *02638*
Geissler DR Edwin N
  ☎ (617) 826-0361 . . 368 Pleasant St, Pembroke, MA *02359*
Gentry MR & MRS Frank L (Sarah E Kildea) . . . . . | ☎ (704) 387-2394
  MR David Y . . . . | 102 Arrowood Rd, Beech Mountain, NC *28604*
George MR & MRS Michael M (Clara E Balfour) . . . | ☎ (516) 288-6124
  MISS Regina E . . . . | 76 Library Av,
  MISS Vivian B . . . . | Westhampton
  MISS Monica R . . . . | Beach, NY *11978*

Gerard MRS James W (Jean B Shevlin)
  "Sol's Cliff" Bar Harbor, ME *04609*
Gerard MR James W 5th
  ☎ (207) 288-4990 . . "Sol's Cliff" Bar Harbor, ME *04609*
Gerard MR & MRS Peter H (Elizabeth W Browning)
  ☎ (207) 374-2863 . . "Brightly" Parker Point, Blue Hill, ME *04614*
Gerard MR & MRS Robert A (Johnston—Philippa C | ☎ (516) 283-7662
  W Groves) . . . . | 611 Hill St,
  MISS Celia C . . . . | PO Box 2365,
  MR Robert G . . . . | Southampton, NY
  JUNIORS MR William A . . . . | *11969*
Gerdsen MR & MRS James N (Cynthia C Clegg) . . . | Black Island,
  MISS Margot S . . . . | Rice Lake, Ontario,
  MR James T . . . . | Canada
Gerli MR & MRS David C (Gram—Anne W Harvey)
  ☎ (516) 324-0757 . . "Maya" Ocean Av & Crossways, Box 153, East Hampton, NY *11937*
Germic MR & MRS Stephen A (Catherine R Boomer)
  ☎ (517) 738-6389 . . 2015 Cliff Rd, Port Austin, MI *48467*
Gerrity MR & MRS Edward M (Joe Ann C Thatcher) | Sundowner,
  MISS Corrigan T . . . . | Breckenridge, CO
  MISS Ryan K . . . . | *80424*
  MR E Michael 4th . . . . |
Gerrity MR & MRS J Frank 2d (Ruth Mathes)
  ☎ (207) 363-5200 . . "Mainescape" Box 77, York Harbor, ME *03911*
Gerry MR & MRS Henry A (Nancy Whitney)
  ☎ (516) 788-7423 . . "Five Winds" Box 367, Fishers Island, NY *06390*
Geupel MRS John C (Hamilton—Ann H Mulville)
  ☎ (614) 252-0487 . . 135 Preston Rd, Columbus, OH *43209*
Gevalt MR & MRS Peter Y (Lorene C Stefan)
  ☎ (508) 228-2590 . . Old Cliff Rd, Nantucket, MA *02554*
Geyelin MR Henry R
  ☎ (207) 276-3647 . . "Passage West" Seal Harbor, ME *04675*
Ghriskey MR & MRS H Williamson (Flora Roberts)
  ☎ (207) 276-5409 . . "Nantibi" Seal Harbor, ME *04675*
Giacomuzzi-Moore MR & MRS Lorenzo (Giovanna | ☎ (011-39-566)
  Coccitto) . . . . | 940206
  MISS Carolina . . . . | via Verdi 46,
  MR Marco . . . . | Massa Marittima, Grosseto, Italy
Giard MR & MRS George P JR (Thomas—Wendell Adams)
  ☎ (516) 283-2861 . . Meadow Club, First Neck Lane, Southampton, NY *11968*
Gibb MR John B
  ☎ (207) 276-3357 . . Northeast Harbor, ME *04662*
Gibian MR & MRS Paul P (Schneider—Martha P Parke)
  ☎ (508) 257-9867 . . "Star Hill" 47 Chuck Hollow Rd, Siasconset, MA *02564*
Gibson MR & MRS George W (Diana Marvin)
  ☎ (207) 622-9831 . . "The Vaughan Homestead" 1 Litchfield Rd, Hallowell, ME *04347*
Gibson MR & MRS Gregory L (Priscilla H Cook)
  ☎ (908) 899-0360 . . 735 East Av, Bay Head, NJ *08742*
Gifford MR & MRS Stephen W (Enid Fessenden)
  ☎ (508) 945-0485 . . 66 Harding Lane, Chatham, MA *02633*

Gignoux MR & MRS Reginald (Newberry—Joan F Landon) . . . . | ☎ (518) 523-9262 "Cobble View Too" Lake Placid, NY *12946*
    JUNIORS MR Christopher C . . . . |
        MR Gardner C Newberry . . . . |
        JUNIORS MR James W Newberry . . . . |

Gilbert MR & MRS Clinton JR (Paton—Jane S Treman)
    ☎ (802) 867-4147 . . Box 152, Dorset Orchard, Dorset, VT *05251*
Gilbert MR & MRS Dudley A (Johnson—Katharine McK Olyphant)
    ☎ (860) 739-7170 . . 12 Great Wight Way, Niantic, CT *06357*
Gilbert MR Francis H . . see G Rublee 2d
Gilbert MR John
    ☎ (717) 525-3246 . . "Eagles Edge Road House" Box 186, Eagles Mere, PA *17731*
Gilbert MR & MRS Richard C (Dorothy F Perkins)
    ☎ (516) 788-7732 . . "Cathy's Place" Fishers Island, NY *06390*
Gilbert MR & MRS Thomas S (Shelley S Rea)
    ☎ (516) 537-7862 . . 8 Georgica Association, PO Box 1028, Wainscott, NY *11975*
Gilchrist MISS Stephanie S . . see H Fiorato
Gill MR & MRS Robert Lee (Melanie Snyder)
    Connaught Hotel, Carlos Place, London, England
Gill MR & MRS Robert M (Joan Tucker)
    ☎ (508) 428-6274 . . 60 Great Bay Rd, Osterville, MA *02655*
Gillespie MR & MRS Charles A (Fuller—Osgood—Jane Hewlett)
    ☎ (415) 851-0894 . . 160 Greer Rd, Woodside, CA *94062*
Gillespie MRS Lee D (Nancy Lee Day)
    ☎ (508) 228-2137 . . "Irrelephant" 40 Easton St, Nantucket, MA *02554*
Gillet MR & MRS F Warrington JR (Boykin—Elesabeth Ridgely Ingalls)
    ☎ (207) 276-3604 . . "Litchfield Cottage" Peabody Dv, Northeast Harbor, ME *04662*
Gillett MISS Marian N . . see W L Brookfield
Gillette MR Hyde
    ☎ (508) 748-2456 . . "Holly House" 10 Holly Rd, Marion, MA *02738*
Gillies MRS William B JR (Mary Lee Rust)
    87 Granite Point Rd, Biddeford, ME *04005*
Gilligan MRS Francis S (Fernanda M Kellogg) . . . . . | ☎ (914) 677-3271 "Fitch's Corner" 154 N Mabbettsville Rd, Millbrook, NY *12545*
    MISS Fernanda K . . . . |
Gilligan MR Francis S
    770 Boylston St, Boston, MA *02199*
Gillmore MR & MRS Frederick H JR (Dolores N Airey)
    ☎ (518) 589-5210 . . Onteora Club, Tannersville, NY *12485*
Gilmor MR Christopher C . . see F A Irwin
Gilmor MR Mark C . . see F A Irwin
Gilmour MR & MRS Andrew S (Carol R Hansen)
    "Evergreen Prairie" FS107 N Government Prairie, Parks, AZ *86012*
Giroux MR & MRS Paul A (Margaret R Hester)
    ☎ (516) 676-2332 . . Piping Rock Club, Piping Rock Rd, Locust Valley, NY *11560*
Glascock MRS Elizabeth W (Boyer—Elizabeth B White)
    ☎ (410) 239-7887 . . 5200 Old Quarter Rd, Upperco, MD *21155-9378*
Glasgow MR & MRS W Merrill (Elizabeth P Fauntleroy) . . . . | ☎ (713) 559-2780 2120 Park Av, Kemah, TX *77565*
    MISS Virginia S . . . . |
    MISS Julia M M . . . . |

Glass MR & MRS Charles F (Susan B Grace) . . . . | ☎ (616) 526-9563 Pineyrie, 3445 N Lake Shore Dv, Harbor Springs, MI *49740*
    MR Charles F JR . . . . |
    MR D Carter . . . . |
    JUNIORS MR William J . . . . |
Glass MRS J Hall (Joannah C Hall)
    ☎ (610) 869-3993 . . "Bryn Lea" Hood Rd, Box 39, Chatham, PA *19318*
Glass MR & MRS John B JR (Martha K Vietor)
    ☎ (508) 627-3281 . . "Summertime" 31 S Water St, Edgartown, MA *02539*
Glazebrook MRS James R (Rebeckah DuBois)
    ☎ (508) 548-0651 . . Box 64, Woods Hole, MA *02543*
Glendinning MR & MRS Robert 2d (Sandra E Dufort) | ☎ (518) 483-4668 "Great Rock Camp" Owls Head, NY *12969*
    MISS Gray R . . . . |
Glenn MRS Joan W (Joan L Woolman) . . . . | see H N Woolman JR
    MISS Holly T . . . . |
    MR George S JR . . . . |
Glidden MRS William Townsend (Jane J Walsh)
    ☎ (508) 526-4017 . . 79 Bridge St, Manchester-By-The-Sea, MA *01944*
Gloeckner MRS Frederick H (Mudd—Emily B Hartshorne)
    ☎ (603) 367-4734 . . "Back-O-Beyond" Silver Lake, NH *03875*
Glynn MR & MRS Thomas A JR (Julia A Devereux) . | ☎ (207) VI6-4034 "Sunset Hill" Box 102, Chebeague Island, ME *04017*
    JUNIORS MR T Anthony 3d . . . . |
Gober MR & MRS Glenn D (Margaret W Parke)
    "Deerfields Run" Happy Rd, Dushore, PA *18614*
Goddard MR & MRS C Convers (Katherine Van I Downey)
    ☎ (518) 327-3254 . . "Fenacres" Upper St Regis, NY *12945*
Goddard MR & MRS Edward Q (Nancy J Poerstel)
    ☎ (302) 539-7926 . . "Cloud Nine" 8 Ocean Dv, South Bethany Beach, DE *19930*
Goddard MR & MRS Robert H I (Hope L Drury) . . . | ☎ (401) 847-3734 74 Bridge St, Newport, RI *02840*
    MR Robert H I 3d . . . . |
Goddard MR & MRS William H D (Katharine W Ferris) . . . . | ☎ (603) 542-6488 RFD 2, Box 468, Claremont, NH *03743*
    MISS Charlotte I . . . . |
Godfrey MRS Ellwood W (Sophia Moore)
    ☎ (207) 374-5697 . . HC 64, Box 242, Blue Hill, ME *04614*
Godfrey MR Lincoln 3d . . . . | "Cricket Hill" Blowing Point, Anguilla
    JUNIORS MISS Emily . . . . |
    JUNIORS MR Lincoln 5th . . . . |
Godfrey MR & MRS Peter (Margaret K Meister)
    ☎ (207) 276-3692 . . "Stony Point" Northeast Harbor, ME *04662*
Goff MRS James M (del Val—Jennifer J Anderson)
    ☎ (910) 754-7359 . . Inlet Wacche, Brick Landing Plantation, Ocean Isle Beach, NC *28469*
Goffinet MR François M P J
    "Château de Reux" 5590 Conneux, Belgium

Gogolak MR & MRS Charles P (Marion Madeira) . . .
JUNIORS MR Stephen S . . . . | ☎ (207) 276-3715
"Time Out"
Northeast Harbor,
ME *04662*

Goiran MR Philip de la H
"Wynburg" Brightwater, Phippsburg, ME *04562*

Golden MR William T . . . .
MISS Sibyl R . . . .
MISS (DR) Pamela P . . . . | ☎ (914) 657-8983
"Rock Ledge"
Olive Bridge, NY
12461

Goldman DR & MRS Allen S (Kise—Rachel Bok) ⚓
☎ (207) 236-3878 . . "Ogier Point" PO Box 906, Camden, ME *04843*

Goldsborough MR Nicholas Tilghman
☎ (508) 945-2790 . . 80 Main St, Chatham, MA *02633*

Goldwater MISS Carolyn (Sexson—Thompson—Erskine—
Carolyn Goldwater)
☎ (520) 525-9528 . . 289 Forest Highlands Dv, Flagstaff, AZ *86001*

Goltra MR & MRS O Renard (Smith—Alice B
Cotsworth) . . . .
JUNIORS MISS Carolyn S . . . .
JUNIORS MR Andrew R . . . . | ☎ (715) 356-1643
9276 Country Club
Rd, Box 914,
Minocqua, WI
54548

González MR Eugene R
☎ (703) 273-9303 . . 9229 Arlington Blvd, Fairfax, VA *22031*

Gonzalez MRS Richard I (Mary C Miller)
☎ (011-34-7) 276-9329 . . "Mas Rajoleriá" Foixá, 17132 Gerona, Spain

Goodall MR & MRS Herbert W 3d (Susan E
Gallagher) ⚓ . . . .
MISS Eliza H S . . . .
MR Robert D 2d . . . . | ☎ (508) 228-1848
34 Orange St,
Nantucket, MA
02554

Goodall MISS Mary E
☎ (508) 228-2222 . . "Shimmo" Nantucket, MA *02554*

Goodan MRS William (Mary E Phleger)
☎ (619) 433-5724 . . St Malo Beach, 2041 S Pacific St, Oceanside, CA *92054*

Goodenough MR & MRS Oliver R (Alison H Clarkson)
☎ (518) 251-4073 . . "Hill House" Windover, North Creek, NY *12853*

Goodhue MRS Albert (Pulitzer—S Helen Dempwolf)
☎ (207) 276-5607 . . "Rose Lane Cottage" PO Box 494, Northeast Harbor, ME *04662*

Gooding MR & MRS Judson (Françoise T Ridoux) . . of
☎ (011-33-1) 45-53-36-32 . . 16 rue Spontini, 75116 Paris, France
☎ (603) 756-4162 . . N Main St, Box 745, Walpole, NH *03608*

Goodman MR David P . . . .
MR Nicholas D . . . . | ☎ (809) 332-2207
"Goodwind"
Box 1, Governor's
Harbour, Eleuthera,
Bahamas

Goodman MR & MRS Edward T (Carolyn V Cutler) .
MISS Samantha W . . . .
MISS Beverly P . . . .
MISS Allison C . . . . | ☎ (508) 627-9918
96 S Water St,
Edgartown, MA
02539

Goodman MR & MRS Maurice JR (Georgine L Rake)
☎ (207) 967-4991 . . "Grey Gull Cottage" PO Box 608, Kennebunkport, ME *04046*

Goodman MR & MRS William E 4th (Manette L Carpenter)
☎ (908) 899-8959 . . 35 Bay Point Harbour, Point Pleasant, NJ *08742*

Goodrich MISS Catherine D . . see J W Mettler III

Goodrich MR & MRS John Alden (H R Valaer
van Roijen) . . . .
JUNIORS MISS Lauren V . . . . | ☎ (203) 972-1618
720 West Rd,
PO Box 1714,
New Canaan, CT
06840

Goodwin DR & MRS Charles B (Anne Cunningham)
☎ (516) 624-9174 . . 367 Split Rock Rd, Syosset, NY *11791*

Goodwin MRS Macdonald (Hope Erwin) . . . .
MR Macdonald E . . . .
MR Bruce N . . . .
MR Norton . . . . | ☎ (906) 847-3810
"Casa Verano"
Mackinac Island, MI
49757

Goodyear MR & MRS David L (Sally L Chapman) . .
MISS Ella C . . . .
MISS Julianna R . . . . | ☎ (504) 892-0569
"Money Hill
Plantation" Rte 1,
Bush, LA *70431*

Gordan MR & MRS John D 3d (Catherine H
Morot-Sir) . . . .
MISS Elizabeth LeS . . . .
JUNIORS MR John D . . . . | ☎ (203) 838-1511
54 Shorehaven Rd,
East Norwalk, CT
06855

Gordon MR & MRS John R (Alice L Brady) . . . .
MISS Amanda R . . . .
JUNIORS MR Nicholas R . . . . | ☎ (518) 589-6540
"Clove Lodge"
Twilight Park,
Haines Falls, NY
12436

Gordon MISS Katharine G . . see P J Davidson

Gordon MR & MRS Kilbourn JR (Mary E S Butler)
HC 1, Box 1134, Blakeslee, PA *18610*

Gordon MR & MRS Lewis H JR (Nadel—Elizabeth E Dunham)
☎ (207) 276-3734 . . PO Box 294, Seal Harbor, ME *04675*

Gordon MRS Patricia P (Patricia B Powell)
☎ (516) EA4-0782 . . Cove Hollow Rd, East Hampton, NY *11937*

Gordon MR & MRS William D (Herrick—Gibbons—Denny—Lee Coney)
☎ (705) 764-1908 . . "St Brandon's Isle" Beaumaris, Ontario P0B 1B0, Canada

Gorham DR & MRS George W (Ann F Willens) . . . .
MISS Sarah C . . . .
MR John W . . . . | ☎ (860) 567-9387
Litchfield, CT *06759*

Gorham MRS Nathaniel (Mary L Budik)
"Elbon" Twitchell Lake, Big Moose, Eagle Bay, NY *13331*

Gorham MR & MRS Nathaniel 8th (Janalin M Shuler)
☎ (315) 357-4108 . . Twitchell Lake, Big Moose, Eagle Bay, NY *13331*

Goriansky MR Alexander Yale
☎ (207) 276-3956 . . "Pebble Beach" Seal Harbor Rd, Northeast Harbor, ME *04662*

Goriansky MR Michael E
☎ (207) 276-3956 . . "Pebble Beach" Peabody Dv, PO Box 673, Northeast Harbor, ME *04662*

Gorman MR & MRS Kernan F (Mardie Madden) . . . .
MISS Annabel C . . . . | ☎ (516) 329-0276
40 Dunemere Lane,
East Hampton, NY
11937

Gorman MRS Paul A (Richards—Althea D Robinson)
☎ (412) 741-4521 . . Merriman Rd, Box 33, Sewickley, PA *15143*

Gorog MR & MRS William Christopher (Ellen MacMillan)
☎ (805) 962-8310 . . 430 Corona Del Mar, Santa Barbara, CA *93103*

Gorog MR & MRS William F (Gretchen E Meister)
☎ (970) 925-9232 . . Box 1273, Aspen, CO *81612*

Goss MR & MRS Richard W 2d (Michele W du Pont) . . . . | ☎ (516) 788-7649
MISS Holland H . . . . | Fishers Island, NY
MR Jared du P . . . . | *06390*

Gottschalk MR Adam W H . . see A Cushman JR

Gould MR & MRS George D (Jane C Mack)
☎ (516) 283-5712 . . Meadowmere Lane, Southampton, NY *11968*

Gourlay MR & MRS Lawrence (Harris—M Elizabeth Parkinson) . . . . | ☎ (516) 537-0534
MISS Diana H . . . . | Beach Lane,
MISS Brooke J Harris . . . . | Wainscott, NY *11975*

Gowen MR & MRS George W 2d (Marcia A Fennelly)
☎ (516) 324-4029 . . Box 763, Lily Pond Lane, East Hampton, NY *11937*

Grace MR Eric W . . see MRS W P Wood
Grace MR Jeremy B . . see MRS W P Wood
Grace MRS Morgan H (Natalie O Watts)
☎ (516) 324-0313 . . 85 Lee Av, Box 594, East Hampton, NY *11937*

Grace MR & MRS Morgan H JR (Robin W Rutherfurd)
☎ (516) 287-4740 . . "High Hedges" 292 Ox Pasture Rd, Southampton, NY *11968*

Grace MR & MRS Patrick P (Margaret P McMenamin)
"Jordan Cottage" Northeast Harbor, ME *04662*

Graff MR & MRS Austin B (Evans—Kathleen A Horne)
☎ (508) 775-1383 . . "Windward" 25 Maywood Av, Hyannis Port, MA *02647*

Graff MR & MRS William E (Murray—Eddy—Pakenham—Fairly—Mary M Connelly)
☎ (518) 873-2219 . . Underwood Club, New Russia, NY *12964*

Graham MR & MRS Gordon (Phillips—Kirby E Smith)
☎ (718) 885-0861 . . 5 Deepwater Way, Bronx, NY *10464*

Graham MR & MRS Gordon JR (Cathleen A Colella)
☎ (508) 771-4855 . . "le Vieux Nid" 42 Bradford Rd, West Yarmouth, MA *02673*

Graham MRS R Hilles (Conkling—Claire L Wentworth Rump)
☎ (011-44-170) 546-3011 . . "Little Whinhurst House" Seafront, Hampshire PO11 0AW, England

Graham MR R Hilles
☎ (202) 333-5124 . . 2801 New Mexico Av NW, Apt 207, Washington, DC *20007*

Granbery MR & MRS W Preston (Ann R Hoffman) . | ☎ (401) 635-2528
JUNIORS MR J Hastings . . . . | "Harbor Edge"
JUNIORS MR C Weld . . . . | 8 Minnesota Rd,
 | Little Compton, RI *02837*

Grand MRS Gordon (Ruth Young) . . . . | ☎ (207) 244-3238
MR Timothy W . . . . | Box 1392,
 | Southwest Harbor, ME *04679*

Grandin MR & MRS John L (Susanne P Wilson)
☎ (508) 693-0416 . . West Chop, MA *02573*

Granger MR & MRS David (Clyde—M Lee Mason)
☎ (516) 283-2286 . . 41 Great Plains Rd, PO Box 823, Southampton, NY *11969*

Grannis MRS Arthur E 3d (Jerri J Ziegenhein) . . . . . | ☎ (508) 627-4614
MISS Lindsey W . . . . | "Hurricane House"
MISS Hilary E (Wendland—Hilary E Grannis) . . | Box 5271,
 | Edgartown, MA *02539*

Grant DR & MRS Joseph L (Mary Drayton) ⚓
☎ (207) 244-7703 . . "Grant Camp" Mt Desert, ME *04660*

Grant MR & MRS Richard R H 3d (Mary E Brainard)
☎ (517) 821-8951 . . "Grant Cottage" Cottage Grove, Higgins Lake, Roscommon, MI *48653*

Grassi MR & MRS Marco (Cristina Sanpaolesi) . . . . . | ☎ (011-39-55)
MISS Irene . . . . | 247-7677
MR Matteo . . . . | via San Niccolo 28, 50125 Florence, Italy

Grassi MR & MRS Temple (Eleuthèra B Smith) . . . . . | ☎ (207) 276-3312
JUNIORS MISS Melissa S . . . . | "Northern Lodge"
JUNIORS MISS Charlotte McC . . . . | Northeast Harbor, ME *04662*

Gratwick MISS Katharine . . see MRS L McDill
Gratwick MISS Laura B . . see MRS L McDill
Graves MR & MRS Harry Hammond (Lynne E Reichart)
"Belcaro" 193 W Shore Rd, Grand Isle, VT *05458*

Graves MRS Jonathan K (Sara Grey Terry) . . . . | ☎ (207) 389-1427
MISS Laura M . . . . | PO Box 235, Phippsburg, ME *04562*

Graves MRS Sidney C (Harris—Alice D Brown)
☎ (603) 253-4457 . . "Cotton Farm" Center Harbor, NH *03226*

Gray MR & MRS Austen T (Beatrice Milo Gray)
☎ (207) 734-2243 . . Dark Harbor, Islesboro, ME *04848*

Gray MR & MRS Austen T JR (Lynn Merrill) . . . . | ☎ (208) 622-3157
JUNIORS MISS Lily Merrill . . . . | Box 1598,
JUNIORS MR Austen T 3d . . . . | Ketchum, ID *83340*

Gray MRS Bowman 3d (Kimberly—Josephine Whitman) . . . . | Aug 1 . .
MR Oliver A Kimberly 3d . . . . | ☎ (516) 788-7609
 | "Collins House" Fishers Island, NY *06390*

Gray MR Bowman 4th . . see T O Moore JR
Gray MRS Burton C (Dorothy C Stephens)
Northeast Harbor, ME *04662*

Gray MRS Carl A (Kenan—Harriet Du Bose)
☎ (207) 276-3754 . . "Cedar Cliff" Seal Harbor, ME *04675*

Gray MR & MRS Harvey L (Margaret C Bartlett) . . . . | ☎ (802) 457-1328
MR Elliot W . . . . | "Brookside" Stage Rd, South Pomfret, VT *05067*

Gray MR Jeb . . see MRS M T Harrison
Gray MR & MRS John B (Virginia H Tripp)
☎ (508) 996-6807 . . "Eden Run" 95 De Garis Av, South Dartmouth, MA *02748*

Gray MRS Mark F (Curtin—Ellen W Manganaro) see MRS E M Manganaro

Gray MR & MRS Robert B (Elizabeth C Lord)
☎ (516) 922-0620 . . 367 Split Rock Rd, Syosset, NY *11791*

Gray MR & MRS Robert L 3d (Elizabeth D Elkins)
☎ (603) 544-7339 . . Colony Cottage, Bald Peak Colony Club, Melvin Village, NH *03850*
Gray MR & MRS Samuel P M (Margaret G Zink) ⚓
  MISS Alicia L
  MISS Caroline G
☎ (508) 295-7842 Bourne's Point, Wareham, MA *02571*
Gray MR & MRS Sherman (Barbara C Bintz)
☎ (518) 251-3946 . . "The Clearing" North Woods Club, Minerva, NY *12851*
Gray MR & MRS Walter F (Susan A Mair)
☎ (314) 991-2728 . . 27 Briarcliff, St Louis, MO *63124*
Gray MRS William A (Hulick—Smith—Elizabeth F Lewis)
☎ (201) 736-1855 . . Llewellyn Park, West Orange, NJ *07052*
Grayson MISS Maud M P
☎ (214) 234-8678 . . 517 Brookshire, Richardson, TX *75080*
Grazioli-Venier JUNIORS MISS Assia . . see K C Chen
Grazioli-Venier JUNIORS MR Saverio E . . see K C Chen
Greeff MRS Theodore (Hurd—Catherine M Stevens)
☎ (802) 867-5522 . . Box 544, Dorset, VT *05251*
Greely MR & MRS John C (Jane C Grimball)
☎ (603) 447-2290 . . "Hidden Harbor" Box 16, Center Conway, NH *03813*
Green MR Ashbel
  MISS Alison McK
☎ (860) 535-1691 223 Wamphassuc Point, Stonington, CT *06378*
Green MR & MRS Edwin B III (Anne K Du Vivier) see P F Du Vivier
Green MRS Joseph C (Gertrude H Norris)
"Eagles Nest" Pointe-au-Baril, Ontario P0G 1K0, Canada
Green MR & MRS Marshall (Lispenard S Crocker) . . of
☎ (207) 439-3745 . . "Bayberry Rocks" 44 Pocahontas Rd, Kittery Point, ME *03905*
☎ (207) 439-2953 . . 28 Goose Point Rd, Kittery Point, ME *03905*
Green MRS Martha T (Martha F Tilford) Fishers Island, NY *06390*
Greenan MISS Eleanor J
☎ (207) 276-3915 . . "Christmas Trees" Seal Harbor, ME *04675*
Greene MR & MRS James C (Elizabeth Rollins)
☎ (805) 965-4638 . . 103 Mesa Lane, Santa Barbara, CA *93109*
Greene MR & MRS Thurston (Davies—Norris—Marta Brodie)
☎ (508) 257-6200 . . "Admiral Benbow" Box 614, 19 McKinley Av, Siasconset, MA *02564*
Greenfield DR & MRS Paul S (Pratt—Sandra C Steele)
☎ (207) 363-8967 . . "The Custom House" 82 Lindsay Rd, York, ME *03909*
Greenough MR & MRS Malcolm W (Catherine R MacKenna)
  MR Charles W
  MR Andrew S
  JUNIORS MR George P
☎ (441) 293-2150 "Outlook" 14 Knapton Estates Rd, Smiths, Bermuda
Greenough MR & MRS Peter B (Beverly Sills)
  MISS Meredith H
  MR Peter B JR
☎ (508) 693-3936 Box 323, RFD, Vineyard Haven, MA *02568*

Greenway MR & MRS Hugh D S (Joy B Brooks) ⚓
☎ (207) 867-4814 . . "Mill Farm" North Haven, ME *04853*
Greenwood MR & MRS Richard H (Jean E MacPhee)
☎ (508) 746-1122 . . 7 Blackmer Lane, Plymouth, MA *02360*
Greenwood MR & MRS Robert S (Patricia A Griffin)
☎ (702) 749-5233 . . 165 The Back Rd, PO Box 46, Glenbrook, NV *89413*
Gregg MR & MRS Robert E JR (Mary W Williams) . .
  MISS Robina K
  MR Walter H
☎ (518) 654-6280 "Brier-Patch" Box 662, County Rte 10, Corinth, NY *12822*
Gregory MR & MRS Quintard (Patricia W Hunter) . .
  MISS Diana H
  MR William W
  JUNIORS MISS Lilla B
☎ (408) 628-3219 "Rancho Cienega del Gabilan" 1636 Thomas Rd, Hollister, CA *95023*
Grenier MR & MRS G Thomas (Vieva F Christy) . . .
  MISS Jennifer B
  JUNIORS MISS Emilie F
☎ (011-44-1862) 811-062 "Ord House" 22 Elizabeth Crescent, Dornoch, Sutherland IV25 3NN, Scotland
Grew MR & MRS Edward S (Dudley—Priscilla C Perkins)
☎ (207) 581-2169 . . "Dissakisite" 2 N Main St, Orono, ME *04473*
Grew RT REV & MRS J Clark (Jones—Sarah W Loomis)
  MISS Sarah W
☎ (207) 276-3793 "Gruvie" Northeast Harbor, ME *04662*
Griffin MR & MRS Andrew (Wyman—Sharon Crary)
  MR Sherman G
  MR Mark C
☎ (208) 787-2341 "The Rockin' G" PO Box 451, Victor, ID *83455*
Griffin MR & MRS Anthony (Jennifer Barnes)
☎ (415) 669-1231 . . 2 Cameron, Inverness, CA *94937*
Griffin MR & MRS Christopher A F (M Calvert C Saunders)
☎ (516) 759-5022 . . 230 Piping Rock Rd, Locust Valley, NY *11560*
Griffin MR & MRS Nathaniel M (Jane E Boudreau) . .
  MISS Natalie B
  MR Andrew W
  JUNIORS MR James H
☎ (616) 843-4225 "Dixieland Cottage" Epworth Heights, Ludington, MI *49431*
Griffin MR & MRS William J 4th (Geraldine M Nager)
☎ (401) 596-4129 . . 22 E Hills Rd, Watch Hill, RI *02891*
Griffith MISS Caroline C . . see M Fenton JR
Griscom MR & MRS Lloyd P SR (Abby A K T Van Pelt)
☎ (207) 639-2711 . . "The Red House" E Madrid Rd, PO Box 117, Phillips, ME *04966*
Griscom MR Lloyd P JR
☎ (207) 639-5555 . . "Greenfield Hill" PO Box 360, Phillips, ME *04966*
Griswold MRS A Whitney (Mary M Brooks)
☎ (508) 693-0680 . . RD 409, Lambert's Cove Rd, Vineyard Haven, MA *02568*
Griswold REV & MRS Brendan (Heyniger—Adelaide Cole) ⚓
☎ (508) 993-0708 . . "The Meadows" 189 Smith Neck Rd, South Dartmouth, MA *02748*

Griswold REV DR & MRS Lincoln T (Jean S Coghlan)
☎ (717) 868-6780.. "Happy House" 70 N End Rd, Lake Nuangola, Mountain Top, PA *18707*

Groman MR & MRS (DR) Phillip S (Sarah R Newell-Price)..................... ☎ (207) 967-2374
  JUNIORS MR Christopher H .... "The Grayling" Kennebunkport, ME *04046*

Grose MR & MRS Thomas Pierpont (Herlin—Eleanor F Evans) ⛵ .... ☎ (207) 644-8150
  MISS Signe P........................ "Seascape"
  MISS Vanessa P...................... Christmas Cove, ME
  MISS Heather B...................... *04568*
  JUNIORS MR William F P ....

Gross MRS George Mason (Hanley—McAlpin—McDevitt—Jean I J Brown)
  ☎ (401) 635-8509.. 100 Sakonnet Point Rd, Little Compton, RI *02837*

Gross MR & MRS Rainer (Cynthia Cannell).. see P B Cannell

Gross MR & MRS William A O (Abby M Minot).... ☎ (207) 725-6025
  MR Bayard M .... 3089 Mere Point Rd, Brunswick, ME *04011*

Grosvenor MR & MRS Charles B (Louise B Wheeler) ☎ (401) 847-4817.. "Windswept" 208 Ocean Av, Newport, RI *02840*

Grosvenor MRS Melville Bell (Anne E Revis)..... ☎ (902) 295-2654
  MISS Sara A .... "Beinn Bhreagh"
                                       Baddeck,
                                       Nova Scotia
                                       B0E 1B0, Canada

Grove MR & MRS Henry S 3d (Joan Hemmerly) ⛵ ☎ (609) 492-8911
  MR Donald H .... "The Ship"
  MR David D .... 217 Norwood Av, Beach Haven, NJ *08008*

Grummon MR & MRS John H (Klaussmann—Elizabeth M Chapin) .... ☎ (508) 758-4291
  MISS Elizabeth M Klaussmann........... Box 333,
  MR Eric K Klaussmann .... Mattapoisett, MA *02739*

Gruner MR & MRS Otto Harry III (Nancy V Evans)
  ☎ (516) 788-7369.. Fishers Island, NY *06390*

Grunwald MR & MRS Henry (Savitt—Melhado—Louise Liberman)
  ☎ (516) 283-2365.. Dune Rd, Southampton, NY *11968*

Gubelmann MR & MRS James B (Kate C Crichton) . ☎ (401) 846-9797
  MISS Tantivy A....................... "Greywalls"
  MISS Phoebe G .... Beacon Hill Rd,
  JUNIORS MR James A .... Newport, RI *02840*

Gubelmann MISS Marjorie Barton
  ☎ (401) 847-6434.. "Starboard House" 138 Narragansett Av, Newport, RI *02840*

Gubelmann MRS Walter S (Barton Green)
  ☎ (401) 847-6210.. "Starboard House" 138 Narragansett Av, Newport, RI *02840*

Gubelmann MR & MRS William S (Shelley Page)
  ☎ (011-44-171) 351-3475.. 8 Swan Walk, London SW3 4JJ, England

Guernsey MR & MRS David T (Jacqueline A Chapman)
  ☎ (508) 627-4278.. "Kent Bunk Port" Box 1151, Edgartown, MA *02539*

Guernsey MR & MRS Peter E (Barbara Thurston)
  ☎ (508) 627-4342.. Kent Harbor, RFD 149, Edgartown, MA *02539*

Guest MR & MRS John S C (Margaret H Houck)
  ☎ (516) 788-7883.. "North Hill" Fishers Island, NY *06390*

Guest MR & MRS Richard L (Cynthia R Vaiden).... of ☎ (516)788-7883
  JUNIORS MISS Sarah F V .... "North Hill"
                                              Fishers Island, NY
                                              06390
                                              Aug 1..
                                              ☎ (805) 772-9452
                                              700 Sierra,
                                              Morro Bay, CA
                                              93442

Guild MR & MRS Bayard S (Kay T Dunlap)
  ☎ (508) 945-2340.. 125 Seaview St, Chatham, MA *02633*

Guild MR & MRS Henry R JR (Gale A Robb)
  ☎ (508) 283-7631.. "Essex River Point" 171 Concord St, West Gloucester, MA *01930*

Gummere MR & MRS F Barton (McWilliam—Claire Miller)
  ☎ (617) 631-1592.. Eustis Rd, Peach's Point, Marblehead, MA *01945*

Gummere MR & MRS Richard M (Janet B Kelly)... ☎ (315) 947-5127
  JUNIORS MISS Margaret B .... 8905 Howland Rd,
  JUNIORS MR George W K .... Fair Haven, NY *13064*

Gund MR & MRS Graham de Conde (Ann S Landreth)
  ☎ (508) 228-0133.. 14 Washing Pond Rd, Nantucket, MA *02554*

Gundlach MR Andrew S.. see J French 3d
Gundlach MISS Annabelle K.. see J French 3d

Gunn MR & MRS Robert G (Carrie G Newton) ..... ☎ (210) 238-4044
  MR & MRS Robert G 3d (Elizabeth S Rockwood). "Windy Hill"
                                              FM 1340, Hunt, TX *78024*

Gunness MR & MRS Robert Charles (Beverly Osterberger)
  ☎ (616) 352-4298.. "Linksmere" 224 E Crystal Downs Dv, Frankfort, MI *49635*

Gunter MRS W Davis (Wightman—Taylor—Margaret Cabell)
  ☎ (616) 526-5225.. 580 Arbor St, Harbor Springs, MI *49740*

Guntharp MR Alfred B JR.. see MRS E Van R Stires

Gurney MR & MRS William H JR
  ☎ (508) 228-2617.. "The Cobbles" 89 Main St, Nantucket, MA *02554*

Gutcheon MR David S.. see R M Clements JR

Guth MR & MRS John H J (Davidson—Polly Wheeler)
  ☎ (207) 276-3058.. "The White Hen" Sutton Island, ME *04662*

Guthans MR & MRS Robert A (Barbara A Taylor) .. ☎ (334) 973-2462
  MR & MRS Robert A JR (Patricia L Turner) ..... "Edgewater"
                                                Mobile, AL *36608*

Guthrie MR & MRS Alexander D (Elizabeth J Ashcroft)
  ☎ (207) 282-6343.. Biddeford Pool, ME *04006*

Guthrie MR & MRS Lucien S Yokana (Caroline E Wood)
  ☎ (207) 282-0360.. Biddeford Pool, ME *04006*

Guthrie DR & MRS Randolph H JR (Beatrice M Holden) .... ☎ (307) 733-0997
  MR Randolph H 3d .... Box 25006, Jackson,
  MR Michael P .... WY *83001*
  JUNIORS MR Philip H ....

Guthrie MR & MRS Robert D (Rogers—Tremaine—Beatrice R Brown)
  ☎ (860) 536-1281.. 10 Skiff Lane, Mystic, CT *06355*

H

Haack MR & MRS Frederick L (Hobson—Ann Kendall)
Northeast Harbor, ME *04662*
Haack MR & MRS Frederick L 3d (Mary Lita Kean)
☎ (207) 276-5220 .. "Squirrel's Nest" Northeast Harbor, ME *04662*
Haas MRS Walter A JR (Evelyn Danzig)
☎ (406) 932-6105 .. Beaver Meadow Ranch, Big H, Box 967, Big Timber, MT *59011*
Habenicht MR & MRS Frederick K JR (Rebecca A Sample) .... | ☎ (716) 357-8442
  MISS Helen H .... | 16 Emerson St,
  MISS Gratia M............................ | Chautauqua, NY
  MR Fritz .... | *14722*
  MR William L .... |
Hackley MRS Helena J (May—Helena Johnson)
☎ (516) 671-0670 .. 89 Duck Pond Rd, Glen Cove, NY *11542*
Haddad MR & MRS Robert M (Helen C Rogerson) .. | of ☎ (508)544-3409
  MISS Leila H .... | Jennison Rd,
  MISS Josette H........................... | Wendell, MA *01379*
  MR George R .... | ☎ (508) 992-4279
                                         | Box 4, Nonquitt, MA *02748*
Hadden DR & MRS David Rodney (Margaret H Ledford)
"Shangri La" Georgetown, CA *95634*
Hadden MR & MRS Hamilton (Sarah M Russell)
☎ (802) 362-1965 .. "The Homestead" Box 383, Manchester Center, VT *05255*
Hadden DR & MRS John W (Elba L Más) .... | ☎ (516) 367-3502
  JUNIORS MR Paul J .... | 428 Harbor Rd,
       | Cold Spring Harbor, NY *11724*
Hadden MR & MRS John W 2d (Victoria S Hillebrand)
☎ (516) 692-6319 .. "Laurel Brake" 428 Harbor Rd, Cold Spring Harbor, NY *11724*
Hadley MRS Willis D (Jacqueline B Jones)
☎ (607) 547-2702 .. Fox Run Hill Farm, W Lake Rd, Three Mile Point, Cooperstown, NY *13326*
Hafkenschiel DR & MRS Joseph H (Rush—Carol MacD Smith)
☎ (207) 276-3984 .. "Woodlark" Box 191, Northeast Harbor, ME *04662*
Hagan MR & MRS John W (Alice N Neel) .... | ☎ (401) 624-1525
  MR Brooks W .... | 440 East Rd,
       | Tiverton, RI *02878*
Hagen MR & MRS Lee R (Mary G Mead)
"Little Boy Lake Cabin" Little Boy Lake Access Rd, Longville, MN *56655*
Haggie MR Michael R
"Red Lion Mill House" PO Box 195, Crumpton, MD *21658*
Haggin MR Ben Ali .... | ☎ (914) 351-4401
  MISS Leslie B .... | Club House Rd,
       | Tuxedo Park, NY *10987*
Hague REV & MRS William (Jane P Milliken)
☎ (207) 288-2356 .. "Heaven Cent" Box 511, Mt Desert, ME *04660*

Hahn MR & MRS Charles J (Anne H Davey)
☎ (905) 894-4890 .. Abino Dunes, Point Abino, Ridgeway, Ontario L0S 1N0, Canada
Haight MR David C .. see N H Miller
Haight MR & MRS John McV JR (Deborah D Smith)
☎ (705) 782-6729 .. Killaly Point, Desbarats, Ontario P0R 1E0, Canada
Haight MR & MRS Sherman P JR (Margaret E Grahame)
☎ (860) 567-8840 .. "East-A-Mile" 32 Chestnut Hill, Litchfield, CT *06759*
Hailand MR & MRS Arthur G JR (Mildred Bunn)
☎ (616) 526-5342 .. 11 First Av, Wequetonsing, MI *49740*
Hailand MR & MRS Arthur G 3d (Rebecca C Howe)
☎ (616) 526-2177 .. 415½ Glenn Dv, Harbor Springs, MI *49740*
Haines MRS J Barr (Isobel Y Sheppard)
☎ (906) 484-2263 .. "Tree Tops" Box 53, Cedarville, MI *49719*
Haines DR & MRS James B (Martha M Scull) ⚓ .. | ☎ (906) 484-3619
  MR Thomas W .... | "The Far Side"
       | Sheppard Bay,
       | RR 1, Box 52A,
       | Cedarville, MI
       | *49719*
Haines MR & MRS Thomas D (Stephany Warick) ... | ☎ (860) 542-5921
  MR Samuel H .... | Box 249, Norfolk,
  MR Thomas D JR......................... | CT *06058*
Hale MR & MRS Bradley H (Mary E Henderson)
☎ (601) 982-5383 .. 2153 Eastover Dv, Jackson, MS *39211*
Hale MR & MRS George N JR (Ann A Thoron)
☎ (508) 693-3424 .. "Beech House" 7 Gates Farm, Vineyard Haven, MA *02568*
Hale MRS Prentis Cobb (Gigante—Minnelli—Denise Radosavljevic)
☎ (707) 894-5465 .. "H-E Ranch" 4401 Geysers Rd, Cloverdale, CA *95425*
Hale MR & MRS Richard T JR (Eleanor A Gibson)... | ☎ (508) 257-6269
  MISS Delia T .... | 6 Hedge Row,
  JUNIORS MR Richard T 3d .... | PO Box 762,
       | Siasconset, MA
       | *02564*
Hale MR & MRS Thomas H (Nancy Brooks) .... | PO Box 72,
  MR Mark C .... | Telluride, CO *81435*
  JUNIORS MR Christopher R F ....|
Hale VERY REV & MRS William M (Helen H Frost)
☎ (207) 371-2120 .. "Nemenikuk" MacMahan Island, ME *04548*
Hall DR Arthur P
☎ (617) 580-1515 .. "The Boathouse" 211 Willow Rd, Nahant, MA *01908*
Hall MR & MRS C Barrows (Eleanor L Crosby) ..... | ☎ (516) 788-5518
  JUNIORS MISS Letitia L.................... | Fishers Island, NY
       | *06390*
Hall MR & MRS Eben C (Jane E Terhune)
☎ (401) 635-8918 .. "Red Rock" 102 Round Pond Rd, Little Compton, RI *02837*
Hall MISS Elizabeth B .. see B G Waters 3d
Hall MRS F Bailey (Josephine B Dawes)
☎ (860) 542-5883 .. Golf Dv, Norfolk, CT *06058*
Hall MR Gregory J
☎ (908) 782-0044 .. "Hunterdon" 680 Sidney Rd, Pittstown, NJ *08867*

Hall MR & MRS John H (Erika E M Pick)
  ☎ (607) 263-5643 . . "The Elms" PO Box 218, Morris, NY *13808*
Hall MR & MRS John L 2d (Ann S Tuckerman) . . . . . | ☎ (508) 526-4049
  MISS Emily . . . . | "Garage"
  MISS Daphne . . . . | 20R Masconomo St,
  MISS Sarah . . . . | Manchester, MA
  | *01944*
Hall MR & MRS John M (Jane B Shiverick)
  ☎ (508) 526-4973 . . "The Maples" Masconomo St, Manchester, MA *01944*
Hall MRS Julia T (Julia T McLane)
  ☎ (207) 276-3090 . . "Rock End" Northeast Harbor, ME *04662*
Hall MRS Melville W (Jaffe—Evelyn Annenberg)
  ☎ (401) 847-4189 . . 452 Bellevue Av, Newport, RI *02840*
Hall MR & MRS Philip von P (V Jane Price)
  ☎ (616) 543-4396 . . "Pier Cove" 2256—70 St, Fennville, MI *49408*
Hall MRS Ridgway M (Lucy E Wayland)
  Jly 1 . . 28 W Point Rd, Stony Creek, Branford, CT *06405*
Hall MRS Rodney D (Carol Benedict)
  ☎ (908) 899-1277 . . "The Roost" Box 626, 1547 Ocean Av, Mantoloking, NJ *08738*
Hall MRS Stella E (Stella E Reeves) . . . . | ☎ (802) 457-2855
  MISS Lynne D . . . . | Flying Heels Farm,
  | South Woodstock,
  | VT *05071*
Hall MR & MRS Thomas Cartwright (Garber—Louise C Simrall)
  Ojibway Island, Pointe au Baril, Ontario P0G 1K0, Canada
Hall MR & MRS Thomas J (Ada McI Huffman)
  ☎ (616) 627-2450 . . 1215 Mullett Lake Rd, Mullett Lake, MI *49761*
Hall MRS Thomas S (Tompkins—Mary B Taussig)
  ☎ (207) 276-3900 . . "Landfall" Box 594, Northeast Harbor, ME *04662*
Hall MR Winthrop T . . see B G Waters 3d
Hallahan MR & MRS Donald G (Cynthia K Harkness)
  ☎ (414) 275-2665 . . "The Lake House" 390 N Lake Shore Dv, Rte 1, Box 607, Fontana, WI *53125*
Hallanan MR Paul K
  ☎ (011-353-27) 67184 . . "Leana's" Ahakista, Durrus, Co Cork, Ireland
Halle MRS Chisholm (Cynthia A White)
  ☎ (216) 942-8808 . . 7090 Waite Hill Rd, Waite Hill, OH *44094*
Hallen MR & MRS John R (Laurie E P Grenley) . . . . | ☎ (516) 653-6013
  MISS D Alexandra . . . . | "Boxwood"
  JUNIORS MR John R JR . . . . | PO Box 288,
  | Quogue, NY *11959*
Hallowell MRS Alfred B (Priest—Francine N Bull)
  ☎ (207) 867-4626 . . Bowditch Cottage, Box 235, North Haven, ME *04853*
Hallowell MR & MRS Frederick H (Maureen A | ☎ (508) 228-0482
  Slowik) . . . . | 24 Fair St,
  MISS Marion H . . . . | Nantucket, MA
  MR Christian H . . . . | *02554*
Hallowell MR & MRS Roger H JR (Anderson-Bell—Elinor B Lamont)
  ☎ (207) 867-4463 . . "The Lookout" North Haven, ME *04853*
Halperson MR Michael A
  ☎ (508) 896-2031 . . "Hillside" off Long Pond Rd, PO Box 10, Brewster, MA *02631*

Hambleton MR George B E—⛵
  ☎ (207) 244-0148 . . "Zavidovo" Turner Rd, Seal Cove, PO Box 744, Mt Desert, ME *04660*
Hamersley MR & MRS L Gordon JR (Mihok—Madeline H Hellum)
  ☎ (207) 422-3608 . . "Ledgelands" Treasure Island, Sorrento, ME *04677*
Hamill MR & MRS Samuel M JR (Mary R Townsend) | ☎ (207) 244-7719
  MR Samuel . . . . | "Goose Gables"
  | Seal Cove, ME
  | *04674*
Hamill MR William D
  ☎ (207) 833-5980 . . Curtis Cove, South Harpswell, ME *04079*
Hamilton MR & MRS Daniel H (Nicholson—Jane S | ☎ (508) 775-1611
  Evans) . . . . | "The Playhouse"
  MR T Heyward M . . . . | PO Box 106,
  | Centerville, MA
  | *02632*
Hamilton MR & MRS David R (H Catharine Cline) . . | ☎ (011-33)
  MISS Catharine E . . . . | 37-43-50-01
  | St Georges, France
Hamilton MRS Ferris F (Mary Ann Stevens)
  ☎ (401) 847-5262 . . "Sea Edge" Price's Neck, Newport, RI *02840*
Hamilton MR & MRS Frederic C (Jane Murchison)
  ☎ (516) 788-7672 . . "Teal Pond House" Fishers Island, NY *06390*
Hamilton MRS Frederick J (Olivia K Walker)
  ☎ (203) 264-2569 . . 356B Heritage Village, Southbury, CT *06488*
Hamilton MRS H Marim Pew (H Marim Pew)
  ☎ (970) 586-2184 . . "Crocker Ranch" PO Box 720, Estes Park, CO *80517*
Hamilton MR & MRS John Craig (Monica C MacNamara)
  ☎ (302) 227-0338 . . 124 Hickman St, Rehoboth Beach, DE *19971*
Hamilton MR Lewis Thorne . . see J M Marrin
Hamilton JUNIORS MR Rylan . . see T G Stemberg
Hamilton MR & MRS S Matthews V JR (Anne H | ☎ (401) 849-8712
  Fritchman) . . . . | "Beacon Ledge"
  JUNIORS MISS Dorrance H . . . . | 58 Beacon Hill Rd,
  | Newport, RI *02840*
Hamilton MR & MRS Samuel M V (Dorrance Hill)
  ☎ (401) 846-2104 . . Beacon Ridge S, 58 Beacon Hill Rd, Newport, RI *02840*
Hamilton MR & MRS William G 3d (Nan W Whitridge)
  ☎ (603) 544-3634 . . Bald Peak Colony Club, Melvin Village, NH *03850*
Hamlen MR & MRS William T (Lynn Northwood) . . | ☎ (207) 867-4681
  MISS Anna N . . . . | "Kent Cottage"
  JUNIORS MR William T JR . . . . | North Haven, ME
  | *04853*
Hamlin MR Jerome F—⛵
  Cliff Island, Joseph River Marina, Peninsula Rd, RR 2, Port Carling, Ontario P0B 1J0, Canada
Hammer MR & MRS James S (Joan B Moore) . . . . . | PO Box 1,
  MISS Bess W . . . . | McLeod, MT *59052*
  MR James G . . . . |
Hammer MRS John L JR (Josephine L Wilson) . . . . | ☎ (609) 492-2666
  MISS Judith A (Ladd—Judith A Hammer) . . . . . . | 100 Ocean St,
  | Beach Haven, NJ
  | *08008*

Hammett MR & MRS Philip M (Palmer—Mary Jane Dowd)
 ☎ (201) 579-3839.. "Great Oak Cottage" 274 Newton-Swartswood Rd, Newton, NJ *07860*
Hammond MR Frank H
 ☎ (540) 856-2488.. "Hill Top" 5432 Supinlick Ridge Rd, Mt Jackson, VA *22842*
Hammond MR & MRS Harry S JR (Constance P Johnston) . . . . | ☎ (508) 228-5123
MISS Jane W . . . . | "Mistover"
MISS Helen J . . . . | Monomoy, Nantucket, MA *02554*
Hammond MRS Ogden H (Montgomerie—Marsyl Stokes)
 ☎ (401) 847-0340.. 128 Mill St, Newport, RI *02840*
Hammond MRS William C JR (Gertrude Green)
 ☎ (207) 422-3205.. "Hammondwood" Hancock Point, ME *04640*
Hammond MR & MRS William C 3d (Victoria C Karel)
 ☎ (207) 422-3577.. W Shore Rd, Hancock Point, ME *04640*
Hamon MRS Jake Louis (Taylor—Nancy L Blackburn)
 ☎ (415) 441-3828.. Royal Tower 1601, 1750 Taylor St, San Francisco, CA *94133*
Hamrick MR & MRS Charles F (Marguerite J Darnell).. of
 ☎ (704) 274-2017.. 7 Bourne Lane, Asheville, NC *28803*
 ☎ (561) 276-6648.. 2000 S Ocean Blvd, Apt 704, Delray Beach, FL *33483*
Hancock MR & MRS F Woodson 3d (Poll—Leslie B Tompkins)
 ☎ (207) 867-4666.. "Blue Point" Pulpit Harbor, North Haven, ME *04853*
Hand MRS Alfred (Elizabeth A Grant)
 ☎ (860) 739-8645.. 12 West Lane, Old Black Point, Niantic, CT *06357*
Handler MR & MRS Steven B (Elizabeth C Pyle)
 ☎ (508) 526-4263.. 2 Boardman Av, Manchester-By-The-Sea, MA *01944*
Hanes MISS Allison P.. see M de V Flinn
Hanes MR Jonathan Y.. see M de V Flinn
Hanes MR & MRS R Philip JR (M Charlotte Metz)
 ☎ (910) 363-2440.. Roaring Gap, NC *28668*
Hanley MR & MRS William Lee JR (Alice A Hoffman) . . . . | ☎ (516) 788-5533
MISS Brooke F . . . . | "White Caps"
MISS Nicole . . . . | Fishers Island, NY *06390*
JUNIORS MR Merrill . . . . |
Hannum MR & MRS John B JR (Menocal—Bradford —Anne Stroud) . . . . | ☎ (207) 276-3783
MISS Christianna P . . . . | Sargent Head, Northeast Harbor, ME *04662*
MISS Curtiss P S . . . . |
MR George D . . . . |
 JUNIORS MR Seth Bradford . . . . |
 JUNIORS MR Luke Bradford . . . . |
Hansen MR & MRS Carl L (Norma L Warren)
 ☎ (408) 624-9056.. Box 5501, Carmel, CA *93921*
Hansen MR & MRS Frederick F (Huebing—Annelore J Schaefer)
 ☎ (414) 351-2006.. 8990 N Range Line Rd, Milwaukee, WI *53217*
Hansen MRS H Leighton (Katharine D Baird)
 ☎ (315) 655-8273.. "Westerlea" 4502 Syracuse Rd, Cazenovia, NY *13035*

Hanson MR & MRS Harry A JR (E Terry Ponvert)
 ☎ (408) 685-3540.. "Los Robles" 175 Halton Lane, Watsonville, CA *95076*
Hanson MR & MRS Maurice F (Margaret E Hixon)
 ☎ (203) 531-5244.. 204 W Lyon Farm Dv, Greenwich, CT *06831*
Hanson MISS Phaedra A.. see MRS M B Annan
Harbison MR & MRS James W JR (Margaret G Morgan) . . . . | ☎ (914) 534-9884
MR James W 3d . . . . | Box 225, Deer Hill Rd, Cornwall-on-Hudson, NY *12520*
Hard MR & MRS Michael W (Kathryn L Lockett) . . . | ☎ (520) 774-1018
MISS Jennifer S . . . . | Rte 4, Box 985, Flagstaff, AZ *86002*
MR Christopher L . . . . |
Harder MR & MRS Henry U (Calista Lincoln)
 ☎ (518) 891-1304.. "Red Pine Point" Box 259, Lake Clear, NY *12945*
Hardin MRS B Lauriston JR (Dorcas F Hull)
 Aug 1.. ☎ (508) 639-0981.. Box 11, West Chop, MA *02573*
Harding MRS Deborah S (Deborah S Schust)
 ☎ (207) 865-1896.. 11 Flying Point Way, Freeport, ME *04032*
Harding MR & MRS John Mason (Margaret Riker).. | ☎ (413) 243-4715
MISS Katherine W . . . . | Webster Rd, Tyringham, MA *01264*
MR Thomas H . . . . |
Harding MR L Branch 4th
 ☎ (207) 338-5815.. 74 Union St, Belfast, ME *04915*
Harding MRS Nancy J (Nancy J Dickey).. of
 ☎ (352) 403-0411.. "Querencia" 13530 SW Airport Rd, Cedar Key, FL *32625*
 Villa 164, Pacific Harbor, Fiji, Oceania
Hardwick MRS Elizabeth T (Johnson—Elizabeth I Townsend)
 ☎ (207) 363-6269.. PO Box 451, York Harbor, ME *03911*
Hardy MR & MRS John A JR (June Dorflinger)
 ☎ (518) 589-5203.. Onteora Club, PO Box 57, Tannersville, NY *12485*
Hare MISS Elizabeth B.. see N T Callaway
Hare MR Hobart N.. see N T Callaway
Hare MISS Katherine W.. see N T Callaway
Harfield MR & MRS Henry (Marion G Bussang)
 ☎ (516) 288-2811.. "Cornerhouse" 49 South Rd, Westhampton, NY *11977*
Harmsworth HON Esmond V
 ☎ (401) 847-7742.. "Four Winds" Bellevue Av, Newport, RI *02840*
Harnes DR & MRS Jack R (Joan F Tomick) . . . . | ☎ (914) 855-1204
MISS Anne E . . . . | 64 S Quaker Hill Rd, Pawling, NY *12564*
Harper MRS Harry H JR (Mary H Jopling) ⚓
 ☎ (902) 756-2326.. St Patrick's Channel, Rte 4, Whycocomagh, Nova Scotia B0E 3M0, Canada
Harper MR & MRS James A (Mai Duane)
 ☎ (908) 291-3058.. "Woodland Farm" 555 Cooper Rd, Red Bank, NJ *07701*
Harper MR James G
 ☎ (717) 646-0187.. Pocono Lake Preserve, PA *18348*

Harper MR & MRS James R (Annette E Fogo) ..... | ☎ (717) 646-3293
MISS Hadley R .... | Camp Tamarack,
MR Alexander W .... | Pocono Lake
 | Preserve, PA *18348*
Harper REV DR & MRS John C (Barbara J Quarles)
☎ (508) 385-3536 . . ''Beach Run'' Box 92, Dennis, MA *02638*
Harrington MR & MRS Charles J (Hoopes—Dewart—Elinore I Hoelzel)
☎ (516) 788-7414 . . ''Harrington House'' Fishers Island, NY *06390*
Harrington MR & MRS Dennis L (Margaret A Lukens)
☎ (609) 967-4591 . . 14 E 17 St, Avalon, NJ *08202*
Harrington MR & MRS Edward A (Ashley P Riegel) ⚓
PO Box 575, Fishers Island, NY *06390*
Harris MISS Brooke J . . see L Gourlay
Harris MRS Charles D (Janet B Jeffery)
☎ (302) 227-4442 . . 75 Tidewaters, Henlopen Acres, Rehoboth Beach, DE *19971*
Harris MRS Francis M (Barbara L Sharpe)
☎ (408) 423-6833 . . ''Empress Ranch'' 2500 Empire Grade Rd, Santa Cruz, CA *95060*
Harris MR & MRS George B (Florence Butcher) ⚓
☎ (508) 693-1468 . . Box 153 RFD, Hatch Rd, Vineyard Haven, MA *02568*
Harris MR & MRS George I E (Kate B Webb)...... | ☎ (802) 985-2263
JUNIORS MISS Amanda H .... | ''High Acres Farm''
JUNIORS MR Jonathan J .... | PO Box 235,
 | Shelburne, VT
 | *05482*
Harris MRS Gwathmey (Nancy Gwathmey)
☎ (207) 276-3651 . . Manchester Rd, Northeast Harbor, ME *04662*
Harris MR & MRS Henry F (A J Penelope Parsons).. | ☎ (207) 276-3791
MISS Elizabeth H .... | ''The Ledge''
MR Henry F JR .... | Northeast Harbor,
 | ME *04662*
Harris MR & MRS Henry P U JR (Mary Jeanne Johnston)
☎ (603) 968-3635 . . ''Loon Rock'' PO Box 193, Holdnerness, NH *03245*
Harris MR & MRS Henry P U 3d (Eleanor M Magruder) ⚓ .... | ☎ (603) 968-7046
JUNIORS MR Gregory M .... | ''Loon Rock''
 | PO Box 193,
 | Holderness, NH
 | *03245*
Harris MR & MRS James Hoban (Anne Reuther)
☎ (203) 866-2017 . . ''Bois Joli'' 10 Woodland Rd, Wilson Point, South Norwalk, CT *06854*
Harris MR & MRS John A 4th (Annie L Ryerson)
☎ (207) 276-5576 . . ''Moss Hill'' Box 553, Northeast Harbor, ME *04662*
Harris MR & MRS Jonathan M (Cynthia A Bidart)
☎ (603) 968-7046 . . ''Loon Rock'' PO Box 193, Holderness, NH *03245*
Harris MR Lamont B P
''The Ledge'' Northeast Harbor, ME *04662*
Harris MR & MRS R Macy 3d (Louise B Ward)
☎ (716) 374-2045 . . Semple Hill Rd, Longs Point, Naples, NY *14512*
Harrison MRS Edward T (Carkener—Gallowhur—Mary L Gary)
☎ (415) 459-7016 . . 2 Madrone Av, Kentfield, CA *94904*

Harrison MR & MRS James B (Holderness—Jane R Munson)
☎ (207) 244-5543 . . ''Pine Ledge'' Herrick Rd, Southeast Harbor, ME *04679*
Harrison MRS James S 3d (Free—Medlen—Mary A T T Phillips)
☎ (207) 276-0570 . . PO Box 865, Northeast Harbor, ME *04662*
Harrison MR & MRS John T (Patricia Wood)
☎ (802) 442-4292 . . ''Four Corners'' RR 2, Box 72, Shaftsbury, VT *05262*
Harrison MRS June A (Wells—June F Auslander)
☎ (516) 653-4436 . . ''Bug House'' Drawer JJ-5034, 57 Quogue St, Quogue, NY *11959*
Harrison MRS Melissa T (Gray—Melissa A Travis) | ☎ (908) 730-7626
MR Jeb Gray ..... | Travis Hill Farm,
 | 5 Travis Hill Rd,
 | Hampton, NJ *08827*
Harrison MR & MRS R Brandon JR (Agnes W Smith) | ☎ (508) 627-5928
MISS Sarah C .... | 56 Cottage St,
MISS Emily D .... | Edgartown, MA
MISS Catherine W .... | *02539*
Harrison MR & MRS Ridgely W (Cozad—Johnson—Josephine E Streeter).. |
☎ (516) 283-7823 . . ''Ivy Cottage'' 350 Hill St, Southampton, NY *11968*
☎ (616) 526-5704 . . ''Windward'' Box 726, Harbor Springs, MI *49740*
Harrison MR & MRS William R (Karen C Graham) . | ☎ (860) 691-1727
MR William R JR...................... | 11 Hemingway Rd,
MR Christopher W .... | Old Black Point,
MR Kenneth G .... | Niantic, CT *06357*
Harrity MR & MRS (DR) Robert J JR (Janet A Madigan)
☎ (603) 253-9921 . . Squam Lake, Old Harvard Rd, Box 177K, Center Harbor, NH *03226*
Harrower MRS Lyle (Léontine Lyle)
☎ (207) 867-4640 . . ''Custom House'' North Haven, ME *04853*
Harsch MR & MRS Paul A 3d (Merry Anderson).... | ☎ (401) 423-0690
MISS Sarah W .... | ''Windswept''
MR Caleb C .... | Highland Dv,
JUNIORS MISS Katherine A .... | Jamestown, RI
JUNIORS MISS Jessica L .... | *02835*
Hart DR & MRS Brandon B (Katrina V N O Bogert) . | ☎ (207) 244-3568
MISS Eliza W .... | ''Grey Havens''
 | Pretty Marsh,
 | Mt Desert, ME
 | *04660*
Hart MR & MRS Bruce W (Anne Elizabeth Jones)
☎ (207) 397-2681 . . ''Liberty Camp'' Water Rte 41, Belgrade Lakes, ME *04918*
Hart MR & MRS Douglas E (Lydia Melville Day) ... | ☎ (207) 644-8207
JUNIORS MISS Caroline B .... | W Side Rd,
JUNIORS MR Andrew E .... | PO Box 72,
 | South Bristol, ME
 | *04568*
Hart MR & MRS George D (Jessica W Ely)
☎ (617) 934-2432 . . ''Powder House'' Box 378, Duxbury, MA *02331*
Hart MISS Hilary B . . see S H Brainerd
Hart MR Howard S . . see S H Brainerd
Hart MR & MRS John H (Sarah R Miller)
☎ (516) 569-7090 . . ''Haywood'' 2 Village Way, Lawrence, NY *11559*

Hart MR & MRS Todd C (Zoé de Ropp-Weinman)
☎ (516) 653-5198 . . "Pine Neck" Box 63, East Quogue, NY *11942*

Hartshorne MR Harold
☎ (414) 248-3319 . . Flowerside Farms, W 3601 Hartshorne Lane, Lake Geneva, WI *53147*

Harvey MR & MRS Curran W JR (Marjorie J Simons)
☎ (410) 296-8035 . . 1866 Circle Rd, Ruxton, MD *21204*

Harvey MR & MRS Cyrus I JR (Rebecca P Miller) . . . | ☎ (011-44-1285)
MISS Natasha . . . . | 654-518
 | Daglingworth,
 | nr Cirencester,
 | Gloucestershire,
 | England

Harvey MR & MRS F Barton JR (Grace W Locke) . . . | "Dimi House"
MR F Barton 3d . . . . | Fishers Island, NY
 | *06390*

Harvey JUNIORS MR Nathan A . . see MISS A C Toogood

Harvey MR & MRS Robert E (Karen N Simpson) . . . | ☎ (908) 899-6093
JUNIORS MISS Jennifer S . . . . | 401 Lake Av,
JUNIORS MR James R S . . . . | Bay Head, NJ *08742*

Harvie MR & MRS J Beverly (Faith G Hall)
☎ (508) 945-0820 . . 112 Inlet Rd, Chatham, MA *02633*

Hasell MRS Samuel M (Annie B Simons) . . . . | ☎ (704) 693-4809
MISS Ann Simons . . . . | "Prospect Hill"
 | 540 Fairway Dv,
 | Hendersonville, NC
 | *28739*

Hasen MR & MRS George M (Charlotte H Binger)
☎ (802) 533-2277 . . Greensboro, VT *05841*

Haskell MRS Francis W (M Noelle Delafield Finch)
☎ (516) 288-1145 . . "Callendar" 11 Delafield Dv, Westhampton Beach, NY *11978*

Haskell MR & MRS John H F JR (Francine G | ☎ (011-33-33)
Le Roux) . . . . | 47-06-58
MISS Diana F T . . . . | "Villa Le Perron"
 | 29 Le Feugre, 50230
 | Agon-Coutainville,
 | France

Haskell MR Macdonald T
☎ (508) 645-3130 . . Lot 3, Lighthouse Rd, Lobsterville Beach, Chilmark, MA *02535*

Haskell MR & MRS William P (Helen B Park)
☎ (508) 693-0835 . . 788 Main St, PO Box 6006, West Chop, MA *02573-6006*

Haskins MR & MRS William Chandler (Elizabeth Ivins)
☎ (508) 428-2943 . . Box 617, Osterville, MA *02655*

Hastie MR & MRS J Drayton (Fernanda deMohrenschildt)
☎ (704) 692-7343 . . "The Cottage" Woodfields Rd, Flat Rock, NC *28731*

Hastings MRS Ellison (Mary Ellison)
Squirrel Island, ME *04570*

Hastings MR & MRS Matthew T (Linda F Steele)
"Stone Cottage" Isle au Haut, ME *04645*

Hastings MRS T Mitchell JR (Thacher—Margot L Campbell)
☎ (603) 563-8610 . . Box 266, Page Rd, Dublin, NH *03444*

Hatchette DR & MRS James B 3d (Mary Farrar) . . . | ☎ (970) 586-5348
MISS Constance McC . . . . | 825 Longs Peak Rd,
MR Charles V 2d . . . . | Estes Park, CO
 | *80517*

Hately MISS Jennifer W . . see F F Seidler

Hatfield MR & MRS Charles J 2d (Nancy Nicholas) . . | ☎ (207) 374-2402
MR Charles J 3d . . . . | "Leese House"
 | East Blue Hill, ME
 | *04629*

Havemeyer MR & MRS Harry W (Eugénie Aiguier)
☎ (516) 665-1843 . . 90 S Saxon Av, Bay Shore, NY *11706*

Havemeyer MRS Horace JR (Rosalind Everdell)
☎ (410) 778-4588 . . "The Reward" 24031 Walnut Point Rd, Chestertown, MD *21620*

Havens MR & MRS Richard W (Bettle—Sally A Atwater)
☎ (401) 635-8965 . . "Mizzentop" 32 Sakonnet Point Rd, Little Compton, RI *02837-1043*

Havre MR Jay P . . see J E Pierce

Hawes MRS Alexander B (Breed—Rosilla M Hornblower)
☎ (401) 635-4894 . . 6 Taylors Lane N, Little Compton, RI *02837*

Hawes MRS Louis (Diana W Mallory) . . . . | ☎ (207) 348-7718
MR Christopher M . . . . | 604 Pressey Village
MR Daniel . . . . | Rd, Deer Isle, ME
 | *04627*

Hawkings MISS Parish H (Bogliaccini—Parish H Hawkings)
☎ (908) 899-4338 . . 936 Barnegat Lane, Mantoloking, NJ *08738*

Hawtin MRS Raymond F (Ware—Elise H Fay)
☎ (207) 276-5440 . . Sutton Island, Northeast Harbor, ME *04662*

Haxall MRS Bolling W (Rainsford—Elizabeth | ☎ (315) 686-5223
Dodge) . . . . | "Club Island"
MR D Barton—☎ (315) 686-2197 . . . . | PO Box 66, Clayton,
 | NY *13624-0066*

Hayes MR Nicholas
☎ (516) CE9-3325 . . 7 Stable Lane, Lawrence, NY *11559*

Haygood MR & MRS Paul M (Charlotte S Smither) . . | ☎ (504) 635-4208
JUNIORS MISS Charlotte H . . . . | Hazelwood
JUNIORS MISS Katherine S . . . . | Plantation, Old
 | Laurel Hill Rd,
 | St Francisville, LA
 | *70775*

Haynes MR Robert B
☎ (516) 283-0425 . . Meadow Club, First Neck Lane, Drawer F, Southampton, NY *11969*

Haynes MRS Sophy P-Q (Soutter—Sophy | ☎ (516) 283-6552
Pellegrini-Quarantotti) . . . . | "Hopeland 3d"
MR Schuyler B . . . . | 134 Herrick Rd,
MR Robert Van R . . . . | Southampton, NY
 | *11968*

Hays DR & MRS F Whiting (Helen D Hibbard) . . . . | ☎ (401) 635-2249
MISS Daphne D . . . . | "Rocky Beach
MR Frederick W JR . . . . | House" 45 Atlantic
MR William S . . . . | Av, Little Compton,
 | RI *02837*

Hays MR & MRS Thomas A (Julia P Kinloch) . . . . . | ☎ (302) 539-5825
MR Thomas A 3d . . . . | 24 Short Rd,
 | South Bethany, DE
 | *19930*

Hayward MRS Johnston (Patricia M Johnston) . . . . . | ☎ (518) 523-9339
   MISS Barbara A . . . . | Camp Gordon,
                                                                        Lake Placid, NY
                                                                        12946

Haywood MR & MRS T Holt JR (Nancy A Ahern)
   ☎ (011-33-93) 61-39-26 . . ''Villa Jacane'' 142 blvd du Cap, 06600 Cap d'Antibes, France

Hazard MR & MRS Oliver C (Pell—Sarah E Halsey) ⚓
   ☎ (508) 228-0739 . . 15 Gardner St, Nantucket, MA *02554*

Heald MRS William E (Anne S Haydock)
   ☎ (616) 223-4454 . . ''The Maples'' 14540 Prospect, Traverse City, MI *49684*

Healy MR & MRS Harold H JR (Elizabeth A Debevoise)
   ☎ (201) 377-5325 . . ''Hidden Springs'' Green Village, NJ *07935*

Healy MR & MRS William T (Gail F Hull) . . . . | ☎ (619) 435-2858
   MR William T JR . . . . | 1100 Adella,
   MR Sean P . . . . | Coronado, CA
                                                         92118

Heaphy MRS Edward T JR (Candace Wilder) . . . . . . | ☎ (207) 967-3806
   MISS Emily D . . . . | Kennebunkport, ME
   MISS Christina M . . . . | *04046*

Heaphy MR Edward T JR
   ☎ (207) 967-5828 . . 104 Kings H'way, Kennebunkport, ME *04046*

Heard MR & MRS Charles W (Corina S Higginson) . | ''Aurora''
   MISS Sarah . . . . | Lower Bragdon Rd,
   MR Drayton . . . . | Wells, ME *04090*

Heard MR & MRS Edwin Anthony JR (Phyllis M Gregory)
   ☎ (860) 354-6319 . . 3 Timber Lake Rd, Sherman, CT *06784*

Heard MISS Susan E
   ☎ (508) 228-0340 . . 10 Fulling Mill Rd, Box 448, Nantucket, MA *02554*

Hebard MR & MRS Morgan JR (Wells—Jean T Ballard)
   ☎ (207) 763-3394 . . ''Loon Point'' RD 1, Box 4331, Lincolnville, ME *04849*

Heckman MR & MRS Guy C (Margaret I Jenks) . . . . | ☎ (207) 276-5448
   JUNIORS MR William A M . . . . | ''The Willows''
                                                                 Northeast Harbor,
                                                                 ME *04662*

Heckman MRS William Guy (Moulton—Margaret L Carter)
   ☎ (616) 526-6570 . . 1047 Beach Dv, Harbor Springs, MI *49740*

Heckscher MR & MRS August (Claude Chevreux)
   ☎ (207) 276-3267 . . ''High Loft'' Seal Harbor, ME *04675*

Heckscher MR & MRS Benjamin H (Pratt—Nancy B | ☎ (508) 428-2484
   Turner) . . . . | Peppercorn Lane,
   MR Benjamin H JR . . . . | Cotuit, MA *02635*
   MR David M . . . . |
   MR Christopher D . . . . |

Heckscher MR & MRS Morrison H (M A Fenella Greig)
   Louds Island, Round Pond, ME *04564*

Heimbecker DR & MRS Raymond O (Kathleen H H | ☎ (705) 762-0174
   Jensen) ⚓ . . . . | ''Log House''
   MISS Dorothy A T . . . . | Holliday Bay,
   MISS Constance M H . . . . | Lake Muskoka,
   MR Harry O 2d . . . . | Bala, Ontario
                                                                     P0C 1A0, Canada

Heintz MR & MRS Paul C A (Jane Develin) . . . . | ☎ (508) 228-8576
   MR Robert B D . . . . | ''Woxof''
   MR Edward S A . . . . | 12 Irving St,
                                                                     Nantucket, MA
                                                                   02554

Heitner MR & MRS Norman E (Georgia R Morse)
   ☎ (616) 547-9886 . . 9 Belvedere Club, Charlevoix, MI *49720*

Helfenstein MR J Gouverneur M
   ☎ (914) 876-3849 . . ''The Belfry'' 34 Salisbury Tpke, Rhinebeck, NY *12572*

Helfet MR & MRS Anthony B (Marjorie H McMahon)
   ☎ (516) 788-7704 . . Greenwood Av, Fishers Island, NY *06390*

Heller MRS Homer K (Frances McC Kennedy)
   ☎ (207) 374-2237 . . ''Shoreby'' Box 279, Blue Hill, ME *04614*

Helling MR & MRS Robert E (Clare Hudson)
   ☎ (203) 762-3723 . . 45 Boulder Brook Rd, Wilton, CT *06897*

Hellmuth MR & MRS Joseph A (Katherine B Gatch) . | ☎ (508) 432-4947
   MISS Harriet . . . . | 456 Long Pond Dv,
                                                            East Harwich, MA
                                                           02645

Hellmuth MR & MRS William K (Nancy R Le Sage)
   ☎ (401) 596-6394 . . Round Hill Rd, Watch Hill, RI *02891*

Hellyer MR & MRS Walter 2d (Jeanne A Vidal)
   ''Up-Away'' 9229 Gibraltar Bluff Rd, Fish Creek, WI *54212*

Helm MR & MRS William L JR (Eleanor Lloyd) . . . . . | ☎ (603) 323-8647
   MR William L 3d . . . . | ''The Deck House''
                                                        Fowlers Mill Rd,
                                                        Box 26, Chocorua,
                                                       NH *03817*

Helme MISS Elizabeth S E
   ☎ (516) 749-0121 . . 8 Clinton Av, Shelter Island Heights, NY *11965*

Helme MR & MRS Jay E JR (Nancy M Gleske)
   ☎ (516) 749-3398 . . 8 Clinton Av, Shelter Island Heights, NY *11965*

Helmsing MR & MRS Frederick G (Margaret S | ☎ (334) 990-9888
   Oswalt) . . . . | ''Over the Bay''
   MISS Margaret S . . . . | Point Clear, AL
   MR Frederick G JR . . . . | *36564*
   MR Joseph G . . . . |

Hemingway MR & MRS Patrick (Carol Thompson)
   ☎ (406) 235-4208 . . Craig Rte, Wolf Creek, MT *59648*

Heminway MR John H JR . . of
   ☎ (406) 222-0041 . . ''Bar 20'' West Boulder Reserve, McLeod, MT *59052*
   ☎ (406) 947-2161 . . ''Bull Mountain Ranch'' Worden, MT *59088*

Hemphill MR & MRS John JR (Wenche Smith)
   ☎ (011-47-370) 95684 . . ''Nesset'' Skarpnestangen, 4875 Nedenes, Norway

Henchey MISS Hope G
   ☎ (603) 586-4372 . . Cottage Rd, Jefferson, NH *03583*

Henckels MR Kirk
   ☎ (914) 868-1543 . . ''Pondfields Farm'' Box 628, Bangall, NY *12506*

Henderson MR & MRS Dan F (Carol D Hardin)
   ☎ (509) 687-3721 . . Halmalka 509, Wapato Point Resort, Lake Chelan, WA *98831*

Henderson MR & MRS David R (Cassandra F Hyland)..........................
MISS Consuelo C.......................
JUNIORS MR G L Cabot ....
☎ (508) 228-8771
6 Winter St, Nantucket, MA *02554*

Henderson MR & MRS Ernest F 3d (Mary L Campbell)...........................
MISS Roberta C........................
☎ (508) 775-2057
"The Elms" 35 Linden Av, Centerville, MA *02632*

Henderson MR & MRS Gerald van S (Joan A Bristol)
☎ (401) 322-7032 .. "The Seabreeze Cottage" 10 Seabreeze Av, Quonochontaug, RI *02813*

Henderson MR & MRS J Welles (Hannah L Bradley)
☎ (508) 526-7900 .. "Whimsey" 19 Old Neck Rd, Manchester, MA *01944*

Henderson MR & MRS Joseph W 3d (M Lucia Bosqui)............................
MISS Lucia R ....
JUNIORS MR J Welles 4th ....
☎ (516) 788-7128
"Scot Free" PO Box 673, Fishers Island, NY *06390*

Henderson MRS Wellington S (Harriet E Walker)
☎ (916) 525-7726 .. Lone Pine Point, Tahoma, CA *96142*

Hendrick MR Robert E P
☎ (516) 537-3889 .. "Kildobbin" Georgica Association, Wainscott, NY *11975*

Hennessy MRS B Rial (Doherty—Kelley—Bruce Rial).............................
MR John E T Kelley...................
☎ (516) 283-4644
56 Linden Lane, Southampton, NY *11968*

Henningsen MR & MRS Victor W JR (Mary F B Ludington)
☎ (441) 236-2136 .. 7 Mizzentop, 14 Harbour Rd, Warwick WK 06, Bermuda

Henshaw MR & MRS William G 3d (Patricia A Madigan)
☎ (702) 749-5228 .. 2173 W W Bliss Dirt Rd, Glenbrook, NV *89413*

Hensley MR & MRS Robert T JR (Mower—Frances Newhard)
☎ (517) 738-5935 .. Cottage 38, Pointe-aux-Barques, Port Austin, MI *48467*

Hepburn MR & MRS Austin B (Taylor—Huber—Adele Hunter)....................
MR Martin H..........................
MR Douglas P........................
☎ (609) 368-5925
190—75 St, Avalon, NJ *08202*

Heppenheimer MR & MRS William S (Martha J Ball)
☎ (516) 324-6279 .. PO Box 144, Amagansett, NY *11930*

Hepting MR & MRS G Carleton (Diana Duncan) ....
MISS Caroline S ....
MR Dyson D ....
☎ (401) 849-3217
25 Bridge St, Newport, RI *02840*

Hermann MR & MRS Robert R JR (Signa V Merrill) .
JUNIORS MISS Elizabeth L B ....
☎ (616) 526-6510
"Windswept" 405 Glenn Dv, Harbor Springs, MI *49740*

Herrick MRS Anita G (Kearns—Anita G Herrick) ..
MISS Jessica G Kearns ....
MR J Nicholas Kearns ....
PO Box 226, Islesboro, ME *04848*

Herrick MRS Harold E JR (Mary H Williams)
☎ (315) 654-2036 .. "Point of View" Box 92, Cape Vincent, NY *13618*

Herrick MR & MRS Peter (Beatricia Bierau) ⚓ ...
MR David S ....
☎ (516) 878-1677
"The Cottage" East Moriches, NY *11940*

Herrick MISS Robin F .. see J D Phyfe
Herrick MR Trevor S .. see J D Phyfe

Herrlinger MR & MRS Edward F 2d (Herrlinger—Gail A Hathaway) ⚓ ....
MR David H ....
☎ (401) 848-0233
"Brenton's Cove" Harrison Av, Newport, RI *02840*

Herrmann MR & MRS R Leith (Susan A Speers)....
JUNIORS MISS Virginia G ....
JUNIORS MR William deW ....
☎ (207) 647-9488
Highland Ridge Rd, Bridgton, ME *04009*

Herschede MRS Mark P (Huffman—Joan Roth)....
MISS Deborah L Huffman ....
☎ (616) 547-9295
"Cedar Crest" 403 Belvedere Av, Charlevoix, MI *49720*

Hesser MR & MRS Terry A (Helene H Hartenstein)
☎ (413) 566-8926 .. "Rocky Hill" 20 Old Coach Circle, Hampden, MA *01036*

Heuer MRS Scott JR (Spender—Ann F Lynch) .....
MISS Catherine A ....
☎ (504) 486-5196
6550 Oakland Dv, New Orleans, LA *70118*

Hewes MR & MRS Laurence I 3d (Mary C Darling) ..
MISS Mary C D........................
MR Laurence I 4th ....
MR H Patrick D ....
☎ (802) 533-2303
"Aspenhurst" Greensboro, VT *05841*

Hewitt MR Edward Cooper JR .. see S B Colt
Hewson MRS Charlotte W (Charlotte M Wolf)
"Windward" 60 First Av, Avon-By-The-Sea, NJ *07717*

Heyward MR & MRS Allan McA (Marianna C Marshall)
☎ (207) 244-5343 .. "Fairway" Causeway Lane, Southwest Harbor, ME *04679*

Heyward MR & MRS Robert B (Jacqueline McCormick)
☎ (412) 593-7011 .. Pike Run Country Club, Jones Mills, PA *15646*

Hiam MR & MRS Edwin W (Katharine C Watson)
☎ (508) 548-5903 .. 224 Quissett Av, Falmouth, MA *02540*

Hickman MRS Norman Gilbert (James—D'Oench—Wood—Donovan—Minnie Fell Cassatt)
☎ (516) 283-1684 .. 496 First Neck Lane, Southampton, NY *11968*

Hickok MR Daniel H (Mary Isabel Voorhees)
☎ (717) 525-3364 .. "Altament" Eagles Mere, PA *17731*

Hickox MR & MRS Charles C (Moulton—Linda L Janien) .. of
☎ (616) 526-2944 .. Cottage 12, Harbor Point, MI *49740*
☎ (203) 629-4346 .. 79 Harbor Dv, Greenwich, CT *06830*

Hickox MR & MRS Charles R (Walker—Edith L Porter)
☎ (819) 842-2402 .. "Kilby Cottage" North Hatley, Quebec J0B 2C0, Canada

Hickox MRS James P (Barbara J Raymond).......
MISS Polly C.........................
MR James P JR ....
☎ (508) 636-4923
3 Hurricane Lane, Westport, MA *02790*

Hickox MRS Louise F (Louise C Fitzhugh) . . . . ☎ (616) 526-6660
MR George F. . . . . "Shintangle"
PO Box 4414,
3 Trillium Walk,
Wequetonsing, MI
49740

Hidalgo MR & MRS Alfonso (Elizabeth S Hall)
☎ (609) 466-1517 . . "Justa Caixinha" 225 Amwell Rd, Hopewell, NJ *08525*

Hiestand MR & MRS Harry K (Nancy M Price) . . . . . ☎ (207) 244-7108
MR Philip M . . . . Sail Mountain Rd,
PO Box 1292,
Southwest Harbor,
ME *04679*

Higgins MR & MRS James H 3d (Martha M Robinson)
☎ (508) 945-3284 . . 1 Wapoos Trail, Chatham, MA *02633*

Higgins MRS Raymond M (Joan S Griess)
☎ (508) 228-2106 . . "Lot One" 15 Jefferson Av, Nantucket, MA *02554*

Higginson MR & MRS Charles (Genevra A Osborn)
☎ (617) 383-9427 . . "Cedar Ledges" 159 Atlantic Av, Cohasset, MA *02025*

Hildebrandt MRS Donald H (Mary Helen Detrick) . ☎ (520) 527-4087
MR & MRS David D (Mary Maguire) . . . . 6081 E Laurel Loop
Rd, Flagstaff, AZ
86004

Hilgenberg MR & MRS John C (Twells—Evelyn B ☎ (207) 642-2645
Handy) . . . . "Pokomoke"
MISS Elizabeth Crady . . . . Sebago Lake, ME
04075

Hill MISS Ann . . see L E MacElree

Hill MR & MRS Charles B 3d (Sheila J Brewster) . . . ☎ (414) 868-3772
MR Charles B 4th . . . . PO Box 635,
MR Robert J . . . . Fish Creek, WI
54212

Hill MISS Charlotte . . see L E MacElree

Hill DR & MRS (DR) George J (Helene Zimmermann) . ☎ (603) 447-4214
MISS Sarah . . . . Paul Hill Rd, Eaton,
MISS Helena R . . . . NH *03832*
MR James W . . . .

Hill MR & MRS J Tomilson 3d (Janine A Wolf) . . . . . ☎ (516) 759-9169
JUNIORS MISS Margot. . . . . Piping Rock Rd,
JUNIORS MISS Astrid . . . . Locust Valley, NY
11560

Hill MRS James T JR (Dorothy H Kutcher)
☎ (508) 428-2907 . . 25 Vineyard Rd, Box 565, Cotuit, MA *02635*

Hill MR & MRS Jefferson B (Gabrielle M Tourville) . ☎ (508) 693-9426
MISS Corinna B. . . . . "Barnard's Inn
JUNIORS MISS Lydia R . . . . Farm" Vineyard
Haven, MA *02568*

Hill MR & MRS Joseph J (Elizabeth Van H Bartlett) ☎ (902) 275-3832
⚓. . . . . "Fat City" Chester,
MISS Susannah B . . . . Nova Scotia
MR Alexander McC . . . . B0J 1J0, Canada
MR Michael H. . . . .

Hill MRS Ray R (Jessie H Leonard)
☎ (207) 734-6785 . . PO Box 236, Islesboro, ME *04848*

Hill MRS William E (Jane E Herrmann) . . . . ☎ (860) 739-5553
MISS Sarah K . . . . Old Black Point Rd,
Niantic, CT *06357*

Hillman MRS Howard B (Sandra Fales)
☎ (203) 661-3698 . . "Stoneybrook" 29 Taconic Rd, Greenwich, CT *06830*

Hillman MR Howard B . . . . ☎ (508) 645-2573
MR Howard B JR. . . . . "Water Wheel
Farm" RFD Box
297, Middle Rd,
Chilmark, MA
02535

Hills MR & MRS Austin E (Erika M Brunar) . . . . . . ☎ (707) 963-4577
JUNIORS MR Austin . . . . PO Box 139,
JUNIORS MR Justin . . . . Rutherford, CA
94573

Hillsmith MRS Fannie L (Welchman—Fannie L Hillsmith)
☎ (603) 532-7132 . . "Wedgwood" Jaffrey, NH *03452*

Hilton MR & MRS John A JR (Julia L Hansen) . . . . . ☎ (508) 228-3398
MISS Julia H . . . . "Crosswinds"
MISS Katharine B . . . . 6 Fargo Way,
JUNIORS MISS Ashley S . . . . Nantucket, MA
02554

Hinckley MR & MRS Samuel H (Nancy A Frohan) ⚓
☎ (415) 669-1369 . . "Toad Hall" 13 Laurel View Rd, Inverness, CA *94937*

Hind MR James M
☎ (702) 749-5262 . . 18 Golf Links Rd, Glenbrook, NV *89413*

Hines MR & MRS Edward M W (Caroline M Knapp) . North Haven, ME
MISS Alexandra E *04853*
JUNIORS MISS Laura L . . . .

Hines MR & MRS Marion E (Julie W Viele)
☎ (508) 428-5345 . . Inner Harbor, Box 1074, Cotuit, MA *02635*

Hird MR & MRS Samuel Ainsworth JR (Drogoul—Benacerraf—Webb—Diane C Meentemeier) ⚓
☎ (516) 749-0037 . . Box 254, 8 Shore Rd, Dering Harbor, Shelter Island Heights, NY *11965*

Hirsh MRS Willard (Sarah F Cole)
☎ (216) 286-7268 . . "Vengreen Farm" 12987 GAR H'way, Chardon, OH *44024*

Hitchcock MISS Margaret Mellon (Scarrone— "Shangri-La"
Bowart—Margaret Mellon Hitchcock) . . . . Paradise Valley, AZ
MISS Sophia J Bowart *85253*
MISS Nuria L Bowart . . . .

Hitchcock MR Nelson B
☎ (802) 457-2469 . . Moore Place, Woodstock, VT *05091*

Hitchcock MR & MRS Peter T (Cecily G Kohlsaat) . . "Thurtilperk Hill"
MISS Courtney A. . . . . Beech Plain Rd,
New Boston, MA
01255

Hitchcock MRS Thomas (Laughlin—Margaret Mellon)
☎ (705) 764-1129 . . Camp Vagabondia, Beaumaris, Lake Muskoka, Ontario P0B 1B0, Canada

Hoagland MRS Henry W JR (Biehl—A Ray Watkin)
☎ (207) 967-4934 . . PO Box 2737, Kennebunkport, ME *04046*

Hobart MR & MRS Aaron A (Swan—Selina Strong) ⚓
☎ (802) 297-1497 . . "West Hill" Bondville, VT *05340*

Hobart MR & MRS William H (Julia R De Camp)... ☎ (508) 257-6668
   MISS J N Surridge........................ "The Power House" 25 Morey Lane, Siasconset, MA *02564*
   MR W Harrison 3d......................

Hobbs MR & MRS Franklin W (Margery G Baird)
   ☎ (508) 993-1060.. "Eden Voe" Box P231, South Dartmouth, MA *02748*

Hobbs MR & MRS Franklin W 4th (Linda B Read).. ☎ (508) 999-4157 Nonquitt, MA *02748*
   JUNIORS MISS Ashley R....................
   JUNIORS MR Nicholas B..................

Hobbs JUDGE & MRS Truman McG (Joyce D Cummings)
   ☎ (704) 733-5508.. "Hobbs Hollow" Box 722, Linville, NC *28646*

Hoblitzell MR & MRS Alan P JR (Prentice—M Louise Perkins)
   ☎ (508) 457-6469.. 124 Moorland Rd, Falmouth, MA *02540*

Hobson REV DR & MRS George H JR (Dearborn—Victoria A Lewis)
   ☎ (011-33-65) 33-66-81.. Puy del Claux, Gintrac, 46130 Bretenoux, France

Hobson MR & MRS Henry Wise JR (Elizabeth Balch)
   ☎ (516) 788-7381.. "Playhouse" Box 85, Fishers Island, NY *06390*

Hobson MR & MRS J Kendall (Ketchum—Kathleen L Friel)................ ☎ (516) 726-4757 Cobb Isle, Cobb Rd, Water Mill, NY *11976*
   JUNIORS MR John K JR....................

Hodges MISS Elizabeth J
   ☎ (603) 526-6620.. 10 Burpee Lane, New London, NH *03257*

Hodges MR & MRS Fletcher III (Chantal Leroy).... ☎ (508) 627-5450 Box 211, Edgartown, MA *02539*
   MISS Rebecca........................

Hodges MR & MRS Lorin C (Eleanor M Lyman).... ☎ (207) 563-2010 PO Box 1288, Damariscotta, ME *04543*
   MISS Orlanda C........................

Hodges MR & MRS Thomas V (Elizabeth N Wilbur)
   ☎ (207) 348-2532.. Box 222, Little Deer Isle, ME *04650*

Hodgkins MR & MRS Thomas D (Mary A BonDurant)........................ ☎ (705) 782-6251 Box 124, Desbarats, Ontario P0R 1E0, Canada
   MISS Katherine E....................
   MR Thomas S........................

Hoerle MR & MRS Robert F (Sheila S Armstrong)... ☎ (508) 627-8261 118 S Water St, Edgartown, MA *02539*
   MR Jeffrey........................
   MR W Scott....................
   MR Alexander F....................

Hoffman MRS Albert L JR (Florence C Meyer) ⚓
   ☎ (207) 244-7881.. "The Play Ground" PO Box 252, 102A S Seawall Rd, Manset, ME *04656*

Hoffman MR & MRS Eric (Pope—Ronna C Hitchcock).. of
   ☎ (503) 635-1434.. 11625 SW Military Rd, Portland, OR *97219*
   ☎ (619) 773-1045.. 47-000 E Eldorado Dr, Indian Wells, CA *92210*

Hoffman MR & MRS Harrison B W (Martin—Louise E Sinkler)........................ ☎ (207) 389-1598 Small Point, ME *04567*
   MR Nicholas O........................
   MR Crozer W Martin....................

Hoffman MRS J Gordon (Elizabeth J Gibson)
   ☎ (203) 637-2770.. 31 Lake Dv S, Riverside, CT *06878*

Hoffman MR & MRS Peter K (Lindsey A Murkland)
   ☎ (508) 228-1361.. Gull Island, Nantucket, MA *02554*

Hoffstot MR Henry P
   ☎ (216) 457-7216.. "Henphip House" 3060 Waterford Rd, New Waterford, OH *44445*

Hofheins MR Robert F
   "Shaki Shanti" Cranberry Lake, NY *12927*

Hoge MRS Francis H (Shafer—Helene S Gales)
   ☎ (516) 283-1084.. Whitefield, 155 Hill St, Southampton, NY *11968*

Hoguet MISS Diana L.. see G E Wantz

Hoguet MR Geoffrey R
   ☎ (011-43-7480) 248.. 3294 Langau bei Gaming, NÖ, Austria

Hoguet MRS Robert L (Condon—Alice Berry)
   ☎ (207) 734-6950.. "Eastridge" Dark Harbor, Islesboro, ME *04848*

Hoguet MRS Roland H (Billings—Aileen C Jackson)
   ☎ (609) 896-1283.. 9 Maple Av, Lawrenceville, NJ *08648*

Hokin MISS Alexandra.. see MRS D Coudert

Hokin MISS Dana.. see MRS D Coudert

Holbrook MR & MRS Christopher C (Alice B Hager)
   ☎ (607) 547-4110.. "Busch House" Box 163, Cooperstown, NY *13326*

Holbrook MR & MRS David D (Holly C Gales)
   ☎ (207) 846-0875.. 20 Sligo Rd, Yarmouth, ME *04096*

Holbrook MR & MRS Dean (Christina Flander)
   ☎ (518) 623-3567.. "Crane View" Henry Wescott Rd, Thurman, NY *12885*

Holbrook DR & MRS John P (Weed—Hibner—Jane Wraith)
   ☎ (406) 837-5578.. "Eagle Bend" 80 Rock Place, Bigfork, MT *59911*

Holbrook MR & MRS William Sumner 3d (Sally A Davis) ⚓
   ☎ (310) 435-7839.. Shoreline Terrace Apt 303, 1230 E Ocean Blvd, Long Beach, CA *90802*

Holch MR & MRS Eric S (Elspeth M Royster)...... ☎ (508) 228-7654 11 Wauwinet Rd, Nantucket, MA *02554*
   MISS Serena B........................
   MR Sven C........................

Holcombe MR & MRS Shepherd M JR (Elizabeth S Cammann)
   ☎ (603) 823-5285.. Grandview Rd, Sugar Hill, NH *03585*

Holden MR & MRS Richmond Y (Mary Jane S Muzzy)
   ☎ (516) 653-4276.. "Holdune" 152 Dune Rd, Box 4, Quogue, NY *11959*

Holder MRS Richmond (Marcia S Black)
   ☎ (603) 823-5348.. "The Snuggery" Church St, Franconia, NH *03580*

Holdsworth MRS David Bethune (Lorraine G Bacon)
   ☎ (508) 645-2864.. Box 185, Chilmark, MA *02535*

Holland MRS William King (Dorothy Garesché)... ☎ (616) 857-4578 "Ravinedge" 278 Lake Shore Dv, Douglas, MI *49406*
   MR Garesché W F........................

Hollenback MR & MRS William M JR (Worrall—Patterson—Mae G Cadwalader)
   ☎ (207) 867-2251.. PO Box 222, North Haven, ME *04853*

Hollingsworth MR & MRS Amor (Eleanor Gibson)
   ☎ (508) 693-1458.. West Chop Club, PO Box 6011, West Chop, MA *02573*

Hollister MR & MRS Buell 4th (Margaret F Russell) ⚓
   ☎ (508) 994-1838.. "Blue Chantey" 5 Gladys St, Padanaram, MA *02748*

Holloway MR & MRS Edward JR (Kennedy—Gail Fiske) . . . . ☎ (717) 595-2478 "Quintessense" PO Box 211, Buck Hill Falls, PA 18323
   MISS Hope L . . . .

Holloway MR & MRS John Ennis (Ann S Clegg)
   ☎ (702) 847-9087 . . Box 429, Virginia City, NV 89440
Holloway MR & MRS R Marcus (Leslie R Grosvenor)
   ☎ (401) 847-4817 . . "Windswept" 208 Ocean Av, Newport, RI 02840
Hollyday MR & MRS Richard C JR (Jane B Perry) . . . ☎ (902) 295-2175 Box 315, Baddeck, Nova Scotia B0E 1B0, Canada
   MISS Anne B . . . .
   MR Richard C 3d . . . .
   MR Thomas P . . . .

Holmes COL & MRS Frederick S JR (Elisabeth B Nicholson) USA.
   ☎ (717) 525-3622 . . "Sunset House" Eagles Mere, PA 17731
Holmes MR & MRS George B (K Nancy Trowbridge)
   ☎ (207) 348-2479 . . Deer Isle, ME 04627
Holmes MR & MRS Gordon (Willis—Nancy Hooe)
   ☎ (508) 945-1055 . . 384 Fox Hill Rd, Box 608, Chatham, MA 02633
Holmes MR & MRS John G (Lord—Ruth Ellen du Pont)
   ☎ (860) 739-0311 . . White Gate Farm, Box 253, East Lyme, CT 06333
Holmes MR Richard F
   ☎ (603) 964-5233 . . Beach Club, Box 292, Rye Beach, NH 03871
Holmes MRS Stanley A (Blake—Mary A Blake)
   ☎ (802) 365-4092 . . "The Last Resort" Townshend, VT 05353
Holton MISS Alexandra C . . see MRS A P Curran
Holton MR John M 3d . . see MRS A P Curran
Holton MR & MRS Richard C (Carlota C C Hermann) | ☎ (616) 526-6510 "Windswept" 405 Glenn Dv, Harbor Springs, MI 49740
   MISS Christy Busch . . . .
   MR Richard C JR . . . .
   JUNIORS MR Robert H B . . . .

Homans MRS George C (Nancy P Cooper) . . . . | ☎ (506) 752-2502 North Rd, Welsh Pool, Campobello Island, NB E0G 3H0, Canada ⛵
   MISS Elizabeth C . . . .

Honan MR & MRS William Holmes (Nancy L Burton) ⛵
   ☎ (860) 536-0457 . . 4 Allyn's Alley, Mason's Island, Mystic, CT 06355
Honeyman MR & MRS R Stewart JR (Cochran—Barbara J Taylor)
   ☎ (714) 548-3438 . . 2480 Arbor Dv, Newport Beach, CA 92663
Hooe MR & MRS Nelson D JR (Susanne Shaw) . . . . . | Squirrel Island, ME 04570
   MR Nelson S . . . .
Hooker MR Philip O'D
   ☎ (414) 728-2084 . . "Hyllgarth" 2946 N Shore Dv, Delavan, WI 53115
Hooper MR & MRS Adrian S (Elizabeth W Shober) . . | "Morningside" Shore Lane, Tucker's Town HS 02, Bermuda
   MISS Elizabeth H . . . .
Hooper MR & MRS Lawrence L (Oliver—Marion D Marshall)
   ☎ (301) 229-9097 . . 4940 Sentinel Dv, Apt 403, Bethesda, MD 20816
Hooper MR & MRS Robert C (Gulielma Tyler)
   ☎ (508) 546-6295 . . "Haulabout House" Halibut Point, Pigeon Cove, MA 01966

Hoopes MR David M . . . . ☎ (418) 665-4713 "Les Cerceaux" Pointe-au-Pic, Quebec G0T 1M0, Canada
   MISS Helen M . . . .
   MISS Martha F . . . .
   MISS Nancy M . . . .
   MISS Wendy A . . . .
   MISS Rachel M . . . .

Hoopes MR & MRS Joseph C JR (Lesley W Bissell) | ☎ (441) 236-9623 Belt's Island, 8 Inwood Close, Paget PG 05, Bermuda
   ⛵ . . . .
   MISS Elliott T . . . .
   MR Joseph C 3d . . . .

Hooton MRS Bruce D (Higginson—Theodora Winthrop)
   ☎ (516) 626-1345 . . 55 Wheatley Rd, Upper Brookville, Glen Head, NY 11545
Hoover MR F Herbert . . . . ☎ (707) 996-3375 Meadow Gardens, Apt 26, 225—2 St E, Sonoma, CA 95476
   MR Cleveland P . . . .

Hopkins MR & MRS David L JR (Suzanne Bunker) . . | ☎ (207) 276-5355 Northeast Harbor, ME 04662
   MISS Suzanne B . . . .
Hopkins DR & MRS John E (Mary K Bazemore)
   ☎ (717) 925-2090 . . Spring Valley Farm, RD 3, Box 43, Benton, PA 17814
Hopkins MRS Kendal C (Nancy Pemberton)
   Little Island, Medomak, ME 04551
Hopkins MRS Mark (Fenno—Virginia Chapman)
   ☎ (207) 288-3908 . . "Fenwold" Harbor Lane, Bar Harbor, ME 04609
Hopkins MR & MRS Robert D (Jean D Griffith)
   ☎ (207) 276-5355 . . "Tree Tops" Northeast Harbor, ME 04662
Hopkins MR & MRS Samuel (Anne E Dankmeyer)
   ☎ (410) 255-4656 . . Box 114, Gibson Island, MD 21056
Hopkins MR Thayer . . . . ☎ (415) 669-1258 150 Keith Way, Inverness, CA 94937
   MR Charles A . . . .
   MR David P . . . .
Horan MISS Honora
   ☎ (860) 672-6056 . . 7 Hurlburt Place, Cornwall Hollow, RFD, Falls Village, CT 06031
Horan MR & MRS John R (Damaris S S Smith) . . . . . | ☎ (860) 672-0085 Rexford Rd, West Cornwall, CT 06796
   MR Quincy . . . .
   MR Patrick . . . .

Horan JUNIORS MR T Bramwell Welch . . see MISS (DR) M G Welch
Horchow MISS Regen (Pillsbury—Regen Horchow)
   ☎ (508) 228-5222 . . 33 Cliff Rd, Nantucket, MA 02554
Horchow MR & MRS S Roger (Carolyn Pfeifer) . . . . . | ☎ (508) 228-5222 33 Cliff Rd, Nantucket, MA 02554
   MISS Sally . . . .
Hord MR & MRS William T (Elizabeth Anne Edwards)
   ☎ (518) 647-8080 . . "Rappahannock Lodge" 71 N Shore Lane, Silver Lake, Au Sable Forks, NY 12912
Hornblower MR Alexander W . . see D K Thorne
Hornblower MR Josiah C . . see D K Thorne

Hornblower MRS Ralph JR (Phoebe M Blumer).... | ☎ (508) 645-2262
MR James W............................. | RFD Box 67,
 | Chilmark, MA
 | *02535*

Hornor MR & MRS DeWitt (Edith Sterrett) ⚓
☎ (508) 428-6415 . . 194 Eel River Rd, Osterville, MA *02655*

Hornung MRS Robert M (Gertrude Seymour)
☎ (216) 283-5636 . . 13801 Shaker Blvd, Apt 4B, Cleveland, OH *44120*

Horsey MRS Outerbridge (Mary H Lee)
☎ (304) 897-6483 . . "Squirrel Nest" Lost River Valley, Lost River, WV *26810*

Horst MR & MRS Jesse B (Diane Tappan)
"Needle Rush Point" Perdido Key Dv, Pensacola, FL *32507*

Horwitz DR & MRS Orville (Nataline B Dulles)
☎ (609) 494-5575 . . "Fishmonger's Hall" Box 402, Barnegat Light, NJ *08006*

Host MR & MRS Stig (Jeanne Grinnell) ⚓
☎ (603) 272-5876 . . "The Pond" Indian Pond Rd, Orford, NH *03777*

Hotchkiss MR & MRS John F (Potts—Mary W Eggert)
☎ (516) 653-4552 . . 5 Assop's Neck Lane, PO Box 1523, Quogue, NY *11959*

Hotchkiss MR & MRS Winchester F (Jane H Ellsworth)
☎ (516) 788-7853 . . "Windex" Box 702, Fishers Island, NY *06390*

Houghton MR & MRS Amory JR (Dewey—Priscilla Blackett)
☎ (617) 383-0554 . . 91 Atlantic Av, Cohasset, MA *02025*

Houghton MR & MRS Arthur A 3d (Davis—Linda B Livingston)
☎ (516) 788-7391 . . "Money Pond" Fishers Island, NY *06390*

Houghton MR & MRS H Arnold (Helen W Tiers)
☎ (518) 963-7747 . . RR 1, Box 83, Essex, NY *12936*

Houghton MR & MRS Neil L (Mary W Tompkins) . . | ☎ (207) 276-5641
MISS Katherine T .... | Northeast Harbor,
MR Neil L JR............................ | ME *04662*

Houghton MRS Ruth W (Ruth West)
☎ (413) 528-0686 . . 310 Monument Valley Rd, Great Barrington, MA *01230*

Houghton MR & MRS William M (Elizabeth B Richards)
☎ (603) 526-2671 . . 33 Camp Sunapee Rd, Box 1906, New London, NH *03257*

Houston MR & MRS James A (Alice D Watson)
☎ (604) 557-4431 . . "Bridge Cottage" Queen Charlotte Islands, Tlell, BC V0T 1Y0, Canada

Hover MR John C 2d .... | ☎ (215) 794-2074
MISS Margaret B .... | "Glenloch"
 | 3039 Durham Rd,
 | PO Box 676,
 | Buckingham, PA
 | *18912*

Hovey MRS Charles F (Anita C Hinckley) .... | ☎ (401) 783-8194
MR Benjamin .... | Whale Rock Point,
 | Narragansett, RI
 | *02882*

Hovey MR William C . . see J H Walton JR

Howard HON Barnaby J
☎ (902) 929-2829 . . St Ann's Bay, Englishtown, Nova Scotia B0C 1H0, Canada

Howard MR & MRS Jack R (Eleanor S Harris) . . of
☎ (212) 737-1157 . . 120 East End Av, New York, NY *10028*
☎ (516) 922-7524 . . "Bagamoyo" 214 Centre Island Rd, Centre Island, Oyster Bay, NY *11771*

Howard MR & MRS John L (Susan W Hunsiker)
☎ (508) 255-0481 . . "Taffrail" Tonset Rd, Orleans, MA *02653*

Howard MR & MRS Philip K (Alexandra C Cushing) | ☎ (516) 626-1589
MISS Charlotte I C...................... | 154 Wheatley Rd,
JUNIORS MISS Olivia C.................... | Old Brookville, NY
 | *11545*

Howard MR & MRS Reese Evans JR (Janet A Schierloh)
☎ (908) 830-9230 . . 5 & Broad Sts, Normandy Beach, NJ *08739*

Howard MRS Suzette A (Suzette Alger)
☎ (908) 234-1028 . . PO Box 233, Far Hills, NJ *07931*

Howard-Smith MR Stuart S
☎ (315) 686-3063 . . "Grindstone" General Delivery, Clayton, NY *13624*

Howe MRS James C (Lockwood—Barbara Batchelder)
☎ (508) 994-0219 . . "Birchfield Farm" 4 South Lane, South Dartmouth, MA *02748*

Howe MR & MRS James H 3d (Elizabeth C Scudder)
☎ (616) 526-2073 . . 9252 Sylvan Av, Harbor Springs, MI *49740*

Howe MR & MRS John S (Frances F Hovey) .... | ☎ (508) 922-0017
MISS Emily D .... | "Beach House"
 | Box 238,
 | Prides Crossing, MA
 | *01965*

Howe MR & MRS Lawrence (Ellen G Vaughan)
☎ (207) 348-2313 . . "Eight Bells" Box 81, Sunset, ME *04683*

Howe MR & MRS Nathaniel S (Alison Gilman)
☎ (401) 635-2296 . . Round Pond Rd, Little Compton, RI *02837*

Howe MR & MRS Richard O (Sadie R H Hall)...... | ☎ (401) 635-4485
MR Reginald H 2d .... | 20 Old Bull Lane,
MR Richard O JR........................ | Little Compton, RI
 | *02837*

Howell MR & MRS Hampton P (Katharine E Van Buren)
☎ (516) 288-1162 . . 4 Howell Lane, Box 889, Westhampton Beach, NY *11978*

Howell MRS Thomas Paull (Mary C Simmons)
☎ (906) 484-3365 . . "Howell's Tee Pee" Cedarville, MI *49719*

Howells MR & MRS William Dean (Benitha C | ☎ (207) 439-4651
Lindeman) .... | Kittery Point, ME
MISS Rose Marie........................ | *03905*
MR Edward S .... |
MR John M .... |

Howland MR & MRS Abbett P (Mary A Hall)
☎ (914) 373-7019 . . "Troutbeck" Green Rd, Amenia, NY *12501*

Howland MR & MRS Cornelius De F 3d (Colleen F Gibbs)
☎ (914) 868-7231 . . "Well-Nigh" PO Box 370, Millbrook, NY *12545*

Howland MR & MRS Edward M 2d (Marianna H Cooper)
☎ (401) 635-9585 . . "The Farmhouse" 40 Pottersville Rd, Little Compton, RI *02837*

Howland MRS George (Margaret C Clarke)
☎ (508) 748-0425 . . 14 Planting Island Rd, Marion, MA *02738*

Hoyt MR & MRS William V (Nancy P Hale)
☎ (540) 854-5333 . . Mill Run Farm, 9221 Zachary Taylor H'way, Unionville, VA *22567*

Hoyt MR & MRS William W (Julie L Smith) . . . . | ☎ (802) 824-5055
  MISS Kimberly M . . . . | "Ballavitchel"
  MISS Ashley S . . . . | Londonderry, VT
  MISS Allison L . . . . | *05148*
  JUNIORS MR Winthrop S . . . .
Hubbard MR & MRS Cortlandt van D (Kampmann— | of ☎ (207)236-4351
  Pepper—Lillian H Schwartz) . . . . | "Frogwood"
  MISS Margaret D . . . . | 10 Calderwood
    MISS Megan H Kampmann . . . . | Lane, Rockport, ME
      | *04856*
      | ☎ (207) 963-7702
      | "Tower House"
      | Grindstone Neck,
      | Winter Harbor, ME
      | *04693*
Hubbard MR & MRS Eliot 3d (Margaret Van Hook)
  ☎ (207) 439-2908 . . "Stone Cottage" 12 Thaxter Lane, Cutts Island, Kittery Point, ME *03905*
Hubbard MR & MRS Ralph H JR (Gibson—Mary Henry)
  ☎ (203) 531-1819 . . 415 W Lyon Farm Dv, Greenwich, CT *06831*
Hubbard MR & MRS William N 3d (Whitney—Robin Davies)
  ☎ (203) 259-7781 . . 534 Harbor Rd, Southport, CT *06490*
Huber MR & MRS Daniel (Pamela W Hamrick) ⚓
  on board Acceptance II" Dana Point Marina, Box 624, Dana Point, CA *92629*
Huber MR & MRS Timothy B (Susan C Ware) . . . . . | ☎ (508) 997-3702
  MISS Kathleen E . . . . | "Round Hill"
  MR Timothy B JR . . . . | 307 Smith Neck Rd,
      | South Dartmouth,
      | MA *02748*
Hubner MR & MRS Robert W (Katherine L Huick)
  ☎ (508) 627-5604 . . "Windswept" 112 Tower Hill, Edgartown, MA *02539*
Hudnut MRS William H (Elizabeth A Kilborne)
  ☎ (518) 251-2601 . . "Windover" North Creek, NY *12853*
Hudson MR & MRS Edward R JR (Ann Frasher)
  ☎ (970) 925-8269 . . 750 Castle Creek Dv, Aspen, CO *81611*
Hudson MR & MRS William H (Elizabeth E | ☎ (406) 682-4498
  Van Upton) . . . . | "Wonder Ranch"
  MR Andrew C . . . . | Cameron, MT *59720*
  MR James C C . . . . |
Hudson MR & MRS William P C (Kolowitz—M | "Amazing Grace"
  Antonia R Ramirez) . . . . | Huletts Landing, NY
  JUNIORS MISS Vanessa L . . . . | *12841*
  JUNIORS MR John H P . . . . |
  JUNIORS MR Michael R H . . . . |
    MISS Emma H Kolowitz . . . . |
Huey MR & MRS G H Harris (Edith C MacVeagh) ⚓
  Cuttyhunk Island, MA *02713*
Huffman MISS Deborah L . . see MRS M P Herschede
Huggins MR Charles N
  ☎ (360) 375-6412 . . Blakely Island, WA *98222*
Hughes MISS Frances M D'O . . see MRS F S Allis JR
Hughes MRS Joseph D (Jane S Blackistone) . . . . | ☎ (301) 769-4088
  MR Gerard B . . . . | "River Springs"
      | Avenue, MD *20609*

Hume MR & MRS R Stuart JR (Elisabeth W Hull) . . . | ☎ (914) 361-3111
  MR Douglas A . . . . | Hollyrood Farm,
  MR David M . . . . | RD 3, Middletown,
      | NY *10940*
Humes MR & MRS William O (Frick—Heidi E Bramwell)
  ☎ (518) 576-4411 . . Ausable Club, St Huberts, NY *12943*
Humphrey MRS Frank J (C Frances Sise) . . . . | ☎ (516) 283-0289
  MISS Susan A . . . . | PO Box 321,
      | 520 Hampton Rd,
      | Apt 22,
      | Southampton, NY
      | *11968*
Humphrey MR & MRS G Watts JR (Sally H Schriber) | ☎ (606) 734-3325
  MISS Victoria . . . . | Shawnee Farm,
  MR G Watts 3d . . . . | Harrodsburg, KY
      | *40330*
Humphrey MRS Gilbert W (Louise Ireland)
  ☎ (207) 677-2311 . . "Fircroft" HC 62, Box 143, Pemaquid, ME *04558*
Humphrey MR & MRS Joseph J H (Katherine N | ☎ (603) 744-2428
  Reed) . . . . | "Wind Bell Farm"
  MISS Abigail A . . . . | Washburn Rd,
  MR Pieter R . . . . | Bristol, NH *03222*
Humphreys MR & MRS William Y 3d (Brooks—Suzanne E White)
  ☎ (207) 734-6942 . . W Shore Rd, PO Box 316, Islesboro, ME *04848*
Humpstone MRS John H (Maribel Cheney)
  ☎ (802) 368-2845 . . "Wake Robin Farm" Box 95, Rte 1, Whitingham, VT *05361*
Hundley MR & MRS James W JR (Virginia C Baird) . | ☎ (401) 348-8907
  MR James W 3d . . . . | "Bayridge"
      | 8 Aquidneck Av,
      | Watch Hill, RI
      | *02891*
Hungerford MISS Sally-Byrd (Breeney—Sally-Byrd Hungerford)
  Queen Anne Rd, North Eastham, MA *02651*
Hunn MR & MRS David T (Florence deM Urban)
  Aug 1 . . General Delivery, Siasconset, MA *02564*
Hunnewell MR & MRS James F (Eleanor W McClurg)
  ☎ (207) 883-2673 . . Box 3027, Prouts Neck, ME *04074*
Hunnewell MR Richard F
  ☎ (401) 847-0207 . . . "The Brambles" 20 Atlantic Av, Newport, RI *02840*
Hunsaker MR & MRS Jerome C III (Marcie Gunnell)
  ☎ (518) 576-4378 . . "Wildwood" Ausable Club, St Huberts, NY *12943*
Hunsicker MRS J Quincy 3d (Johnson—Brown—Janet B Pierce)
  ☎ (413) 229-7785 . . "Farm Fatale" Brewer Hill, Mill River, MA *01244*
Hunsiker MR Harold W . . . . | 25 Windsor Av,
  MISS Marguerite H B . . . . | Cape May, NJ
  MISS Mary B . . . . | *08204*
Hunt DR & MRS Andrew D (Lotta H Mayberry)
  ☎ (616) 894-8785 . . 8265 S Scenic Dv, Rte 1, Montague, MI *49437*
Hunt CDR & MRS C Lansdowne (Ethel A Klima) | ☎ (301) 656-8360
  USN. . . . . | 5225 Westpath Way,
  MISS Jennifer R . . . . | Bethesda, MD
  MR Elliott L . . . . | *20816*

Hunt MR & MRS David P (F Randall Chanler)...... ☎ (315) 369-3810
  MISS Elizabeth W .... Little Moose Lake,
  MISS Frances R .... Old Forge, NY
  MISS Lucy St J *13420*
Hunt VERY REV DR & MRS Ernest E 3d (Elsie Beard)
  ☎ (518) 589-6122.. "Crowfoot" Onteora Club, Tannersville, NY *12485*
Hunt MRS George P (Anita C Eller)
  ☎ (207) 667-6169.. Newbury Neck Rd, Surry, ME *04684*
Hunt MR & MRS R Peter (Barbara K Borland)
  ☎ (207) 422-3817.. "Pine Pillow" Sorrento, ME *04677*
Hunt MR & MRS Torrence M (Joan Kilner)
  ☎ (412) 238-9664.. "Sporting Hill" Old Forbes Rd, Box 27, Laughlintown, PA *15655*
Hunt MR & MRS William B (Susan E Creswell)
  ☎ (413) 684-0334.. 121 Hemlock Hill, Dalton, MA *01226*
Hunt MR & MRS William H G (Mary A H Scheetz) . | ☎ (304) 765-2401
  MR William H G JR...................... | "Bug Ridge"
  JUNIORS MR Thomas H .... | 957 Bug Ridge,
  | Sutton, WV *26601*
Hunter MR & MRS Derek K (Fredericka Haswell)
  ☎ (805) 684-1927.. 3266 Beach Club Rd, Carpinteria, CA *93013*
Hunter MR & MRS Harold James JR (Sally Logan)
  ☎ (714) 494-2218.. 960 Cliff Dv, Laguna Beach, CA *92651*
Huntington MR & MRS (DR) Francis C (Patricia F | ☎ (516) 862-9185
  Skinner)............................... | "Rassapeague"
  MR David S .... | 98 Long Beach Rd,
  MR Thomas P .... | St James, NY *11780*
Huntington MR & MRS Lawrence S (Ballard— | ☎ (914) 232-7245
  Caroline C A Hankey) .... | Nash Rd,
  MR Alexander R F R Ballard .... | Goldens Bridge, NY
  | *10526*
Hunton MR & MRS Eppa 5th (Mary B Peters)...... | "Chesloma"
  MISS Eleanor B .... | Irvington, VA *22480*
  JUNIORS MR Eppa 6th .... |
Hupper MR & MRS David R (Marian N Faesy)
  Conary Island, RR 1, Box 429, Deer Isle, ME *04627*
Huppman MR & MRS L Reed (Susan T Wolfe)
  Little Island Camp, PO Box 2, Greenville, ME *04441*
Hurd JUDGE & MRS George N JR (Elizabeth B Cunningham)
  ☎ (508) 295-0747.. "On the Rocks" 49 Warren Point Rd, Wareham, MA *02571*
Hurley MR & MRS Stephen Nash (Phyliss P | ☎ (508) 645-2570
  Meaders)............................. | "Quitsa Mooring"
  MISS Kimberly T........................ | 135 South Rd,
  MR Stephen Nash JR .... | RFD 29, Chilmark,
  | MA *02535*
Huston MR & MRS Aubrey JR (Katharine W Myers)
  ☎ (518) 963-7742.. "The Cedars" 296 Lake Shore Rd, PO Box 386, Willsboro, NY *12996*
Huston MR & MRS Morrison C JR (Elizabeth C | ☎ (908) 899-9164
  Hillman).............................. | "Shingletop"
  MR M Coates 3d .... | 1339 Ocean Av,
  MR Churchill H........................ | Mantoloking, NJ
  | *08738*
Hutchings MR & MRS C H Ford (Elizabeth Preston)
  Jly 1.. ☎ (802) 362-1207.. "Carriage House" Box 536, Manchester, VT *05254-0536*

Hutchings MR & MRS Robert E (Christine H Hagen) | ☎ (516) 676-1503
  MISS Christine R........................ | "Fox Brae"
  MR William H.......................... | Box 305,
  | Locust Valley, NY
  | *11560*
Hutchinson MR & MRS Pemberton (Elizabeth P Townsend)
  ☎ (809) 336-2078.. Jollie Hall, George Town, Great Exuma, Bahamas
Hutner MR Nathaniel C
  ☎ (802) 388-6543.. "Dragon Farm" Box 48, East Middlebury, VT *05740*
Hutton MR & MRS William E (Joan K Chapin)
  Jly 1.. ☎ (508) 228-0858.. 84 Polpis Rd, Nantucket, MA *02554*
  Sep 1.. ☎ (516) 676-2211.. 680 Chicken Valley Rd, Locust Valley, NY *11560*
Hutton-Miller MR & MRS William E (Wiklund—Lydia A Iversen)
  SDR Seierslev, PR Hojer, Denmark
Hutz MR & MRS Rudolf E (Elizabeth M Hall)
  ☎ (207) 985-6285.. "Tara" Kennebunk, ME *04043*
Huxley MRS Charles G (Frederica L Huxley)...... | Middlegaer,
  MR Josceline G .... | Lower Cwmyoy,
  MR Hugh G G .... | Abergavenny,
  MR Alexander R G .... | Gwent, Wales, UK
Huxley MR Charles G
  ☎ (011-44-171) 735-5105.. 82 Claylands Rd, London SW8 1NJ, England
Hyde MR & MRS Alexis L (Helen A Stickel)....... | ☎ (011-33)
  JUNIORS MISS Sandrine L.................... | 66-22-70-98
  | "Foussargues"
  | Aigaliers,
  | F30700 Uzes,
  | France
Hyde MR & MRS Benjamin D (Mildred H Brown)
  ☎ (207) 372-6674.. Box 98, Tenants Harbor, ME *04860*
Hyde MR & MRS George H (Barbara A Cowan)
  ☎ (716) 627-7304.. 6070 Old Lakeshore Rd, Lake View, NY *14085*
Hynson MR & MRS Richard (Beck—Eloise R | ☎ (908) 899-1679
  Fullerton) .... | 1053 Ocean Av,
  MR Peter D............................ | Mantoloking, NJ
  MISS Elizabeth R F Beck .... | *08738*
  MR Robert L Beck .... |

I

Iglehart MR & MRS Iredell W (Courtney Garland)
  ☎ (518) 576-4540.. St Huberts, NY *12943*
Iglehart MR & MRS Philip C (Susan Lonsdale) ..... | ☎ (508) 228-0235
  MISS Laura C .... | "The Knoll"
  MR Philip L .... | 74 Monomoy Rd,
  | Nantucket, MA
  | *02554*
Ijams MR & MRS Porter (Cabot—Naneen S Cutler)
  ☎ (516) 759-1617.. 12 Ryefield Rd, Locust Valley, NY *11560*
Ijams MRS Seton (Nancy Mellen)
  ☎ (207) 389-1283.. "Manley Cottage" HCR 32, Box 228, Small Point, ME *04562*

Inch MR & MRS Robert W (Oliver—Hester—Jennie R Thomas) ⛵
☎ (209) 965-3642 . . 159 Rustic Rd, Pinecrest, CA *95364*

Inches MR & MRS Henderson JR (M Joanna Ray)
☎ (508) 758-2016 . . ''The Paddock'' 12 Ned's Point Rd, Mattapoisett, MA *02739*

Ingalls MR & MRS Melville E JR (Barbara M Moore)
☎ (719) 447-1066 . . 3430 Camels Ridge Lane, Colorado Springs, CO *80904*

Into MR & MRS A Norman JR (Jane S Timberman)
''Indian House'' Herring Rd, PO Box 784, Rangeley, ME *04970*

Ireland MISS Kate— ⛵
☎ (207) 677-2595 . . ''Sandy Cove'' HC 62, Box 145, Pemaquid, ME *04558*

Ireland MR & MRS Robert L III (Gray—Anne C Sweetser) ⛵
☎ (207) 677-2888 . . ''The Ship'' HC 62, Box 144, Pemaquid, ME *04558*

Irish MR Charles F JR
☎ (860) 364-0015 . . Herrick Rd, Sharon, CT *06069*

Irving MR & MRS Christopher C (Jeanne E Achorn)
☎ (401) 423-3899 . . 78 Columbia Lane, Jamestown, RI *02835*

Irving COL & MRS Frederick F (Alice T G Blue) USA.
☎ (904) 246-1575 . . 3515 S Ocean Dv, Jacksonville Beach, FL *32050*

Irving MR & MRS Malcolm D W (Roberta R C Marshall)
☎ (207) 244-5243 . . ''Fairways'' Causeway Lane, Southwest Harbor, ME *04679*

Irwin MAJ & MRS Charles J (Jane R Darlington) USMC.
☎ (516) 922-4194 . . ''Seven Pillars'' 75 Cove Neck Rd, Oyster Bay, NY *11771*

Irwin MR & MRS Fred A (Gilmor—Janet B Clarke) | ☎ (819) 686-1164
MISS Maria B . . . . | ''Lac Dauphinen''
MR C Russell . . . . | RR 2, Labelle,
   MR Christopher C Gilmor . . . . | Quebec J0T 1H0,
   MR Mark C Gilmor . . . . | Canada

Isaacs MRS Kenneth L (Helen C Adams)
☎ (508) 636-2098 . . ''Cuttyhunk Farm'' 92 Allens Neck Rd, Box 110, Dartmouth, MA *02714*

Iselin MR & MRS Frederick D (Sallie C B Drury) . . . | 1101 Middle St,
JUNIORS MR Charles O . . . . | Sullivans Island, SC
    | *29482*

Iselin MR & MRS John J (J Lea Barnes)
☎ (207) 867-4669 . . Vinalhaven, ME *04863*

Iselin MRS Lewis (Sarah C Curtis) ⛵ . . of
☎ (207) 236-3093 . . Belfast Rd, Box 838, Camden, ME *04843*
☎ (011-33-1) 45-51-91-27 . . 8 Place du Palais Bourbon, 75007 Paris, France

Iselin MR & MRS Peter (Margaretta S L Duane)
☎ (207) 276-5592 . . ''Sylvanora'' Seal Harbor, ME *04675*

Isham MR & MRS George S (Sally Ann O McPherson)
☎ (847) 234-3145 . . 1070 N Elm Tree Rd, Lake Forest, IL *60045*

Isham MR & MRS Heyward (Sheila B Eaton)
☎ (516) 537-1222 . . ''Skyfields'' 872 Sagg Main St, Box 418, Sagaponack, NY *11962-0418*

Isham MR & MRS Ralph H (Kneissl—Annie-Laurie von Auersperg) . . of
☎ (516) 537-7566 . . ''Hilltop'' Noyac Path, Bridgehampton, NY *11932*
☎ (401) 846-3561 . . ''Sea Garden'' Price's Neck, Newport, RI *02840*

Israel MR & MRS Thomas C (Barbara Frelinghuysen) | 9 Starbuck Neck,
MISS Emily F . . . . | Edgartown, MA
MR Peter C . . . . | *02539*
JUNIORS MISS Wendy V R . . . . |

Istel MR & MRS Jacques-Andre (Felicia J Lee)
''Felicity'' Bundorragha, Leenane, Co Galway, Ireland

Ittmann MR & MRS Robert W (Sarah J Barlow) . . . . | ☎ (207) 282-2567
MISS Sarah McC . . . . | General Delivery,
MR Daniel McL . . . . | Biddeford Pool, ME
JUNIORS MR George W . . . . | *04006*

Ivanoff MR & MRS Ivan V (Thorn T Welden)
☎ (860) 435-3503 . . 379 Taconic Rd, PO Box 605, Salisbury, CT *06068*

J

Jacks MISS Elizabeth B . . see A L Scott
Jacks MR Robert LeRoy JR . . see A L Scott

Jackson MR & MRS D Eldredge JR (Mary J Hilliard)
☎ (802) 457-1537 . . ''High Time'' South Woodstock, VT *05071*

Jackson MRS Edmund B (Willauer—Louise K Russell)
☎ (508) 228-1275 . . ''Westcliff'' Nantucket, MA *02554*

Jackson MR & MRS F Gardner JR (Pamela G Hardee) | ☎ (508) 759-4233
MR Patrick G . . . . | ''The Barn''
MR William C . . . . | 118 Emmons Rd,
  | Tobey Island,
  | Monument Beach,
  | MA *02553*

Jackson MR & MRS Gilder D 3d (Truesdale—Suzanne C Havens)
☎ (207) 348-6868 . . ''Brontë'' Bridge St, Deer Isle, ME *04627*

Jackson MR J Hamilton
☎ (516) 288-6365 . . 47 Sunswyck Lane, Westhampton Beach, NY *11978*

Jackson MR & MRS John T (Suzanne H Bartley) . . of
☎ (610) 642-4653 . . 155 Rose Lane, Haverford, PA *19041*
☎ (407) 863-1634 . . 210 Ocean Terr, Palm Beach, FL *33480*

Jackson MR & MRS John T 3d (Frazier—Biddle—M | ☎ (208) 263-0754
Latimer Coleman) . . . . | ''Whiskey Jack''
MR Stephen C Frazier . . . . | Box 1948,
  | Sandpoint, ID *83864*

Jackson MRS Katharine E (Patty—Davis— | ☎ (914) 679-6094
Katharine F Evans) . . . . | ''Acorn Hill''
MR William A Patty 4th . . . . | Bearsville, NY
MR Robert E Davis . . . . | *12409*

Jackson MR & MRS Orton P (Butcher—Parker—Noël H Smyth)
☎ (207) 374-5602 . . ''Left Bank'' PO Box 809, Blue Hill, ME *04614*

Jackson MR Orton P JR
☎ (207) 276-3223 . . ''Pine Ledge'' PO Box 725, Northeast Harbor, ME *04662*

Jackson MRS Peter A (Joan D Benkard) . . . . | Biddeford Pool, ME
MISS Vivian L . . . . | *04006*
MISS Jeannie U . . . . |
MR Peter A JR . . . . |

Jackson MR & MRS Richard S (Mary F Mathes)
☎ (207) 363-2706 . . ''The Moorings'' PO Box 78, York Harbor, ME *03911*

Jackson MR & MRS Robert H (Hope M Clark)
☎ (508) 627-8620 . . "Hidden House" Edgartown Bay Rd, Edgartown, MA *02539*
Jackson MR & MRS Timothy (Susan J Olson) . . . . | ☎ (508) 759-3676
MISS Sally M . . . . | Tobey Island,
MR Nicholas C . . . . | Monument Beach,
MR Samuel B . . . . | MA *02553*
JUNIORS MISS Susannah E . . . . |
Jackson MR & MRS William E (Nancy D Roosevelt)
☎ (516) 692-7434 . . "Turkey Lane House" Box 23, Cold Spring Harbor, NY *11724*
Jacob MR & MRS William Le G (Rhonda McComas)
☎ (860) 542-5038 . . "The Wigwam" 98 Deerfield Rd, Norfolk, CT *06058*
Jacobi MR & MRS Jan de G (Virginia P Newton)
☎ (508) 228-9517 . . "Blueberry Patch" 64 Wauwinet Rd, Nantucket, MA *02554*
Jacobs MR & MRS George M (Jacqueline B Sperow)
☎ (401) 847-6292 . . "Rock Pasture" PO Box 4251, Middletown, RI *02842*
Jacobs MR & MRS Ted S (Romney—Janet S Adams)
☎ (516) 267-6042 . . 272 Old Stone H'way, East Hampton, NY *11937*
James MRS Denis N R (Miles—M Elizabeth Horner)
☎ (860) 535-0762 . . 14 Main St, Stonington, CT *06378*
James MR & MRS Hamilton E (Amabel G Boyce) . . . | ☎ (616) 526-9901
JUNIORS MISS Meredith E . . . . | Box 4334,
JUNIORS MISS Rebecca L . . . . | 5 Fifth Av,
| Wequetonsing, MI
| *49740*
James DR Nathaniel W 4th
☎ (207) 863-4313 . . Vinalhaven, ME *04863*
James MR & MRS Oliver B JR (Cassidy—Norma E McNeill)
☎ (619) 454-4519 . . 1504 Buckingham Dv, La Jolla, CA *92037*
James MR & MRS Philip R (Colla—Mai Wood Zara)
☎ (516) 283-6580 . . "Breezeway Cottage" 14 Old Town Crossing, Southampton, NY *11968*
James MR R Campbell
☎ (011-44-171) 493-6671 . . White's, 37 St James's, London SW1A 1JG, England
James MR William D . . see R C Wallis
Jameson MR Owen
☎ (415) 851-7449 . . "Oakleigh" 680 Mountain Home Rd, Woodside, CA *94062*
Janin MR & MRS Blaine C (Susan J York)
☎ (707) 865-1244 . . "The Kremlin" 21361 Monte Cristo Av, Monte Rio, CA *95462*
Jannetta DR & MRS Peter J (Davant—Rose—Diana L Risien)
☎ (412) 593-6652 . . "High Meadow Farm" Box 55, Rte 381 S, Rector, PA *15677*
Janney MRS Jervis S JR (Macy B Putnam) . . . . | ☎ (802) 372-5606
MR Henry L . . . . | "Hyde Point"
| PO Box 75,
| Grand Isle, VT
| *05458*
Janney MR Jervis S JR
31 Tecumseh St, Dayton, OH *45402*

Jansing MR & MRS John C (Flora S Bush)
☎ (616) 526-7395 . . Cottage 65, Box 256, Harbor Springs, MI *49740*
Janvier MRS Charles 2d (L Joy Bagnell)
☎ (704) 526-2847 . . "Finally" PO Box 723, Highlands, NC *28741-0723*
Jarratt MR & MRS James H 3d (Roslyn M Potter) . . . | ☎ (011-61-2)
MISS Katrina J . . . . | 601541
MR Timothy C . . . . | 45 Pretty Beach Rd,
JUNIORS MISS Penelope K . . . . | Pretty Beach,
JUNIORS MR Ross A . . . . | NSW 2256,
| Australia
Jay MR & MRS Robert D (Cynthia M White)
☎ (508) 228-2923 . . "Quaise Pastures" Nantucket, MA *02554*
Jeffery MRS Ann Folliss (Ann V Folliss)
Southampton, NY *11968*
Jeffords MRS Walter M (Kathleen McLaughlin) . . . | ☎ (518) 584-1866
MR George McL . . . . | 719 N Broadway,
MR John D . . . . | Saratoga Springs,
| NY *12866*
Jelinek MR & MRS (REV DR) Richard U (Allen—Bonnie Scott) . . . . | ☎ (508) 255-2006
MISS Jennifer S Allen . . . . | "Beachcroft"
MR Barton B Allen . . . . | 646 Shore Rd,
MR Joshua C Allen . . . . | South Orleans, MA
| *02662*
Jellinghaus MRS C Butler (Carol C Green) . . . . | ☎ (914) 679-8383
MISS Catherine P . . . . | 40 Coopers Lake
| Rd, Bearsville, NY
| *12409*
Jenkins MR & MRS A Diehl (Patricia A Hurlbut) . . . . | of ☎ (508)996-6888
MISS Patricia D . . . . | "Summertide"
MR Jonathan P . . . . | Naushon Av,
JUNIORS MR David W . . . . | Salters Point,
| South Dartmouth,
| MA *02748*
| ☎ (617) 631-2459
| "Rock End" Davis
| Rd, Marblehead,
| MA *01945*
Jenkins MRS Alan N (Barbara Hoffstot)
☎ (540) 347-1529 . . "Leeton Hill" PO Box 191, Warrenton, VA *22186-0191*
Jenkins MISS Alexandra . . see J W Wastcoat
Jenkins MR & MRS David N JR (J Lailey H Roudebush)
☎ (508) 997-5455 . . "Bayberry Hill" Cuttyhunk Island, MA *02713*
Jenkins MR Jonathan W . . see J W Wastcoat
Jenkins MR William P JR . . see J W Wastcoat
Jenney MR John L K JR
☎ (302) 227-3544 . . "Seabreeze" 318 Salisbury St, Rehoboth Beach, DE *19971*
Jenney MRS Meredith T (Dougherty—Meredith Townsend) . . . . | ☎ (302) 227-2374
MISS Caroline K . . . . | 69 Henlopen Av,
JUNIORS MR John L K 3d . . . . | Rehoboth Beach, DE
JUNIORS MR Marshall T . . . . | *19971*
MISS Ann S Dougherty . . . . |
Jennings MRS A Gould (Grace V N Swackhamer)
☎ (203) 655-4879 . . "The Cottage" Box 3034, Noroton, CT *06820*

Jennings MRS Sara L (Sara E Lupton)
☎ (804) 266-4496 . . 5618 Crenshaw Rd, Apt 822, Richmond, VA *23227-2561*

Jenrette MR Richard H
☎ (914) 758-8784 . . ''Edgewater'' Dock Rd, Barrytown, NY *12507*

Jensen MRS Philip J (M Anne McCarthy) . . . . | Hope Town, Abaco,
MR Philip J 3d | Bahamas

Jerauld MR & MRS Anthony B (Kahle—Melinda A Smith)
☎ (508) 228-3049 . . 19 India St, Nantucket, MA *02554*

Jewell MR & MRS Pliny 3d (J Sue Shelly)
☎ (518) 576-4229 . . ''Noonmark Cottage'' Ausable Club, St Huberts, NY *12943*

Jewell MR & MRS Samuel R (Sheila F Balding)
☎ (303) 765-0980 . . 90 Corona St, Apt 706, Denver, CO *80218*

Jewett MR & MRS Edgar B 3d (Frances B Appleton)
☎ (518) 576-4368 . . ''Summerbrook'' Hurricane Rd, Keene, NY *12942*

Jewett MR & MRS Freeborn G JR (Joan Sanford Lewis) ⛵
☎ (914) 986-4925 . . Van Duzer Place, Warwick, NY *10990*
Aug 1 . . ☎ (207) 367-2630 . . Bay View Av, Stonington, ME *04681*

Jewett MR & MRS George F JR (Lucille W McIntyre)
☎ (808) 882-7796 . . ''Beachbound'' HC 01, Box 578, Mauna Kea Beach, Kamuela, HI *96743*

Jewett MR & MRS Jonathan (Nancy M Robertson) . . | ☎ (860) 434-7787
JUNIORS MR Ian S . . . . | 100-1 Joshuatown Rd, Lyme, CT *06371*

Jewett MRS Margaret N (Margaret R Nichols) . . . . . | ☎ (516) 324-9146
JUNIORS MR Lamon H . . . . | PO Box 1987, 14 Pondview Lane, East Hampton, NY *11937*

Johnson MRS Alexander B (H Louise Huntting) . . of
☎ (914) 439-3693 . . ''The Mead Place'' Balsam Lake Anglers Club, Livingston Manor, NY *12758*
☎ (203) 966-4143 . . 16 Mead St, New Canaan, CT *06840*

Johnson MR & MRS Broaddus (Kate de F Chamberlin)
☎ (518) 589-6119 . . ''Quaker Lady'' Onteora Club, Tannersville, NY *12485*

Johnson MR & MRS Collister (Eleanor W Muir)
☎ (508) 693-1631 . . ''Watcha'' West Tisbury, MA *02575*

Johnson MR & MRS David C JR (Caroline H Davenport)
☎ (860) 434-5357 . . ''Edge Lea'' South Lyme, CT *06376*

Johnson MR & MRS Edward C 3d (Elizabeth B Hodges)
☎ (617) 581-0020 . . ''Wharf Cottage'' 35 Vernon St, Nahant, MA *01908*

Johnson MR & MRS Edward M (Elizabeth B Childs)
☎ (914) 583-5239 . . RD 1, Box 52, Swan Lake, NY *12783*

Johnson MR & MRS Edward R (Kimberley W Graff) | ☎ (860) 536-1589
⛵ . . . . | ''Quirk Island''
MISS Lacy K—⛵ . . . . | Box 9174, Noank, CT *06340*

Johnson MRS F Lincoln (Le Boutillier—Ayres—Patterson—Deirdre G Jones)
☎ (518) 589-6351 . . ''The Meadow'' Onteora Club, Tannersville, NY *12485*

Johnson MR & MRS Francis E (Helena N Edey)
☎ (508) 627-3605 . . ''Eel Pond House'' Edgartown, MA *02539*

Johnson MR & MRS Hallett JR (Mary Ellen Cooke)
☎ (207) 244-5674 . . Box 166, Pretty Marsh, Mt Desert, ME *04660*

Johnson MR & MRS John B (Margaret G Scott)
''Devil Island'' Box 418, Stonington, ME *04681*

Johnson MR & MRS John G (Bahnson—de Bragança—Katharine King)
☎ (910) 363-2357 . . Roaring Gap Club, Mountain View Rd, Roaring Gap, NC *28668*

Johnson MR & MRS L Oakley (Frances B Wells) . . . | ☎ (207) 422-9593
MR Parker W . . . . | ''Summersalt''
JUNIORS MR O Tod . . . . | Sorrento, ME *04677*

Johnson MRS Mildred T (Mildred F Thornton) . . . . | ☎ (704) 526-3013
MISS Shannon E . . . . | Box 472, Highlands,
MR M Maynard 4th . . . . | NC *28741*
MR Lewis B . . . . |

Johnson MR & MRS Norman Dudley (Virginia H Couper)
☎ (508) 627-4895 . . ''Capt Morse House'' 80 N Water St, PO Box 34, Edgartown, MA *02539-0034*

Johnson MR Richard M W
212 Scraggy Neck Rd, Cataumet, MA *02534*

Johnson MISS Sally B
☎ (203) 938-2090 . . 88 Cross H'way, Redding, CT *06875*

Johnson MRS Samuel S (Elizabeth A Hill)
☎ (541) 595-6544 . . ''Seekseekwa Neshuppa'' Camp Sherman, OR *97730*

Johnson MR Stephen S 2d . . of
☎ (860) 739-7170 . . 12 Great Wight Way, Old Black Point, Niantic, CT *06357*
☎ (516) 749-0761 . . 68 Tuthill Dv, Shelter Island, NY *11964*

Johnson MR Timothy C
Burke Rd, Orwell, VT *05760*

Johnson MR & MRS William L (Marjory Bruce Hughes)
☎ (518) 873-2090 . . Underwood Club, New Russia, NY *12964*

Johnston MR & MRS Alan R (Eleanor C Smith)
☎ (847) 251-6160 . . 504 Park Dv, Kenilworth, IL *60043*

Johnston MR & MRS Alfred M (Eleanor C Tierney)
☎ (609) 492-2411 . . 121 Ocean St, Beach Haven, NJ *08008*

Johnston MR & MRS G Sim 3d (Lisa Ferwerda)
☎ (516) 283-7850 . . PO Box 41, Southampton, NY *11969*

Johnston MR & MRS Henry O (Sally F Curby)
☎ (919) 553-2671 . . 3527 Baltusrol Court, Clayton, NC *27520*

Johnston MR & MRS Hugh McB (Sheffield—Ellen J Wacker)
☎ (508) 693-6740 . . Box 256, Vineyard Haven, MA *02568*

Johnston MR & MRS J Murray (Nancy Gill Wylie)
☎ (207) 244-3437 . . Southwest Harbor, ME *04679*

Johnston MR John W . . . . | ☎ (207) 244-3437
MISS Dana C . . . . | Manset Rd,
MISS Alix V . . . . | Southwest Harbor, ME *04679*

Johnston MRS Toulson (Helen I Toulson) . . . . | ☎ (804) 678-5820
MISS Elizabeth S . . . . | ''Oak Grove'' Eastville, VA *23347*

Johnston MR & MRS Waldo C M (Weyburn—Chapman—Anschutz—Renze Wilshire)
☎ (607) 547-9472 . . Fox Meadow Farm, PO Box 616, Cooperstown, NY *13326*

Jonas MR & MRS Robert P JR (Peck—Louise D Irons)
☎ (802) 867-0118 . . 4 Myrickview, PO Box 785, Dorset, VT *05251*

Jones MR & MRS Benjamin C 3d (Anne W C Smith)
MR Benjamin B C . . . . ☎ (508) 945-0420
517 Old Harbor Rd,
North Chatham, MA
02650

Jones MR & MRS Charles H JR (Hope Haskell)
☎ (908) 842-6816 . . PO Box 441, 90 Ridge Rd, Rumson, NJ *07760*

Jones MR & MRS David Lloyd (Flagg—Hattie—Hildegard Schneider)
☎ (516) 283-0116 . . "Homeport" PO Box 1546, Southampton, NY *11969*

Jones MR & MRS Dryden JR (Wendy V Collinson) . .
MISS Millicent H . . . .
MISS Alison F . . . .
JUNIORS MISS Christen C . . . . ☎ (508) 693-8341
"Cove House"
Brook Hollow Rd,
West Tisbury, MA
02575

Jones MR & MRS Edward S (Patricia H Bleecker)
☎ (516) 922-5417 . . Box 127A, Cove Rd, Oyster Bay, NY *11771*

Jones JUNIORS MR Frederick K . . see W J Evans

Jones MR Gilbert E
☎ (508) 748-2795 . . 538 Point Rd, Marion, MA *02738*

Jones MR & MRS Glenn D (Patricia J Van Andel)
"The Little House" 149 W Avenida Palizada, San Clemente, CA *92672*

Jones MR & MRS Horace C (Helen M Allen)
☎ (508) 994-0456 . . "Buzzards Nest" PO Box P153, Nonquitt, MA *02748*

Jones MRS Horace G (Hardin—Betty Smith)
☎ (702) 588-6863 . . "The Jones Buoy" Lake Tahoe, Zephyr Cove, NV *89448*

Jones MR J Turner
☎ (404) 231-0474 . . 67 Blackland Rd NW, Atlanta, GA *30342*

Jones MR & MRS Kaye Harding (Anne M Churchill)
☎ (508) 295-3535 . . Codman Point, Wareham, MA *02571*

Jones MRS Linda R (Grant—Linda C Ryan) . . . . . .
MISS Virginia R . . . .
JUNIORS MISS Alexandra D . . . . ☎ (401) 846-2004
"Harborview"
1 Harborview Dv,
Newport, RI *02840*

Jones JUNIORS MR Oliver H . . see W J Evans
Jones MISS Palmer D . . see W J Evans
Jones MR & MRS Peter D (Leslie R Murphy)
☎ (516) 653-4190 . . 11 Ocean Av, Quogue, NY *11959*

Jones MR & MRS Proctor P (Martha E Martin) . . . . .
MISS Jessica H . . . . ☎ (415) 868-1874
"Mersoleil"
332 Seadrift Rd,
Stinson Beach,
CA *94970*

Jones MR & MRS Richard W (Sarah S Bartlett) . . . . .
MR Philip B . . . . ☎ (508) 888-0377
167 Main St,
Sandwich, MA
02563

Jones MR & MRS Richard W S (Grace J Ellicott) . . . .
MR Andrew E . . . .
MR Purnell M . . . . "Ellicott Cottage"
Eagles Mere, PA
17731

Jones DR & MRS Robert E (Florence B V Vaught)
☎ (619) 274-9643 . . "Villa Vacanze Missione Mare" 1327 La Palma St, San Diego, CA *92109*

Jones MR & MRS Roger M (F Margaret Taylor)
Sleeth Island B581, Georgian Bay, care McIsaac Bros Dock, 13 Bay St, Parry Sound, Ontario P2A 1S4, Canada

Jones MR & MRS Samuel B 4th (Patricia Starr) . . . . .
MR Samuel Bancroft . . . .
MR Christopher S . . . . ☎ (860) 388-9723
"Buck Pal"
31 Pettipaug Av,
Fenwick, CT *06475*

Jones MR & MRS Winfield P (Davis—Miller—Madeleine D Burns) . . . .
MISS Kirsten M Davis . . . .
JUNIORS MR Robert B Miller . . . . ☎ (011-33)
94-47-85-20
rte de Claviers,
83830 Bargemon,
France

Jonson MISS Dana A . . see H B Satterthwaite
Jonson MR Randolph S . . see H B Satterthwaite
Jordan MRS F Peter (Beatrice L Renwick)
☎ (207) 276-5420 . . "Dim View" Northeast Harbor, ME *04662*

Jordan DR & MRS Henry A (West—Barbara J McNeil) . . . .
MISS Gretchen McN . . . .
MR Michael H . . . .
JUNIORS MR Douglas L . . . . ☎ (802) 472-5090
Box 918,
Hardwick, VT
05843

Jordan MR & MRS Philip H JR (Sheila A Gray) . . . . .
MR Philip H 3d . . . .
MR John G 2d . . . . ☎ (207) 846-5618
"Stone Sloop"
Chebeague Island,
ME *04017*

Jordan MRS R Bennett (Ruth A Bennett)
Jly 1 . . ☎ (516) 367-7516 . . 1348 Ridge Rd, Laurel Hollow, Syosset, NY *11791*

Jordan MR & MRS William JR (Burton—Sheila A Garside)
☎ (203) 438-8667 . . "Old Oaks" 31 Whipstick Rd, Ridgefield, CT *06877*

Jorgensen MR Edvard
☎ (516) 325-0507 . . "Vildanden" 15 Seatuck Lane, Remsenberg, NY *11960*

Joy MRS Frederick van B (Edith L P Greacen)
☎ (201) 538-0838 . . "Half-a-Nickel" 2 Spruce Lane, Morristown, NJ *07960*

Joyce MR & MRS Douglas Henry (Sue M Smythe)
☎ (704) 733-2833 . . "Trillium Cottage" Grandson Hill Rd, Linville, NC *28646*

Joyce MR & MRS William R JR (Mary-Hoyt Sherman) . . . .
MISS Helen Floyd-Jones . . . . ☎ (607) 547-5123
"The Distillery"
11 River St,
Cooperstown, NY
13326-1051

Justi MR & MRS Henry K (Helen B Milne)
☎ (809) 366-0365 . . "Surf Song" Hope Town, Abaco, Bahamas

Justi MR & MRS Thomas R (Rebecca J Spratt) . . . . .
MR David M . . . . ☎ (610) 783-7122
507 Richards Rd,
Wayne, PA
19087-1005

K

Kaiser MR & MRS Franck H (Beverly J Hurt)
☎ (011-61-755) 335-310 . . "Eagle Crest" Springbrook Rd, Springbrook, Queensland 4213, Australia

Kales MR & MRS William R 2d (Nancy B Ely)
☎ (207) 288-2250 .. Green Island, Mt Desert, ME *04660*
Kallop MR & MRS William M (Deborah B Farber) .. | ☎ (516) 324-2939
JUNIORS MR Brooks M................... | "Fairways"
JUNIORS MR Brent McK.................. | 18 Further Lane,
 | East Hampton, NY
 | *11937*
Kaltenbach MRS Henry J (Read—Waterworth—Laura Dean)
☎ (401) 635-4609 .. "Little Gatherem" Little Compton, RI *02837*
Kamihachi MR & MRS James D (Louise L Henry) .. | ☎ (410) 287-2853
JUNIORS MISS Caroline H.................. | 700 Piney Creek
JUNIORS MISS Catherine G .... | Lane, North East,
 | MD *21901*
Kaminer MR Stevenson S—⚓
☎ (410) 268-1238 .. 14B2 President Point Dv, Annapolis, MD *21403*
Kampmann MISS Megan H .. see C van D Hubbard
Kane MR & MRS Charles F JR (Anne W Eldridge)
Great Cranberry Island, Cranberry Isles, ME *04625*
Kane MR & MRS Louis I (Katharine F Daniels)
☎ (207) 646-7471 .. River Rd, Ogunquit, ME *03907*
Kassebaum MR & MRS John Philip (Sinkler— | ☎ (508) 228-4680
Llewellyn H Hood) .... | 289 Hummock Pond
MISS Linda J .... | Rd, Nantucket, MA
MR John P JR .... | *02554*
MR Richard L ....
MR William A..........................
 MR G Dana Sinkler JR ....
 MR Huger Sinkler 2d ....
Katzenbach MR & MRS L Emery (Marley Marseilles)
☎ (508) 636-8754 .. Box 533, Adamsville, RI *02801*
Kauffmann MRS Godfrey W (Jane L Knapp)
☎ (401) 635-4238 .. 120B Sakonnet Point Rd, Little Compton, RI *02837*
Kauffmann MRS John H (Chamberlain—Patricia Bellinger)
☎ (011-33-93) 93-75-48-17 .. 40 av de Reale, Porte La Galère, PO Theoule-sur-Mer, 06598 Cannes, France
Kauffmann MR John M
☎ (603) 636-1079 .. "Waterside Lodge" Percy Summer Club, Groveton, NH *03582*
Kay MRS William G JR (Chellis—Marcia Quale) ... | "Round Hill"
MR Bradford A Chellis.................. | 307 Smith Neck Rd,
 | South Dartmouth,
 | MA *02748*
Kayes MR & MRS Alan (Bruckner—Crawford—Cecily Elmes)
☎ (516) 537-0973 .. 16 Bay Lane, Water Mill, NY *11976*
Kean MR & MRS Hamilton F (Bacon—Edith M Williamson)
☎ (508) 992-6056 .. Mishaum Point, South Dartmouth, MA *02748*
Kearns MR J Nicholas .. see MRS A G Herrick
Kearns MISS Jessica G .. see MRS A G Herrick
Keating MR & MRS Brian E (Anne C Ginther) .... | ☎ (905) 894-5674
JUNIORS MR Brennan E .... | Holloway Bay,
JUNIORS MR Ryan E....................... | Humberstone,
 | Ontario L3K 5V3,
 | Canada
Keech MR & MRS Gilbert W (Mary G L Murray)
☎ (902) 295-2626 .. Baddeck, Nova Scotia B0E 1B0, Canada

Keech MR & MRS Gilbert W JR (Anne M Callahan)
☎ (919) 261-8912 .. 101 High Dune Loop, Southern Shores, NC *27949*
Keefe MR & MRS Harry V JR (de Lesseps—Anita H Lihme) ⚓
☎ (203) 869-8339 .. 21 Aiken Rd, Greenwich, CT *06831*
Keefe MRS Roger M (Nancy Hunter)
☎ (207) 276-3962 .. "Ledgelawn" Northeast Harbor, ME *04662*
Keefe MISS Victoria M
☎ (203) 866-4824 .. Wilson Point, South Norwalk, CT *06854*
Keeler MR & MRS Robert T (Mithoefer—Buxton—Margaret A Palmer)
☎ (802) 867-4482 .. "Fine Hollow" Dorset, VT *05251*
Keene MISS Katharine
"Hilltop" Menemsha, MA *02552*
Keevil MR & MRS Philip C (Augusta D McGrail) ... | ☎ (516) 624-8268
MISS Augusta H .... | "Mill Brook"
JUNIORS MR Adrian A C .... | 155 Cove Rd,
 | Oyster Bay, NY
 | *11771*
Kehl MR & MRS David C (Jane C Everett) .... | ☎ (916) 581-5775
MR Jonathan E .... | 36 Observation Dv,
 | Dollar Point,
 | Tahoe City, CA
 | *95730*
Kehoe MR & MRS Richard G (Zingg—Elizabeth C Foulk)
☎ (860) 526-5844 .. "Merry Farm" 332 Joshuatown Rd, Lyme, CT *06371*
Keidel MR & MRS Albert JR (Justine F Lewis) ⚓
Isle au Haut, ME *04645*
Keiser MR David M (Sylvia S Kodjbanoff)
☎ (802) 877-3364 .. "Grosse Pointe" Ferrisburg, VT *05456*
Keith MR & MRS Alastair J (Jayne W Teagle) ..... | ☎ (914) 677-3558
JUNIORS MISS Serena B .... | PO Box 60,
JUNIORS MR Alexander T .... | South Rd,
 | Millbrook, NY
 | *12545*
Keith MR & MRS Allan R (Winifred A Ward)
"Turtle Brook Farm" South Rd, Chilmark, MA *02535*
Keith MR & MRS Frederick W JR (Sidney P Meeker)
☎ (802) 644-5653 .. "Far Forty" RD 1, Box 62, Jeffersonville, VT *05464*
Kelham MR & MRS Rawson (Nicholsen—Susanna P | of Seadrift,
 B Rogers)............................. | 269 Seadrift Rd,
 MR Ronald C Nicholsen................. | Stinson Beach, CA
 MR Hamilton R Nicholsen .... | *94970*
 | ☎ (406) 825-3839
 | Red Pepper Jack
 | Ranch, HCR 85,
 | Box 973, Clinton,
 | MT *59825*
Keller MR & MRS David W (Sharon L Smith) ...... | ☎ (307) 739-1724
MR Michael R .... | "Wise Acres"
 | PO Box 7420,
 | Jackson, WY *83001*
Kellett MR & MRS Morris C (Anne O Bacon)
☎ (207) 276-3772 .. "Forest Ledge" Seal Harbor, ME *04675*
Kelley MR Augustus W III
5 Putnam Hill, Greenwich, CT *06380*

Kelley MR & MRS Edmund R T (Rollins—Maureen Sullivan)
 ☎ (860) 379-6001 . . "Little Kingdom" Colebrook, CT *06021*
Kelley MRS Edmund S JR (Elizabeth P Emery)
 ☎ (617) 585-6032 . . F3 Tree Top Lane, Kingston, MA *02364*
Kelley MR John E T . . see MRS B R Hennessy
Kellogg MR Francis L
 ☎ (914) 234-3526 . . "Mill Pond Farm" Bedford Village, NY *10506*
Kellogg MR & MRS Howard (Frances S Perkins)
 ☎ (603) 968-3671 . . Box 322, Holderness, NH *03245*
Kellogg MR & MRS James McN (Sally A Schlesinger)
 ☎ (207) 244-5958 . . Mt Desert, ME *04660*
Kellogg MR & MRS John M JR (Ann L Willet) . . . . . . | ☎ (508) 228-9680
 MR Daniel C . . . . | West Shack,
 | PO Box 1224,
 | Nantucket, MA
 | *02554*
Kellogg MR & MRS Stephen (Carolyn Karcher)
 ☎ (716) 947-5516 . . "The Garden House" Lochevan,
 7220 Old Lake Shore Rd, Derby, NY *14047*
Kelly MR & MRS Arthur L (Cain—Diane J Rex)
 ☎ (508) 257-6755 . . "Milestone" 22 Main St, Siasconset, MA *02564*
Kelly MR Edward J JR . . . . | ☎ (610) 581-0343
 MR Michael McL . . . . | "Wrenfield"
 | 1017 Canterbury
 | Lane, Villanova, PA
 | *19085*
Kelly MR & MRS William Cody (Garrison—Karen L Brown)
 ☎ (513) 271-4072 . . 5910 Rettig Lane, Cincinnati, OH *45243*
Kelsey MRS John D (Swift—Rosamond Whitney)
 ☎ (617) 828-2646 . . 53 Green St, Milton, MA *02186*
Kelso LT COL & MRS Robert Earl (Roberts—Betty Ann Stieren) USA.
 ☎ (719) 630-7550 . . 3110 Sheik's Place, Colorado Springs, CO *80904*
Kemmerer MR & MRS John L JR (Mary E Halbach)
 ☎ (208) 726-3795 . . Box 661, Sun Valley, ID *83353*
Kenady MR & MRS Charles W (Williamson—Elizabeth Case)
 ☎ (707) 965-2256 . . "Dalraddy Vineyards" 3928 Chiles Valley Rd,
 St Helena, CA *94574*
Kendall MR Henry W
 ☎ (508) 748-0070 . . 35 Water St, Marion, MA *02738*
Kendall MR & MRS John P (Nancy N Feick) . . . . . . | ☎ (508) 748-1092
 MR David F . . . . | 29 Water St,
 | Marion, MA *02738*
Kendrick MR & MRS Edmund H (Mayotta Southworth)
 ☎ (207) 348-2441 . . "Salmon Point" RR 1, Box 627, Deer Isle,
 ME *04627*
Kendrick DR & MRS Marvin H JR (Kathleen Snow) . | "Blueberry Hill"
 JUNIORS MISS Julia B . . . . | 1 Pancake Hollow,
 JUNIORS MR Jeffrey . . . . | Lighthouse Rd,
 | Gay Head, MA
 | *02535*
Kenefick MR & MRS John C (Ryan—Helen P Walker)
 ☎ (207) 766-2527 . . Northeast Cove, Cliff Island, ME *04019*
Kennard MR & MRS Samuel M 3d (Mildred K Hill) . | ☎ (908) 892-4864
 MISS Anne M . . . . | "Bedlam by the
 | Bay" 968 S Lagoon
 | Lane, Mantoloking,
 | NJ *08738*

Kennedy MR & MRS (DR) Kevin W (Karen E | ☎ (508) 693-9439
 Andresen) . . . . | 573 Main St,
 MR Coleman W . . . . | Vineyard Haven,
 JUNIORS MR William F . . . . | MA *02568*
Kennedy MR & MRS Mark B (Cantrell—Heath | ☎ (609) 967-5164
 Mirick) . . . . | 10601 Golden Gate
 MISS Devon W . . . . | Dv, Stone Harbor,
 JUNIORS MISS Ashley L . . . . | NJ *08247*
 JUNIORS MR Christopher R . . . . |
Kennedy MRS Stuart R (Frances C Judson) . . . . . . | ☎ (801) 647-3380
 MISS Martha C . . . . | Aspen Hollow 11,
 | PO Box 2603,
 | Park City, UT
 | *84060-0914*
Kennelly MISS Ellen L (Brown—Ellen L Kennelly)
 ☎ (603) 563-8419 . . Charcoal Rd, PO Box 55, Dublin, NH *03444*
Kennelly MRS R Grice (Ellen Lee Bayard)
 ☎ (603) 563-8419 . . Charcoal Rd, PO Box 55, Dublin, NH *03444*
Kenney MR & MRS Charles C II (Judith A Braber) . . | ☎ (707) 833-6802
 JUNIORS MISS Theresa A . . . . | "Redwood Springs
 | Ranch" 7639
 | Sonoma H'way,
 | Santa Rosa, CA
 | *95409*
Kent MR & MRS Geoffrey J W (Shober—Kendall— | Bahati,
 Richardson—Jorie F Butler) . . . . | PO Box 59749,
 MR Hugo J A . . . . | Nairobi, Kenya
Kent MRS (DR) Gerald T (Janet T Dingle)
 ☎ (216) 321-2939 . . 12526 Cedar Rd, Apt 1, Cleveland Heights,
 OH *44106*
Kent MR Peter A . . see J W Annan
Kent MRS W Thompson (P Elaine Baruch)
 ☎ (803) 768-9370 . . 2250 Rolling Dune Rd, Seabrook Island,
 Johns Island, SC *29455*
Kenyon MR & MRS Geoffrey R T (Sidney W Anderson)
 ☎ (802) 672-3047 . . "Boxford Cottage" Bridgewater, VT *05034*
Keogh MISS Adele C
 ☎ (302) 227-7918 . . 17 Columbia Av, Rehoboth Beach, DE *19971*
Keppel MRS Francis (Edith M Sawin)
 ☎ (819) 842-2824 . . North Hatley, Quebec J0B 2C0, Canada
Kernan MR Benjamin T . . . . | ☎ (518) 576-4394
 MISS Sophia R . . . . | "High Meadows"
 MISS Maud T . . . . | Keene Valley, NY
 | *12943*
Kernan MRS Francis K (Maud T Tilton)
 ☎ (516) 788-7579 . . "Sky High" Box 221, Fishers Island, NY *06390*
Kerr MR & MRS Alexander (Margaret C Wilson) . . . | ☎ (508) 693-5429
 MISS Cecily W . . . . | "Tashmoo East"
 MISS Suzannah W . . . . | Vineyard Haven,
 | MA *02568*
Kerr REV DR & MRS Donald C (Nora M Lloyd)
 ☎ (705) 765-3948 . . "Totem Hill" Port Sandfield, Ontario P0B 1K0,
 Canada
Kerr MR John Hoare
 "Oppnehrn Park" 876 Poonamallee High Rd, Madras 600084, India
Kerr MRS Wendell (Soule—Barbara Wendell)
 Aug 1 . . ☎ (508) 693-5609 . . Box 953, Vineyard Haven, MA *02568*

Kerry MR & MRS John F (Heinz—M Teresa Simóes Ferreira)
"Rosemont Farm" 1950 Squaw Run Rd, Pittsburgh, PA *15258*

Ketcham MR William T JR
☎ (516) 569-0763 . . "Willow Edge" 3 Meadow Dv, Lawrence, NY *11559*

Ketner MR & MRS D Scott (Elizabeth Brown) . . . . . . | ☎ (516) 788-7663
   MISS Barbara L . . . . | Fishers Island, NY
   MR D Scott JR . . . . | *06390*
   JUNIORS MISS Elizabeth P . . . . |

Kew MISS Christina E . . see MISS L B Watson

Key MR & MRS Albert L (Julia I Bowdoin)
☎ (802) 824-5456 . . "Winhollow Farm" South Londonderry, VT *05155*

Keyes MR Austin D . . see P H Briger

Keyes MR Eben Wight 2d
☎ (508) 548-1789 . . "Sunset Hill" Gunning Point, Falmouth, MA *02540*

Keyes MR & MRS Jonathan M (Judith S Button)
☎ (802) 372-6644 . . "The Button House" Box 47, S End Rd, North Hero, VT *04574*

Kidder MR & MRS Howard C (Bettibelle Heslop) . . . | ☎ (802) 765-4462
   MISS Elizabeth K . . . . | "By the River"
   MR Christopher H . . . . | South Strafford, VT
   MR James T . . . . | *05070*

Kidder MRS Jerome H T (Frances L Turnbull)
☎ (802) 765-4521 . . "Three Fields" South Strafford, VT *05070*

Kiendl MR & MRS Philip R (Audrey G Ochs)
☎ (508) 288-9447 . . 11 Fair St, Nantucket, MA *02554*

Kiernan MISS M Carroll . . see R F Callahan

Kiernan DR Michael J . . see R F Callahan

Kiernan MR & MRS Peter de L 3d (R Eaddy W Hayes)
☎ (704) 693-5779 . . "Wileywood" Lake Summit, Tuxedo, NC *28784*

Kilborne MR & MRS George B (Mahoney—Jean W W Bronson)
☎ (508) 428-7121 . . "Briskaven" 871 Sea View Av, PO Box 252, Osterville, MA *02655*

Kiley MRS Eugene J (H Jessie Hadley)
☎ (414) 748-7438 . . 690 Sandstone Rd, Rte 2, Ripon, WI *54971*

Kilgore MISS Constance P
☎ (860) 599-0906 . . 14 Pinewoods Rd, North Stonington, CT *06359*

Kilgore MRS Emilie S (Gilbreath—Emilie de Mun Smith) . . . . | ☎ (011-33-53) 29-51-05
   MR Alexander G . . . . | "Château de Goursac"
   | St Cybranet, 24250 Domme, France

Killion MRS Marion P (Marion M Payne) . . . . | ☎ (508) 228-2268
   MISS Karen L . . . . | 7 Summer St,
   MISS (DR) Susan L . . . . | Nantucket, MA *02554*

Kilmer MR & MRS Joyce P (M Catesby Halsey)
☎ (516) 283-0088 . . "The Banks" 64 S Magee St, Southampton, NY *11968*

Kilmer MRS Norman Joyce (Margaret E S Prentice)
☎ (615) 268-2310 . . "Fox Crossing" Hornbeck Farm, 1354 Morrison Creek Rd, Gainesboro, TN *38562*

Kimball MR & MRS Daniel M (Lydia C Fitler)
☎ (207) 276-3700 . . PO Box 514, Northeast Harbor, ME *04662*

Kimball MRS Mary Eliza (Stanley—Mary Eliza Kimball) . . . . | ☎ (860) 928-7689
   JUNIORS MR Arthur E Kimball Stanley . . . . . . | "Jericho"
   | Seth Kimball Rd, Pomfret Center, CT *06259*

Kimberly MR Oliver A 3d . . see MRS B Gray 3d

Kindred MR John J III
☎ (518) 589-5939 . . "Kindred Spirits" Twilight Park, Haines Falls, NY *12436*

King MRS Alfred F JR (Gorman—Frances P Barton)
Eagle Rise 4, PO Box 308, Dorset, VT *05251*

King MR & MRS Clarence H JR (Toni Richards) ⚓
☎ (207) 282-1287 . . "Little House" 9 Stonecliffe St, Biddeford Pool, ME *04006*

King MR & MRS Frank-Paul A (Eugenia Hudson)
"Wonder Ranch" General Delivery, Cameron, MT *59720*

King MR & MRS Henry L (Sokolov—Margaret Gram)
☎ (516) 788-7167 . . Fishers Island, NY *06390*

King MR & MRS John Andrews JR (Rheault—M Cristina Carega)
☎ (011-39-577) 793-076 . . Podere Doglio, 53030 Belforte, Siena, Italy

King MR & MRS Kimball (Harriet R Lowry) . . . . | ☎ (603) 934-4923
   MISS Virginia F . . . . | "Maryland Lodge" New Boston Rd, RD 1, Franklin, NH *03235*

King MISS Kristina van B . . . . | ☎ (719) 657-3593
   MISS (DR) Victoria van B . . . . | 12888 County Rd 15, Del Norte, CO *81132*

King MR & MRS MacLellan E JR (Elizabeth C Hellyer) . . . . | ☎ (616) 223-4857
   MISS Stephanie L . . . . | "Beach Cottage"
   MR Blair M . . . . | Box 1, Old Mission, MI *49673*

King MR Michael B
☎ (603) 563-8066 . . "Stonefields" Box 374, Dublin, NH *03444*

King MR & MRS Paul K (Edith H G Joy) . . . . | ☎ (207) 596-7349
   MISS Melissa van B . . . . | Rockport, ME *04856*
   JUNIORS MISS Sarah H J . . . . |

King MR & MRS Richard H (Reta P Schoonmaker) ⚓
☎ (508) 548-3635 . . "Sea Barker" 11 Snug Harbor Lane, West Falmouth, MA *02574*

King MR Samuel G JR
☎ (508) 548-0130 . . 300 Quissett Av, Falmouth, MA *02540*

King MR & MRS W Griffin JR (Mary C Floyd) ⚓
☎ (216) 451-6519 . . 1 Bratenahl Place, Apt 107, Bratenahl, OH *44108*

Kingsbury MRS Frederick H JR (O'Donnell—Eleanor Bried)
☎ (717) 226-9222 . . "Tall Trees" Tafton, PA *18464*

Kingsbury MR H Neal . . see F M Pope

Kingsbury MRS Howard T (Ellen M Wales)
☎ (207) 867-4813 . . "The Boat House" RD 1, Vinalhaven, ME *04863*

Kingsbury MISS Macy T . . see F M Pope

Kingsland MRS Elizabeth C (Finlay—Elizabeth E Corbin) . . . . | ☎ (516) 267-6551
   MR Nicholas C . . . . | 18 Sandpiper Lane, Amagansett, NY *11930*

Kingsland MR & MRS James A (Auchincloss—Eve Grantham)
☎ (011-33-65) 41-04-63 . . "L'Ancien Presbytère" St Cirq-Souillaguet, 46300 Gourdon, France
Kinney MR & MRS Douglas M (Smyth—Elizabeth Hummel) . . . .
  MISS Martha S . . . .
  MISS Hilary S . . . .
    MISS Elizabeth E Smyth . . . .
    MR John E Smyth
☎ (847) 234-0832
920 E Deerpath Rd, Lake Forest, IL *60045*

Kinney MR & MRS Gilbert H (Ann B Rasmussen) . . .
  MISS Eleanor H . . . .
☎ (207) 244-5186
"TOP" Pretty Marsh, Mt Desert, ME *04660*

Kinnicutt MRS Roger JR (Janet Heywood)
☎ (508) 432-0883 . . 21 Pilgrim Rd, Harwich Port, MA *02646*
Kinsella MR & MRS Eugene Benoist (Lindsey—Ethel P du Pont)
"Adam's Cottage" Rock End Rd, Northeast Harbor, ME *04662*
Kinsolving MR & MRS Augustus B (Monique O H Bérard) ⚓ . . . .
  JUNIORS MISS Isabelle . . . .
  JUNIORS MR Arthur B . . . .
☎ (516) 788-7561
Fishers Island, NY *06390*

Kipp MRS Donald B (Jessup—Kellogg—Wilhelmina van Neyenhoff)
Jly 10 . . Box 982, Northeast Harbor, ME *04662*
Kipp MR & MRS Wilson (Jean M Creely)
Box 366, East Boothbay, ME *04544*
Kirby MR & MRS James Lewis JR (Ann S Kirby)
☎ (804) 866-8910 . . "Montclare House" Claremont, VA *23899*
Kirk MRS Donald G (Maureen V Shanley)
☎ (516) 324-4075 . . Further Lane, East Hampton, NY *11937*
Kirkham MR & MRS Francis R (Ellis Musser)
☎ (707) 944-2505 . . "Little Farm" 1591 Oakville Grade Rd, Oakville, CA *94562*
Kirkland MR Charles McM
☎ (207) 646-3303 . . "Sea Urchins" Cape Neddick, ME *03902*
Kirkland MR & MRS David S (Lila Wilmerding) . . . .
  MISS Amanda R . . . .
☎ (207) 276-5615
"Old Homestead" Manchester Rd, Northeast Harbor, ME *04662*

Kirkpatrick MR & MRS Thomas W (Anne G More)
☎ (401) 789-9675 . . Galilee Beach Club, Sand Hill Cove, Narragansett, RI *02882*
Kise MR & MRS James Nelson (Sarah L O Smith) . . .
  MISS L L Susanna . . . .
  JUNIORS MR A L Triplett . . . .
☎ (207) 865-0539
"Twin Coves" 152 Wolfe's Neck Rd, Freeport, ME *04032*

Kissel MR & MRS Michael Case (Elena M Thornton)
☎ (401) 847-7745 . . "Lily Pad" 175 Carroll Av, Newport, RI *02840*
Kitchel MR & MRS Denison (Naomi M Douglas)
☎ (619) 454-7850 . . 7950 La Jota Way, La Jolla, CA *92037*
Kittredge MR & MRS Harvey Gaylord JR (Elizabeth J Houston)
☎ (011-33-33) 52-46-88 . . "La Bergerie" Siouville-Hague, 50340 Les Pieux, France
Klapp MRS Nina S (Nina C Scheidt)
☎ (609) 492-9672 . . 325 Essex Av, Beach Haven, NJ *08008*

Klaussmann MISS Elizabeth M . . see J H Grummon
Klaussmann MR Eric K . . see J H Grummon
Klebnikov MR & MRS George (Sarah D Coffin)
☎ (518) 576-4411 . . Ausable Club, St Huberts, NY *12943*
Klein MR & MRS Gilbert W (Marybelle P Ziesing) . .
  MR Thomas H . . . .
☎ (603) 284-7723
"Yellow Cottage" Coolidge Farm Rd, Center Sandwich, NH *03227*

Kline MR & MRS C Tomlinson 3d (Catherine Hanlon W Zaro) . . . .
  JUNIORS MISS Laura L . . . .
  JUNIORS MR C Tomlinson 4th . . . .
☎ (908) 892-7548
"Windfall" 1520 Runyon Lane, Mantoloking, NJ *08738*

Kline MR Charles T JR
☎ (908) 892-7548 . . "Windfall" 1520 Runyon Lane, Mantoloking, NJ *08738*
Kling MR Daniel W
Five Pines Island, Ojibway, Keewaydin Camp, Temagami, Ontario P0H 2H0, Canada
Kloman MR & MRS Christopher R (Pamela W Brown) . . . .
  MISS Sibyl W . . . .
  MR Christopher A T . . . .
  JUNIORS MR Peter J . . . .
☎ (207) 372-8260
Harts Neck Rd, Tenants Harbor, ME *04860*

Kloman MRS E Felix (Olivia R Pragoff)
☎ (207) 372-6239 . . "The Barn" Harts Neck Rd, Tenants Harbor, ME *04860*
Kloman MR & MRS H Felix 2d (Ann B Stern) ⚓
☎ (207) 372-8008 . . "Seawrack" PO Box 550, Harts Neck Rd, Tenants Harbor, ME *04860*
Klots MRS Trafford P (Isabel S Hulings)
Château de Rochefort-en-Terre, 56220 Malansac, France
Knable MR & MRS John P 2d (M Cynthia Boyle) . . .
  MISS Eliza M . . . .
  MR John P 3d . . . .
  MR Geoffrey L
☎ (410) 641-7869
150 Teal Circle, Berlin, MD *21811*

Knapp MR & MRS George F (Mary Ann Hofheins)
  MISS Katharine K . . . .
  MR Robert H . . . .
  MR George F JR . . . .
  MR Geoffrey L . . . .
"Shaki Shanti" Cranberry Lake, NY *12927*

Knapp MR & MRS Lawrence W 3d (Genoveva de Carvalho Dias)
☎ (011-55-11) 826-7460 . . Rua Gabriel dos Santos 493, São Paulo, SP 01-231, Brazil
Knechtle MR & MRS Emilio B (Ann Johnston) . . . . .
  MISS Heidi P . . . .
  MISS Grace A . . . .
  MR John C . . . .
  MR David M . . . .
"The Highlands" RR 2, Baddeck, Nova Scotia B0E 1B0, Canada

Kneen MR & MRS Thomas Beaudry (Sturges—Elizabeth W Betz)
☎ (508) 775-9097 . . Box 225, West Hyannisport, MA *02672*
Knight MR & MRS Lawrence A (Linda J Augustine)
☎ (717) 775-7566 . . Blooming Grove Hunt & Fish Club, Hawley, PA *18428*

Knight MR & MRS Richard N JR (Ann H Philbrick)
☎ (207) 846-4167 . . "Tall Beaches" Box 407, Chebeague Island, ME *04017*

Knight MR & MRS Ridgway B (Dupont—Christine Saint-Léger)
☎ (011-33) 21-90-70-83 . . Inxent, 62170 Montreuil-sur-Mer, France

Knight MR & MRS Robert H (Gibson—Rosemary Costikyan)
☎ (203) 869-8997 . . "The Knoll" 12 Knollwood Dv, Greenwich, CT *06830*

Knight MR & MRS Robert P (Andrea Saladine)
☎ (616) 547-9926 . . "Sailors' Rest" 3647 Hemingway Pointe Rd, East Jordan, MI *49727*

Knight MRS Roma W (Roma L Wickwire)
☎ (717) 775-7566 . . "The Little House" Blooming Grove Hunt & Fish Club, Hawley, PA *18428*

Knipe MR & MRS T Wetherill (Gilchrist—Wainwright—Mary G Harris)
☎ (516) 324-2666 . . Box 289, Pudding Hill Lane, East Hampton, NY *11937*

Knoop MR & MRS Frederick G (Grace E Gilmore) . . | ☎ (541) 595-6515
MISS Katherine D . . . . | Black Butte Ranch,
MR Robert G . . . . | Sisters, OR *97759*

Knop MR Peter J . . . . | ☎ (703) 754-4484
MR Peter R Q . . . . | Ticonderoga Farm,
                                                                 | 26175 Ticonderoga
                                                                 | Rd, Chantilly, VA
                                                                 | *22021*

Knowles MR & MRS Gorham B (Hickingbotham—Diana Dollar)
Jly 1 . . ☎ (916) 525-5051 . . "Tamarack Cove" Tahoma, Lake Tahoe, CA *95733*

Knowles MRS James H (Reed—Elizabeth McCullough)
☎ (412) 238-6261 . . "Three Chimneys" RR 2, Box 343, Ligonier, PA *15658*

Knowles MR & MRS James H JR (Sherin Hetherington)
☎ (412) 238-6400 . . "Dragonswood" Box 36, Ligonier, PA *15658*

Knowlton MRS Eben (Helen M Foote)
☎ (860) 824-7321 . . "The Chimneys" 71 Beldon St, Falls Village, CT *06031*

Knowlton MR & MRS Frank W (Hélène Sigourney)
☎ (508) 563-3216 . . "High Lee Sea's End" 381 Scraggy Neck Rd, Box 331, Cataumet, MA *02534*

Knowlton GEN & MRS William A (Marjorie A Downey) USA.
☎ (603) 763-5448 . . George Hill Rd, West Springfield, NH *03284*

Knox MRS Arthur JR (Hubby—Margaret N Fisher)
☎ (860) 542-5731 . . "Cabaña Basque" Doolittle Lake, Box 344, Norfolk, CT *06058*

Knox MRS D Thoma (Kaiser—Diana Thoma)
Landlocked Lodge, Short Rd, East Aurora, NY *14052*

Knox-Johnston MR & MRS John A (Lovell—Beatrice Sweney-Borden)
☎ (508) 228-5090 . . "Corner House" 49 Center St, Box 1828, Nantucket, MA *02554*

Kobusch MR Nicholas Cabell
☎ (616) 526-2510 . . Cottage 81, Harbor Point, Harbor Springs, MI *49740*

Koch MR David H
☎ (516) 287-3508 . . "Aspen East" 880 Meadow Lane, Southampton, NY *11968*

Koch MR Frederick R
"Schloss Blühnbach" A5451 Tenneck, Land Salzburg, Austria

Kohle MR Christopher F . . see La Besse CTE de

Kohle MISS Patricia J . . see La Besse CTE de

Kohlmeyer MR Carter S . . see G F Phillips JR

Kole MR & MRS Michael U (Kelly A Murray)
☎ (516) 288-1183 . . "Serendipity" 1 Apaucuck Point Lane, Westhampton, NY *11977*

Kolowitz MISS Emma H . . see W P C Hudson

Koons MRS Benjamin H B JR (Violette R Mann) . . . | ☎ (609) 884-4417
MR Charles B . . . . | "Slightly
MR Garner M . . . . | Shipshape"
                                                             | 1200 New York Av,
                                                             | Cape May, NJ
                                                             | *08204*

Kopp MR & MRS Bradford B (Jean S Rath)
☎ (401) 596-5625 . . 10 Sunset Av, Watch Hill, RI *02891*

Kopper MRS Juliette Starr (Bidlack—Juliette Starr Kopper)
☎ (207) 255-4363 . . Box 194, RD 1, Rogue Bluffs, Machias, ME *04654*

Korff BRNSS Serge A (Mittendorf—Brett—Marcella C Heron)
☎ (516) 537-3694 . . Beach Lane, Wainscott, NY *11975*

Korosi MR & MRS Dana A (Johnston—Barbara C Caldwell)
☎ (716) 386-2165 . . Warner Bay Rd, Bemus Point, NY *14712*

Kouwenhoven MR & MRS William G (Alexandra | ☎ (410) 360-1612
Stein) . . . . | Skywater Rd,
MR William B . . . . | Gibson Island, MD
                                                                | *21056*

Kovas MR & MRS Ronald A (Patricia L Bond) . . . . . | 34 Sierra Crest
MISS Allyson E . . . . | Trail, Olympia
JUNIORS MR Peter B . . . . | Valley, CA *96146*
JUNIORS MR Charles A . . . . |
JUNIORS MR Joseph S . . . . |

Kraft MRS John F JR (Mary S Gordon)
☎ (412) 782-3145 . . 43 Oakhurst Circle, Pittsburgh, PA *15215*

Kraft MR & MRS John F 3d (Mary J West) . . . . | ☎ (508) 627-5841
MR Peter A . . . . | "Mattakesett"
                                                                 | Edgartown, MA
                                                                 | *02539*

Kraftson MR & MRS Donald W (Ann H Madara)
"Water's Edge" Southwest Harbor, ME *04679*

Krag MR & MRS W Brace JR (Kristen B Peterson)
☎ (517) 738-8532 . . "Oak Bluff" Cliff Rd, Pointe-Aux-Barques, MI *48467*

Kratovil MR Emil A JR
PO Box 1250, Edgartown, MA *02539*

Krech DR & MRS Shepard (Nora Potter)
☎ (207) 359-8888 . . Sedgwick, ME *04676*

Kreger MR & MRS Charles S (Lynch—Whitaker— | ☎ (401) 348-0035
Mary B Brown) . . . . | "Caboose II"
MISS Mary B Lynch . . . . | 4 Camelback Way,
MISS Elizabeth W Lynch . . . . | Watch Hill, RI
                                                               | *02891*

Kremer MRS J Lee (Joan F Lee)
☎ (207) 963-4051 . . "Beyond the Pale" Winter Harbor, ME *04693*

Krimendahl MISS (DR) Elizabeth K (Wolf—Elizabeth K Krimendahl)
☎ (516) 324-4552 . . Box 218, East Hampton, NY *11937*

Krimendahl MR H Frederick 2d
☎ (516) 324-4552 . . Box 218, 40 West End Rd, East Hampton, NY *11937*

Krisel MR & MRS William E (Donna S Zilkha)
☎ (516) 283-4686 . . 310 First Neck Lane, Southampton, NY *11968*
Kriz MR Christopher J
☎ (860) 923-2298 . . ''Graystone Farm'' Thompson, CT *06277*
Kroeger MR & MRS Arthur F (Hammond—Alexa C Daley)
☎ (704) 963-6732 . . Hound Ears Club, Shulls Mill Rd, Blowing Rock, NC *28605*
Kroeger MR & MRS Harold A JR (Carole D Ferris) . . | ☎ (970) 925-4115
MR Hal R . . . . | ''Broken Rock''
JUNIORS MR George F . . . . | 0103 Oak Ridge Dv, Aspen, CO *81612*
Krulak LT GEN & MRS Victor H (Amy Chandler) USMC.
☎ (619) 767-5531 . . 215 Montezuma Rd, Borrego Springs, CA *92004*
Krulak REV & MRS William M (Mae M Spence) . . . | ''The Barracks''
MR William M JR . . . . | Corolla, NC *27927*
Kuczynski MR Pedro P de G . . . . | ☎ (608) 524-5555
MR John-Michael . . . . | Elder Ridge Farm, E 7082 County H'way W, Rock Springs, WI *53961*
Kuehn MR Alfred L
☎ (508) 228-4984 . . 4 Fayette St, Nantucket, MA *02554*
Kuehn MR & MRS George W (Katherine Rust)
☎ (508) 748-0105 . . ''The Cedars'' 456 Point Rd, Marion, MA *02738*
Kuhn MRS Spencer F (Ada M Dixon)
32 Resort Rd, Harbor Beach, MI *48411*
Kunhardt MRS Edith W (Edith L Woodruff) . . . . . . | ☎ (603) 284-7046
MR Timothy W . . . . | Long Point, Coolidge Farm Rd, Center Sandwich, NH *03227*
Kuper MR & MRS George Henry (Danielle E Pienaar) ⚓
☎ (508) 775-4972 . . Great Island, PO Box 987, West Yarmouth, MA *02673*
Kyle MR Robert J JR . . see J R Sherwood 3d
Kysely MR & MRS Arvy F (Elizabeth G Coxe)
☎ (715) 693-3528 . . Kysely Farm, 731 S H'way X, Mosinee, WI *54455*
Kyser MR & MRS Emery K (Judith C Clark) . . . . | ☎ (205) 857-2298
MISS Kristin C . . . . | Lake Martin,
MR E Kyle JR . . . . | Alexander City, AL
JUNIORS MISS Caroline C . . . . | *35010*

L

La Besse CTE & CTSSE de (Kohle—Jane B | ☎ (011-33-55)
Boardman) . . . . | 25-60-71
MISS Patricia J Kohle . . . . | Château de
MR Christopher F Kohle . . . . | Chabrignac, 19350 Chabrignac par Juillac, France
Labouisse MRS Henry R (Eve D Curie)
☎ (516) 537-7719 . . Beach Lane, Box 616, Wainscott, NY *11975*

La Branche MISS Elizabeth
☎ (516) 283-6597 . . ''Side Door'' 62 Culver Hill, Southampton, NY *11968*
Labrot MR & MRS Andrew G (Marguerite E | ☎ (803) 757-2618
Wilford) . . . . | 844 May River Rd,
JUNIORS MISS Sarah H . . . . | Bluffton, SC *29910*
JUNIORS MR William H . . . . |
Ladd MR & MRS Charles Haven (Phyllis A Howe)
☎ (207) 734-2284 . . HC 60, Box 85, Islesboro, ME *04848*
La Farge MR & MRS Edward T (E F Maida Williams) . . of
☎ (860) 421-3624 . . ''Woodcock'' 214 Greenhill Rd, Killingworth, CT *06417*
''La Farge House'' Tuckernuck Island, Nantucket, MA *02554*
La Farge MISS Louisa R H
☎ (401) 294-2516 . . ''The River Farm'' Saunderstown, RI *02874*
Laffon MRS Penrose S (Penrose Stovell) . . . . | ☎ (441) 29-30615
MISS Alexandra P . . . . | ''Nonesuch'' 55 Tucker's Town Rd, St George 1-22 HS 02, Bermuda
Laflin MRS Lloyd Alan (Brady—Patricia A Sweeney)
☎ (715) 356-3133 . . ''Indian Summer'' Box 600, Minocqua, WI *54548*
Laflin MRS Louis E 3d (Carolyn Robbins)
☎ (360) 842-0266 . . Box 4591, Rolling Bay, WA *98061*
Laird MR & MRS Walter J JR (Antonia V Bissell)
☎ (518) 891-2537 . . HCR 1, Box 42, Saranac Lake, NY *12983*
Lake MISS Amanda R . . see B B Woodger
Lake MR Whitney B . . see B B Woodger
Lakin MR & MRS Charles B (Mary Wight)
''Burnt Island'' Isle au Haut, ME *04645*
Lalire MR & MRS Rex P (Greta S Nettleton)
Mountainy Pond Club, East Holden, ME *04429*
Lamb MR & MRS James R (Brigid Shanley)
☎ (516) 324-7931 . . 44 Egypt Lane, East Hampton, NY *11937*
Lamb MR & MRS Lawton S (H Heathcote McIlvaine) | ☎ (508) 228-5934
MR Dana L . . . . | 73 Cliff Rd, Nantucket, MA *02554*
Lambert MR & MRS Adrian JR (Sandia E Dain)
☎ (860) 739-0753 . . 20 Great Wight Way, Old Black Point, Niantic, CT *06357*
Lambert MR & MRS J Laird (M Susan Mahoney)
☎ (414) 839-2010 . . ''Black Acre'' 7336 Kangaroo Lake Rd, Baileys Harbor, WI *54202*
Lamberton MR & MRS Ian K (M Lewis Barroll)
☎ (609) 884-3779 . . ''Geranium Cottage'' 25 Windsor Av, Cape May, NJ *08204*
Lamont MR Donald B
☎ (415) 441-6644 . . 1100 Sacramento St, San Francisco, CA *94108*
Lamont MR & MRS Edward M (Camille H Buzby)
☎ (207) 867-4622 . . ''Sky Farm'' North Haven, ME *04853*
Lamont MR & MRS Lansing (Ada Jung)
☎ (207) 867-4706 . . ''Sky Farm'' North Haven, ME *04853*
La Motte MRS Ferdinand 3d (June Mitchell)
☎ (302) 575-1604 . . Stonegates, Box 18, 4031 Kennett Pike, Greenville, DE *19807-2031*

Lampson MRS Edward T (Mary C Wright)
Dipper Cove Point, Box 42, Orrs Island, ME *04066*

Lamy MISS Julia M (Anstey—Julia M Lamy) . . . . . ☎ (970) 586-3334
    JUNIORS MR Christopher L Anstey . . . .   "Moonridge"
PO Box 1647,
Estes Park, CO
80517

Land MR & MRS William G (McAvoy—Frances B Chisolm)
☎ (207) 244-3909 . . "Rugged Rocks" Box 55, Islesford, ME *04646*

Lander DR & MRS William W (Nancy G Bomberger)
☎ (603) 763-2894 . . "Hastings" New London, NH *03256*

Landreth MRS Diana C (Childs—Altschul—Diana C Landreth)
☎ (516) 537-7724 . . 14 Halsey St, Bridgehampton, NY *11932*

Landreth MR John Colt
☎ (847) 234-1799 . . 1750 Shoreacres Rd, Lake Bluff, IL *60044*

Landstreet MR & MRS Beverly W IV (Julia N Fry)
☎ (401) 596-1304 . . "Sunset Hill" 5 Aquidneck Av, Watch Hill,
RI *02891*

Lane REV DR & MRS Warren W (Virginia Penney)
☎ (905) 468-3475 . . "Far End" 369 Niagara Blvd, Niagara-on-the-Lake,
Ontario L0S 1J0, Canada

Langhorne MR & MRS W Keene (Skillern—Jane T Cobb)
☎ (208) 622-3098 . . Villager 1321, Sun Valley, ID *83353*

Langmann DR & MRS Robert D (Toulmin—Saraellen Merritt) . . of
☎ (860) 535-8210 . . 46 Main St, Stonington, CT *06378*
☎ (518) 576-4573 . . Hulls Falls Rd, Keene Valley, NY *12943*

Langworthy MRS David C (Norma J Shea)
☎ (802) 297-9756 . . Fairway Meadow 12, Stratton Mountain,
VT *05155*

Lankenau MR & MRS John C (Alison D Lanckton) . .   ☎ (518) 537-4430
    MISS Christine R . . . .   Banks Lane,
Germantown, NY
12526

Lansing MR & MRS Gerrit L (M Suydam   ☎ (207) 276-5500
Rosengarten) ⛵ . . . .   "Summer
    MR Gerrit L JR . . . .   Afternoon"
PO Box 73,
Northeast Harbor,
ME *04662*

Laplante MR & MRS Paul A (Elizabeth A Wiley) . . .   ☎ (401) 683-1765
    MR Andrew P . . . .   "The Hummocks"
    MR David A . . . .   194 Cliff Av,
    MR John P . . . .   Portsmouth, RI
    MR Christopher S *02871*

Laporte MR & MRS William F (Ruth W Hillard)
☎ (717) 595-2298 . . "The Spruces" Buck Hill Falls, PA *18323*

Lapsley MR & MRS John W (Hope Whitney) . . . .   ☎ (207) 276-5520
    MR Howard . . . .   Northeast Harbor,
ME *04662*

Lardi MR & MRS (DR) Paul F (Elizabeth Coryllos) . . .   ☎ (518) 672-7368
    MR Gordon C . . . .   "Mountain Brook
Farm" 106 Clum
Rd, Hillsdale, NY
12529

Larkin MR & MRS Frank Y (Smith—June Noble)
☎ (516) 324-1777 . . "Outermost House" PO Box 1351, Spaeth Lane,
East Hampton, NY *11937*

Larm MR & MRS Richard P (Jona C Vieta)
☎ (703) 765-1364 . . "Nap's Retreat" 7715 Elba Rd, Alexandria,
VA *22306*

La Rochefoucauld CTE Patrice de & CTSSE de (Stephanie W Parrish)
☎ (011-33) 54-98-01-04 . . "Château de Douy" 41320 Chatres-sur-Cher,
France

Larrabee MR & MRS Stephen F (Marka H Truesdale)   ☎ (207) 967-3460
    MISS Elizabeth M . . . .   "Beachwood"
    MR Jonathan F . . . .   RFD 2, Box 5,
Kennebunkport, ME
04046

Larsen MR & MRS Robert R (Vaast—Constance L Cheney)
☎ (508) 228-6164 . . 4 Summer St, Nantucket, MA *02554*

Larson MR & MRS Daniel M (Catherine L McNeal)
☎ (207) 359-8377 . . "Kill Kare Kamp" PO Box 281,
Camp Four Winds, Sargentville, ME *04673*

Larson MRS E Carruthers (Rebhun—Minor—Elizabeth P Carruthers)
☎ (616) 526-5938 . . Box 800, Cottage 41, Harbor Point, MI *49740*

Larson MR & MRS Wilfred J (Joan J Tilford)
☎ (616) 256-9598 . . 822 Juniper Trail, Leland, MI *49654*

Larzelere MR & MRS William E JR (Kathleen F Chace)
☎ (518) 644-9400 . . Sagamore 6A5, Bolton Landing, NY *12814*

Laserson MR & MRS Stephen A (Frances M Griffith)   of ☎ (705)746-8239
    JUNIORS MISS Tenley L . . . .   "Ermyn Island"
    JUNIORS MISS Galen G . . . .   Sans Souci, Ontario
P0G 1L0, Canada
☎ (516) 653-9555
"Tuckaway"
Ocean Av, Quogue,
NY *11959*

Lassen MR & MRS John Kai (Flanagan—Marion duP McConnell)
☎ (302) 227-4040 . . "Shore Winds" 19 Hall Av, Rehoboth Beach,
DE *19971*

Lauder MRS George (Bedford—DuPuy—Jessie Cook)
☎ (516) 283-8735 . . 545 Hampton Rd, Apt 17, Southampton,
NY *11968*

Laughlin MR & MRS Alexander M (Judith Walker)
☎ (516) 324-1361 . . Box 325, Ocean Av, East Hampton, NY *11937*

Laughlin MR & MRS Leighton H (Carin E Moore)
☎ (508) 778-0391 . . 70 Irving Av, Hyannis Port, MA *02647*

Laumont MR & MRS Philippe E (Anne C Adams)
☎ (518) 576-2206 . . "Crystal Brook Cottage" Ausable Club,
St Huberts, NY *12943*

Laverack MR & MRS William (Persis E Gleason)
☎ (207) 422-3969 . . Box 62, Sorrento, ME *04677*

Laveran-Stiebar DR & MRS Rudolf L (Harriet J Peabody)
Harbor Springs, MI *49740*

Lavin MR Peter C
"Shaki Shanti" Cranberry Lake, NY *12927*

Lavino MRS E George (Virginia Vail)
☎ (802) 823-7738 . . Ladd Brook Rd, Pownal, VT *05261*

Lawrence MR Arthur Burtis . . . .   ☎ (603) 284-6979
    MR Reed K . . . .   School House Rd,
Sandwich, NH
03227

Lawrence MR & MRS David B (Hannele Robinson) . ☎ (516) 288-1735
  MR George F 2d . . . . "Ambunti"
  MR David B JR . . . . 8 Delafield St, Box 1368, Westhampton Beach, NY *11978*
Lawrence MR & MRS David T (Susan L Hadden) . . . ☎ (516) 364-2995
  MISS Katharine P . . . . "Orchard House"
  MR John H . . . . 202 Brookville Rd,
  JUNIORS MISS Sarah T . . . . Glen Head, NY *11545*
Lawrence MR & MRS James R (Jill A Owesny)
  ☎ (401) 466-5935 . . "The Bluff" Block Island, RI *02807*
Lawrence MR & MRS John W (Reba R Carruthers) . . ☎ (616) 526-2495
  JUNIORS MISS Elizabeth R . . . . "The Pines" Cottage 82, Harbor Point, MI *49740*
Lawrence MR & MRS Peter G (Sandra Bartolini)
  ☎ (508) 548-5633 . . Box 26, Woods Hole, MA *02543*
Lawrence MR & MRS Solon L N (Matlack—Elizabeth Buchanan)
  ☎ (802) 496-2680 . . Mad River Glen, Ridge Rd, Faxston, VT *05673*
Lawrence MR & MRS Wayne B (Elizabeth B Smith)
  ☎ (207) 372-8445 . . "Red House" Harts Neck Rd, Tenants Harbor, ME *04860*
Lawrence MR William
  ☎ (207) 244-5128 . . off Claremont Hotel Rd, Southwest Harbor, ME *04679*
Lawrence MRS William Van D (Jones—Downer—Jean Hibbard)
  Adirondack League Club, Old Forge, NY *13420*
Lawson MRS Carol S (Carol H Skinner) . . . . Box 282B,
  MISS Susanna V R . . . . St George, ME *04857*
Lawson MR & MRS Joel S JR (Libbey—Ann Koover)
  ☎ (301) 652-2840 . . 5301 Westbard Circle, 118, Bethesda, MD *20816*
Layng MR & MRS John G (Amanda La M Barney) . . ☎ (207) 846-4033
  JUNIORS MISS Katherine S . . . . Chebeague Island,
  JUNIORS MR Andrew G . . . . ME *04017*
Layton MRS Buxton Lawn JR (Ruth D Ellis)
  ☎ (704) 526-2365 . . "The Cottage" Satulah Mountain, Highlands, NC *28741*
Lea MR Churchill P
  220 Artesian Way, Harbor Springs, MI *49740*
Lea MR Edward E
  ☎ (616) 223-4486 . . 13958 Bay View Av, Neahtawanta, Traverse City, MI *49684*
Lea MR & MRS Robert C JR (Nancy H Kellogg)
  ☎ (207) 244-5988 . . "Leaway" Cranberry Isles, ME *04625*
Leach MR & MRS Paul C (Dorsey—Bates—Sheila W Jackson) . . . . ☎ (707) 938-5860
  MISS Barclay P Bates . . . . "Pool House" 1221 Sobre Vista Dv, Sonoma, CA *95476*
Leach MR & MRS Peter T (Lee H Davidson) . . . . . . ☎ (518) 584-9294
  JUNIORS MR Alexander D . . . . "River Run Farm"
  JUNIORS MR Christopher T . . . . 149 Fitch Rd, Saratoga Springs, NY *12866*
Leach MRS Richard P (Katherine Thatcher)
  ☎ (518) 584-9294 . . "River Run Farm" 149 Fitch Rd, Saratoga Springs, NY *12866*
Leachman MR & MRS William H 3d (Kelsy K Drowne)
  "Elmore Farm" PO Box 316, Markham, VA *22643*
Le Blanc MRS Bertrand (Noël Kennerly)
  ☎ (408) 688-4759 . . "Chanteclair" 525 Quail Run Rd, Aptos, CA *95003*
LeBrecht MRS Brown (Maxwell—Sheila T Brown)
  ☎ (516) 324-0025 . . 35 Meadow Way, East Hampton, NY *11937*
Leclerc MR & MRS Ivor (Thayer—Joan Pirie) . . . . . . ☎ (610) 942-9675
  MISS Margaret P Thayer . . . . Box 337, Lyndell, PA *19354*
Leddy MR & MRS Thomas F (Studebaker—Newell—Tamara L B Newell) . . . . ☎ (207) 244-0207
  JUNIORS MISS Alexandra Newell . . . . Camp Tam Tom, Fernald Point Rd, Southwest Harbor, ME *04679*
Lederer MRS Henry A 3d (Maria S Gamble)
  ☎ (410) 828-6806 . . 7505 L'Hirondelle Club Rd, Ruxton, MD *21204*
Ledoux MR & MRS L Pierre (Joan Fernegg) . . . . ☎ (914) 534-3487
  MISS Jeanne-Nicole (Chase—Jeanne-Nicole Ledoux) . . . . Deer Hill Rd, Box 397, Cornwall-on-Hudson, NY *12520*
Lee MRS Augustus W (E Brooke Conley)
  ☎ (502) 895-2880 . . "New Guilford" 6507 Longview Lane, Louisville, KY *40222*
Lee MR & MRS Charles C (Sally S White)
  ☎ (207) 883-2136 . . "The Wasnuts" PO Box 3163, Prouts Neck, ME *04070*
Lee MR & MRS Charles P (Camilla Wall) . . . . ☎ (401) 783-6591
  MR Christopher . . . . "Grove Cottage"
  MR John . . . . 15 Hazard Av, Narragansett, RI *02882*
Lee MR & MRS D Day (Nancy A Mills)
  ☎ (518) 576-4457 . . Ausable Club, St Huberts, NY *12943*
Lee MR & MRS David S (M Lucinda Hopkins) . . . . . ☎ (603) 569-3573
  MISS Madeline J . . . . "Blue Goose
  MISS Alice I . . . . Lodge" Lakeside at
  MR Alexander P . . . . Winnipesaukee, Piper's Point Rd, Alton, NH *03809*
Lee MISS Denise M S
  ☎ (011-33-93) 76-13-97 . . Grand Hotel, 06230 St Jean-Cap-Ferrat, France
Lee MR & MRS Edward F (Tracie Anne Morrissey)
  Back Cove, Sorrento, ME *04677*
Lee MRS Frederick B (Jane Pillow Rightor)
  ☎ (802) 457-1608 . . Cloudland Rd, Box 11, Woodstock, VT *05091*
Lee MR & MRS John N (Mary H Subers)
  ☎ (717) 325-4724 . . "Bear Creek Lakes" 113 Lake Dv, Jim Thorpe, PA *18229*
Lee MRS John P (Nancy G Peabody)
  ☎ (508) 997-0865 . . 170 Smith Neck Rd, South Dartmouth, MA *02748*
Lee MISS Latané Lisle (Martini—Latané Lisle Lee)
  ☎ (516) 653-6842 . . Midland St, Quogue, NY *11959*

Lee MR & MRS Robert E IV (Rice—Jane C Cotton)
☎ (207) 563-3580 . . "Cotterbrook" Walpole, ME *04573*
Lee MR & MRS Robert H JR (Holt—Mary Clay Platt)
☎ (207) 963-7145 . . "Crossroads" Winter Harbor, ME *04693*
Lee MR & MRS W Ashton (Barbara E Whiting) ⛵
☎ (970) 468-2762 . . The Moorings, Apt B, PO Box 1513, 316 E LaBonte St, Dillon, CO *80435*
Leeds MR & MRS Roland O (Mary D L Boersma) . . . | ☎ (616) 889-4073
  JUNIORS MR Anthony R L . . . . | 8141 Portage Point Dv, Onekama, MI *49675*
Leeds MR & MRS Ronald P E (Damgard—Darcy A Mead). . . | ☎ (516) 283-4157
  MISS Natalie . . . . | "Wee Bairn"
    MISS Julie M Damgard . . . . | Fairlea Lane,
    MR & MRS Michael T Damgard (Lucy G Siewers) . . . . | Southampton, NY *11968*
Leeper MR & MRS Harry G JR (Rossana M Sollitto)
☎ (860) 379-6910 . . "Overledge" New Hartford, CT *06057*
Leeson MR & MRS A Dix (Nancy A Browne)
☎ (508) 994-4304 . . 16 Broadway, Cuttyhunk, MA *02713*
Lefferts MISS Kate C
☎ (516) JU4-5348 . . "Harbor East" Box 326, St James, NY *11780*
Legendre MRS Sidney J (Weeks—Gertrude Sanford)
☎ (516) 788-7364 . . "Chocomount House" Fishers Island, NY *06390*
Leggett MRS Mary Lee (M Lee Fahnestock)
☎ (508) 526-1994 . . 227 Summer St, Manchester, MA *01944*
Lehrman MR & MRS Lewis E (Louise L Stillman) . . | ☎ (717) 697-4308
  MISS Eliza D . . . . | 1024 Boiling
  MR Leland . . . . | Springs Rd,
  MR John S . . . . | Mechanicsburg, PA
  MR Thomas D . . . . | *17055*
  JUNIORS MR Peter R . . . . |
Leib MR G Bruce . . . . | ☎ (516) 283-0500
  MISS Cara I . . . . | Southampton Club,
  MR G B Eric . . . . | 10 First Neck Lane, Southampton, NY *11968*
Leib MR & MRS John H (Danforth—Du Bois—Mary I Bryan)
☎ (516) 626-3948 . . Wolver Hollow Rd, Oyster Bay, NY *11771*
Leighton MR & MRS Charles M (Vaughan—Sanderson—Roxanna B McCormick) ⛵
☎ (207) 734-6730 . . Point Comfort, Islesboro, ME *04848*
Leisure MR & MRS Peter K (Kathleen Blair) . . . . . . | ☎ (212) 791-0927
  MISS M Blair . . . . | 608 US Courthouse,
  MISS Kathleen K . . . . | 40 Centre St, New York, NY *10007*
Leitch MR & MRS Dynes L (Mochwart—Mary Jane Offutt)
☎ (301) 229-3813 . . 4411 Chalfont Place, Bethesda, MD *20816*
Lejeune MRS Patrick A (Mary C Carleton)
☎ (714) 494-1461 . . "Georgian-Cot" 52 Emerald Bay, Laguna Beach, CA *92651*
Lemaitre MRS Victor A (Jean R Spencer)
☎ (518) 589-5238 . . "Diquini" Twilight Park, Haines Falls, NY *12436*

Lembo MR & MRS Gregory L (Carole R Neri) . . . . . . | ☎ (908) 449-6882
  MISS Joanne G . . . . | 100 Madison Av,
  MISS Eleanor R . . . . | Spring Lake, NJ *07762*
Lenahan MR & MRS Sheldon T (Jacobs—M Kathryn Milks)
☎ (716) 688-6508 . . 155 Briarhill Rd, Williamsville, NY *14221*
Leness MR & MRS Anthony V (Beuerlein—Maureen F Geraty) . . . . | ☎ (516) 653-4031
  MISS Susan B . . . . | 23 Penniman Point
  MR Anthony H . . . . | Rd, PO Box 669, Quogue, NY *11959*
    MISS Pamela Beuerlein . . . . |
    MISS Sandra Beuerlein . . . . |
    MR Robert Beuerlein . . . . |
Leness MRS George J (Christine C Gibbs)
☎ (516) 653-4365 . . 17 Penniman Point Rd, PO Box 993, Quogue, NY *11959*
Leness MR & MRS John G (Jean R Southworth) . . . | ☎ (516) 653-4661
  MR Thomas G . . . . | Penniman Point Rd, PO Box 192, Quogue, NY *11959*
Lennon MR & MRS Kenneth N (Catharine R Pilling)
☎ (908) 899-8545 . . "Seahorse" 553 Lake Av, Bay Head, NJ *08742*
Lenssen MRS Nicholas F JR (Madlene C E von Glasow)
☎ (011-49) 2443-8321 . . Marienau 9, Mechernich 5353, Germany
Leonard MR Anthony N
PO Box 1353, Southampton, NY *11969*
Leonard MISS Cynthia Elyse
☎ (508) 748-1960 . . 185 Converse Rd, Marion, MA *02738*
Leonard MR & MRS Daniel (S May Morey)
☎ (518) 891-2538 . . "Wa A Wa" 19 Gabriels Onchiota Rd, Box 143, Onchiota, NY *12968*
Leonard MR & MRS Daniel JR (Elizabeth D Chamberlain)
☎ (518) 891-2538 . . "Wa A Wa" 19 Gabriels Onchiota Rd, Onchiota, NY *12968*
Leonard MR & MRS Edward M (Victoria A Fay) . . . | ☎ (916) 583-3169
  MISS Cynthia H . . . . | 1370 W Lake Blvd,
  MR Andrew W . . . . | Tahoe City, CA *96145*
Leonard MR & MRS James G (Henning—Cavanagh—Anne Butler)
☎ (203) 245-4020 . . 20 Kingsbridge Way, Madison, CT *06443*
Leonard MR & MRS Nelson J (Phelps—Margaret Taylor)
☎ (619) 433-7943 . . 70 St Malo St, Oceanside, CA *92054*
Leonard MR Spencer H . . see G W Smith
Leonards MR & MRS Thomas C JR (Barbara Baketel) | ☎ (603) 423-4210
  MISS Sherry K . . . . | "Stone House"
  MR James B . . . . | Canaan, NH *03741*
Le Pelletier MR & MRS Franck (Monica Behn) . . MR absent
see W C Behn
Lerch MR & MRS Dana Thompson (Gretchen A Young) . . . . | ☎ (518) 674-3217
  MR Robert Bond . . . . | "Lerches Birches"
  MR Richard Jones T . . . . | Bowman Lake, Taborton Rd, Sand Lake, NY *12153*

LeRoux MR & MRS Jacques J (E Shelley Earhart) . . . ☎ (207) 633-3710 "Bay Ledge" Boothbay Harbor, ME *04538*
   MR James J 3d . . . .

Le Roy MR & MRS G Palmer (Kyra Hawkins)
   ☎ (508) 228-0465 . . 7 Hussey St, Nantucket, MA *02554*

Leschen MR & MRS Harry J 3d (Anne H Goddard) . . ☎ (561) 234-1138 1616 S Ocean Dv, Vero Beach, FL *32963*
   MR H John 4th . . . .
   MR Elliott F . . . .

Lesher MR Stephen H
   ☎ (619) 435-2640 . . 804 F Av, Coronado, CA *92118*

Leslie MR & MRS George R (Smith—Catherine M McIntire)
   ☎ (516) 788-7478 . . Fishers Island, NY *06390*

Lester MR & MRS Robin D (Helen S Doughty) . . . . . "Trespassers W" Old Rte 55, Pawling, NY *12564*
   MR Robin D . . . .
   MR James R . . . .

Letchworth MR & MRS Geoffrey J JR (Margaret S Fry) . . . . ☎ (315) 364-8309 4004 W Lake Rd, Auburn, NY *13021*
   MR Thomas F . . . .

Levering MRS C Rowland (Cornelia Rowland)
   ☎ (705) 387-4310 . . "Sequoia" Magnetawan, Ontario P0A 1P0, Canada

Levering MR & MRS C Tilghman (Rebecca H Cromwell)
   ☎ (410) 822-4965 . . "Little Gross Coate" 11249 Gross Coate Rd, Easton, MD *21601*

Levering MR & MRS J P Wade (Hundley—Davis—L Louise La Montagne)
   ☎ (410) 825-0822 . . Box 18, Stevenson, MD *21153*

Levick MR & MRS Dudley A JR (Lucy D Dunham) . . ☎ (508) 627-5862 17 Meshacket Wood Rd, Edgartown, MA *02539*
   MISS Stephanie S . . . .

Le Viness MRS G Denmead (Hamilton—Barbara A Tulloch)
   "Beach House" 22 Henlopen Av, Rehoboth Beach, DE *19971*

Lewin MR & MRS John H JR (Jean T T Brown) . . . . . ☎ (302) 539-1408 "Somersault" 36 Cove Way, Cotton Patch Hills, Bethany Beach, DE *19930*
   MISS Janet T . . . .
   MR John H 3d . . . .

Lewis MR & MRS Edward D (Elvira Bonaccorsi di Patti)
   ☎ (011-39-90) 922-1375 . . via Addolorata 57, 98057 Milazzo, Italy

Lewis MR Frederick W 3d
   ☎ (910) 256-4843 . . "The Patio" 121 Cypress Av, Wrightsville Beach, NC *28480*

Lewis MRS Geoffrey W (Elizabeth M Locke)
   ☎ (207) 354-6670 . . Rte 68, Box 104, Cushing, ME *04563*

Lewis MR & MRS H H Walker (Eleanor R Nelson)
   ☎ (508) 693-0588 . . Box 784, Vineyard Haven, MA *02568*

Lewis MRS Henry 3d (Meyer—Georgie Williams)
   ☎ (401) 348-8944 . . "Sunnyledge Cottage" Watch Hill, RI *02891*

Lewis DR & MRS J Eugene (Elizabeth B McKee)
   ☎ (203) 272-5741 . . "Brooks Homestead" 532 S Brooksvale Rd, Cheshire, CT *06410*

Lewis MR & MRS James E 3d (Kenna M Bratcher)
   ☎ (203) 272-5741 . . "Brooks Homestead" 532 S Brooksvale Rd, Cheshire, CT *06410*

Lewis MR & MRS John B JR (Kirsten N Hansen) . . . . ☎ (516) 749-1290 Box 359, Shelter Island Heights, NY *11965*
   MR David L . . . .

Lewis MR & MRS Ogden Northrop (Adams—Susan S High) . . . . ☎ (516) 653-4665 Box 798, 21 Ocean Av, Quogue, NY *11959*
   JUNIORS MR Ogden N JR . . . .

Lewis MR & MRS Orme JR (Elizabeth Bruening)
   ☎ (520) 778-4723 . . "Highland Pines" 5973 Oak Ridge, Prescott, AZ *86301*

Lewis MR & MRS Perry (Kerr—Elizabeth Wright)
   ☎ (207) 244-3515 . . HCR 62, Box 106, Mt Desert, ME *04660*

Lewis MR & MRS R Brian (Sarah M Wood)
   Kirk Lake Rd, Texada Island, BC, Canada

Lewisohn MISS (DR) Marjorie G
   ☎ (516) 324-4432 . . "Rowdy Hall" 111 Egypt Lane, East Hampton, NY *11937*

LickDyke MR & MRS Jay C (Nagle—Priscilla Cunningham)
   ☎ (207) 867-4677 . . "Capriccio" Pulpit Harbor Rd, North Haven, ME *04853*

Lickle MR & MRS William C (Renee C Kitchell)
   ☎ (302) 652-5457 . . 300 Rockland Rd, Montchanin, DE *19710*

Liddell MR & MRS D Roger B (Florence J Wofford) . ☎ (860) 435-4566 202 Wells Hill Rd, Lakeville, CT *06039*
   MISS Alice E E . . . .
   JUNIORS MR Torrey B W . . . .

Liebolt MR & MRS Frederick Lee JR (Suzanne L Lloyd)
   ☎ (914) 677-8055 . . Verbank Rd, Millbrook, NY *12545*

Liggett MRS Alexander C (Priscilla W Watson)
   ☎ (860) 567-8190 . . 71 South St, PO Box 156, Litchfield, CT *06759*

Liggett MR & MRS Frank R 3d (Mildred L Le Blond) . . . . ☎ (919) 247-6294 G5 Westport-Beacon's Reach, Morehead City, NC *28557*
   MISS Louise H . . . .

Lillard MR & MRS John S (Paula L Polk)
   ☎ (705) 285-5015 . . McGregor Bay, Ontario P0P 1K0, Canada

Lillard MRS Margarita F (Margarita Fuller)
   ☎ (616) 526-2672 . . Cottage 19, Box 4082, Harbor Point, MI *49740*

Lilley MRS Genevieve G (Abberley—Genevieve G Caldecutt)
   ☎ (203) 655-2260 . . 99 Long Neck Point Rd, Darien, CT *06820*

Lilley MR & MRS William 3d (Eve La G Auchincloss) . . . . "Wadsworth Cottage" Northeast Harbor, ME *04662*
   MR Buchanan M . . . .
   MR Justin W . . . .

Limberg MR & MRS Edward A (Sarah B Perry)
   ☎ (314) 997-2694 . . 12 Robindale Dv, St Louis, MO *63124*

Limbocker MR & MRS Derek L (Nicole du Pont) . . . ☎ (401) 846-6311 "Trois Coops" 545 Ocean Av, Newport, RI *02840*
   MISS Ridgely . . . .

Lincoln MR Alexander JR
   ☎ (207) 244-3488 . . Dirigo Rd, Southwest Harbor, ME *04679*

Lincoln MR & MRS Gilbert (Le Boutillier—Polly Kinnear)
   ☎ (860) 739-6315 . . Old Black Point, Niantic, CT *06357*

Lincoln MR & MRS J Alden (Elaine E Fairman) . . . . ☎ (207) 276-5146
  MISS Lista A . . . . "Quarry Cove"
  MR Stephen E Sargent Dv,
  MR Benjamin B . . . . Northeast Harbor, ME *04662*
Lind MR & MRS Gerard G (Carolyn C Rittenour) . . . ☎ (516) 324-9121
  MISS Elizabeth L . . . . 33 Hither Lane,
  MISS Alexandra G . . . . East Hampton, NY *11937*
Linden MRS Carvel C (Jones—Oakes—Knight— ☎ (908) 449-5488
  Mary Sue McCulloch) . . . . "Green Gables"
    MISS Daphne V N Oakes . . . . 1401 Ocean Av, Spring Lake, NJ *07762*
Linderman MR & MRS Robert P 3d (Greeff—Arrel ☎ (508) 283-8632
  Parson) "Head of the Cove"
  MISS Nicole F S . . . . 4 Lane Rd, Annisquam, MA *01930*
Lindgren MR & MRS Robert K (Victoria T Cleveland)
  ☎ (508) 325-5239 . . 4 New Mill St, Nantucket, MA *02554*
Lindh MR & MRS David E P (Lynda Yost) . . . . ☎ (401) 847-3471
  MR Kenneth M P . . . . "Le Marais" Commonwealth Av, Newport, RI *02840*
Lindsay MRS George N (Mary S Dickey)
  ☎ (516) 692-7388 . . PO Box 1462, Laurel Hollow, Syosset, NY *11791*
Lindsey MISS Anne Y
  ☎ (705) 764-1302 . . Vernon Island, Beaumaris, Ontario P0B 1B0, Canada
Lindsey MRS Chisholm (Jean G Chisholm)
  ☎ (601) 649-2261 . . "Green Barn" 726 Fifth Av, Box 2766, Laurel, MS *39440*
Lineberger MRS Walter F JR (Coakley—Patricia Hunkin)
  ☎ (208) 622-8224 . . Sun Valley, ID *83340*
Link MR & MRS George H (Betsy Leland) . . of
  ☎ (805) 521-1556 . . "Rancho Eslabon" 3183 E Telegraph Rd, Fillmore, CA *93015*
  ☎ (916) 795-2006 . . "Rancho Inviernos" 31187 Russell Blvd, Winters, CA *95694*
Lins MR & MRS John P (Marion K Stewart)
  ☎ (717) 595-2834 . . Box 114, Buck Hill Falls, PA *18323*
Linthicum MRS Edward D (Murchison—C Virginia Long)
  Jly 1 . . 8052 Calle de Cielo, La Jolla, CA *92037*
Lionberger MR & MRS John S JR (Erle T Lund)
  ☎ (508) 748-2524 . . Point Rd, Marion, MA *02738*
Lippincott MR & MRS Bertram JR (Margaret Bruun)
  ☎ (401) 423-1013 . . 272 Highland Dv, Box 404, Jamestown, RI *02835*
Lippincott MRS Eleanor H (Lapsley—Boucher—Eleanor H Hallowell)
  ☎ (207) 276-5007 . . Northeast Harbor, ME *04662*
Lippincott MR & MRS Joseph W JR (Thomas—Marie L Beck)
  ☎ (610) 525-0782 . . 22 Pond Lane, Bryn Mawr, PA *19010*
Lippincott MR Walter H JR . . . . Northeast Harbor,
  MISS Sophie E . . . . ME *04662*
  JUNIORS MR Hugh . . . .
Lippman MR & MRS L Max JR (Fordyce—Zoé Desloge)
  ☎ (314) 485-8922 . . "Oak Hill Farms" Eolia, MO *63344*

Lirakis MR & MRS W Stephen (Bernadette Sabatier) . ☎ (011-33-62)
  JUNIORS MISS Isabelle 95-00-72
  JUNIORS MR Stefan . . . . "Villa les Roses" 38 rue Georges la Salle, 65200 Bagnères-de-Bigorre, France
Lischer MRS Carl E (Noel—Christine C Jones)
  ☎ (517) 479-9191 . . "Din's Dip" 19 Resort Rd, Harbor Beach, MI *48441*
Littell MR Walter D
  ☎ (207) 867-4685 . . North Haven, ME *04853*
Little MRS David B (Goldsborough—Marjorie English)
  ☎ (508) 945-2790 . . 80 Main St, Chatham, MA *02633*
Little MR & MRS Warren M (Jean E Hardy)
  ☎ (603) 279-7050 . . "Wren's Nest" 56 Little Rd, Meredith, NH *03253*
Littlefield MR & MRS Edmund W (Jeannik M C Méquet)
  ☎ (415) 348-1166 . . 405 Chapin Lane, Burlingame, CA *94010-5126*
Littlefield MR John S . . see D M Payne
Littlejohn MR & MRS Angus C JR (Leslie W Butcher)
  ☎ (508) 526-8709 . . 3 Cobb Av, Manchester, MA *01944*
Livens MR John H . . . . ☎ (617) 720-4590
  MISS Elizabeth Ann . . . . 27 Beaver Place,
  MR John H JR Boston, MA *02108*
Livens MRS M A Harris (Mary Ann Harris)
  ☎ (603) 968-7140 . . "Willoughby Point" Box 573, Holderness, NH *03245*
Livermore MR George S
  ☎ (707) 942-4320 . . "Montesol" 5500 Lake County H'way, Calistoga, CA *94515*
Livermore MR & MRS Richard C (Patricia A Mulford)
  ☎ (707) 942-4320 . . "Montesol" Lake County H'way, Middletown, CA *95461*
Livingston MR & MRS Ralph E (Lucia B Buchanan)
  ☎ (508) 369-3948 . . 106 Milldam Square, 100 Keyes Rd, Concord, MA *01742*
Llopis MR & MRS Jose Maria (Garrigues—Frances G Aldrich)
  ☎ (011-34-71) 316896 . . PO Box 848, 07800 Ibiza, Spain
Lloyd MR & MRS Charles E G JR (Sally B Hill) . . . . . ☎ (516) 537-3509
  MISS Jennifer H . . . . Oak St,
  JUNIORS MR Ewing McA . . . . PO Box 1983, Bridgehampton, NY *11932*
Lloyd MR & MRS David (Hollenbeck—Susan B ☎ (401) 348-8989
  Lattner) . . . . "Bluffit"
  JUNIORS MR Oliver M . . . . 8 Bluff Av, Watch Hill, RI *02891*
Lloyd MR & MRS Francis V 3d (Lida L Thompson) . ☎ (508) 394-0746
  MISS Lida L . . . . 34 Aunt Jane's Rd,
  MR Stratton C . . . . South Yarmouth, MA *02664*
Lloyd MR H Gates
  ☎ (508) 428-8936 . . "Sandanwood" PO Box 221, Cotuit, MA *02635*
Lloyd MR H Gates 4th
  ☎ (508) 428-8930 . . PO Box 221, Cotuit, MA *02635*

Lloyd MRS Richard W (Margaret C P Hebard) . . . . . ☎ (508) 428-7133
  MR O H Perry . . . . 1617 Main St, Box 193, Cotuit, MA *02635*

Lloyd MR & MRS Robin M (Georges—Tamara L Hall) . . . . ☎ (207) 236-4826 "Jabberwalk" Sherman's Point Rd, Box 834, Camden, ME *04843*
  JUNIORS MISS Marisa E D . . . .

Lloyd MR Stacy B 3d . . . . ☎ (508) 428-8942 Oyster Harbors, Osterville, MA *02655*
  MR Thomas L . . . .
  JUNIORS MR Stacy B 4th . . . .

Lloyd MRS Tangley C (Quinn—DeLaney—Tangley C Lloyd) . . . . ☎ (508) 771-7099 "C-Syde" Box 455, 23 Park Place, Hyannis Port, MA *02647*
    MISS Demarest L Quinn . . . .
    MR James P Quinn . . . .

Lloyd MR & MRS Wingate (Janet West)
  ☎ (508) 428-6791 . . 42 Bailey Rd, Box 1651, Cotuit, MA *02635*

Lobkowicz PRC Edouard A de & PRCSS de (PRCSS Françoise de Bourbon de Parme) . . . . ☎ (011-33) 35-27-71-54 Manoir d'Ujezd, Grainville Ymauville, 76110 Goderville, France
  PRCSS Marie-Gabrielle de . . . .
  PRC Charles-Henri de . . . .

Lockhart MISS A Whitney . . see F L Patterson 3d

Lockwood MR & MRS George S JR (Lee Wilson)
  ☎ (508) 693-2295 . . RR 1, Box 328, Vineyard Haven, MA *02568*

Lockwood MR Hamilton de F JR
  ☎ (207) 867-4636 . . "Cracroft" North Haven, ME *04853*

Lockwood MRS John Edwards (Henrietta E Sedgwick)
  ☎ (914) 234-7173 . . St Mary's Church Rd, RD 2, Box 192, Bedford, NY *10506*

Lockwood MR Thomas W—⚓
  ☎ (518) 891-3474 . . "Stone House" Turtle Pond Park, Saranac Lake, NY *12983*

Löfberg MR & MRS Per G H (Margaret P McDowell) . . . . ☎ (508) 992-5501 "Ricketson's Point" 110 Elm St, South Dartmouth, MA *02748*
  JUNIORS MR John P . . . .

Loizeaux MISS Christine
  ☎ (616) 895-6456 . . 7270 Pierce St, Allendale, MI *49401*

Loizeaux DR & MRS Theodore (Cecily W Flanagan)
  ☎ (508) 394-7004 . . "Granada" 246B Pleasant St, South Yarmouth, MA *02664*

Lombard MRS Barbara C (Twaddell—Barbara C Hooton)
  North Haven, ME *04853*

Lombard MR James M . . . . ☎ (603) 838-6633 Parker Hill Rd, Lyman, NH *03585*
  MISS Hillary S . . . .
  MR Laurence M 2d . . . .

Londen MR & MRS Jack W (Dodie M Isaacson)
  31015 Coast H'way, Laguna Beach, CA *92677*

Loney MR & MRS Frederick R (Nancy H Shevers)
  ☎ (401) 596-5657 . . "The Lookout" 17 Misquamicut Hills, Westerly, RI *02891*

Long MR Claxton A (O'Connell—Judith G Shepard) . . . . ☎ (707) 252-1501 "Rancho Valdera" 1300 Wooden Valley Rd, Napa, CA *94558*
  JUNIORS MISS Lydia S . . . .
    MR Courtney O'Connell . . . .
    MR Robin S O'Connell . . . .

Long MR & MRS Phillip C (M Whitney Rowe) . . . . . ☎ (508) 548-1089 PO Box 414, Woods Hole, MA *02543*
  MISS Charlotte C . . . .
  MR Elisha W . . . .
  JUNIORS MR Elliot S . . . .

Long MR & MRS Thad G (Carolyn F Wilson) . . . . . . ☎ (603) 253-6321 PO Box 784, Center Harbor, NH *03226*
  MISS Louisa F . . . .
  MR Wilson A . . . .

Longcope MR & MRS Thomas M 3d (Elizabeth Lefferts)
  ☎ (207) 244-5908 . . Clark Point, Southwest Harbor, ME *04679*

Longmaid MR & MRS John H (Penelope J Shumaker) of "Spectacle Island" Winter Harbor, ME *04693* ☎ (207) 244-5772 "Invermeade" Fernald Point Rd, PO Box 765, Southwest Harbor, ME *04679-0765* . . MR absent
  JUNIORS MR Ashley J S . . . .

Longmire MISS Helen M
  2915 Pilgrim H'way, Frankfort, MI *49635*

Longstreth MR & MRS Richard W (Lucinda E Train)
  ☎ (518) 576-4339 . . "Hamersley" Keene Valley, NY *12943*

Loomis MR & MRS Thomas H (Lorenz—Alice W Ingraham)
  ☎ (207) 832-4089 . . "Sea Fields" Friendship Island, PO Box 45, Friendship, ME *04547*

Lorber JUNIORS MISS Augusta H B . . see MISS J de M Foster
Lorber JUNIORS MR Giraud van N F . . see MISS J de M Foster

Lord MRS Charles E (Margaret A Plunkett)
  ☎ (203) 255-0808 . . 50 Southport Woods Dv, Southport, CT *06490*

Lord MRS Paul E (Mabel A Strong) . . . . ☎ (207) 622-2653 Webber Pond Rd, RFD 1, Box 786, Augusta, ME *04330*
  MISS Barbara Gile . . . .

Lorentzen MRS Hans L (Morris—Gerd K Wiese)
  ☎ (011-47-2) 449391 . . 5 Nordraaks Gate, Oslo 2, Norway

Lorenz MRS Barbara S (Barbara P Strong) . . . . ☎ (207) 255-6231 "Sea Bluff" Johnson Cove Rd, RR 1, Box 220, Machias, ME *04654*
  MISS Anne E . . . .

Lorenz MR Keith JR
  ☎ (207) 342-5156 . . "Gudanya House" Box 123, Morrill, ME *04952*

Lorenze DR & MRS Edward J 3d (Margit Hintz)
  ☎ (516) 288-1958 . . "Quantuck Bay Farm" Box 546, Quogue, NY *11959*

Lorillard MRS Alice C (Augustus—Alice Cavedon)
 ☎ (401) 847-3767 . . "Belair" 50 Old Beach Rd, Newport, RI *02840*
Lorillard MRS Screven (Alice Whitney) . . of
 ☎ (908) 234-0951 . . "Bindon Farm" PO Box 219, Larger Cross Rd, Far Hills, NJ *07931*
 ☎ (970) 728-5289 . . 150 Elk Way, Raspberry Patch, Telluride, CO *81435*
Loring MR & MRS Robert W (Elizabeth Madeira) . . . | ☎ (207) 276-5619
 JUNIORS MISS E Amory . . . . | "Jibe Ho"
 | Northeast Harbor, ME *04662*
Loughlin JUNIORS MISS Anna M . . see J T Witherspoon
Loughlin MISS Clare M . . see J T Witherspoon
Loughlin MR John J JR . . see J T Witherspoon
Louthan MR & MRS Thomas C (Paige R Gillette)
 ☎ (516) 283-1622 . . "Southside" 425 Hampton Rd, Southampton, NY *11968*
Love MRS George H (Lindenmeyr—McClintic—Lorraine McArthur)
 ☎ (412) 238-2565 . . 1 Franklin Ext, Ligonier, PA *13658*
Love MR & MRS Howard McC (Jane Vaughn)
 ☎ (518) 523-2702 . . Camp Woodland, 65 Victor Herbert Rd, Lake Placid, NY *12946*
Love MRS Robert M (MacLaren—Knowles—Elizabeth Morgan Firth)
 ☎ (860) 928-3647 . . "Tyrone Farm" 89 Tyrone Rd, Pomfret, CT *06258*
Love MISS Suzanna P (Lommel—Suzanna P Love)
 ☎ (207) 734-8891 . . "The Jap House" PO Box 62, Dark Harbor, Islesboro, ME *04848*
Lovejoy MR & MRS George M JR (Ellen W Childs)
 ☎ (603) 269-8641 . . "The Ridge" HC 74, Box 10D, Center Strafford, NH *03815*
Lovelace MR & MRS Richard S (Whitney—Caroline S Oveson)
 ☎ (508) 228-1807 . . 6 Old North Wharf, Nantucket, MA *02554*
Lovell MR & MRS A Buffum (Amanda L Norris) . . . . | ☎ (516) 765-3658
 MR Jonathan R . . . . | "Little House"
 MR William B N . . . . | Private Rd, Foot of Town Creek, Southold, NY *11971*
Lovering MR & MRS Joseph S (Eleanor T Dunning)
 ☎ (908) 899-1197 . . "The Clews" 1313 Bay Av, Mantoloking, NJ *08738*
Lovett MR Laurence Dow
 ☎ (011-39-41) 528-7942 . . "Palazzo Sernagiotto" Canareggio 5723, 30131 Venice, Italy
Lovett MRS Robert S 2d (Dorothy deHaven) . . . . . . | ☎ (508) 945-9031
 MISS Virginia Q . . . . | "Robins' Haven"
 MR Robert A 2d . . . . | 122 Champlain Rd, Chatham, MA *02633*
Low MR & MRS Anthony (Pauline I Mills) . . . . | ☎ (207) 734-2280
 MISS Elizabeth . . . . | Dark Harbor,
 MISS Catherine . . . . | Islesboro, ME *04848*
 JUNIORS MISS Alexandra . . . . |
 JUNIORS MR Nicholas . . . . |
Low MR & MRS K Prescott (Susan Tucker Boaz) . . . . | ☎ (508) 428-3095
 MISS Lisa Tucker . . . . | "Scottfree"
 MR Seth Prescott . . . . | 22 Sea View Av, Osterville, MA *02655*
Low MRS W Gilman JR (Frances J Larrabee) . . . . . . | ☎ (207) 799-0002
 MR David B . . . . | "Spurwink House"
 MR Abbot F . . . . | Ram Island Farm, Cape Elizabeth, ME *04107*
Lowe MR & MRS William L (Margaret Sloss)
 ☎ (702) 749-5384 . . 2045 Pray Meadow Rd, Glenbrook, NV *89413*
Lowell MR & MRS Ralph JR (Joan MacDuffie)
 ☎ (617) 581-0126 . . 11 Swallow Cave Rd, Nahant, MA *01908*
Lowrey MR & MRS Charles F (Mary C Rentschler) ⚓
 ☎ (415) 868-1286 . . 284 Seadrift Rd, Stinson Beach, CA *94970*
Luce MRS Ann R (Baird—Campbell—Ann Raymond)
 ☎ (303) 443-9039 . . 9302 E Ridge Rd, Golden, CO *80403*
Luce MR & MRS Henry 3d (Hadley—Smitter—Musham—Leila Eliott Burton) . . . . | ☎ (516) 788-7421
 DR Matthew S Eliott . . . . | "Brillig" Fishers Island, NY *06390*
Ludington MR & MRS Martin L (Baum—Betty L Carico)
 ☎ (314) 454-0067 . . 5290 Waterman Av, St Louis, MO *63108*
Ludington MR Nicholas L . . . . | ☎ (516) 583-8218
 MR Leland H . . . . | 75 Ridge Rd, Point O'Woods, NY *11706*
Ludington MR & MRS William F (van Otterloo—Betty A Erickson)
 ☎ (508) 696-8719 . . "East View" RFD 475D, Edgartown, MA *02539*
Ludlow MR & MRS George C (Louise H McGuinness) . . . . | ☎ (518) 576-4738
 MISS Amy C . . . . | "Highland Cottage" Keene Valley, NY *12943*
Luebke MISS Marie K . . see G Schwab 5th
Luers MR & MRS William H (Turnbull—Wendy W Woods) . . . . | ☎ (508) 693-4929
 MISS Ramsay F Turnbull . . . . | Main St at Owen Little Way,
 MISS Connor E Turnbull . . . . | Vineyard Haven, MA *02568*
Luke MR & MRS David L 3d (Sweetser—Fanny R Curtis)
 ☎ (516) 676-2799 . . 34 Shelter Lane, Locust Valley, NY *11560*
Luke MR & MRS Douglas S (Sarah C Mullen)
 ☎ (518) 576-4411 . . "The Lean-To" Ausable Club, St Huberts, NY *12943*
Luke MR & MRS John A (Joy Carter)
 ☎ (508) 693-3269 . . West Chop, MA *02573*
Lukens MR & MRS Alan W (Susan Atkinson)
 ☎ (802) 533-7453 . . Aspenhurst Farm, Greensboro, VT *05841*
Lukens MR E Benjamin C . . . . | ☎ (207) 276-3929
 MR Peter G . . . . | "Golf Course Bungalow" Somes Sound, Northeast Harbor, ME *04662*
Lukens MRS John Brockie (Amy Austin)
 ☎ (609) 967-4591 . . 14 E 17 St, Avalon, NJ *08202*
Lukens MR & MRS Robert A (Elizabeth S Taylor) . . . | ☎ (207) 276-5404
 MISS Alice L . . . . | Northeast Harbor,
 MR David C . . . . | ME *04662*
 JUNIORS MR J Nicholas . . . . |

Lupton MR & MRS John Thomas 2d (Alice M Probasco)
☎ (423) 821-6561 . . ''Stonedge Point'' Lookout Mountain, TN *37350*

Lurie MR & MRS David V (Sally W Johnson)
☎ (508) 228-7647 . . ''Peek-a-View'' 11 New St, Nantucket, MA *02554*

Lyden DR & MRS John P (Engelhardt—Carol S Murphy)
☎ (914) 332-7812 . . Gory Brook Rd, North Tarrytown, NY *10591*

Lyman MRS Arthur T (Joan M Lincoln)
☎ (617) 934-2888 . . 54 Crooked Lane, Powder Point, Duxbury, MA *02331*

Lyman MR & MRS Frederick W (Mary S Freeman)
☎ (508) 283-3744 . . Norwood Heights, Annisquam, MA *01930*

Lyman MR & MRS Lincoln P (Barbara L Putnam) . . . | ☎ (207) 276-5717
JUNIORS MISS Daphne W . . . . | Sinclair Rd, Northeast Harbor, ME *04662*

Lyman MR Ronald T
☎ (207) 244-5220 . . ''Cranstone'' Great Cranberry Island, Cranberry Isles, ME *04625*

Lyman MRS Ronald T JR (Shaw—Susan J Storey) . . of Box 207, 45 Ring Rd, Plympton, MA *02367* Great Cranberry Island, Cranberry Isles, ME *04625*

Lynch MRS Edmund A (Florence D Sullivan)
☎ (802) 824-6049 . . ''Content'' South Londonderry, VT *05515*

Lynch MR & MRS Edmund C JR (Braff—Teller—Alice Treibick)
☎ (401) 847-1285 . . ''Horizons'' 221 Ocean Av, Newport, RI *02840*

Lynch MR & MRS Edmund C 3d (Deborah A Brown)
☎ (307) 733-5545 . . Box 1173, Jackson Hole, WY *83001*

Lynch MISS Elizabeth W . . see C S Kreger
Lynch MISS Mary B . . see C S Kreger
Lynch MR & MRS Michael P (Catherine R Parker) Ocean City, NJ *21842*

Lynn MISS Letitia C . . see D R Valiunas

Lyons MR & MRS Henry W (Winifred Runton) . . . . . | ☎ (603) 253-6304
MR David A . . . . | Black Cat Island,
MR Robert W . . . . | Box 571, Center Harbor, NH *03226*

M

McAfee MR & MRS W Gage (Linda Ho) . . . . | ''Highmeadows''
JUNIORS MISS Dallas . . . . | 73 Sterling Rd,
JUNIORS MR Zachary R G . . . . | Greenwich, CT *06830*

McAleenan MRS Clifford C (Stewart—Sheronas— | Apr 1 . .
Marian Farrel) ⛵ . . . . | ☎ (207) 594-0660
MISS Marian Stewart . . . . | ''Bear House'' 38 Wellington Dv, Rockport, ME *04856-4022*

McAllister MRS Walter W JR (Edith L Scott)
☎ (512) 749-5755 . . ''Heron Rock'' Port Aransas, TX *78573*

McAllister MRS William B (Nancy B Barth)
☎ (203) 488-5434 . . Dogfish Island, Stony Creek, CT *06405*

McAlpin MR & MRS Benjamin B 3d (Jeanie P Gerst)
☎ (705) 764-1938 . . Fairholm Island, Beaumaris, Ontario P0B 1B0, Canada

McAlpin MR & MRS Charles N (Anne M Stupp)
Aug 1 . . ☎ (315) 354-4325 . . ''Log Lodge'' Brandreth Park, Long Lake, NY *12847*

McAlpin MR & MRS Malcolm M (Judith A | ☎ (717) 775-6890
Rohrbacher) . . . . | ''Turkey Tracks''
MISS Joann C . . . . | Blooming Grove
MISS Marian M . . . . | Hunt & Fish Club,
MR Andrew M . . . . | Hawley, PA *18428*

McAlpin MRS William R (Williams—Lawrence—Kathleen E Middleton)
☎ (860) 542-5794 . . ''High Meadow'' Golf Dv, Norfolk, CT *06058*

McAshan MRS Samuel A (Phelps—Marie C Lee)
☎ (409) 836-6489 . . Rte 2, Box 500, Brenham, TX *77833*

McAuliffe MRS Dorothy Buck (Dorothy Weekes | ☎ (516) 725-8843
Buck) . . . . | PO Box 895,
MISS Thirza D . . . . | Sag Harbor, NY
MISS Dorothy L . . . . | *11963*
MR George B 3d . . . . |

McBean MR & MRS Peter (Helmer—Nancy N Hoguet)
☎ (401) 847-0421 . . ''Chepstow'' Narragansett Av, Newport, RI *02840*

McBurney MRS Andrew M (Lidie L Sloan)
☎ (518) 523-3245 . . ''River Ranch'' Adirondack Loj Rd, Box 1271, Lake Placid, NY *12946*

McCabe MR & MRS James L (Louise Beachboard) . . | ☎ (207) 276-3282
MISS Sarah B . . . . | ''Pyne Cottage''
JUNIORS MR William L . . . . | Northeast Harbor, ME *04662*

McCall MR & MRS David B JR (Abigail F Stackpole)
☎ (516) 788-7373 . . Fishers Island, NY *06390*

McCall MR & MRS Jonathan C (Jane A Walker) . . . . | ☎ (207) 563-3420
MISS Alston W . . . . | Barroll's Point,
MR Jonathan C JR . . . . | Newcastle, ME *04553*

McCall MR & MRS Peter C (de St Phalle—Susan K Collingwood)
☎ (860) 434-0016 . . ''Maison Skootee'' 25 Johnny Cake Hill Rd, Old Lyme, CT *06731*

McCall MR Robert D
☎ (516) 788-7373 . . General Delivery, Fishers Island, NY *06390*

McCance MR & MRS Thomas JR (Francine Jaques)
☎ (516) 788-7801 . . ''The Ark'' Fishers Island, NY *06390*

McCann MR & MRS Donald Fraser (Fairchild—Joy E Vietor)
☎ (307) 733-6677 . . Box 14, Wilson, WY *83014*

McCargo MR & MRS Grant (McLean—Chew—Audrey S Holding) ⛵
☎ (508) 627-5072 . . Box 699, Katama Rd, Edgartown, MA *02539*

McCarrens MRS Arthur D (Constance Alexander)
☎ (508) 994-2890 . . Salter's Point, South Dartmouth, MA *02748*

McCarter MR Thomas N 3d
☎ (516) 283-0425 . . Meadow Club, 555 First Neck Lane, PO Box 5005, Southampton, NY *11969*

McCarthy MR & MRS John G (Fleming—Lily Lambert)
☎ (610) 527-2269 . . 74 Pasture Lane, Apt 214, Bryn Mawr, PA *19010*

McCay MR Andrew T . . see W G von Weise JR
McCleary MR Benjamin P . . see R E Watson
McCleary MR & MRS Benjamin W (Jean L Muchmore)
☎ (401) 783-6223 . . PO Box 5236, Wakefield, RI *02880*

McCleary MISS Katherine C . . see R E Watson
McClellan MRS Emilie S (Wood—Emilie R Stevenson)
  ☎ (401) 789-6435 . . 1 Seagate Dv, Narragansett, RI 02882
McClellan MR & MRS Robert (A Jeanette Banta) . . . | ☎ (518) 677-3158
  MR Robert 3d . . . . | "Northwood"
  MR Gordon B . . . . | 41 N Union St, Cambridge, NY 12816
McClelland MR & MRS Donald R (Janet N Legendre) . . . . | ☎ (410) 651-0426 "School Ridge Farm" Box 137, Upper Fairmount, MD 21867
  MISS Sylvia Marina . . . . |
  MISS Janet Newbold . . . . |
McClintock MR & MRS John T (Mary B Mitchell)
  ☎ (860) 435-2266 . . "The Little House" Prospect Mountain Rd, Salisbury, CT 06068
McCloskey MR & MRS Paul N JR (Helen V Hooper)
  ☎ (916) 796-2124 . . Box 3, Rumsey, CA 95679
McCloud MR & MRS Kimball P (Claire Swain Huntington) . . . . | 1 Huntington Rd, Glenbrook, Lake Tahoe, NV 89413
  MISS Casey H . . . . |
  MISS Ashley H . . . . |
McClughan DR & MRS Joseph F (Annette M Stahl)
  ☎ (207) 264-3673 . . "Driftwood Lodge" Rangeley, ME 04970
McCluney MR & MRS Henry N (Carolyn Lansing)
  ☎ (314) 991-2479 . . 6 Sunny Meade Lane, St Louis, MO 63124
McClung MR & MRS S Alfred 3d (Adelaide B Smith)
  ☎ (508) 255-3179 . . 345 Tonset Rd, Box 1077, Orleans, MA 02653
McColley MR Sutherland
  ☎ (516) 324-3373 . . Box 155, Wainscott, NY 11975-0155
McComas MR & MRS Oliver P JR (Chamberlain—Goodnow—Peggy B Caldwell)
  ☎ (860) 542-5038 . . "The Wigwam" PO Box 181, Norfolk, CT 06058
McConihe MRS F Moran (Marguerite C Hagner)
  ☎ (508) 996-1608 . . "Eagle's Nest" Nonquitt, MA 02748
McConnell MRS Julia C (Waterbury—Julia L Chieppo)
  ☎ (516) 626-1327 . . "Nido d'Ucello" 1065 Friendly Rd, Upper Brookville, Oyster Bay, NY 11771
McCormick MR Brooks
  ☎ (708) 393-9416 . . "St James Farm" 2-S-601 Winfield Rd, Warrenville, IL 60555
McCormick MR & MRS Ernest O 3d (Cynthia Romaneck) . . . . | ☎ (408) 688-5626 767 Las Olas Dv, Sea Cliff Beach, Aptos, CA 95003
  MISS Laura L . . . . |
  JUNIORS MR Christopher R . . . . |
McCormick MR & MRS John S (Bertha B Brooks)
  ☎ (518) 359-3732 . . Follensby Park, Tupper Lake, NY 12986
McCown MR John A . . see MRS P T Stowe
McCreery MR & MRS Lawrence K (Lorraine Sampson) Orchards Town Stud, Clonmel, Co Tipperary, Ireland
McCrindle MR Joseph F R
  ☎ (011-44-171) 937-2155 . . 32 Kensington Court, London W8, England
McCuaig MR & MRS Victor C JR (Robb—Fell—Cordelia D Reid)
  ☎ (516) 325-0546 . . "West Point Cottage" PO Box 161, Eastport, NY 11941

McCue MRS Allen L (Gertrude L Peabody)
  ☎ (207) 244-7402 . . "Sunset Farm" HCR 62, Box 308, Mt Desert, ME 04660
McCulloch MR & MRS Andrew C (Joan G Houston)
  ☎ (802) 254-5998 . . "Meadowbrook Maples" 166 Meadowbrook Rd, West Brattleboro, VT 05301
McCulloch MRS John I B (Van Devere—Patricia Robineau)
  ☎ (516) 324-4319 . . "Children at Play" 77 Lily Pond Lane, PO Box 1556, East Hampton, NY 11937
McCulloch MRS Paul L (Helen E Widmaier)
  ☎ (847) 724-2189 . . "Carriage Hill on the West Fork" 1500 Palmgren Dv, Glenview, IL 60025
McCullough MR & MRS George R (Henshaw—Elisabeth G Briant)
  ☎ (412) 238-7733 . . "Deer Springs" Box 7, Rector, PA 15677
McCurdy DR & MRS Alexander 3d (Tyson—Stroud—Patricia J Peterson)
  ☎ (207) 276-5408 . . "Deer Rock" Peabody Dv, Box 512, Northeast Harbor, ME 04662
McCutcheon MR & MRS George Barr 2d (Paula E Wilms) . . . . | ☎ (803) 524-5242 601 Prince St, Beaufort, SC 29902
  MR Ian . . . . |
McDaniel MR & MRS R Chase 2d (Barbara Santora) . | ☎ (717) 646-3779 Pocono Lake Preserve, PA 18348
  MISS Sarah D . . . . |
  MR R Chase 4th . . . . |
McDermott DR William V JR
  ☎ (207) 582-4044 . . "Orchard House" PO Box 26, Gardiner, ME 04345
McDevitt MRS Gwynne C G (Rhodes—Severance—Gwynne C Garbisch)
  ☎ (302) 227-4926 . . 46 Pine Reach Rd, Henlopen Acres, DE 19971
McDevitt MR & MRS John J 3d (Elkins—Elizabeth Downes)
  ☎ (603) 544-7338 . . Bald Peak Colony Club, Melvin Village, NH 03850
McDill MRS Laura (Gratwick—Laura McDill) . . . . . | ☎ (802) 457-1725 "Line Farm" Woodstock, VT 05091
  MISS Laura B Gratwick . . . . |
  MISS Katharine Gratwick . . . . |
McDonough MR John R
  ☎ (519) 592-5873 . . "Cedar Lodge" 1 Misty Glen Vale, Stokes Bay, Ontario, Canada
McDonough MR & MRS Michael P (Florence T Strawbridge) . . . . | ☎ (401) 847-3266 "Beachmound" Bellevue Av, Newport, RI 02840
  MR Michael L . . . . |
  MR David Lucas . . . . |
McDowell MR & MRS Putnam B (Lee—Lee—Rosamond Brooks)
  ☎ (508) 999-5082 . . Box P283, Nonquitt, MA 02748
McEvoy MRS Nan Tucker (Phyllis A Tucker)
  ☎ (707) 769-1878 . . 5935 Red Hill Rd, Petaluma, CA 94952
McFadden MR & MRS George (Moreton—Carol Owsley)
  ☎ (516) 283-4844 . . 300 First Neck Lane, Southampton, NY 11968
McFadden MR & MRS John H (Deirdre M Whiteside) . . . . | ☎ (011-39-584) 975196 "Sassella" Compignano, 55045 Lucca, Italy
  JUNIORS MR William V W . . . . |
McFarland MR & MRS Alan R JR (Kathleen M Troia)
  ☎ (516) 283-9660 . . "The Pump House" Ram Island, PO Box 825, Southampton, NY 11969

McFerran MR & MRS Alexander Y (Frederica P French).................... ☎ (508) 994-8108
  MISS Brooke A........................ 94 Nonquitt Av S,
  MR Alexander Y JR.................... Nonquitt, MA 02748
  MR Christopher D.....................
  JUNIORS MR Frederick P ....
McGehee MRS C Coleman (Caroline Y Casey)
  ☎ (804) 529-6642.. "Faunroy" Bon Harbors, Lottsburg, VA 22511
McGennis MR & MRS William J (Winifred J Wetherald)
  ☎ (905) 894-1126.. "The School House" 929 Cherry Hill Blvd, Ridgeway, Ontario L0S 1N0, Canada
McGeorge MR & MRS Arthur JR (Patricia L Fenn)
  ☎ (207) 667-7933.. PO Box 213, Ellsworth, ME 04605
McGeorge MRS Edward B JR (Oberweiser—Ambler—Dorothy L Newsome)
  ☎ (516) 324-1274.. 67 Davids Lane, East Hampton, NY 11937
McGovern MR & MRS David T (Owen—Margery White)....................... ☎ (207) 883-6084
  MISS M Alexandra .... Prouts Neck, ME 04074
McGowan MR & MRS Gerard F (Claire M Miller)... ☎ (905) 894-1984
  MISS Claire K .... "Grey Grove Farm"
  MR Gerard A......................... Erie Rd, Bay Beach,
  MR Edwin M.......................... Ridgeway, Ontario L0S 1B0, Canada
McGraw MRS Diana Dent (Diana G Dent)
  ☎ (914) 351-3485.. "The Bird Nest" Tuxedo Park, NY 10987
McGraw MR & MRS Theodore A (Helen R Stoepel)
  Huron Mountain Club, Big Bay, MI 49808
McGugan MR & MRS Vincent J (Joyce H Wyman)
  ☎ (508) 563-7364.. 550 Scraggy Neck Rd, Cataumet, MA 02534
McGuire DR & MRS Hunter H JR (Alice B Reed)
  ☎ (516) 788-7449.. PO Box 91, Fishers Island, NY 06390
McIlvain MR & MRS Alan (Elizabeth L Claghorn)
  ☎ (508) 228-9817.. "Thorn Hill" 76 Millbrook Rd, Box 3247, Nantucket, MA 02584
McIlvain MR & MRS T Baird (Mary L Boles)
  ☎ (610) 645-8696.. 1400 Waverly Rd, Villa 47, Gladwyne, PA 19035
McIlvaine MR & MRS Leighton H JR (Probst—Karin M Rose)............................ ☎ (207) 833-5898
  MR L Reed .... "Sora" South Harpswell, ME 04079
McIntosh MR & MRS Henry P 4th (Susan D Riggs)
  ☎ (970) 925-1788.. Aspen Alps Club, Aspen, CO 81611
McIntyre MR & MRS James Bigelow (Juliana S Cuyler)............................ ☎ (802) 533-2247
  MISS Juliana S C....................... "Weathervane"
  MR James B.......................... Main St, Greensboro, VT 05841
McKay MRS George F (Marybeth O'Reilly)....... ☎ (616) 547-6880
  MR George F JR .... 215 Belvedere Club, Charlevoix, MI 49720
McKay MRS James C (Thompson—E Jane Reeves)
  Aug 1 .. ☎ (705) 764-1902.. Beaumaris, Ontario P0B 1B0, Canada
McKay MR & MRS Lawrence (Elizabeth A Slocum)
  ☎ (705) 765-3362.. "Raspberry Island" Beaumaris, Ontario P0B 1B0, Canada

McKean MR John W
  ☎ (508) 922-4657.. 15 Miller Rd, Beverly, MA 01915
McKean MRS Q A Shaw (Katharine Winthrop)
  ☎ (508) 468-2922.. "Savin Hill" Box 2067, South Hamilton, MA 01982
McKenrick MRS Stratford Eyre (Keith McC Price)
  ☎ (410) 224-5668.. 930 Astern Way, Apt 407, Annapolis, MD 21401
McKinney MR & MRS James E (Ann M Marrow) ... ☎ (860) 567-5648
  JUNIORS MR Robin L .... "Kilbourn Farm" 37 Saw Mill Rd, Litchfield, CT 06759
McKinney MR & MRS Robert M (de Montmollin—Marie Louise Ehrmann-Egry)
  ☎ (505) 986-3001.. PO Box 2048, Santa Fe, NM 87501-2048
McKinnie MRS Ralph E (Everett—Gwendolen Shethar)
  ☎ (802) 824-6020.. PO Box 235, Derry Woods, Londonderry, VT 05148
McKinnon MR & MRS Ian Neil (Rebecca Webster).. ☎ (705) 765-3188
  MISS Michelle........................ Olive Island,
  MISS Laura .... Muskoka Lakes Golf & Country Club, Port Carling, Ontario P0B 1J0, Canada
McKinnon MR & MRS James M (Marthe W Tribble)
  ☎ (508) 362-1194.. "The Old Mill" 122 Thacher Shore Rd, Yarmouth Port, MA 02675
McKleroy MR & MRS Bruce G (Mary Jo Gioviné) .. ☎ (203) 795-9054
  JUNIORS MR B Gardiner JR................ "The Court" 249 Charles Court, Orange, CT 06477
McKnight MRS William G JR (Le Brun C Rhinelander)
  ☎ (516) 283-1201.. "Suncoast" PO Box 1528, Gin Lane, Southampton, NY 11968
McKnight MR & MRS William G 3d (Katherine W Ewart)............................. ☎ (516) 283-8377
  MR William R......................... 24 Gin Lane, Southampton, NY 11968
McKown MR & MRS David R (Ann F Gasque) ..... ☎ (516) 788-7810
  MISS Hilary B .... Fishers Island, NY
  MR Matthew W....................... 06390
McKown MRS Frank B (Helen M Pendleton)
  ☎ (516) 788-7810.. "Miramette" Fishers Island, NY 06390
McLanahan MR & MRS Bruce (Ellen J Mahoney)... ☎ (518) 891-0728
  MISS Elizabeth S .... "Camp of the
  MR John H B .... Winds" Star Rte,
  MR Jeremiah B .... Box 4, Saranac Inn, NY 12983
McLanahan MRS Duer (Martha M Bloch)......... ☎ (516) 283-9388
  MR & MRS Morgan C (Elizabeth A Markham) ... 1 Gin Lane,
  MR & MRS William D (Lara B Schefler)........ Box 1017, Southampton, NY 11969
McLane MRS Allan (Jean Marianne Spottiswoode)
  ☎ (401) 849-6887.. "The Glen House" Glen Farm Rd, Portsmouth, RI 02871

McLane MRS Elizabeth (Jennison—Elizabeth Heed)
  ☎ (011-44-171) 837-8888 . . Fellowship House,
  23 Mecklenburgh Square, London W61N 2AB, England
McLaughlin MR & MRS George H 2d (Charlotte Heyl)
  ☎ (802) 375-9975 . . Arlington, VT *05250*
McLaughlin MR & MRS Ian M W (Mary G Makrianes) . . . . ☎ (207) 763-3839
  JUNIORS MR Gavin M K . . . . "Woodcock Farm"
  JUNIORS MR Callum M W . . . . Lincolnville, ME
  JUNIORS MR Ian A Van D *04849*
McLean MR & MRS Donald G (Kennedy—Mona Townsend)
  ☎ (207) 276-3238 . . "Ship's In" Peabody Dv, Northeast Harbor, ME *04662*
McLean DR & MRS Ephraim R 3d (Jane J Ruckert) . ☎ (706) 268-3753
  MISS Janet . . . . 433 Chestnut Rise,
  JUNIORS MISS Susan . . . . Big Canoe, GA
                                                                30143
McLean MRS Gale (Mary P Gibson)
  ☎ (207) 363-8920 . . "Hilltop" York Harbor, ME *03911*
McLean MR & MRS Locke (Sara P Ridgway) . . . . . . ☎ (516) 788-7613
  JUNIORS MISS Emily R . . . . Box 219,
  JUNIORS MR George R . . . . Fishers Island, NY
                                                                06390
McLean COL (RET) & MRS Robert L (Linda K Durfee) USA . . . . ☎ (516) 283-8698
  MISS Elissa S . . . . 18 Ochre Lane,
  MISS Margaret T . . . . Southampton, NY
                                                                11968
McLean MRS Stafford (Manice—Josephine Coster)
  ☎ (518) 589-5316 . . "Nearma" Onteora Club, Tannersville, NY *12485*
McLucas MR & MRS Don H JR (Pepper—Lloyd—Anne Emmet) ⚓ . . . . Box 413,
    MISS Edith M Pepper . . . . Norwood Lane,
                                                                Southwest Harbor,
                                                                ME *04679*
McMahon MR & MRS Frederic G (Elizabeth A Pflug) ☎ (516) 288-3102
  MR Frederic C . . . . Box 363,
                                                                Westhampton, NY
                                                                11977
McManus MR & MRS Charles J JR (Press—Esther T Azran)
  ☎ (954) 462-1579 . . Point of Americas II, Apt 202, 2200 S Ocean Lane, Ft Lauderdale, FL *33316*
McMeel DR & MRS J Wallace (Elizabeth C Wetherill) . . . . Nonquitt, MA *02748*
  MR W Cortright . . . .
McMillan MR & MRS S Sterling 3d (Judith E Knight) ☎ (207) 367-5159
  MISS Victoria M . . . . 3450 Sand Beach
  MR S Sterling 4th . . . . Rd, Stonington, ME
                                                                04681
McMullen MRS George R (Jane T Garesché) . . . . . . ☎ (517) 738-7138
  MR George R JR . . . . Pointe-Aux-Barques,
                                                                Port Austin, MI
                                                                48467
McNally MR & MRS Edward C (Margaret McGann) . ☎ (315) 482-2598
  MISS Heather C . . . . Island Royal,
  JUNIORS MR E Gray . . . . PO Box 55,
                                                                Alexandria Bay, NY
                                                                13607

McNeal MRS Thomas F (Grace H Smith)
  ☎ (207) 359-8377 . . "Kill Kare Kamp" Rte 15-175, Box 281, Sargentville, ME *04673*
McNeely MR & MRS Prentice J 3d (Susan H Finney) . | Chester,
  MISS Melissa F . . . . | Nova Scotia
  MR Prentice J 4th . . . . | B0J 1J0, Canada
  MR Grayson C . . . . |
  JUNIORS MR John W . . . . |
McNeil MRS Henry S (Lois A Fernley) ⚓
  ☎ (610) 828-1706 . . "Hickory Farm" Plymouth Meeting, PA *19462*
McNeil MR & MRS Robert D (Jennifer P Cox)
  ☎ (717) 595-2368 . . High View, Cottage 319, Buck Hill Falls, PA *18323*
McPherson MR & MRS J Bruce (Susan H Shea) . . . . ☎ (508) 775-1368
  JUNIORS MISS Ellen B . . . . PO Box 506,
                                                                Hyannis Port, MA
                                                                02647
McQuade MR & MRS Lawrence C (Margaret Osmer) PO Box 746,
  MR Andrew P . . . . Siasconset, MA
                                                                02564
McQuilkin MR G J Geoffrey . . see MRS S A Barngrove
McQuilkin MISS Hilary B . . see MRS S A Barngrove
McSweeney MISS A Thayer . . see W J Strawbridge JR
McSweeney JUNIORS MISS Catherine B D . . see W J Strawbridge JR
McSweeney MISS Christine S . . see W J Strawbridge JR
McSweeney MRS Edward F (Ramsay—Newman—Eleanor Walton Newman)
  ☎ (804) 484-7151 . . 3101 Riveredge Dv, Portsmouth, VA *23702*
McVitty MRS Reginald L M (Honoria A Livingston)
  ☎ (518) 537-6103 . . "Sylvan Cottage" Rte 1, Box 216, Germantown, NY *12526*
McWilliams MR & MRS James K (Anne M Giannini) ☎ (707) 944-2045
  MR Kevin S . . . . "Mt Eden Ranch"
                                                                Box 147, Oakville,
                                                                CA *94562*
MacArthur MRS Cynthia W (Preble—Hutchison—Cynthia W Wirtz)
  ☎ (847) 234-2116 . . 85 E Laurel St, Apt 2B, Lake Forest, IL *60045*
MacArthur MR & MRS Edward S (Wright—Billie S Rowley) ⚓
  ☎ (705) 246-2986 . . Coulter Island, Desbarats, Ontario P0R 1E0, Canada
Macauley MR & MRS John C W (Margaret A Long)
  ☎ (011-41-22) 751-29-14 . . "Apres Mai" 7A Chemin des Hutins, CH 1247 Anieres, Switzerland
Macbeth MR Pierre de StJ . . of
  "Reekie Lum" Box 461, Port Townsend, WA *98368*
  Box 787, Kathmandu, Nepal
MacCallum MR & MRS David H (N Lee Neill) . . . . . ☎ (516) 324-5549
  JUNIORS MISS Alexandra Y . . . . 19 Amy's Lane,
  JUNIORS MR Neill McL . . . . East Hampton, NY
                                                                11937
MacColl MR & MRS N Alexander JR (Nancy F Herron)
  ☎ (508) 428-5231 . . "Blithe Bit" Box 236, Osterville, MA *02655*
MacCracken MRS Eleanor D (Eleanor G Dickson)
  ☎ (516) 267-3684 . . Box 296, Amagansett, NY *11930*
MacDonald MISS Catherine . . see MRS S A Trundle JR
MacDonald DR & MRS Douglas G (Diane Driscoll)
  ☎ (516) 583-8630 . . PO Box 82, Point O'Woods, NY *11706*

MacDonald MR Joseph . . see MRS S A Trundle JR
MacDonald MR & MRS Kirkpatrick (Jory—Lee A Fahey) . . . .
    MR Bryce E A . . . .
    JUNIORS MISS Alexis A . . . .
☎ (914) 534-9690
"Deerhill Point"
Cornwall-on-Hudson, NY *12520*

Macdonald MR & MRS Robert S JR (Leola Armour) .
    MR Ian R . . . .
    JUNIORS MR Colin S . . . .
☎ (516) 324-6559
Middle Lane, Box 2019, East Hampton, NY *11937*

MacElree MR & MRS Lawrence E (Hill—Jane Cox) .
    MISS Charlotte Hill . . . .
    MISS Ann Hill . . . .
☎ (207) 374-5465
Box 792, Chase House, Union St, Blue Hill, ME *04614*

MacEwan MR & MRS Nigel S (Elliman—Beavers—Judith G Sperry) ⚓
    ☎ (207) 734-6654 . . "Indian Head" Dark Harbor, Islesboro, ME *04848*

Machold MR & MRS Roland M (Pamela W Pulleyn) .
    MISS Alyssa M . . . .
    MR Roland P . . . .
    MR Robert P . . . .
☎ (518) 576-4319
Box 771, Keene Valley, NY *12943*

Mack MR & MRS John D (Etter—Lorna U Carey)
    ☎ (508) 945-0306 . . 195 Bridge St, Chatham, MA *02633*

Mack MR Norman E 2d
    ☎ (508) 228-2617 . . 89 Main St, Nantucket, MA *02554*

Mack MR & MRS William L (Jennifer L McLean)
    ☎ (315) 348-8773 . . Brantingham Lake, Brantingham, NY *13312*

Mackay MRS Jacqueline deF (Jacqueline deF Meyler)
    ☎ (914) 276-2425 . . "Stone House Farm" Box 533, Somers, NY *10589*

MacKay MR & MRS (DR) Malcolm (Cynthia N Johnson) . . . .
    MISS Hope W . . . .
    MR Robert L . . . .
☎ (516) 628-2619
206 Centre Island Rd, Centre Island, Oyster Bay, NY *11771*

MacKenzie MR & MRS David O (Deborah W Williams) . . . .
    MR David W . . . .
☎ (307) 733-6288
Red Rock Ranch, Box 38, Kelly, WY *83011*

Mackenzie MRS William G (Weaver—Shirley E Fetterolf)
    ☎ (215) 643-6362 . . 453 Skippack Pike, Box 246, Blue Bell, PA *19422*

MacLean MR & MRS Babcock (M Cynthia Gannon) ⚓
    ☎ (516) 424-5675 . . 44 Knollwood Av, Huntington, NY *11743*

MacLean MRS Charles C (Lee S Howe)
    ☎ (516) 423-3258 . . 40 Lloyd Lane, Lloyd Neck, Huntington, NY *11743*

Maclean REV CANON & MRS Dougald L (Mary W Patterson)
    ☎ (860) 536-3028 . . "Waukeya" 24 Whitehall Landing, Mystic, CT *06355*

MacLear MR & MRS Frank R (Suzanne G Gardner) .
    MISS Lydia A . . . .
    MR Malcolm G . . . .
    MR Bruce A . . . .
☎ (401) 348-8145
"Moana" Watch Hill, RI *02891-5710*

Maclennan MR & MRS Robert A R (Noyes—Helen Cutter) . . . .
    MISS Ruth B I . . . .
    MR Adam L R . . . .
    MR Nicholas H Noyes . . . .
☎ (603) 466-3857
"Little House" Durand Rd, Randolph, NH *03570*

Macleod MR & MRS Robert W (Barbara B Wilmerding) . . . .
    MISS Avery W . . . .
    MR Ian R . . . .
    MR Morris W . . . .
☎ (516) 788-7368
"The Point" Fishers Island, NY *06390*

MacMillan MR & MRS Richard J (Josephine B Worcester) . . . .
    MISS Josephine B . . . .
    MR Donald S . . . .
"Head Hollow" Squam Lake, Holderness, NH *03254*

MacNeish MR & MRS William Jack JR (Marion S Madara) . . . .
    MISS Marion Madara . . . .
    MISS Anna Jack . . . .
☎ (207) 244-4164
"Meadow's Edge" Southwest Harbor, ME *04679*

Macomber MR & MRS John De W (Caroline Morgan) . . . .
    MISS Elizabeth C . . . .
    MR William B 2d . . . .
☎ (207) 867-2283
Crabtree Point Rd, Box 723, North Haven, ME *04853*

MacPherson MR & MRS Gordon B (Baiter—Welsh—Barbara D Baker)
    ☎ (401) 635-4482 . . 19 Baileys Ledge Rd, Little Compton, RI *02837*

MacPherson MR & MRS Robert W B (Joan B Wallace)
    ☎ (617) 631-0948 . . "The Cottage" 34 Foster St, Marblehead Neck, MA *01945*

MacRae MR & MRS Cameron F 3d (Ann W Bedell) .
    MISS Catherine F . . . .
    JUNIORS MISS Ann C . . . .
☎ (516) 283-5792
Meadow Lane, Southampton, NY *11968*

Macrae MRS John (Solley—Niedringhaus—Jane Switzler)
    ☎ (508) 228-1760 . . 45 Cliff Rd, Nantucket, MA *02554*

Madara MRS Edward S (Ann W Hessenbruch)
    ☎ (207) 244-3279 . . "Water's Edge" Southwest Harbor, ME *04679*

Madara MR & MRS Edward S JR (Rosalinda B Roberts) . . . .
    MR Edward S III . . . .
☎ (207) 244-3279
"Water's Edge" Southwest Harbor, ME *04679*

Madeira MISS Elizabeth
    ☎ (207) 276-5452 . . "Greenaway" Northeast Harbor, ME *04662*

Madeira MR & MRS Lewis N (Hay—Joan Dillon)
    ☎ (802) 867-4128 . . "Trillium" RR 2, Box 1644, Lower Hollow Rd, Dorset, VT *05251*

Madeira MRS Louis C (Helen Tyson)
    ☎ (207) 244-3432 . . "Manset House" 37 Shore Rd, Southwest Harbor, ME *04679-1070*

Maechling MR & MRS Charles JR (Janet G Leighton)
    ☎ (506) 529-3341 . . "Bar House" Bar Rd, St Andrews-by-the-Sea, NB E0G 2X0, Canada

Magee MR & MRS Jerome (Barbara J Hansen)
    ☎ (916) 546-2565 . . Box 327, Carnelian Bay, Lake Tahoe, CA *96140*

Magnuson MR & MRS Mark G (Elise C Gray) . . .
    MR & MRS Charles L Siemon (Laura S Magnuson) . . . .
☎ (704) 526-5275
1441 Falls Dv W, Highlands, NC *28741*

Magowan MRS Robert A (Doris Merrill)
    ☎ (516) 283-1087 . . "Swan House" PO Box 1355, 563 Ox Pasture Rd, Southampton, NY *11969*

Maguire MR & MRS J Robert (Pauline Thayer) . . . . . ☎ (207) 288-3246
　MISS Pauline T . . . . "Cover Farm"
　　Hulls Cove, ME
　　04644

Maher MR & MRS John Francis (Helen Lee Stillman)
　☎ (805) 684-2983 . . 4561 Del Mar Av, Carpinteria, CA *93013*

Mahoney MR & MRS David J (Merrill—Hildegarde M W Ercklentz)
　☎ (516) 537-3744 . . "Twin Eagles" Box 1560, Ocean Rd, Bridgehampton, NY *11932*

Major MR & MRS Howard B JR (Eleanor Gontier)
　☎ (216) 247-4553 . . 15005 County Line Rd, Chagrin Falls, OH *44022*

Makepeace MRS Lloyd B (Jean Thompson)
　☎ (508) 627-5209 . . Box 1159, Cummings Way, Edgartown, MA *02539*

Makrianes MR & MRS James K (Judith A Erdmann)
　☎ (516) 324-6646 . . Jericho Lane, Box 434, East Hampton, NY *11937*

Mali MR & MRS Frederick J (Lucretia Simmons)
　☎ (860) 379-8927 . . "Wendigo" Grantville Rd, Winchester, CT *06098*

Mallery MR & MRS Bayard M (Virginia Reichenbach) . . . . ☎ (603) 823-5950
　MR John C . . . . PO Box 547,
　　Franconia, NH
　　03580

Mallery MR & MRS David (Judith Chappell)
　☎ (603) 823-5231 . . Sugar Hill, NH *03585*

Mallory MR & MRS C King (Smith—Florence B Marshall) . . . . ☎ (717) 794-5301
　MR Raburn M . . . . Monterey Circle,
　JUNIORS MR Richard C M . . . . Blue Ridge Summit,
　　PA *17214*

Malone MRS Frederick R (Jean Hamilton)
　Fieldway Lane, Prouts Neck, ME *04074*

Malone DR Laurence A . . . . ☎ (301) 387-6571
　MR Michael H L . . . . "Meadowood"
　　Deep Creek Lake,
　　Swanton, MD *21561*

Maloney MR & MRS Paul (Virginia Wells)
　☎ (518) 352-7360 . . "Minnewawa" Blue Mountain Lake, NY *12812*

Manchester DOWAGER DUCHESS OF (Coleman—Crocker—Elizabeth Fullerton)
　☎ (011-39-41) 5207-746 . . "Ca Vendramin" 13 Giudecca, 30123 Venice, Italy

Manganaro MRS E Morris (Ellen N W Morris) . . . . ☎ (207) 374-2232
　MR Nicholas W . . . . "Fernrock"
　　MRS Nina V M Watson (Robertson—Nina V Manganaro) . . . . Blue Hill, ME
　　　04614
　　MRS Mark F Gray (Curtin—Ellen W Manganaro) . . . .

Manger DR & MRS William M (Lynn S Sheppard) . . ☎ (516) 283-3365
　MR William M JR . . . . "Top O'Dunes"
　MR S Sheppard . . . . Fairlea Rd,
　MR Charles S . . . . Southampton, NY
　　11968

Manheim MR Grant C
　☎ (508) 645-9550 . . Box 26, Menemsha, MA *02552*

Mann MRS J Herbert (de Mello—Joyce Herbert) . . . ☎ (516) 283-1204
　MISS Joanne—☎ (516) 283-4102 . . . . "Mayday"
　　Box 600,
　　Halsey Neck Lane,
　　Southampton, NY
　　11968

Mann MR & MRS Thomas D JR (Susan T Porter) . . . . ☎ (508) 430-0080
　MISS Lauren P . . . . 1 Colonial Way,
　JUNIORS MISS Leslie C . . . . Harwich Port, MA
　　02646

Manoogian MR & MRS Richard A (Jane A Cameron)
　☎ (906) 847-6433 . . Cottage 24, W Bluff Rd, Mackinac Island, MI *49757*

Mansbridge MR & MRS F Ronald (van Duyn—Janet Dunning)
　☎ (203) 227-2324 . . "Corner House" 306 Lyons Plain Rd, Weston, CT *06883*

Mansell MR & MRS Frank L (Miller—Edmona Lyman)
　☎ (516) 324-0836 . . Box 1244, East Hampton, NY *11937*

Marburg MR & MRS Charles L (Louise D White)
　440 Joshuatown Rd, Lyme, CT *06371*

Marckwald MRS Andrew K (Clarissa T Price)
　☎ (616) 223-7777 . . 1100 Neahtawanta Point Rd, RD 1, Traverse City, MI *49684*

Maricle MR John F
　5 Lower Baggott St, Dublin 2, Ireland

Mark MR & MRS Gordon St G (Barbara L Wedelstaedt) . . . . ☎ (508) 228-1233
　MR Gordon Griffith . . . . "High Water Mark"
　　13 Hallowell Lane,
　　Nantucket, MA
　　02554

Marks MR & MRS C Caldwell (Jeanne A Vigeant)
　☎ (334) 857-2271 . . Lake Martin, 19 Trailing W, Trillium, Eclectic, AL *36024*

Marks MRS Laurence M (de Bosdari—Martin—Herzer—Marjorie Greenan)
　☎ (207) 276-3915 . . "Christmas Trees" Upland Rd, Seal Harbor, ME *04675*

Marlette MRS John E (Rosemary H Smith) . . . . ☎ (905) 894-2512
　MISS Mary C . . . . "Wychwood"
　　2077 MacDonald
　　Dv, Bertie Bay,
　　Ontario L0S 1N0,
　　Canada

Marran MR & MRS Jack F (Theodora W Morris)
　☎ (516) 329-1305 . . 40 E Hollow Rd, East Hampton, NY *11937*

Marrin MR & MRS James M (Hamilton—Phebe E Thorne) . . . . ☎ (518) 576-4306
　MR John P T . . . . "The Uplands"
　JUNIORS MISS Helena Thorne . . . . Keene Valley, NY
　　MR Lewis Thorne Hamilton *12943*

Marron MR & MRS Donald B (Catherine D Calligar) ☎ (516) 283-7744
　MR Donald B JR . . . . Box 2573,
　　174 Coopers Neck
　　Lane, Southampton,
　　NY *11968*

Marsh MR & MRS H Newman JR (Marion Carhart)
☎ (902) 637-3742 . . "Mara Mia Farm" 142 Bayside Rd, Barrington, Nova Scotia B0W 1E0, Canada
Marsh MR & MRS Tom Fariss (Charlene Cline) . . . . . ☎ (505) 454-8251
JUNIORS MISS Charlene C . . . . "Marsh Ranch"
JUNIORS MR Charles . . . . Box 13, Valmora, NM 87750
Marshall MRS Dwight (Gertrude A Nolan)
☎ (508) 228-2725 . . "Sun Dune" PO Box 1305, Nantucket, MA 02554
Marshall MRS Fenton (Elinor S Fenton) . . . . ☎ (302) 539-6459
MR Edward T F . . . . "Bent Anchor"
MR Ragan S . . . . Box 1010, Bethany Beach, DE 19930
Marshall MR & MRS Harry R JR (Claire S Whitman) ☎ (508) 228-9239
MISS Katharine S . . . . 5 Wannacomet Rd,
MR Harrison R . . . . Nantucket, MA 02584
Marshall DR & MRS James S (Elizabeth Rockwell)
☎ (207) 236-2066 . . "Owl House" PO Box 912, Beaucaire Rd, Camden, ME 04843
Marshall MR & MRS John (Cynthia G Churchman)
Acoaxet, MA 02071
Marshall MR John A JR
Box 2557, Sun Valley, ID 83353
Marshall MRS Pendleton (MacDonald—Frances Townsend)
☎ (802) 824-6309 . . Riverside Farm, Boynton Rd, RR 1, Box 97B, Londonderry, VT 05148
Marshall MR & MRS Peter E (Wood—Laurette B ☎ (516) 676-2745
Milask) . . . . "The Barn"
JUNIORS MR Jonathan P . . . . 10 Frost Pond Rd, Locust Valley, NY 11560
Marshall MR & MRS Thornton W (Farrell—Carolann ☎ (602) 814-7852
Frost) . . . . "High Noon"
MISS Courtney D'E . . . . 961 N Criss St,
MISS Kristin A Farrell . . . . Chandler, AZ 85226
Marston MR & MRS Hunter S 3d (Helen D Williams)
☎ (401) 348-8904 . . "Aloha Cottage" Aloha Rd, Watch Hill, RI 02891
Marston MR & MRS Thomas Atherton (Josephine Heron Jellett)
☎ (704) 274-8528 . . 4 Briarknoll Court, Park Av, Asheville, NC 28803
Martin MR Benjamin . . . . ☎ (860) 442-3004
MISS Anne T . . . . "The Quail's Nest"
MISS Roberta E . . . . 62 Shore Rd,
MR Briton . . . . Waterford, CT 06385
Martin MR Crozer W . . see H B W Hoffman
Martin MISS Duart M . . see MRS E M Pollock
Martin MR & MRS Edward J (Schwefel—Chambers—Grace L Beer)
☎ (516) 665-5555 . . "The Admiralty" 73 Harbour Lane, Bay Shore, NY 11706
Martin MR & MRS Guy (Edith K Gould) . . . . ☎ (914) 586-2892
MISS Theodosia Burr . . . . "Kingslodge"
Dry Brook Rd, Arkville, NY 12406
Martin MR & MRS H Curtiss (Virginia W Drewry)
☎ (516) 537-1190 . . Georgica Association, Wainscott, NY 11975
Martin MRS Hollinshead T (Abbott—Elinor R Hay)
☎ (303) 670-9811 . . 2338 Hearth Dv, Evergreen, CO 80439
Martin MISS Josephine C
☎ (540) 687-4147 . . "Sweet Grass" Rte 1, Box 165, Middleburg, VA 22117
Martin MR Lee Gwynne
☎ (516) 537-1190 . . "Lane's Turning" Wainscott, NY 11975
Martin MR & MRS Malcolm Van D (Moffit—Nancy B Webb)
☎ (441) 293-2479 . . "Calico House" 7 Glebe Hill, Tucker's Town HS 02, Bermuda
Martin MR & MRS Middleton Ansley (Anne K ☎ (406) 995-4908
Newhard) . . . . Trapper's Cabin
MISS Anne W . . . . Ranch,
MISS Virginia U . . . . Gallatin Gateway,
MISS Margot H . . . . MT 59730
MR Middleton A JR . . . .
Martin MR & MRS Oliver (Ellen Allen)
☎ (508) 428-6138 . . "Bayberry" 1267 Main St, Cotuit, MA 02635
Martin MRS Robert W (Black—Virginia Uihlein)
☎ (406) 995-4908 . . Trapper's Cabin Ranch, PO Box 267, Gallatin Gateway, MT 59730
Martin LT COL & MRS W Swift (Ellen M Wills) USA.
☎ (302) 227-4365 . . "Cedar Knoll" 21 Rolling Rd, Henlopen Acres, Rehoboth Beach, DE 19971
Martinez MR & MRS Roman 4th (Helena E Hackley) ☎ (516) 922-2149
JUNIOR MISS Helena C . . . . Planting Fields Rd,
JUNIOR MR Roman 5th . . . . Upper Brookville, NY 11771
Marvel MR & MRS Hunter M (Camilla S McKisson) . ☎ (401) 322-8989
MISS Genevieve M . . . . 47 Chapman Rd,
MR Hunter M JR . . . . Weekapaug, RI 02891
Marvel MR James M D . . see W B Denham JR
Marvel MISS Jennifer V
☎ (401) 596-5990 . . "Robin's Nest" 1 Turtleback Rd, Watch Hill, RI 02891
Marvin MRS Camilla (Behn—Weinmann—Camilla Marvin)
☎ (603) 563-8488 . . Box 313, Dublin, NH 03444
Marx MR & MRS Graham A (Louise McVickar) . . . . ☎ (508) 627-8688
MISS Elizabeth McK . . . . Edgartown, MA
MR Alexander R 02539
Marx MR Graham E
Port Sandfield, Muskoka, Ontario P0B 1K0, Canada
Marx MR & MRS Louis JR (Helen Zanetti)
☎ (914) 232-5024 . . Nash Rd, Goldens Bridge, NY 10526
Maschal MR & MRS John R (Maribell R Whetstone) ☎ (609) 492-2872
⚓ 1100 West Av,
MR John Bell . . . . Beach Haven, NJ
MR Peter Roberts 08008
Mashek MRS Chandler C (Montgomery—A ☎ (516) 283-5895
Chandler Cox) . . . . PO Box 2610,
JUNIORS MR Grant E . . . . Southampton, NY 11969
Mashek MR John D JR . . . . ☎ (505) 986-8627
MISS Lauren L . . . . 213 Tano Rd, Santa Fe, NM 87501

Mason MRS Mary T (Mary E Terry) . . . . ☎ (302) 227-7965
  MISS Alexandra T . . . . 20 Park Av,
  MISS Peyton R . . . . Rehoboth Beach, DE *19971*

Mason MR & MRS Robert C (Martha A Goodyear)
  ☎ (207) 644-8141 . . Box 153, Christmas Cove, South Bristol, ME *04568*

Mason MR & MRS Scott C (Carolyn Amos)
  ☎ (508) 281-0980 . . 10 Highland Av, Annisquam, MA *01930*

Massey MR & MRS Calvin R (Martha C Miller)
  ☎ (604) 335-2031 . . Hornby Island, BC V0R 1Z0, Canada

Massey MR Jay Richardson JR
  ☎ (011-44-171) 835-1234 . . 17F Nevern Square, London SW5 9PD, England

Masten MR John E
  ☎ (716) 394-4734 . . 3650 E Lake Rd, Canandaigua, NY *14424*

Masters DR & MRS William H (Becker—Oliver—Geraldine H Baker)
  ☎ (518) 891-0988 . . ''Serenescene'' Gabriels Rd, Box 10, Onchiota, NY *12989*

Mastin MRS Carroll S (Laura Baumgarten)
  ☎ (414) 868-3378 . . PO Box 76, Fish Creek, WI *54212*

Mateer MR & MRS G Diehl JR (Hentz—Eldredge—Ann N Lohmann)
  ☎ (540) 364-3101 . . ''Tirvelda Farms'' Box 111, Middleburg, VA *22117*

Mather MRS Charles E 2d (Miller—Catherine M Haas)
  ☎ (518) 587-2292 . . ''Overlook'' Trombly Rd, RD 1, Stillwater, NY *12170*

Mather MR & MRS Thomas W (Gatch—Brodhead—Elizabeth A Lamy)
  ☎ (704) 526-3256 . . ''Snailspace'' Rte 1, Box 226, Highlands, NC *28741*

Matheson MR & MRS Finlay L (Lucretia G Brooks)
  ☎ (207) 276-5072 . . Seal Harbor, ME *04675*

Matheson MR & MRS William L (Bard—Marjorie Anderson)
  ☎ (516) 922-4407 . . 147 Heather Lane, Mill Neck, NY *11765*

Mathews MISS Barbara R . . see D R Arthur

Mathews MR & MRS Charles P (Wendy E Graham)
  ☎ (717) 646-2434 . . Pocono Lake Preserve, PA *18348*

Mathews MR & MRS Richard A (Anne P Powell)
  ☎ (908) 774-6196 . . ''Whimsea'' 320 First Av, Avon-By-The-Sea, NJ *07717*

Mathews MR & MRS Robert W (Margaret B Prindle)
  ☎ (207) 729-3681 . . Cundys Harbor, ME *04011*

Mathias MR & MRS Charles McC JR (Ann Hickling Bradford)
  Birch Point, Isle au Haut, ME *04645*

Mathieu MRS Charles L JR (Barbara Bedford)
  ☎ (516) 283-1835 . . 21 Huntting St, Southampton, NY *11968*

Mathieu MR Charles L JR
  ☎ (516) 287-5681 . . 214 Hill St, Southampton, NY *11968*

Mattei MR & MRS Peter O (Shewell—Carmelita Romano)
  ''Mattei's Aspen House'' Squaw Valley, CA *93675*

Matthews MR & MRS Charles L 3d (Barbara S Standish) . . ☎ (517) 738-8787
  MISS Mary B . . . . 1973 Cliff Rd,
  MR Charles L . . . . Pointe-Aux-Barques, Port Austin, MI *48467*

Matthiessen MR Erard A
  ☎ (516) 788-7434 . . PO Box 396, Fishers Island, NY *06390*

Mattis MR & MRS Stephen van S (Mary Christy Bohn) . . . . ☎ (314) 365-6319
  JUNIORS MISS Virginia B . . . . 602 Carol Rd,
  JUNIORS MISS Hilary H . . . . Lake Ozark, MO *65049*

Mattison MR & MRS Joseph JR (Elizabeth Moir)
  ☎ (508) 428-2848 . . 936 Sea View Av, Osterville, MA *02655*

Mattison MR & MRS Joseph 3d (Alice C Donahue) ⚓
  Box 965, Edgartown, MA *02539*

Mattison MR & MRS Mark H (Karel D Oliver) . . . . . ☎ (508) 627-8179
  MISS Delphine . . . . ''Sweetened Water
  MISS Alissa . . . . Farm'' Edgartown,
  MR Graham . . . . MA *02539*

Mattison MR & MRS Peter D (Rebecca G Wells)
  ☎ (603) 367-8261 . . ''Joy Farm'' Silver Lake, NH *03875*

Mattsson MR & MRS N Christer (Lynch—Deborah W Lippincott)
  ☎ (401) 423-0886 . . Box 197, Jamestown, RI *02835*

Mawicke MR Frederick H . . see S E Brinckerhoff

Maxwell MR George L—⚓
  ☎ (207) 460-2683 . . on board Tristram'' PO Box 386, Bass Harbor, ME *04653-0386*

Maxwell MR & MRS John C JR (Adrienne d'A Leichtle)
  ☎ (207) 244-9073 . . ''Linn Mor'' Mt Desert, ME *04660*

Maxwell MISS Linda S
  ☎ (203) 938-8770 . . 117 Umpawaug Rd, West Redding, CT *06896*

May DR & MRS George A JR (Beth H Butler)
  ☎ (207) 244-3404 . . Manset, ME *04656*

May MR & MRS J Denny (Meriam—Kathryn Arns)
  ☎ (216) 975-9691 . . ''Pepperidge Farm'' 189 Northridge Dv, Willoughby, OH *44094*

May MR & MRS James G G (Michele M Georger)
  ⚓ . . . . ☎ (905) 894-2287
                                                                          753 Point Abino Rd,
  MISS Michele G . . . . South Ridgeway,
  MR James G G JR . . . . Ontario L0S 1N0, Canada

May MR & MRS William B JR (Wiles—Jeanne C Atkinson) . . . . ☎ (516) 788-7498
                                                                         ''Spinnaker Run''
  MR William T . . . . Fishers Island, NY *06390*

May MR & MRS William F (Kathleen H Thompson) ⚓
  ☎ (207) 236-8157 . . ''Liberty Cottage'' 90 Beauchamp Point Rd, PO Box 62, Rockport, ME *04856*

Maybank MR Francis P . . . . Box 52, Flat Rock,
  MISS Alexis M . . . . NC *28731*
  JUNIORS MISS Helena E R . . . .

Maybank MR & MRS John P F (Marina Rancic)
  ☎ (704) 692-0900 . . 33 Trenholm Rd, Flat Rock, NC *28731*

Mayer MRS John (Helen E Shumway)
  ☎ (802) 484-3380 . . ''Spring Brook Farm'' RR 1, Box 141, Reading, VT *05062*

Mayer MRS John A (Effie F Disston)
☎ (412) 593-2410 . . "Woodridge" Box 633, Ligonier, PA *15658*
Mayfield MR & MRS Glover B (Soule—Gale Smith)
☎ (508) 526-1428 . . "Edgewood" 26 Old Neck Rd, Manchester, MA *01944*
Maynard DR & MRS Edwin P (Elizabeth S Simonds)
☎ (207) 883-6649 . . Checkley Point, Prouts Neck, ME *04074*
Maynard MR & MRS Walter JR (Swords—Jane F Henderson) ⚓ . . . .
    MISS Deirdre H Swords . . . .
    ☎ (516) 324-6123 Box 1382, Georgica Rd, East Hampton, NY *11937*
Mayne MR & MRS Stephen S (Linda Furst) . . . .
    MR Michael . . . .
    ☎ (415) 461-5477 41 Elizabeth Circle, Greenbrae, CA *94904*
Mead MRS Nelson S (Ruth D Cummings)
☎ (513) 299-4225 . . 680 W David Rd, Dayton, OH *45429*
Meaders MR & MRS Paul Le Sourd (Jane Dickely) . .
    MR Paul Le S 3d . . . .
    ☎ (516) 283-3253 PO Box 2623, 120 Bishops Lane, Southampton, NY *11969*
Means MRS Marian D (Marian Donald)
☎ (508) 994-5824 . . Nonquitt, MA *02748*
Medina MR & MRS Harold R 3d (Pamela C Huck)
☎ (516) 288-3148 . . 9 Apaucuck Point Lane, Westhampton, NY *11977*
Medina MR Standish Forde— ⚓
☎ (516) 288-1655 . . 1 Apaucuck Point Lane, Westhampton, NY *11977*
Medina MR & MRS Standish Forde JR (Kathryn L Bach)
☎ (516) 288-3873 . . "Still To Windward" Box 210, 5 Apaucuck Point Lane, Westhampton, NY *11977*
Meehan MR & MRS Michael J 2d (Jenkins—Carr—Sandra Gotham)
☎ (516) 283-7585 . . "Mungo Hall" 451 Hill St, Southampton, NY *11968*
Meek MR & MRS George H (Cynthia A Martin) . . . .
    MISS Lissa H . . . .
    MISS Tally A . . . .
    JUNIORS MR John M . . . .
    ☎ (916) 541-2993 2088 Cascade Rd, South Lake Tahoe, CA *95731*
Meek MR & MRS Samuel W JR (Dunn—Appleby—Marjorie Meacham)
☎ (203) 661-5604 . . Box 7732, Greenwich, CT *06836-7732*
Meem MR & MRS Gilbert S JR (Knight Patterson) . . .
    JUNIORS MR Gilbert S 3d . . . .
    ☎ (516) 283-0503 "Four Walls" 30 Wall St, Southampton, NY *11968*
Megowen MR & MRS William J (Alicia Barbour)
"Sea Fields" Chester, Nova Scotia B0J 1J0, Canada
Mehegan MRS Gay (Gay Griscom) . . . .
    MISS Tara B . . . .
    MR Sean C . . . .
    MR Eben J . . . .
    ☎ (207) 639-2781 "The Yellow House" E Madrid Rd, Phillips, ME *04966*
Mehlman DR & MRS Robert D (Mary A Caner)
☎ (508) 526-4644 . . 373 Summer St, Manchester, MA *01944*
Mehran JUNIORS MR Alexander R JR . . see MISS L B Watson
Mehran MISS Annabel M . . see MISS L B Watson

Mehta MR & MRS Ved P (Linn F C Cary) ⚓
☎ (207) 734-8185 . . HC 60, Box 93, Dark Harbor, Islesboro, ME *04848*
Meier CAPT & MRS Louis L (DONNA Eleonora Tomacelli-Filomarino) USN.
☎ (401) 849-4136 . . "Black Point Farm" 715 Indian Av, Portsmouth, RI *02871*
Meigs MR & MRS Henry (Sara L Willis) . . . .
    MR John B Averell . . . .
    ☎ (516) 653-8117 "Creek Cottage" 116 Montauk H'way, Quogue, NY *11959*
Meigs DR & MRS J Wister (Camilla K Riggs)
☎ (508) 548-0709 . . "Juniper" Box 33, Woods Hole, MA *02543*
Meigs MR & MRS S Willis (Deborah R Wyatt) . . . . .
    JUNIORS MISS Lauren W . . . .
    ☎ (516) 653-8117 "Creek Cottage" 116 Montauk H'way, Quogue, NY *11959*
Meihuizen MR Nicolaas J van
☎ (011-44-1252) 7133-58 . . "Oak Trees" Echo Barn Lane, Farnham, Surrey GU10 4NL, England
Meinfelder MR & MRS Edmond L 2d (Anderson—Edith S Blake) . . . .
    MISS Elizabeth S Anderson . . . .
    ☎ (610) 933-3597 "Gunncroft" PO Box 61, Kimberton, PA *19442*
Melen DR & MRS Roger D (Williams—Arlene H Camm) . . . .
    JUNIORS MISS Michelle A . . . .
    JUNIORS MR Samuel A F Williams . . . .
    JUNIORS MR Nicholas C Williams . . . .
    ☎ (707) 994-0399 Windflower Point, Clearlake, CA *95422*
Mellgard MR & MRS David M (Georgiana J Slade)
☎ (516) 324-0145 . . Middle Lane, East Hampton, NY *11937*
Mellon MR & MRS Armour N (Sophie C Annibali)
☎ (412) 238-8418 . . Rte 381, Rector, PA *15657*
Mellon MRS Charles H 3d (Katherine P Hopkins) . .
    MR Charles H JR . . . .
    ☎ (207) 276-5094 "Forestay" Northeast Harbor, ME *04662*
Mellon MR Henry C S— ⚓
☎ (207) 244-5035 . . Greyweather Farm, Seal Cove, ME *04674*
Mellon MR Matthew T . . see J R Bright
Melville MR & MRS John A (Lee A Deters)
☎ (616) 386-5288 . . Fire Lane 7, Omena, MI *49674*
Melville MR & MRS John W (Jane Akin)
☎ (616) 386-5288 . . Fire Lane 7, Omena, MI *49674*
Menges MR & MRS Carl B (Cordelia Sykes) . . . .
    MR Benjamin W . . . .
    MR Samuel G . . . .
    ☎ (516) 324-3435 "Hook Pond House" Box 447, East Hampton, NY *11937*
Menocal MR & MRS Enrique V (Rosa E Delmás)
☎ (809) 772-0495 . . "Castaways" Cottages-by-the-Sea, Frederiksted, St Croix, VI *00840*
Menzies MR & MRS John T 3d (Julia M Baker) . . . . .
    JUNIORS MISS Mary C . . . .
    JUNIORS MR John B . . . .
    ☎ (518) 891-4719 Camp Sunrise, Boat Rte, Saranac Lake, NY *12983*

Merck MR & MRS Albert W (Katharine M Evarts)
 ☎ (508) 758-6227 . . ''Gull Barn'' 16 Ned's Point Rd, Mattapoisett, MA *02739*
Meredith MR William Morris
 ☎ (860) 848-8486 . . ''Riverrun'' 337 Kitemaug Rd, Uncasville, CT *06382*
Merle-Smith REV & MRS Van Santvoord JR (Combs—Katherine P N Smith)
 ☎ (518) 576-4748 . . ''Pinecrest'' Keene Valley, NY *12943*
Merrill MR & MRS Arthur C JR (Monique J Vos)
 ☎ (516) 283-0805 . . 2 Whitefields, 155 Hill St, Southampton, NY *11968*
Merrill MR & MRS Barrant V (Martha E Page)
 ☎ (401) 348-3036 . . ''Crows Nest'' 11 Nepun Rd, Watch Hill, RI *02891*
Merrill MR & MRS John L JR (Helen B R Swan)
 ☎ (207) 244-3426 . . ''Mile End'' Islesford, ME *04646*
Merrill MR & MRS Robert A (Christina O Bushkin)
 ☎ (516) 671-4402 . . 11 Valley Rd, Locust Valley, NY *11560*
Merrill MR & MRS Robert G (Vernon Lynch)
 ☎ (518) 359-9316 . . Big Wolf, Tupper Lake, NY *12986*

Merrill MR & MRS Steven L (Judy P Stewart) . . . . . . JUNIORS MR John S	☎ (916) 583-3333 PO Box 661, Tahoe City, CA *96145*

Merriman MR & MRS David W (Virginia Anderson)
  MISS Serena A . . . .
  JUNIORS MR Charles A . . . .
	☎ (401) 635-8579
	''Sealands''
	82 Warren's Point
	Rd, Little Compton,
	RI *02837*

Merriman MRS M Heminway (Natalie-Smith Rowbottom) . . . . MISS Natalie-Smith	☎ (401) 322-8875 ''Windfall'' 3 Waxcadowa Av, Weekapaug, RI *02891*

Merriman MR & MRS M Heminway 2d (Linda J Lane) . . . .
  MISS Hillary C . . . .
  MR M Heminway 3d . . . .
	☎ (401) 322-0270
	''Shady Lane''
	Waxcadowa Av,
	Weekapaug, RI
	02891

Merritt CAPT Robert G—USN.
 ☎ (413) 528-4913 . . ''White Pines'' Box 131, South Egremont, MA *01258*
Merryman MR & MRS Adrian H (Moylan—Joan M Corrigan)
 ☎ (410) 886-2579 . . Sherwood, MD *21665*
Merwin MR David U
 ☎ (309) 378-2561 . . ''Hopewell'' RR 1, Box 184, Bloomington, IL *61704*
Mesnard DR & MRS (DR) William J (Ann W Lucas)
 ☎ (908) 899-1078 . . 1219 Bay Av, Mantoloking, NJ *08738*
Messimer MRS W Gilbert (Juliet W Harrison)
 ☎ (802) 375-9716 . . ''Tory Lane'' PO Box 556, Arlington, VT *05250*
Mestres MR & MRS Ricardo A JR (Ann Farnsworth)
 ☎ (908) 899-1889 . . 757 East Av, Bay Head, NJ *08742*
Metcalf MR & MRS John R (Catherine J Rolph)
 ☎ (916) 525-7778 . . Homewood, CA *95718*
Metcalf MR & MRS Manton B 3d (Teresa D Peabody)
 ☎ (603) 924-7220 . . 161 E Mountain Rd, Peterborough, NH *03458*
Metcalf MRS Richard G (Dorothy R Anson)
 ☎ (802) 253-8807 . . Elmore Mountain Rd, Morrisville, VT *05661*
Metcalf MR & MRS S Warren (Joan Pressprich)
 ☎ (203) 259-1399 . . 92 Center St, Southport, CT *06490*
Metcalf MR & MRS Thomas N JR (Patricia A Thompson)
 ☎ (508) 993-8527 . . PO Box P15, South Dartmouth, MA *02748*

Metcalfe MR & MRS James W (Elizabeth C Brokaw)
  MISS Elizabeth C . . . .
  MR James K B . . . .
	Blackberry Hill,
	Defiance, MO *63341*

Mettler MR & MRS John W III (Goodrich—Cornelia Daley) . . . .
  MISS Melinda W . . . .
  MISS Catherine D Goodrich . . . .
	☎ (516) 788-7334
	Fishers Island, NY
	06390

Mettler MRS Nancy K (Nancy K King)
 Aug 1 . . ☎ (516) 788-7854 . . Fishers Island, NY *06390*
Metz MR & MRS Richard E (Muriel Gurdon Howells)
 ☎ (207) 439-4364 . . 9 Lawrence Lane, Kittery Point, ME *03905*
Metz REV & MRS Ronald I (Helen Chapin)
 ☎ (207) 276-5473 . . ''Runningpoint'' Seal Harbor, ME *04675*

Metzger MR & MRS J William JR (Perry—Anne D Grant) . . . .
  MR Nathaniel D Perry . . . .
  JUNIORS MR David H Perry . . . .
	Northeast Harbor,
	ME *04662*

Meyer MR Christopher H . . see MRS R Ducas
Meyer MISS Eliza F . . see W G von Weise JR
Meyer MR & MRS Henry von L JR (Babinski—Barbara E Osborn)
 ☎ (516) 537-0972 . . 20 Beach Lane, Box 660, Wainscott, NY *11975*

Meyer MR & MRS Ulrich D (Marion C Schoellkopf) . MISS Ulrike A	of ☎ (011-41-81) 341294 ''Cresta Stquoira'' 7078 Lenzerheide, Switzerland ☎ (011-41-1) 781-38-33 Halbinsel Au, 8804 Au, Zürich, Switzerland

Meynell MR & MRS David B (Margaret A Shotton) . .
  MISS Andrea M . . . .
  MISS Christina M . . . .
  MR Robert A S . . . .
	''d'Marc Farm''
	Cobourg, Ontario,
	Canada

Michahelles MRS Caroline Burton E (Caroline B Ewing)
 ☎ (011-39-55) 225-478 . . via Bellosguardo 20, 50124 Florence, Italy

Michel MR & MRS Clifford L (Betsy Shirley) . . . . . .
  MISS Katherine B . . . .
  MR Jason L . . . .
	☎ (508) 257-4128
	Box 231,
	Siasconset, MA
	02564

Michel MISS Julienne M
 ☎ (505) 982-5782 . . 215 Paseo De La Tierra, Santa Fe, NM *87501*
Michelsen MRS Katherine K (Katherine Ann Killgallon)
 ☎ (912) 638-4238 . . ''Ballie Nicol Jarvie'' Cottage 238, Sea Island, GA *31561*
Middleton MR & MRS David (Reed—Joan Bartlett)
 ☎ (508) 432-5035 . . 13 Harbor Rd, Harwich Port, MA *02646*
Middleton MR & MRS Henry B (Condon—Payne W Payson)
 ☎ (011-39-55) 854-7970 . . ''Le Caselle'' 50022 Greve in Chianti, Italy

Milbank MRS Robbins (Helen P Kirkpatrick)
☎ (603) 847-3292 . . Box 620, Nelson Village, Munsonville, NH *03457*
Milbank MR & MRS Samuel L (Dominique Detay) . . | ☎ (518) 589-6272
MISS Nathalie . . . . | Onteora Park,
JUNIORS MR Thomas . . . . | Tannersville, NY *12485*
Milbury MR & MRS Edwin Van R (Henderson—Cassandra K Mellon)
☎ (508) 548-1710 . . Long House, Penzance Point, Woods Hole, MA *02543*
Milbury MR & MRS K David (Edith E Nelson)
☎ (207) 288-9544 . . "Villa Mary" 77 Eden St, Bar Harbor, ME *04609*
Millard MR & MRS John A (Carey B French) . . . . . . | ☎ (516) 537-0337
MR John A JR . . . . | Matthews Lane,
MR James G . . . . | Bridgehampton,
MR Alexander F . . . . | NY *11932*
Millard MR & MRS Richard D (Kathleen S Traynor)
☎ (516) 749-4261 . . "Crosspatch" 32 S Menantic St, Box 339, Shelter Island Heights, NY *11965*
Miller MRS Andrew Otterson JR (Jeanne L White)
☎ (516) 692-2893 . . "Ducks Landing" 1452 Ridge Rd, Laurel Hollow, Syosset, NY *11791*
Miller MR & MRS Barton H (Marion J Becker)
☎ (413) 243-0112 . . "Red House" Spring St, Lee, MA *01238*
Miller MRS Carroll T (Inganni—Sachs—Carroll R | ☎ (401) 783-5530
Townsend) . . . . | 1591 Commodore
MISS Sarah T . . . . | Perry H'way,
JUNIORS MR Andrew D . . . . | Wakefield, RI *02879*
JUNIORS MR Jared W . . . . |
Miller MR & MRS Clay Lowell (Ellen E Green)
Boonethea Hill, Ukiah Rd, Comptche, CA *95427*
Miller MR & MRS Courtlandt G (Gina M Salvatore)
☎ (516) 692-6889 . . "Unstable" 1448 Ridge Rd, Laurel Hollow, Syosset, NY *11791*
Miller DR & MRS David H (Patricia C Hancock)
☎ (802) 824-4330 . . Box 143, Peru, VT *05152*
Miller MR & MRS Donald K (Priscilla C Barker) . . . . | ☎ (203) 622-0544
MR Prescott C . . . . | "Jamais Fini"
JUNIORS MR Barclay St J . . . . | 588 Round Hill Rd, Greenwich, CT *06831*
Miller REV & MRS Edward O (Ann H Lackman)
☎ (207) 326-4367 . . Perkins St, Castine, ME *04421*
Miller MR & MRS Edward Terhune (Noël C Clark) . . | ☎ (518) 576-4385
MISS Virginia C . . . . | Box 678,
MR Edward G S . . . . | Keene Valley, NY *12943*
Miller MR & MRS Eric T (Spencer—Susan Williams)
☎ (508) 255-2148 . . Box 206, East Orleans, MA *02643*
Miller MRS H Wisner JR (Riley—Palmer—Barbara Clapp)
☎ (508) 945-3974 . . "Harbor View" 15 Barcliff Av Ext, Chatham, MA *02633*
Miller MR & MRS Leigh M (Lynden R Breed) . . . . . | ☎ (860) 364-0244
MR Marshall L . . . . | Calkinstown Rd, Sharon, CT *06069*

Miller MR & MRS Michael (Edith duP Riegel) . . . . . | ☎ (410) 778-5717
MISS Edith H . . . . | 5268 Quaker Neck Rd, Chestertown, MD *21620*
Miller MR & MRS Norman H (Haight—Nellie I | Kennebunkport, ME
Fitzgerald) . . . . | *04046*
MR David C Haight . . . . |
Miller MR & MRS Paul L (Adèle Olyphant) ⚓
Aug 1 . . ☎ (207) 276-5516 . . "Aerie" Northeast Harbor, ME *04662*
Miller MR & MRS Peter F (Ridgely—Julie D S | ☎ (860) 567-4667
Ripley) . . . . | 55 Duck Pond Rd,
JUNIORS MISS Mary McN . . . . | Litchfield, CT *06759*
JUNIORS MR Peter D . . . . |
JUNIORS MISS Laura L Ridgely . . . . |
Miller MR & MRS Randolph L (Janet K Warner) . . . . | ☎ (503) 738-9330
MISS Kelsey A . . . . | 101—5 St, Gearhart,
MISS Haley E . . . . | OR *97138*
Miller MRS Robert (Victoria E Pearson) . . . . | ☎ (518) 589-5870
MR Robert P . . . . | "The Birches"
MR Christopher Y . . . . | Onteora Park, Tannersville, NY *12485*
Miller JUNIORS MR Robert B . . see W P Jones
Miller MR & MRS Robert J (Adrienne Agardy)
Box 58, Fishers Island, NY *06390*
Miller MR Robert J 3d . . see D G Anderson
Miller MR & MRS Robert N 3d (Elizabeth T Broome) . . . . | ☎ (508) 428-2318
MR & MRS James J Chrismen (Leslie S Miller) | "Breezy Bluff" 135 Bridge St, Osterville, MA *02655*
Miller MR & MRS Stanley R JR (Stillman—Frances M Mason)
☎ (207) 359-4468 . . "Rice Cottage" Hamilton Shore, Rte 175, Blue Hill Falls, ME *04615*
Miller MR & MRS Thomas W C (Miller—Loraine | ☎ (401) 348-8106
Laughlin MacDougall) . . . . | "East Dunes"
MISS Katherine A . . . . | Watch Hill, RI *02891*
MR T Wilson C . . . . |
MR Jason E B . . . . |
Miller MR & MRS Walter R JR (Joan M Groark) . . . . | ☎ (516) 537-0872
MISS Kathryn A . . . . | Bridge Lane,
MISS Meghan E . . . . | Bridgehampton, NY
MISS Jennifer M . . . . | *11932*
JUNIORS MR Walter R 3d . . . . |
Miller MR & MRS William R (Fowler—Black—Emma Gillespie)
☎ (516) 239-5823 . . 121 Berkshire Place, Lawrence, NY *11559*
Miller MR Willis McCook JR
☎ (705) 764-1393 . . Beaumaris, Lake Muskoka, Ontario P0B 1B0, Canada
Millet MR & MRS David F (Christina W Moore) ⚓ | ☎ (207) 283-1373
MR Alexander C . . . . | 22 Lester B Orcutt
JUNIORS MISS Katharine W . . . . | Blvd, Biddeford Pool, ME *04006*
Milliken MR & MRS Christopher C (Nancy Ryerson) . . | ☎ (516) 788-7428
MISS Kate R . . . . | East End Rd,
MR Christopher C JR . . . . | Fishers Island, NY *06390*

Milliken Mr & Mrs Gerrish H (Winslow—Phoebe T Goodhue)
 ☎ (207) 276-5436 . . "The Haven" Northeast Harbor, ME *04662*
Milliken Mr & Mrs Minot K (Hovey—Clark—Norris—Armene Lamson)
 ☎ (207) 288-3303 . . "Northern Lights" Hulls Cove, ME *04644*
Milliken Mrs Seth M (Knapp—Gloria Walker)
 ☎ (207) 633-4747 . . "Two Deck Wonder" West Southport, ME *04576*
Millington Mr & Mrs George P Jr (Patricia Cooney)
 ☎ (610) 645-8678 . . Waverly Heights Villa 29, 1400 Waverly Rd, Gladwyne, PA *19035*
Mills Mrs James Paul (Alice F du Pont)
 ☎ (540) 687-6209 . . "Hickory Tree Farm" Box 125, Middleburg, VA *20118*

Milton Mr & Mrs A Fenner (Stanton—Ina M Orwicz)	☎ (207) 276-5450 "Norman"
Miss Elizabeth H	804 Dodge Point Rd, Seal Harbor, ME *04675*

Miner Mr & Mrs Charles Jr (Mae D Hoffman)
 ☎ (203) 655-4145 . . 40 Horseshoe Rd, Darien, CT *06820*
Minevitz Mr & Mrs Bruce H (Katherine R Cunningham)
 ☎ (508) 758-2759 . . "Weetucket" 5 Freeman St, Mattapoisett, MA *02739*
Minor Mr & Mrs R Lance (Mary H Gregg)
 ☎ (518) 654-6280 . . "Brier Patch" Box 662, County Rte 10, Corinth, NY *12822*
Minot Mr & Mrs Henry W Jr (Elizabeth M Cabot)
 ☎ (207) 867-4655 . . North Haven, ME *04853*
Minot Mrs Otis N (E Louise Gross)
 ☎ (207) 725-6025 . . 1082 Merepoint Rd, Brunswick, ME *04011*

Minott Mr & Mrs Joseph A Jr (Lorraine D Lukens) .	☎ (207) 276-5404
Miss Elizabeth	Northeast Harbor,
Mr John H C	ME *04662*

Minton Mr & Mrs Dwight C (Marian H Haines)
 ☎ (406) 995-2632 . . Elkhorn Ranch, 33133 Gallatin Rd, Gallatin Gateway, MT *59730*
Minton Mr & Mrs G V Morton (Lloyd McKee)
 ☎ (970) 641-1032 . . 12855 Taylor River Rd, H'way 742, Almont, CO *81210*
Miranda Mr César
 Seal Harbor, ME *04675*

Mitchell Mr & Mrs Henry B (Diana C H Learmonth).	☎ (401) 635-4512 PO Box 26,
Mr James L	Adamsville, RI *02801*

Mitchell Mr & Mrs MacNeil (Katherine McGowin)
 ☎ (516) AM7-3610 . . "Elmshade" Meeting House Lane, Amagansett, NY *11930*

Mitchell Mr & Mrs Roland G (Virginia S Watkins) .	☎ (207) 244-5873
Miss Virginia P	"Little Eagle Point" Box 120, Mt Desert, ME *04660*

Mitchell Mr & Mrs Walter B (Nancy A Denebeim)
 28 F R Lillie Rd, Woods Hole, MA *02540*
Mittendorf Mrs W Frederick (Canham—Eleanor S Shaw)
 ☎ (508) 295-6338 . . Cedar Point, Wareham, MA *02571*

Mitton Mr & Mrs Michael A (Marilyn K Bowen)
 ☎ (541) 994-9539 . . "Casa Pacifica" PO Box 982, Lincoln City, OR *97367*
Mitton Mrs Ralph W (Stone—Ann-Louise von Pilarz)
 ☎ (802) 496-2326 . . "Cider Hill" Box 135, Warren, VT *05674*
Mixter Mr & Mrs Peter J (Nancy G Schaefer)
 ☎ (516) 583-7043 . . House 135, Point O'Woods, NY *11706*
Moffitt Dr & Mrs Herbert C (Gwynne Reed)
 ☎ (707) 944-2391 . . "M-Ranch" Box 2588, Yountville, CA *94599*
Mogan Mr & Mrs Richard F 3d (Gross—Keon—Sally Tuttle)
 ☎ (307) 733-7380 . . 6625 Upper Cascades Dv, Jackson, WY *83001*
Mohun Mr & Mrs Charles Leon (Ann C Harris)
 ☎ (011-61-66) 857-513 . . "The Hawk" Pandanus Place, Wategos Beach, Byron Bay, NSW, Australia
Moller Mr & Mrs Kenneth Jr (Marion Collin)
 ☎ (207) 967-5700 . . Haverhill St, Kennebunkport, ME *04046*
Moncrief Mr & Mrs William Alvin Jr (Johnson—Deborah Beggs)
 ☎ (970) 641-0168 . . Moncrief River Ranch, Gunnison, CO *81230*

Mongendre Mr & Mrs Gérard (Sandra P Smith) . . .	☎ (011-33)
Juniors Miss Nina.	30-55-94-34 4 rue Maurice Barrés La Boissière, 78370 Plaisir, France

Montague Mr & Mrs Edward (Dianne C Tankoos)
 ☎ (914) 677-5306 . . "Milesend" Milewood Rd, RD 2, Box 140, Millbrook, NY *12545*

Montague Mr Robert L 3d	☎ (804) 758-2663
Miss Anne S M.	"Sandwich"
Mr Robert L 4th	PO Box 327, Urbanna, VA *23175*

Montgomery Mr & Mrs Archibald R 3d (Anita C Packard)	☎ (518) 891-3489 "Heron's Landing"
Mr & Mrs Archibald R 4th (Phyllis C Sponberg)	Saranac Lake, NY *12983*

Montgomery Mr & Mrs J Anthony (Virginia E Haynes)
 ☎ (914) 666-5611 . . "Crows Nest" Crow Hill Rd, Mt Kisco, NY *10549*
Montgomery Mr & Mrs John L 2d (Natalie M Moore)
 ☎ (516) 583-8712 . . Cottage 68, Point O'Woods, NY *11706*
Montgomery Mr & Mrs Parker G (Yorke—Lane Harvey)
 ☎ (805) 684-0877 . . 4036 Foothill Rd, Carpinteria, CA *93013*
Montross Mr & Mrs Franklin 3d (Helen L Mohr)
 ☎ (508) 945-4145 . . Box 215, North Chatham, MA *02650*
Montross Mr & Mrs Franklin 4th (Laura Lee Eifert)
 ☎ (508) 945-5665 . . 168 Stage Harbor Rd, Chatham, MA *02633*
Moore Mr & Mrs A Preston (Nathalie C Hague)
 ☎ (508) 349-2783 . . 975 Chequesset Neck Rd, Wellfleet, MA *02667*
Moore Mr C Wickham
 ☎ (011-33-1) 45-51-63-91 . . 5 rue de Champagny, 75007 Paris, France
Moore Mrs Charles A 3d (Hon Sheila Digby)
 ☎ (011-353-22) 21568 . . Bearforest House, Mallow, Co Cork, Ireland

Moore Mr & Mrs Douglas G (Margaret G Gibbs) . .	☎ (415) 663-9360
Mr Mark A	Inverness, CA *94937*

Moore Mr & Mrs George C (Audrey Connell)
 ☎ (401) 348-8258 . . "Cove Cottage" 7 Pawcatuck Av, Watch Hill, RI *02891*

Moore MR & MRS John L JR (Hope Trumbull)
☎ (508) 758-3669 . . 8 Ned's Point Rd, Mattapoisett, MA *02739*
Moore MRS Maurice T (Elisabeth M Luce) . . . . | ☎ (203) 227-2026
MR M Thompson JR . . . . | 100 Davis Hill Rd,
MR Michael . . . . | Weston, CT *06883*
Moore DR & MRS Peter Van C (Pamela P Harris)
☎ (508) 228-9854 . . 8 Crooked Lane, Box 882, Nantucket, MA *02554*
Moore MR & MRS Sumner Kittelle JR (Ann Hollister Hamilton)
☎ (508) 775-1611 . . "The Playhouse" Box 106, Centerville, MA *02632*
Moore MR & MRS Thomas O JR (Gray—Katherine T | ☎ (910) 372-2448
Condon) . . . . | "Bearlocks"
MR Bowman Gray 4th . . . . | Sparta, NC *28675*
Moore MR & MRS Thomas R (Margaret C King)
☎ (516) JU3-8011 . . "Moorish Castle" Point O'Woods, NY *11706*
Moore MR & MRS Willard S (Margaret E Nelson)
☎ (516) 583-8011 . . Point O'Woods, NY *11706*
Moore MR & MRS William C (Helga Davis) . . . . . . | ☎ (404) 896-3724
MISS Andrea E . . . . | Windjammer Rte 1,
MISS Sabrina G . . . . | Box 17, Hiawassee,
MR Charles W . . . . | GA *30546*
Moore MR & MRS William H (Edith McKnight)
☎ (207) 326-4826 . . Box 208, Breezemere Rd, Brooksville, ME *04617*
Moore MRS William H 3d (Mabelle Symington)
☎ (410) 377-9344 . . 7A Devon Hill Rd, Baltimore, MD *21210*
Moorhead MR & MRS J Upshur 2d (Mari A Kilroy)
☎ (516) 674-3666 . . Locust Valley, NY *11560*
Moorhouse MR & MRS William H JR (Margaret C | ☎ (908) 892-3704
Pew) . . . . | "East Mooring"
MISS Nina E . . . . | 1307 Ocean Av,
 | Mantoloking, NJ
 | *08738*
Moot MR & MRS John R (Ellen Guild)
☎ (603) 323-8863 . . Fowler's Mill Rd, Chocorua, NH *03817*
Moran MR & MRS John P (Margaretta B Knorr) . . . . | ☎ (616) 347-2968
MISS Margaretta G . . . . | "Fugly"
MR John P JR . . . . | 509 Woodland Av,
 | PO Box 1252,
 | Bay View, MI
 | *49770*
Moran MR Joseph H 2d
☎ (516) 283-7050 . . 300 Montauk H'way, Southampton, NY *11968*
Morey MR Joseph H JR
☎ (905) 894-1027 . . Ft Erie, Ontario L0S 1N0, Canada
Morgan MR & MRS Alfred Y 3d (Virginia E | ☎ (516) 324-6730
Toomey) . . . . | "The Tyler House"
MISS Muriel C . . . . | 217 Main St,
MISS Charlotte M . . . . | East Hampton, NY
 | *11937*
Morgan MR & MRS G Frederick (Paula Deitz)
☎ (207) 374-5618 . . "Trailwood" East Blue Hill, ME *04629*
Morgan MR & MRS George O JR (Marianela | ☎ (809) 775-1157
Martinez de Eguiluz) . . . . | Pineapple Village
MR George O 5th . . . . | 3500-3503,
JUNIORS MISS Marianela . . . . | Stouffer Resort,
 | St Thomas, VI
 | *00802*

Morgan MRS H Vaughan JR (Susan E Manimon)
☎ (603) 436-1171 . . 2 Bay Shore Dv, Greenland, NH *03840*
Morgan MR & MRS Howard R (Elizabeth B Trudeau) | ☎ (207) 348-2724
MISS Anna E . . . . | "Loon's Landing"
MR H Randall JR . . . . | Rte 15, Deer Isle,
MR Carl G . . . . | ME *04627*
Morgan MR & MRS John M (Andrew—Elizabeth M McPherson)
☎ (410) 255-6771 . . "Out of Bounds" Box 167, Skippers Row, Gibson Island, MD *21056*
Morgan MR John S
☎ (860) KI2-5050 . . "Spofford Pond" 462 Mountain Rd, Box 453, Norfolk, CT *06058*
Morgan MISS Margaret Eiluned
Bartlett's Harbor, North Haven, ME *04853*
Morley MR & MRS Daniel F (Evans—Ruth F Oliver) | ☎ (508) 758-6469
JUNIORS MISS Amanda W . . . . | "The Lesser
MR Jeremy A M Evans . . . . | Parsonage"
 | 36 Water St,
 | Mattapoisett, MA
 | *02739*
Morosani MR & MRS John W (Joan C Devine)
☎ (860) 567-0233 . . 160 Wigwam Rd, Litchfield, CT *06759*
Morphy MR & MRS James C (Priscilla W Plimpton)
"Honey Bunny Hill" 432 Wianno Av, Osterville, MA *02655*
Morrill MR & MRS Henry Leighton (Irene N Randolph)
☎ (508) 428-2184 . . Box 307, 31 Old Shore Rd, Cotuit, MA *02635*
Morris MRS Edward W (Ruth Gibson)
☎ (508) 693-1942 . . West Chop, MA *02573*
Morris MR & MRS Martin Van B (Sara E Layman) . . | ☎ (516) 288-8676
MISS Heather de R . . . . | 47 Beach Rd,
MR Martin Van B 3d . . . . | Westhampton
JUNIORS MR Courtney de R . . . . | Beach, NY *11978*
Morris MRS Nicholas W (Margaret Pancoast)
☎ (609) 492-2465 . . 1304 S Beach Av, Beach Haven, NJ *08008*
Morris MR & MRS Robert M (Nellie Terzian)
☎ (207) 374-2232 . . "Fernrock" Blue Hill Falls, ME *04164*
Morris MR & MRS Roland (Sally J Fageol)
☎ (518) 962-4975 . . "Meadow Springs" Rte 1, Box 1140A, Westport, NY *12993*
Morris MR William B
☎ (860) 535-1107 . . 8 Broad St, Stonington, CT *06378*
Morris MR & MRS William H (Arvia B Crosby)
☎ (914) 876-3231 . . "Cedar Heights Orchards" Crosby Lane, Rhinebeck, NY *12572*
Morrison MR D Craig JR . . . . | "Ravens' Retreat"
MISS Heather E . . . . | Jacks River, GA
MR Donald C 3d . . . . | *30541*
Morrison MR David J
☎ (717) 646-0818 . . Pocono Lake Preserve, PA *18348*
Morrison MR & MRS Gordon M (Barbara J Lee)
☎ (207) 284-6478 . . 5 Neptune Lane, Fortunes Rocks, Biddeford, ME *04005*
Morrison MR & MRS James A (Anne N Wilbur)
☎ (916) 426-3773 . . The Cedars, Soda Springs, CA *95728*
Morrison MR Reid B
☎ (207) 282-3236 . . 3 Neptune Lane, Biddeford, ME *04005*

Morrow MR & MRS A J Donelson (Sears—Suzanne Roy)......................... ☎ (208) 727-7444
  MR Andrew J............................ "Fish Creek Ranch" Carey, ID
    MR Nathaniel R Sears.................. 83320
    MR Sebastian C Sears..................
Morse MRS David Hunnewell (Nancy M Balis)
  ☎ (508) 255-2147.. Box 732, East Orleans, MA 02643
Morse MR & MRS Edmond H (Barbara R White)
  ☎ (207) 846-4393.. Chebeague Island, ME 04017
Morse MR & MRS Edmond N (Sidney H Phillips)
  ☎ (207) 846-9500.. "Sunset Hill" Chebeague Island, ME 04017
Morse MRS Edward Clarke (Neally—Eleanor L Scott)
  "The Doll's House" Deacon Hill, Bread Loaf, VT 05753
Morse MRS Thomas R JR (Suzanne Rice)
  ☎ (802) 485-8972.. "Tzothy Farm" RR 2, Randolph, VT 05060
Morsman MR & MRS Joseph J 3d (Laura C DeYoung)........................ ☎ (508) 627-4460
  MISS Laura W........................... Box 520,
  MISS Virginia H........................ Edgartown, MA
  MR Joseph J 4th....................... 02539
Morss MR & MRS Anthony W (Carolyn Charles)
  ☎ (860) 567-4007.. 86 Brooks Rd, Litchfield, CT 06759
Mortimer MR & MRS Henry T (Linda M Metcalfe)...... ☎ (011-44-171)
  MR John M............................. 589-9604
  MR Alexander D........................ 14 Elvaston Place,
                                         London SW7 5QF,
                                         England
Mortimer MR & MRS Henry T JR (Bierbaum—Susan E Lewis)........................... ☎ (516) 283-7937
  MISS Caroline E........................ 56 S Main St,
  MR Henry T 3d......................... PO Box 2612,
    JUNIORS MR Richard L Bierbaum........ Southampton, NY
                                         11969
Mortimer MR & MRS Richard (Coulter—Madeline H Brown)
  ☎ (516) 283-3778.. 590 Halsey Neck Lane, PO Box 1089, Southampton, NY 11969
Mortimer MR & MRS Stanley G (Kathleen L Harriman)
  ☎ (914) 351-4692.. PO Box 321, Harriman, NY 10926
Morton MR & MRS Robert S (Elizabeth V Evans)
  ☎ (516) 788-7369.. Fishers Island, NY 06390
Morton MR & MRS W Hugh M (Diana H Manton).. ☎ (508) 636-2538
  MISS Sandra T.......................... 39 Atlantic Av,
                                         Westport, MA
                                         02790
Moseley MRS David Bogue (Fernow—M Carolyn Roberg)
  ☎ (716) 884-3664.. 624 W Ferry St, Buffalo, NY 14222
Moseley MR & MRS Frederick S 3d (Elizabeth H Perkins)
  ☎ (207) 734-8880.. Seal Island, Islesboro, ME 04848
Moskey MR Stamatis
  Molyvos, Lesbos, Greece
Moss MR & MRS George K (Joyce K Leonard)
  ☎ (207) 867-2005.. "Turner Farm" North Haven, ME 04853
Moss MR & MRS Robert A JR (Laurie McL Watson).. ☎ (508) 945-2806
  MISS Laurie McL........................ 204 Countryside Dv,
  MISS Sarah B........................... Chatham, MA 02633
Motley MRS Herbert J (Catharine A Little)
  ☎ (207) 867-2053.. Box 448, North Haven, ME 04853
Motley MR Thomas........................ ☎ (207) 389-1997
  MISS Sarah P........................... "The Cuddy"
  MISS Elisabeth C....................... Small Point, ME
  MR Thomas 3d.......................... 04567
Mott MR & MRS Colter W (Steffanie R Griffis)
  ☎ (206) 884-9862.. "Tu Tucy" 5012 Mahncke Rd KPS, Longbranch, WA 98349
Muckerman COL (RET) & MRS Joseph E 2d (Anne J Butler) USA.
  ☎ (302) 645-4952.. "Stack Arms" Box 627, 309 W 3 St, Lewes, DE 19958
Muckerman DR & MRS Richard I C (Barbara L Hagnauer)
  ☎ (970) 949-3290.. 918 Deer Blvd, Eagle, Vail, CO 81657
Mucklé MR & MRS Craig W JR (Amanda E Barnes)
  ☎ (508) 563-3234.. 37 Squeteague Harbor Rd, PO Box 287, Cataumet, MA 02534-0287
Mudd MR & MRS Dayton H (Dorothy R Morse).... ☎ (616) 547-2670
  MR Dayton H JR........................ 210 Belvedere Club,
                                         Charlevoix, MI
                                         49720
Mueller MR Bret A.. see E T H Talmage 3d
Mueller MR J Adrian.. see E T H Talmage 3d
Muenter MRS Knud B (Eirin T Münter)
  ☎ (716) 941-5909.. "Knudahei" 8009 Lower E Hill Rd, Colden, NY 14033
Muhlenberg MR & MRS Kobi (Mary E Kearns)
  ☎ (011-353-61) 76151.. "Kincora Lodge" Killaloe, Co Clare, Ireland
Muir MR & MRS James JR (Marjorie Flynt)........ ☎ (908) TW2-1627
  MISS Helen G........................... 915 East Av,
  MR Henry F............................ Mantoloking, NJ
  MR Frederick G........................ 08738
Muir MRS Malcolm JR (Nancy H Jones)
  ☎ (508) 627-8241.. 9 Oliver St, Edgartown, MA 02539
Mullan MRS Nancy D (Nancy De V Field)....... ☎ (516) 653-4315
  MR Peter D............................ 49 Quaquanantuck
                                         Lane, Box 47,
                                         Quogue, NY 11959
Mulliken MR & MRS Alfred D (Margaret Kelly)
  ☎ (802) 253-3989.. PO Box 501, Stowe, VT 05672
Mullins MR & MRS Thomas D 2d (Corinne A McLaughlin) ⚓.................... ☎ (508) 693-9609
  MR William E G........................ Lambert's Cove Rd,
                                         RFD Box 408,
                                         Vineyard Haven,
                                         MA 02568
Muma MRS John R (Edith Smith Noyes)
  ☎ (516) 727-0145.. "Chain Hill" 41½ Sound Av, PO Box 1048, Riverhead, NY 11901
Mungall MR & MRS Daniel JR (Edith D Smith)
  ☎ (401) 635-2288.. 51D Warren's Point Rd, Little Compton, RI 02837
Munn MRS Mark S (McKelvy—Patricia M Pyke).. ☎ (717) 775-6501
  MISS Mary L............................ Blooming Grove
                                         Hunt & Fish Club,
                                         Hawley, PA 18428
Munn MR & MRS Orson D (Patricia A Geoghegan)
  ☎ (516) 283-2501.. "Dividend" Gin Lane, Southampton, NY 11968
Munn MR & MRS Orson D 3d (Christine Jue)
  ☎ (516) 287-4526.. 43 Foster Crossing, Southampton, NY 11968

Munroe MRS Andrew T H (Susan H Spalding) . . . . ☎ (505) 983-2339
  MISS Nicoletta L . . . . 244 Casados St,
  MR Antonio W . . . . Santa Fe, NM 87501
Munson MR & MRS Charles S JR (Harts—Celia B Deming)
  ☎ (203) 259-0843 . . Box 507, Southport, CT 06490
Munson MRS John H G (Ruth F Blake) . . . . ☎ (508) 758-3357
  JUNIORS MISS Marianna C A . . . . 2 Ship St,
  Mattapoisett, MA 02739
Murdoch MRS Lawrence C (Barbara M Boyd)
  ☎ (609) 492-2937 . . 214 Berkeley Av, Beach Haven, NJ 08008
Murley MR & MRS Robert S (Mary B Pivirotto)
  ☎ (603) 544-2229 . . "Pine Point House" Bald Peak Colony Club,
  Melvin Village, NH 03850
Murphy MISS Esmé C . . see E E Vose
Murphy MR & MRS Grayson M P (Mary E Warren)
  ☎ (516) 788-7304 . . Fishers Island, NY 06390
Murphy MISS Margaret J . . . . ☎ (847) 356-5175
  MR George J 3d . . . . PO Box 186,
  Lake Villa, IL 60046
Murray MR & MRS A Brean (Sands—Bettina B   of ☎ (914)534-7154
  Patterson) . . . . "Sengen"
  MR Stephen F . . . . Deer Hill Rd,
  MR Christopher B . . . . Box 234, Cornwall-
  on-Hudson, NY 12520
  ☎ (208) 622-4506
  Box 2594,
  Sun Valley, ID 83353
  ☎ (516) 653-9658
  Box 1163, Quogue, NY 11959
Murray MR & MRS John V A (Francesca P Hersloff)
  ☎ (516) 653-4354 . . Quaquanantuck Lane, Quogue, NY 11959
Murray MR & MRS Robert A (Meredith H Medina)
  ☎ (516) 288-1183 . . "Serendipity" 1 Apaucuck Point Lane, Westhampton, NY 11977
Murray MR & MRS Russell 2d (Sally T Gardiner)
  ☎ (804) 336-4018 . . "The Catbird Seat" 5319 Sunrise Shore, Chincoteague, VA 23336
Murray MR William E—⚓
  ☎ (914) 351-5218 . . Pine Hill Rd, Tuxedo Park, NY 10987
Murrie MR & MRS Richard W (Finley—Rita R Toohey)
  ☎ (516) 653-4684 . . "Thistledune" 100 Dune Rd, Box 2, Quogue, NY 11959
Muse MR & MRS Albert C (Nancy B Trainer)
  ☎ (705) 765-5963 . . RR 2, Port Carling, Ontario P0B 1J0, Canada
Muse MISS Martha T
  312 Harvest Commons, Westport, CT 06880
Musgrave MR & MRS William G (Elizabeth R   Box 242,
  Sweetland) . . . . Truro, MA 02666
  MISS Jane G R . . . .
Musser MISS Lisa D . . see R B Ewart

Myer MR & MRS Samuel C (M Josefa C Whitman)
  ☎ (608) 231-9654 . . "White Oaks" 125 S Owen Dv, Madison, WI 53705-5034
Myer MR & MRS Theodore H (Mary E Hartmann)   ☎ (207) 882-6076
  ⚓ . . . . Shore Rd,
  MR John W . . . . North Edgecomb,
  MR Frederick H . . . . ME 04556
  MR Arthur R . . . .
Myers MR C Twiggs
  ☎ (518) 963-7227 . . "Topstone" Crater Club, Essex, NY 12936
Myers COL & MRS Eugene E (Ritchie—Florence M Hutchinson) USAF.
  ☎ (304) 366-3329 . . "Tanglewood" 721 Mt Vernon Av, Fairmont, WV 26554
Myers MR Paul D . . . . ☎ (401) 596-5036
  MR James A . . . . "Pomme de Mer"
  7 Niantic Av,
  Watch Hill, RI 02891
Myers MRS Walter K (E Carol Grosvenor)
  Jly 1 . . ☎ (902) 295-2638 . . "Beinn Bhreagh" Baddeck, Nova Scotia B0E 1B0, Canada
Myers MR & MRS William A (Harriet L Robey) . . . . ☎ (508) 283-5386
  MR William T . . . . "Cardinal House"
  876R Washington St, Gloucester, MA 01930
Myles MR & MRS Robert C (Francine P Berth) . . . . . ☎ (860) 536-1414
  MISS Robin P . . . . 4 Peck St,
  Groton Long Point, CT 06340

N

Nadherny MR & MRS Ferdinand (Elinor N Case)
  ☎ (847) 251-2470 . . 1630 Sheridan Rd, Apt 4A, Wilmette, IL 60091
Nagel MRS Frederick W (Lisa Gratwick)
  ☎ (705) 765-3430 . . "The Cabin" Minett, Muskoka, Ontario P0B 1B0, Canada
Nager DR & MRS George T (Mathilde Hofstetter)
  Piazza al Lago, 6987 Caslano, Ticino, Switzerland
Nagy MR & MRS Gregory B (Olga M Davidson) . . . . ☎ (603) 563-8926
  JUNIORS MISS Antonia . . . . "Owlsnest"
  JUNIORS MR Laszlo . . . . Dublin, NH 03444
Naimi DR & MRS Shapur (Amy C Simonds) . . . . ☎ (617) 383-1466
  MISS Susan L . . . . 55 Lothrop Lane,
  DR Timothy S . . . . Cohasset, MA 02025
  MR Cameron L . . . .
Nalle MR & MRS David (Dickey—Margaret B   ☎ (207) 244-7084
  Shumaker) . . . . Box 243,
  MISS Susan T . . . . Mt Desert, ME 04660
Nalle MR & MRS Jesse (Alice H Scott) ⚓
  ☎ (401) 295-0474 . . "Appledore" Saunderstown, RI 02874

Nash DR & MRS (DR) A E Keir (Marguerite
 Bou-Raad) ⚓ . . . .
 MR William E . . . .
☎ (208) 263-0765
"Swn-y-Don West"
Lake Pend Creille,
PO Box 492,
Sagle, ID *83860*

Nash MR & MRS John 2d (Hellyer—Joan G Le Grand)
 ☎ (508) 249-9014 . . Royalston Common, Royalston, MA *01368*
Nason MR & MRS John W (Knapp—Elizabeth Mercer)
 ☎ (518) 576-4506 . . "Rocky Point" Keene, NY *12942*
Navarro MR & MRS Rául A (Marta Cabané)
 ☎ (011-34-3) 200-1691 . . Amigo 71, 08021 Barcelona, Spain
Naylon MRS Henry M 3d (Patricia A Hopkins)
 ☎ (716) 652-8667 . . 138 The Meadow, East Aurora, NY *14052*
Neagle MRS Francis E JR (Julia M Snow)
 ☎ (516) 324-1717 . . 72 James Lane, East Hampton, NY *11937*
Neal MR & MRS Bernard N JR (Elizabeth D Kennard)
 MISS Elizabeth F . . . .
☎ (704) 526-3315
"Rabbit Hole"
Box 337, Highlands,
NC *28741*

Neblett MRS Cary H (Mary H G West) . . . .
 MISS Berkeley H . . . .
 MISS Dabney C H . . . .
 MR Brandon H . . . .
☎ (508) 228-3110
"Sunnyport"
24 E Lincoln Av,
Nantucket, MA
02554

Neel MR & MRS Richard (Constance M Hoguet) . . . .
 MISS Olivia D . . . .
 MISS Antonia H . . . .
 MISS Alexandra H . . . .
 JUNIORS MISS Victoria A . . . .
☎ (516) 653-8157
Box 1434,
Quogue, NY *11959*

Neel MR & MRS Samuel E (Mary Wilson)
 ☎ (603) 968-7873 . . "Camp Owls Nest" Red Lodge Rd, Holderness,
 NH *03245*
Neff MR & MRS James L (Barney—Frederica S
 Auerbach) . . . .
 MISS Hilary H . . . .
 MR Christopher W . . . .
☎ (518) 589-5761
"Skyhigh"
Onteora Park,
Tannersville, NY
12485

Neff MR & MRS W Perry (Michele D Dubois) . . . . . .
 MR Taylor E . . . .
 MR Michael W P . . . .
☎ (802) 824-6485
Little Holden Farm,
Holden Hill Rd,
Weston, VT *05161*

Neill MR Michael S de L
 ☎ (901) 276-9709 . . 2277 Union Av, Memphis, TN *38104*
Neilson MRS Harry R JR (Haack—Janneke Seton-Jansen)
 ☎ (207) 276-5093 . . "Over-The-Way" PO Box 465, Northeast Harbor,
 ME *04662*
Neilson MRS Lewis L (Barbara S Leech)
 ☎ (518) 576-9846 . . "Windy Brow" Ausable Club, St Huberts,
 NY *12943*
Nelson MR & MRS Arthur H (Eleanor Thomas)
 Box 194, Cataumet, MA *02534*
Nelson MR & MRS Norman F 2d (Sally L Hutt) ⚓
 ☎ (516) 286-0206 . . Meadow Lane, Brookhaven, NY *11719*
Nelson MR Robert M— ⚓
 ☎ (207) 644-8214 . . "Nelson Cottage" McFarlands Cove, South Bristol,
 ME *04568*

Ness MR & MRS Philip W (Anne T F Semple)
 ☎ (508) 428-6779 . . 449 Eel River Rd, Osterville, MA *02655*
Nettl MR & MRS Stephen A (Pratt—Noël S Butcher)
 ☎ (207) 374-5529 . . "Lobster Lodge" Box 240, Blue Hill, ME *04614*
Neuhaus MR & MRS James Harrison (Kathryn H Gaffney)
 ☎ (704) 479-3933 . . 744 Cherokee Trail, Robbinsville, NC *28771*
Neuhaus MR & MRS William O 3d (E Kay Ficklen)
 461 Acequia Madre St, 2, Santa Fe, NM *87501*
Neumann MRS Anne Rittershofer (Anne F
 Rittershofer) . . . .
 MISS Helen K . . . .
☎ (508) 645-9934
"Studio House"
Middle Rd,
PO Box 148,
Chilmark, MA
02535

Neumann MRS Charles P (Saranne King)
 ☎ (805) 969-1468 . . 1341 Plaza De Sonadores, Santa Barbara,
 CA *93108*
Neville MR & MRS James D (Anne McM Biggar)
 ☎ (716) 789-5395 . . Manor Dv, Chautauqua, NY *14722*
Newbegin MRS Robert (Katharine Slade)
 ☎ (603) 532-6672 . . 43 Thorndike Pond Rd, Jaffrey, NH *03452*
Newberry MR Alexander S
 ☎ (508) 927-0264 . . "Windemere" 175 West St, Beverly Farms,
 MA *01915*
Newberry MR Gardner C . . see R Gignoux
Newberry JUNIORS MR James W . . see R Gignoux
Newberry MR & MRS John S IV (MacGuigan—Edith McBean) . . of
 ☎ (508) 927-0264 . . "Lee's Crossing" 175 West St, PO Box 5620,
 Beverly Farms, MA *01915*
 ☎ (401) 847-1027 . . "Saltmarsh" Hazard Rd, Newport, RI *02840*
Newberry MR Stevenson . . of
 ☎ (508) 927-0264 . . "Lee's Crossing" 175 West St, PO Box 5620,
 Beverly Farms, MA *01915*
 ☎ (941) 964-2682 . . "Pink House" 361 Gilchrist Av, Boca Grande,
 FL *33921*
Newbold MR & MRS Arthur E 3d (Swartley—Emily
 Trefz) ⚓ . . . .
 MR J Christopher Swartley . . . .
☎ (207) 276-5645
"Rising Gorge"
Northeast Harbor,
ME *04662*

Newbold MR & MRS Clement B JR (Virginia A
 Dunkerton) . . . .
 MISS Pamela deW . . . .
 MR Clement B 3d . . . .
☎ (704) 295-4441
"Eastern View"
Box 1910,
1125 Old John's
River Rd,
Blowing Rock, NC
28605

Newbold MR & MRS John L (Judith A Bourne) . . . . .
 MR Timothy B . . . .
☎ (508) 645-2201
Abel's Hill, RR 1,
Box 373, Chilmark,
MA *02535*

Newbold MR & MRS William F (Wolf—Elinor Kemper)
 ☎ (207) 244-7815 . . "Tern II" Indian Point Rd, Mt Desert, ME *04660*
Newcomer MR & MRS Waldo (Linda L Moon) . . . . .
 MR John W . . . .
☎ (508) 281-2611
29 Rockholm Rd,
Annisquam, MA
01930

Newell JUNIORS MISS Alexandra . . see T F Leddy

Newhall MR & MRS Charles Mercer (Brock—Priscilla Jenks)
☎ (207) 276-3689 . . Northeast Harbor, ME *04662*
Newhall MR & MRS John H (Jane C Ward) . . . . | ☎ (207) 276-5149
  MR Daniel W . . . . | "Ilfracombe"
                                         | Seal Harbor, ME
                                         | *04675*
Newhall MR & MRS Thomas B (Sarah S Shelburne) ⚓
☎ (207) 276-5149 . . "Ilfracombe" General Delivery, Seal Harbor, ME *04675*
Newlin MR & MRS William V P (Louisa Lawrence | ☎ (207) 276-3736
  Foulke). . . . . | "Four Winds"
  MR Nicholas . . . . | Northeast Harbor,
                                         | ME *04662*
Newman REV & MRS Andrew H (Carmichael—Mary M Allen)
☎ (705) 762-3237 . . "Pewabic Island" Box 226, Bala, Ontario P0C 1A0, Canada
Newman MR & MRS Charles I (Anglesea A Parkhurst)
☎ (413) 528-2288 . . "Anglesea" Hillsdale Rd, South Egremont, MA *01258*
Newman MR & MRS George W 3d (Mary E Kyte) . . | ☎ (508) 526-7916
  MR George W 4th . . . . | "Glendyne"
  JUNIORS MISS Mary E K . . . . | Manchester, MA
  JUNIORS MR Charles L . . . . | *01944*
Newman MRS Leslie H (Walker—Leslie M Hailand) | ☎ (616) 526-2177
  MISS Whitney H Walker . . . . | 415½ Glenn Dv,
                                         | Harbor Springs, MI
                                         | *49740*
Newton MR & MRS Harold R (Margaret A Turner)
☎ (714) 494-1303 . . "El Parador" 156 Emerald Bay, Laguna Beach, CA *92651*
Newton MR & MRS Matthew K (Victoria L Carver)
☎ (207) 374-5537 . . "Sunset Cliff" Blue Hill, ME *04614*
Nicholas MR Frederick S
☎ (207) 374-2230 . . "1798" East Blue Hill, ME *04629*
Nicholas MRS Peter H (Mattison—Gretchen Ridder)
☎ (860) 739-8457 . . "White Shutters" 5 Francis Lane, Old Black Point, Niantic, CT *06357*
Nicholas MR & MRS Robert C 3d (Lynn C Holman) . | ☎ (508) 775-1543
  MR William C . . . . | Box 885,
  MR R Carter . . . . | Great Island,
  MR Philip H . . . . | West Yarmouth, MA
                                         | *02673*
Nicholls MR Samuel S 3d
110 E 57 St, Apt 3B, New York, NY *10022*
Nichols MRS (DR) Charles W (Chrysler—Marguerite P Sykes)
☎ (802) 362-1320 . . "Bunker Hill" Prospect St, Manchester, VT *05254*
Nichols MR & MRS Clifford JR (Edson—Mary M Butler)
"Puckerbush" Sargentville, ME *04673*
Nichols MRS Elizabeth M (O'Keefe—Elizabeth M | ☎ (516) 324-1421
  Nichols) . . . . | Lee Av &
  MISS Shannon E O'Keefe . . . . | Crossways,
  MR Michael T O'Keefe 2d . . . . | East Hampton, NY
  MR Berkeley H O'Keefe . . . . | *11937*
Nichols MR & MRS H Gilman (Swigert—Ellen Ford) ⚓
☎ (207) 867-4609 . . Box 352, Crabtree Point, North Haven, ME *04853*
Nichols MR & MRS J Donald (Hackett—Elizabeth G Litterer)
"Point of View" 117 Wayne Creek Dv, Beaver Creek, CO *81620*

Nichols MRS Katharine M (Katharine F Merriman) . | ☎ (413) 258-4419
  MISS Ashley M . . . . | Tunxis Club,
  JUNIORS MR C Houk . . . . | HC 60, Box 150,
                                           | 288 S Trail, Tolland,
                                           | MA *01034*
Nichols MR & MRS Milton G (Margaret J Adams) . . . | ☎ (207) 867-4487
  MR M Griggs JR . . . . | Crabtree Point,
  MR Peter A . . . . | North Haven, ME
                                           | *04853*
Nicholsen MR Hamilton R . . see R Kelham
Nicholsen MR Ronald C . . see R Kelham
Nicholson MR & MRS Oliver P (Caroline A Smitter)
☎ (011-44-1884) 255-877 . . "Lark Hill" Washfield, Tiverton, Devon, England
Nickel MR & MRS James L (Kathleen M McGrath) | ☎ (805) 871-8447
  MISS Erin D . . . . | 8651 Rancheria Rd,
  MISS Heidi K . . . . | Bakersfield, CA
  MR James C . . . . | *93306*
Nickerson MRS Albert L (Elizabeth Perkins)
☎ (207) 594-7565 . . Clark Island, Spruce Head, ME *04859*
Niedringhaus MRS W Delafield (Effie V Zeibig) . . . | ☎ (616) 526-9389
  MR W Delafield JR (Linda Van Eck) . . . . . | 3 Cedar Lane,
  MISS Alicia A . . . . | Wequetonsing, MI
                                           | *49740*
Niehoff MR K Richard B JR . . see MRS L S Walker
Niehoff MISS Kelly B . . see MRS L S Walker
Nigra DR & MRS Thomas P (Jane H Brawley) . . . . . . | ☎ (518) 576-4418
  MISS Jane H . . . . | Keene Valley, NY
  MR Peter T . . . . | *12943*
Niles MRS Barbara E (Barbara H Elliott) . . . . | ☎ (860) 435-9994
  MR Andrew E . . . . | "Sow's Ear"
                                           | Selleck Hill Rd,
                                           | Salisbury, CT *06068*
Niles MR & MRS Nicholas JR (Varick Katzenbach)
☎ (508) 636-4488 . . 300 Cornell Rd, Westport, MA *02790*
Niles MR & MRS Robert L (Virginia A Moore) . . . . . | ☎ (603) 563-8575
  MR Jonathan B . . . . | Upper Jaffrey Rd,
                                           | Dublin, NH *03444*
Nimick MRS A Corkran (Anne S Corkran)
☎ (207) 276-5426 . . "Sound Mill" Northeast Harbor, ME *04662*
Nimick MR & MRS Thomas M H JR (Whiteside—Hunt—Theresa M Listowska)
☎ (407) 627-0728 . . 996 Lake House Dv, Lost Tree Village, FL *33408*
Nitze MISS Heidi
Aug 1 . . ☎ (207) 276-5453 . . "Rockridge" Northeast Harbor, ME *04662*
Nitze MR & MRS William A 2d (Ann K Richards) . . . | ☎ (970) 920-1179
  JUNIORS MR Paul K . . . . | 420 W North St,
                                           | Aspen, CO *81611*
Nixon MISS Diane A
☎ (717) 595-2393 . . Box 112, Skytop, PA *18357*
Noble MR & MRS Daniel S (Elizabeth A Ream)
Northport Point, Northport, MI *49670*
Noble MR & MRS Henry S (Elizabeth L Brewer)
☎ (207) 422-3646 . . Sorrento, ME *04677*

Noble MR Lawrence M JR
 ☎ (616) 386-5561 . . "Stony Point" 100 Northport Point, Northport, MI *49670*
Noble MR Timothy E
 ☎ (516) 537-0742 . . Georgica Association, Wainscott, NY *11975*
Noell MR Charles Preston 3d
 ☎ (717) 225-7147 . . RD 2, Box 2015, Spring Grove, PA *17362*
Nolan MR & MRS Gaillard R (Meryl E Richardson) . . | ☎ (302) 227-8551
 MR Merlyn R . . . . | 23 Tidewaters, Henlopen Acres, Rehoboth Beach, DE *19971*
Nolen MR & MRS Wilson (Eliot Chace)
 ☎ (508) 775-0705 . . Box 516, Great Island, West Yarmouth, MA *02673*
Noojin MR & MRS Ray O JR (Janice D Skinner) . . . . | ☎ (904) 492-1575
 MISS Catherine E | "Seafarer"
 MISS Allison D . . . . | 16401 Pedido Key
 MR Ray O 3d . . . . | Dv, Pensacola, FL *32507*
Noone MRS Robert Scott (Johnson—Hallock—Ruth H Gordon)
 "Ish-Pop-Kah" Pointe au Baril, Ontario P0G 1K0, Canada
Nordeman MR & MRS Jacques C (Anne W Stillman) | ☎ (516) 283-6688
 MR Landon S | "Sunnyside"
 MR John H . . . . | Pond Lane,
 JUNIORS MISS Eliza P . . . . | Southampton, NY *11968*
Norden MR & MRS Carl F (Archer—Vivian Nichol)
 ☎ (207) 947-3030 . . Mountainy Pond Club, East Holden, ME *04429*
Norfleet MR & MRS John V R SR (Sarah F Edwards)
 ☎ (508) 487-2253 . . The Cottage at Captain Lysander Inn, 96 Commercial St, Provincetown, MA *02657*
Norfleet MISS Valerie W . . see M Blow
Norling MR & MRS Barry Allen (Abigail B Chandler) | ☎ (207) 389-2818
 MISS Alesia Fay . . . . | "Eastwinds"
 JUNIORS MISS Rebecca M . . . . | HC 32, Box 450, Small Point, ME *04567*
Norman MR Frederick C
 ☎ (203) 633-6081 . . Box 246, Riverside, CT *06878*
Norman MR & MRS James T (Bierman—Caroline T Hooff)
 ☎ (804) 435-0148 . . "Willow Oaks" Rte 1, Box 6755, White Stone, VA *22578*
Norris MR & MRS Alfred D JR (Marguerite A Scadding)
 ☎ (609) 368-5333 . . 197—66 St, Avalon, NJ *08202*
Norris MR Charles H
 ☎ (970) 476-2801 . . Forest Rd, Vail, CO *81657*
Norris MISS Margaret D . . see W R Wister JR
Northrop MR & MRS Johnston F (Gray—Lucile R Ralston) . . of
 ☎ (508) 228-0956 . . 22 Orange St, Nantucket, MA *02554*
 ☎ (508) 228-1395 . . "Shimmo" PO Box 248, Nantucket, MA *02554*
Northrop MR & MRS Johnston W (Jill L Weissinger)
 ☎ (508) 228-0956 . . 22 Orange St, Nantucket, MA *02554*
Norton MRS Garrison (Emily E McMullan)
 ☎ (207) 867-4616 . . Pulpit Harbor, North Haven, ME *04853*
Norweb MRS R Henry JR (Elizabeth Gardner)
 ☎ (207) 633-2002 . . Road's End, PO Box 545, Boothbay Harbor, ME *04538*

Notz MR & MRS John K JR (Janis L Wellin) . . . . | ☎ (414) 248-1315
 MISS Jane Elinor . . . . | N 1609 Countryside
 MR John Wellin . . . . | Rd, Lake Geneva, WI *53147*
Nouri MR & MRS Edmond J (Redington—Diana H Crocker) . . . . | ☎ (516) 671-1945
 MISS Ruth M Redington . . . . | Chicken Valley Rd, Oyster Bay, NY *11771*
Nourie MR Bruce L
 ☎ (401) 635-4636 . . "Harbourside" Rhode Island Av, Little Compton, RI *02837*
Noyes MR & MRS Jansen JR (M Dorothy O'Day) ⛵
 ☎ (516) 788-7202 . . "Sea Swept" Fishers Island, NY *06390*
Noyes MR & MRS José W (Grace E Gammino) . . . . . | ☎ (860) 364-5941
 MR José W JR | "Monte-Sol Farm"
 JUNIORS MR Prentiss G . . . . | 12 Herb Rd, Sharon, CT *06069-2326*
Noyes MR Nicholas H . . see R A R Maclennan
Nunan MR & MRS Alfred B (Beverly E McLaughlin) | ☎ (717) 289-4561
 MISS Elizabeth D . . . . | "Meadowbound"
 MR Alfred B JR . . . . | Box 37, Hop Bottom, PA *18824*
Nype MR & MRS Russell H (Mander—Diantha Lawrence)
 ☎ (207) 967-3531 . . "Pear Tree Farm" PO Box 805, Kennebunkport, ME *04046*
Nype MR & MRS Russell L (Martha E Foley)
 ☎ (207) 967-3531 . . "Pear Tree Farm" Kennebunkport, ME *04046*

O

Oakes MISS Daphne V N . . see MRS C C Linden
Oakes MRS Thomas F (Elinor Righter)
 ☎ (516) 788-7627 . . "Hawks Nest" Box 434, Fishers Island, NY *06390*
Ober MR & MRS David G (Polly F Norris)
 ☎ (207) 276-5078 . . PO Box 8, Northeast Harbor, ME *04662*
Obolensky MRS Serge (Breer—Marilyn F Wall)
 ☎ (313) 886-5848 . . "Rose Hill House" 45 Preston Place, Grosse Pointe Farms, MI *48236*
O'Brien MRS Catherine L (James—Noel—Catherine L O'Brien) ⛵
 ☎ (516) 324-1045 . . "Sea Cote" Lily Pond Lane, Box 1488, East Hampton, NY *11937*
O'Brien MRS Francis T (Stone—Frances Dunn McKee)
 ☎ (508) 993-8284 . . Nonquitt, MA *02748*
O'Brien MR & MRS Frank JR (Marianna H Mead)
 ☎ (508) 627-4261 . . "Havoc House" N Water St, Edgartown, MA *02539*
O'Brien MR & MRS Jonathan B (Joan Dominick)
 ☎ (508) 636-3265 . . "Potlatch" 606 River Rd, Westport, MA *02790*
O'Brien MR & MRS Lawrence F 3d (Helen M Powell) . . . . | Cotuit, MA *02635*
 JUNIORS MR Luke . . . . |
 JUNIORS MR Peter . . . . |
O'Brien MR & MRS Robert E (Smith—Marian S Achilles)
 ☎ (011-44-171) 235-4164 . . 82 Eaton Square, London SW1, England

Ocampo MR & MRS Juan M (Anne K O'Neil)
☎ (516) 537-0776 . . Wainscott Stone Rd, Wainscott, NY *11975*
O'Connell MR Courtney . . see MRS C A Long
O'Connell MR & MRS J Ryan (Janet B Keyes)
☎ (516) 324-4152 . . Box 286, East Hampton, NY *11937*
O'Connell MR Robin S . . see MRS C A Long
O'Connor MR & MRS Anthony M (Suzanne De G Perry)
☎ (508) 627-8902 . . RFD 298, Edgartown, MA *02539*
O'Connor MR & MRS Richard D (Korybut—Unger—Katherine C Maffitt)
☎ (810) 748-9931 . . Boardwalk 2, Old Club, Harsens Island, MI *48028*
O'Day MR & MRS John C (Coyne—Sheila G Doyle)
☎ (916) 581-4003 . . PO Box 1046, Carnelian Bay, Lake Tahoe, CA *95140*
Odell MISS Alison W . . see J A Evans
Odell MR & MRS I Gordon (Jane A Schaff)
☎ (616) 386-5067 . . 3 Northport Point, Northport, MI *49670*
Odell MISS Suzanne W . . see J A Evans
O'Donnell MR & MRS Robert J (Sue L Dodson) . . . . | ☎ (401) 846-0075
MISS Nancy S . . . . | "Crossways"
| 83 Ocean Av,
| Newport, RI *02840*
O'Dunne MRS Eugene (Elsie W Ekengren)
Edgartown, MA *02539*
Oelsner MR & MRS W James (Carol Perkins) . . . . . . | ☎ (516) 922-7417
MISS Christine E . . . . | "Seacroft"
MR W James E—☎ (516) 624-3200 . . . . | Centre Island,
| Oyster Bay, NY
| *11771*
O'Farrell MR & MRS William J (E M Noreen Drexel)
☎ (401) 847-3323 . . "Stonor Lodge" 479 Bellevue Av, Newport, RI *02840*
Off MR Robert W
☎ (508) 775-5991 . . "Hawthorne" Box 143, Washington Av, Hyannis Port, MA *02647*
Off MR & MRS Samuel W (Mary D Hays)
☎ (705) 764-1906 . . "Bay Point" Beaumaris, Lake Muskoka, Ontario P0B 1B0, Canada
Offield MRS Wrigley (Edna J Headley)
☎ (616) 526-2187 . . Box 395, Harbor Springs, MI *49740*
Ogden MR Alfred
☎ (860) 599-4880 . . "Anguilla" PO Box 214, Stonington, CT *06378*
Ogden MR & MRS Alfred T 2d (Tyler—Susan R | ☎ (860) 599-4880
Clark) ⚓ . . . . | "Anguilla"
MISS Alix R . . . . | PO Box 214,
MISS Mary Fell P . . . . | Stonington, CT
MR Alfred T 3d . . . . | *06378*
  MISS Mary T Tyler . . . . |
  MISS Cecily W Tyler . . . . |
  JUNIORS MR Wat H Tyler . . . . |
Ogden MR & MRS Dayton JR (Margaret P Reid) . . . . | ☎ (401) 322-7077
MISS Margaret P . . . . | 40 Ocean View Av,
MR Dayton R . . . . | Charlestown, RI
| *02813*
O'Hara MR & MRS Robert S JR (McSweeney— | ☎ (516) 583-5346
Bonnie Ann Durkin) ⚓ . . . . | Point O'Woods, NY
MISSES Alison & Jennifer L . . . . | *11706*
MISSES Katherine D & A Brett . . . . |

Ohrstrom MR Kenneth M
☎ (401) 848-5932 . . 208 Cogshell Av, Newport, RI *02840*
Ohrstrom MRS Ricard R (Rosse—Allen G Dunnington)
☎ (208) 726-8657 . . Box 1213, Sun Valley, ID *83533*
Ohrstrom MR & MRS Ricard R JR (Rochelle Steiner)
☎ (401) 847-7742 . . "Four Winds" Bellevue Av, Newport, RI *02840*
Ohrstrom MISS Winifred E A . . see MRS S S Wright
Ohrstrom MR Wright R S . . see MRS S S Wright
O'Keefe MR Berkeley H . . see MRS E M Nichols
O'Keefe MR Michael T 2d . . see MRS E M Nichols
O'Keefe MISS Shannon E . . see MRS E M Nichols
Olcott MRS A Van Santvoord JR (Diana M Morgan) | ☎ (802) 362-1570
MISS Leslie H . . . . | "Glebelands"
| Rte 7A, Box 476,
| Manchester, VT
| *05254*
Oldenburg MR & MRS Richard E (H Lisa Turnure)
☎ (516) 267-8913 . . Handy Lane, Amagansett, NY *11930*
Olds MR & MRS John T (Candace Rose) . . . . | ☎ (802) 293-5028
MISS Samantha . . . . | Raymond Rd,
| Danby, VT *05739*
O'Leary MR & MRS Robert S (Eleanor M Ruggles)
☎ (508) 228-0428 . . "The Coop" Chicken Hill, Nantucket, MA *02554*
Oliphant MR & MRS Bryan M (Katherine H Maguire)
☎ (508) 945-2234 . . Box 685, North Chatham, MA *02650*
Oliphant MR & MRS Robert T (Diana A Marston) | ☎ (207) 288-4948
MR Alexander M . . . . | "Blue Horizon"
| PO Box 222,
| Mt Desert, ME
| *04660*
Oliva MR George JR
☎ (216) 256-0717 . . "Apple Hill" 8954 Booth Rd, Kirtland Hills, OH *44060*
Oliva MR & MRS Mark (Victoria McKittrick)
☎ (315) 369-3275 . . "Panther Camp" Little Moose Lake, Old Forge, NY *13420*
Olive MR & MRS John C (Patricia L Paul) . . . . | ☎ (508) 428-9081
JUNIORS MISS Elizabeth L . . . . | 19 Great Bay Rd,
| Osterville, MA
| *02655*
Oliver MR & MRS Andrew JR (Diana Buitron)
☎ (011-357) 5-233-965 . . 25 Kourion St, Episkopi Village, CY 4620 Limassol, Cyprus
Oliver MR & MRS Daniel (A Louise Vietor) . . . . . . | ☎ (508) 627-4263
MISS A Louise . . . . | S Water St,
MISS Susan F . . . . | Edgartown, MA
MR Andrew II . . . . | *02539*
MR Daniel JR . . . . |
JUNIORS MR Peter A . . . . |
Olmstead MR & MRS William W (Higgins—Marilynn M Maxted)
☎ (410) 275-1246 . . "Mt Harmon" Earleville, MD *21919*
Olmsted MR & MRS Robert G (Louise MacCracken) | ☎ (203) 661-1632
MISS (DR) Nancy . . . . | 680 Steamboat Rd,
| Greenwich, CT
| *06830*
Olsen MR & MRS Burton A JR (Hughes—Mary P Ziel)
☎ (916) 525-5311 . . 3935 W Lake Rd, Tahoe Pines, CA *95718*

Olson MR & MRS John F (Elizabeth H Callard) . . . . . ☎ (617) 581-0868
   MISS Emily M . . . . 35 Cliff St,
   MR Timothy C . . . . Nahant, MA *01908*
   MR Peter J . . . .
   MR Matthew E . . . .
   JUNIORS MR Nicholas P . . . .
Olson DR & MRS Robert M (Megan E Thomas) . . . . ☎ (603) 863-1545
   JUNIORS MR Robert H . . . . Anderson Pond Bight, Eastman, Grantham, NH *03753*
O'Malley MR & MRS Cormac K H (Moira Kennedy) . . ☎ (860) 535-2798
   MISS Bergin . . . . 16 Diving St, Stonington, CT *06378*
O'Malley MR Hilaire . . . . ☎ (207) 276-3759
   MISS Justine B . . . . "van Alen Cottage"
   MISS Alixine F . . . . Northeast Harbor, ME *04662*
O'Malley MR & MRS John P (Hutchinson—Margaret L Parlin)
   ☎ (616) 548-5048 . . Burt Lake, MI *49717*
O'Neill MR & MRS Bertram L (Lea—E Jane Jordan)
   ☎ (207) 796-2908 . . Munson Island, Grand Lake Stream, ME *04637*
O'Neill DR Hugh . . . . ☎ (401) 423-0166
   MISS Maria L . . . . 177 Beavertail Rd, Jamestown, RI *02835*
O'Neill MR & MRS W Paul JR (Caroline K Slutter) . . ☎ (401) 423-1495
   MISS Phebe W . . . . 177 Beavertail Rd, Jamestown, RI *02835*
Oppenheimer MR & MRS Jesse H (Susan Rosenthal)
   ☎ (210) 224-2855 . . "Halycion Place" Pearsall, TX *78206*
Oppmann MR & MRS Harvey G (Patricia H Coakley) . . ☎ (216) 423-3500
   MR Justin C . . . . "Sunshine Farm"
   JUNIORS MISS Alexandra F . . . . Foxboro Rd,
   JUNIORS MR Patrick P . . . . Gates Mills, OH *44040*
Ordway MRS Samuel H (Anna Wheatland)
   ☎ (914) 402-4353 . . 1695 Croton Lake Rd, Yorktown Heights, NY *10598*
O'Reilly MR & MRS Terence J (Katharine van D Wallace) . . . . ☎ (702) 749-5435
   MR Tobin C . . . . "The Rock Pile" PO Box 503,
   JUNIORS MR Matthew W . . . . Glenbrook, NV *89413*
Oriel MRS S Parsons (Sarah L Parsons)
   ☎ (212) 759-8060 . . 10 Mitchell Place, New York, NY *10017*
   Jly 24 . . West Chop Club, Cedars Inn, West Chop, MA *02573*
Orme MR & MRS Edgar J JR (Nancy L Luttrell)
   ☎ (302) 227-7856 . . "Orménage" 18 Bedford Av, Indian Beach, Rehoboth Beach, DE *19971*
Orr MR & MRS Charles P (Paula G Welles)
   ☎ (705) 764-1978 . . "Outlook" Beaumaris, Ontario P0B 1B0, Canada
Orr MR & MRS P Welles (Ann S Young)
   ☎ (508) 228-5438 . . "The Shack" 0 Hulbert Av, Nantucket, MA *02554*

Orr MR & MRS William Pratt (Sullivan—Pauline Gerli)
   Jly 1 . . PO Box 341, Southampton, NY *11969*
Orrick MR & MRS A Downey (Marjorie H Soule) . . . ☎ (408) 624-3958
   MR Andrew D JR . . . . "Pinewood Edge"
   MR Winsor S . . . . 17 Mile Dv,
   MR Murray S . . . . Pebble Beach, CA
   MR Samuel W *93953*
Orth MR & MRS Philip W (Mariette R Clark)
   ☎ (715) 856-5898 . . Wausaukee Club, Athelstane, WI *54104*
Orthwein MR & MRS James B JR (Jane R Ross)
   ☎ (401) 348-8973 . . "West Cottage" Meadow Lane, Watch Hill, RI *02891*
Osborn MR & MRS Frederick H 3d (Anne H de P Todd) ⚓ . . . . ☎ (207) 422-6713
   MISS Alice-Elisabeth Van C . . . . Tranquillity Farm,
   MR F Henry 4th . . . . Gouldsboro, ME
   JUNIORS MR Graham L *04607*
Osborn MR & MRS (DR) John J JR (Emilie H Sisson)
   ☎ (207) 422-6854 . . Tranquillity Farm, Gouldsboro, ME *04607*
Osborne MR & MRS Frederik R-L (May Minturn Sedgwick)
   ☎ (418) 665-2041 . . Pointe-au-Pic, Quebec G0T 1M0, Canada
Osborne MR Stanley de J
   ☎ (802) 533-2364 . . E Craftsbury Rd, Greensboro, VT *05841*
Osgood MRS Alice C K (Keeble—Alice O Collins) . . ☎ (705) 764-1932
   MR G Hudson . . . . "Lowbridge" Beaumaris, Milford Bay, Ontario P0B 1E0, Canada
Oshei MRS Mary B (Dillaway—Mary E Bayliss) . . . ☎ (905) 894-3039
   MISS Mary E B . . . . 2147 Macdonald Dv,
   MR William B . . . . Bertie Bay, Ontario
   MISS Kimberly H . . . . L0S 1N0, Canada
Oswald MRS Clinton (Pile—Audrey G Clinton) . . . . ☎ (401) 849-7246
   MISS Diana S T . . . . "Treehaven" Ledge Rd, Newport, RI *02840*
Otis MRS J Sanford (Spencer—Violetta L Berry)
   ☎ (207) 781-5574 . . "Fairways" 17 Foreside Rd, Falmouth Foreside, ME *04105-1925*
O'Toole MR & MRS John J 3d (Suzanne Black)
   ☎ (508) 257-4521 . . 15 Sconset Av, Nantucket, MA *02564*
Ott MR & MRS Lambert B (Suzanne Austin)
   ☎ (207) 359-8384 . . "Aloha" Byard Point, Sargentville, ME *04673*
Otter MR & MRS Richard C (Sibyl A Wiper) . . . . . . ☎ (707) 996-4266
   MISS Sibyl A . . . . 901 Moon Mountain Dv, Glen Ellen, CA *95442*
Ottley MR & MRS Philip G (Glenna R Holleran) ⚓
   ☎ (208) 726-9447 . . PO Box 1444, Sun Valley, ID *83353*
Oudin MR C Folger JR
   ☎ (607) 547-6216 . . 2 Elm St, Cooperstown, NY *13326*
Ourusoff MRS Leonide (Katherine Carlisle)
   ☎ (603) 526-4247 . . Burpee Hill Rd, New London, NH *03257*

Outerbridge MR & MRS Yeaton D (Betsey Coste) . . | ☎ (401) 423-1710
   MISS Louisa Y. . . . . | "Clove Hitch"
   MISS Elizabeth W (McMenamin—Elizabeth W | 28 Hawthorne Rd,
   Outerbridge). . . . . | Jamestown, RI
    | *02835*

Outwater MR & MRS John O (Alice H Davidson)
   ☎ (802) 425-2012 . . "Pebble Beach" Thompson's Point, Charlotte, VT *05445*

Owen MRS Frederick H JR (Dayton—Jeanne P Comey)
   ☎ (516) 324-4535 . . 195 Main St, East Hampton, NY *11937*

Owen MR & MRS H Martyn (Candace C Benjamin) . | ☎ (207) 389-2206
   MR Douglas P. . . . . | "Quintet"
    | Small Point, ME
    | *04567*

Owen MR & MRS John G (Hope Henshaw)
   Lake Owen, Cable, WI *54821*

Owen MR & MRS Mitchell (Alma F Chapin)
   ☎ (315) 392-4908 . . Adirondack League Club, Honnedaga Lodge, RD 1, Box 256, Forestport, NY *13338*

Owen MR & MRS Stephen C JR (Evelyn D Bates)
   ☎ (516) 239-2673 . . Breezy Way, Lawrence, NY *11516*

Owsley MR David T
   ☎ (516) 537-7713 . . "Dune House" Dune Rd, Bridgehampton, NY *11932*

Owsley REV & MRS Randolph Gibson JR (Barbara A | ☎ (704) 669-8185
   Jones) . . . . | Texas Rd,
   MISS Laura A . . . . | Montreat, NC *28757*
   MISS Barbara A . . . . |
   MR R Gibson 3d . . . . |

Owsley MRS Richard P (Clark—Alexander—Anne Paul)
   ☎ (207) 734-2275 . . Islesboro, ME *04848*

P

Page MR & MRS Allison F (Margaret B Lucas)
   ☎ (717) 646-3554 . . Pocono Lake Preserve, PA *18348*

Page MR Blakely C . . see C T Cudlip

Page MR & MRS Charles H (Mayer—Garril C Goss) . | ☎ (541) 822-3333
   MISS Atlantic F . . . . | "Riverdendrons"
   MR Charles 3d . . . . | 56905 McKenzie
    | H'way, McKenzie
    | Bridge, OR *97413*

Page MR Jay J
   ☎ (401) 847-8142 . . 34 Golden Hill St, Newport, RI *02840*

Page MISS Olivia M . . see C T Cudlip

Pagel MR & MRS Alex B (Luisa M LaViola) . . . . | ☎ (516) 324-0886
   JUNIORS MISS Allegra LaV . . . . | "Elsufral"
    | 67 Woods Lane,
    | East Hampton, NY
    | *11937*

Pagel MRS Alex J (Elinor R Bronaugh)
   ☎ (516) 324-0886 . . "Elsufral" 67 Woods Lane, East Hampton, NY *11937*

Paine MR & MRS Peter S (Ellen C Lea)
   ☎ (518) 963-8354 . . "Boquette Farm" 77 River Rd, Willsboro, NY *12996*

Paine MR & MRS Peter S JR (Constance M Murphy) . | ☎ (518) 963-4081
   MR Alexander G . . . . | "Red Farm"
    | 30 River Rd,
    | Willsboro, NY
    | *12996*

Paine MR & MRS Richard P (Dickison— | ☎ (207) 371-2229
   Dragonas—Martha L Parsons) . . . . | "Timberlea"
   MR David L . . . . | MacMahan Island,
   MISS Sara E Dickison. | ME *04548*
   MR Matthew P Dickison . . . . |

Paine MR & MRS Richard P JR (Cathleen F Ross)
   ☎ (603) 876-3810 . . "Colonial Hall" Frost Hill, Marlborough, NH *03455*

Painter MR & MRS Richard W (Karen J Lindsley)
   ☎ (603) 643-5849 . . 34 MacDonald Dv, Hanover, NH *03755*

Pakradooni MR & MRS Dikran S (Ann L Jacobs)
   ☎ (508) KI8-2549 . . "Cromlech" Woods Hole, MA *02543*

Palen MR & MRS Frederick P (Harriette H Adams)
   ☎ (518) 963-4521 . . "Skyfield" Crater Club, Box 35, Essex, NY *12936*

Palfrey MR & MRS George G (Martha A Macdonald)
   Saquish Head, Plymouth, MA *02360*

Palmer MRS Arthur E (Julia C Reed)
   ☎ (207) 244-3915 . . HCR 62, Box 76, Pretty Marsh Pond, Mt Desert, ME *04660*

Palmer MISS Blair W . . see H L Bogert 3d

Palmer MRS Elisabeth G (CTSS Elisabeth Gatterburg)
   ☎ (011-37-6281) 6292-232 . . "Schloss Eberstadt" 6967 Buchen, Odenwald, Germany

Palmer MR & MRS Everett A JR (Margaret A Niedringhaus) . . of
   ☎ (316) 843-2551 . . Palmer Ranch, Beaumont, KS *67012*
   700 W Bay Av, Balboa, CA *92661*

Palmer MR F Timothy . . . . | ☎ (516) 472-3360
   MR Brett T . . . . | 72 Oak Rd, Bayport,
   MR Todd C . . . . | NY *11705*

Palmer MR H Meredith
   ☎ (302) 539-0891 . . PO Box 1297, Bethany Beach, DE *19930*

Palmer MRS James K (Mickelson—E Joan Ramsay) . | ☎ (707) 433-3790
   MISS Elizabeth W . . . . | Palmer Ridge
   JUNIORS MR James R . . . . | Ranch, 3369
    | Westside Rd,
    | Healdsburg, CA
    | *95448*

Palmer MR Lansing R JR . . see H L Bogert 3d

Palmer MR & MRS Raymond N (Joan M Starkey)
   ☎ (860) 542-5409 . . Doolittle Lake, Norfolk, CT *06058*

Palmer MRS Vincent (Lucie C Mackay)
   ☎ (603) 964-8496 . . 31 Atlantic Av, North Hampton, NH *03862*

Palumbo MR & MRS Jonathan B (Leslie K Hunt)
   117 Pump Lane, Guilford, CT *06437*

Pantaleoni MR & MRS Anthony (Emily A Patterson) . | ☎ (508) 993-3187
   MR Michael T . . . . | Old Wharf Rd,
    | Nonquitt, MA *02748*

Pape JUNIORS MISS Katrina V . . see MISS M T Vitagliano

Papin MRS Pierre L (Lilly Allen)
☎ (603) 964-5370 . . "Rose Cottage" 190 South Rd, Rye Beach, NH *03871*

Parish MR & MRS Richard Laurence JR (Lowther—Joan H Reijmers)
☎ (203) 637-0226 . . Lowther Point, Riverside, CT *06878*

Parisot MR & MRS Ricardo (Katherine Throckmorton)
"Manawaki" PO Box 2, Severance, NY *12872*

Park MR & MRS H Halsted JR (Virginia G Semlow)
☎ (914) 234-3598 . . Box 284, Bedford, NY *10506*

Parker MRS Allan D (Elizabeth Chick)
☎ (617) 566-6063 . . 56 Fairgreen Place, Chestnut Hill, MA *02167*

Parker MR & MRS Anthony W (Margaret C Alexander) . . . . | ☎ (410) 267-0249
JUNIORS MR Preston W . . . . | 7011 Bay Front Dv, Annapolis, MD *21403*

Parker MRS Augustin H (Reynolds—Judith McKean) ⚓ . . . . | ☎ (207) 326-4677
MISS Pamela D . . . . | Box 11, Rte 1, Brooksville, ME *04617*

Parker MR & MRS Cortlandt (Nancy Knowles)
☎ (401) 847-3268 . . "Greenvale Farm" 582 Wapping Rd, Portsmouth, RI *02871*

Parker MR & MRS Ellis J 3d (Haase—Nancy E Bealer) . . . . | of ☎ (301) 627-4487
MR Ellis S . . . . | "Mount Pleasant" 3401 Mt Pleasant Rd, Upper Marlboro, MD *20772*
 | ☎ (302) 537-4023 306 S Edgewater, Bethany Beach, DE *19930*

Parker MR & MRS Frederick A JR (Susan N Embree)
☎ (203) CI5-4333 . . 91 Middle Beach Rd, Madison, CT *06443*

Parker MR & MRS Harry S 3d (Ellen M McCance) . . | ☎ (516) 788-7352
MISS Elizabeth Day . . . . | "The Barn"
MISS Catherine A . . . . | Box 426,
MR Thomas B . . . . | Fishers Island, NY
MR Samuel F . . . . | *06390*

Parker MRS Henry S JR (Ruth Weyburn)
☎ (207) 596-0866 . . 11 Jameson Point Rd, Rockland, ME *04841*

Parker CAPT & MRS Jefferson D (Louisa B Barbour) USN.
☎ (508) 945-9404 . . 79 Atwood Lane, Chatham, MA *02633*

Parker MRS Judith A (Westin—Judith A Parker) . . . | ☎ (802) 728-5718
MISS Anne M . . . . | "Chase House"
JUNIORS MR William S . . . . | Ridge Rd, Randolph Center, VT *05061*

Parker MRS Patricia Gross (Dempsey—Patricia L Gross) . . . . | ☎ (505) 473-7963
MISS Victoria D . . . . | Box 166B, Rte 6,
MISS Elizabeth S . . . . | Santa Fe, NM *87501*
MR John E JR . . . . |

Parker MR & MRS Richard S JR (Kirstie L Alley) ⚓ . . .
"Mitchell Cottage" W Shore Rd, Dark Harbor, Islesboro, ME *04848*

Parker MR & MRS (DR) Stephen W (Elizabeth V Hillyer)
☎ (401) 847-3268 . . "Greenvale Farm" 582 Wapping Rd, Portsmouth, RI *02871*

Parker MR & MRS Thomas J (Hilary B Higgins)
☎ (508) 945-3549 . . 8 Cranberry Knoll, Chatham, MA *02633*

Parker MR & MRS William E (Rowland—Ruth Bentley)
☎ (207) 967-2509 . . 11 Haverhill St, Kennebunkport, ME *04046*

Parker MR & MRS William Merrick (Mackall—Virginia Lawrence)
☎ (301) 824-2451 . . "The Willows" 11310 Mapleville Rd, Smithsburg, MD *21783*

Parkinson MR & MRS James T 3d (Molly O Owens)
☎ (717) 646-3271 . . Pocono Lake Preserve, PA *18348*

Parkman MR & MRS Samuel (Mary K Simonds)
☎ (207) 244-3182 . . Dodge Point, Seal Cove, ME *04674*

Parkman MR & MRS Theodore B (Winslow—G Floyd-Jones Harrison)
☎ (207) 244-3182 . . Seal Cove, ME *04674*

Parlee MISS Elizabeth J . . see J A Bauer JR

Parmley MR & MRS John R (Shyamala Murugesan)
Papaaloa Rd, Laupahoehoe, HI *96764*

Parrott MR & MRS Thomas A (Barbara Brown)
☎ (516) 788-7552 . . "Driftwood" Fishers Island, NY *06390*

Parshall MR C Ward
☎ (508) 775-2190 . . 4 Wachusett Av, Hyannis Port, MA *02647*

Parsons MR David McI
☎ (207) 867-2255 . . "Bonnie Brae" North Haven, ME *04853*

Parsons MR & MRS I Manning 3d (Fehsenfeld—Cynthia Riley)
☎ (508) 993-7686 . . Salters Point, South Dartmouth, MA *02748*

Parsons MR & MRS J Lester 3d (Estella P Day) . . . . | ☎ (516) 788-7327
MR James S . . . . | Fishers Island, NY
MR Charles S . . . . | *06390*

Parsons MR & MRS Robert White (Suzanne de C Warner) . . . . | ☎ (516) 788-7360
JUNIORS MISS Rebecca H . . . . | "Neau Vue"
JUNIORS MISS Emily W . . . . | PO Box 667, Fishers Island, NY *06390*

Passano MR & MRS Edward M JR (Helen C Marikle) | ☎ (860) 536-1415
MISS Catherine M . . . . | "EMPrest"
JUNIORS MISS Tamara A . . . . | 8 Weston Rd,
JUNIORS MISS Sarah R . . . . | Groton Long Point, CT *06340*

Passano MR & MRS William M JR (Helen V Addington)
☎ (410) 255-6776 . . Cooley's Pond Rd, Box 40, Gibson Island, MD *21056*

Paston-Bedingfeld MR & MRS Henry E (Mary K Ambrose) . . . . | ☎ (011-44-171) 236-6420
MISS Katherine M . . . . | College of Arms,
MISS Charlotte A . . . . | Queen Victoria St,
MR Richard E A . . . . | London EC4V 4BT,
JUNIORS MR Thomas H . . . . | England

Patch MR Peter B
☎ (508) 627-5536 . . Main St, Edgartown, MA *02539*

Patel MR & MRS Sanjay H (Leslie S Dickey)
☎ (203) 438-6063 . . "Rippowam Farm" 177 Rippowam Rd, Box 538, Ridgefield, CT *06877*

Paternotte MR & MRS William L (Nancy D Brewster) . . . . | ☎ (518) 576-9734
MISS Nancy M . . . . | "Bear-in-Mind"
MR William B . . . . | Rte 73, Box 567,
MR Christopher B . . . . | Keene Valley, NY *12943*

Paton MR Kenneth H
☎ (607) 547-9470 .. "Lion's Toe" PO Box 184, Springfield Center, NY *13468*

Pattee MR & MRS Gordon B (Dailey Jones) . . . . ☎ (516) 283-3718
JUNIORS MISS Mary D . . . .
275 Ox Pasture Rd, Southampton, NY *11968*

Patterson MR & MRS Ellmore C (Anne H Choate)
☎ (516) 788-7523 .. Fishers Island, NY *06390*

Patterson MR & MRS F Lytton 3d (Betty L Leggett) . ☎ (207) 667-4312
MISS A Whitney Lockhart . . . .
Toddy Pond, Surry, ME *04684*

Patterson MR Henry Stuart 2d
☎ (508) 693-2694 .. Seven Gates Farm, Vineyard Haven, MA *02568*

Patterson MR & MRS James B (Audrey R Hagen) . . . ☎ (207) 853-4629
MISS Dorothy H . . . .
"Blueberry Point" Robbinston, ME *04671*

Patterson MR James G
454 Jerusalem Rd, Cohasset, MA *07025*

Patterson MRS Jefferson (M Marvin Breckinridge)
☎ (207) 363-3620 .. "River House" 201 US Rte 1, York, ME *03909-1635*

Patterson MR & MRS Jere W (Healey—Betty Muggleton)
☎ (516) 283-7050 .. 30 Wall St, Southampton, NY *11968*

Patterson MR & MRS Lloyd A (Judith I Carroll)
"The Stone House" Great Island, West Yarmouth, MA *02673*

Patterson MR & MRS Oliver M (Donnelley—Cynthia K Coffey)
☎ (847) 486-9190 .. Glen View Club, Golf, IL *60029*

Patterson MRS Patricia S (Norris—Patricia Shephard)
☎ (516) 283-9397 .. "Chapter XI" Box 1344, Coopers Neck Lane, Southampton, NY *11968*

Patterson MR & MRS Robert E (Jane E Manopoli)
☎ (516) 788-7757 .. Crescent Av, Fishers Island, NY *06390*

Patterson MR & MRS Robert R (Edith B Sheerin)
☎ (508) 228-4254 .. "Ducking In" 16 W Chester St, Nantucket, MA *02554*

Patterson MRS Rushmore (Peyton S Kirk)
☎ (516) WA2-0539 .. "Little House" East Norwich, NY *11732*

Patterson MISS Shirley C
☎ (508) 228-4254 .. 24 W Chester St, Nantucket, MA *02554*

Pattishall MR & MRS Beverly W (Mashek—Dorothy M Daniels)
☎ (616) 469-0448 .. "Swift Cottage" 14156 Swift Lane, Lakeside, MI *49116*

Patton MR & MRS Paul L (Kimble—Judith A Thomas) . . . . ☎ (916) 583-3004
JUNIORS MISS Jennifer L . . . .
JUNIORS MR Nicholas B . . . .
"Ly-Inn" 553 River Rd, Tahoe City, CA *95730*

Patty MISS Eleanor J
"Acorn Hill" Bearsville, NY *12409*

Patty MR William A 4th .. see MRS K E Jackson

Paul MR & MRS Douglas L (McMullen—Elizabeth A Curtis-Setchell) . . . . ☎ (516) 671-9284
JUNIORS MR Nicholas L . . . .
"Meadow Farm" Sheep Lane, Lattingtown, NY *11560*

Paul MRS J H Haywood-Reuben (J Hope Haywood-Reuben)
☎ (219) 787-8282 .. "Elephants Rest" 84 West Rd, Dune Acres, IN *46304*

Paul DR & MRS Oglesby (Hatch—Paul—Jean D Lithgow)
☎ (508) 428-9081 .. 19 Great Bay Rd, Little Island, Osterville, MA *02655*

Paumgarten MR & MRS Nicholas B (Carol Marshall) . ☎ (516) 624-8141
MR Nicholas B JR . . . .
MR Alexander M . . . .
411 Centre Island Rd, Oyster Bay, NY *11771*

Paumgarten-Hohenschwangau-Erbach MR & MRS Harald (Barbara Rowinska) . . . . ☎ (207) 276-3631
MISS Christina . . . .
Point Rd, Northeast Harbor, ME *04662*

Paxton MRS Frank Roberts (Stein—Prowell—Leonora H Parsons)
☎ (860) 526-9089 .. "Highover" 153 Ferry Rd, Hadlyme, CT *06439*

Payne MR & MRS David M (Littlefield—Sally Shore) . ☎ (207) 372-6615
MR John S Littlefield . . . .
CR 35, Box 765, Glenmere Rd, Tenants Harbor, ME *04860*

Payne DR & MRS John W (Jane Champe) . . . . ☎ (207) 364-4726
JUNIORS MR David F C . . . .
JUNIORS MR J Kimball C . . . .
Howard Pond Rd, Hanover, ME *04237*

Paynter MR & MRS Grenville H (Tehan—Sally Gooch) . . . . ☎ (860) 868-0062
MR Nathaniel C . . . .
"Cold Spring Hill" New Preston, CT *06777*

Peabody MR & MRS Endicott (Barbara W Gibbons) ⚓
☎ (207) 276-5241 .. "Aunt Hannah's Pasture" Northeast Harbor, ME *04662*

Peabody MR & MRS Francis W (Ward—Swetzoff—Sara T Weeks)
☎ (207) 276-3204 .. "The Shell Heap" Peabody Dv, Northeast Harbor, ME *04662*

Peabody MR & MRS Julian L (Bowles—Hart—Constance E Crowley)
☎ (209) 826-3175 .. "Water Tower" 11609 S Hereford Rd, Los Banos, CA *93635*

Peabody MR & MRS Malcolm E (Pamela O Rowe) . . ☎ (207) 276-5241
MR Carter E . . . .
Northeast Harbor, ME *04662*

Peake MR & MRS David W (Ann D Journeay)
☎ (210) 238-4380 .. "Twin Gates" Box 397, Hunt, TX *78024*

Pearce MR & MRS John I JR (Jane S Ely) . . . . ☎ (516) 267-3651
JUNIORS MISS Sarah E . . . .
JUNIORS MR James I . . . .
"Hedge-Gate" Further Lane, Amagansett, NY *11930*

Pearson MR & MRS G Burton JR (Riegel—Edith du Pont)
☎ (516) 788-7424 .. "Rocky Ledge" Box 441, Fishers Island, NY *06390*

Pearson MR & MRS Nathan W (Kathleen P McMurtry)
☎ (860) 536-3644 .. "Gallup Hill Farm" Box 272, Ledyard, CT *06339*

Pearson MR & MRS Stephen (Margaret Y Newbold) . ☎ (207) 276-3307
  MR & MRS Stephen JR (Irwin—Elizabeth N Dunning) . . . . "Sea Flat"
  MR & MRS Arthur N (Barbara Harris) . . . . Northeast Harbor,
  MR & MRS Alexander C (Kristin A Lindgren) . . . ME *04662*
  MR & MRS Joshua L (Tracy M Brown) . . . .
  MR & MRS Philip Y (Stephanie E LoRusso) . . . . .
Peck MR Arthur K (Coleman—Jane Cochran)
  ☎ (516) 569-4151 . . "Eastview" 221 Polo Lane, Lawrence, NY *11559*
Peck MR & MRS David W JR (Leness—Susan B Harfield)
  ☎ (516) 653-9641 . . "Brigadune" PO Box 349, Quogue, NY *11959*
Peck MRS Hubert R (Barbara F Smith)
  4206 Mariners Watch, Kiawah Island, SC *29455*
Peck MR & MRS Jeffrey E (Abigale H McKean)
  ☎ (516) 788-7508 . . "Apecks" PO Box 56, Fishers Island, NY *06390*
Peck MR Philip F W . . . . ☎ (516) 788-7508
  MISS Pamela S . . . . "Apecks"
                                                                 PO Box 56,
                                                                 Fishers Island, NY
                                                                 06390
Peck MR Robert McC
  ☎ (717) 646-2551 . . Pocono Lake Preserve, PA *18348*
Pedersen MISS Amy R
  ☎ (207) 326-8708 . . "The Cottage" PO Box 312, Main St, Castine, ME *04421*
Pedersen MR & MRS (DR) Matthew H (Theresa T Kudlak) ⚓
  ☎ (207) 326-8708 . . Main St, Castine, ME *04421*
Pedley MR & MRS Eric A (Jane Leland) . . . . ☎ (415) 868-0590
  MISS Alison . . . . 59 Dipsea Rd,
  MR Dean A . . . . Stinson Beach, CA
                                                                 94970
Peirce MR John W
  ☎ (508) 295-0863 . . "Nucleus" Bourne Point, Wareham, MA *02571*
Peirce MR & MRS William H (Jamesina Bathgate) . . . ☎ (207) 864-3726
  MISS Margaret H . . . . "Loon Camp"
  MISS Kittson B . . . . PO Box 1008,
                                                                 Rangeley, ME
                                                                 04970
Pell MRS Allison M . . see E N Cutler 3d
Pell MR & MRS Claiborne (Nuala O'Donnell)
  ☎ (401) 847-0003 . . "Pelican Ledge" Ledge Rd, Newport, RI *02840*
Pell MR & MRS Herbert C 3d (Eugenia S Diehl) . . . . ☎ (401) 847-0057
  MISS Christina O'D . . . . "Pelican Nest"
                                                                 3 Ledge Rd,
                                                                 Newport, RI *02840*
Pell MR John Bigelow
  ☎ (401) 847-2462 . . "Pelican Place" 579 Bellevue Av, Newport, RI *02840*
Pell MRS L Jeffcott (Lucy B Jeffcott)
  "Pell-bei Ghertsos" Schübel Strasse 5, CH 8700 Küsnacht, ZH Switzerland
Pell JUNIORS MR Peter J JR . . see E N Cutler 3d
Pellenc BRNSS (Frances M Kier)
  ☎ (011-33-93) 77-23-68 . . "Prè L'Evêque" OP10 06650 Le Rouret, France

Pelzer MR & MRS Felix C (Carol N Cole) . . . . ☎ (616) 845-1054
  MR Felix C JR . . . . "Time Out
  MR Arthur C . . . . Cottage" Epworth
                                                                 Heights, Ludington,
                                                                 MI *49431*
Pemberton MRS John C (Catherine Watjen)
  ☎ (508) 693-0844 . . Lambert's Cove Rd, RFD 325, Vineyard Haven, MA *02568*
Pendergrass DR & MRS Henry P (Roberts—Carol Y Minster)
  ☎ (207) 244-3551 . . "Tidal Watch" Southwest Harbor, ME *04679*
Pendl MR & MRS Ulrich G (Mary Van R Cruger)
  ☎ (914) 351-4470 . . Ridge Rd, Tuxedo Park, NY *10987*
Pendleton MR & MRS Miles S JR (Elisabeth A Morgan) . . . . ☎ (207) 867-4606
  MISS Constance M . . . . Deacon Brown's
  MR Nathaniel P . . . . Point, North Haven,
                                                                 ME *04853*
Penfield MRS Elizabeth F (Elizabeth V Few)
  ☎ (970) 963-3206 . . 1204 County Rd 170, Carbondale, CO *81623*
Peniston MR & MRS E Winchester (S Lyerly Spöngberg)
  see E de Cordova JR
Penniman MR & MRS H Dawson (Eleanor L Thompson)
  ☎ (508) 758-9496 . . 2 Shipyard Lane, Mattapoisett, MA *02739*
Penniman MRS Nicholas G 3d (Foster—Pattie Symington)
  ☎ (207) 276-5050 . . "The Havoc" Northeast Harbor, ME *04662*
Pennington MR & MRS James S JR (Eleanor Wetten)
  ☎ (715) 547-3870 . . 6921 Thousand Island Lake Rd, Land O'Lakes, WI *54540*
Pennoyer MR & MRS Russell P (Helen E Bearn) . . . . of ☎ (508)994-5619
  JUNIORS MR Gordon S . . . . 164 Mishaum Point,
                                                                 South Dartmouth,
                                                                 MA *02748*
                                                                 ☎ (860) 535-1374
                                                                 "Pentways"
                                                                 Wyassup Rd,
                                                                 North Stonington,
                                                                 CT *06359*
Pennypacker MISS Joanna
  ☎ (610) 647-6854 . . 220 W First Av, Malvern, PA *19355*
Penovich MISS Katherine Redwood
  34 Cunliffe Close, Oxford OX2 7BL, England
Penrose MR & MRS Charles JR (Ann L Cantwell)
  ☎ (603) 323-7703 . . "Briar Farm" North Sandwich, NH *03259*
Penrose MR & MRS James C (Mary Buff Hunter)
  ☎ (914) 225-3205 . . Gipsy Trail Club, Carmel, NY *10512*
Penrose MRS Julian d'E (Elvia Martin) . . . . ☎ (860) 442-3004
  MISS Christine . . . . "The Quail's Nest"
  MR Timothy . . . . 62 Shore Rd,
  MR Julian d'Este JR . . . . Waterford, CT
                                                                 06385
Penson MR & MRS John Gordon (Nancy E Penn)
  ☎ (970) 920-2462 . . 0348 Johnson Dv, Starwood, Aspen, CO *81611*
Pepper MISS Edith M . . see D H McLucas JR
Pepper MRS George W 3d (Whitman—Meyer—Margaret E Morgan)
  ☎ (207) 244-7226 . . "Causeway House" Causeway Lane N, Box 1253, Southwest Harbor, ME *04679*

Pereira MR & MRS Gaston E (Claire S Benacerraf) . . | ☎ (516) 749-0037
  JUNIORS MR Alejandro E . . . . | 8 Shore Rd,
                                                                            Dering Harbor,
                                                                           Shelter Island
                                                                           Heights, NY *11965*

Perera MR Guido R
  ☎ (508) 362-3137 . . "The Homestead" 17 Strawberry Lane, Yarmouth Port, MA *02675*

Perera MR & MRS Guido R JR (Joan W Hulme) . . . . | ☎ (508) 362-3971
  MISS Jessica H . . . . | 18 Strawberry Lane,
  MISS Helen T . . . . | Yarmouth Port, MA
  MISS Margaret S . . . . | *02675*

Perera MR & MRS Lawrence T (Elizabeth A | ☎ (508) FO2-6350
  Wentworth) . . . . | "Hamblen House"
  MISS Lucy E . . . . | Strawberry Lane,
  JUNIORS MR Lawrence T JR . . . . | Yarmouth Port, MA
                                                                            | *02675*

Perera MRS Phillips (Frederica P Drinkwater) . . . . . | ☎ (508) 362-3693
  MISS Frederica S . . . . | 126 Thacher Shore
  MR Phillips JR . . . . | Rd, Yarmouth Port,
  MR Christopher D . . . . | MA *02675*
  MR Alexander L . . . . |

Perera MR & MRS Ronald C (Judith A Weed) . . . . . . | ☎ (508) 362-6937
  MISS Lisa D . . . . | 114 Wharf Lane,
  MISS Katherine T . . . . | Yarmouth Port, MA
  MISS Rosalind P . . . . | *02675*

Perin MRS Lawrence (Smith—Margaret G Vogel)
  ☎ (603) 464-5696 . . "Hillside" Loon Pond, Hillsborough, NH *03244*

Perkins MR & MRS Edward C (Louise D DuBois)
  ☎ (413) 243-0681 . . "Glencote" Box 365, Tyringham, MA *01264*

Perkins MR & MRS Eric B (A Joyce Cottrell) . . . . . . | Edgartown, MA
  JUNIORS MISS Carolyne B . . . . | *02539*
  JUNIORS MISS Alison J . . . . |
  JUNIORS MR Eric H T . . . . |

Perkins MR & MRS Francis E JR (Edith M Bradley) . . | ☎ (207) 963-7628
  MR William S . . . . | West Gouldsboro,
                                                                             | ME *04607*

Perkins MR & MRS Gilman (Rebecca D Mastin)
  ☎ (207) 967-3003 . . "Green Lane Cottage" 2 Dover Lane, Box 1384, Kennebunkport, ME *04046*

Perkins MR & MRS Gilman C (Deborah S Hower)
  ☎ (207) 967-0027 . . RR 2, Box 985, Kennebunkport, ME *04046*

Perkins MR & MRS John A (Lydia B Cobb)
  ☎ (207) 867-4618 . . Crabtree Point, Box 748, North Haven, ME *04853*

Perkins MRS Palfrey (Linda Wellington)
  ☎ (207) 244-3181 . . "Woodfield" Southwest Harbor, ME *04679*

Perkins MR & MRS Richard S (Newell—Audrey T Walker) . . of
  ☎ (908) 842-2270 . . 4 Navesink Av, Rumson, NJ *07760*
  ☎ (860) 535-1464 . . 21 Front St, Stonington, CT *06378*

Perkins MR Robert F JR
  "Loon" Back River, Northwest Territories, Canada

Perkins MR & MRS Roswell B (Joan Titcomb)
  ☎ (401) 635-4444 . . 125 Sakonnet Point Rd, Little Compton, RI *02837*

Perlberg MR Edward B
  ☎ (516) 537-0614 . . Sagaponack, NY *11962*

Pernoud DR & MRS Michael J (Christine Costello) . . | ☎ (705) 842-5366
  MISS Cathleen . . . . | "Grey House"
  JUNIORS MISS Elizabeth . . . . | Thessalon, Ontario
  JUNIORS MR Michael J . . . . | P0L 1L0, Canada

Perrin MRS John (Gardner—Esther Coffin)
  ☎ (207) 326-8223 . . "Perkins-Brooks House" The Common, Castine, ME *04421*

Perry JUNIORS MR David H . . see J W Metzger JR

Perry MR & MRS H Bradlee (Virginia Reimers)
  ☎ (207) 348-2836 . . "Harborside Farm" Dow Rd, Deer Isle, ME *04627*

Perry MR Henry E . . . . | "Winter Sun"
  MR Henry E 3d . . . . | Winthrop, WA
  MR George F . . . . | *98862*

Perry MR & MRS Lyman S A (Kate T Driggs)
  ☎ (508) 228-3340 . . "Bayberry Wind" 78 Polpis Rd, Nantucket, MA *02554*

Perry MR Nathaniel D . . see J W Metzger JR

Perry MRS Oliver H (Woods—Louise H Colie)
  ☎ (410) 494-0214 . . Blakehurst 209, 1055 W Joppa Rd, Towson, MD *21204*

Perry MR & MRS Walter E 3d (Mary G Kennard) . . . | ☎ (908) 892-4864
  JUNIORS MISS Diana B . . . . | "Bedlam by the
  JUNIORS MR Sam H P . . . . | Bay" Box 233,
                                                                             | Bay Head, NJ *08742*

Perry MR William Haggin JR
  ☎ (860) MO3-3262 . . "Maple Hill" 67 Roast Meat Hill Rd, Killingworth, CT *06419*

Persons MR & MRS Alan R (Rosa C Miller) . . . . | ☎ (716) 394-1939
  MISS Elizabeth A . . . . | 18 Fallbrook Rd,
  MR Robert D . . . . | Canandaigua, NY
  MR William S . . . . | *14424*

Persse MR John W 3d—⛵
  "Spruce Tops" Juniper Point, Boothbay Harbor, ME *04538*

Peters MR & MRS Alton E (Fisher—Elizabeth I | ☎ (860) 824-5206
  Berlin) . . . . | Falls Village, CT
  MISS Rachel C . . . . | *06031*

Peters MR & MRS Frederick W (Alexandra T Lally) . | ☎ (914) 763-8685
  MISS Clelia W . . . . | 137 Boway Rd,
  JUNIORS MR John F . . . . | South Salem, NY
                                                                             | *10590*

Peters MRS Horace W (Edith C Colt)
  ☎ (207) 799-0010 . . "Ram Island Farm" Box 55, Charles E Jordan Rd, Cape Elizabeth, ME *04107*

Peters MRS John L D (Eleanor T Carpenter)
  ☎ (203) 259-7290 . . 105 Southport Woods Dv, Southport, CT *06490*

Peters MR & MRS Ralph F (Threatt—Diana J | of ☎ (406)235-4430
  Clayton) . . . . | "Lucky Dizzy
  MR Richard C . . . . | Ranch" Craig Rte,
                                                                             | Wolf Creek, MT
                                                                             | *59648*
                                                                             | ☎ (518) 251-4060
                                                                             | North Woods Club,
                                                                             | Minerva, NY *12851*

Peters MR & MRS Richard (Gribbel—Elizabeth T | ☎ (804) 428-1195
  Fehr) . . . . | 114—52 St,
  MISS Julie . . . . | Virginia Beach, VA
                                                                             | *23451*

Petersen MR & MRS Erroll M (Romaine—Elisabeth S Howe)
☎ (307) 455-2266 . . CM Ranch, Dubois, WY *82513*

Peterson MR & MRS Frederick A (Elisabeth McC Thomas) . . . .
MR John T . . . .
☎ (207) 627-4335
Box 5035, RFD 1, Oxford, ME *04270*

Petrasch MR & MRS John G (Olivia H Rutter) . . . . . .
JUNIORS MISS Anne S . . . .
JUNIORS MR John G JR . . . .
☎ (508) 228-2585
"Shawkemo" 10 Berkeley Av, Monomoy, Nantucket, MA *02554*

Petrie MR & MRS John E (Gribbel—Katherine E Wiedersheim)
☎ (508) 228-1593 . . 3 Mulberry St, Nantucket, MA *02554*

Pettengill MR & MRS Kroger (Kathryn W Mitchell)
☎ (513) 561-6732 . . 4750 Willow Hills Lane, Cincinnati, OH *45243*

Pettit MR & MRS William D (Stetson—Elizabeth J McChristie)
☎ (508) 627-5869 . . 4 Armstrong Lane, PO Box 5037, Edgartown, MA *02539*

Pettus MRS Charles P (Stella R Cartwright) . . . .
MISS Georgia . . . .
MR Charles P JR . . . .
Jly 1 . .
☎ (616) 526-2067
2 Park Walk, Wequetonsing, MI *49740*

Pettus MR & MRS Robert C (Sharon A Wright)
☎ (314) 968-8631 . . 6 Daniel Rd, St Louis, MO *63124*

Pew MR & MRS G Thompson JR (Sandra L Kennedy)
⚓ . . . .
JUNIORS MR G Thompson 3d . . . .
☎ (410) 255-7632
on board Anodyne" Gibson Island Club, Gibson Island, MD *21056*

Pflueger MR & MRS Edward M (Neighbour—Kathleen I Powers)
☎ (914) 221-2692 . . "Kiyiwana Farm" 440 Hosner Mountain Rd, Stormville, NY *12582-5326*

Phelan MR & MRS Arthur J JR (Kathleen A Butler) . .
MISS Margaret A . . . .
MR Arthur J 3d . . . .
☎ (860) 739-8212
66 S Washington Av, Crescent Beach, CT *06357*

Phelps MR Mason JR
"Block House" Campment d'Ours Island, Desbarats, Ontario P0R 1E0, Canada

Phelps MR & MRS Stowe C (Charlton Y Jacobs)
☎ (516) 788-7610 . . Fishers Island, NY *06390*

Philbin MRS Brisbane (Kelley—Elinor Brisbane)
☎ (516) 324-2142 . . 43A Dunemere Lane, East Hampton, NY *11937*

Philip MR & MRS Peter S (Victoria S Rockefeller)
☎ (207) 885-0224 . . "Greywalls" 494 Black Point Rd, Box 3055, Prouts Neck, ME *04074*

Philip MR & MRS William V N (Jennifer C Brainard)
☎ (802) 867-5365 . . West Rd, Dorset, VT *05251*

Phillips MRS (DR) Asa E JR (Anne Wight)
☎ (207) 276-5182 . . "Westover" PO Box 227, Seal Harbor, ME *04675-0227*

Phillips MR Christopher H
☎ (508) 768-6319 . . 74 Eastern Av, Essex, MA *01929*

Phillips MR & MRS (REV) Daniel A (Diana Walcott) . .
MR Bradford L . . . .
MISS Lisa W (Meyer—Lisa W Phillips) . . . .
☎ (508) 996-5258
"Treehouse" Shore Acres Rd, South Darmouth, MA *02748*

Phillips MR & MRS Ellis L JR (Marion E Grumman)
☎ (508) 359-7922 . . "Rien de Vue" 279 North St, Medfield, MA *02052*

Phillips MR & MRS George F JR (Kohlmeyer—Carin Wyckoff) . . . .
MR Carter S Kohlmeyer . . . .
☎ (905) 468-7718
228 Queen St, Niagara-on-the-Lake, Ontario L0S 1J0, Canada

Phillips DR & MRS Gerald B (Maria B Lewis) . . . . . .
MISS Abigail S . . . .
MISS Elizabeth B . . . .
☎ (203) 259-5031
1081 Redding Rd, Fairfield, CT *06430*

Phillips MRS Harry H S JR (Munson—Marr—Martha J Potter)
☎ (207) 244-5543 . . "Pine Ledge" Box 154, Southwest Harbor, ME *04679*

Phillips MRS Lewis G (Butler—Jessie V Ewing)
48 Sammy's Beach Rd, East Hampton, NY *11937*

Phillips MR & MRS Silas B JR (Frances M Rau) . . of
☎ (210) 896-4851 . . 551 Fairway Dv, Kerrville, TX *78028*
☎ (011-52-465) 2-24-30 . . Revueltas 19, San Miguel de Allende, GTO, Mexico

Phillips MRS Stephen (Bessie G Wright)
Burpee Hill Rd, New London, NH *03257*

Philson DR & MRS Arthur De L (Pogue—Gourd—Nancy W Hadra)
3 Trumbull St, Stonington, CT *06378*

Phipps MR & MRS Frank H 3d (Averyl B McComb)
☎ (508) 993-7674 . . "The Patch" Nonquitt, MA *02748*

Phipps MR Ogden . . . .
MISS Cynthia . . . .
717 N Broadway, Saratoga Springs, NY *12866*

Phyfe MR & MRS Churchill B (Bloom—Jean Corris) .
MR Duncan A . . . .
☎ (203) 966-5647
145 Kimberly Place, New Canaan, CT *06840*

Phyfe MR Henry Pinkney JR . . see D Roberts

Phyfe MR & MRS James D (Herrick—Winifred Swoyer) ⚓ . . . .
MISS Gaelen B . . . .
MR James D 3d . . . .
 MISS Robin F Herrick . . . .
 MR Trevor S Herrick . . . .
☎ (508) 992-0240
Nonquitt, MA *02748*

Pierce MR & MRS Benjamin T (Josephine Wells Browning)
☎ (011-33) 59-26-13-72 . . "Menda Belateia" Vieille rte de St Pée, 64500 St Jean-de-Luz, France

Pierce MR & MRS Daniel (May P Harding)
Box 362, Northeast Harbor, ME *04662*

Pierce MRS Frederick S (Phyllis E Wendt)
☎ (716) 947-4626 . . Century House, Derby, NY *14047*

Pierce MR John B JR
☎ (207) 371-2673 . . Marrtown Rd, Georgetown, ME *04548*

Pierce MR Julius E . . . . | ☎ (705) 633-5578
    MR Jay P Havre . . . . | Bartlett Lodge, Cache Lake, Algonquin Park, Huntsville, Ontario P0A 1K0, Canada

Pierce MR & MRS Roger (Felicia P Havre)
    ☎ (705) 633-5578 . . "Skymount Cove" Cache Lake, Algonquin Park, Huntsville, Ontario P0A 1K0, Canada

Pierce MR & MRS Stephen B (Catherine Calvé) . . . . . | ☎ (011-33-3)
    MISS Pauline C . . . . | 44-07-68-77
    JUNIORS MISS Susan P . . . . | 60 rue Nicolas
    JUNIORS MR Philip C . . . . | Fortin, 60250 Mouchy-la-Ville, France

Pierce MR & MRS William Curtis (Elizabeth N Gay)
    ☎ (207) 625-3942 . . "The Pierce Place" Rte 1, Box 5140, West Baldwin, ME 04091

Pierce MRS William G (Bunting—Susan H Sayen)
    ☎ (207) 359-8596 . . "The Yellow House" Carter Point Rd, Box 111, Sedgwick, ME 04676

Pierpoint MR & MRS Powell (Margaret S Sagar)
    ☎ (203) 245-9820 . . 23 Chapman Av, Madison, CT 06443

Pierpont MR & MRS Harlan T JR (Georgia W Simmons)
    ☎ (617) 934-6786 . . 70 Peterson Rd, Duxbury, MA 02332

Pierrepont MR & MRS John (Dewey—Nancy Weller)
    ☎ (207) 276-5248 . . "The Elms" PO Box 866, Northeast Harbor, ME 04662

Pierrepont MRS R Stuyvesant JR (Mary O Shriver)
    ☎ (516) 671-4291 . . 336 Duck Pond Rd, Locust Valley, NY 11560

Pierrepont MR & MRS Seth Low (Consuelo D Wilson)
    ☎ (616) 526-7486 . . 461 Glenn Dv, Harbor Springs, MI 49740

Pierson DR & MRS Richard N JR (Dunn—Alice W Roberts)⚓
    ☎ (207) 244-5732 . . "Bold Shores" Great Cranberry Island, Cranberry Isles, ME 04625

Pigott MR & MRS James S G (Wyckoff—Oscarsson —Constance A H Robinsson) . . . . | ☎ (207) 236-8410
    MR Richard I . . . . | 3 Spruce St, Rockport, ME 04856

Pike REV & MRS Thomas F (Lys McLaughlin) . . . . . | ☎ (207) 763-3839
    MISS Jean L . . . . | "Woodcock Farm"
    CAPT Thomas F JR—USA. . . . . | Lincolnville, ME 04849

Pilling MRS George Platt 4th (Barbara Bosworth)
    ☎ (717) 646-2722 . . "Lake's End" Pocono Lake Preserve, PA 18348

Pilling MR & MRS Robert B (Elizabeth J Ludzinski)
    "Lake's End" Pocono Lake Preserve, PA 18348

Pillsbury MR Charles S B . . see J B Britton

Pillsbury MR & MRS Philip W JR (Caroline E Hannaford) . . . . | of ☎ (612)473-4705
    MISS Caroline H . . . . | "The Cottage"
    MR Philip W 3d . . . . | 302 W Ferndale Rd, Wayzata, MN 55391
    | ☎ (218) 226-4545 "La Chouette" Beaver Bay Club, Beaver Bay, MN 55601

Pillsbury MR W Caleb JR
    8672 Loch Levon, Kings Beach, CA 96143

Pinckney MISS Elizabeth R
    ☎ (704) 692-1908 . . "Hemlocks" Box 664, Flat Rock, NC 28731

Pingeon DR & MRS René A (Frances D Parsons)
    ☎ (508) 996-9968 . . "Les Hurle-Vents" Mishaum Point, South Dartmouth, MA 02748

Pinkham MR & MRS Richard A R (Mary G Struthers)
    ☎ (203) 531-1543 . . 618 W Lyon Farm Dv, Greenwich, CT 06831

Piñon MR & MRS Horacio J (Maria V Sanchez-Elia)
    ☎ (011-598-42) 70643 . . "Del Mar" Punta Del Este, Maldonado, Uruguay

Pinson MR & MRS Pablo C (Winifred Wisner) . . . . . . | ☎ (011-52-5)
    MISS Cecilia . . . . | 282-5542
    MR Pablo . . . . | Alencastre 99, 202,
    MR George . . . . | Lomas Virreyes, Mexico DF 11000, Mexico

Pinto MR & MRS Maurice E (Elizabeth A Cooley) . . . | ☎ (516) 749-7870
    MISS Lisa . . . . | 9 Seagull Lane, Shelter Island, NY 11964

Piro DR & MRS Philip A JR (Marion W Jones)
    ☎ (516) 283-3936 . . "Why Not" 339 Captain's Neck Lane, Southampton, NY 11968

Pirrung MR & MRS C Mark (Mary D Gargaro)
    ☎ (616) 526-2651 . . "The Columns" 56 Beach Dv, Wequetonsing, MI 49740

Pistell MR & MRS Christopher A (Louise H Wharton)
    ☎ (207) 787-2854 . . East Sebago, ME 04029

Pitarys MR & MRS Peter S (Nancy H Leggett) . . . . . . | ☎ (508) 945-4670
    MISS Katherine . . . . | 40 Gladen Lane,
    JUNIORS MISS Laura . . . . | Chatham, MA 02633

Pitt MR William H
    ☎ (203) 869-1811 . . 449 Round Hill Rd, Greenwich, CT 06830

Pivirotto MR & MRS David H (Brenda T Brophy)
    ☎ (603) 569-3630 . . PO Box 20, Tuftonboro Rd, Mirror Lake, NH 03853

Pivirotto MR & MRS Richard R (Mary P Burchfield) . | ☎ (603) 544-2229
    MISS Jennifer P . . . . | "Pine Point" Bald Peak Colony Club, Melvin Village, NH 03850

Pizzicaria MRS Jean H (Jean E Hope)
    ☎ (011-39-81) 837-1538 . . "Cassetta Artimo" via Vignola 40, Anacapri, Italy

Pizzinat MR & MRS Arthur Franklin (Julia Wingfield)
    ☎ (808) 882-7936 . . "Pu'uhonua" 13 Leihulu Place, Mauna Kea Fairways, Kohala Coast, HI 96743

Place MR & MRS David E (Susanna M Badgley) ⚓
    ☎ (207) 371-2333 . . "Robin Hood Cove" N End Rd, PO Box 209, Georgetown, ME 04548

Place MRS Julie L (Julie C Lewis) . . . . | ☎ (508) 771-5538
    MR H Calvin JR . . . . | "Strawberry
    MR Jonathan C . . . . | Cottage" Scudder Av, Hyannis Port, MA 02647

Plater MR & MRS David D (Sheela G Burke) ...... | "Ballingrobe"
    MISS Juliana H .... | Covington, LA
    MR Bryan B .... | *70433*
    MR Christopher S ....|
Platt MR & MRS David N (Marguerite L E Beer).... | ☎ (516) 653-6630
    MISS Marguerite F........................... | 25 Quaquanantuck
    MR David S .... | Lane, Quogue, NY
     | *11959*
Platt MR & MRS Geoffrey JR (Hope G Forsyth) ..... | ☎ (207) 867-4685
    JUNIORS MISS Lucy F....................... | North Haven, ME
     | *04853*
Platt MR Henry .. of
    ☎ (516) 283-0425 .. Meadow Club, First Neck Lane, Southampton, NY *11968*
    ☎ (212) 838-0800 .. 825 Fifth Av, New York, NY *10021*
Platt MR Hermann K
    ☎ (603) 744-5620 .. "Allonby Orchard" East Hebron, NH *03232*
Platt MR & MRS Nicholas (Sheila Maynard)
    ☎ (207) 867-2242 .. North Haven, ME *04853*
Platt MR Richard B .... | ☎ (616) 547-4083
    JUNIORS MISS Anne D .... | "North Depot"
    JUNIORS MR R Booth JR .... | Platt Cottage,
     | Chicago Club,
     | Charlevoix, MI
     | *49720*
Platt MR William
    ☎ (902) 643-2787 .. Ardnamurchan Club, Glenwood RR 1, Central Argyle, Nova Scotia B0W 1W0, Canada
Plimpton DR & MRS Calvin H (Ruth Talbot)
    ☎ (508) 428-2150 .. "Lands End" 979 Sea View Av, Osterville, MA *02655*
Plimpton MR & MRS George A (Sarah W Dudley) .. | ☎ (516) 267-3638
    MISS Medora A............................. | 73 Louse Point Rd,
    MR Taylor A .... | East Hampton, NY
     | *11937*
Plimpton REV DR & MRS Hollis W JR (Peggy Lucas)
    ☎ (508) 428-7255 .. "Gone with the Wind" 191 Sea View Av, Osterville, MA *02655*
Plowden-Wardlaw MR & MRS Thomas C (Mason—Stanton—Mary D Francis)
    ☎ (508) 992-0862 .. "Boxwood House" Box 164P, South Dartmouth, MA *02748*
Plum MR & MRS John E (Mimi Kim) .... | ☎ (201) 445-7161
    JUNIORS MISS Sabrina M .... | 531 Eastgate Rd,
    JUNIORS MISS Tamina M .... | Ho Ho Kus, NJ
     | *07423-1707*
Plum MR & MRS Matthias JR (Morris—Margaret E R White) .... | ☎ (508) 945-0286
    MISS Arabella G .... | "Appleway"
    MR Matthias M .... | 114 Cedar St,
     | Chatham, MA *02633*
Plumer MR & MRS William R (Audrey Capen) .... | ☎ (508) 945-9460
    MISS Julie .... | 252 Stage Harbor
     | Rd, Chatham, MA
     | *02633*
Plummer MRS H Pierson (Atherton—Roberta Stevenson)
    ☎ (408) 625-5730 .. 1412 Riata Rd, Box 1273, Pebble Beach, CA *93953*

Plummer MR & MRS Morgan H JR (Jean MacHale)
    ☎ (508) 758-2833 .. "Tupelo House" 13 Shipyard Lane, Mattapoisett, MA *02739*
Plunkett MRS William C (Eleanore A Kennedy)
    ☎ (203) 255-2216 .. 50 Southport Woods Dv, Southport, CT *06490*
Poe MR & MRS Edgar A 3d (Rojahn—Christina F Zuray)
    "Ravens Cliff" Tesuque, NM *87574*
Poinier MRS John (Lawrence—Lois P Wodell)
    ☎ (401) 322-7768 .. "The Covey" Fenway Rd, Weekapaug, RI *02891*
Poitevent MR & MRS Eads 3d (Deborah Roulhac) .... | ☎ (615) 924-2488
    MISS Evelyn S............................. | "Wayside Cottage"
    MR Eads 4th .... | Monteagle
     | Assembly,
     | Monteagle, TN
     | *37356*
Polk MR & MRS David C S (Amy Brown) .... | "Land's End"
    MISS Julia M P .... | Cragsmoor, NY
     | *12420*
Polk MR & MRS Samuel S (Anne Page Homer) ..... | ☎ (516) 788-7708
    MR Thomas S .... | "Top O'
    MR Samuel H .... | World"
     | Fishers Island, NY
     | *06390*
Pollock MRS Elizabeth Maclean (Martin—Elizabeth O Maclean) .... | ☎ (011-44-1452)
    MISS Duart M Martin .... | 81-3013
     | "Holcombe House"
     | Painswick,
     | Gloucestershire
     | GL6 6RG, England
Pomeroy MR & MRS Robert W 3d (Giblin—Jane G A Ramsay)
    ☎ (207) 526-4346 .. Swans Island, ME *04685*
Pons MR & MRS John P (Yvonne G Archer) .... | ☎ (609) 368-5529
    MISS Louise B............................. | 184—70 St,
     | Avalon, NJ *08202*
Ponti MRS Ettore (Anne K Riggins)
    ☎ (203) 853-7322 .. 20 Shorehaven Rd, Norwalk, CT *06855*
Ponvert MRS Nancy B (Wilkinson—Nancy Borger). | ☎ (802) 297-3519
    MR Kent K Wilkinson JR .... | "Stonewalls"
     | PO Box 521,
     | Winhall Hollow Rd,
     | Bondville, VT
     | *05340*
Pool MR & MRS Eugene H (L Parrish Dobson) ..... | ☎ (207) 867-4409
    MR Nathan B .... | "Point House"
     | Pulpit Harbor,
     | North Haven, ME
     | *04853*
Poole MR & MRS Peter A (Rosemary F Sullivan)
    ☎ (603) 823-8120 .. "The Farmhouse" Franconia, NH *03580*
Poor MR & MRS Charles L (Greene—Edith F Cowles) ⚜
    ☎ (508) 992-4696 .. Box P290, Nonquitt, MA *02748*
Pope MISS Adrianna M
    ☎ (209) 674-8506 .. "El Peco Ranch" 10462 Rd 21, Madera, CA *93637*
Pope MRS Edward J (Horkan—McConnell—Evelyn H Maddox)
    ☎ (540) 687-5884 .. "Rockmere" PO Box 915, Middleburg, VA *22117*

Pope MR & MRS Frank M (Kingsbury—Sylvia M Thorndike) . . . . ☎ (603) 529-2313
MISS Rosamond T . . . . "Red House"
JUNIORS MR Albert A . . . . 396 Memorial Dv,
    MISS Macy T Kingsbury . . . . Weare, NH 03281
    MR H Neal Kingsbury . . . .
Pope MR & MRS John A (Nancy Mabrey)
  ☎ (508) 768-6000 . . "Sea Dunes" 71 John Wise Av, Essex, MA 01929
Pope MR & MRS Wilmot T (Margery P Montgomery) ☎ (508) 526-4063
MR Geoffrey J . . . . 465 Summer St,
    PO Box 281,
    Manchester, MA
    01944
Porteous MISS Alexandra K . . see W J Thomas JR
Porteous MRS Jane D (Vale—Jane B Drexel) . . . . . ☎ (207) 288-2348
MR Louis D . . . . Acadian Farm,
    1 Youngs Mountain
    Rd, Bar Harbor, ME
    04609
Porteous MR William D . . see W J Thomas JR
Porter DR & MRS George H 3d (Virginia Pillow)
  "Villa Pliny" Tremezzo, Lake Como, Italy
Porter MISS Linda M
  ☎ (715) 385-2760 . . Camp Osoha, 11019 Big Muskellunge Lake Rd, Boulder Junction, WI 54512
Porter MISS Mary K
  ☎ (413) 637-0638 . . 80 Undermountain Rd, Lenox, MA 01240
Portner MRS John A D (Erveane D Massey) . . . . . ☎ (919) 441-2565
MR John A D JR . . . . "Marslanding"
    Kill Devil Hills, NC
    27948
Posselius MR Edward J JR . . . . ☎ (517) 738-8333
MISS M Christy . . . . Cottage 50,
MISS Patricia E . . . . 1929 Cliff Rd,
    Pointe Aux Barques,
    MI 48467
Post MISS Diana
  Ensign Island, Islesboro, ME 04848
Postley MRS Clarence S (Kebaili—Marilynn L Dinneen)
  ☎ (415) 771-4286 . . 1980 Jackson St, San Francisco, CA 94109
Potter MR & MRS Charles S (Barbara O McClurg)
  ☎ (847) 362-0103 . . "Widgeon Hill" 32315 N Almond Rd, Libertyville, IL 60048
Potter MR & MRS Eugene W JR (M Melinda Rice) . . ☎ (508) 228-0534
MISS Peyson W . . . . Box 15, Nantucket,
    MA 02554
Potter MR & MRS H David (Elizabeth F Stone) . . . . ☎ (860) 542-5448
MR Nicholas F . . . . 220 Mountain Rd,
    Norfolk, CT 06058
Potter MR & MRS Hamilton F JR (Maureen E Cotter) . . of
  ☎ (212) 737-4225 . . 325 E 65 St, New York, NY 10021
  ☎ (516) 584-7589 . . 99 Long Beach Rd, RFD 1, Box 99, St James, NY 11780
Potter MR & MRS John H N 2d (Kimberly D McKinley)
  ☎ (401) 423-1369 . . 191 Narragansett Av, Jamestown, RI 02835

Potter MR & MRS John S JR (Joan C Wall) . . . . ☎ (508) 693-0190
MR John S 3d . . . . "Breakwater
MR William N H . . . . Lodge" Box 1475,
MR Robert L C . . . . East Chop,
    Oak Bluffs, MA
    02557
Potter MR & MRS Spencer W (Cornelia V H Ferber) . ☎ (401) 423-1369
JUNIORS MISS Diana L . . . . 191 Narragansett
JUNIORS MISS Lydia L . . . . Av, Jamestown, RI
    02853
Potter DR & MRS William H (Lighthill—Agnes E Hawkins)
  ☎ (203) 637-1091 . . "Primrose Cottage" 49 Edgewater Dv, Old Greenwich, CT 06870
Potts MR & MRS Robert H (E Halsey Ligget) . . . . . . ☎ (603) 253-4537
MR David L . . . . RR 1, Box 185,
    Center Harbor, NH
    03226
Pough MR Richard H
  ☎ (508) 645-9750 . . "The Eyrie" RR 1, Box 462, South Rd, Chilmark, MA 02535
Powell MRS Charles S (Marguerite B Shannon)
  ☎ (201) 664-2455 . . 7 Humphrey Rd, Morristown, NJ 07960
Powell MRS Irwin A (Myles—Edith B Harlan)
  ☎ (516) OR6-8306 . . "Woods Harbor" 40 Frost Creek Dv, Lattingtown, NY 11560
  Aug 1 . . ☎ (418) 665-2728 . . "Jardin Joyeux" Pointe-au-Pic, Quebec G0T 1M0, Canada
Powell MRS John G (Alcorn—Sara A Deacon)
  ☎ (908) 714-0827 . . 976 Barnegat Lane, Mantoloking, NJ 08738
Powell MR Robert F JR . . . . ☎ (609) 884-0325
MISS Margot McCoy . . . . 1321 New York Av,
JUNIORS MISS Laura Johnson . . . . Cape May, NJ
    08204
Powers MRS John M JR (Marian B Stevens)
  ☎ (860) 669-9821 . . 28 Sol's Point Rd, Beach Park, Clinton, CT 06413
Pratt MR & MRS Carl E (M Julie Hogan) . . . . ☎ (508) 888-8745
JUNIORS MR Carl E JR . . . . "Freeman Farm"
    Sandwich, MA
    02563
Pratt MR & MRS Charles McC (Helen H Forson) . . . ☎ (418) 665-7609
MR Eliot F . . . . "Steepways"
JUNIORS MR Charles E . . . . Pointe-au-Pic,
    Quebec G0T 1M0,
    Canada
Pratt MR & MRS John T (Jane S Stone)
  ☎ (207) 734-6443 . . HC 60, Box 340, Islesboro, ME 04848
Pratt MRS M Melville (Mary M Melville) . . . . ☎ (616) 386-5288
MR Lanier W 3d . . . . Omena, MI 49674
JUNIORS MR Jonathan M . . . .
JUNIORS MR Charles A . . . .
Pratt MR & MRS Vaughan W (Caroline W Malone) . ☎ (207) 883-4656
⚓ . . . . "Knoll Lea"
MISS Katherine B . . . . Fieldways,
MR Jon V M . . . . Prouts Neck, ME
JUNIORS MISS Chauncey H 04074
Pratt MRS William C JR (Patricia C Morey)
  ☎ (413) 269-4639 . . East Otis, MA 01029

Preble MR & MRS Wallace L (Elizabeth L Ward)
⛵ . . . . ☎ (503) 738-0937
   MR Thomas Ward . . . . 4780 Fairway Dv,
   MR Mark E Gearhart, OR 97138

Prentice MR & MRS Sheldon E (Nancy M Reilly) . . . ☎ (516) 283-7708
   MISS Alison P PO Box 2261,
   JUNIORS MISS Katherine S . . . . First Neck Lane,
   JUNIORS MR James E . . . . Southampton, NY 11969

Prentice MR & MRS William C H (Elsie B Doty)
   ☎ (508) 636-8934 . . 646 River Rd, Westport, MA 02790

Prescott DR & MRS Richmond (Dwight—Pamela Sedgwick)
   ☎ (508) 993-5747 . . 93 Nonquitt Av, Nonquitt, MA 02748

Preston MR Kendall JR
   ☎ (520) 795-3160 . . 3180 N Hill Farm Dv, Tucson, AZ 85712

Preston MR & MRS Seymour JR (Suzanne Gregory) . . ☎ (518) 576-4459
   JUNIORS MISS Eliot . . . . Rte 73,
Keene Valley, NY 12943

Preston MR & MRS Thomas P (Helen C Davis) . . . . . ☎ (508) 432-6060
   JUNIORS MISS Barbara P . . . . 629 Main St,
Harwich Port, MA 02646

Prewitt MRS Russe (Prewitt—Eaton—Ann H Russe)
   ☎ (705) 633-5709 . . ''Wolf-Pass'' Camp Northway, Algonquin Park, Ontario P0A 1K0, Canada

Prezioso MR & MRS Michael S (Miranda Griscom Smith)
   ☎ (401) 348-8585 . . ''The Folly'' 12 Meadow Lane, Watch Hill, RI 02891

Price MRS Hickman JR (Meacham—Eyre—Dorothy Hurt)
   ☎ (516) 283-0094 . . ''Boxwood'' Foster Crossing, PO Box 1230, Southampton, NY 11969

Price MR & MRS John S (Martha E Stokes)
   ☎ (508) 540-7034 . . 54 Carey Lane, Quissett, Falmouth, MA 02540

Price MR & MRS Joseph A (Weeks—Barbara A Benedict)
   ☎ (802) 824-3916 . . 111 Landgrove Rd, Weston, VT 05161

Price MR & MRS Philip JR (Sarah B Dolan) . . . . ☎ (207) 366-3600
   MISS Alexandra G . . . . Matinicus Island,
   MISS Emilie A . . . . ME 04851
   MR Philip 3d . . . .

Price MR & MRS Richard H SR (Mary K Beecher)
   Box 131, Barnard, VT 05031

Price MR & MRS Robert M (O'Hara—Mary C Arkell) ⛵
   ☎ (908) 899-1567 . . 84 Bay Point Harbour, Point Pleasant, NJ 08742

Price MR & MRS William R (Christine C Goodman)
   ☎ (516) 288-6387 . . 52 Griffing Av, Westhampton Beach, NY 11978

Prideaux-Brune MR & MRS Rowland D C . . . . ☎ (408) 625-9756
   (Genevieve P McLaren) . . . . PO Box 1761,
   MISS Diana E . . . . Pebble Beach, CA 93953

Priestley MR & MRS William T 3d (Gina B Arsena)
   ☎ (414) 243-3663 . . ''Seymour Tracey Castle'' 13322 N Lakewood Dv, Mequon, WI 53097-2409

Prince MR & MRS Frederick H (Diana A Cochrane) . . ☎ (401) 847-0177
   MISS Daisy . . . . ''Swan's Way''
   JUNIORS MR Octavius . . . . Hazard Rd,
Newport, RI 02840

Prince MR William N W
   ☎ (401) 846-4495 . . ''The Villa'' Annandale Rd, Newport, RI 02840

Prince MR & MRS William Wood (de Ricou—Eleanor Edwards)
   ☎ (401) 846-4494 . . ''Beech Lawn'' Annandale Rd, Newport, RI 02840

Prioleau MR & MRS Charles H (Miriam W Payne)
   ☎ (713) 559-2385 . . 123 Park Circle, Kemah, TX 77565

Prosser MR & MRS Robert L (Stanley—Judith L . . . . ☎ (401) 322-1925
   McKinlay) . . . . ''Sou'west''
   MISS Lindsay B Stanley . . . . 30 Spring Av,
   MR Edwin J C Stanley . . . . Westerly, RI 02891

Prout MR & MRS William W (Betts—Evelyn Ohman)
   ☎ (802) 362-1716 . . Long View Dv, Manchester, VT 05254

Prouty MR & MRS Charles N 3d (Wright—Thorne—Helen P Ellis)
   ☎ (518) 576-4433 . . ''The Uplands'' Box 792, Keene Valley, NY 12943

Prouty MR & MRS Richard (Ann Jenkins)
   ☎ (508) 758-2105 . . Ned's Point Rd, Mattapoisett, MA 02739

Pugh MRS Charlotte R (Charlotte C Reed) . . . . ☎ (616) 223-7294
   MR R Reed . . . . 14495 Linwood Av,
Neahtawanta,
Traverse City, MI 49684

Pugh MR & MRS William W (Elizabeth J Ritter)
   ☎ (704) 926-8024 . . 5 Blackberry Trace, Maggie Valley, NC 28751

Pujol MR & MRS Raoul H (Evgenia Gagarin)
   ☎ (860) 567-0143 . . ''Prospect Mountain Farm'' PO Box 1055, Litchfield, CT 06759

Pulitzer MRS Joseph JR (Emily S Rauh)
   ☎ (314) 993-2002 . . 9501 Clayton Rd, St Louis, MO 63124

Pulitzer MR & MRS Joseph 4th (Delano—Flynn— . . . ☎ (207) 288-5405
   Jennifer A Williams) . . . . ''Beechcroft''
   MISS Elkhanah . . . . Lower Main St,
   MISS Bianca . . . . Bar Harbor, ME
   MISS Abigail W Flynn 04609

Pulling MRS S Sonne (Sheila B A Sonne) . . . . Jun 24 . .
   MISS Diana D . . . . ☎ (516) 537-5890
   JUNIORS MR Christopher C . . . . ''Higgledy''
Box 456,
Bridgehampton, NY 11932
Aug 1 . .
☎ (207) 276-5374
Box 181,
Northeast Harbor, ME 04662

Pulsifer MR & MRS Nathaniel (F Holliday Miller) . . . ☎ (207) 725-2243
   MISS Alicia H . . . . ''Natrimac''
   MR Nathaniel M . . . . Bethel Point RFD,
Brunswick, ME 04011

Pulver MR & MRS George M (Penelope A Spencer) on board
⛵ Bluejacket''
   MISS Caroline . . . . River Yealm,
Newton Ferrers,
Devon, England

Purdy MR & MRS Peter J (Susan S Fisher) . . . . | ☎ (413) 339-4301
  MISS Mary S . . . . | "Brooklands"
  MR Christopher H . . . . | 45 Middle Rd,
                                                           Hawley, MA *01339*
Purnell MR & MRS Richard I (Marguerite W Hillman)
  ☎ (516) 788-7539 . . Fishers Island, NY *06390*
Purves MR & MRS Alexander (Drika N Agnew)
  "Cricket Hollow" PO Box 179, Washington Depot, CT *06794*
Putnam MR & MRS Augustus L (Schmitz—Barbara Blake)
  ☎ (207) 867-4416 . . Box 204, North Haven, ME *04853*
Putnam MR & MRS Frederic P (Penny C Johnson)
  ☎ (914) 266-4546 . . "Penny Pond" 311A Fallkill Rd, Hyde Park, NY *12538*
Putnam MR & MRS George (Boardman—Nancy
  Burrows) . . . . | ☎ (207) 244-3091
  MISS Susan W . . . . | "Cape Farm"
                                                           Mt Desert, ME *04660*
Putnam MRS Gerald R (Nancy A Darsie) . . . . | ☎ (518) 576-4445
  MR Gerald R JR . . . . | "Hielan Home"
  MR John D . . . . | Ausable Club,
                                                           St Huberts, NY *12943*
Putnam MR & MRS Sumner C (Jane H Bishop) . . . . . | ☎ (508) 627-6026
  JUNIORS MISS Katherine P . . . . | 80 S Summer St,
  JUNIORS MR Sumner C JR . . . . | Edgartown, MA
  JUNIORS MR Nicholas B . . . . | *02539*
Putnam MR William L
  ☎ (508) 645-9226 . . "Gladsmuir" Tea Lane, Chilmark, MA *02535*
Putnam-Farr JUNIORS MISS Eleanor L . . see T G Delaney
Putney MR & MRS Lacey E JR (Laura M Mason)
  ☎ (508) 281-0980 . . 10 Highland Av, Annisquam, MA *01930*
Pyle MRS Charles McA JR (Margot H Copeland) . . . | ☎ (508) 526-4263
  MR Stuart H . . . . | 2 Boardman Av,
  MR Russell T . . . . | Manchester-By-The-
                                                           Sea, MA *01944*
Pyle MR & MRS James Tolman (Ann Finlay)
  ☎ (207) 276-3794 . . "Over Sea" Seal Harbor, ME *04675*
Pyle MR & MRS Robert M JR (C Page Neville) . . . . . | ☎ (908) 892-3680
  MISS Cynthia N . . . . | 876 East Av,
  MISS Laura C . . . . | Mantoloking, NJ
                                                           08738
Pyle MR & MRS Robert N (Crosier—Claire Thoron) . | ☎ (603) 563-8312
  MR Louis M Crosier . . . . | Dublin, NH *03444*
Pyne MR & MRS Eben W (Beebe—Gray—Nancy Maguire)
  ☎ (207) 276-3381 . . "Brookwood" PO Box 417, Northeast Harbor, ME *04662*
Pyne MRS H Rivington JR (Lydia M Fulweiler)
  ☎ (207) 529-5564 . . "Pine Island" Box 200, Medomak, ME *04551*
Pyne MR & MRS John S (Ann Wilkinson Sherrill) . . . | ☎ (516) 283-8971
  JUNIORS MISS Elizabeth S . . . . | 449 Hill St,
  JUNIORS MR John S JR . . . . | Southampton, NY
                                                           11968

Q

Quasha MR & MRS Alan G (Diana V Ronan)
  ☎ (011-33-93) 76-05-38 . . "La Pointe du Cap" av de la Corniche, 06230 St Jean-Cap-Ferrat, France
Quasha MISS Jennifer C . . see J R French
Quinn MR Christopher W . . see D B Stott
Quinn MISS Demarest L . . see MRS T C Lloyd
Quinn MR & MRS J Eugene (Trevor—I Marguerite | ☎ (401) 847-0968
  Slocum) . . . . | "The Cottage"
  MISS Tara E . . . . | 2 Hazard Av,
    MISS Evelyn J B Trevor . . . . | Newport, RI *02840*
    MISS Sophia A B Trevor . . . .
    MISS Irene S Trevor . . . .
Quinn MR James P . . see MRS T C Lloyd
Quinn MR Nicholas D . . see D B Stott

R

Rabbe MR & MRS George W (Theodora V Aspegren)
  ☎ (516) 283-1324 . . "Sunnymeade" Ox Pasture Rd, PO Box 643, Southampton, NY *11969*
Radcliffe MR & MRS Charles E C (Sarah D F Jeffords)
  ☎ (717) 529-2337 . . 1897 Georgetown Rd, Christiana, PA *17509*
Raley MR & MRS Robert L (Mary C Fenn)
  Aug 3 . . ☎ (508) 228-5765 . . 53 Cliff Rd, Nantucket, MA *02554*
Ramsing MR & MRS Byron L (Annette H Reynolds)
  ☎ (307) 587-3960 . . A2Z Ranch, 289 Hunter Creek Rd, Cody, WY *82414*
Rand MRS Adaline H (Perkins—Adaline Havemeyer)
  ☎ (508) 997-4421 . . "Whale House" 112 Mishaum Point Rd, South Dartmouth, MA *02748-1294*
Rand MRS Mary F (Troy—Mary F Rand)
  ☎ (516) 283-3777 . . 5 Maylen Dv, Southampton, NY *11968*
Rand MR & MRS William (Paula M Coudert) . . . . . . | ☎ (516) 922-4458
  MISS Paula B . . . . | 73 Cove Neck Rd,
  MR William C . . . . | Oyster Bay, NY *11771*
Randall DR & MRS Peter (Rose G Johnson)
  ☎ (401) 295-5129 . . 449 Old Boston Neck Rd, PO Box 202, Saunderstown, RI *02874*
Randolph MR & MRS Evan (Frances L Beale)
  ☎ (207) 244-5064 . . PO Box 911, Southwest Harbor, ME *04679-0911*
Randolph MR & MRS Evan 4th (Penelope H Dixon) . | Rte 175, Thornton,
  MISS Camilla C . . . . | NH *03228*
  MISS Lisa L . . . . |
Randolph MR & MRS Francis F JR (Dickey—Catherine A Meyers)
  ☎ (203) 438-8995 . . "Rippowam Farm" 177 Rippowam Rd, Box 538, Ridgefield, CT *06877*
Randolph DR & MRS Peter B F (Helen Garside) . . . . | ☎ (508) 295-0725
  MISS Helen Tod . . . . | "Indian Neck
  MISS Sarah French Robinson . . . . | House" 53 Warren
  MISS Eliza C F . . . . | Point Rd, Indian
  MR Christopher B F . . . . | Neck, Wareham,
  MR Nicholas D F . . . . | MA *02571*

Randolph MR & MRS Richard R IV (Patricia A Farmer)
  ☎ (704) 526-5135 . . "Homewoods" Highlands, NC *28741*
Randolph MR Ryland M
  ☎ (704) 526-5135 . . "Homewoods" Highlands, NC *28741*
Randt MR Thomas A
  ☎ (619) 456-6678 . . 253 Bonair St, La Jolla, CA *92037*
Rankin MR & MRS Henry P JR (Clark—Hook—Louise C Morgan)
  ☎ (216) 423-4556 . . "Rake Mill Farm" 7545 Old Mill Rd, Box 336, Gates Mills, OH *44040*
Ranlet MR & MRS Robert (Suzanne Hanckel)
  ☎ (804) 286-2369 . . "The Rectory" Keene, VA *22946*
Ransom MISS Ashley B . . see V H Brown JR
Rappleye MR & MRS Willard C JR (Doherty—Tankoos—Marita Crofton)
  ☎ (207) 989-3636 . . Mountainy Pond Club, East Holden, ME *04429*
Rasin MR & MRS Rudolph S (Joy Peterkin) . . . . | ☎ (414) 248-8011
  MR James Stenning . . . . | "Flowerside Inn"
  | N2261 Mallory
  | Lane, Lake Geneva,
  | WI *53147*
Rastetter DR & MRS William H (Lucy S Dillon)
  ☎ (508) 257-6517 . . "Rugosa Cottage" Baxter Rd, Siasconset, MA *02564*
Ratcliff MR & MRS John P (Katherine A Joy)
  ☎ (707) 884-3433 . . Slick Rock Creek Ranch, 31101 S Coast H'way 1, Gualala, CA *95445*
Ratcliffe MRS Myron F (Margaret E Archibald)
  ☎ (847) 251-7126 . . 82 Indian Hill Rd, Winnetka, IL *60093*
Rathbone MR & MRS Peter B (Teissier—G Alanna Chesebro)
  ☎ (508) 790-1964 . . "Osprey Cottage" PO Box 987, Great Island, West Yarmouth, MA *02673*
Rathborne MRS Carol S (Carol Simmons)
  ☎ (516) 329-1212 . . "Thither 'n Yon" 54 Hither Lane, East Hampton, NY *11937*
Ratliff MR & MRS Thomas A JR (Lucy L Graydon)
  ☎ (609) 361-0594 . . 29 E 40 St, Brant Beach, NJ *08008*
Rauch MR & MRS Alfred JR (Mary Belle Scott) . . . . . | ☎ (864) 836-3453
  MISS M Brearley . . . . | Caesar's Head,
  MR J Scott . . . . | Cedar Mountain, NC
  | *28718*
Rauch MR & MRS R Stewart (Frances S Brewster)
  ☎ (516) 788-7331 . . Fishers Island, NY *06390*
Ravenel MR & MRS Daniel (Linda Compton) ⛵ . . | ☎ (704) 692-7087
  JUNIORS MISS Elizabeth H . . . . | "Piedmont"
  | Middleton Rd,
  | Box 147,
  | Flat Rock, NC
  | *28731*
Rawson MRS Kennett L (MacMannis—Eleanor Stierhem) ⛵
  ☎ (516) 941-4133 . . "Blueberry Bay Farm" 23 Brewster Lane E, Setauket, NY *11733*
Ray MR & MRS William F (Helen A Payne) . . . . . . | ☎ (516) 788-7729
  MISS Susan E . . . . | "Woodcock Cove"
  | Fishers Island, NY
  | *06390*
Raymond MR & MRS David A (Dorothy C Dillon)
  ☎ (508) 257-6517 . . "Rugosa Cottage" Baxter Rd, Siasconset, MA *02564*

Raymond MR & MRS Edward H (Katherine B Channing)
  ☎ (508) 990-8221 . . 686 Potomska Rd, South Dartmouth, MA *02748*
Raymond MRS Irving W (Henrietta D Skinner)
  ☎ (207) 363-5047 . . PO Box 238, York Harbor, ME *03911*
Rea MRS James C JR (Mary C Cary)
  ☎ (207) 460-0422 . . Trafton Island, PO Box 248, Milbridge, ME *04658*
Read MRS Charles A (Green—Katherine H Ayers)
  96 Seniola, Javea, Alicante, Spain
Read MR & MRS Robert O JR (Alden H Calmer) . . . . | ☎ (401) 635-4609
  MR Jonathan B . . . . | 24 Grinnell Rd,
  | Little Compton, RI
  | *02837*
Read MR & MRS William A JR (Collier—Isabel Uppercu)
  ☎ (307) 587-9844 . . 391 Hunter Creek Rd, Cody, WY *82414*
Ream MRS John W (Barbara Borden)
  ☎ (508) 775-3058 . . 85 Ocean Av, Hyannis Port, MA *02647*
Reardon DR & MRS James J JR (Miller—Robin A | ☎ (516) 676-0380
  Arbon) . . . . | "Cymbidium"
  JUNIORS MISS J Alexes . . . . | Box 188,
  JUNIORS MR J Ashe . . . . | Locust Valley, NY
  | *11560*
Reath MRS George (Isabel D West)
  ☎ (207) 963-2283 . . "Dirigo" Winter Harbor, ME *04693*
Reath MR & MRS Thomas JR (E Joyce Borie)
  ☎ (207) 276-5200 . . "Little House" Box 817, Northeast Harbor, ME *04662*
Reback MR & MRS Forbes R (Charlotte D Buttrick)
  ☎ (401) 423-0078 . . 24 Prudence Lane, Jamestown, RI *02835*
Rebmann MRS Paul C (F Irene Jackson)
  ☎ (717) 775-7073 . . "Black Feet Lodge" Blooming Grove Hunt & Fish Club, Hawley, PA *18428*
Reboul MR & MRS John W (Josée Vrignon) . . . . . . | ☎ (518) 589-5611
  JUNIORS MISS Alexandra . . . . | "Grayledge"
  JUNIORS MR John M . . . . | Onteora Park,
  | Tannersville, NY
  | *12485*
Redington MISS Ruth M . . see E J Nouri
Redmond MR & MRS J Woodward (Elizabeth B Aldrich)
  ☎ (207) 734-6479 . . "One Way" Dark Harbor, Islesboro, ME *04848*
Redmond MRS Roland L (Macy—di San Faustino—Lydia P Bodrero)
  ☎ (914) 757-2521 . . Box 100, Tivoli, NY *12583*
Redpath MR & MRS Frederick L (Long—Deborah B | ☎ (717) 643-3049
  Law) . . . . | Pocono Lake
  MR Bruce L . . . . | Preserve, PA *18348*
Redpath MRS Robert U JR (Nancy S Miller)
  123 Lincoln Rd, Lincoln, MA *01773*
Reece MR & MRS Christopher S (Elizabeth L Riemer)
  ☎ (207) 276-5376 . . "Stone's Throw" Northeast Harbor, ME *04662*
Reece MRS John B (Helm—Peabody—Barbara Ginn)
  ☎ (508) 748-0783 . . 114 Point Rd, Marion, MA *02738*
Reed MR & MRS A Lachlan (Martha W Sweatt) . . of
  ☎ (612) 473-4262 . . "Thistledor" 1500 Brackett's Point Rd, Wayzata, MN *55391*
  ☎ (218) 675-6535 . . "Midpines" RR 1, Box 10, Hackensack, MN *56452*
Reed MR Charles V . . see O de la Renta

Reed MR & MRS Frank Fremont 2d (Matthiessen—Cox—Jaquelin Silverthorne)................ of ☎ (715)385-2359 6375 High Lake Rd, Boulder Junction, WI *54512*
  MISS Nancy de F.......................
  MISS Sarah C ....
  ☎ (715) 856-5809 Wausaukee Club, Athelstane, WI *54104*

Reed MR & MRS Joseph Verner JR (Marie M Byers) . ☎ (207) 276-5333 "Jordan House" Rte 3-198, Seal Harbor, ME *04675*
  MISS Electra ....

Reed MR & MRS Nathaniel (G Dabney Freeman).... PO Box 1421, Southampton, NY *11969*
  MR Timothy N ....

Reed MR & MRS Nathaniel P (Alita D Weaver)..... ☎ (207) 963-5509 "Owl's Ledge" Winter Harbor, ME *04693*
  MISS Alita D ....

Reed MR & MRS Nathaniel P JR (Emily K Thomas)
  ☎ (207) 963-7741 . . Winter Harbor, ME *04693*

Reed MISS P J Eliza . . see O de la Renta

Reed MR & MRS P Loring JR (Truesdale—Ann M Soule)
  ☎ (207) 846-4142 . . Littlejohn Island, Yarmouth, ME *04096*

Reed MISS Phyllis A
  ☎ (516) 329-1165 . . 14 Cross H'way, East Hampton, NY *11937*

Reeder MR & MRS Henry S (Susan B Carnes)...... ☎ (508) 228-2007 "Sea-Nip" Wauwinet, Nantucket, MA *02554*
  MISS Liza C ....
  MR Nathaniel S......................

Rees MRS Richard Lee SR (Jane Davis) .... of ☎ (011-81-3) 265-1111 New Otani Hotel, 4 Kioi-cho, Tokyo, Japan ☎ (808) 221-8834 on board The Mizu" Hawaii Yacht Club, Ala Wai Marina, Honolulu, HI *96815*
  MR Richard L JR ....

Reese MR & MRS Algernon B 3d (Lyman—Catherine S Mallinckrodt)
  ☎ (207) 276-5447 . . "Seawoods" PO Box 435, Northeast Harbor, ME *04662*

Reese MR & MRS George B (Elizabeth A Stolba)
  ☎ (914) 234-7808 . . RR 3, Box 418, Hook Rd, Bedford, NY *10506*

Reese MR & MRS William Willis (Sonia L van Voorhees)
  ☎ (516) 283-0020 . . 118 Harvest Lane, Southampton, NY *11968*

Reeves MR & MRS William H 4th (Suzanne Evans)
  ☎ (415) 775-8848 . . 1895 Jackson St, Apt 506, San Francisco, CA *94109*

Regan MRS Gordon S (Baltazar—Elba V Campos) . ☎ (540) 832-3343 "Inverness" 10226 Inverness Dv, Gordonsville, VA *22942-8355*
  MR Gordon B ....
  MR J Rafael Baltazar-Campos ....

Regan MR & MRS William J JR (Barbara Leahy)
  ☎ (905) 894-0458 . . Abino Hills, Ridgeway, Ontario L0S 1N0, Canada

Reich MR & MRS Christopher V (Eleanor M Paschal)
  ☎ (516) 583-8769 . . House 144, Point O'Woods, NY *11706*

Reichel MR & MRS Frank H JR (Beatrice A Hinson)
  ☎ (541) 298-4151 . . 6023 Rowena River Rd, The Dalles, OR *97058*

Reid MR Bagley
  ☎ (516) 788-7882 . . PO Box 475, Fishers Island, NY *06390*

Reid MR & MRS C Nash (Perrault—Elizabeth T Willis) ⚓
  ☎ (914) 273-3123 . . "Dier Hill" 31 N Greenwich Rd, Armonk, NY *10504*

Reid MR & MRS James G (Elizabeth D Key)
  Fishers Island, NY *06390*

Reid MRS John (Denyse E Van Hove)
  84 Egypt Lane, East Hampton, NY *11937*

Reid MR & MRS Samuel S (Juliet C Weber)
  ☎ (207) 439-0118 . . "Heron Hill" PO Box 161, Kittery Point, ME *03905*

Reidy MR John S
  ☎ (508) 295-1140 . . Sherburne House, Green Gate Lane, Box 368, Wareham, MA *02571-0368*

Reigeluth MR & MRS Robert S (Mary C Applegate)
  ☎ (860) 388-2061 . . "Fenwick" Old Saybrook, CT *06475*

Reily MR & MRS W Boatner III (Edwinna Griswold) ⚓
  ☎ (508) 627-4820 . . "Green Hollow" Katama Rd, Edgartown, MA *02539*

Reimer MR & MRS J Squier (Donna V Webster)
  ☎ (401) 466-3190 . . Corn Neck Rd, Block Island, RI *02807*

Reiner MR & MRS John P (Mary E Wells)......... ☎ (914) 351-2673 Tuxedo Club, W Lake Rd, Tuxedo Park, NY *10987*
  MISS Mary E A ....
  MR Clark B..........................

Reiniger MR & MRS Harlan deC (Jane D Maurer)
  ☎ (508) 325-4307 . . 4 Barnabus Lane, Nantucket, MA *02554*

Reisinger MR & MRS Ronald B (Carolyn J Gall) .... ☎ (616) 846-1738 25 Stickney Ridge Rd, Grand Haven, MI *49417*
  MISS Hope B........................
  MR Christopher B ....

Reitter MR & MRS Frank R (Gail G Linzee) .... ☎ (802) 422-8067 "Villa Reitter" Weathervane Rd, Killington, VT *05751*
  MISS Stefani A ....
  MISS Kirsten M ....

Remer MR & MRS John H (Ketcham—Frances C Edmunds)
  ☎ (506) 529-4257 . . "Craignish" PO Box 561, St Andrews, NB E0G 2X0, Canada

Remer MRS John H JR (Mary F Scott)
  ☎ (610) 688-0516 . . "Ardrossan" 811 Newtown Rd, Villanova, PA *19085*

Remer MR John H JR
  ☎ (506) 529-4257 . . "Anderson Cottage" PO Box 561, St Andrews, NB E0G 2X0, Canada

Rentschler MR & MRS Charles E M (Suzanne S Snowden) . . . . | ☎ (516) 788-7624
MISS Marie K . . . . | "Osprey Hill"
MR Adam S . . . . | Fishers Island, NY
MR Charles F . . . . | *06390*

Rentschler MRS Frances B (Krumbhaar—Frances D Banes)
☎ (207) 963-7302 . . Winter Harbor, ME *04693*

Repp MRS Herbert N (Rike—Catharine B Conklin)
☎ (616) 386-5672 . . "Afterglow" 105 Northport Point, Northport, MI *49670*

ReQua MRS Patrick A (Joan Smith)
Squirrel Island, ME *04570*

Resnik MR & MRS Michael D (Janet M Depping) . . . | ☎ (704) 295-9374
MISS Sarah L. . . . . | "Pegasus West"
MR Dimitri . . . . | Blackberry Rd,
 | Blowing Rock, NC
 | *28605*

Ressler MR & MRS Harold Kirkby (Gabriella Plimpton)
☎ (516) 749-3095 . . Shore Rd, PO Box 293, Dering Harbor, Shelter Island Heights, NY *11965*

Reuter MRS Walter H JR (Roberta T Speller)
Box 475, Chautauqua, NY *14722*

Reventlow CTSS Court Haugwitz (Van Laer—Davis—Brent—Margaret A Drayton)
☎ (860) 567-9000 . . "Pineholm Farm" Duck Pond Rd, PO Box 1046, Litchfield, CT *06759*

Rex MRS Robert McC (Struthers—Lilly S Ferrell) . . of 5 Sessions Dv, Columbus, OH *43209*
☎ (561) 272-1456 . . 200 Little Club Rd, Apt 9, Delray Beach, FL *33483-7556*

Reynolds MR & MRS A William (Joanne McCormick)
229 Greenhorn Rd, Box 4226, Ketchum, ID *83340*

Reynolds MRS Bartow (Prudence M Bartow) ⚓ . . | ☎ (508) 548-0611
MR Philip B . . . . | "The Boat House"
 | 46 Penzance Point,
 | Woods Hole, MA
 | *02543*

Reynolds MR & MRS George I (Love—Royds—Nancy R Sullivan) . . . . | ☎ (607) 547-5208
MISS Janet . . . . | 96 Lake St,
 | Cooperstown, NY
 | *13326*

Reynolds MR & MRS Hal W (Elizabeth I McLean)
☎ (207) 348-2877 . . Little Deer Isle, ME *04650*

Reynolds MR Oliver C (Mildred Ellis)
☎ (860) 868-7585 . . Old Litchfield Rd, Washington, CT *06793*

Reynolds MRS Richard S (Virginia Sargeant)
☎ (304) 536-9272 . . The Greenbrier, Station A, White Sulphur Springs, WV *24986*

Reynolds MR & MRS Russell A 3d (Lynda C Low)
☎ (415) 579-4444 . . "Leicestershire Manor" Hobbs on Ferry, RD 1, Burlingame, CA *94010*

Rhea MR & MRS Alexander D 3d (Suzanne Menocal)
☎ (304) 536-4730 . . The Greenbrier, Creekside, White Sulphur Springs, WV *24986*

Rhein MRS Francis B (Jane A Foster) . . . . | ☎ (401) 294-2724
MISS Jane F. . . . . | "South Meadow"
 | Box 403,
 | Saunderstown, RI
 | *02874*

Rhein MRS Jean-Pierre F (Wills—BRNSS Ludmilla M Forani)
☎ (011-33-16) 92-18-95-91 . . "Les Terrasses du Soleil" 40 rte des Bréguières, 06110 Le Cannet, France

Rhein MR & MRS John H W 3d (Phyllis J Betz)
☎ (401) 294-9225 . . "Bittersweet" 168 Willett Rd, Box 313, Saunderstown, RI *02874*

Rhein MR Peter Van R
☎ (401) 294-2724 . . "Bayberry Cottage" 195 Waterway, Saunderstown, RI *02874*

Rhett MR & MRS H Moore 3d (Lynne Smith)
☎ (508) 945-5683 . . 61 Shore Rd, Chatham, MA *02633*

Rhett MR Harry M . . . . | ☎ (508) 945-1689
MR & MRS W Warren B (L Ellen MacElvain) . . . | "East Lawn"
 | 63 Shore Rd,
 | Chatham, MA *02633*

Rhinelander MR & MRS John B (Jeanne E Cattell) . . | ☎ (508) 283-1478
MISS Margaret T . . . . | 10 Cove Way,
MISS Katherine P . . . . | Rust Island,
 | Gloucester, MA
 | *01930*

Rhoades MRS John H (Bird—Alice M Heye). . . . . . | ☎ (518) 523-3281
MR & MRS James C (Mary B Rogers) . . . . | Camp Birch Point,
 | PO Box 1315,
 | Lake Placid, NY
 | *12946*

Rhoads MRS Owen B (Brooks—Emily C Scott)
☎ (610) 644-2077 . . "Hollystone" 333 S Valley Rd, Paoli, PA *19301*

Rhodes MRS Augustine J (McKinney—Augustine W Janeway)
☎ (609) 884-9498 . . 1016 Stockton Av, Cape May, NJ *08204*

Rhodes MR & MRS Clarence J (Hellmuth—Dorothy A Marshall)
☎ (207) 644-8271 . . "Gray Gables" Christmas Cove, ME *04568*

Rianhard MR & MRS Lockwood (Mary E Wurst) . . . | ☎ (508) 457-5085
MISS Elizabeth B . . . . | "Menauhant"
MR Edward N . . . . | 3 Bob White Way,
 | East Falmouth, MA
 | *02536*

Rice MR & MRS Donald S (M Edgenie Higgins) ⚓ | ☎ (508) 758-2525
MISS Alice H. . . . . | 26 Ned's Point Rd,
MISS Edgenie R . . . . | Mattapoisett, MA
 | *02739*

Rich MR & MRS Robert S (Myra Lakoff) . . . . | ☎ (970) 925-2498
MISS Rebecca A . . . . | "The Little Green
MR David M . . . . | Pea" 0408 W Reds
JUNIORS MISS Sarah C . . . . | Rd, Aspen, CO
 | *81611*

Richard MR & MRS Harold Van B (Jane Schmeltzer)
☎ (207) 363-3455 . . Box 1195, 23 Aldis Lane, York Harbor, ME *03911*

Richard MR & MRS Peter L (Virginia A Rynne) . . . . | ☎ (207) 363-6735
MR W Zachary . . . . | 21 Aldis Lane,
JUNIORS MISS Cecily J C . . . . | York Harbor, ME
JUNIORS MR Travis Van B . . . . | *03911*

Richards MR & MRS John H JR (Mary E Melville)
☎ (508) 228-0522 . . "Peril Point" Box 1827, Nantucket, MA *02554*

Richards MRS John L (Sanford—Elizabeth W Prosser)
☎ (203) 869-8730 . . 98 Valley Rd, Apt 8, Cos Cob, CT *06807-2224*

Richards MR & MRS John T L (Nancy J Gascoigne)
☎ (207) 563-5195 . . High St, Newcastle, ME *04553*

Richards MR & MRS Rowland JR (Martha L Marcy) . | ☎ (802) 496-2113
  MISS Christine K . . . . | "Floodwoods"
  MISS Jean L . . . . | Waitsfield, VT
  MR Rowland 3d . . . . | *05673*
  LT George M—USA. . . . . |

Richardson MR & MRS Charles S JR (Janet Bane) . . . | ☎ (207) 244-7731
  MR Samuel S . . . . | "Beech Meadows"
  JUNIORS MISS Hannah B . . . . | Beech Hill Rd,
  | Mt Desert, ME
  | *04660*

Richardson MR & MRS Donald H (Plumley—Charlotte A Brown) . . of
☎ (202) 337-1001 . . 2700 Virginia Av NW, Apt 1001, Washington, DC *20037*
East Hampton, NY *11937*

Richardson DR & MRS Edward P JR (Margaret S Eustis)
☎ (207) 374-5281 . . Blue Hill, ME *04614*

Richardson MR & MRS Frank E JR (Rosamound T Fitch)
☎ (207) 374-2490 . . "Red Fox Cove" Blue Hill, ME *04614*

Richardson MRS Frederick L W (Hughes—Ross—Rebecca G Brock)
☎ (802) 234-9162 . . Barnard, VT *05031*

Richardson MR Harris S JR
☎ (508) 945-0417 . . "Salt Hill" 25 Hammond Lane, Chatham, MA *02633*

Richardson BRIG GEN & MRS Robert C 3d (Anne W Taylor) USAF.
☎ (603) 747-2494 . . "Upper Village" Bath, NH *03740*

Richey MR & MRS John M (Barbara Bray)
☎ (516) 324-0637 . . 1 Egypt Close, East Hampton, NY *11937*

Richmond MR & MRS Thomas T (Eleanor Angle)
☎ (802) 457-4625 . . 3 Linden Hill, Woodstock, VT *05091*

Rick MRS Alan J (Nancy B Moss) . . . . | Donner Lake, LA
  MISS Margaret M . . . . | *70352*

Ridder MR L Michael
☎ (518) 672-4647 . . "Villa Antibes" 179 Soller Heights Rd, Ghent, NY *12075*

Ridder MRS Tucker (Ethelette Tucker)
☎ (516) 283-5473 . . "Small Potatoes" Narrow Lane, PO Box 1045, Southampton, NY *11969*

Ridgely JUNIORS MISS Laura L . . see P F Miller

Ridgway MRS William C JR (Emily F Parsons)
☎ (516) 788-7413 . . Box 251, Fishers Island, NY *06390*

Ridruejo MR & MRS Epifanio (Monique B Timbal) . . | ☎ (011-34-75)
  MISS Susana . . . . | 22-20-22
  MR Ignacio . . . . | "Los Royales"
  | Soria, Spain

Riefler MR & MRS Donald B (Patricia A Hawley) . . . | of ☎ (516)676-2959
  MISS Barbara A . . . . | The Creek, Box 427,
  | Locust Valley, NY
  | *11560*
  | ☎ (970) 926-3779
  | "The Greens-
  | Arrowhead" 0306
  | Windermere Circle,
  | PO Box 98,
  | Edwards, CO *81632*

Riegel MR & MRS John E (A Deborah du Pont) . . . . . | ☎ (516) 788-7707
  MISS Deborah du P . . . . | PO Box 707,
  MR John E JR . . . . | Fishers Island, NY
  | *06390*

Riegel MR & MRS Richard E JR (Law—Barbara C | ☎ (516) 788-5678
  Ives) . . . . | "The Rectory"
  MISS Laura Cushing . . . . | PO Box 567,
  MISS Anne Alexandrine de M . . . . | Fishers Island, NY
  | *06390*

Riegel MR & MRS William M JR (Elizabeth A Lyman)
☎ (860) 868-9381 . . "Achness" 29 Mallory Brook Rd, Washington, CT *06794*

Riemer MRS Karl (Louise Crowninshield)
☎ (508) 748-2942 . . "Water's Edge" 108 Point Rd, Marion, MA *02738*

Riepe REV Charles K
☎ (207) 526-4464 . . "The Cedars" Swans Island, ME *04685*

Rigby MR & MRS Henry S (MacMullan—Marjorie S Holt)
☎ (609) 492-6511 . . "Clam Cottage" 134 Belvoir Av, Beach Haven, NJ *08008*

Righter MR & MRS James V (Alice A Robinson)
☎ (516) 788-7531 . . Fishers Island, NY *06390*

Riginos MR & MRS Vasilis E (Alice Swift) . . . . | "Kalami"
  MISS Cynthia . . . . | Sámos, Greece
  MISS Corinna . . . . |

Riker MISS Audrey
☎ (908) 389-8465 . . "Patchwork North" 132 Hockhockson Rd, Colts Neck, NJ *07722*

Riker MR John L
☎ (908) 291-4194 . . 440 Locust Point Rd, PO Box 236, Locust, NJ *07760-0236*

Riley MR & MRS C Madison 3d (Laura Alden Hewitt)
☎ (508) 349-2417 . . "Long View" Long Pond Rd, Box 373, Wellfleet, MA *02667*

Riley MR & MRS J Barton (Martha Gretchen Pfaff) . . | ☎ (508) 228-4817
  JUNIORS MISS M Quincy . . . . | "Beyond Hope"
  JUNIORS MR H Barton . . . . | 6 Eat Fire Spring
  | Rd, Nantucket, MA
  | *02554*

Riley MR & MRS Phelps T (Mary L Pacent) . . . . | ☎ (207) 963-2253
  MISS Eleanor W . . . . | "Ruthven Rocks"
  MR Phelps T JR . . . . | Grindstone Av,
  | Winter Harbor, ME
  | *04693*

Rinaldini MR & MRS Luis E (Talbert—Julie S Short)
☎ (516) 759-2784 . . "Two Sheds" West Island, Glen Cove, NY *11542*

Ring DR & MRS Edward M (Wilson—Claudine M Vincent)
Villa Le Récif, av Edouard VII, Biarritz, France

Ripley MISS Rosemary L (Lanius—Rosemary L Ripley)
  ☎ (860) 567-4375 . . 32 Duck Pond Rd, Litchfield, CT *06759*
Ripley MR & MRS S Dillon 2d (Eddy—Mary M Livingston)
  ☎ (860) 567-8208 . . ''Paddling Ponds'' PO Box 210, 63 Duck Pond Rd, Litchfield, CT *06759*
Ritchie MR & MRS John B (Suzanne Raisin) . . . . | ☎ (702) 749-5333
  MR Randolph B . . . . | ''Shakespeare House''
  MISS Charlotte S (Hogan—Charlotte S Ritchie) . | 209 S Meadow Rd, Glenbrook, NV *89413*
Ritchie MR & MRS Thomas M JR (Jean W Baldwin) . | ☎ (603) 523-4814
  MISS Katherine W . . . . | ''Perry House''
  MR Robert B . . . . | Canaan St, Canaan, NH *03741*
Rittenhouse MR Peter D
  ☎ (302) 645-5343 . . ''Sand Castles'' 114 E 4 St, Lewes, DE *19958*
Rittenour MR & MRS Charles A (Calder—Maralyn Christie-Miller)
  ☎ (516) 324-3817 . . 151 Waterhole Rd, East Hampton, NY *11937*
Ritter MISS Deborah C
  ☎ (401) 423-2784 . . 4 Prudence Lane, Jamestown, RI *02835*
Ritter MR & MRS Edmund U (Priscilla Rich)
  ☎ (508) 746-8425 . . ''Longview'' Warren Av, Plymouth, MA *02360*
Ritter MR & MRS William B (Barbara T Barclay)
  ☎ (401) 423-2975 . . 30 Whittier Rd, Jamestown, RI *02835*
Rittershofer MRS Clare R (Mary C Swing)
  ☎ (508) 645-9934 . . ''Studio House'' Middle Rd, Chilmark, MA *02535*
Rivers MR & MRS John M JR (Elebash—M Kathleen Hudson)
  ☎ (704) 743-5768 . . ''Hickory House'' Box 1885, Cashiers, NC *28717*
Rizzo MRS Joan N (Joan Nichols)
  ☎ (914) 763-9384 . . 1 Hunt Farm, Waccabuc, NY *10597*
Roach MRS Caryl L M (Caryl L Miller) . . . . | ☎ (508) 428-3988
  MISS Janis E . . . . | 19 Woodland Av, Osterville, MA *02655*
Robbins MRS Edward C (Hatfield—Mary Stewart Hodge)
  ☎ (207) 244-5550 . . HCR 3, Box 34A, Rte 102A, Manset, ME *04656*
Robbins MR & MRS James M (Schwartzburg—Mary Brooks)
  ☎ (802) 362-1486 . . ''No Vacancy'' Dorset, VT *05251*
Robbins MR & MRS James O (Deborah H Clark) . . . . | ☎ (704) 884-5999
  MISS Jane B . . . . | Lake Toxaway, NC *28747*
  MISS Payson C . . . . |
  MISS Hilary C . . . . |
Robbins MR & MRS Kip M (Glenaan M Elliott)
  ☎ (508) 228-5802 . . ''Mandalay'' 13 Goldfinch Dv, Nantucket, MA *02554*
Robbins MRS Louise N (Louise S Nash)
  ☎ (203) 629-5952 . . 37 Midwood Dv, Greenwich, CT *06831*
Robbins MRS Rowland Ames (Margaret C Paterson)
  ☎ (516) 788-7663 . . Fishers Island, NY *06390*
Robbins MRS Sabin (Harriet T Galt) . . . . | ☎ (616) 386-5571
  MR Sabin 4th . . . . | 16 Northport Point, Northport, MI *49670*
Robbins MR & MRS Thomas N (Elizabeth W Custis)
  Camp Virginia, Grindstone Island, Clayton, NY *13624*
Robbins REV DR William Randolph . . . . | Oxford University,
  MR Henry C . . . . | Oxford, England
Roberts MRS A Addison (Doris L Lawrence)
  ☎ (717) 595-3247 . . ''End View'' Dutch Hill Rd, Box 222, Skytop, PA *18357*
Roberts MR & MRS A Sydney (Andrews—Baird—Mary S Dempwolf)
  ☎ (508) 636-4012 . . 684 River Rd, Westport, MA *02790*
Roberts MR & MRS A Sydney JR (Christine E Gibbons) ⚓
  ☎ (508) 636-4960 . . ''Indian Spring Farm'' PO Box 3909, Westport, MA *02790*
Roberts MR & MRS Alan Y (Sally W Gordon)
  ☎ (914) 763-8372 . . Box 69, 41 Chapel Rd, Waccabuc, NY *10597*
Roberts MISS Anne C
  ☎ (616) 469-5657 . . ''Rest and Be Thankful'' 46109 Glenwood, Grand Beach, New Buffalo, MI *49117*
Roberts MR & MRS Bayard H (M Louise McIlhenny)
  ☎ (207) 276-5427 . . ''Grasslands'' Box 523, Northeast Harbor, ME *04662*
Roberts MR & MRS Curtis M (Susan B Kalat) . . . . . . | ☎ (401) 783-5754
  MISS Blair M . . . . | ''Windsong''
  MR E Hunter . . . . | 681 Main St, Wakefield, RI *02879*
Roberts MR & MRS Dudley (Fitch—Phyfe—Laura Serra-Garibaldi) ⚓ . . . . | ☎ (516) 324-0330
  MR Henry Pinkney Phyfe JR . . . . | Box 1077, Further Lane, East Hampton, NY *11937*
Roberts MISS George-Anne
  ☎ (505) 986-2040 . . 30 Old Arroyo Chamiso, Santa Fe, NM *87505*
Roberts MR & MRS Harold M (Jill L Curry) . . . . | ☎ (516) 283-5392
  MISS Stephanie E B . . . . | ''Bay Chalet'' Meadow Lane, Southampton, NY *11968*
Roberts MR & MRS John L M (Irène E Crofut)
  ☎ (518) 483-3211 . . Mat-A-Mek Preserve, Owls Head, NY *12969*
Robertson MR Charles S JR—⚓ . . . . | ☎ (508) 548-3036
  MR Charles S 3d . . . . | ''Handy House'' 337 Scranton Av, Falmouth, MA *02540*
Robertson MRS Charles Stuart (Elizabeth Swing)
  ☎ (508) 548-0807 . . ''Brier Patch'' 45 Swing Lane, Falmouth, MA *02540*
Robertson MR & MRS Harrison M JR (Burnham—Barbara N Bumgarner) . . . . | ☎ (410) 435-8903
  MR Harrison M 3d . . . . | 124C E Melrose Av, Baltimore, MD *21212*
  MISS Kim N Burnham . . . . |
Robertson DR & MRS James F 3d (Anne B Richardson) . . . . | ☎ (401) 294-9184
  JUNIORS MISS Katharine A . . . . | 75 Willett Rd, Saunderstown, RI *02874*
  JUNIORS MR William F . . . . |
Robertson MR & MRS James L 3d (Sanford—Genevieve B Sullivan)
  ☎ (508) 428-6981 . . Wianno Club, Sea View Av, PO Box 249, Osterville, MA *02655*
Robertson MRS James Y (Sara R Stewart)
  ☎ (407) 832-4081 . . 122 Peruvian Av, PH, Palm Beach, FL *33480-4477*
Robertson MR & MRS Jaquelin T (Marianna Neese)
  ☎ (516) 323-1906 . . 11 Dunemere Lane, East Hampton, NY *11937*

Robertson MR & MRS R Bruce (Sarah O Wells)
☎ (860) 485-9588 . . "Horseshoe Hill Farm" 765 South Rd, Harwinton, CT *06791*
Robertson MR R Emmett 3d
☎ (804) 784-2668 . . "Liberty Hill" PO Box 27281, Richmond, VA *23261*
Robertson MR & MRS William D (D Scarlett Leas) . . | ☎ (516) 283-5560
  MISS Scarlett Leas . . . . | 445 Hill St,
  JUNIORS MISS Alexis Virginia . . . . | Southampton, NY *11968*
Robins MR & MRS Seth S (Sarah J Scrymser)
☎ (908) 741-7214 . . "Cheymerd" Barley Point, Rumson, NJ *07760*
Robinson MRS Alexander C 4th (Patricia R Davin)
☎ (616) 533-8094 . . North Arms, Bellaire, MI *49615*
Robinson MR & MRS Barclay JR (Katharine H | ☎ (860) 535-4433
  McCagg) . . . . | Box 229,
  MISS Elizabeth H . . . . | Wamphassuc Point
  MISS Anne W . . . . | Rd, Stonington, CT *06378*
Robinson MR & MRS Beverley (Hattler—Rosélène | ☎ (401) 846-2504
  Briceño) . . . . | 114 Sachuest Way,
  MR John B . . . . | Middletown, RI *02842*
Robinson MR & MRS Blake W (Marjorie F Merritt)
☎ (910) 686-0051 . . 232 Beach Rd N, Wilmington, NC *28405*
Robinson MR & MRS D Patrick M (Elisabeth T Howell)
☎ (603) 253-6241 . . "Witch Haven" PO Box 1108, Center Harbor, NH *03226*
Robinson MR & MRS David G (M Susan de Gruchy) | ☎ (603) 569-6226
  MISS Anne Fisher . . . . | PO Box 2148,
  MR D Graham JR . . . . | Campfire Lane, Wolfeboro, NH *03894*
Robinson MRS Dwight E (Anne S Grosvenor)
☎ (360) 468-2426 . . "Bergerie" Rte 1, Box 1416, Lopez Island, WA *98161*
Robinson MR & MRS Hamilton JR (Alger—Roxana Barry)
☎ (207) 276-3775 . . "Seal Ledge" Northeast Harbor, ME *04662*
Robinson MRS Mary L K (Mary L Kendall)
☎ (516) 726-4757 . . 91 Cobb Isle Rd, Water Mill, NY *11976*
Robinson MR Michael W
☎ (401) 322-1315 . . "Swan's Way" 55 Noyes Neck Rd, Weekapaug, RI *02891*
Robinson MRS Sanger P (Baur—Martha Fishback)
25 Atwood Circle, Edgartown, MA *02539*
Robinson DR & MRS Thomas D (Anne S Jeffers)
☎ (508) 645-2254 . . "Lookout Hill" Box 225, Chilmark, MA *02535*
Robinson MRS W Champlin (Olivia E Frick)
☎ (207) 282-1498 . . Biddeford Pool, ME *04006*
Rockefeller MR & MRS Godfrey A (Margaret N Kuhn) ⚓
☎ (207) 883-2676 . . 4 Harmon St, Box 3147, Prouts Neck, ME *04074*
Rockefeller MR & MRS Rodman C (Sascha von Metzler)
☎ (914) 631-0910 . . "Winterburn" 48 Raafenberg Rd, Pocantico Hills, Tarrytown, NY *10591*
Rockefeller MRS William (Mary D Gillett)
☎ (518) 327-3540 . . "Bay Pond" Paul Smiths, NY *12970*

Rockwell MR & MRS Robin Markle (Barbara J | ☎ (516) 584-5324
  Russell) . . . . | "Woodcrest"
  MISS Stephanie O . . . . | 43R Moriches Rd, St James, NY *11780-9709*
Rockwell MR & MRS Stuart W (Rosalind H Morgan) | ☎ (413) 566-3353
  MISS Susan C . . . . | "Maidstone Farm"
  MR Stephen W . . . . | Rockadundee Rd,
  MR Geoffrey M . . . . | Hampden, MA *01036*
Rode MR & MRS Stephen W (Sletvold—Patricia L Bryant)
☎ (609) 368-2542 . . "End of the Rode" 121—115 St, Stone Harbor, NJ *08247*
Rodemyer MISS Jeannette C
☎ (616) 526-2666 . . Wequetonsing, MI *49740*
Rodgers MR & MRS Christopher R P (Parson—Katharine S Bolton)
☎ (207) 359-8525 . . Rte 175, PO Box 132, Brooklin, ME *04616*
Rodgers MRS John B (Ruth Easton)
☎ (415) 669-1101 . . 115 Forres Way, Inverness, CA *94937*
Rodiger MR & MRS Walter G JR (Elizabeth D King)
Jly 1 . . ☎ (207) 967-3777 . . "Gable Cottage" PO Box 309, 12 Arlington Av, Kennebunkport, ME *04046*
Rodner MR & MRS James O (Felicity A | ☎ (212) 223-0245
  Maxwell-Bresler) . . . . | 36 Sutton Place S,
  MISS Maria R . . . . | New York, NY
  MISS Victoria L . . . . | *10022*
Roe MR & MRS Ralph C (Stacy N Wardrop)
☎ (508) 228-4618 . . "Holly Ridge" Pocomo Rd, Nantucket, MA *02554*
Rogers MR & MRS Arthur M JR (Barbara Whitney) | ☎ (207) 244-3481
  ⚓ . . . . | "West View"
  MISS Whitney M . . . . | Bernard, ME *04612*
  MR Arthur M 3d . . . . |
Rogers MR & MRS Bernard F 3d (Woods—Leslie J | ☎ (970) 923-5124
  Pasch) . . . . | Box 176,
  MR Anthony H Woods . . . . | Woody Creek, CO *81656*
Rogers MRS C Boyd (Ruth Donnell)
☎ (616) 845-6888 . . "Anchorage" Epworth Heights, Ludington, MI *49431*
Rogers MRS James Gamble 2d (Evelyn C Smith)
☎ (770) 878-2420 . . "Hill Creek Farm" Sautee Nacoochee, GA *30571*
Rogers MRS James Webb (Anna P Clarke) . . . . | ☎ (301) 627-4511
  MR Joseph Shepperd . . . . | Montpelier of Moores Plains, Box 273, Upper Marlboro, MD *20772*
Rogers MR John A
☎ (714) 497-2999 . . 676 Glenneyre St, Laguna Beach, CA *92651*
Rogers MR & MRS John C (Anne C Read) . . . . | ☎ (603) 447-5208
  MISS Amy R . . . . | South Conway, NH *03813*
Rogers DR & MRS Malcolm P (Susan E Atkins) . . . . | ☎ (603) 764-5246
  MISS Lauren A . . . . | "Studio Barn"
  MR Stuart A . . . . | Warren, NH *03279*

Rogers MR & MRS Robert G JR (Dora S Lewis)..... ☎ (516) 653-6975
   MISS Dorothy B....................... Box 774, Old Depot
   JUNIORS MR Robert G 3d................. Rd, Quogue, NY
   11959

Rohner MR & MRS Franklin B (C Vanya Foster).... ☎ (707) 677-0419
   MISS Boyden E......................... "Windsong"
   294 Roundhouse
   Creek Rd, Trinidad,
   CA *95570*

Rollhaus MR & MRS Philip E JR (Childs—Barbara L ☎ (516) 749-4291
   Walker)........................ 68 Ram Island Dv,
   MR Philip E 3d....................... Shelter Island
   Heights, NY *11965*

Rollow MR & MRS J Douglas JR (Miesse—Loblein—Bergen—
   Marie D Lawrence)
   ☎ (704) 898-8941.. "Trails End" Grandfather Golf & Country Club,
   Box 785, Linville, NC *28646*

Rolph JUDGE & MRS Henry R (Barbara D Sherwood) ☎ (707) 226-9798
   MISS Barbara J........................ Casita 26,
   100 Fairways Dv,
   Silverado, Napa, CA
   94558

Rom MR & MRS Paul R (Helen Gray)............ "Rom's Roost"
   JUNIORS MISS Holly G................... Navajo Court,
   La Valle, WI *53941*

Romaine MR David F
   ☎ (508) 548-1081.. "Windymoor" Box 35, West Falmouth, MA *02574*

Romley MR Frederick J JR
   ☎ (508) 394-8894.. 100 Centre St, RR 1, South Dennis, MA *02660*

Ronan MRS Monica V (Montoya—Nourie—Monica V Ronan)
   ☎ (011-33-93) 76-08-65.. "La Pointe du Cap" 30 av de la Corniche,
   06230 St Jean-Cap-Ferrat, France

Ronan MR & MRS William J (Elena V de Poblet y Vinadé)
   ☎ (011-33-93) 76-08-65.. "La Pointe du Cap" 30 av de la Corniche,
   06230 St Jean-Cap-Ferrat, France

Roome MR & MRS Peter W (Hartranft—Stitzer—Phyllis D Jones)
   105 Parker Rd, Osterville, MA *02655*

Roosevelt MR & MRS Peter K (Marjorie Snyder).... ☎ (508) 228-5060
   MISS Christine......................... 43 India St,
   MISS Margaret......................... Nantucket, MA
   02554

Roosevelt MR & MRS Tweed (Candace C MacGuigan)
   ☎ (508) 693-5609.. "Tashmoo" Vineyard Haven, MA *02568*

Root MR & MRS Henry W (Marilyn B Seabury)
   "The Boathouse" PO Box 357, Mt Desert, ME *04660*

Rorer MR & MRS Edward C (Sarah H Bradbury).... ☎ (508) 627-3306
   MISS Amélie Marshall.................. "Summerhill"
   Box 855,
   Edgartown, MA
   02539

Rorer MR & MRS Gerald B (Elizabeth A Keator).... ☎ (717) 646-2771
   ⚓.................................. Pocono Lake
   MISS Carrie A......................... Preserve, PA *18348*
   JUNIORS MISS Elizabeth C................
   JUNIORS MR Jonathan B..................
   JUNIORS MR Christopher K...............

Rorer MR & MRS Herbert T (Linda M Hibbins).... ☎ (717) 595-0635
   MISS Heather A........................ Skytop, PA *18357*
   JUNIORS MR Edward T...................

Rorick MR & MRS Richard P (Herrlinger—Marcia Van E Pearsall)
   ☎ (860) 567-4031.. "Riverbend" 116 Headquarters Rd, Litchfield,
   CT *06759*

Rorimer MRS James J (Katherine N Serrell)
   ☎ (216) 543-4419.. "Bigsbluff" 18173 Geauga Lake Rd, Chagrin Falls,
   OH *44023*

Rorimer MRS & MRS Louis (Helen Savery Fitz-Gerald)
   ☎ (216) 543-4419.. 18173 Geauga Lake Rd, Chagrin Falls, OH *44023*

Rose MR & MRS Andrew C (Ann S Copeland)
   ☎ (516) 329-1684.. "The Rosery" 146 Main St, East Hampton,
   NY *11937*

Rose MR & MRS C Bowie (Mary J Scally) ⚓..... ☎ (410) 723-2278
   MISS Margaret C....................... "Seaway"
   MISS Elizabeth A...................... 17—72 St,
   Ocean City,
   MD *21842*

Rose MR & MRS J Harden (Georgia S Rockefeller)
   ☎ (516) 537-0511.. "Sandford Homestead" Bridgehampton, NY *11932*

Rose MR & MRS James McK JR (Anne L Bourne)... ☎ (207) 883-4253
   MISS Anne C........................... "The Clearing"
   MISS Louise B......................... Winslow Homer Rd,
   Prouts Neck, ME
   04074

Rose MR & MRS Milton C (Emily W Mason)
   ☎ (315) 482-2692.. "River House" Alexandria Bay, NY *13607*

Rose MR & MRS William Duncan (Juliette C Loizeaux)
   ☎ (508) 394-7004.. 246B Pleasant St, Bass River, MA *02664*

Rosekrans MR & MRS John N JR (Topham—Georgette Naify)
   ☎ (415) 851-0523.. 555 Albion Rd, Woodside, CA *94062*

Rosenberry MRS Samuel L (Cicely L Kershaw)
   ☎ (508) 945-0381.. "The Port House" Box 612, Chatham, MA *02633*

Ross MR & MRS Donald F (Elizabeth H Boardman)
   ☎ (916) 583-4705.. 2065 Big John Rd, Alpine Meadows, Tahoe City,
   CA *95730*

Ross MR Donald P JR
   ☎ (970) 476-1809.. 1297 Vail Valley Dv, Vail, CO *81657*

Ross MR E Burke JR...................... ☎ (508) 627-7301
   MISS Allyson H........................ "Tower Hill"
   Box 1543,
   39 Dunham Rd,
   Edgartown, MA
   02539

Ross MR & MRS Edmund B (Margaret R Haskell)
   ☎ (508) 627-4621.. 65 Davis Lane, Box 5276, Edgartown, MA *02539*

Ross MRS J Clifford (Marjorie D Rhoades)
   ☎ (508) 548-3435.. "Old Field" Little Island Rd, West Falmouth,
   MA *02574*

Ross MR & MRS John G (Patricia A Edgar)........ ☎ (908) 766-0593
   MR Louis B............................ 66 Childsworth Av,
   Bernardsville, NJ
   07924

Ross MR & MRS Llewellyn G (Katharine C Leyman)
   ☎ (616) 526-2944.. Cottage 4, Harbor Point, MI *49740*

Ross MR & MRS Paul H (Patricia S Allen)
 ☎ (516) 653-8058 . . 27 Ogden Lane, Box 1383, Quogue, NY *11959*
Ross MRS Robert S (Janet Burk)
 ☎ (508) 994-0641 . . ''The Farm House'' Nonquitt, MA *02748*
Ross MRS Walter L 2d (Sarane B Hickox)
 ☎ (616) 526-9997 . . 2632 Pennsylvania Av, Harbor Springs, MI *49740*
Rossi DR & MRS Joseph G (Cornelia L Cogswell)
 ☎ (207) 276-3986 . . ''Westacre'' Northeast Harbor, ME *04662*
Rossmassler MR & MRS Peter R (Frances B Scott) . . | ☎ (315) 686-4388
 MR William R III . . . . | ''Hermit Port''
 MR Thomas B S . . . . | Box 341, Clayton,
 MR Richard R . . . . | NY *13624*
Rotch MR & MRS William (Jane C Whitehill) ⚓
 ☎ (508) 999-5483 . . ''Marshes'' Nonquitt, MA *02748*
Rothe MR & MRS Ernst (Nancy Louise Eberhart) . . . | ☎ (401) 849-6281
 MR Ernst JR . . . . | ''Posapaug''
 JUNIORS MR Alden Augustus . . . . | 80 John St,
  | Newport, RI *02840*
Roulette REV & MRS Philip Burwell (Clover D | ☎ (302) 684-3271
 Purvis) . . . . | ''Preserve Landing''
 MR Carter B . . . . | 33 Texas Av,
 MR Randolph B D . . . . | Broadkill Beach,
  | Milton, DE *19968*
Roulston MR & MRS Thomas H (Lois E Mueller)
 ☎ (970) 926-3233 . . ''Arrowhead at Vail'' 97 Hillside Court, Edwards, CO *81632*
Rouse DR & MRS Ernest T (Eleanor Scott)
 ☎ (314) 725-5978 . . 710 S Hanley Rd, Apt 5C, St Louis, MO *63105*
Rousseau MR Henry H (Mary Bullard)
 ☎ (207) 374-5017 . . ''Bay View'' Blue Hill, ME *04614*
Rowan DR & MRS Joseph E (Diana M Pyle) . . . . | ☎ (860) 868-0282
 MISS Victoria C . . . . | ''Knoll''
 MR Ian McA . . . . | 7 North Shore Rd,
 MR Edward Van S . . . . | New Preston, CT
  | *06777*
Rowe MR & MRS A Loring (Barbara A Bastien)
 ☎ (508) 627-5003 . . 82 N Water St, Box 595, Edgartown, MA *02539*
Rowe MR & MRS George W (Kate R Munson) . . of
 ☎ (207) 883-2351 . . Prouts Neck, ME *04074*
 ☎ (508) 548-1089 . . Woods Hole, MA *02543*
Rowe MR Peter J
 ☎ (941) 748-3193 . . 1610—30 St W, Bradenton, FL *34205*
Rowe MR & MRS William S (Martha P Whitney)
 ☎ (508) 548-1089 . . Box 414, Woods Hole, MA *02543*
Rowe MRS William Wallace (Elizabeth F Woodin)
 ☎ (513) 561-7388 . . 8605 Camargo Club Dv, Cincinnati, OH *45243*
Rowland MR & MRS George R (Carolyn C Crossett)
 ☎ (508) 428-6348 . . ''Innisfree'' Box 246, Fox Island Rd, Osterville, MA *02655*
Rowley MR & MRS Edward D (Lusk—Adelaide E Storer)
 ☎ (802) 583-2416 . . Golf Course Rd, West Hill, Warren, VT *05674*
Rowley MR John C
 1351 Meadow Lane, Southampton, NY *11968*
Rowley MR & MRS Peter W (Terez De Tuboly)
 ☎ (518) 589-5118 . . 63 Thurber Rd, Onteora Park, Tannersville, NY *12485*
Rowse MISS Flavia . . see G L Smith

Roxby MAJ GEN (RET) & MRS William C JR (Corinne | Box 30022,
 T Romig) USAF . . . . | Sea Island, GA
 MISS Elisabeth C . . . . | *31561*
 MISS Susanna T . . . . |
Royce MISS Amanda B . . see T F Bundy JR
Royce MR & MRS Charles M (Karen P Free)
 ☎ (401) 322-7732 . . ''Anchorage'' 13 Spring Av, Weekapaug, RI *06891*
Royce MR Charles M JR . . see T F Bundy JR
Royce MISS Jennifer H . . see T F Bundy JR
Royce MR & MRS Stephen W 2d (Brigitte Bernhardt) ⚓
 on board Coaster'' Port Vauban, 06600 Antibes, France
Royster DR & MRS Thomas S JR (Caroline M Henry)
 ☎ (516) 653-4214 . . 52 Dune Rd, PO Box 383, Quogue, NY *11959*
Rublee MR & MRS George 2d (Gallagher—Gilbert— | ☎ (603) 675-2778
 Ellen M MacVeagh) . . . . | ''The Crossways''
 MR Francis H Gilbert . . . . | HCR 75, Box 6,
  | Platt Rd, Cornish,
  | NH *03745*
Rudkin MRS Dorothy S (Dorothy S Smith)
 ☎ (203) 259-7372 . . Box N, Southport, CT *06490*
Ruebhausen MR Oscar M
 ☎ (619) 756-1834 . . PO Box 1955, Rancho Santa Fe, CA *92067*
Rueckert DR & MRS Frederic (Joan Dodge)
 ☎ (315) 686-0025 . . ''Mid-River'' Box 9, Clayton, NY *13624*
Rueter MR & MRS William G JR (Sarah L Edwards) . | ☎ (508) 362-1930
 MISS Margaret B . . . . | ''The Barn''
 MISS Katherine B . . . . | Box 852, Barnstable,
 MR Matthew C . . . . | MA *02630*
Rugg MRS J Samuel (Sara S Lewis)
 ☎ (307) 733-8697 . . ''Teton Shadows'' 470 Sagebrush Dv, Jackson, WY *83001*
Rugg MR & MRS Peter (Meredith C Phelps) . . . . | ☎ (516) 788-7762
 MISS C Caroline . . . . | Fishers Island, NY
 MR Charlton A . . . . | *06390*
Rumbough MR & MRS Stanley M JR (Janson—Janne Herlow)
 ☎ (516) 324-0563 . . Box 1053, 22 Terbell Lane, East Hampton, NY *11937*
Rumery MR & MRS John R (Hall—Nancy Kluge)
 ☎ (603) 763-9642 . . ''Fernwood Point'' Box 73, Sunapee, NH *03782*
Runnells MR & MRS Clive (Firestone—Garwood— | ☎ (705) 375-5188
 Nancy J Morgan) . . . . | Iron City Fishing
 MR Thomas Pierce . . . . | Club, Parry Sound,
 MR David M Firestone . . . . | Ontario P2A 2X4,
 MR John M Garwood . . . . | Canada
Runnells MR & MRS John S 2d (Louise O Gale)
 ☎ (847) 234-3636 . . 89 Warrington Dv, Lake Bluff, IL *60044*
Rupp MRS Albert G (Rupp—Lowell—Baxter—Cynthia C Foy)
 ☎ (207) 546-7161 . . ''Gull Haven'' RFD 1, Box 85B, Milbridge, ME *04658*
Russell MR & MRS A Douglas JR (Marie-Caroline M | Mimosa Villa 777,
 Masson) . . . . | Val do Lobo,
 MISS Eugenie Isabelle C . . . . | Almansil, Algarve,
 MR Alexis A Douglas . . . . | Portugal
 JUNIORS MR Adrien Philippe M M . . . . |
 JUNIORS MR Pierre-Alexandre O . . . . |
Russell MR & MRS Charles T JR (Catharine Olney)
 ☎ (508) 945-0324 . . Box 433, Chatham, MA *02633*

Russell MISS Diana . . see MRS A Farwell
Russell MR & MRS Edward T JR (M Charlotte Emery) . . . . | ☎ (508) 224-2007 Long Pond, Plymouth, MA 02360
   MISS Aldis . . . .
   MISS Bradley . . . .
Russell MR & MRS Harold S (Margo Stratford) . . . . . | ☎ (616) 469-2533 "The Hig" 14200 Lake Shore Rd, Lakeside, MI 49116
   MR Nathan W . . . .
   MR Peter L . . . .

Russell MR & MRS James B (Joan Anderson)
   "Strawberry Fields" 34 Bourne Lane, PO Box 2082, Ogunquit, ME 03907
Russell MR & MRS James S (Léonore Upham)
   ☎ (415) 669-1073 . . Inverness, CA 94937
Russell MR & MRS John B JR (Cynthia Lee) . . . . | ☎ (914) 254-5737 Winnisook Club Big Indian, NY 12410
   MISS Jenny de W . . . .

Russell MR John Mosby
   ☎ (401) 783-8552 . . 2595 Kingston Rd, Kingston, RI 02881
Russell MRS Renouf (Lily Warren)
   ☎ (603) 532-7023 . . "Wesselhoeft Farm" 4 Gilson Rd, Jaffrey, NH 03452
Russell MR & MRS Thomas W JR (Mary Ferguson)
   ☎ (516) 788-7474 . . "Holiday House" Fishers Island, NY 06390
Rust MR David E . . . . | ☎ (305) 294-9833 306 Elizabeth St, Key West, FL 33040
   MISS Marina M . . . .

Rust MR & MRS S Murray JR (Hill—Elinor Q Cowdrey)
   ☎ (508) 255-1446 . . 18 Meg's Lane, Orleans, MA 02653
Rutan MR & MRS Frank E 3d (Crandall—Beverly A Tuthill)
   ☎ (401) 348-8279 . . "The Lodge" 7 Yosemite Valley Rd, Watch Hill, RI 02891
Rutherfurd MR & MRS Guy G (Georgette Whelan)
   ☎ (516) 788-7272 . . Fishers Island, NY 06390
Rutherfurd MR & MRS Guy G JR (CTSS Marie T Seilern-Aspang) . . . . | ☎ (516) 283-3150 "Wooley Pond" 1201 Noyac Rd, Southampton, NY 11968
   MISS Elizabeth F . . . .
   MR Guy Christopher . . . .

Rutherfurd MR & MRS John JR (Caroline L Gordon)
   ☎ (518) 576-9816 . . "Hill Station" St Huberts, NY 12943
Rutherfurd MR Lewis P . . . . | ☎ (516) 788-7687 Box I, Fishers Island, NY 06390
   MR Lewis S . . . .
   JUNIORS MR Andrew H A . . . .

Rutherfurd MRS Winthrop (Alice Polk)
   ☎ (516) 788-7640 . . Fishers Island, NY 06390
Rutter MR J Wood 2d
   ☎ (508) 228-2585 . . "Shawkemo" Monomoy, Nantucket, MA 02554
Ruykhaver MR & MRS Charles G JR (Jane Currier)
   ☎ (508) 349-3420 . . Chequesset Neck Rd, Wellfleet, MA 02667
Ryan MR Allan A 3d . . . . | ☎ (516) 288-6391 15 Shore Rd, Westhampton Beach, NY 11978
   MISS Melissa R F . . . .

Ryan MRS John T JR (M Irene O'Brien)
   ☎ (508) 945-1082 . . Whistler Lane, North Chatham, MA 02650
Ryan MRS McA Donald (Madeleine C Hemingway)
   Cow Island, Medomak, ME 04551
Ryan MR & MRS Michael (Debora D Gilbert)
   ☎ (518) 851-9140 . . RD 1, Box 171, Craryville, NY 12521
Ryan MISS Saville
   ☎ (970) 925-3678 . . Royal Cabin, Ashcroft, 300 Puppy Smith St, Apt 205-175, Aspen, CO 81611
Ryburn MR & MRS Samuel M (M Beverly Huse)
   ☎ (517) 479-3433 . . "The Outlook" 29 Resort Rd, Harbor Beach, MI 48441
Ryerson MR & MRS Joseph T 3d (Barbara I Hyde)
   "Lilac Ledge" Northeast Harbor, ME 04662
Ryerson MRS M Ducey (Maria B Ducey)
   ☎ (207) 276-5010 . . "Lilac Ledge" Northeast Harbor, ME 04662
Ryland MR W Bradford 2d
   ☎ (619) 360-9139 . . "Sea View" Box 1565, La Jolla, CA 92038
Ryland MR & MRS William H (George Ann H Doty)
   ☎ (607) 547-2860 . . Box 324, Cooperstown, NY 13326
Ryle MRS Robert W (Anne L Thouron)
   ☎ (207) 288-5482 . . "Sea Urchins" Bar Harbor, ME 04609
Rynning MR & MRS Eivind P (Baker—Virginia L Busser) ⚓ . . . . | "Gusteglova" Tveitan i Sandefjord, Norway
   MR Ralph E . . . .
   JUNIORS MR Lars E . . . .

Ryon MR & MRS Mortimer (Cornell—E Sandra Lipson)
   ☎ (508) 257-6677 . . "Double Decker" Box 389, Siasconset, MA 02564

S

Sabet JUNIORS MR Amman H . . see MRS S H Cole
Sachs MR Stephen F . . . . | ☎ (508) 228-1958 "Dionis Cottage" PO Box 492, Nantucket, MA 02554
   MISS Natasha . . . .
   MR Shamus F . . . .

Sachs MR & MRS William R JR (Elizabeth Le D Kidd)
   Fishers Island, NY 06390
Sadler MR & MRS Julius T JR (Jacquelin D Jones)
   ☎ (819) 463-4507 . . Gatineau Fish & Game Club, RR 1, Gracefield, Quebec J0X 1W0, Canada
   MR at . . ☎ (860) 567-8804 . . Carolina House, PO Box 55, Litchfield, CT 06759
Sadron MRS Alexandra (Alexandra Sellar) . . . . | ☎ (401) 847-5362 "Seaweed" Bellevue Av, Newport, RI 02840
   MR Nicholas . . . .

Sadtler MR & MRS Stephen C (Jean A Johnson) . . . . | ☎ (804) 787-7320 Folly Creek, PO Box 614, Accomac, VA 23301
   MR Stephen C JR . . . .
   MR Thomas MacL . . . .
   MR Benjamin B . . . .

Safrin MR & MRS Robert W (Darlington—Silvana R A Lubini)
   ☎ (011-41-22) 346-60-59 . . 14 Bis Av Peschier, 1206 Geneva, Switzerland

Sailer MR & MRS Christopher A (C Christina Berg) . ☎ (207) 236-2246
  MR Christopher A JR
  JUNIORS MR Samuel C
  2 Highland Av, Camden, ME *04843*
Sailer MR & MRS John JR (Pamela W Steffens) . . . . . ☎ (207) 236-4343
  JUNIORS MR John 3d
  "The Ledges" Rte 105 & Molyneaux Rd, Camden, ME *04843*
Saint-Amand DR & MRS Nathan E (Cynthia W Chisholm) . . . . ☎ (914) 666-2518
  MISS Elizabeth
  MR Alexander
  Guard Hill Farm, Bedford Hills, NY *10507*
  Aug 1 . . ☎ (516) 788-7033 Fishers Island, NY *06390*
St John MR & MRS Fordyce B JR (Lisa S Polhemus)
  ☎ (516) 537-0369 . . Box 344, Sagaponack, NY *11962*
St John MR & MRS Warren Jackson (Irma Claire Frech) ⚓ . . . . ☎ (205) 234-3161
  MISS Mary C
  MISS Susanna H
  MR Warren J JR
  "Finmar Cottage" Willow Point Rd, Alexander City, AL *35010*
St Lewis MRS Roy (Taylor—Peggy Hammond)
  4 Matinecock Farms Rd, Glen Cove, NY *11542*
Salembier MRS Harold P (Townsend—Anita van L Higgins)
  ☎ (516) 324-8802 . . 95 Egypt Lane, East Hampton, NY *11937*
Salisbury MR D Austin JR
  ☎ (516) 324-5731 . . 105 Main St, East Hampton, NY *11937*
Salisbury MR & MRS John F (Nancy W Furlong)
  47 Elm St, Stonington, CT *06878*
Saltonstall MR & MRS William L (Jane Chandler)
  ☎ (508) 693-0477 . . "Seven Gates Farm" Vineyard Haven, MA *02568*
Saltsman MR & MRS James A (E Brooks Johnstone)
  ☎ (207) 244-5548 . . Box 695, Southwest Harbor, ME *04679*
Saltus MR Ralph W H
  Box 184, Rockland, ME *04841*
Saman MR & MRS Alain-Constantin (Anita E Alig)
  ☎ (860) 542-5112 . . "Torrington House" 127 Old Goshen Rd, Norfolk, CT *06058*
Sammis MR & MRS Jesse F 3d (Jean McA Tilt). . . . . ☎ (802) 728-9122
  MISS Suzanne Tilt
  MR Jesse F 4th
  "Stoneleigh" Green Mountain Stock Farm, Randolph, VT *05060*
Sample MR & MRS Joseph S (Willing—Miriam Tyler)
  ☎ (406) 252-8662 . . 606 Highland Park Dv, Billings, MT *59102-1909*
Sanders MR & MRS David I (Hatfield—H Celeste Pogue) ⚓ . . . .
  MISS Susan E
  MR David I JR
  Edgewood Lane, Snowmass, CO *81654*
Sant MR & MRS John T (Almira S Baldwin)
  ☎ (616) 526-2474 . . 43 Beach Dv, Wequetonsing, MI *49740*
Sargent MR & MRS Christopher S (Anne MacGaffin) . . . . ☎ (401) 635-2272
  JUNIORS MISS Thayer A
  JUNIORS MR Christopher S 3d
  99D Sakonnet Point Rd, Little Compton, RI *02837*
Sargent MRS Edward C (Nancy B Lawrence)
  ☎ (518) 359-3009 . . "Witch Island" Big Wolf Lake, Tupper Lake, NY *12986*
Sargent MRS F Porter (Jane K Culver) . . . . ☎ (603) 542-6600
  MISS Cornelia E
  MISS Roslyn
  "The Uplands" RD 2, Box 466A, Claremont, NH *03743*
Sargent MR & MRS Fitzwilliam (Mercedes Muguiro) . . . . . ☎ (508) 526-4438
  MR Antonio M
  202 Beach St, Manchester, MA *01944*
Sargent MRS George Lee (Hester Lloyd Jones)
  ☎ (508) 295-2608 . . Great Neck Rd, Wareham, MA *02571*
Sargent MR & MRS Thomas A (Allison D Ijams)
  ☎ (516) 788-7126 . . "Rago" Box 236, Fishers Island, NY *06390*
Satterthwaite MR & MRS Henry B (Jonson—Anne W Stambaugh) . . . . ☎ (011-353-65) 74351
  MR James D
  MISS Dana A Jonson
  MR Randolph S Jonson
  "Luogh South" Coast Rd, Doolin, Co Clare, Ireland
Satterthwaite MRS T Wilkinson (Anne T Stewart)
  ☎ (508) 627-8932 . . Box 393, Oliver St, Edgartown, MA *02539*
Saul MR & MRS B Francis 2d (Elizabeth Patricia English) ⚓ . . . . ☎ (508) 428-6519
  MISS Elizabeth W
  MISS Patricia E
  MR B Francis 3d
  "Tempo" 355 Eel River Rd, Osterville, MA *02655*
Saunders MR & MRS Donald H (Eleanor F Hall) . . . . ☎ (401) 847-4683
  MISS Patricia G—⚓
  42 Elm St, Newport, RI *02840*
Saunders MR & MRS Thomas A III (M Jordan Horner) . . . . ☎ (804) 971-8031
  MR Thomas A IV
  University of Virginia, Lower Mews, West Lawn, Charlottesville, VA *22903*
Saurel MRS Paul (Louise R Hoguet)
  ☎ (413) 298-4877 . . "Council Grove" E Main St, Box 853, Stockbridge, MA *01262*
Savage MR & MRS Arthur V (Harriet B Hawes)
  ☎ (518) 576-2223 . . "All Seasons" St Huberts, NY *12943*
Savage MR & MRS Michael D (Remp—Ann S Tweedy) . . of
  ☎ (011-44-14) 645-263 . . Harthill Castle, Oyne, Insch, Aberdeenshire AB52 6QU, Scotland
  44 rue St Louis en l'Ile, 75004 Paris, France
Savage MR William Halsted
  ☎ (518) 251-3816 . . North Woods Club, PO Box 905, Minerva, NY *12851*
Savory MR & MRS Wallace E (Charlotte Macy) . . . . . ☎ (207) 354-2593
  MR Richard
  JUNIORS MISS Caroline
  Hathorn Point Rd, Cushing, ME *04563*
Sawyer MRS Geoffrey A (Knowles—Elizabeth C Pennock)
  ☎ (207) 883-2485 . . "The Sea Urchin" Prouts Neck, ME *04074*
Sawyer MRS William B H (Fannette B Horner)
  ☎ (508) 228-1954 . . 37 Hulbert Av, Nantucket, MA *02554*

Saylor MR & MRS Harold D 2d (Genevieve M Gutt)
☎ (717) 698-5594 . . Lake Ariel, PA *18436*
Scaife MRS Frances G (Frances L Gilmore) . . . . | ☎ (508) 228-4024
   MISS Jennie K . . . . | 53 Easton St,
                                           | Nantucket, MA
  | *02554*
Scaife MR & MRS Richard Mellon (Battle—Margaret | ☎ (508) 228-5983
   Ritchie Rhea) . . . . | 9 Kimball Av,
      MR T Westray Battle . . . . | Nantucket, MA
  | *02554*
Scannell MR & MRS David G (Susan M Lloyd) . . . . . | ☎ (508) 420-0247
   MISS Anik E . . . . | 101 Vineyard Rd,
   MISS Kirsten M . . . . | Cotuit, MA *02635*
Scarlett MR & MRS Lindley C (Christine P | ☎ (717) 646-8767
   Kenworthy) . . . . | Pocono Lake
   MISS Whitney B . . . . | Preserve, PA *18348*
   MR Beecher C . . . . |
Schade MR & MRS Wilbert C JR (Florence M Allen)
☎ (616) 547-6405 . . 11000 Evergreen Lane, Charlevoix, MI *49720*
Schaefer MR & MRS Herman A (Montaldo—Marie-France Fosset)
☎ (516) 283-3059 . . 200 Captain's Neck Lane, Southampton, NY *11968*
Schaeffer MRS Marcia M (Marcia A Meehan) . . . . . | ☎ (516) 283-4211
   MISS Georgina B . . . . | Box 593, First Neck
  | Lane, Southampton,
  | NY *11968*
Schafer MR & MRS John H (Edith T Nalle) . . . . | ☎ (207) 276-5541
   MISS Alison T . . . . | "Juniper Ledge"
   MISS Nancy C . . . . | Northeast Harbor,
   MR John R . . . . | ME *04662*
Schaff MR & MRS David S 3d (Sarah I Hosack) . . . | ☎ (616) 386-5405
   MR & MRS John H (Mary Elder) . . . . | Box 67,
  | Northport Point,
  | Northport, MI *49670*
Schaupp DR & MRS Willis C (Pinger—Joan H Whitney)
☎ (415) 868-1657 . . Box 641, Stinson Beach, CA *94970*
Scheerer MR & MRS William 2d (Idoline W Crabbe) | ☎ (516) 324-0586
   MR Thomas I . . . . | Box 1248, West End
  | Rd, East Hampton,
  | NY *11937*
Scheetz MRS Edwin Freed (Eleanor Baton)
☎ (412) 235-2372 . . Ross Mountain Club, New Florence, PA *15944*
Scheetz MR & MRS J Paul (Alice C Rust)
Jly 15 . . ☎ (207) 282-2940 . . 89 Granite Point Rd, Fortunes Rocks, RD 2, Biddeford, ME *04005*
Schefer MR Anton E B
The Mill House at Auburn, Box 217, Casanova, VA *22017*
Scherer MRS Albert G (Clara Legg)
☎ (413) 229-2024 . . "Old Meadow Farm" Box 162, Kellogg Rd, Sheffield, MA *01257*
Schieffelin MRS William Jay (Annette Markoe)
☎ (207) 422-6441 . . "Point of View" Rte 1, Box 61, Gouldsboro, ME *04607*
Schiff MR & MRS David T (Martha E Lawler) . . . . . . | ☎ (970) 925-1340
   MISS Ashley R . . . . | "Serendipity"
   DR Andrew N . . . . | 214 Lake Av,
   MR David B . . . . | Aspen, CO *81611*

Schipper MR & MRS Howard P (Alice C Evarts)
see W M Evarts JR
Schlafly MR & MRS Robert F (Maie B Kimball)
☎ (616) 526-2947 . . Cottage 51, Harbor Point, MI *49740*
Schleussner MRS Robert C JR (Grehan—Elisabeth G | ☎ (315) 859-0980
   Stevens) ⚓ . . . . | "Bardscroft"
   MISS Laura S . . . . | 15 Marvin St,
  | Clinton, NY *13323*
Schley MRS Diana R (Clucas—Diana A Reeder)
☎ (011-39-81) 837-0764 . . "Casa Arbace" via Valentino 22, Capri, Italy
Schley MRS Reeve JR (Elizabeth D Boies)
☎ (508) 693-1590 . . West Tisbury, MA *02539*
Schley MR & MRS Reeve 3d (Georgia R Terry) . . . . . | "The Studio"
   MISS Marie B . . . . | Pointe-au-Pic,
   JUNIORS MR Reeve T . . . . | Quebec G0T 1M0,
  | Canada
Schmitt MR Roger M L . . . . | "Brooklands"
   MR John F 2d . . . . | Aldwich by the
   MR James E . . . . | Water,
  | Gloucestershire,
  | England
Schmitz MR & MRS Richard D (Ellen T Goodwin) . . | ☎ (518) 392-6046
   MISS Catherine . . . . | RD 165, Rte 9,
   JUNIORS MR Jeffrey D . . . . | New Concord, NY
  | *12060*
Schoeffer MR & MRS Peter A V (Jeannine B | ☎ (011-33-93)
   Rhinelander) . . . . | 01-16-80
   JUNIORS MR Frederic B R . . . . | "La Jearena" blvd
   JUNIORS MR Peter A S . . . . | Settimelli-Lazare,
  | 06 Villefranche-
  | sur-Mer, France
Schoeller MR & MRS K Christian (C Brewer Mullins)
☎ (508) 693-9609 . . RFD 408, Lambert's Cove Rd, Vineyard Haven, MA *02568*
Schoettle MR & MRS Karl R JR (Katherine Illoway) | ☎ (207) 359-2757
   ⚓ | PO Box 292,
   JUNIORS MISS Sarah E . . . . | Center Harbor,
  | Brooklin, ME *04616*
Schoettle MR & MRS Philip A (Merritt—Adele Biddle)
☎ (908) TW9-0257 . . 510 East Av, Bay Head, NJ *08742*
Schoettle MRS Robert M (Elisabeth D Abbott)
☎ (514) 292-5804 . . "Camp Point" RR 2, Mansonville, Quebec, Canada
Schofield MR & MRS Robert H (Barbara F Porter)
☎ (401) 635-8631 . . 662 W Main Rd, Little Compton, RI *02837*
Scholle MR & MRS Oliver C JR (Elizabeth R Haffenreffer)
☎ (516) 788-7156 . . Greenwood Rd, Fishers Island, NY *06390*
Schoyer MR Timothy R
☎ (207) 282-2379 . . "Willow Lawn" 124 Mile Stretch Rd, PO Box 163, Biddeford Pool, ME *04006*
Schrade MR & MRS Robert W (Rolande M Young) . . | ☎ (413) 238-5854
   MISS Rhonda-Lee . . . . | Sevenars Music
   MISS Rolisa M . . . . | Festival,
   MISS Rorianne C . . . . | Worthington, MA
  | *01098*
Schroeder MR & MRS A Reed (Ann H Williams)
Ojibway Island, Pointe-au-Baril, Ontario P0G 1K0, Canada

Schultz MR & MRS John F (Patricia A Kelsey) ..... ☎ (910) 256-2027
    MISS Frances E .... 24 W Oxford St,
    MR Christopher B .... Wrightsville Beach,
    JUNIORS MISS Joanna K .... NC *28480*
Schwab MR & MRS Gustav 5th (Luebke—Mary E   ☎ (860) 535-4568
  Klein)................................. 21 Quanaduck Cove
    MISS Marie K Luebke .... Rd, Stonington, CT
      06378
Schwartz MR & MRS Alexander C JR (Perry—Glorvina H Rodewald)
  ☎ (914) 351-2494 . . Ridge Rd, Tuxedo Park, NY *10987*
Schwartz MR & MRS Edwin J (Elisa K Escamilla)
  ☎ (415) 669-7566 . . 200 Via De La Vista, Inverness, CA *94937*
Schwartz MR & MRS James P (Mary L Moseley) ... ☎ (302) 653-9458
    MR Marshall L .... 4261 Sudlersville
      Rd, Clayton, DE
      19978
Schwartz MRS Philip W (Seabury—Bright—Mary L Peck)
  ☎ (860) 434-3200 . . "Eight Mile River House" 20 Old Hamburg Rd,
  Lyme, CT *06371*
Schwarz DR & MRS Fred R (Carol Larner) .... 5 Back Court,
    MISS Lesley A......................... Wild Dunes,
    MR Jeffrey R.......................... Charleston, SC
    MR Jason B........................... *29451*
    JUNIORS MISS Allyson L ....
Schwarz MR & MRS Horace W (Ann Haydock)
  ☎ (717) 685-2348 . . Forest Lake Club, RR 1, Box 333, Hawley,
  PA *18428*
Scott MRS A Thornton (Catherine Little)
  ☎ (617) 383-0708 . . 428 Atlantic Av, Cohasset, MA *02025*
Scott MR & MRS Alfred L (Jacks—Elizabeth Bond   of ☎ (207)372-8153
  Hunter)................................ "Sail Loft"
    MR Alexander L .... Tenants Harbor, ME
    MISS Elizabeth B Jacks *04860*
    MR Robert LeRoy Jacks JR.............. ☎ (518) 851-6220
      "The Hill"
      65 Bells Pond Rd,
      Hudson, NY *12534*
Scott MR & MRS Donald JR (Margaret J Dilworth)
  ☎ (207) 326-4416 . . 20 Acre Point, Harborside, ME *04642*
Scott MR & MRS George C JR (Boyle—Helen R Shepard)
  ☎ (617) 631-6498 . . 1 Kimbal St, Marblehead, MA *01945*
Scott MR & MRS Harlan (Skelly—Ann S Layton)
  ☎ (302) 227-2254 . . "Drake's Folly" 149 Silver Lake Dv, Rte 1A,
  Rehoboth Beach, DE *19971*
Scott MR & MRS Hugh N (Alexandra Korff) .... ☎ (518) 576-4548
    MISS Eliza R .... "Freiheit Schloss"
    MISS Laura H .... Keene Valley, NY
      12943
Scott MR & MRS John H (Avern—Jean McDougall) . ☎ (508) 228-2651
    MR Hugh McD .... 4 Capaum Rd,
      Nantucket, MA
      02554
Scott MR & MRS John J (Evelyn Attwood)
  ☎ (203) 869-5518 . . 8 Beechcroft Rd, Greenwich, CT *06830*
Scott MR & MRS John T JR (Karen W Fraley)
  "Overflow" Rockport, ME *04856*

Scott MR Norman
  17105 Sonoma H'way, Sonoma, CA *95476*
Scott MR & MRS R Stewart (Bowman—Sheila Williams)
  ☎ (412) 781-6614 . . 3 Oakhurst Circle, Pittsburgh, PA *15215*
Scott MRS Robert Montgomery (H Gay Elliot)
  ☎ (610) 688-7010 . . "Hopelands" 705 Church Rd, Wayne, PA *19087*
Scott MR Robert Montgomery
  ☎ (508) 228-0596 . . E Hallowell Lane, Box 992, Nantucket, MA *02554*
Scott MRS S Lytton (Underhill—Dorothy Sullivan)
  ☎ (860) 663-2259 . . "Fox Meadow" 80 Chestnut Hill Rd, Killingworth,
  CT *06419*
Scott MISS Sheila N
  ☎ (516) 537-2426 . . 526 Hedges Lane, Sagaponack, NY *11962*
Scribner MRS Charles JR (Joan Sunderland)
  ☎ (908) 953-8296 . . 109 Countryside Dv, Basking Ridge, NJ *07920*
Scribner MR & MRS Charles 3d (Ritchie H Markoe)
  ☎ (516) 671-1517 . . PO Box 347, Locust Valley, NY *11560*
Scripps MR & MRS Edward W (McDonnell—Betty J Knight)
  ☎ (804) 973-3345 . . "Eagle Hill Farm" HCR 1, Box 38, Charlottesville,
  VA *22901*
Scudder MR & MRS Barrett (Hyde—Aljean Thomas)
  ☎ (802) 362-4245 . . PO Box 705, W Union St Ext,
  Manchester Village, VT *05254*
Scudder MR & MRS Edward W JR (Perrin—Louise B Fry)
  ☎ (518) 523-3833 . . "Birchgate" Victor Herbert Dv, Lake Placid,
  NY *12946*
Scudder MRS Mason (Celia Vandermark)
  ☎ (617) 354-0249 . . 14 Elmwood Av, Cambridge, MA *02138-4740*
Sculley MR & MRS John S 3d (Hersh—Carol L Adams)
  ☎ (207) 236-4491 . . 64 Chestnut St, Camden, ME *04843*
Scullin MR & MRS John R (McAdams—Janice J Micka)
  ☎ (508) 420-3052 . . "Pebble Cove" 110 Pine Ridge Rd, Cotuit,
  MA *02635*
Scully MR & MRS John A (Josephine W Pepper) .... ☎ (207) 883-6218
    MR Benjamin P........................ Prouts Neck, ME
      04074
Scully MR & MRS Leonard Tyson (Jean T Jackson)
  ☎ (914) PO4-5180 . . "Home Station" Fancher Rd, Pound Ridge,
  NY *10576*
Seale MR & MRS William (Lucinda L Smith). . . . . . . ☎ (409) 384-5269
    MR William 3d .... "Ant Hill"
    MR John Henry B .... Rte 2, Box 507,
      Jasper, TX *75951*
Seaman MRS Dixon (Madeleine C Dixon)
  ☎ (516) 324-4723 . . Town House East, 18 Cross H'way, East Hampton,
  NY *11937*
Searle MR & MRS Robert S (Davie—Urling S Iselin)
  ☎ (518) 624-2973 . . "Aldebaran" Long Lake, NY *12847*
Sears MR & MRS Herbert T (Ann G Mason)
  ☎ (207) 563-3881 . . Clarks Cove Rd, Walpole, ME *04573*
Sears MR Nathaniel R . . see A J D Morrow
Sears MR & MRS R Buford (Suzanne H Marlette)
  ☎ (905) 894-2512 . . 2077 McDonald Rd, Bertie Bay,
  Ontario L0S 1N0, Canada

Sears MR Richard . . . . ☎ (011-33-94)
    MISS Stephanie 05-64-77
    Le Dattier, Cavalaire, Var, France

Sears MRS Sally (Wechsler—Sally S Thayer)
    ☎ (415) 388-4493 . . 53 Woodbine Dv, Mill Valley, CA *94941*

Sears MR Sebastian C . . see A J D Morrow

Seaton MR & MRS Hugh Van (Lucille C Pendleton) . 79 Harbor Dv,
    MISS Dana A . . . . Apt 304, Stamford,
    MR Hugh G . . . . CT *06902*

Sednaoui MR & MRS M Kent (Jennifer S Wettlaufer)
    Fishers Island, NY *06390*

Seeley MR & MRS Franklin M (Suzanne E Fotterall) . ☎ (207) 695-2942
    MISS Olivia F . . . . ''On the Rocks''
    JUNIORS MISS Cordelia M . . . . Box 316,
    Greenville Junction, ME *04442*

Segerstrom MRS Yvonne de C (Yvonne de C Perry) . ☎ (011-33-1)
    MR Toren H 43-29-01-99
    MR Anton D . . . . 9 rue Poulletier, 75004 Paris, France

Seidler MR & MRS Francis F (Hately—Patricia C . ☎ (707) 257-3866
    Martin) 170 Westgate Dv,
    MISS Jennifer W Hately . . . . Napa, CA *94558*

Sekera MR Jeffrey O . . see E H Bennett 3d
Sekera MISS Katherine H . . see E H Bennett 3d

Selby MR Frederick P
    ☎ (516) 287-3508 . . 880 Meadow Lane, Southampton, NY *11968*

Selby MRS Linn Howard (Linn Howard) . . . . ☎ (307) 587-3917
    MISS Andrea H . . . . ''Hawkeye Ranch''
    MISS Stephanie M . . . . 4148 S Fork Rd, Cody, WY *82414*

Selby MR & MRS Norman C (Melissa G Vail)
    ☎ (914) 234-7168 . . 156 E Middle Patent Rd, Bedford, NY *10506*

Selden MR & MRS George L (Ann L Arnold)
    ☎ (518) 589-6527 . . Onteora Club, Tannersville, NY *12485*

Selleck DR & MRS Nathaniel (Ross—Emily C Lanier)
    ☎ (518) 576-9472 . . ''Owls' Nest'' Keene, NY *12942*

Sellers MR & MRS Emory R JR (MinnieBelle Fry)
    ☎ (904) 428-3686 . . Golden Arms, 601 N Atlantic Av, New Smyrna Beach, FL *32069*

Sellers MR & MRS William B (Lucille L Grant)
    ☎ (904) 837-8637 . . 5084 Shoreline Towers W, Destin, FL *32541*

Semans MR & MRS Truman T (Nellie M Merrick) . . ☎ (540) 839-2039
    MR Truman T JR . . . . ''Hobby Horse
    MR William M . . . . Farm'' Hot Springs, VA *24445*

Semerjian MR George G
    ☎ (516) 283-0264 . . ''Brigadune'' Gin Lane, PO Box 112, Southampton, NY *11969*

Semple MR & MRS Nathaniel M (Patricia Maguire) . . ☎ (517) 479-3525
    JUNIORS MR Nathaniel M JR . . . . Cottage 40, Harbor Beach Resort Rd, Harbor Beach, MI *48441*

Sengelmann MR Erich P
    Triangle F Ranch, Bondurant, WY *82922*

Sengelmann MISS (DR) Roberta D
    ☎ (310) 476-7651 . . 12303-3 Helena Dv, Los Angeles, CA *90049*

Senior MR & MRS Richard J L (Diana T Morgan) . . . ☎ (715) 547-3812
    MISS Alicia M . . . . ''Headwaters''
    MISS Amanda T . . . . 3280 County Trunk
    MR Alden L . . . . E, Land O'Lakes, WI *54540*

Sensenbrenner MR & MRS F James JR (Cheryl L ''The Shack''
    Warren) . . . . Box 6, Nashotah,
    JUNIORS MR F James 3d . . . . WI *53058*

Servick MRS K Hannah (Katharine M Hannah) . . . . ☎ (705) 764-1079
    MR Edward Ross 2d . . . . ''Cahannahda''
    MR Douglas Todd . . . . Beaumaris, Lake Muskoka, Ontario P0B 1B0, Canada

Sethness MRS Charles H JR (Mary G Buckley) . . . . . ☎ (715) 544-2316
    MR & MRS Daniel B (Marilyn Noe) . . . . ''Duck Lake'' Land O'Lakes, WI *54540*

Sewall MRS George T (Mary H Bossidy)
    ☎ (413) 243-0618 . . South Lee, MA *01260*

Sexson MR & MRS Timothy J (Elizabeth Wilmer)
    ☎ (520) 367-1731 . . 3244 Bullfrog Loop, Pinetop, AZ *85935*

Seybolt MR & MRS G Crossan JR (Margaret McC Meyer)
    ☎ (508) 945-9508 . . 205 Champlain Rd, Chatham, MA *02633*

Seymour MR Peter A
    ☎ (207) 276-3237 . . ''Eastward Way'' Clifton Dock Rd, Northeast Harbor, ME *04662*

Shafer MR & MRS George C JR (Louise S Hoopes) . . ☎ (717) 553-2343
    MISS Elizabeth T . . . . Camp
    MAJ G Carlton 3d—USMCR . . . . Susquehannock, Lake Choconut, Friendsville, PA *18818*

Shafer MR & MRS J Bradley (Cynthia A Cozad)
    ☎ (616) 526-2859 . . ''The Annex'' 348 Glenn Dv, Harbor Springs, MI *49740*

Shafer MR & MRS Robert L (Ellen A Schlafly) . . . . . ☎ (207) 276-5584
    MISS Adelaide . . . . ''Rocky Pasture''
    MISS Katherine . . . . Harborside Rd,
    JUNIORS MR Daniel . . . . Northeast Harbor, ME *04662*

Shaffer MR & MRS William B JR (Law—Mary F ☎ (616) 223-4816
    Morrison) . . . . Neahtawanta,
    MISS Dorothy P . . . . Traverse City, MI
    MR M Bakewell 3d *49684*
    MR Robert M M . . . .

Shand MR & MRS James JR (Corina C Guild)
    ☎ (508) 228-2038 . . 31 Pilgrim Rd, Box 1406, Nantucket, MA *02554*

Shands MR & MRS Courtney JR (Nancy B Lewis)
    ''Blackacre'' General Delivery, Watersmeet, MI *49969*

Shands MR & MRS E F Berkley (Pamela M Leahy)
    General Delivery, Watersmeet, MI *49969*

Shank MR & MRS Howard C (Pattou—Hollis L McLaughlin)
    ☎ (847) 234-1660 . . 777 Washington Rd, Lake Forest, IL *60045*

Shanley MR & MRS Kevin (Eleanor S Canham)..... of ☎ (717)775-7165 "Timberdoodle" Blooming Grove Hunt & Fish Club, Hawley, PA *18428*
   MISS Alison P..........................
   MISS Katy S............................
   MISS Julie S............................
   MISS Elizabeth S.......................
☎ (508) 295-6338 "The Folly" Great Neck Rd, Wareham, MA *02571*

Sharp MRS George C (Ruth Baldwin)
   ☎ (914) 232-3566.. "Cantitoe Corners" Box L, Katonah, NY *10536*

Sharp MR & MRS Robert W (Naquin—Mary G Miller) ⚓ .. of
   ☎ (508) 548-2115.. Chapoquoit, West Falmouth, MA *02574*
   ☎ (410) 255-1881.. Gibson Island, MD *21056*

Sharpe MR & MRS William P (Soule—Emily F Moser)..........................
   MR Timothy W Soule ....
Hewett's Island, General Delivery, Spruce Head, ME *04859*

Sharples MR & MRS Thomas D (Renate H A Backhausen)
   ☎ (541) 998-6090.. 91448 Steinmetz Rd, Junction City, OR *97448-9540*

Shattuck MR & MRS George H JR (Isabel D Closson)
   ☎ (508) 693-2362.. "East Hill" RD 305, Lambert's Cove Rd, Vineyard Haven, MA *02568*

Shattuck MR H Francis JR
   ☎ (802) 824-5955.. Box 240, Landgrove, VT *05148*

Shattuck MR & MRS Mayo A 3d (Jennifer W Budge) Chebeague Island, ME *04017*

Shattuck MR & MRS Peter H (Elizabeth J Horr)
   ☎ (707) 964-9548.. "Ojala" Mendocino, CA *95460*

Shaw MR & MRS Harry L (Jocelyn Thomas)
   ☎ (401) 423-0022.. "Gray Rocks" 6 Blueberry Lane, Jamestown, RI *02835*

Shaw MR & MRS L Edward JR (Irene M Ryan) .....
   MISS Hope E...........................
   MISS Hillary A ....
   MISS Julia J............................
   MR Christopher B ....
   JUNIORS MR Rory E......................
☎ (516) 329-2331 PO Box 416, Middle Lane, East Hampton, NY *11937*

Shaw MR & MRS Robert J (Davis—Patricia N French)
   ☎ (508) 748-0539.. 406 Point Rd, Marion, MA *02738*

Shaw MR & MRS S Parkman JR (Lisa A Geissenhainer)
   ☎ (207) 244-3819.. Great Cranberry Island, Cranberry Isles, ME *04625*

Shaw MR & MRS William D JR (C Tobey Gilmore)..
   JUNIORS MISS Carroll G ....
   JUNIORS MISS Katherine B ....
☎ (508) 257-9811 117 Baxter Rd, Nantucket, MA *02554*

Shaw MR & MRS William V (Osborne—Mary Morse)
   ☎ (408) 659-3666.. "River Ranch" Carmel Valley, CA *93924*

Shea MR & MRS Peter L (Nancy W Sage) ....
   JUNIORS MR James DeW ....
☎ (516) 676-8863 Box 384, Locust Valley, NY *11560*

Shedd MR & MRS Carl B Ely (Barton—Isabel McIlvain)..............................
   JUNIORS MISS Elisabeth H Ely ....
☎ (518) 327-3227 "Björn" Upper St Regis, NY *12945*

Sheehan MR & MRS Robert W (Pauline O Vietor)...
   MR William B..........................
   MR Thomas V ....
   JUNIORS MR Arthur W ....
☎ (508) 627-8566 41 S Water St, Box 498, Edgartown, MA *02539*

Sheerin REV & MRS Charles W JR (Edith P Barton)
   ☎ (518) 891-5215.. HCR 1, Box 3C, Saranac Lake, NY *12983*

Sheerin MR & MRS J Laurence (Halff—Betty L Burton)...............................
   MISS Andrea Kate......................
   MR J Laurence JR ....
☎ (401) 847-3963 "Nearsea" Ocean Dv, Newport, RI *02840*

Sheffield MR & MRS Edwin S (Dorothy G Yerger) ..
   MR Edwin S JR ....
☎ (401) 846-8548 "Daisyfield" 315 Indian Av, Middletown, RI *02842*

Sheffield MRS Sandra S (Sandra W Shelvey)
   ☎ (508) 228-0888.. "Miramar" 11 Jefferson Av, Nantucket, MA *02554*

Shelly MR & MRS James N JR (Julia E Jorgensen)
   ☎ (516) 324-5507.. 74 Fireplace Rd, East Hampton, NY *11937*

Shelnutt MRS Budd (Martha L Budd)
   ☎ (206) 232-5292.. 7705—89 Place SE, Mercer Island, WA *98040*

Shelton MRS Richard D (Catherine P McKay)
   ☎ (616) 547-6365.. 37 Belvedere Club, Charlevoix, MI *49720*

Shennan MR & MRS James G JR (Janna L Osmond) .
   MISS Elizabeth R.......................
   JUNIORS MR William G ....
☎ (208) 772-4188 Rte 2, Box 284, Hayden Lake, ID *83835*

Shephard MISS Geraldine L
   ☎ (516) 283-5722.. "Tucked Away" PO Box 1024, Southampton, NY *11969*

Sheppard MR & MRS Carl F JR (Carroll A Hogan) ⚓
   ☎ (609) HY2-2591.. "The Big House" 214—3 St, Beach Haven, NJ *08008*

Sheppard MR & MRS Edgar M JR (Mary A Smythe)
   ☎ (207) 374-5597.. "Manor House" HCR 64, Box 482, Blue Hill, ME *04614*

Sheppard MR & MRS W Stevens (Bloom—Patricia Gillis) ⚓
   ☎ (207) 867-2049.. "Stonecrop" North Haven, ME *04853*

Sheppard MR & MRS Winston C (Olive C Pearson)
   ☎ (207) 244-3230.. "Grey Gulls" Southwest Harbor, ME *04679*

Sheridan MR & MRS John Edward (Herbert—Mary A Hemry) ⚓
   ☎ (441) 292-6415.. "Up Top" 39 Bostock Hill E, Paget PG 01, Bermuda

Sheriff MISS Nathalie H .. see MRS B T Reid

Sherley MR Thomas H
   ☎ (705) 387-4298.. Magnetawan, Ontario P0A 1P0, Canada

Sherman MRS Dallas B (Glass—Beatrice Schaenen)
   ☎ (516) 283-4263.. 64 Down East Lane, Southampton, NY *11968*

Sherman MR Edward D
   ☎ (508) 526-1719.. "Round Top" 100 Beach St, Manchester-By-The-Sea, MA *01944*

Sherman MRS George C JR (Natalie Hyde)
   Aug 1.. ☎ (516) 283-0425.. Meadow Club, Box 5005, Southampton, NY *11968*

Sherman MRS William B (Catherine B McKecknie)
   ☎ (508) 228-2199.. 27 W Chester St, Nantucket, MA *02554*

Sherrer MR & MRS Roland C JR (Moss—Thelma T Cremer) . . . . | ☎ (516) 788-7637
MR Charles D . . . . | "White Wings" Fishers Island, NY 06390

Sherrerd MR & MRS John J F (Kathleen Compton)
☎ (603) 544-2121 . . Elkins Point, Bald Peak Colony Club, Melvin Village, NH 03850

Sherrill MR & MRS H Virgil (Betty L Stevens)
217 Pond Lane, Southampton, NY 11968

Sherrill REV & MRS Henry W (Martha S Weeks)
☎ (603) 788-3579 . . Weeks Rd, RR 2, Box 561, Lancaster, NH 03584

Sherwood MR & MRS John R 3d (Kyle—Elisabeth L Dobbin) . . . . | ☎ (908) 892-1224
MISS Anne D . . . . | 1053 Ocean Av, Mantoloking, NJ
MR Robert J Kyle JR . . . . | 08738

Shettle MR & MRS William M 2d (Renée M Wellford)
☎ (302) 226-3656 . . 12 Oak Av, Rehoboth Beach, DE 19971

Shields MR & MRS David V (Margaret Barney) ⚓ . | ☎ (401) 596-2522
MISS Elizabeth L . . . . | "Sunnyridge"
MR D Larus . . . . | Valley Path, Watch Hill, RI 02891

Shields DR & MRS Joseph Dunbar JR (Kendall—Goodrich—Mary L Netterville)
☎ (516) 726-4757 . . "Cobb Isle" 91 Cobb Rd, Water Mill, NY 11976

Shields MISS Katharine . . see MRS R G Blaine

Shields MISS Victoria G
☎ (011-33-1) 30-99-06-15 . . 134 av de Paris, 78740 Vaux-sur-Seine, France

Shinn VICE ADM & MRS Allen M (Sevilla H Shuey) USN.
☎ (508) 627-8693 . . 46 Cooke St, Box 9, Edgartown, MA 02539

Shinn MR & MRS Jonathan H (Yates—Isabel B Lenssen) ⚓ . . . . | ☎ (508) 627-8693
MR Alexander L . . . . | 46 Cooke St, Edgartown, MA
JUNIORS MR Jonathan M . . . . | 02539

Shipley MR & MRS Samuel R 3d (Hannah Hope Randolph) . . . . | ☎ (508) 228-6240
MISS Julia R . . . . | "The Kennel"
MR Upton S . . . . | 19 Shimmo Pond Rd, Nantucket, MA 02554

Shiras MR & MRS Winfield 3d (Sherrill L Joyce)
☎ (847) 446-0057 . . 42 Indian Hill Rd, Winnetka, IL 60093

Shoemaker DR & MRS B Dawson (Cheryl H Linn) . . | ☎ (802) 765-4008
MISS Elizabeth J . . . . | "Rolling Pastures" Rte 132, PO Box 111, South Strafford, VT 05070

Short MRS J Simonds (Hurd—Janet Simonds)
☎ (603) 772-1717 . . Dixville Village D110, 7 River Woods Dv, Exeter, NH 03833-4375

Shrady MR Henry M 3d
☎ (516) 676-8985 . . "The Rainsplitter" 52 Factory Pond Rd, Locust Valley, NY 11560

Shriver MR & MRS Robert Sargent JR (Eunice M Kennedy)
1 Atlantic Av, Hyannis Port, MA 02647

Shutt MR & MRS George Austin (Nancy W Perkins)
☎ (505) 983-1422 . . 511B Armijo St, Santa Fe, NM 87501

Sibley MAJ GEN & MRS Alden K (Drake—V Elvira Trowbridge) USA.
☎ (207) 935-2798 . . "Pearson House" Brownfield, ME 04010

Sibley MR & MRS Stephen T (Lisa A Czarick) ⚓
"Eagle Aerie" HC 65, Box 925, Cloudland, GA 30731

Sidamon-Eristoff MR Andrew
☎ (914) 446-8566 . . Box 181, Highland Falls, NY 10928

Sidamon-Eristoff MR & MRS Constantine (Anne Phipps)
☎ (914) 446-2034 . . "Ananouri" S Main St, Highland Falls, NY 10928

Siedler DR & MRS H Duane (Nancy C Miller) . . . . . | "Melmouth"
MISS Bridget A . . . . | Ugak Bay, Kodiak, AK 99603

Siemon MR & MRS Charles L (Laura S Magnuson) . . see M G Magnuson JR

Sierck MR & MRS Alexander W (Susan S Arthur) . . . | ☎ (207) 359-4664
MISS Sarah S . . . . | Brooklin, ME 04616

Siglow MR Jesse W JR . . see D N Adams JR

Siglow MR Zachary H . . see D N Adams JR

Silverthorne MRS John H (Mary L Rose) ⚓
☎ (715) 385-3253 . . "North Fork" High Lake, 6381 High Lake Rd, Boulder Junction, WI 54512

Simmons MR & MRS Grant G JR (Darlington—F Elizabeth Richardson)
☎ (518) 891-3167 . . Camp Onaway, HCR 1, Box 27E, Saranac Lake, NY 12983

Simmons MRS Harry C B (Mary O Blair) . . . . | Mac Mac Island,
MISS Lisabeth B . . . . | Ojibway Island,
MISS Nancy L . . . . | Pointe-au-Baril,
MR John T B . . . . | Ontario P0G 1K0,
MR Harry C . . . . | Canada

Simmons MR & MRS James L (Annison—Urbahn—Allyn D Smith)
☎ (508) 428-5706 . . 10 Crossway, Osterville, MA 02655

Simmons MRS John Farr (Caroline H Thompson)
☎ (207) 244-3291 . . Box 634, Southwest Harbor, ME 04679

Simmons MR & MRS Richard De L (Mary De W Bleecker)
☎ (508) 645-9470 . . South Rd, Box 75, Chilmark, MA 02535

Simonds MRS John H (Patricia T Spencer)
☎ (207) 846-9228 . . "Cove" Box 119, Yarmouth, ME 04096

Simonds MR & MRS Robert L (Ann S Bainbridge) . . | ☎ (508) 945-2472
JUNIORS MISS Caroline F . . . . | "Turtle Hill"
JUNIORS MISS Rebecca T . . . . | 353 Barnhill Rd,
JUNIORS MR Alden B . . . . | West Chatham, MA 02669

Simpkins DR & MRS (DR) C Alexander (Annellen Minkin) . . . . | ☎ (207) 236-2579
MISS Alura L . . . . | "Wishbone Point"
JUNIORS MR Charles A JR . . . . | RR 1, Box 4250, Beaucaire Rd, Camden, ME 04843

Simpkins MRS Nathaniel S 3d (Carmen E Zitelmann)
☎ (207) 236-2579 . . "Wishbone Point" RR 1, Box 4250, Beaucaire Rd, Camden, ME 04843

Simpson JUNIORS MISS Melanie S . . see MRS M Trevor

Simpson MR & MRS Michael H (Marion H Brown)
Stagecoach Rd, Sunapee, NH 03782

Sims MRS John C (Lucile Caldwell)
☎ (207) 734-6718 . . "The Birches" CR 60, Box 169, Islesboro, ME 04848

Simson MRS Prudence G (Prudence A Goodman)
 ☎ (207) 967-4991 . . "Grey Gull Cottage" PO Box 608, Kennebunkport, ME *04046*
Singer MR & MRS F R Forbes (Anne M de Lapeyrouse). . . . . | ☎ (011-33-59) 03-76-58
 JUNIORS MR Mortimer M . . . . | "La Grange"
 JUNIORS MR Oliver G L . . . . | 64600 Anglet, France
Sinkler MR G Dana JR . . see J P Kassebaum
Sinkler MR Huger 2d . . see J P Kassebaum
Sinton MRS Stanley H JR (Gantner—Florence W Erskine)
 ☎ (707) 963-7330 . . 3600 Spring Mountain Rd, St Helena, CA *94574*
Siphron MR & MRS Joseph R (Mary John Wilson)
 ☎ (516) 653-6749 . . Box 814, Quogue, NY *11959*
Sise MRS Charles Carpenter (Anna Belle Sewell)
 Aug 1 . . Stage Neck Inn, York Harbor, ME *03911*
Sizemore MR & MRS James M JR (Smith—Brenda K Champlin) . . . . | ☎ (205) 234-6647
 MISS Rebecca L . . . . | "Pleasure Island"
 MISS Charlotte C Smith | Rte 1, Box 225,
 JUNIORS MR John A Smith 5th . . . . | Alexander City, AL *35010*
Skidmore MR & MRS Louis H JR (Margaret B Cooke) . . . . | ☎ (207) 529-5536
 MISS Heather C . . . . | "Mainestay" Box 111, Round Pond, ME *04564*
Skinner MRS Claiborne A (Meeker—E Olivia Little)
 ☎ (906) 484-3486 . . "Romancoke" Hessell, MI *49745*
Slade MR & MRS Jarvis J JR (Carmen B Torruella)
 ☎ (516) 329-3196 . . Middle Lane, Box 702, East Hampton, NY *11937*
Slater MR & MRS Alexander B (Murray—Steinmann—Dionne K Ryan) . . . . | ☎ (970) 925-7665
 MR Alexander B JR . . . . | 112 Aspen Alps, 700 Ute Av, Aspen, CO *81611*
Slidell MRS John R (Hallie M Brooke)
 ☎ (717) 794-2721 . . Blue Ridge Summit, PA *17214*
Slingluff MRS Patricia K (Patricia D'A de Koranyi) . . . . | ☎ (401) 846-1969 on board Nani Ola II" Ida Lewis Yacht Club, Box 479, Wellington Av, Newport, RI *02840*
 MR Peter de K—at ☎ (401) 423-2468 "Old Green Farm" 55 Longfellow Rd, Jamestown, RI *02835* . . . . |
Slingluff MRS T Rowland (Gibson—Pamela Lloyd)
 ☎ (207) 244-5801 . . "Rock Point" Box 124, Mt Desert, ME *04660*
Sloan MRS (REV) M Treadway (Margaret M Treadway)
 ☎ (520) 720-4218 . . "Spirit Journey" 56 Sabin St, St David, AZ *85630*
Sloan MR & MRS Samuel (Titus—Marion D Baker)
 ☎ (908) 741-3434 . . 65A Cheshire Square, Little Silver, NJ *07739*
Sloat MR & MRS Jonathan W (DeGraff—Jane E Roberts)
 ☎ (508) 775-7608 . . 2 Vacation Lane, West Yarmouth, MA *02673*
Slocum MR John J 3d . . see N L D Firth
Slocum MISS M Olivia J . . see N L D Firth
Slocum MISS Marie-Louise C . . see N L D Firth
Slowinski MRS Walter A (Annette C Roberts)
 ☎ (301) 259-2392 . . "Yatten" Mt Victoria, MD *20661*

Smith MR & MRS A Warren JR (Bloss—Gretchen A Leeds)
 ☎ (905) 468-3100 . . "Petit Trianon" 303 Niagara Blvd, Niagara-on-the-Lake, Ontario L0S 1J0, Canada
Smith DR & MRS Alexander B (Emily B Griffin)
 ☎ (914) 723-1533 . . 26 Walworth Av, Scarsdale, NY *10583-1434*
Smith MR & MRS Alexander J (Alice L Grau) . . . . . | ☎ (516) 583-7218
 JUNIORS MISS Katherine M . . . . | Point O'Woods, NY
 JUNIORS MR Cameron A . . . . | *11706*
Smith DR & MRS Barry H (Carley Eldredge) . . . | ☎ (207) 883-2018
 MR Christopher R . . . . | 79 Sandpiper Cove,
 JUNIORS MISS Sara R . . . . | Scarborough, ME *04074*
Smith MR & MRS Bayard W (Susanna A McClary) . . | ☎ (207) 372-8201
 MR Nathaniel A . . . . | "Goose Cottage" Harts Neck Rd, Tenants Harbor, ME *04860*
Smith MR & MRS Blair W (C Stirling Cassidy)
 ☎ (914) 351-3360 . . "La Bagatelle" Tuxedo Park, NY *10987*
Smith MR & MRS Bradley W . . . . | ☎ (207) 925-6253
 JUNIORS MR Bradley W JR . . . . | "Pinecrest"
 JUNIORS MR Malcolm P . . . . | Severance Lodge Club, Center Lovell, ME *04016*
Smith MISS Charlotte C . . see J M Sizemore JR
Smith MR & MRS Colin L M (Diana M Dennison) . . | West Chop, MA *02573*
 MISS F Isabel
 MR Adrian C M . . . . |
Smith MR & MRS David Shiverick (Mary H Edson)
 ☎ (516) 283-0324 . . "Herons' Point" PO Box 366, Southampton, NY *11969*
Smith MISS Elizabeth Curtiss
 ☎ (508) 645-2668 . . Box 78, Blacksmith Valley, Chilmark, MA *02535*
Smith MR & MRS Endicott (Steele—Jeanne E Fellows)
 ☎ (508) 432-1244 . . "Sumestate" 41 Walther Rd, Harwich Port, MA *02646*
Smith MRS Everett Ware (Ruth H Tyler)
 ☎ (207) 644-8312 . . PO Box 75, Christmas Cove, South Bristol, ME *04568*
Smith MR & MRS G E Kidder (Dorothea F Wilder)
 ☎ (607) 547-9298 . . The Manor House, Springfield Center, NY *13468*
Smith MR & MRS Geoffrey W (Leonard—Nancy W Spencer) . . . . | ☎ (603) 522-3373
 MR Spencer H Leonard . . . . | "Corner House" Wakefield, Sanbornville, NH *03872*
Smith MR & MRS George D (Carolyn S E Koenig) . . | ☎ (314) 637-2489
 MISS Cynthia E . . . . | "Taum Sauk"
 MR Charles F . . . . | Rte 1, Box 26,
 MR Nicholas E . . . . | Lesterville, MO *63654*
Smith MR & MRS Gerard L (Carr—Rowse—Isabel de Rancougne) . . . . | ☎ (516) 283-2425
 MISS Hadley L . . . . | 108 Toylsome Lane,
 MISS Flavia Rowse . . . . | Southampton, NY
 MR Michael Carr . . . . | *11968*

Smith MR & MRS Gregory Little 2d (Frazer—Clara H Little)
Gulf Shores, AL *36542*
Smith MR & MRS H Morgan (Katharine V Darmanin) | ☎ (609) 967-4203
⛵ . . . . | Avalon 411,
  MISS Julia T . . . . | 700 First Av,
  MR H Morgan JR . . . . | Avalon, NJ *08202*
Smith MRS H Webster (Coffin—Sallie O Gorman)
☎ (207) 372-8843 . . "Hart House" Box 555, Tenants Harbor,
ME *04860*
Smith MR & MRS Howard W JR (Marion H Norris)
☎ (540) 347-0003 . . Cedar Hill Farm, Broad Run, VA *22014*
Smith MR & MRS James P JR (Catherine T Wilson) . . | ☎ (207) 633-0818
  MISS Catherine H . . . . | PO Box 516,
  MR James P 3d . . . . | 127 Atlantic Av,
  | Boothbay Harbor,
  | ME *04537*
Smith JUNIORS MR John A 5th . . see J M Sizemore JR
Smith REV & MRS John Cutrer (Mary A Gregg) . . . . | ☎ (518) 589-5041
  MISS Alexandra G . . . . | "Skylark"
  MR John Clark . . . . | Onteora Park,
  | Tannersville, NY
  | *12485*
Smith MR & MRS Kennedy (Mary E Rutter)
☎ (410) 745-9523 . . "Waterhole Cove" 8021 Tilghman Island Rd,
Sherwood, MD *21665*
Smith MR & MRS Langhorne B (Valerie G Lamb) . . . | ☎ (207) 734-6415
  MISS Averil S . . . . | "Bright Meadows"
  MR Philip R . . . . | Box 32, Islesboro,
  | ME *04848*
Smith MR Lloyd H
☎ (516) 283-2196 . . "Linden" 160 Ox Pasture Rd, PO Box 978,
Southampton, NY *11969*
Smith MR & MRS Marcus W (Strawbridge— | ☎ (207) 883-2751
  Alexandra White) | 25 Massacre Lane,
  MR Robert E Strawbridge 4th—at | Prouts Neck, ME
  ☎ (207) 883-4382 . . 21 Massacre Lane, | *04074*
  Prouts Neck, ME *04074* . . . . |
Smith MR & MRS Michael S (Anne M Murray)
"Street House" Harts Neck Rd, Box 549, Tenants Harbor, ME *04860*
Smith MRS Morgan K (Beatrice Stewart)
☎ (518) 576-4702 . . Ausable Club, St Huberts, NY *12943*
Smith MR & MRS Page W (Teagle—Boggs—Jane Will)
☎ (410) 822-2390 . . "Crowe Point Farm" Box 1192, Easton,
MD *21601*
Smith MR & MRS Peter L (Marie L Shrady) . . . . | ☎ (516) 537-3560
  MISS Maria Alexandra . . . . | "Hearthstone"
  JUNIORS MISS Maria Elizabeth . . . . | PO Box 81,
  | Sagg Main St,
  | Sagaponack, NY
  | *11962*
Smith MR & MRS Philip C F (Stevenson—G G Meredith Smith)
☎ (207) 865-3569 . . "The River House" 151 Wolf Neck Rd, Freeport,
ME *04032*
Smith MR & MRS Philip W JR (Sheila M Scott)
☎ (207) 372-8070 . . "Marsh Point" Box 549, Tenants Harbor,
ME *04860*

Smith MR & MRS Philip W III (Hillary C Bailey)
☎ (207) 372-8666 . . "Ledge House" Harts Neck Rd, Tenants Harbor,
ME *04860*
Smith MR & MRS Prentice K (Patricia Ford)
☎ (508) 627-5965 . . Pierce Lane, Edgartown, MA *02539*
Smith MR & MRS R Andrew (Karen A Grace)
☎ (314) 637-2321 . . "Meadowbrook" Rte 1, Box 26, Lesterville,
MO *63654*
Smith MR & MRS Rodney W (Phyllis G Fiske) ⛵
☎ (804) 438-5807 . . "Déjà Vu" PO Box 187, King Carter Dv,
Irvington, VA *22480*
Smith MRS Roger D (Kathleen W Tener) . . . . | ☎ (914) 255-7435
  MISS Jocelyn T . . . . | "LeFevre Bontecou
  MR Silas W . . . . | Farm"
  JUNIORS MR Luke E T . . . . | 454 Rte 32 N,
  | New Paltz, NY
  | *12561*
Smith MISS Sallie Dorsey— ⛵
☎ (207) 372-8167 . . "Singing Beach" Harts Neck Rd, Tenants Harbor,
ME *04860*
Smith MRS Sarah D (Sarah D Schumacher)
☎ (315) 942-3665 . . "The Stable" Miller Woods Rd, Boonville,
NY *13309*
Smith MR & MRS Stockton N (Sallie B Spence)
☎ (207) 276-4127 . . "The Stockyard" Kimball Rd, Northeast Harbor,
ME *40662*
Smith MR & MRS T Gunter (Bradley Goodyear) . . . . | ☎ (607) 547-9375
  MISS Jeanette G . . . . | "Cary Mede"
  MISS Susanne R . . . . | PO Box 188,
  | Springfield Center,
  | NY *13468*
Smith MRS Taylor R (Jean N Dunn)
☎ (516) JU3-8632 . . House 25, Point O'Woods, NY *11706*
Smith MRS Thurston H (Ruth F Mooney)
☎ (508) 468-3868 . . 310 Old Country Rd, Wenham, MA *01984*
Smith MR & MRS W N Harrell 4th (Mary Oakes | ☎ (540) 775-7373
  Skinner) . . . . | Nanzatico, Rte 698,
  MISS Caroline Doswell . . . . | King George, VA
  MR W N Harrell 5th . . . . | *22485*
Smith MRS Wallace H (Mary A Kelsey) . . . . | ☎ (616) 526-2057
  MR Jay Herndon . . . . | Harbor Springs, MI
  | *49740*
Smith MR & MRS Winthrop D (Claire V A de Tarr)
☎ (011-39-584) 91-38-44 . . Monteggiori 43, Camaiore, 55041 Lucca,
Italy
Smithers MR & MRS Austin L (Bartram—Anstiss H McCormick-Goodhart)
☎ (208) 456-2701 . . "Chicken Hill" 22 E Dry Ridge Rd, Tetonia,
ID *83452*
Smithers MR & MRS Francis C (Virginia L Pearson)
☎ (410) 822-2919 . . "Holly Point" 5734 Pirate's Cove Rd, Oxford,
MD *21654*
Smithers MRS Ruth H (Ruth A Hall) . . . . | ☎ (860) 739-9723
  MISS Claire H . . . . | 14 Great White
  | Way, Niantic, CT
  | *06357*
Smith-Petersen MRS Pettengill (Mary E Pettengill)
☎ (540) 839-2002 . . North Ridge, PO Box 901, Hot Springs, VA *24445*

Smithwick MR Reginald H
 ☎ (617) 631-0555 . . "Boat House" Foster St, Marblehead Neck, MA *01945*
Smylie MR & MRS Charles A (Green—Marguerette S Sheridan)
 ☎ (603) 284-6681 . . Box 122, Center Sandwich, NH *03227*
Smyth MISS Elizabeth E . . see D M Kinney
Smyth MR John E . . see D M Kinney
Smythe MR & MRS J L Nevill (Ann V Stout)
 ☎ (207) 374-5597 . . "Manor House" HCR 64, Box 482, Blue Hill, ME *04614*
Snedeker MR & MRS Sedgwick (McGrath—Elizabeth G Naudin)
 ☎ (516) 367-9172 . . 568 Cold Spring Rd, Laurel Hollow, Syosset, NY *11791*
Snodgrass MR & MRS Francis R (Anne L Darneille) . | ☎ (207) 647-2072
 JUNIORS MISS Virginia W . . . . | "Nawandyn"
 JUNIORS MISS Anne W . . . . | Rte 3, Box 1075,
 JUNIORS MR Francis D . . . . | Bridgton, ME *04009*
Snow MRS E Douglas (Gucker—Ellen H Douglas)
 ☎ (603) 323-8039 . . "The Shelter" Box 8, Chocorua, NH *03817*
Snowden MR & MRS James M JR (Katherine B G | ☎ (401) 348-8973
 Orthwein) . . . . | "West Cottage"
 MISS Katherine K . . . . | Meadow Lane,
 MISS Suzanne O'F . . . . | Watch Hill, RI
 | *02891*
Snyder MR & MRS Paul H H (Margaret G Whiteman)
 ☎ (508) 627-9069 . . "Cuff's Cove" PO Box 1984, Edgartown, MA *02539*
Snyder MR & MRS William P 3d (Jean E Rose)
 ☎ (705) 764-1375 . . "Columbia" Beaumaris, Lake Muskoka, Ontario P0B 1B0, Canada
Soffel MISS Christie A . . of
 ☎ (716) 789-3804 . . RD 1, Woodlawn, Ashville, NY *14710*
 ☎ (516) 537-7185 . . Box 45, Sagg Main St, Sagaponack, NY *11962*
Sohier MRS William D JR (Gladys E Arias)
 ☎ (508) 526-1944 . . 43 Proctor St, PO Box 1542, Manchester, MA *01944*
Sokoloff MRS Boris T (Bijur—Lee—Alice St J Hunt)
 ☎ (315) 369-3610 . . Little Moose Lake, Old Forge, NY *13420*
Soleri MR Paolo
 ☎ (520) 632-7135 . . Arcosanti, HC 74, Box 4136, Mayer, AZ *86333*
Solley MR Robert L
 ☎ (305) 531-6951 . . 1621 Collins Av, Apt 918, Miami Beach, FL *33139-3142*
Sommaripa MR & MRS George (Eva A Coifman) . . . | ☎ (508) 636-5869
 MR Leo M . . . . | "Eva's Garden"
 JUNIORS MR Nicholas C R . . . . | 105 Jordan Rd,
 | South Dartmouth,
 | MA *02748*
Sonntag MR Joseph K
 "Heritage Glen" 36 Library Lane, Simsbury, CT *06070*
Soper MR & MRS Brian McK (Vaughan—F Jane Todd)
 PO Box 1494, Easton, MD *21601*
Sortwell MR & MRS Daniel R JR (Nancy H Bascom)
 ☎ (207) 882-7193 . . "Willow Lane Farm" Wiscasset, ME *04578*

Soule MR & MRS Richard H (Cooper—Virginia L | ☎ (603) 763-5824
 Anthony) . . . . | "Rockwall Farm"
 MR Alan A Cooper . . . . | 100 Rolling Rock
 MR Douglas C Cooper . . . . | Rd, Burkehaven,
 | Sunapee, NH *03782*
Soule MR & MRS Richard H JR (Kimberly Anne Beede) . . of
 ☎ (508) 636-4750 . . River Rd, Westport, MA *02790*
 on board Gypsy II" 79 St Boat Basin, New York, NY *10024*
Soule MR Timothy W . . see W P Sharpe
Southworth MRS Hamilton (Katharine R Jones)
 ☎ (516) 653-4369 . . Quogue St, Quogue, NY *11959*
Southworth MR & MRS Hamilton JR (Eleanor W Ewart)
 ☎ (516) 653-4369 . . Box 277, Quogue, NY *11959*
Spahr MR Boyd Lee
 ☎ (902) 275-3751 . . "Brigadoon" Chester, Nova Scotia B0J 1J0, Canada
Spahr MR & MRS Robert N (Julia W Darling) . . . . . | ☎ (207) 244-7406
 MISS Stephanie N . . . . | Latty Cove,
 MISS Noël W . . . . | West Tremont, ME
 | *04690*
Spangler MR & MRS John L JR (Elsie M Lindeman)
 ☎ (401) 423-0064 . . "Longwood" 9 Bryer Av, Jamestown, RI *02835*
Speers REV & MRS T Guthrie JR (Susan Savage)
 ☎ (603) 284-6409 . . Squaw Cove, Center Sandwich, NH *03227*
Speese MR & MRS John JR (Margaret C Clark)
 ☎ (706) 896-4371 . . 7066 Speese Dv, Hiawasse, GA *30546*
Speight MR & MRS Randolph L (June P Danglade) . . | ☎ (441) 293-8088
 MISS June Jacqueline D . . . . | "Camalot"
 MR Randolph L 2d . . . . | 39 Knapton Estates
 MR Craig M P . . . . | Rd, Smith's Parish
 | HS 01, Bermuda
Speir MRS Lydia P (Elissabide—Lydia M Pratt) . . . | ☎ (518) 589-6263
 MR R Wade JR . . . . | "Bergheim"
 | Twilight Park,
 | Haines Falls, NY
 | *12436*
Spencer MR Carlton W
 ☎ (603) 522-3373 . . "Corner House" Wakefield, NH *03888*
Spencer MR & MRS Clayton B (Susan J Fischer)
 ☎ (860) 388-9834 . . 6 Agawam Av, Fenwick, CT *06475*
Spencer MR & MRS Duncan C (Megan D Rosenfeld)
 ☎ (804) 454-7475 . . "Do-Better" Saxe, VA *23967*
Spencer MR & MRS Henry B 2d (Phillips—Helen M Walker)
 ☎ (401) 295-1619 . . 131 W Main St, Wickford, RI *02852*
Spencer MR & MRS John (Cushing—Natalie L Fell) . | ☎ (516) 537-1232
 MISS Natalie C . . . . | PO Box 207,
 | Beach Lane,
 | Wainscott, *11975*
Spencer MR & MRS John M (Diana C Davis) . . . . . | of ☎ (207)276-5519
 MISS Kimberly F . . . . | "Crestwood"
 | Northeast Harbor,
 | ME *04662*
 | ☎ (508) 867-2941
 | "Elm Hill Farm"
 | Brookfield, MA
 | *01506*

Spencer MR & MRS Samuel (Byrne—June Beakes).. of
   ☎ (401) 783-4962.. "Shore Leave" 404 Ocean Rd, Narragansett, RI *02882*
   ☎ (207) 276-3270.. "Tenedos" Northeast Harbor, ME *04662*
Spencer MR Samuel 3d
   ☎ (401) 294-1356.. 129 W Main St, Wickford, RI *02852*
Spofford MR & MRS John S W (Mélie B Truesdale).
   MISS Daphne B . . . .
   MR Jeremy S W . . . .
   ☎ (516) 788-7377 "Winthrop House" Fishers Island, NY *06390*
Spofford MRS Margaret W (Margaret M Walker) Fishers Island, NY *06390*
Sprague MR Charles G JR
   ☎ (207) 883-4080.. Beach Rd, Prouts Neck, ME *04074*
Sprague MR & MRS George R (R Lee Thorndike)...
   MISS Lucy R . . . .
   MISS Cynthia N . . . .
   MR Alexander T . . . .
   ☎ (207) 883-2200 "May-Den" Prouts Neck, ME *04074*
Sprague MR & MRS J Christopher (Margot A Lyman)
   ☎ (508) 283-3744.. 41 Norwood Heights, Annisquam, MA *01930*
Sprague MR Juan H
   ☎ (603) 447-5717.. Briant Dv, PO Box 236, Center Conway, NH *03813*
Sprague MRS Julie H (Minot—Talmage—Julie H Sprague). . . . .
   JUNIORS MISS Julie H Talmage . . . .
   ☎ (207) 799-0007 "The Odessey" Ram Island Farm, Cape Elizabeth, ME *04107*
Sprague MRS Penelope A (Penelope Andrews).. see MRS W E Andrews
Spring MR & MRS William C (Barbara R Lovejoy)
   ☎ (508) 228-1291.. "Sandrift" 19 Hulbert Av, Nantucket, MA *02554*
Springs MISS Clare H
   ☎ (941) 591-1667.. St Maarten Apt 1805, 6101 Pelican Bay Blvd, Naples, FL *33963*
Spurdle MR & MRS John William JR (Cynthia W Stauffer)
   ☎ (908) 842-6128.. "The Ark" 3 Tennis Court Lane, Rumson, NJ *07760*
Spurgeon MR & MRS Edward V R (Patricia T Flynn)
   ☎ (541) 386-6644.. 700 Cascade, Apt 6, Hood River, OR *97031*
Squibb MR & MRS George R (C Fay Irving)
   ☎ (616) 526-2444.. "Squibnocket" 48 Beach Dv, Wequetonsing, MI *49740*
Squiers MR & MRS James D (Virginia M Barrie)
   ☎ (902) 245-4200.. "Ballantrae" Smith's Cove, Nova Scotia B0S 1S0, Canada
Stafford DR & MRS Sam 3d (Ann M Webb) . . . .
   MISS Adele P . . . .
   MISS Ann L . . . .
   ☎ (803) 559-1421 Rockville, SC *29670*
Stahl MR & MRS William W JR (Nancy Ireland) . . . .
   JUNIORS MISS Jacqueline McN . . . .
   ☎ (914) 677-8006 "Rose Cottage" PO Box 1031, Millbrook, NY *12545*
Stallworth MR Nicholas Jack
   ☎ (904) 654-5320.. Casa Bendall, 39 Rue Caribe, Sandestin, FL *32540*

Stamm MRS John D (Sara B Babbitt)
   ☎ (516) 537-5124.. 1 Montauk H'way, Box 1113, Bridgehampton, NY *11932*
Staneluis MR & MRS James M (Kim Ely Peck) . . . . .
   MR Christian N . . . .
   Twin Pine Camp, RR 1, Peterborough, Ontario K9J 6X2, Canada
Staniford MR & MRS Foye F JR (Williams—Ellen W Breed) . . . .
   MR William M . . . .
   MISS Louise B Williams . . . .
   ☎ (516) 239-2674 264 Victoria Place, Lawrence, NY *11559*
Stanley JUNIORS MR Arthur E Kimball.. see M E Kimball
Stanley MR Edwin J C.. see R L Prosser
Stanley MR & MRS Justin A (Helen L Fletcher)
   ☎ (715) 856-5211.. Wausaukee Club, Athelstane, WI *54104*
Stanley MISS Lindsay B.. see R L Prosser
Stanton MR & MRS L Lee 3d (Elizabeth R Rose) . . .
   JUNIORS MISS Penelope R . . . .
   11 Promenade Way, Crystal Beach, Ontario L0S 1B0, Canada
Stanton MR & MRS Myron E (Ann C Dawson) . . . . .
   MISS Sarah A . . . .
   MISS Margaret A . . . .
   MR John R . . . .
   ☎ (207) 647-8130 RR 1, Box 738, Pleasant Mountain Rd, Bridgton, ME *04009*
Stanton MR & MRS Peter W (Judith A Crawford) . . .
   MISS Cornelia C . . . .
   MR Peter W JR . . . .
   ☎ (508) 997-8340 Rabbit Hill, Nonquitt, MA *02748*
Stanton MRS Phoebe R (Phoebe Rentschler)
   ☎ (203) 853-0046.. "South Wind" Woodland Rd, Wilson Point, South Norwalk, CT *06854*
Starkey DR & MRS George W B (Lois Van A MacMurray)
   ☎ (860) 542-5409.. "Greenshore" 110 Deerfield Rd, Norfolk, CT *06058*
Starr MRS Donald Carter (Polly R Thayer)
   ☎ (617) 749-1684.. 140 Turkey Hill Lane, Hingham, MA *02043*
Starr MR & MRS Edward 3d (Antoinette Nolan)
   ☎ (508) 627-8465.. "Tower Gate" Edgartown, MA *02539*
Starr MR & MRS I Tatnall 2d (Mary M Detweiler)
   ☎ (508) 228-5966.. "Starrgazer" 19 E Creek Rd, Nantucket, MA *02554*
Starr MRS Nathan C (Nina Howell)
   ☎ (603) 827-3298.. 12 Brown Rd, Chesham, Marlborough, NH *03455*
Starr MR & MRS Ogden P (Patricia Morrill)
   ☎ (908) 766-0480.. Mt Harmony Rd, Bernardsville, NJ *07924*
Starring MR & MRS Mason B 3d (Nancy B Donaldson)
   ☎ (603) 431-2327.. Tidewatch 9, 579 Sagamore Av, Portsmouth, NH *03801*
Stason MR E Blythe JR
   ☎ (617) 259-8939.. Sandy Pond Rd, Lincoln, MA *01773*
Stautberg MR & MRS Aubrey Theodore JR (Susan Berwind Schiffer)
   ☎ (401) 847-2393.. "Carriage House" 30 Chastellux Av, Newport, RI *02840*
Stearns MR & MRS John P (Winifred C Anthony) Point O'Woods, NY *11706*

Stebbins MRS H Lyman (Madeleine Froelicher)
☎ (819) 842-2691 . . "Bagatelle" North Hatley, Quebec J0B 2C0, Canada
Stedman MR & MRS Theodore W (McDonell—Patricia Hallowell)
☎ (516) 788-7568 . . Box 371, Fishers Island, NY *06390*
Steel MR & MRS Francis P (Sinkler—Nina Knowles)
☎ (401) 253-8490 . . "Lee Shore" 24 Monkey Wrench Lane, Box 108, Bristol, RI *02809*
Steele MR & MRS Edward C (Joan Markey)
☎ (516) 283-4711 . . PO Box 5055, Southampton, NY *11969*
Steele MR & MRS Kilman (Carol L Knowles) . . . . . . | ☎ (207) 883-2218
MR Lockhart . . . . | "Eastways"
JUNIORS MR George F . . . . | Prouts Neck, ME *04074*
Steere MR & MRS Bruce M (Harper—Anne MacC S Bullivant)
☎ (508) 432-3747 . . "Rabbit Hill" 44 Snow Inn Rd, Harwich Port, MA *02646*
Steers MR & MRS Charles R C JR (Margaret L Hamilton)
☎ (518) 589-5430 . . "Stone Acres" Onteora Park, Tannersville, NY *12485*
Stefani MR & MRS Jeffrey J (Emily E Todd)
☎ (616) 223-7279 . . "Somerset" 940 Neahtawanta Rd, Traverse City, MI *49684*
Steffan MR & MRS Andrew P (Patricia V Andrews) . | ☎ (516) 537-1659
MR Alexander P . . . . | Bull Head Court, Bridgehampton, NY *11932*
Steffens MR & MRS George V 3d (Virginia G Golden) . . . . | ☎ (501) 856-2668
JUNIORS MR George V 4th . . . . | 7 Pecan Grove E, Hardy, AR *72542*
JUNIORS MR Andrew G . . . . |
Stein MR & MRS Julian S JR (Schwab—Emory B Phillips) . . . . | ☎ (207) 864-3653
MISS Sarah E . . . . | "Kemankeag" Oquossoc, ME *04964*
Steinmetz MR & MRS William Q (Judith J Chapman) | ☎ (508) 428-6511
MISS Melinda . . . . | Sea View Av,
MR Robert . . . . | Osterville, MA
MR James . . . . | *02665*
JUNIORS MISS Liana . . . . |
Stemberg MR & MRS Thomas G (Hamilton—Zarins—Dola S Davis) . . . . | ☎ (508) 748-2206
JUNIORS MR Rylan Hamilton . . . . | 99 Moorings Rd, Marion, MA *02738*
Stenbeck MR & MRS Jan H (Scott—Merrill MacLeod) . . . . | ☎ (011-46-175) 633-11
MISS Cristina M . . . . | "Christineholm"
JUNIORS MISS Sophie M . . . . | 76031 Edsbro,
JUNIORS MR Hugo E . . . . | Sweden
Stephaich MRS Louise H (Louise E Hitchcock)
☎ (212) 734-9510 . . 117 E 72 St, New York, NY *10021*
Stephens MR & MRS F Scott (Woodruff—Joanna D Beal) . . . . | ☎ (508) 999-6015
MISS Darrow A . . . . | Salters Point,
MISS Joanna B . . . . | 45 Naushon Av,
MR Clayton L . . . . | South Dartmouth, MA *02748*

Stephenson MR & MRS Garrick C (Obolensky—Claire McGinnis) . . . . | ☎ (516) 283-6555
MISS Claire E . . . . | Millstone Brook Rd,
MISS Christina C . . . . | Southampton, NY *11968*
Stephenson MRS John G 3d (Elizabeth Cashman)
☎ (610) 388-7124 . . Crosslands 78, Kennett Square, PA *19348*
Sterling MR Warner S
65 rue Pierre Julier, 26200 Montélimar, France
Sterling MR & MRS William Lee (Renée L Sands)
☎ (914) 534-7154 . . "Sengen" PO Box 234, Cornwall-on-Hudson, NY *12520*
Stern DR W Eugene
☎ (916) 426-3591 . . The Cedars, PO Box 909, Soda Springs, CA *95728*
Sterne MR & MRS Richard J (Nicholas—Eleanor M Moore)
☎ (516) 283-7268 . . 23 Gin Lane, Southampton, NY *11968*
Stetson MRS Brewster (Nancy K Andrews)
☎ (617) 934-6535 . . 228 Crescent St, Duxbury, MA *02332*
Stetson MR & MRS Eugene W JR (Nicoll—Walbridge—Kathryna H Ray) . . of
☎ (410) 226-5929 . . PO Box 376, Oxford, MD *21654*
☎ (207) 863-4383 . . Calderwood Neck, Vinalhaven, ME *04863*
Stevens MR & MRS James H (Joan H Coulborn) . . . | ☎ (802) 533-2695
MR J Alexander . . . . | Greensboro, VT
MR Russell McI . . . . | *05841*
JUNIORS MR Geoffrey F . . . . |
Stevens MR & MRS Norton (Wright—Margaret McC Love)
☎ (914) 763-8369 . . "Wold Wind Farm" 106 Mead St, PO Box 229, Waccabuc, NY *10597*
Stevens MR & MRS Robert L (Sydney A Davis) . . . . | ☎ (609) 492-2118
MISS Dina B . . . . | "Holiday House" 201 Coral St, Beach Haven, NJ *08008*
Stevenson MRS Anne H (Anne M Hollister)
☎ (401) 348-8210 . . "Surfside" Misquamicut Club, Ninigret Av, Watch Hill, RI *02891*
Stevenson MR Borden W
☎ (208) 726-9591 . . 108 Walnut St, Box 3114, Ketchum, ID *83340*
Stevenson MR & MRS Charles P (Rogers—Barbara J Franklin)
☎ (516) 283-4089 . . "Lake View" 25 Gin Lane, PO Box 402, Southampton, NY *11969*
Stevenson MR & MRS Frederick J JR (Sally B Wheat) | Yoctangee Island,
⚓ | Georgian Bay,
MISS Elizabeth B . . . . | Pointe-au-Baril,
MR William E . . . . | Ontario P0G 1K0, Canada
Stevenson MR & MRS John R (Johnson—Ruth Carter)
☎ (910) 363-2343 . . "No Deer" Box 219, Roaring Gap, NC *28668*
Stevenson MRS Stuart D (Margaret D Roberts) . . . . | ☎ (717) 646-2050
MISS Irene D . . . . | Pine Log Camp, Pocono Lake Preserve, PA *18348*
Steves MISS Gale C (Stocker—Gale C Steves)
☎ (914) 439-4341 . . "Troutbrook" Berry Brook Rd, Roscoe, NY *12776*
Steward MRS Gilbert L (Coolidge—Victoria S Tytus)
☎ (508) 741-5700 . . Grosvenor Park, 7 Loring Hills Av, Salem, MA *01970-4267*

Steward MR Scott C
 ☎ (508) 887-3901 . . "Grasslands" 65 Asbury St, Topsfield, MA *01983*
Stewardson MISS Caroline C . . see J Ford 3d
Stewart MRS Anne Lee (Anne Lee Rose) . . . . | Edgartown, MA
 MISS Amy H . . . . | *02539*
Stewart MRS Charles L (Sharon P Campbell) . . . . . . | ☎ (516) 569-0172
 MISS Marjorie L . . . . | 566 Atlantic Av,
 MR Charles L 3d . . . . | Lawrence, NY
 JUNIORS MR Campbell L . . . . | *11559-2804*
Stewart MR & MRS Charles P 3d (Frances H Todd)
 ☎ (412) 238-5665 . . "Midfield" Ligonier, PA *15658*
Stewart MR & MRS James M (Hunter—Joly Walton)
 ☎ (508) 228-4101 . . "Low Shimmo" 42 Shimmo Pond Rd, Nantucket, MA *02554*
Stewart MR & MRS James P (Hackl—Faith D Severance)
 ☎ (516) 324-4931 . . Three Mile Harbor Rd, PO Box 26, East Hampton, NY *11937*
Stewart MISS Marian . . see MRS C C McAleenan
Stewart MRS Potter (Mary A Bertles)
 ☎ (603) 823-5500 . . "Bowen Brook Farm" Franconia, NH *03580*
Stewart MRS Thomas C (McIlvaine—Katherine E Mein)
 ☎ (908) 892-7603 . . 1032 Barnegat Lane, Mantoloking, NJ *08738*
Stewart MR & MRS William A W 3d (Cutter— | ☎ (518) 576-4593
 Elizabeth H Whittemore) . . . . | "Aucére"
 MR Christian A S . . . . | Ausable Club,
  MISS Kimberly E Cutter . . . . | St Huberts, NY
  MISS Amanda H Cutter . . . . | *12943*
Stickney MR & MRS Albert 3d (Susan K King) . . . . . | ☎ (516) 788-7038
 MISS Katharine K . . . . | Fishers Island, NY
 JUNIORS MISS Anna N | *06390*
Stiles MR & MRS Ned B (Deborah Fiedler) . . . . | ☎ (516) 653-4120
 MR Andrew J . . . . | 58 Quaquanantuck
 MR Peter S . . . . | Lane, Quogue, NY
 JUNIORS MISS Jessica B . . . . | *11959*
Stillman MR & MRS John S (Jackson—Amelia di C | ☎ (207) 276-5342
 Pasquini) . . . . | "Nebbioso"
 MR John J . . . . | PO Box 261,
 | Seal Harbor, ME
 | *04675-0261*
Stillman MRS Margaret R (Margaret D Riley)
 ☎ (914) 359-5571 . . "The Acorn" Box 682, Oak Tree Rd, Palisades, NY *10964*
Stillman MRS Peter Gordon B (Eugenia Watters)
 ☎ (910) 256-2834 . . 14 Birmingham St, Wrightsville Beach, NC *28480*
Stimpson MR & MRS Phillip E (Brita E Schlosser)
 ☎ (516) 287-0564 . . 201 Towd Point Rd, Southampton, NY *11968*
Stinchcomb MR Carl J . . of
 ☎ (212) 838-4910 . . 14 Sutton Place S, New York, NY *10022*
 ☎ (407) 863-5267 . . 231 Southland Rd, Palm Beach, FL *33480*
Stinchcomb MRS Elizabeth H (Elizabeth P Haneman)
 ☎ (516) 374-4076 . . 600 Ocean Av, Lawrence, NY *11519*
Stinson MISS (DR) Nell L
 Aug 1 . . ☎ (208) 788-2535 . . "Chaney Creek Ranch" Rte 1, Bellevue, ID *83313*

Stires MRS Ernest Van R (Guntharp—Nell Kilgore) . | ☎ (518) 644-9657
 MR Alfred E Guntharp JR . . . . | "Edgemere"
 | PO Box 413,
 | Bolton Landing, NY
 | *12814*
Stobs MRS Constance W (Constance Wick) . . . . . . | ☎ (520) 368-8354
 MISS Wendy W . . . . | "The Shores"
 MISS Natalie . . . . | Box 2342, Pinetop,
 | AZ *85935*
Stock DR & MRS Richard J (Eleanor M Schwarz)
 ☎ (516) 537-0425 . . Sagg Main St, Sagaponack, NY *11962*
Stockman MR & MRS Robert B (Lisa A Russell)
 ☎ (401) 847-4476 . . "Wood's Castle" 195 Indian Av, Newport, RI *02840*
Stockmar MR J Brian . . of
 ☎ (970) 476-4833 . . "Stream Side" 4096 Columbine Lane, Vail, CO *81657*
 ☎ (303) 778-8593 . . 400 Lafayette St, Denver, CO *80218*
Stockwell MR & MRS John F (Dorothea C Baker) . . . | Cedar Island,
 MISS Stephanie R . . . . | Vinalhaven, ME
 MR John F JR . . . . | *04863*
 MR William A . . . . |
Stoddard MISS Alexandra B . . see P M Brown
Stoddard MISS Brooke G . . see P M Brown
Stoddart MR & MRS Alexander N (Emilie M Cole)
 ☎ (603) 823-5352 . . Center District Rd, Sugar Hill, NH *03585*
Stokes MRS Anson Phelps JR (Hope Procter)
 ☎ (413) 298-3554 . . "Orleton Farm" Box 801, Prospect Hill, Stockbridge, MA *01262*
Stokes MRS J Tyson (L Gurney Fuguet)
 ☎ (603) 744-3338 . . "High Fields" East Hebron, NH *03232*
Stokes MR & MRS John W 2d (Alice H Enos) . . . . . | ☎ (401) 294-3165
 MISS Ellery T . . . . | "Wister House"
 MISS Anne Kemble . . . . | PO Box 363,
 | Saunderstown, RI
 | *02874*
Stokes MR & MRS William S 3d (Mary F Merchant) . | ☎ (609) 884-3416
 MR Claiborne M . . . . | "Thunderbolt II"
 | 1123 Beach Av,
 | Cape May, NJ
 | *08204*
Stokes MR & MRS William Standley (Sarah Lee Biddle)
 ☎ (401) 423-1134 . . "Stowaway" Beavertail Rd, Jamestown, RI *02835*
Stone MRS Alexander Graham (Hagan—Dolly O'Neile Corbin)
 ☎ (202) 338-3856 . . Colonnade Apt 1422, 2801 New Mexico Av NW, Washington, DC *20007*
Stone MR & MRS Charles Lanier (Jacqueline B Hekma)
 ☎ (508) 993-8284 . . Nonquitt, MA *02748*
Stone MR & MRS Edward L (Cassandra S Reeve)
 ☎ (401) 847-8883 . . "The Poplars" 12 Leroy Av, Newport, RI *02840*
Stone MR & MRS Franz T (Katherine D Jones)
 ☎ (304) 536-3566 . . The Greenbriar, Creekside Cottage 342, White Sulphur Springs, WV *24986*
Stone MR & MRS Galen L (Anne Brewer)
 ☎ (508) 748-0293 . . Great Hill, Marion, MA *02738*
Stookey MR & MRS John Hoyt (Katherine E Emory)
 ☎ (413) 229-2882 . . S Egremont Rd, Sheffield, MA *01257*

Storer MR & MRS Francis E (Dinet—Bankier—Nancy Bruce Fulton)
☎ (802) 434-2979 .. "Shaker Hill" Starksboro, VT *05487*
Storey MR & MRS Anderson (Joan A Butkowsky)
☎ (207) 244-7791 .. Cranberry Isles, ME *04625*
Storey MR & MRS James M (von Steiger—Evans—Isabelle H Boeschenstein) ⚓
☎ (207) 244-5210 .. Cranberry Isles, ME *04625*
Stork MR Francis Wharton
☎ (508) MI5-2590 .. Box 61, Chilmark, MA *02535*
Storrow MRS James J (Stephenson—Brooke—Edythe M Geissinger)
☎ (508) 744-1933 .. "The End Place" 34-1 America Way, Salem, MA *01970*
Story CAPT & MRS William F (Martha van Beuren) USN. ⚓
☎ (304) 339-2424 .. "Holly Bush Farm" Holly Bush Rd, PO Box 251, Valley Head, WV *26294*
Stott MR & MRS Donald B (Quinn—Joan W Johnson)..................
   MR Christopher W Quinn................
   MR Nicholas D Quinn.................
☎ (908) 273-3470
111 Bellevue Av, Summit, NJ *07901*
Stott MR & MRS Robert L JR (Fell—Heidi M Bingham)
☎ (516) 765-3138 .. 750 Paradise Point Rd, Southold, NY *11971*
Stout MRS J Jeppson (Julie Jeppson) ....
   MISS Antonia A...............
   MISS Julie S ....
   MR Carder J ....
☎ (508) 867-4006
"Timberock" RR 1, Box 94, Lake Rd, Brookfield, MA *01506*
Stout MR Mark W H
☎ (412) 238-9517 .. Box K, Huntland Downs, Ligonier, PA *15658*
Stovell MR & MRS James B (Snyder—Thompson—Katharine G Randolph)
☎ (203) 255-2177 .. 94 Beachside Av, Greens Farms, CT *06436*
Stowe MRS Putnam T (McCown—Juliana Wright) .
   MR John A McCown ....
☎ (717) 828-7297
Edgemere Club, Silver Lake Rd, Dingmans Ferry, PA *18328*
Stradella MRS Charles G (Marilyn Carter)
☎ (212) 838-8000 .. 2 E 61 St, New York, NY *10021*
Stralem MR Pierre
☎ (819) 986-3641 .. Blanche Lake Fish & Game Club, RR 3, Buckingham, Quebec J8L 2W8, Canada
Strange MR Robert H
☎ (208) 558-9919 .. North Fork Club, PO Box 108, Macks Inn, ID *83433*
Strasenburgh MR & MRS J Griffin (Suzanne C Thompson)......................
   MR John G JR
   JUNIORS MISS Allison W
   JUNIORS MR Blair B...................
☎ (508) 257-6270
"Multiflora" PO Box 704, Siasconset, MA *02564*
Straton MR & MRS John C JR (Marion S Holder) ...
   MISS Ashley H ....
☎ (914) 351-4424
Ledge Rd, Tuxedo Park, NY *10987*

Straus DR & MRS Francis H 2d (Helen L Puttkammer)......................
   MISS (DR) Helen E ....
   MR Francis H 3d..................
   DR Christopher M.................
   MR Michael W ....
☎ (906) 847-3846
"Maple Lodge" Mackinac Island, MI *49757*
Straus MRS Ralph I (Maffitt—Katherine Mulvane)
☎ (516) 283-5644 .. PO Box 853, Southampton, NY *11969*
Strauss MR & MRS Elliott MacGregor (Tower—Luise E von Mayrhauser) ....
   MISS Caroline H Tower ....
   MISS Lydia M Tower ....
☎ (401) 847-1786
"Bridge House" 485 Paradise Av, Middletown, RI *02842*
Strawbridge MR Robert E 4th .. see M W Smith
Strawbridge MR & MRS William J JR (McSweeney—Christine S Penniman)..................
   MISS Sabrina V ....
   MR Geoffrey T ....
   MR Michael R ....
   MISS A Thayer McSweeney ....
   MISS Christine S McSweeney.......
   JUNIORS MISS Catherine B D McSweeney....
☎ (207) 276-5170
"Green Gables" PO Box 984, Northeast Harbor, ME *04662*
Strekalovsky MR & MRS Vcevold O (M Jane Cram) .
   MISS Anna B ....
☎ (802) 545-2241
"Gooseneck Bend" Box 172, RD 1, Middlebury, VT *05753*
Strickler MR & MRS Richard S JR (Diana B Hole)...
   JUNIORS MISS Margaret E H.................
☎ (203) 245-7093
20 Grove Av, Madison, CT *06443*
Stringham MR Elliott L
☎ (516) 283-0314 .. "Elsmere" 80 Harvest Lane, Southampton, NY *11968*
Strong MR & MRS Frederick S 3d (White—Leary—Elizabeth N Shontz) .. of
☎ (516) 676-2599 .. Piping Rock Rd, Locust Valley, NY *11560*
56 Vaughn Ridge, Bloomfield Hills, MI *48304*
Strong MR & MRS Trowbridge (Alice T Wadsworth)
☎ (860) 739-6594 .. "Wong Way" 39 Great Wight Way, Niantic, CT *06357*
Stroud MR & MRS Samuel S (Judith M Chamberlin)
☎ (518) 589-5432 .. "The Boulders" Onteora Club, Tannersville, NY *12485*
Struse MR & MRS C Richard (Frederica G K Richards) ....
   JUNIORS MISS Elizabeth L K ....
☎ (207) 563-5195
High St, Newcastle, ME *04553*
Stuart MR & MRS Mose W 3d (Eva M Stuckey) ....
   MR William B ....
☎ (334) 857-3450
Nero's Point, Elmore, AL *36025*
Stuart MR Robert W W
☎ (011-34-52) 448-206 .. "Villa Monterrey" Benalmadena, Malaga, Spain
Stubbins MR Hugh A JR
☎ (617) 354-0073 .. 199 Brattle St, Cambridge, MA *02138*

Stubbs MR & MRS Michael B (Veronica S Mallory) ⛵ . . . . | ☎ (207) 326-4934
MISS A Merrill . . . . | "Quiet Harbor"
MISS Abigail M . . . . | Box 14, Brooksville, ME *04617*
Stubenbord DR & MRS William T (Jane C MacDougall) . . . . | ☎ (860) 388-1533
MISS Elizabeth J . . . . | Oyster River Landing 9,
MISS Pamela T . . . . | Old Saybrook, CT *06475*
Stuebe MR & MRS William H (Isabel M Combs) . . . . | ☎ (516) 283-0875
MISS Alison M . . . . | "The Trumpet Vines" Art Village, 21 Ochre Lane, Southampton, NY *11968*
JUNIORS MR David A . . . . |
Sturges MR George David
☎ (805) 684-3663 . . 4587 Sandyland Rd, Sandyland Cove, Carpinteria, CA *93013*
Sturgis MR & MRS John C (Loretta M Howard)
☎ (414) 248-1812 . . "Panacea Farm" Box 149, Lyons, WI *53148*
Sturgis MR & MRS Nathaniel R (Ecaterini Satolias)
☎ (011-30-1) 895-2142 . . Leof Vasileos Pavleu 129, Voula 16673, Athens, Greece
MR at 53 Greer St, Waltham, MA *02154*
Sturgis MR & MRS Norman R (Linda Terry)
☎ (207) 389-2368 . . HC 32, Box 452, Phippsburg, ME *04562*
Sturtevant MR & MRS Peter A (Marriott—Linda L Webber) ⛵
☎ (207) 359-2243 . . Brooklin, ME *04616*
Sudler MRS Louis C (Virginia F Brown)
☎ (616) 526-2184 . . Cottage 44, Harbor Point, Harbor Springs, MI *49740*
Sudler MR & MRS Louis C JR (Ames—Laura Fairbank) . . . . | ☎ (219) 232-4044
MR S Zachariah . . . . | 62322 Oak Rd, South Bend, IN *46614*
Sullivan MR & MRS A Michael JR (Beverly S Bissell)
☎ (401) 849-8211 . . "Fourth Wind" Barclay Square, Newport, RI *02840*
Sullivan MR & MRS Henry P (Joan G Blair) . . . . | ☎ (902) 295-2650
MR Jeremiah J 4th . . . . | "Beinn Bhreagh"
MR H Paul JR . . . . | Baddeck, Nova Scotia B0E 1B0, Canada
Sullivan MR & MRS J Langdon (Griswold—Denny Prager)
☎ (203) 227-3082 . . "Kettle Creek Farm" 127 Kettle Creek Rd, Weston, CT *06883*
Sullivan MR & MRS Walter H (Dagmar dePins)
☎ (707) 963-3789 . . "The Elms" 1901 St Helena H'way, Rutherford, CA *94573*
Sunderland REV & MRS Edwin S S (Choumenkovitch—Phyllis Gardner)
☎ (207) 734-6662 . . PO Box 55, Heald Rd, Islesboro, ME *04848*
Sunderland MRS Thomas E (Mary L Allyn)
☎ (617) 734-4144 . . 66 Fernwood Rd, Chestnut Hill, MA *02167*
Supper MRS Frederick M (Green—Chace—Patricia McKeon)
☎ (203) 661-1250 . . "Round Island" 50 Pear Lane, Field Point Park, Greenwich, CT *06830*

Sutherland REV & MRS Malcolm R JR (Mary Anne Beaumont)
☎ (207) 326-4743 . . "Dunrobin" Timothys Lane, South Brooksville, ME *04617*
Sutor MR & MRS James F (Helme—Flora Van Sciver)
☎ (717) 595-7691 . . PO Box 206, Skytop, PA *18357*
Sutphin MR & MRS Stuart B JR (Jean C Webber)
☎ (508) 627-5090 . . "The Boat House" 25 Dunham Rd, Box 982, Edgartown, MA *02539*
Sutro MRS John A (Elizabeth L Hiss)
☎ (707) 226-8672 . . "Horseshoe S Ranch" 4578 Atlas Peak Rd, Napa, CA *94558*
Sutro MRS Katharine B (Katharine S Barbour)
☎ (516) 324-0029 . . "Easterlea" 2 Pony Ramble, East Hampton, NY *11937*
Sutro MR & MRS Ogden W (Nettleton—G Susanna Small) . . . . | ☎ (207) 947-3030
MR Curtis de W . . . . | Mountainy Pond Club, Box 1241, East Holden, ME *04429*
Sutter MR & MRS William P (Helen Y Stebbins)
☎ (847) 446-6637 . . 96 Woodley Rd, Winnetka, IL *60093*
Sutton MR & MRS Howard D (D Selden Womrath)
☎ (860) 535-9221 . . 13 School St, Stonington, CT *06378*
Sutton MR & MRS John B JR (Knipe—Salvesen—Ann D Gross)
☎ (412) 238-2816 . . "Sutton Place" 212 West Rd, Ligonier, PA *15658*
Sutton MR & MRS Roger B (Caroline H Craig) . . . . . | ☎ (516) 749-1925
MISS Judith C . . . . | 12 Crab Creek Rd, Shelter Island, NY *11964*
Swain MR & MRS Thomas S (Anne Mehan)
☎ (908) 295-8261 . . 946 East Av, Mantoloking, NJ *08738*
Swartley MR J Christopher . . see A E Newbold 3d
Swartwood MR & MRS Charles B 3d (Judith K Farrington) . . . . | ☎ (508) 428-6524
MR Alexander B . . . . | "Gifford Cottage"
MR Thayer F . . . . | Ocean View Av, Cotuit, MA *02635*
Swartwood MR & MRS Slater W (Kathryn H Pécot) . | ☎ (508) 428-1423
MISS Heather W . . . . | 1262 Main St,
MR Slater W JR . . . . | Cotuit, MA *02635*
JUNIORS MISS Effie B . . . . |
Swartz MR & MRS A Wakelee JR (Deborah Disston)
☎ (207) 244-3076 . . "Tide Race" Mt Desert, ME *04660*
Swartz MR & MRS Thomas B (Ann Wright) . . . . . . | ☎ (916) 583-2294
MR Anthony C . . . . | 50 The Northshore, Lake Tahoe, CA *95730*
Swartz MRS W Hamilton (Margaret Mac I Farmer)
☎ (516) 288-1039 . . "Cricket Hill" Westhampton Beach, NY *11978*
Swayze MR & MRS Douglas A 2d (Van Hecke—Marie E Holman)
☎ (601) 388-1231 . . 134 Barq Av, Biloxi, MS *39531*
Sweeney MR & MRS John F JR (Rhetta A Boyd) . . . | Jordan Island,
MISS Alicia B . . . . | Frenchman's Bay,
MISS Faith A . . . . | Bar Harbor, ME *04609*
Sweetser MR & MRS John A 3d (Druanne Blackmore)
Box 97, Madeline Island, La Pointe, WI *54850*

Swetland MR & MRS Eli B (Michelle Garnette) . . . . . ☎ (941) 793-1598
  MR Eli B JR . . . . 2216 Curtis St,
  JUNIORS MR Luke V . . . . Naples, FL *33962*
Swetland MR & MRS Frederick L JR (Anita M Fellner)
  ☎ (508) 228-1327 . . 16 N Liberty St, Nantucket, MA *02554*
Swift MR & MRS Hampden M (Margaret ☎ (616) 526-2578
  Muckerman) . . . . "Moon Hill"
  MISS Laura C . . . . 16 Bluff Walk,
  MISS Maria M . . . . Wequetonsing, MI
  MISS Constance J *49740*
  MR Stephen M . . . .
  MR Stewart G . . . .
Swift MR & MRS Humphrey H (Pamela A Whitney) ☎ (508) 996-4773
  ⚓ . . . . "Arrowhead
  MISS Edith S . . . . Cottage"
  MISS Alison C . . . . Mishaum Point,
                                                                 South Dartmouth,
                                                                 MA *02748*
Swift MISS Lindsay C . . see G R Wright
Swift MR William F
  ☎ (207) 867-4855 . . North Haven, ME *04853*
Swindell MR & MRS Robert H JR (Nancy D Cotton) . ☎ (207) 563-3580
  MR Douglas C . . . . "Cottesbrook"
                                                                 Walpole, ME *04573*
Swinerton MR & MRS William A (Mary N Clark)
  "The Catchall" Box 105, Wolf Creek, MT *59483*
Swope MR & MRS Gerard L (Mary G Carlton) . . . . . . ☎ (508) 548-0625
  MR Timothy W C . . . . 90 Church St,
  MR Ian G . . . . Woods Hole, MA
                                                                 02543
Swords MISS Deirdre H . . see W Maynard JR
Symington MRS M Frick (Martha H Frick)
  ☎ (410) 583-8005 . . 2 Old Boxwood Lane, Lutherville, MD *21093*
Symington MRS Stuart (Watson—Ann C Hemingway)
  ☎ (207) 236-2018 . . 96 Bay View St, Box 575, Camden, ME *04843*
Symonds MR & MRS George W D (Margaret Preston)
  ☎ (508) 693-2189 . . 120 Barnes Rd, RD 3, Vineyard Haven, MA *02568*
Symonds MRS Samuel M (Anderson—Deborah S ☎ (315) 354-4312
  Lee) . . . . "Thumbs Up"
  JUNIORS MISS Courtenay B . . . . Brandreth Park,
  JUNIORS MISS Samantha L . . . . Long Lake, NY
                                                                 12847
Szabo-Imrey MRS Diane L (Diane B D Leroy) . . . . ☎ (508) 627-9263
  MISS Celia C A . . . . "Witchwood
  MR G Christopher . . . . Cottage" Katama
  MR Thomas R . . . . Way, Edgartown,
                                                                 MA *02539*

T

Taber MR & MRS George H (Janet Beebe) . . . . ☎ (207) 374-2721
  MR John . . . . "Roads End"
                                                                 Blue Hill, ME
                                                                 04614
Taft MR & MRS David D (Sara Leonard) . . . . ☎ (616) 223-7773
  MISS Elisabeth K . . . . Neahtawanta Point,
                                                                 Traverse City, MI
                                                                 49684
Tailer MRS T Suffern (Thompson—Clark—Jean Sinclair)
  ☎ (516) 283-5080 . . "Serendipity" 405 Ox Pasture Rd, PO Box 1148,
  Southampton, NY *11969*
Talbot MISS Lorna (Atkins—Lorna Talbot)
  ☎ (540) 592-9545 . . "Ross Farm" 10821 Trappe Rd, Upperville,
  VA *22176*
Talbot MRS Nathan B (Anne Perry)
  ☎ (207) 354-9216 . . "Pointed Firs" PO Box 87, Cushing, ME *04563*
Talbot MR & MRS Robert B (Caroline Allen)
  ☎ (516) 788-7886 . . Fishers Island, NY *06390*
Talmage MR & MRS E T Hunt 3d (Mueller—Kathrin ☎ (916) 546-7305
  L Johnson) . . . . 5845 Sudan Rd,
  MR E Taylor H . . . . Box 241,
  MR J Adrian Mueller . . . . Carnelian Bay, CA
  MR Bret A Mueller *96140*
Talmage JUNIORS MISS Julie H . . see MRS J H Sprague
Tankersley MR & MRS Garvin E (Miller—Ruth E McCormick)
  ☎ (520) 635-2314 . . "The Hat Ranch" Box 584, Williams, AZ *86046*
Tasman DR & MRS William (Alice Lea Mast) . . . . . . ☎ (410) 348-2155
  MISS Alice L M . . . . Kentmore,
  MR James B . . . . Kennedyville, MD
                                                                 21645
Taussig MR & MRS Frederick (Browne—Ferriss— ☎ (314) 239-1955
  Jean A Overstreet) ⚓ . . . . "Bluff House"
  MISS Susan C . . . . St John's Rd,
                                                                 Washington, MO
                                                                 63090
Taves DR Ernest H
  ☎ (603) 876-3359 . . "Westover Farm" Marlborough, NH *03455*
Taylor MR A Thomas
  ☎ (847) 234-0170 . . 435 N Thorne Lane, Lake Forest, IL *60045*
Taylor MR & MRS B Loyall JR (Nancy S Harkins) . . . ☎ (910) 457-4300
  MISS Brooke S . . . . Bald Head Island,
  JUNIORS MR B Loyall 3d . . . . 50 S Bald Head
                                                                 Wynd, Southport,
                                                                 NC *28461*
Taylor MRS C Harold (Juliet C Baldwin)
  ☎ (508) 228-1695 . . 33 Quaise Rd, Nantucket, MA *02554*
Taylor MR & MRS David H JR (Milbrey T Rennie) . . ☎ (516) 626-5531
  JUNIORS MISS Rennie M . . . . 1053 Friendly Rd,
                                                                 Upper Brookville,
                                                                 NY *11771*
Taylor MR & MRS Duncan R (Deeds—E Kathleen ☎ (360) 376-5744
  Brewer) . . . . "Soundings"
  MR Duncan R JR . . . . PO Box 31,
  MR Nathaniel B . . . . Orcas, WA *98280*
  JUNIORS MR Blake Deeds . . . .
Taylor MR & MRS Frank H 2d (Eve L Hebbard)
  ☎ (802) 464-5664 . . "Negus Place" HCR 63, Box 59, West Dover,
  VT *05356*

Taylor MR & MRS Frederic F (Blodgett—Judith T McCormick) . . . . ☎ (508) 548-0865
   MISS Suzanne H . . . . 136 Old Dock Rd,
   MR Charles M . . . . West Falmouth, MA *02574*

Taylor MR & MRS H Furness 3d (Fantauzzi—Sheila W Reath) . . . . ☎ (609) 399-0802
   MISS Samantha F Fantauzzi . . . . 5321 West Av, Ocean City, NJ *08226*

Taylor MR & MRS Henry W JR (Sekula—Ann L Dayton)
   ☎ (208) 726-5498 . . 12694 H'way 75 S, Ketchum, ID *83340-2247*

Taylor MRS James C (Cecilia A Baldner)
   425 Cameron Av, Chapel Hill, NC *27516*

Taylor MRS James Spear (Helen L MacG Strauss)
   ☎ (518) 576-4503 . . "The Runway" Keene Valley, NY *12943*

Taylor MR & MRS John I JR (E Carson Custer)
   ☎ (970) 349-7305 . . 509—2 St, Crested Butte, CO *81224*

Taylor MR & MRS Nicholas C (Catherine H Blaffer) . ☎ (518) 576-4503
   MISS Katherine C . . . . "The Runway"
   MR Nicholas Van C . . . . Keene Valley, NY *12943*

Taylor MR Quinby
   "Cedar Crest" 100 Garnett Av, North Falmouth, MA *02556*

Taylor MR & MRS Richard S (Waterman—Belle S Kilborne) ⚓ . . . . ☎ (508) 428-2276
   MR Richard S . . . . 713 Sea View Av, PO Box 117, Osterville, MA *02655-0117*

Taylor MR Robert E L
   Jly 1 . . "Thomaston House" Northeast Harbor, ME *04662*

Taylor MRS Robert G (Gates—Phyllis C Lueders)
   ☎ (704) 526-4607 . . PO Box 2321, Highlands, NC *28741*

Taylor MRS Sandra B (Sandra S Brown) . . . . ☎ (516) 537-3583
   MISS Louise T . . . . PO Box 176, Sagaponack, NY *11962*

Taylor DR & MRS Talbot J 2d (Rosemary A Furse)
   ☎ (516) 788-7243 . . Fishers Island, NY *06390*

Taylor MRS William Davis (Ann C Macy)
   ☎ (508) 627-3776 . . 48 Mill St, PO Box 2370, Edgartown, MA *02539*

Taylor MR William Davis
   Burrage House, 314 Commonwealth Av, Boston, MA *02116*

Taylor MR & MRS William O (Sally P Coxe)
   ☎ (508) 993-0123 . . 307 Smith Neck Rd, South Dartmouth MA *02748*

Taylor MR & MRS William T (Elizabeth N Todd)
   ☎ (603) 585-6673 . . Box 52, Fitzwilliam, NH *03447*

Tenney MR & MRS Daniel G JR (Constance L Franchot)
   ☎ (518) 327-3187 . . "Wanakiwin" Box 268, Paul Smiths, NY *12970*

Terrell MR & MRS Allen M (Josephine H Peters)
   "Hemlock Woods" La Anna Rd, RD 2, Cresco, PA *18326*

Terry MISS Elizabeth
   ☎ (616) 526-2583 . . Wequetonsing, MI *49740*

Terry MR & MRS Robert L (Ellen McH Bruce)
   ☎ (609) 924-0954 . . Box 9, Princeton, NJ *08540*

Terry MRS Whitelaw T (Julia Wells)
   ☎ (616) 526-2583 . . Wequetonsing, MI *49740*

Terry MRS Wyllys (Elena Howell)
   ☎ (207) 326-4663 . . "Wilson Point" RD 1, Penobscot, ME *04476*

Thacher MR & MRS John H JR (Carol A Saam) . . . . . ☎ (908) 295-0307
   MISS Ashley B . . . . 1224 Ocean Av,
   MISS Kimberly B . . . . Mantoloking, NJ *08738*

Thacher MR & MRS Thomas (Barbara Auchincloss)
   ☎ (207) 867-4872 . . "Deacon Brown's Point" North Haven, ME *04853*

Thatcher MR & MRS John M P JR (Dorothy Riddell)
   ☎ (802) 824-6511 . . "Snowcroft" RR 1, Box 234, Londonderry, VT *05148*

Thayer MRS Frederick M JR (Barbara Russell)
   ☎ (207) 766-2536 . . Cushing Island, Portland, ME *04109*

Thayer MRS Gordon B (Lydia C Prescott)
   ☎ (508) 283-3147 . . 69 Leonard St, Annisquam, MA *01930*

Thayer MISS Margaret P . . see I Leclerc

Thayer MR & MRS Seth A (Frances F Macy) . . . . . . ☎ (516) 626-0844
   MISS Jennifer M . . . . 897 Remsens Lane,
   MISS Ann W . . . . Oyster Bay, NY
   MR Seth A JR *11771*

Thayer MRS Sydney 3d (Drayton—Edith M Bettle) . ☎ (401) 635-8371
   MR Frederick R Drayton 3d . . . . "Windward Farm" 466 W Main Rd, Little Compton, RI *02837*

Thibault MR Robert G . . see H D Tiffany 3d
Thibault MISS Tammy M . . see H D Tiffany 3d

Thiele MR Kenneth W
   ☎ (513) 294-3700 . . 4518 Troon Trail, Dayton, OH *45429*

Thierry MR & MRS Charles A (Diana R Laing)
   ☎ (603) 744-3540 . . "The Lichens" Murray Hill Rd, Hill, NH *03243*

Thomas MRS Alfred (Frances Flood)
   ☎ (508) 563-2909 . . "The Cape" 251 Scraggy Neck Rd, Cataumet, MA *02534*

Thomas MR B Brooks— ⚓
   ☎ (860) 767-0219 . . "Cove's End" Essex, CT *06426*

Thomas MR Charles D (Nancy Kenney)
   ☎ (717) 676-0500 . . "Feather Fin Farm" La Anna Rd, RD 2, Cresco, PA *18326*

Thomas COL & MRS Dudley E JR (Susan A Horne) USMC . . . . ☎ (516) 323-2778
   MISS Dorothy D E . . . . 800 Village Lane,
   MISS Sarah-Grace H . . . . Orient, NY *11957*

Thomas MR & MRS Edward C P (Marjorie M Prince)
   ☎ (508) 356-3867 . . PO Box 705, 190 Argilla Rd, Ipswich, MA *01938*

Thomas MISS Hilleary T . . see H H Chappell

Thomas MR & MRS Jeffrey F (Evelyne Champin) . . ☎ (011-33-50)
   MISS Fiona de F 60-22-17
   MR Patrick J . . . . 22 rte du Port, 74290 Veyrier-du-lac, France

Thomas MR & MRS Jeremiah L 3d (Clara E Ruthrauff)
   ☎ (914) 855-5957 . . 282 Quaker Hill Rd, Pawling, NY *12564*

Thomas MR Landon
   ☎ (207) 734-6455 . . Dark Harbor, Islesboro, ME *04848*

Thomas MR & MRS Lowell S JR (Judith K Evans) ⚓
   ☎ (207) 348-2583 . . "Pen Bryn" Little Deer Isle, ME *04650*

Thomas MR Stephen L JR . . see H H Chappell

Thomas MRS Weston L (Kaemmerer—Weston S Linn)
☎ (860) 739-2538 . . 22 Hemingway Rd, Old Black Point, Niantic, CT *06357*

Thomas MR & MRS Wilmer J JR (Porteous—K Douglas Dockery) . . . .
    MISS Alexandra K Porteous . . . .
    MR William D Porteous . . . .
☎ (860) 435-2546 ''Hope Hill Farm'' 272 Undermountain Rd, Salisbury, CT *06068-1510*

Thomasson MR Nelson 3d
☎ (301) 334-4173 . . ''Little Monte Vista'' General Delivery, Mountain Lake Park, MD *21550*

Thompson MR & MRS Charles I (Woods—Judith Johnson)
☎ (207) 244-5360 . . PO Box 1362, 461 Seawall Rd, Southwest Harbor, ME *04679*

Thompson MR Charles W JR . . of
☎ (301) 229-2094 . . 7906 Riverside Dv, Cabin John, MD *20818*
☎ (406) 222-1350 . . 201 W Park St, Livingston, MT *59047*

Thompson MRS D G Brinton (Anne H Bigelow)
☎ (207) 288-3576 . . ''Westfield Cottage'' West St, Bar Harbor, ME *04609*

Thompson MISS Deborah H
☎ (617) 934-2446 . . ''Four Rooves'' 151 King Caesar Rd, PO Box 114, Duxbury, MA *02331*

Thompson MR & MRS Donald G (Miller—Ella Mae Mathis)
☎ (603) 329-5262 . . Governor's Island, PO Box 780, Hampstead, NH *03841*

Thompson MR & MRS Edward P (Margot R Levis)
☎ (207) 529-5675 . . ''Cedar Oaks'' Shore Rd, Round Pond, ME *04564*

Thompson MR & MRS George W (Margaret H Cooper)
☎ (508) 349-2034 . . ''Uplands'' Truro, MA *02666*

Thompson MR & MRS Gerard M JR (Barbara A Wilcox)
☎ (011-44-171) 838-9811 . . 29 Cadogan Square, London SW3, England

Thompson MR & MRS Grant McM (Helen E Morrison)
☎ (508) 228-0795 . . ''Wheelhouse'' 20 Lincoln Av, Nantucket, MA *02554*

Thompson MR & MRS Henry F (Elizabeth M Cross) .
    MISS Grace B . . . .
    MISS Elizabeth C . . . .
    MR Berkeley F . . . .
    MR Henry F JR . . . .
    MR John M D . . . .
☎ (207) 366-3460 ''Lizzie's'' Matinicus Island, ME *04851*

Thompson MRS James E (Ethel H Bartlett)
☎ (860) 567-8474 . . N Lake St, Litchfield, CT *06759*

Thompson MR & MRS John E JR (Julia A Forster)
☎ (717) 775-6799 . . Blooming Grove Hunt & Fish Club, Box 380, Hawley, PA *18428*

Thompson MRS Josephine M (Josephine U Merwin)
☎ (011-44-147) 032-305 . . 4 Eyre by Portree, Isle of Skye IV51 9XE, Scotland

Thompson MR & MRS Lawrence B (Louise M Blanchard)
☎ (207) 288-3576 . . ''Westfield Cottage'' West St, Bar Harbor, ME *04609*

Thompson MISS Maris Wistar
☎ (518) 286-2833 . . ''Windward'' Old Troy Rd, Rensselaer, NY *12144*

Thompson MR & MRS Mark J (Alison Mary Wilbur)
☎ (203) 255-3318 . . ''Quayside'' 648 Harbor Rd, Southport, CT *06490*

Thompson MR & MRS Neil L (Kathleen Cox) . . . . . .
    JUNIORS MISS Caroline R . . . .
☎ (802) 387-4456 PO Box 1020, Old Athens Rd, Westminster West, Putney, VT *05346*

Thompson MR & MRS O David (Nancy L Hooper) . .
    MISS Jennifer L . . . .
    MISS Kate G . . . .
    JUNIORS MISS Sarah B . . . .
Box 155, Old Shore Rd, Bremen, Medomak, ME *04551*

Thompson MRS Phyllis A (Phyllis A Nitze) . . . .
    MISS Phyllis E P . . . .
    MISS Heidi A N . . . .
    MR Nicholas E S . . . .
☎ (207) 276-5453 ''Rockridge'' Schoolhouse Ledge, Northeast Harbor, ME *04662*

Thompson MR & MRS Rodman E JR (Ana C Davidson)
☎ (207) 276-3951 . . ''Cow Cove'' Peabody Dv, Northeast Harbor, ME *04662*

Thompson MR & MRS Stephen E (Helen L Malarkey)
☎ (503) 738-7500 . . General Delivery, Gearhart, OR *97138*

Thompson DR W Scott . . of
☎ (540) 937-5189 . . ''Storybrook Farm'' Rte 1, Box 2150, Amissville, VA *22002*
☎ (302) 227-1578 . . ''The Pines'' 82 Oak Av, Rehoboth Beach, DE *19971*

Thompson MR & MRS William (Potter—Thieriot—Julia K Macy)
☎ (604) 598-4829 . . 1211 Beach Dv, Victoria, BC V8R 2N4, Canada

Thomson MR & MRS A Lindsay (Emily A Bannard)
☎ (802) 824-6070 . . South Londonderry, VT *05155*

Thomson MR & MRS George G (Sylvia Grove-Palmer)
☎ (207) 832-4274 . . Waldoboro, ME *04572*

Thomson SIR John A & LADY (Cabot—Bullitt—O Judith Ogden)
☎ (011-44-155) 665-0271 . . Lochpatrick Mill, Kirkpatrick Durham, Castle Douglas OG7 3HT, Scotland

Thomson MR Richard S
☎ (601) 466-3300 . . ''The Farm'' 11191 Cazaubon Rd, Bay St Louis, MS *39520*

Thorndike MR & MRS Richard K (Archibald—M Mercy Bours)
☎ (508) 526-7804 . . ''Maison Masconomo'' 6 Masconomo St, Manchester-By-The-Sea, MA *01944*

Thorne MR & MRS Daniel K (Hornblower—Alexandra C Tower) ⚓ . . . .
    MR Josiah C Hornblower . . . .
    JUNIORS MR Alexander W Hornblower . . . . . .
☎ (207) 734-8300 Shipyard Point, Islesboro, ME *04848*

Thorne MR & MRS Oakleigh B (Forg—Felicitas Selter) . . . .
    MISS Eliza . . . .
    MR Jonathan . . . .
''Thorndale West'' 9 Parkdale Court, Ft Smith, MT *59035*

Thorne MRS Oakleigh Lewis (Akin—Dorothy M Forbes)
☎ (516) 626-0389 . . 68 Linden Lane, Glen Head, NY *11545*

Thorne MR & MRS Samuel JR (See—Elizabeth B Jones)
☎ (508) 526-8274 . . 31 Harbor St, Manchester, MA *01944*

Thornhill MR & MRS Arthur H JR (Dorothy M Matheis)
☎ (508) 627-9538 . . PO Box 5016, Edgartown, MA *02539*

Thoron MRS Benjamin Warder (Violet Spencer)
☎ (508) 693-1287 . . RFD 900, Vineyard Haven, MA *02568*

Thoron MRS J Lloyd (Janeth Lloyd) . . . . | ☎ (516) 537-1332
   MISS Elise . . . . | 88 Sayre's Path, Wainscott, NY *11975*

Thorsen MR & MRS J Gwynne (Frances G Woods) ⚓
   ☎ (508) 257-4424 . . 32 Beach Club Rd, Siasconset, MA *02564*

Thouron SIR John R H
   ☎ (610) 384-5542 . . ''Doe Run'' Thouron Rd, Unionville, PA *19375*

Throop MRS Enos T 4th (Barbara Williams)
   ☎ (518) 582-3501 . . ''Rock Bottom'' Tahawus, NY *12879*

Thurston MRS E Ladd JR (Hulley—Laura F Broeksmit) . . . . | ''Sounion'' Cuttyhunk Island, MA *02713*
   MR Elliott S . . . . |
   MR David L . . . . |
   MR Zachary J . . . . |

Tiernan MR & MRS Charles W JR (Carol H Stark)
   ☎ (516) 749-1485 . . 12 Burro Hall Lane, Shelter Island, NY *11964*

Tiffany MR & MRS Edwin P (Joan Thacher) ⚓ . . . | ☎ (508) 748-0490
   JUNIORS MISS Kathrene B . . . . | 67 Holly Rd,
   JUNIORS MR Thacher B . . . . | Marion, MA *02738*

Tiffany MR & MRS Gordon MacL (Ellen Auchincloss)
   ☎ (603) 529-2812 . . ''Tiffany Hill Farm'' 197 Tiffany Hill Rd, Weare, NH *03281*

Tiffany MR & MRS Henry D 3d (Thibault—Mary E Keegan) . . . . | ☎ (603) 547-8794
   MR Henry D 4th . . . . | ''Mill Village House'' Box 86, Francestown, NH *03043*
   MR Edwin F . . . . |
   MISS Tammy M Thibault . . . . |
   MR Robert G Thibault . . . . |

Tifft MR & MRS Henry N (Suzanne N McCarter)
   ☎ (508) 748-0292 . . 31 Pawkechatt Way, Marion, MA *02738*

Tilghman MR & MRS Benjamin C JR (Margo R Taggart) . . . . | ☎ (410) 758-1813
   MISS Emily DeY . . . . | ''The Hermitage'' 120 Hermitage Farm Lane, Centreville, MD *21617*
   MISS Eliza C . . . . |
   JUNIORS MR Benjamin C 3d . . . . |

Tilghman MR & MRS George H (Elizabeth B Easton)
   ☎ (508) 228-3309 . . 38 Cliff Rd, Nantucket, MA *02554*

Tilghman MR & MRS Henry R (Cordelia R Hodges)
   ☎ (508) 627-5450 . . Box 211, Edgartown, MA *02539*

Tilghman MR & MRS Richard A (Joan McA Shiland)
   ☎ (203) 259-9854 . . 842 Redding Rd, Fairfield, CT *06430*

Tilghman MR & MRS William F (Juliette Deleuze-Dordron) . . . . | Villa Maria, rte du Lac, 31510 Barbazon, France
   MISS Isabelle F . . . . |
   MR Christian D . . . . |

Tilney MRS Norcross S (C Kane Merritt)
   ☎ (802) 867-4135 . . Box 924, Danby Mountain Rd, Dorset, VT *05251*

Tilt MRS Rodman King (Putnam—Frances Catlin)
   ☎ (914) 234-7133 . . 33 The Hook Rd, Bedford, NY *10506*

Tilt MR Rodman King
   ☎ (516) 788-7525 . . ''Monatucket I'' Box 711, Fishers Island, NY *06390*

Timpson MR & MRS Carl W JR (Patricia White) ⚓
   ☎ (207) 883-1232 . . ''Bohemia II'' 526 Black Point Rd, Scarborough, ME *04074*

Timpson MR & MRS James (Barnard—Rea—M Priscilla Goodrich) ⚓ . . . . | ☎ (207) 734-8335
   MISS Anne Barnard . . . . | Pendleton Point, Islesboro, ME *04848*
   MISS Phoebe Barnard . . . . |

Tippit MR & MRS C Carlisle (Margaret Mayo)
   ☎ (216) 247-4260 . . 37035 Shaker Blvd, Chagrin Falls, OH *44022*

Tirrell MR David J . . . . | ☎ (415) 669-7219
   MISS Angela . . . . | 70 Callender Way, Inverness, CA *94937*

Titus MR David C
   ☎ (516) 922-6200 . . 314 Yacht Club Rd, Centre Island, Oyster Bay, NY *11771*

Tobias MR & MRS Terrence A (Cynthia du Pont)
   ☎ (505) 984-8471 . . 576 Camino del Monte Sol, Santa Fe, NM *87501*

Tobin MR & MRS James E (A Laura Dalley)
   ☎ (508) 693-3966 . . 7 Holly Tree Lane, Vineyard Haven, MA *02568*

Tobin MR & MRS Joseph O 2d (Dant—Edith T Andrews)
   ☎ (916) 546-4874 . . ''Stone House'' 9620 Brockway Springs Rd, Kings Beach, CA *95734*

Tobin MR & MRS Joshua (Medina—Janet B Williams)
   ☎ (516) 653-5055 . . Box 853, Quogue, NY *11959*

Tobin MISS Katherine O (Whipple—Katherine O Tobin)
   ☎ (415) 344-8079 . . 888 Irwin Dv, Hillsborough, CA *94010*

Tobin MR & MRS Maurice B (Joan K Fleischmann)
   ☎ (970) 925-2414 . . 210 W Francis St, Aspen, CO *81611*

Todd MR & MRS Burt K (Frances Hayes)
   ☎ (705) 375-5003 . . ''Twin Pines'' Iron City Fishing Club, Parry Sound, Ontario P2A 2X4, Canada

Todd MR & MRS Frederic de P (Laura F Knox-Dick)
   ☎ (508) 627-5606 . . ''High Tide'' 110 N Water St, PO Box 1268, Edgartown, MA *02539*

Todd MR James
   ☎ (508) 627-5606 . . ''High Tide'' 110 N Water St, PO Box 1268, Edgartown, MA *02539*

Todd MR & MRS John K (Downes—Charlotte Golden)
   ☎ (705) 387-4307 . . General Delivery, Magnetawan, Ontario P0A 1P0, Canada

Todd MRS Joseph Z (Bliss—Hatherly Brittain)
   ☎ (702) 749-5288 . . ''High Meadows'' Glenbrook, NV *89413*

Todd DR & MRS Samuel P JR (Emily L Gest)
   ''Somerset'' 940 Neahtawanta Rd, Traverse City, MI *49684*

Todd MR Verser (Chase—Sally L Dickinson)
   ☎ (508) 693-0524 . . West Chop, MA *02573*

Toland MR & MRS Asheton C (Judith E Beckanstin) . | ☎ (401) 847-5595
   MISS Lisa G . . . . | 441 Tuckerman Av, Middletown, RI *02842*
   MISS J Jessie . . . . |
   MR M Maximillian . . . . |
   MR Samuel C . . . . |

Toland MR & MRS John G (Lita B Wicksey)
   ☎ (508) 228-6172 . . 4 Pleasant St, Nantucket, MA *02554*

Toland MR & MRS Richard H R JR (Diane L Adams)
   ☎ (516) 653-4640 . . Box 919, Quogue, NY *11959*

Told MR William H JR
   ☎ (215) 862-9215 . . ''The Villa'' 186 S Main St, New Hope, PA *18938*

Tolles MR & MRS Bryant F JR (Carolyn C Kimball).. ☎ (603) 284-7028
MR Bryant F 3d .... Coolidge Farm Rd, Center Sandwich, NH *03227*

Tompkins MR & MRS Frederick K (Odile H Delente) ☎ (011-33-31) 91-00-59
MISS Anne-Cecile .... "Ferme d'Osseville" 14390 Cabourg, France

Toogood MISS Anna Coxe (Harvey—Anna Coxe Toogood).......................... ☎ (207) 276-5882 Northeast Harbor, ME *04662*
JUNIORS MR Nathan A Harvey

Toogood MR & MRS Granville N (Patricia A Dale).. ☎ (207) 276-5695
MISS Heather D........................ "Ebbtide"
MR Chase .... Northeast Harbor, ME *04662*

Tooker MISS Tracey
☎ (516) 287-3556.. 81 Jobs Lane, Southampton, NY *11968*

Toole MR & MRS William F (Battey—Bertha B Lee)
☎ (704) 743-3419.. PO Box 1274, Cashiers, NC *28717*

Torbert MR & MRS Clement C JR (Gene D Hurt)
☎ (904) 492-0130.. "Windward" 16777 Perdido Key Dv, Pensacola, FL *32507*

Totten MR & MRS Michael W (Alexandra C Train).. ☎ (207) 644-8384
JUNIORS MISS Ellen A C .... PO Box 205, South Bristol, ME *04568*

Toulmin MR & MRS Peter N (Olga Sturtevant) ..... ☎ (207) 359-8501
MR Steven W .... "The Maxie" Brooklin, ME *04616*

Tower MISS Caroline H .. see E M Strauss
Tower MISS Lydia M .. see E M Strauss
Towers MR & MRS Charles S (Lois W Mason)
☎ (802) 229-5630.. PO Box 15, Calais, VT *05648*

Townes MR & MRS Charles H (Frances H Brown)
☎ (603) 487-2442.. "Hillcroft" S Hill Rd, New Boston, NH *03070*

Townsend MRS Charles Coe (von Wiesenthal—Ruth E Scott)
☎ (518) 851-9151.. "Pict Bush" Snowberry Farm, Box 92, RD 4, Hudson, NY *12534*
Aug 1 .. ☎ (518) 584-5514.. 27 Wedgewood Dv, Saratoga Springs, NY *12866*

Townsend MRS Edward (Andrade—Felicia C Thomas)
☎ (516) 427-2179.. "Far Afield" 9 Count Rumford Lane, Lloyd Neck, Huntington, NY *11743*

Townsend MR Edward L
☎ (704) 375-4701.. 2331 Mecklenburg Av, Charlotte, NC *28205*

Townsend MR & MRS P Coleman JR (Susan Marshall)............................. ☎ (603) 563-8805 "Tiadnock"
MR John M .... PO Box 141, Dublin, NH *03444-0141*

Townsend MR & MRS Thomas H (Mary F Friedmann) ⚓ .... ☎ (508) 356-2716 "Merula Farm"
MISS Katharine C .... Argilla Rd, Ipswich, MA *01938*
MISS Elizabeth P......................
MISS Caroline H ....

Townsend MRS Wisner H (Edith W Richard)
☎ (401) 783-4050.. "Commodore Perry Farm" 1591 Commodore Perry H'way, Wakefield, RI *02879*

Tozer MR & MRS W James JR (Elizabeth Farran).... ☎ (914) 868-2265
MISS Farran V......................... "Uplands Farm"
MISS Katharine C .... Hunns Lake Rd, Stanfordville, NY *12581*

Tracy MR Phelps K
☎ (508) 432-1732.. "Mistover" 113 Riverside Dv, Box 190, West Harwich, MA *02671*

Tracy MRS William T (Marylin R Noble) .... ☎ (516) 288-1938
MR Paul W .... 64 Aspatuck Rd, Westhampton Beach, NY *11978*

Tracy MR William T
☎ (212) 535-1468.. 35 E 84 St, New York, NY *10028*

Train MRS Cuthbert R (Clark—Noël Hall)
18 Old Neck Rd, Manchester-By-The-Sea, MA *01944*

Train MR & MRS John (Tower—Fosburgh—Frances D Cheston) ⚓ .... ☎ (207) 734-2277 Islesboro, ME *04848*
MISS Lisa ....

Train MRS Middleton G C (Audrey N Campbell)
☎ (508) 526-1724.. "Port Regis" 43 Coolidge Point, Manchester, MA *01944*

Traina MR & MRS Albert S (C Vail Devereux) ..... ☎ (207) 846-4462
MR R Brooks .... RR 1, Box 627, Chebeague Island, ME *04017*

Traina MR Todd B .. see A S Wilsey
Traina MR Trevor D .. see A S Wilsey
Trainer MR David P JR
☎ (609) 823-7719.. 30 N Jerome Av, Margate City, NJ *08402*

Trainer MR & MRS John N (Alice T Stone)
"Nigunak" Great Pubnico Lake, Nova Scotia B0W 2W0, Canada

Trask MR & MRS Frederick K (Samuelson—Sarah A Whittinghill)
Jun 1 .. ☎ (802) 899-2528.. RR 1, Box 1400, Underhill, VT *05489*

Treadway MR & MRS William L (Anderson—Elizabeth G M Coale)
☎ (910) 686-0227.. 176 Beach Rd S, Wilmington, NC *28405*

Treadwell MR & MRS Louis Mead 2d (Carol A Walsh)
☎ (616) 256-9763.. "Lovelylee" 1064 N Manitou Trail, Leland, MI *49654*

Treherne-Thomas MRS V Osborn (Hunt—Virginia B Osborn)............................ ☎ (508) 627-4851 "Child's Play"
JUNIORS MR Samuel A.................... Rte 62, Edgartown, MA *02539*

Trench MR & MRS Archer W P (Hope T Humphreys)
☎ (508) 775-0368.. 11 Maywood Av, Hyannis Port, MA *02647*

Trevor MR & MRS Bronson (Eleanor D Fisher)
☎ (518) 327-3258.. "Trevallyn" Paul Smiths, NY *12970*

Trevor MISS Evelyn J B .. see J E Quinn
Trevor MISS Irene S .. see J E Quinn
Trevor MRS Michele (Simpson—Michele M Safley) ☎ (401) 846-2828
JUNIORS MISS Melanie S Simpson .... 372 Indian Av, Middletown, RI *02842*

Trevor MISS Sophia A B .. see J E Quinn

Trigg MRS R C Ballard 3d (Helen B Milman)
  ☎ (713) 531-8859 . . 2410 Briarview Dv, Houston, TX *77077*
Trimble MRS John T (Marie E Gibbon)
  "Blue Orchids" First Neck Lane, Southampton, NY *11968*
Trimble MR & MRS William C JR (Barbara Janney)
  ☎ (207) 276-5070 . . "Sweet Briar" Northeast Harbor, ME *04662*
Trimmier MR & MRS C Stephen (Rae E Wade) . . . . | ☎ (334) 928-4893
  MR C Stephen 3d . . . . | 9 Point Clear Landing, Point Clear, AL *36532*
Trincal MR & MRS Alain J (Vivian B Vose)
  1 rue Jeanne D'Arc, Nouan-le-Fuzelier, France
Trippe MR & MRS Charles W (Pamela J Reid)
  ☎ (508) 636-5427 . . 24 Valentine Lane, PO Box 156, Westport Point, MA *02791*
Trott MR & MRS Elliott C (Gertrude M Singer)
  ☎ (441) 236-0717 . . "Salt Winds" 3 Salt Kettle Lane, Paget PG 01, Bermuda
Trotter MR & MRS Gordon Trumbull (Jean M Oberg) . . . . | ☎ (410) 723-4196
  MISS Laura J . . . . | "Calypso"
  MISS Linda M . . . . | 6201 Atlantic Av, Ocean City, MD *21842*
Trowbridge MR & MRS Thomas R JR (Eunice W Herrick)
  ☎ (860) 364-5464 . . "Nequitamauk" S Main St, Sharon, CT *06069*
True MR Edward Russell JR
  ☎ (508) 428-8496 . . "Wind Song" 395 Eel River Rd, Osterville, MA *02655*
Truesdale MISS Suzanne C . . see G D Jackson 3d
Truitt MRS S Stokes (Allen—Louise B Grayson)
  ☎ (819) 842-2142 . . "Lakeside Cottage" North Hatley, Quebec J0B 2C0, Canada
Trump MR & MRS Robert Townshend (Sandra F Snowden) . . . . | ☎ (401) 624-7427
  MISS Lillie F . . . . | "Nonquit's Little Greek Revival"
  MR Michael . . . . | 42 Punkateest Neck Rd, Tiverton, RI *02878*
Trundle MRS Sidney A JR (MacDonald—Charmian Campbell) . . . . | Tory Hill Rd, Alstead, NH *03602*
  MISS Catherine MacDonald . . . . |
  MR Joseph MacDonald . . . . |
Truscott MR & MRS George B (Edith R Howe)
  ☎ (401) 635-2902 . . 50 Taylor's Lane, Little Compton, RI *02837*
Truslow MR & MRS Godfrey G (Olivia H Van Norden) . . . . | ☎ (207) 734-2294
  MR Edward D . . . . | Dark Harbor, Islesboro, ME *04848*
Truslow MR & MRS Peter C (Andrea K Schaefer)
  ☎ (207) 734-2294 . . Dark Harbor, Islesboro, ME *04848*
Truslow MR & MRS William A (Miriam P Kellogg) | ☎ (207) 867-4656
  MR Hugh K . . . . | Iron Point Rd, North Haven, ME *04853*
  MR Samuel B . . . . |
Tucker REV & MRS Luther (Josephine L Pullman)
  ☎ (860) 767-8145 . . 26 Prospect St, Essex, CT *06426*

Tucker MRS Toinette (Randell—King—Toinette Tucker)
  ☎ (802) 297-9358 . . Piper Ridge, Bondville, VT *05340*
Tucker MR & MRS William Hollingsworth (Nute—Sandra J Bernard) . . . . | ☎ (609) 884-4692
  MR Christopher S . . . . | "Clearview" 1001 New Jersey Av, Cape May, NJ *08204*
Tucker MR & MRS William R (Carol M O Exnicios) | ☎ (860) 739-2430
  MISS Elinor D W . . . . | 258 Old Black Point Rd, Niantic, CT *06357*
  MR Michael W . . . . |
Tuckerman MR & MRS Roger W (Edith D Fenton) . . | ☎ (914) 234-7886
  JUNIORS MISS Katharine F . . . . | Box 174, Bedford Hills, NY *10507*
  JUNIORS MR Oliver W . . . . |
Tudor MR & MRS Daniel H (Jeanice Eddy) . . . . | ☎ (619) 247-1635
  MR Geoffrey W . . . . | 14611 Flathead Rd, Apple Valley, CA *92307*
Tunnell MR & MRS Kenneth W (Joanne Huntington)
  ☎ (508) 693-3262 . . RFD 476T, Edgartown, MA *02539*
Turnbull MISS Connor E . . see W H Luers
Turnbull MRS Mary S (Mary M Slingluff)
  Camp Low Gear, Adirondack League Club, Little Moose Lake, Old Forge, NY *13420*
Turnbull MISS Ramsay F . . see W H Luers
Turnbull MRS Thomas 3d (Clara Howard)
  ☎ (315) 369-6537 . . "Overlook" Bisby Lake, Thendara, NY *13472*
Turner MR & MRS Arthur N (Anne L Grove) . . . . . | ☎ (207) 389-2586
  MR Arthur N JR . . . . | "Hidden Ledge" Small Point Rd, Phippsburg, ME *04562*
Turner MR & MRS Clifford O (Louise B Evans)
  ☎ (508) 325-4773 . . 1 Plumb Lane, Nantucket, MA *02554*
Turner MR & MRS James J 3d (Anica B Walker) . . . | ☎ (609) 492-2146
  MR David H . . . . | 121 Glendola Av, Beach Haven, NJ *08008*
Turner LT COL (RET) & MRS Robert F 3d (Patricia B Rhein) USA.
  ☎ (401) 294-2724 . . "South Meadow" Box 403, Saunderstown, RI *02874*
Turner MRS Theodore Francis (de Rham—Ruxton—Jackson—Ruth E Ledyard)
  ☎ (516) WA1-1175 . . Box 303, East Norwich, NY *11732*
Turner DR Thomas B
  ☎ (410) 255-0515 . . Gibson Island, MD *21056*
Turnure MRS David A (Marian V Wilson)
  ☎ (860) 435-2928 . . Box 33, Salisbury, CT *06068*
Turpin MR & MRS John K (Bigio—Margery S Dillon) . . . . | ☎ (508) 228-6510
  MR John D . . . . | 27 India St, Nantucket, MA *02554*
Tuten MR & MRS John C JR (Margaret G Evans) . . . | ☎ (508) 775-0487
  MISS Virginia E . . . . | "Merview" Hyannis Port, MA *02647*
  JUNIORS MR John C III . . . . |

Tuthill MR & MRS John B (Hillis—Elizabeth A Rice)
  ☎ (219) 753-3248 . . 7 Hickory Lane, Logansport, IN *46947*

Tutt MR & MRS William Bullard (Frances Campbell) | ☎ (970) 668-5590
  MR William Benjamin . . . . | "Uneva Lake"
                                                             | 1221 H'way 6,
                                                             | Frisco, CO *80443*

Twining MR & MRS Alexander C (Nell M Willis)
  ☎ (860) 434-2844 . . "Toad Hall" Sill Lane, Old Lyme, CT *06371*

Twining MR Edmund S 4th . . see M D Wheelock JR

Twining MR Taylor P . . see M D Wheelock JR

Twiss MR & MRS John R JR (Mary H Sheldon) . . . . . | ☎ (508) 563-3284
  MISS Alison M . . . . | 528 Scraggy Neck
  MISS Emily E . . . . | Rd, Scraggy Neck,
  MR John S . . . . | Cataumet, MA
                                                         | *02534*

Tyler MRS C Perin (Burling—Carnealia A Perin)
  ☎ (401) 348-8234 . . "Sea Crest" 7 Ninigret Av, Watch Hill, RI *02891*

Tyler MISS Cecily W . . see A T Ogden 2d

Tyler MISS Mary T . . see A T Ogden 2d

Tyler JUNIORS MR Wat H . . see A T Ogden 2d

Tyson MRS Anna Starr (Anna N Starr) . . . . | Aug 1 . .
  MISS Anna B . . . . | ☎ (401) 348-8833
                                                            | "Catlin Cottage"
                                                            | Watch Hill, RI
                                                            | *02891*

Tyson MR & MRS Charles R (Barbara Kurtz)
  ☎ (207) 244-3414 . . Box 36, Mt Desert, ME *04660*

Tyson MR & MRS Christopher G (Christiane J E Muller)
  ☎ (011-41-2) 154-1249 . . "Villa Mycena" Rte de St Maurice 146,
  1814 La Tour de Peilz, Switzerland

U

Ufford MR & MRS Charles W JR (I Letitia Wheeler)
  ☎ (207) 644-8864 . . High Island, South Bristol, ME *04568*

Uhle MRS Charles A W (Janet G Patterson)
  ☎ (603) 284-6693 . . "Boulder Brook Farm" 98 Range Rd,
  Center Sandwich, NH *03227*

Umstattd MR & MRS James M (Elizabeth M Coles)
  Ausable Club, Upper Lake, St Huberts, NY *12943*

Unger MR & MRS Peter J (Monica L Smith)
  ☎ (516) 283-5745 . . Hill St, PO Box 732, Southampton, NY *11969*

Upson MRS J Warren (Grace S Fisher)
  ☎ (508) 645-2293 . . "Upson Dunes" Chilmark, MA *02535*

Upton MR & MRS J Gordon (Barbara Allen) . . of
  ☎ (516) 583-8962 . . Ridge Cottage 76, Point O'Woods, NY *11706*
  ☎ (207) 439-1341 . . "The Creek" 76 Chauncey Creek Rd,
  Kittery Point, ME *03905*

Upton MR Richard W
  ☎ (860) 567-9272 . . 153 Norfolk Rd, PO Box 372, Litchfield, CT *06759*

Urban MR & MRS Henry Z (Ruth de M Wickwire)
  ☎ (508) 257-6264 . . Pitman Lane, Siasconset, MA *02564*

Urfer MR & MRS Richard P (Cynthia L Vaughan) . . . | ☎ (207) 276-3734
  MISS Jocelyn L . . . . | Seal Harbor, ME
  MISS Courtney V . . . . | *04675*
  MR Gilbert C F . . . . |

Urstadt MR & MRS James Jeffrey (Susan H Powers) . | ☎ (802) 763-7224
  MR Bryant E . . . . | Balla Machree Farm,
  MR Jeffrey J . . . . | Broad Brook Rd,
  JUNIORS MISS Elizabeth C . . . . | South Royalton, VT
                                                             | *05068*

Utgoff CAPT & MRS Vadym V (Miriam D Scott) USN.
  ☎ (207) 734-6740 . . "Crow Cove" Box 217, Islesboro,
  ME *04848-0217*

V

Vail MR & MRS Donald (Priscilla A Luke)
  ☎ (860) 535-1792 . . 100 Water St, Stonington, CT *06378*

Vail MRS Herman Lansing (Gleason—Mary L Frackelton)
  ☎ (616) 386-5255 . . "Indigo Reach" Box 95, Omena Point, MI *49674*

Vaill MR John A
  ☎ (860) 567-9240 . . 49 Old Mt Tom Rd, Bantam, CT *06750*

Valentine MR & MRS E Massie (Van Alen—Virginia Guest)
  ☎ (207) 734-6642 . . Dark Harbor, Islesboro, ME *04848*

Valentine MR & MRS John H (Elizabeth H Hiam)
  ☎ (603) 968-3363 . . "Burleigh Brae" Box 205, Holderness, NH *03245*

Valenzuela-Bock MR & MRS Alejandro (Anne A | ☎ (207) 276-3975
  Du Bois) . . . . | High Camp,
  MR Carroll A . . . . | PO Box 957,
  JUNIORS MR Andres . . . . | Peabody Dv,
                                                             | Northeast Harbor,
                                                             | ME *04662*

Valiunas, Dominicus R & Lynn, Letitia C
  Aug 1 . . ☎ (516) 283-2104 . . 45 Gin Lane, Southampton, NY *11968*

Van Alen MRS James H (Vanderlip—Candace B Alig)
  ☎ (401) 846-6564 . . "Avalon" Ocean Av, Newport, RI *02840*

Van Alen MR & MRS William L JR (Kanzler—Judith A Frost)
  ☎ (207) 276-3650 . . "Ox Ledge" Seal Harbor, ME *04675*

Van Antwerp MR & MRS Thomas B (Gypsie B Bear) | ☎ (334) 962-2446
  JUNIORS MISS Virginia O . . . . | "Perdido"
  JUNIORS MR Thomas B JR . . . . | 31490 Randolph Rd,
                                                            | Lillian, AL *36549*

van Buren MRS Elizabeth P (Elizabeth P Prince)
  ☎ (508) 356-3867 . . Argilla Rd, Ipswich, MA *01938*

van Daalen MR & MRS M Anthony E (Amy B Crocker)
  ☎ (516) 283-1874 . . 86 Post Lane, Southampton, NY *11968*

VandenBerg MR & MRS Peter H (Nancy G Todd)
  "Summerset" Neahtawanta, Traverse City, MI *49684*

Vanderbilt MR & MRS O De Gray (Frances M Philips)
  ☎ (516) 324-8314 . . Box 1251, East Hampton, NY *11937*

van der Burgh MR & MRS Charles E 3d (Marielle M Nijdam)
  ☎ (011-33-4) 440-97-32 . . "Château du Soupiseau" St Sauveur,
  60320 Béthisy-Ste Pierre, France

van der Hoeven MR & MRS Bernard J C JR
 (Josephine W Lane) . . . . | PO Box 18,
 MISS Annette W . . . . | Walpole, ME *04573*
 MISS Katrien J. . . . . |
Vanderlip MR & MRS Henrik N (Christina J Hoyt) ⚓
 ☎ (970) 925-2515 . . 35 Ute Place, Aspen, CO *81611*
Vanderpoel MR & MRS Wynant D 3d (Bishop—S Barrie Osborn)
 ☎ (518) 576-4574 . . Camp Comfort, Interbrook Rd, Keene Valley, NY *12943*
van der Voort MR & MRS Michael V M (Helen E Crane)
 ☎ (516) 286-4884 . . 18 Academy Lane, Bellport, NY *11713*
Van Dine MR & MRS Vance (Isabel E Brewster) ⚓
 ☎ (516) OR1-6091 . . Crescent Beach Rd, Glen Cove, NY *11542*
Van Dusen MR & MRS Lewis H 3d (Curtiss W Richardson)
 ☎ (717) 646-2588 . . Tiger Camp, Pocono Lake Preserve, PA *18348*
Van Ingen MR & MRS Lawrence B (Evelyn G Harris)
 ☎ (518) 327-3240 . . Good Hope Camp, Upper St Regis, NY *12945*
Van Lennep MRS Frederick Leas (Sprow—Mary E Hazen)
 ☎ (606) 231-6333 . . "Castleton House" 2469 Iron Works Pike, Lexington, KY *40511*
Van Natta MR Jason . . see MRS K H Buchanan
Vanneck MR & MRS William P (Scroggins—Margaret R Heffington)
 ☎ (203) 661-9606 . . 521 Riversville Rd, Greenwich, CT *06831*
Van Nest MR & MRS Dean G (Reigeluth—Joan A | ☎ (508) 945-9135
 Houlihan) . . . . | "The Bluff"
 MISS Kathleen F . . . . | Cove Hill,
  | Box 155,
  | North Chatham, MA
  | *02650*
Van Nest MR & MRS Dean G JR (Virginia K Kegg)
 ☎ (516) 583-5198 . . House 21, Point O'Woods, NY *11706*
van Orman MR & MRS Chandler L (Kendall | ☎ (406) 888-5649
 Wheeler) . . . . | "Oqui"
 MISS Robin . . . . | Box 210027,
 MR Cameron . . . . | Lake McDonald,
  | MT *59921*
  | . . MR absent
Van Rensselaer MR Charles A
 ☎ (970) 845-7500 . . "Poste Montane" Box 959, Avon, CO *81620*
Van Rensselaer MRS Knauth (Botsford—Anne W | 75 Dunemere Lane,
 Knauth) . . . . | East Hampton, NY
 MR Blake Botsford. . . . . | *11937*
van Roijen MR Christopher T . . of
 ☎ (540) 347-2407 . . "St Leonard's Farm" Rte 211, PO Box 814, Warrenton, VA *22186*
 ☎ (302) 539-6501 . . 95H Campbell Place, Ocean 8, Bethany Beach, DE *19930*
van Roijen MISS Laura W (de Vogel—Laura W van Roijen)
 ☎ (540) 347-6476 . . "St Leonard's Farm" Rte 211, PO Box 814, Warrenton, VA *22186*
Van Schoonhoven MR William L
 ☎ (905) 382-3876 . . "River House" 3999 Niagara P'kway, Stevensville, Ontario L0S 1S0, Canada

van Voorhees MR & MRS Clifford I III (Kathryn A | ☎ (516) 287-1489
 Mercer) . . . . | "Finbur Cottage"
 MISS Kathryn M . . . . | 26 Lenape Rd,
 JUNIORS MR Alexander P . . . . | Southampton,
  | NY *11968*
van Wagenberg MR & MRS Hannes F (Susan T Long)
 "Pigs in Clover" Polks Rd, Princess Anne, MD *21853*
Van Winkle MR & MRS Edgar B 2d (Staempfli—E Fordyce Ewing)
 ☎ (207) 422-3235 . . Sorrento, ME *04677*
Van Winkle MR & MRS Peter K (Prudence A | ☎ (603) 253-9011
 Bridges) . . . . | "Feng Shui"
 MISS Trintje A. . . . . | Harvard Point Rd,
 MISS Elizabeth P . . . . | Center Harbor, NH
  | *03226*
Vartanian MR & MRS Paul D (Christabel Kelly) . . . . | ☎ (516) 788-7770
 MISS Annabel K . . . . | "Beach Haven"
 MR Nishan P . . . . | Fishers Island, NY
  | *06390*
Vaughan MR & MRS Alan C (Patricia A Peterson) . . | ☎ (508) 257-4456
 MR Brian C . . . . | "Patience"
  | Box 245, Siasconset,
  | MA *02554*
Vaughan MR & MRS Curtis T 3d (Karen L McHugh)
 ☎ (210) 896-8034 . . 213 Lakewood Dv, Kerrville, TX *78028*
Vaughan MRS William L (Margaret Driggs)
 ☎ (207) 867-4643 . . "Choatside" North Haven, ME *04853*
Velge MR & MRS Bertrand (Catherine C Wright)
 ☎ (011-32-3) 685-1851 . . R M Van Havrelaan 405, 2900 Schoten, Belgium
Verkuil MRS Frances G (Frances H Gibson) . . . . . . | ☎ (910) 363-9178
 JUNIORS MR J Gibson. . . . . | 505 Ridge Rd,
  | Roaring Gap, NC
  | *28668*
Verkuil MR & MRS (DR) Paul R (Rodin—Niejelow—Judith Seitz)
 ☎ (410) 827-9407 . . "Wyefield" 701 Wye Hall Dv, Queenstown, MD *21658*
Vermeule MR & MRS Cornelius C 3d (Emily D | ☎ (201) 379-3818
 Townsend) . . . . | "Chatswold"
 MISS Emily D B . . . . | 75 Coniston Rd,
 MR C Adrian C . . . . | Short Hills, NJ
  | *07078*
Verner MR & MRS Elliott K (Joan S Howard)
 ☎ (518) 624-3845 . . Long Lake, NY *12847*
Verner MRS William K (Abbie L Sunde). . . . . | ☎ (518) 624-3840
 MISS Victoria S . . . . | The Camp,
  | Long Lake, NY
  | *12847*
Victor MR & MRS David (Copeland—Judith M | ☎ (520) 735-7252
 James) . . . . | Box 232, Greer, AZ
 MISS Laurie. . . . . | *85927*
 MR David . . . . |
 MR Andrew. . . . . |
Victor MRS Martin (Helene L Peters)
 ☎ (516) 676-1935 . . 15 Quail Ridge Rd, Glen Cove, NY *11542*
Vieta MRS John O (Henrietta E Countiss)
 ☎ (203) 259-4436 . . "Mine Acres" 2300 Bronson Rd, Fairfield, CT *06430*

Vietor MRS Alexander O (Anna G Butler) . . . . ☎ (508) 627-4654
    MR Andreas H . . . . "Grandma's
    JUNIORS MR Edward M . . . . House"
    31 S Water St, Edgartown, MA *02539*

Vietor MR & MRS Alexander W (Carol L Bancker) . . ☎ (508) 627-8586
    MISS Cornelia O . . . . S Water St,
    MISS Lindsay J . . . . Edgartown, MA
    JUNIORS MISS Anna B *02539*

Vietor MRS Julia B (Julia G Bastedo) . . . . ☎ (916) 587-0143
    MR John R . . . . "Cottage on Donner Lake" 15843 Southshore Dv, PO Box 10178, Truckee, CA *96162*

Vietor MR & MRS Richard R (Nicholls—Rosemary Schmitt) . . . . ☎ (508) 627-9519
    MISS Abigail F . . . . "Pagoda House" S Water St, Edgartown, MA *02539*

Villa MR & MRS G Paolo (Elena Bertozzi)
    ☎ (011-39) 321-518450 . . Via Madonna 13, Cameri, 28016 Novara, Italy

Vilter MRS Carl F (Elder—Barbara H Wood) . . . . . . ☎ (616) 256-7341
    MISS Alice L Elder . . . . "Whitegate" Box 713, Leland, MI *49654*

Vitagliano MISS Maria T (Pape—Skillin—Maria T Vitagliano) . . . . ☎ (203) 661-2722
    JUNIORS MISS Katrina V Pape . . . . "Villa Vitagliano" 52 Upland Dv, Greenwich, CT *06831-4451*

Vlietstra MR & MRS Klaas F (Dorothy T Royce)
    158 Emerald Bay, Laguna Beach, CA *92651*

Vogt MR & MRS Peter A (Nancy R Scharff)
    ☎ (401) 596-3074 . . "Out-of-Bounds" 150 Watch Hill Rd, Watch Hill, RI *02891*

Vogt MR William T JR
    ☎ (401) 348-8276 . . 3 Lighthouse Rd, Watch Hill, RI *02891*

Volkmann MRS William G JR (Smith—Orabelle S Carter)
    ☎ (805) 995-1450 . . 2780 Studio Dv, Cayucos, CA *93430*

von Gontard MR & MRS Adalbert JR (Marie E W Williams)
    ☎ (401) 348-8944 . . Sunnyledge Cottage, Ridge Rd, Watch Hill, RI *02891*

von Stade MR & MRS Frederick H (Carolyn L Carrier)
    ☎ (616) 386-7286 . . 64 Northport Point, Northport, MI *49670*

von Stade MR & MRS John T (Sandra K Carnahan)
    ☎ (518) 583-1332 . . "Birch Run" 17 Saratoga Circle, Saratoga, NY *12866*

von Waldow MR & MRS Bernd (Maria Theresia Shrady) . . . . "Doniesenhof" Altaussee 26, Styria, Austria
    MISS Maria Donata
    JUNIORS MISS Maria Christina . . . .
    JUNIORS MISS Maria Benedicta . . . .

von Weise MR Bradford L
    "Wendy's Way" 11 York St, Nantucket, MA *02554*

von Weise MR & MRS W Gage JR (McCay—Meyer—June C Oltmans) . . . . ☎ (314) 629-3626
    MISS Eliza F Meyer . . . . "Piney" 1655 Michie Lane,
    MR Andrew T McCay . . . . St Clair, MO *63077*

von Zweck MR & MRS Heimart (Laura B Pollock) ⚓
    ☎ (617) 354-3385 . . on board Allegra" Marion, MA *02738*

Vose MR & MRS Elliott E (Murphy—Ann Cogswell) . ☎ (516) 653-4574
    MISS Esmé C Murphy . . . . Old Point Rd, Box 442, Quogue, NY *11959*

W

Wack MR & MRS Patrick J JR (Laura H Sculley)
    ☎ (207) 236-2965 . . 152 Bayview St, Camden, ME *04843*

Wacker MR & MRS Frederick G JR (Ursula Comandatore) . . . . ☎ (847) 234-2833
    MISS Wendy . . . . 1600 Green Bay Rd, Lake Bluff, IL
    MR Joseph C *60044*

Wade MR & MRS George J (Gwendolen B Livermore) . . . . ☎ (802) 496-2839
    MISS Barbara C . . . . "Forest Hill" Box 487, Waitsfield,
    MR George J . . . . VT *05660*

Wadsworth MR & MRS Dyer S (Beverley A D Barringer) . . . . ☎ (207) 422-3830
    MISS Sophia B . . . . "Bayview" PO Box 52, Bay Av, Hancock Point, ME
    MISS Jennifer S *04640*

Wadsworth MR & MRS Eugene D (Elizabeth E Frothingham)
    ☎ (802) 362-3326 . . Box 641, River Rd, Manchester, VT *05254*

Waggaman MRS Robert M (Welles—Le Breton—Adèle Harman)
    ☎ (508) 627-5545 . . "The Growlery" PO Box 5093, Edgartown, MA *02539*

Waggaman MR & MRS William (Daphne H Geary)
    ☎ (508) 627-8886 . . "The Roadhouse" PO Box 5093, Edgartown, MA *02539*

Wagner MR & MRS Samuel (Mary Ann G G Baker) . ☎ (508) 228-2628
    MR Michael C . . . . Nantucket, MA *02554*

Wainwright MR & MRS Carroll L (Nina Walker)
    ☎ (516) 324-0312 . . 57 Dunemere Lane, East Hampton, NY *11937*

Wainwright MRS Parsons (Janet I Parsons) . . . . ☎ (516) 537-1509
    MISS Belle B Waring . . . . "Cove Cottage"
    MR Benjamin A Waring . . . . PO Box 199, Wainscott, NY *11975*

Wainwright MR & MRS Peter S (Gerri F Jordan)
    ☎ (520) 526-9344 . . "Duckwood" 4849 E Hightimber Lane, Flagstaff, AZ *86004*

Wainwright MR & MRS Stuyvesant 3d (Marcella C Mittendorf)
    ☎ (516) 324-0139 . . 16 Fithian Lane, East Hampton, NY *11937*

Wait MRS William G (Ann B Frothingham)
    ☎ (518) 644-9674 . . "Eagle's Nest" Bolton Landing, NY *12814*

Wakefield MRS G Kennard (Mary M Binney)
    "Knollcroft" Rte 113A, Wonalancet, Tamworth, NH *03886*

Walbridge MR & MRS Kenneth M (Jean Palmer)
☎ (207) 633-2096 . . PO Box 131, Boothbay, ME *04537*

Walbridge MR & MRS Ryckman R (Karen R Monaghan) . . . .
  MISS Kimberly W . . . .
☎ (207) 863-4983 Calderwood Neck, Vinalhaven, ME *04863*

Walcott MISS Alexandra (Wahl—Alexandra Walcott)
☎ (860) 542-5292 . . Windrow Rd, Norfolk, CT *06058*

Walker MRS Bayard (Maud Tilghman)
☎ (516) 324-1095 . . ''Normandie'' Lily Pond Lane, Box 139, East Hampton, NY *11937*

Walker MRS Benjamin H (Elizabeth Sillcocks)
Bayberry Hill Rd, Cuttyhunk, MA *02713*

Walker MR & MRS Brian D (Abby M Gross)
☎ (207) 725-6025 . . 3089 Mere Point Rd, Brunswick, ME *04011*

Walker MRS Brooks (Marjory E Walker)
☎ (916) 583-3211 . . ''Brookswood'' Box 56, Tahoe City, CA *95730*

Walker MR & MRS C Carter JR (Julia B Armour) . . .
  MISS Julia B . . . .
☎ (518) 576-4572 ''Lone Pine'' PO Box 731, Keene Valley, NY *12943*

Walker MR & MRS James A S (Alexandra R Forbes)
☎ (207) 867-2271 . . ''Mouse House'' Pulpit Harbor, North Haven, ME *04853*

Walker MR & MRS John D (Roskam—Schaedtler—Helen Hoogerwerff)
''The Salt Box'' Tuckernuck Island, Nantucket, MA *02554*

Walker MRS L Gordon 3d (Cara C Smith) . . . .
  MISS Page E . . . .
  MR L Gordon 4th . . . .
☎ (207) 534-7355 ''Flatlander Lodge'' Rockwood, ME *04478*

Walker MR & MRS Louis (Grace B White)
☎ (207) 967-5759 . . ''Inglesea'' Box 1508, Kennebunkport, ME *04046*

Walker MRS Lucinda S (Niehoff—Lucinda K Schaefer) . . . .
    MISS Kelly B Niehoff . . . .
    MR K Richard B Niehoff JR . . . .
☎ (508) 775-4755 67 Irving Av, Hyannis Port, MA *02647*

Walker MR & MRS Mallory (Diana Hardin)
☎ (208) 726-8095 . . 140 River Rock Rd, Ketchum, ID *83340-1206*

Walker DR & MRS Michael D (E Katherine Law)
☎ (617) 545-2496 . . The Glades, Glades Rd, Minot, MA *02055*

Walker MR & MRS Norman S (Marie Eve Cournand)
  MISS Anne . . . .
  MR Norman S JR . . . .
  MR Alan S . . . .
☎ (413) 628-3387 ''Farmhouse'' Hawley Rd, Ashfield, MA *01330*

Walker MISS Pamela Buchanan (Potts—Pamela Buchanan Walker)
☎ (516) 283-7454 . . ''Tides End'' Gin Lane, Southampton, NY *11968*

Walker MR & MRS Robert A JR (Monique M Briend)
  JUNIORS MISS Charlotte M E . . . .
☎ (011-33) 96-31-02-85 3 rue du Jeu-de-Paume, PO Box 541, 22400 Lamballe, France

Walker MR & MRS W Wyatt JR (Wood—Hunter—Daphne Dodge)
☎ (508) 257-6354 . . ''Sea Wing'' 17 Low Beach Rd, Box 222, Siasconset, MA *02564*

Walker MISS Whitney H . . see MRS L H Newman

Walker MR & MRS William B (Ruth E Lennard)
☎ (011-39-564) 82-40-38 . . ''Villa Le Mimose'' Porto Santo Stefano, Italy

Walkup MR & MRS Richard L (Jean L Gilbert)
☎ (717) 525-3246 . . ''Eagles Edge Roadhouse'' Allegheny Av, Eagles Mere, PA *17731*

Wall MRS Albert Carey (Fincke—Virginia D Gardner)
☎ (516) 788-7545 . . Halcyon Av, Fishers Island, NY *06390*

Wall MR & MRS H Peter (Patricia Allen) . . . .
  MR Alexander M . . . .
☎ (609) 924-2850 130 Westcott Rd, Princeton, NJ *08540*

Wallace MRS Constance H (Rockefeller—Constance V Hamilton)
☎ (302) 658-4096 . . Box 4451, 122 Brook Valley Rd, Greenville, DE *19807*

Wallace MR & MRS J Berry (McAdam—Anne C Harrison)
☎ (508) 526-1740 . . ''Old Tree House'' 4 Boardman Av, Manchester-By-The-Sea, MA *01944*

Wallace MR & MRS John C (Mary O Willson)
☎ (716) 789-3715 . . 4417 Canterbury Dv, Chautauqua Shores, Mayville, NY *14757*

Wallace MR & MRS Neil W (Elise Raymond)
''Highlands Farm'' Vaill Rd, Yarmouth, ME *04096*

Waller MR & MRS Harold E JR (M Lisa Bowen)
☎ (011-51-1) 992-8584 . . ''Punta Hermosa'' Playa Blanca, Punta Hermosa, Peru

Waller MR & MRS John W 3d (Alexis P Robinson)
☎ (908) 892-5884 . . 15 Harris St, Bay Head, NJ *08742*

Waller MRS Thomas M (Wilhelmine S Kirby)
☎ (914) 666-5965 . . ''Tanrackin Farm'' Box 457, Bedford Hills, NY *10507*
Aug 1 . . ☎ (518) 583-4546 . . 3 Ward St, Saratoga Springs, NY *12866*

Wallick MR & MRS Philip B (Joan A M Carnevali)
☎ (603) 323-8837 . . 313 Quaker-Whiteface Rd, North Sandwich, NH *03259*

Wallis MR James T 2d
☎ (207) 460-4045 . . ''Round Island'' Box 370, Bass Harbor, ME *04653*

Wallis MR & MRS Robert C (James—Margaret P Bodine) . . . .
  MR Nathaniel T . . . .
    MR William D James . . . .
☎ (508) 281-2385 6 Leonard St, Gloucester, MA *01930*

Wallop MR & MRS Malcolm (Goodwyn—French C Gamble)
☎ (307) 674-6086 . . ''Canyon Ranch'' Big Horn, WY *82833*

Walmsley MRS Robert M (Virginia Johnston)
☎ (207) 276-5060 . . ''Ledge Rock'' Northeast Harbor, ME *04662*

Walsh MR & MRS Edward F (Grace H Salt)
☎ (905) 835-8544 . . Lorraine, RR 1, Port Colborne, Ontario L3K 5V3, Canada

Walsh CAPT & MRS Eric F (Caroline E McK Earle) USMC.
☎ (401) 783-8920 . . . ''Twin Gables'' 352 Ocean Rd, Narragansett, RI *02882*

Walsh MR & MRS Frederick R JR (Hope I Mauran)
☎ (207) 363-0570 . . General Delivery, York Harbor, ME *03911*

Walsh MR & MRS Laurence S (Ellen Scott) . . . .
  MISS Margaret L . . . .
  MR James H . . . .
109 Featherbed Lane, Nonquitt, MA *02748*

Webb MR & MRS William M (Bottomley—Patricia Diamond)
☎ (609) 368-2371 . . 234—121 St, Stone Harbor, NJ *08247*

Weber MR & MRS Douglas J (Carey U Mack)
☎ (508) 945-0306 . . 195 Bridge St, Chatham, MA *02633*

Weber MRS John J (Levenson—Helen B Freeman)
☎ (860) 399-5264 . . "Witch Wood" 489 Stevenstown Rd, Westbrook, CT *06498*

Webster MRS Bethuel M (Case—M Elizabeth Wylie)
☎ (860) 379-2946 . . "Windrush" RR 1, 152 Grantville Rd, Winsted, CT *06098*

Webster MR & MRS Daniel E (Mollie E K Cooper) . . | Manor Farm,
MISS Camilla E . . . . | Framingham, Woodbridge, Suffolk, England

Webster MR & MRS David Z (Janie S Huntley) . . . . . | ☎ (603) 526-2216
MR C Scott . . . . | 25 Highland Ridge, New London, NH *03257*

Webster MR & MRS Henry C (Elizabeth Slater)
☎ (717) 646-8042 . . "Salt Lick" Stoddardsville, Star Rte, Blakeslee, PA *18610*

Webster MR & MRS James G 4th (Valerie H Minton)
Aug 1 . . ☎ (406) 995-2632 . . "Elkhorn Ranch" 33133 Gallatin Rd, Gallatin Gateway, MT *59715*

Webster MR & MRS Jerome P JR (Patterson— | ☎ (809) 639-8613
Rockefeller—Anne C Sammis) . . . . | "Southern Cruz
MISS Marcella D . . . . | Plantation" Great
MISS Brooke E . . . . | Cruz Bay, Box 37,
MR Hunter McA . . . . | St John, VI *00831*

Webster DR & MRS (DR) John C (Jancar—Barbara Wolfe)
☎ (518) 494-4442 . . Donovan Farm, Chestertown, NY *12817*

Webster MR & MRS Richard G (Marguerite A Brush)
☎ (609) 492-2023 . . "Come Aboard" 704 S Beach Av, Beach Haven, NJ *08008-1612*

Weed MR & MRS Arthur H (Karoleonko—Natalia S Akulinichev)
☎ (011-7-812) 268-70-46 . . Turku St 26-105, St Petersburg, Russia

Weed MRS Barbara L (Barbara McD Lewis) . . . . . . | ☎ (508) 771-5538
MR Joseph J 2d . . . . | "Strawberry
MR Edward L . . . . | Cottage" 649 Scudder Av, Hyannis Port, MA *02647*

Weedon MR & MRS Alexander R (Elizabeth L Warner)
☎ (508) 627-4468 . . PO Box 635, 9 Lenssen Way, Edgartown, MA *02539*

Weedon MRS William Stone (Elizabeth du P Bayard)
3 Cliff Rd, Nantucket, MA *02554*

Weekley MR & MRS Richard W (Margaret E Neuhaus)
☎ (409) 737-2804 . . 4246 Sandpiper Lane, Galveston, TX *77553*

Weeks MR & MRS Gerald C (Nancy K Allen)
☎ (516) 367-8428 . . 1592 Laurel Hollow Rd, Laurel Hollow, NY *11791*

Weems MR & MRS F Carrington 2d (Mary Ann | ☎ (713) 471-6455
Sledge) . . . . | "Mildendo"
MISS Mathilde S . . . . | 2019 Broadway, La Porte, TX *77571*

Weicker MRS Marie Godfrey (Marie Louise | ☎ (508) 748-2374
Godfrey) . . . . | 91 Water St,
MR Brian B . . . . | Marion, MA *02738*

Weil MR & MRS Frank A (Denie P Sandison) . . . . . | ☎ (207) 367-5008
MISS Amanda E . . . . | Grog Island,
MR Sandison E . . . . | Stonington, ME
MR William S . . . . | *04681*

Weil MRS Peter (Susan S F Cooper) . . . . | ☎ (607) 547-8433
MISS Sara S . . . . | RD 2, Box 72,
MR Henry F C . . . . | Cooperstown, NY *13326*

Weinberger MR & MRS Caspar W (Jane Dalton)
☎ (207) 244-7149 . . "Windswept" Somesville, Mt Desert, ME *04660*

Weiss MR & MRS William D (Robin B Martin) . . . . . | ☎ (616) 238-9321
MR William U . . . . | "Bide-A-Wee"
JUNIORS MISS Katrina D . . . . | Columbus Beach Club, 3698 W Loren St, Indian River, MI *49749*

Welch MISS (DR) Martha G (Horan—Martha G | ☎ (716) 357-2483
Welch) . . . . | "Kimball House"
JUNIORS MR T Bramwell Welch Horan . . . . . . | 23 Morris Av, Chautauqua, NY *14722*

Weld MRS A Matthew (Jacqueline Bograd)
☎ (914) 763-8258 . . 128 Kitchawan Rd, Pound Ridge, NY *10576*

Weld MR A Matthew
"Bocaditos" 2305 Ponce De Leon Blvd, Coral Gables, FL *33134*

Weld MR & MRS Christopher (Mary E D'Aprix)
☎ (508) 526-1532 . . "Harbor View Hill" 21A School St, Manchester, MA *01944*

Weld MR & MRS William G JR (Ellen L Carleton) . . . | ☎ (508) 420-0503
MR William G 3d . . . . | "Wind 'n Sea"
MR Edward K . . . . | 878 Sea View Av, Wianno, MA *02655*

Wellborn MR & MRS John Bennett (Kelly G Dunnam)
☎ (616) 256-9619 . . "Wildwood" Box 13, Leland, MI *49654*

Wellborn MR & MRS Robert H (Sylvia P Palmer)
☎ (616) 256-9619 . . "Wildwood" Box 13, Leland, MI *49654*

Wellborn MR & MRS Robert H JR (Kathryn S Brockett) . . of
☎ (616) 256-9619 . . 385 Birdsong Rd, Leland, MI *49654*
☎ (904) 363-0252 . . 9915 Vineyard Lake Lane, Jacksonville, FL *32256*

Weller MR & MRS Frank H JR (Keyser—Eleanor J | ☎ (508) 228-0140
Constable) . . . . | 41 India St,
MISS Eleanor W . . . . | Nantucket, MA *02554*

Welles MR & MRS Arnold (Dana E Ogden)
☎ (508) 627-9281 . . Star Rte 178, Edgartown, MA *02539*

Welles MR & MRS Edward R 3d (Anne E La Hines) . . | ☎ (207) 244-5015
⚓ . . . . | Oceanus,
MISS Laura . . . . | Southwest Harbor,
MR William B v A . . . . | ME *04679*

Welles MR & MRS Jeffrey F (Maud D Iselin)
☎ (516) 624-6817 . . 202 Sunset Rd, Oyster Bay Cove, NY *11771*

Welles MR & MRS Peter de L (Anna Roberts) ⛵ .. | ☎ (207) 244-3941
  MISS Suzanne R .... | "Heron View"
  JUNIORS MR Peter de L JR .... | 355 Seawall Rd,
  | Manset, ME *04679*
Wellesley MR & MRS Robin A (Marianne McDonald)
  ☎ (011-44-1732) 86-2251.. "Shingle Barn" Dwelly Lane, Edenbridge, Kent, England
Welling MR & MRS W Lambert (Louise A Partridge) | ☎ (401) 884-5905
  MR Andrew L .... | "Waremoana"
  MR C David .... | Pojac Point,
  | North Kingstown, RI
  | *02852*
Wells MR Christopher J
  "The Grange" Melbourne, Yorkshire YO4 4SX, England
Wells MR David Q (Jean Kiley)
  ☎ (508) 428-6269.. 207 Crystal Lake Rd, Osterville, MA *02655*
Wells MRS James L 3d (Ann V P Radcliff) .... | ☎ (908) 899-6612
  MISS Lee R .... | 32 Strickland St,
  | Bay Head, NJ *08742*
Wells MR & MRS Peter Scoville (Patricia A Trent)
  ☎ (610) 388-6286.. "Firefly" PO Box 244, Chadds Ford, PA *19317*
Welsh MR & MRS Donald E (Elizabeth B Floyd).... | ☎ (518) 329-4832
  MISS Leah B .... | Boston Corners,
  | Millerton, NY *12546*
Welsh MR & MRS John E 3d (Dreyfous—Andrée E Devendorf)
  ☎ (516) 537-5456.. Wheaton Way, Water Mill, NY *11976*
Welsh MR & MRS John L JR (Phoebe Cook) ⛵
  ☎ (207) 633-4725.. "Timothy Hill" River Rd, Box 505, Boothbay, ME *04537*
Wendell MR David R
  ☎ (508) 768-7868.. Conomo Point, Essex, MA *01929*
Wendell MR & MRS Harlan L P (Dorothea Richardson)
  ☎ (508) 768-7868.. Conomo Point, Essex, MA *01929*
Wendell MRS John W (Nancy W Crompton)
  ☎ (508) 548-1261.. Box 363, Chapoquoit Island, West Falmouth, MA *02574*
Werner MR & MRS Charles P (Shelby I | ☎ (914) 855-9080
  Schoonmaker) .... | 111 N Quaker Hill
  JUNIORS MR Nicholas B .... | Rd, Pawling, NY
  | *12564*
Werner MRS Charles S (Mary E Portfolio)
  ☎ (516) 283-4260.. Shinnecock Hills Golf Club, 2 North H'way, Southampton, NY *11968*
Werner MRS L Matthews (Margaret Steele)
  ☎ (207) 583-4700.. Camp Ironwood, Rte 2, Box 716, Harrison, ME *04040*
Werwaiss MR & MRS John A (Beth Nielsen)....... | ☎ (516) 671-5105
  MISS Gretchen N .... | Peacock Point,
  MR John A JR .... | Lattingtown, NY
  JUNIORS MR Christian W .... | *11560*
West MISS Anne N
  ☎ (717) 646-2252.. S Shore Rd, Pocono Lake Preserve, PA *18348*
West MR & MRS Ralph O'Neal (Mary D Anthony)
  "Rock Point Landing" New London, NH *03257*

West MR & MRS Stephen K (Ann L Wick) .... | ☎ (508) 257-4003
  MR Daniel W—☎ (508) 257-4549 .... | Box 56, McKinley
  | Av, Siasconset, MA
  | *02564*
West MRS William Nelson (Edith T Harris)
  ☎ (307) 455-2705.. Trail Lake Ranch, Dubois, WY *82513*
Westerfield MR F Bradford
  ☎ (401) 348-1002.. "Wickiup" 12 Westerly Rd, Watch Hill, RI *02891*
Westervelt MR & MRS Peter J (Alice F Brown)..... | ☎ (401) 463-8781
  MR Dirck E............................ | "White House"
  | 600 Spring Green
  | Rd, Warwick, RI
  | *02888*
Westfeldt MR & MRS Thomas D 2d (Linda S Hawthorne)
  ☎ (704) 687-2935.. "Rugby Grange" Fannings Bridge Rd, Fletcher, NC *28732*
Westmoreland GEN & MRS William C (Katherine S Van Deusen) USA.
  ☎ (704) 733-2912.. "Caisson" Box 1168, Linville, NC *28646*
Wetherill MRS Leonore S (Smith—Gibson—Leonore Smart)
  ☎ (508) 228-5620.. 4 School St, Nantucket, MA *02554*
Wetherill MR Peter W
  Apr 1.. ☎ (610) 356-1805.. "Happy Hill Farm" 912 N Providence Rd, Newtown Square, PA *19073*
Wetherill MR Ramsay
  ☎ (401) 423-0385.. "Spindrift" 50 Bayview Dv, PO Box 475, Jamestown, RI *02835*
Wetherill MRS Samuel P (Jewett—Alice Groom Constable)
  ☎ (508) 228-0611.. "Beach Plum" 45 Hulbert Av, Nantucket, MA *02554*
Wetherill MR & MRS Stephen H (Hatter—Susan Sallada)
  ☎ (207) 832-4275.. 860 Deaver Rd, Waldoboro, ME *04572*
Wharton DR & MRS Lawrence R JR (Alison A de Ropp)
  ☎ (207) 787-2854.. East Sebago, ME *04029*
Wheatland MR & MRS Richard (Cynthia N McAdoo)
  ☎ (207) 422-6760.. "Grey Deck" Sorrento, ME *04677*
Wheeler MR & MRS Alexander B JR (Parry—Deborah N Trench).. of
  ☎ (207) 244-3389.. "Rest Harrow" Mt Desert, ME *04660*
  ☎ (508) 775-0368.. PO Box 395, Hyannis Port, MA *02467*
Wheeler MISS Deirdre W
  ☎ (315) 369-6410.. Adirondack League Club, PO Box 8, Little Moose Lake, Old Forge, NY *13420*
Wheeler MR & MRS George Y 2d (Orthwein—Katherine B Gatch)
  ☎ (401) 348-8920.. "Aerie" 12 Ridge Rd, Watch Hill, RI *02891*
Wheeler MR & MRS James G (Mary E Lowell) ..... | ☎ (617) 581-0826
  MR William H .... | 9 Swallow Cave Rd,
  MR Jonathan L .... | Nahant, MA *01908*
Wheeler MRS Leonard (Cornelia Balch)
  ☎ (603) 323-8823.. Chocorua, NH *03817*
Wheeler MR Murray JR
  ☎ (315) 369-6410.. Adirondack League Club, PO Box 8, Little Moose Lake, Old Forge, NY *13420*
Wheeler DR & MRS Paul S (Barbara J Bradley)..... | ☎ (508) 548-2389
  MR Bradley E .... | 9 Quissett Av,
  | Woods Hole, MA
  | *02543*

Wheeler MR & MRS Thomas B (Anne T Robertson) .
 MISS Wendy B . . . . | ☎ (508) 540-2244
"Snug Harbor House"
22 Nashawena St,
PO Box 33,
Falmouth, MA
02574

Wheeler DR & MRS William M (Beatrice B Nickerson)
 ☎ (508) 548-2917 . . 3 Quissett Av, Woods Hole, MA *02543*

Wheelock DR & MRS E Frederick (M Jean Lowery)
 ☎ (609) 494-3423 . . 351 Dusty Miller Dv, Lovelladies, NJ *08008*

Wheelock MR & MRS George F (Elisabeth A Martin)
 MR Austin W . . . .
 MR Philippe M . . . . | "Santa Clara"
Estartit, Gerona,
Spain

Wheelock MR & MRS Morgan Dix JR (Twining—
 Judith K Taylor) . . . .
 MR Edmund S Twining 4th . . . .
 MR Taylor P Twining . . . . | ☎ (207) 276-5204
"Isis"
Harborside Rd,
Northeast Harbor,
ME *04662*

Wheelock MR Thomas G B
 ☎ (516) 537-3648 . . Bridgehampton, NY *11932*

Wheelwright MISS Elizabeth B
 ☎ (508) 228-0633 . . 49 Squam Rd, Nantucket, MA *02554*

Wheelwright MR & MRS Henry C (Celeste M Adams)
 ☎ (207) 363-7665 . . "Rock Ledge" Box 1193, York Harbor, ME *03911*

Whipple MRS Hope A (Hope Auchincloss)
 ☎ (508) 627-9567 . . 114 N Water St, Edgartown, MA *02539*

Whitaker MRS John T (Patricia C Pettengill)
 ☎ (508) 945-9537 . . Box 1235, 86 Plum Daffy Lane, West Chatham, MA *02669*

Whitbeck MR & MRS B Hunt JR (S Katherine
 Oechler) . . . .
 JUNIORS MISS Caroline N . . . .
 JUNIORS MR Brainerd H 3d . . . . | ☎ (516) 653-4625
"Far East"
Box 672, Quogue,
NY *11959*

Whitcraft MR & MRS Edward T (Susan K Runyon) .
 MISS Samantha R . . . . | "Grouse House"
North Woods Club,
Minerva, NY *12851*

White MR & MRS Alexander W (Anne H Meissner) .
 MISS Cynthia N . . . .
 JUNIORS MR Alexander W JR . . . . | ☎ (802) 453-3991
Rte 17,
South Starksboro,
VT *05487*

White MR & MRS C Stuart JR (Matilda B Romaine) . .
 MISS Laura B . . . .
 MR Cleveland S 3d . . . . | ☎ (508) 548-1081
"Windymoor"
34 Chapoquoit Rd,
Box 35,
West Falmouth, MA
02574

White MR & MRS Edgar P E (Dorothy Jeanne Fuhrer)
 ☎ (908) 295-1836 . . "Overflow" 1225 Bay Av, Mantoloking, NJ *08738*

White MR & MRS Harold T (Penelope Weld) ⚓
 ☎ (508) 540-1104 . . 40 Associates Rd, Box 11, West Falmouth, MA *02574*

White MISS Mary B
 1793—12 St, Oakland, CA *94607*

White MR & MRS Michael B (Virginia G Burke)
 ☎ (401) 635-4402 . . 26 Atlantic Av, Little Compton, RI *02837*

White MR & MRS Michael M (Vignes—Nadège de Brantes)
 Rum Point, Grindstone Island, Clayton, NY *13624*

White MR & MRS Ogden JR (Bonnie Donnell Richardson)
 ☎ (207) 883-7020 . . "Eastern Point" 26 Jocelyn Rd, Prouts Neck, ME *04074*

White MR & MRS Pendleton P (Julia S Clarke) . . . . .
 MISS Anne C . . . . | ☎ (508) 627-5397
Box 5131,
Edgartown, MA
02539

White MR & MRS R Quincy JR (D Joyce Caldwell) . .
 MISS Annelia E . . . . | ☎ (616) 469-5127
10945 Marquette
Rd, New Buffalo,
MI *49117*

White MR & MRS Robert H 2d (Katherine S West)
 ☎ (516) 788-1439 . . "West Harbor House" Fishers Island, NY *06390*

White MRS Sumner W JR (Virginia Earle)
 ☎ (908) 899-0084 . . "Midway" 1317 Bay Av, Box 901, Mantoloking, NJ *08738*

White MRS Sumner W 3d (Eleanor C Phillips) . . . . .
 MR Timothy P . . . . | ☎ (908) 295-1836
"Overflow"
1225 Bay Av,
Mantoloking, NJ
08738

White MR & MRS Thomas W 4th (Joan W Woods)
 Hulbert Av, Nantucket, MA *02554*

White MRS William B (Virginia L Rutter)
 ☎ (860) 667-9714 . . 95 Mountain View Dv, Newington, CT *06111*

Whitehurst DR Walter R 3d
 ☎ (011-44-1225) 317964 . . 14 Marlborough Bldg, Bath, Avon BA1 2LX, England

Whiteley MR & MRS George C 3d (Hamilton—Jeanne E Stockman)
 ☎ (508) 257-6187 . . "What Odds" 93 Sankaty Rd, PO Box 451, Siasconset, MA *02564*

Whiteman MR & MRS Daniel S JR (Dorothy H Ritterbush)
 ☎ (603) 569-5337 . . "Loon Lodge" Box 1919, Wolfeboro, NH *03894*

Whiteman MR & MRS H Clifton (Leib—Joan E Coffin)
 ☎ (518) 589-5583 . . "Southerly" Onteora Club, Tannersville, NY *12485*

Whiting MRS Richard G (Rosemary Menzies-Wilson)
 ☎ (508) 693-0591 . . 12 Cleveland Av, Vineyard Haven, MA *02568*

Whitman MR & MRS Charles S JR (Janet Russell) . . .
 MISS Janet . . . . | ☎ (401) 348-8750
"Snug Harbor"
15 Breen Rd,
Watch Hill, RI
02891

Whitman MR & MRS Ian M (Marie P de Valois
 de St Aymour) . . . .
 MR Edouard . . . .
 JUNIORS MR Alfred . . . . | ☎ (011-33)
21-85-70-32
"Château de la
Palme" 62370
Nortkerque, France

Whitman MR & MRS Johnston de F (Christina B
 Rand) . . . .
 MISS Susan D . . . .
 MR Johnston de F JR . . . . | ☎ (207) 963-5858
Main St,
Winter Harbor, ME
04693

Whitman MR Lawrence B
 ☎ (516) 584-5508 . . Driftwood Lane, RR 1, Box 110-3, St James, NY *11780*

Whitman MRS Peter M (F Elizabeth Blodget)
☎ (508) 228-9239 . . "Hawk Moor" PO Box 2266, Nantucket, MA 02584

Whitman MR & MRS R Eugene (Daphne Tewksbury) | ☎ (508) 996-5901
MR Ralph E JR . . . . | "The Rock"
| Washburn Lane,
| Nonquitt, MA 02748

Whitman MR & MRS Robert F (Marina von Neumann)
☎ (508) 295-8222 . . 34 Long Beach Way, Wareham, MA 02571

Whitman MR & MRS Stephen L (Susan C Watson)
☎ (207) 867-2019 . . "Oak Hill Farm" North Haven, ME 04853

Whitmer MR & MRS Robert F 3d (Mary Leigh Pell) . | ☎ (516) 653-6813
MR Robert F 4th . . . . | General Delivery,
MR Walden P . . . . | Quogue, NY 11959
MR John L . . . . |

Whitney MRS Alexandra E (Alexandra Ewing)
☎ (207) 422-9030 . . "Captain's House" Sorrento, ME 04677

Whitney MRS Cornelius Vanderbilt (Hosford—Marie L Schroeder)
☎ (518) 584-2166 . . "Cady Hill House" 40 Geyser Rd, Saratoga Springs, NY 12866

Whitney MR & MRS Edward B (Stover—Martha C Howell) . . . . | ☎ (802) 525-3571
JUNIORS MR William H . . . . | "New Dublin
JUNIORS MR John H . . . . | Farm" RR 3,
| Box 111, Barton,
| VT 05822

Whitney MRS Frances J (Frances J Lannon)
☎ (860) 355-0722 . . Evan's Hill Rd, Sherman, CT 06784

Whitney MR & MRS Gifford C (Francine C Douwes)
Sorrento, ME 04677

Whitney MR & MRS Thomas H P (Horst—Remick—Margaret Boney)
☎ (508) 758-3356 . . 2 Ship St, Box 483, Mattapoisett, MA 02739-0483

Whitridge MR & MRS Roland W (Sarah E Lincoln) . | ☎ (603) 544-3893
MR Bradford S . . . . | "On the Rocks"
JUNIORS MR Stoddard L . . . . | Bald Peak Colony
| Club, Box 163,
| Melvin Village, NH
| 03850

Whitridge MRS William C (Emmy L Phillips)
☎ (409) 597-4641 . . "Dobbins Farm" Dobbin, TX 77333

Whittelsey MR & MRS Frank C 3d (Margaret A Gerli)
☎ (802) 496-2088 . . PO Box 419, Waitsfield, VT 05673

Whittemore MR & MRS Allen W (Terry A McIlvaney)
☎ (616) 526-2492 . . 5229 Windward Passage, Harbor Springs, MI 49740

Whittemore MR & MRS Frederick B (Marion Willi) . . of
☎ (401) 322-7595 . . 29 Knowles Av, Weekapaug, RI 02891
☎ (401) 348-8392 . . 72 Ocean View H'way, Watch Hill, RI 02891

Whittemore MR & MRS Laurence F 3d (Kathleen A Mackay)
☎ (401) 322-7595 . . 29 Knowles Av, Weekapaug, RI 02891

Whittemore CAPT & MRS Robert M (Margaret A Burrows) USN.
☎ (508) 283-0634 . . "The Homestead" 125 Cole's Island Rd, West Gloucester, MA 01930-1507

Wick MR & MRS Henry C 3d (Hart—Barbara A Ireland) . . . . | ☎ (714) 376-9073
MISS Virginia Chandler . . . . | "Glory Be II"
MISS Alyssa . . . . | Emerald Bay,
MR Alexander Henry . . . . | Laguna Beach, CA
| 92651

Wick MR & MRS Kent D (Jerre L Barber)
☎ (520) 368-5739 . . Misty Mountain Estates, Lakeside, Pinetop, AZ 85935

Wick MRS Myron A JR (Elizabeth L Dillingham)
☎ (203) 531-0062 . . 216 W Lyon Farm Dv, Greenwich, CT 06831

Wick MR & MRS Peter A (Kathleen Lord)
☎ (011-33-32) 57-31-30 . . "Les Maillis" 27350 La Haye Aubrée, France

Wick MRS Philip JR (Marguerite Merrick)
☎ (860) 767-2341 . . 123 Essex Meadows, Essex, CT 06426

Wickes MR Nicholas du P . . see D R Carse JR

Wickser MR & MRS John P (Frances M Halsey) . . . . | ☎ (508) 228-5157
MR Philip J 2d—☎ (508) 228-1276 . . . . | "Champ Fleur"
| 68 Madaket Rd,
| Nantucket, MA
| 02554

Widdoes MR & MRS W Peirce (Barbara R Landauer) | ☎ (508) 257-6634
MR William P JR . . . . | "Widdoes Walk"
| Box 277, Siasconset,
| MA 02564

Widing MR & MRS Eric P (Laura K Todd)
☎ (412) 238-7784 . . "Log Cabin Farm" Box 720, Ligonier, PA 15658

Wiedemann MR & MRS (DR) Frederic Franklin (Florence Leachman)
"Moon Reach" Sea Ranch, CA 95497

Wieler MR & MRS Scott A (Mary M Baily)
☎ (516) 239-0639 . . 115 Ocean Av, Lawrence, NY 11559

Wiesen MR Gavin B . . see MRS B A Brackenridge

Wiggers MRS Thomas C (Helen Baker)
☎ (513) 321-3698 . . 3536 Bayard Dv, Cincinnati, OH 45208

Wiggin MRS Morrill (Margaret Patterson)
☎ (508) 283-1309 . . Norwood Heights, Annisquam, MA 01930

Wiggin MR & MRS Rollin H JR (Whelpley—Emilie O'D Iselin)
☎ (207) 374-9907 . . Wood's Point Rd, Blue Hill, ME 04614

Wightman MR & MRS Orrin S 3d (Letitia A Stephens) . . . . | ☎ (208) 622-5606
MR Orrin S 4th . . . . | Box 2510,
| Sun Valley, ID
| 83353

Wilberding MR & MRS Stephen Van C (Ann S Spaulding) . . . . | ☎ (518) 576-4422
MISS Ashley McL-B . . . . | "Hurricane Farm"
MR Augustus Van C—USA . . . . | Keene, NY 12942
MR Robert R . . . . |

Wilbur MR & MRS Colburn S (Mary G Verburg)
☎ (916) 426-3773 . . The Cedars, PO Box 909, Soda Springs, CA 95728

Wilbur DR & MRS Richard S (Betty L Fannin) . . . . | ☎ (916) 426-9244
MR Thomas S . . . . | The Cedars,
| PO Box 96,
| Soda Springs, CA
| 95728

Wilcox MRS F Samuel JR (Mary E Stine)
Stonegates 60, 4031 Kennett Pike, Greenville, DE 19807

Wilcox MR Gordon Cumnock
☎ (516) 283-4117 . . 80 Post Crossing, Southampton, NY 11968

Wild MR & MRS Henry S (Anne O Russell) . . . . | ☎ (203) 754-2224
MISS Anna . . . . | 54 Hillside Av,
MR Wellesley . . . . | Waterbury, CT
| 06710

Wilder MRS David (Coleman—Nancy Nye)
☎ (401) 635-8669 . . Taylor's Lane S, Little Compton, RI *02837*
Wilds MR & MRS Peter G (Sara R Wetherill). . . . . . . | ☎ (207) 374-2008
MISS Jennifer K. . . . . | "The Mooring II"
MISS Grayson W . . . . | Blue Hill, ME *04614*
Wilkie MRS John (Morrow—Margot Loines)
☎ (508) 693-0771 . . "Seven Gates Farm" RD 900, Vineyard Haven, MA *02568*
Wilking DR & MRS Leo F J (Virginia C Nichols)
☎ (508) 228-2937 . . "Parade Rest" Squam Rd, Quidnet, Nantucket, MA *02554*
Wilking REV DR & MRS Spencer Van B (Louisa Dennis). . . . . | ☎ (508) 228-9365
MISS Nina D. . . . . | "1799 House"
MISS Anna V W . . . . | 3 Joy St, Nantucket,
JUNIORS MR Spencer Van B JR. . . . . | MA *02554*
Wilkins MR & MRS Fraser Bryan (Katherine M Grayson)
"Moxley Farm" Box 395, Shelbyville, KY *40066*
Wilkins MR Henry Hepburn
☎ (808) 885-6228 . . E201 Mauna Lani Terr, Kawaihae, HI *96743*
Wilkinson MR Kent K JR . . see MR S N B Ponvert
Wilkinson MR & MRS Leland (Ruth E VanDemark) . | ☎ (508) 349-9688
MISS Anne M . . . . | Depot Rd, Truro,
MISS Caroline C . . . . | MA *02666*
Wilkinson-Gould MRS Josephine (Gould—Josephine Diana Wilkinson)
☎ (207) 236-6530 . . Harbor House, 1 Ocean Way, Camden, ME *04843*
Willard MR & MRS Daniel 3d (Linda R Zeller)
"Arbacia" 45 Forest Lane, Mollusk, VA *22517*
Willard MRS William Bradley (Florence Fatio Keys) | ☎ (603) 756-3270
LT COL (RET) William B JR—USA. . . . . | "Stephen Rowe
 | Bradley House"
 | Westminster St,
 | Walpole, NH *03608*
Willauer MR Whiting R
☎ (508) 228-1276 . . "Westcliff" Box 1106, Nantucket, MA *02554*
Willcox MR & MRS J Taney JR (Catherine E Goldschmidt) . . . . | ☎ (609) 967-4472
MR Bryan C . . . . | 74 E 15 St,
 | Avalon, NJ *08202*
Williams MR & MRS Albert D JR (Gary—Joyce McC Hadley)
☎ (715) 686-2235 . . Crab Bay Rd, Presque Isle, WI *54557*
Williams MR & MRS Ben A JR (Jessie A Marshall)
☎ (508) 283-8032 . . "The Dolphins" Davis Neck, Bay View, Gloucester, MA *01930*
Williams MRS Burdick F (Barbara M Taylor)
☎ (714) 494-6076 . . 434 Emerald Bay, Laguna Beach, CA *92651*
Williams MR & MRS Christopher Sewall (Sarah C Cecil)
☎ (207) 389-2567 . . "Honeymoon" Small Point, ME *04567*
Williams MR & MRS Daniel H III (Sue B McGrattan) | ☎ (905) 894-4525
MISS Jennifer B . . . . | Bay Beach,
MR Daniel H IV . . . . | Ridgeway,
 | Ontario L0S 1B0,
 | Canada
Williams MR & MRS Dave H (Reba J White)
135 Zaccheus Mead Lane, Greenwich, CT *06831*
Williams MRS David B (Edith C Huntington)
☎ (516) 583-5580 . . Box 112, Point O'Woods, NY *11706*

Williams MR & MRS David R JR (Baxter—Kerr—Anne Wright)
☎ (516) 324-0750 . . 68 Woods Lane, East Hampton, NY *11937*
Williams MR & MRS Eugene F (Evelyn D Niedringhaus). . . . . | ☎ (516) 324-4254
MR Edward W . . . . | Box 1205,
 | Apaquogue Rd,
 | East Hampton, NY
 | *11937*
Williams MR & MRS Eugene F 3d (Jacqueline D Russell)
☎ (516) 324-4819 . . Jones Rd, East Hampton, NY *11937*
Williams MR & MRS Francis H (Susan B Martin) . . . | ☎ (603) 487-5121
MR Francis H JR . . . . | "South Hill Farm"
 | New Boston, NH
 | *03070*
Williams DR & MRS Howard C (Marian L Vejvoda) ⚓
☎ (516) 583-5580 . . House 112, Point O'Woods, NY *11706*
Williams MR & MRS Hoyt H (Judith A George)
☎ (716) 745-3468 . . 1809 Lake Rd, Youngstown, NY *14174*
Williams MRS Ichabod Thomas (Eda M Dunstan)
☎ (518) 325-3846 . . Box 245, Texas Hill Rd, Hillsdale, NY *12529*
Williams MR & MRS John C (Patricia O'Connell) . . . | ☎ (707) 938-9278
MISS Lorna . . . . | 19205—7 St E,
MISS Samantha . . . . | Sonoma, CA *95476*
MR Douglas P . . . . |
Williams MISS Louise B . . see F F Staniford JR
Williams DR & MRS M Lee (Brune—Katherine H Ryland) . . . . | ☎ (804) 438-6352
MR Phillip L . . . . | "Huckleberry
 | Point" Box 214,
 | Steamboat Rd,
 | Irvington, VA *22480*
Williams MRS Moses (Mary B Holden)
☎ (207) 363-4586 . . PO Box 274, York Harbor, ME *03911*
Williams JUNIORS MR Nicholas C . . see R D Melen
Williams MRS Ralph B (Margaret Creighton)
☎ (617) 383-1057 . . "Boat House" 214 Atlantic Av, Cohasset, MA *02025-1413*
Williams MR Richard P JR
☎ (703) 777-1353 . . "Little Oatlands" Rte 2, Box 365, Leesburg, VA *22075*
Williams MR & MRS Robert W JR (Rosetta M Adams) ⚓
on board Ishtar" Ft Myers, FL *33908*
Williams MR & MRS Rufus M G (Sheila Janney)
☎ (207) 276-3987 . . "Gull Cove" Northeast Harbor, ME *04662*
Williams JUNIORS MR Samuel A F . . see R D Melen
Williams MRS Thomas (Nadia Iungerich)
☎ (508) 546-7216 . . "The Studio" 55 Phillips Av, Pigeon Cove, MA *01966*
Williams MR & MRS Thomas J C (Maude B Anderson)
☎ (804) 422-2510 . . 7216 Atlantic Av, Virginia Beach, VA *23451*
Williams MR & MRS W Grant (Betty J Tarlton)
☎ (970) 476-3555 . . 302 Mill Creek Circle, Vail, CO *81657*
Williams MR & MRS Walworth B (Mary Louise French)
☎ (603) 329-5078 . . "Tall Timbers" Governors Island, PO Box 97, Hampstead, NH *03841*
Williamson MR & MRS Edwin D (M Kathe Gates) . . | ☎ (516) 288-5382
MISS Sara E. . . . . | 40 Beach Rd,
LT Samuel G—USMCR. . . . . | Westhampton
MR Edwin D JR . . . . | Beach, NY *11978*

Williamson MRS Harold L JR (Jacqueline L Lanérès)
☎ (516) 788-7895 . . Fishers Island, NY *06390*
Williamson MR & MRS John F (Emily G Damon)
☎ (410) 348-2160 . . ''Kiteman's Place'' 28740 Valley Rd, Kennedyville, MD *21645*
Williamson MR & MRS Norman B (Victoria W Andrew) ⛵
1130 W Bay Av, Newport Beach, CA *92663*
Williamson MR & MRS Samuel H (Janet M Macomber)
☎ (207) 867-2283 . . Crabtree Point Rd, North Haven, ME *04853*
Willis MR & MRS Gregory T (Lois M Cross)
''Edgecliff'' Seal Harbor, ME *04675*
Willis MR & MRS Richard S (Bowers—Cynthia Gardner)
☎ (516) 653-4155 . . 30 Elizabeth Lane, Quogue, NY *11959*
Willis MR & MRS William H JR (Pauline S Smith)
☎ (207) 276-3682 . . ''Edgecliff'' Seal Harbor, ME *04675*
Wilmer MR & MRS John Whittingham (Jean R Smith)
☎ (819) 842-2621 . . ''Cedar Hedges'' 4265 rue Main, North Hatley, Quebec J0B 2C0, Canada
Wilmer REV DR & MRS Richard H JR (Sarah King)
☎ (415) 851-0141 . . 360 King's Mountain Rd, Woodside, CA *94062*

Wilmerding MR Henry A JR	☎ (970) 925-3574
MISS Kathryn H	PO Box 3484,
MISS Patsy R	1034 Red Mountain
MISS Daphne H	Rd, Aspen, CO
	81612

Wilmerding MR John
☎ (207) 276-3979 . . ''Ever Green'' Sargent Dv, PO Box 108, Northeast Harbor, ME *04662-0108*
Wilmerding MR Lucius JR
☎ (207) 244-3192 . . ''Indian Head'' Bernard, ME *04612*

Wilmerding MR & MRS Patrick R (Elsie Storm) ⛵	☎ (207) 374-2514
MISS Eliza R	''Fiddler's Green''
MR Patrick S	Rte 15, Blue Hill,
MR Michael R	ME *04614*

Wilsey MR & MRS Alfred S (Traina—Diane D Buchanan)	☎ (707) 963-9407
MR Trevor D Traina	''Rutherford River Ranch''
MR Todd B Traina	999 Rutherford Rd, Rutherford, CA *94573*

Wilshire MR & MRS W Murray (Beresford—Kingsbury—Charlotte E Meyer)
☎ (508) 627-4670 . . ''Compass House'' 115 Pease's Point Way, Box 803, Edgartown, MA *02539*
Wilson MR Benjamin V M
☎ (609) 492-2935 . . 211 Berkeley Av, Beach Haven, NJ *08008*
Wilson MRS Charles H (Tolles—Ysabel Angulo)
☎ (203) 259-7304 . . 215 Lansdowne, Westport, CT *06880*

| **Wilson** MISS Dorothy D | ☎ (717) 436-9852 |
| MISS Dorothy V | ''Wilson Farms'' Star Rte, Box 34, Mifflin, PA *17058* |

Wilson MR & MRS G Ross (Mary Jane L Browne)
☎ (609) 884-3505 . . 20 Queen St, Cape May, NJ *08204*
Wilson MR & MRS Gordon (April Donald)
☎ (616) LI7-6696 . . Chicago Club, Charlevoix, MI *49720*

Wilson MR & MRS John C (Mona B Dick)	The Meadows P3,
JUNIORS MR Angus M B	Beaver Creek, CO
JUNIORS MR Joshua E B	*81620*

Wilson MRS Kathryn L (Cuevas—Kathryn T Loud)
☎ (441) 238-8801 . . ''Little Sound Cottage'' Southampton SN 02, Bermuda
Wilson MR & MRS Kendrick R (Van Cott—Katharine F Gordon)
☎ (203) 655-6808 . . ''White Gate Farm'' 580 Middlesex Rd, Darien, CT *06820*

Wilson MR & MRS Kendrick R 3d (Linda K Babcock)	☎ (406) 222-8310
JUNIORS MISS Jane D	Eightmile Ranch, Rte 38, Box 2247,
JUNIORS MISS Olivia T	Livingston, MT *59047*

Wilson MR & MRS Marvel JR (Sara J Bingham)	☎ (302) 227-8274
MISS Elizabeth J	74 Pine Reach,
MISS Sara Jane G	Henlopen Acres,
MR Garrett M	Rehoboth Beach, DE *19971*

Wilson MR & MRS Milton JR (Barbara Hixon)
☎ (916) 645-3644 . . Box 157, Lincoln, CA *95648*
Wilson MR & MRS Percy H JR (Virginia Raycroft)
☎ (610) 558-3675 . . White Horse Village, 535 Gradyville Rd, Newtown Square, PA *19073*
Wilson MR & MRS Robert Letchworth (Comstock—Sarah Y Buck)
☎ (716) 941-3536 . . ''Lintemar-Ho'' 10001 Emerling Rd, Boston, NY *14025*
Wilson MR & MRS William B (Weitzman—Cramer—Joan M Erickson)
☎ (315) 369-3368 . . ''Rough House'' Adirondack League Club, Box 8, Little Moose Lake, Old Forge, NY *13420*
Wilson MR & MRS William F (Nancy G Parker)
☎ (401) 847-3268 . . Greenvale Farm, 582 Wapping Rd, Portsmouth, RI *02871*

Wilson MR & MRS William N (Barbara M Lane)	☎ (908) 899-4638
MISS Katherine N	839 Clayton Av,
MISS Margaret L	Bay Head, NJ *08742*
JUNIORS MR Samuel W	

Winans MR & MRS Walter E (Pauline L Harrison)
☎ (914) 234-7090 . . Box 572, Middle Patent Rd, Bedford, NY *10506*
Winburn MR & MRS William A 3d (Emily W Coxe)
☎ (912) 786-7772 . . 9A Oceanview Court, Tybee Island, GA *31328*

| **Winkelman** MR & MRS Mark O (Dorinda J P Cruickshank) | ☎ (860) 767-7903 |
| JUNIORS MISS Victoria P | ''Hayden's Point'' PO Box 362, Essex, CT *06426* |

Winship MR & MRS Frederick M (Thompson—Joanne Tree)
☎ (011-39-789) 96309 . . Pevero Golf Club, Porto Cervo, Sardinia, Italy
Winslow MR & MRS John G (Baldwin—Helen V Michalis)
☎ (401) 847-2664 . . ''Windward'' 236 Coggeshall Av, Newport, RI *02840*
Winsor MR & MRS James D 3d (Sally Wistar Waterman)
☎ (207) 244-3180 . . ''Seawall'' Manset, ME *04656*

| **Winstead** MR & MRS David L (Louise T Vietor) ⛵ | ☎ (302) 539-4216 |
| JUNIORS MR Trevor V | 49 Cotton Patch, Bethany Beach, DE *19930* |

Winter MR & MRS John W (Jeanne A Rozier)
  ☎ (704) 743-1677 . . Meadow Ridge Farm, PO Box 628, Glenville, NC *28736*

Winter MR & MRS Thomas G (Josephine E Grasselli) | ☎ (970) 728-5110
  MISS Clare McG . . . . | PO Box 2310,
  MR Thomas A . . . . | 215 N Fir St,
  MR Frank C . . . . | Telluride, CO *81435*
  MR William H . . . . |

Wintersteen REV DR & MRS Prescott B (Storey—Sheila Mills)
  ☎ (802) 334-6953 . . Lake Rd, PO Box 27, Newport, VT *05855*

Winthrop MRS Deborah H (Deborah Holbrook)
  ☎ (207) 374-2409 . . ''Birch Rocks'' East Blue Hill, ME *04629*

Winthrop MR & MRS Grant F (Hope H Brock)
  ☎ (508) 283-1349 . . Adams Hill Rd, Annisquam, MA *01930*

Winthrop MR & MRS Nathaniel T (Eleanor R Beane)
  ☎ (207) 359-8577 . . ''Willfan Lodge'' HC 64, Box 302, Brooklin, ME *04616*

Wirtz MR Willem K
  ☎ (516) 725-2111 . . ''The Summer House'' 44 Jesse Halsey Lane, Sag Harbor, NY *11963*

Wise MR & MRS D Scott (Linden Havemeyer)
  ☎ (516) 665-0561 . . 96 S Saxon Av, Bay Shore, NY *11706*

Wise DR & MRS Henry A 2d (Joshan R Backus) . . . . | ☎ (614) 766-1511
  MISS J Ridgely . . . . | 5420 Muirfield
   | Court, Dublin, OH
   | *43017*

Wise MRS James A (Drum—Isabel Davis)
  ☎ (616) 386-5424 . . ''Stoney Ledge'' 19 Northport Point, Northport, MI *49670*

Wise MR & MRS John H JR (Margaret R Hinckley)
  ☎ (207) 883-9296 . . ''The Lodges'' 588A Black Point Rd, Scarborough, ME *04074*

Wise MR & MRS William A (Marie C Figge) . . . . | 269 N Starwood Dv,
  MISS Vivian M . . . . | Aspen, CO *86211*
  MISS Genevieve M . . . . |
  JUNIORS MISS Mary E . . . . |

Wiseman MR & MRS William F (Linda F White)
  ☎ (508) 432-3392 . . Harwich Port, MA *02646*

Wistar MR & MRS James B (Elaine D Flanagan)
  ''Over the Rainbow'' Box 141C, Warren, VT *05674*

Wister MR & MRS Caspar (Cass—Uta G Schlegel)
  ☎ (518) 891-0287 . . ''Log Cove'' PO Box 887, Saranac Lake, NY *12983-0887*

Wister MR & MRS Malcolm L (Rosato—Lillian A Hirschbeck)
  ☎ (518) 891-0819 . . Windfall Camp, Saranac Lake, NY *12983*

Wister MR & MRS William R JR (Crompton—Norris | Box 496,
  —Diana D Strawbridge) . . . . | Northeast Harbor,
  MISS Margaret D Norris . . . . | ME *04662*

Witherbee MR & MRS John Hemenway (Downing—Beckwith—Mary I Osborne)
  ☎ (802) 533-2971 . . ''Partridge Hill'' Greensboro, VT *05841*

Witherby MR & MRS Frederick R H (Anne B Reed)
  ☎ (401) 789-9191 . . Box 188, Narragansett, RI *02882*

Witherby MR & MRS Frederick R H JR (Margaret C | PO Box 647,
  Pratt) . . . . | Vinalhaven, ME
  MR Frederick R H 3d . . . . | *04863*

Witherspoon MR & MRS John T (Loughlin—Dorothy | ☎ (616) 547-6793
  M Mudd) . . . . | 1 Belvedere Club,
  MISS Clare M Loughlin . . . . | Charlevoix, MI
  MR John J Loughlin JR . . . . | *49720*
  JUNIORS MISS Anna M Loughlin . . . . |

Withington MR & MRS Lothrop JR (Millican—Dorothy Shedd)
  ☎ (508) 224-6666 . . Holmes Rd, Manomet, MA *02345*

Witsell MR & MRS Frederick C JR (Daphne V Towne)
  ☎ (516) 671-0704 . . Lattingtown Ponds, 16 Swan Court, Glen Cove, NY *11542*

Witter MR & MRS Wendell W (Harkins—Gooding—Evelyn Grinter)
  ☎ (707) 224-9027 . . 303 Deer Hollow Dv, Napa, CA *94558*

Wodell MR W Page . . . . | ☎ (516) 788-7337
  MR Willis C Arndt JR . . . . | ''Harbor Haven''
   | Hedge St,
   | Fishers Island, NY
   | *06390*

Wolbach MR & MRS William W (Emma D Crispin)
  ☎ (508) 526-7185 . . ''Marshlands'' 377 Summer St, Manchester, MA *01944*

Wolcott MR Oliver III
  72 Wingaersheek Beach Rd, Gloucester, MA *01930*

Wolf MR Christopher R
  ☎ (516) 283-5911 . . 30 White Oak Lane, Southampton, NY *11968*

Wolf MR & MRS Richard A (Christine Marburg)
  ☎ (207) 276-4018 . . ''Garden Court'' Northeast Harbor, ME *04662*

Wolfe MR & MRS John J JR (Elizabeth L Moser) . . . . | ☎ (011-33-32)
  MISS Elizabeth . . . . | 56-25-14
  MR John J 3d . . . . | ''La Vacherie''
  MR Mathew S . . . . | Fiancourt-Catelon,
   | 27310 Bourg-
   | Achard, France

Wolfe MR & MRS Townsend D 3d (Jane R Lee)
  ☎ (802) 457-1608 . . Upper Line Farm, PO Box 11, Woodstock, VT *05091*

Wolfsberger MR & MRS Donald L (Joyce E Reith)
  ☎ (314) 725-9506 . . 211 N Bemiston Av, St Louis, MO *63105*

Wolkonsky DR & MRS Peter (Ward—Mary G Van Etten)
  ☎ (847) 234-2269 . . 1596 N Green Bay Rd, Lake Forest, IL *60045*

Wood MRS Arnold (Cornelia A Ely)
  ☎ (717) 278-9341 . . ''A House'' RR 4, Box 238A, Montrose, PA *18801-9804*

Wood MR Arthur M
  ☎ (847) 234-3112 . . 1050 N Green Bay Rd, Lake Forest, IL *60045*

Wood MR Edward F R JR
  ☎ (508) 758-3588 . . 44 Ned's Point Rd, Box 412, Mattapoisett, MA *02739-0412*

Wood MRS Harleston R (Emily N Campbell) . . . . . . | Haverford Village
  MR Ross G . . . . | 315, 700 Ardmore
  MR M Campbell . . . . | Av, Ardmore, PA
   | *19003*

Wood MR & MRS Harrison Wilson JR (Sabina S Adamson)
  ☎ (207) 276-5388 . . ''Benguet'' Tennis Club Rd, Northeast Harbor, ME *04662*

Wood MR & MRS Leighton C JR (Sarah L Hall)
☎ (401) 423-2006 . . "Tiffany Cottage" 22 Old Walcott Av, Jamestown, RI *02835*

Wood MR & MRS Peter H (Nina K Stuart) . . . . ☎ (207) 867-4860
 MISS Daphne F . . . . "Nabby House"
 MISS David P . . . . 727 Crabtree Point
 MR Michael H H . . . . Rd, North Haven, ME *04853*

Wood MR & MRS Rawson L (Elizabeth F Ford)
☎ (603) 253-4479 . . High Haith, PO Box 502, Center Harbor, NH *03226*

Wood MRS Richard Gilpin 3d (Martha W Thayer) . . "Gul Hus"
 MISS Margaretta D . . . . Kungsbacka, Sweden

Wood MR & MRS Robert E 2d (Susan Mayer)
☎ (847) 295-0699 . . "Thornhurst" 1167 N Sheridan Rd, Lake Forest, IL *60045*

Wood MR & MRS Theodore V JR (Betty S Deming) . . ☎ (609) 399-2762
 ⚓ . . . . 45 Arkansas Av,
 MISS Betty-Schuyler . . . . Ocean City, NJ
 MR Theodore V 3d *08226*

Wood MR & MRS Thomas W (Martha McA Borie)
☎ (616) 348-1902 . . 58 L'Arbre Croche, Harbor Springs, MI *49740*

Wood MRS Valentine (Vera Van B Richard)
☎ (207) 363-4690 . . "Windover" Roaring Rock Rd, PO Box 123, York Harbor, ME *03911*

Wood MRS William P (Grace—Sara E Wadsworth) . ☎ (716) 243-3862
 MR Jeremy B Grace . . . . "Swann Manor"
 MR Eric W Grace . . . . 4060 Roots Tavern Rd, Geneseo, NY *14454*

Woodbridge MRS M Brooks (Mary C Brooks) . . . . ☎ (809) 429-3570
 MISS Calista H . . . . Villa dei Felici,
 MISS Amelia N . . . . Second Av, Strathclyde, St Michael, Barbados

Woodger MR & MRS Bruce B (Lake—Cynthia R Bullock) . . . . ☎ (508) 627-4089
 MISS Amanda R Lake . . . . "The Lighthouse"
 MR Whitney B Lake . . . . Star Rte 52, Edgartown, MA *02539*

Woodhouse MR & MRS Henry Macauley (Joan K Neuberger)
☎ (508) 548-0484 . . 100 Moorland Rd, Falmouth, MA *02540*

Woods MR Anthony H . . see B F Rogers 3d

Woods MR & MRS Edward L A (Virginia D Simpson)
Bisby Lodge, Thendara, NY *13472*

Woods MRS Patricia Fay (Woods—Guiberson—Patricia O Fay)
Aug 1 . . 32 Windward, Belvedere, CA *94920*

Woods MR & MRS Richard M (Robin E Brown) ⚓ . . "The Shack"
 MISS Whitney S . . . . Green River,
 MISS Ashley E . . . . Leyden, MA *02038*
 MR Richard S . . . .

Woodward MR Bruce A
☎ (802) 496-2921 . . Rte 17, Fayston, VT *05673*

Woodward MRS Hiram W (Letitia R McKenrick)
"Second Wind" Deer Isle, ME *04627*

Woodwell MR & MRS J Knowles JR (Martha L Reed)
☎ (412) 238-2748 . . "Sunny Ridge Farm" Barron Rd, RD 2, Ligonier, PA *15658*

Woodworth MR & MRS J Gordon (Sally R Coleman)
☎ (207) 846-3255 . . 64 Blueberry Cove, Yarmouth, ME *04096*

Woollam MR & MRS Philip M (Anacker—Tina L Freeman) ⚓
☎ (601) 452-7570 . . "Yellow House" 611 St Louis St, Pass Christian, MS *39571*

Woolwine MR & MRS Woodrum E (Susanne B Phillips)
☎ (805) 688-9795 . . "Mountain View" 839 Ballard Canyon Rd, PO Box 546, Solvang, CA *93463*

Wooten MR & MRS Harry C JR (Dorothy M Caroé) . . . . . . ☎ (919) 726-5539
 MR T Sheffield . . . . 915 Ocean Ridge, Box 62, Atlantic Beach, NC *28512*

Wooten MAJ GEN & MRS Sidney C (Mary W Gibson) USA.
☎ (508) 228-0471 . . 35 Cliff Rd, Nantucket, MA *02554*

Worrell MR Granville 3d . . . . ☎ (609) 399-5523
 MISS Carolyn E . . . . 1106 Ocean Av, Ocean City, NJ *08226*

Worsley MR & MRS James R JR (Cornelia Cheston)
☎ (207) 867-4716 . . Pulpit Harbor, North Haven, ME *04853*

Worth MR James H
☎ (860) 355-4811 . . 46 Battle Swamp Rd, Roxbury, CT *06783*

Worth MR William A JR
☎ (610) 388-2293 . . 1219 Fairville Rd, Chadds Ford, PA *19317*

Worthington MR & MRS Ralph 4th (Lucinda E Morrisey) . . of
☎ (516) 653-6614 . . 25 Edgewood Rd, Box 1399, Quogue, NY *11959*
☎ (315) 357-3133 . . "Camp Wabun" Seventh Lake, Inlet, NY *13360*

Wray MR & MRS Michael B (Reid—Mary Denny Scott)
☎ (516) 788-7969 . . Fishers Island, NY *06390*

Wright MR & MRS Charles P JR (Holly McIntire)
Basin Creek Ranch, Basin Creek Rd, Troy, MT *59935*

Wright MR & MRS Gordon R (Swift—Margaret C Whipple) . . . . Edgartown, MA *02539*
 MR Gordon W . . . .
 MISS Lindsay C Swift . . . .
 MISS Helen S Brown . . . .

Wright MR & MRS Kenneth T (Judith B Atwood) . . . Trude Ranch,
 MISS Kimberly T . . . . Box 241,
 MISS Cameron M . . . . Island Park, ID
 MR Kenneth T JR *83429*

Wright CAPT (RET) & MRS (DR) Richard T (Pierson— Anne Bingham) USN. . . . . ☎ (315) 324-5851
 MISS Christian L . . . . Brush Island, Chippewa Bay, NY
 MISS Elizabeth T *13623*

Wright MRS Sandra S (Tower—Ohrstrom— Houghton—Sandra S Wright) . . . . ☎ (518) 644-9414
 MISS Winifred E A Ohrstrom . . . . "Farelight"
 MR Wright R S Ohrstrom . . . . Bolton Landing, NY *12814*

Wright MRS Thruston JR (Patricia M Bahen)
☎ (508) 228-6374 . . "Kielley Cottage" 26 Gosnold Rd, Nantucket, MA *02554*

Wright MR & MRS Whitney (Anne Wigglesworth)
☎ (508) 775-0484 . . Box 185, Hyannis Port, MA *02647*

Wriston MR & MRS Walter B (Kathryn A Dineen)
"Deer Pond Farm" 57 Wakeman Rd, Sherman, CT *06784*

Wulfing MR & MRS Charles 4th (A Barbara Fritze) . . ☎ (314) 798-2412
MISS Andrea G . . . . 129 Brushy Fork Lane, Augusta, MO *63332-1452*

Wulsin DR & MRS John H (Rosamond F Reed) . . . . . Campment d'Ours Island, Desbarats,
MISS Rosamond R . . . . Ontario P0R 1E0, Canada

Wuorinen MR Charles P
☎ (908) 832-7973 . . RD 3, Middle Valley Rd, Long Valley, NJ *07853*

Wurts MR & MRS Clarence Z (Patricia E Weaver) . . . ☎ (902) 275-3145
⛵ . . . . 94 Golf Course Rd,
MR Charles S . . . . Chester,
MR Benjamin W . . . . Nova Scotia B0J 1J0, Canada

Wurts MR & MRS John S (Roberta P Ray)
☎ (508) 748-3060 . . 260 Converse Rd, Marion, MA *02738*

Wyatt MR & MRS Felton Mark (Ann A Storrow)
☎ (916) 583-3157 . . "Dolce Far Niente" PO Box 176, Carnelian Bay, CA *96140*

Wyatt MRS Joseph W (Dorothy Georgens)
☎ (302) 539-9778 . . Sussex Shores, Bethany Beach, DE *19930*

Wyckoff MR & MRS Ferdinand L JR (Mary L Bayles)
☎ (207) 967-5690 . . 308 Kings H'way, Kennebunkport, ME *04046*

Y

Yancey MRS Charles S (Anne Richardson) . . . . ☎ (207) 833-2951
MISS Sherod A . . . . Merriconeag Rd,
MR C Stephen JR . . . . South Harpswell, ME *04079*

Yandell MR Lunsford P
☎ (207) 359-2034 . . Oakland House, Sargentville, ME *04673*

Yarnall MR & MRS Richard A (Dolan—Margaret M Knight)
☎ (011-353-64) 84255 . . "Llanray" Derrylough, Tuosist, Killarney, Co Kerry, Ireland

Yassukovich MRS Dimitri M (Denise Henry)
☎ (516) 759-2326 . . 75 Weir Lane, Locust Valley, NY *11560*

Yassukovich MR & MRS Stanislas M (Diana V O Townsend) . . . . ☎ (011-44-128) 5740-346
MRS Tatyana Y Dubow (Tatyana Yassukovich) "Malt House" Bibury, Cirencester, Gloucestershire GL7 5NT, England

Yates DR & MRS C Michael (Katherine R Babcock)
☎ (011-33-79) 08-63-72 . . Meribel-Les-Allues, 73550 Savoie, France

Yates MR & MRS Douglas T (Margaret L Titus)
☎ (516) 581-5616 . . Bayberry Point, Islip, NY *11751*

Yates MRS John Sellers (Marguerite K Tabor) . . . . . ☎ (717) 646-3268
MR Christopher M R . . . . Yates Camp, Pocono
MR Jeremy S . . . . Lake Preserve, PA *18348*

Yerkes MR & MRS David N (Satterlee—Sarah M Hitchcock)
☎ (508) 636-3626 . . 220 Howland Rd, Westport, MA *02790*

Yerkes MR & MRS Harry Estile 3d (Nancy Spofford) | ☎ (516) 788-7538
⛵ . . . . "The Zoo"
MISS Nathalie S . . . . Box 444,
MR J Nicholas . . . . Fishers Island, NY *06390*

Ylvisaker MRS Jane P M (Jane P Mitchell)
☎ (011-44-171) 727-1589 . . 5A Lansdowne Rd, London W11 3AL, England

Ylvisaker MR William T . . . . ☎ (540) 364-3996
MR Jon A . . . . 3074 Zulla Rd,
MISS Laurie E (Koehler—Laurie E Ylvisaker) . . The Plains, VA *22171*

Yokana MR & MRS Lucien D (Anne D Guthrie)
☎ (207) 282-0360 . . 41 Lester Orcutt St, Biddeford Pool, ME *04006*

York MRS Barney H (Newell—Mary S Foster)
☎ (216) 423-4811 . . Chagrin Valley Hunt Club, Old Mill Rd, Gates Mills, OH *44040*

York MRS Janet B (Janet L Brewster) . . . . ☎ (914) 452-8506
MISS Torrance Brewster . . . . "Walkabout" Melville Rd, Hyde Park, NY *12538*

York MR & MRS John C (Judith A Carmack) . . . . . ☎ (616) 429-1664
MISS Charlotte B . . . . "Watermelon
MR George E C . . . . House" 3965 Lake
JUNIORS MISS Alice M . . . . Forest Path, Stevensville, MI *49127*

Young MRS Andrew P (Elizabeth J S Newton)
☎ (508) 945-4216 . . 102 Lake Shore Dv, Chatham, MA *02633-1711*

Young MRS Brinton Coxe (Hilda M Osterhout)
☎ (508) 325-5094 . . "House of the Three Lights" 7 Eat Fire Spring Rd, Nantucket, MA *02554*

Young MR & MRS Charles T 3d (Milliken—Nancy H Cooper)
"Red House" 127 Elys Ferry Rd, Lyme, CT *06371*

Young MR Edward H
☎ (011-44-171) 930-1000 . . East India Club, 16 St James's Square, London SW1, England

Young MRS George B (Mary S Adams)
☎ (847) 234-0509 . . 130 E Onwentsia Rd, Lake Forest, IL *60045*

Young MR & MRS H Peyton (Fernanda F Toueg)
☎ (614) 655-2528 . . "Applethorpe Farm" Hallsville, OH *45633*

Young MR Henry Knowlton
Box 1033, Greenwich, CT *06830*

Young MRS Jane S (Toland—McDermott—Jane Stewart)
☎ (508) 299-8016 . . Uncatena Lodge, PO Box 87, Woods Hole, MA *02543*

Young MRS John Randolph (MacLeod—Elizabeth T McMullin)
☎ (610) 525-4018 . . 19 Pond Lane, Bryn Mawr, PA *19010*

Young MR & MRS Ledlie W JR (Edson—Joan McKay)
☎ (609) 884-3895 . . "Seawall" 1507 Beach Av, Cape May, NJ *08204*

Young MRS Susan B (Victor—Susan S Beaty) . . . . . ☎ (914) 253-9248
MISS Stephanie Morgan . . . . 60 Lincoln Av,
MR Alexander Morgan . . . . Purchase, NY *10577*

Young MR & MRS Thomas G 3d (K Beverley Whiting) . . . . | ☎ (410) 833-2218
JUNIORS MISS Brooke W . . . . | "Huntly Farm"
3940 Butler Rd,
Glyndon, MD *21071*
Youngman MR & MRS Robert P (Barbara G Pollock) | ☎ (914) 241-0418
MISS Eloise P . . . . | "Shady Tree Farm"
W Patent Rd,
Mt Kisco, NY
10549

Z

Zacharias MR & MRS Thomas E (Clelia LeBoutillier)
☎ (516) 283-1136 . . 65 Post Crossing, Southampton, NY *11968*
Zachrisson MR & MRS Carl U (Adele L Hall) . . . . . . | ☎ (415) 879-0790
MR Carl F . . . . | "Sans Souci"
JUNIORS MR Christopher D . . . . | Butano Canyon,
Pescadero, CA
94060
Zaldastani MR & MRS Othar (Elizabeth R Bailey) . . . | ☎ (717) 525-3402
MR Alexander G B . . . . | "Bailiwick"
Eagles Mere, PA
17731
Zantzinger MRS C Clark (Mary A Cook)
☎ (207) 244-3069 . . "Tinker Hill" PO Box 81, West Tremont, ME *04690-0081*
Zapffe MRS Carl A (A C Denise du Pont)
☎ (218) 963-2218 . . "Villa Z" 1324 Mission Rd, Nisswa, MN *56468*
Zeisler MR Richard S
☎ (516) 324-6754 . . Ocean Av, East Hampton, NY *11937*
Zellerbach MR & MRS Stephen A (Beaumont—Cecile M Nervo)
☎ (707) 431-2249 . . 14625 McDonough Heights Rd, Healdsburg, CA *95448*
Zelov MR Peter E
☎ (717) 646-7521 . . Pocono Lake Preserve, PA *18348*
Zelov MR & MRS Randolph D (Josephine E Frank)
☎ (717) 643-7674 . . "Dalibarda" 6 S Shore, Pocono Lake Preserve, PA *18348*
Zembrzuski CAPT & MRS Michael A (Wendy L Phillips) USA.
☎ (818) 796-1747 . . 787 S Euclid Av, Pasadena, CA *91106*
Zick MR & MRS John W (Mary A Sutter)
☎ (203) 531-0569 . . 418 W Lyon Farm Dv, Greenwich, CT *06831*
Ziegler MR & MRS Henry S (Hoffman—Jourdan Arpelle)
☎ (860) 491-3456 . . Box 140, Thompson Rd, Goshen, CT *06756*
Ziesing MISS Heather W . . see MRS J W Eckman
Ziesing MISS Jane D . . see MRS J W Eckman
Ziesing MR & MRS Robert A (M Sinclair Adams)
☎ (603) 284-7025 . . Bear Cove Camp, Metcalf Rd, Center Sandwich, NH *03227*
Zilkha MISS Bettina L (Trink—Bettina L Zilkha)
☎ (212) 288-2885 . . 1001 Fifth Av, Apt 14D, New York, NY *10028*
Zilkha MR & MRS Daniel A (Frances P Rogers) . . . . | ☎ (207) 883-5466
MISS Leonora R . . . . | 1 Library Lane,
JUNIORS MISS Rebecca R . . . . | Prouts Neck, ME
JUNIORS MR Nathaniel M . . . . | *04074*

Zilkha MR & MRS Ezra K (Cecile Iny)
☎ (516) 283-4686 . . 310 First Neck Lane, Southampton, NY *11968*
Zimmerman MR & MRS Christian B (Garroway—Sarah Lee Lippincott)
☎ (609) 967-3768 . . "Open House" 5299 Dune Dv, Avalon, NJ *08202*
Zouck MR & MRS Peter G (Katharine Symington)
☎ (410) 377-0869 . . 6109 Bellinham Court, Baltimore, MD *21210*
Zoullas MR Nicholas S
☎ (516) 283-0706 . . "Fairwinds" 145 Ox Pasture Rd, Box 2454, Southampton, NY *11968*
Zug MR & MRS Harry Coover (Anne W Mayer)
☎ (717) 646-2601 . . "Mereside" Pocono Lake Preserve, PA *18348*
Zug MR & MRS James W (Debora W Collier) . . . . . . | ☎ (717) 646-2601
MR James W JR . . . . | "Bird's Nest"
Pocono Lake
Preserve, PA *18348*

Yachts in Commission and their Owners

YACHT CLUB ABBREVIATIONS

Aga	Agamenticus Yacht
Ayc	Annapolis Yacht
Bhy	Bar Harbor Yacht
Buf	Buffalo Yacht
Bvl	Beverly Yacht
Co	Corinthians
Cry	Corinthian Yacht
Cyc	Chicago Yacht
DelB	Delray Beach Yacht
Dy	Dillon Yacht
Dyc	Devon Yacht
Exy	Essex Yacht
Ey	Eastern Yacht
Eyc	Edgartown Yacht
Fb	Fishing Bay Yacht
Fiy	Fishers Island Yacht
Glc	Great Lakes Cruising
Ihy	Indian Harbor Yacht
Il	Ida Lewis Yacht
Myc	Manchester Yacht
Nf	Northeast Harbor Fleet
Ny	New York Yacht
Nyc	Nantucket Yacht
Pqt	Pequot Yacht
Rby	Royal Bermuda Yacht
Rk	Rappahannock River Yacht
S	Seawanhaka Corinthian Yacht
Sdy	San Diego Yacht
Sfy	St Francis Yacht
Syc	Southampton Yacht
Why	Watch Hill Yacht

YACHT OWNERS

A

Abernethy MR & MRS Samuel F .... *Berwyn*
Adams MR & MRS Charles F .... *Auk VI*
Allison MR & MRS Walter R .... *Miss Wiggins*
Ames MR & MRS Alden III .... *Tripper II*
Anderson MR & MRS William G .... *Rumrunner*
Anderson-Bell MR Andrew .... *Fiona*
Andrew MR & MRS Thomas G JR .... *Sakana*
Andrews MR & MRS Stockton A .... *Takeover*
Andrews MR & MRS William T .... *Physalia*
Angle MR & MRS Richard W .... *Tickled Too*
Anthony MR & MRS Silas R JR .... *Abracadabra*
Arnold MR & MRS David B JR .... *Alpha*
Austin MR & MRS Stephen D W .... *Intrepid*
Avery MRS Victoria J .... *Mama Safari*
Ayer MR James C .... *Promise*

B

Baer MR & MRS Gordon R JR .... *BaerCat*
Bailey MR & MRS Samuel JR .... *Kehaar*
Baillière MR & MRS Thomas H G JR .... *Soirèe*
Baker MR & MRS Anthony K .... *Red Witch*
Baker MR & MRS Benjamin M III .... *Nora*
Baker MR & MRS Hollis MacL .... *Whisper VIII*
                                                                                Whisper X
Baker MR & MRS John Milnes .... *Howkola*
Baker MR Talbot JR .... *Torch*
Baker MR & MRS William C .... *Mimika*
Bakewell MR & MRS Henry P JR .... *Sixpence*
Balch DR & MRS Henry H .... *Blue Goose*
Baldwin MR & MRS Michael .... *The Sicilian*
Barker MR & MRS James R .... *Shuh-Shuh-Gah*
Barker MR & MRS Morgan R .... *Gazebo*
Barneson MR & MRS Lee H .... *Drummuir*
Barnum MR & MRS John W .... *Miles To Go*
                                                                                Waterloo
Barrett MRS (DR) Beatrice H .... *Aphrodite*
Barrow MR & MRS Kenneth P JR .... *Shearwater IV*
Barton MR & MRS Alexander K .... *Trianon*
Bates MR & MRS Richard J *QE3*
Beadleston MR & MRS William L .... *Callooh Callay*
Beckner MR Bruce A .... *Perdida*
Belknap MR & MRS Thomas H .... *Radiant*
Bender MR & MRS Robert G .... *Whirlwind*
Benjamin MR & MRS Edward B JR .... *Wind Lass*
Benjamin MR & MRS Henry Rogers .... *Reflection*
Benney MR & MRS J B Neil JR .... *Ballad*
Berger MR & MRS William M B .... *Triton*
Bering MRS Edgar A JR .... *Voyager*
Biays MR & MRS W Tuckerman .... *Aquacolor*
Bicket MR & MRS Robert M .... *Phoebe*
Bidwell MR & MRS Miles O JR .... *Touché*

Bishop DR & MRS Harry C .... *Lyn Dee*
                                                                                Skoal
Bissell MR & MRS Frank S .... *Champ*
Black MR & MRS Peter .... *Caroline*
Blagden MR & MRS George .... *Mime*
Boerke MR & MRS Richard E .... *Tickidyboo*
Boersma MR & MRS Milford .... *Marymil IV*
Bogart MR & MRS Adrian T JR .... *Altair*
Boggs MR & MRS George T .... *Solitude*
Boyd MR & MRS Nicholas G K JR .... *Margy B*
Boynton MR & MRS Oren K .... *Fiddler's Green*
Braham MR & MRS W Walter JR .... *Manatee*
Brewer MRS Ann W .... *Jacques Coeur*
Brewer MR & MRS Charles H .... *Postcard*
Brewer MR William C .... *Periwinkle*
Brewster MR & MRS Benjamin H .... *Evenstar*
Brooks MR & MRS W Denison .... *Shangri-La*
Brown MRS George Estabrook JR .... *Pyrite*
Brown MR & MRS James M III .... *Freedom*
Brown MRS John A .... *Samantha*
Brown MR John R JR .... *Dawn Treader*
Brown DR & MRS Lloyd .... *Panacea*
Brown CAPT & MRS Nicholas .... *Quadrille*
Brown MR & MRS William J W .... *Regaelia*
Brune MR J T Terry .... *Rum Runner*
Buck MR Roswell S .... *Tanamera*
Buckley MR & MRS Christopher T .... *Traveller*
Burden MRS William A M .... *Spindrift IV*
Burger MR & MRS F Gregg .... *Electra*
Burke MR & MRS Duncan G .... *Breathless*
Burke MR & MRS Peter G .... *Lorelei*
Burns MR & MRS Edward E JR .... *Winburn*
Burr MR & MRS Robert Page .... *Betsy B*
Burrage MR & MRS Walter S JR .... *Wind Song*
Butt MR Charles C .... *Volador*
Byers MR & MRS Randolph K JR .... *Granny Carr*

C

Camp MRS Frederic E .... *Thistledown*
Carpenter MRS Francis F .... *Pleiades*
Carr MR Dayton T .... *Gunga Din*
Carroll MR & MRS Barry J .... *Katy*
Carroll MR & MRS Lucius W II .... *Lagniappe IV*
Carruthers MR & MRS Thomas H IV .... *Gosling*
Carter MR & MRS J Newman .... *Victoria*
Catlin MR & MRS Avery .... *Dorado*
Chance MR Britton .... *Complex VII*
                                                                                Complex X
Chance MR Edwin M .... *Chiriqui*
                                                                             La Jolie Rousse
Chandler MR & MRS Henry T .... *Avant-Garde*
Chandor MR & MRS Jeffrey F .... *Bluechip*
Chanler MR & MRS Bronson W .... *Highlight*

YACHT OWNERS | 175

Chapin MR & MRS Charles A .... *Voyager*
Chew MR & MRS H Richard .... *Fair Witness*
Clagett MR C Thomas JR .... *Moonraker*
Clark MR & MRS James H JR .... *Sea Lion*
Clark MR & MRS Laurance R .... *Uncle Bob*
Clark MRS Reuben B III .... *Naraka II*
Claytor MR Warren Ingersoll .... *Caroline*
Clinnin MR John W .... *Dancer*
Clough MR Walter J .... *Tight Lines*
Cluett MR & MRS Mark S .... *Shearwater*
Coates MR & MRS Benjamin .... *Queen Nefertiti*
Cobbs MR & MRS James W JR .... *Red Shift*
Colburn MR & MRS Kenneth H .... *Fraulein*
Coleman MR & MRS Wilfrid W .... *Sea Hunter*
Conklin MR & MRS Louis H .... *Iron Duke*
Conklin MR & MRS Theodore B .... *Kahlua III*
                Minx V
Cook MR & MRS Stephen A .... *Pre-Emptive Bid*
Cooke MR & MRS Dudley P .... *Quiescence*
Corcoran MR & MRS Thomas A .... *Snow Dance*
Coxe MR Weld .... *Toge II*
Crans MR & MRS Robert R .... *Swamp Fire*
Crawford MR & MRS Harden L III .... *Caviar*
Crew MR & MRS William W .... *Pelican Express*
Crispin MR & MRS Frederick E .... *Manana*
Crocker MR & MRS Davenport B .... *Valeehi II*
Crocker MRS U Haskell .... *Crocodile*
Crozer MRS Betsy Carlyle .... *Tropicbird*
Cullen MR & MRS Craig W .... *Windwalker*
Cushman MR & MRS Allerton JR .... *Means of Grace*

D

Dall MR Henry A .... *Allegra*
Dann MR E Webster .... *Skidbladnir*
Darlington MR & MRS Harry .... *Yakut*
Davis MR David O .... *Reef Runner*
Davison MR & MRS Daniel P .... *Matuta*
Dayton MR & MRS S Grey JR .... *September Song*
de Bullet MR & MRS Eugene G JR .... *Bessie Baby V*
de Castro MR & MRS J Edmund JR .... *Wenonah*
Deméré MR & MRS Raymond S .... *My Fair Lady*
Deming MR & MRS David H .... *Adagio*
Dennis MR & MRS Samuel S III .... *Respite III*
Dennis-Browne MR John F .... *She*
Dennison MR & MRS E Allen .... *Mandala*
de Roulet MRS Vincent .... *Patrina III*
Devaney MR & MRS Richard T .... *Miss Midge*
Devine MR & MRS Kevin J .... *Ned Kelly*
Dewhurst MR & MRS Walter Albert .... *Calypso*
Dickey MRS Lucy Baker .... *Murana*
Dickey MR & MRS Paul B JR .... *Souwest*
Dimsey MR & MRS Peter S P .... *Cheers*
Dinning MR E Lawrence III .... *Teetotaler*
Dinning MR & MRS E Lawrence IV .... *Bay Monarch*

Donham MR & MRS Paul JR .... *Resolute*
Donnan MR & MRS David Hibbs .... *Quindaro*
Donovan MR & MRS Lee M .... *Shenanigans*
Dorsey DR & MRS J Henderson .... *Trilogy*
Dougherty MR & MRS Geoffrey B .... *Cat's Whiskers*
                Morning Mist
                Robin
                Segar
Dow MR & MRS Peter A .... *Shifting Wind*
Downey MR & MRS Dixon P .... *Mon Rêve*
Dudley MR & MRS Wesley C .... *Donald Duck*
du Pont MR Henry B IV .... *Nor'Easter*

E

Earle MR & MRS Francis III .... *Countess*
Eberhart MR & MRS Frank III .... *Hound*
Eddy MR & MRS Selwyn II .... *Hale-Kai II*
Ellis MRS D Rowland .... *Southern Comfort II*
Emerson MR & MRS Jonathan E .... *Cheers*
Emery MR Willard .... *Jubilation*
Emory MR Dennis S .... *Spindrift*
Eshleman MR & MRS Charles L JR .... *Sybarite*
Espinosa de los Monteros MR & MRS Alvaro F .... *Sea Sharp*
Eustis MR & MRS William E C .... *Moonwind*

F

Fairbank MR & MRS (DR) David E .... *Häxan*
Fairburn MR & MRS David H .... *Meltemi*
Fanjul MR & MRS Alexander L .... *Osceola*
Feder MR & MRS Andrew M .... *Cassiopeia*
Fegela MR & MRS John R .... *Wings*
Ferrarini CAPT & MRS Richard L .... *Runaway*
Fetter MR & MRS Trevor .... *La Réserve*
Ficks MRS Gerald J .... *The General III*
Field MR & MRS Henry F .... *Ramblin' Rose*
Fischer DR & MRS Edwin G .... *Tempo*
Flaccus MR & MRS Charles L III .... *Windmar*
Flower MR & MRS Walter C III .... *Ragtime*
Flynn MR & MRS Allan A A .... *Adios*
Foley MR Thomas C .... *Glory*
Forbes MR & MRS John Douglas .... *Annie T*
Ford MR & MRS Peter B .... *Starling*
Foulke MR & MRS William G .... *Schoodic II*
Fowler LT COL & MRS C Worthington II .... *Valldemosa*
Fox MR & MRS Richard Ottley Beaufort .... *Hot Chocolate*
Fraker MR & MRS Harrison S .... *Riptide V*
Frantz MR & MRS L Scott .... *Arrivaderci*
                Ticonderoga
Frantz MR & MRS Leroy JR .... *Camaruche*
Freeman MR & MRS Louis M JR .... *Blizzard*
Fuller MR & MRS Robert Gorham .... *Tringa III*
Fulweiler MRS Spencer B .... *Airdrie*

G

Gallatin MR & MRS Thomas G JR .... *Euphoria*
Galpin MR & MRS Stephen K .... *Astrea*
Galston MR & MRS John W .... *Escapade*
Gaston MR & MRS Benjamin McT JR .... *Dawn*
Gelette MR & MRS Grantland W .... *Tern To*
Gibson MR & MRS John McCullough .... *Festive Mood*
Gildred MR & MRS George Lewis .... *La Vida*
Gillespie MR & MRS Stuart P SR .... *Highland Fling*
Gillette MR & MRS Edwin .... *Misty Isle*
Goldman DR & MRS Allen S .... *Nepenthe*
Goldsborough MR & MRS Nicholas .... *Wahoo*
Goodall MR & MRS Herbert W III .... *Eliza*
Goodhue MR & MRS Albert III .... *Quadrille*
Goodyear MR & MRS (DR) Austin .... *Mermaid*
Grant DR & MRS Joseph L .... *Fair Lead*
Gray MR & MRS Samuel P M &
   Gray MR & MRS W Latimer JR .... *Clarion*
Greenway MR & MRS Hugh D S .... *Mary Oakes*
Griswold REV & MRS Brendan .... *Venture IV*
Grose MR & MRS Thomas Pierpont .... *Arturus*
   Dido
Grove MR & MRS Henry S III .... *Stavidon*
Guimont MR & MRS Maurice S .... *Galatea*
Gurin MR & MRS Richard S .... *Nereus*

H

Haas MR Edward T .... *Pegasus*
Haines DR & MRS James B .... *Farsider*
Hall MR & MRS R Tucker .... *Panache*
Hambleton MR George B E .... *Abrazos*
Hamlin MR Jerome F .... *Wendigo*
Harper MRS Harry H JR .... *Kuan Yin III*
Harrington MR & MRS Edward A .... *Rumblefish*
Harris MR & MRS George B .... *Dido*
Harris MR Gregory S .... *Xanadu*
Harris MR & MRS Henry P U III .... *Riding Hood*
Harsch MR & MRS Joseph C .... *Sea Fever*
Hart MR & MRS Robert J K .... *Serendipity II*
Hazard MR & MRS Oliver C .... *Telluride*
Healy MR & MRS William T .... *Weatherbird*
Heimbecker DR & MRS Raymond O .... *Magic Dragon*
   Maia
   Our Pleasure
Heller MR Anthony K .... *Hello*
Hentic MR & MRS Yves F M .... *Send It In*
Herrick MR & MRS Peter .... *Bea Happy*
Herrlinger MR & MRS Edward F II .... *Kimsong*
Hicks MR & MRS Edward L III .... *Ladybeth*
Hill MR & MRS Joseph J .... *Issy "B" II*
Hill MR & MRS T Bowen III .... *Legal Ease*
Hinckley CAPT & MRS Robert M .... *Kahala III*
Hinckley MR Samuel H .... *Tahawus*
Hird MR & MRS Samuel Ainsworth JR .... *Blueflower*

Hobart MR & MRS Aaron A .... *Sleigh Ride*
Hoffman MRS Albert L JR .... *Windless*
Hogen MR Timothy L .... *Whale*
Holbrook MR & MRS William Sumner III .... *Sundowner*
Hollister MR & MRS Buell IV .... *Blue Chantey*
Holmes MISS (REV) Olivia .... *Liberty*
Holt MR & MRS Charles C III .... *Merrilil*
Honan MR & MRS William Holmes .... *Wind's Fool*
Hoopes MR & MRS Joseph C JR .... *Hot Water*
Hornor MR & MRS DeWitt .... *Hotel Splendide*
Host MR & MRS Stig .... *Hostess*
Hubbard MRS D Seeley .... *Red, Inc*
Huber MR & MRS Daniel .... *Acceptance II*
Hucks MR & MRS Herbert deM III .... *Spring Tide*
Huebner MR & MRS J Stephen .... *Magic X*
Huey MR & MRS G H Harris .... *Iroquois*
Hunnewell MISS Sarah F .... *Suddenly*
Hunt MR William O JR .... *Alfalfa*

I

Inch MR & MRS Robert W .... *Jennie Rose*
Ireland MISS Kate .... *Perseverance*
Ireland MR & MRS Robert L III .... *Pastime*
Irving MR & MRS Pierre duP .... *Shalamar*
Irwin MR & MRS Robert J A JR .... *Bateleur*
Iselin MRS Lewis .... *L'Avenir*

J

Jewett MR & MRS Freeborn G JR .... *Cincuenta*
Johns MR & MRS Lionel S .... *Blithe Spirit*
Johnson MR & MRS Edward R &
   Johnson MISS Lacy K .... *Flying Buttress II*
Jones MR & MRS Howland B JR .... *Hawksbill*

K

Kaminer MR Stevenson S .... *Heretic*
   Predator
Kastendike MR & MRS T Graham R .... *Re-Treat*
Kean MR & MRS John .... *Guillemot*
Keefe MR & MRS Harry V JR .... *Nita*
Keidel MR & MRS Albert JR .... *Highland Mist II*
Kennedy MR & MRS Grafton S .... *Blues Chaser*
   Wave Dancer II
Ker MR & MRS Davis S I .... *Thalia*
Kilroy MR & MRS Edward A JR .... *Kimari*
King MR & MRS Clarence H JR .... *Crucero*
King MR & MRS Richard H .... *Barseeker*
King MR & MRS W Griffin JR .... *Ice Bucket*
King MR & MRS William A .... *Caramba*
Kinsolving MR & MRS Augustus B .... *Seabird*
Klapp MR Joseph W .... *Christina*
Kloman MR & MRS H Felix II .... *Anemone*
Kniffin MR & MRS Robert S .... *Swan Song*

Kratovil MR & MRS Stephen C .... Fat Chance
Kuper MR & MRS George Henry .... Satori

L

Lane MR William N III .... Rocinante
Lansing MR & MRS Gerrit L .... Chicken of the Sea
Leale MR & MRS Douglas M .... Pea Pod
Lee MR & MRS W Ashton .... Silver Queen II
Leeson MR & MRS Robert JR .... Hope-San
Leggett MR & MRS Anthony L .... White Arrow
Leib MR Franklin A .... Antares
Leighton MR & MRS Charles M .... Whitecap
Leonard MR Nicholas A .... Mistral
Livingston MR & MRS Deryck Van V .... Alerion
Lockwood MR Thomas W .... Gasparilla
Lorenzen MR & MRS Phillip H JR .... Matia
Loring MR & MRS William C .... Samar
Lowrey MR & MRS Charles F .... Mako

M

McAleenan MRS Clifford C .... Dawn Mist
McCargo MR & MRS Grant .... Sacajawea
McComic MR & MRS R Barry .... Scylla
McCormick MR & MRS Peter H .... Bright Thread
McCreary MR & MRS Pierce N .... Malaga
McCurdy DR & MRS Alexander III .... Fermina Daza
McCurdy MRS James A .... Selkie
McGraw MR & MRS Theodore A JR .... Hyper Borealis
McKenrick MR S Eyre JR .... Aimless Lady
McLane MR & MRS Thomas L .... Chasseur
McLean MR James H III .... Searcher
McLucas MR & MRS Don H JR .... Picaroon
McNeil MRS Henry S .... Yes, Dear
MacArthur MR & MRS Edward S .... Jolly Sixpence
MacEwan MR & MRS Nigel S .... Aurora
MacLean MR & MRS Babcock .... Lee Selden
MacLean MR & MRS Malcolm O .... Honor M
Madeira MR & MRS Edward W JR .... Sagamore
Madeira MR Harry R .... Daybreak
Mallory MR Charles .... Fancy
Maresi MR & MRS Henry J .... Moonshine
Marshall MR & MRS Allerton D .... Growler
Marshall MR John Hunt .... Prowler
Maschal MR & MRS John R .... HGS
Mattison MR & MRS Joseph III .... Cybèle
Maxwell MR George L .... Tristram
May MR & MRS James G G .... Vitesse
May MR & MRS William F .... Arcturus
Mayer MR & MRS Frederick R .... White Eagle
Maynard MR & MRS Walter JR .... Albicore
Medina MR Standish Forde .... Tembototo
Mehta MR & MRS Ved P .... Natty Bumppo
Mellon MR Henry C S .... WaterMellon
Metzger MR & MRS Kurt P .... Four Gulls

Meyer MR & MRS George S .... Halcyon
Miller MR & MRS Jo Zach IV .... Sanriel
Miller MR & MRS Paul L .... Peregrine II
Millet MR & MRS David F .... Capella
Millspaugh MR & MRS S Kirk .... Sardonic
Mitchell MR & MRS Paul R .... Elenoa
Mohlman MR & MRS Theodore A .... Trident III
Moncrieff MR & MRS Ernest V JR .... Vintage
Moore DR & MRS Matthew R .... Alliegator
Moorhouse MR & MRS Leslie C .... Sea Dancer
Morrin DR & MRS Peter A F .... Star of Isis
Morris MR & MRS Frederic H .... Chime
Mortensen MR & MRS Dan S .... Lady Bug
Mott MR Lawrence H .... Ellen
Muller MR & MRS Scott W .... Mischief
Mullins MR & MRS Thomas D II .... Nakhoda
Murphy MR & MRS Mark .... Brer' Fox
Murray MR & MRS William E .... Escort
Myer MR & MRS Theodore H .... Argo

N

Nalle MR & MRS Jesse .... Naushon
Nash DR & MRS (DR) A E Keir .... Britannia Serena
Nelson MR & MRS Norman F II .... Peaconnet
Nelson MR Robert M .... Noel
Newbold MR & MRS Arthur E III .... Adagio
Newburg MR & MRS Andre W G .... Typhoon
Newhall MR George A III .... Rubicon
Newhall MR & MRS Thomas B .... Stat
Nichols MR & MRS H Gilman .... Pèlerin
Nobel MR & MRS Robert D .... Mystère
Norweb MR & MRS R Henry III .... Rapture
Nottingham MR & MRS R Kendall .... Rover
Noyes MR & MRS Jansen JR .... The Gray Gull
Noyes MR William M .... Lita

O

O'Brien MRS Catherine L .... Ariel
Ogburn MR & MRS Hugh B .... Lucky Haole III
Ogden MR & MRS Alfred T II .... Dawn Treader
O'Hara MR & MRS David O .... Theodora
O'Hara MR & MRS Robert S JR .... Sand Wedge
Olmi MR Eugene J JR .... Fantasia
Osborn MR & MRS Frederick H III .... Amphitrite
Osgood MR & MRS Edward H JR .... Brief Candle
Ottley MR & MRS Philip G .... Noble Falcon

P

Paddock MR & MRS Anthony C .... Starfire
Pagenstecher MR & MRS John A .... Saratoga II
Pardee MR & MRS S Trevor .... Talaria
Pardee MR S Trevor JR .... Coriolis
Parker MRS Augustin H .... Portunus

YACHT OWNERS

Parker MR & MRS Richard S JR ... *Sister*
Passano MR & MRS William M JR &
Passano MR & MRS William M III ... *Carina*
Peabody MR & MRS Endicott ... *Long Haul*
Pedersen MR & MRS (DR) Matthew H ... *Emma T*
Truth B
Peet MR & MRS E Chester JR ... *Wicked Lady*
Pennoyer MR & MRS Paul G JR ... *Arabella*
Persse MR John W III ... *Grace*
Pew MR & MRS G Thompson JR ... *Anodyne*
Two Tender
Pew MR & MRS Richard Ford ... *Cross Wave*
Pfaelzer MR Carter P ... *Resolution*
Pfeffer MR & MRS James L ... *Katama*
Phyfe MR & MRS James D ... *Aristea*
Pierce REV & MRS Nathaniel W ... *La Mer*
Piersol MR George Morris JR ... *Whim*
Pierson DR & MRS Richard N JR ... *Lady Jane*
Pitts MR & MRS Henry C ... *Tempest*
Place MR & MRS David E ... *Arabella*
Platt MR & MRS Thomas C ... *Whim*
Poor MR & MRS Charles L ... *Down East*
Poutiatine MR & MRS Michael ... *Simply Divine*
Pratt MR & MRS Vaughan W ... *Halcyon*
Preble MR & MRS Wallace L ... *Sir Walter Wally*
Price MR & MRS Robert M ... *Xanthippe III*
Price MR & MRS Robert R III ... *Sara B²*
Prien MR & MRS Henry I ... *Maya IV*
Prioleau MR & MRS H Frost ... *Tonopah*
Pulver MR & MRS George M ... *Bluejacket*
Purdon MR & MRS Henry P ... *Renegade*

R

Rando MR John S JR ... *Agincourt*
Ravenel MR & MRS Daniel ... *Fly By Night*
Rawson MRS Kennett L ... *Aurora*
Rea MR & MRS C Cary ... *Plotter*
Reeder MR & MRS Oliver H ... *Ishmael*
Reeve MR & MRS Lawrence Lowell ... *Narcissus*
Reilly MR John H JR ... *Kinsale*
Reily MR & MRS W Boatner III ... *Bounder IV*
Edwinna B
Reksten MRS Astrid J ... *Endeavor*
Reynolds MRS Bartow ... *Reynegade*
Reynolds MR & MRS Russell S JR ... *Windsong*
Rhame DR & MRS Harold E JR ... *Wisp*
Rice MR & MRS Donald S ... *Snow Goose*
Ridley MR & MRS Frank M ... *Enspignant II*
Riggs MR & MRS Richard C JR ... *Outrigger*
Riker CDR & MRS Robert T ... *Upbeat*
Roberson MR & MRS Robert S ... *Kibosh*
Roberts MR & MRS A Sydney JR ... *Elena*
Roberts MR & MRS Dudley ... *Shady Lady*
Roberts CHAPLAIN (COL) & MRS Malcolm III ... *Tyme N Tyde*
Robertson MR Charles S JR ... *Rebel Too*

Robertson MR & MRS John O ... *Pickle II*
Robertson MR & MRS John T III ... *No Problem*
Robins MR & MRS Alfred LeC ... *Robin's Nest*
Robinson MR & MRS Hamilton JR ... *Summer Light*
Roche MR & MRS Thomas K ... *Lilliput*
Rockefeller MR & MRS Godfrey A ... *Kirana III*
Rodner MR & MRS Henry F JR ... *Eureka III*
Rogers MR & MRS Arthur M JR ... *Katahdin*
Rogerson MR & MRS Thomas C ... *Baluke*
Rogerson MR William G ... *Windsong*
Rollhaus MR & MRS Philip E JR ... *Dulcinea*
Rorer MR & MRS Gerald B ... *Rag Time*
Rose MR & MRS C Bowie ... *Sandy C III*
Rotch MR & MRS A Lawrence ... *Phoenix*
Rotch MR & MRS William ... *Swallow*
Royce MR & MRS Stephen W II ... *Coaster*
Rulon-Miller MR Berkeley T ... *Seahorse*
Russell MRS Angelica L ... *Arielle*
Rynning MR & MRS Eivind P ... *Ternen*

S

Sadtler MR & MRS Samuel B ... *Laura June*
St John MR & MRS Warren Jackson ... *Wishful Thinking*
Sanders MR & MRS David I ... *Pelee Player*
Saul MR & MRS B Francis II ... *Gamine*
Saunders MISS Patricia G ... *Stargazer*
Schaefer MR & MRS Frederic M ... *Paquet V*
Schleussner MRS Robert C JR ... *Bardscraft*
Schoellerman MR & MRS Jack L ... *Bora Bora*
Schoettle MR & MRS Karl J JR ... *Integrity*
Schutt MR & MRS Charles P JR ... *Safari*
Scott MR & MRS George C JR ... *Dipper*
Heeltapper
Seamans DR & MRS Robert C JR ... *Viva*
Senior MR & MRS Enrique F ... *Circe*
Shafer MRS Gail P ... *Virgil P Gibney*
Sharp MR & MRS Robert W ... *Tarantella*
Sheppard MR & MRS Carl F JR ... *Sand Witch*
Sheppard MR & MRS W Stevens ... *Mainstay*
Shenemere
Sheridan MR & MRS John Edward ... *Passage East*
Shields MR & MRS David V ... *Zephyr*
Shinn MR & MRS Jonathan H ... *Symphony*
Sibley MR & MRS Stephen T ... *Louvoyeur*
Sigety MR & MRS Cornelius E ... *Ketchup*
Silver MR Duncan M ... *Silver Lining*
Silverthorne MRS John H ... *Duckplucker*
Slingluff MR David D JR ... *Sugarbush*
Slingluff MRS Patricia K ... *Nani Ola II*
Slingluff MRS T Rowland ... *Cruzan*
Smith DR & MRS Alexander B ... *Joie de Vivre*
Smith DR & MRS Barry H ... *Spirit*
Smith MR & MRS Blair W ... *Sara B*
Smith MR & MRS H Morgan ... *Malta*
Smith MR K Hart ... *Hasty Heart*

Smith MR & MRS Rodney W	*Déjà Vu*
Smith MISS Sallie Dorsey	*Dyon*
Smith MR William G S	*Grey Goose*
Smythe LT CDR & MRS T H Butler II	*Caerulean*
Spencer MR & MRS Duncan C	*Cosa II*
Stafford MR & MRS Robert T	*Full Moon*
Stein MR & MRS Charles F III	*Snallygaster*
Stevenson MR & MRS Frederick J JR	*Yoctangee*
Stewart MR David E	*Blue Point*
Stewart MR & MRS John A JR	*Oyster Stew*
Stone MR & MRS Charles Lanier	*Astra III*
Storey MR & MRS James M	*Isola*
Story CAPT & MRS William F	*Fabula*
Stovell DR & MRS Peter B	*Esprit III*
Strong MR Steven W	*Pandora*
Stubbs MR & MRS Michael B	*Desperate Lark*
Sturtevant MR & MRS Peter A	*Cachalot*
Sumner MR Jason	*No Name*
Sutton MRS F Michael	*Maria IV*
Swift MR & MRS Humphrey H	*Sea Horse*
Swift MR & MRS Nathan B	*Sandpiper II*

T

Taussig MR & MRS Frederick	*Rampant*
Taylor MR & MRS Richard S	*Owl*
Tetzeli MR Frederick E	*Ahchung*
Thatcher MR & MRS John M P III	*Song 'N Dance*
Thomas MR B Brooks	*Teal*
Thomas MR & MRS Donald W	*Yonder*
Thomas MR & MRS Lowell S JR	*Fox Trot II*
Thomas MR & MRS William P	*Makai*
Thompson MR & MRS Ralph F JR	*Halcyon II*
Thorington MR & MRS James II	*Conflict*
Thorne MR & MRS Daniel K	*Cristobal*
Thorsen MR & MRS J Gwynne	*Private Lives*
Thys MR Thierry N	*Favorite Daughter*
Tiffany MR & MRS Edwin P	*Patience*
Timpson MR & MRS Carl W JR	*Timper*
Timpson MR & MRS James	*Flying Colors Traveller*
Tonissi MR & MRS M Pierre	*Splashy Dog*
Townsend MR & MRS Thomas H	*Windslipper V*
Train MR & MRS John	*Iona*
Tucker DR Samuel H	*Loriinae*
Turpin MR Traynter B	*Rudee's Rendezvous*

U

Urbahn MR & MRS Eric M	*Finback*
Utgoff CAPT & MRS Vadym V	*Vami*

V

van Buren MR & MRS Harold S JR	*Halcyon*
Vanderlip MR & MRS Henrik N	*The Other Line*
Van Dine MR & MRS Vance	*Bel Canto*
van Heerden MR & MRS Christiaan I	*Electra*
Van Rensselaer MR & MRS Alexander T	*Cancan*
Van Sciver MR Wesley J	*Friendship*
Voevodsky MR & MRS Peter	*Nana III*
von Wentzel MRS Elizabeth Cabot	*Cats Pyjamas*
von Zweck MR & MRS Heimart	*Allegra*

W

Wainwright MR Stuyvesant II	*Wainscott Wind*
Walling MR Alexander R H	*Republic of Vermont*
Waring MR & MRS Bradish J	*Damtootin*
Warner MR Irving JR	*Zephyr*
Warren MR William S	*Vorlage*
Watkins MR Lowry Rush II	*Justifiable*
Watson MISS Olive F	*Oz Ocean*
Watts MR & MRS James Harrison	*Molly Jane*
Waud MR & MRS Cornelius Byron	*Hawk*
Webb DR & MRS Charles A	*Hollyday*
Welch MR Noble	*Four Belles*
Welch MR & MRS W Perry	*Lady Catherine*
Weld REV & MRS George F II	*Grace*
Welles MR & MRS Edward R III	*Dream*
Welles MR & MRS Peter de L	*Heron Southern Cross*
Welsh MR & MRS John L JR	*Phoebe C*
Wesley MR & MRS Timothy A	*Tinker Toy*
Wheeler MR & MRS Thomas B	*Off The Hook*
White MR & MRS Christopher M	*Spirit*
White MR & MRS Harold T	*Gadfly*
Whitmore MR & MRS John R	*Sundowner*
Whittaker MR & MRS Philip N	*Whit's End*
Wickser MISS M Melissa	*Telluride*
Wiehl MR & MRS Ernest A JR	*Magic*
Willcox MR & MRS J Keating	*Ebb Tide*
Williams DR & MRS Howard C	*Bandit*
Williams MR & MRS John M	*Lord Jeff*
Williams MR & MRS Robert W JR	*Ishtar*
Williams MR & MRS Thomas A	*Grayling*
Williamson MR & MRS Norman B	*Concorde*
Willits MR & MRS Christopher N	*Sarah*
Wilmerding MR & MRS Patrick R	*Minstrel*
Wilson MR & MRS Frederick E	*Vindalf*
Wilson MR & MRS Milton III	*Escargo*
Winstead MR & MRS David L	*On Time*
Wirtz MR & MRS William W	*Blackhawk IV*
Wladyka MR & MRS William J	*Altair*
Wolcott MR & MRS Frank E III	*Panda*
Wood MR & MRS Theodore V JR	*Woodshed*
Woodland MR Henry T JR	*Shawna*
Woods MR & MRS James A	*Whimsey*
Woods MR & MRS Richard M	*Eventide*
Woollam MR & MRS Philip M	*Timy*
Worm de Geldern MR & MRS Vagn	*Dulcibella*
Wurts MR & MRS Clarence Z	*The Third Wave*

Wyman MR & MRS Parker D .... *Whim*

Y

Yarington DR & MRS Charles T JR .... *Endurance II*
Yerkes MR & MRS Harry Estile III .... *Predator*
York MR & MRS B Hamlin III .... *Little Chum II*

YACHTS AND TENDERS

Type	Name Owner	Length	Beam	Draft	Gross Tonnage	Builder	Year Launched	Home Port	Club Affiliations
	ABRACADABRA MR & MRS Silas R Anthony JR	22'	—	—	—	Mako Marine, Inc	1979	Quogue, NY	
	ABRAZOS MR George B E Hambleton	30'	12'	3'	—	Cape Dory Yachts, Inc	1990	Seal Cove, ME	Nf
	ACCEPTANCE II MR & MRS Daniel Huber	32'	11'	3'6"	—	Bayliner Marine Corp	1984	Dana Point Harbor, CA	
	ADAGIO MR & MRS David H Deming	40'9"	11'9"	4'3"	8.9	Henry R Hinckley & Co	1974	Oyster Bay, NY	S
	ADAGIO MR & MRS Arthur E Newbold III	26'	8'	4'	2	Bayfield	1983	Northeast Harbor, ME	Nf
	ADIOS MR & MRS Allan A A Flynn	31'	11'2"	3'	10	Bertram Yacht	1974	Plandome, NY	
	AGINCOURT MR John S Rando JR	30'	5'10"	3'11"	—	Obscure Boats	1985	Gloucester, MA	Ey, Rby, Sfy
	AHCHUNG MR Frederick E Tetzeli	23'	9'	3'	—	Pro-Line, Inc	1984	Boca Grande, FL	
	AIMLESS LADY MR S Eyre McKenrick JR	24'	8'6"	2'6"	1.25	Thunder Craft	1993	Annapolis, MD	
	AIRDRIE MRS Spencer B Fulweiler	25'	8'	3'	6	Bayliner Marine Corp	1981	Wilmington, DE	Ny
	ALBICORE MR & MRS Walter Maynard JR	41'	10'9"	5'9"	11	Luder Marine Construction Co	1955	Sag Harbor, NY	
	ALERION MR & MRS Deryck Van V Livingston	25'	8'	3'11"	—	Hunter Marine	1982	Rye, NY	
	ALFALFA MR William O Hunt JR	28'	7'	4'9"	3	Rice Lake Boatworks	1964	Cedarville, MI	
	ALLEGRA MR Henry A Dall	26'	8'	4'	3.25	Einar Ohlson	1969	False Whitehead Harbor, ME	
	ALLEGRA MR & MRS Heimart von Zweck	30'	9'	5'	4.2	Cape Cod Ship Building Co	1982	Marion, MA	Bvl
	ALLIEGATOR DR & MRS Matthew R Moore	41'5"	12'4"	2'5"	7	Sea Ray Boats, Inc	1992	Boca Raton, FL	

182 | YACHTS AND TENDERS

Type	Name / Owner	Length	Beam	Draft	Gross Tonnage	Builder	Year Launched	Home Port	Club Affiliations
	ALPHA MR & MRS David B Arnold JR	29′	6′	2′6″	4	Anchorage, Inc—Dyer Boats	1982	Gloucester, MA	
	ALTAIR MR & MRS Adrian T Bogart JR & MR & MRS William J Wladyka	30′3¾″	6′6″	4′9″	2.08	Shields	1964	Oyster Bay, NY	S
	AMPHITRITE MR & MRS Frederick H Osborn III	28′6″	8′4″	4′8″	7.6	Pearson Yachts	1964	Gouldsboro, ME	Ny
	ANEMONE MR & MRS H Felix Kloman II	36′	12′6″	6′	6	Tillotson-Pearson, Inc	1987	Tenants Harbor, ME	
	ANNIE T MR & MRS John Douglas Forbes	26′	8′	—	—	R W Stanley	1963	Southwest Harbor, ME	
	ANODYNE MR & MRS G Thompson Pew JR	43′9″	13′10″	8′3″	23	Jeanneau	1989	Philadelphia, PA	Cry
	ANTARES MR Franklin A Leib	41′	12′9″	6′6″	—	Cheoy Lee Shipyards, Ltd	1978	New York, NY	
	APHRODITE MRS (DR) Beatrice H Barrett	28′6″	8′4″	3′	—	Soverel Marine, Inc	1963	Chatham, MA	
	AQUACOLOR MR & MRS W Tuckerman Biays	33′	12′	2′6″	8	Penn-Yan Marine Mfg Corp	1983	Key Largo, FL	
	ARABELLA MR & MRS Paul G Pennoyer JR	48′	12′6″	6′6″	9.6	Jacobs	1936	Cohasset, MA	Ny
	ARABELLA MR & MRS David E Place	47′	12′	6′	28	Jacobs	1937	Robinhood Cove, ME	
	ARCTURUS MR & MRS William F May	36′	11′	4′	14	Webbers Cove Boat Yard	1980	Rockport, ME	
	ARGO MR & MRS Theodore H Myer	38′6″	11′	4′	7.5	Alden Yachts	1962	Wiscasset, ME	S
	ARIEL MRS Catherine L O'Brien	30′	10′	6′	5.6	Foster	1948	Southampton, NY	Dyc, Syc
	ARIELLE MRS Angelica L Russell	45′5″	13′2½″	4′11″	26.91	Bristol Yacht Co	1982	Padanaram, MA	
	ARISTEA MR & MRS James D Phyfe	47′11″	13′9″	7′10″	28	Nautor	1981	New York, NY	Co, Ny

Type	Name Owner	Length	Beam	Draft	Gross Tonnage	Builder	Year Launched	Home Port	Club Affiliations
⛵	**ARRIVADERCI** MR & MRS L Scott Frantz	29'	10'	2'	6	Riva of Italy	1959	Greenwich, CT	
⛵	**ARTURUS** MR & MRS Thomas Pierpont Grose	21'	5'10"	3'6"	2	J M Williams Co	1989	Christmas Cove, ME	
⛵	**ASTRA III** MR & MRS Charles Lanier Stone	33'	11'	4'	—	Hunter Marine	1980	Greenwich, CT	
⛵	**ASTREA** MR & MRS Stephen K Galpin	36'	11'	3'	10	Hinckley-Newman	1988	Southport, CT	Pqt
⛵	**AUK VI** MR & MRS Charles F Adams	60'	17'	5'4"	54	Lyman-Morse Boatbuilding Co	1992	Portsmouth, RI	Ny
⛵	**AURORA** MR & MRS Nigel S MacEwan	46'11"	13'3"	5'	16.5	Alden/Molich, Denmark	1973	Dark Harbor, ME	Ny
⛵	**AURORA** MRS Kennett L Rawson	44'	12'	5'6"	20	Pearson Yachts	1965	Setauket, NY	
⛵	**AVANT-GARDE** MR & MRS Henry T Chandler	35'1"	11'7"	6'	6.5	H Wauquiez	1984	Lake Forest, IL	Glc
⛵	**BAERCAT** MR & MRS Gordon R Baer JR	22'	10'	2'	—	Marshall Cat	1986	Oxford, MD	
⛵	**BALLAD** MR & MRS J B Neil Benney JR	31'	8'10"	3'9"	5.2	Cheoy Lee Shipyards, Ltd	1969	Marblehead, MA	Co, Ey
⛵	**BALUKE** MR & MRS Thomas C Rogerson	22'	7'	2'	—	G Patten	1983	Duxbury, MA	
⛵	**BANDIT** DR & MRS Howard C Williams	20'	5'	2'	1.5	O'Day Corp	1973	West Islip, NY	
⛵	**BARDSCRAFT** MRS Robert C Schleussner JR	24'	12'	3'	1.5	Bayliner Marine Corp	1984	Gibson Island, MD	
⛵	**BARSEEKER** MR & MRS Richard H King	28'	9'	4'	5	Sabre Yachts	1976	West Falmouth, MA	
⛵	**BATELEUR** MR & MRS Robert J A Irwin JR	30'3"	11'8"	4'3"	7'	Hinterhoeller Yachts	1994	Niagara-on-the-Lake, Ontario, Canada	
⛵	**BAY MONARCH** MR & MRS E Lawrence Dinning IV	39'	13'	3'	—	Topaz Marine Corp	1990	Bush River, MD	

YACHTS AND TENDERS

Type	Name / Owner	Length	Beam	Draft	Gross Tonnage	Builder	Year Launched	Home Port	Club Affiliations
	BEA HAPPY *MR & MRS Peter Herrick*	36'	11'7"	2'10"	5.7	Carver Boat Co	1989	City Island, NY	
	BEL CANTO *MR & MRS Vance Van Dine*	45'	13'6"	4'6"	12.5	Irwin Yacht Marine Corp	1983	Glen Cove, NY	Ny, S
	BERWYN *MR & MRS Samuel F Abernethy*	38'	9'6"	2'6"	—	R Wiley	1952	Oxford, MD	
	BESSIE BABY V *MR & MRS Eugene G de Bullet JR*	36'	12'	3'	14	Trojan Yachts	1979	Ft Worth, TX	
	BETSY B *MR & MRS Robert Page Burr*	38'	13'	4'	10	M L Pettegrow, Inc	1990	Matinicus, ME	
	BLACKHAWK IV *MR & MRS William W Wirtz*	123'2"	23'3"	12'8"	244	DeVries, Scheepsbouw Aalsmeer, The Netherlands	1971	Chicago, IL	Cyc
	BLITHE SPIRIT *MR & MRS Lionel S Johns*	40'	11'6"	5'6"	11.5	Ketch	1977	Solomons, MD	
	BLIZZARD *MR & MRS Louis M Freeman JR*	36'	13'6"	2'6"	12	Topaz Marine Corp	1984	New Orleans, LA	
	BLUE CHANTEY *MR & MRS Buell Hollister IV*	40'9"	11'9"	4'3"	12	Henry R Hinckley & Co	1960	South Dartmouth, MA	Rby
	BLUECHIP *MR & MRS Jeffrey F Chandor*	40'	12'	5'	—	Bristol Yacht Co	1984	Little Compton, RI	
	BLUEFLOWER *MR & MRS Samuel Ainsworth Hird JR*	34'	10'3"	3'11"	5.3	Douglas & MacLeod	1969	Shelter Island, NY	
	BLUE GOOSE *DR & MRS Henry H Balch*	43'4"	13'	3'4"	26	Matthews Co	1964	Washington, DC	Ayc
	BLUEJACKET *MR & MRS George M Pulver*	36'	11'4"	3'9"	10.49	Bowman/Emsworth	1970	River Exe Canal, Exeter, Devon, England	
	BLUE POINT *MR David E Stewart*	33'9"	10'6"	5'	6	Allied Boat Co	1968	Newport, RI	Il, Ny
	BLUES CHASER *MR & MRS Grafton S Kennedy*	25'	8'	2'	—	Sea Ray Boats, Inc	1986	Dover, NH	
	BORA BORA *MR & MRS Jack L Schoellerman*	32'	12'	—	—	Beneteau, Ltd	1990	Newport Beach, CA	

Type	Name / Owner	Length	Beam	Draft	Gross Tonnage	Builder	Year Launched	Home Port	Club Affiliations
	BOUNDER IV MR & MRS W Boatner Reily III	31'	—	—	—	Bertram Yacht	1969	Edgartown, MA	Eyc, Ny
	BREATHLESS MR & MRS Duncan G Burke	21'	8'2"	2'6"	1.2	Mako Marine, Inc	1996	Greenwich, CT	Ihy
	BRER' FOX MR & MRS Mark Murphy	30'10"	11'9"	2'4"	5.1	Chris-Craft	1986	Erie, PA	
	BRIEF CANDLE MR & MRS Edward H Osgood JR	36'	11'3"	6'4"	11	Sabre Yachts	1987	Essex, CT	Exy
	BRIGHT THREAD MR & MRS Peter H McCormick	26'	10'	2'	3	Rogers Marine Corp	1985	Padanaram, MA	
	BRITANNIA SERENA DR & MRS (DR) A E Keir Nash	36'7"	12'	5'9"	7	Catalina Yachts	1988	Santa Barbara, CA	
	CACHALOT MR & MRS Peter A Sturtevant	35'3"	11'3"	5'6"	9	J White	1970	Brooklin, ME	
	CAERULEAN LT CDR & MRS T H Butler Smythe II	38'	12'	4'6"	—	Island Packet	1994	San Diego, CA	
	CALLOOH CALLAY MR & MRS William L Beadleston	40'	12'10"	6'	14.5	Tashiba	1989	Bass Harbor, ME	Nf
	CALYPSO MR & MRS Walter Albert Dewhurst	36'	12'6"	3'11"	—	Kong & Halvorsen	1984	San Diego, CA	Sdy
	CAMARUCHE MR & MRS Leroy Frantz JR	49'6"	15'	4'3"	—	Albin Marine, Inc	1987	Stamford, CT	Ny, Why
	CANCAN MR & MRS Alexander T Rensselaer	47'	14'8"	5'10"	15	H Wauquiez	1985	Westport, CT	Ny, Pqt
	CAPELLA MR & MRS David F Millet	36'	12'	6'6"	21	Sabre Yachts	1995	Biddeford Pool, ME	Cry
	CARAMBA MR & MRS William A King	40'	14'	6'	10.5	Tania Yacht Co	1989	Riverside, CT	Ny
	CARINA MR & MRS William M Passano JR & MR & MRS William M Passano III	37'6"	12'6"	7'	—	J-Boats, Inc	1989	Gibson Island, MD	
	CAROLINE MR & MRS Peter Black	50'6"	15'5"	5'	—	Grand Banks Yachts, Ltd	1995	Portsmouth, NH	Ny
	CAROLINE MR Warren Ingersoll Claytor	24'	8'6"	3'6"	1.5	Bristol Yacht Co	1966	Radnor, PA	

YACHTS AND TENDERS

Type	Name / Owner	Length	Beam	Draft	Gross Tonnage	Builder	Year Launched	Home Port	Club Affiliations
	CASSIOPEIA MR & MRS Andrew M Feder	38'3"	10'11"	5'4"	17	LeComte Co, A, Inc	1970	Oyster Bay, NY	Co, Ny, S
	CATS PYJAMAS MRS Elizabeth Cabot von Wentzel	39'	18'4"	2'6"	—	Prout	1992	South Harpswell, ME	Myc
	CAT'S WHISKERS MR & MRS Geoffrey B Dougherty	42'	12'	4'	12	Bunker & Ellis	1958	Mantoloking, NJ	Cry
	CAVIAR MR & MRS Harden L Crawford III	65'	15'	5'6"	31	Wellington Boats	1986	Far Hills, NJ	Myc, Ny
	CHAMP MR & MRS Frank S Bissell	27'	9'6"	2'	—	Grady-White Boats, Inc	1995	Easton, MD	Ny
	CHASSEUR MR & MRS Thomas L McLane	38'	11'6"	6'6"	—	Sabre Yachts	1984	Norwalk, CT	Ny
	CHEERS MR & MRS Peter S P Dimsey	40'	12'8"	7'	8.5	C & C Yachts, Ltd	1982	Wilson Point, CT	
	CHEERS MR & MRS Jonathan E Emerson	39'6"	10'6"	5'2"	14	Kaiser Yachts, Inc	1979	Farmington, CT	
	CHICKEN OF THE SEA MR & MRS Gerrit L Lansing	32'	9'6"	3'4"	—	R Rich	1952	Northeast Harbor, ME	Nf
	CHIME MR & MRS Frederic H Morris	35'	10'6"	5'	12	De Visser NV, The Netherlands	1970	Manchester, MA	Myc
	CHIRIQUI MR Edwin M Chance	37'	12'	4'2"	15	Tartan Marine Co	1979	Baltimore, MD	
	CHRISTINA MR Joseph W Klapp	53'	15'5"	5'	40	Hatteras Yachts	1971	Philadelphia, PA	
	CINCUENTA MR & MRS Freeborn G Jewett JR	30'	9'6"	5'	4	Pearson Yachts	1978	Gibson Island, MD	
	CIRCE MR & MRS Enrique F Senior	36'	13'	3'6"	—	John Rybovich & Sons	1957	—	
	CLARION MR & MRS Samuel P M Gray & MR & MRS W Latimer Gray JR	35'	10'10"	4'	10	Bristol Yacht Co	1978	Marion, MA	Bvl
	COASTER MR & MRS Stephen W Royce II	41'3"	12'	6'3"	17	M Peterson	1935	Boston, MA	

Type	Name / Owner	Length	Beam	Draft	Gross Tonnage	Builder	Year Launched	Home Port	Club Affiliations
⛵	**COMPLEX VII** MR Britton Chance	22'	7'	3'	2	Plas-Trend	1970	Mantoloking, NJ	Cry
⛵	**COMPLEX X** MR Britton Chance	32'	8'	2'	3	Marine Innovations	1975	Marathon, FL	Cry
⛵	**CONCORDE** MR & MRS Norman B Williamson	44'	14'	8'	11	J-Boats, Inc	1990	Newport Beach, CA	
⛵	**CONFLICT** MR & MRS James Thorington II	35'6"	10'	4'	13	Bristol Yacht Co	1983	Easton, MD	Cry
⛵	**CORIOLIS** MR S Trevor Pardee JR	30'2"	6'	4'5"	2.25	Chris-Craft	1971	Oyster Bay, NY	S
🚤	**COSA II** MR & MRS Duncan C Spencer	42'	12'	3'6"	13	Matthews Co	1955	Deltaville, VA	Fb
🚤	**COUNTESS** MR & MRS Francis Earle III	36'	12'	4'	13	Grand Banks Yachts, Ltd	1980	Sandy Point, WA	
⛵	**CRISTOBAL** MR & MRS Daniel K Thorne	70'	13'	7'	37	Seaglass Yachts	1977	Galveston, TX	Ny
⛵	**CROCODILE** MRS U Haskell Crocker	39'10"	10'	5'8"	—	Abeking & Rasmussen	1959	Manchester, MA	Myc
⛵	**CROSS WAVE** MR & MRS Richard Ford Pew	40'9"	11'9"	3'11"	12	Henry R Hinckley & Co	1987	Jackson Hole, WY	Bvl, Ny
⛵	**CRUCERO** MR & MRS Clarence H King JR	42'	15'	4'7"	—	Kady-Krogen Yachts, Inc	1988	Boca Grande, FL	
⛵	**CRUZAN** MRS T Rowland Slingluff	65'5"	17'	7'	76	Sparkman & Stevens, Inc	1966	Wilmington, DE	Nf
⛵	**CYBÈLE** MR & MRS Joseph Mattison III	37'5"	10'3"	5'6"	15.48	Ohlson Brothers, Gothenburg, Sweden	1971	Edgartown, MA	Eyc, Ny
🚤	**DAMTOOTIN** MR & MRS Bradish J Waring	36'	11'9"	3'9"	—	Willard	1965	Charleston, SC	
⛵	**DANCER** MR John W Clinnin	43'10"	14'	8'3"	10.5	C & C Yachts, Ltd	1980	Gibson Island, MD	
🚤	**DAWN** MR & MRS Benjamin McT Gaston JR	44'	14'6"	3'6"	15	Cruisers, Inc	1988	Marathon, FL	
🚤	**DAWN MIST** MRS Clifford C McAleenan	24'	9'6"	1'5"	—	Hinterhoeller Yachts	1989	Rockport, ME	

YACHTS AND TENDERS

Type	Name / Owner	Length	Beam	Draft	Gross Tonnage	Builder	Year Launched	Home Port	Club Affiliations
	DAWN TREADER MR John R Brown JR	44'	11'3"	4'6"	11	Morgan Yachts	1971	Urbanna, VA	
	DAWN TREADER MR & MRS Alfred T Ogden II	33'	11'	5'11"	6.2	Pearson Yachts	1974	Stonington, CT	
	DAYBREAK MR Harry R Madeira	41'2"	10'2"	6'1"	—	Henry R Hinckley & Co	1965	Northeast Harbor, ME	Nf
	DÉJÀ VU MR & MRS Rodney W Smith	34'	8'6"	3'	—	Elco, Inc	1931	Irvington, VA	
	DESPERATE LARK MR & MRS Michael B Stubbs	48'10"	10'6"	7'6"	—	Herreshoff Mfg Co	1903	Orcutts Harbor, ME	Ny
	DIDO MR & MRS Thomas Pierpont Grose	23'	8'	2'	1.5	Seaway Boats, Inc	1983	Christmas Cove, ME	
	DIDO MR & MRS George B Harris	30'	8'6"	4'	6	Pearson Yachts	1962	Vineyard Haven, MA	Co
	DIPPER MR & MRS George C Scott JR	26'	7'11"	5'	6	Seafarer Yachts, Inc	1962	Ipswich, MA	Ey
	DONALD DUCK MR & MRS Wesley C Dudley	46'7"	16'	5'	22	Bertram Yacht	1981	Philadelphia, PA	
	DORADO MR & MRS Avery Catlin	41'	—	—	—	Tiger Marine	—	Edgartown, MA	Eyc
	DOWN EAST MR & MRS Charles L Poor	36'	10'	4'	18	J Newman, Inc	1979	Washington, DC	Ayc
	DREAM MR & MRS Edward R Welles III	37'	12'	5'	15	Gulfstar, Inc	1979	Bar Harbor, ME	
	DRUMMUIR MR & MRS Lee H Barneson	65'	18'	7'6"	—	Skallerud	1968	Los Angeles, CA	
	DUCKPLUCKER MRS John H Silverthorne	53'	—	5'	27	Hatteras Yachts	1977	Lake Texoma, TX	
	DULCIBELLA MR & MRS Vagn Worm de Geldern	44'2"	12'6"	4'11"	—	Alden Yachts	1978	Old Saybrook, CT	Co, Exy, Ny
	DULCINEA MR & MRS Philip E Rollhaus JR	48'6"	16'4"	4'	25.5	Ocean Yachts, Inc	1989	Shelter Island, NY	
	DYON MISS Sallie Dorsey Smith	52'6"	13'	7'6"	20	Luder Marine Construction Co	1924	Tenants Harbor, ME	

Type	Name / Owner	Length	Beam	Draft	Gross Tonnage	Builder	Year Launched	Home Port	Club Affiliations
⛵	**EBB TIDE** MR & MRS J Keating Willcox	40'	8'	4'	4	Legnos Boatbuilding, Inc	1971	Eastern Point, MA	
⛵	**EDWINNA B** MR & MRS W Boatner Reily III	22'	—	—	—	M Schwarz	1932	Edgartown, MA	Eyc, Ny
⛵	**ELECTRA** MR & MRS F Gregg Burger	24'	9'	2'	—	Starboard Yacht Co	1986	Bay Head, NJ	
⛵	**ELECTRA** MR & MRS Christiaan I van Heerden	25'5"	7'9"	2'9"	1.5	Mt Desert Yacht Yard	1958	Northeast Harbor, ME	Nf
🚤	**ELENA** MR & MRS A Sydney Roberts JR	44'	13'	4'	—	Garlington	1989	Palm Beach, FL	
⛵	**ELENOA** MR & MRS Paul R Mitchell	36'	10'6"	5'6"	9	R S Gilbert	1988	Sydney, Australia	Ny
⛵	**ELIZA** MR & MRS Herbert W Goodall III	80'	20'6"	9'10"	—	Southern Ocean Shipyards	1981	Ponte Vedra Beach, FL	Nyc
⛵	**ELLEN** MR Lawrence H Mott	15'	4'6"	—	—	U Fox	1959	Charlotte, VT	
🚤	**EMMA T** MR & MRS (DR) Matthew H Pedersen	20'	7'	18"	1	Mako Marine, Inc	1993	Cumberland Foreside, ME	
⛵	**ENDEAVOR** MRS Astrid J Reksten	40'	13'	4'3"	9.5	Pearson Yachts	1980	Newburyport, MA	
🚤	**ENDURANCE II** DR & MRS Charles T Yarington JR	50'	16'	4'	16	Ocean-Alexander	1985	Seattle, WA	
🚤	**ENSPIGNANT II** MR & MRS Frank M Ridley	24'	9'6"	1'6"	—	Morgan Yachts	1988	Naples, FL	
🚤	**ESCAPADE** MR & MRS John W Galston	30'	12'10"	2'10"	9	Egg Harbor Boat Co	1976	Cold Spring Harbor, NY	Ny
🚤	**ESCARGO** MR & MRS Milton Wilson III	33'	8'	18"	3.5	Fountain Power Boats	1986	San Rafael, CA	
🚤	**ESCORT** MR William E Murray	39'9"	9'6"	2'9"	—	H B Nevins, Inc	1940	Charleston, SC	
⛵	**ESPRIT III** DR & MRS Peter B Stovell	37'	11'9"	7'9"	7.75	Tartan Marine Co	1981	Fairfield, CT	Ny, Pqt, Rby
🚤	**EUPHORIA** MR & MRS Thomas G Gallatin JR	35'8"	12'6"	3'	7	Tiara Yachts	1994	Manhasset Bay, NY	Ny

190 | YACHTS AND TENDERS

Type	Name Owner	Length	Beam	Draft	Gross Tonnage	Builder	Year Launched	Home Port	Club Affiliations
	EUREKA III MR & MRS Henry F Rodner JR	54'	15'	5'	50	Hatteras Yachts	1976	La Guaira, Venezuela	
	EVENSTAR MR & MRS Benjamin H Brewster	34'	11'	4'8"	—	Tartan Marine Co	1976	Charlevoix, MI	
	EVENTIDE MR & MRS Richard M Woods	38'	11'6"	4'11"	8	Morris Yachts	1994	Darien, CT	Co
	FABULA CAPT & MRS William F Story	32'	11'	4'	6	Morgan Yachts	1983	Hudgins, VA	Ny
	FAIR LEAD DR & MRS Joseph L Grant	40'	11'4"	5'	10	Yokosuka Marine	1961	Sawyer Cove, ME	Nf
	FAIR WITNESS MR & MRS H Richard Chew	40'9"	11'9"	4'3"	12	Henry R Hinckley & Co	1969	Annapolis, MD	Rby
	FANCY MR Charles Mallory	52'	13'6"	7'	18	Sanford Wood	1987	Key West, FL	Ihy, Ny
	FANTASIA MR Eugene J Olmi JR	58'4"	15'10"	4'	43	Hatteras Yachts	1972	Tantallon, MD	
	FARSIDER DR & MRS James B Haines	23'10"	8'6"	3'	2	Sea Ray Boats, Inc	1996	Cedarville, MI	
	FAT CHANCE MR & MRS Stephen C Kratovil	22'7"	8'	1'2"	1	Mako Marine, Inc	1980	Dover, DE	Eyc, Ny
	FAVORITE DAUGHTER MR Thierry N Thys	50'	14'	6'	17	Gulfstar, Inc	1978	San Francisco, CA	
	FERMINA DAZA DR & MRS Alexander McCurdy III	40'	10'9"	6'	17	Bristol Yacht Co	1972	Northeast Harbor, ME	Nf
	FESTIVE MOOD MR & MRS John McCullough Gibson	43'3"	13'4"	7'4"	23.24	Nautor Ky, Finland	1976	Wilmington, DE	Cry, Ny
	FIDDLER'S GREEN MR & MRS Oren K Boynton	32'	11'2"	3'4"	8	Transpacific	1986	Stonington, CT	
	FINBACK MR & MRS Eric M Urbahn	51'	15'	12'	36	Lyman-Morse Boatbuilding Co	1990	Siasconset, MA	Ny, Nyc
	FIONA MR Andrew Anderson-Bell	39'	31'	6'	12	Jensen Marine Corp	1972	North Haven, ME	Ny
	FLY BY NIGHT MR & MRS Daniel Ravenel	25'	8'	3'6"	—	Hunter Marine	1983	Charleston, SC	

YACHTS AND TENDERS | 191

Type	Name / Owner	Length	Beam	Draft	Gross Tonnage	Builder	Year Launched	Home Port	Club Affiliations
⛵	**FLYING BUTTRESS II** MR & MRS *Edward R Johnson* & MISS *Lacy K Johnson*	31′	9′	—	—	Golden Era Boats	1996	Noank, CT	
⛵	**FLYING COLORS** MR & MRS *James Timpson*	20′9″	7′1½″	3′1½″	—	Golden Era Boats	1981	Dark Harbor, ME	Ny, Pqt
⛵	**FOUR BELLES** MR *Noble Welch*	34′5″	10′2″	3′11″	5.6	Tartan Marine Co	1972	Greenwich, CT	Ihy
⛵	**FOUR GULLS** MR & MRS *Kurt P Metzger*	30′3″	8′9″	4′3″	4.5	Whitby Boat Works, Ltd	1971	East Greenwich, RI	
🚤	**FOX TROT II** MR & MRS *Lowell S Thomas* JR	28′	9′	3′	—	Ellis Boat Co	1987	Eggemoggin, ME	
⛵	**FRAULEIN** MR & MRS *Kenneth H Colburn*	21′	6′	5′	1.5	Boothbay Design	1938	Southport, ME	Why
⛵	**FREEDOM** MR & MRS *James M Brown III*	35′6″	10′10″	4′	8	Bristol Yacht Co	1994	Padanaram, MA	
⛵	**FRIENDSHIP** MR *Wesley J Van Sciver*	27′	10′	3′6″	4	Glen L-Custom	1980	Falmouth, ME	Co
🚤	**FULL MOON** MR & MRS *Robert T Stafford*	55′	14′9″	4′	28	Chris-Craft	1956	Shelburne, VT	
⛵	**GADFLY** MR & MRS *Harold T White*	30′	9′	5′	4	Hinterhoeller Yachts	1969	West Falmouth, MA	
⛵	**GALATEA** MR & MRS *Maurice S Guimont*	44′	13′6″	5′6″	16	Little Harbor Custom Yachts	1986	Gloucester, VA	
⛵	**GAMINE** MR & MRS *B Francis Saul II*	40′7″	11′7″	4′3″	17.38	Henry R Hinckley & Co	1979	Wianno, MA	
🚤	**GASPARILLA** MR *Thomas W Lockwood*	60′	18′6″	5′	40.4	Hatteras Yachts	1986	Ft Pierce, FL	
⛵	**GAZEBO** MR & MRS *Morgan R Barker*	52′	15′6″	5′	23	Little Harbor Custom Yachts	1991	Philadelphia, PA	Cry
🚤	**GLORY** MR *Thomas C Foley*	68′	16′	4′6″	58	J Trumpy & Sons	1955	Greenwich, CT	Ny
⛵	**GOSLING** MR & MRS *Thomas H Carruthers IV*	35′5″	11′6″	6′10″	—	Schlageter	1990	Harbor Point, MI	

YACHTS AND TENDERS

Type	Name Owner	Length	Beam	Draft	Gross Tonnage	Builder	Year Launched	Home Port	Club Affiliations
	GRACE MR John W Persse III	28'2"	9'4"	5'	6	E Rochester	1978	Branford, CT	
	GRACE REV & MRS George F Weld II	25'	6'	3'6"	—	Cape Dory Yachts, Inc	1987	Charleston, SC	
	GRANNY CARR MR & MRS Randolph K Byers JR	24'	6'	4'	2	Brownell Boat Works	1961	Sakonnet, RI	
	GRAYLING MR & MRS Thomas A Williams	44'2"	12'6"	4'9"	12.5	Alden Yachts	1985	Rye, NY	Ny
	GREY GOOSE MR William G S Smith	25'	8'8"	4'6"	—	C & C Yachts, Ltd	1983	Five Mile River, CT	
	GROWLER MR & MRS Allerton D Marshall	36'11"	13'2"	3'6"	18	Lord Nelson Yachts	1985	New York, NY	
	GUILLEMOT MR & MRS John Kean	41'1"	12'11"	4'6"	21	Bristol Yacht Co	1981	Wilmington, DE	S
	GUNGA DIN MR Dayton T Carr	41'	12'9"	5'9"	15	Sweden Yachts	1988	Newport, RI	Ny
	HALCYON MR & MRS George S Meyer	38'	11'6"	4'	—	Sabre Yachts	1987	Oyster Bay, NY	S
	HALCYON MR & MRS Vaughan W Pratt	32'	10'6"	4'	8.5	Grand Banks Yachts, Ltd	1980	Prouts Neck, ME	
	HALCYON MR & MRS Harold S van Buren JR	36'	12'6"	3'2"	9	Nauset Marine, Inc	1996	Harwich Port, MA	
	HALCYON II MR & MRS Ralph F Thompson JR	38'6"	11'	6'	12	Pearson Yachts	1983	Annapolis, MD	
	HALE-KAI III MR & MRS Selwyn Eddy II	44'	15'	3'	5.25	Kings Craft, Inc	1973	San Rafael, CA	
	HASTY HEART MR K Hart Smith	48'	15'	9'2"	22	H Wauquiez	1986	San Francisco, CA	
	HAWK MR & MRS Cornelius Byron Waud	44'	12'6"	7'3"	19	Nautor Ky, Finland	1974	Chicago, IL	Glc, Nf
	HAWKSBILL MR & MRS Howland B Jones JR	56'	15'	5'	30	Hodgeson Brothers	1965	Harwich Port, MA	
	HÄXAN MR & MRS (DR) David E Fairbank	26'4"	9'	5'	.25	Spillersboda, Sweden	1974	Lake Lanier, GA	

Type	Name / Owner	Length	Beam	Draft	Gross Tonnage	Builder	Year Launched	Home Port	Club Affiliations
⛵	**HEELTAPPER** / MR & MRS George C Scott JR	36′	11′	5′6″	10	Graves Yacht Yard	—	Marblehead, MA	Ey
⛵	**HELLO** / MR Anthony K Heller	23′	7′	2′6″	1.25	Seacraft	1967	Blue Hill, ME	
🚤	**HERETIC** / MR Stevenson S Kaminer	28′	11′	—	5	Bertram Yacht	1993	Annapolis, MD	Ayc
⛵	**HERON** / MR & MRS Peter de L Welles	21′8″	7′2″	4′3″	2	O'Day Corp	1983	Manset, ME	
🚤	**HGS** / MR & MRS John R Maschal	26′	8′	2′4″	1.17	Tonnison	1973	Beach Haven, NJ	
⛵	**HIGHLAND FLING** / MR & MRS Stuart P Gillespie SR	37′	10′	5′6″	8.4	Whitby Boat Works, Ltd	1971	Pemaquid, ME	
🚤	**HIGHLAND MIST II** / MR & MRS Albert Keidel JR	34′	10′9½″	3′	17	Webbers Cove Boat Yard	1980	Isle au Haut, ME	
⛵	**HIGHLIGHT** / MR & MRS Bronson W Chanler	42′	12′	6′	12	Alden Yachts	1965	New York, NY	
⛵	**HOLLYDAY** / DR & MRS Charles A Webb	26′	8′	2′5″	2.25	S2 Yachts, Inc	1975	Oxford, MD	
🚤	**HONOR M** / MR & MRS Malcolm O MacLean	42′	15′	3′6″	29	M W Willis & Sons	1966	Lawrence, NY	
⛵	**HOPE-SAN** / MR & MRS Robert Leeson JR	42′	11′1″	6′1″	11	Cheoy Lee Shipyards, Ltd	1959	Wickford, RI	
🚤	**HOSTESS** / MR & MRS Stig Host	27′	9′6″	3′6″	3.45	Albin Marine, Inc	1990	Greenwich, CT	Ihy, Ny
🚤	**HOT CHOCOLATE** / MR & MRS Richard Ottley Beaufort Fox	25′	—	—	—	Bertram Yacht	1968	New Orleans, LA	
🚤	**HOTEL SPLENDIDE** / MR & MRS DeWitt Hornor	42′6″	15′	4′	17	Bertram Yacht	1977	Osterville, MA	DelB, Ny
⛵	**HOT WATER** / MR & MRS Joseph C Hoopes JR	54′	15′1″	5′6″	25	Little Harbor Custom Yachts	1990	Wilmington, DE	Ny
⛵	**HOUND** / MR & MRS Frank Eberhart III	59′11″	13′4″	9′9″	35	Abeking & Rasmussen	1970	Vinalhaven, ME	Ny
⛵	**HOWKOLA** / MR & MRS John Milnes Baker	23′	8′	2′6″	—	O'Day Corp	1974	Norwalk, CT	Co

YACHTS AND TENDERS

Type	Name / Owner	Length	Beam	Draft	Gross Tonnage	Builder	Year Launched	Home Port	Club Affiliations
	HYPER BOREALIS MR & MRS Theodore A McGraw JR	20'	4'	—	1	Feathercraft	1991	Fishers Island, NY	
	ICE BUCKET MR & MRS W Griffin King JR	25'6"	8'	2'6"	—	Mako Marine, Inc	1977	Key Largo, FL	
	INTEGRITY MR & MRS Karl R Schoettle JR	41'	12'	6'6"	12	Nautor Swan	1974	Brooklin, ME	
	INTREPID MR & MRS Stephen D W Austin	48'	15'2"	3'8"	20	Ocean Yachts, Inc	1989	Osterville, MA	
	IONA MR & MRS John Train	34'	10'9"	4'7"	12.7	Victoria Marine	1986	Dark Harbor, ME	
	IRON DUKE MR & MRS Louis H Conklin	25'6"	8'6"	1'6"	4	Stamas Yachts, Inc	1987	Greenland Cove, ME	
	IROQUOIS MR & MRS G H Harris Huey	41'6"	12'8"	5'10"	—	Passport Yachts	1990	Camden, ME	Ny
	ISHMAEL MR & MRS Oliver H Reeder	42'	13'	5'	24	Whitby Boat Works, Ltd	1975	Gibson Island, MD	Ny
	ISHTAR MR & MRS Robert W Williams JR	24'	8'7"	3'10"	3.2	Pacific Seacraft Corp	1989	Ft Myers, FL	
	ISOLA MR & MRS James M Storey	26'	8'2"	3'10"	5	Victoria Marine	1986	Cranberry Isles, ME	Nf
	ISSY "B" II MR & MRS Joseph J Hill	32'	8'	2'	2	D Stevens	1958	Chester, Nova Scotia, Canada	
	JACQUES COEUR MRS Ann W Brewer	32'	10'	3'5"	9	Triangle	1962	Manchester, MA	Myc, Ny
	JENNIE ROSE MR & MRS Robert W Inch	50'	14'6"	4'6"	16.5	CHB	1982	San Francisco, CA	
	JOIE de VIVRE DR & MRS Alexander B Smith	32'	14'	4'	10	Luhrs Corp	1975	Larchmont, NY	
	JOLLY SIXPENCE MR & MRS Edward S MacArthur	36'	12'6"	3'6"	—	American Marine	1980	Racine, WI	Cyc
	JUBILATION MR Willard Emery	41'	13'	8'	9.5	W D Schock Corp	1984	Wilmington, DE	
	JUSTIFIABLE MR Lowry Rush Watkins II	32'	12'	3'	7	Burns Craft	1974	Louisville, KY	

Type	Name / Owner	Length	Beam	Draft	Gross Tonnage	Builder	Year Launched	Home Port	Club Affiliations
⛵	KAHALA III CAPT & MRS Robert M Hinckley	41'	12'	6'	14	—	1980	Altea, Alicante, Spain	Ny
🚤	KAHLUA III MR & MRS Theodore B Conklin	36'	—	12'	—	Grand Banks Yachts, Ltd	1972	Boca Grande, FL	Ny
🚤	KATAHDIN MR & MRS Arthur M Rogers JR	32'	12'	4'	12	J Newman, Inc	1977	Bass Harbor, ME	
⛵	KATAMA MR & MRS James L Pfeffer	40'	12'1"	5'	7.7	Tillotson-Pearson, Inc	1989	Essex, CT	Ny
⛵	KATY MR & MRS Barry J Carroll	41'	13'	4'2"	18	Morgan Marine	1979	Lake Forest, IL	
⛵	KEHAAR MR & MRS Samuel Bailey JR	24'	8'	4'	—	Tillotson-Pearson, Inc	1980	Nantucket, MA	Ny, Nyc
⛵	KETCHUP MR & MRS Cornelius E Sigety	51'3"	14'	5'10"	21.5	Henry R Hinckley & Co	1985	Pipersville, PA	
⛵	KIBOSH MR & MRS Robert S Roberson	30'2"	9'	5'	6	Jensen Marine Corp	1969	Norfolk, VA	Fiy, Ny
🚤	KIMARI MR & MRS Edward A Kilroy JR	70'	18'3"	5'	51	Hatteras Yachts	1989	Cleveland, OH	
🚤	KIMSONG MR & MRS Edward F Herrlinger II	46'	14'	4'7"	19.5	American Marine	1991	Cincinnati, OH	Eyc, Ny
⛵	KINSALE MR John H Reilly JR	41'	11'3"	4'2"	—	Morgan Yachts	1969	New York, NY	Ihy, Ny, S
⛵	KIRANA III MR & MRS Godfrey A Rockefeller	42'8"	12'6"	5'9"	—	Henry R Hinckley & Co	1987	Gibson Island, MD	
⛵	KUAN YIN III MRS Harry H Harper JR	26'4"	8'6"	2'10"	2	Nimble Boats, Inc	1996	Gwynedd, PA	
⛵	LADYBETH MR & MRS Edward L Hicks III	38'8"	12'4"	4'3"	9	Sabre Yachts	1988	Greenwich, CT	
🚤	LADY BUG MR & MRS Dan S Mortensen	43'	15'6"	3'8"	27	Hatteras Yachts	1972	Vero Beach, FL	
🚤	LADY CATHERINE MR & MRS W Perry Welch	40'10"	13'7"	4'4"	15	Hatteras Yachts	1989	Oyster Bay, NY	
⛵	LADY JANE DR & MRS Richard N Pierson JR	27'	—	4'6"	—	Tartan Marine Co	1963	Cranberry Isles, ME	

YACHTS AND TENDERS

Type	Name / Owner	Length	Beam	Draft	Gross Tonnage	Builder	Year Launched	Home Port	Club Affiliations
	LAGNIAPPE IV MR & MRS Lucius W Carroll II	47'	—	—	—	Carver Boat Co	1994	Nashville, TN	
	LA JOLIE ROUSSE MR Edwin M Chance	30'	11'	3'6"	7.26	Westerly Yachts, Ltd	1986	London, England	
	LA MER REV & MRS Nathaniel W Pierce	35'	12'2"	4'11"	6.6	Endeavour Yacht Corp	1984	Cambridge, MD	
	LA RÉSERVE MR & MRS Trevor Fetter	35'	—	—	—	Jeffries	1962	Los Angeles, CA	Sdy
	LAURA JUNE MR & MRS Samuel B Sadtler	31'	10'3½"	4'6"	4.1	Gera Yachts	1990	Philadelphia, PA	Cry
	L'AVENIR MRS Lewis Iselin	29'7"	8'	4'	—	Martha's Vineyard Shipyard, Inc	1978	Camden, ME	
	LA VIDA MR & MRS George Lewis Gildred	44'	15'4"	4'3"	17.5	Kong & Halvorsen	1988	San Diego, CA	Sdy
	LEE SELDEN MR & MRS Babcock MacLean	30'4"	11'10"	5'	8	Hinterhoeller Yachts	1981	Oyster Bay, NY	
	LEGAL EASE MR & MRS T Bowen Hill III	28'6"	11'	27½"	7	Bertram Yacht	1986	Montgomery, AL	
	LIBERTY MISS (REV) Olivia Holmes	36'	12'	6'6"	5	W D Schock Corp	1980	Wilmington, DE	Ny
	LILLIPUT MR & MRS Thomas K Roche	28'	9'11"	5'	2.2	Islander Yachts	1975	Oyster Bay, NY	S
	LITA MR William M Noyes	30'	10'	3'	8	Sunseeker Int'l	1991	Key Biscayne, FL	
	LITTLE CHUM II MR & MRS B Hamlin York III	48'	14'6"	4'	27	Gillikin Brothers	1955	Jupiter, FL	
	LONG HAUL MR & MRS Endicott Peabody	35'	11'	5'	8	Fuji Ketch	1975	Northeast Harbor, ME	
	LORD JEFF MR & MRS John M Williams	32'	10'	5'	—	American Yacht Builders	1968	Oyster Bay, NY	S
	LORELEI MR & MRS Peter G Burke	42'	11'	8'6"	9	Allied Marine	1970	New Orleans, LA	Syc
	LORIINAE DR Samuel H Tucker	45'	13'	5'	20	Columbia Yacht Corp	1973	Philadelphia, PA	

Type	Name Owner	Length	Beam	Draft	Gross Tonnage	Builder	Year Launched	Home Port	Club Affiliations
⛵	**LOUVOYEUR** MR & MRS Stephen T Sibley	29'	9'6"	4'6"	4.5	CAL Boats	1977	Flowery Branch, GA	
🚤	**LUCKY HAOLE III** MR & MRS Hugh B Ogburn	27'	9'6"	3'6"	3.1	Bayliner Marine Corp	1988	Honolulu, HI	
⛵	**LYN DEE** DR & MRS Harry C Bishop	34'	—	4'6"	—	Columbia Yacht Corp	1967	Philadelphia, PA	Co
⛵	**MAGIC** MR & MRS Ernest A Wiehl JR	38'8"	11'	4'	—	Alden Yachts	1962	Southport, CT	Ny, Pqt
🚤	**MAGIC DRAGON** DR & MRS Raymond O Heimbecker	34'	11'	4'	8	Marine Trader Co, Ltd	1973	Georgian Bay, Ontario, Canada	
⛵	**MAGIC X** MR & MRS J Stephen Huebner	30'3"	10'6"	5'9"	9.5	X-Yachts, Denmark	1986	Annapolis, MD	
⛵	**MAIA** DR & MRS Raymond O Heimbecker	30'	9'	7'	7	Morgan Yachts	1969	Hope Town, Abaco, Bahamas	
⛵	**MAINSTAY** MR & MRS W Stevens Sheppard	33'	12'	2'6"	3.75	Stuart Marine Corp	1976	North Haven, ME	Ny, Pqt
⛵	**MAKAI** MR & MRS William P Thomas	28'	8'3"	3'6"	5	Herreshoff Mfg Co	1956	Oxford, MD	Co, Cry
🚤	**MAKO** MR & MRS Charles F Lowrey	41'	14'	3'	9	Hatteras Yachts	1962	San Francisco, CA	Sfy
⛵	**MALAGA** MR & MRS Pierce N McCreary	30'	9'6"	5'9"	8.12	Columbia Yacht Corp	1972	Larchmont, NY	Ny
🚤	**MALTA** MR & MRS H Morgan Smith	35'	11'6"	3'	8.5	Nauset Marine, Inc	1985	Rock Hall, MD	Cry
🚤	**MAMA SAFARI** MRS Victoria J Avery	26'5"	9'	1'5"	3.1	S2 Yachts, Inc	1990	Newport, RI	Il
🚤	**MANANA** MR & MRS Frederick E Crispin	60'	15'3"	4'6"	47	Chris-Craft	1968	Casey Key, FL	
🚤	**MANATEE** MR & MRS W Walter Braham JR	22'	—	—	—	Chris-Craft	1947	Cedarville, MI	
⛵	**MANDALA** MR & MRS E Allen Dennison	34'	10'	3'3"	6	Morgan Yachts	1966	Rye, NY	

198 | YACHTS AND TENDERS

Type	Name / Owner	Length	Beam	Draft	Gross Tonnage	Builder	Year Launched	Home Port	Club Affiliations
	MARGY B MR & MRS Nicholas G K Boyd JR	32'	11'6"	3'6"	—	American Marine, Singapore	1972	San Francisco, CA	Sfy
	MARIA IV MRS F Michael Sutton	45'	13'9"	6'6"	19	Lancer Boats, Inc	1982	Carmel-by-the-Sea, CA	
	MARYMIL IV MR & MRS Milford Boersma	34'8"	10'	4'11"	5.8	Ericson Yachts, Inc	1977	Onekama, MI	
	MARY OAKES MR & MRS Hugh D S Greenway	31'	—	5'6"	—	Concordia Co	1967	North Haven, ME	
	MATIA MR & MRS Phillip H Lorenzen JR	36'	11'	6'	9	Islander Yachts	1975	Seattle, WA	
	MATUTA MR & MRS Daniel P Davison	32'	10'	5'	—	Pacific Seacraft Corp	1994	Peacock Point, NY	Ny, S
	MAYA IV MR & MRS Henry I Prien	44'	14'	3'	20	Bluewater Marine	1986	Belvedere, CA	Sfy
	MEANS OF GRACE MR & MRS Allerton Cushman JR	28'6"	10'	5'2"	—	Devlin Designing Boatbuilders	1995	Olympia, WA	
	MELTEMI MR & MRS David H Fairburn	44'3"	13'8"	5'6"	15	Little Harbor Custom Yachts	1985	Greenwich, CT	Ihy, Ny
	MERMAID MR & MRS (DR) Austin Goodyear	45'8"	11'6"	6'10"	11	P E Luke	1957	Brooklin, ME	
	MERRILIL MR & MRS Charles C Holt III	47'	12'	3'	15	Kenner Mfg Co, Inc	1970	Palm Beach, FL	Why
	MILES TO GO MR & MRS John W Barnum	40'	12'1"	5'2"	20	Tillotson-Pearson, Inc	1988	Colijnsplaat, The Netherlands	Ny
	MIME MR & MRS George Blagden	32'	8'	5'6"	3.7	Lindsay	1986	Blue Hill, ME	Myc
	MIMIKA MR & MRS William C Baker	40'	10'6"	4'	9	Bristol Yacht Co	1979	Annapolis, MD	Ayc
	MINSTREL MR & MRS Patrick R Wilmerding	42'7"	12'8"	8'6"	—	J 130	1994	Blue Hill, ME	Nf

Type	Name / Owner	Length	Beam	Draft	Gross Tonnage	Builder	Year Launched	Home Port	Club Affiliations
	MINX V MR & MRS Theodore B Conklin	41'	—	—	14	Consolidated Ship Building	1946	Westhampton Beach, NY	Ny
	MISCHIEF MR & MRS Scott W Muller	44'	12'8"	5'6"	15	Lyman-Morse Boatbuilders Co	1982	Oxford, MD	Ny, Nyc
	MISS MIDGE MR & MRS Richard T Devaney	29'	10'11"	2'	—	Strike Powerboats	1996	Stuart, FL	
	MISS WIGGINS MR & MRS Walter R Allison	34'	11'	3'	—	Custom Marine	1983	Lighthouse Point, FL	
	MISTRAL MR Nicholas A Leonard	33'	9'3"	4'7"	7	Pearson Yachts	1967	Almería, Spain	
	MISTY ISLE MR & MRS Edwin Gillette	48'	14'	5'	25	G Sutton	1962	Newport Beach, CA	
	MOLLY JANE MR & MRS James Harrison Watts	24'	8'11"	4'1"	1.5	J-Boats, Inc	1979	San Diego, CA	Sdy
	MON RÊVE MR & MRS Dixon P Downey	60'	14'4"	3'	60	Antique Dutch Tjalk	—	Paris, France	
	MOONRAKER MR C Thomas Clagett JR	48'	15'	4'6"	34	M L Pettegrow, Inc	1989	Norfolk, VA	Ayc, Il, Ny, S
	MOONSHINE MR & MRS Henry J Maresi	46'	15'	4'	36	Golden Star	1987	Vero Beach, FL	
	MOONWIND MR & MRS William E C Eustis	31'	9'4"	5'6"	6	Hallberg Rassy	1974	Boston, MA	
	MORNING MIST MR & MRS Geoffrey B Dougherty	24'	8'	2'	1	F Baay, The Netherlands	1951	Mantoloking, NJ	Cry
	MURANA MRS Lucy Baker Dickey	44'6"	14'	5'	27	Lowland Yachts, The Netherlands	1980	St Maarten, Netherlands Antilles	
	MY FAIR LADY MR & MRS Raymond S Deméré	35'	—	—	—	Johnstone	—	Savannah, GA	
	MYSTÈRE MR & MRS Robert D Nobel	35'5"	12'	4'	12.03	Heritage Yacht Corp	1976	Shipshead Creek, MD	Cry

200 | YACHTS AND TENDERS

Type	Name Owner	Length	Beam	Draft	Gross Tonnage	Builder	Year Launched	Home Port	Club Affiliations
⛵	**NAKHODA** MR & MRS *Thomas D Mullins II*	34'4"	10'6"	5'2"	14	Martha's Vineyard Shipyard, Inc	1982	Lamberts Cove, MA	
🛥	**NANA III** MR & MRS *Peter Voevodsky*	31'6"	11'11"	2'8"	6.2	Maritimer	1978	Bahia San Carlos, Guaymas, Mexico	
⛵	**NANI OLA II** MRS *Patricia K Slingluff*	62'	15'9"	8'3"	36	Tyler Boat	1986	Dover, DE	Il
⛵	**NARAKA III** MRS *Reuben B Clark III*	41'	13'6"	4'6"	—	Morgan Yachts	1972	Philadelphia, PA	
⛵	**NARCISSUS** MR & MRS *Lawrence Lowell Reeve*	48'6"	—	—	—	Henry R Hinckley & Co	1967	Mt Desert, ME	Nf
🛥	**NATTY BUMPPO** MR & MRS *Ved P Mehta*	22'	—	—	—	Mako Marine, Inc	1993	Dark Harbor, ME	
🛥	**NAUSHON** MR & MRS *Jesse Nalle*	37'	13'	3'	—	Eldrege/McInnis/Brownell	1969	Saunderstown, RI	Pqt
⛵	**NED KELLY** MR & MRS *Kevin J Devine*	40'	19'9"	2'6"	7.5	Western Boat Works	1975	Berkeley, CA	
⛵	**NEPENTHE** DR & MRS *Allen S Goldman*	33'9"	10'10"	5'	9	Mason	1985	Chicago, IL	
⛵	**NEREUS** MR & MRS *Richard S Gurin*	40'9"	11'9"	4'1"	9.5	Henry R Hinckley & Co	1974	Philadelphia, PA	
🛥	**NITA** MR & MRS *Harry V Keefe JR*	65'	18'	4'	—	Azimut	—	Greenwich, CT	Ny
⛵	**NOBLE FALCON** MR & MRS *Philip G Ottley*	82'	20'	8'	114	D Brooke	1981	Jupiter Island, FL	
⛵	**NOEL** MR *Robert M Nelson*	21'	6'	4'	1	G & Stevens	1930	South Bristol, ME	
🛥	**NO NAME** MR *Jason Sumner*	43'	14'3"	4'9"	15	F T Merrill	1973	Old Greenwich, CT	
🛥	**NO PROBLEM** MR & MRS *John T Robertson III*	26'	—	—	—	Mako Marine, Inc	1989	Cambridge, MD	
⛵	**NORA** MR & MRS *Benjamin M Baker III*	40'5"	10'10"	5'10"	9	W Healy	1961	Southport, CT	Ny, Pqt

Type	Name Owner	Length	Beam	Draft	Gross Tonnage	Builder	Year Launched	Home Port	Club Affiliations
	NOR'EASTER MR Henry B du Pont IV	59'	16'	6'6"	—	C Anderson	1927	Wilmington, DE	Cry, DelB, Ny, Pqt
	OFF THE HOOK MR & MRS Thomas B Wheeler	31'	11'6"	2'6"	7.5	Crosby Yacht Yard, Inc	1994	West Falmouth, MA	
	ON TIME MR & MRS David L Winstead	28'	8'2"	6'6"	7.7	Pearson Yachts	1966	Gibson Island, MD	
	OSCEOLA MR & MRS Alexander L Fanjul	52'	16'4"	4'6"	30	Hatteras Yachts	1986	Palm Beach, FL	
	OUR PLEASURE DR & MRS Raymond O Heimbecker	31'	11'	2'6"	6	Phoenix Products, Inc	—	Hope Town, Abaco, Bahamas	
	OUTRIGGER MR & MRS Richard C Riggs JR	38'6"	—	4'2"	1.8	Bertram Yacht	—	Baltimore, MD	
	OWL MR & MRS Richard S Taylor	25'	8'	5'	2.5	Crosby Yacht Yard, Inc	1974	Osterville, MA	Sfy
	OYSTER STEW MR & MRS John A Stewart JR	32'2"	10'2"	2'5"	4.5	Vineyard Haven Shipyard	1978	Annapolis, MD	Ayc, Co
	OZ OCEAN MISS Olive F Watson	24'	7'5"	1'2"	1.3	Boston Whaler, Inc	1989	North Haven, ME	
	PANACEA DR & MRS Lloyd Brown	34'	10'2"	3'11"	—	Tartan Marine Co	1970	Bucks Harbor, ME	
	PANACHE MR & MRS R Tucker Hall	33'4"	10'	5'	—	CAL Boats	1969	Bristol, RI	
	PANDA MR & MRS Frank E Wolcott III	45'	14'	3'	—	Huckins Yacht Corp	1955	Essex, CT	Exy, Ny
	PANDORA MR Stephen W Strong	48'	14'	4'5"	36	Chris-Craft	1986	Cos Cob, CT	
	PAQUET V MR & MRS Frederic M Schaefer	43'	—	—	—	Hodgen Brothers	1981	Yarmouth, ME	Ny
	PASSAGE EAST MR & MRS John Edward Sheridan	26'4"	9'6"	4'6"	3.2	Alcort Sailboats	1978	Southport, CT	Pqt
	PASTIME MR & MRS Robert L Ireland III	48'4"	17'4"	5'	30	Lyman-Morse Boatbuilding Co	1992	George Town, Grand Cayman	

YACHTS AND TENDERS

Type	Name Owner	Length	Beam	Draft	Gross Tonnage	Builder	Year Launched	Home Port	Club Affiliations
	PATIENCE MR & MRS Edwin P Tiffany	30'	6'5½"	4'9"	2.3	Cape Cod Ship Building Co	1961	Marion, MA	Bvl
	PATRINA III MRS Vincent de Roulet	62'	17'6"	5'6"	80	Durbeck's, Inc	1983	Manhasset, NY	Ny
	PEACONNET MR & MRS Norman F Nelson II	28'	8'	3'6"	—	Edey & Duff, Stonehorse	1986	New Suffolk, NY	
	PEA POD MR & MRS Douglas M Leale	25'	8'	3'	3	Wellcraft Marine Corp	1992	Orcas Island, WA	
	PEGASUS MR Edward T Haas	23'	4'6"	6"	1	E T Haas	1986	Goleta, CA	
	PELEE PLAYER MR & MRS David I Sanders	25'	8'6"	1'6"	—	Lyman Mfg Co, Inc	1965	Pelee Island, Ontario, Canada	Eyc
	PÈLERIN MR & MRS H Gilman Nichols	36'	11'5"	5'	8.5	Cape Dory Yachts, Inc	1981	North Haven, ME	
	PELICAN EXPRESS MR & MRS William W Crew	42'	12'	7'	10	Glass	1982	Ventura, CA	
	PERDIDA MR Bruce A Beckner	35'	10'3"	3'10"	10	Allied Marine	1972	Annapolis, MD	Ayc
	PEREGRINE II MR & MRS Paul L Miller	39'	13'5"	4'5"	15.33	M L Pettegrow, Inc	1986	Northeast Harbor, ME	Nf
	PERIWINKLE MR William C Brewer	33'	25'	2'	4	Quorning Boats, Inc	1994	Galesville, MD	
	PERSEVERANCE MISS Kate Ireland	42'	14'2"	5'6"	20	K N Hodgdon	1963	Pemaquid, ME	
	PHOEBE MR & MRS Robert M Bicket	30'6"	6'11½"	4'6"	1.7	Bashford Boatbuilders	1993	Cowes, Isle of Wight, UK	
	PHOEBE C MR & MRS John L Welsh JR	38'	12'6"	4'	—	Young Brothers	1984	Boothbay, ME	
	PHOENIX MR & MRS A Lawrence Rotch	27'	6'6"	4'	1.6	South Liberty Boatworks	1982	Round Pond Harbor, ME	
	PHYSALIA MR & MRS William T Andrews	32'	9'6"	4'9"	9	Dutch Mill, The Netherlands	1961	Rock Hall, MD	

Type	Name Owner	Length	Beam	Draft	Gross Tonnage	Builder	Year Launched	Home Port	Club Affiliations
⛵	**PICAROON** MR & MRS Don H McLucas JR	42'9"	12'6"	5'	12	Henry R Hinckley & Co	1990	Washington, DC	S
🚤	**PICKLE II** MR & MRS John O Robertson	19'6"	3'6"	2'6"	.5	Luder Marine Construction Co	1988	Mosquito Island, ME	
⛵	**PLEIADES** MRS Francis F Carpenter	44'	12'	9'10"	11	Turku, Finland	1973	Pittsburgh, PA	
⛵	**PLOTTER** MR & MRS C Cary Rea	24'	—	—	—	Dyer Boats	1987	Annapolis, MD	
⛵	**PORTUNUS** MRS Augustin H Parker	39'10"	10'6"	5'8"	8.5	Abeking & Rasmussen	1959	Bucks Harbor, ME	
⛵	**POSTCARD** MR & MRS Charles H Brewer	44'	14'	6'	—	Marion	1993	Boston, MA	
⛵	**PREDATOR** MR Stevenson S Kaminer	39'	12'8"	8'8"	5	M Lindsay	1995	Annapolis, MD	Ayc
🚤	**PREDATOR** MR & MRS Harry Estile Yerkes III	31'	—	—	—	Mako Marine, Inc	1984	Fishers Island, NY	
⛵	**PRE-EMPTIVE BID** MR & MRS Stephen A Cook	33'5"	6'9"	5'4"	3.56	Bjarne Aas, Norway	1959	Fishers Island, NY	Fiy, Ny
🚤	**PRIVATE LIVES** MR & MRS J Gwynne Thorsen	36'	13'6"	3'6"	—	—	1984	Jupiter Island, FL	Nyc
⛵	**PROMISE** MR James C Ayer	40'	12'	5'	8.5	Tillotson-Pearson, Inc	1986	Marblehead, MA	Ey
🚤	**PROWLER** MR John Hunt Marshall	42'	13'7"	4'6"	24	Grand Banks Yachts, Ltd	1972	Boca Grande, FL	Ny
🚤	**PYRITE** MRS George Estabrook Brown JR	32'	9'6"	3'	10	Chris-Craft	1958	Naples, FL	
⛵	**QE3** MR & MRS Richard J Bates	33'	9'3"	5'10"	3.35	Tartan Ten	1979	Belvedere, CA	
⛵	**QUADRILLE** CAPT & MRS Nicholas Brown	45'	13'4"	5'9"	—	Goetz Custom Sailboats, Inc	1993	Newport, RI	Ayc, Il, Ny
⛵	**QUADRILLE** MR & MRS Albert Goodhue III	42'	11'6"	4'6"	—	Allied Boat Co	1969	Marblehead, MA	Ey, Myc

YACHTS AND TENDERS

Type	Name / Owner	Length	Beam	Draft	Gross Tonnage	Builder	Year Launched	Home Port	Club Affiliations
⛵	**QUEEN NEFERTITI** *MR & MRS Benjamin Coates*	129'	27'8"	11'	209	Astilleros y Talleres Celaya, Spain	1986	Monte Carlo, Monaco	
⛵	**QUIESCENCE** *MR & MRS Dudley P Cooke*	47'7"	13'2"	5'	17	Bristol Yacht Co	1990	Philadelphia, PA	Cry
⛵	**QUINDARO** *MR & MRS David Hibbs Donnan*	38'	11'7"	5'9"	9	Morris Yachts	1995	Northeast Harbor, ME	Nf
⛵	**RADIANT** *MR & MRS Thomas H Belknap*	36'	10'8"	5'	8.05	Cape Dory Yachts, Inc	1980	Manchester, MA	Myc
⛵	**RAGTIME** *MR & MRS Walter C Flower III*	35'	9'	4'	4.8	Bristol Yacht Co	1983	New Orleans, LA	
⛵	**RAG TIME** *MR & MRS Gerald B Rorer*	47'7"	13'3"	4'11"	17.3	Bristol Yacht Co	1986	Philadelphia, PA	Cry
⛵	**RAMBLIN' ROSE** *MR & MRS Henry F Field*	40'	13'	3'6"	8	Freedom Yachts	1980	Chicago, IL	
⛵	**RAMPANT** *MR & MRS Frederick Taussig*	57'	15'	7'6"	22	Bowman Yachts	1983	St Louis, MO	Nf
🚤	**RAPTURE** *MR & MRS R Henry Norweb III*	33'	13'	3'	—	Egg Harbor Boat Co	1978	Marion, MA	Bvl
🚤	**REBEL TOO** *MR Charles S Robertson JR*	29'6"	11'8"	2'8"	—	Crosby Yacht Yard, Inc	1980	Falmouth, MA	
⛵	**RED, INC** *MRS D Seeley Hubbard*	36'6"	11'8"	—	1.85	P Norlin	1979	Noroton, CT	Ny
⛵	**RED SHIFT** *MR & MRS James W Cobbs JR*	25'	9'	4'6"	1.5	Mirage Marine Corp	1979	Greenwich, CT	Ihy
🚤	**RED WITCH** *MR & MRS Anthony K Baker*	38'	9'	3'6"	2.25	Chris-Craft	1929	Oyster Bay, NY	Ny, S
⛵	**REEF RUNNER** *MR David O Davis*	26'	8'8"	4'5"	2.5	Columbia Yacht Corp	1968	Kaneohe, HI	
🚤	**REFLECTION** *MR & MRS Henry Rogers Benjamin*	43'3"	14'	3'5"	29.51	Gulfstar, Inc	1975	Southampton, NY	Syc
⛵	**REGAELIA** *MR & MRS William J W Brown*	40'9"	11'9"	4'3"	10	Henry R Hinckley & Co	1977	Southwest Harbor, ME	
⛵	**RENEGADE** *MR & MRS Henry P Purdon*	37'	11'	6'	2.5	Geraghty Marine	1977	San Diego, CA	Sdy

YACHTS AND TENDERS | 205

Type	Name / Owner	Length	Beam	Draft	Gross Tonnage	Builder	Year Launched	Home Port	Club Affiliations
	REPUBLIC OF VERMONT MR Alexander R H Walling	34'	11'6"	6'6"	9	C & C Yachts, Ltd	1980	Mystic, CT	
	RESOLUTE MR & MRS Paul Donham JR	32'	9'9"	2'6"	6.5	Vineyard Haven Yachts	1983	Camden, ME	
	RESOLUTION MR Carter P Pfaelzer	34'	13'	—	—	Phoenix Marine, Inc	1988	Osterville, MA	
	RESPITE III MR & MRS Samuel S Dennis III	42'	14'	4'4"	17	Uniflite, Inc	1977	Duxbury, MA	
	RE-TREAT MR & MRS T Graham R Kastendike	35'4"	10'6"	5'3"	—	C & C Yachts, Ltd	—	Gibson Island, MD	
	REYNEGADE MRS Bartow Reynolds	25'	10'	3'	—	Chris-Craft	1987	Penzance Point, MA	
	RIDING HOOD MR & MRS Henry P U Harris III	37'	13'	4'6"	12	Egg Harbor Boat Co	1967	Norfolk, VA	
	RIPTIDE V MR & MRS Harrison S Fraker	24'	9'	3'6"	2.25	Mako Marine, Inc	1986	Nantucket, MA	Nyc
	ROBIN MR & MRS Geoffrey B Dougherty	24'	8'	2'	1.5	Chris-Craft	1932	Mantoloking, NJ	Cry
	ROBIN'S NEST MR & MRS Alfred LeC Robins	27'	—	—	—	Hunter Marine	1978	Houston, TX	
	ROCINANTE MR William N Lane III	46'	13'8"	5'	—	Little Harbor Custom Yachts	1991	Naples, FL	
	ROVER MR & MRS R Kendall Nottingham	31'	11'	4'	4.5	Herreshoff Mfg Co	1982	Bay Head, NJ	
	RUBICON MR George A Newhall III	42'	15'	4'	—	Ocean Alexander	1988	Sausalito, CA	Sfy
	RUDEE'S RENDEZVOUS MR Traynter B Turpin	35'9"	13'5"	3'5"	21	Trojan Yachts	1977	Virginia Beach, VA	
	RUMBLEFISH MR & MRS Edward A Harrington	23'	—	—	—	Mako Marine, Inc	—	Fishers Island, NY	Fiy
	RUMRUNNER MR & MRS William G Anderson	43'	13'	5'	15	R Rich	1977	Boston, MA	
	RUM RUNNER MR J T Terry Brune	33'	11'	3'	5	Owens Yacht	1949	White Stone, VA	

YACHTS AND TENDERS

Type	Name / Owner	Length	Beam	Draft	Gross Tonnage	Builder	Year Launched	Home Port	Club Affiliations
	RUNAWAY CAPT & MRS Richard L Ferrarini	30'	10'	3'	4.5	Bayliner Marine Corp	1982	La Conner, WA	
	SACAJAWEA MR & MRS Grant McCargo	43'	12'	6'9"	5	Tillotson-Pearson, Inc	1994	Edgartown, MA	Eyc
	SAFARI MR & MRS Charles P Schutt JR	42'	12'8"	5'8"	15	Sabre Yachts	1987	St Michaels, MD	Cry, Nf
	SAGAMORE MR & MRS Edward W Madeira JR	38'	13'	6'	—	Sabre Yachts	1984	Freeport, ME	Cry, Nf
	SAKANA MR & MRS Thomas G Andrew JR	30'	11'	6'	4	Yamaha Corp, USA	1981	Seattle, WA	
	SAMANTHA MRS John A Brown	46'	15'	4'6"	—	J Newman, Inc	1981	Philadelphia, PA	Cry
	SAMAR MR & MRS William C Loring	35'9"	9'	5'	6	Henry R Hinckley & Co	1967	Manchester, MA	Myc
	SANDPIPER II MR & MRS Nathan B Swift	32'6"	11'	5'11"	10	Pearson Yachts	1986	Chicago, IL	
	SAND WEDGE MR & MRS Robert S O'Hara JR	35'	12'6"	2'6"	6	S2 Yachts, Inc	1990	Point O'Woods, NY	
	SAND WITCH MR & MRS Carl F Sheppard JR	27'	10'	3'	3.5	Fortier Boats	1984	Beach Haven, NJ	
	SANDY C III MR & MRS C Bowie Rose	20'	8'	2'	—	Shamrock Marine	1982	Annapolis, MD	Ayc
	SANRIEL MR & MRS Jo Zach Miller IV	29'	9'5"	3'	4	Dyer Boats	1983	Sarasota, FL	Ny, S
	SARA B MR & MRS Blair W Smith	34'	—	—	—	C & C Yachts, Ltd	1988	Solomons, MD	
	SARA B² MR & MRS Robert R Price III	41'5"	13'	7'10"	8	Barberis Med Yard, Ltd	1985	Wye River, MD	
	SARAH MR & MRS Christopher N Willits	42'3"	13'8"	4'	—	Bruno & Stillman	1975	Peachblossom Creek, MD	Cry
	SARATOGA II MR & MRS John A Pagenstecher	37'3"	11'9"	7'9"	—	Tartan Marine Co	1984	Potomac, MD	
	SARDONIC MR & MRS S Kirk Millspaugh	26'	—	4'11"	—	Ranger Boats	1977	Gibson Island, MD	

Type	Name / Owner	Length	Beam	Draft	Gross Tonnage	Builder	Year Launched	Home Port	Club Affiliations
⛵	**SATORI** MR & MRS George Henry Kuper	42'	11'	6'	15	J G Alden/Halmatic, Ltd	1967	Southport, CT	Ny, Pqt
🚤	**SCHOODIC II** MR & MRS William G Foulke	29'	9'6"	2'6"	8	Dyer Boats	1987	Seal Harbor, ME	
⛵	**SCYLLA** MR & MRS R Barry McComic	40'	13'6"	6'6"	8.5	Hunter Marine	1984	San Diego, CA	Sdy
⛵	**SEABIRD** MR & MRS Augustus B Kinsolving	36'	11'	3'6"	9	International Marine Corp	1961	New York, NY	Ny
⛵	**SEA DANCER** MR & MRS Leslie C Moorhouse	34'	—	—	—	Columbia Yacht Corp	1969	Philadelphia, PA	
⛵	**SEA FEVER** MR & MRS Joseph C Harsch	22'	—	—		Bristol Yacht Co	—	Jamestown, RI	
⛵	**SEAHORSE** MR Berkeley T Rulon-Miller	26'	7'	4'	—	Cape Dory Yachts, Inc	1980	Annapolis, MD	
⛵	**SEA HORSE** MR & MRS Humphrey H Swift	36'	10'6"	5'8"	—	Casey Yawl	1941	South Dartmouth, MA	Co
🚤	**SEA HUNTER** MR & MRS Wilfrid W Coleman	46'6"	—	—	—	Bertram Yacht	1987	North East, MD	
🚤	**SEA LION** MR & MRS James H Clark JR	61'	—	—		Gladding-Hearn	1994	Ft Lauderdale, FL	
🚤	**SEARCHER** MR James H McLean III	42'4"	15'	4'7"	19.75	Kadey-Krogen Yachts, Inc	1984	Mantoloking, NJ	Ny
⛵	**SEA SHARP** MR & MRS Alvaro F Espinosa de los Monteros	22'	8'	3'4"	—	Columbia Yacht Corp	1980	Dillon, CO	Dy
🚤	**SEGAR** MR & MRS Geoffrey B Dougherty	25'	6'5"	2'5"	1.5	G L Watson, Scotland	1896	Mantoloking, NJ	Cry
⛵	**SELKIE** MRS James A McCurdy	38'6"	11'3"	6'8"	—	Concordia Co	1986	Oyster Bay, NY	S
🚤	**SEND IT IN** MR & MRS Yves F M Hentic	36'	12'	2'6"	11	Runaway Offshore Sportfishing Boats, Inc	1985	Ft Pierce, FL	
⛵	**SEPTEMBER SONG** MR & MRS S Grey Dayton JR	41'8"	11'	6'	10	Alden/Molich, Denmark	1965	Philadelphia, PA	Cry

YACHTS AND TENDERS

Type	Name / Owner	Length	Beam	Draft	Gross Tonnage	Builder	Year Launched	Home Port	Club Affiliations
	SERENDIPITY II MR & MRS Robert J K Hart	42'6"	13'	3'6"	—	Matthews Co	1959	Lawrence, NY	Ny
	SHADY LADY MR & MRS Dudley Roberts	37'6"	14'	4'5"	—	Topaz Marine Corp	1987	East Hampton, NY	Dyc
	SHALAMAR MR & MRS Pierre duP Irving	47'	15'	5'	25	Cheoy Lee Shipyards, Ltd	1973	Newport, RI	Il
	SHANGRI-LA MR & MRS W Denison Brooks	28'	9'	4'	—	Bunker & Ellis	1960	Cranberry Isles, ME	
	SHAWNA MR Henry T Woodland JR	33'	11'6"	2'8"	—	Fortier Boats	1985	Newport, RI	Eyc, Ny
	SHE MR John F Dennis-Browne	31'	10'11"	3'	6	Black Watch Corp	1987	Freeport, NY	
	SHEARWATER MR & MRS Mark S Cluett	42'	12'2"	6'6"	7	J Boats, Inc	1996	Blue Hill, ME	
	SHEARWATER IV MR & MRS Kenneth P Barrow JR	25'	9'6"	3'6"	2.8	Bayliner Marine Corp	1987	Charlestown, MD	
	SHENANIGANS MR & MRS Lee M Donovan	25'	10'	3'	—	Bertram Yacht	1962	Annapolis, MD	Ayc
	SHENEMERE MR & MRS W Stevens Sheppard	51'	14'6"	6'	—	Beneteau, Ltd	1985	Road Town, Tortola	Ny, Pqt
	SHIFTING WIND MR & MRS Peter A Dow	22'	—	—	—	Boston Whaler, Inc	1987	Harsens Island, MI	
	SHUH-SHUH-GAH MR & MRS James R Barker	40'	13'5"	5'2"	—	Freedom Yachts	1994	Darien, CT	Ny
	SILVER LINING MR Duncan M Silver	34'	—	4'	—	Seidelmann Yachts	1985	Sarasota, FL	
	SILVER QUEEN II MR & MRS W Ashton Lee	22'	7'4"	—	—	W D Schock Corp	1970	Dillon, CO	Dy
	SIMPLY DIVINE MR & MRS Michael Poutiatine	25'4"	9'6"	1'6"	4.8	Grady-White Boats, Inc	1994	Vero Beach, FL	
	SIR WALTER WALLY MR & MRS Wallace L Preble	40'	13'	7'	14	Standfast Const, The Netherlands	1983	St Vincent and Grenadines	

Type	Name Owner	Length	Beam	Draft	Gross Tonnage	Builder	Year Launched	Home Port	Club Affiliations
	SISTER MR & MRS Richard S Parker JR	40′	12′	3′9″	21	J Cochran	1963	Dark Harbor, ME	
	SIXPENCE MR & MRS Henry P Bakewell JR	31′	9′	3′3″	8.6	Belleville Marine, Ltd	1970	Old Saybrook, CT	
	SKOAL DR & MRS Harry C Bishop	44′	—	5′	—	CS Yachts, Ltd	1977	St Thomas, VI	Co
	SKIDBLADNIR MR E Webster Dann	44′	12′	6′	10	Camper & Nicholsons	1934	Freswick Harbour, Scotland	
	SLEIGH RIDE MR & MRS Aaron A Hobart	23′	8′	3′6″	2	Mako Marine, Inc	1976	Dataw Island, SC	Ny
	SNALLYGASTER MR & MRS Charles F Stein III	39′7″	11′10″	7′3″	9	Islander Yachts	1979	Gibson Island, MD	
	SNOW DANCE MR & MRS Thomas A Corcoran	45′	12′3″	7′	30	LeComte, The Netherlands	1968	Boothbay Harbor, ME	
	SNOW GOOSE MR & MRS Donald S Rice	34′4″	10′6″	5′2″	13.87	Martha's Vineyard Shipyard, Inc	1981	Mattapoisett, MA	Ny
	SOIRÈE MR & MRS Thomas H G Baillière JR	40′	11′	5′7″	6	CAL Boats	1967	Baltimore, MD	
	SOLITUDE MR & MRS George T Boggs	35′	9′8″	5′2″	13.5	Pearson Yachts	1964	Gibson Island, MD	
	SONG 'N DANCE MR & MRS John M P Thatcher III	36′	12′	6′10″	6	W D Schock Corp	1981	Wilmington, DE	Eyc, Ihy, Ny
	SOUTHERN COMFORT II MRS D Rowland Ellis	35′3″	12′	3′2″	—	Sea Rover	1970	Islamorada, FL	
	SOUTHERN CROSS MR & MRS Peter de L Welles	22′	7′1″	5′	1.2	South Coast Seacraft	1972	Atlanta, GA	
	SOUWEST MR & MRS Paul B Dickey JR	24′	8′8″	4′	1.5	Tillotson-Pearson, Inc	1981	Greenwich, CT	Ihy
	SPINDRIFT MR Dennis S Emory	29′11″	10′	5′	8.2	Sabre Yachts	1981	Bass Harbor, ME	
	SPINDRIFT IV MRS William A M Burden	38′9″	13′6″	4′	24	J Newman, Inc	1984	Northeast Harbor, ME	

210 | YACHTS AND TENDERS

Type	Name / Owner	Length	Beam	Draft	Gross Tonnage	Builder	Year Launched	Home Port	Club Affiliations
⛵	**SPIRIT** DR & MRS Barry H Smith	30'	10'6"	6'3"	9	Sabre Yachts	1988	Prouts Neck, ME	
⛵	**SPIRIT** MR & MRS Christopher M White	34'	11'	4'6"	6	Sabre Yachts	1986	Stonington, CT	
⛵	**SPLASHY DOG** MR & MRS M Pierre Tonissi	39'9"	12'9"	5'4"	13	Beneteau, Ltd	1992	Boston, MA	Bvl
⛵	**SPRING TIDE** MR & MRS Herbert deM Hucks III	44'	12'11"	6'4"	17	Kelly-Peterson	1979	Philadelphia, PA	
⛵	**STARFIRE** MR & MRS Anthony C Paddock	38'	12'	7'	7.5	C & C Yachts, Ltd	1985	Larchmont, NY	
⛵	**STARGAZER** MISS Patricia G Saunders	24'2"	7'8"	3'	2.5	Yankee Yachts	1971	Washington, DC	Il
⛵	**STARLING** MR & MRS Peter B Ford	27'	9'6"	5'2"	—	US Yacht Building Corp	1983	Vero Beach, FL	
⛵	**STAR OF ISIS** DR & MRS Peter A F Morrin	28'	9'8"	4'4"	—	Vandestadt & McGruder, Ltd	1983	Kingston, Ontario, Canada	
⛵	**STAT** MR & MRS Thomas B Newhall	38'	12'8"	6'	10	Hinterhoeller Yachts	1986	Scituate, MA	
🛥	**STAVIDON** MR & MRS Henry S Grove III	31'	11'6"	3'	6	Pacemaker Yachts	1978	Beach Haven, NJ	
⛵	**SUDDENLY** MISS Sarah F Hunnewell	44'	12'6"	4'11"	12	Alden Yachts	1979	Newport, RI	
⛵	**SUGARBUSH** MR David D Slingluff JR	30'	5'	5'	—	—	—	Jamestown, RI	
⛵	**SUMMER LIGHT** MR & MRS Hamilton Robinson JR	31'	—	4'6"	—	Vindo, Sweden	1976	Northeast Harbor, ME	Nf
⛵	**SUNDOWNER** MR & MRS William Sumner Holbrook III	27'	8'6"	7'	—	Catalina Yachts	1975	Long Beach, CA	
🛥	**SUNDOWNER** MR & MRS John R Whitmore	49'	14'	5'6"	—	American Marine	1991	Greenwich, CT	
⛵	**SWALLOW** MR & MRS William Rotch	28'	—	4'10"	—	Sabre Yachts	1984	South Dartmouth, MA	
🛥	**SWAMP FIRE** MR & MRS Robert R Crans	50'	16'6"	5'	—	Hatteras Yachts	1996	Annapolis, MD	

Type	Name Owner	Length	Beam	Draft	Gross Tonnage	Builder	Year Launched	Home Port	Club Affiliations
⛵	SWAN SONG MR & MRS Robert S Kniffin	31'	10'11"	4'4"	5.2	Pearson Yachts	1985	Marblehead, MA	Ny
⛵	SYBARITE MR & MRS Charles L Eshleman JR	26'	—	4'	—	Luder Marine Construction Co	—	—	
⛵	SYMPHONY MR & MRS Jonathan H Shinn	50'	14'6"	7'6"	—	Morgan Yachts	1983	San Francisco, CA	Sfy
⛵	TAHAWUS MR Samuel H Hinckley	24'	—	3'	—	—	1961	Inverness, CA	
🚤	TAKEOVER MR & MRS Stockton A Andrews	28'	9'6"	2'6"	5.5	Lee S Wilbur & Co	1984	Northeast Harbor, ME	Bhy, Nf
⛵	TALARIA MR & MRS S Trevor Pardee	35'	10'	3'9"	13	Pearson Yachts	1977	Newport, RI	S
⛵	TANAMERA MR Roswell S Buck	40'	11'3"	4'9"	10	Belleville Marine, Ltd	1968	Point Abino, Ontario, Canada	Buf
⛵	TARANTELLA MR & MRS Robert W Sharp	39'9"	8'6"	6'	12	T Holm	1955	Gibson Island, MD	
⛵	TEAL MR B Brooks Thomas	38'	11'6"	5'	19.3	Shannon Boat Co, Inc	1984	New York, NY	Exy, Ny
🚤	TEETOTALER MR E Lawrence Dinning III	46'	16'	4'	—	J Newman, Inc	1982	Bethany Beach, DE	
⛵	TELLURIDE MR & MRS Oliver C Hazard	24'	5'	4'	.9	—	1979	Nantucket, MA	Nyc
⛵	TELLURIDE MISS M Melissa Wickser	24'	9'6"	4'	1.8	Tillotson-Pearson, Inc	1979	Nantucket, MA	Nyc
🚤	TEMBOTOTO MR Standish Forde Medina	22'	9'	3'	—	Cobia Boat Co	1969	Westhampton, NY	
⛵	TEMPEST MR & MRS Henry C Pitts	40'	12'6"	4'4"	20	Pearson Yachts	1979	Monkton, MD	
⛵	TEMPO DR & MRS Edwin G Fischer	39'	12'	6'	—	Ocean Cruising Yachts	1985	Newport, RI	Il, Ny
⛵	TERNEN MR & MRS Eivind P Rynning	28'	7'8"	5'	1.5	Jan Herman Linge, Norway	1976	Fairfield Co, CT	

YACHTS AND TENDERS

Type	Name / Owner	Length	Beam	Draft	Gross Tonnage	Builder	Year Launched	Home Port	Club Affiliations
	TERN TO MR & MRS Grantland W Gelette	34'	13'	3'6"	21	Uniflite, Inc	—	South Dartmouth, MA	
	THALIA MR & MRS David S I Ker	36'	11'8"	4'9"	11.88	Cabotcraft Industries	1978	Hamilton, Ontario, Canada	
	THE GENERAL III MRS Gerald J Ficks	31'	11'	3'	—	Bertram Yacht	1973	Edgartown, MA	Eyc
	THE GRAY GULL MR & MRS Jansen Noyes JR	31'9"	11'6"	3'6"	—	Flye Point Marine	1987	Brooklin, ME	Fiy
	THEODORA MR & MRS David O O'Hara	32'5"	8'6"	4'8"	—	Norge Boats & C Baadebyggeri	1955	Manchester, MA	
	THE OTHER LINE MR & MRS Henrik N Vanderlip	37'	13'	3'6"	—	Sea Ray Boats, Inc	1995	Cos Cob, CT	
	THE SICILIAN MR & MRS Michael Baldwin	31'	10'10"	3'3"	—	Maine Way Boats	1988	Beaufort, SC	
	THE THIRD WAVE MR & MRS Clarence Z Wurts	39'6"	12'	7'10"	—	C & C Yachts, Ltd	1988	Chester, Nova Scotia, Canada	
	THISTLEDOWN MRS Frederic E Camp	39'10"	10'	5'8"	8	Abeking & Rasmussen	1958	East Blue Hill, ME	Ey
	TICKIDYBOO MR & MRS Richard E Boerke	34'	11'	4'6"	6.8	Sabre Yachts	1989	North Palm Beach, FL	
	TICKLED TOO MR & MRS Richard W Angle	26'8"	10'	2'6"	8	Fortier Boats	1979	Marion, MA	Bvl, Ny
	TICONDEROGA MR & MRS L Scott Frantz	72'	16'7"	8'	—	Herreshoff Mfg Co	1936	Greenwich, CT	
	TIGHT LINES MR Walter J Clough	38'	13'6"	4'6"	15	Bertram Yacht	1985	Rumson, NJ	
	TIMPER MR & MRS Carl W Timpson JR	25'8"	8'6"	4'5"	2.4	Tillotson-Pearson, Inc	1981	Prouts Neck, ME	
	TIMY MR & MRS Philip M Woollam	36'	12'	4'6"	7.5	LeGuen Hemidy, France	1982	New Orleans, LA	
	TINKER TOY MR & MRS Timothy A Wesley	62'	19'	5'	37	Striker Yachts Corp	1974	San Diego, CA	

Type	Name / Owner	Length	Beam	Draft	Gross Tonnage	Builder	Year Launched	Home Port	Club Affiliations
⛵	**TOGE II** / MR Weld Coxe	35'	10'9"	4'11"	5	Scanmar	1985	Block Island, RI	
⛵	**TONOPAH** / MR & MRS H Frost Prioleau	37'	—	—	—	C & C Yachts, Ltd	1985	Emeryville, CA	
⛵	**TORCH** / MR Talbot Baker JR	40'	11'6"	5'9"	17	Camper & Nicholsons	1980	Marion, MA	Bvl
⛵	**TOUCHÉ** / MR & MRS Miles O Bidwell JR	34'	11'	4'6"	5.5	Tartan Marine Co	1986	Greenwich, CT	Ihy, Ny
⛵	**TRAVELLER** / MR & MRS Christopher T Buckley	27'	6'	4'	1.5	S Crocker	1938	Blue Hill, ME	
⛵	**TRAVELLER** / MR & MRS James Timpson	33'2"	9'7"	5'	—	Ranger Boats	1975	Dark Harbor, ME	Ny, Pqt
⛵	**TRIANON** / MR & MRS Alexander K Barton	35'	12'	5'	8	Vindo, Sweden	1976	Annapolis, MD	Ayc
🚤	**TRIDENT III** / MR & MRS Theodore A Mohlman	45'	12'	3'6"	29	Whittaker	1972	St Michaels, MD	
⛵	**TRILOGY** / DR & MRS J Henderson Dorsey	60'	15'7"	7'9"	50	Camper & Nicholsons	1985	Norfolk, VA	
🚤	**TRINGA III** / MR & MRS Robert Gorham Fuller	25'	6'	2'	1	Boston Whaler, Inc	1988	York Harbor, ME	Aga
⛵	**TRIPPER II** / MR & MRS Alden Ames III	34'	12'	5'	6	Jensen Marine Corp	1978	Tiburon, CA	Sfy
⛵	**TRISTRAM** / MR George L Maxwell	44'	13'	7'	16	Ta'Shing	1991	Bass Harbor, ME	Co, Ny
⛵	**TRITON** / MR William M B Berger	28'	6'11"	5'6"	2	E & D Stuart, Inc	1996	Prouts Neck, ME	
⛵	**TROPICBIRD** / MRS Betsy Carlyle Crozer	39'2"	13'2"	5'7"	11	Lavronos	1989	Annapolis, MD	
⛵	**TRUTH B** / MR & MRS (DR) Matthew H Pedersen	18'	7'	1'6"	1	Eatons Boat Yard	1943	Castine, ME	
🚤	**TWO TENDER** / MR & MRS G Thompson Pew JR	22'4"	8'	2'6"	3	Mako Marine, Inc	1982	Gibson Island, MD	Cry
🚤	**TYME N TYDE** / CHAPLAIN (COL) & MRS Malcolm Roberts III	27'	9'8"	2'6"	9	Albin Marine, Inc	1989	New York, NY	

YACHTS AND TENDERS

Type	Name / Owner	Length	Beam	Draft	Gross Tonnage	Builder	Year Launched	Home Port	Club Affiliations
⛵	**TYPHOON** MR & MRS Andre W G Newburg	33'	9'3"	4'6"	10	Emsworth, Ltd	1977	Lyme, CT	
🚤	**UNCLE BOB** MR & MRS Laurance R Clark	21'	—	1'	—	Boston Whaler, Inc	1989	Nantucket, MA	
⛵	**UPBEAT** CDR & MRS Robert T Riker	27'	9'6"	4'	2	Hunter Marine	1988	Siesta Key, FL	
⛵	**VALEEHI II** MR & MRS Davenport B Crocker	40'	11'6"	4'6"	9.6	Pearson Yachts	1972	Cohasset, MA	Co
⛵	**VALLDEMOSA** LT COL & MRS C Worthington Fowler II	26'3"	6'3"	2'6"	2.8	Tylercraft	1973	Virginia Beach, VA	
⛵	**VAMI** CAPT & MRS Vadym V Utgoff	26'	9'	3'	8	V V Utgoff	1979	Islesboro, ME	
⛵	**VENTURE IV** REV & MRS Brendan Griswold	35'	—	—	—	Duffy & Duffy	1988	South Dartmouth, MA	
⛵	**VICTORIA** MR & MRS J Newman Carter	30'2½"	9'	4'2"	8	Cape Dory Yachts, Inc	1980	McLean, VA	
⛵	**VINDALF** MR & MRS Frederick E Wilson	32'	8'9"	4'10"	5	Dan Boat, Aeroskobing, Denmark	1960	Worton Creek, MD	Co
🚤	**VINTAGE** MR & MRS Ernest V Moncrieff JR	30'	9'6"	2'4"	—	Scout	1989	Wickford, RI	Ny
🚤	**VIRGIL P GIBNEY** MRS Gail P Shafer	43'	14'	3'6"	—	Nautiline	1972	Osprey, FL	
⛵	**VITESSE** MR & MRS James G G May	30'4"	8'4"	5'	4	Hinterhoeller Yachts	1970	Point Abino, Ontario, Canada	
⛵	**VIVA** DR & MRS Robert C Seamans JR	42'	12'11"	4'6"	—	Bristol Yacht Co	1988	Manchester, MA	Myc
⛵	**VOLADOR** MR Charles C Butt	82'	19'	10'5"	—	Royal Huisman Shipyard	1982	Northeast Harbor, ME	Nf, Ny, Nyc
🚤	**VORLAGE** MR William S Warren	60'	—	4'	—	Huckins Yacht Corp	1970	Prindle, WA	
🚤	**VOYAGER** MRS Edgar A Bering JR	34'	11'	3'6"	6	Albin Marine, Inc	1987	Oxford, MD	

YACHTS AND TENDERS | 215

Type	Name Owner	Length	Beam	Draft	Gross Tonnage	Builder	Year Launched	Home Port	Club Affiliations
	VOYAGER MR & MRS Charles A Chapin	34'	12'	3'2"	—	Chung Hwa	1975	San Diego, CA	Sdy
	WAHOO MR & MRS Nicholas Goldsborough	39'9"	13'	6'	—	Concept Holding Corp	1984	Annapolis, MD	Ayc
	WAINSCOTT WIND MR Stuyvesant Wainwright II	36'	11'6"	6'2"	15	Sabre Yachts	1985	Somes Sound, ME	
	WATERLOO MR & MRS John W Barnum	25'	7'5"	3'	2.5	Fairhaven Marine	1971	Waquoit, MA	Ny
	WATERMELLON MR Henry C S Mellon	52'	16'	4'6"	—	Hatteras Yachts	1986	Delray Beach, FL	DelB
	WAVE DANCER II MR & MRS Grafton S Kennedy	42'	14'	4'8"	—	Catalina Yachts	1991	Dover, NH	
	WEATHERBIRD MR & MRS William T Healy	40'9"	11'9"	8'9"	17	Henry R Hinckley & Co	1984	Coronado, CA	
	WENDIGO MR Jerome F Hamlin	25'	6'	2'	2	—	1889	Cliff Island, Muskoka, Ontario, Canada	
	WENONAH MR & MRS J Edmund de Castro JR	28'6"	8'3"	4'	7	Pearson Yachts	1965	Buffalo, NY	Buf
	WHALE MR Timothy L Hogen	30'	12'	5'	—	Nonsuch	1980	Stonington, CT	
	WHIM MR George Morris Piersol JR	26'4"	10'4"	3'	4.5	Crosby Yacht Yard, Inc	1985	Shelter Island, NY	Co, Cry
	WHIM MR & MRS Thomas C Platt	28'6"	8'	4'	4	Pearson Yachts	1960	Cold Spring Harbor, NY	
	WHIM MR & MRS Parker D Wyman	28'5"	9'2"	4'4"	4	Sabre Yachts	1981	Gibson Island, MD	
	WHIMSEY MR & MRS James A Woods	40'1"	12'6"	3'4"	10	Sabre Yachts	1991	Cold Spring Harbor, NY	
	WHIRLWIND MR & MRS Robert G Bender	27'	7'6"	3'	—	Chris-Craft	1937	Okoboji, IA	
	WHISPER VIII MR & MRS Hollis MacL Baker	55'	16'	4'6"	24	Chris-Craft	1973	Grand Haven, MI	DelB, Ny
	WHISPER X MR & MRS Hollis MacL Baker	64'	16'	4'6"	—	Burger Boat Co, Inc	1972	Palm Beach, FL	DelB, Ny

216 | YACHTS AND TENDERS

Type	Name Owner	Length	Beam	Draft	Gross Tonnage	Builder	Year Launched	Home Port	Club Affiliations
⛵	**WHITE ARROW** MR & MRS Anthony L Leggett	33'5"	6'	6'	3.6	Able Marine	1983	Larchmont, NY	
⛵	**WHITECAP** MR & MRS Charles M Leighton	42'	12'	7'	11	Henry R Hinckley & Co	1986	Islesboro, ME	Ny
⛵	**WHITE EAGLE** MR & MRS Frederick R Mayer	82'5"	17'10"	6'3"	73	Palmer Johnson, Inc	1966	Denver, CO	Ny
⛵	**WHIT'S END** MR & MRS Philip N Whittaker	37'	11'6"	4'6"	8	Dickerson Boat Builders, Inc	1984	Falmouth, MA	
🛥	**WICKED LADY** MR & MRS E Chester Peet JR	38'	12'6"	4'	13	Young Brothers	1994	Shelter Island, NY	
🛥	**WINBURN** MR & MRS Edward E Burns JR	38'	12'10"	3'6"	20	Foley	1988	Kittery Point, ME	
⛵	**WIND LASS** MR & MRS Edward B Benjamin JR	27'	7'	4'	2.6	Pearson Yachts	1965	New Orleans, LA	
🛥	**WINDLESS** MRS Albert L Hoffman JR	38'	13'	4'	18	Lee S Wilbur & Co	1986	Manset, ME	Nf
🛥	**WINDMAR** MR & MRS Charles L Flaccus III	32'	12'	2'6"	7	Pacemaker Yachts	1977	Boca Grande, FL	Ihy
⛵	**WIND'S FOOL** MR & MRS William Holmes Honan	60'	14'	3'	55	—	1952	Mystic, CT	
⛵	**WINDSLIPPER V** MR & MRS Thomas H Townsend	39'2"	12'7"	6'3"	5.3	Jeanneau	1985	Manchester, MA	Myc
⛵	**WIND SONG** MR & MRS Walter S Burrage JR	42'	11'	6'	11	Alden Caravelle	1966	Manchester, MA	Myc
⛵	**WINDSONG** MR & MRS Russell S Reynolds JR	57'	15'	6'6"	27.5	Nautor	1980	Greenwich, CT	Ihy, Ny
⛵	**WINDSONG** MR William G Rogerson	33'8"	10'6"	5'6"	9	Sabre Yachts	1980	Boston, MA	
⛵	**WINDWALKER** MR & MRS Craig W Cullen	46'	12'	6'6"	14	Lyman-Morse Boatbuilding Co	1982	Oxford, MD	Cry
🛥	**WINGS** MR & MRS John R Fegela	28'	8'6"	2'	2	Offshore Yachts	1989	Key Largo, FL	

Type	Name Owner	Length	Beam	Draft	Gross Tonnage	Builder	Year Launched	Home Port	Club Affiliations
⛵	**WISHFUL THINKING** MR & MRS Warren Jackson St John	30'	7'	5'	3	—	1956	Childrens Harbor, AL	
🚤	**WISP** DR & MRS Harold E Rhame JR	43'	14'6"	4'6"	30	Albin Marine, Inc	1980	Southport, CT	Ny, Pqt
🚤	**WOODSHED** MR & MRS Theodore V Wood JR	41'	14'2"	3'	—	Hatteras Yachts	1986	Ocean City, NJ	
⛵	**XANADU** MR Gregory S Harris	34'	11'2"	5'5"	10	O'Day Corp	1981	Boston, MA	
⛵	**XANTHIPPE III** MR & MRS Robert M Price	35'	10'	3'9"	14	Pearson Yachts	1971	Delray Beach, FL	Cry, DelB
⛵	**YAKUT** MR & MRS Harry Darlington	33'	7'8"	5'	3.5	Able Marine	1984	Northeast Harbor, ME	Nf
🚤	**YES, DEAR** MRS Henry S McNeil	53'	16'	4'	40	Hatteras Yachts	1975	Philadelphia, PA	
🚤	**YOCTANGEE** MR & MRS Frederick J Stevenson JR	22'	6'	2'	.5	Greavette Co, Ltd	1949	Pointe-au-Baril, Ontario, Canada	
⛵	**YONDER** MR & MRS Donald W Thomas	36'4"	11'11"	4'5"	—	Catalina Yachts	1996	South Dartmouth, MA	
⛵	**ZEPHYR** MR & MRS David V Shields	38'	11'6"	4'6"	—	Morgan Yachts	1979	Watch Hill, RI	Why
⛵	**ZEPHYR** MR Irving Warner JR	32'6"	9'3"	4'6"	25.1	Pearson Yachts	1965	Vineyard Haven, MA	

YACHT CLUBS AND THEIR OFFICERS

Agamenticus Yacht Club
☎ (207) 363-9814
York Harbor, ME *03911*

Commodore	Marshall N Jarvis II
Vice-Commodore	DR Michael Ciancetta
Secretary	DR Thomas Chassé
Treasurer	MRS John H Finley III

Annapolis Yacht Club
☎ (410) 263-9279
Box 908
Annapolis, MD *21404-0908*

Commodore	Frederick E Bock JR
Vice-Commodore	Karl Von Schwarz
Rear-Commodore	Arthur A Libby

Bar Harbor Yacht Club
☎ (207) 288-3275
5 Stephens Lane
Bar Harbor, ME *04609-1807*

Commodore	Vernon S McFarland JR
Vice-Commodore	Helmut Weber
Rear-Commodore	John E Pelletier
Treasurer	Terrance Kelley

Beverly Yacht Club
☎ (508) 748-0540
99 Water St, PO Box 181
Marion, MA *02738-0181*

Commodore	William S Moonan JR
Vice-Commodore	Graham I Quinn
Rear-Commodore	John Buckley
Secretary	Edwin V Babbitt III
Treasurer	Robert L Rosbe JR

Buffalo Yacht Club
☎ (716) 883-5900
One Porter Av
Buffalo, NY *14201-1097*

Commodore	Daniel C Mullan
Vice-Commodore	Jack Quigley
Rear-Commodore	Frank F Kania
Fleet Captain	R Anthony Daily
Secretary	Homer Fay
Treasurer	MRS Gail J MacCleverty

Chicago Yacht Club
☎ (312) 861-7777
Foot of Monroe St
Chicago, IL *60603*

Commodore	Robin M Demouth
Vice-Commodore	Joseph T Charles
Rear-Commodore	Kurt P Stocker
Secretary	John Regan
Treasurer	Jeffrey H Monger

Corinthian Yacht Club
☎ (610) 521-4705
2d & Taylor Sts
Essington, PA *19029*

Commodore	G Thompson Pew JR
Vice-Commodore	William B Read III
Rear-Commodore	Norman P Robinson
Secretary	John E Zimmermann III
Treasurer	Charles J Horter

The Corinthians
☎ (203) 836-1311
Box 1623
Darien, CT *06820*

Master	MRS Alice Neily Mutch
Master's Mate	Norman Hewitt
Secretary	Harry Curtis
Paymaster	Donald T Relyea
Communications Director	Samuel Suratt

Delray Beach Yacht Club
☎ (561) 272-2700
110 MacFarlane Dv
Delray Beach, FL *33483*

Commodore	H McKee Munnally

Devon Yacht Club
☎ (516) 267-6340
Devon Rd
Amagansett, NY *11930*

Commodore	Jacques P Sibeud
Vice-Commodore	Henry G Parker III
Rear-Commodore	Arthur Becker
Secretary	William Bennington
Treasurer	Michael de Havenon

YACHT CLUBS AND THEIR OFFICERS

Dillon Yacht Club
PO Box 4308
Dillon, CO *80435-4308*

Commodore ....David Helmer
Vice-Commodore ....Charles Rov
Secretary ....Susan Swisher
Treasurer ....Glenn Forsey

Eastern Yacht Club
☎ (617) 631-1400
Foster St
Marblehead, MA *01945*

Commodore ....Richard S Robie JR
Vice-Commodore ....David B Soule
Rear-Commodore ....Jonathan C Wales
Secretary ....Lea Pendleton
Treasurer ....Frank D'Orio JR

Edgartown Yacht Club
☎ (508) 627-4361
Box 1309, One Dock St
Edgartown, MA *02539*

Commodore ....Alexander W Vietor
Vice-Commodore ....Robert D Harrington JR
Rear-Commodore ....Robert F Hoerle
Secretary ....Joan W Wilson
Treasurer ....Earle N Cutler III

Essex Yacht Club
☎ (860) 767-8121
19 Novelty Lane
Essex, CT *06426*

Commodore ....Charles R Moore JR
Vice-Commodore ....William J Cochran
Rear-Commodore ....Edward H Osgood JR
Secretary ....Leon Newburg
Treasurer ....Paul G Page

Fishers Island Yacht Club
☎ (516) 788-7036
Box 141
Fishers Island, NY *06390*

Commodore ....MRS Andrew B Rose
Vice-Commodore ....John S Burnham
Rear-Commodore ....John G Brim
Secretary ....Jennifer J Miller
Treasurer ....Jeffrey J Miller

Fishing Bay Yacht Club
☎ (804) 740-0597
Box 7327
Richmond, VA *23221*

Commodore ....David R Lee
Vice-Commodore ....James O Cobb
Rear-Commodore ....Robert C Wardwell
Secretary ....Judith G Buis
Treasurer ....John F Watlington III

Great Lakes Cruising Club
☎ (312) 372-2344
20 N Wacker Dv, Suite 1540
Chicago, IL *60606*

Commodore ....Richard A Danly
Vice-Commodore ....A John Lobbezoo
Secretary ....Herbert J Kaczmarek
Treasurer ....George S Hender

Ida Lewis Yacht Club
☎ (401) 846-1969
Box 479, Wellington Av
Newport, RI *02840*

Commodore ....Richard Peters
Vice-Commodore ....Earl Stubbs
Rear-Commodore ....Peter Milnes
Secretary ....Sanderson Carney
Treasurer ....Louis Kremer

Indian Harbor Yacht Club, Inc
☎ (203) 869-2484
710 Steamboat Rd
Greenwich, CT *06830*

Commodore ....Donald S Rotzien
Vice-Commodore ....Richard T Carraher
Rear-Commodore ....William J Ferretti
Secretary ....MRS Peter S Godfrey
Treasurer ....Edward L Sinclair JR

Manchester Yacht Club
☎ (508) 526-4595
Tuck's Point Rd
Manchester, MA *01944*

Commodore ....Paul D Shuwall
Vice-Commodore ....Garlan Morse JR
Secretary ....Albert M Creighton III
Treasurer ....Al Ireton

Nantucket Yacht Club
☎ (508) 228-1400
S Beach St
PO Box 667
Nantucket, MA *02554*

Commodore	E Geoffrey Verney
Vice-Commodore	Priscilla G Mleczko
Rear-Commodore	Eric S Holch

New York Yacht Club
☎ (212) 382-1000
37 W 44 St
New York, NY *10036*

Commodore	Alfred L Loomis III
Vice-Commodore	Robert L James
Rear-Commodore	George M Isdale JR
Secretary	Peter M Ward
Treasurer	David K Elwell JR

The Northeast Harbor Fleet
☎ (207) 276-5101
South Shore Rd
Northeast Harbor, ME *04662*

Commodore	Minturn de S V Chace
Vice-Commodore	Thomas R Elkins
Treasurer	Christopher Hutchins

Pequot Yacht Club
☎ (203) 255-5749
669 Harbor Rd
Southport, CT *06490*

Commodore	Hugh R Smith
Vice-Commodore	Benjamin M Baker III
Rear-Commodore	Robert R Larsen
Secretary	MRS M Douglas Bisset
Treasurer	Charles R Sprowl JR

Rappahannock River Yacht Club
☎ (804) 438-6650
Box 55
Irvington, VA *22480*

Commodore	Maurice Dickerson
Vice-Commodore	Henry A Little III
Rear-Commodore	William C Hope III
Secretary	Albert Christensen
Treasurer	Dudley M Patteson

Royal Bermuda Yacht Club
☎ (441) 295-2214
Albouys Point, Box HM 894
Hamilton, Bermuda HM DX

Commodore	Thomas E C Miller
Vice-Commodore	Bruce D Lines
Rear-Commodore	P Somers Cooper
Hon Secretary	Thad A Hollis

St Francis Yacht Club
☎ (415) 563-6363
On the Marina
San Francisco, CA *94123*

Commodore	P Terry Anderlini
Vice-Commodore	Duane M Hines
Rear-Commodore	Terry G Klaus
Secretary	Janet Ann Minar
Treasurer	Mark A McLaughlin

San Diego Yacht Club
☎ (619) 221-8400
1011 Anchorage Lane
San Diego, CA *92106-3005*

Commodore	William R Munster
Vice-Commodore	DR Richard W Virgilio
Secretary	Gordon G T Frost JR
Treasurer	John Driscoll

Seawanhaka Corinthian Yacht Club
☎ (516) 922-6200
314 Yacht Club Rd, Centre Island
Oyster Bay, NY *11771*

Commodore	Clarence F Michalis
Vice-Commodore	DR Donald S Gromisch
Rear-Commodore	Richard H MacDougall
Secretary	John Chamberlain
Treasurer	MISS Jean E Andersen

Southampton Yacht Club
☎ (516) 283-9888
Little Neck Rd, Box 833
Southampton, NY *11968*

Commodore	Richard E Warren
Vice-Commodore	James Ledogar
Rear-Commodore	David Loddengaard
Secretary	Peter B Robinson
Treasurer	John F Van Deventer JR

Watch Hill Yacht Club
☎ (401) 596-4986
Watch Hill, RI *02891*

Commodore	Fred A Allardyce
Vice-Commodore	Judith Lentz
Rear-Commodore	Edwin G Hebb
Secretary	William B Thornton
Treasurer	Robert A Green JR